Oil Paintings in Public Ownership in Nottinghamshire

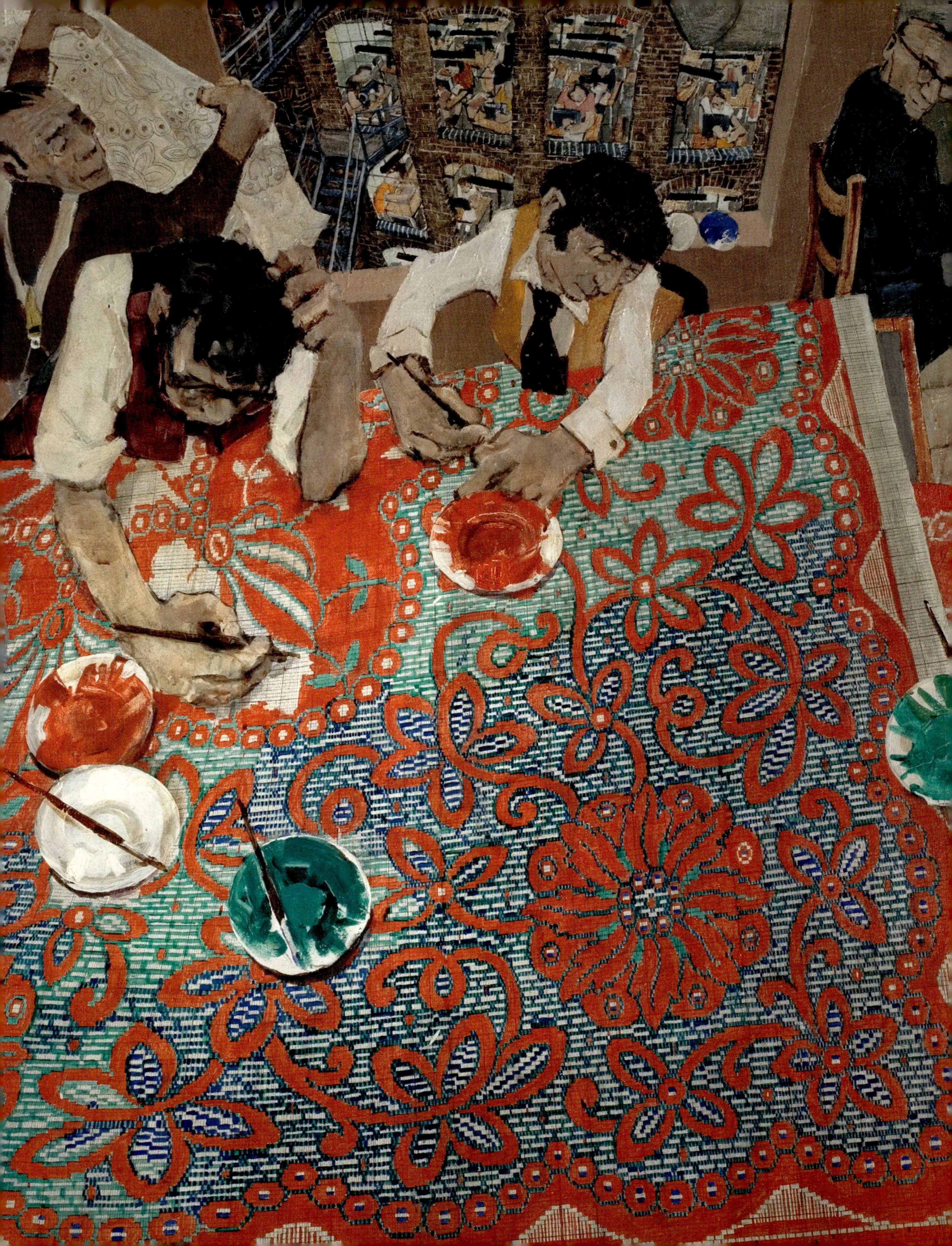

Oil Paintings in Public Ownership in Nottinghamshire

The Public Catalogue Foundation

Andrew Ellis, Director
Sonia Roe, Editor
Angharad Jones, Nottinghamshire Coordinator
John McLean, Photography

First published in 2008 by the Public Catalogue Foundation, 33 Maiden Lane, Covent Garden, London WC2E 7JS.

ISBN 978-1-904931-74-4 (hardback)
ISBN 978-1-904931-75-1 (paperback)

Nottinghamshire photography: John McLean

Designed by Sally Jeffery

Distributed by the Public Catalogue Foundation, 33 Maiden Lane, Covent Garden
London WC2E 7JS
Telephone 020 7395 0330

Printed and bound in China by C&C Offset Printing Co. Ltd

Cover image:

Knight, Harold 1874–1961
Ethel Bartlett, Pianist (detail), c.1935
Nottingham City Museums and Galleries, (see p. 115)

Image opposite title page:

Waplington, Paul b.1938,
The Lace Draughting Room (detail)
Nottingham Central Library, (see p. 54)

Back cover images (from top to bottom):

Phillips, Thomas 1770–1845
6th Lord Byron (1788–1824), 1818
Newstead Abbey, (see p. 39)

Knight, Laura 1877–1970
Lamorna Birch (1869–1955), and His Daughters, 1934
The University of Nottingham, (see p. 211)

Richards, Ceri Geraldus 1903–1971
St Cecilia, 1949
Bassetlaw District Council, (see p. 227)

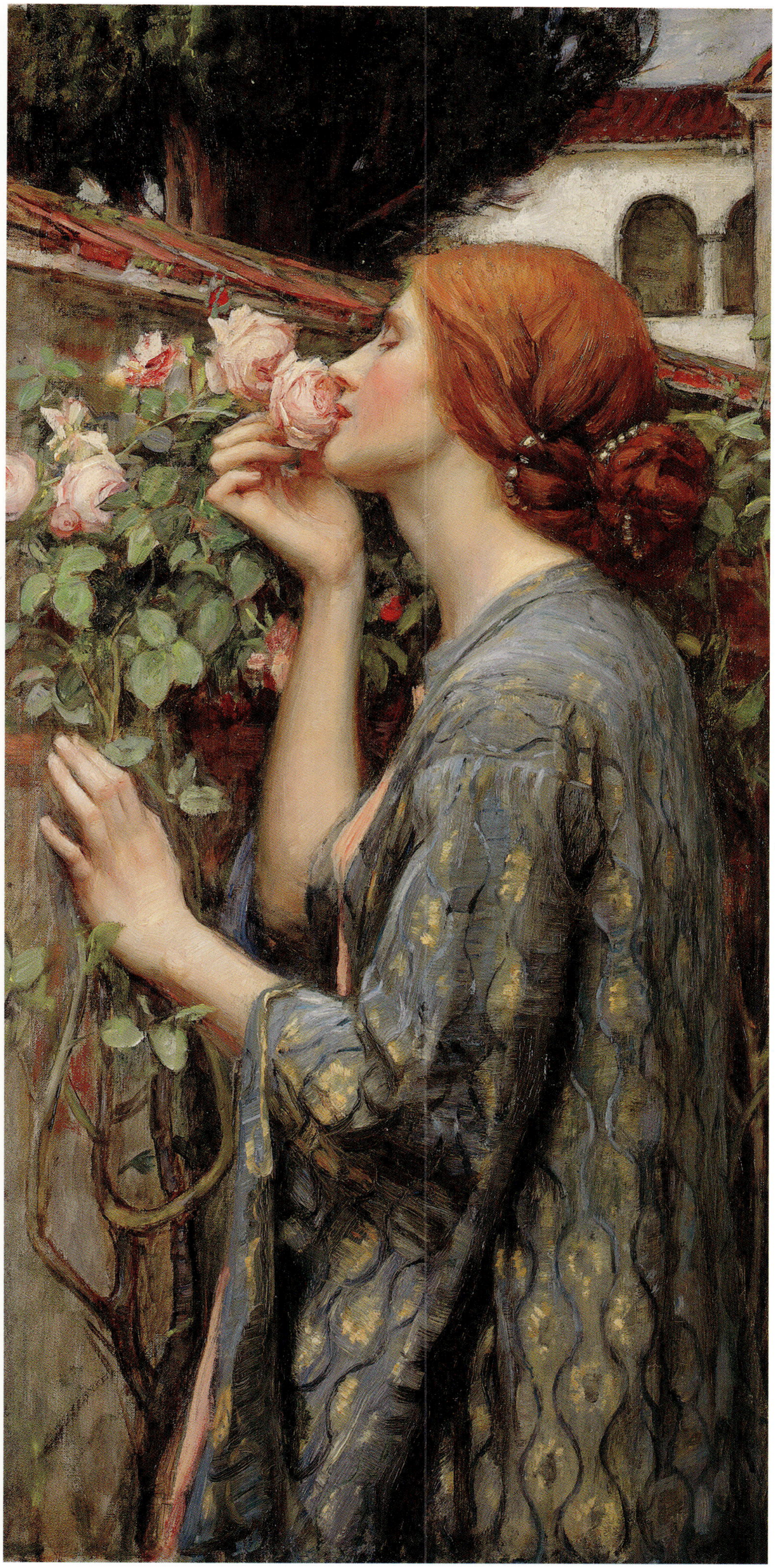

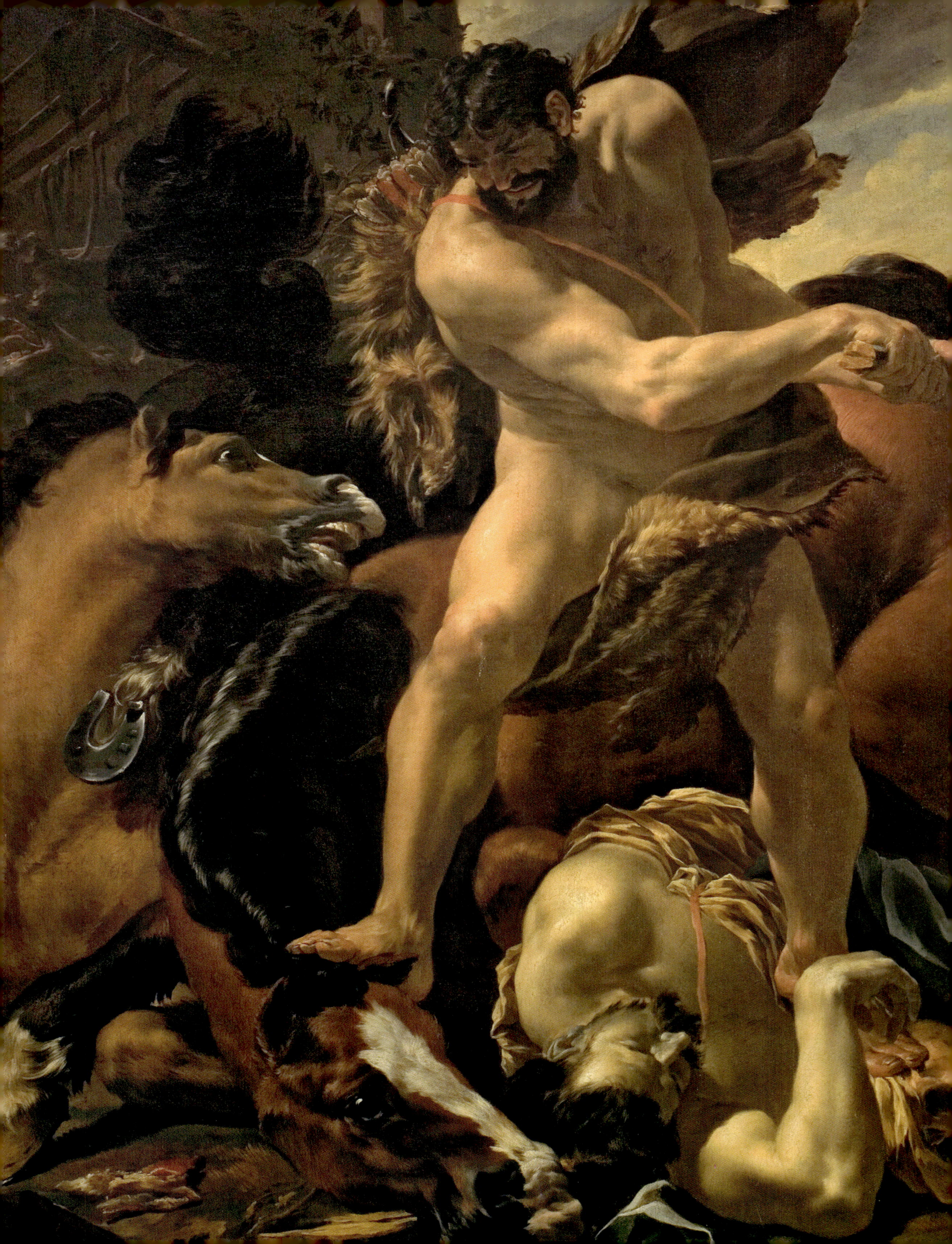

Contents

ix Foreword
x The Public Catalogue Foundation
xi Financial Supporters
xii Acknowledgements
xiii Catalogue Scope and Organisation
xiv Key to Painting Information

THE PAINTINGS

Arnold
3 Gedling Borough Council

Kirkby-in-Ashfield
3 Ashfield District Council

Mansfield
4 Langwith Whaley Thorns Heritage Centre
4 Mansfield District Council:
Mansfield Museum & Art Gallery
13 Mansfield Fire Station Museum
14 Nottinghamshire County Teaching Primary Care Trust:
Ashfield Community Hospital
Mansfield Community Hospital
16 Portland College

Newark-on-Trent
17 Newark and Sherwood Museum Service
26 Newark Town Council:
Newark Town Hall Museum & Art Gallery
32 The Holocaust Centre

Newstead
33 Newstead Abbey

Nottingham
43 Castle College Nottingham
44 Djanogly City Academy Nottingham
48 Galleries of Justice
49 Government Office for the East Midlands
50 Nottingham Central Library[i]
54 Nottingham City Museums and Galleries[i]:
Nottingham Castle Museum and Art Gallery
Nottingham Industrial Museum, Wollaton Park
Nottingham Natural History Museum, Wollaton Hall
The Museum of Nottingham Life at Brewhouse Yard
Wollaton Hall, Wollaton Park
164 Nottingham Magistrates' Court
164 Nottingham Trent University

Facing page: Le Brun, Charles, 1619–1690, *Hercules Vanquishing Diomedes* (detail), 1638–1642, Nottingham City Museums and Galleries (p. 117)

173 Nottinghamshire Archives[ii]
176 Nottinghamshire County Cricket Club
178 Nottinghamshire County Football Club
178 Nottinghamshire County Hall[ii]
183 Nottinghamshire County Library Service[ii]:
Arnold Library
Eastwood Library
Hucknall Library
Ravenshead Library
Retford Library
Stapleford Library
185 Nottinghamshire Police
185 Rushcliffe Borough Council
188 The Congregational Memorial Hall Trust (1978) Limited
196 The Council House[i]
196 The Sherwood Rangers Yeomanry Regimental Association:
Sherwood Rangers Yeomanry Museum
197 The University of Nottingham
219 The Worcestershire and Sherwood Foresters Museum (The Sherwood Foresters Collection) of the Mercian Regiment:
Sherwood Foresters Regimental Museum, Nottingham Castle

Retford
220 Bassetlaw District Council:
Bassetlaw Museum and Percy Laws Memorial Gallery
229 Retford Town Hall[iii]

Ruddington
230 Ruddington Parish Council
231 Ruddington Village Museum

Southwell
231 Southwell Town Council

Sutton-in Ashfield
232 Sherwood Forest Hospitals NHS Foundation Trust:
King's Mill Hospital
Newark Hospital

Upton
238 British Horological Institute:
Upton Hall Museum of Time

Worksop
239 Creswell Crags Museum and Education Centre[iv]

241 Paintings Without Reproductions
242 Further Information
261 Collection Addresses
264 Index
271 Supporters of the Public Catalogue Foundation

i The Council House, Nottingham Central Library and Nottingham City Museums and Galleries are all managed by Nottingham City Council.
ii Nottinghamshire Archives, Nottinghamshire County Hall and Nottinghamshire County Library Service are all managed by Nottinghamshire County Council.
iii Retford Town Hall is managed by Bassetlaw District Council.
iv Creswell Crags Museum and Education Centre is managed by Creswell Heritage Trust.

Foreword

Poor, lame Lord Byron is celebrated internationally as a fine poet and an inspiring libertarian, forever associated with struggles for national independence, a sort of early Che Guevara. For us British however, in our tabloid era, Byron is remembered as an incestuous letcher and in his own home of Newstead Abbey, his poetry is compared to the lyrics of Mr John Mellor, alias Joe Strummer of the punk group The Clash, born ironically the son of a British diplomat serving in Turkey.

That scofflaw, Robin Hood, with Maid Marian, the Bonnie and Clyde of thirteenth century Nottinghamshire, ranks higher than Byron in our register of national heroes. So I tremble to gaze upon the armoury of flintlocks and cannon assembled by Lord Middleton at Wollaton Hall to disperse Luddite attacks or the flayed walls of Nottingham Castle, burned down by deconstructionist citizens in the 1830s.

Yet, as a matter of visible fact, Nottingham is more truly represented by its strong tradition of civilised munificence of the very highest order; consider Sir Jesse Boot and his gift to Nottingham University; or, in our own time, the even more extraordinary Sir Harry Djanogly. Their generosity, of course, extends well beyond Nottingham but Nottingham is their focus, and Nottingham is well worth the attention.

Not least for being the home of Laura Knight, whose theatre pictures are currently (September 2008) the subject of an excellent exhibition at Nottingham Castle, supported by a fine catalogue by Timothy Wilcox. At the end of the month it moves to the Lowry in Salford, and that's that. Surely, that should not be? An important exhibition of the work of Dame Laura Knight, the first woman to be admitted to the Royal Academy since its two founding women members, Angelica Kauffman and Mary Moser, and one of our most brilliant twentieth-century artists, surely merits greater exposure than a few months in Nottingham and Salford. We have wonderful curators in the regions and we must do far more to encourage and support them and to ensure their work is seen and applauded by the widest possible audiences. The Nottingham Castle collection in particular deserves greater. It is a treasure house of splendid paintings that deserves to be far better known. If you doubt this, just look through this catalogue. That said, Nottingham City Museums and Galleries deserves our well-earned respect for their worthy custodianship of Wollaton Hall, Newstead Abbey and the Castle itself.

I would like to thank our Nottinghamshire team for their excellent work and, in particular, to express my deep gratitude to our Master Patron, Mrs Jenny Farr, then Vice Lord-Lieutenant of the County. Her most effective campaign to raise the funds was enthusiastically assisted by a band of 'wise men' that included Tom Huggon, Vic Semmens, Richard Tresidder and Tony Wilkinson together with support from Sir Andrew Buchanan, the Lord Lieutenant of Nottinghamshire. I would like also to add my thanks to those donors who were particularly generous: Sir Harry Djanogly, Nottingham City Council, Mr and Mrs A. H. Wilkinson and Renaissance East Midlands.

Finally, a big thank you to our coordinator on the ground, Angharad Jones, and to our photographer, John McLean. This excellent catalogue is a product of their fine work.

Fred Hohler, Chairman

The Public Catalogue Foundation

The Public Catalogue Foundation is a registered charity. It is publishing a series of illustrated catalogues of all oil paintings in public ownership in the United Kingdom.

The rationale for this project is that whilst the United Kingdom holds in its public galleries and civic buildings arguably the greatest collection of oil paintings in the world, an alarming four in five of these are not on view. Furthermore, few collections have a complete photographic record of their paintings let alone a comprehensive illustrated catalogue. In short, what is publicly owned is not publicly accessible.

The Public Catalogue Foundation has three aims. First, it intends to create a complete record of the nation's collection of oil, tempera and acrylic paintings in public ownership. Second, it intends to make this accessible to the public through a series of affordable catalogues which will later go online. Finally, it aims to raise funds for the conservation and restoration of paintings in participating collections through the sale of catalogues by these collections.

Collections benefit substantially from the work of the Foundation not least from the digital images that are given to them for free following photography and the increased recognition that the catalogues bring. These substantial benefits come at no financial cost to the collections. The Foundation is funded by a combination of support from individuals, companies, the public sector and charitable trusts.

Financial Supporters

The Public Catalogue Foundation would like to express its profound appreciation to the following organisations and individuals who have made the publication of this catalogue possible.

Donations of £10,000 or more

Sir Harry Djanogly, CBE
Nottingham City Council
Mr & Mrs A. H. Wilkinson

Donations of £5,000 or more

Mrs Jenny Farr, MBE, DL
The Lady Hind Trust
Renaissance East Midlands

Donations of £1,000 or more

The Helen Jean Cope Trust
David Crane Trust
J. N. Derbyshire Trust
Dunn Family Charitable Trust
Nottingham Civic Society
P. F. Charitable Trust
Mrs Margaret Pollett
The Portland Family
The Jessie Spencer Trust

Other Donations

Mr & Mrs Peter Allen
Mr & Mrs Gordon K. Asher
Mrs P. F. Bayles
Professor & Mrs R. W. Blamey
Mr Robin Boudard
Mrs J. M. Brook
Andrew Buchanan Charitable Trust
Andrew Cooper & Pippa Marland
Cooper Parry
Laurence Coppel
Paul & Jane Edington
Helen Farr
Mr George & Josephine Fish
Mr & Mrs R. J. Freeston
Mrs B. Harper
Hart Hambleton Plc
Sir Gordon & Lady Hobday
Tom Huggon, DL
Honor Hunt
David Inglefield
Langar Hall
Mrs M. G. Langford
Louis S. Levin
Patrick Mackie
Mrs Jenny Mellors, DL
Commander & Mrs Peter Moore
Derrick & Mary Morley
Sir John & Lady Osborn
Mr & Mrs Trevor Parr
Mr & Mrs M. J. Pearson
Per Pro Poyser Fund
Alan Ripley
Dr Eric Roebuck
Arthur & Kathleen Sandford
Mr & Mrs Tony Scruby
Mrs G. Short
Mrs J. M. Sketchley
Mr & Mrs Edmund Staunton
The Stoney Holme Trust
Mr Ian Sutherland
Professor R. B. Tate
Richard Tresidder
Valerie Truman
The Venerable & Mrs Robin Turner
Mr & Mrs Waine
Sir Frederick & Lady Warner Trust
Mr & Mrs B. C. Weldon
Michael & Nicky Weston
Cynthia R. Whitt
C. G. H. Wilson
Mrs Margery E. C. Wilson
Mr & Mrs C. J. Wood

National Supporters

The Bulldog Trust
The John S. Cohen Foundation
Covent Garden London
Marc Fitch Fund
R. K. Harrison
Hiscox plc
The Monument Trust
National Gallery Trust
Stavros Niarchos Foundation
P. F. Charitable Trust
The Pilgrim Trust
The Bernard Sunley Charitable Foundation
Garfield Weston Foundation

National Sponsor

Christie's

Acknowledgements

The Public Catalogue Foundation would like to thank the individual artists and copyright holders for their permission to reproduce for free the paintings in this catalogue. Exhaustive efforts have been made to locate the copyright owners of all the images included within this catalogue and to meet their requirements. Copyright credit lines for copyright owners who have been traced are listed in the Further Information section.

The Public Catalogue Foundation would like to express its great appreciation to the following organisations for their kind assistance in the preparation of this catalogue:

Bridgeman Art Library
Flowers East
Marlborough Fine Art
National Association of Decorative & Fine Arts Societies (NADFAS)
National Gallery, London
National Portrait Gallery, London
Royal Academy of Arts, London
Tate

The participating collections included in this catalogue would like to express their thanks to the following organisations which have so generously enabled them to acquire paintings featured in this catalogue:

Arts Council England, East Midlands
The Byron Society
Contemporary Art Society
Sir Harry Djanogly
Mr Charles Ian Fraser
The Gulbenkian Foundation
Hazlitt, Gooden & Fox
The Heritage Lottery Fund
The Holbrook Trust (Trustees of the William S. Holbrook Bequest)
The Lammin Bequest Fund
Professor Simon Lewis
The Millns Bequest Fund
MLA/V & A Purchase Grant Fund
MONKS
The Museums and Galleries Commission
National Art Collections Fund (The Art Fund)
Trustees of the Newcastle (Clumber) Collection
The Friends of Newstead Abbey
The Friends of the Nottingham Museums
The Oscroft Bequest Fund
The Pilgrim Trust
Renaissance East Midlands
The Thorpe Perry Bequest Fund
Andrew Wilton
Woodmansterne Publications Limited

Catalogue Scope and Organisation

Medium and Support
The principal focus of this series is oil paintings. However, tempera and acrylic are also included as well as mixed media, where oil is the predominant constituent. Paintings on all forms of support (e.g. canvas, panel, etc.) are included as long as the support is portable. The principal exclusions are miniatures, hatchments or other purely heraldic paintings and wall paintings *in situ*.

Public Ownership
Public ownership has been taken to mean any paintings that are directly owned by the public purse, made accessible to the public by means of public subsidy or generally perceived to be in public ownership. The term 'public' refers to both central government and local government. Paintings held by national museums, local authority museums, English Heritage and independent museums, where there is at least some form of public subsidy, are included. Paintings held in civic buildings such as local government offices, town halls, guildhalls, public libraries, universities, hospitals, crematoria, fire stations and police stations are also included.

Geographical Boundaries of Catalogues
The geographical boundary of each county is the 'ceremonial county' boundary. This county definition includes all unitary authorities. Counties that have a particularly large number of paintings are divided between two or more catalogues on a geographical basis.

Criteria for Inclusion
As long as paintings meet the requirements above, all paintings are included irrespective of their condition and perceived quality. However, painting reproductions can only be included with the agreement of the participating collections and, where appropriate, the relevant copyright owner. It is rare that a collection forbids the inclusion of its paintings. Where this is the case and it is possible to obtain a list of paintings, this list is given in the Paintings Without Reproductions section. Where copyright consent is refused, the paintings are also listed in the Paintings Without Reproductions section. All paintings in collections' stacks and stores are included, as well as those on display. Paintings which have been lent to other institutions, whether for short-term exhibition or long-term loan, are listed under the owner collection. In addition, paintings on long-term loan are also included under the borrowing institution when they are likely to remain there for at least another five years from the date of publication of this catalogue. Information relating to owners and borrowers is listed in the Further Information section.

Layout
Collections are grouped together under their home town. These locations are listed in alphabetical order. In some cases collections that are spread over a number of locations are included under a single owner collection. A number of collections, principally the larger ones, are preceded by curatorial forewords. Within each collection paintings are listed in order of artist surname. Where there is more than one painting by the same artist, the paintings are listed chronologically, according to their execution date.

The few paintings that are not accompanied by photographs are listed in the Paintings Without Reproductions section.

There is additional reference material in the Further Information section at the back of the catalogue. This gives the full names of artists, titles and media if it has not been possible to include these in full in the main section. It also provides acquisition credit lines and information about loans in and out, as well as copyright and photographic credits for each painting. Finally, there is an index of artists' surnames.

Key to Painting Information

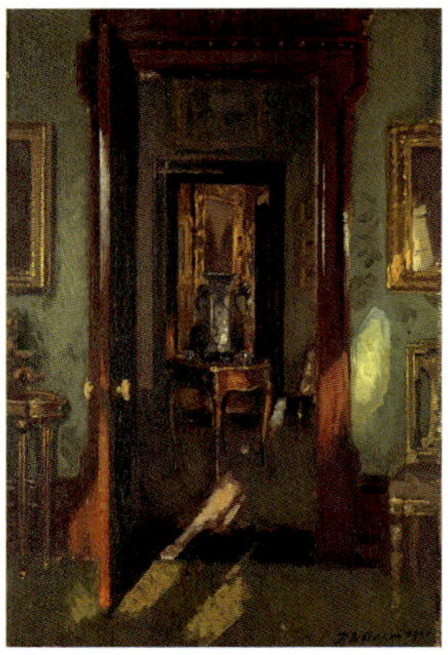

Almost all paintings are reproduced in the catalogue. Where this is not the case they are listed in the Paintings Without Reproductions section. Where paintings are missing or have been stolen, the best possible photograph on record has been reproduced. In some cases this may be black and white. Paintings that have been stolen are highlighted with a red border. Some paintings are shown with conservation tissue attached to parts of the painting surface.

Adam, Patrick William 1854–1929
Interior, Rutland Lodge: Vista through Open Doors 1920
oil on canvas 67.3 × 45.7
LEEAG.PA.1925.0671.LACF ❋

Artist name This is shown with the surname first. Where the artist is listed on the Getty Union List of Artist Names (ULAN), ULAN's preferred presentation of the name is given. In a number of cases the name may not be a firm attribution and this is made clear. Where the artist name is not known, a school may be given instead. Where the school is not known, the painter name is listed as *unknown artist*. If the artist name is too long for the space, as much of the name is given as possible followed by (…). This indicates the full name is given at the rear of the catalogue in the Further Information section.

Painting title A painting title followed by *(?)* indicates that the title is in doubt. Where the alternative title to the painting is considered to be better known than the original, the alternative title is given in parentheses. Where the collection has not given a painting a title, the publisher does so instead and marks this with an asterisk. If the title is too long for the space, as much of the title is given as possible followed by *(…)* and the full title is given in the Further Information section.

Execution date In some cases the precise year of execution may not be known for certain. Instead an approximate date will be given or no date at all.

Artist dates Where known, the years of birth and death of the artist are given. In some cases one or both dates may not be known with certainty, and this is marked. No date indicates that even an approximate date is not known. Where only the period in which the artist was active is known, these dates are given and preceded with the word *active.*

Medium and support Where the precise material used in the support is known, this is given.

Dimensions All measurements refer to the unframed painting and are given in cm with up to one decimal point. In all cases the height is shown before the width. An (E) indicates where a painting has not been measured and its size has been calculated by sight only. If the painting is circular, the single dimension is the diameter. If the painting is oval, the dimensions are height and width.

Collection inventory number In the case of paintings owned by museums, this number will always be the accession number. In all other cases it will be a unique inventory number of the owner institution. (P) indicates that a painting is a private loan. Details can be found in the Further Information section. Accession numbers preceded by 'PCF' indicate that the collection did not have an accession number at the time of catalogue production and therefore the number given has been temporarily allocated by the Public Catalogue Foundation. The ❋ symbol indicates that the reproduction is based on a Bridgeman Art Library transparency (go to www.bridgeman.co.uk) or that Bridgeman administers the copyright for that artist.

Facing page: Weight, Carel Victor Morlais, 1908–1997, *African Girl No.2* (detail), 1965, Nottingham City Museums and Galleries (p. 160)

THE PAINTINGS

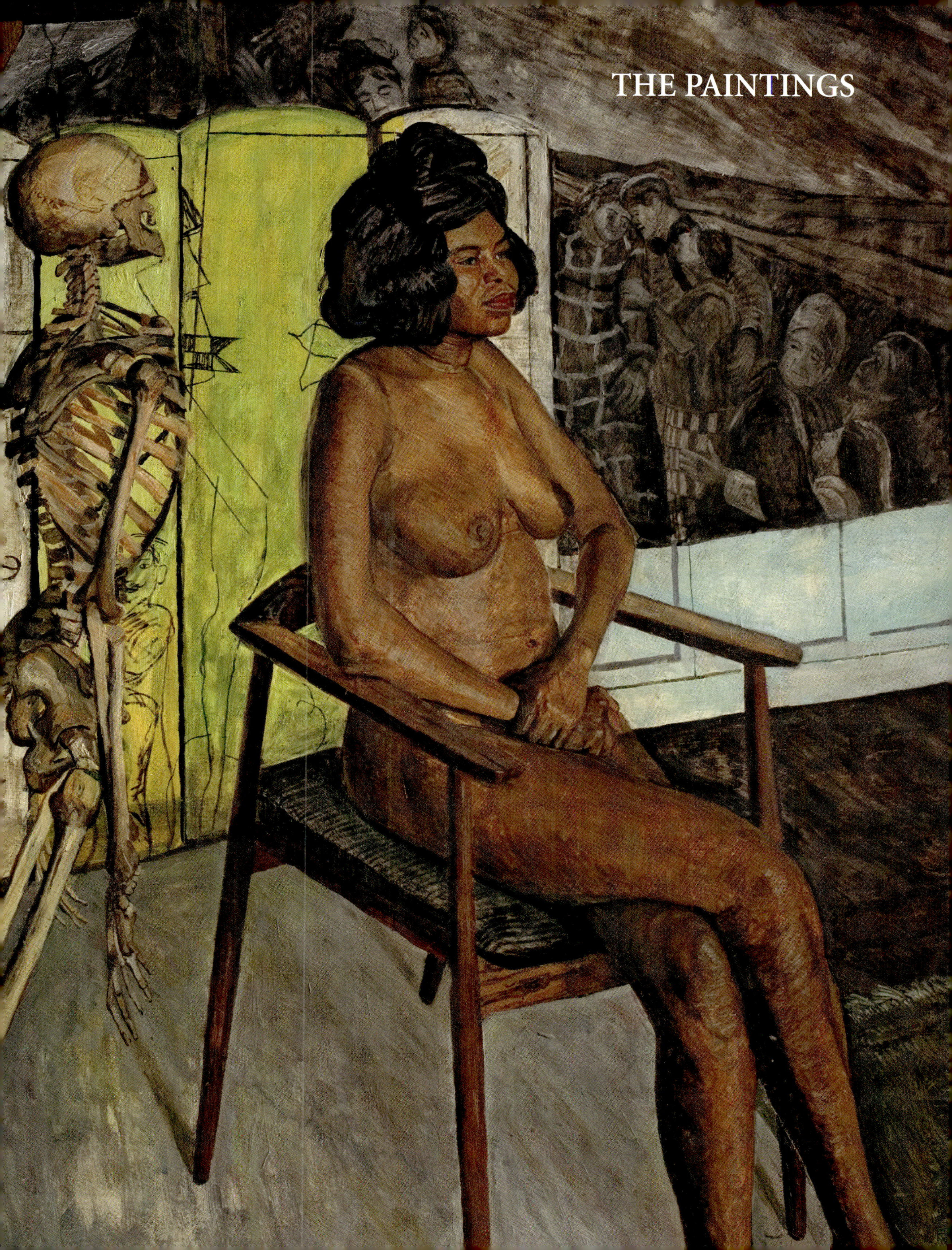

Gedling Borough Council

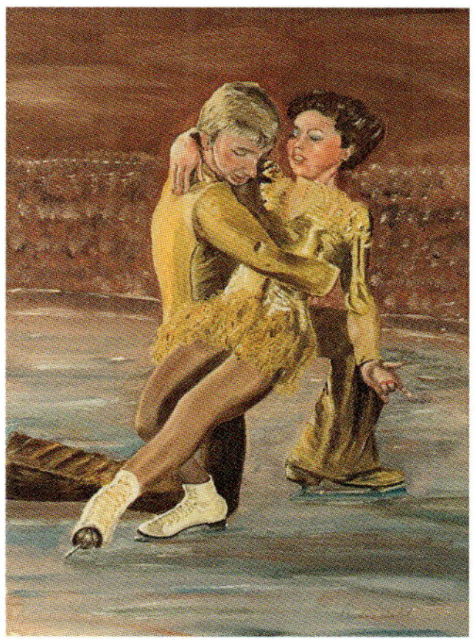

Dodd, Charles J. B.
Jane Torvill and Christopher Dean, Ice Dancing 1984
oil on canvas 40.5 x 30
CV:04

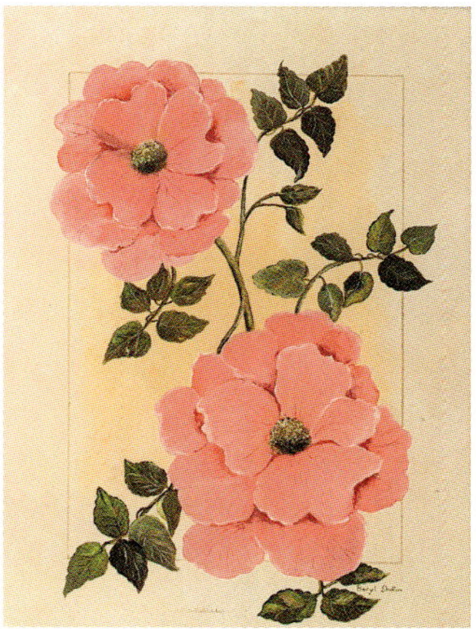

Shelton, Beryl
Camellias
acrylic on board 63.5 x 49
CV:03

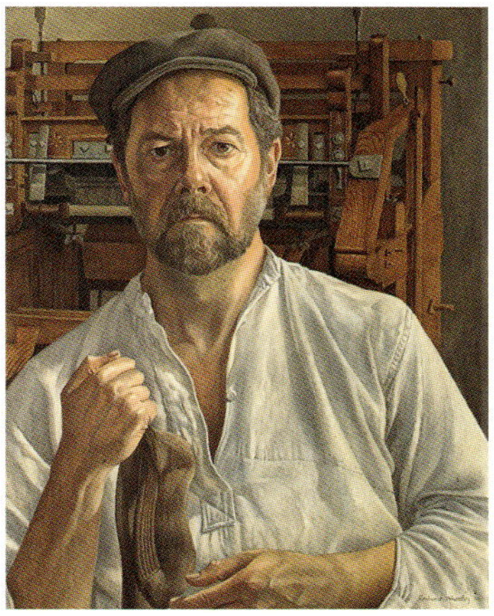

Wheatley, Grahame b.1943
*Self Portrait** 1989
oil on canvas 81.5 x 66.5
CV:01

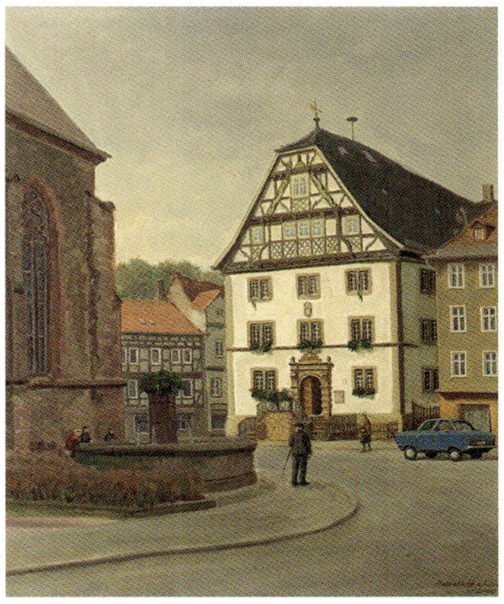

Zirbes, P.
Rothenburg Town Hall, Germany
oil on board 65 x 51.5
CV:02

Ashfield District Council

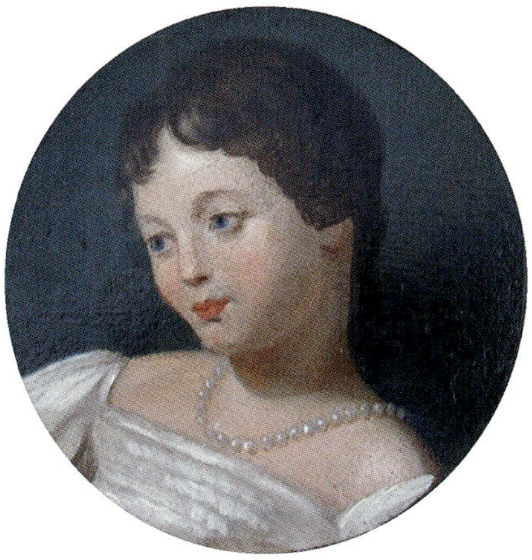

unknown artist
Ada Lovelace (1815–1852)
oil on board 13
PCF1

Langwith Whaley Thorns Heritage Centre

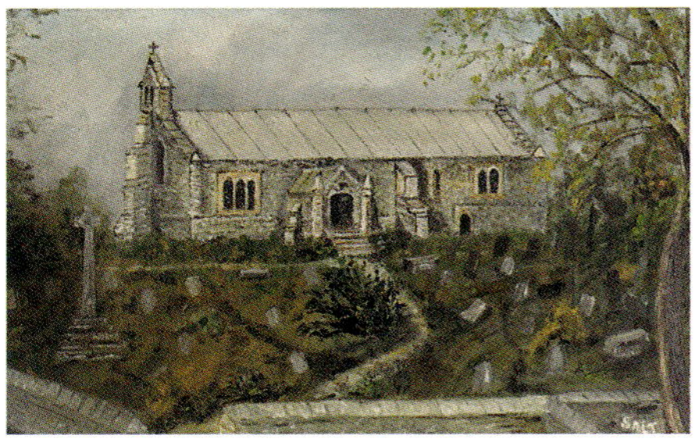

Salt, Les 1916–1986
Holy Cross Church, Upper Langwith, Derbyshire c.1975
oil on canvas 36.5 x 59
AC.002.2008

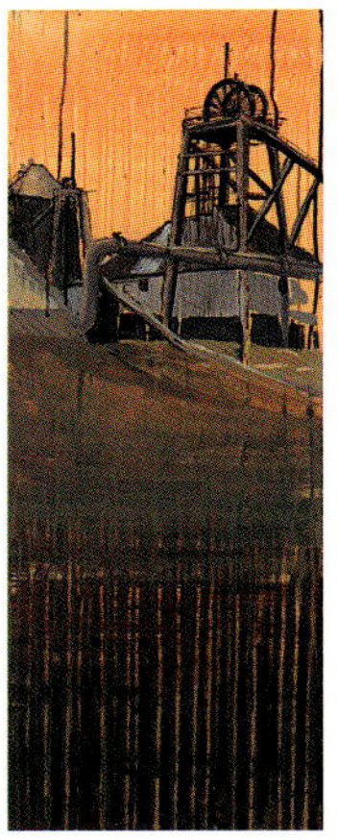

Simons, Stephen b.1984
Pithead Sunset 2007
acrylic & ink on canvas 90.5 x 36
AC.003.2008

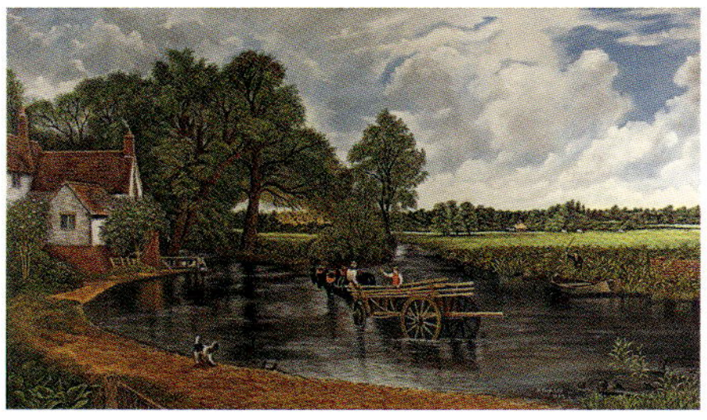

Trolley, Arthur 1914–1985
The Hay Wain (after John Constable) 1983
oil on canvas 71.2 x 122
AC.001.2008

Mansfield District Council

In common with many local museums, Mansfield has an eclectic collection of oil paintings. Acquired over the last century, the paintings range from formal portraits to more naturalistic landscapes, as well as animal studies and still lifes. Numbering some 60 works, they form an important, though minor, part of our collection, which is dominated by the watercolours of Albert Sorby Buxton.

The most recent acquisition is a contemporary representation of an iconic local haberdashery, known affectionately as *Sally Twinkles.* Painted by local artist, Julian Bray, it attracted a lot of attention whilst on display in an exhibition of work by Mansfield painters. As the Museum's collecting policy focuses on items of local interest and manufacture, this painting seemed a natural addition to the Collection.

The larger, older paintings came to the Museum by way of Mansfield District Council who had displayed them in their former offices at Carr Bank

Park. On moving to a purpose-built Civic Centre in 1987 the Council transferred the paintings to the Museum. Of particular note are three examples of the work of Wright Barker who exhibited from 1891 to 1938 at the Royal Academy and who was resident for a time in Mansfield. Of the others it is unfortunate that the Museum has little information about the imposing sitter of *A Lady in a Black Dress* painted by an unknown artist, about whose prestigious local lineage we can only speculate.

Amongst other notable acquisitions are three examples of the work of Hector McDonald Sutton. Born in 1903, this portrait painter and innovator was always looking at new techniques and styles and helped push back the boundaries of Modernism. Before his death in the early 1990s the Museum was fortunate to receive two separate gifts of his work to add to *King John's Palace, Clipstone, Nottinghamshire*, which had been in the Museum's collection a number of years. Again, the local connection is evident in the fact that Sutton was for many years President of the Mansfield Society of Artists, as well as being the Principal of the College of Art and Art Advisor for the County.

At present virtually all the oil paintings are in storage and therefore we are grateful to the Public Catalogue Foundation for the inclusion of our paintings in this publication, which offers the possibility of bringing them to the attention of a wider audience.

Liz Weston, Curator

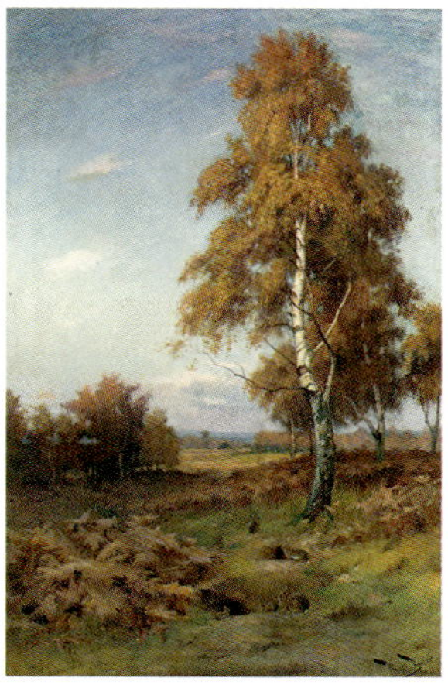

Barker, Wright 1864–1941
Tree and Rabbits 1894
oil on canvas 123.2 x 82.7
MASMG PA 136

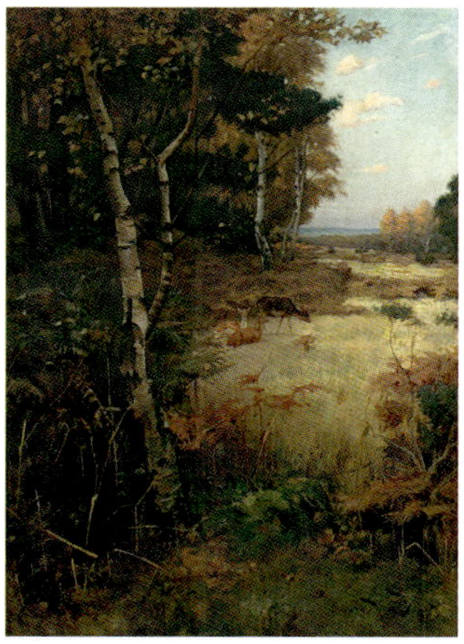

Barker, Wright 1864–1941
Deer in a Forest
oil on canvas 140.4 x 89.8
MASMG PA 137

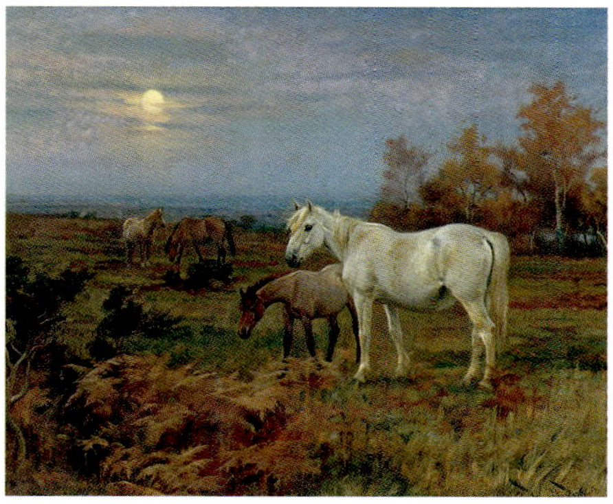

Barker, Wright 1864–1941
*Horses in a Paddock**
oil on canvas 70 x 90.2
MASMG Pa 141

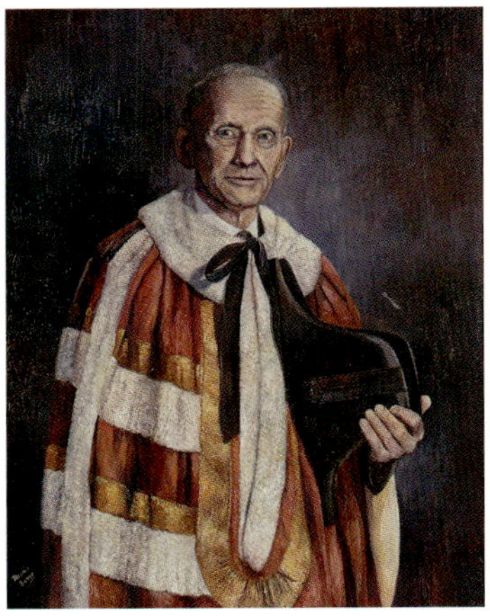

Barron, Dennis active 1999–2001
Baron Taylor of Mansfield (1895–1991), MP for Mansfield (1941–1966)
oil on canvas 60.5 x 51.8
MASMG Pa 507

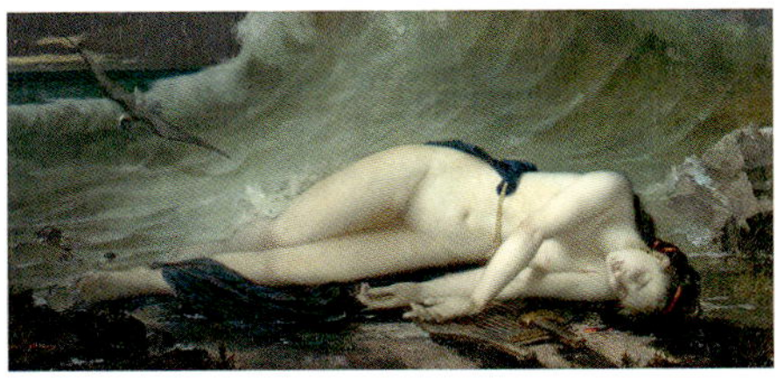

Bertrand, James 1823–1887
Lady on the Beach
oil on canvas 65.2 x 138.3
MASMG Pa 140

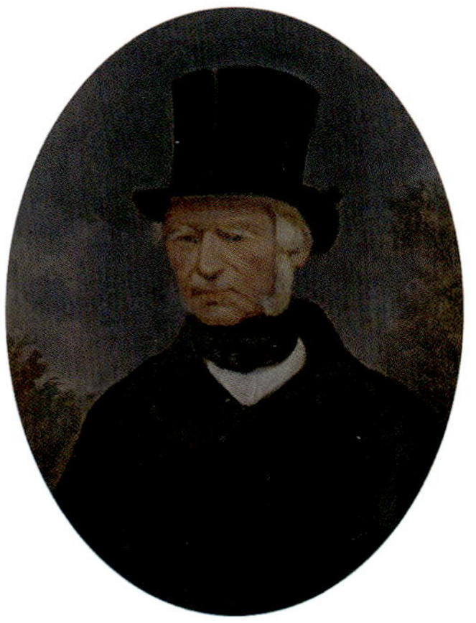

Birks, J.
Sebastian Sales, Official Town Crier for Mansfield (1827–1853) c.1852
oil on board 34.2 x 26.5
MASMG Pa 128

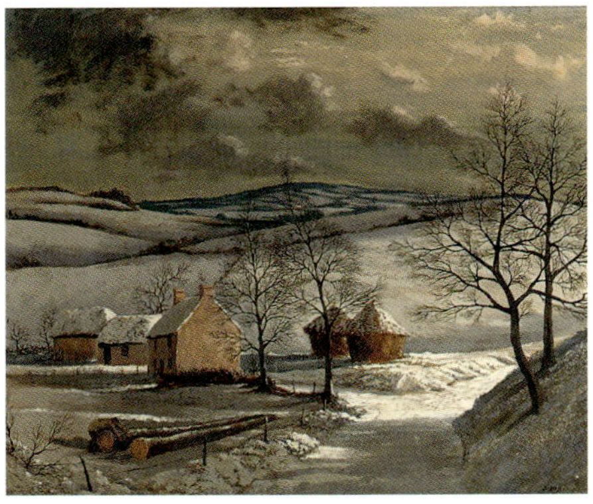

Bissill, George William 1896–1973
Zell's Farm, Winter, Hampshire
oil on canvas 74.6 x 90.1
MASMG Pa 34

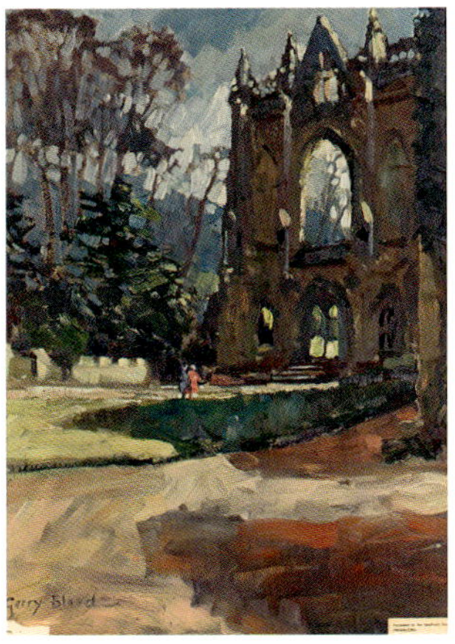

Blood, Gerry 1932–2005
Newstead Abbey, December 1965
oil on board 77.8 x 59.4
MASMG Pa 57

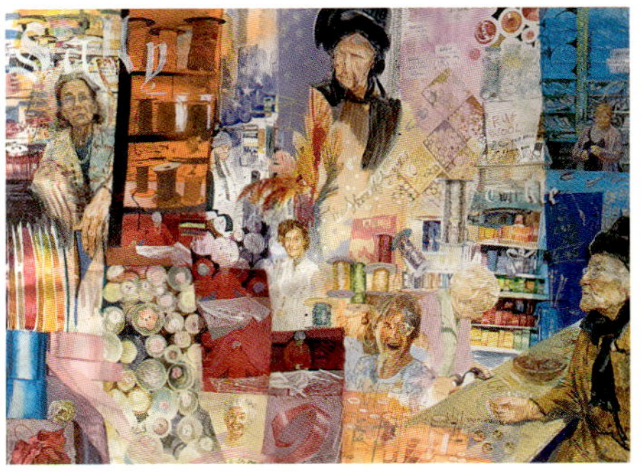

Bray, Julian b.1965
Sally Twinkles 2007
acrylic & mixed media on board 62 x 88
MASMG Pa 508

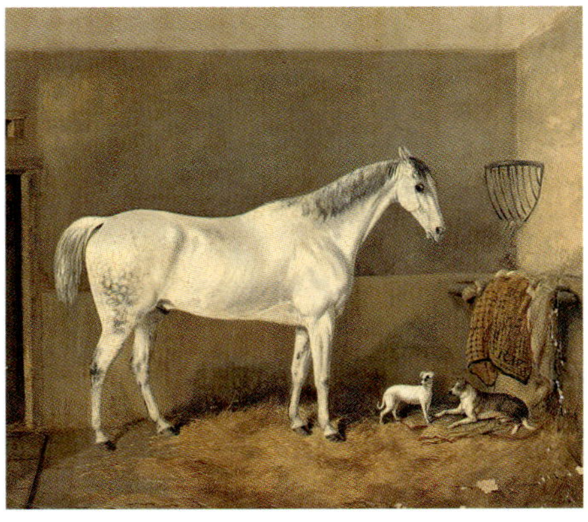

Bretland, Thomas W. 1802–1874
Horse Owned by Mr Robert White 1838
oil on canvas 61.6 x 74.6
MASMG Pa 30a

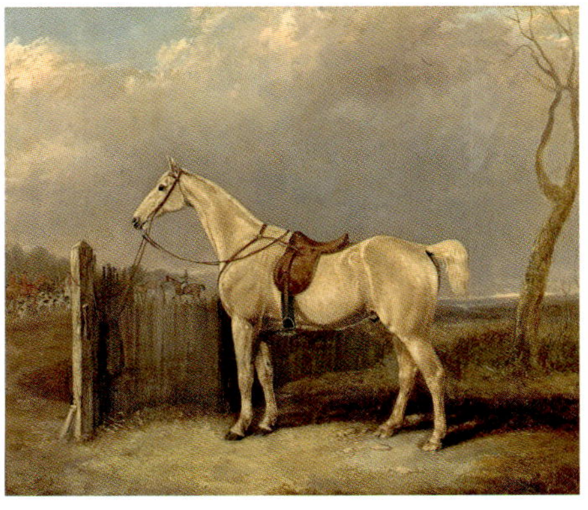

Bretland, Thomas W. 1802–1874
Tethered Horse and Hunt
oil on canvas 61.8 x 74.4
MASMG Pa 30b

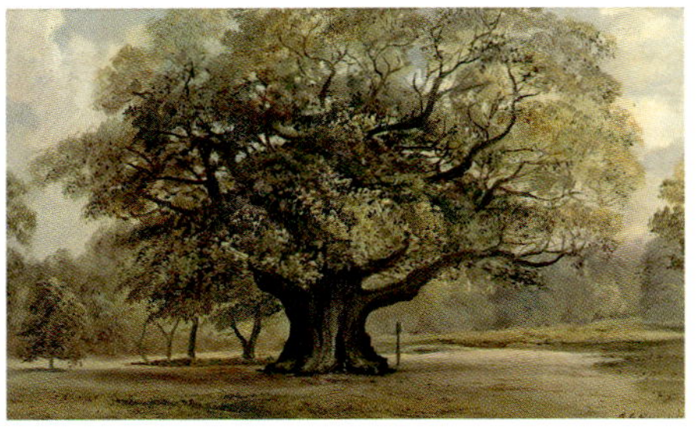

Bywater, J. E.
Major Oak
oil on canvas 29.2 x 49.2
MASMG 45

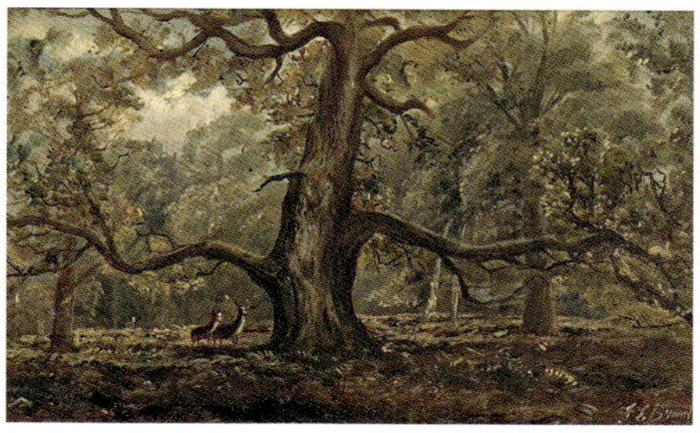

Bywater, J. E.
Oak
oil on canvas 29.2 x 49.2
MASMG 46

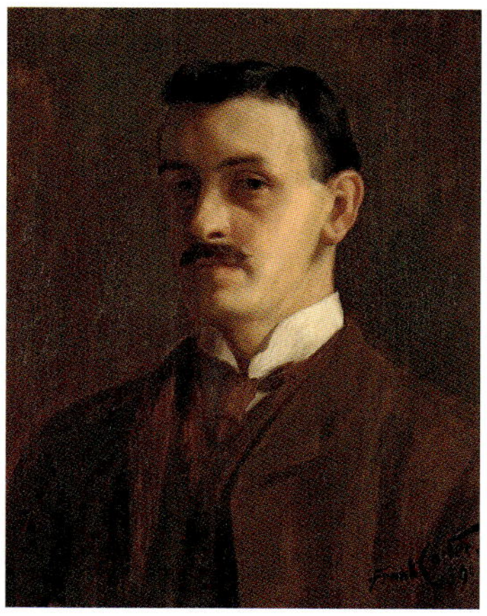

Carter, Frank
Albert Sorby Buxton (1867–1932) 1891
oil on canvas 52 x 42
MASMG Pa 509

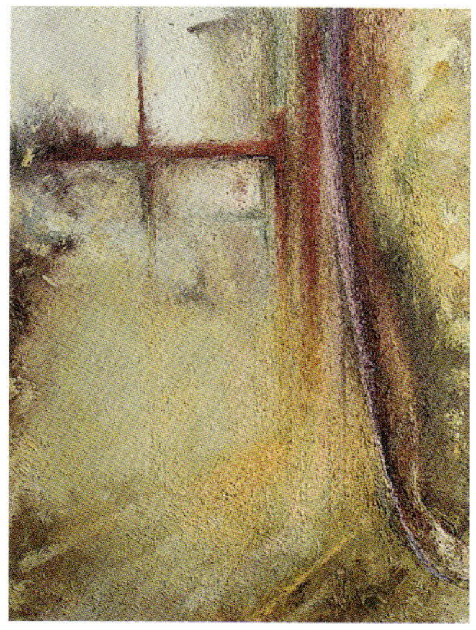

Clark, Heath Richard b.1970
Window II 1996–1997
oil on canvas 136.5 x 104.3
MASMG Pa 490

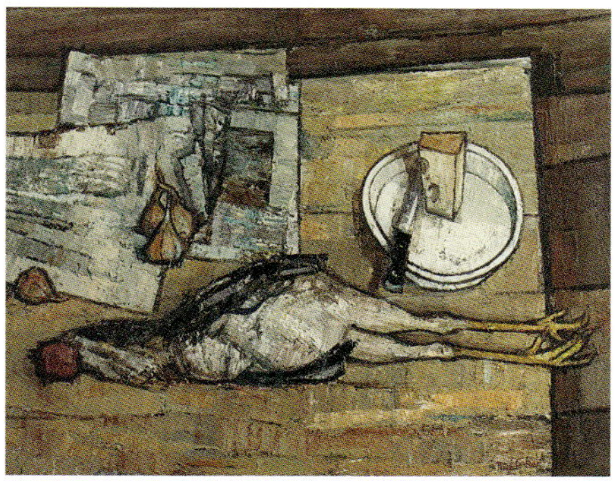

Coker, Peter 1926–2004
Still Life with Chicken
oil on canvas 90.8 x 121.5
MASMG Pa 59

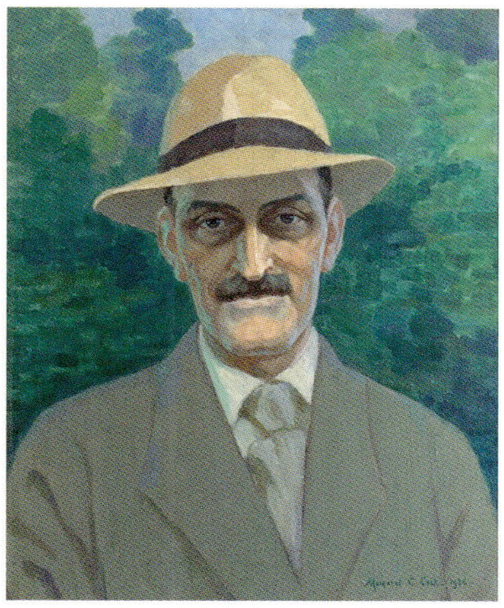

Cook, Margaret C. b.c.1897
Posthumous Portrait of Albert Sorby Buxton (1867–1932) 1936
oil on canvas 57.5 x 49.8
MASMG Pa 94

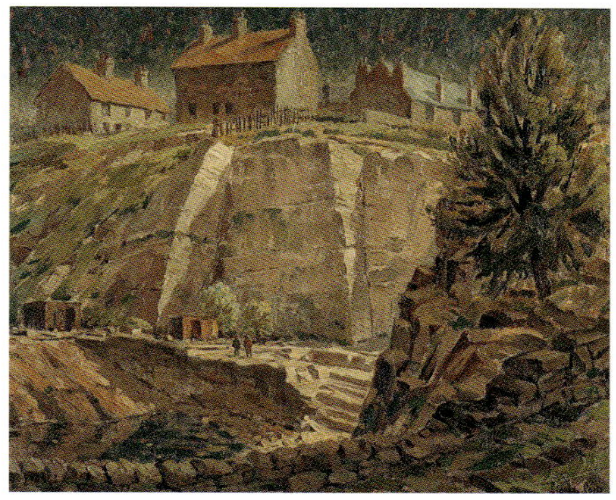

Cooke, Stanley b.1913
Quarry at Mansfield 1952
oil on canvas laid on hardboard 53 x 68.8
MASMG Pa 32

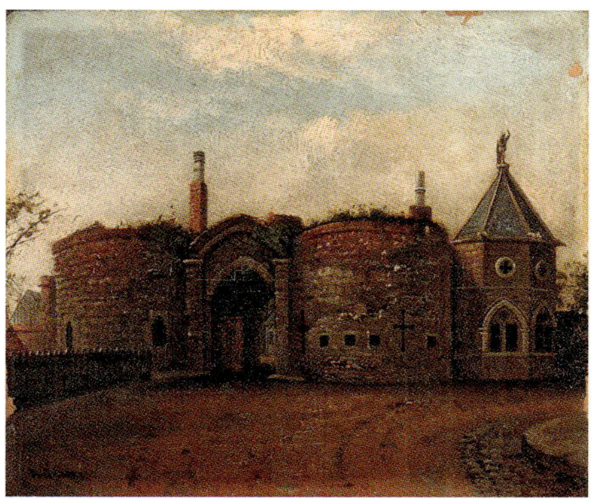

Gilbert, A.
Castle Gateway, Nottingham
oil on board 20.2 x 25.1
MASMG Pa 168

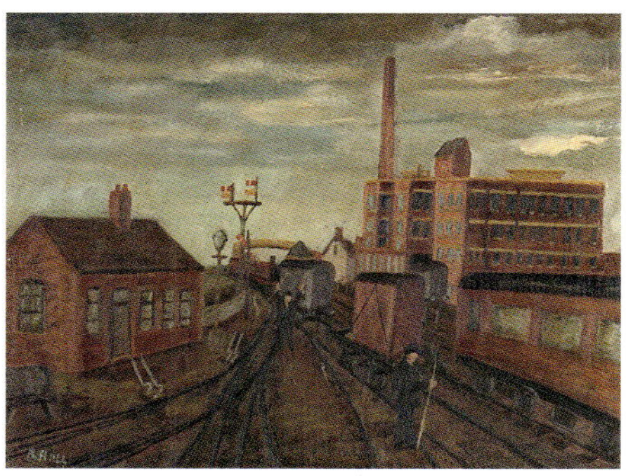

Hall, R. active 1971
Goods Marshalling Yard, Mansfield, London, Midland and Scottish Railway
oil on canvas 49.2 x 68
MASMG Pa 70

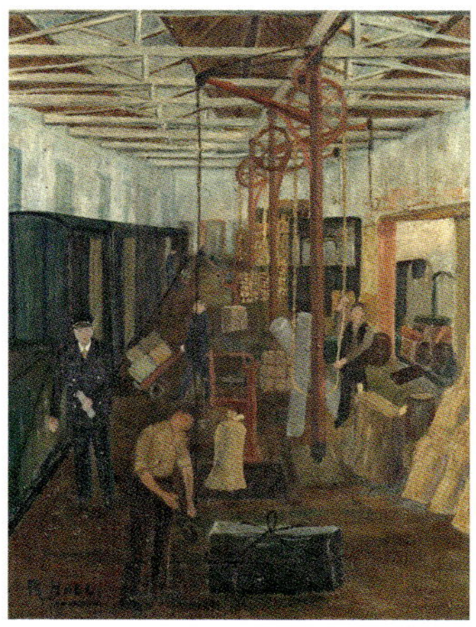

Hall, R. active 1971
Goods Shed, Mansfield, London, Midland and Scottish Railway
oil on canvas 53.1 x 41.3
MASMG Pa 69

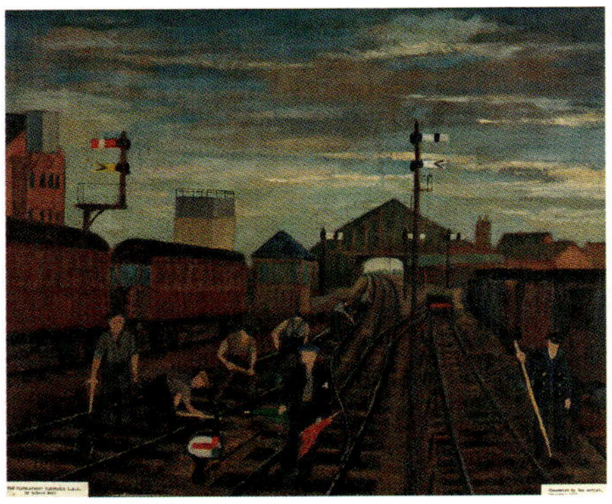

Hall, R. active 1971
The Platelayers, Mansfield, London, Midland and Scottish Railway
oil on canvas 49 x 62.2
MASMG Pa 71

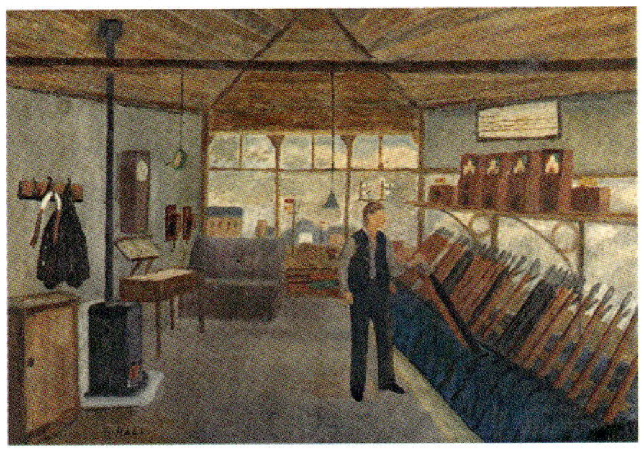

Hall, R. active 1971
The Signal Box, Mansfield, London, Midland and Scottish Railway
oil on canvas 39.7 x 59.1
MASMG Pa 68

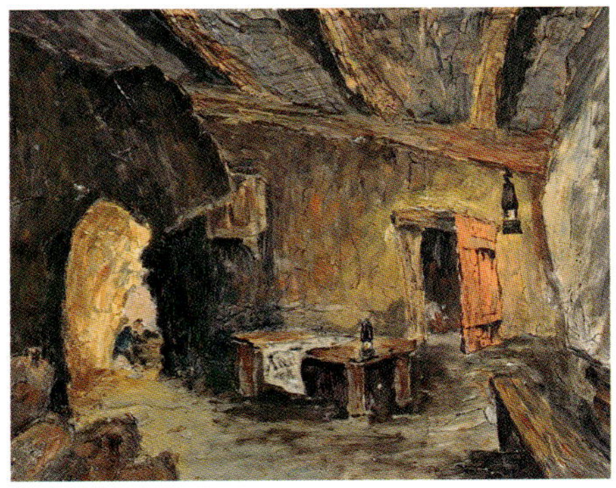

Hampson, John b.1898
Fireman's Cabin
oil on canvas 32.4 x 42.6
MASMG Pa 21

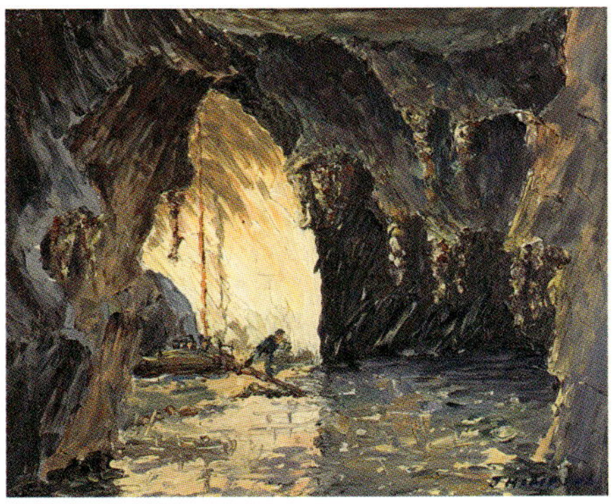

Hampson, John b.1898
Water Level
oil on canvas 39.3 x 49.3
MASMG Pa19

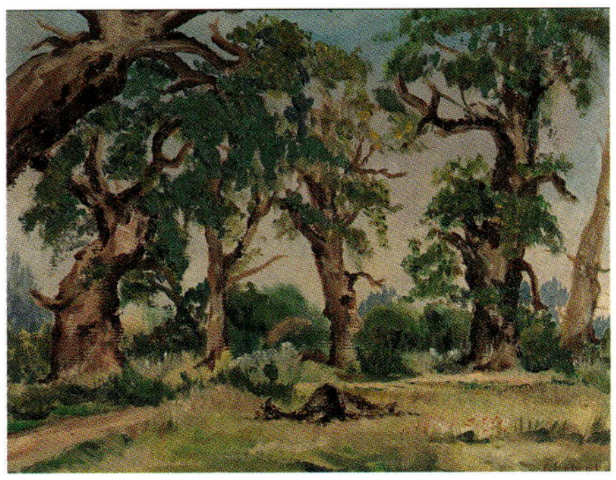

Harbord, R. C.
Old Oaks in Sherwood Forest
oil on hardboard 29.3 x 39.9
MASMG Pa 74

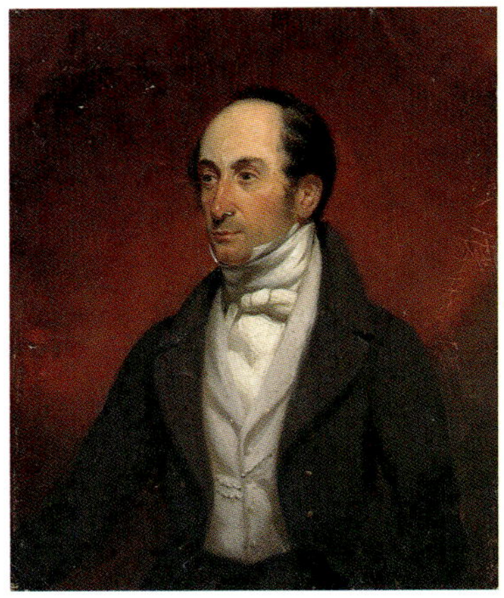

Hill, Chas G.
James Sorby (b.1794) 1836
oil on canvas 29.5 x 24.8
MASMG Pa 129

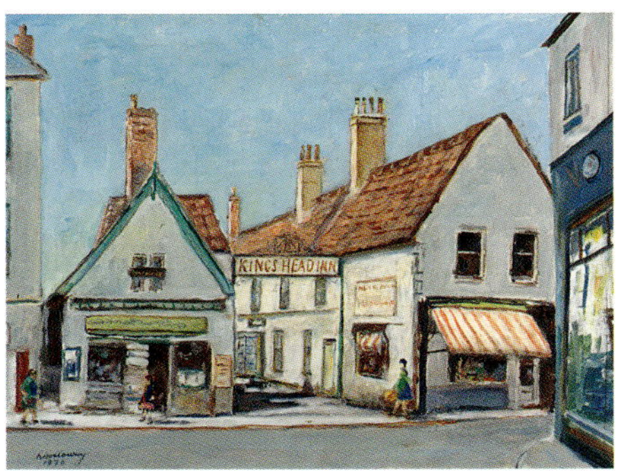

Holloway, Robert 1896–1976
Old Mansfield, Nottinghamshire 1970
oil on hardboard 39.3 x 54.5
MASMG Pa 64

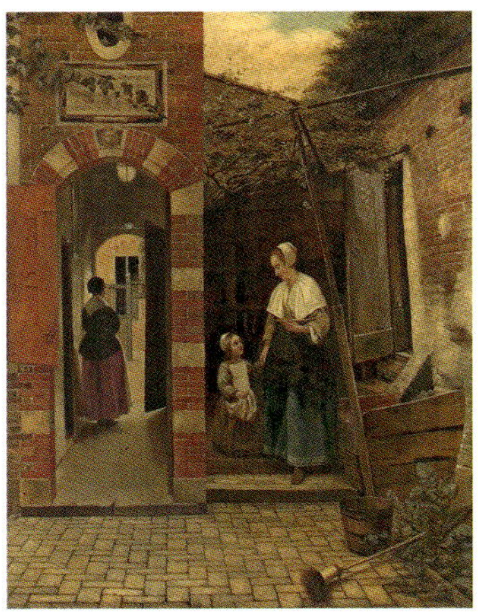

Hooch, Pieter de (copy of) 1629–1684
The Courtyard of a House in Delft
oil on canvas 122.5 x 58.5 (E)
MASMG Pa 495

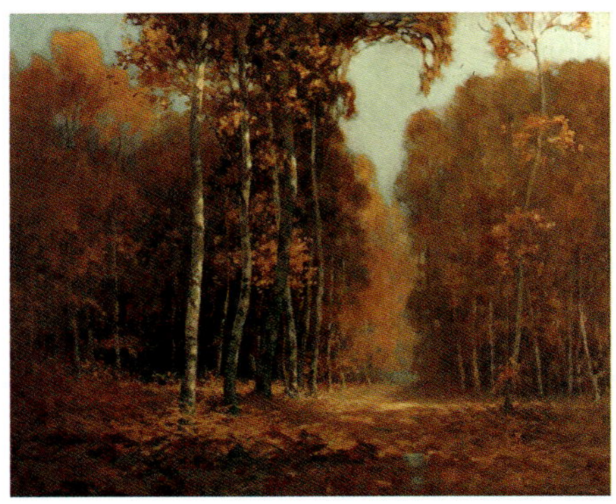

Jones, Tom
Early Autumn, Sherwood Forest, Nottinghamshire
oil on canvas 69.5 x 89.5
MASMG Pa 142

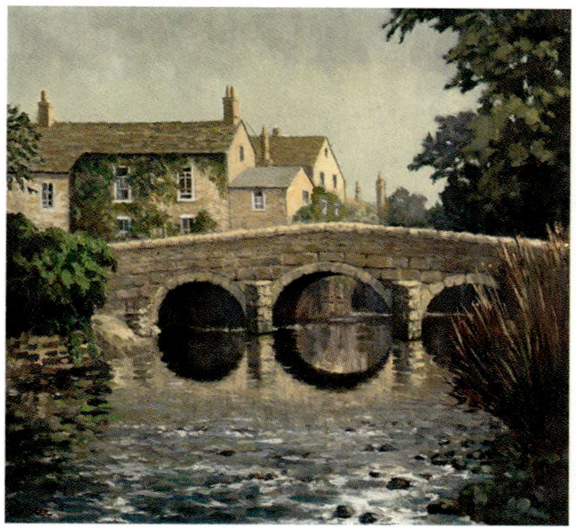

Kidger, C. W.
The Old Bridge, Baslow, Derbyshire
oil on hardboard 44.2 x 49.4
MASMG 54

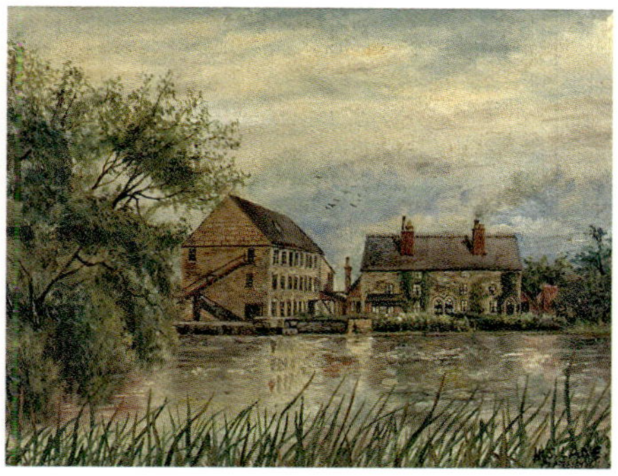

Lane, H. S.
Reed Mill, Mansfield, Nottinghamshire 1916
oil on canvas 24 x 33.6
MASMG Pa 73

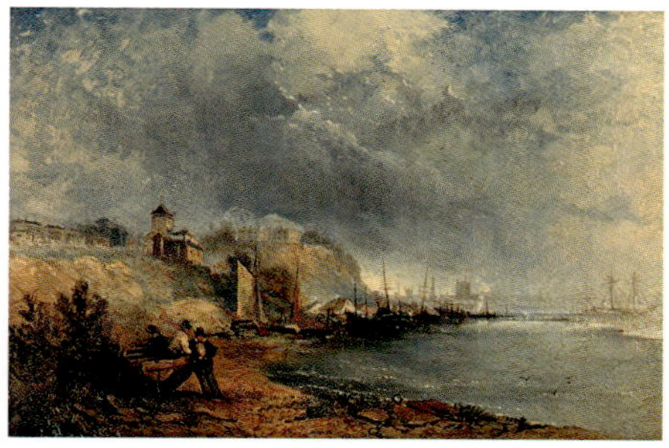

Moore, Thomas Cooper (attributed to)
1827–1901
Harbour and Ships
oil on canvas 29.2 x 44.2
MASMG Pa 191

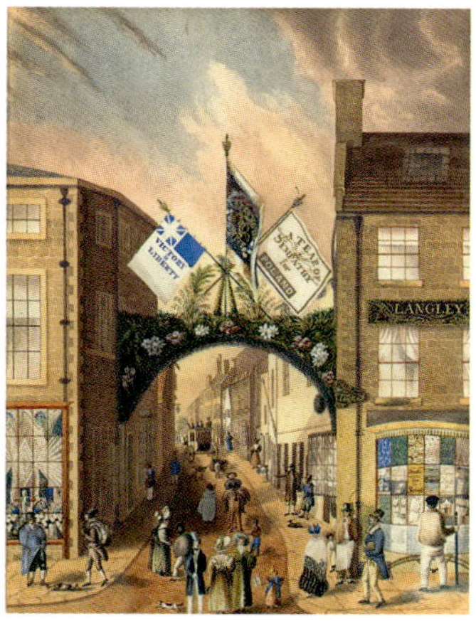

Paulson, Ann 1808–1866
Victory Arch 1833
oil on paper 44.3 x 33.6
MASMG Pa 188

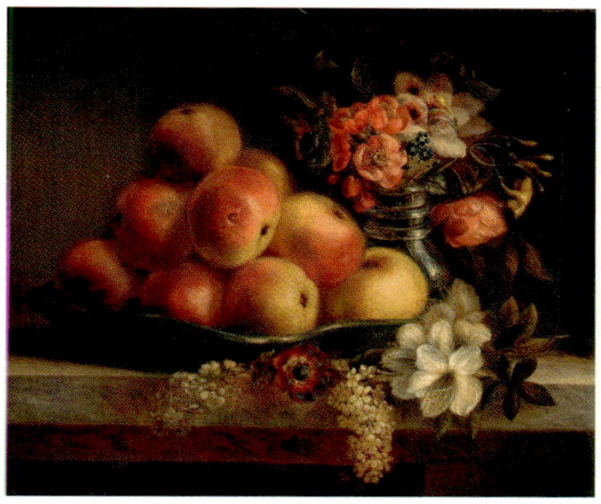

Paulson, Ann 1808–1866
Apples and Flowers
oil on canvas 35.7 x 44
MASMG Pa 30g

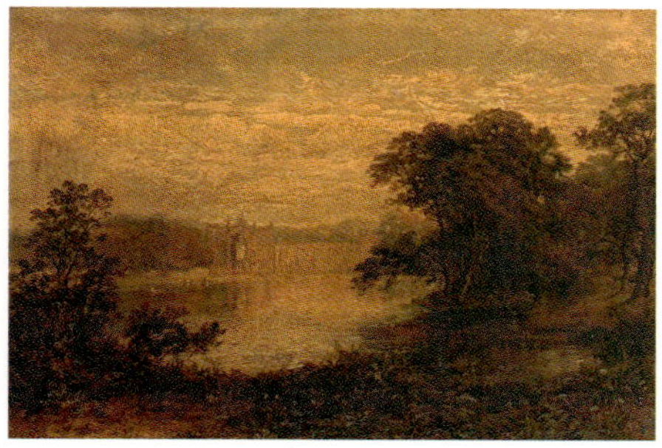

Payne, David c.1844–1891
Newstead Abbey, Nottinghamshire
oil on canvas 49.7 x 75.4
MASMG Pa 96

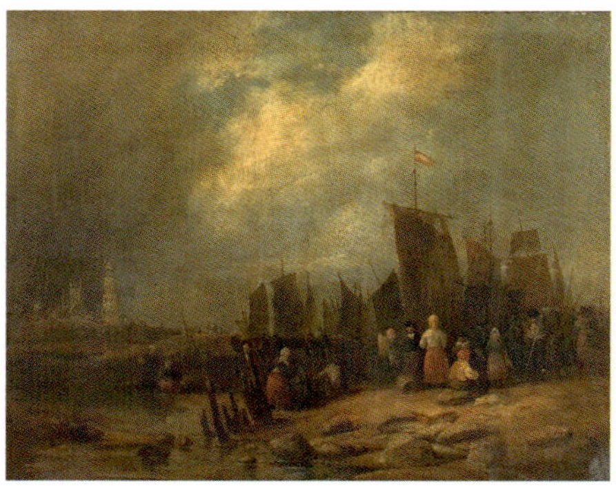

Pickin, E. M. (attributed to)
After the Shipwreck
oil on canvas 82.5 x 118
MASMG Pa 493

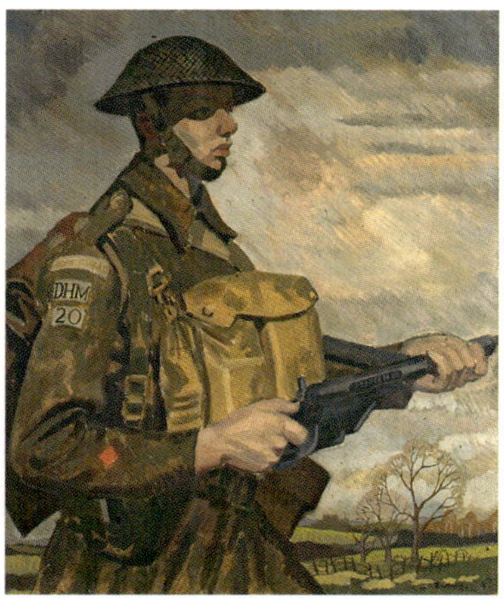

Powell, Ella Ffolliott c.1887–1943
Home Guard 1943
oil on hardboard 67 x 59.8
MASMG Pa 121

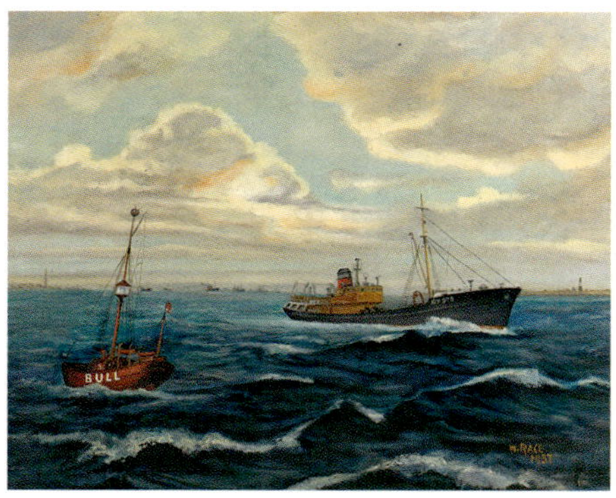

Race, W.
Grimbsy Trawlers Leaving the Humber 1957
oil on canvas 59 x 78
MASMG 38

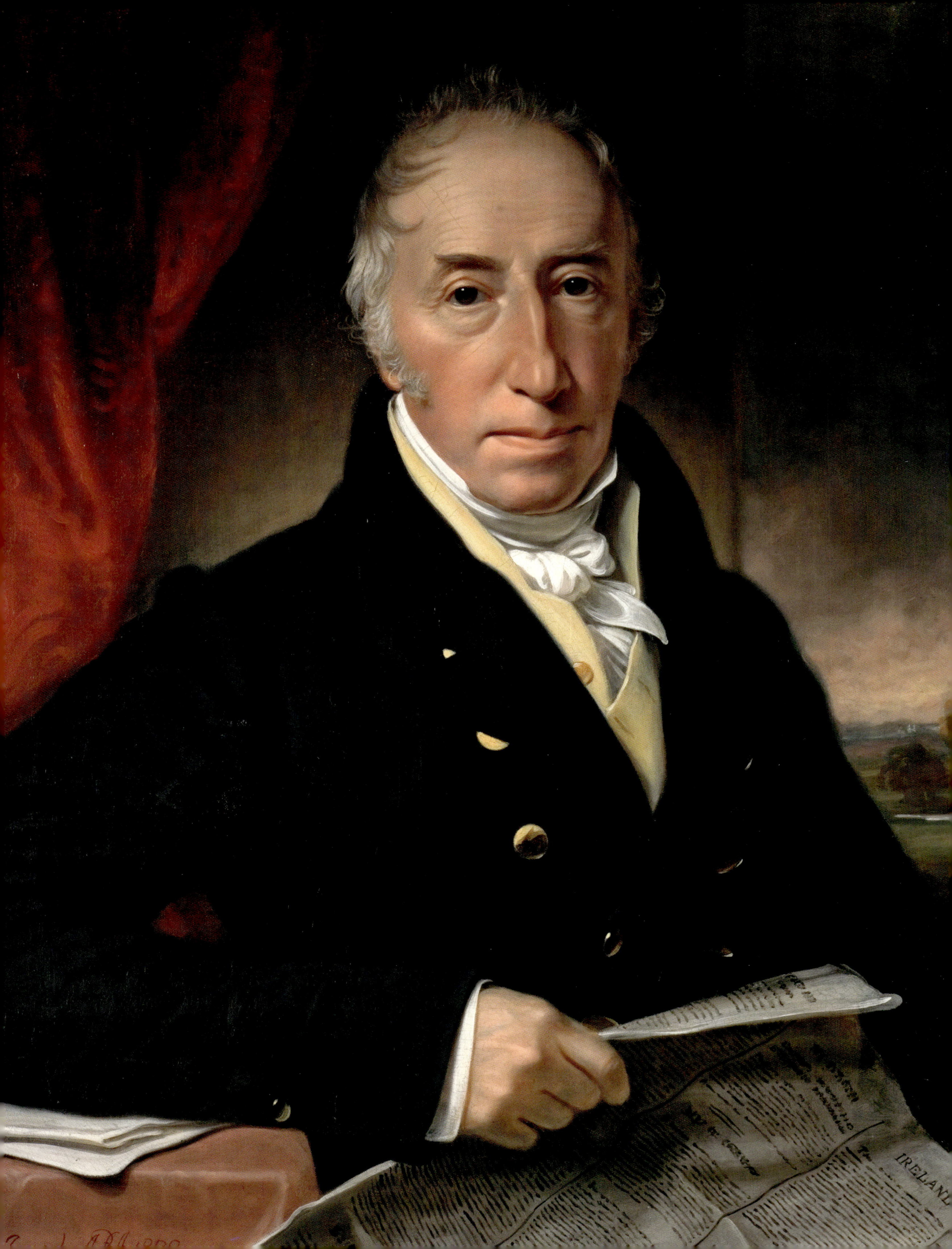
IRELAND

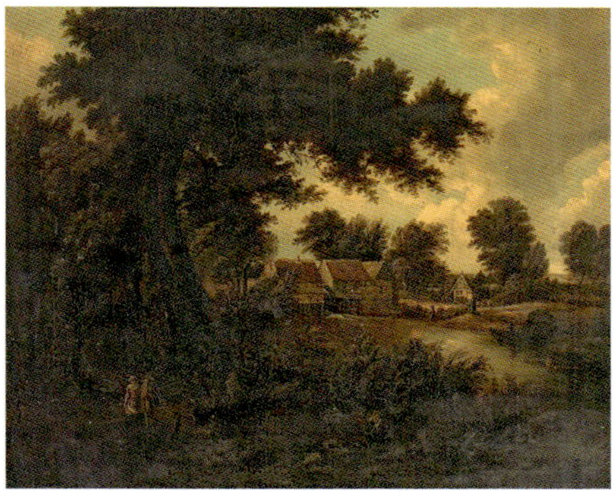

Royce active 19th C
Landscape with Watermill
oil on canvas 58.8 x 74.6
MASMG Pa 143

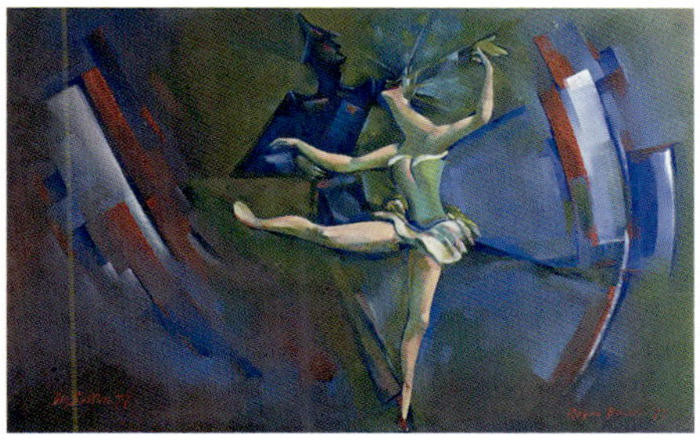

Sutton, Hector McDonald 1903–1992
Royal Ballet 1977
oil on board 94 x 150
MASMG Pa 482

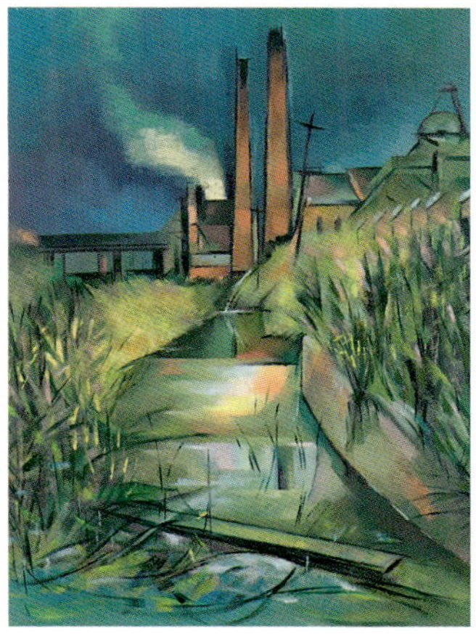

Sutton, Hector McDonald 1903–1992
Brookhill Colliery, Pinxton, Derbyshire
oil on canvas 54.9 x 43.2
MASMG Pa 497

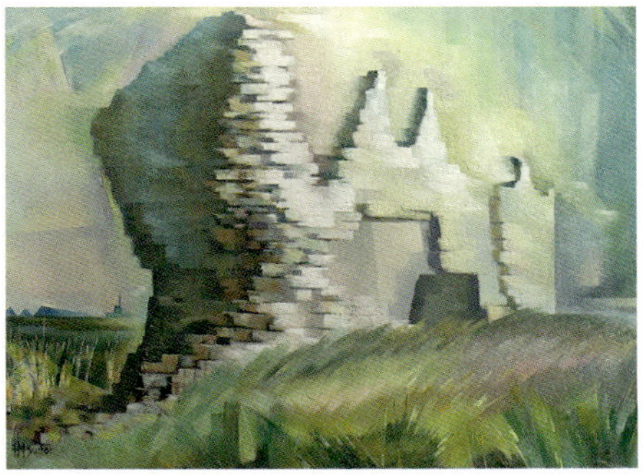

Sutton, Hector McDonald 1903–1992
King John's Palace, Clipstone, Nottinghamshire
oil on hardboard 72.5 x 103.5
MASMG Pa 72

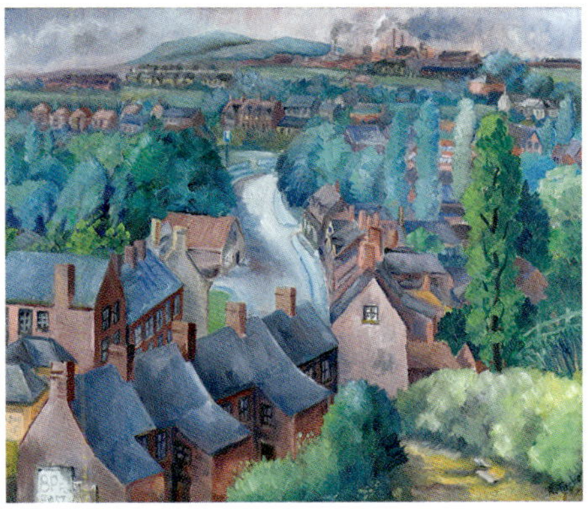

Tucker, R.
Pleasley, Nottinghamshire
oil on canvas 50 x 60
MASMG Pa 58

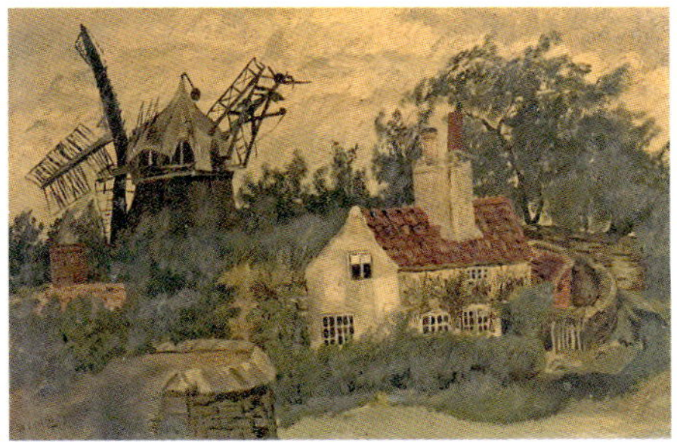

Tyndall, W. Castell
Jackson's Mill, Mansfield, Nottinghamshire
oil on board 30.1 x 46.4
MASMG Pa 56

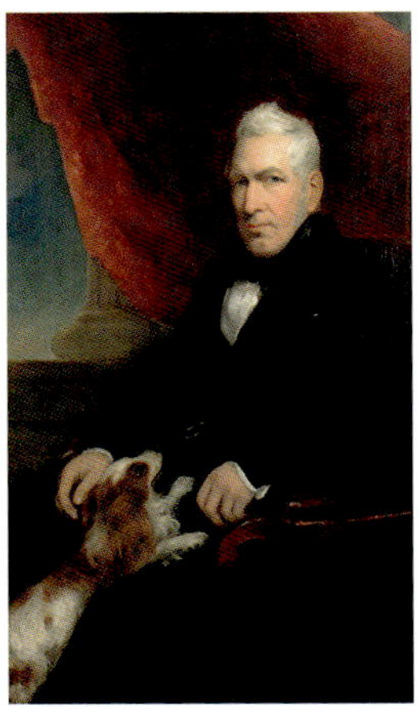

unknown artist early 19th C
Mr Mumford, Former Squire of Mansfield
oil on canvas 137 x 92
MASMG Pa 91

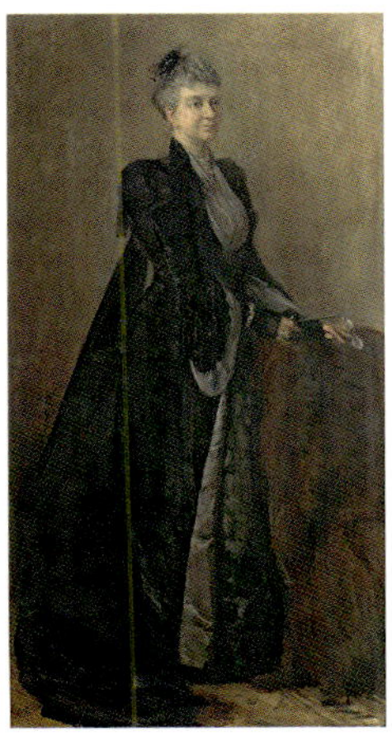

unknown artist
A Lady in a Black Dress
oil on canvas 199.2 x 108
MASMG Pa 494

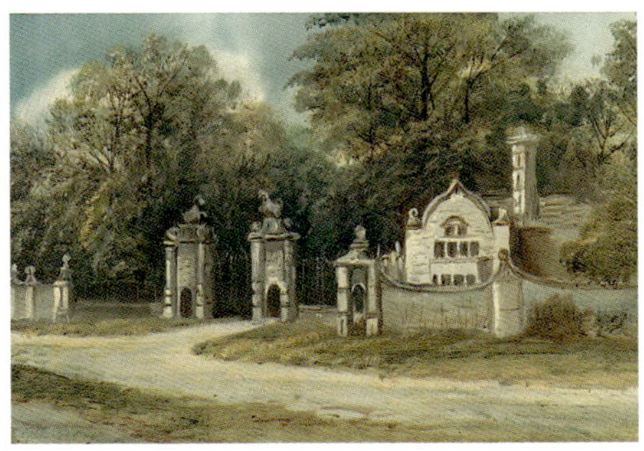

unknown artist
Buck Gates, Thoresby Estate, Nottinghamshire
oil on canvas 19 x 29.2
MASMG Pa 43

Facing page: Joseph, George Francis, 1764–1846, *Unidentified Man from the Bristowe Family* (detail), 1828, Nottinghamshire Archives (p. 173)

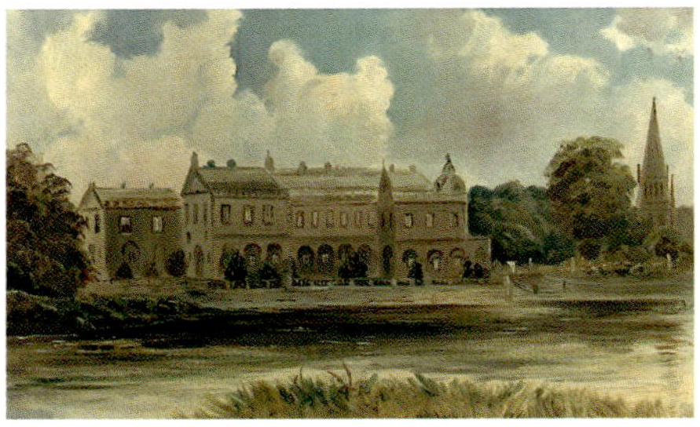

unknown artist
Clumber House, Nottinghamshire
oil on canvas 29.2 x 49.4
MASMG 48

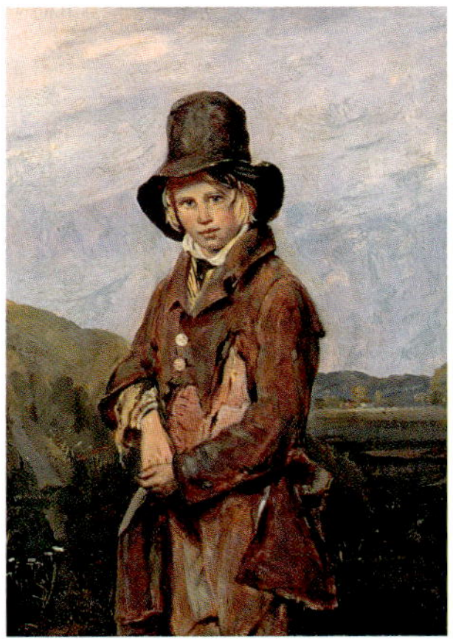

unknown artist
Gypsy Boy
oil on board 30.6 x 22.9
MASMG Pa 30i

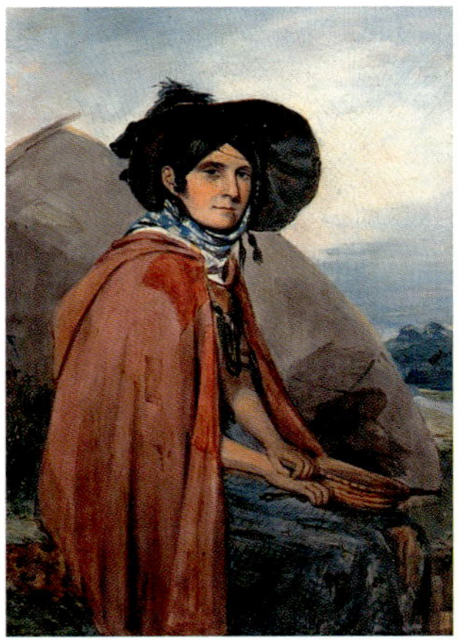

unknown artist
Gypsy Girl
oil on board 30.6 x 22.9
MASMG Pa 30h

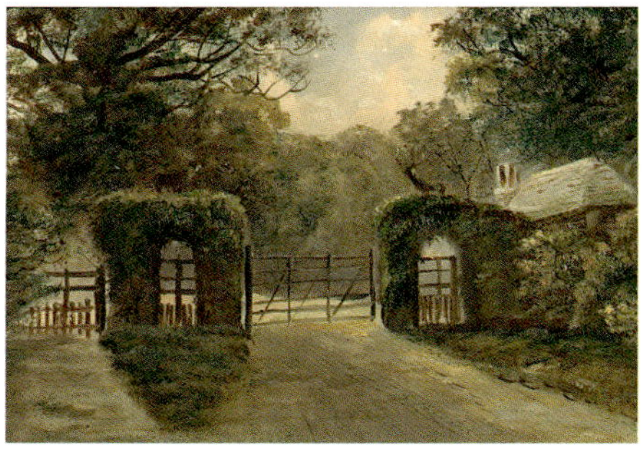

unknown artist
Lodge Gates, Thoresby Estate, Nottinghamshire
oil on canvas 19.2 x 28.9
MASMG Pa 44

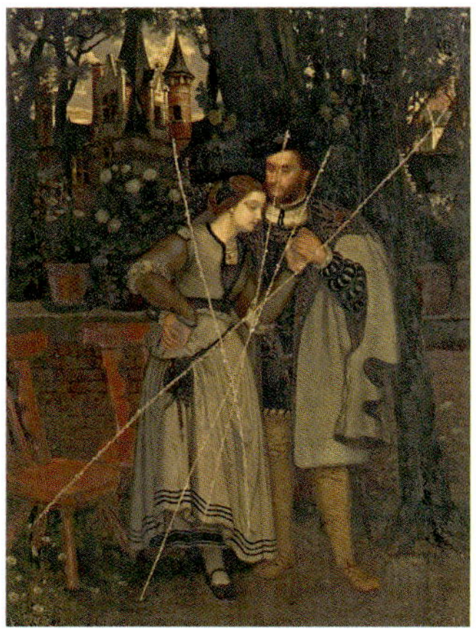

unknown artist
Man and Woman
oil on canvas 57.8 x 43.6
MASMG Pa 496

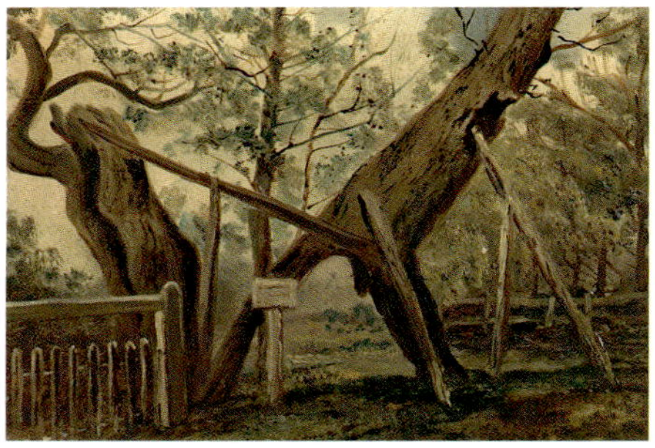

unknown artist
*Oak in Sherwood Forest No.1**
oil on canvas 20.5 x 30.6
MASMG Pa 505

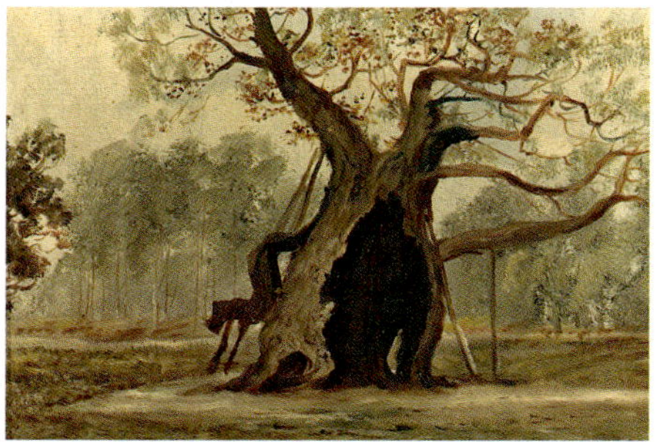

unknown artist
*Oak in Sherwood Forest No.2**
oil on canvas 20.5 x 30.6
MASMG Pa 506

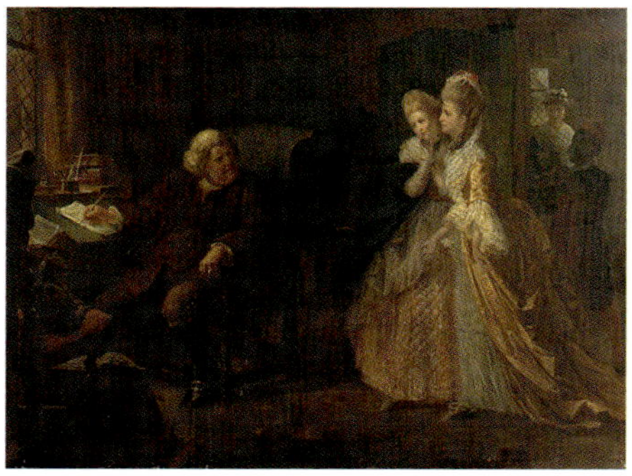

unknown artist
Old Man at a Desk
oil on canvas 101 x 139.6
MASMG Pa 492

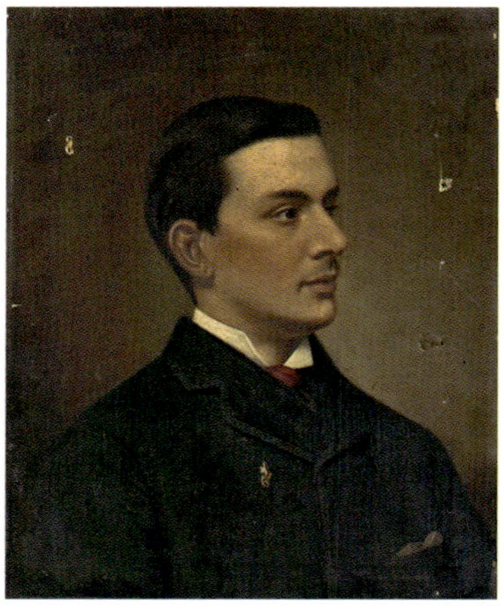

unknown artist
Portrait of an Unknown Man
oil on canvas 47 x 39.4
MASMG Pa 119

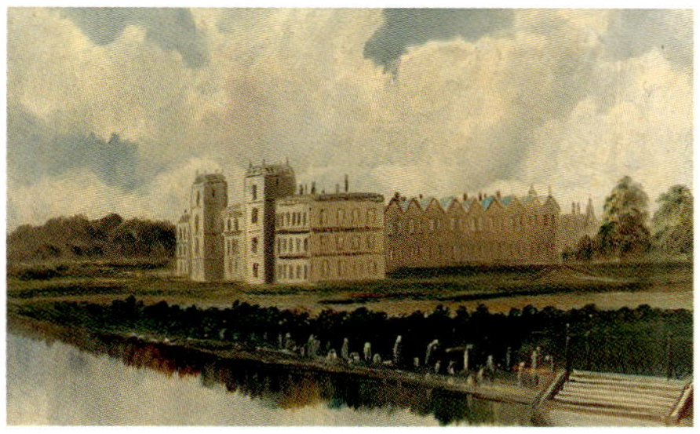

unknown artist
Welbeck Abbey, Nottinghamshire
oil on canvas 29 x 49.3
MASMG 47

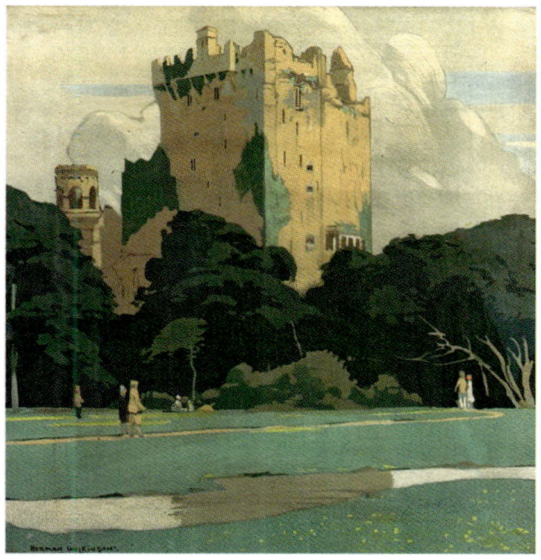

Wilkinson, Norman 1878–1972
*Castle**
oil on canvas 54.7 x 54.7
MASMG Pa 190

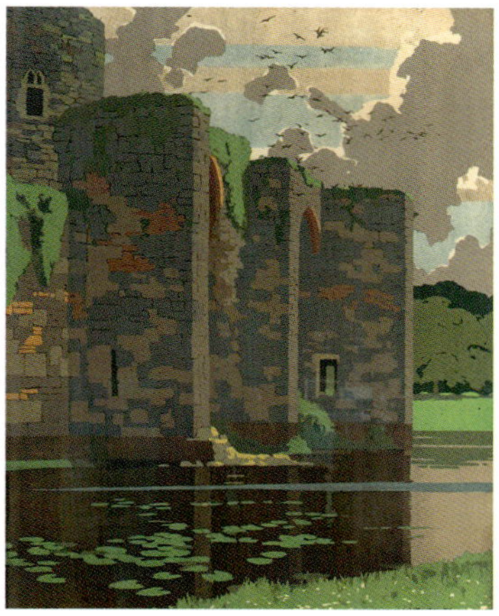

Wilkinson, Norman 1878–1972
Castle and Moat
oil on canvas 71.5 x 59
MASMG Pa 189

Mansfield Fire Station Museum

Mansfield Fire Station Museum, founded and run by a group of volunteers, first opened at the old Mansfield Fire Station in 1977. It transferred to the fire station's new site, the former Nottinghamshire Fire Brigade Training School at the rear of the new Mansfield Fire Station, in 1997. The two paintings by local artist Dennis Barron were commissioned to mark the opening of the new station.

The Museum's aim is to collect, preserve and exhibit to the public. Over the years volunteers have built up an impressive collection of photographs, fire service badges, fire-fighting equipment and memorabilia, as well as a wealth of knowledge of fire-fighting history.

In 1989 the Museum was appointed custodian of the Merryweather Collection, a collection of Fire Service memorabilia from the Merryweather Fire Engineers in London, which included the portrait of Captain Merryweather by Amy Walton.

Another key feature of the Collection is a water squirt once used in the Great Fire of London in 1666. Prior to this historic fire, London had no organised fire protection system. Afterwards, insurance companies formed private fire brigades to protect their clients' property. Painted insurance badges or signs, such as the examples found at the Museum, were placed outside buildings which were insured. Brigades would only fight fires at buildings that displayed their badge.

The Museum can be opened by appointment for anyone who wants to look around and is free of charge.

Terry Spalding, Museum Secretary

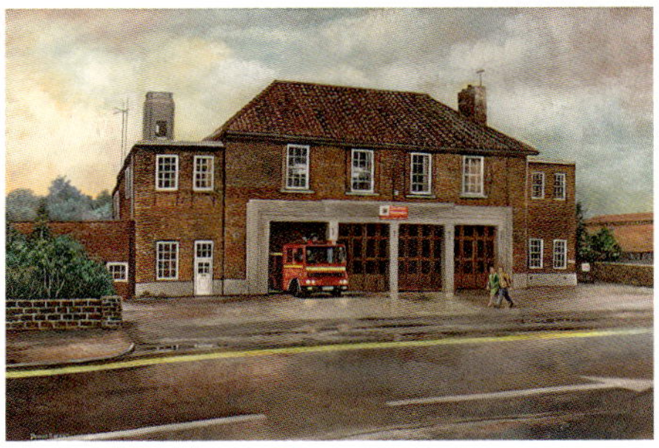

Barron, Dennis active 1999–2001
The Old Borough of Mansfield Fire Station (built in 1939) 1999
oil on canvas 50 x 74.5
MFS.temp2

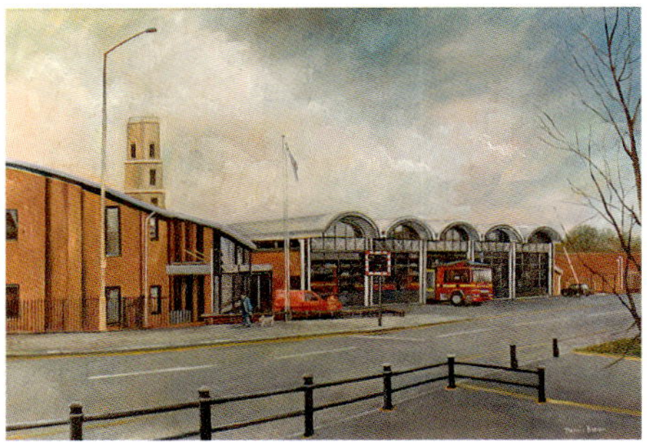

Barron, Dennis active 1999–2001
The New Mansfield Fire Station (built in 1997) 2001
oil on canvas 50 x 74.5
MFS.temp3

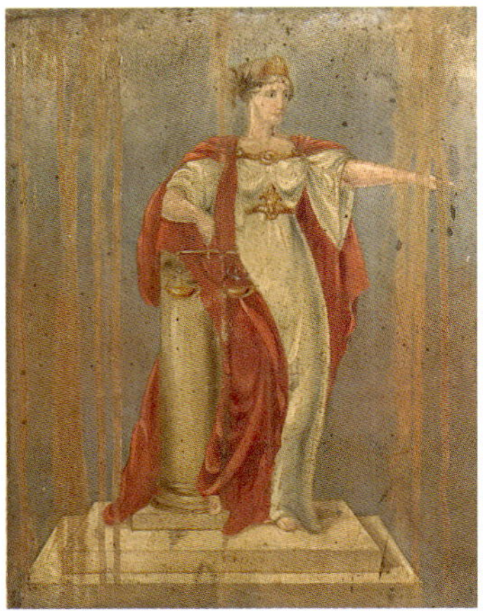

unknown artist
Fire Insurance Badge (1)*
oil on wood 28 x 22
MFS.C47

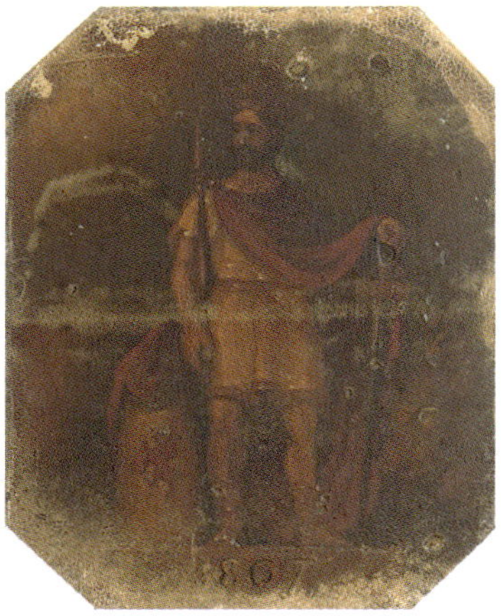

unknown artist
Fire Insurance Badge (2)*
oil on wood 27 x 23
MFS.D1A

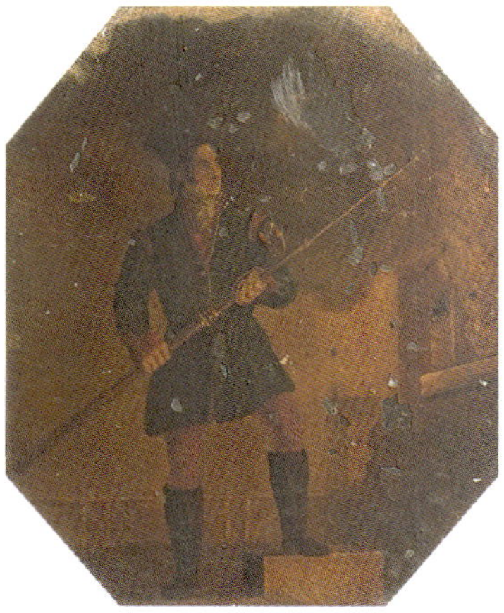

unknown artist
Fire Insurance Badge (3)*
oil on wood 27 x 23
MFS.D1

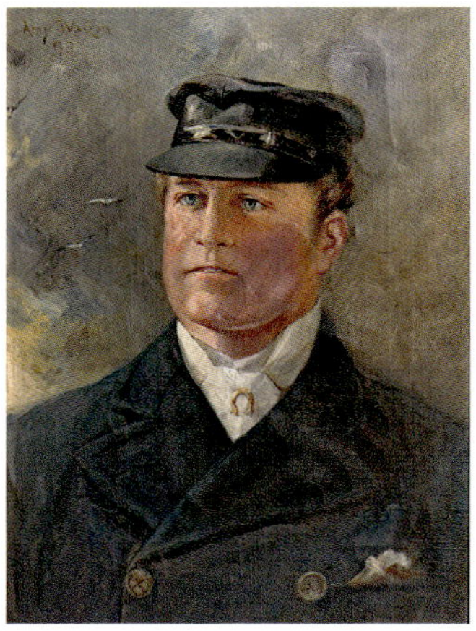

Walton, Amy
Captain Merryweather c.1899
oil on canvas 58 x 43
MFS.temp1

Nottinghamshire County Teaching Primary Care Trust

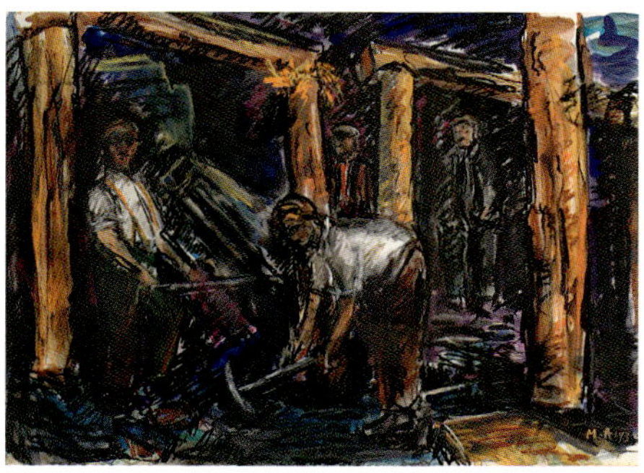

Arnfield, Marjorie 1930–2001
Breaking the Coal (c. 1920) 1993
acrylic on canvas 61 x 78.5
MCH2

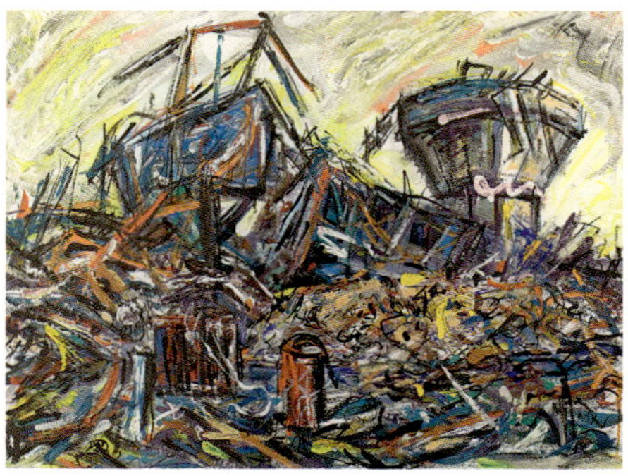

Arnfield, Marjorie 1930–2001
Rufford Colliery Demolition c.1993
acrylic on canvas 72.5 x 79
MCH1

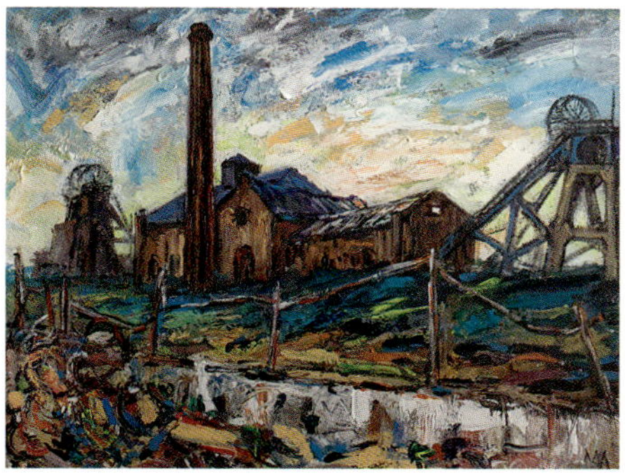

Arnfield, Marjorie 1930–2001
Desolation, Pleasley Colliery, Nottinghamshire
oil on canvas 55 x 73
ACH2

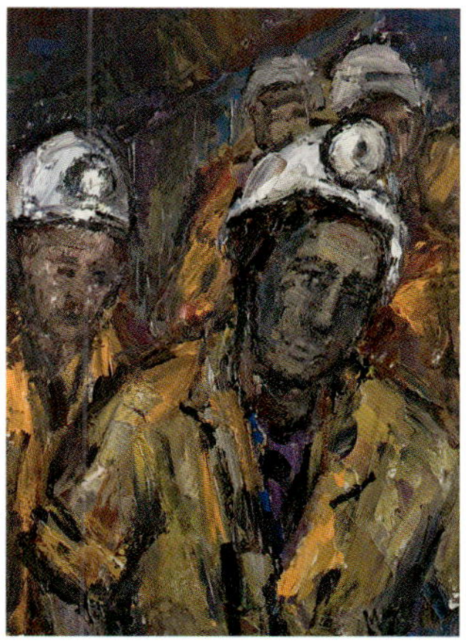

Arnfield, Marjorie 1930–2001
The Last Shift
oil on canvas 59.2 x 43.5
ACH1

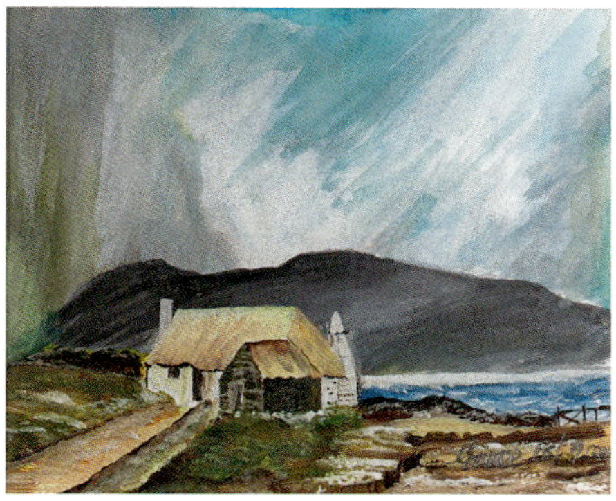

Grace
*Cottage Scene** 2001
acrylic on board 19 x 24
MCH3

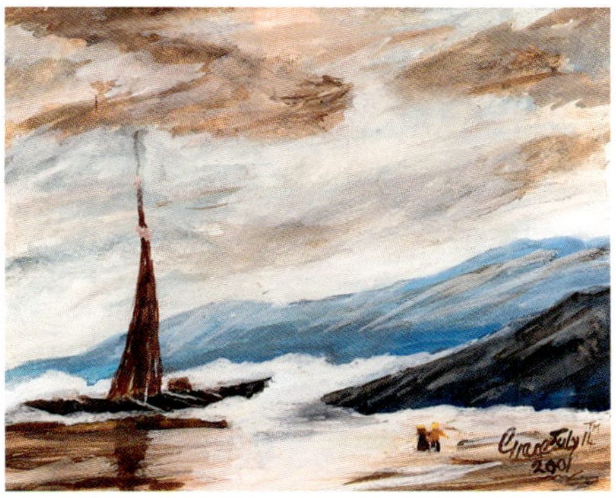

Grace
*Washed Ashore** 2001
acrylic on board 19 x 24
MCH4

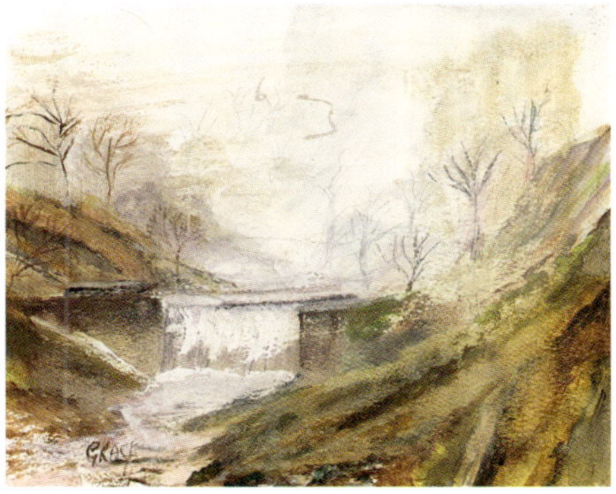

Grace
*Waterfall** 2001
acrylic on board 19.5 x 24.5
MCH5

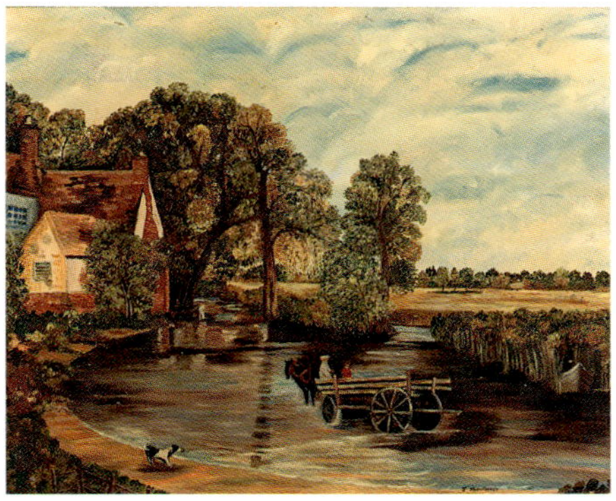

Humphrey, J.
The Hay Wain (copy of John Constable)
oil on board 55 x 69
MCH6

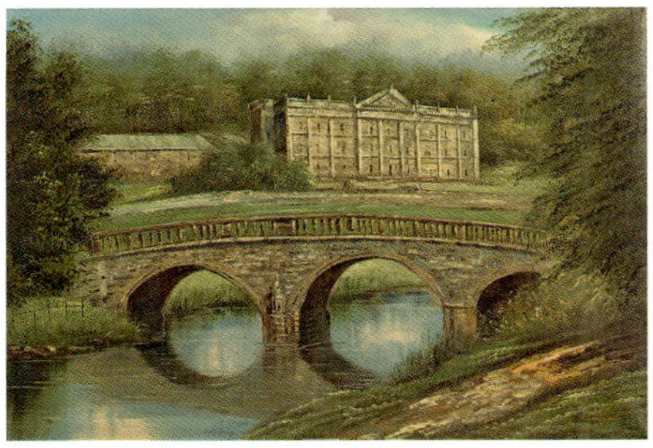

Lambert
Chatsworth House, Derbyshire
oil on canvas 59.5 x 89.5
MCH8

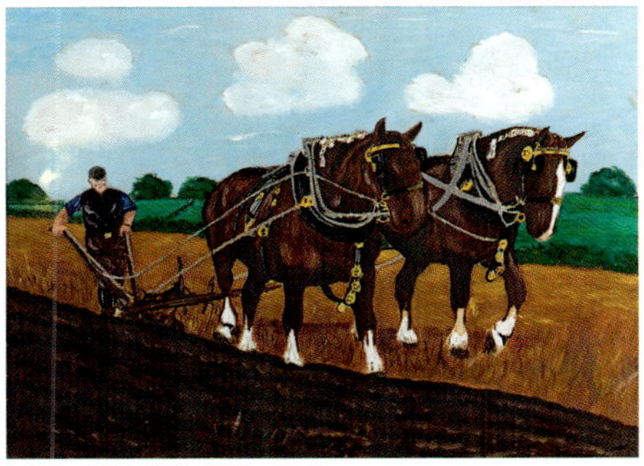

unknown artist
*Ploughing the Field**
acrylic on canvas 41 x 58.5
MCH7

Portland College

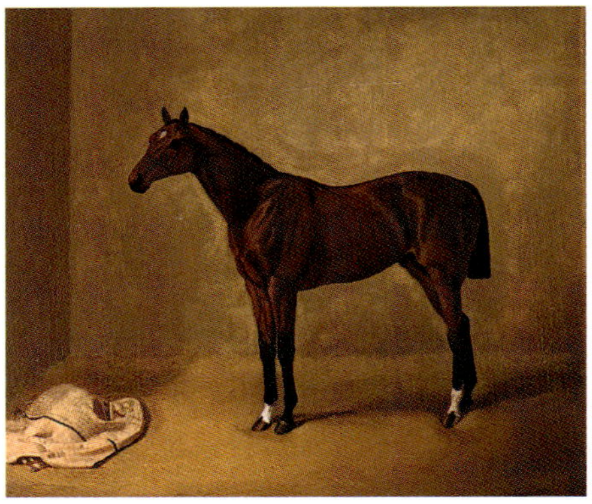

Evans, E. S.
Two of The Duke Of Portland's Racehorses (one of a pair) 1884
oil on canvas 55 x 65
PC:2a (P)

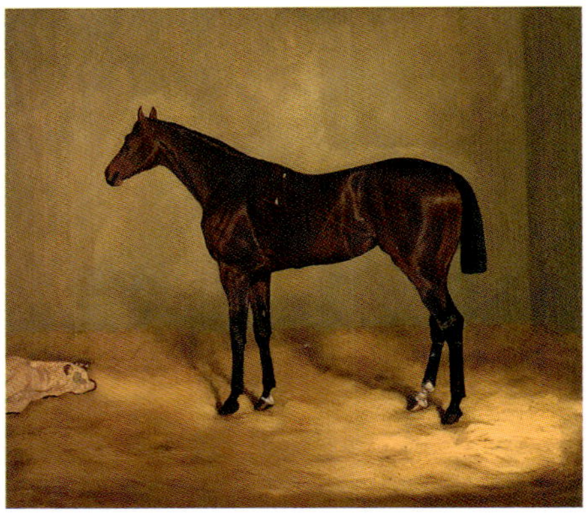

Evans, E. S.
Two of The Duke Of Portland's Racehorses (one of a pair) 1884
oil on canvas 55 x 65
PC:2b (P)

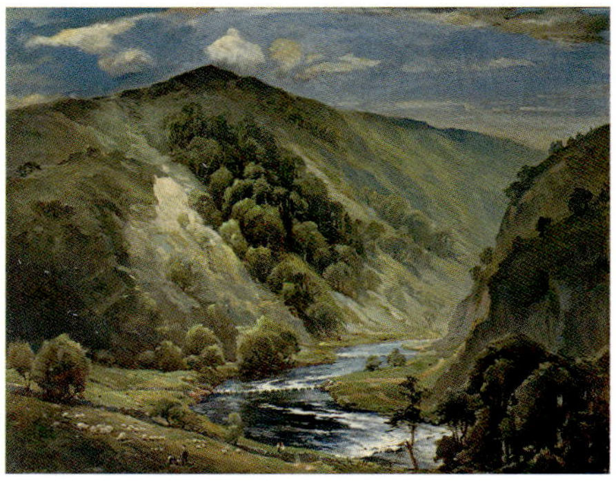

Gresley, Harold 1892–1967
Dovedale, Derbyshire
oil on canvas 70 x 90
PC:4

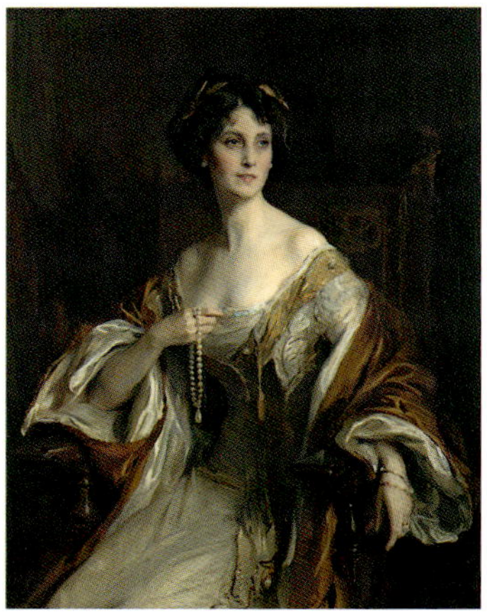

László, Philip Alexius de 1869–1937
The Duchess of Portland 1912
oil on canvas 184 x 126
PC:3 (P)

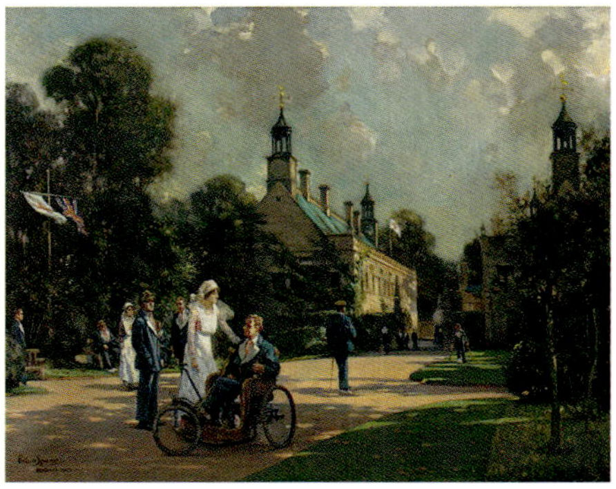

Spooner, Arthur 1873–1961
Welbeck during The Great War (one of a pair) 1918
oil on canvas 70 x 90
PC:1a (P)

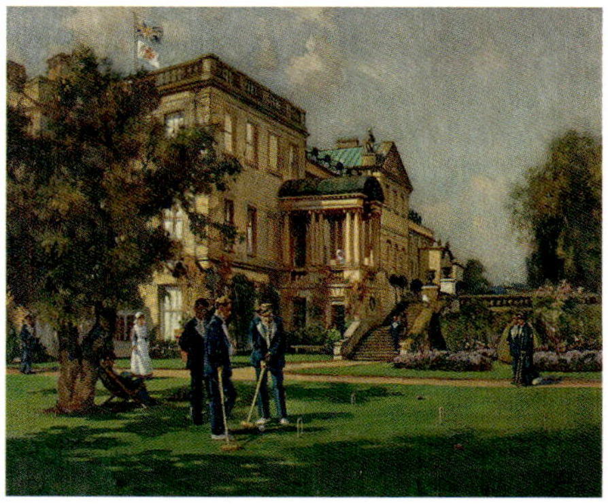

Spooner, Arthur 1873–1961
Welbeck during The Great War (one of a pair) 1918
oil on canvas 70 x 90
PC:1b (P)

Newark and Sherwood Museum Service

Newark and Sherwood Museum Service holds an eclectic and rich collection of over 700 works of art, of which the oils form a small but significant section. Diverse in both its scope and subject matter, the Collection comprises works from national figures such as Vanessa Bell, Winifred Nicholson, Peter Oliver and Renato Guttuso as well as local artists William Harold Cubley and Henry Hadfield Cubley. The Collection also boasts artists such as William Nicholson and Arthur Spooner who comfortably fit both the categories outlined above.

The Collection has been continually added to over the course of the last century since the opening of the first museum in Newark. Previous curators have been selective and astute in their acquisitions and purchases and the Collection contains a pleasing balance featuring landscapes, local views, abstracts, portraits and still lifes. It is with great satisfaction that we now care for the Collection at a purpose-built air conditioned store, which enables us to achieve the right balance between access and care.

The paintings have been acquired by us in various ways. Several key works have been purchased with money from the Victoria and Albert Museum Purchase Grant Fund and the Contemporary Art Society. The Museum Service owes a great debt to these two organisations that have enabled us to acquire works that would otherwise have been beyond our reach.

All paintings, as with all museum objects, have stories behind them; our Collection is no different. Take for instance the portrait painted by an unknown English artist of Lady Ossington, a local notable who railed against the alcohol consumption by men in Newark in Victorian times. Her response was to build the Ossington Coffee Palace in order to dissuade men from the evils of liquor. In the twentieth century as ownership of the coffee house changed and alcohol began to be served, her portrait repeatedly fell down in the night, apparently a symbol of her displeasure from beyond the grave.

From a personal perspective, as a former Thomas Magnus School pupil, it is particularly pleasing to see William Harold Cubley, the former Art Master at the Magnus, reunited with his former pupil William Nicholson; I am sure both would have approved. It is with a measure of regret that as a pupil at the Magnus I never realised the famous footsteps that strolled the same corridors as I did.

This has been a truly wonderful and inspiring project to be involved in and our thanks go to the Public Catalogue Foundation for making it possible to provide increased access to our art. We are, as always, also very grateful to all of the patrons who so generously donate and loan art to our Collection. They are invaluable to the museum service and their generosity never fails to amaze us. Our thanks in particular go to our Documentation Assistant, Richard Paling, and one of our volunteers, Lisa Buswell, for helping us with the background research.

Glyn Hughes, Senior Collections Officer

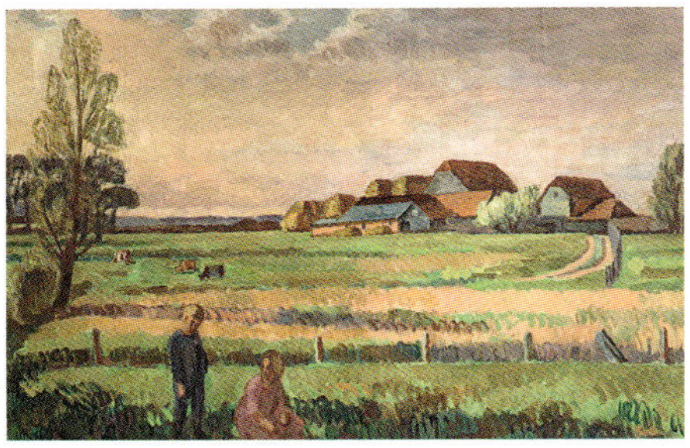

Bell, Vanessa 1879–1961
Jocelyn's Farm, Ripe, East Sussex c.1956
oil on canvas 64 x 99
90.56

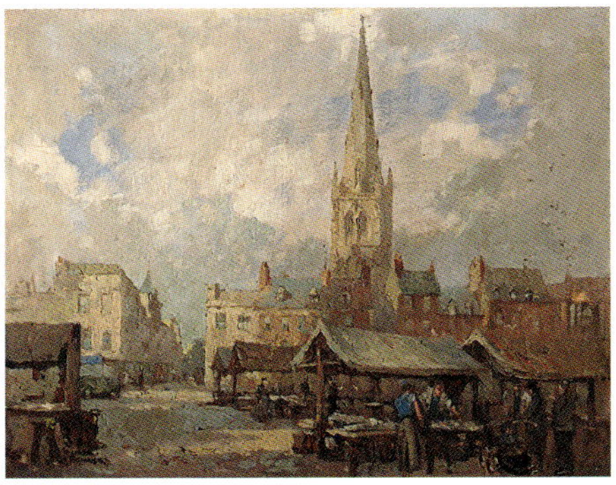

Benner, William 1884–1964
Newark Market Place, Nottinghamshire
oil on panel 59.2 x 75
10/1.74

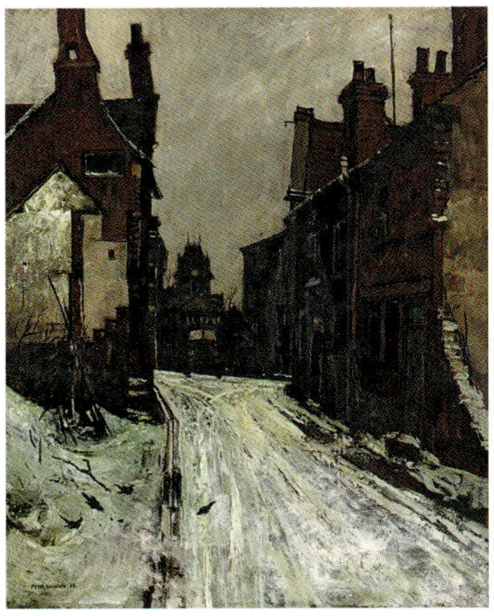

Brannan, Peter 1926–1994
Street Scene, Newark, Nottinghamshire c.1956
oil on board 84 x 60
34/1.89

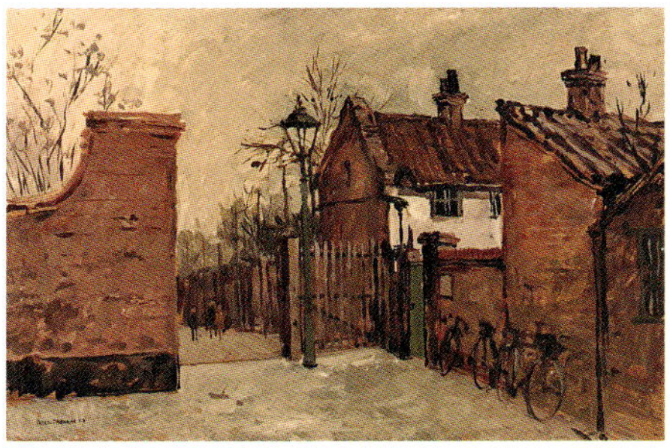

Brannan, Peter 1926–1994
Street Scene, Newark, Nottinghamshire c.1959
oil on board 31 x 40.5
34/2.89

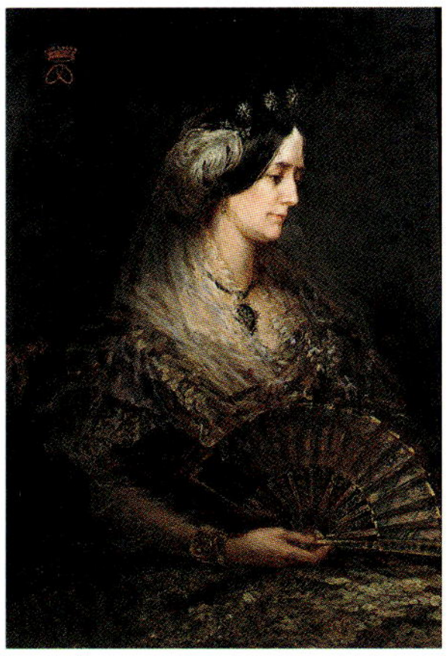

British (English) School
Lady Ossington (1806–1889) 1863
oil on canvas 100 x 70
7.81

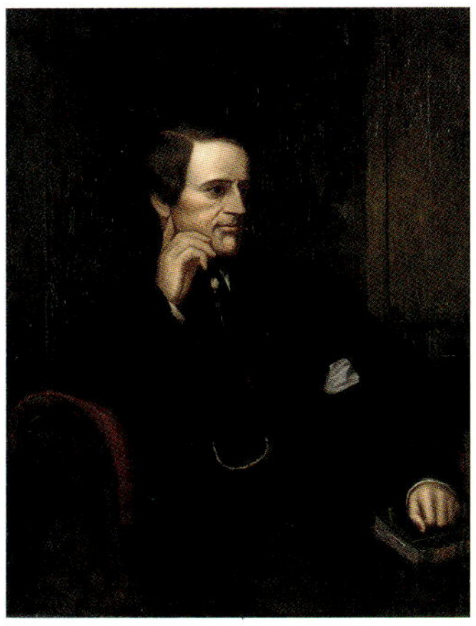

British (English) School 19th C
Portrait of a Man in Black
oil on canvas 85.8 x 67
135.2

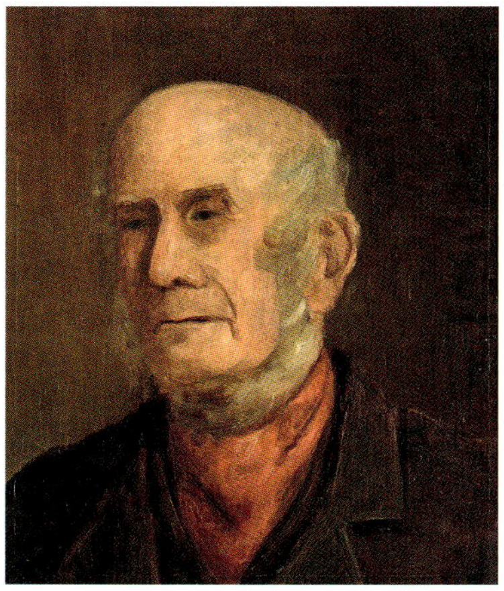

British (English) School 19th C
Portrait of an Old Man
oil on canvas 40 x 34
133.2

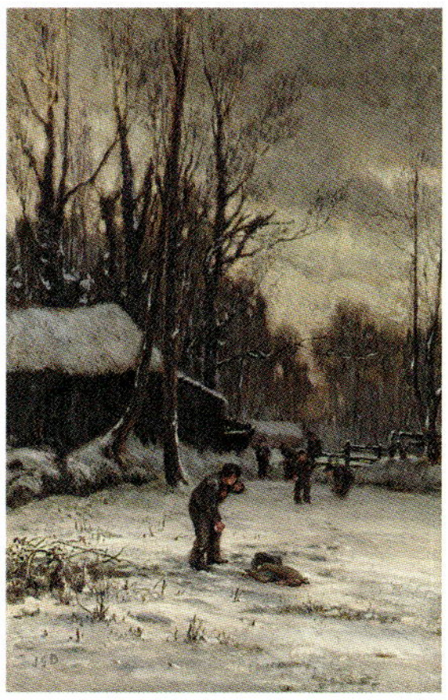

British (English) School late 19th C
Winter Snow Scene
oil on canvas 44.5 x 29
129.2

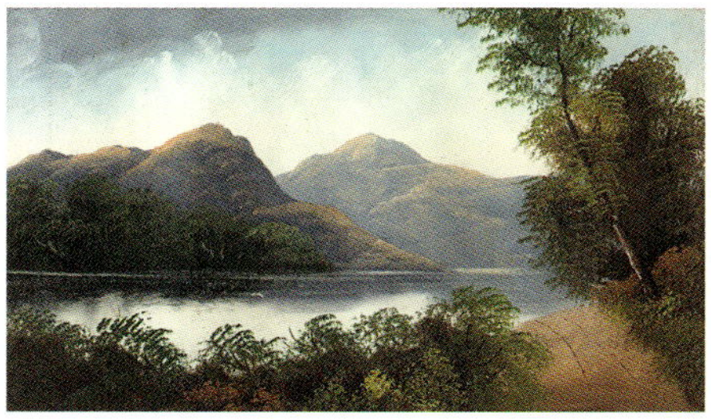

British (English) School
Hills and Lake
oil on board 26.5 x 49
118.2

Facing page: Foster, Herbert Wilson, 1846–1929, *The Belgian Model* (detail), c.1890, Nottingham City Museums and Galleries (p. 97)

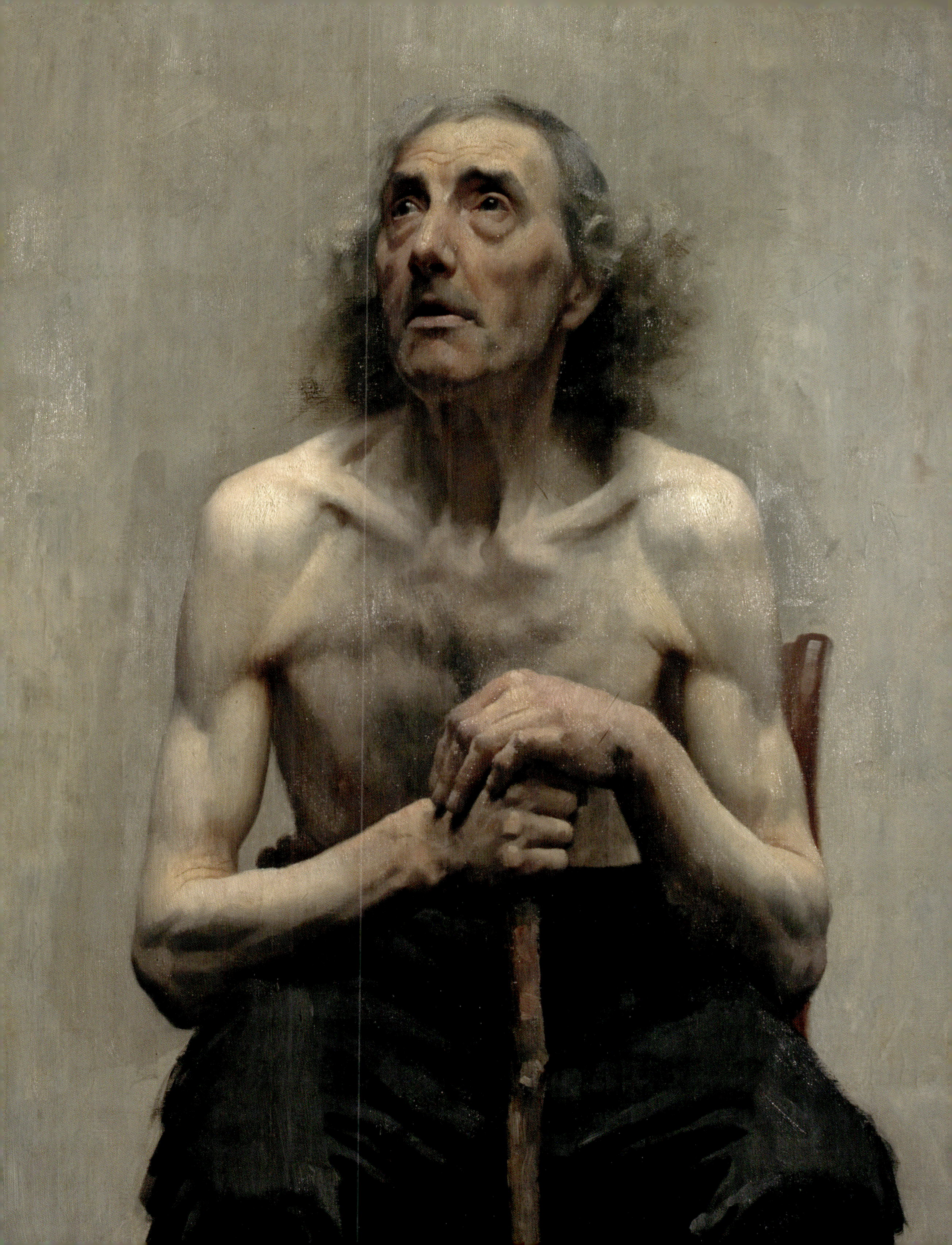

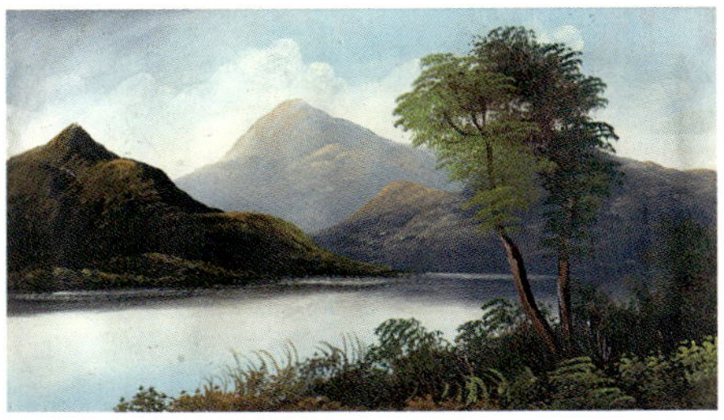

British (English) School
Mountain and Lake Scene
oil on paper 28 x 48
117.2

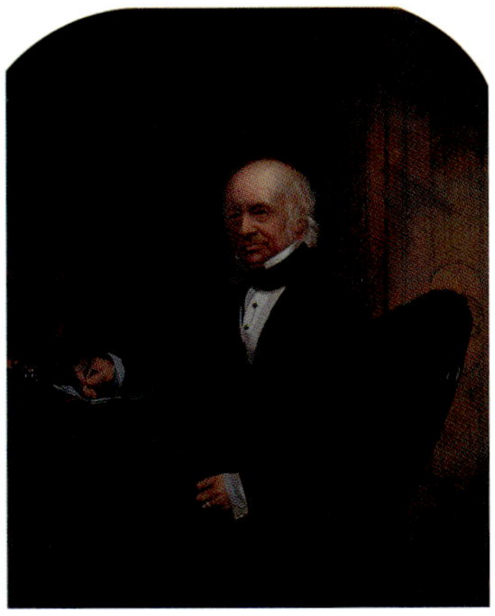

British (English) School
William Ewart Gladstone (1809–1898), MP for Newark (1832), Prime Minister (1868–1874, 1880–1886 & 1892–1894)
oil on canvas 28.7 x 23.7
134.2 T18255

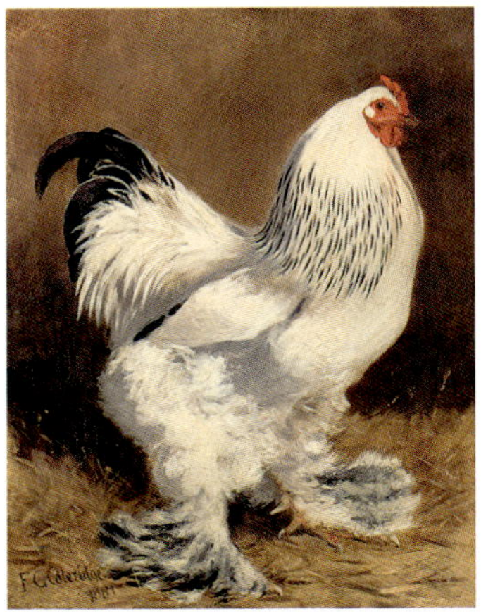

Coleridge, Francis George 1838–1923
Hen 1881
oil on canvas 49.7 x 39.5
74/1.65

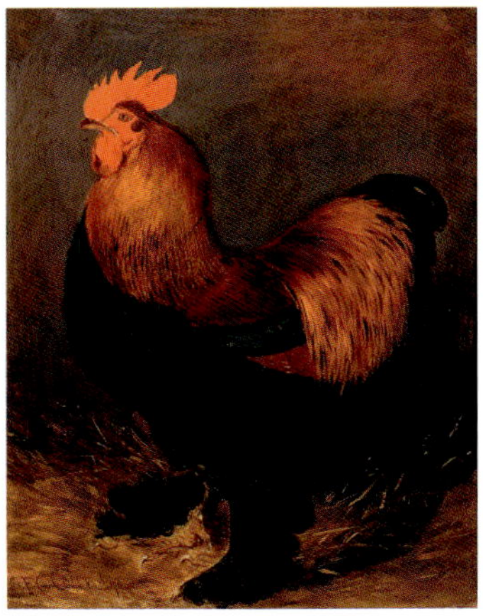

Coleridge, Francis George 1838–1923
Cockbird c.1881
oil on canvas 49.7 x 39.5
75.66

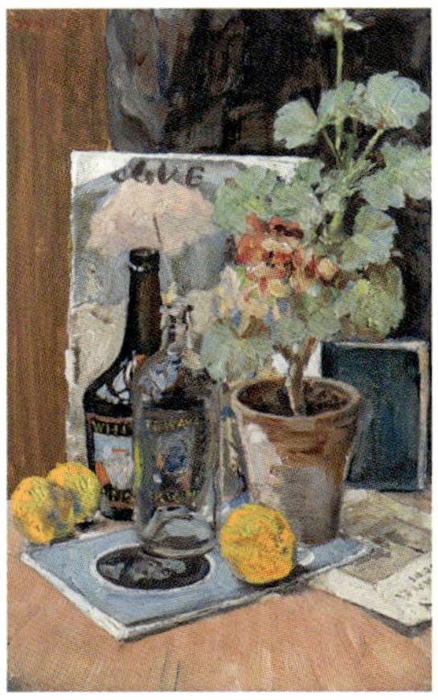

Coyne, Douglas 1930–2008
Still Life with Geraniums, Two Bottles and Fruit 1948
oil on panel 49 x 31.3
95.50

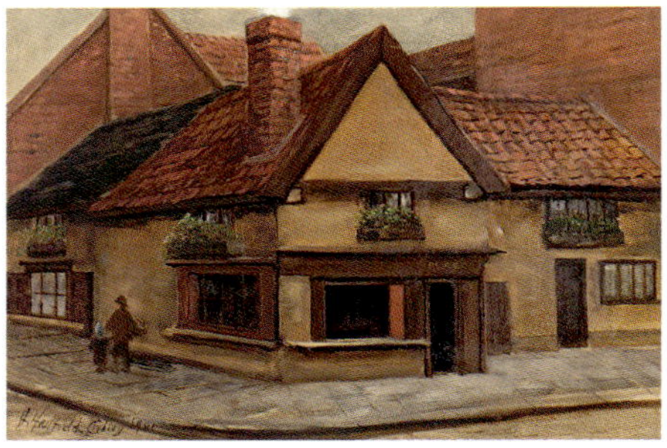

Cubley, Henry Hadfield 1858–1934
The Old Shop, Newark, Nottinghamshire 1901
oil on canvas 39.3 x 59.6
4.54

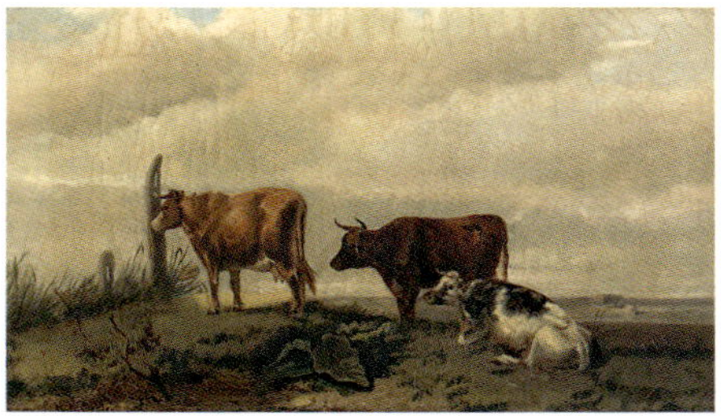

Cubley, Henry Hadfield 1858–1934
Three Cattle on Open Land
oil on canvas 34 x 59.8
NEKMS.2007.37.4 (P)

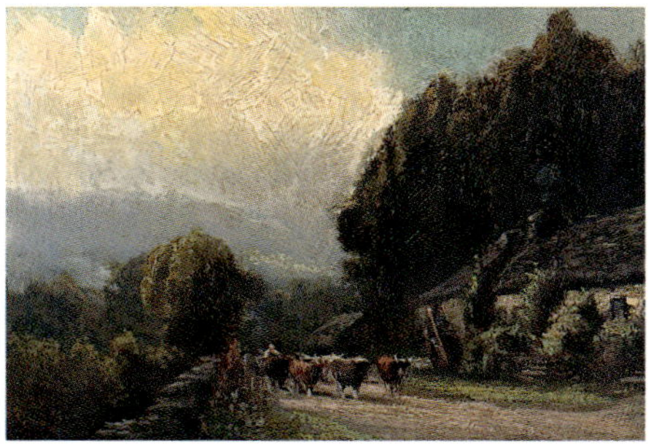

Cubley, Henry Hadfield (attributed to) 1858–1934
Cattle on a Country Road
oil on wood 16.2 x 23.8
131.2

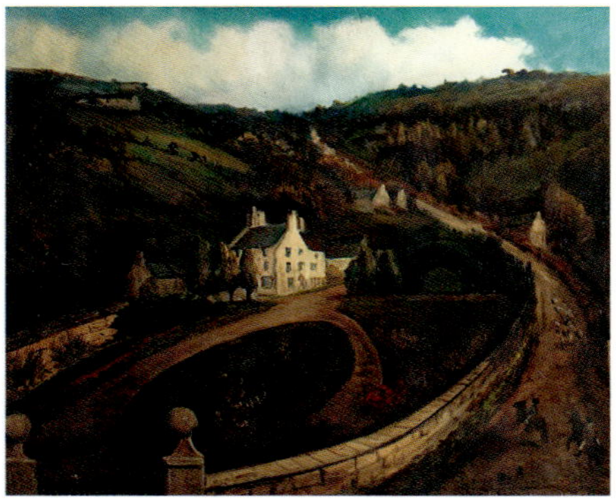

Cubley, Henry Hadfield (copy of) 1858–1934
Norton Hall 1931
oil on canvas 81 x 93
NEKMS.2007.37.5 (P)

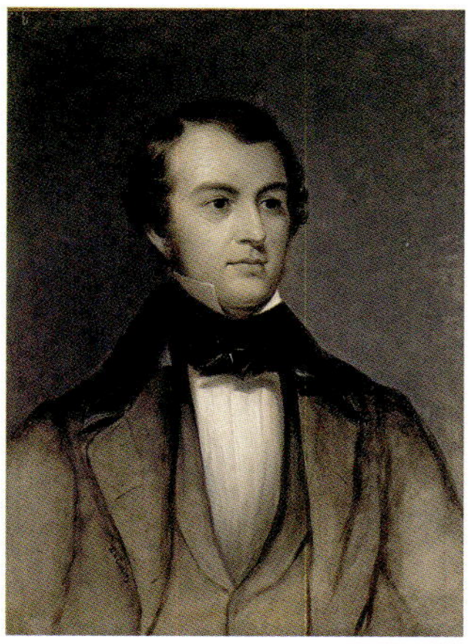

Cubley, William Harold 1814–1896
William Ewart Gladstone (1809–1898), MP for Newark (1832), (…) c.1835–1840
oil on canvas 72.5 x 52
9.47

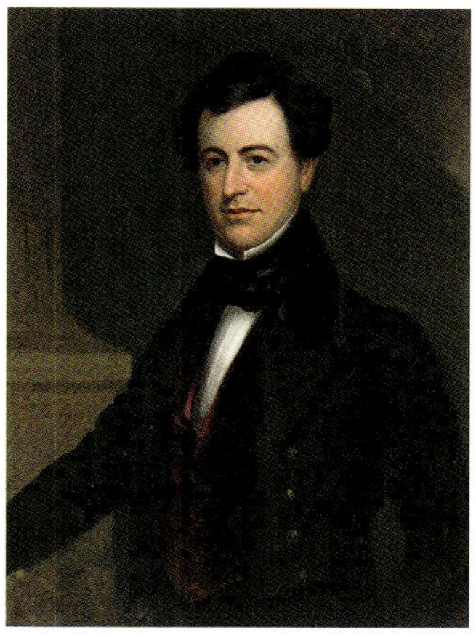

Cubley, William Harold 1814–1896
Frederick Thesiger c.1840
oil on canvas 87.8 x 67.8
14.65

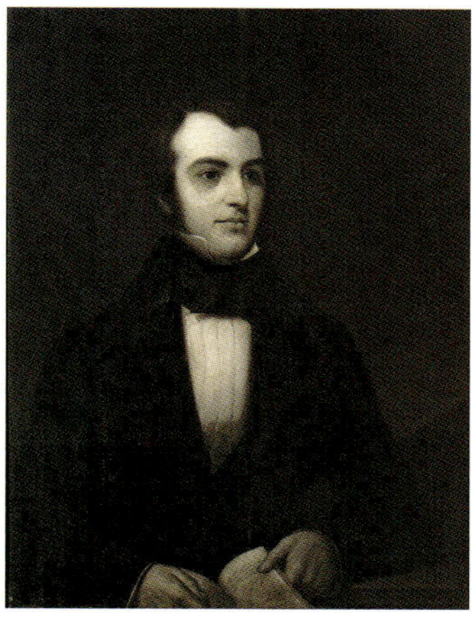

Cubley, William Harold 1814–1896
A Study in Black and White of William Ewart Gladstone (1809–1898), MP for Newark (…) 1840–1841
oil on canvas 89 x 69
10.37

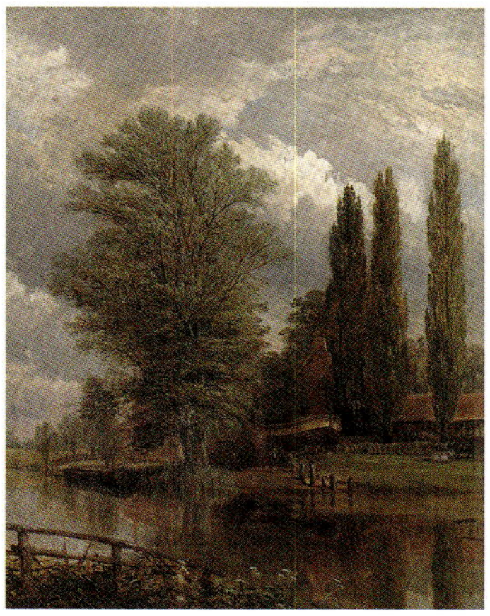

Cubley, William Harold 1814–1896
Flint's Dockyard, Newark, 1850 c.1850
oil on canvas 64.8 x 51.5
110.2

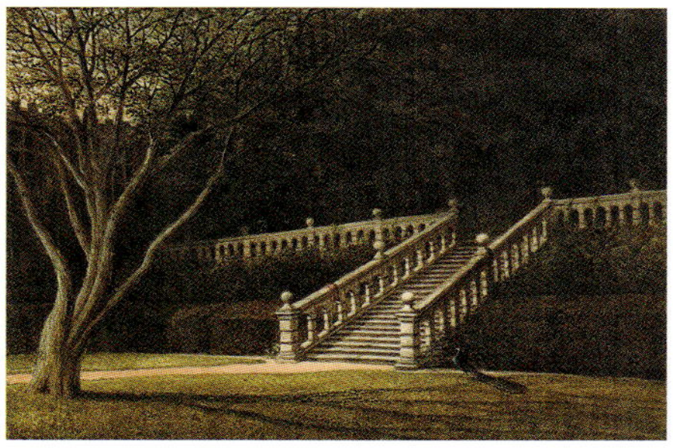

Cubley, William Harold 1814–1896
The Terrace, Haddon Hall, Derbyshire 1888
oil on canvas 52 x 64
108.2

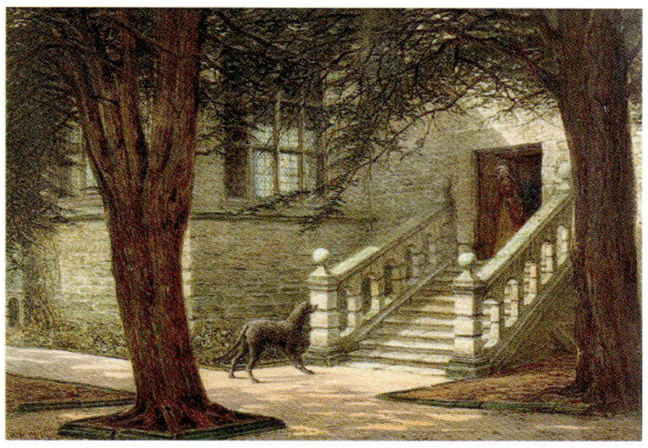

Cubley, William Harold 1814–1896
Dorothy Vernon's Doorway, Haddon Hall, Derbyshire 1890
oil on canvas 35 x 66
109.2

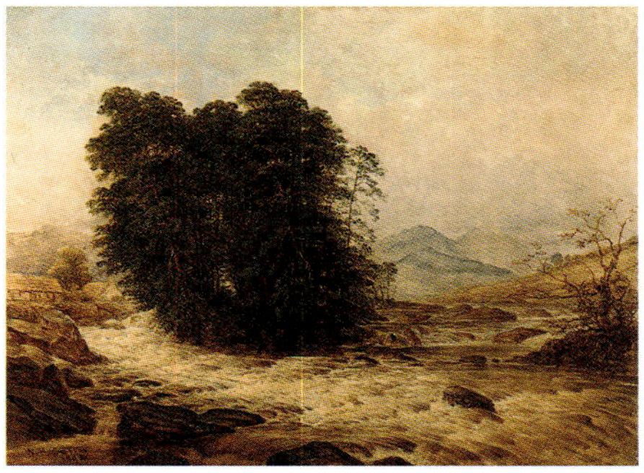

Cubley, William Harold 1814–1896
Killin, Perthshire, Scotland 1893
oil on canvas 84.7 x 90.7
104.2

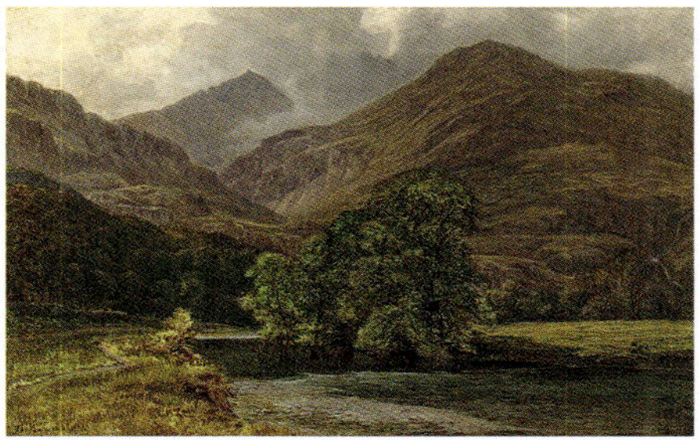

Cubley, William Harold 1814–1896
In the Vale of Gwynant, Wales
oil on canvas 31.8 x 52
t1070

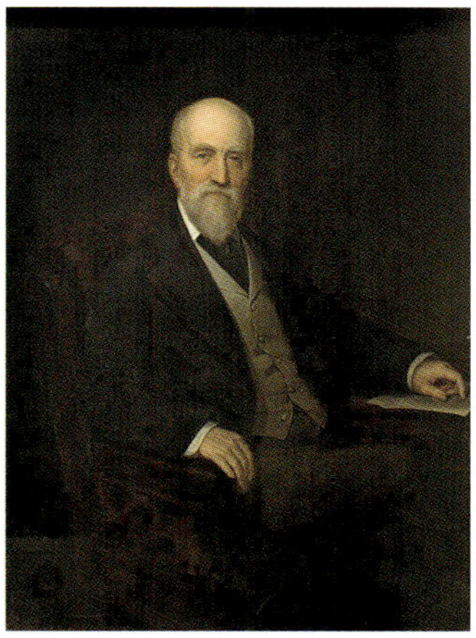

Cubley, William Harold 1814–1896
Joseph Gilstrap (1775–1869)
oil on canvas 288 x 185
51.91

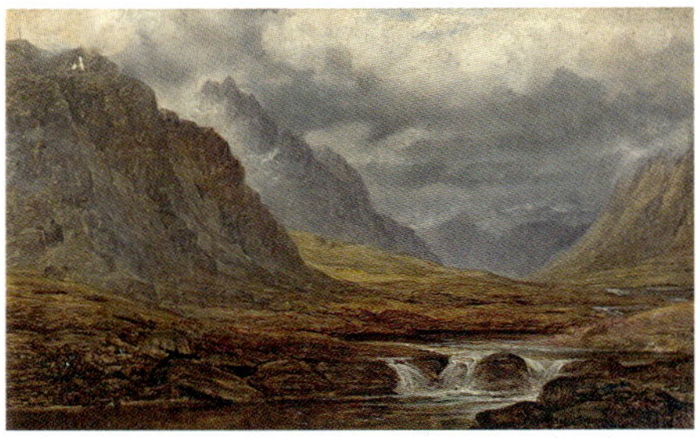

Cubley, William Harold 1814–1896
Near Lake Ogwen, Wales
oil on canvas 24 x 38.5
t994

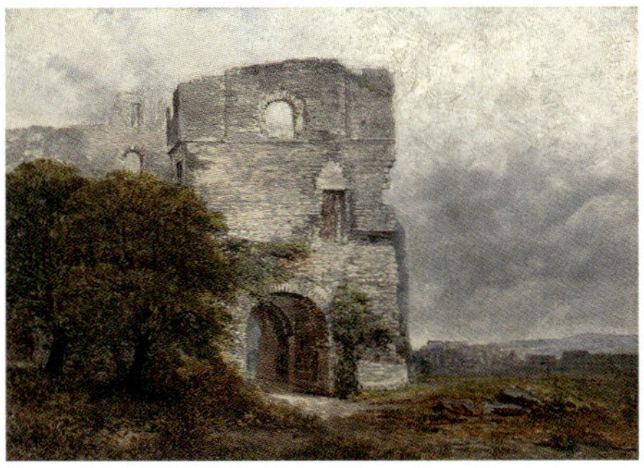

Cubley, William Harold 1814–1896
Newark Castle, Nottinghamshire
oil on canvas 28.1 x 39.4
988.1

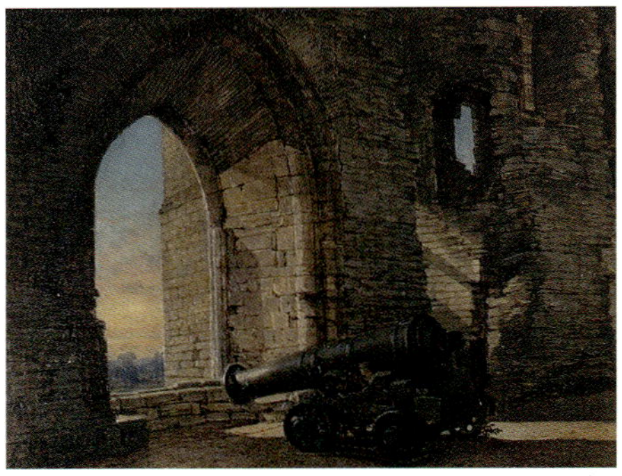

Cubley, William Harold 1814–1896
Newark Castle, Nottinghamshire, with Sebastopol Cannon
oil on canvas 29.2 x 38.3
990.2

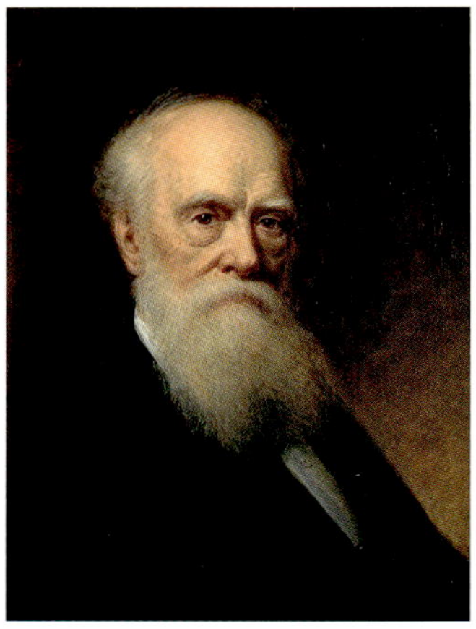

Cubley, William Harold 1814–1896
Self Portrait
oil on canvas 59.3 x 46.5
25.57

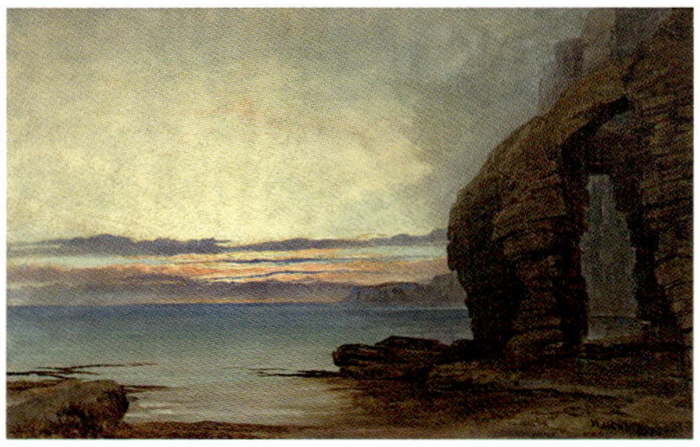

Cubley, William Harold 1814–1896
Sunset at Bridlington, East Yorkshire
oil on canvas 39 x 62
114.2

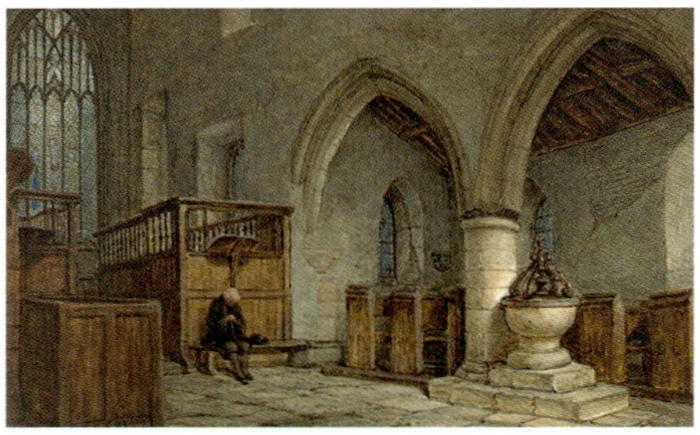

Cubley, William Harold 1814–1896
The Chapel, Haddon Hall, Derbyshire
oil on canvas 31.8 x 52
959.1

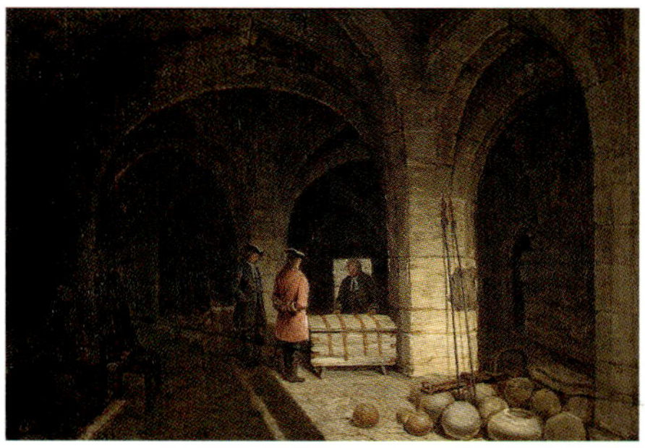

Cubley, William Harold 1814–1896
The Crypt, Knaresborough Castle, Yorkshire
oil on canvas 32 x 52
112.2

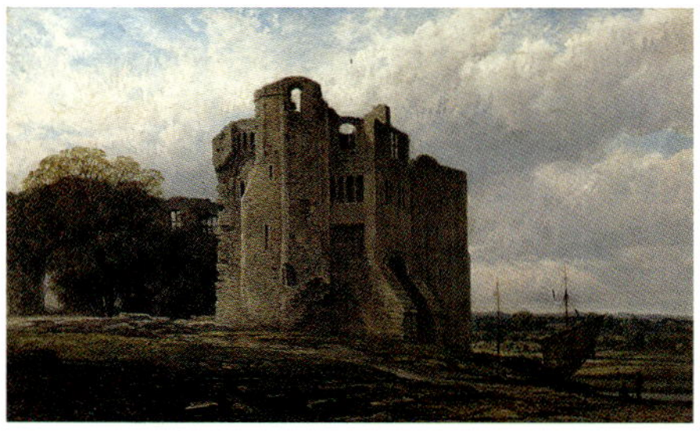

Cubley, William Harold 1814–1896
The Keep, Newark Castle, Nottinghamshire
oil on canvas 38.8 x 64.8
111.2

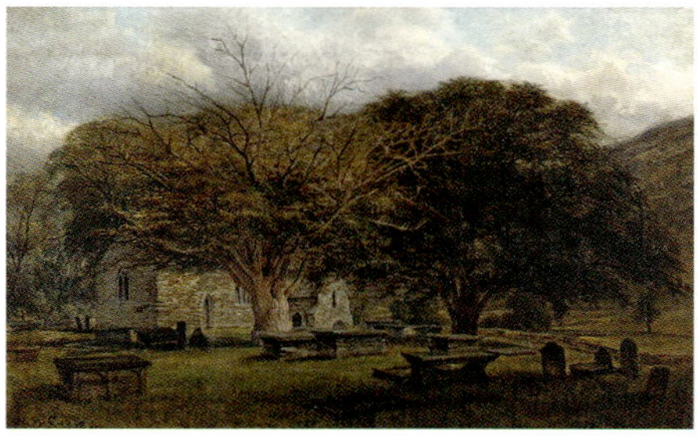

Cubley, William Harold 1814–1896
The Old Churchyard, Betws-y-Coed, Wales
oil on canvas 30 x 52
113.2

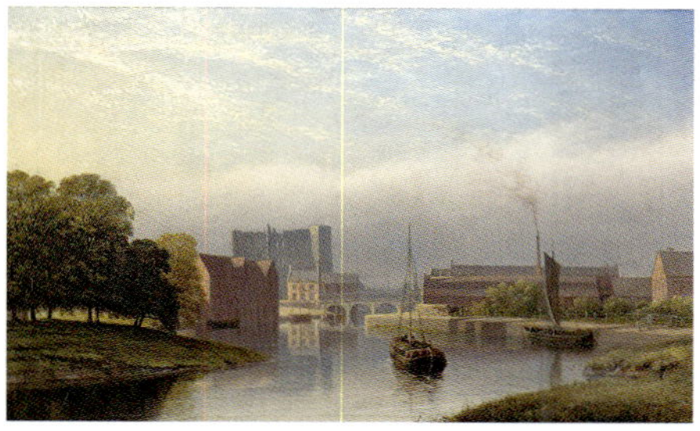

Cubley, William Harold 1814–1896
View of the River Trent
oil on canvas 44 x 63.8
101.2

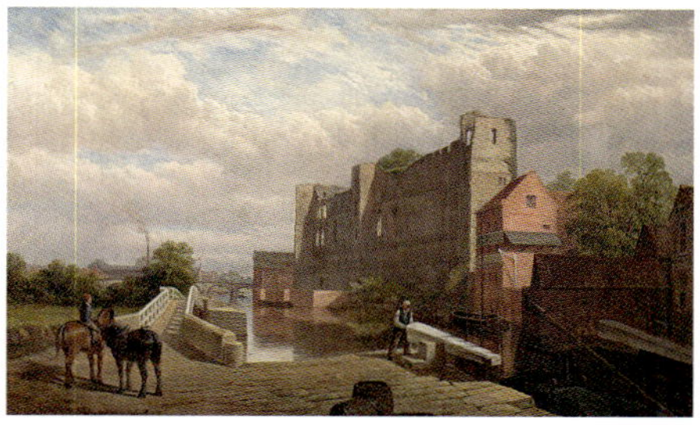

Cubley, William Harold 1814–1896
View of the River Trent and the Old Pack Horse
oil on canvas 53.4 x 89.2
105.2

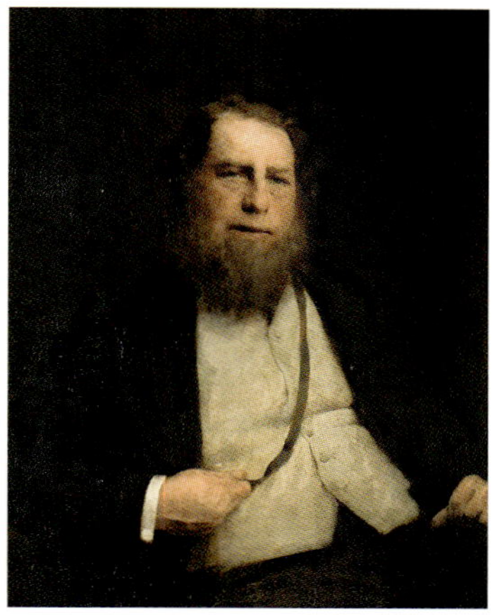

Forbes, Stanhope Alexander 1857–1947
Grosvenor Hodgkinson (1818–1881)
oil on canvas 96 x 78
124.37

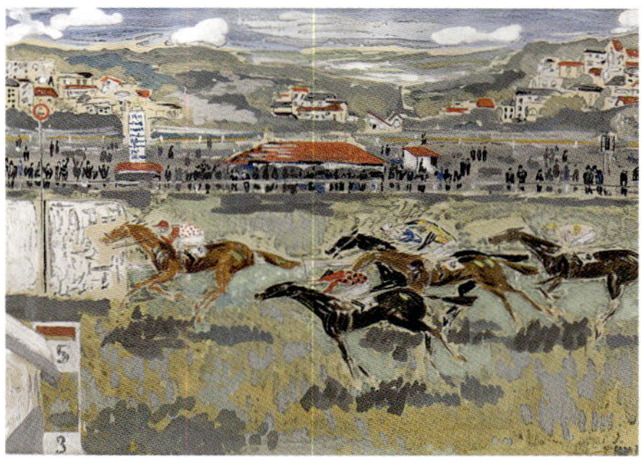

Ganesco, Alexandre 1910–1979
Horse Race 1930
acrylic, wax & pencil on paper 41.5 x 71
76.63

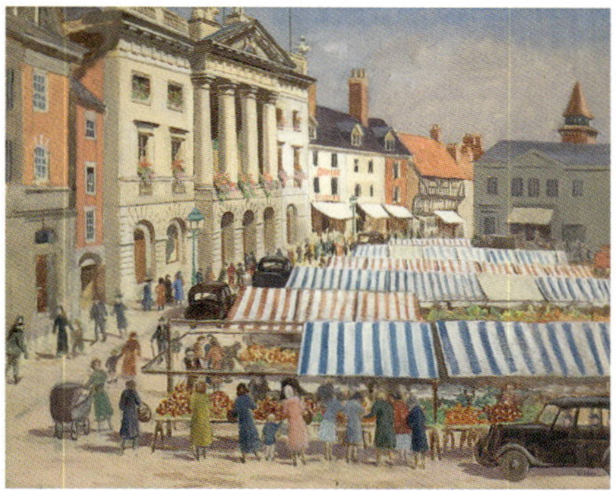

Gibbon, Sidney 1895–1988
Forum Fantasy 1952
oil on canvas 55.5 x 71
121.52

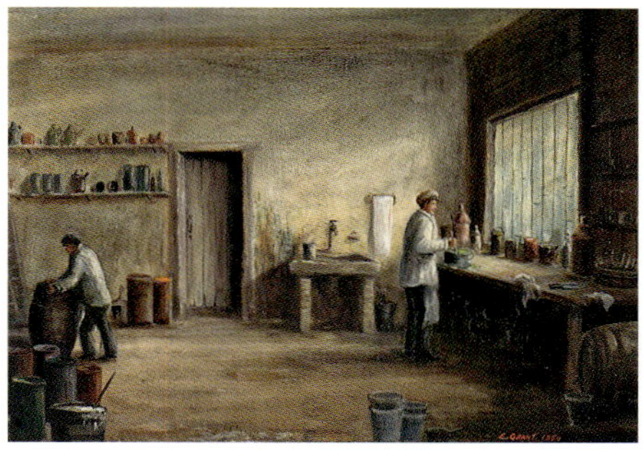

Grant, E. E. d.c.1970
Paintworks 1950
oil on board 30.3 x 44.6
36.7

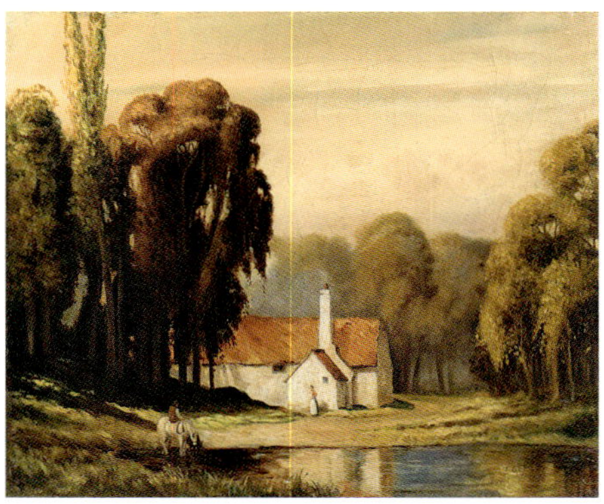

Grant, E. E. d.c.1970
The Farm
oil on canvas 43.8 x 53.5
17.57

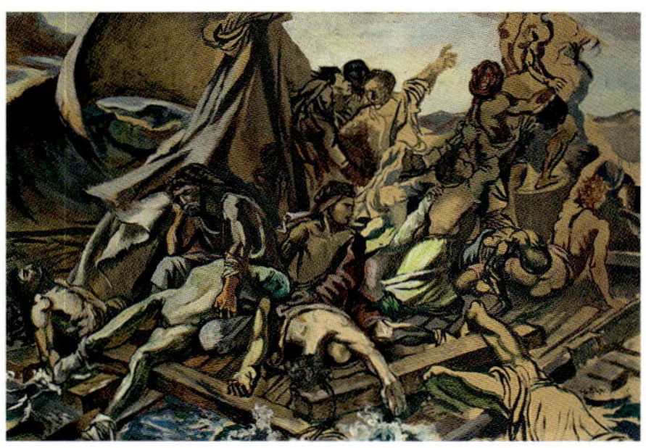

Guttuso, Renato 1912–1987
The Raft of the Medusa (copy after Eugène Delacroix) 1955
oil on paper laid on canvas 108.8 x 158
15.62

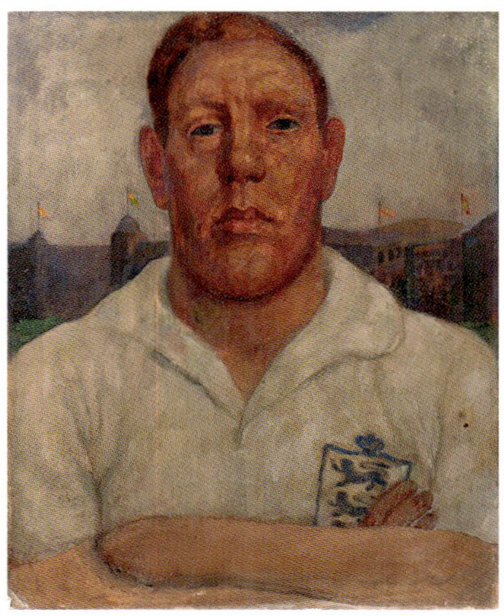

Hall, Lilian Iris 'Betty'
Willie Hall c.1950
oil on canvas 60.6 x 51
t1055

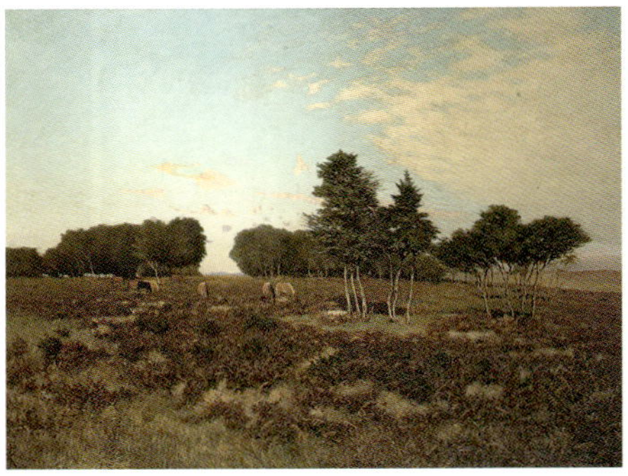

Knowles, William Pitcairn c.1846–c.1904
Heath and Woodlands
oil on canvas 90 x 120
28.36

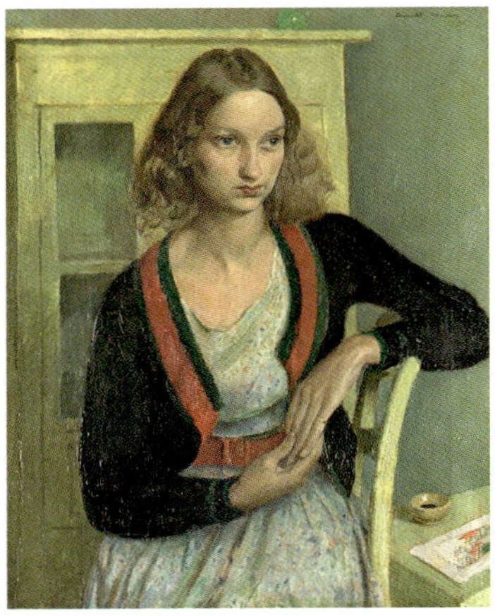

Mason, Arnold 1885–1963
Portrait of a Woman 1931
oil on canvas 42.6 x 36
75.63

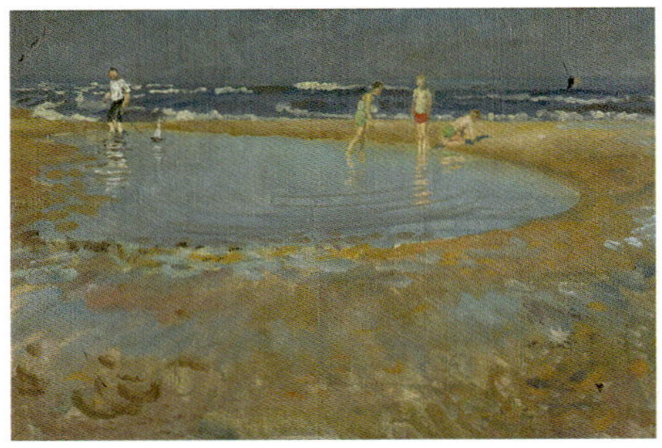

Morrocco, Alberto 1917–1998
Low Tide c.1952
oil on canvas 49.5 x 75
98.52

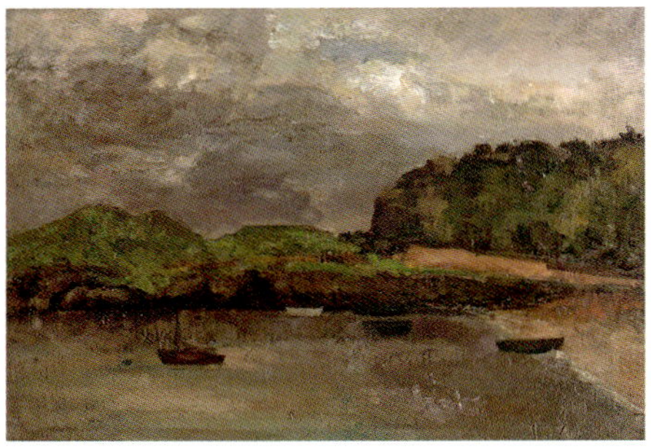

Moynihan, Rodrigo 1910–1990
Rain Clouds, Beached Boats 1944
oil on canvas 50.5 x 74
12.44

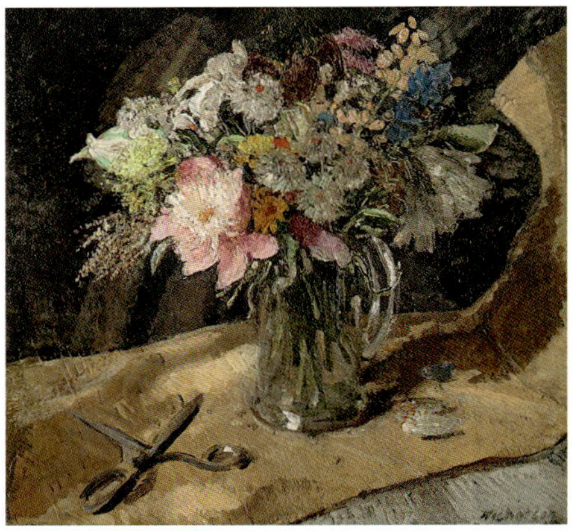

Nicholson, William 1872–1949
Flower Piece 1949
oil on canvas 54.5 x 59.5
9.50

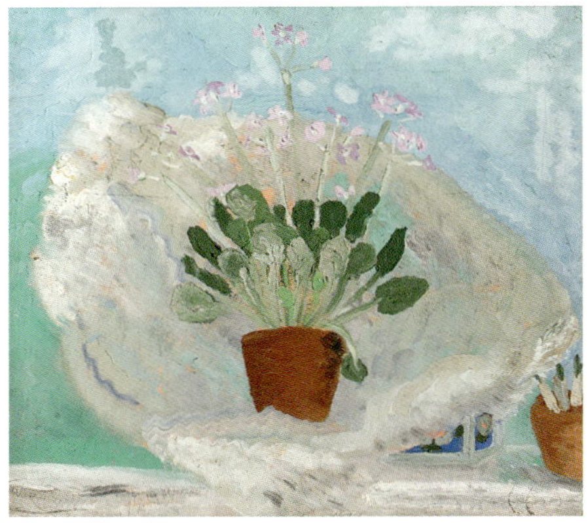

Nicholson, Winifred 1893–1981
Primula stellata 1952
oil on card 47 x 54
97.52

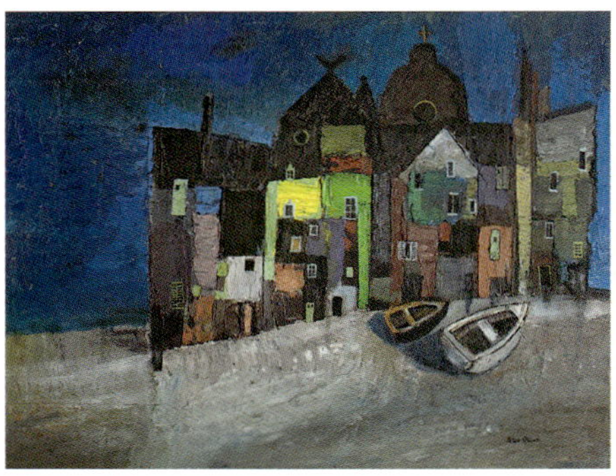

Oliver, Peter 1927–2006
The Strand, Jersey 1957
oil on canvas 85.5 x 117
25.59

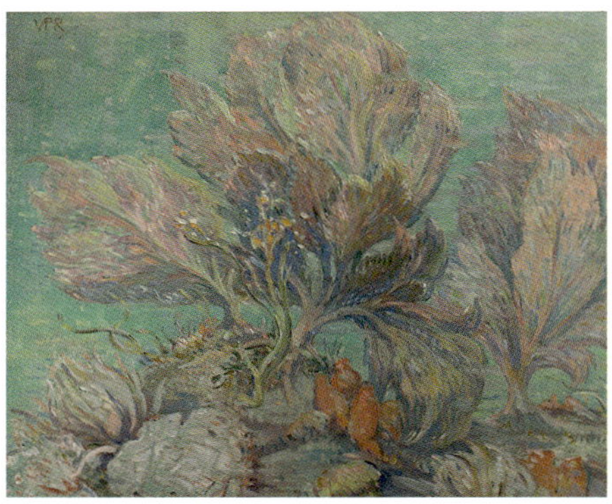

Ramsay, Patricia 1886–1974
Sea Fans, Bermuda
oil on canvas 47 x 50
69.54

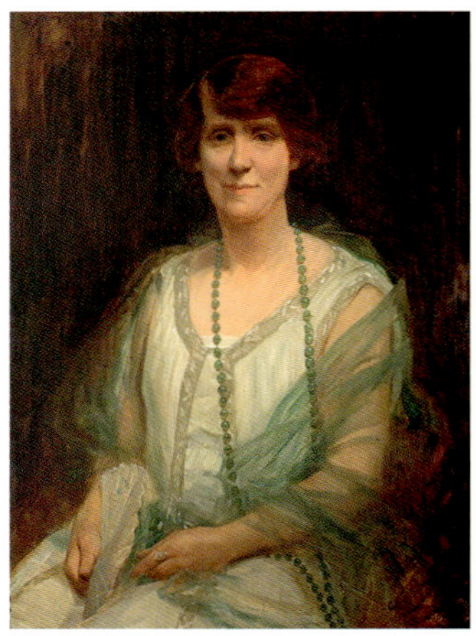

Spooner, Arthur 1873–1961
Mrs J. R. Hole 1925
oil on canvas 88 x 71
9/1.92

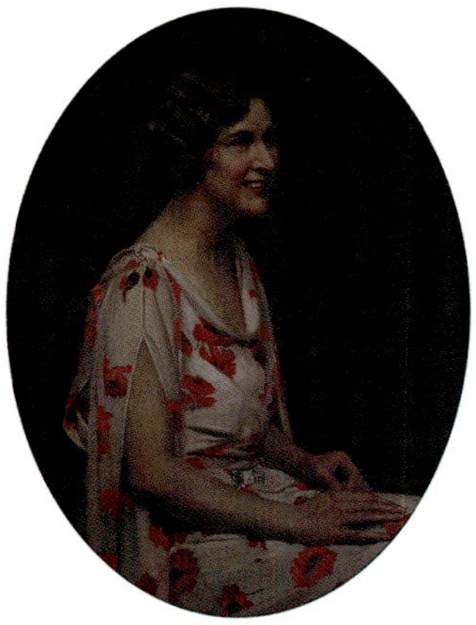

Spooner, Arthur 1873–1961
The Daughter of J. Hole 1925
oil on canvas 87 x 80 (E)
9/2.92

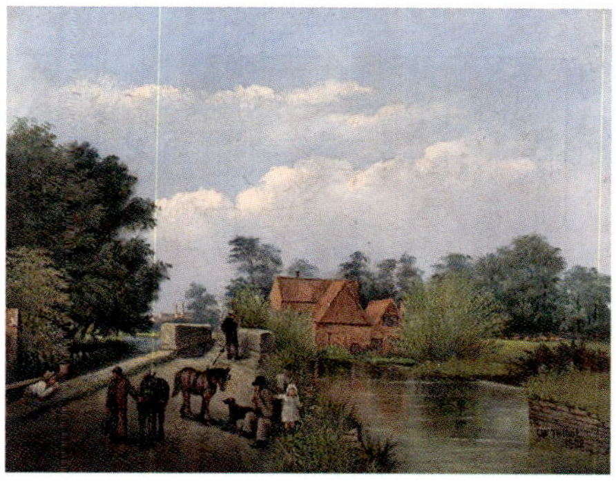

Talbot, William c.1823–1907
Longstone Bridge and Watermill, Derbyshire 1892
oil on canvas 34.6 x 45
18/1.55

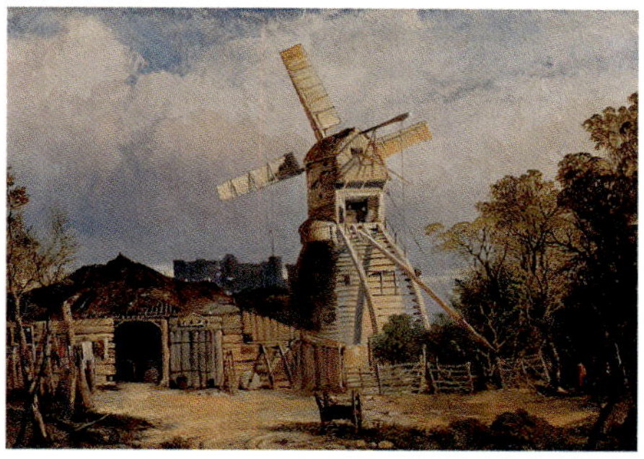

unknown artist
Post Mill, Tolney Lane, Newark, Nottinghamshire c.1840
oil on board 33 x 47
88.37/1

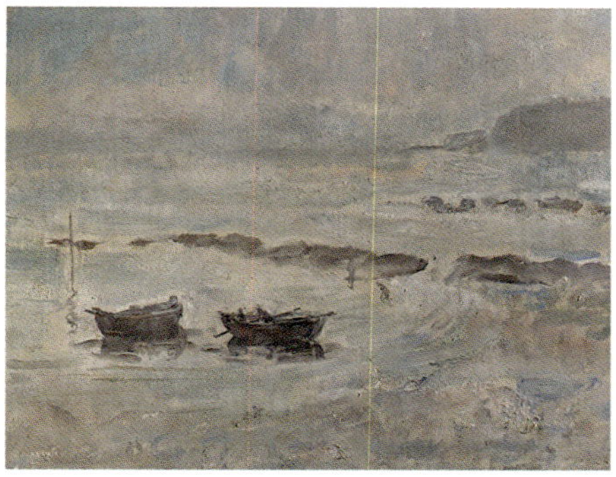

Walker, Ethel 1861–1951
Beached Dinghies on a Storm-Tossed Shore, (Robin Hood's Bay, North Yorkshire) c.1938
oil on canvas 49.5 x 66
52.38

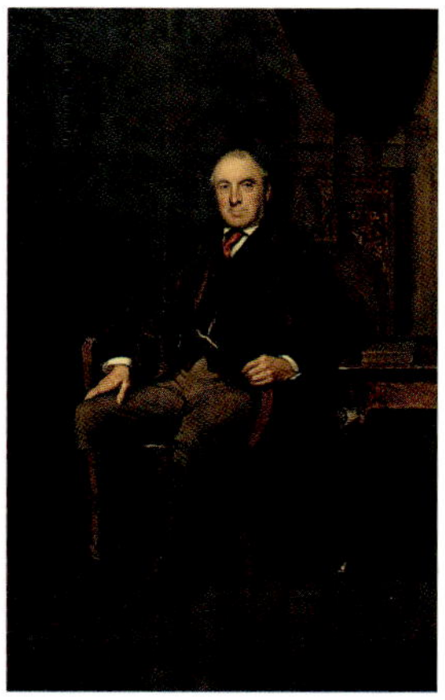

Wehrschmidt, Daniel Albert 1861–1932
Sidney Pierrepont (1826–1900), 3rd Earl Manvers 1891
oil on canvas 316 x 135
22.90

Newark Town Council

Newark Town Council possesses a number of fine oil paintings, some of which came through the Contemporary Art Society (CAS), which was formed in 1910 to promote the collecting of contemporary art. In the 1940s and 1950s, the Council was a member of the CAS enabling it to acquire paintings by Stanley Spencer (1891–1959), William Bernard Adeney (1878–1966) and Gerard Chowne (1875–1917), on behalf of the Town.

Most of the works in the Fine Art Gallery on the second floor of the Town Hall have been given as gifts and many reflect the abundance of local artistic talent in Newark. Amongst these is an artist with an international reputation, William Nicholson (1872–1949) who was born in Newark. *Still Life* was painted when Nicholson was only 13 years old, illustrating his precocious talent. Another painting demonstrating Nicholson's later increasing interest in texture and surface of paint is *Chrysanthemums,* painted in 1934.

Nicholson was tutored by William Harold Cubley (1814–1896), a talented artist who frequently exhibited at the Royal Academy. Many of Newark's aldermen and mayors were painted by Cubley who was himself a member of the Borough Council for some years before being elected Mayor in 1866. A relative of William Cubley, Henry Hadfield Cubley (1858–1934), also has some well-executed oils on display, in particular, *Barmouth Bay, West Wales* and *The Timber Clearing at Matlock, Derbyshire,* both recent acquisitions.

Oil paintings reflecting the civic side of the Town are displayed appropriately in the Council Chamber. A 'star' portrait here is one by Ernest Townsend (1880–1944) of Mayor William Edward Knight (1845–1934) who is wearing the mayoral robes and insignia with great dignity. He was mayor five times and his portrait shows him touching the Peace Proclamation which he read from the Town Hall balcony at the end of the First World War. Other works include those by the Nottingham-born Arthur Spooner (1873–1961). Amongst these is *Godfrey Tallents (1849–1917), Town Clerk,* whose family had a long association with both the legal profession and the Town Council between 1806 and 1918. Another Nottingham-born artist, Harold Knight (1874–1961), married to the artist Laura Knight, painted the distinguished portrait of Thomas Earp (1830–1910) who was Mayor of Newark three times and Liberal MP, and was acquainted with Gladstone and Joseph Chamberlain.

We gratefully appreciate this opportunity to make our collection of fine art better known and are most grateful to the Public Catalogue Foundation for including us in their catalogue.

Patty Temple, Curator

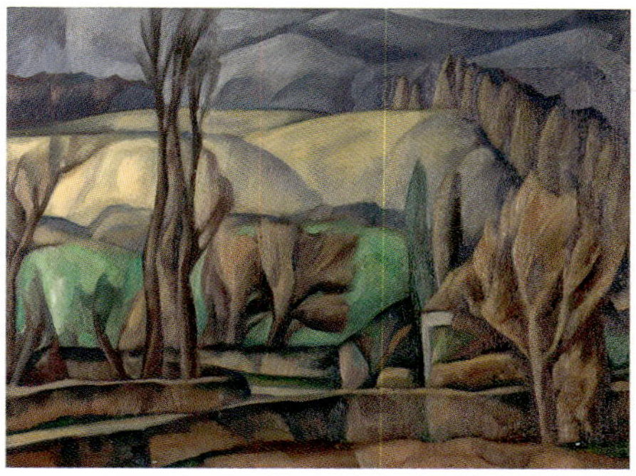

Adeney, William Bernard 1878–1966
Tunley Bottom c.1920
oil on canvas 57 x 77
NTT.1997.6

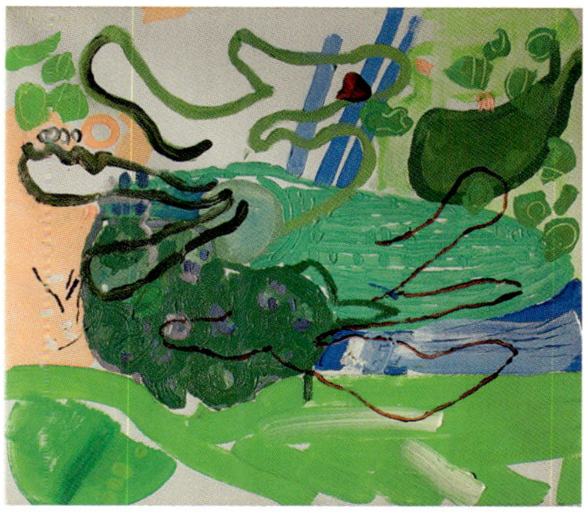

Bearpark, John Victor b.1946
Gill's Garden 2002
oil on canvas 31 x 35
NTT.2002.41

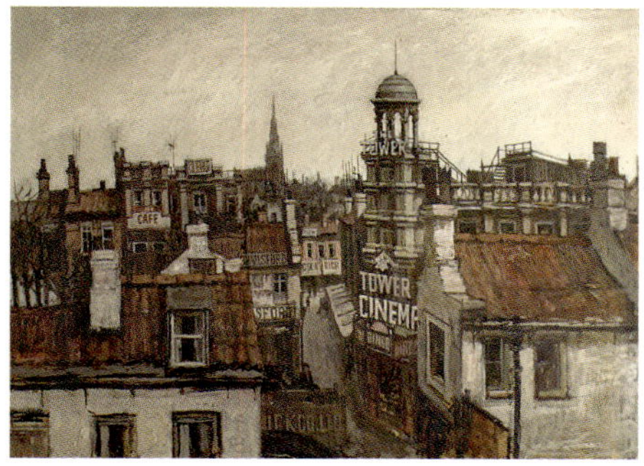

Brannan, Peter 1926–1994
View of a Town 1968
oil on canvas 68 x 93.5
NTT.1997.292

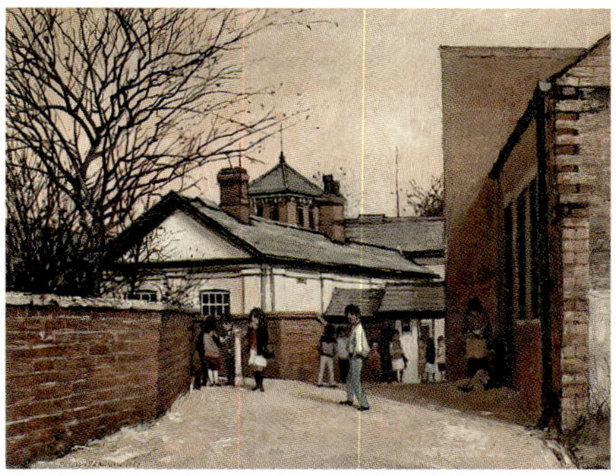

Brannan, Peter 1926–1994
The Mount School, Newark, Nottinghamshire
oil on canvas 25.8 x 34.5
NTT.PCF4 (P)

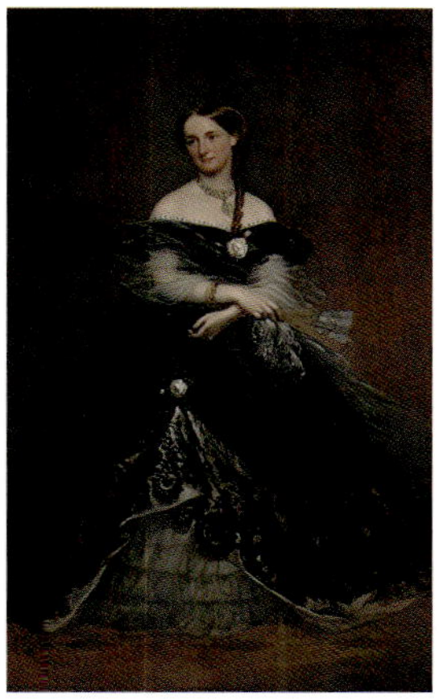

Buckner, Richard 1812–1883
Lady Elizabeth Gilstrap (1822–1891)
oil on canvas 222 x 130
NTT.1997.289

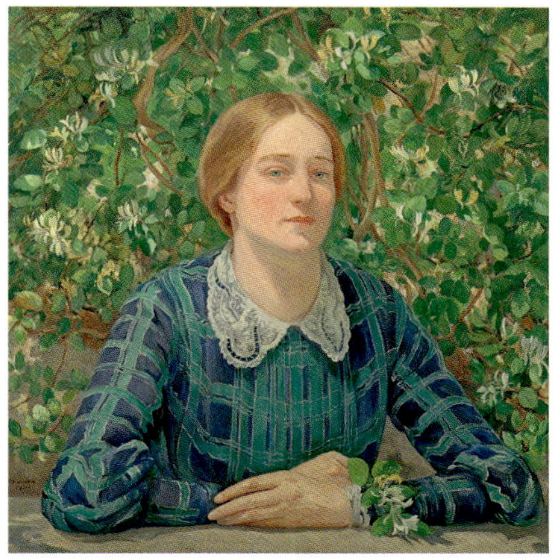

Chowne, Gerard 1875–1917
Honeysuckle 1911
oil on canvas 51 x 51
NTT.1997.19

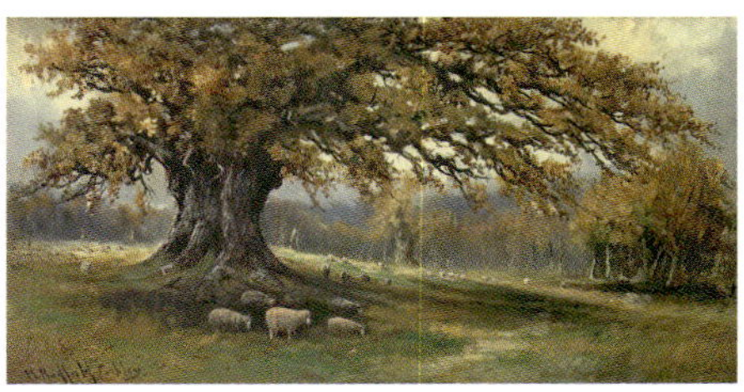

Cubley, Henry Hadfield 1858–1934
Autumn, Albury Park, Surrey 1922
oil on canvas 45 x 91
NTT.2008.17

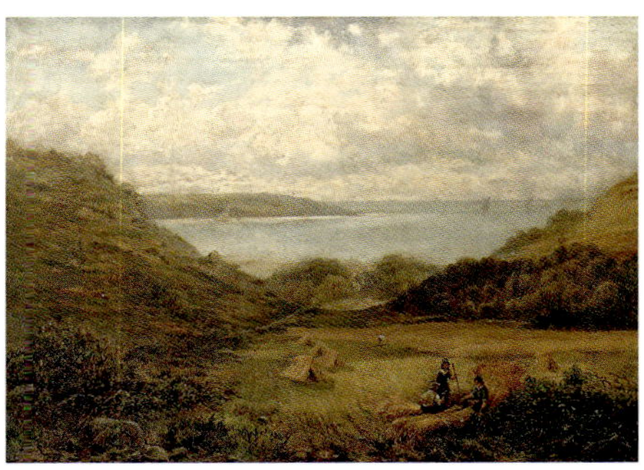

Cubley, Henry Hadfield 1858–1934
Barmouth Bay, West Wales 1931
oil on canvas 63 x 88
NTT.2007.5

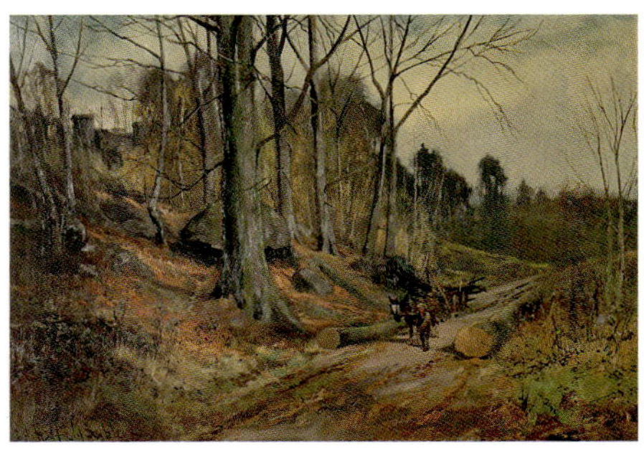

Cubley, Henry Hadfield 1858–1934
The Timber Clearing at Matlock, Derbyshire
oil on canvas 61 x 91
NTT.2007.9

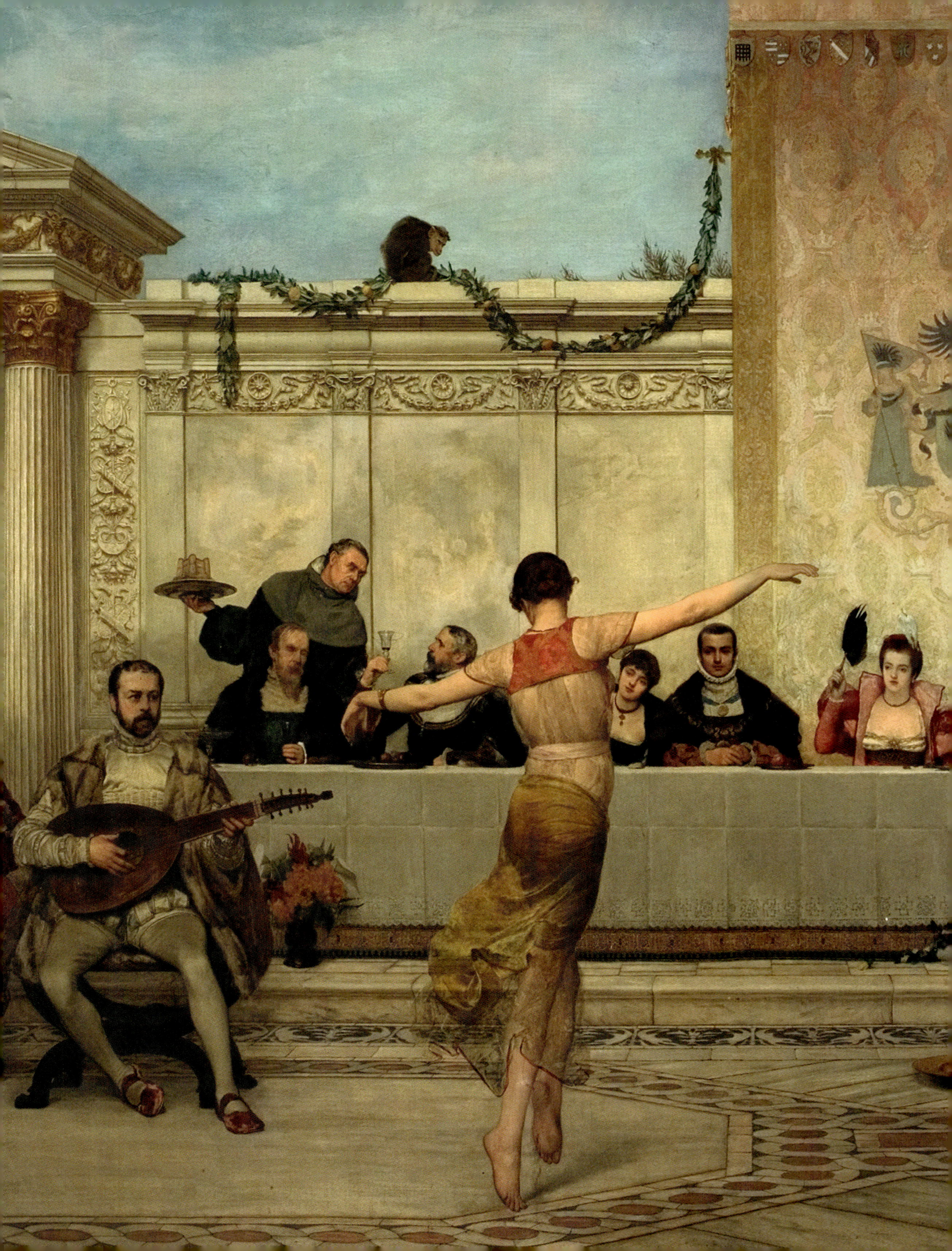

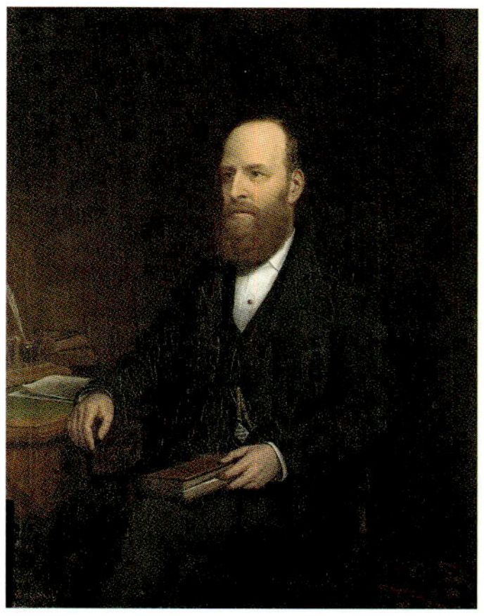

Cubley, William Harold 1814–1896
Becher Tidd Pratt (1826–1901)
oil on canvas 127 x 102
NTT.1997.28

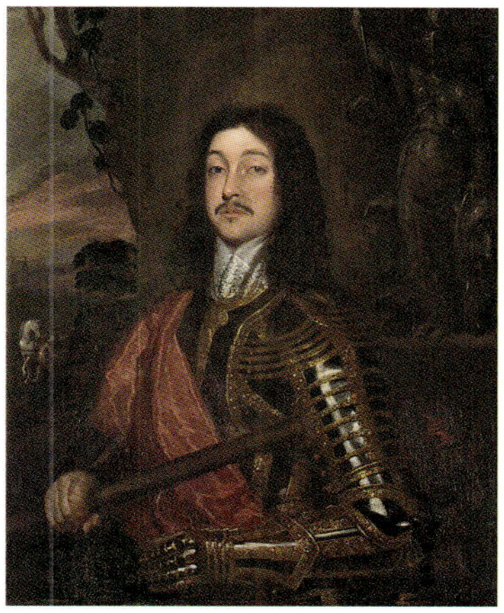

Dobson, William 1611–1646
Sir Richard Willis (1614–1690) 1643
oil on canvas 257 x 168
NTT.1997.293

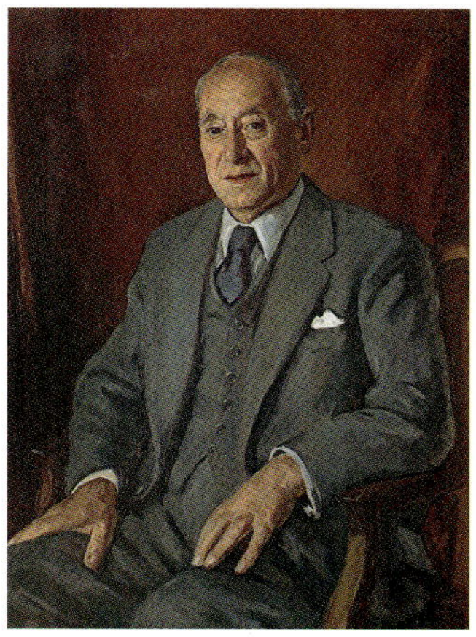

Fuller, Leonard John 1891–1973
John H. Knight (1886–1976) 1959
oil on canvas 89 x 68
NTT.1997.284

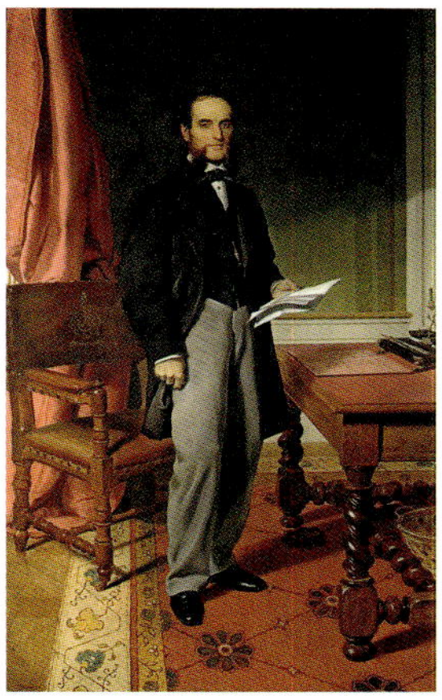

Herbert, John Rogers 1810–1890
Sir William Gilstrap (1816–1896) 1854
oil on canvas 221.5 x 130
NTT.1997.290

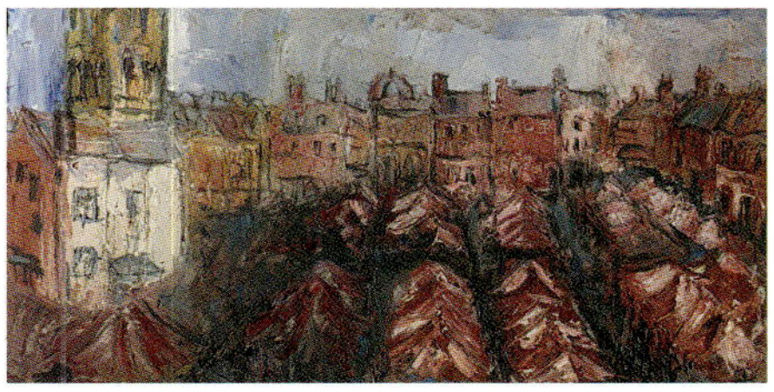

Isaac, Susan b.1961
Market Place, Newark, Nottinghamshire 2007
oil on canvas 30 x 60
NTT.2008.16

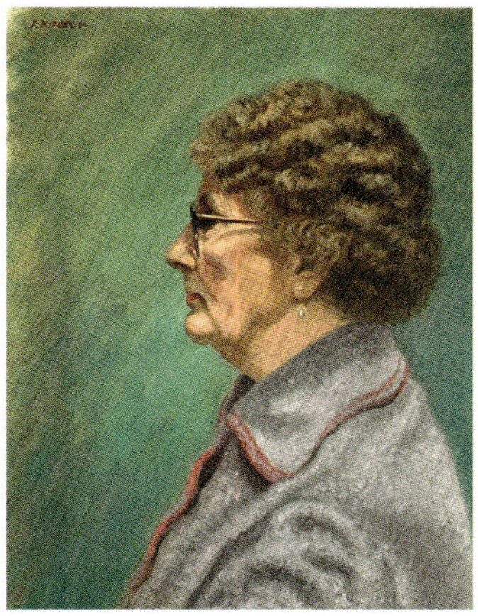

Kiddey, Robert 1900–1984
Hilda Walker 1962
oil on canvas 49 x 39
NTT.1997.26

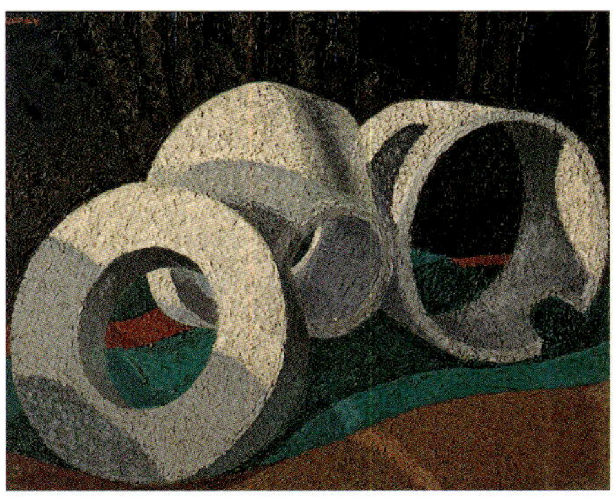

Kiddey, Robert 1900–1984
Night
oil on canvas 64 x 79
NTT.2001.52

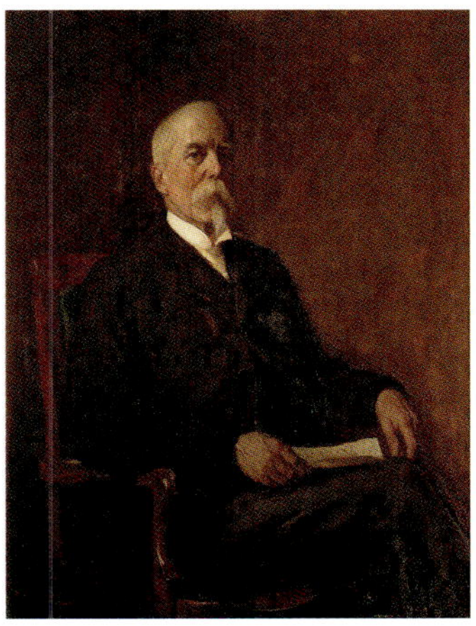

Knight, Harold 1874–1961
Thomas Earp (1830–1910), Mayor of Newark
1903
oil on canvas 127 x 100
NTT.1997.17

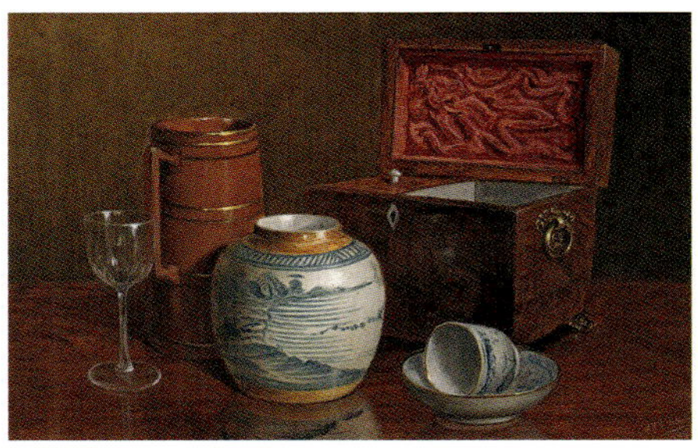

Nicholson, William 1872–1949
Still Life 1885
oil on canvas 33 x 54
NTT.1997.1

Facing page: Linton, James Dromgole, 1840–1916, *The Banquet* (detail), 1882, Nottingham City Museums and Galleries (p. 120)

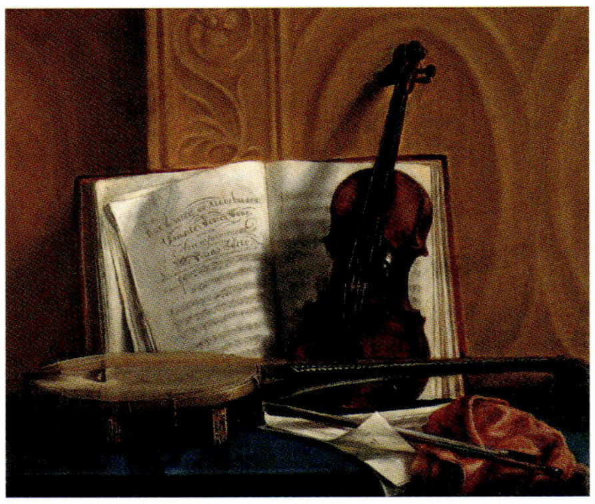

Nicholson, William 1872–1949
Music 1890
oil on canvas 64 x 77
NTT.1997.2

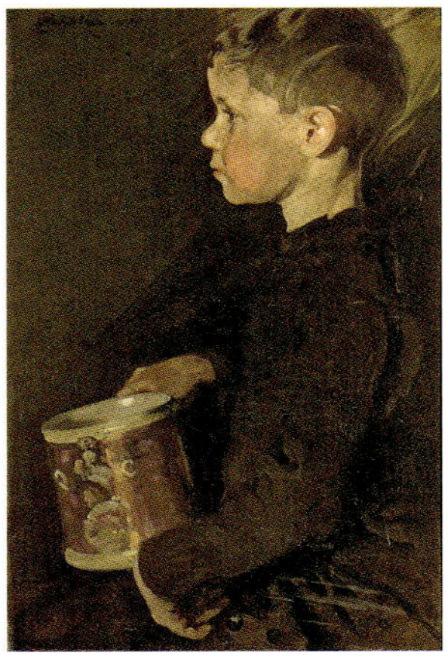

Nicholson, William 1872–1949
Boy with the Caroline Mug 1899
oil on canvas 52.5 x 36.2
NTT.PCF2

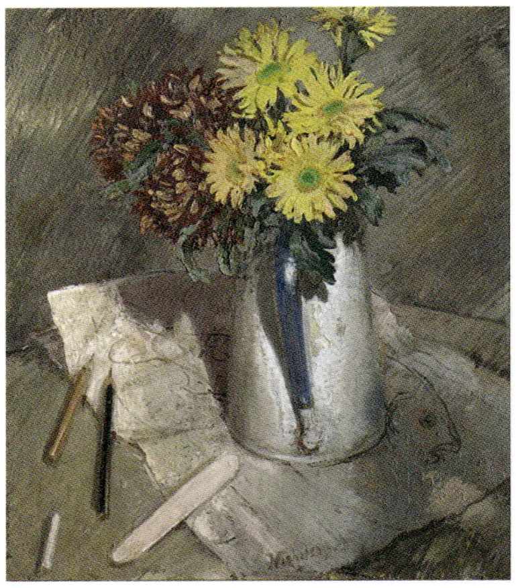

Nicholson, William 1872–1949
Chrysanthemums 1934
oil on canvas 88 x 85.2
NTT.1997.277

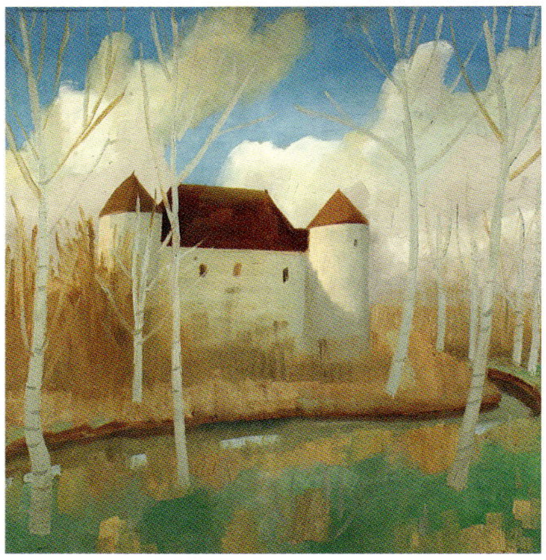

Nicholson, Winifred 1893–1981
Boigneville, Île-de-France, France 1937
oil on canvas 61.5 x 61.5
PCF1

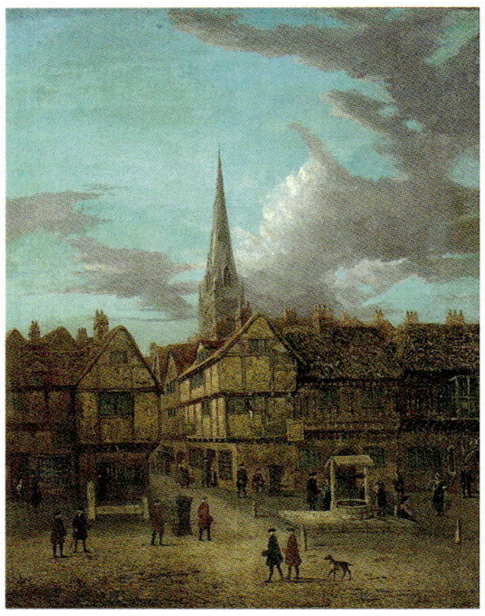

Paul, Joseph (attributed to) 1804–1887
Bridge Street, Newark, Nottinghamshire c.1840
oil on canvas 108.5 x 84
NTT.1997.11

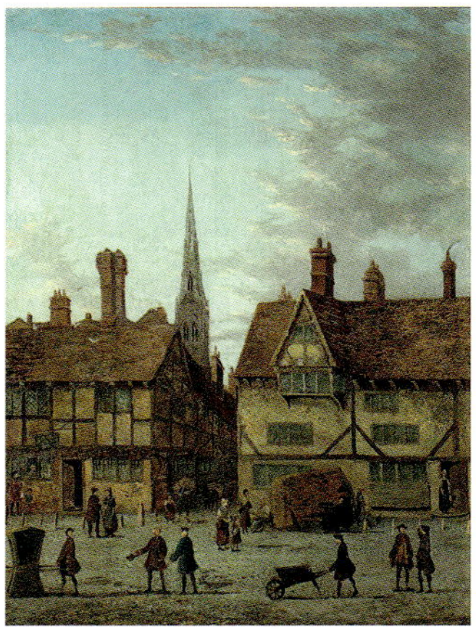

Paul, Joseph (attributed to) 1804–1887
Corner of Market Place, Newark, Nottinghamshire c.1840
oil on canvas 128.5 x 96
NTT.1997.14

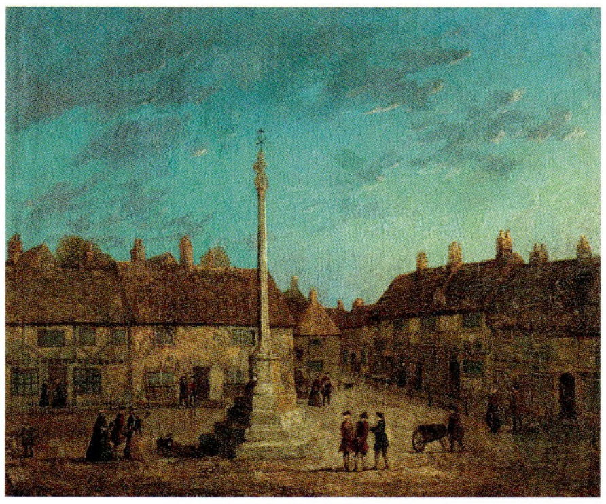

Paul, Joseph (attributed to) 1804–1887
View of Beaumond Cross, Newark, Nottinghamshire c.1840
oil on canvas 94.5 x 117.5
NTT.1997.10

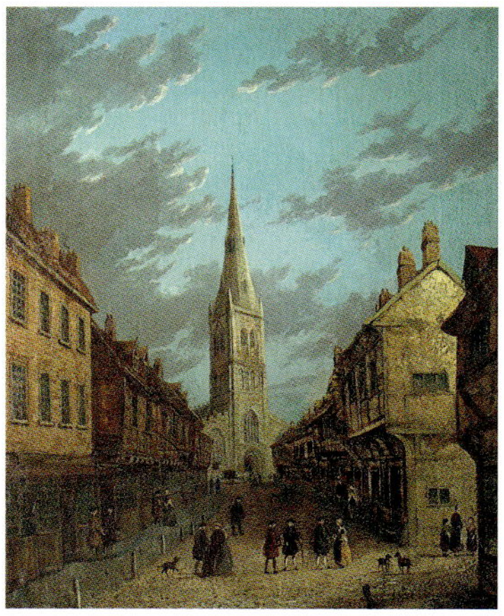

Paul, Joseph (attributed to) 1804–1887
View of Kirkgate, Newark, Nottinghamshire c.1840
oil on canvas 116 x 96
NTT.1997.9

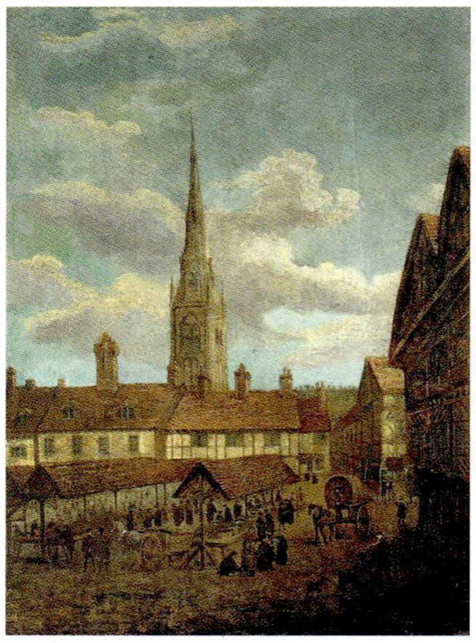

Paul, Joseph (attributed to) 1804–1887
View of Market Place, Newark, Nottinghamshire c.1840
oil on canvas 115.5 x 89
NTT.1997.12

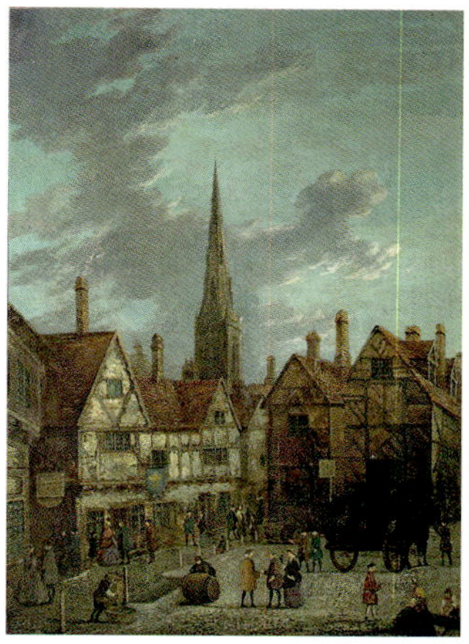

Paul, Joseph (attributed to) 1804–1887
View of the Parish Church, Newark, Nottinghamshire c.1840
oil on canvas 128 x 104
NTT.1997.13

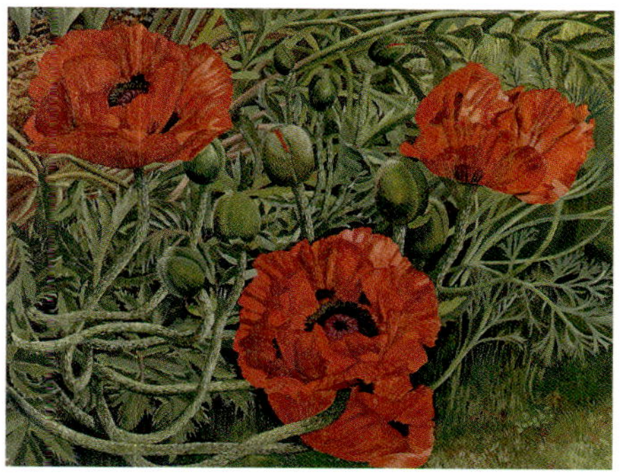

Spencer, Stanley 1891–1959
Poppies 1938
oil on canvas 45 x 60
NTT.1997.18

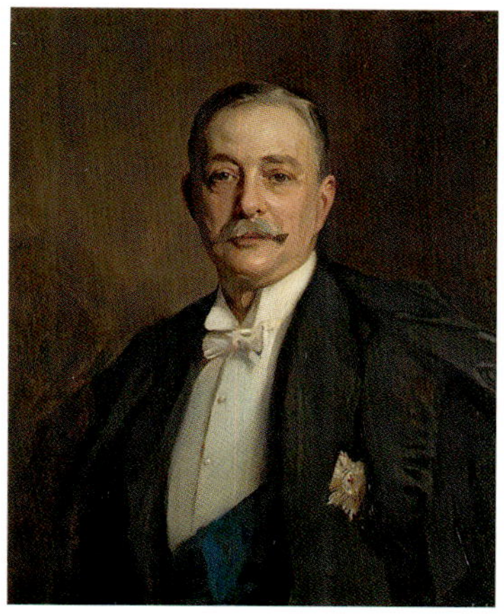

Spooner, Arthur 1873–1961
William Arthur (1857–1943), 6th Duke of Portland, KG, Lord Lieutenant of Nottinghamshire 1914
oil on canvas 74.5 x 62
NTT.1997.3

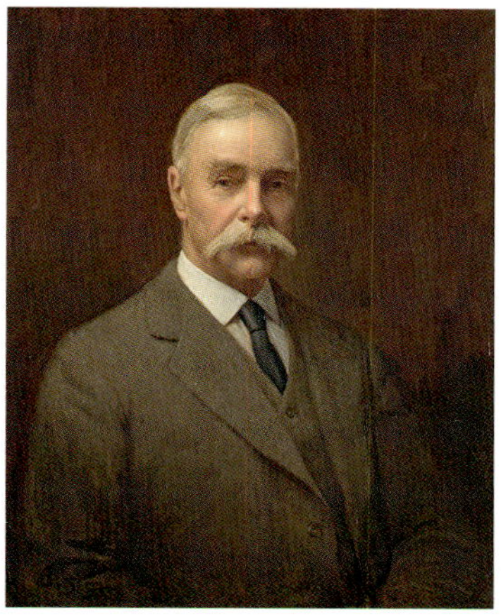

Spooner, Arthur 1873–1961
Godfrey Tallents (1849–1917), Town Clerk 1928
oil on canvas 74 x 62
NTT.1997.283

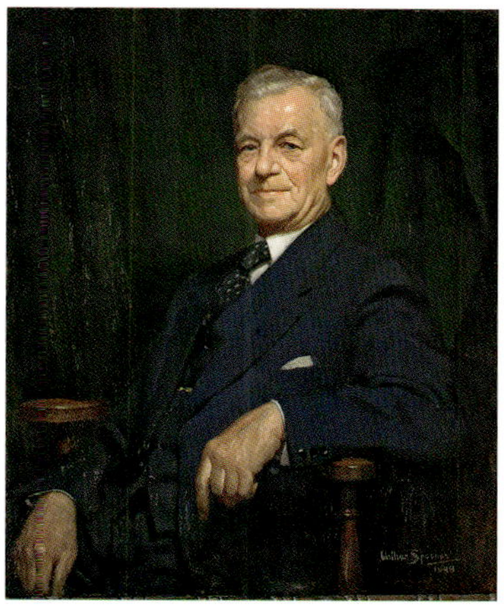

Spooner, Arthur 1873–1961
Percy John Charles Staniland (1880–1961), MBE, JP 1949
oil on canvas 83 x 69
NTT.1997.282

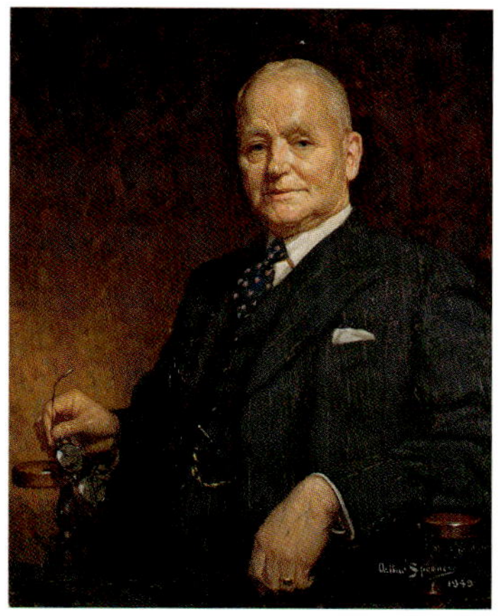

Spooner, Arthur 1873–1961
Richard Pursey Blatherwick (1880–1971), JP 1949
oil on canvas 85 x 72
NTT.1997.4

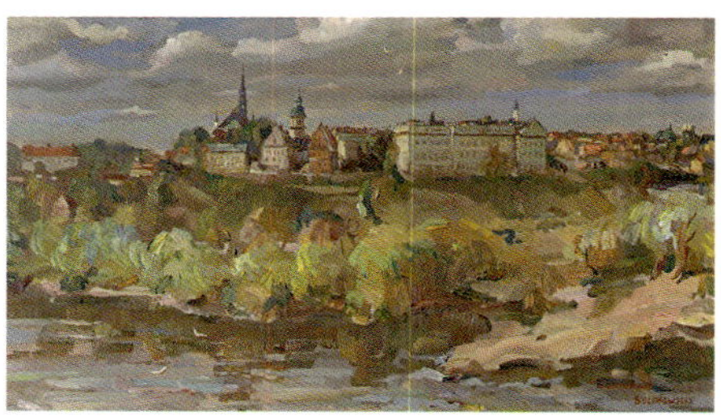

Sulimow, Jurij b.1952
Sandomierz, Poland 2005
oil on canvas 53 x 93
NTT.2006.37

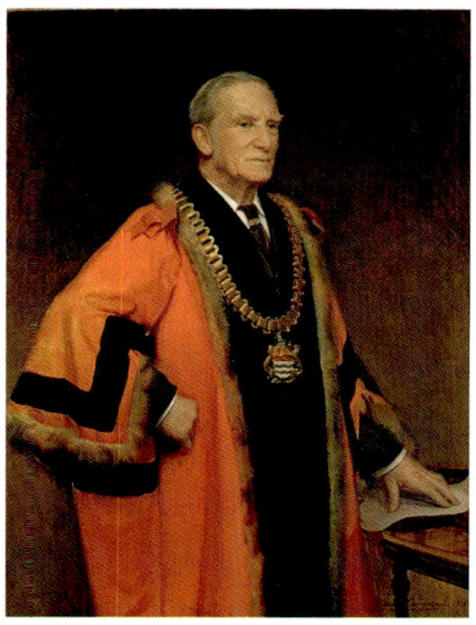

Townsend, Ernest 1880–1944
William Edward Knight (1845–1934), JP, Councillor (1883), Alderman (1904), and Mayor of Newark (1889 & 1915–1918) 1919
oil on canvas 127 x 102
NTT.1997.15

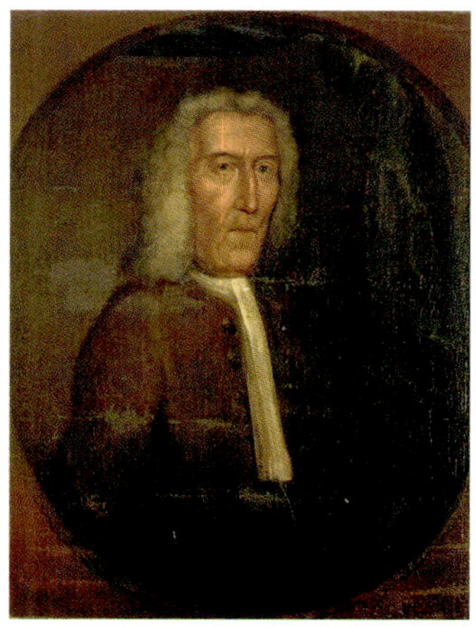

unknown artist
John Clay (1602–1669) 1669
oil on canvas 74 x 59
NTT.PCF3 (P)

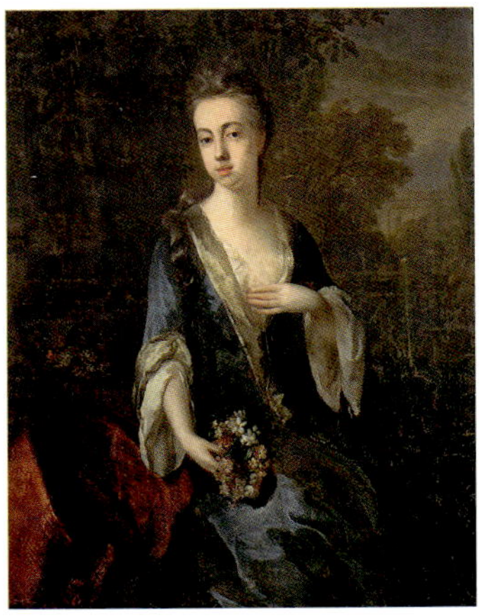

unknown artist
Lady in Blue c.1700
oil on canvas 121 x 97
NTT.1997.16

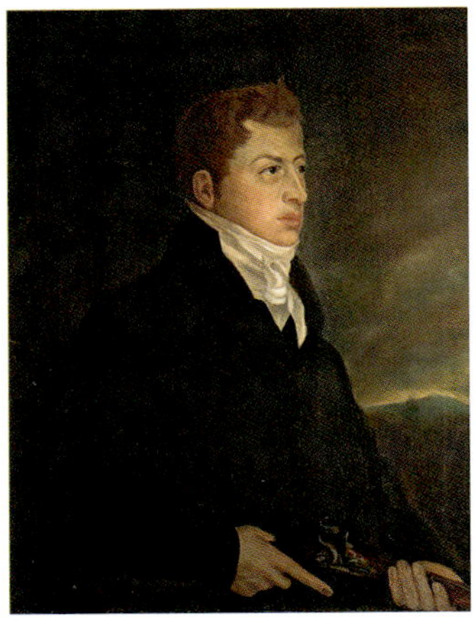

unknown artist
John Hole (b.c.1772), Mayor of Newark (1822) 1822
oil on canvas 89.5 x 68.5
NTT.1997.30

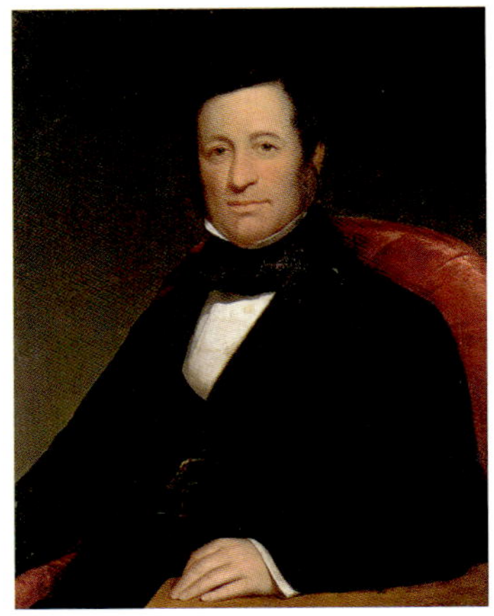

unknown artist
Portrait of an Unknown Gentleman
oil on canvas 71 x 58
NTT.1997.7

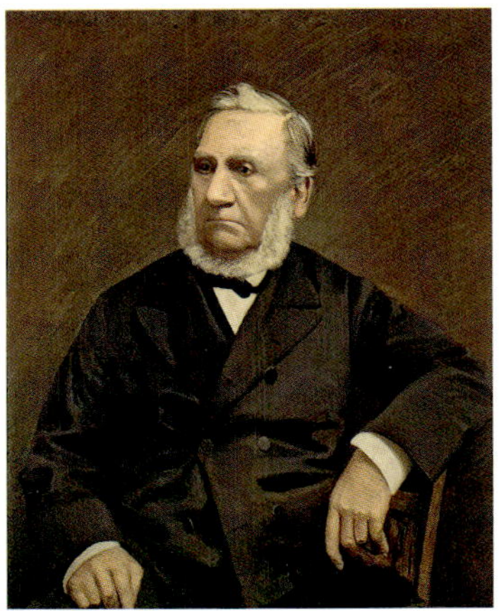

Walton, Henry 1746–1813
Edward Cooper 1811
oil on canvas 70 x 58
NTT.1997.8

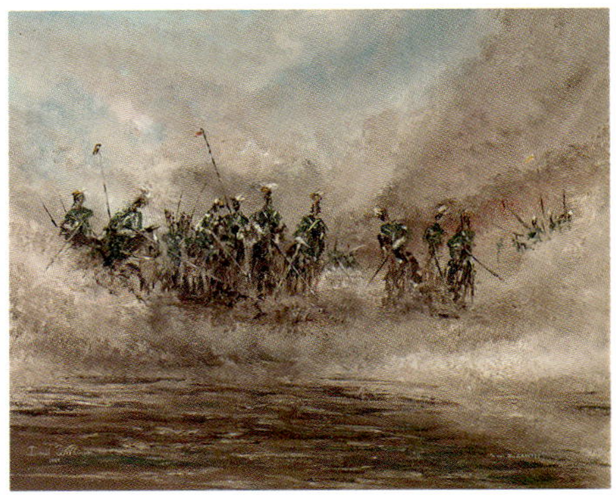

Wilkinson, David
17th and 21st Lancers 1985
oil on canvas 59.5 x 76
NTT.1997.31

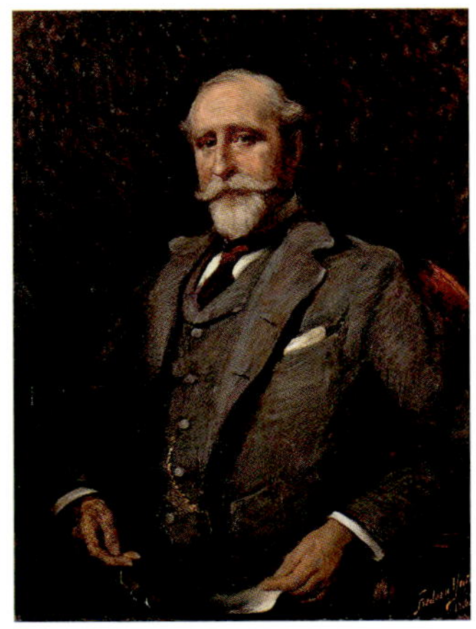

Yates, Edward
Joseph Gilstrap Branston (1838–1926) 1896
oil on canvas 92 x 71
NTT.1997.5

The Holocaust Centre

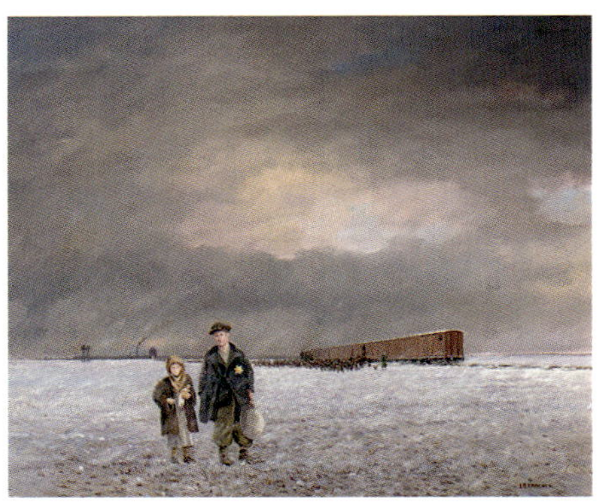

Hancock, K. B.
*Camp Train**
oil on canvas 38.5 x 50
ex.2008.02

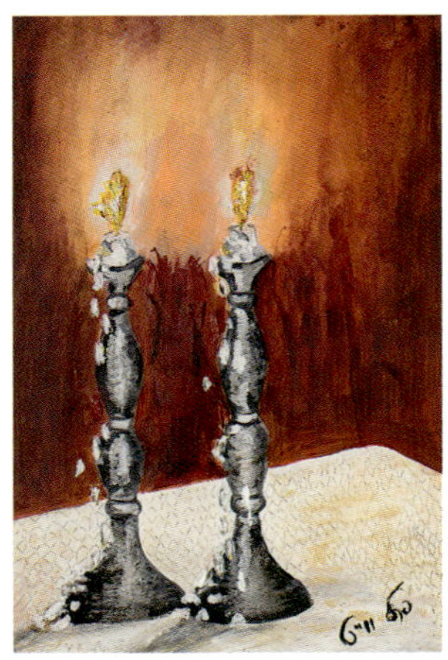

unknown artist
*Jewish Candles**
oil on board 48 x 33
ex.2008.01

Newstead Abbey

When Horace Walpole visited Newstead Abbey in 1760 he found much to admire at that 'beautiful and venerable seat' of the Byron family – but he was particularly impressed by the paintings. William, 4th Lord Byron and great-grandfather of the poet, had formed a collection of art which included what Walpole praised as works 'by the best Flemish hands'. The 4th Lord was both a patron and a pupil of Peter Tillemans, from whom he commissioned views of the Abbey and its park. The artist was a frequent visitor to Newstead where, in Walpole's opinion, 'Tillemans himself must have improved amidst so many fine pictures of animals and huntings'.

The 4th Lord's son, another William, inherited with the title and estates his father's passion for collecting. Following his marriage in 1747, the young 5th Lord spent much of his wife's fortune in the auction houses. Joe Murray, his servant (and later the poet's), recalled that his 'dear late Lord, whenever there were any very costly, rare articles of vertu or art on sale in London, would order horses to his carriage and set out at a moment's notice and bring them down in his carriage with him…'. By all accounts, the results of this enthusiastic acquisitiveness were most impressive. The Duchess of Northumberland, who visited the Abbey in about 1770, thought 'most remarkable… a half-length of Sir Thos More by Holbein… but the pictures which struck me most were one of Tygers and another of Lyons by Rubens'.

Unfortunately, financial difficulties soon obliged the 5th Lord to sell pretty much everything that was not entailed. The first auction took place at Christie's in March 1772. *A Catalogue of all that Grand and Noble Collection of Italian, French, Flemish and Dutch Pictures… collected by his Lordship and noble Father during the Course of a Great Number of Years with Great Speculation and Vast Expense…* lists 429 lots sold in five days. When the 5th Lord died in 1798, the only paintings known to have remained in the Abbey were family portraits and five views of Newstead by Tillemans.

His heir, the poet Byron, while claiming to have no interest in pictures, liked those views well enough to hang them in his private drawing room at Newstead. Soon after he took up residence there, he commissioned three works by local painters: portraits of two of his dogs by Clifton Tomson and a portrait of Joseph Murray by Thomas Barber. The family portraits left the Abbey when Byron sold the estate in 1818. However, Michael Dahl's painting of the poet's great-grandmother was recently returned to Newstead with generous grant aid from the Museums and Galleries Commission/Victoria and Albert Museum Purchase Grant Fund and the National Art Collections Fund, who also made possible the acquisition of Joshua Reynolds' portrait of the poet's grandfather as a young man. We are extremely grateful to them and to the many other organisations who have helped this museum to acquire and conserve paintings. These include the Heritage Lottery Fund, the Pilgrim Trust, the Friends of the Nottingham Museums, Woodmansterne Publications Limited, MONKS and the Byron Society.

Haidee Jackson, Keeper of Collections

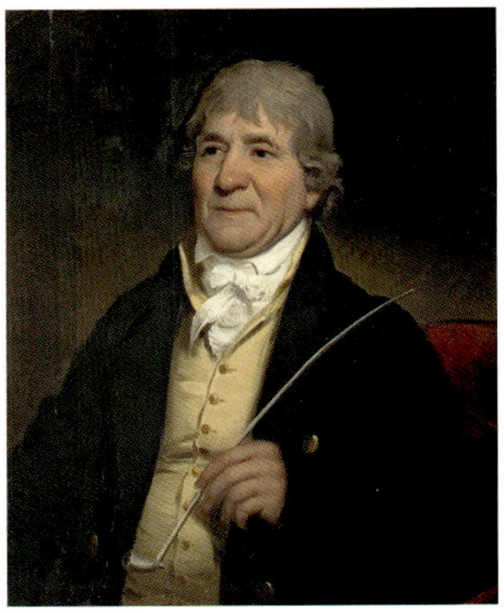

Barber, Thomas 1771–1843
Joseph Murray (1737–1820)
oil on canvas 74.4 x 63.5
NA 341

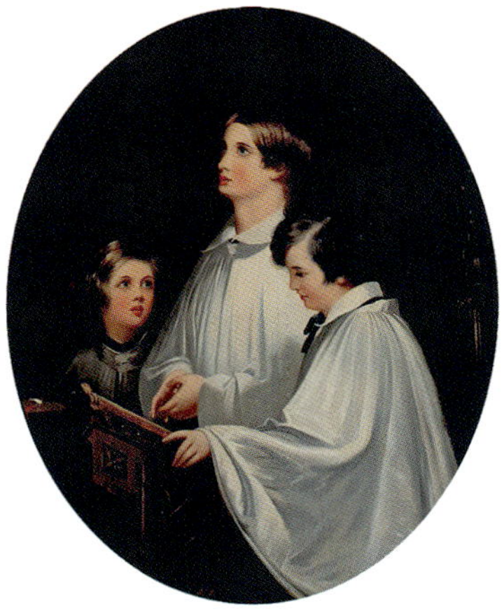

Barraud, Henry 1811–1874
'Lord, have mercy upon us' c.1850
oil on canvas 104 x 87
NA 514

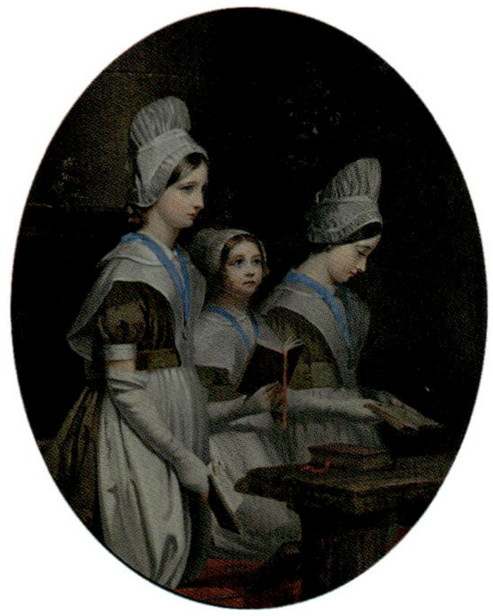

Barraud, Henry 1811–1874
'We praise thee, O Lord' c.1850
oil on canvas 104 x 87
NA 512

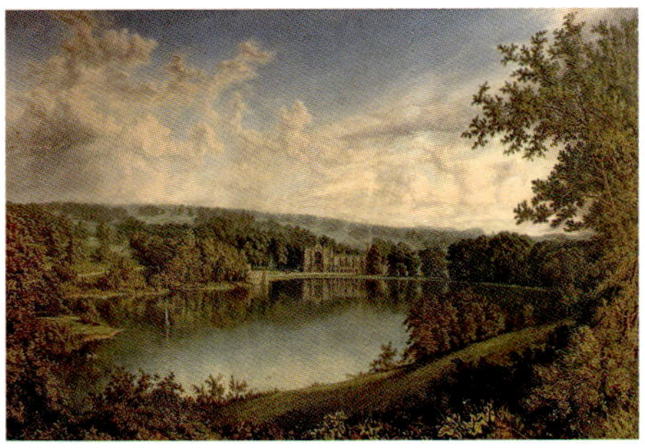

Bell, John 1823–1881
Newstead Abbey, Nottinghamshire, from the Upper Lake 1866
oil on canvas 181 x 305
NA 243

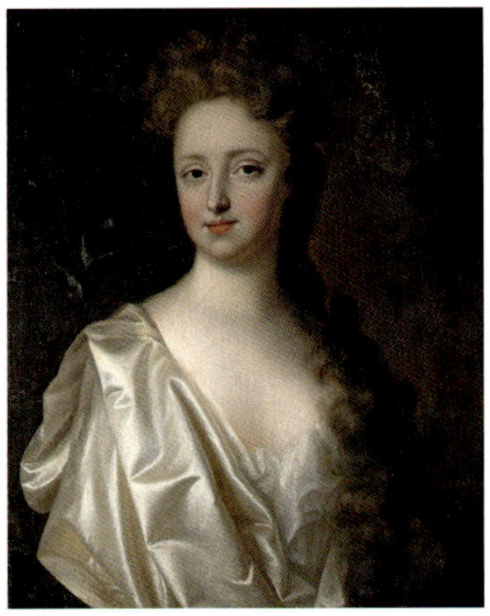

British (English) School late 17th C
Portrait of a Young Woman in White Satin
oil on canvas 86 x 73
NA 516

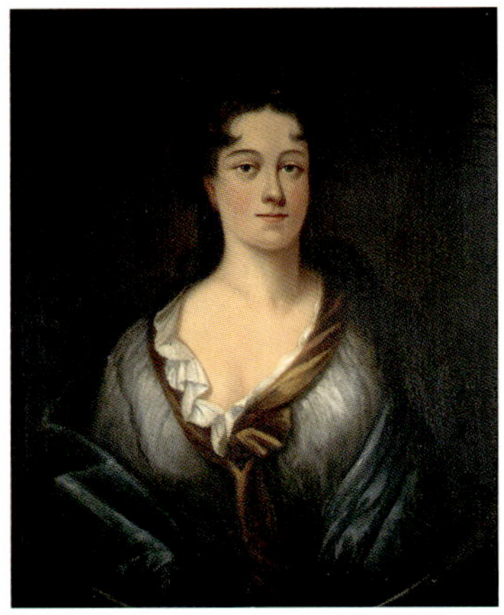

British (English) School early 18th C
Portrait of a Young Woman in a Blue Wrap
oil on canvas 85 x 71.5
NA 518

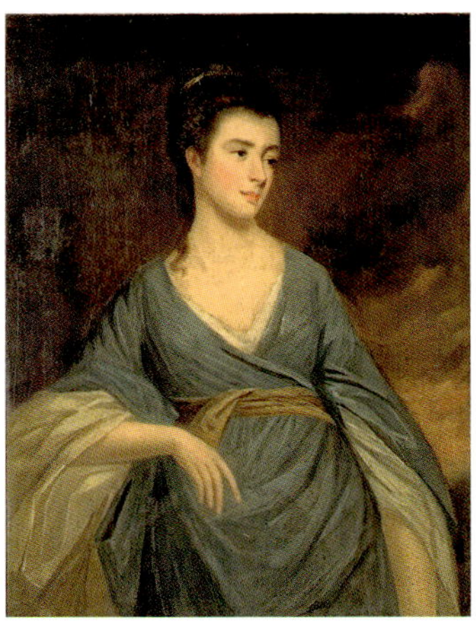

British (English) School 18th C
Young Woman in a Blue Dress
oil on canvas 81.2 x 68.7
NAL 7/25 (P)

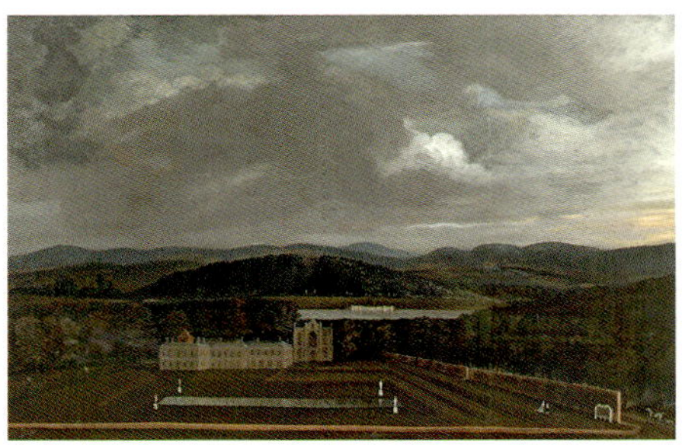

Byron, Richard 1724–1811
East View of Newstead Abbey, Nottinghamshire, and the Great Garden 1758
oil on canvas 49.5 x 80
NA 2245

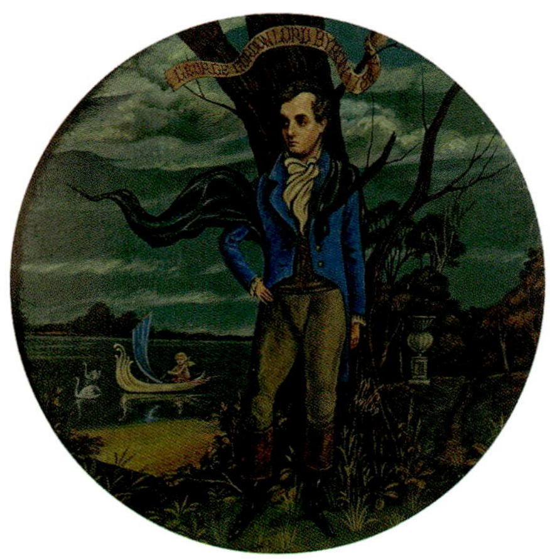

Chaffin, Donald
George Gordon, Lord Byron (1788–1824) 1969
oil on wood 8
NA 996

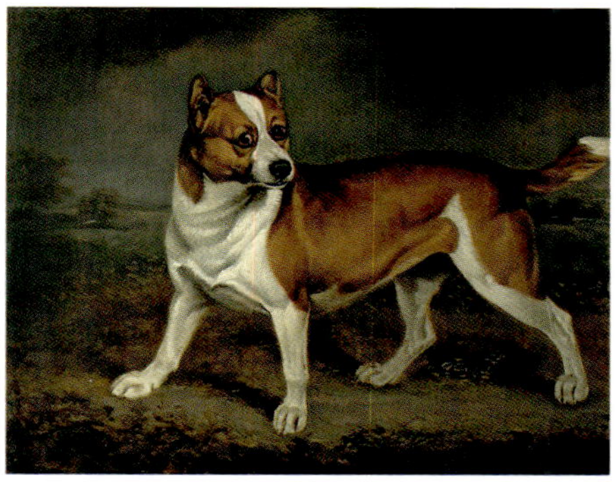

Chalon, Henry Bernard 1771–1849
'Nettle' 1812
oil on canvas 69 x 93.5
NA 601

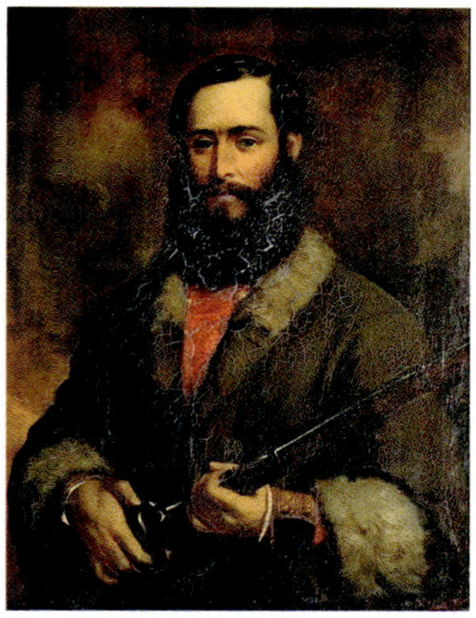

Collins, James Edgell 1819–1895
Colonel Gerald Littlehales Goodlake (1832–1890) c.1857
oil on canvas 120 x 100
NA 508

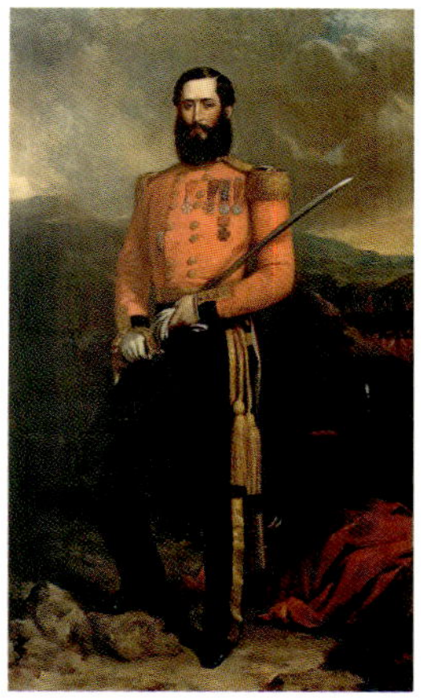

Collins, James Edgell 1819–1895
Colonel Gerald Littlehales Goodlake (1832–1890), Coldstream Guards (1857) c.1857
oil on canvas 270 x 143
NA 242

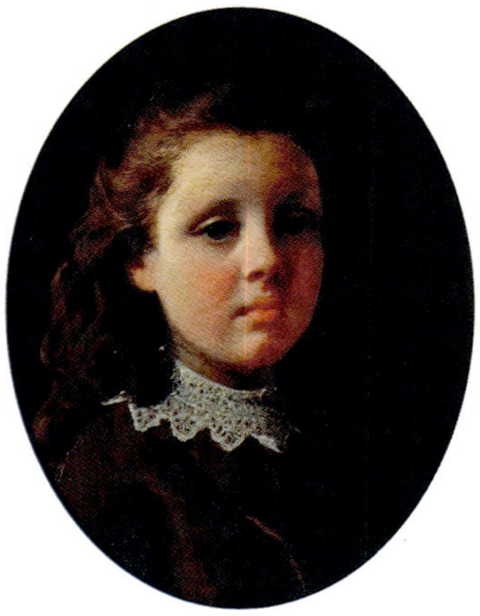

Corbould, Alfred c.1821–1874
Portrait of the Artist's Daughter 1855
oil on canvas 38 x 30
NA 520

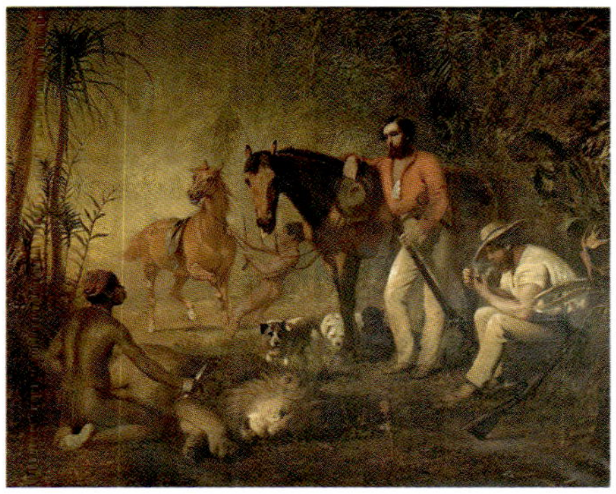

Corbould, Alfred c.1821–1874
After the Lion Hunt (W. F. Webb and Captain W. Codrington, South Africa) 1857
oil on canvas 267 x 334
NA 550

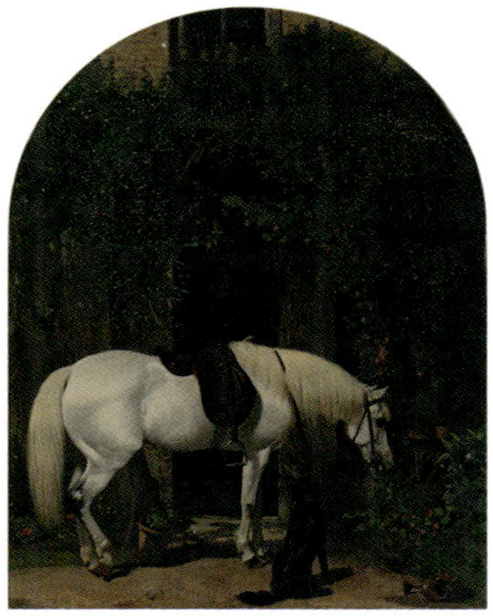

Corbould, Alfred c.1821–1874
White Horse and Retriever
oil on canvas 123 x 99
NA 244

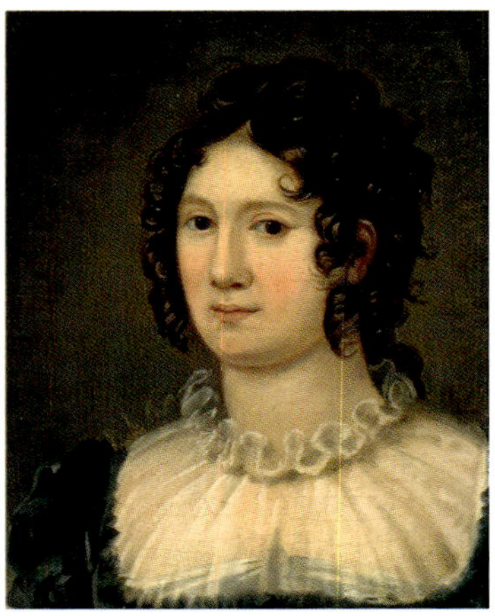

Curran, Amelia 1775–1847
Claire Clairmont (1798–1879) 1819
oil on canvas 47 x 35
NA 271

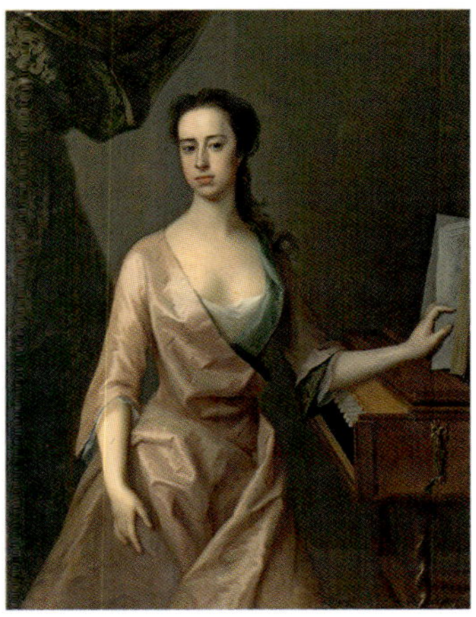

Dahl, Michael I 1656/1659–1743
Frances, Lady Byron (d.1757), Third Wife of the 4th Lord Byron c.1720
oil on canvas 124.4 x 99.5
NA 2164

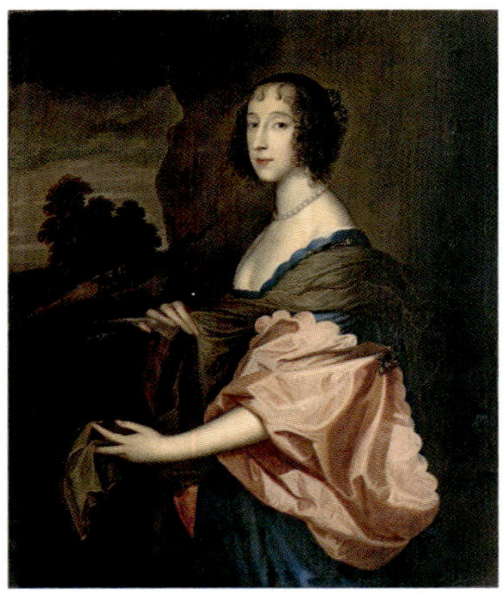

Dahl, Michael I (after) 1656/1659–1743
Penelope, Lady Herbert (1620–1647)
oil on canvas 112.5 x 96.1
NA 511

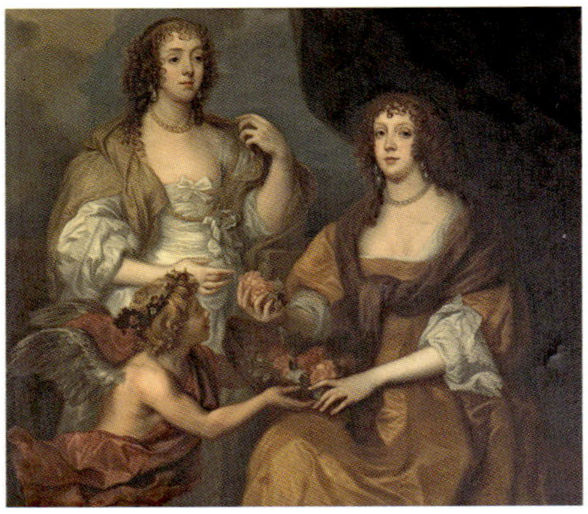

Dyck, Anthony van (after) 1599–1641
Lady Elizabeth Thimbelby and Dorothy, Viscountess Andover
oil on canvas 125 x 144
NA 513

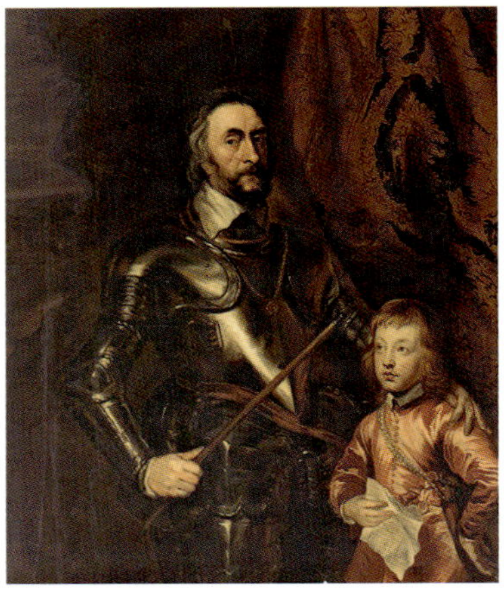

Dyck, Anthony van (after) 1599–1641
Thomas Howard (1585–1646), Earl of Arundel, and His Son Lord Maltravers (1607–1624)
oil on canvas 139 x 120
NA 507

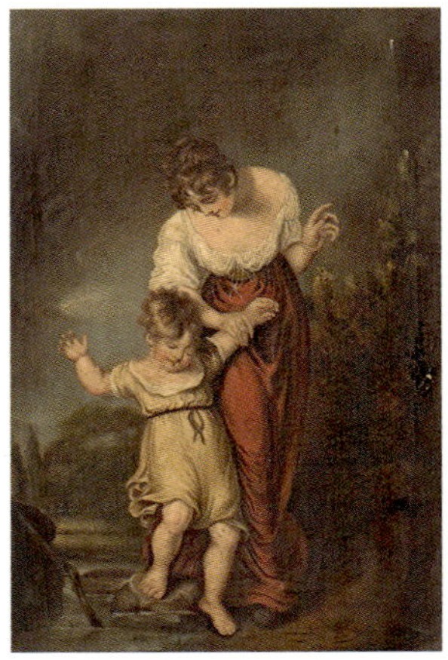

Gainsborough, Thomas (after) 1727–1788
Woman and Child at a Ford
oil on canvas 68.2 x 48.4
NA 602

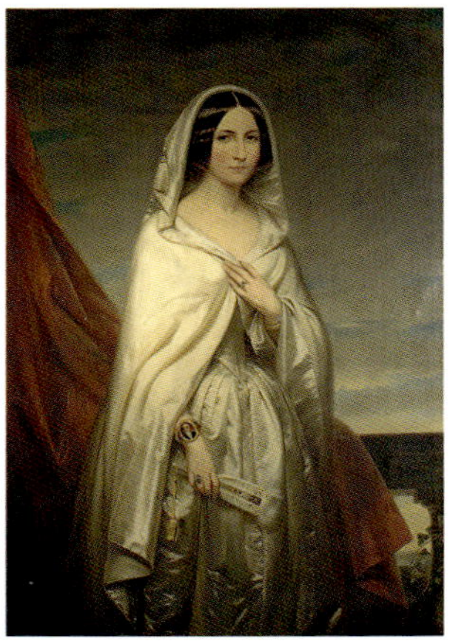

Geefs, Fanny 1807–1883
Katherine Mary Webb Palmer (1824–1890) (later Lady Lambert) 1846
oil on canvas 171.5 x 130
NA 500

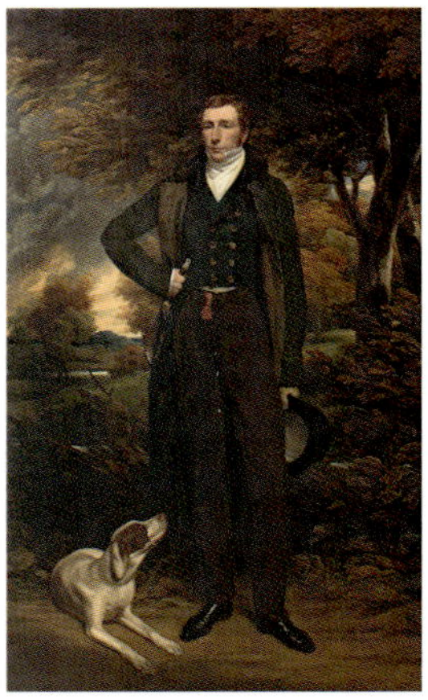

Halls, John James 1776–1853
John Hanson (d.1841)
oil on canvas 238 x 145.5
NA 2093

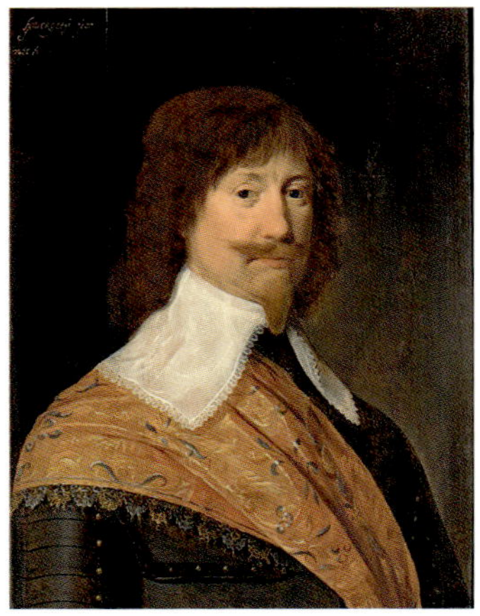

Houckgeest, Joachim Ottensz.
c.1585–before 1645
Sir Nicholas Byron (d.1596) 1631
oil on wood panel 69 x 54
NA 931

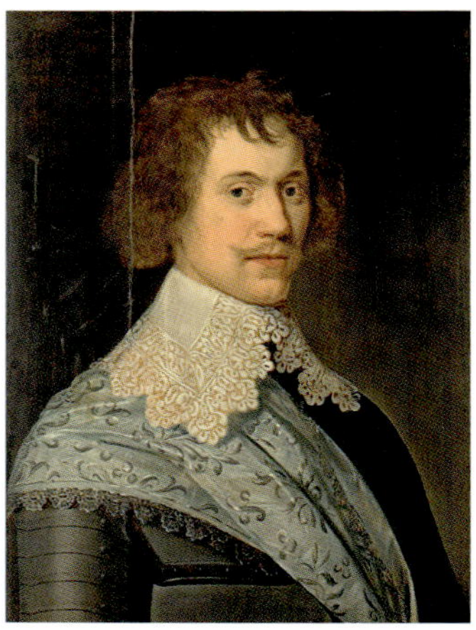

Houckgeest, Joachim Ottensz.
c.1585–before 1645
Sir Thomas Byron (d.1643) 1631
oil on wood panel 69 x 54
NA 930

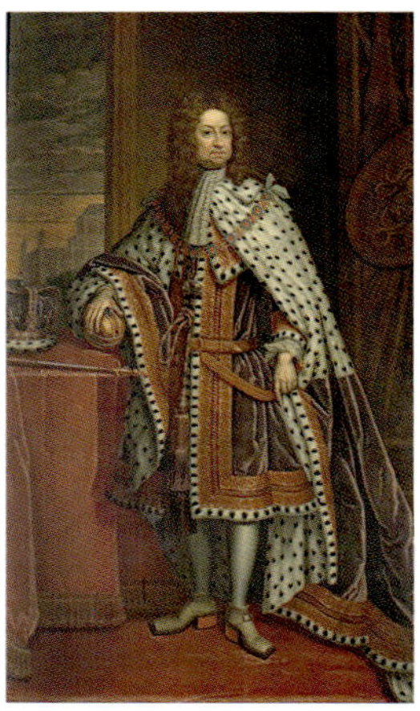

Kneller, Godfrey (after) 1646–1723
George I (1660–1727)
oil on canvas 260 x 140.5
NA 519

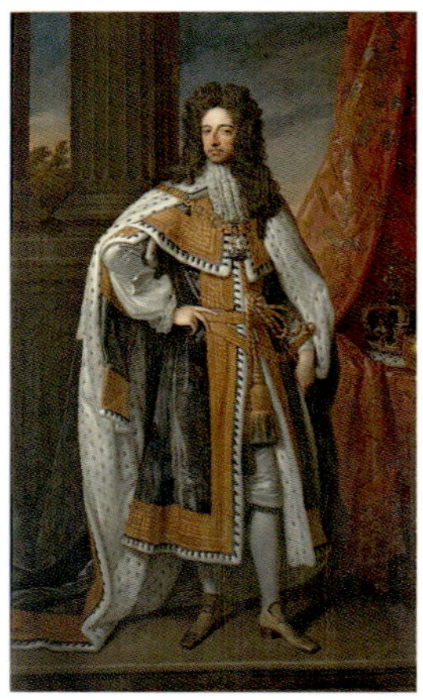

Kneller, Godfrey (after) 1646–1723
William III (1650–1702)
oil on canvas 254 x 137.5
NA 506

Facing page: Royle, Stanley, 1888–1961, *Evening Light, Fishing Village of Prospect, Nova Scotia, Canada* (detail), 1941, Bassetlaw District Council, (p. 227)

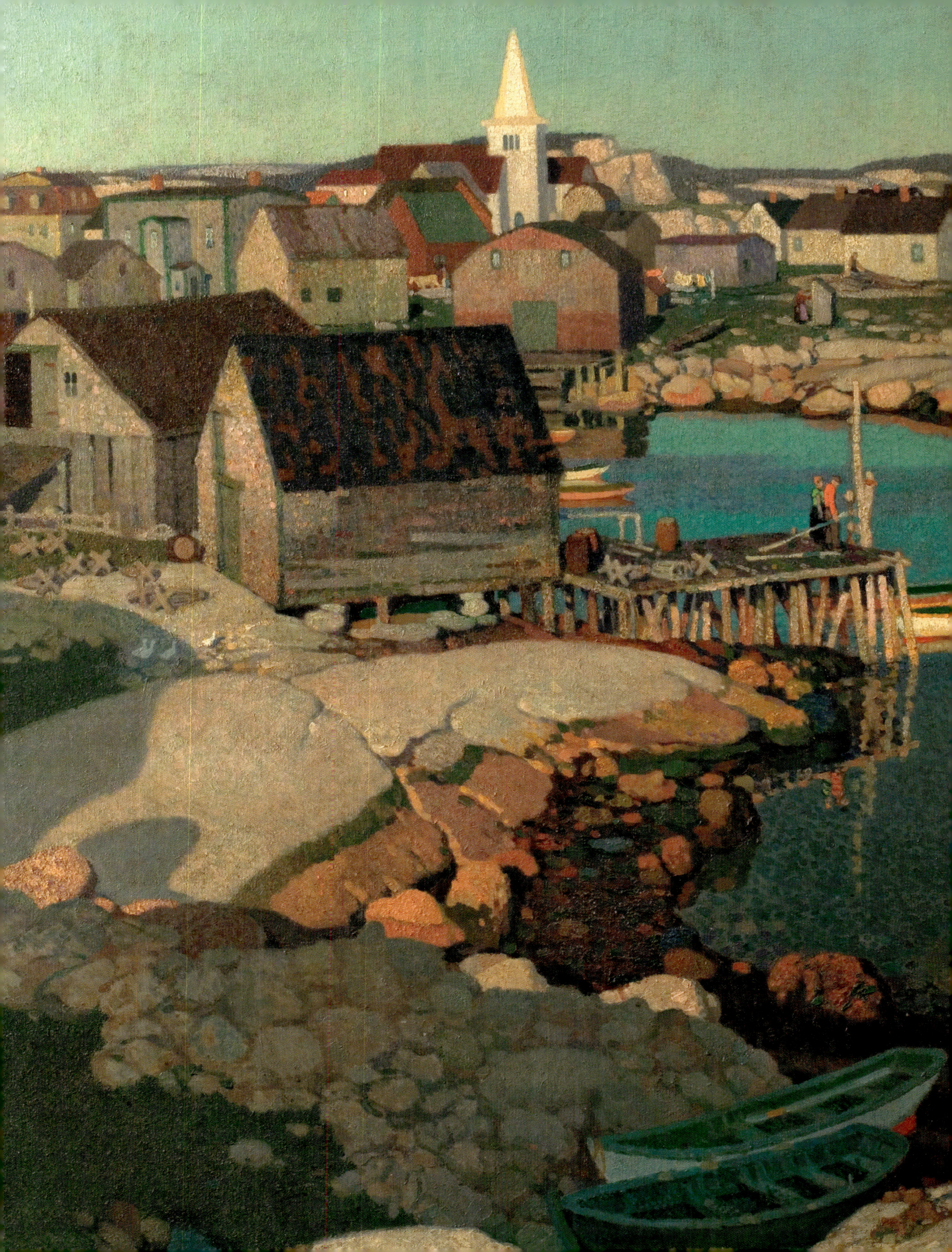

Lawrence, Thomas (style of) 1769–1830
Portrait of a Boy
oil on canvas 58.2 x 50
RB B10

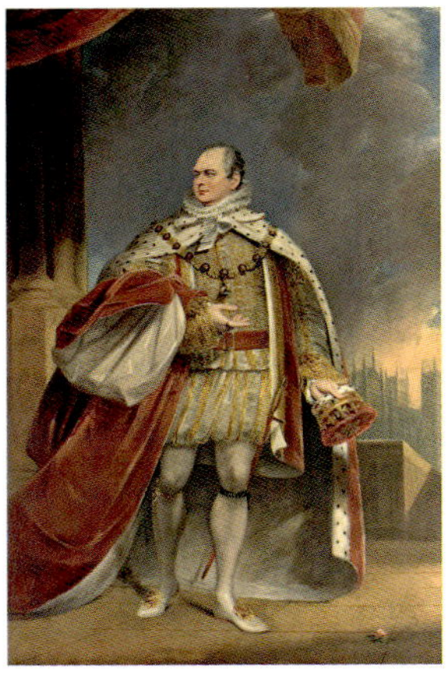

Lonsdale, James 1777–1839
Augustus Frederick (1773–1843), Duke of Sussex
oil on canvas 316 x 172.5
NA 510

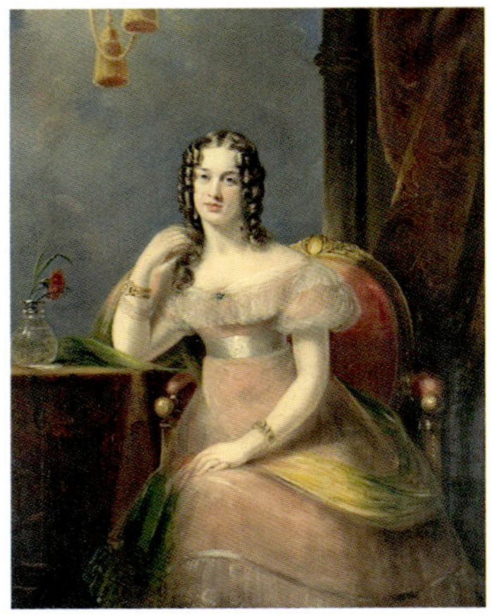

Lonsdale, James 1777–1839
Louisa Wildman (1800–1879)
oil on canvas 127 x 102
NA 562

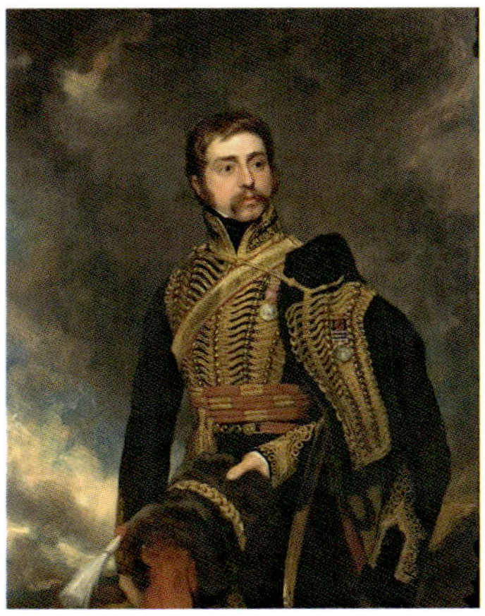

Lonsdale, James 1777–1839
Thomas Wildman (1787–1859)
oil on canvas 125.7 x 100.3
NA 561

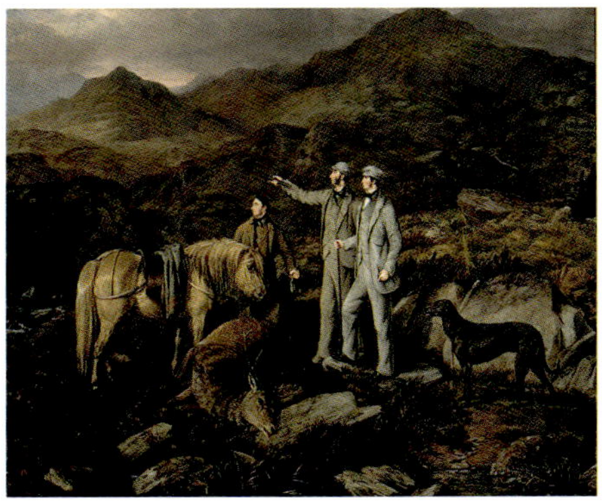

Luker, William c.1820–1892
Stag Hunt in Scotland 1852
oil on canvas 145 x 173
NA 549

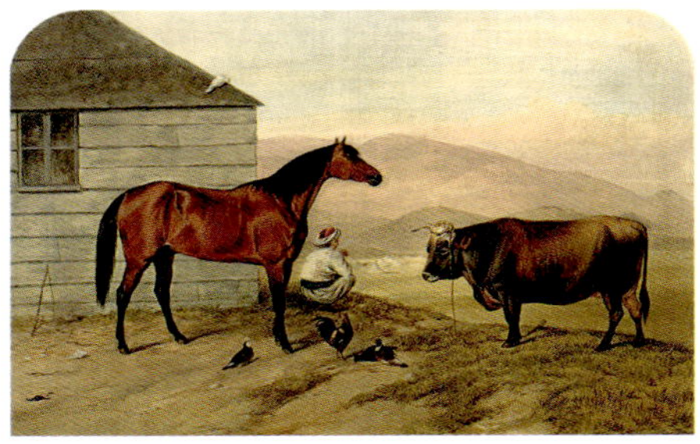

Luker, William (attributed to) c.1820–1892
The Turkish Pony 'Bobby', the Cock from Sebastopol, the Cow from the Valley of Baidar, and the Pigeon (…) 1858
oil on canvas 50 x 75
NA 22

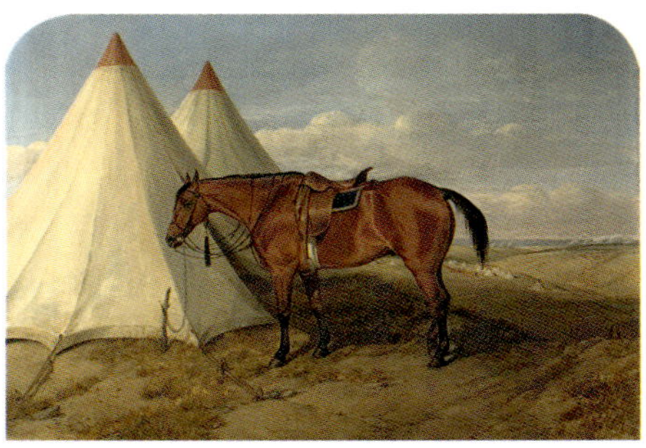

Luker, William (attributed to) c.1820–1892
The Toy c.1858
oil on canvas 49 x 75
NA 25

Reproduction
Rights Refused

Lytton, Neville Stephen 1879–1951
Ralph, 2nd Earl of Lovelace (1839–1906)
oil on canvas 58 x 45.3
NAL 34/16 (P)

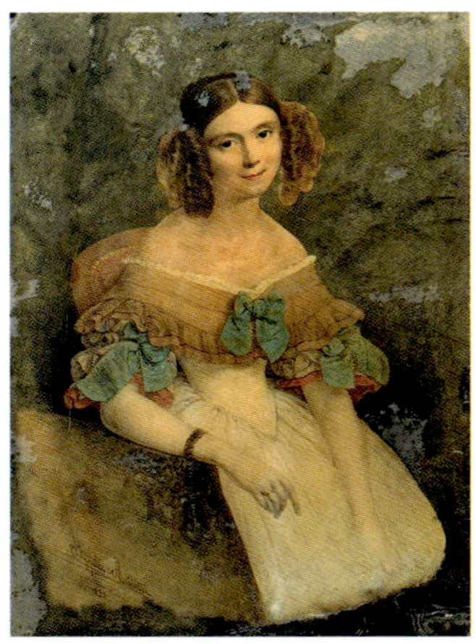

Masson, Hippolyte d.1878
Marguerite, Countess of Blessington (1789–1849) 1838
oil on glass 35.5 x 26.5
RB H11

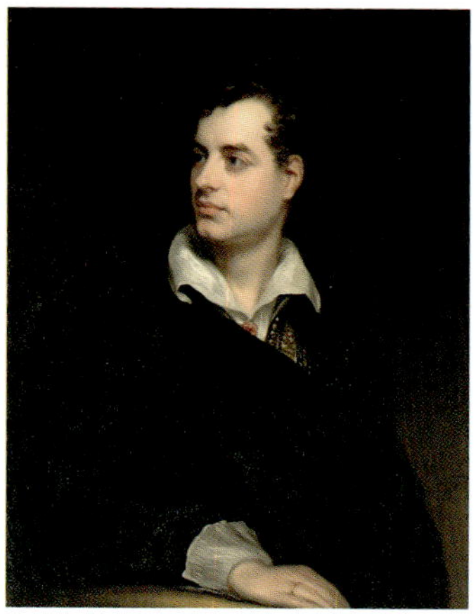

Phillips, Thomas 1770–1845
6th Lord Byron (1788–1824) 1813
oil on canvas 91 x 71
NA 532

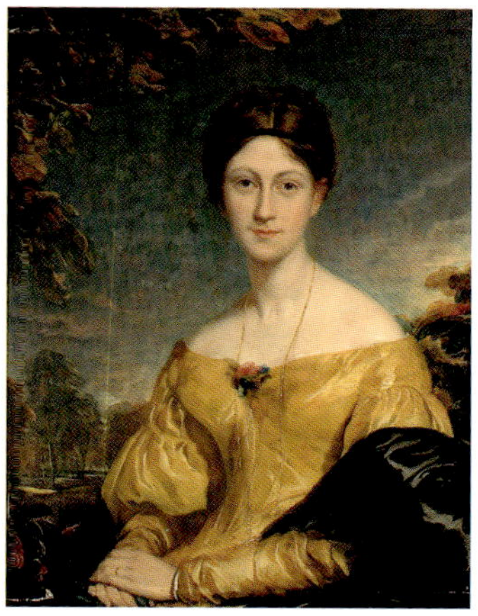

Phillips, Thomas 1770–1845
Mary Chaworth Musters (1786–1832)
oil on canvas 130 x 102
RB B17

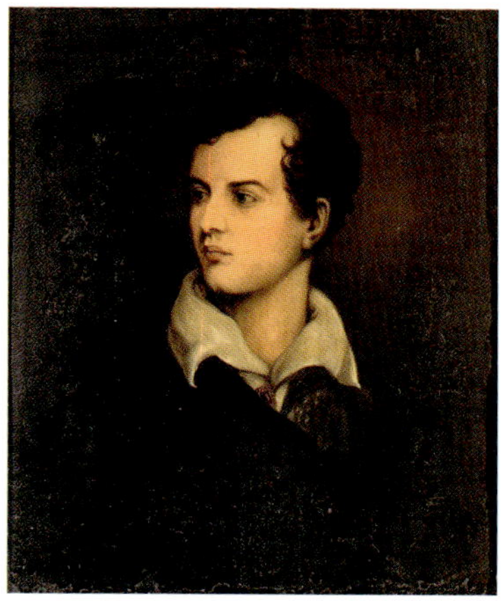

Phillips, Thomas (after) 1770–1845
6th Lord Byron (1788–1824)
oil on canvas 73 x 61.5
NA 364

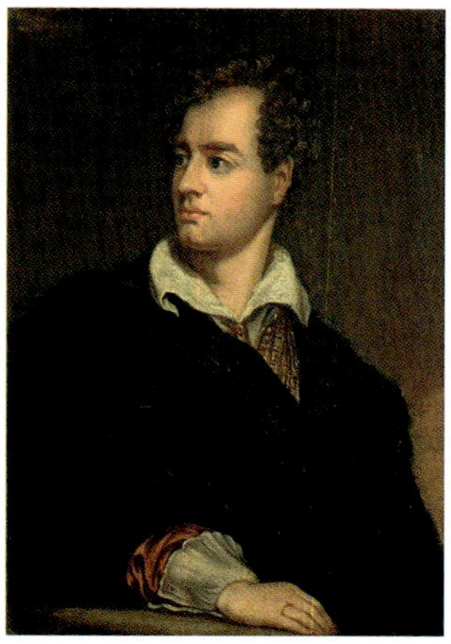

Phillips, Thomas (after) 1770–1845
6th Lord Byron (1788–1824)
oil on canvas 30 x 26.8
RB E23

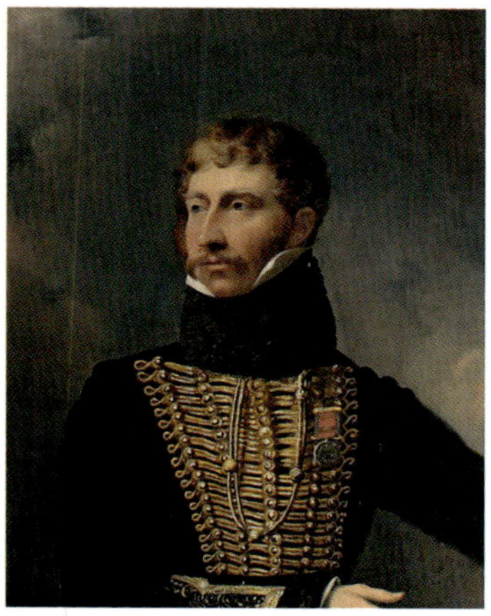

Phillips, Thomas (attributed to) 1770–1845
Thomas Wildman (1787–1859) 1808–1816
oil on canvas 80 x 67
NA 498

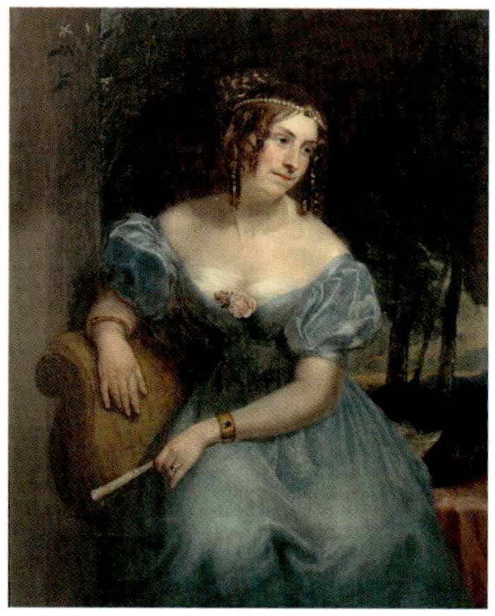

Pickersgill, Henry William 1782–1875
Countess Teresa Guiccioli (c.1800–1873)
oil on canvas 140 x 125
NAL 39/1 (P)

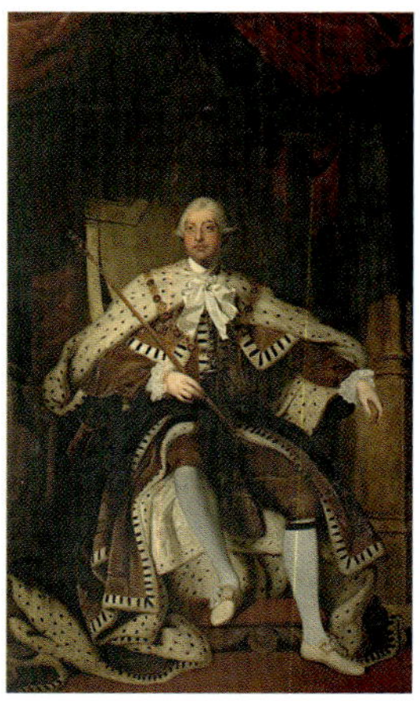

Ramsay, Allan 1713–1784
George III (1738–1820)
oil on canvas 236 x 143
NA 517

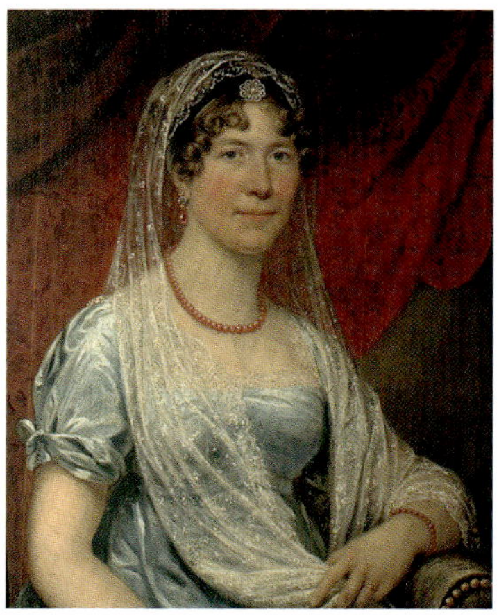

Ramsay, James 1786–1854
Portrait of a Lady 1810–1854
oil on canvas 73.6 x 62.5
NA 497

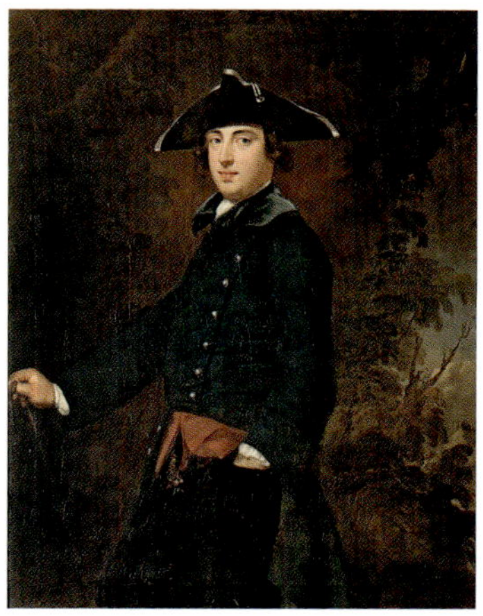

Reynolds, Joshua 1723–1792
Admiral the Honourable John Byron (?) (1723–1786) c.1748
oil on canvas 123.5 x 98
NA 1026

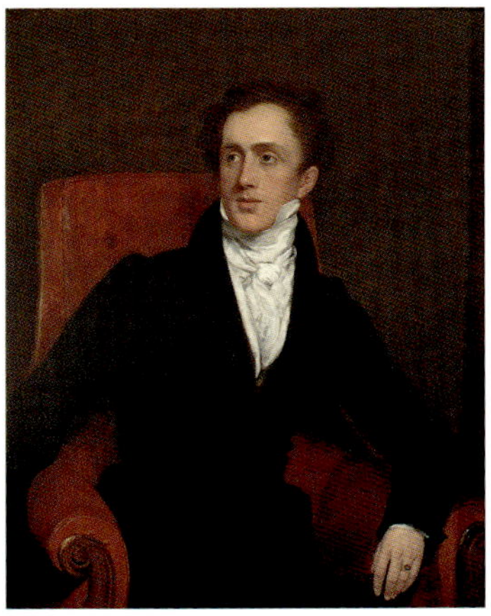

Ross, William Charles 1794–1860
Frederick Webb (1790–1846) c.1822
oil on canvas 136 x 115
NA 501

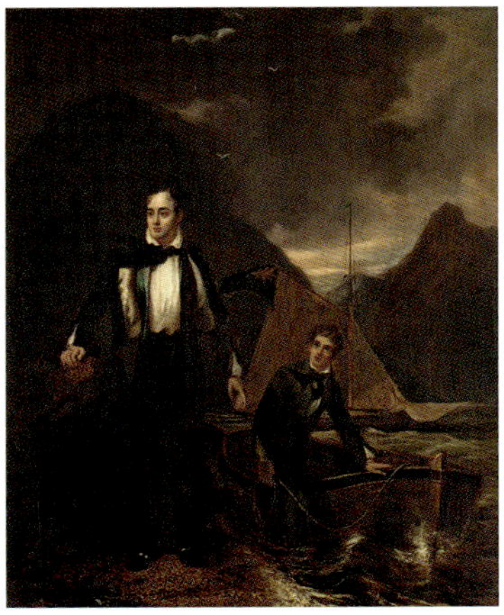

Sanders, George (after) 1774–1846
6th Lord Byron (1788–1824), and His Servant Robert Rushton (1793–1833)
oil on canvas 91 x 75
NA 893

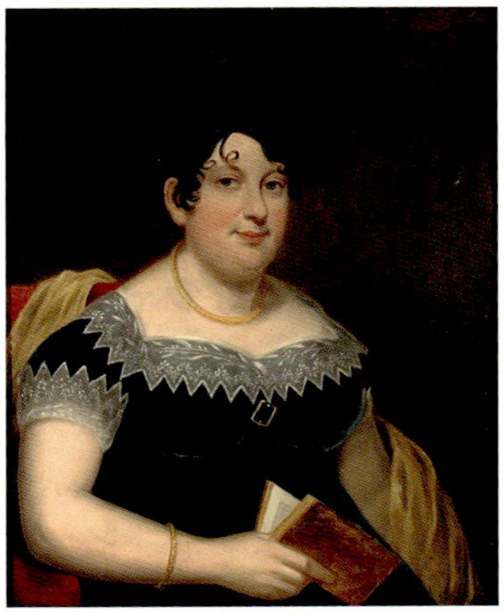

Stewardson, Thomas 1781–1859
Mrs Catherine Gordon Byron (1765–1811)
oil on canvas 73.5 x 65.4
NAL 2/9 (P)

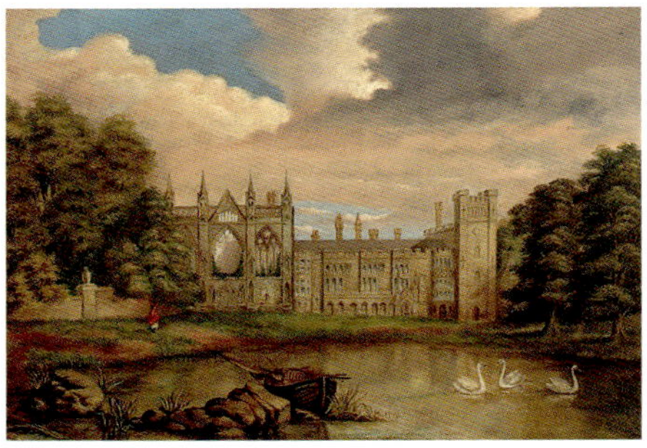

Taylor, George William
Newstead Abbey, Nottinghamshire, from Upper Lake 1884
oil on canvas 68.5 x 98
NA 814

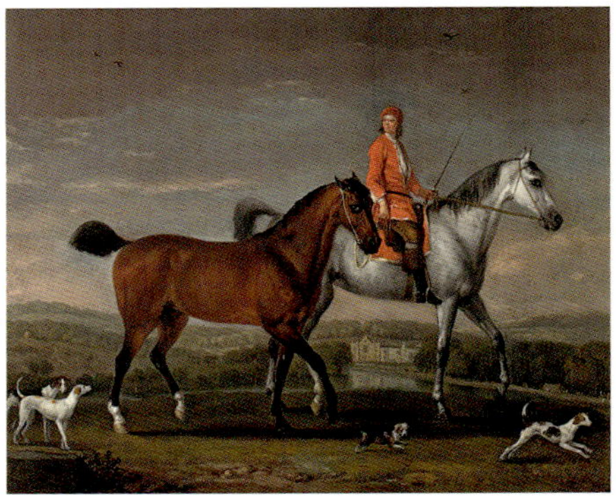

Tillemans, Peter 1684–1734
'Spruce' and 'Bell' 1724
oil on canvas 53 x 67
NA 2246/1

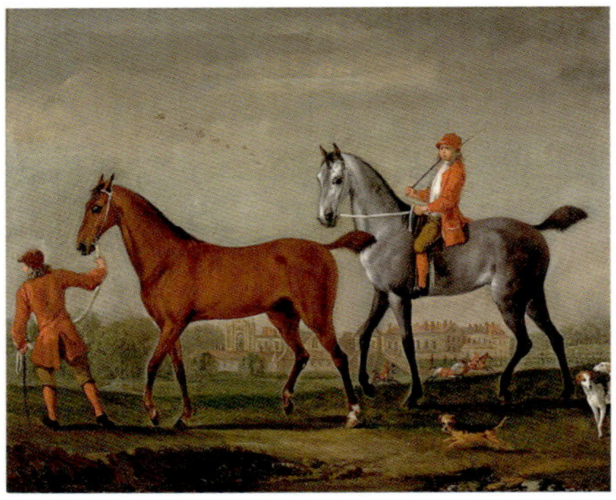

Tillemans, Peter 1684–1734
Two Racehorses with Grooms and Hounds in the Park at Newstead Abbey, Nottinghamshire 1724
oil on canvas 53 x 67
NA 2246/2

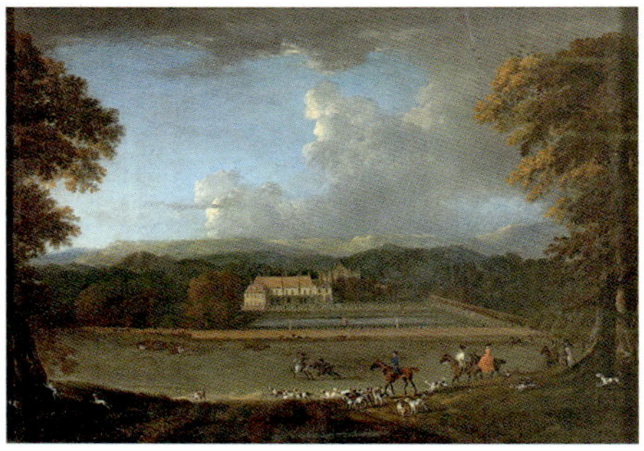

Tillemans, Peter 1684–1734
East View of Newstead Abbey, Nottinghamshire c.1726
oil on canvas 49 x 72
NCMG 2000-35

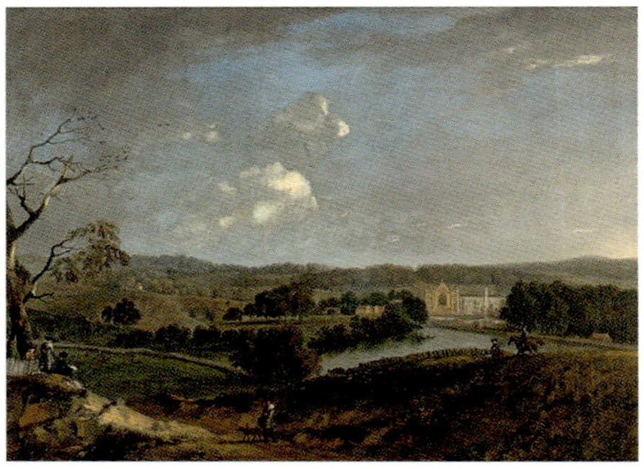

Tillemans, Peter 1684–1734
West View of Newstead Abbey, Nottinghamshire c.1726
oil on canvas 49 x 72
NCMG 2000-36

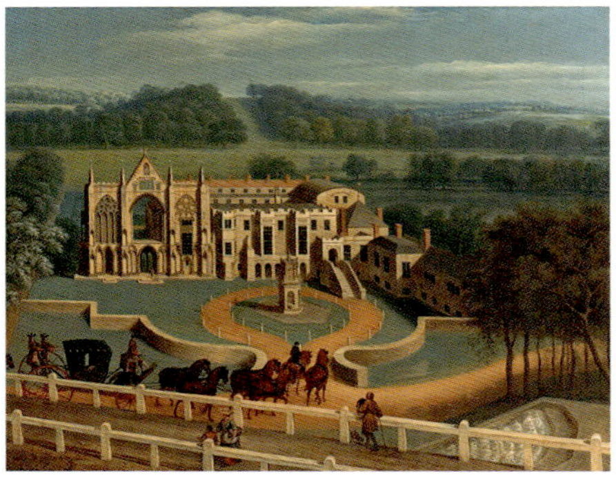

Tillemans, Peter 1684–1734
Newstead Abbey, Nottinghamshire, West Aspect c.1730
oil on canvas 100 x 120 (E)
NA 499

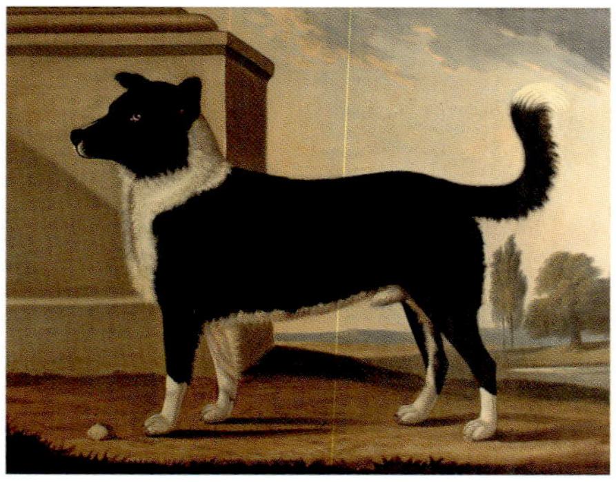

Tomson, Clifton 1775–1835
Lord Byron's Dog 'Boatswain' (1803–1808) (The Newfoundland) 1808
oil on canvas 135 x 171
NA 245

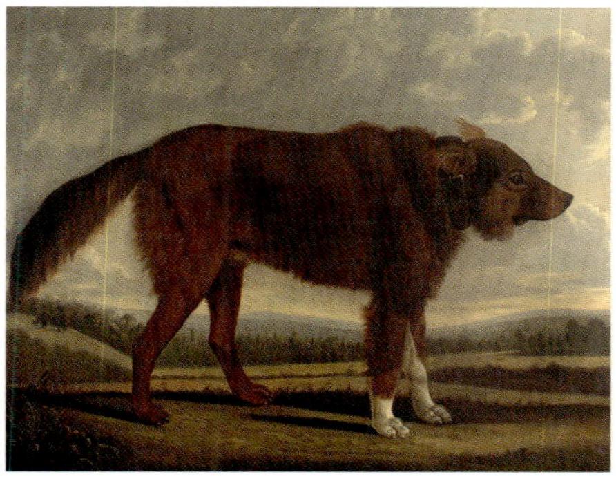

Tomson, Clifton 1775–1835
Lord Byron's Dog 'Lyon' (The Wolf Dog) 1808
oil on canvas 135 x 171
NA 277

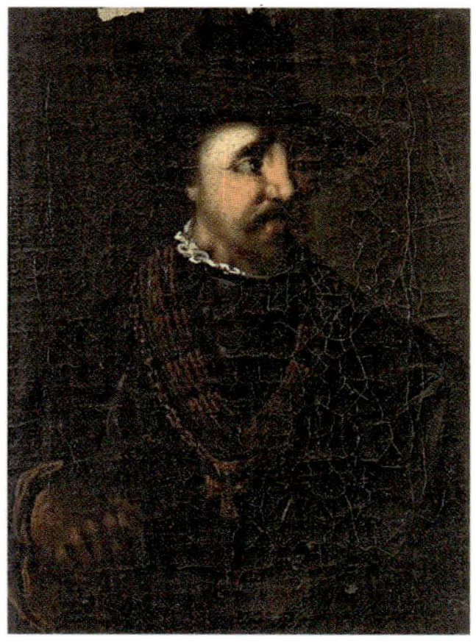

unknown artist 17th C
A Gentleman of the Byron Family
oil on canvas 16.5 x 13
NA 551

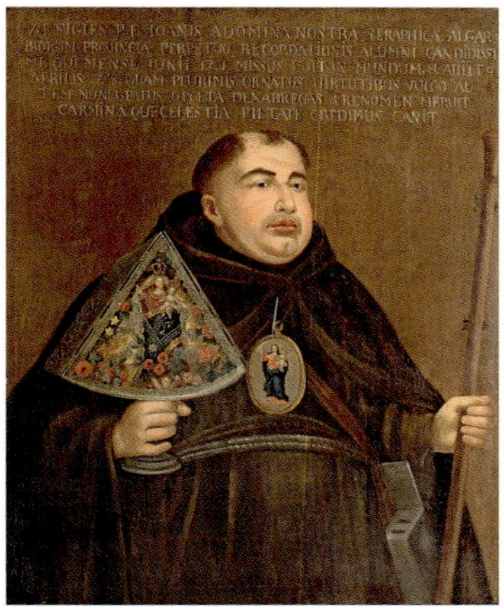

unknown artist 18th C
Brother John of Algarve, Portugal (1701–1758)
oil on canvas 133 x 107
NA 440

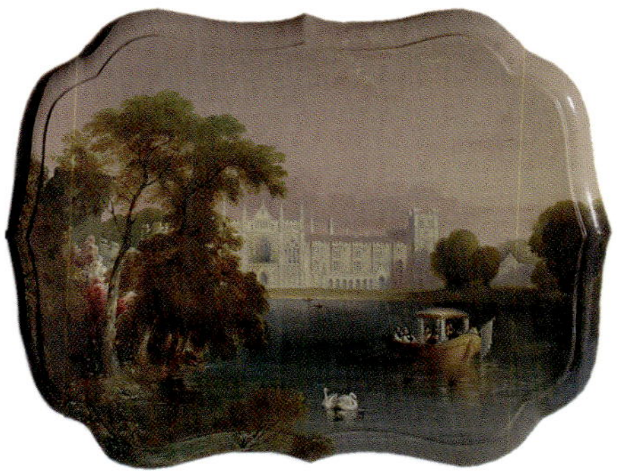

unknown artist 19th C
West View of Newstead Abbey, Nottinghamshire, Including a Boating Party on the Upper Lake
oil on papier-mache 64 x 82
NA 414

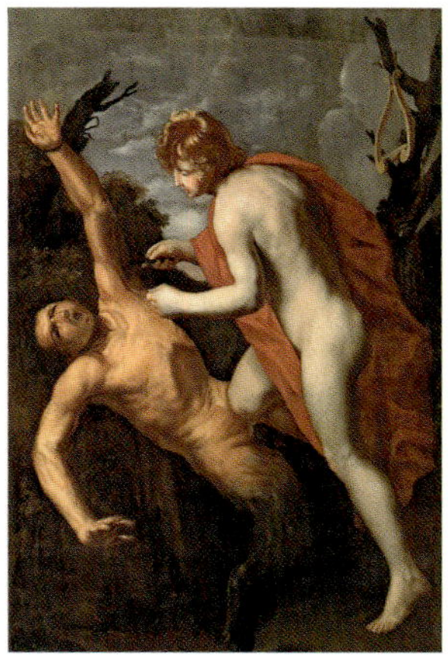

unknown artist
Apollo Flaying Marsyas
oil on canvas 132 x 94
NA 944

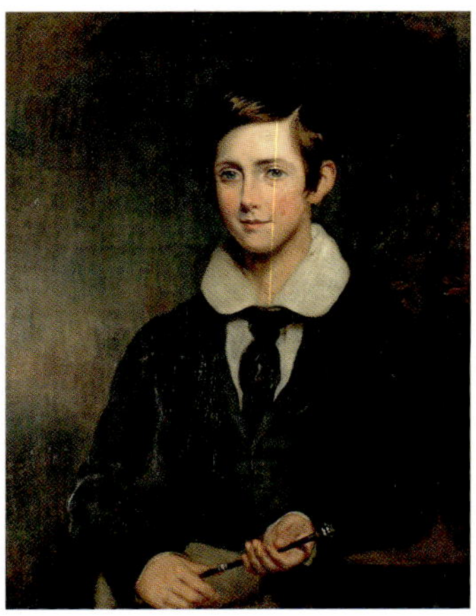

unknown artist
Gerald Littlehales Goodlake (1832–1890)
oil on canvas 103 x 79
NA 613

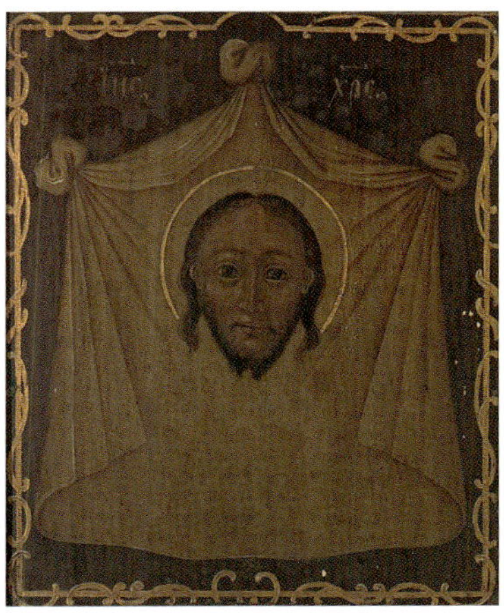

unknown artist
Head of Christ on a Cloth
oil on wood 37 x 31.5
NA 1

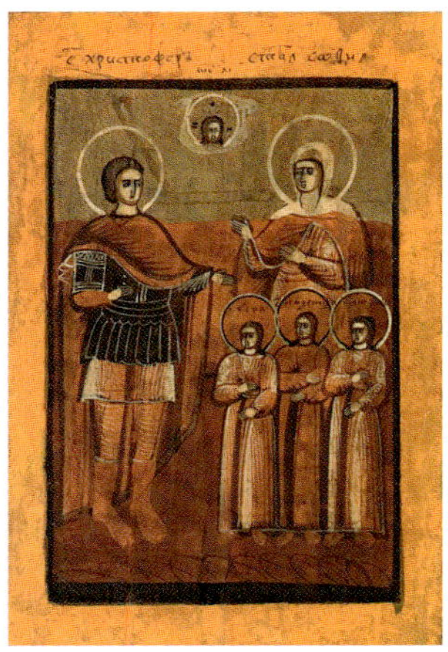

unknown artist
Head of Christ with Figures of Saints
oil on canvas 28 x 20
NA 3

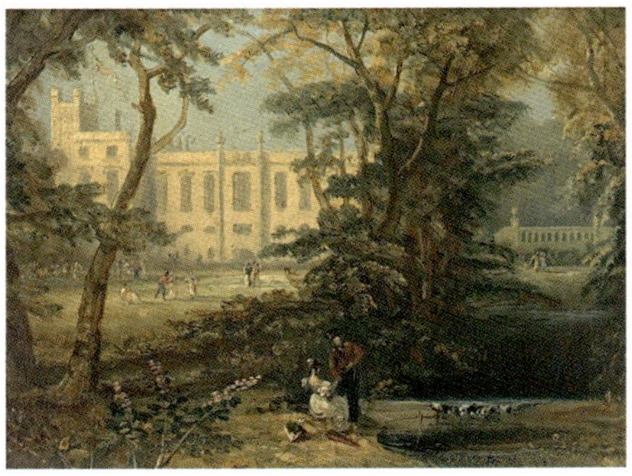

unknown artist
Newstead Abbey, Nottinghamshire, from the South
oil on canvas 21 x 29
NA 19

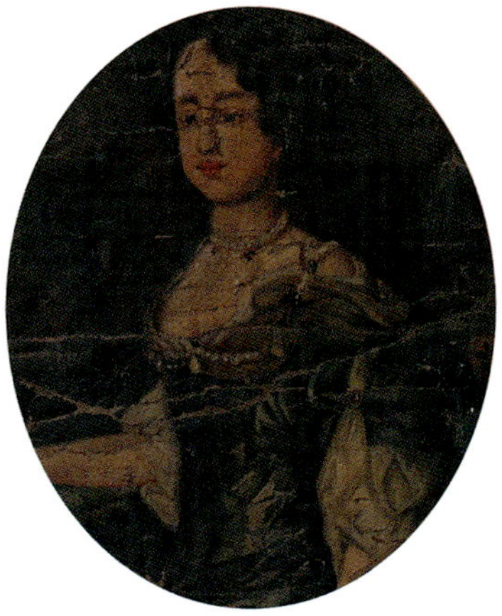

unknown artist
Portrait of an Unidentified Lady
oil on canvas 36 x 30
NA-X 130/(b)

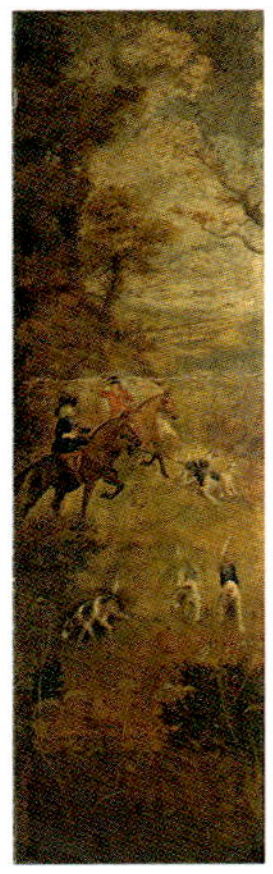

unknown artist
Victorian Foxhunt (far left panel from a folded screen)
oil on canvas 190 x 58
NA 2083A

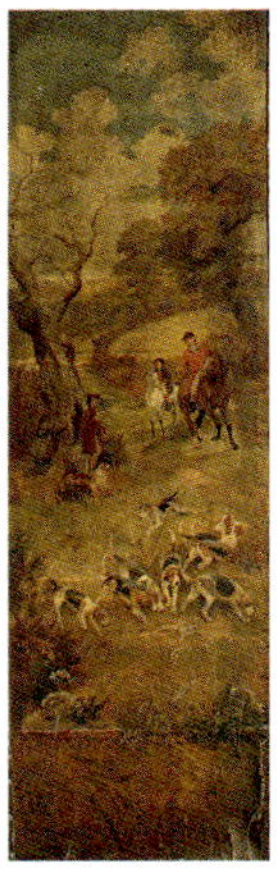

unknown artist
Victorian Foxhunt (left panel from a folded screen)
oil on canvas 190 x 58
NA 2083B

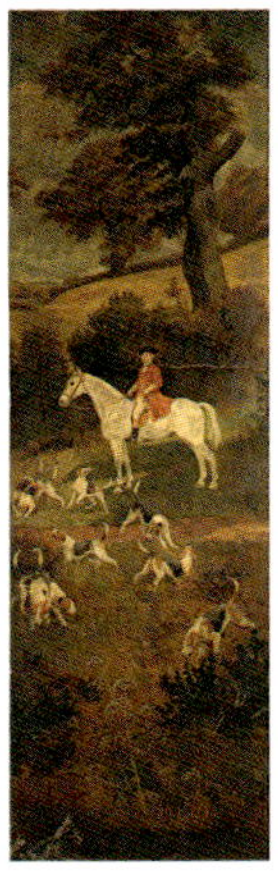

unknown artist
Victorian Foxhunt (right panel from a folded screen)
oil on canvas 190 x 58
NA 2083C

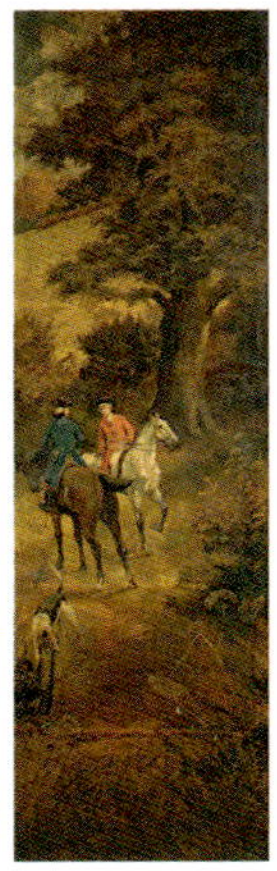

unknown artist
Victorian Foxhunt (far right panel from a folded screen)
oil on canvas 190 x 58
NA 2083D

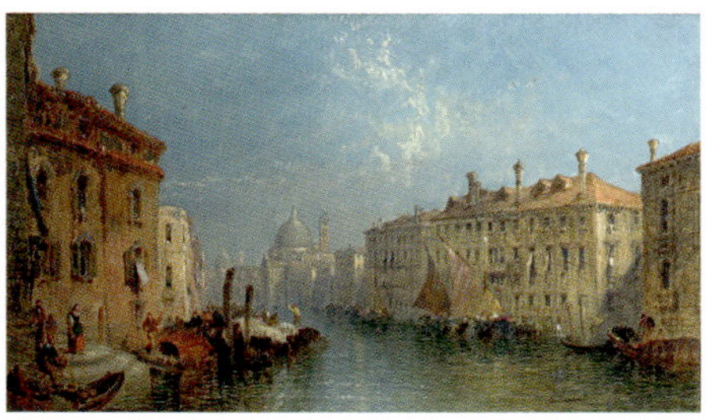

Vivian, Jane active 1861–1877
Grand Canal, Venice, Italy c.1875
oil on canvas 45 x 80
NA 252

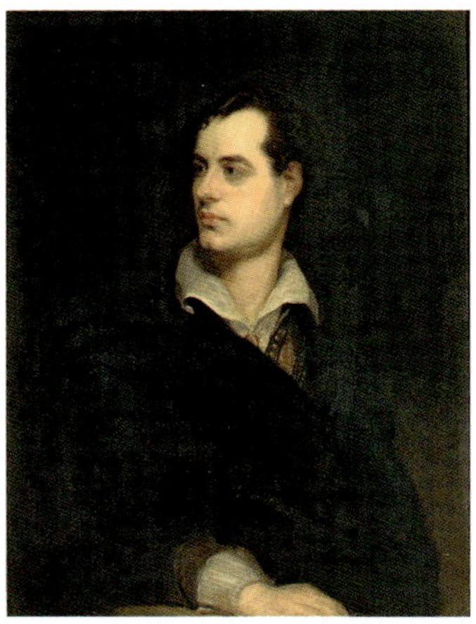

Wainewright, Thomas Francis 1794–1883
6th Lord Byron (1788–1824)
oil on canvas 89 x 69
NA 496

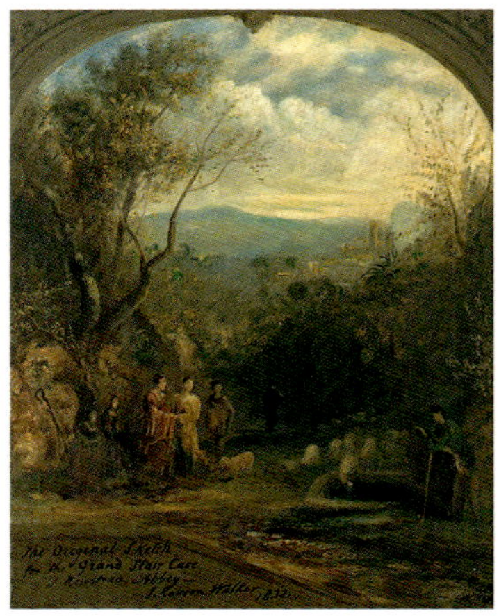

Walker, John Rawson 1796–1873
The Original Sketch for the Grand Staircase at Newstead Abbey, Nottinghamshire 1832
oil on canvas 61 x 51
NCMG 2000-105

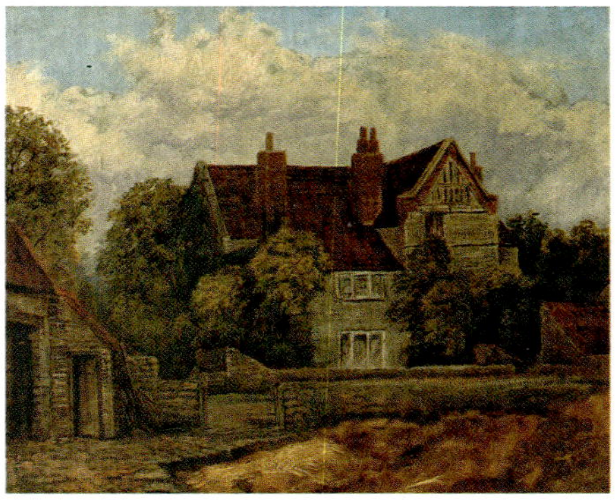

Waplington, Gilbert b.1873
Bulwell Wood Hall, Nottinghamshire c.1890
oil on canvas 39 x 49
NA 1052

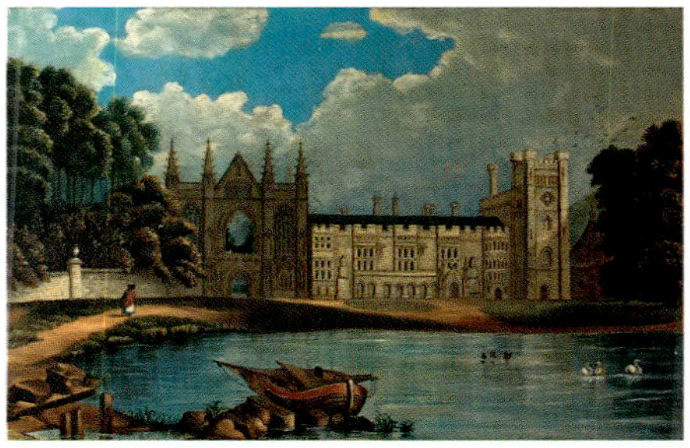

Webster, Moses (after) 1792–1870
West View of Newstead Abbey, Nottinghamshire 1820–1834
oil on wood 65 x 101.5
NA 362

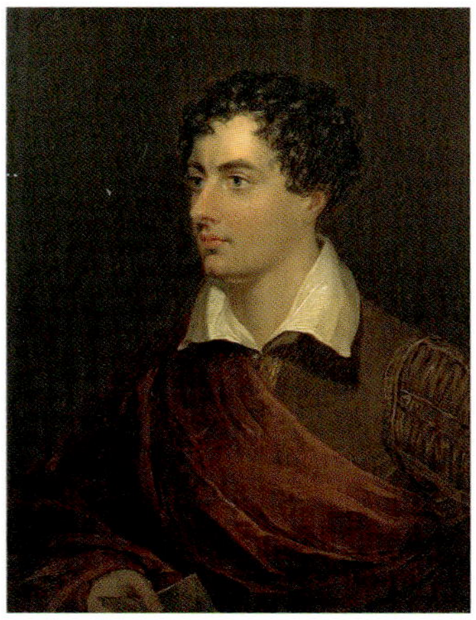

Westall, Richard (attributed to) 1765–1836
6th Lord Byron (1788–1824) c.1825
oil on canvas 26 x 21
NA 249

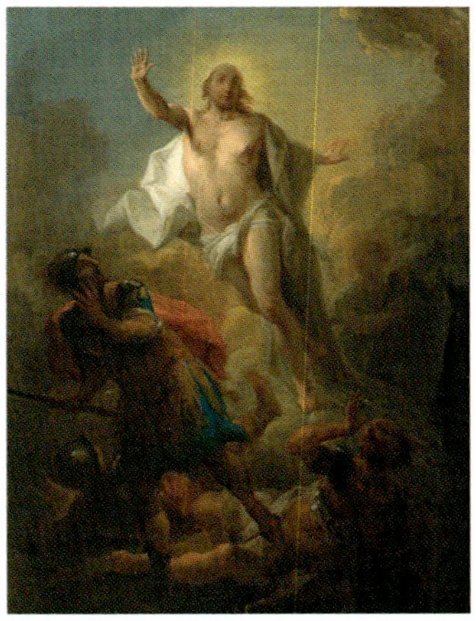

Winck, Christian (attributed to) 1738–1797
Christ Rising from the Tomb and Roman Soldiers Fleeing
oil on board 36 x 27
NA 2

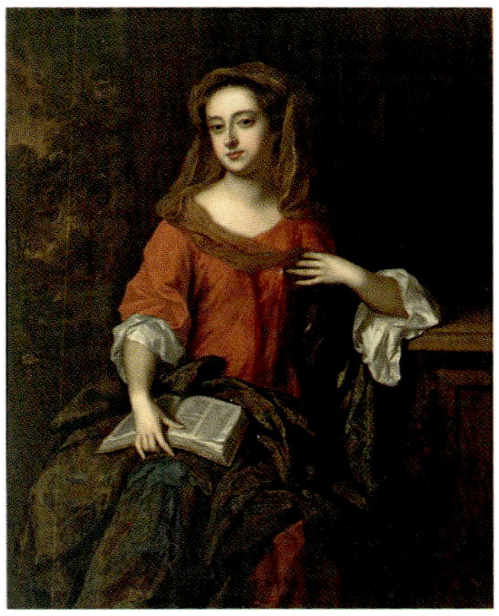

Wissing, Willem (after) 1656–1687
Mrs Knott
oil on canvas 121 x 98 (E)
NA 509

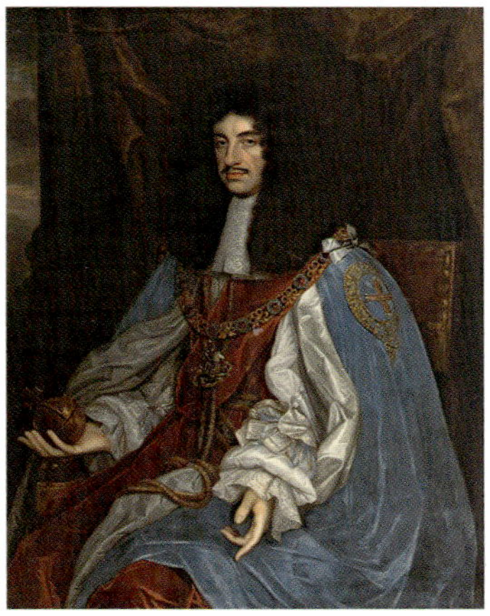

Wright, John Michael (after) 1617–1694
Charles II (1630–1685)
oil on canvas 115 x 96
NA 515

Castle College Nottingham

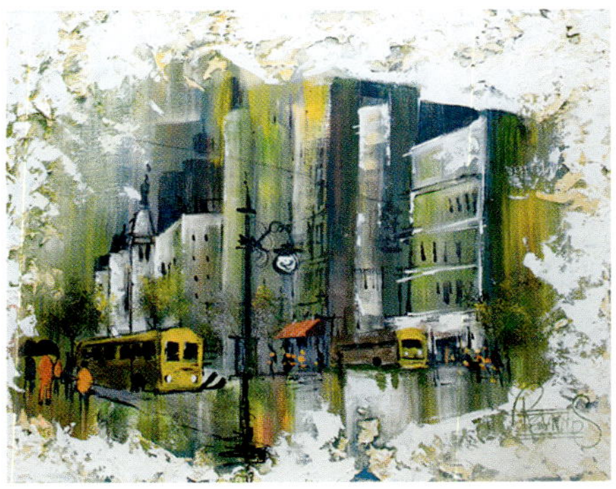

Reynolds, S.
*Rainy Street Scene** c.1980
oil on canvas 101 x 126.5
TPC1

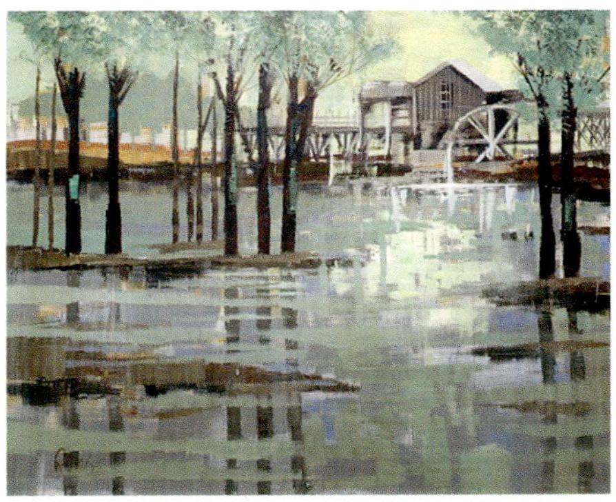

unknown artist
*Watermill** c.1980
oil on canvas 100 x 125.5
TPC2

Djanogly City Academy Nottingham

Djanogly City Academy Nottingham was formed in 2003 from two very different predecessor schools: the Forest School, a Local Authority community school, and Djanogly City Technology College, a state-funded independent school.

Djanogly City Technology College was one of only 15 city technology colleges (CTCs) set up nationally in the late 1980s. Djanogly CTC's major sponsor was Sir Harry Djanogly, CBE and he generously donated several pieces of work to celebrate its opening in 1989. These works are situated in relatively public areas of the Academy, with *John Wayne (1907–1979)*, painted by an unknown artist, having prime location in one of the restaurant areas.

More pieces were introduced when one of the building's original three atria was converted into a theatre space in order for productions to be staged in a more realistic environment and to provide space for assemblies. A series of murals was commissioned for the walls of this newly created space depicting scenes from music, dance and drama, with many of the characters based on real life members of teaching staff.

Following its transition to Academy status in 2003, a new 11 to 14 year old Centre was built. As part of a re-engineering of the original Sherwood Rise site, the theatre space was once again converted, this time into a library for 14 to 16 year olds and the murals continue to adorn its walls.

Sir Harry Djanogly has continued to sponsor the Academy since its transition in 2003 and we are grateful for his generosity and for the opportunity granted to the many youngsters educated here to share his love of art.

Mike Butler, Chief Executive

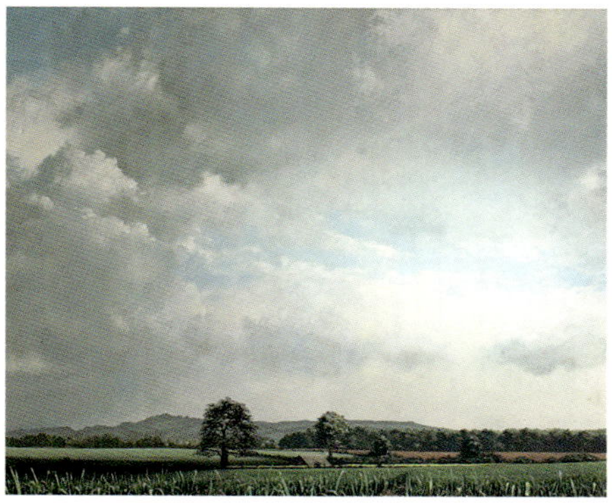

Cheall, John b.1965
Shower, Loughborough, Leicestershire
acrylic on canvas & board 151 x 181
DCA:014

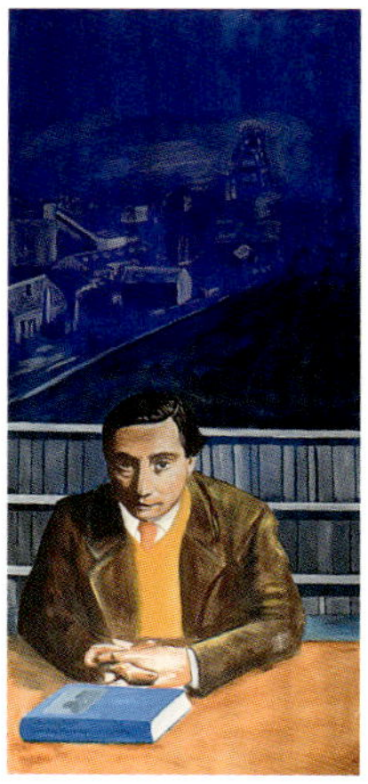

unknown artist
*Alan Sillitoe (b.1928), Author of 'Saturday Night and Sunday Morning'**
acrylic on canvas & board 210 x 90 (E)
DCA:011

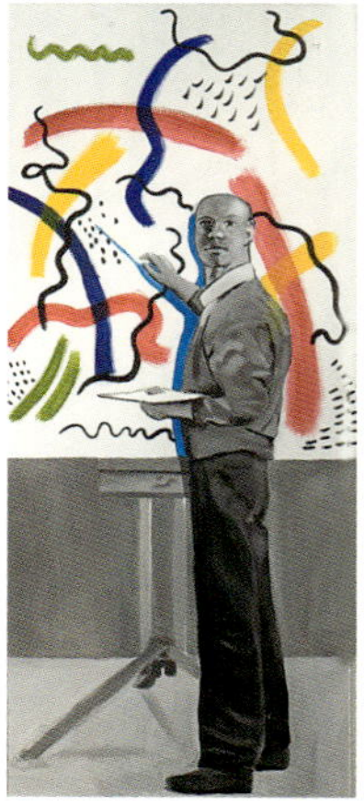

unknown artist
*Art Teacher**
acrylic on canvas & board 210 x 90 (E)
DCA:012

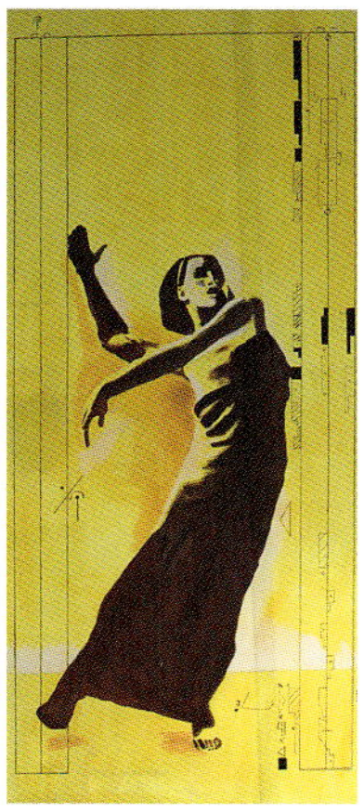

unknown artist
*Dancer**
acrylic on canvas & board 210 x 90 (E)
DCA:009

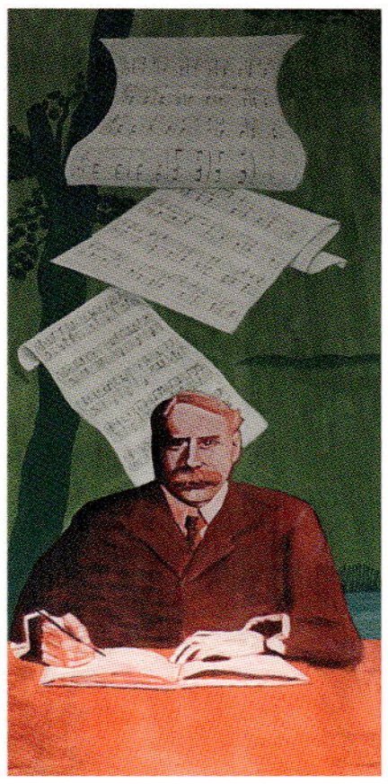

unknown artist
*Edward Elgar (1857-1934), composer**
acrylic on canvas & board 210 x 90 (E)
DCA:010

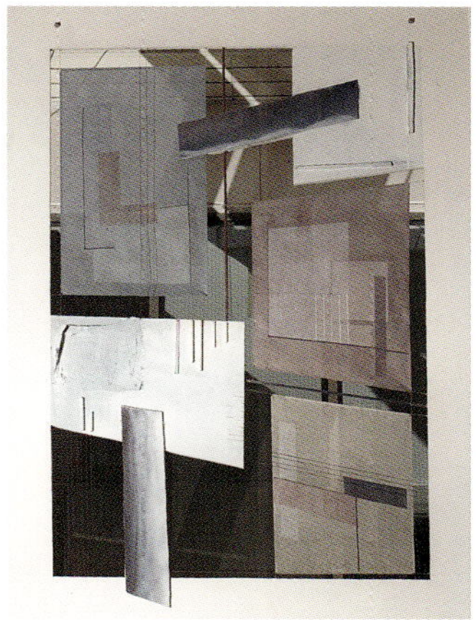

unknown artist
Installation (1)*
oil on wood, cloth, metal & wire 250 x 150
DCA:016

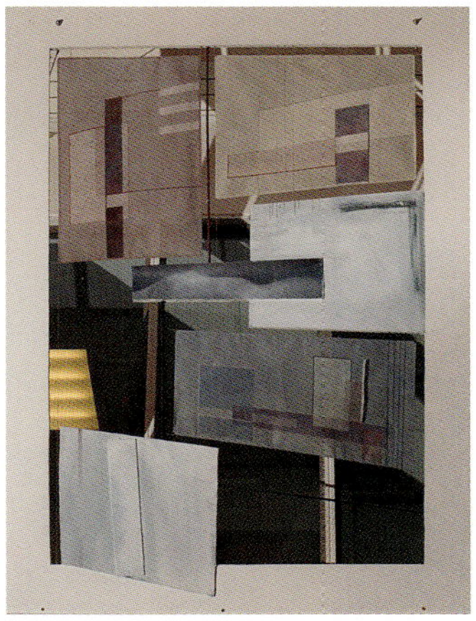

unknown artist
Installation (2)*
oil on wood, cloth, metal & wire 250 x 150
DCA:017

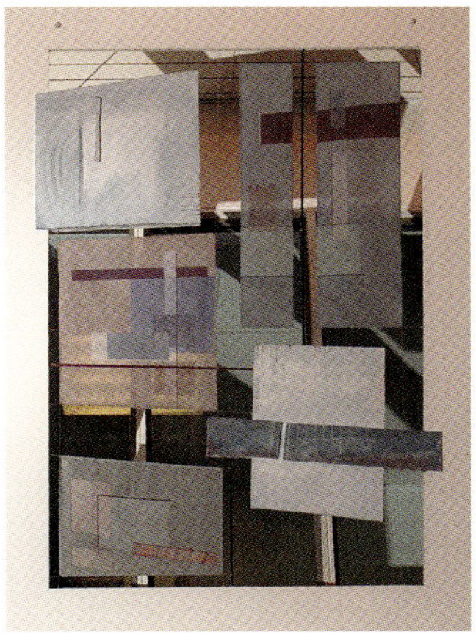

unknown artist
Installation (3)*
oil on wood, cloth, metal & wire 250 x 150
DCA:018

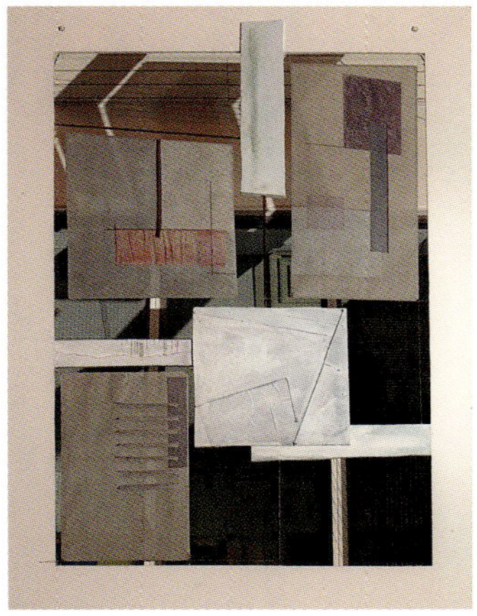

unknown artist
Installation (4)*
oil on wood, cloth, metal & wire 250 x 150
DCA:019

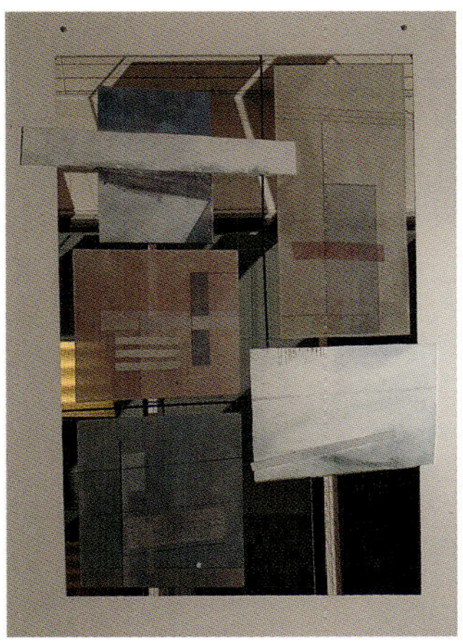

unknown artist
Installation (5)*
oil on wood, cloth, metal & wire 250 x 150
DCA:020

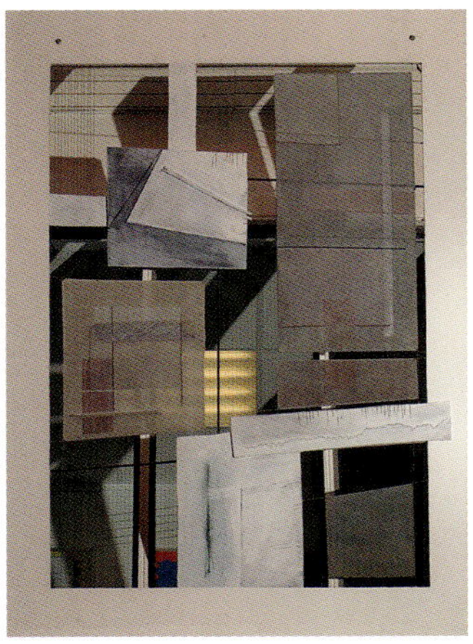

unknown artist
Installation (6)*
oil on wood, cloth, metal & wire 250 x 150
DCA:021

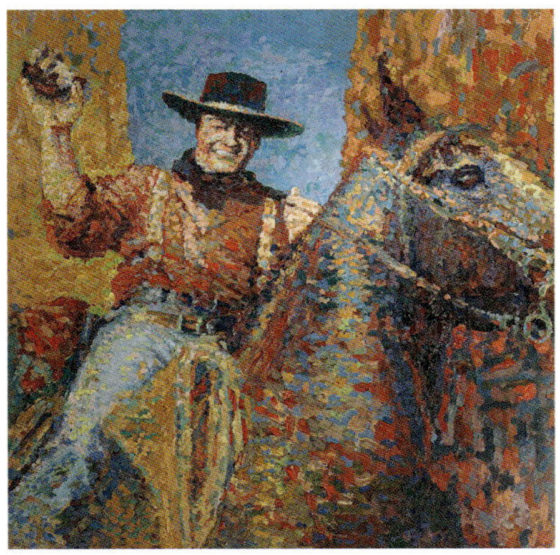

unknown artist
*John Wayne (1907–1979)**
oil on canvas 199.5 x 199.5
DCA:001

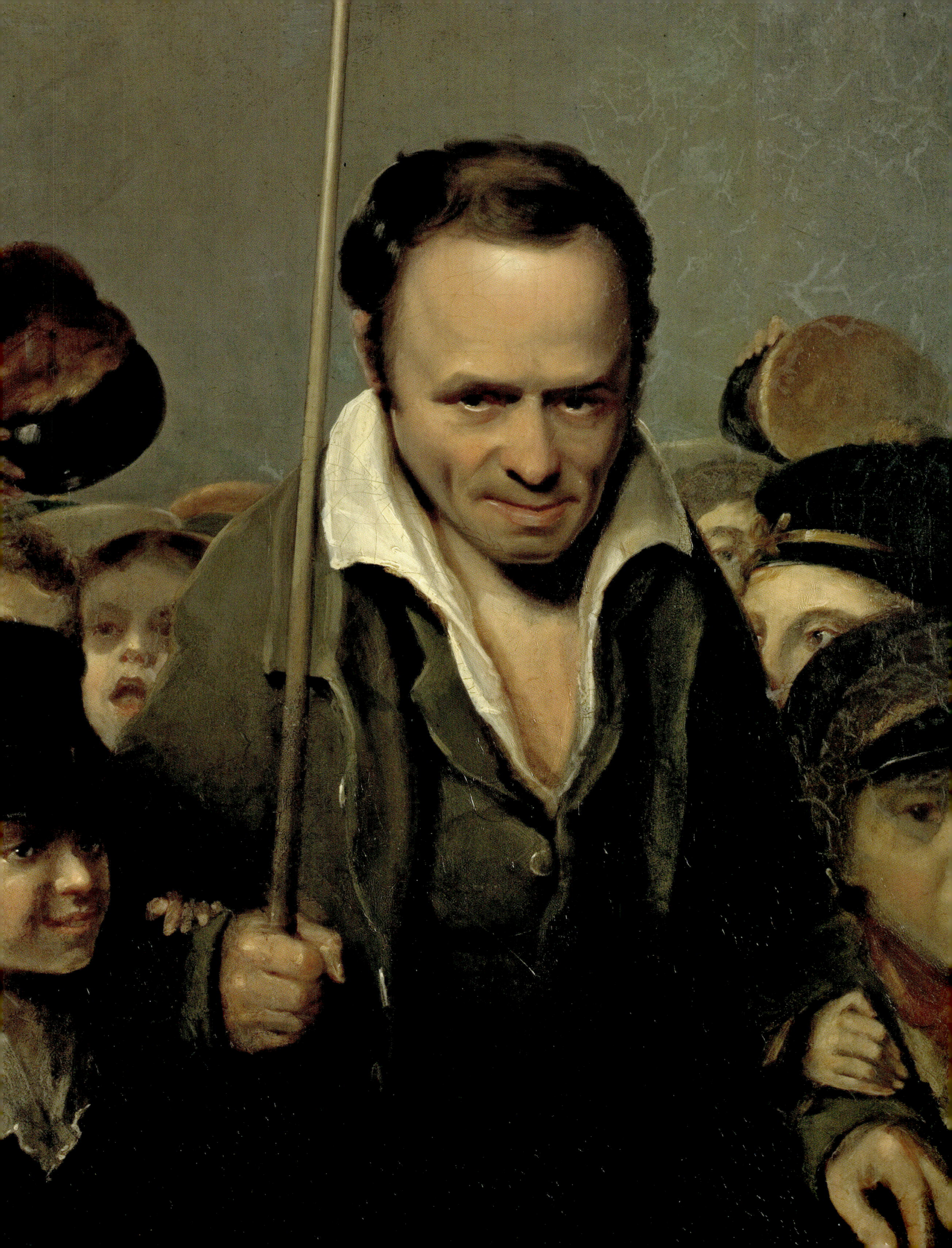

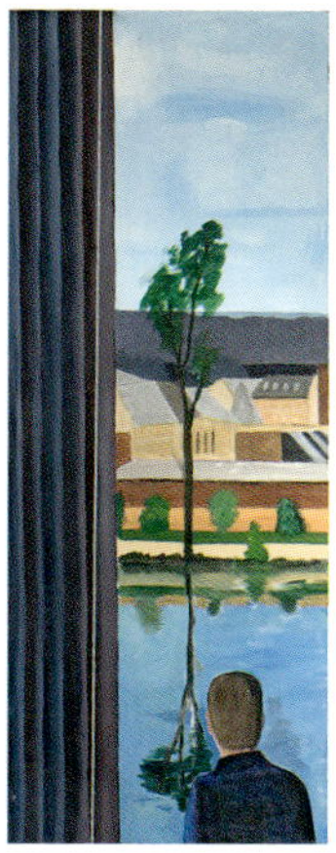

unknown artist
*River View** (panel 1 of 4)
acrylic on canvas & board 210 x 100 (E)
DCA:005

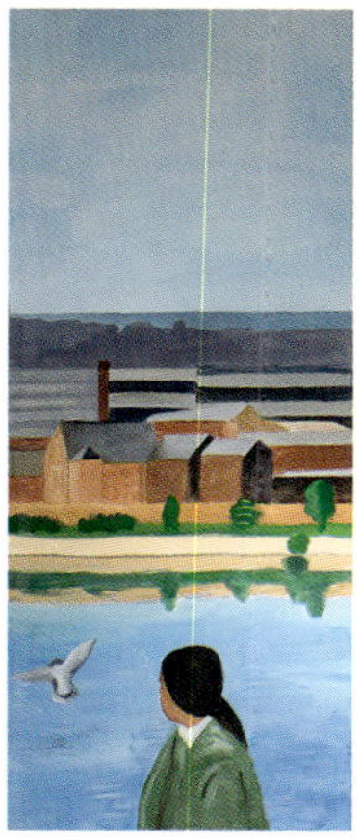

unknown artist
*River View** (panel 2 of 4)
acrylic on canvas & board 210 x 100 (E)
DCA:006

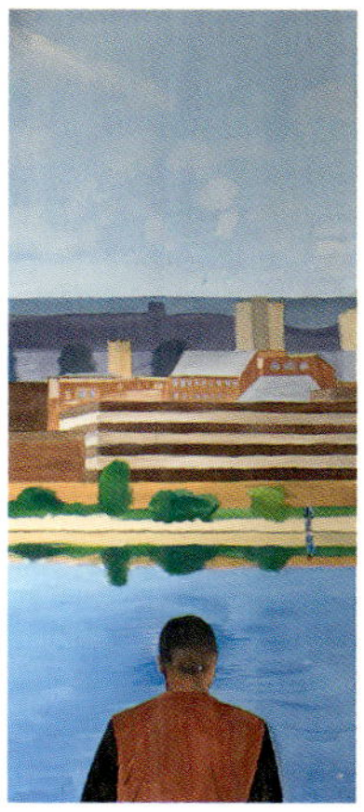

unknown artist
*River View** (panel 3 of 4)
acrylic on canvas & board 210 x 100 (E)
DCA:007

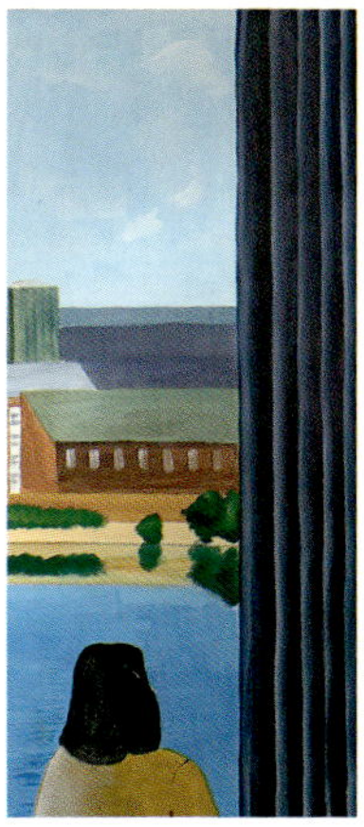

unknown artist
*River View** (panel 4 of 4)
acrylic on canvas & board 210 x 100 (E)
DCA:008

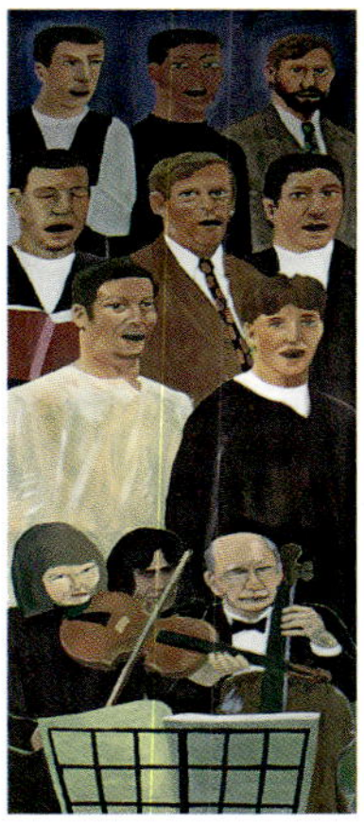

unknown artist
*School Choir** (panel 1 of 3)
acrylic on canvas & board 210 x 90 (E)
DCA:002

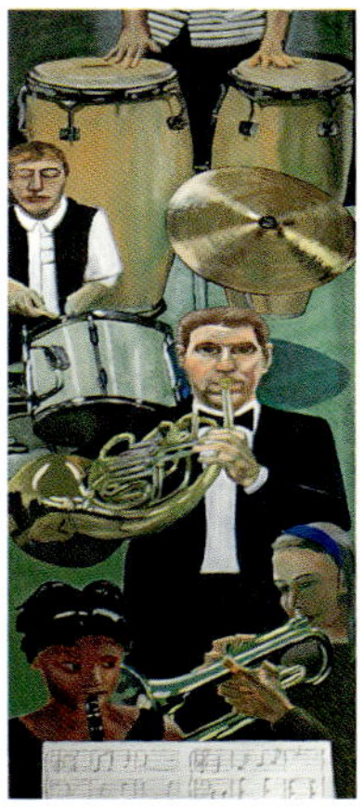

unknown artist
*School Choir** (panel 2 of 3)
acrylic on canvas & board 210 x 90 (E)
DCA:003

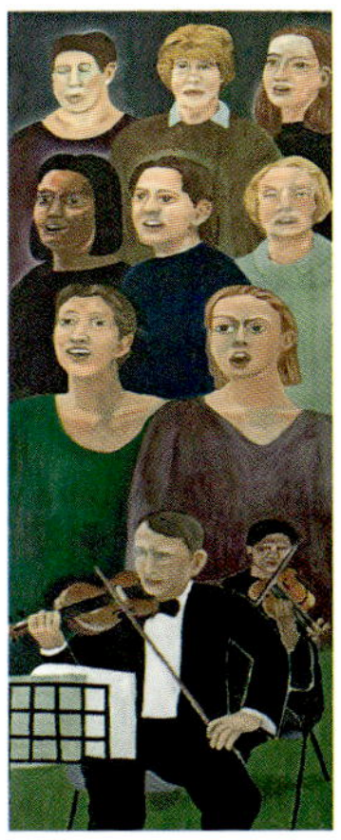

unknown artist
*School Choir** (panel 3 of 3)
acrylic on canvas & board 210 x 90 (E)
DCA:004

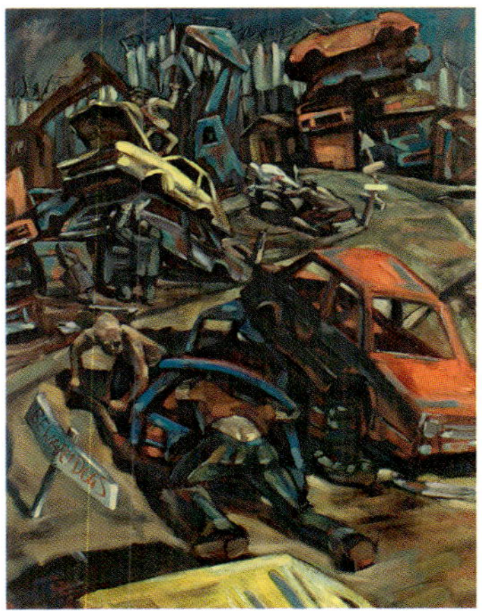

unknown artist
Scrap Yard
oil on canvas 213 x 168
DCA:015

Facing page: Barber, Thomas, 1771–1843, *Benjamin Mayo (c.1779–1843), the Old General* (detail), Nottingham City Museums and Galleries (p. 58)

Galleries of Justice

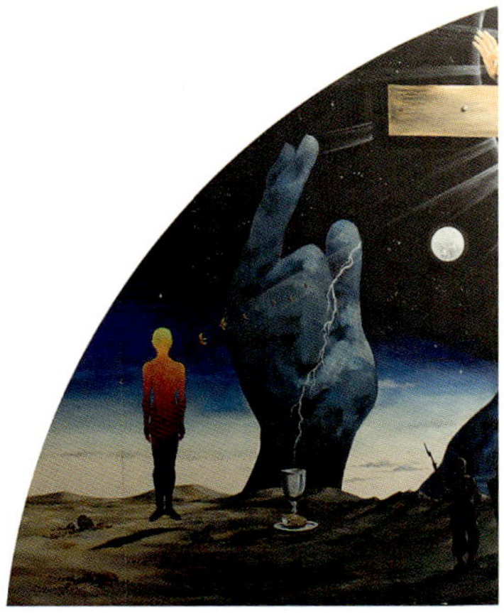

Brickland
PINXIT (triptych left panel) 1981
oil & acrylic on board 193 x 160
2008.1

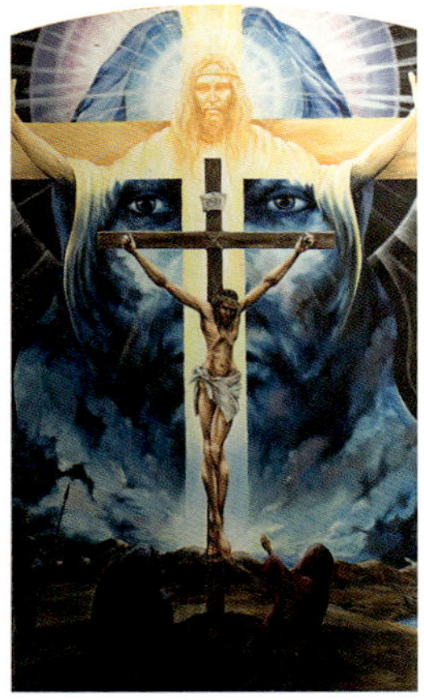

Brickland
PINXIT (triptych centre panel) 1981
oil & acrylic on board 201.9 x 121.9
2008.1

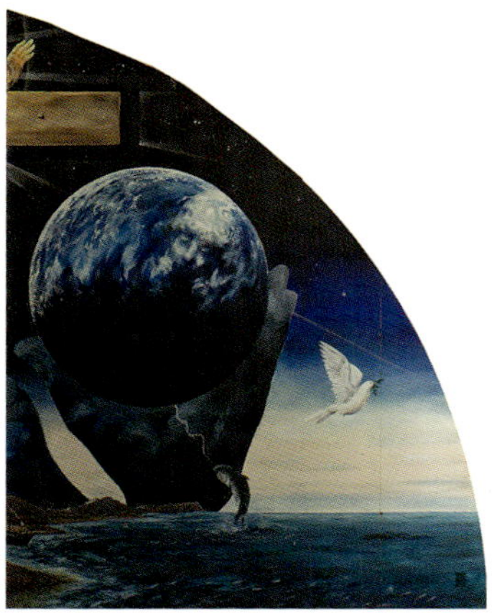

Brickland
PINXIT (right panel of triptych) 1981
oil & acrylic on board 194.3 x 157.5
2008.1

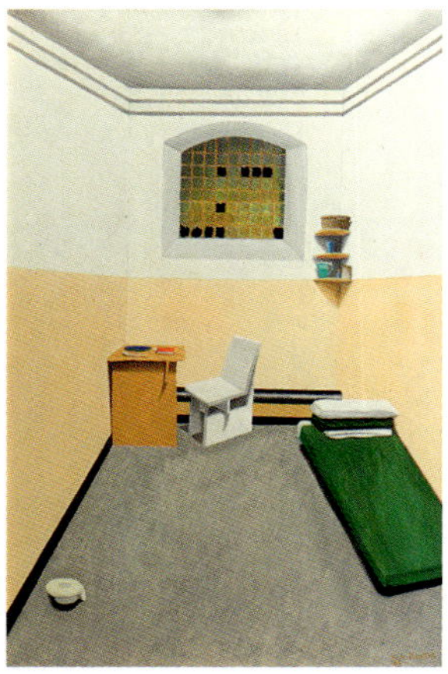

Ross, William A.
Segregation Cell 1993
oil on canvas 85 x 59.7
AAPSM2000.0229

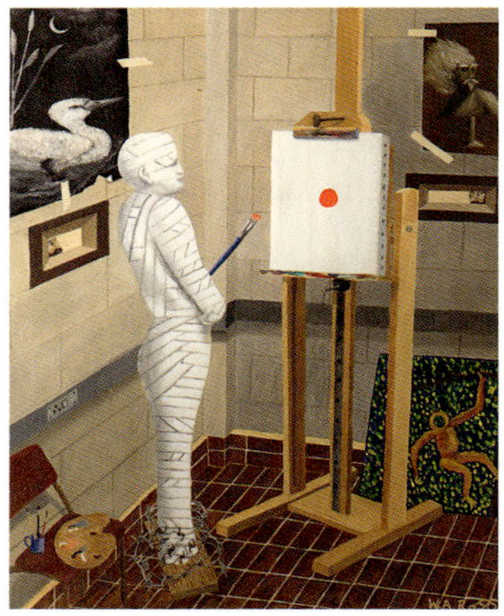

Ross, William A.
Egyptian Mummy
oil on canvas 58.4 x 45.7
PCF1

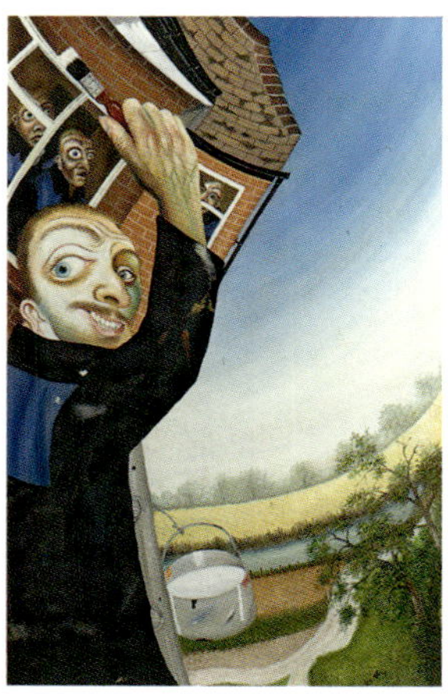

Scobie, Ray active 1995–1997
House Painter 1995
oil on canvas 78.7 x 54.6
AAPSM2000.0228

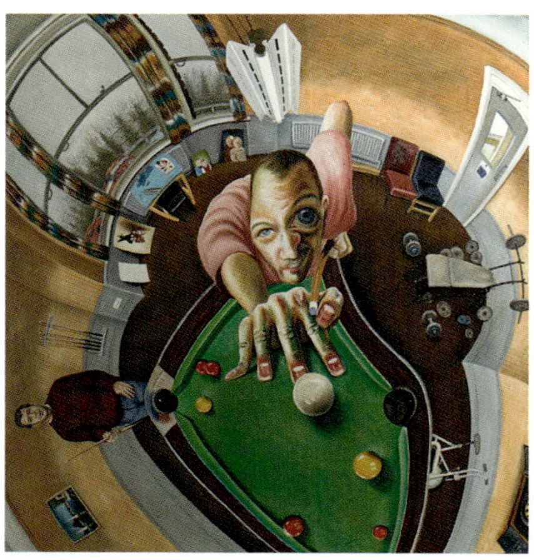

Scobie, Ray active 1995–1997
Billiard Table 1997
oil on canvas 121.9 x 121.9
AAPSM2000.0227

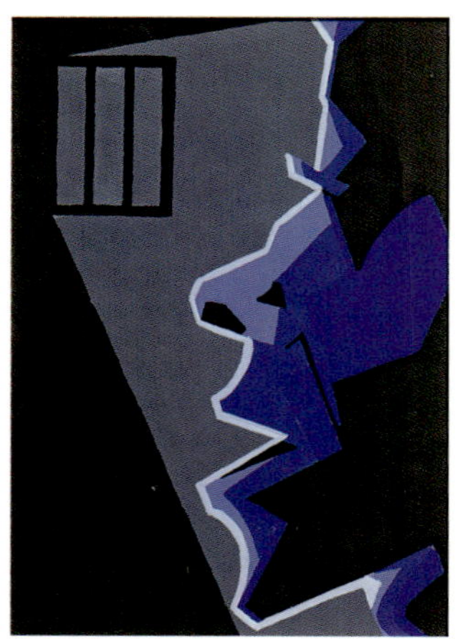

unknown artist
Bang Up 1995
acrylic on board 40.6 x 31.7
AAPSM1997.0168

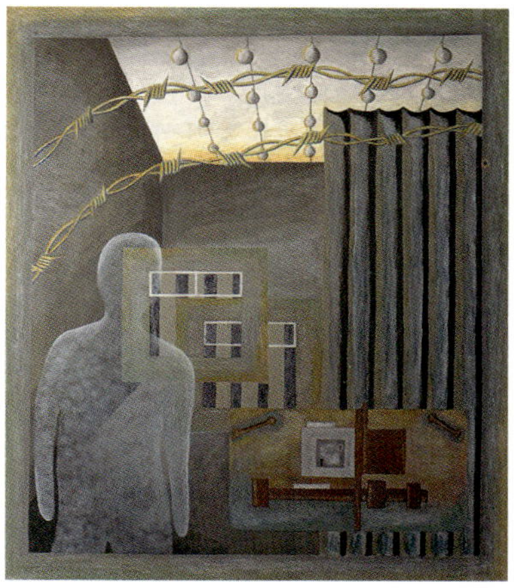

unknown artist
Ghostly Figure
oil on wood 63.5 x 55.9
PCF2

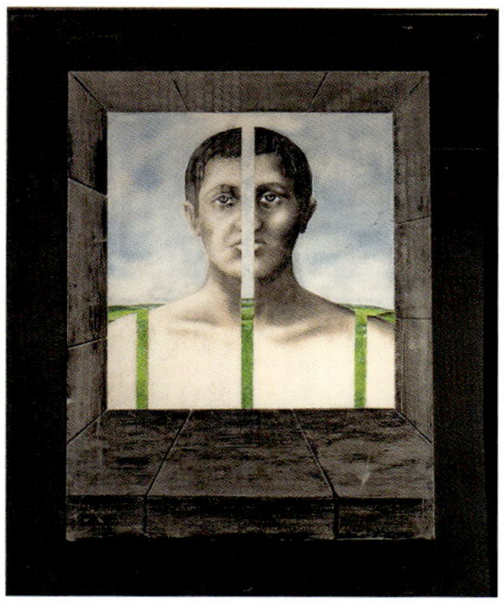

unknown artist
Man behind Bars
oil on paper & wood 72.4 x 71.1 (E)
PCF3

Government Office for the East Midlands

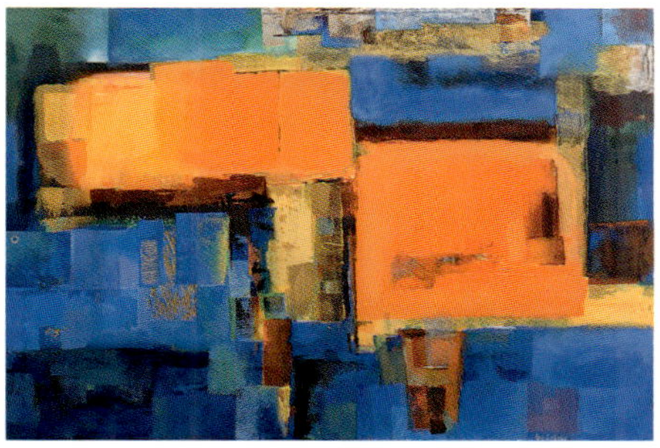

Collaku, B. Y.
*Ocean and Earth No.1**
oil on canvas 100 x 150
PA9

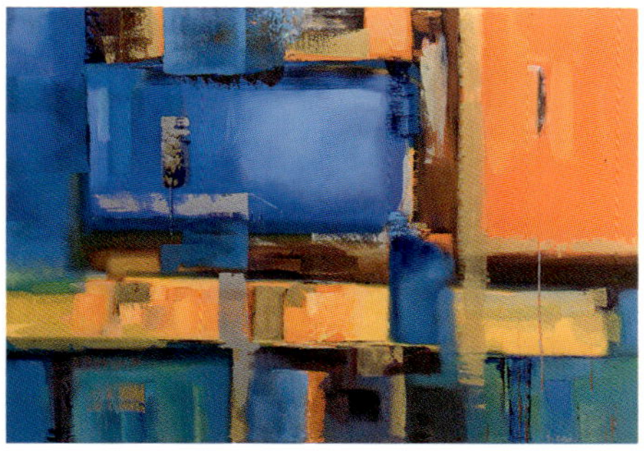

Collaku, B. Y.
*Ocean and Earth No.2**
oil on canvas 100 x 150
PA10

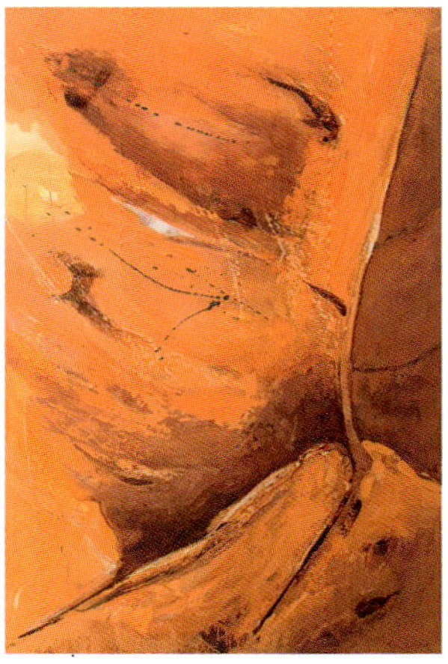

Collaku, B. Y.
*Red Earth**
oil on canvas 146 x 102
PA8

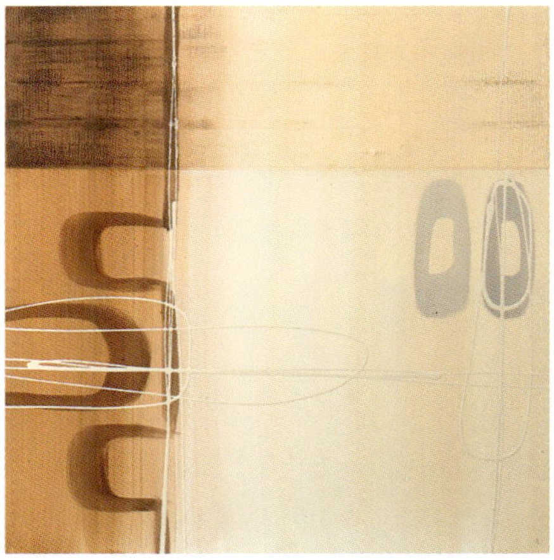

unknown artist
*Brown and Cream**
oil & mixed media on canvas 91 x 91
PA6

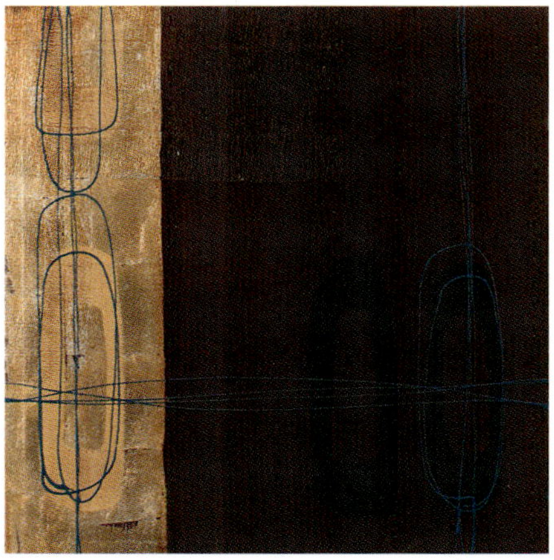

unknown artist
*Brown, Gold and Blue**
oil & mixed media on canvas 90 x 90
PA2

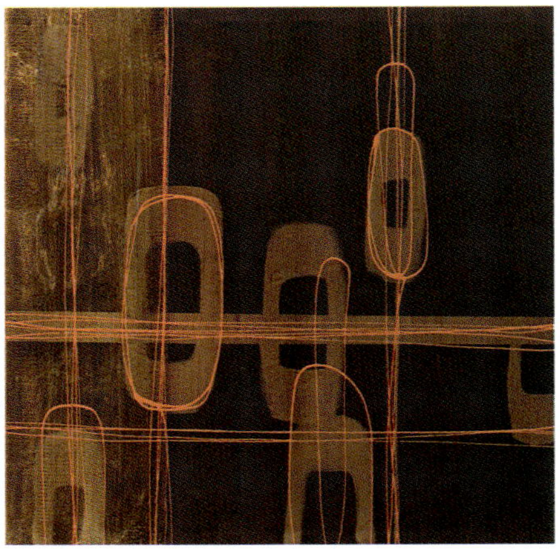

unknown artist
*Brown, Gold and Orange No.1**
oil & mixed media on canvas 90 x 90
PA1

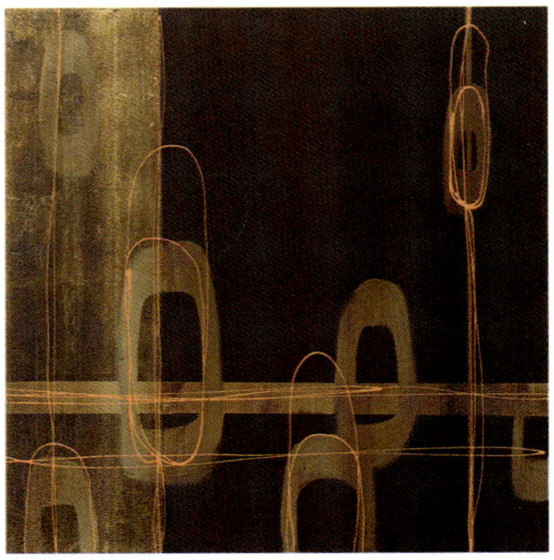

unknown artist
*Brown, Gold and Orange No.2**
oil & mixed media on canvas 90 x 90
PA3

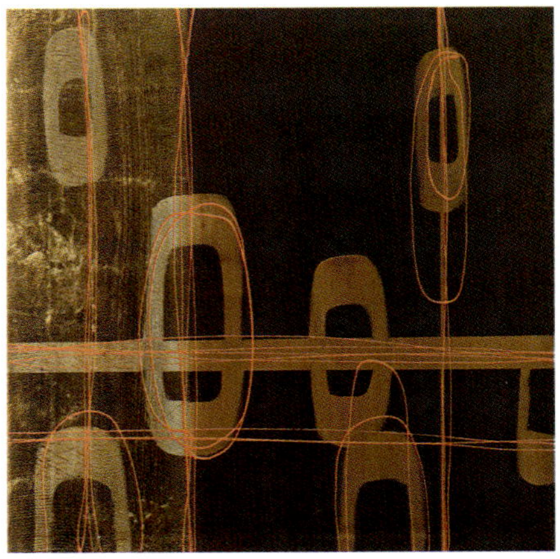

unknown artist
*Brown, Gold and Orange No.3**
oil & mixed media on canvas 90 x 90
PA4

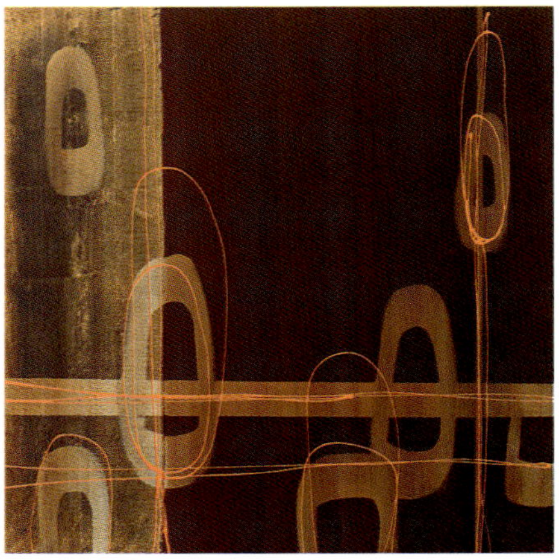

unknown artist
*Brown, Gold and Orange No.4**
oil & mixed media on canvas 90 x 90
PA5

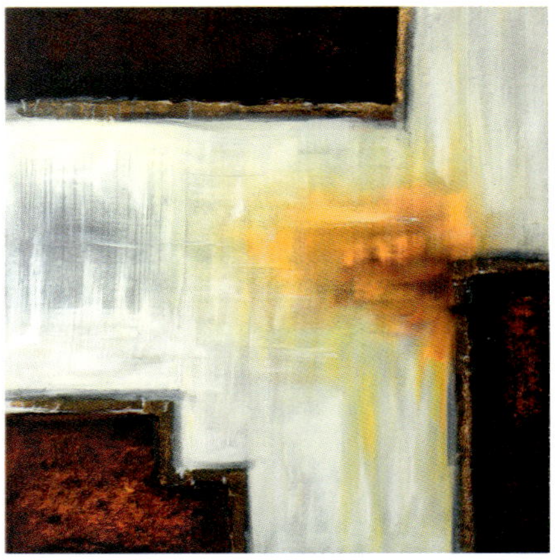

unknown artist
*Brown, Gold, Orange and Cream**
oil, sand & mixed media on canvas 100 x 100
PA7

Nottingham Central Library

The few oil paintings to be found at Nottingham Central Library function as a 'pictorial survey' for the Nottingham Local Studies Collection. The Collection is comprised mostly of photographs, but also includes engravings and original art work, such as etchings, watercolour drawings and oil paintings. Many of the images can be found at the website www.picturethepast.org.uk

The aim of the Collection is to provide an insight into life in Nottingham and Nottinghamshire as well as illustrating the topography of the city and county. Originally the priority was to create a record of buildings and streets, but this has evolved to include the recording of social aspects of life in Nottingham and Nottinghamshire.

All of the paintings have been donated to the library, and they form a small but important part of the Local Studies Collection. Most of the artists are unknown. A number of landscapes are attributed to Thomas Cooper Moore

(1827–1901), who ended his days by struggling to sell his paintings for a few shillings around town. There are also several views of Nottingham by Albert Goodwin (1845–1932), who appears to have wandered around the Charlotte Street area painting the shops, public houses and streets prior to their demolition for the building of the Great Central Railway's Victoria Station.

None of these are masterpieces, but they all contribute to our knowledge and understanding of the history and life of the place where we live.

Dorothy Ritchie, Librarian

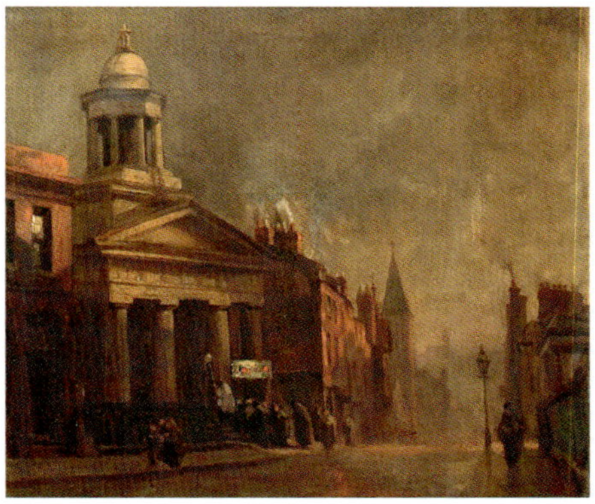

Ball, Henry 1894–1966
St Paul's Church (recto) 1921
oil on canvas 46.7 x 56
tempNCL4

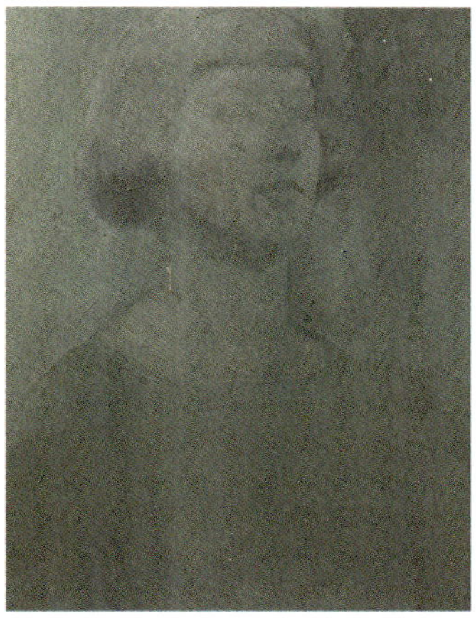

Ball, Henry (attributed to) 1894–1966
*Sketch of an Unidentified Woman** (verso)
oil on canvas 56 x 46.7
tempNCL4R

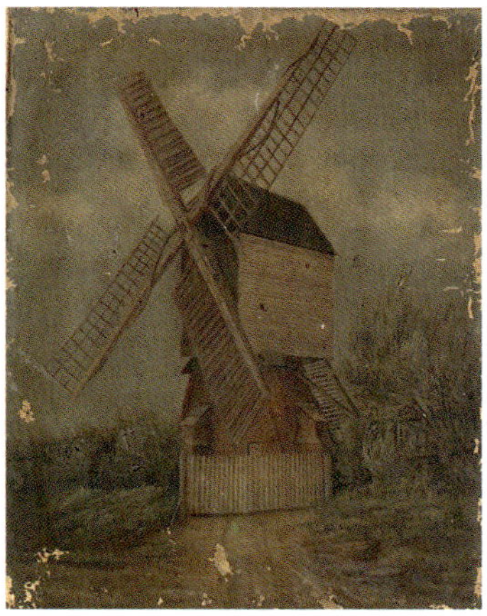

Burrows, Sarah Elisabeth
Oaklands Mill, Sneinton, Nottingham c.1880
oil on canvas 45 x 35
NCL:6474

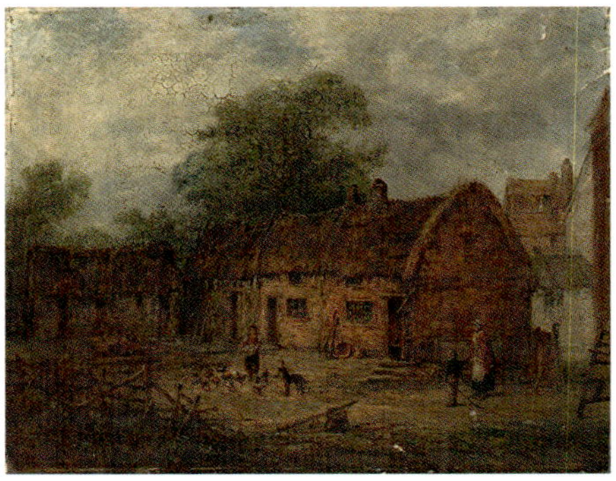

Bussey, Reuben 1818–1893
*Farmyard Scene, Sutton-in-Ashfield, Nottinghamshire** 1892
oil on canvas 33 x 43
tempNCL7

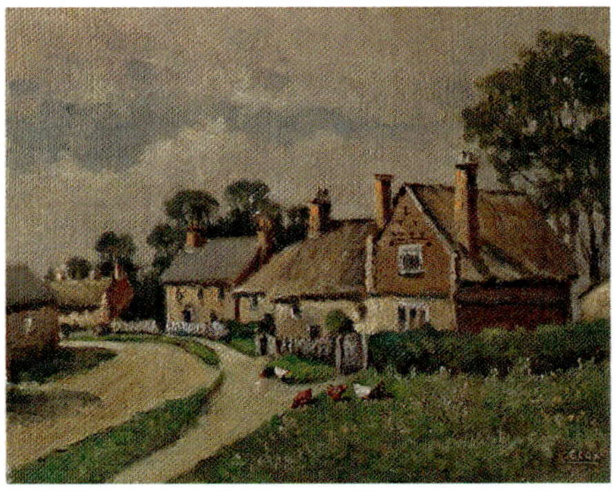

Cox, E.
Clifton Village Green, Nottingham
oil on canvas 26 x 33
tempNCL5

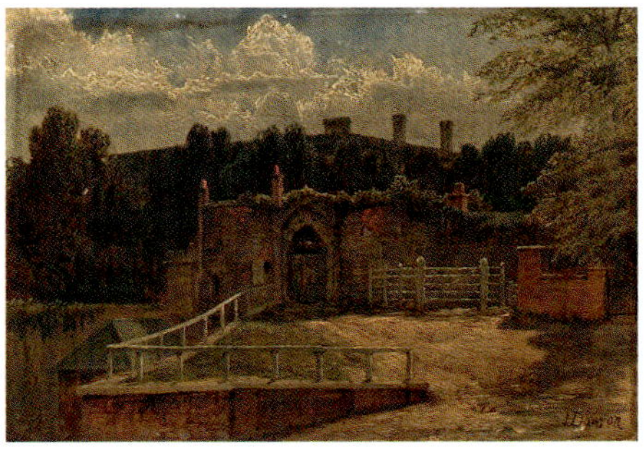

Dawson, Henry 1811–1878
Nottingham Castle Gateway c.1835–1840
oil on canvas 21 x 30.5
NCL:15219

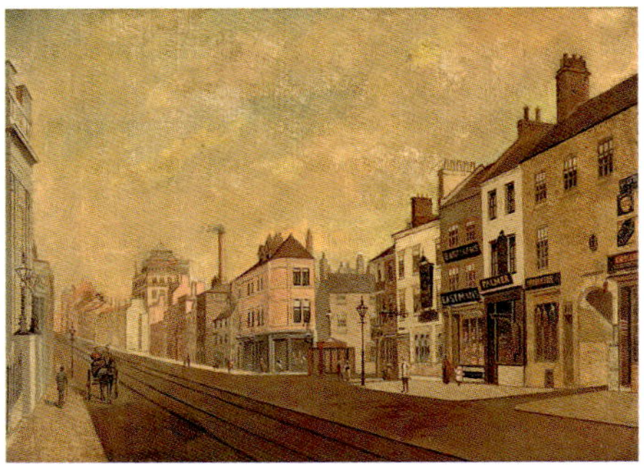

Goodwin, Albert 1845–1932
Mansfield Road, Nottingham
oil on canvas 54.5 x 76
tempNCL12

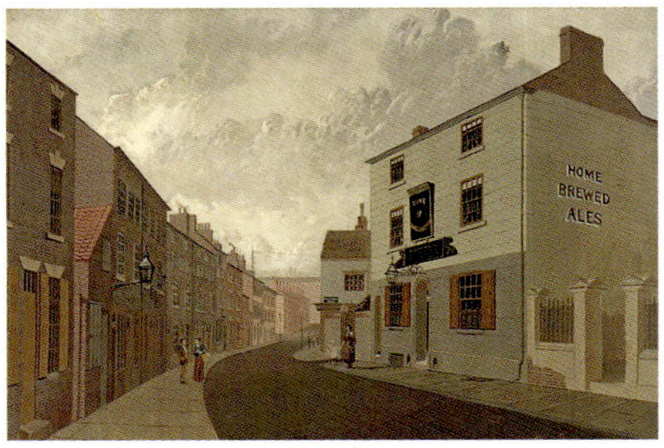

Goodwin, Albert 1845–1932
Mount Street East, Nottingham
oil on canvas 59.5 x 90
tempNCL9

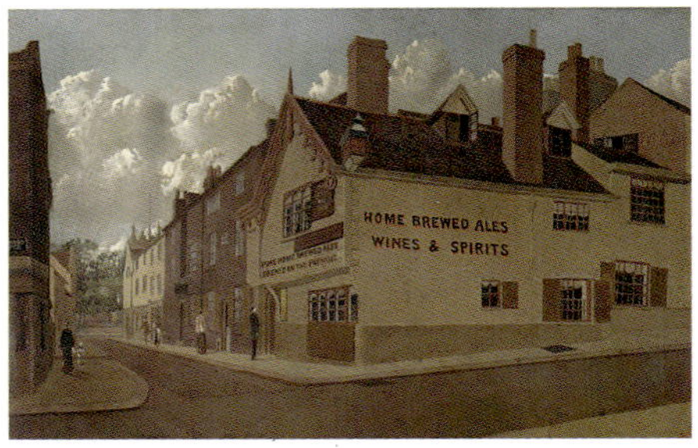

Goodwin, Albert 1845–1932
The 'Salutation Inn', Nottingham
oil on canvas 59 x 95
tempNCL11

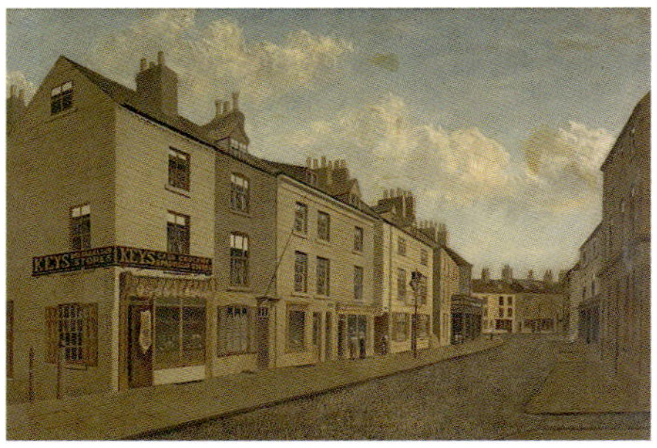

Goodwin, Albert (attributed to) 1845–1932
Charlotte Street, Nottingham
oil on canvas 59.5 x 90
tempNCL10

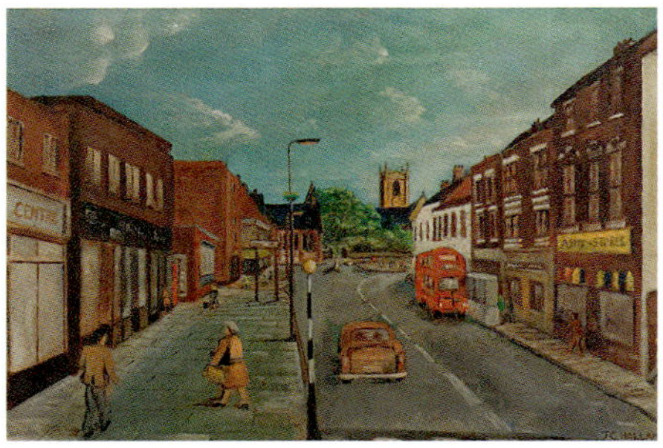

Hallam, J. C.
*High Street, Hucknall, Nottinghamshire** 1973
oil on canvas 39 x 61
tempNCL3

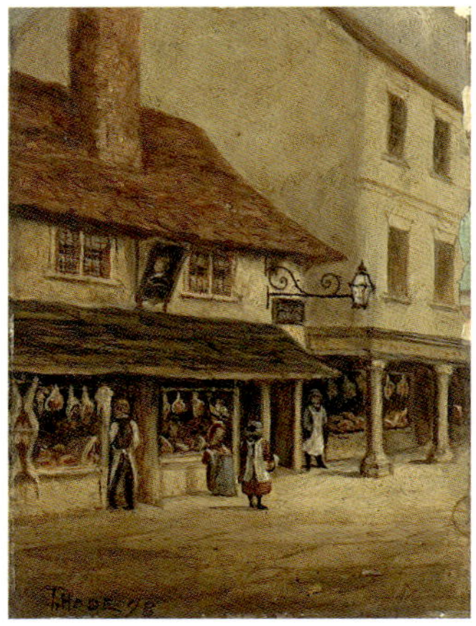

Hode, T.
The Birthplace of Henry Kirke White, Cheapside, Nottingham 1898
oil on board 23 x 17
NCL:31089

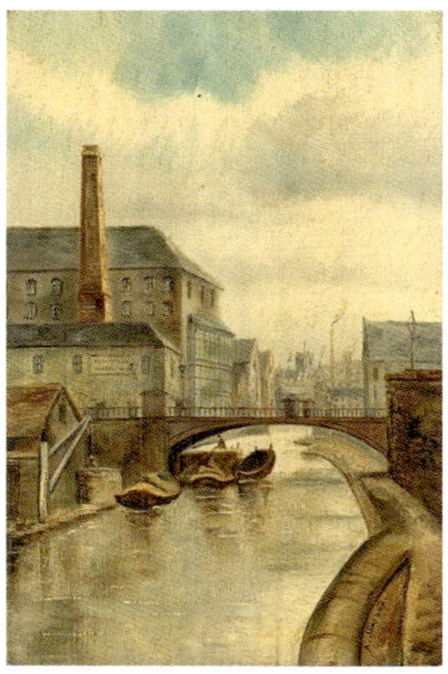

Johnson, A.
Nottingham Canal, View One Kilometre East between Carrington Street Bridge 1894
oil on wood 22 x 15.5
NCL:33754

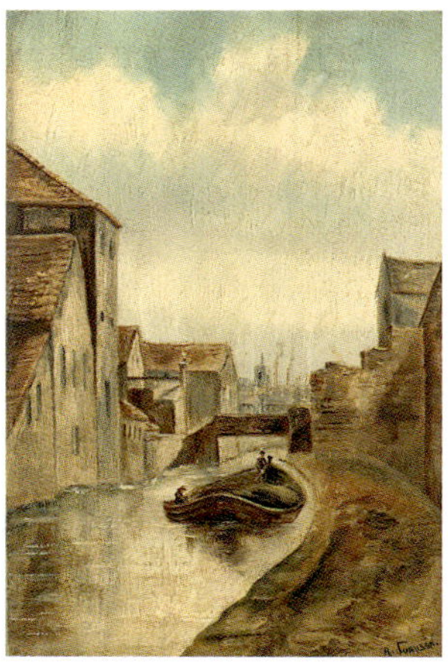

Johnson, A.
Nottingham Canal, View One Kilometre East from Carrington Street Bridge towards Wood Bridge, Trent Street 1894
oil on wood 22 x 15.5
NCL:33753

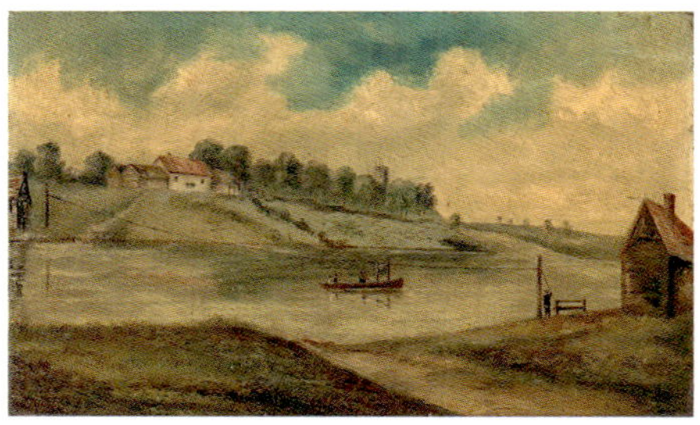

Johnson, A.
Wilford Ferry, Nottinghamshire
oil on wood 18 x 30
NCL:31088

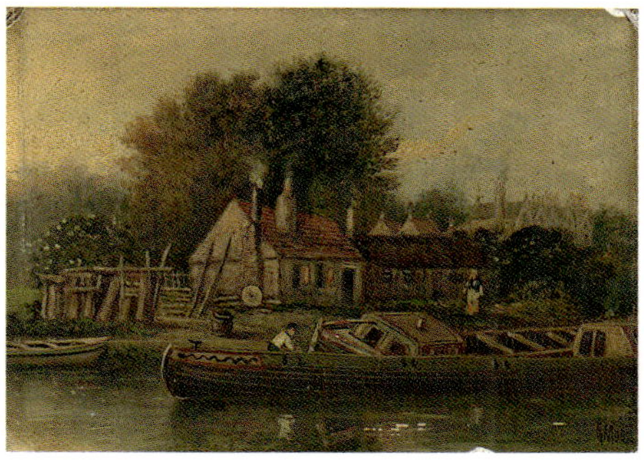

Moore, Thomas Cooper 1827–1901
Lenton Boatyard, Nottingham c.1850
oil on board 18 x 25.5
NCL:68121

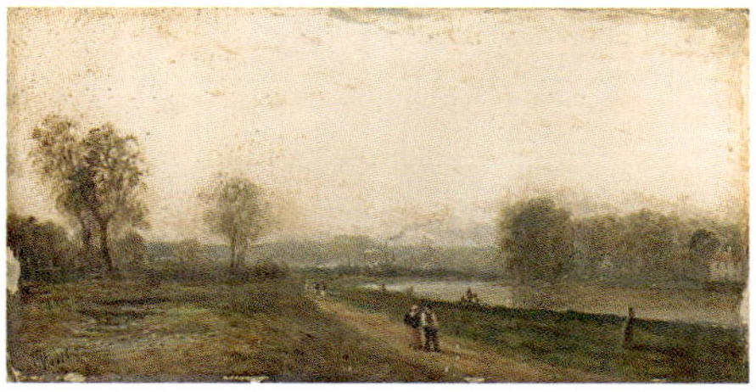

Moore, Thomas Cooper (attributed to)
1827–1901
River Trent, View From the North Bank near Wilford, Nottinghamshire c.1850–1860
oil on board 16 x 31
NCL:24729

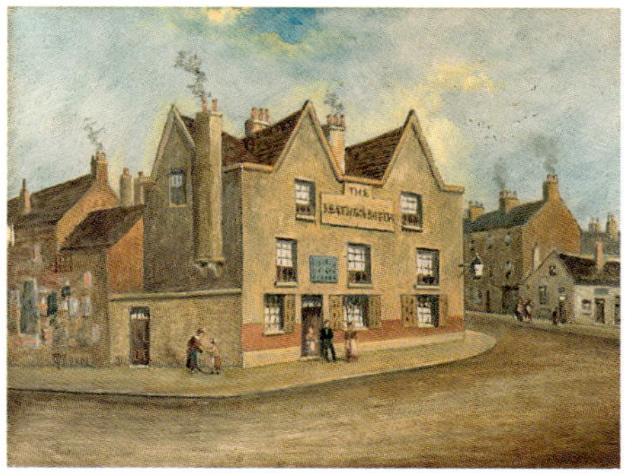

Moore, Thomas Cooper (attributed to)
1827–1901
The 'Leather Bottle Inn', Hockley, Essex c.1896
oil on board 23 x 30
NCL:33381

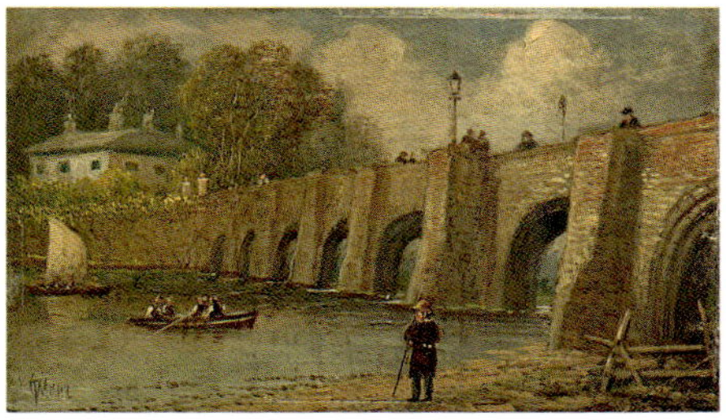

Moore, Thomas Cooper (attributed to
1827–1901
Old Trent Bridge, West Aspect, Nottingham
oil on wood 11.6 x 20.5
NCL:14450

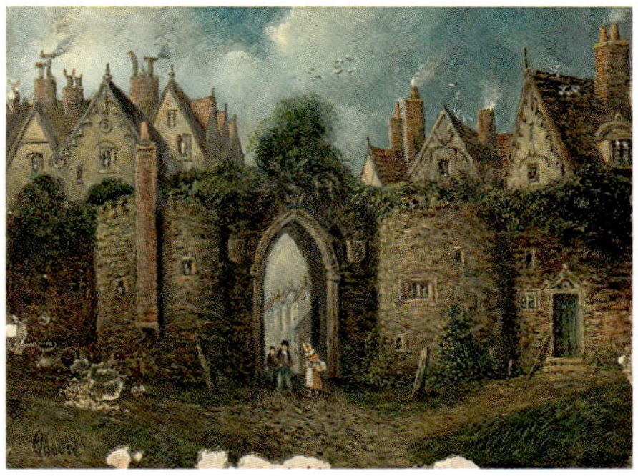

Moore, Thomas Cooper (attributed to)
1827–1901
The Ancient Chapel Bar
oil on board 23 x 30
NCL:33086

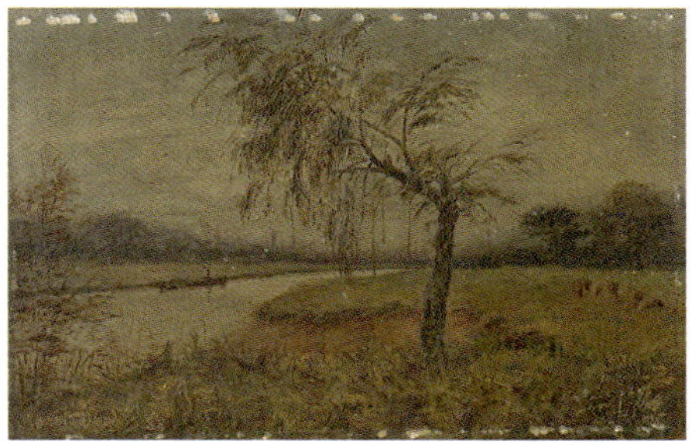

unknown artist
River Trent, View at Colwick, Nottinghamshire 1888
oil on wood 17.5 x 26.5
NCL:33755

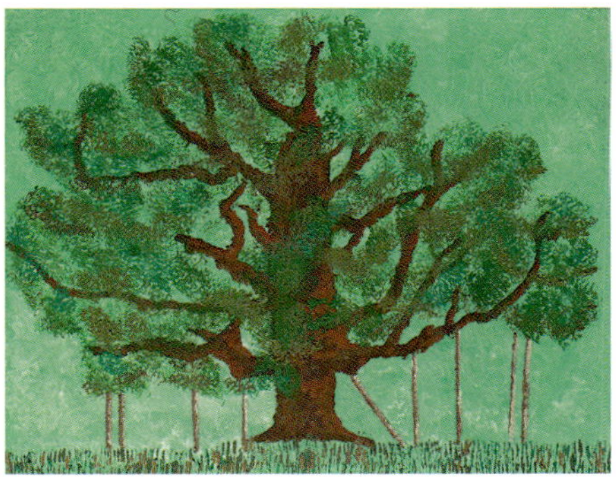

unknown artist
Major Oak 2007
oil on canvas 76 x 101.5
tempNCL6

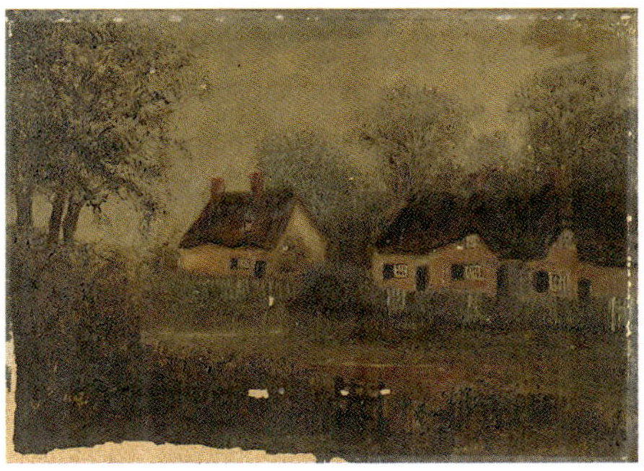

unknown artist
Cottages at Clifton, Nottinghamshire
oil on canvas 18 x 25.5
NCL:33780

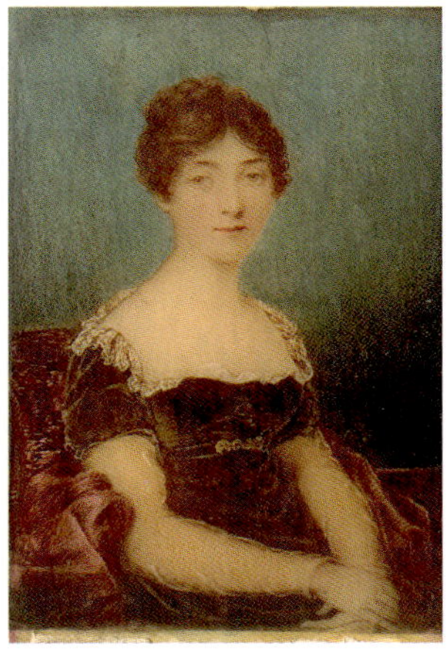

unknown artist
Mrs M. A. Musters, née Chaworth
oil on glass 15 x 12
NCL:31093

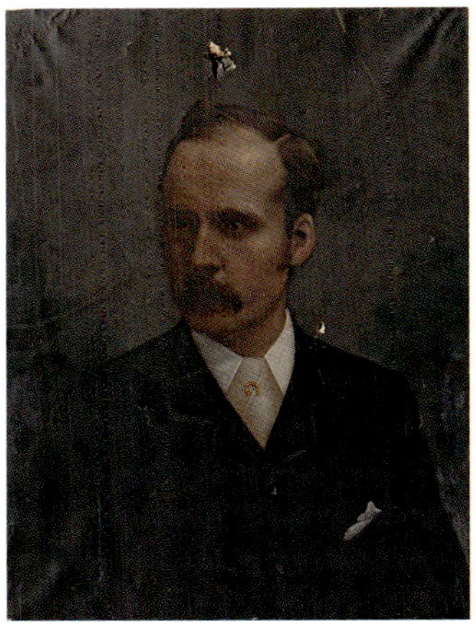

unknown artist
Portrait of an Unidentified Gentleman
oil on canvas 61 x 45.5
tempNCL1

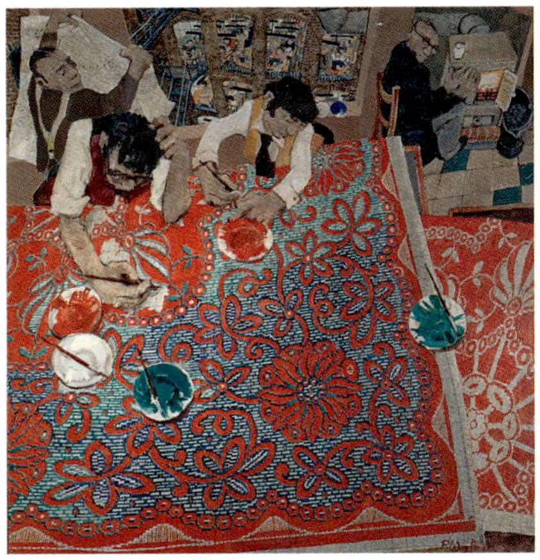

Waplington, Paul b.1938
The Lace Draughting Room
oil on canvas 130 x 130 (E)
tempNCL8

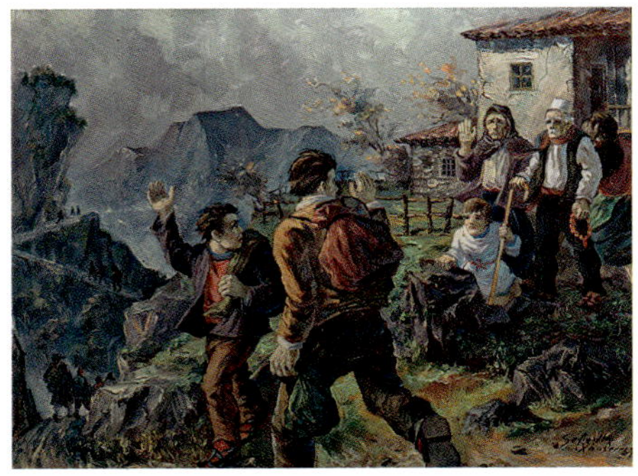

Xhaferin
*The Romanians Departing** 2007
oil on canvas 62 x 82.4
tempNCL2

Nottingham City Museums and Galleries

Nottingham City Museums and Galleries currently consists of Nottingham Castle, The Museum of Nottingham Life at Brewhouse Yard, Wollaton Hall, Nottingham Natural History Museum, Nottingham Industrial Museum, Newstead Abbey (listed separately in this volume) and Green's Windmill. A Collections Access Centre is currently being developed to house the extensive Costume, Lace and Textiles Collection.

Nottingham's museum collections began in 1867, with the donation of the Nottingham Naturalists Society Collection. Since that date, the collections have grown extensively and are now housed across Nottingham City Museums and Galleries' sites.

The largest of these collections is undoubtedly Nottingham Castle Museum and Art Gallery. Its history can be traced back to the first public museum and gallery of art in Nottingham, The Midland Counties Art Museum – a temporary exhibition which opened in the Exchange Buildings in the town square on 20th May 1872. Much of the collection was on loan from the South Kensington Museum (the forerunner of the Victoria and Albert Museum) and from local collections and stately homes. It included a wide range of fine and decorative art, in particular samples reflecting the local machine embroidery and lace industries, with the intention of educating both manufacturers and consumers in the finer points of design and craftsmanship. Its success (an average of 2,500 visitors a week over six years) encouraged the Town Council to establish a permanent collection and museum of its own.

A lease was obtained from the Duke of Newcastle on the burned-out shell of Nottingham Castle, which had been attacked by rioters in 1831 after the Duke refused to support the voting reform. The ruin had been left untouched by the Duke as 'a monument to the folly of the people'.

Forty years on, the conversion of the building to a museum and art gallery was overseen by the local architect Thomas Chambers Hine in consultation with the South Kensington Museum. The Exchange Buildings display closed on 30th March 1878 and the Castle Museum and Art Gallery was opened by

Facing page: Roberts, William Patrick, 1895–1980, *The Return of Ulysses* (detail), c.1913, Nottingham City Museums and Galleries (p. 139)

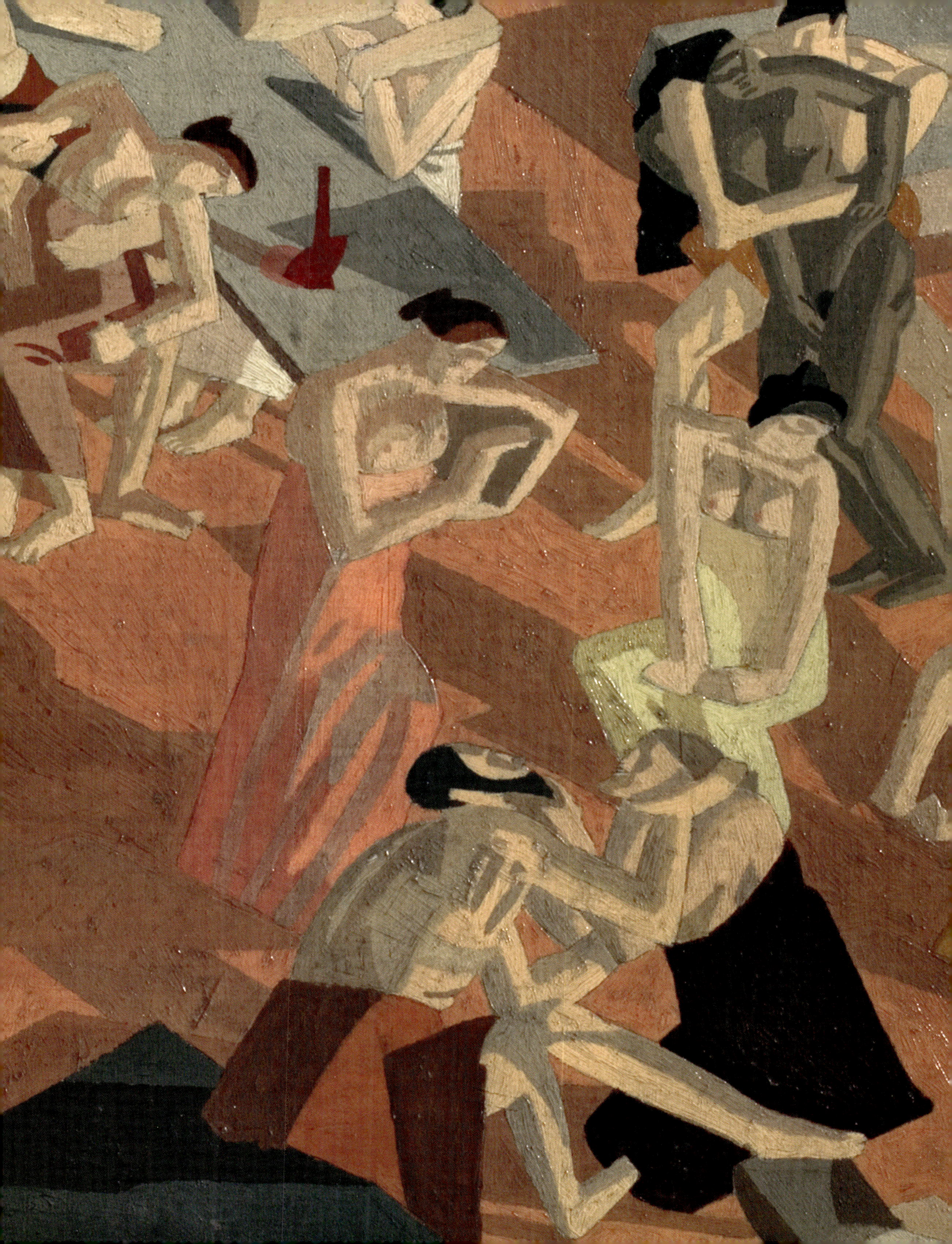

the Prince and Princess of Wales on 3rd July 1878 with a large exhibition of items on loan from many institutional and private collections. It was the first municipal museum and art gallery in the country. G. Harry Wallis, formerly of the South Kensington Museum, was appointed Director and Curator. His brother, Whitworth Wallis, ran Birmingham Museum and Art Gallery and their father was curator at South Kensington. Harry's son Leonard (born in the Castle Museum) went on to become curator of the Whitworth Art Gallery in Manchester.

The Nottingham Castle collections grew quickly through several spectacular donations in the Museum's early years including the donation by Lord Savile of excavated material from the early Roman Temple of Diana at Nemi near Rome and Felix Joseph's donation of his extensive Wedgwood collection. The strengths of the Museum's collections can be seen in numerous items of recent and ancient local origin including archaeological objects and information, numismatics (coin hoards and tokens) and works by local artists and craftspeople. Nottingham machine-made lace, salt-glazed pottery and Medieval alabaster religious sculpture are particular local specialities.

The majority of Nottingham City Museums and Galleries' collection of oil paintings are kept at Nottingham Castle, on display and in store. Some are on display at other museums, some are loaned out to Council offices and institutions within the city and beyond. Around 130 artworks can usually be found on display. Along with the 800 or so oil paintings photographed here, the Fine Art Collection consists of over 4,000 watercolours, drawings and prints, a small collection of sculpture, including the medieval 'Nottingham' alabasters, and a collection of photography and fine art textiles acquired primarily through the Contemporary Art Society Special Collection Scheme.

Important local artists with international reputations whose works are held within the Collection are Paul Sandby, Richard Parkes Bonington and Laura Knight. However the collection of oils is eclectic, highlights range from Charles Le Brun's massive *Hercules Vanquishing Diomedes*, painted for Cardinal Richelieu, to George Morland's small, hard luck painting *The Artist in His Studio and His Man Gibbs*, from William Patrick Roberts' Futurist take on *The Return of Ulysses* to Helena Ben-Zenou's *The Imposition*, a painting inspired by the scaffolded Prospect Room at Wollaton Hall.

The Museum of Nottingham Life at Brewhouse Yard includes the collection of local topography and portraiture which is currently divided between the Fine Art and Community History sections, the latter holding the lion's share. The majority of the printed material and all cartography is kept at Brewhouse Yard. Together with the collections held at the Local Studies Library and the Nottinghamshire Archives, this Collection is a highly important resource for the study of Nottingham's past and the local, natural and man-made environment.

Nottingham City Museums and Galleries hold the only major public collection of works by significant Nottingham artists of the nineteenth and twentieth centuries including Thomas Barber, John Rawson Walker and Henry Dawson. This body of work, apart from its topographical content, tells the story of the rise of Nottingham as a provincial art centre in the last century.

Sarah Skinner, Keeper of Art; Michael Cooper, Registrar; Judith Edgar, Keeper of Community History & Maria Erskine, Keeper of Community History

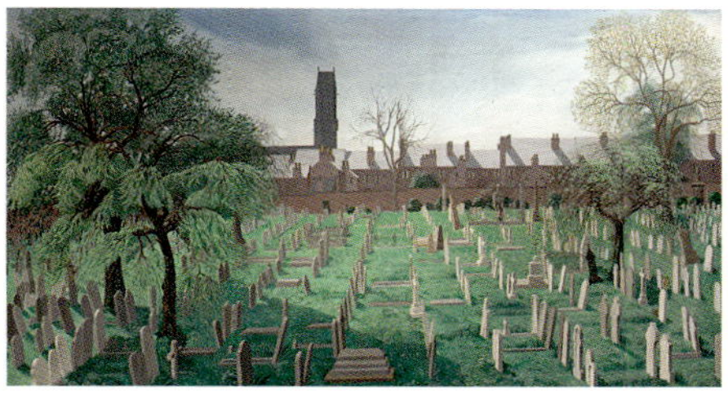

Adnams, Marion 1898–1995
Spring in the Cemetery 1956
oil on board 58.4 x 110.5
NCM 1956-85

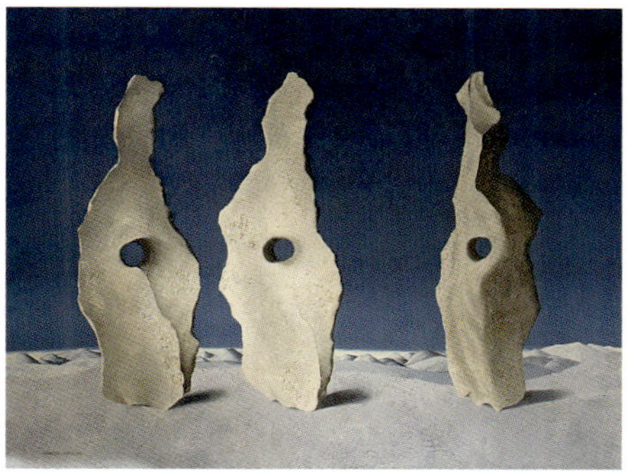

Adnams, Marion 1898–1995
Three Stones 1968
oil on board 75 x 105
NCM 1971-26

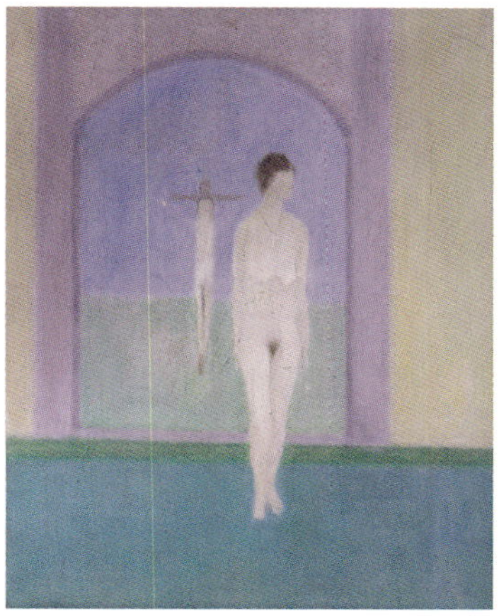

Aitchison, Craigie Ronald John b.1926
Nude Standing in front of a Picture 1963
oil on canvas 65.4 x 54
NCM 1986-1089

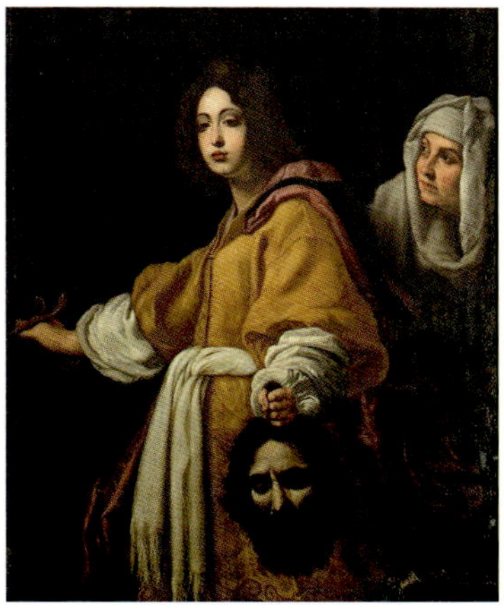

Allori, Cristofano (after) 1577–1621
Judith with the Head of Holofernes c.1620
oil on canvas 142.3 x 116.8
NCM 1878-190

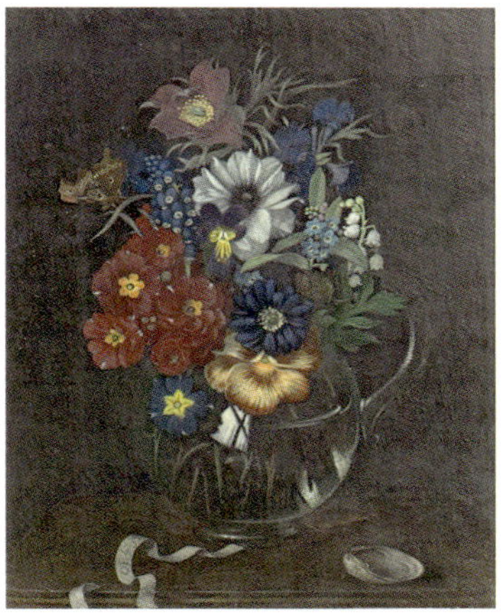

Armfield, Maxwell Ashby 1882–1972
Shell and Comma Butterfly c.1956
tempera on wood 27.9 x 24.2
NCM 1957-7

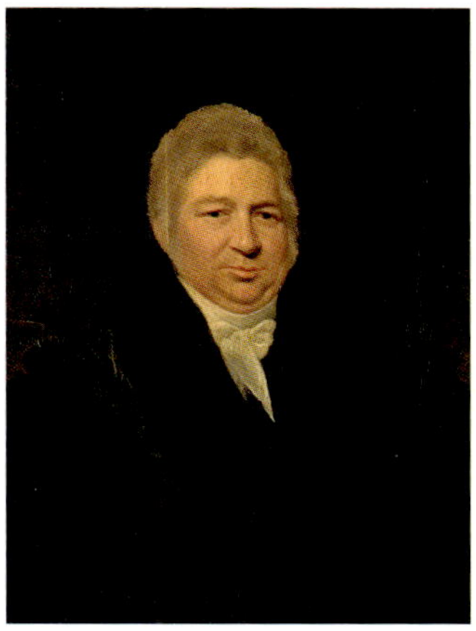

Artaud, William 1763–1823
George Coldham, Town Clerk of Nottingham c.1810
oil on canvas 86.4 x 66
NCM 1879-132

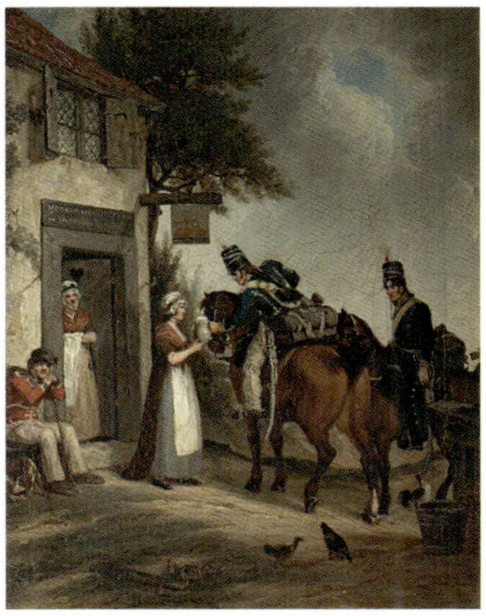

Atkinson, John Augustus 1775–1833
Soldiers Refreshing c.1805
oil on canvas 50.8 x 43.5
NCM 1904-82

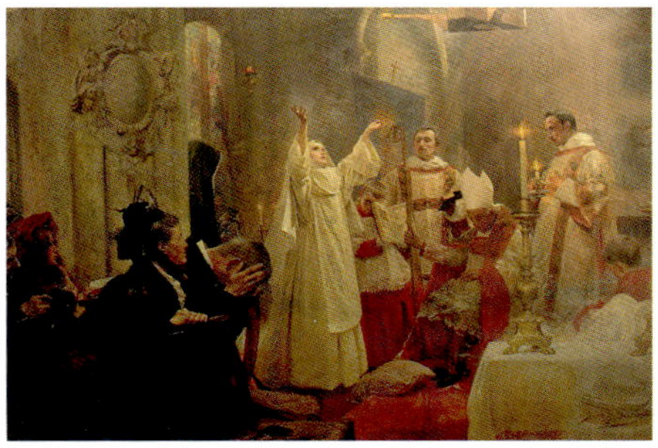

Bacon, John Henry Frederick 1865–1914
'Suscipe me Domine' ('Receive Me O Lord') 1895
oil on canvas 154.9 x 213.4
NCM 1919-1

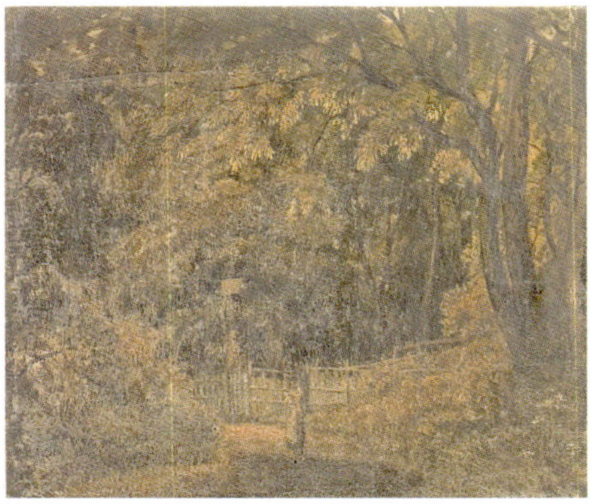

Baker, Thomas 1809–1869
Entrance to Colwick Woods, Nottinghamshire 1840
oil on wood 24.8 x 28.6
NCM 1913-59

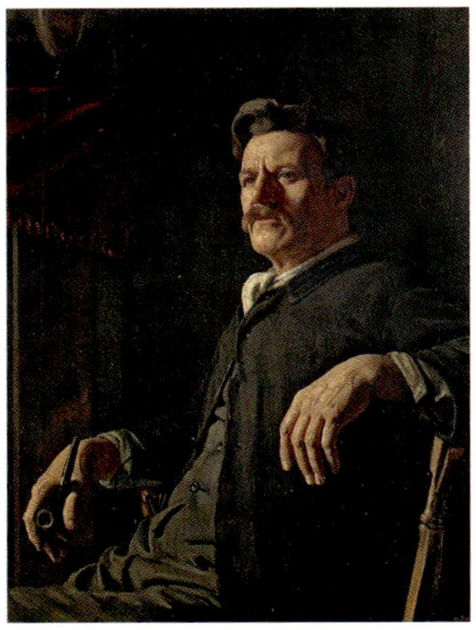

Ball, Henry 1894–1966
Portrait of the Artist's Father (A Quiet Hour) 1926
oil on canvas 91.4 x 71.1
NCM 1956-75

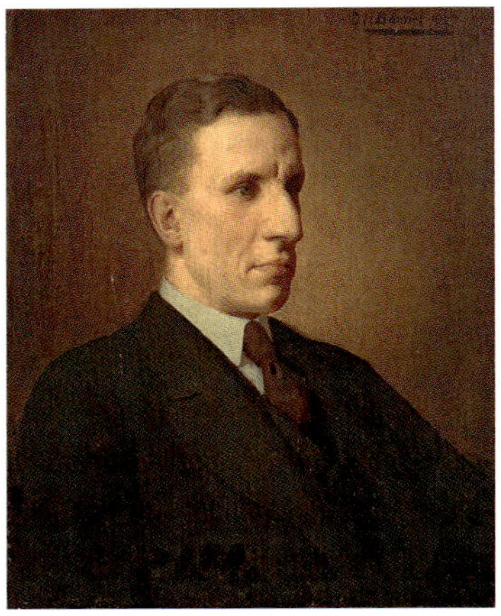

Banner, Delmar Harmond 1896–1983
Clement Fothergill Pitman (d.1973), Art Director and Curator of Nottingham Castle Museum (1930–1959) 1927
oil on canvas 61 x 50.8
NCM 1960-5

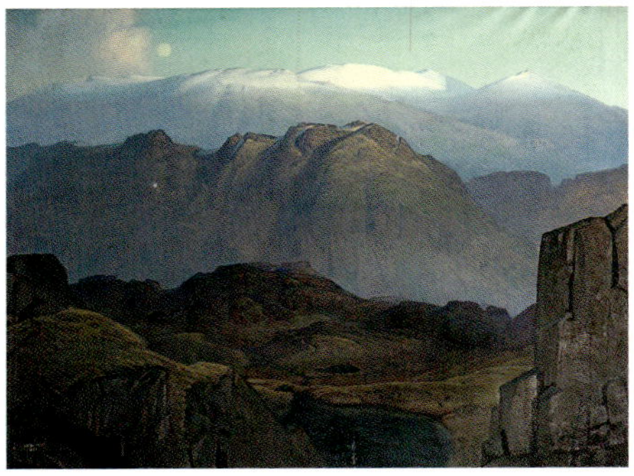

Banner, Delmar Harmond 1896–1983
Coniston Fells from Upper Eskdale, Cumberland (Grey Friar, Old Man, Dow Crag, Hardknott and Upper Eskdale (...)) 1938
oil on canvas 77.5 x 104.1
NCM 1939-4

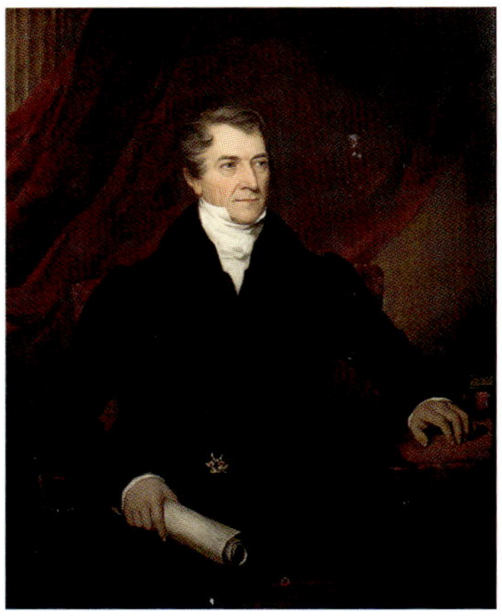

Barber, Thomas 1771–1843
Lord Denman (1779–1854) c.1831–1833
oil on canvas 129.5 x 101.6
NCM 1879-130

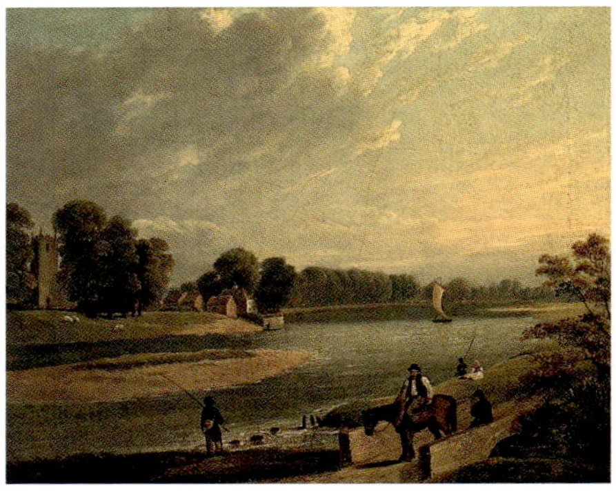

Barber, Thomas 1771–1843
The Trent at Wilford c.1840
oil on canvas 48.9 x 62.2
NCM 1909-69

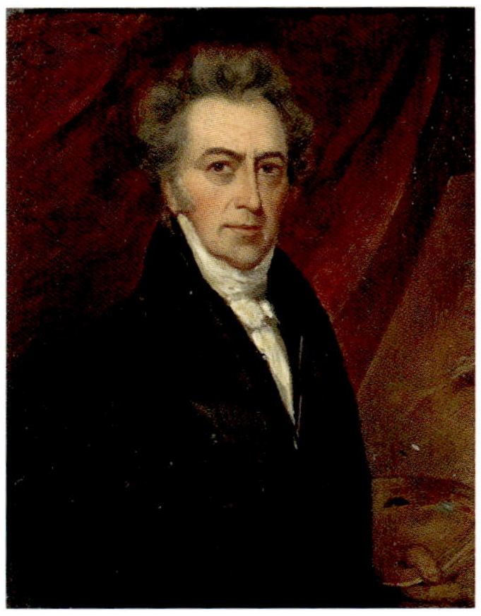

Barber, Thomas 1771–1843
Self Portrait 1841
oil on wood 26 x 21.6
NCM 1909-68

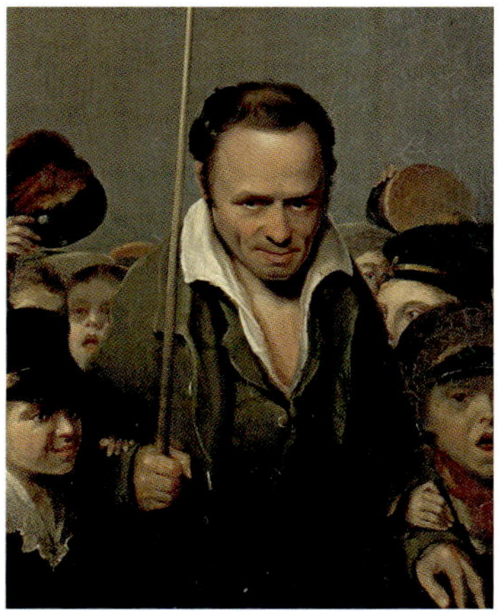

Barber, Thomas 1771–1843
Benjamin Mayo (c.1779–1843), the Old General
oil on canvas 76.2 x 63.5
NCM 1878-195

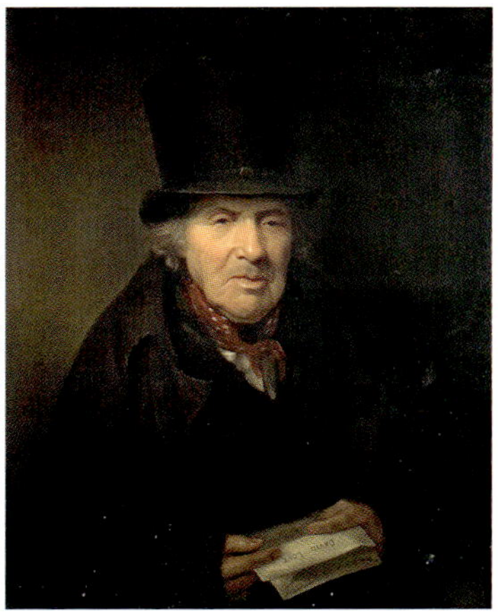

Barber, Thomas 1771–1843
David Love (1750–1827), Ballad-Writer
oil on canvas 76.2 x 63.5
NCM 1946-42

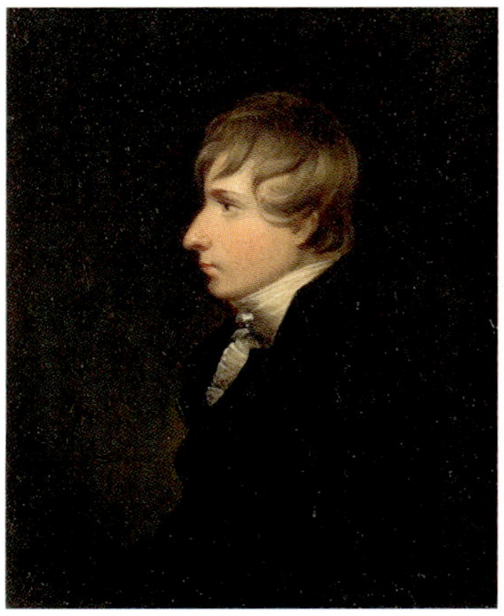

Barber, Thomas 1771–1843
Henry Kirke White (1785–1806), Poet
oil on canvas 24.8 x 21.3
NCM 1894-76

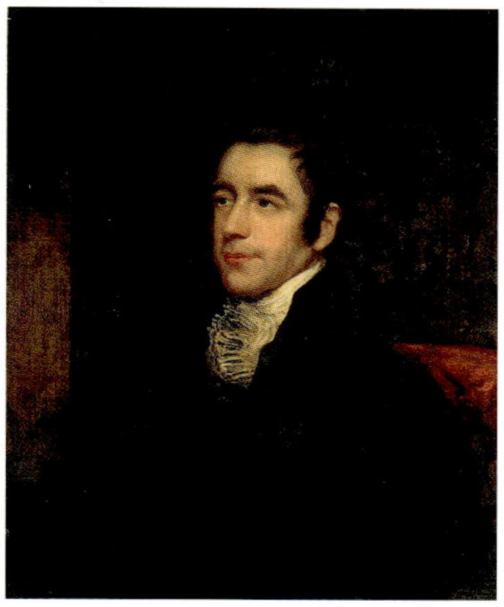

Barber, Thomas 1771–1843
Jonathan Dunn (1771–1857)
oil on canvas 74.9 x 62.2
NCM 1922-70

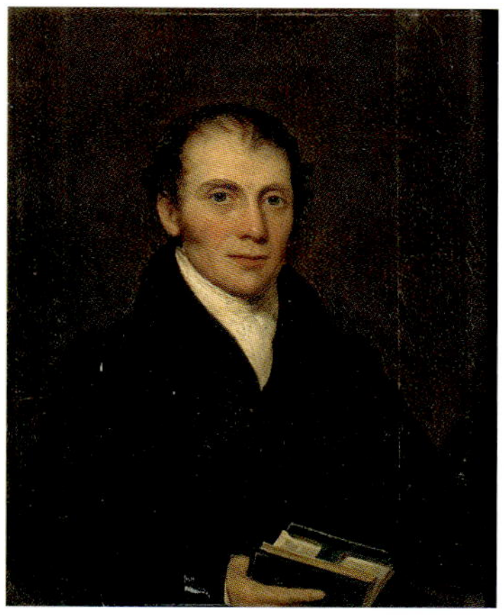

Barber, Thomas 1771–1843
Thomas Stevenson
oil on board 38.1 x 30.5
NCM 1893-49

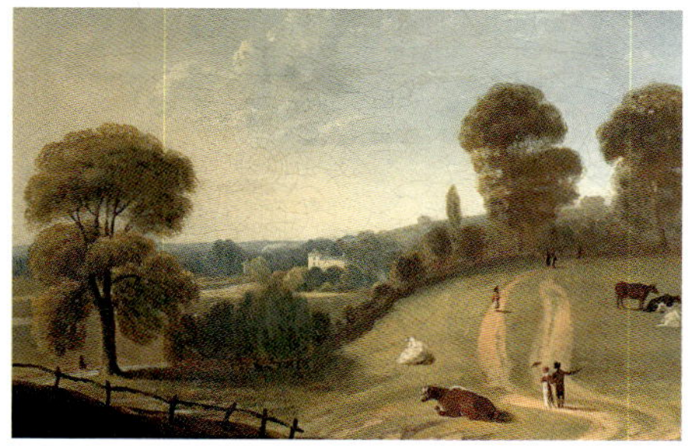

Barber, Thomas 1771–1843
View across Nottingham Park with Lenton Priory in the Distance
oil on canvas 39.4 x 58.4
NCM 1892-59

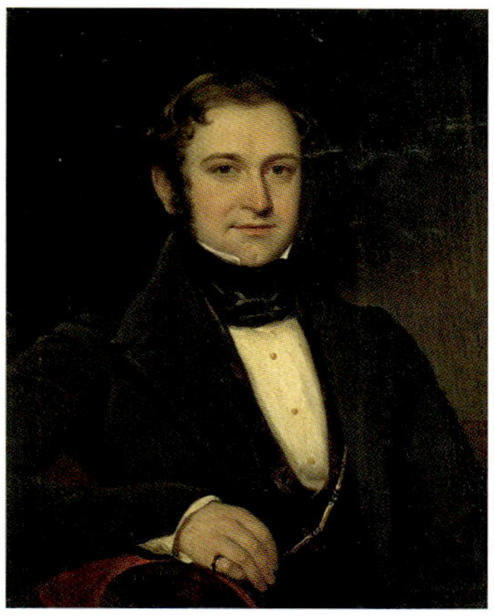

Barber, Thomas 1771–1843
William Chapman (1812–1874)
oil on canvas 76.2 x 62.2
NCM 1894-52

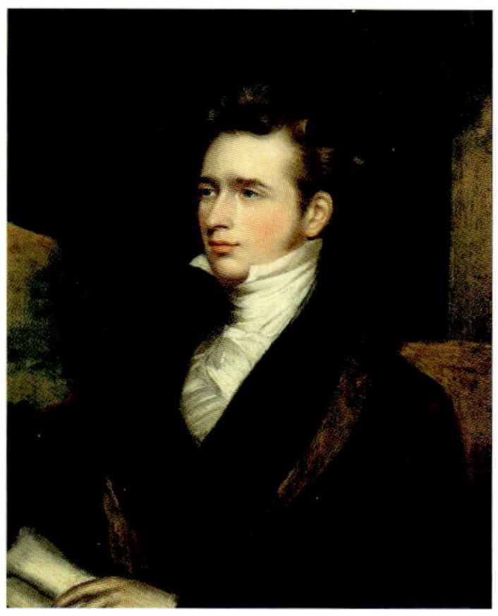

Barber, Thomas (attributed to) 1798–1826
John Rawson Walker (1796–1893) 1822
oil on canvas 74.9 x 62.2
NCM 1898-45

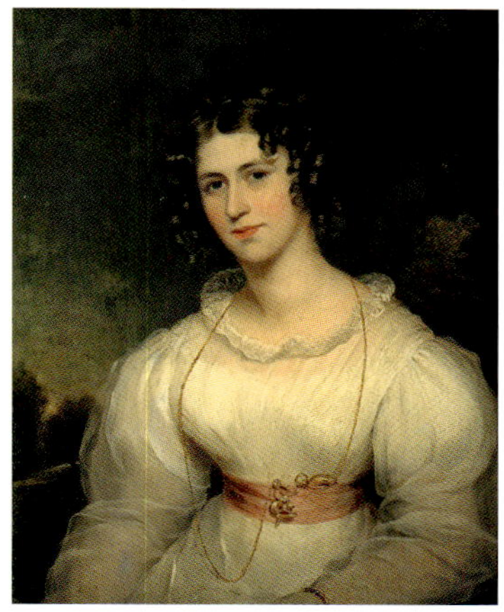

Barber, Thomas (attributed to) 1798–1826
Miss Elizabeth Hoare (later Mrs J. Rawson Walker) 1826
oil on canvas 74.9 x 62.2
NCM 1898-46

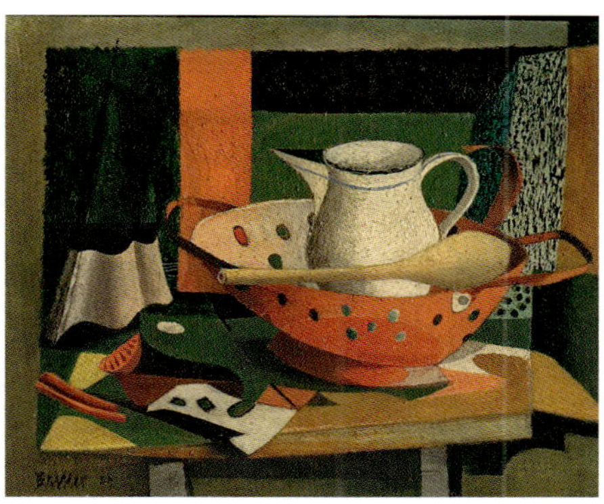

Barker, John Edward 1889–1953
Kitchen Still Life
oil on wood 19.1 x 24.1
NCM 1958-43

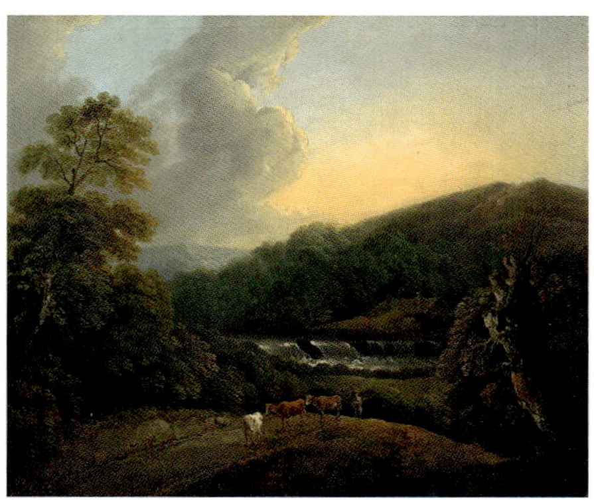

Barker, Thomas 1769–1847
Mountainous Landscape
oil on canvas 62.5 x 76.8
NCM 1890-1165

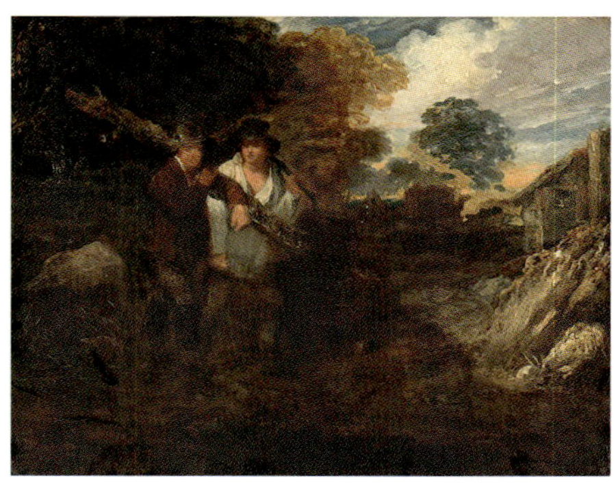

Barker, Thomas (imitator of) 1769–1847
Landscape with Two Figures
oil on board 51.8 x 66.4
NCM 1904-9

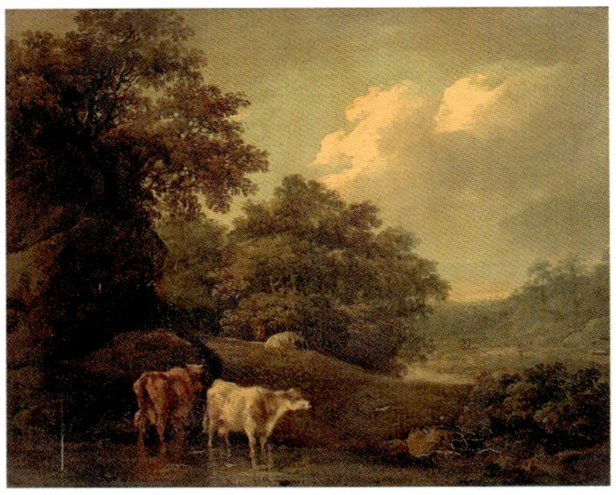

Barker, Thomas Jones 1815–1882
Landscape with Cattle
oil on canvas 51.4 x 67.3
NCM 1890-1195

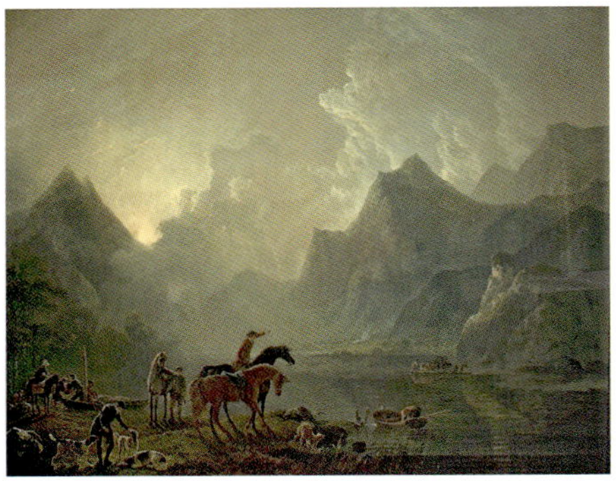

Barret, George 1732–1784
Llanberis Lake and Dolbadarn Castle, North Wales 1777
oil on canvas 121.9 x 170.8
NCM 1904-10

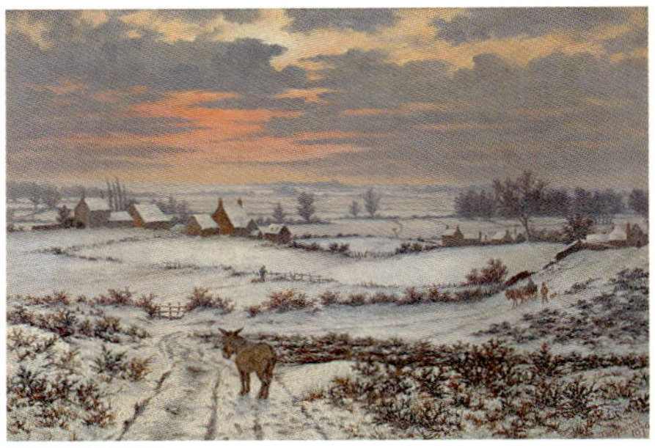

Barrett, Thomas 1845–1924
Snow Piece, Bulwell Forest, Nottinghamshire
oil on canvas 35.6 x 53.3
NCM 1890-1175

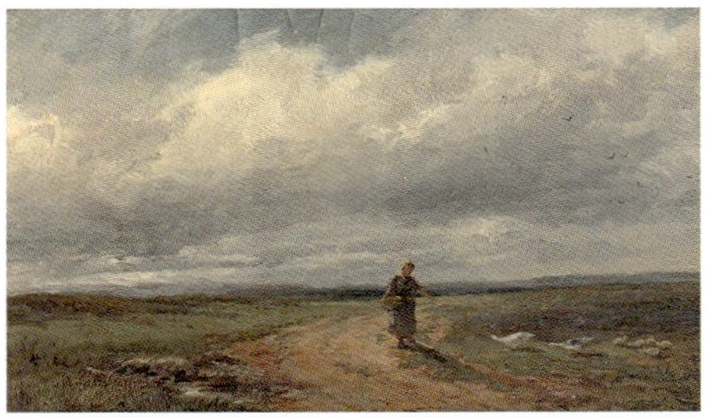

Bates, David 1841–1921
Broadheath Common 1875
oil on canvas 18.4 x 31.1
NCM 1924-27

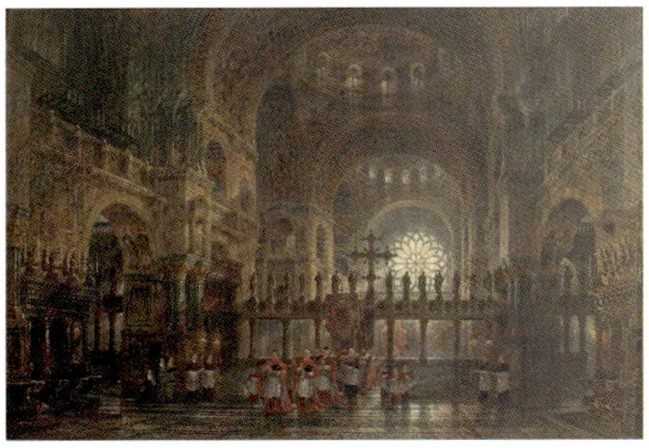

Bayliss, Wyke 1835–1906
Interior of St Mark's Basilica, Venice, Italy 1877
oil on canvas 110.2 x 161
NCM 1882-1

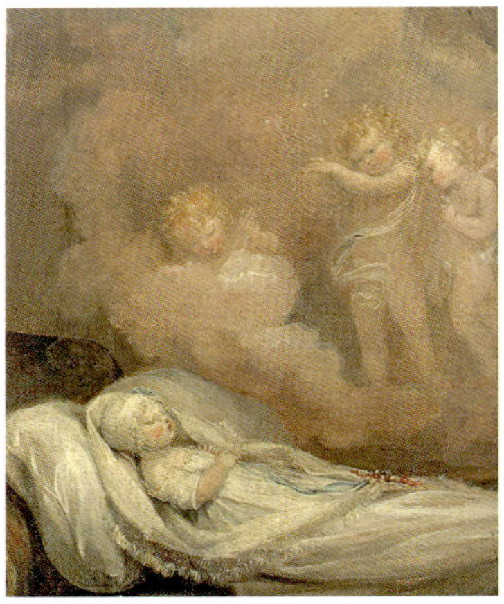

Beechey, William 1753–1839
A Child of Paul Sandby
oil on canvas 24.1 x 19.7
NCM 1945-179

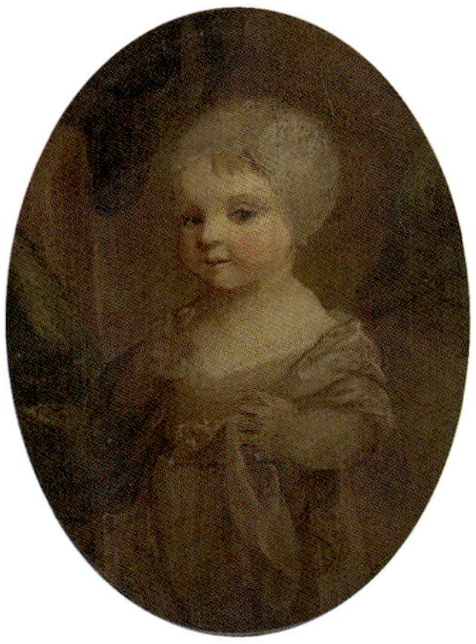

Beechey, William 1753–1839
Portrait of a Young Girl
oil on canvas 23.5 x 19.1
NCM 1945-180

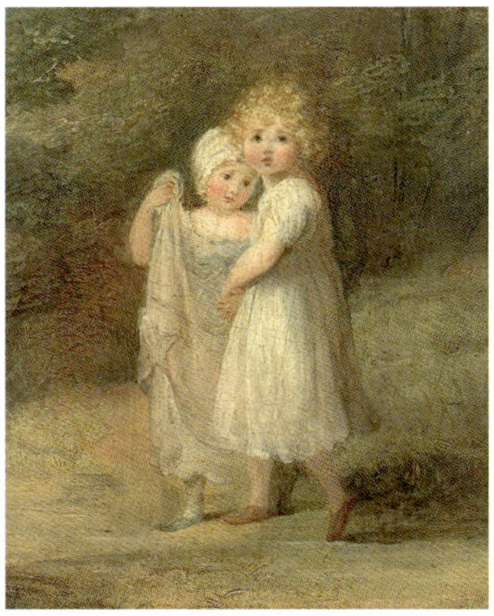

Beechey, William 1753–1839
The Children of Paul Sandby
oil on canvas 23 x 19
NCM 1945-181

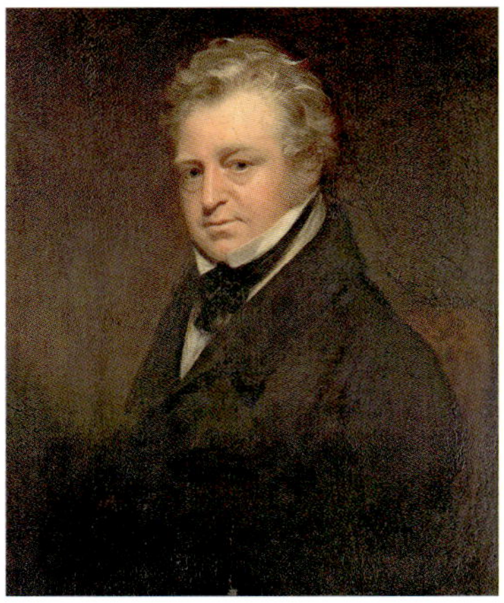

Beechey, William 1753–1839
Thomas Paul Sandby (1766–c.1832)
oil on canvas 76.2 x 63.5
NCM 1945-99

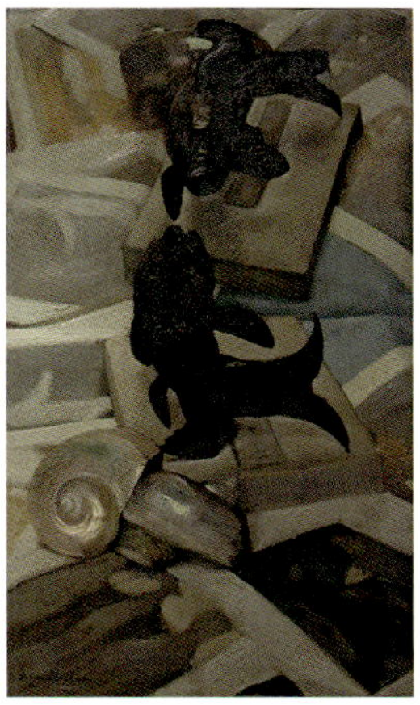

Beeton, Alan 1880–1942
The Black Porcelain Fish (The Bronze Fish)
oil on canvas 76.2 x 45.7
NCM 1939-79

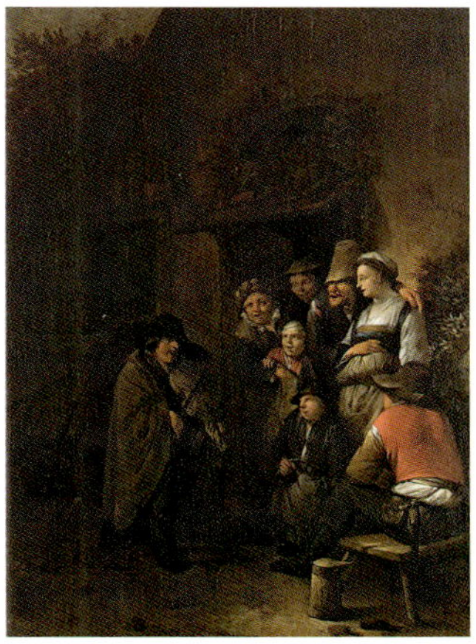

Bega, Cornelis Pietersz. 1631/1632–1664
The Dwarf Fiddler c.1652
oil on wood 28.9 x 23.2
NCM 1904-87

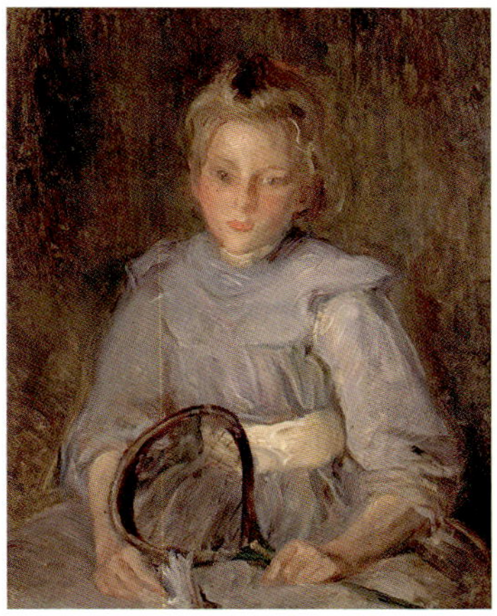

Belleroche, Albert de 1864–1944
A Girl with a Racquet
oil on canvas 73.7 x 60.3
NCM 1952-45

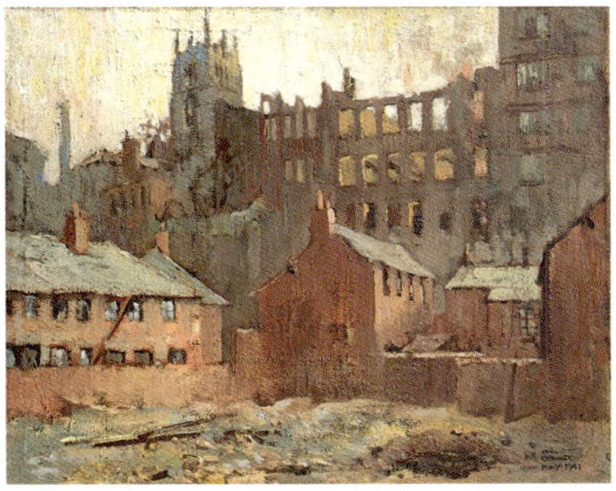

Benner, William 1884–1964
After the Blitz, near Trivett's Works from Cliff Road, Nottingham (painted after the night of enemy aerial attack, 8–9 May 1941) 1941
oil on canvas 48.3 x 38.1
NCM 1943-2

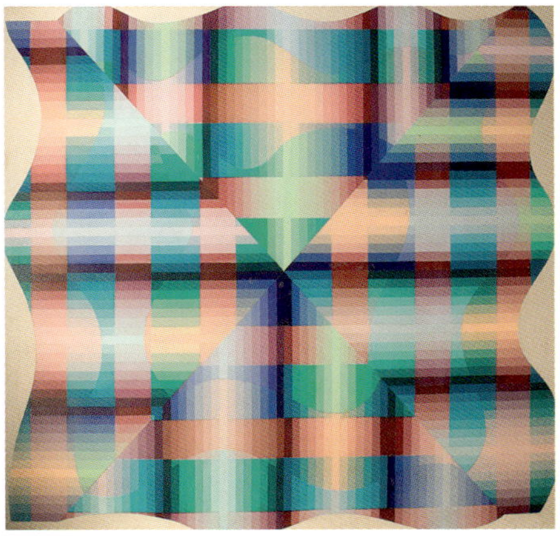

Benyon, Margaret b.1940
Untitled
acrylic on canvas 152.4 x 172.7
NCM 1969-121

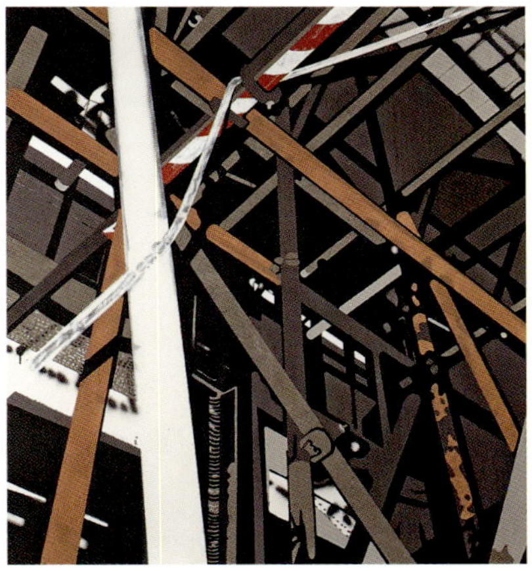

Ben-Zenou, Helena b.1970
The Imposition (Prospect Room, Wollaton Hall, February 2006) 2006
acrylic & mixed media on board 181 x 170.4
NCMG 2006-200

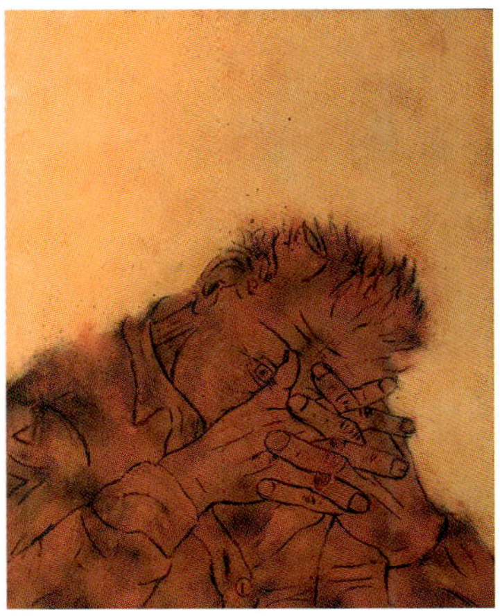

Bevan, Tony b.1951
Condition 1982
acrylic on board 151.3 x 125.1
NCM 1989-905

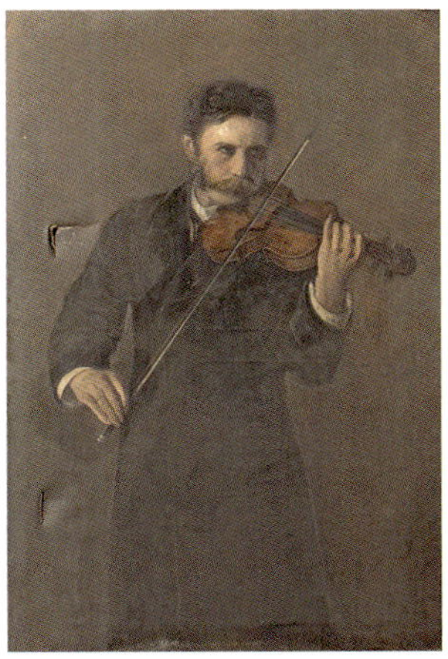

Bilbie, James Lees 1860–1945
An Earnest Movement in Andante (Charles Heywood, Violinist) 1884
oil on canvas 121.9 x 86.4
NCM 1946-243

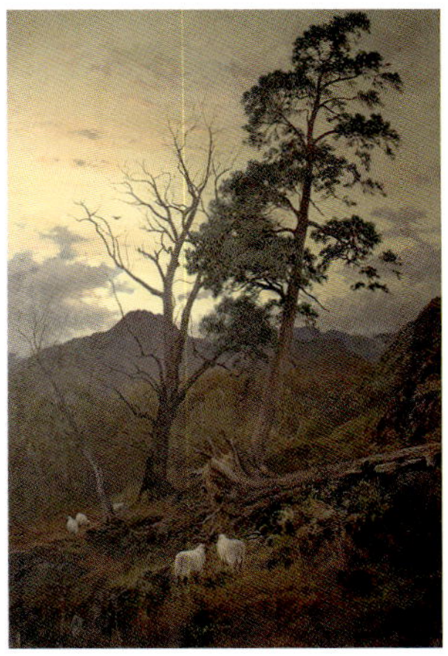

Bilbie, James Lees 1860–1945
Deepening Shades 1889
oil on canvas 157.5 x 127
NCM 1890-1164

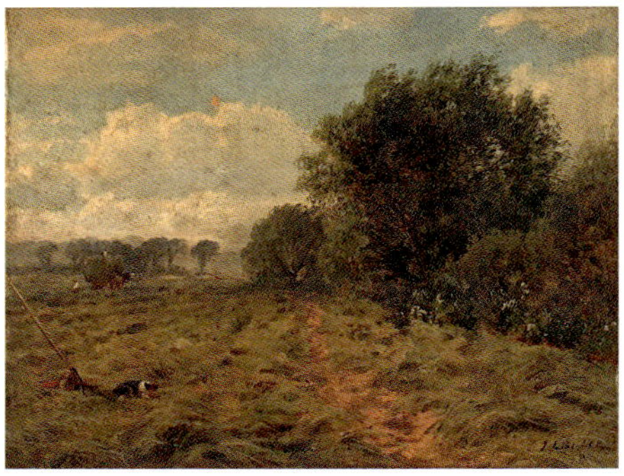

Bilbie, James Lees 1860–1945
Hayfield near Trent Baths at Nottingham
oil on wood 29.8 x 40
NCM 1938-131

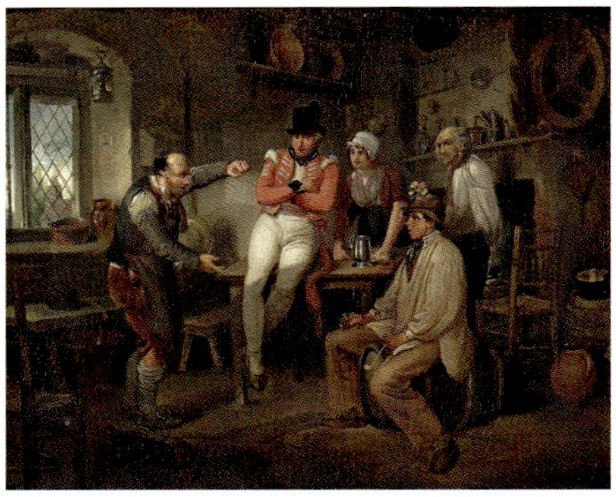

Bird, Edward 1772–1819
The Recruit 1806
oil on canvas 30.5 x 38.1
NCM 1904-11

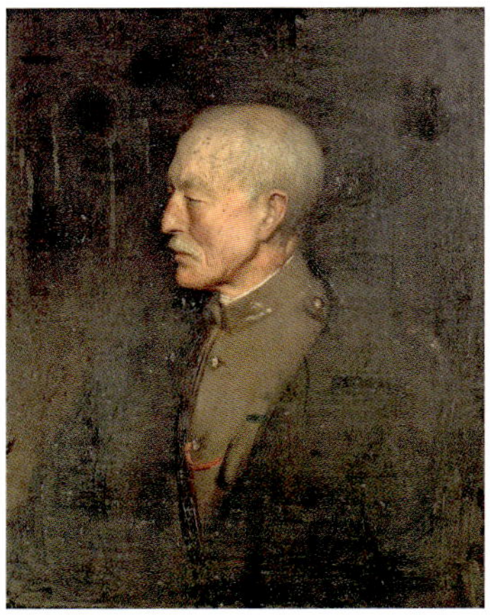

Birley, Oswald Hornby Joseph 1880–1952
Colonel William Frank Wheatley (d.1923)
oil on canvas 81.3 x 66
NCM 1954-27

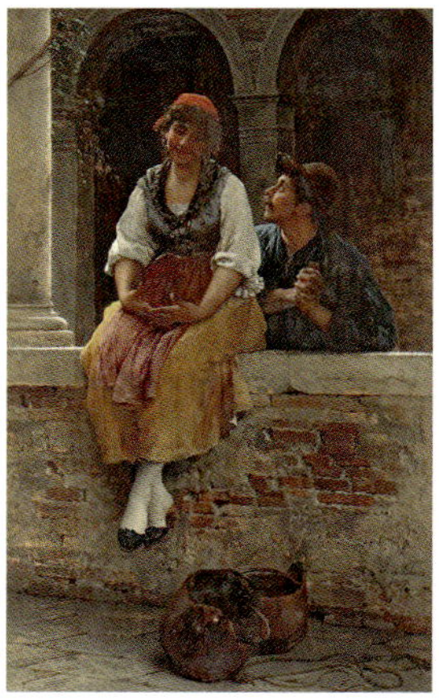

Blaas, Eugen von 1843–1931
The Offer 1887
oil on canvas 93.3 x 61.4
NCM 1899-8

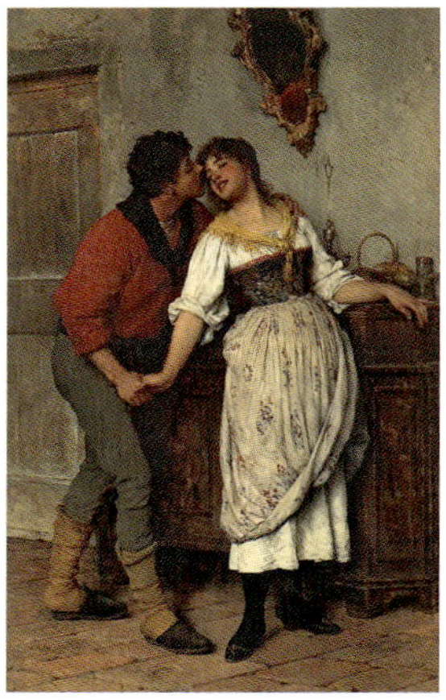

Blaas, Eugen von 1843–1931
Accepted 1887
oil on canvas 93.3 x 61.4
NCM 1899-9

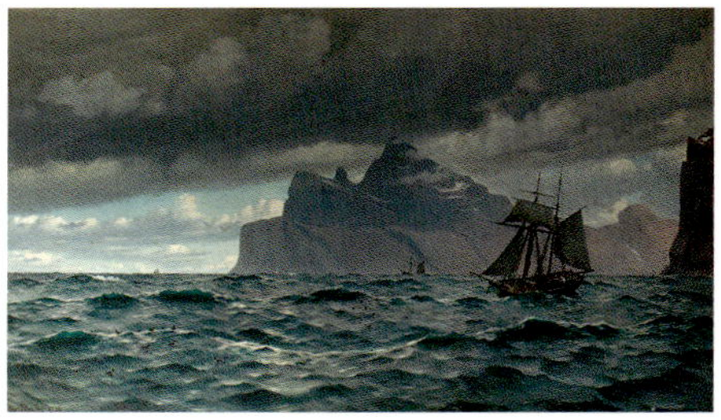

Blache, Christian Vigilius 1838–1920
Cape North, Iceland 1884
oil on canvas 106.7 x 182.9
NCM 1885-3

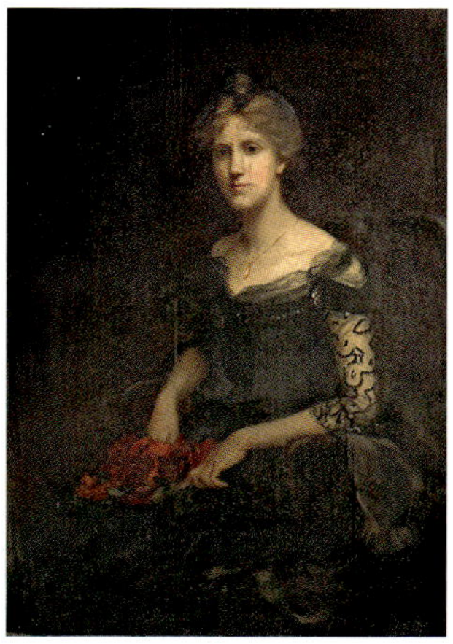

Black, Arthur John 1855–1936
Mrs Mary E. Pennel (Portrait of a Seated Woman Dressed in Black with Red Flowers on Her Lap) 1901
oil on canvas 127 x 91.4
NCM 1945-91

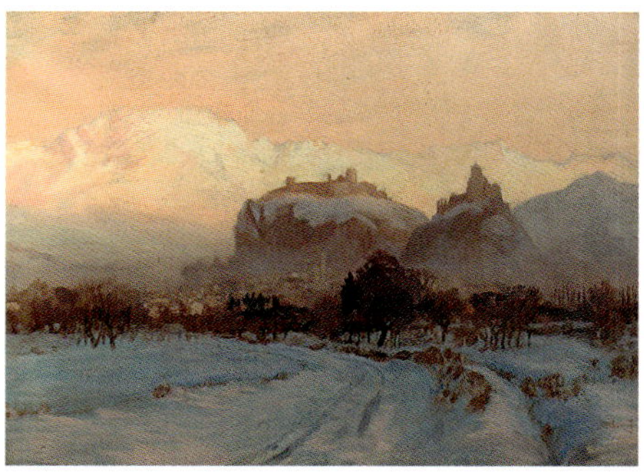

Black, Arthur John 1855–1936
A Winter Scene
oil on canvas 39.4 x 57.2
NCM 1936-22

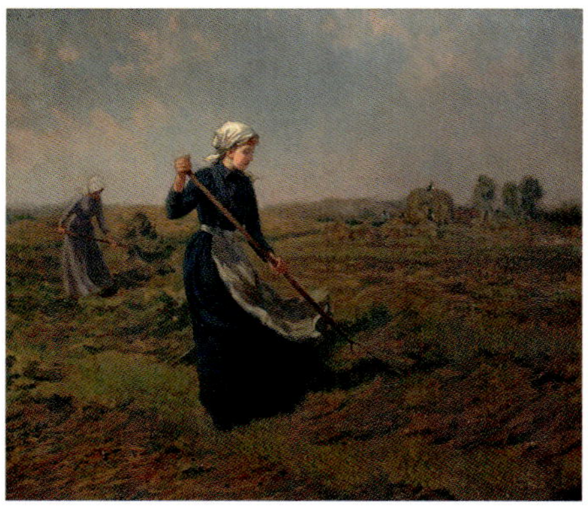

Black, Arthur John 1855–1936
Girl Haymaking
oil on canvas 61 x 76.2
NCM 1936-20

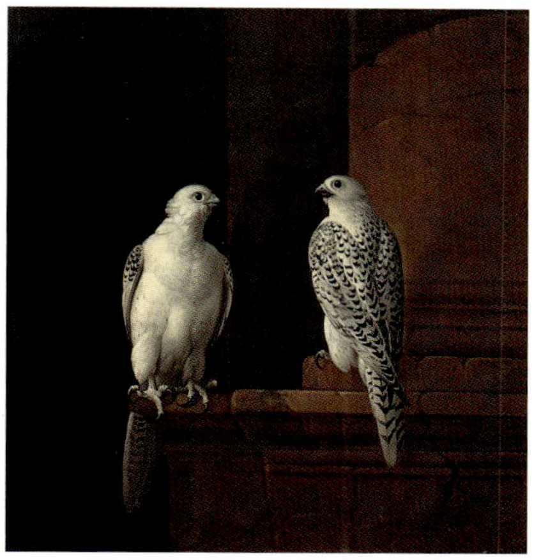

Bogdany, Jakob c.1660–1724
Two Iceland Falcons
oil on canvas 109.2 x 108
NCM 1939-3

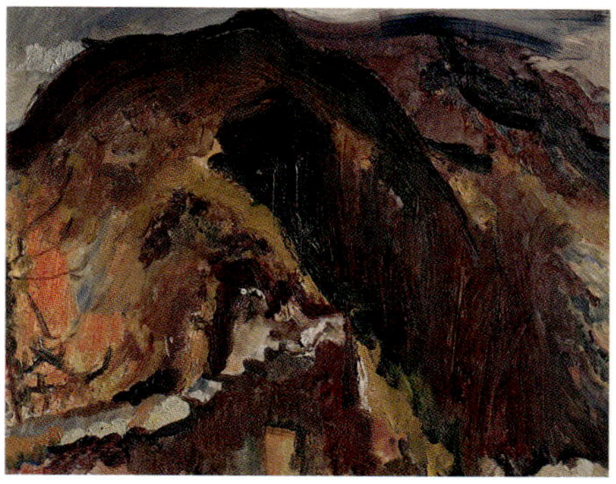

Bomberg, David 1890–1957
The Moorish Wall, Cyprus 1948
oil on canvas 69.5 x 89.9
NCM 1967-279

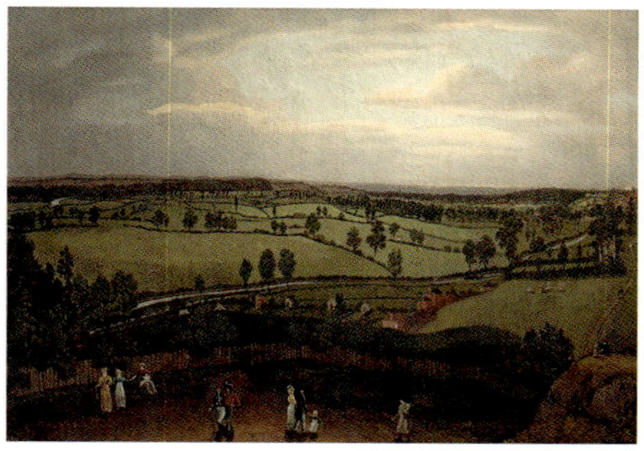

Bonington, Richard 1768–1835
Nottingham Meadows from the Rock Cliff, Where Lenton Road Turns into Park Valley (Nottingham Park from Castle Rock)
oil on canvas 72.3 x 105.4
NCM 1905-65

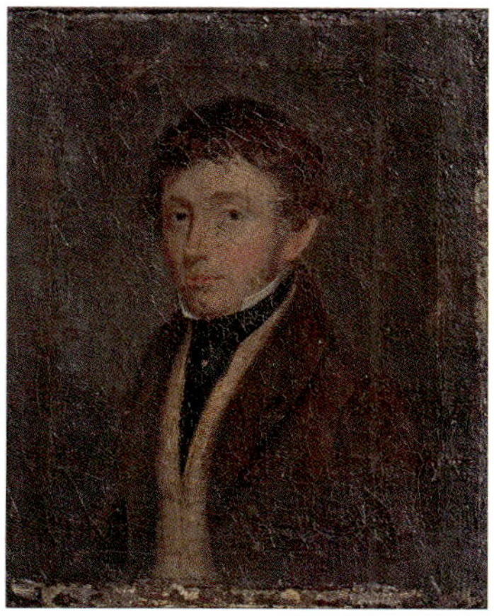

Bonington, Richard 1768–1835
Portrait of One of the Donor's Family (Hodges)
oil on canvas 13.5 x 11.4
NCM 1963-306

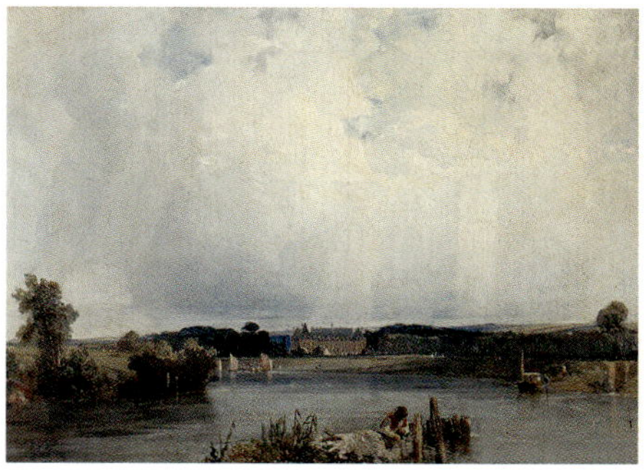

Bonington, Richard Parkes 1802–1828
Le Château de la Duchesse de Berry
1823–1825
oil on canvas 37.5 x 52
FALOAN 96

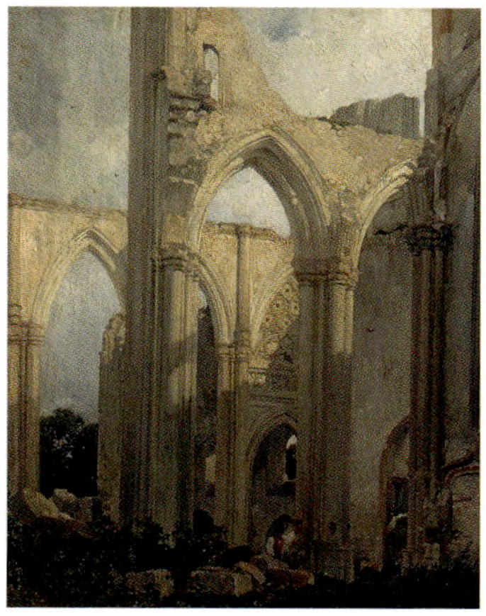

Bonington, Richard Parkes 1802–1828
Ruins of the Abbey St Bertin, St Omer, France (Transept of the Abbey of St Bertin, St Omer, France) c.1824
oil on canvas 59.9 x 48.8
NCM 1907-85

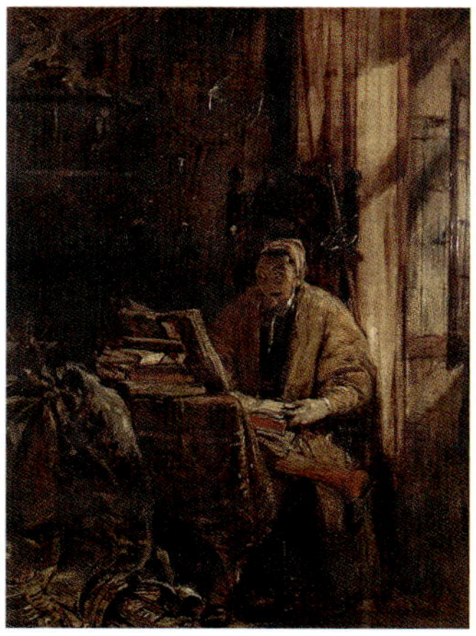

Bonington, Richard Parkes 1802–1828
Don Quixote in His Study c.1825–1826
oil on canvas 40.7 x 33
NCM 1958-56

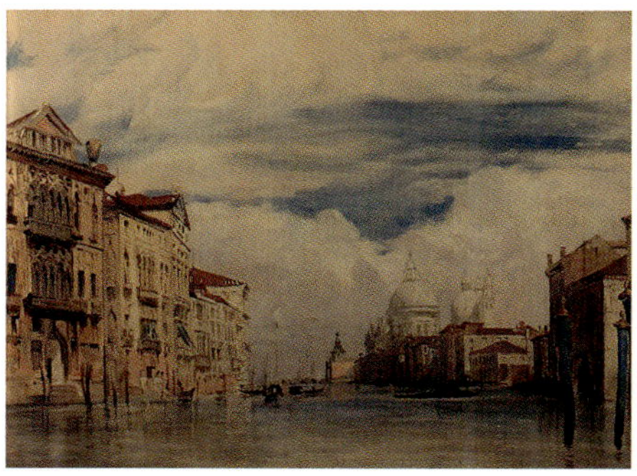

Bonington, Richard Parkes 1802–1828
The Grand Canal, Venice, Italy 1826–1827
oil on canvas 30.5 x 42.6
NCM 1958-55

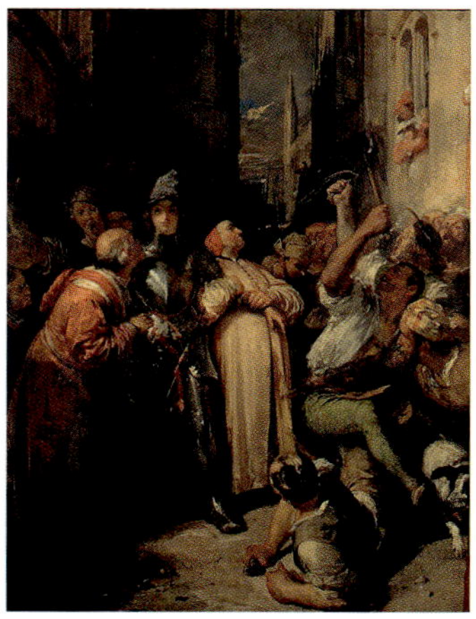

Bonington, Richard Parkes 1802–1828
Quentin Durward at Liège, Belgium
c.1827–1828
oil on canvas 63 x 51.5
NCM 1974-76

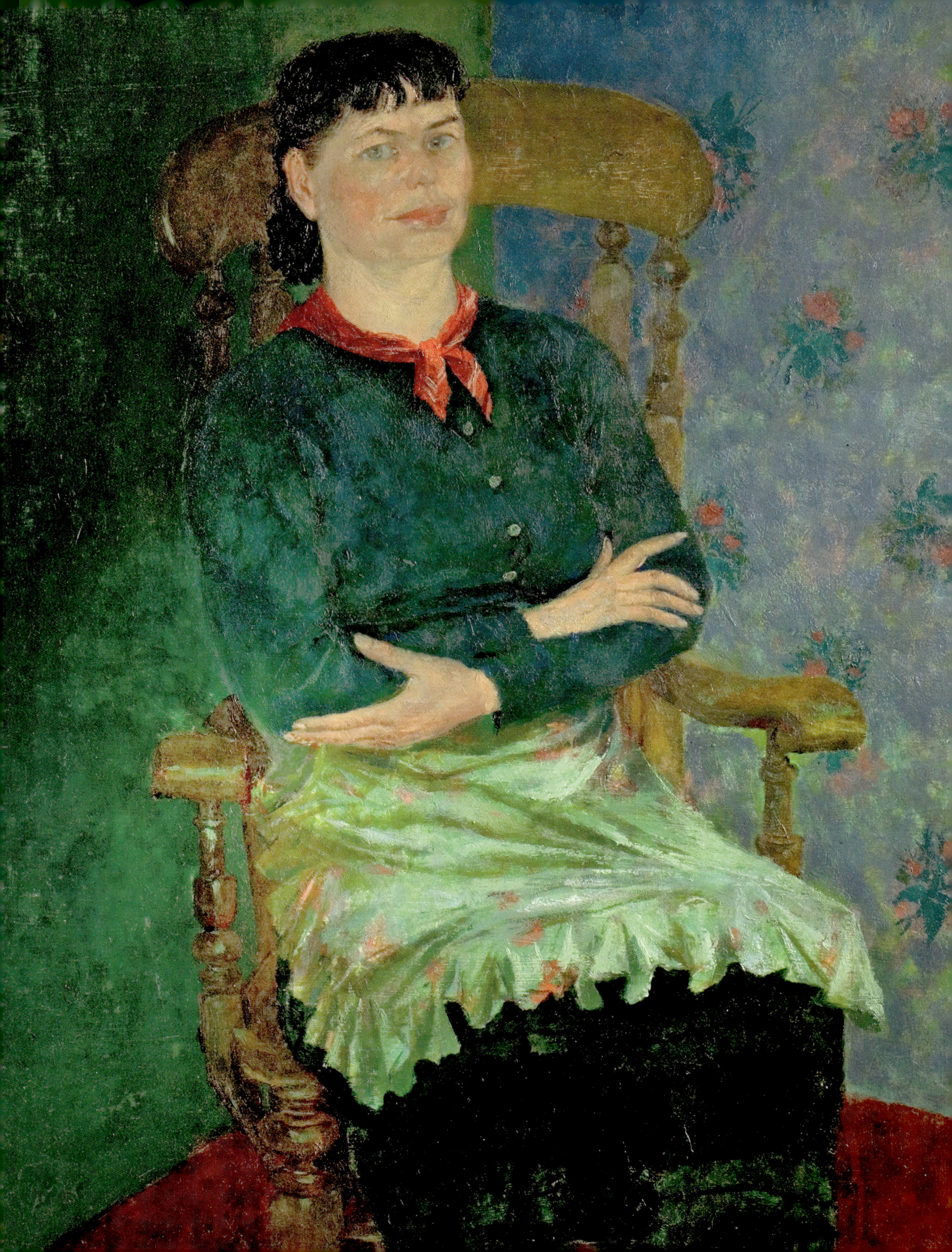

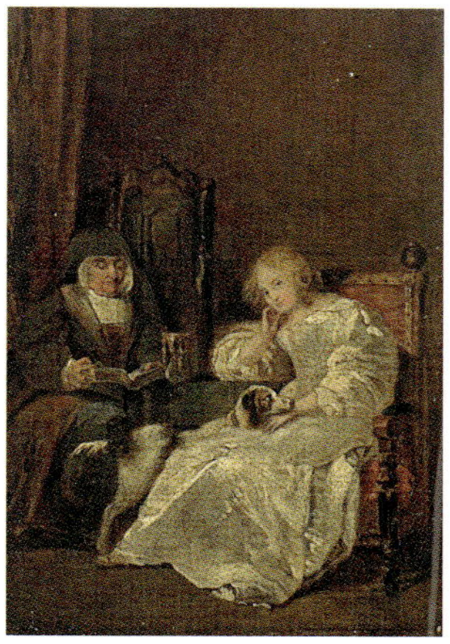

Bonington, Richard Parkes (after)
1802–1828
Meditation
oil on canvas 24.4 x 18.4
NCM 1909-49

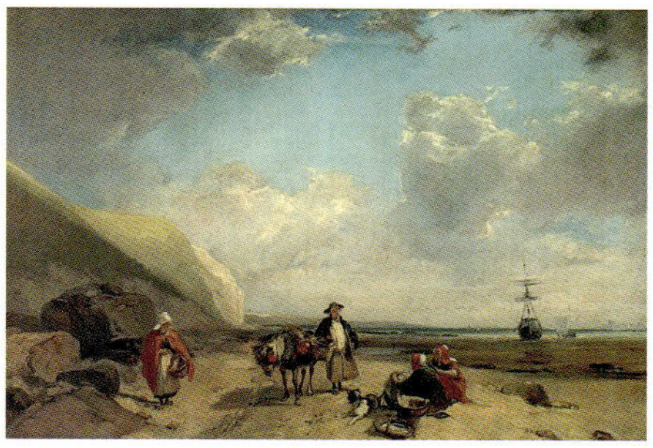

Bonington, Richard Parkes (attributed to)
1802–1828
Fisherfolk on the Coast of Normandy, France c.1824
oil on canvas 66 x 99
NCM 1927-33

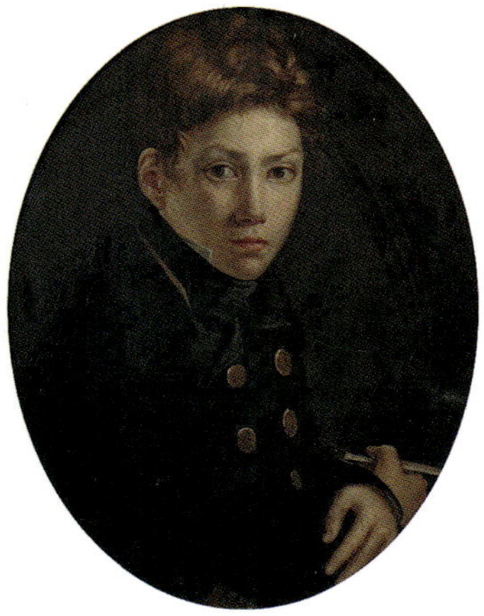

Bonington, Richard Parkes (attributed to)
1802–1828
Self Portrait
oil on canvas 58.8 x 48
NCM 1884-129

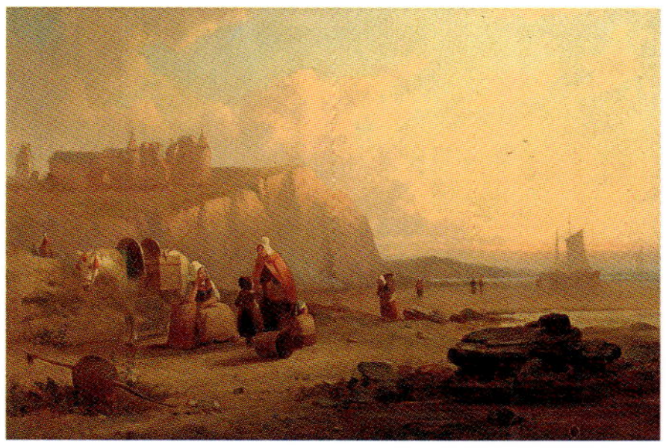

Bonington, Richard Parkes (imitator of)
1802–1828
Scene on the Coast of Normandy, France (The Old Castle of Dieppe on the Coast (...)) c.1825
oil on canvas 51.4 x 76.5
NCM 1895-102

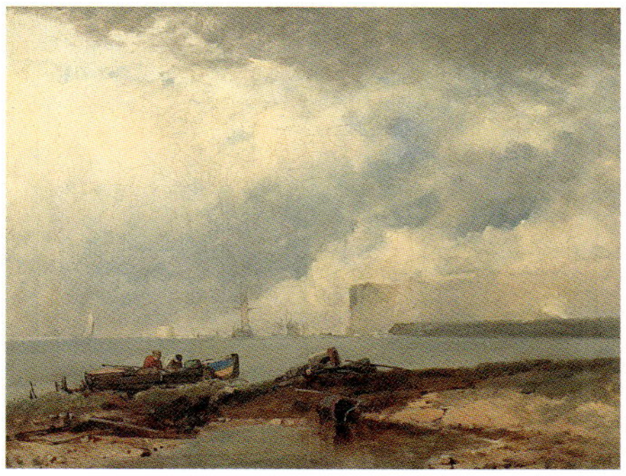

Bonington, Richard Parkes (imitator of)
1802–1828
Coast Scene 1826
oil on canvas 30.5 x 40.6
NCM 1925-190

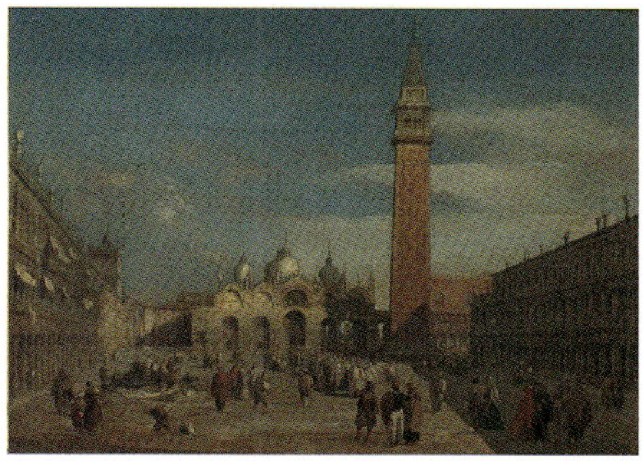

Bonington, Richard Parkes (imitator of)
1802–1828
The Piazza, San Marco, Venice, Italy (View of the Piazza of San Marco (...)) 1826
oil on canvas 24.1 x 34.3
NCM 1892-67

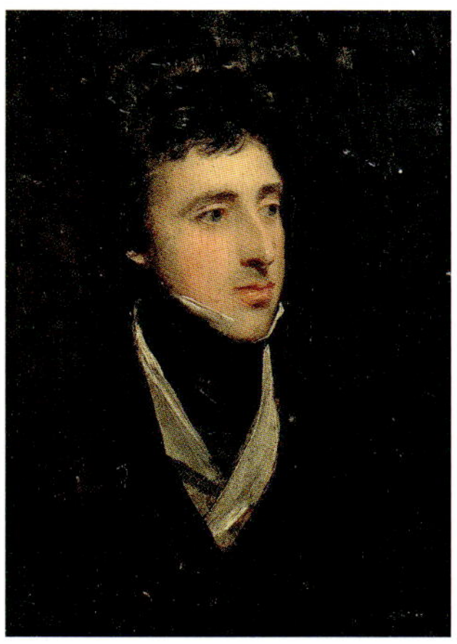

Bonington, Richard Parkes (imitator of)
1802–1828
Self Portrait
oil on wood 39.4 x 33
NCM 1927-23

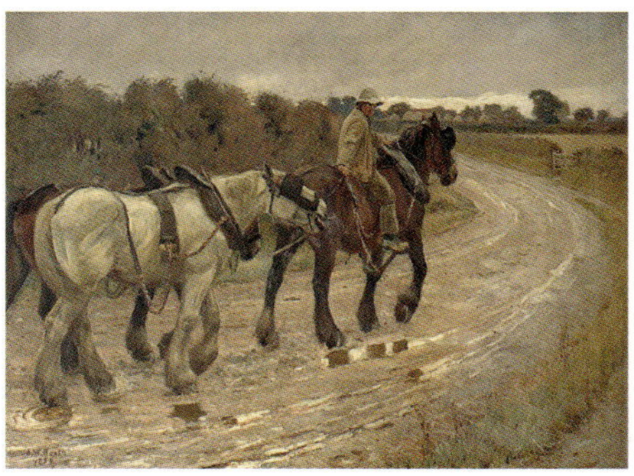

Booth, James William 1867–1953
Homeward Bound 1898
oil on canvas 101.6 x 152.4
NCM 1932-44

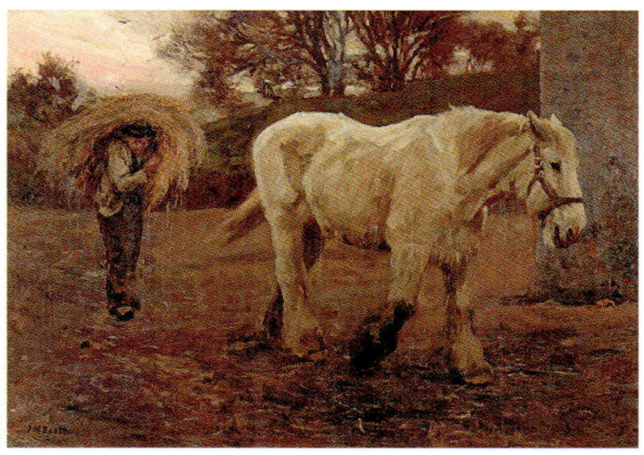

Booth, James William 1867–1953
End O'Day c.1904
oil on canvas 75.1 x 105.4
NCM 1933-249

Facing page: Fitton, James, 1899–1982, *The Painter's Wife* (detail), c.1955, Nottingham City Museums and Galleries (p. 96)

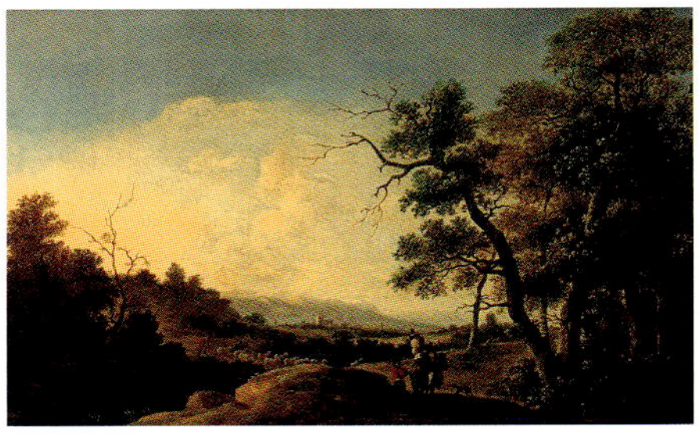

Both, Jan c.1618–1652 & **Both, Andries Dirksz.** 1611/1612–1641
Landscape with Figures
oil on canvas 51.4 x 85.1
NCM 1890-1204

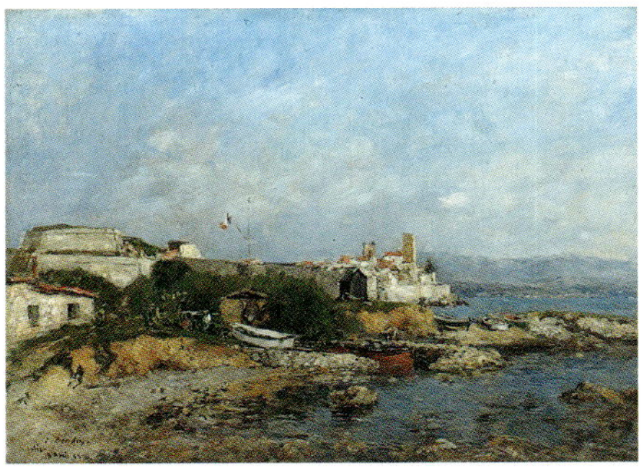

Boudin, Eugène Louis 1824–1898
The Fortifications at Antibes, France 1893
oil on canvas 45.1 x 64.1
NCM 1975-36

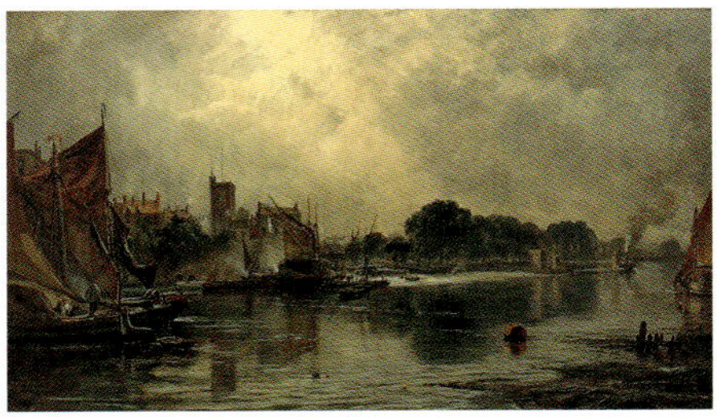

Bough, Samuel 1822–1878
The Thames at Chiswick, London 1865
oil on canvas 38.1 x 68.6
NCM 1904-12

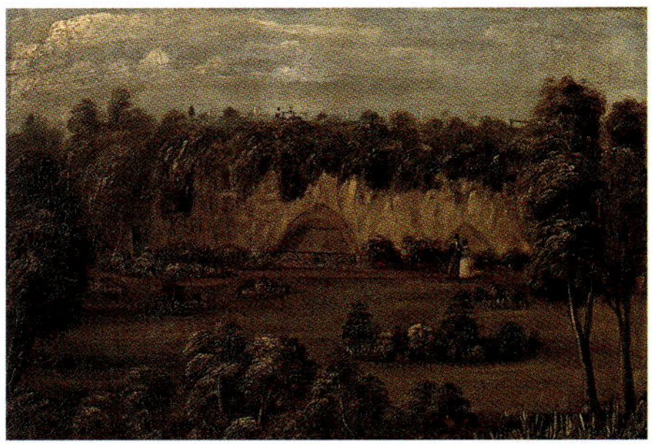

Bradbury, W.
Druidical Remains, Nottingham Park 1849
oil on canvas 30.5 x 45.7
NCM 1960-46

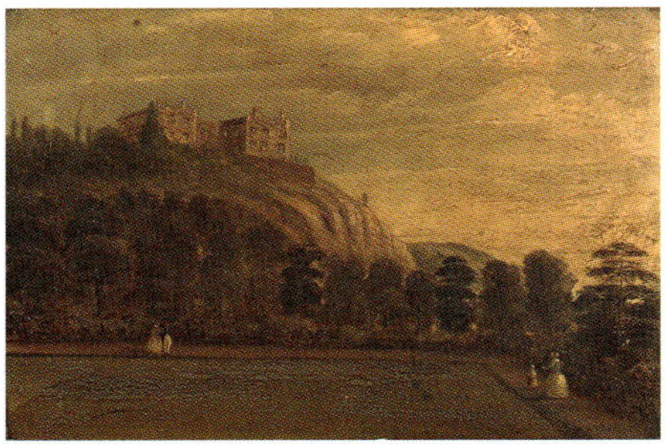

Bradbury, W.
Nottingham Castle from the Park Bowling Green c.1849
oil on canvas 30.8 x 46.3
NCM 1960-45

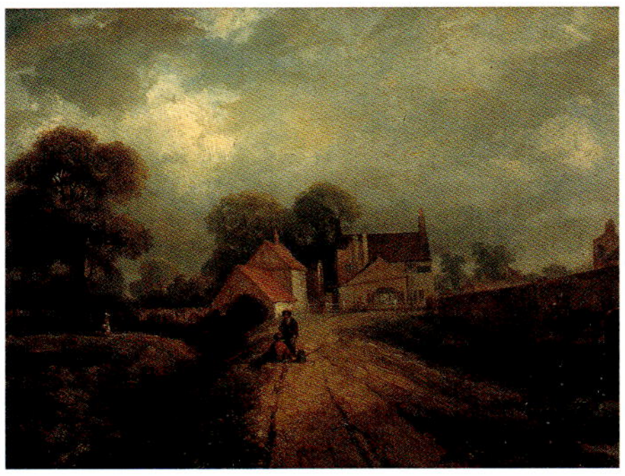

Bradley, Robert 1813–1880
View of the Old Trent Bridge Inn, West Bridgford, Nottingham c.1850
oil on canvas 50.8 x 68.6
NCM 1911-24

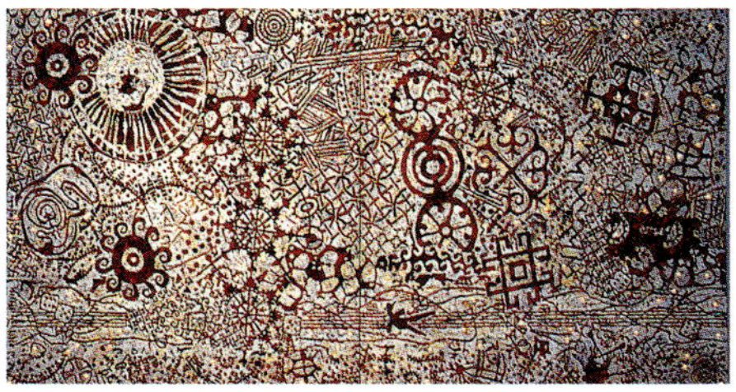

Brennand-Wood, Michael b.1952
You Are Here (joined diptych) 1997
oil, cloth & mixed media on wood 175 x 350
FALOAN 108

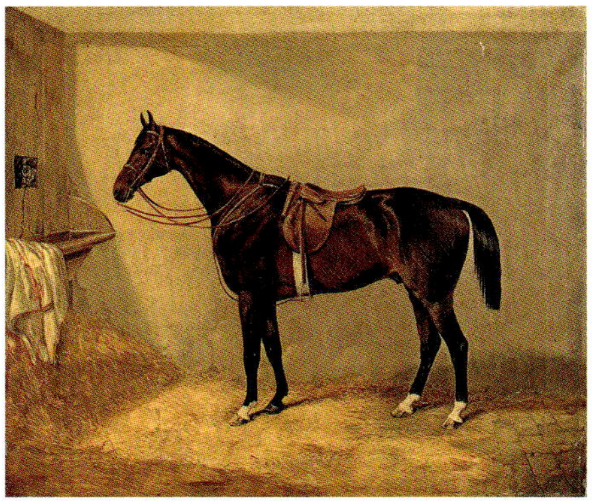

Bretland, Thomas W. 1802–1874
Portrait of the Horse, Which Belonged to Major Burton at the Balaklava Charge
oil on canvas 63.5 x 76.2
NCM 1899-1

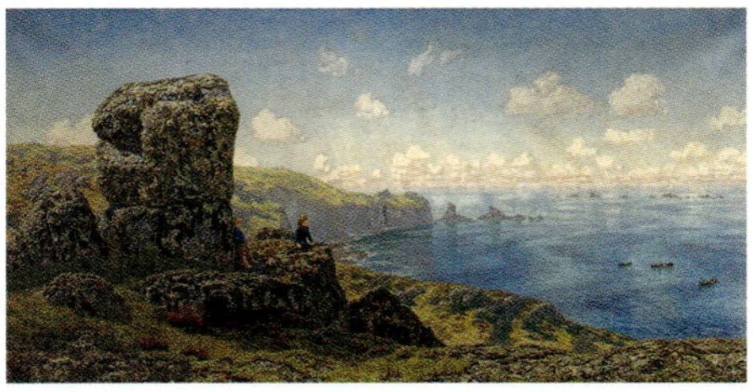

Brett, John 1830–1902
Golden Prospects, St Catherine's Well, Land's End, Cornwall 1881
oil on canvas 106.7 x 214
NCM 1913-65

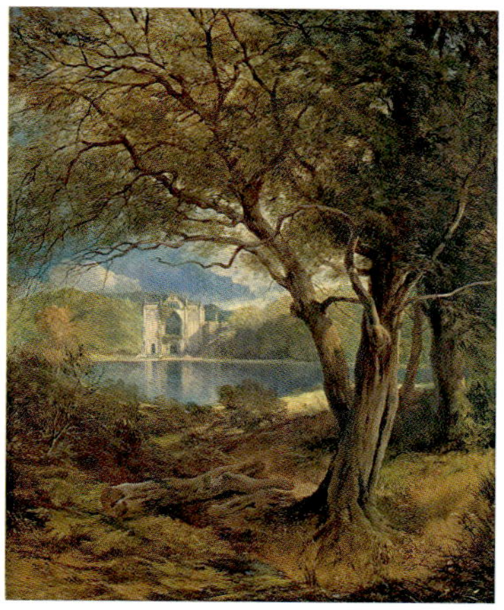

Bright, Henry 1814–1873
Newstead Abbey, Nottinghamshire
oil on canvas 61 x 50.8
NCM 1963-329

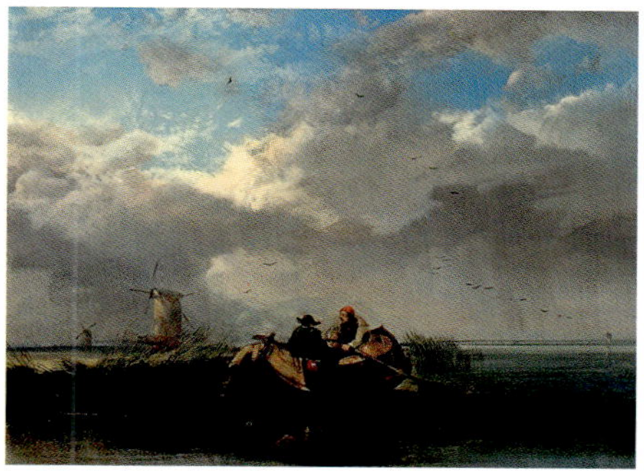

Bright, Henry 1814–1873
Norfolk Broads with Boats
oil on canvas 22.9 x 31.1
NCM 1904-13

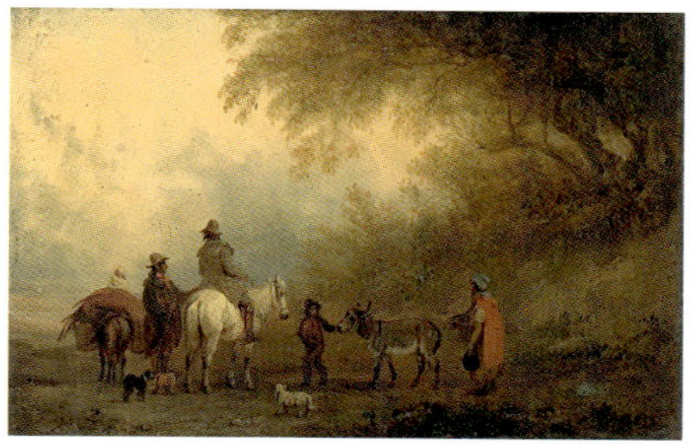

Bristow, Edmund 1787–1876
Gypsies Striking Camp
oil on board 15.6 x 24.1
NCM 1904-16

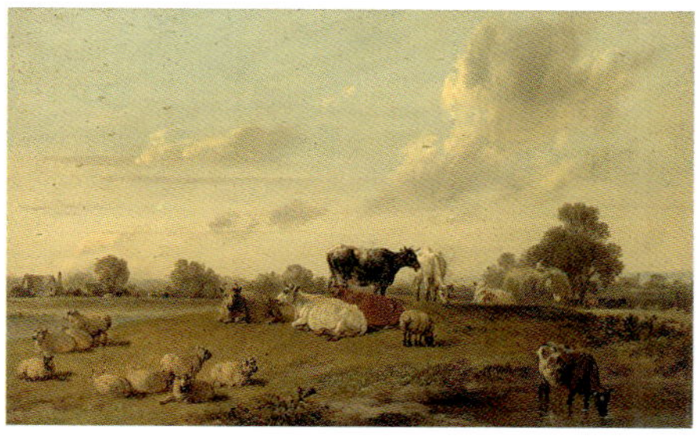

Bristow, Edmund 1787–1876
Landscape with Cattle and Sheep
oil on wood 16.5 x 27.9
NCM 1904-15

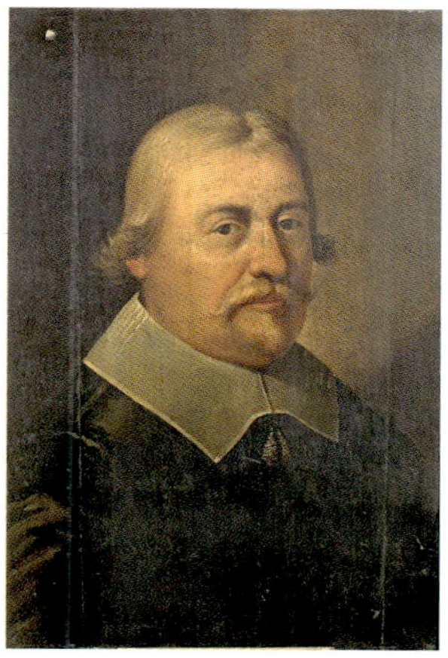

British (English) School 17th C
John Pym (1584–1643)
oil on wood 60.3 x 48.9
NCM 1879-125

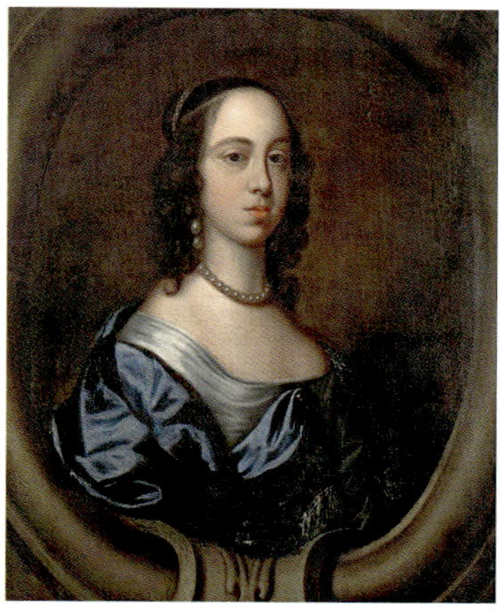

British (English) School 17th C
Lady Sophia Chaworth
oil on canvas 74.9 x 62.2
NCM 1953-17

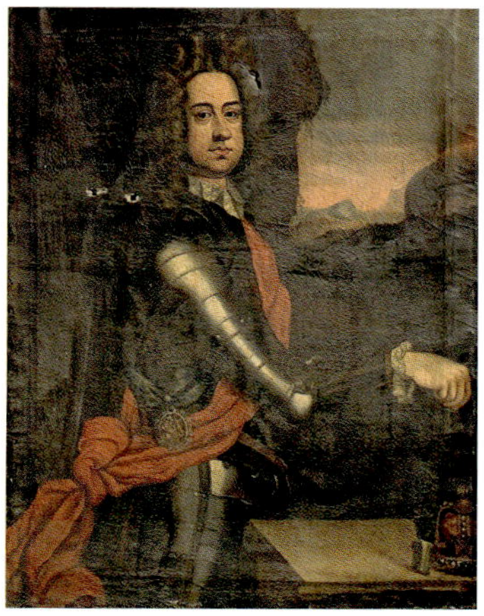

British (English) School 17th C
William Cavendish (1640–1707), 1st Duke of Devonshire
oil on canvas 123.2 x 100.3
NCM 1879-134

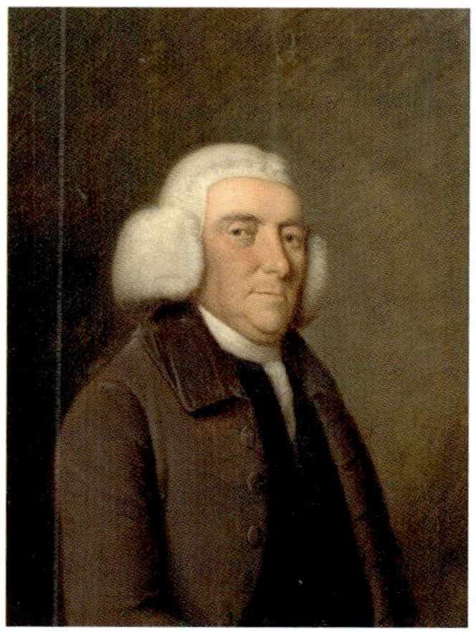

British (English) School
William Elliot (1707–1792) c.1770
oil on canvas 76 x 64
NCMG 2002-13

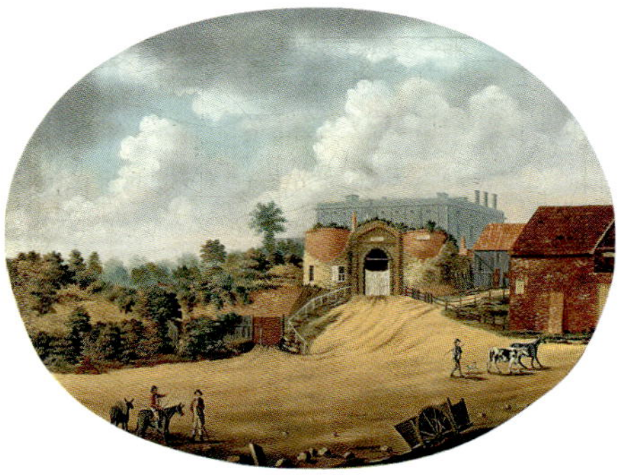

British (English) School
View of the Ancient Gateway and Castle, Nottingham c.1795
oil on wood 48 x 65
NCM 1910-92

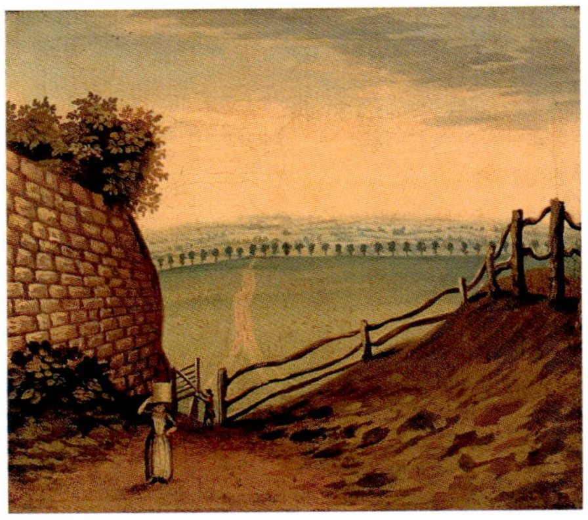

British (English) School
View of the Footpath to Lenton across Nottingham Park c.1795
oil on canvas 30.5 x 35.6
NCM 1910-93

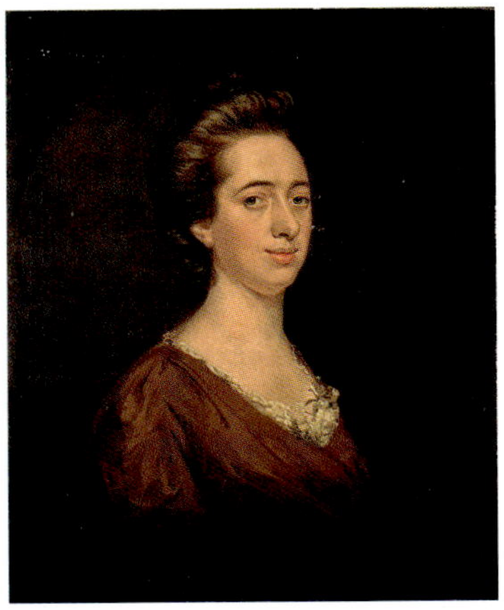

British (English) School 18th C
Portrait of a Lady
oil on canvas 76.2 x 63.5
NCM 1937-40

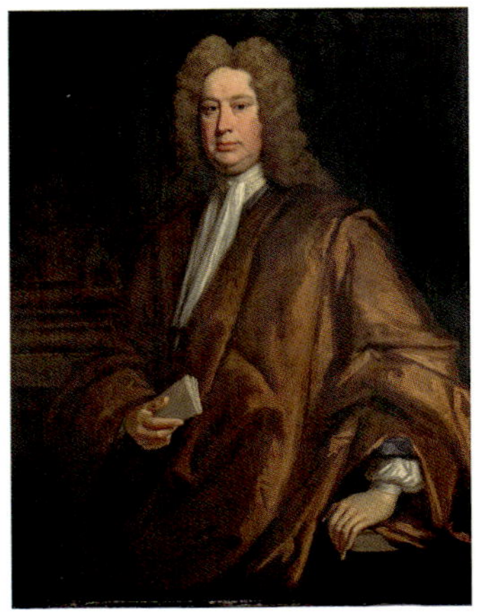

British (English) School 18th C
Portrait of a Man (thought to be Dr Robert Thoroton, 1623–1678)
oil on canvas 127 x 101.6
NCM 1898-9

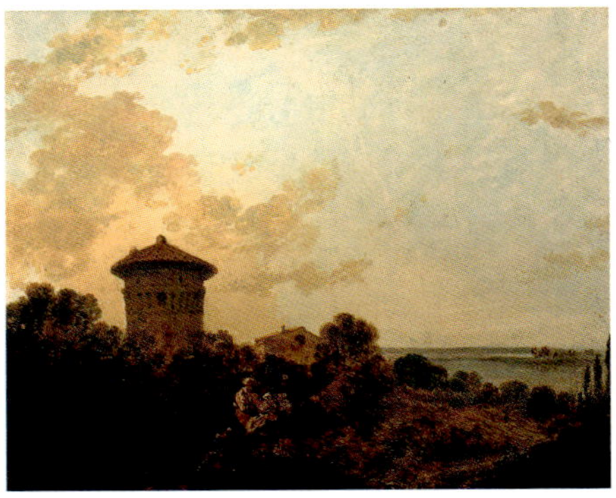

British (English) School 18th C
Ruins near Tivoli, Italy
oil on canvas 41.9 x 52.7
NCM 1924-22

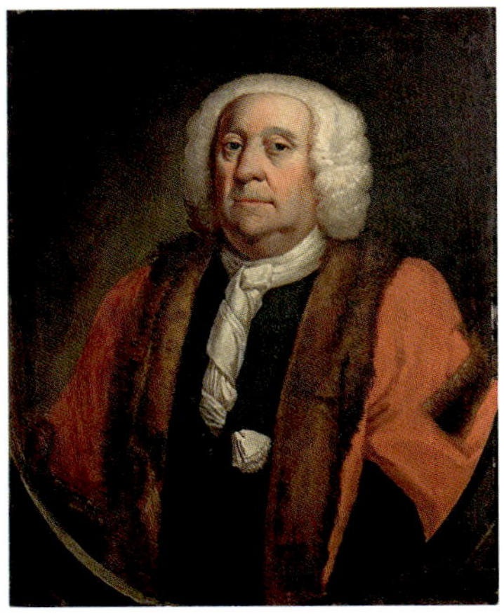

British (English) School 18th C
Thomas Hawksley (1666–1749), Mayor of Nottingham (1715)
oil on canvas 76.2 x 63.5
NCM 1951-69

British (English) School
Nottingham Castle from the Meadows c.1800
oil on iron tray 57 x 73
NCM 1884-153

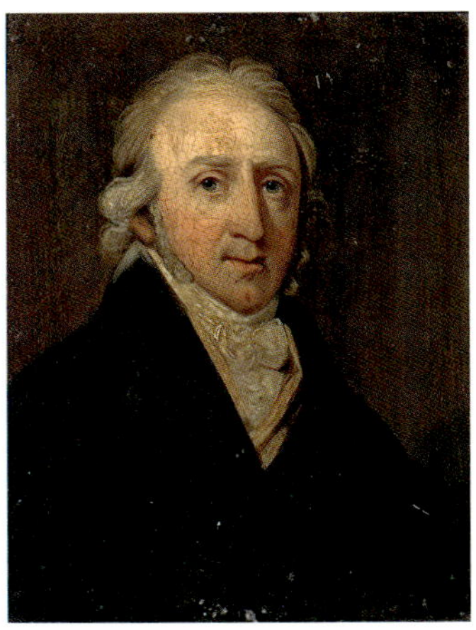

British (English) School
Robert Davison c.1805
oil on wood 25.4 x 20.3
NCM 1959-59

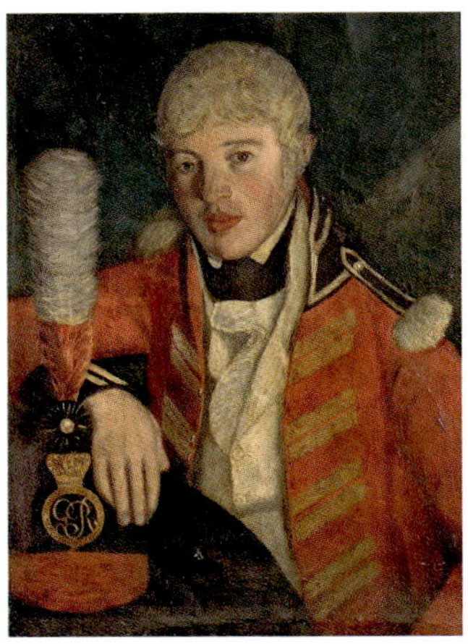

British (English) School
Portrait of an Officer (probably Major William Wylde, 1803–1808, OC, Southwell Volunteer Infantry) c.1806
oil on canvas 75 x 53
NCM 1984-53

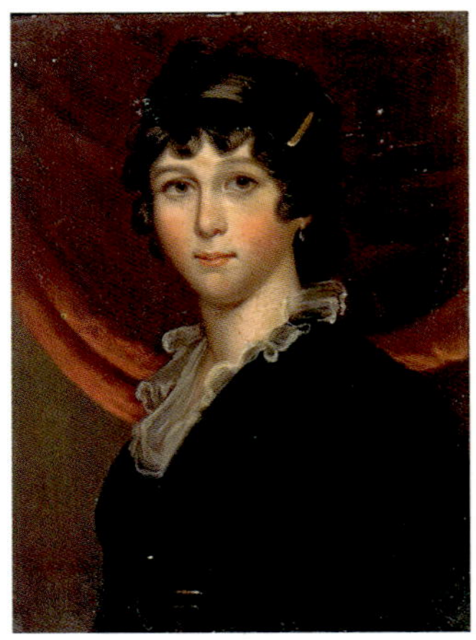

British (English) School
Mrs Birkhead, née Eliza Davison 1810–1815
oil on wood 25.4 x 20.3
NCM 1959-60

British (English) School
View of Nottingham Castle and Rock, Looking East c.1811–1815
oil on canvas 25.4 x 27.9
NCM 1890-858

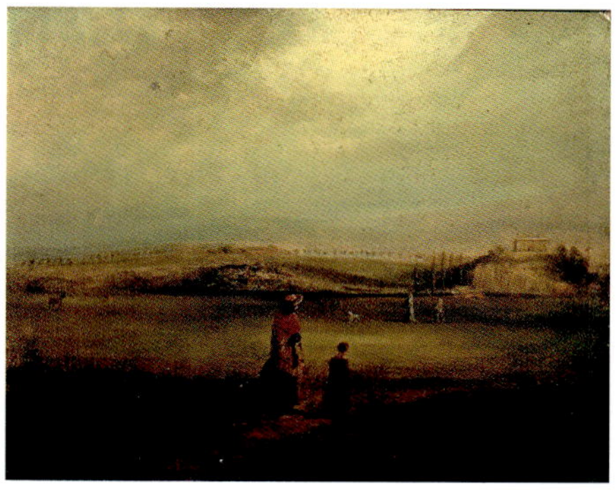

British (English) School
View of Nottingham Castle from the Meadows 1820
oil on wood 76.7 x 90.7
NCM 1889-44

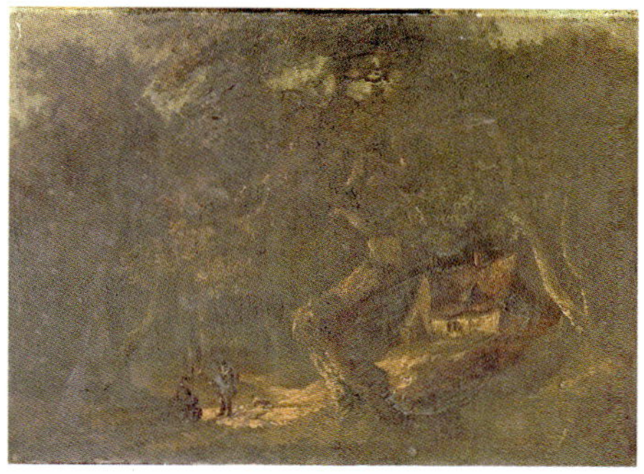

British (English) School 19th C
A Woodland Scene with a Cottage
oil on canvas 31.8 x 40.6
NCM 1890-1211

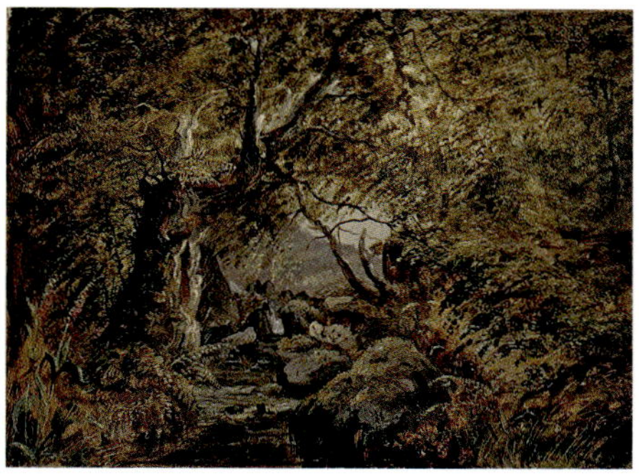

British (English) School 19th C
A Woodland Stream
oil on canvas 22.9 x 31.8
NCM 1890-1209

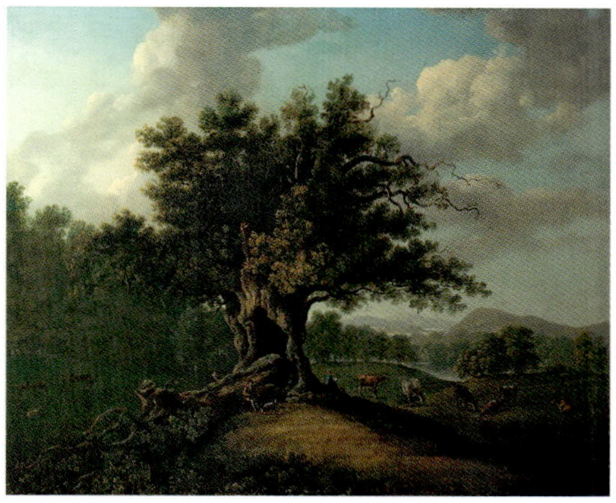

British (English) School 19th C
An Oak in Moccas Park, Herefordshire
oil on canvas 76.2 x 106.7
NCM 1890-1198

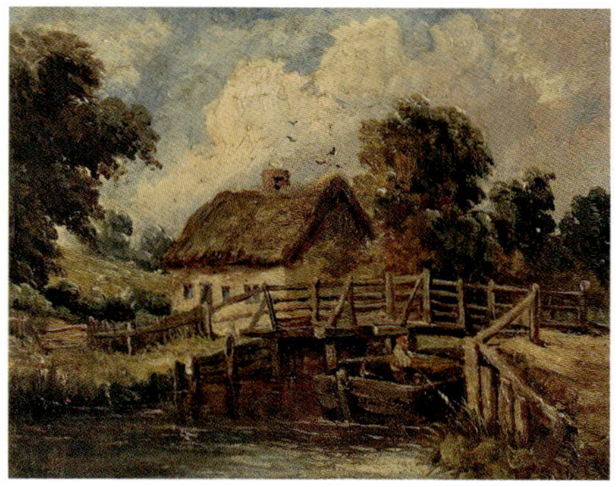

British (English) School 19th C
Cottage near East Bergholt, Suffolk
oil on canvas 24.8 x 31.8
NCM 1909-44

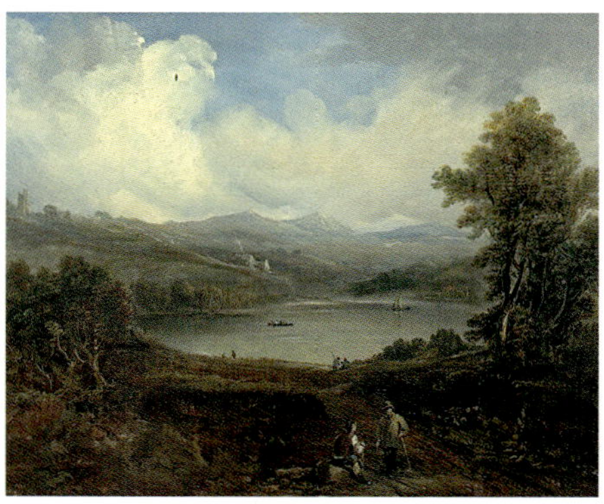

British (English) School 19th C
Grasmere, Westmorland, Cumbria
oil on wood 35.6 x 45.7
NCM 1890-1208

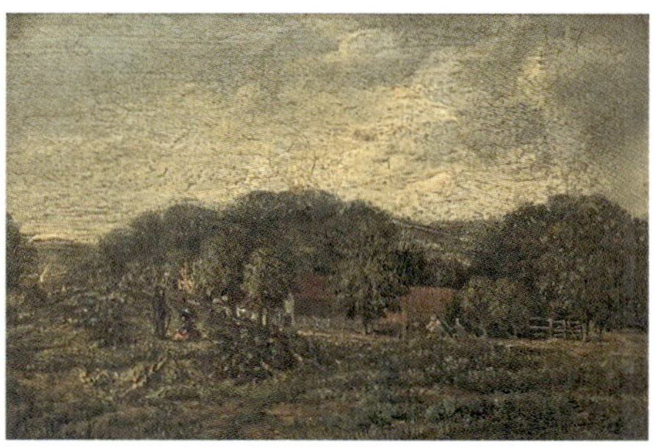

British (English) School 19th C
Hampstead Heath, London
oil on wood 15.5 x 24
NCM 1890-1166

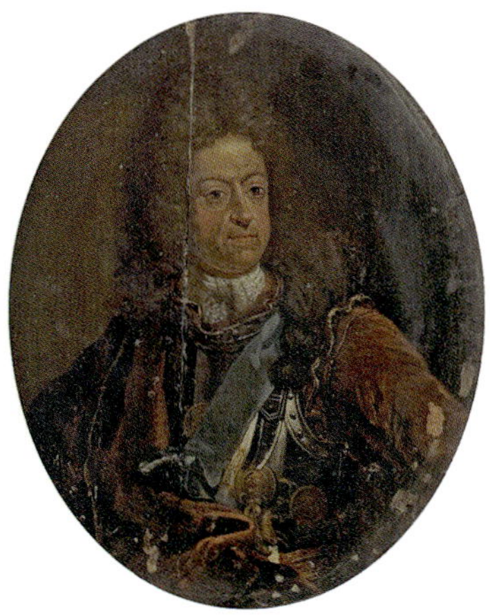

British (English) School 19th C
John Churchill (1650–1722), Duke of Marlborough
oil on wood 25.4 x 21
NCM 1899-5

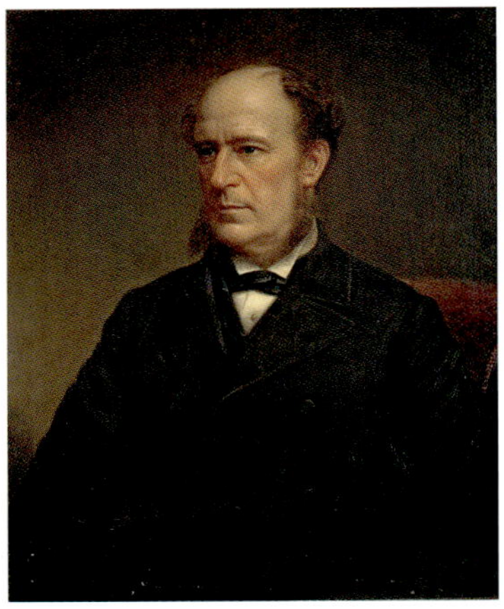

British (English) School 19th C
John Leavers
oil on canvas 76.2 x 63.5
NCM 1970-109

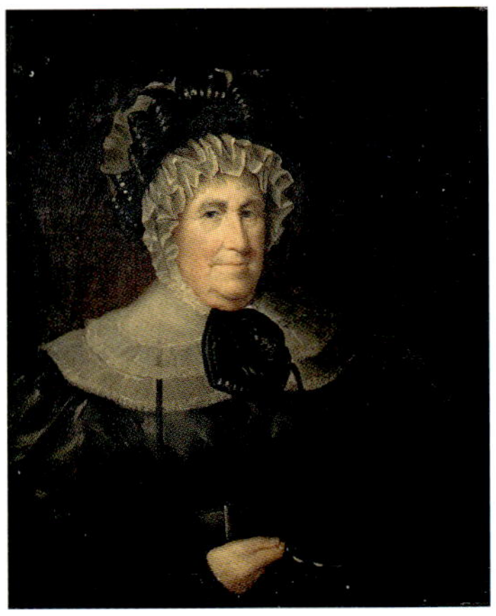

British (English) School 19th C
Lady in a Frilled Cap
oil on canvas 77 x 65
NCM 1966-39

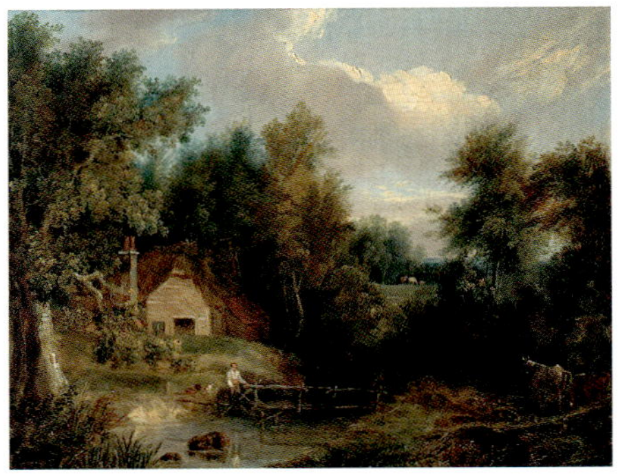

British (English) School 19th C
Landscape, Cottage and Stream with a Figure and a House
oil on canvas 38.1 x 48.3
NCM 1890-1184

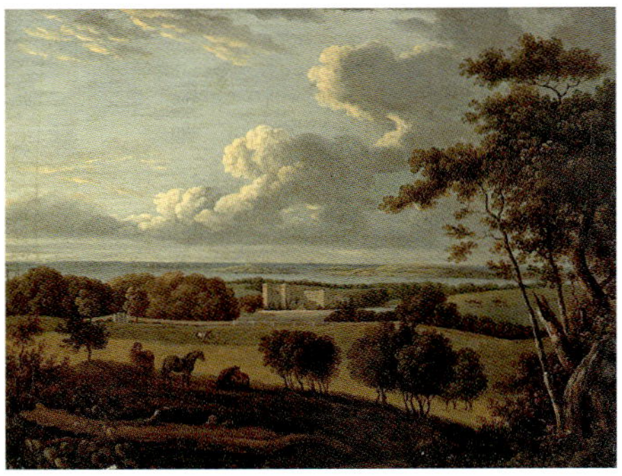

British (English) School 19th C
Landscape near the Coast (View of a Mansion with the Sea in the Distance)
oil on canvas 43.2 x 55.9
NCM 1890-1179

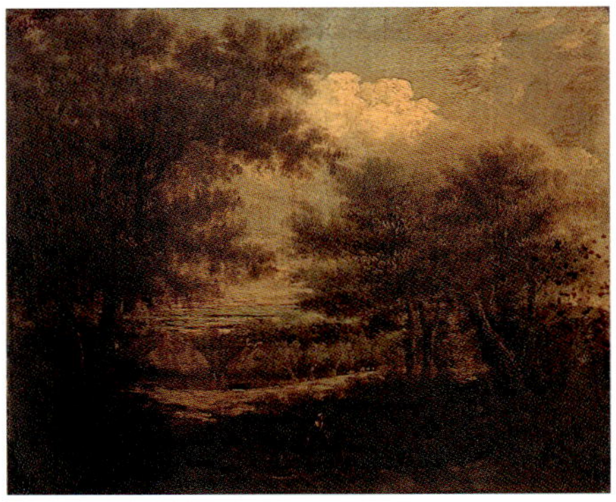

British (English) School 19th C
Landscape, Trees and Cottages
oil on canvas 43.2 x 53.3
NCM 1890-1183

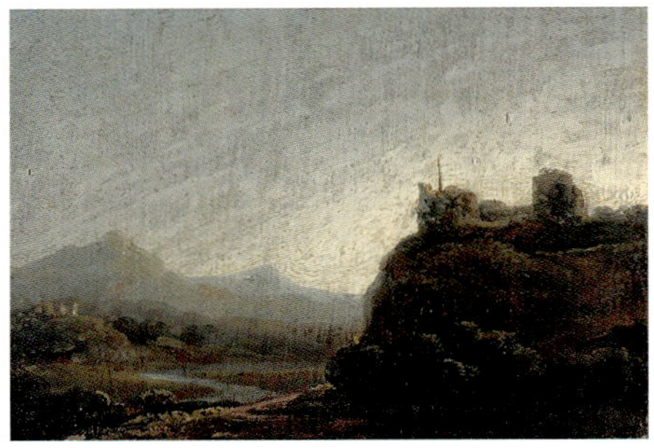

British (English) School 19th C
Mountainous Landscape, Evening
oil on wood 16.5 x 22.9
NCM 1890-1196

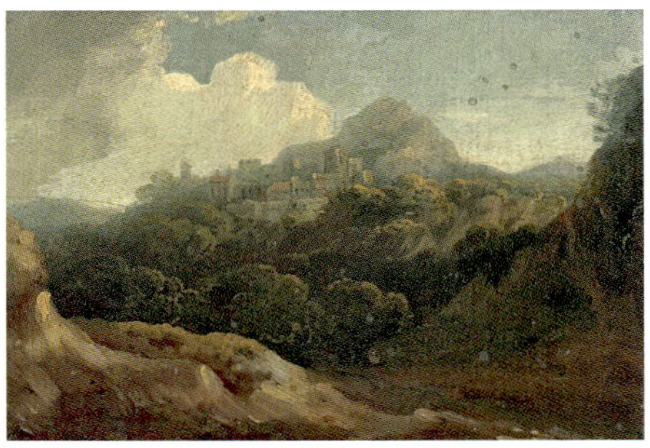

British (English) School 19th C
Mountainous Landscape, Morning
oil on wood 15.2 x 22.9
NCM 1890-1197

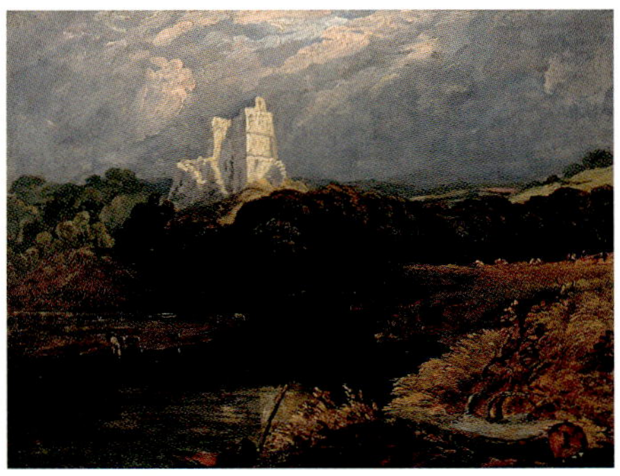

British (English) School 19th C
Norham Castle, Northumberland
oil on canvas 30.5 x 40.6
NCM 1890-1188

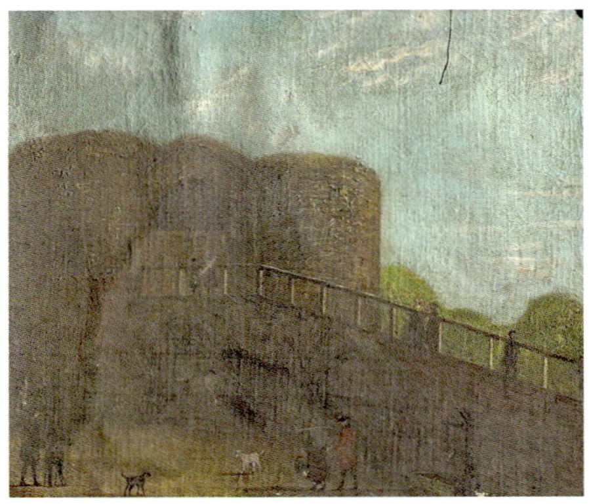

British (English) School 19th C
Nottingham Castle Gateway
oil on canvas 57.2 x 71.1
NCM 1963-173

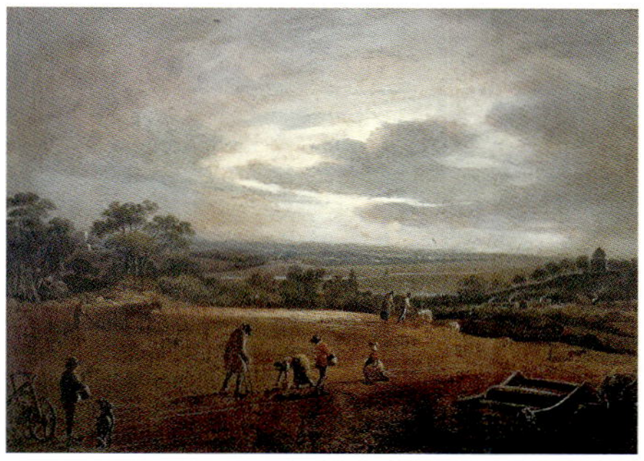

British (English) School 19th C
Ploughing and Dibbling Beans
oil on canvas 43.2 x 61
NCM 1890-1180

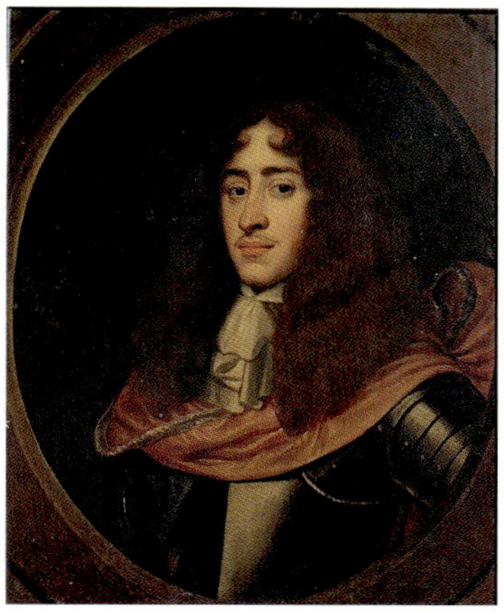

British (English) School 19th C
Portrait of a Gentleman
oil on canvas 73 x 61
NCM 1878-216

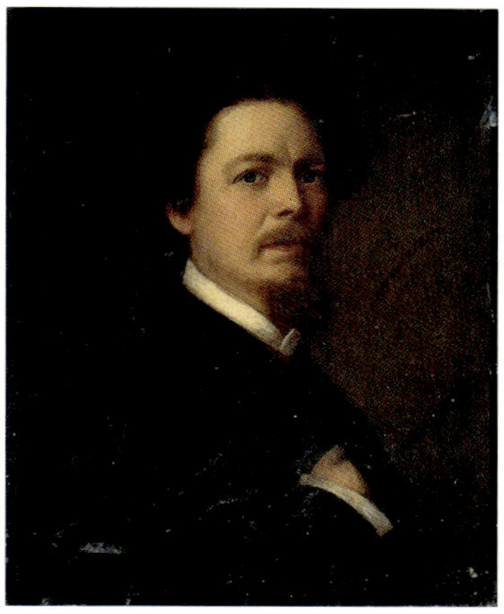

British (English) School 19th C
Portrait of a Gentleman
oil on canvas 61 x 50.8
NCM 1904-119

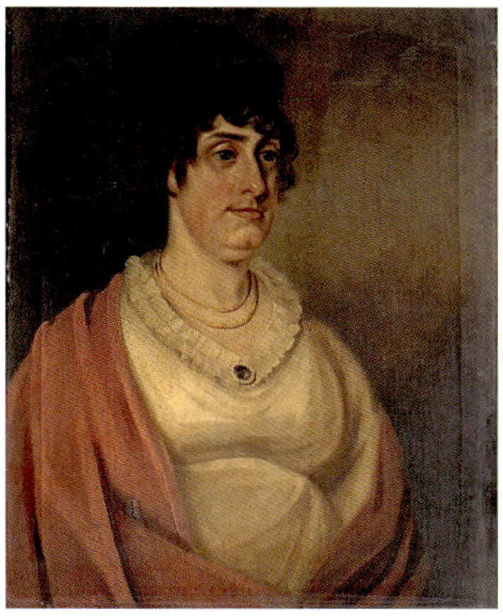

British (English) School 19th C
Portrait of a Lady
oil on canvas 68.6 x 55.9
NCM 1937-41

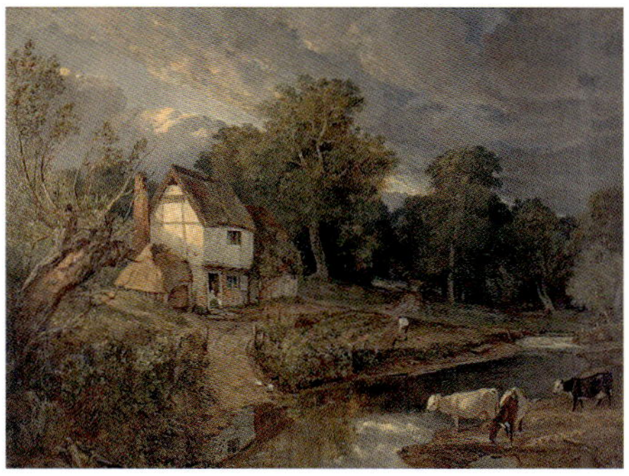

British (English) School 19th C
Ringland Hills, Costessy, Norwich
oil on canvas 95 x 125.5
NCM 1904-28

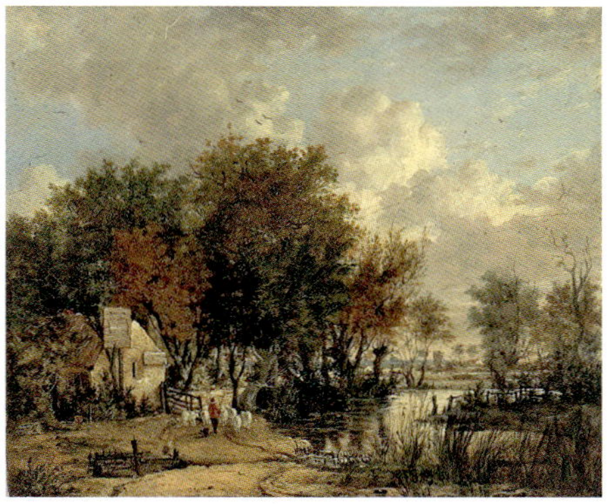

British (English) School 19th C
River Scene, Boy Driving Sheep
oil on wood 25.4 x 30.5
NCM 1904-72

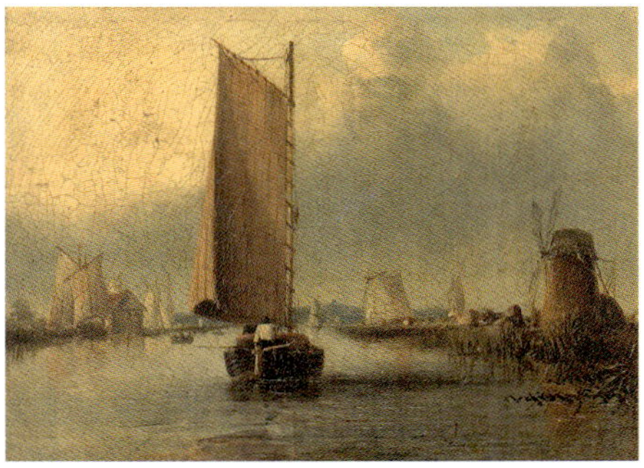

British (English) School 19th C
River Scene with Shipping
oil on canvas 25.4 x 33
NCM 1890-1210

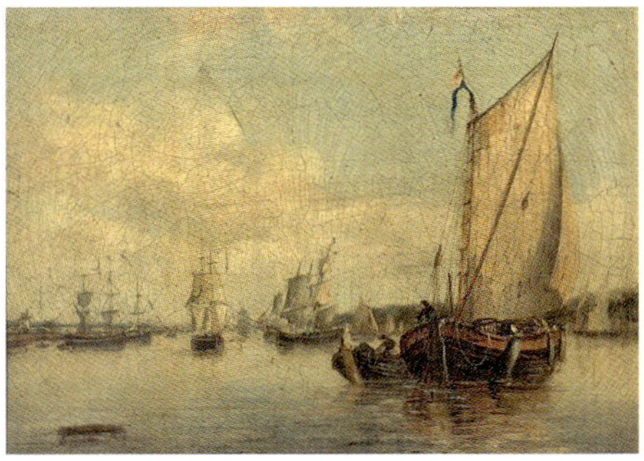

British (English) School 19th C
River Scene with Shipping
oil on canvas 25.4 x 33
NCM 1890-1212

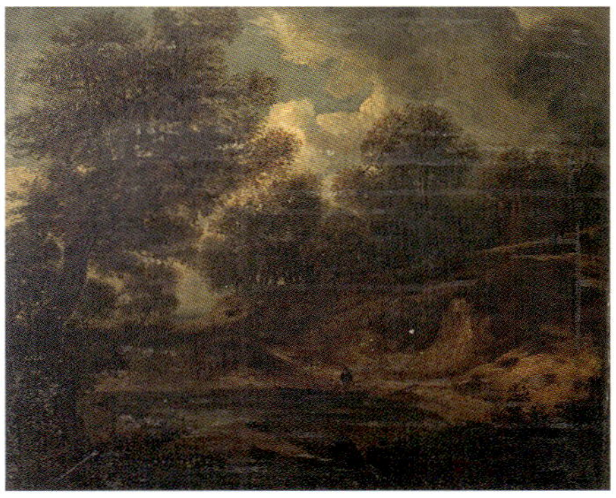

British (English) School 19th C
Wood Scene, Stream and Figures
oil on wood 47 x 60.3
NCM 1890-1178

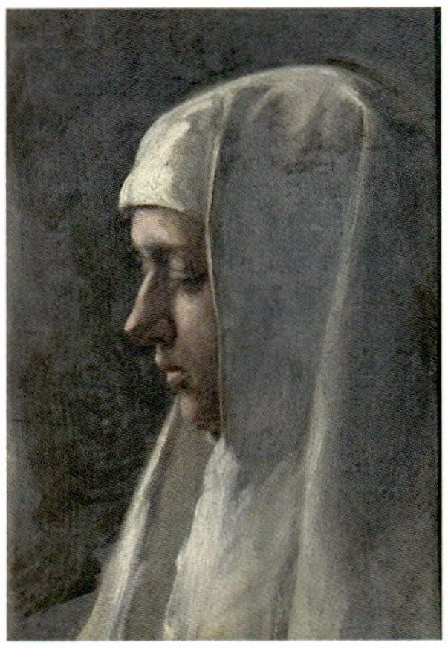

British (English) School
Head of a Woman in Profile 1900–1942
oil on canvas 41.9 x 27.9
NCM 1942-15

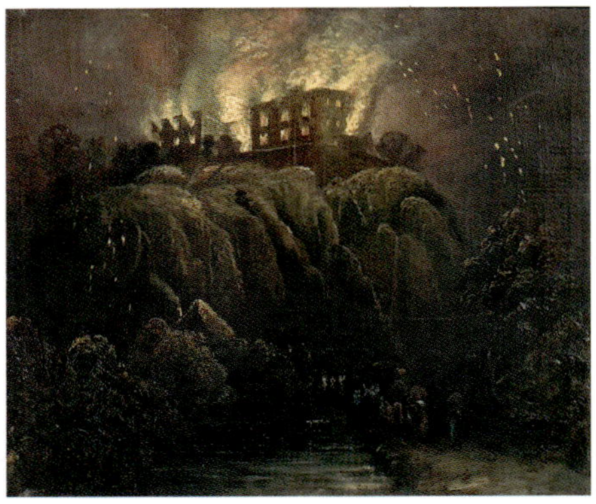

British (English) School
Nottingham Castle on Fire, 1831
oil on canvas 35.6 x 45.7
NCM 1963-391

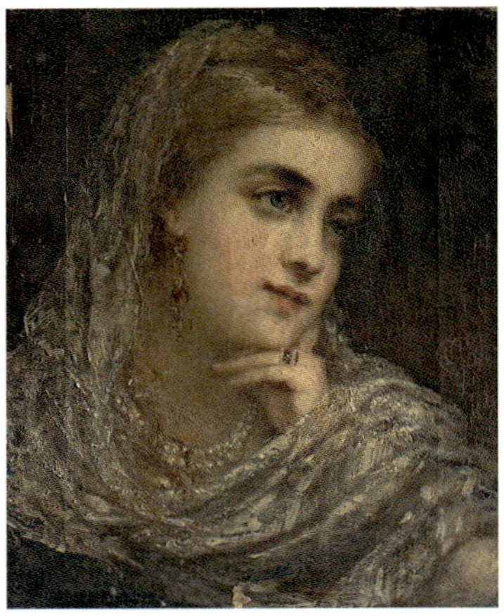

British (English) School
Portrait of a Woman with a Finger on Her Cheek
oil on canvas 30.5 x 25.6
FA-X 11

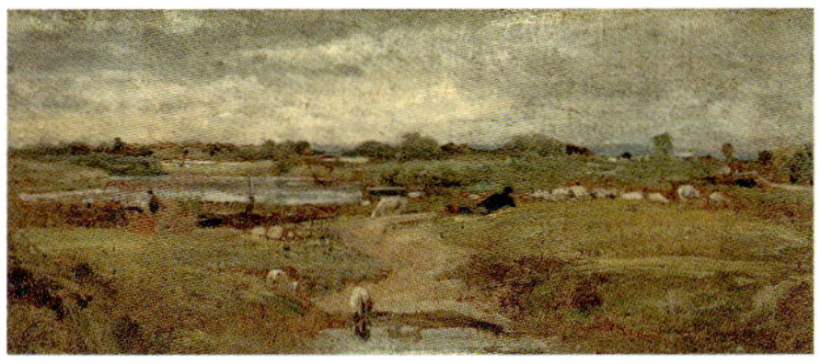

British (English) School
River and Sheep
oil on canvas 11.4 x 26.7
NCM 1924-23

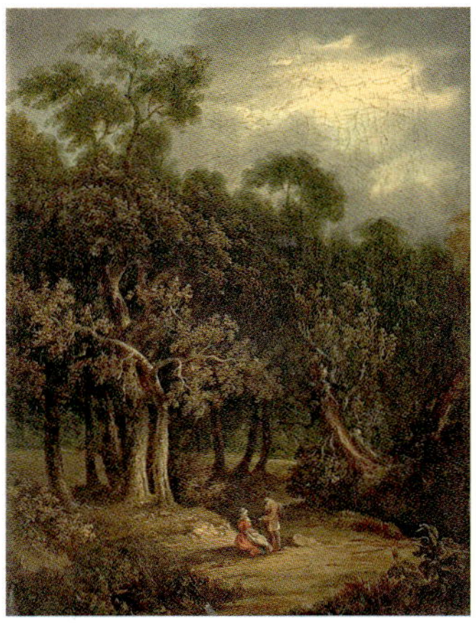

British (Norwich) School 19th C
Lad's Lane, Boy's Hill, Cheltenham
oil on canvas 44.1 x 34.3
NCM 1890-1189

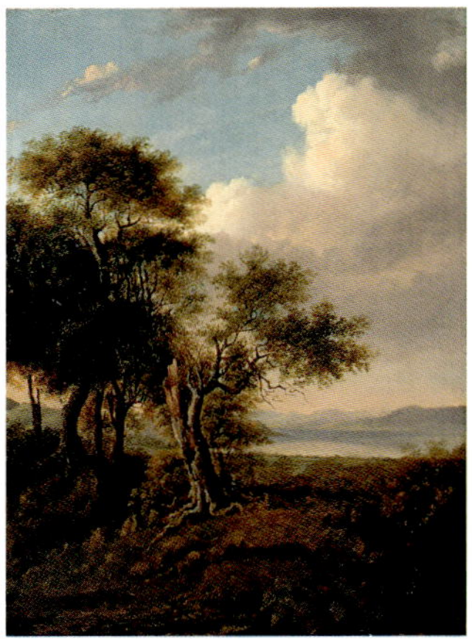

British (Norwich) School 19th C
Landscape, Trees in the Foreground, Lake and Hills in the Distance
oil on canvas 61 x 45.7
NCM 1890-1191

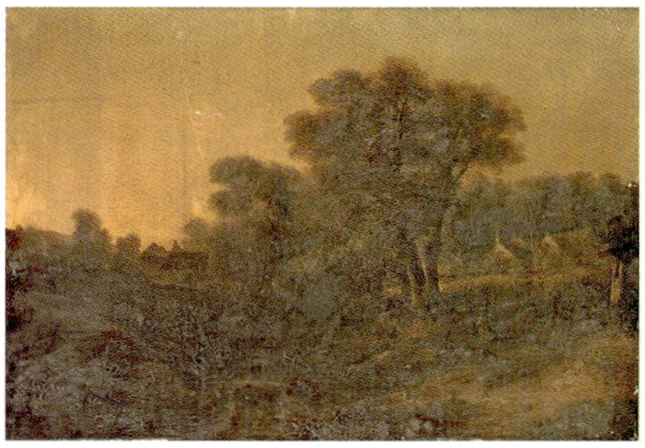

British (Norwich) School 19th C
Landscape with Cottage and Stream
oil on canvas 61 x 91.4
NCM 1890-1193

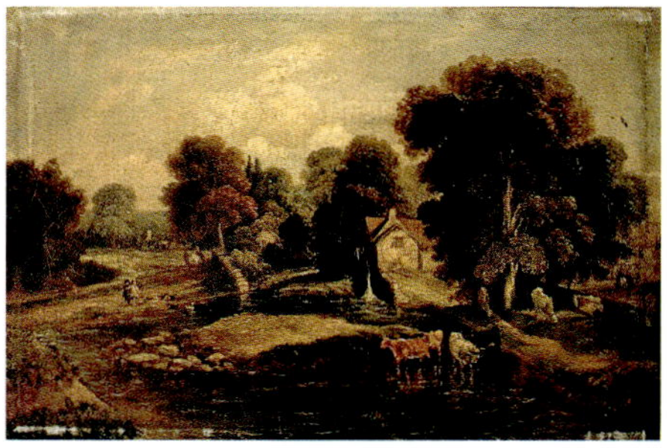

British (Norwich) School 19th C
Old Mill, Norwich, Norfolk
oil on canvas 34.3 x 53.3
NCM 1890-1187

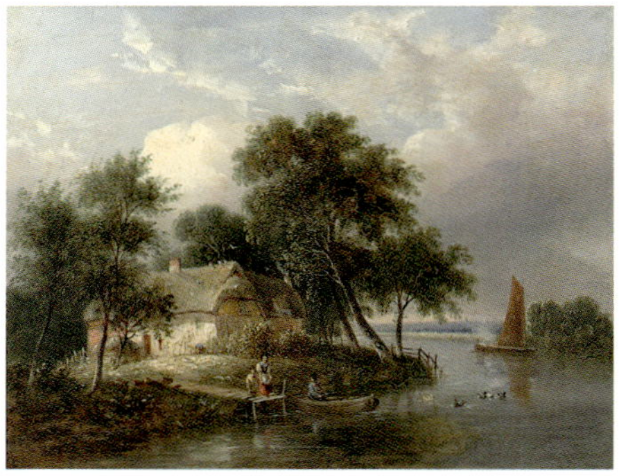

British (Norwich) School 19th C
River Scene (Cottage and Trees)
oil on wood 31.1 x 41.3
NCM 1890-1171

Facing page: Wheatley, Grahame, b.1943, *Self Portrait** (detail), 1989, Gedling Borough Council (p. 3)

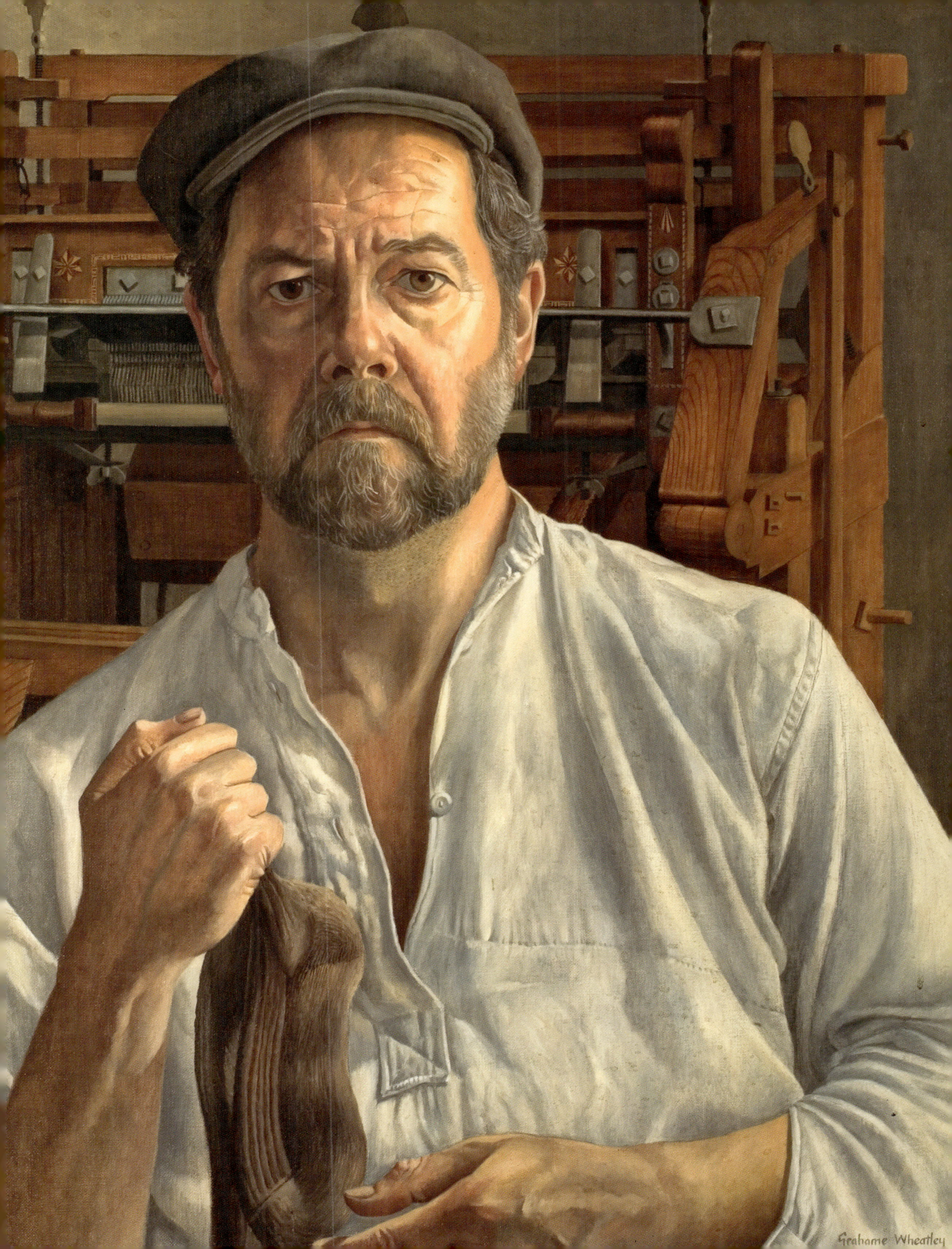
Grahame Wheatley

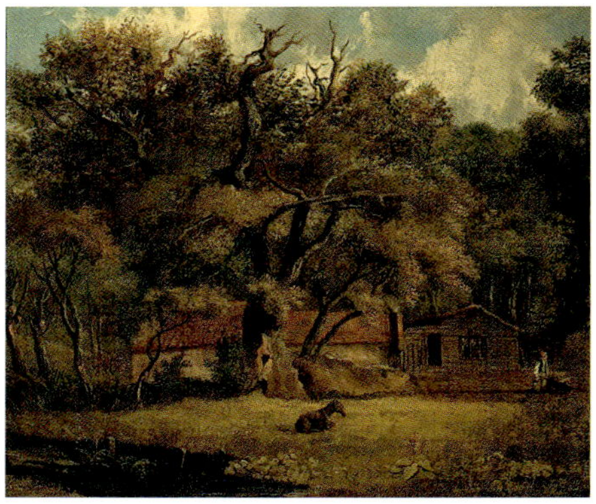

British (Norwich) School 19th C
The Homestead
oil on canvas 50.8 x 62.2
NCM 1890-1181

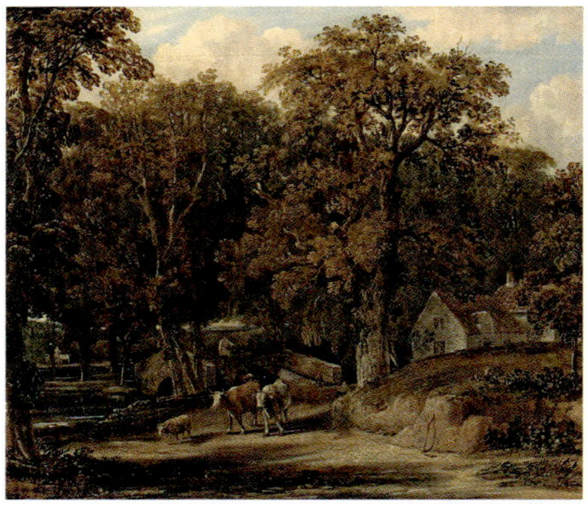

British (Norwich) School 19th C
Woodland Scene with Bridge and Cattle
oil on canvas 41 x 48.6
NCM 1890-1185

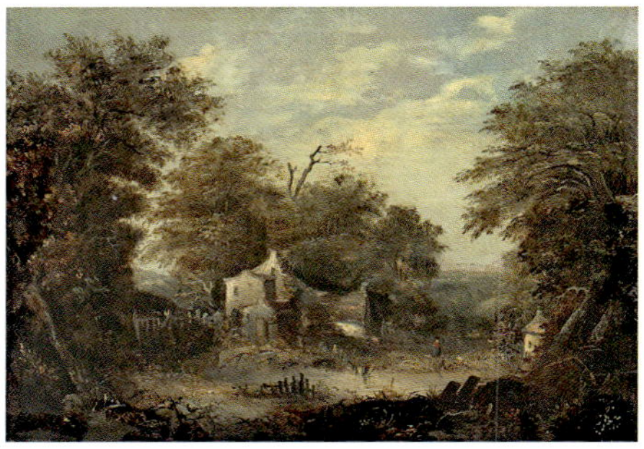

British (Norwich) School 19th C
Woodland Scene with Cottage
oil on wood 40.6 x 59.7
NCM 1890-1176

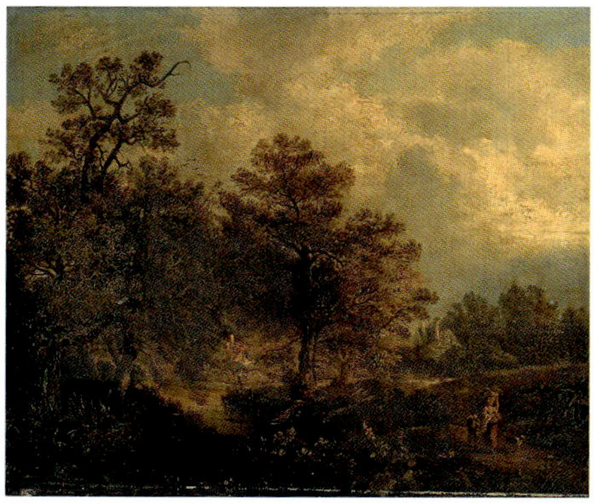

British (Norwich) School 19th C
Woodland Scene with Stream and Cottages
oil on canvas 63.5 x 76.2
NCM 1890-1199

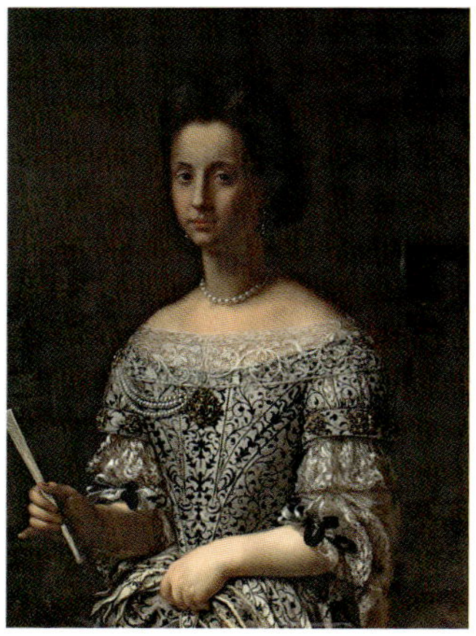

Bronzino, Agnolo (imitator of) 1503–1572
Portrait of an Infanta of Spain
oil on canvas 87.6 x 68
NCM 1893-11

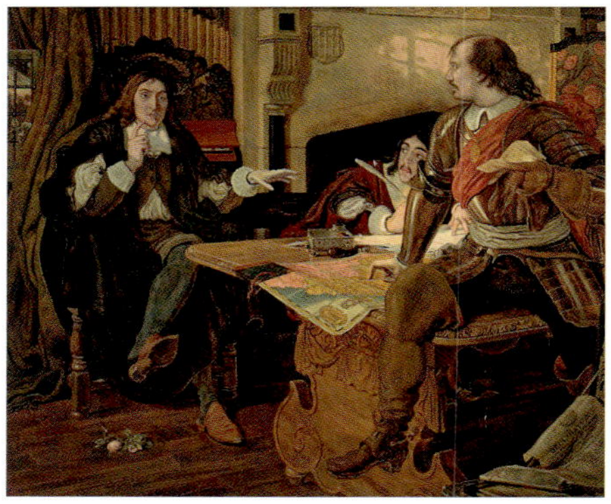

Brown, Ford Madox 1821–1893
Cromwell and the Vaudois (Cromwell, Protector of the Protestants of the Vaudois) 1878
oil on canvas 78.7 x 96.5
NCM 1937-1

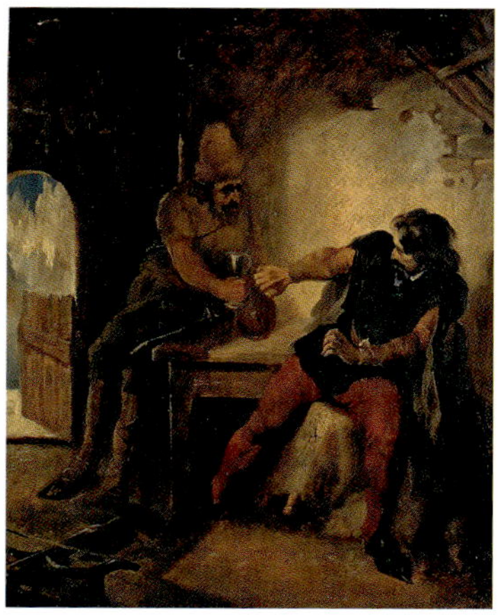

Brown, Ford Madox (attributed to) 1821–1893
Manfred in the Chamois Hunter's Hut c.1850
oil on canvas 56.8 x 47.6
NCM 1927-37

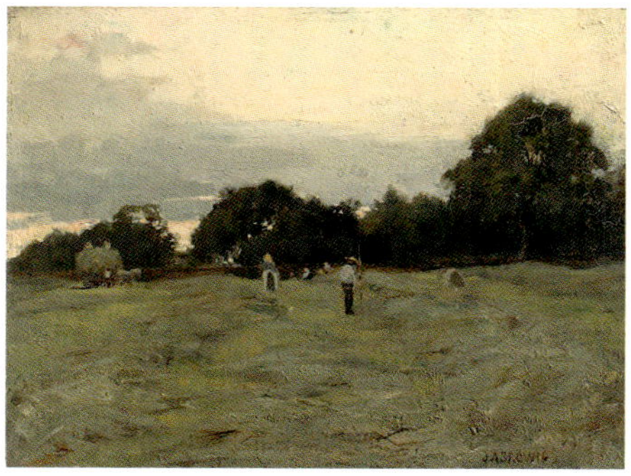

Brown, John Alfred Arnesby 1866–1955
Haymaking (recto) 1880–1890
oil on wood 26.7 x 35.9
NCM 1936-45

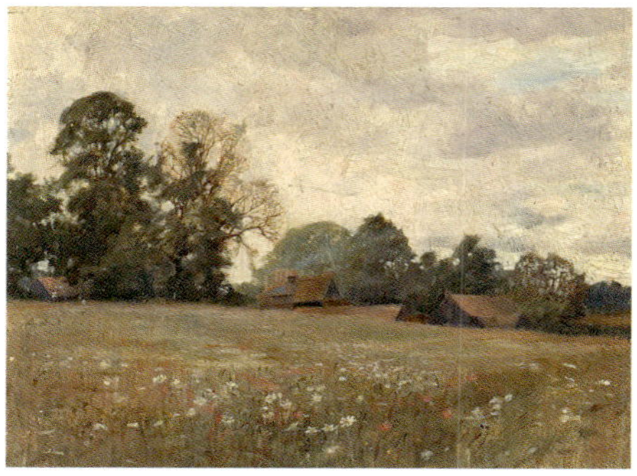

Brown, John Alfred Arnesby 1866–1955
Poppy Field (verso) 1880–1890
oil on wood 26.7 x 35.9
NCM 1936-45

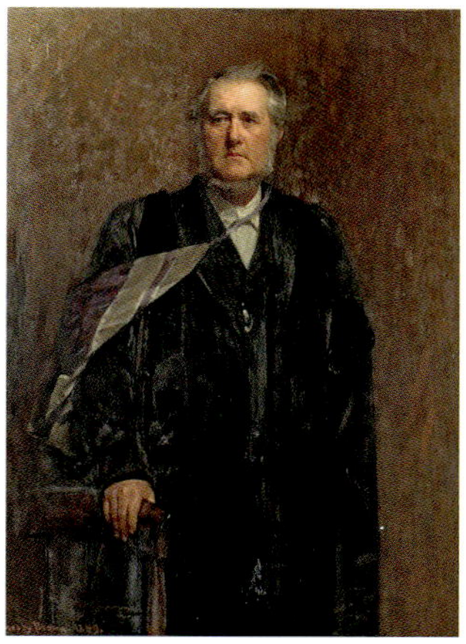

Brown, John Alfred Arnesby 1866–1955
Dr John Brown Paton (1830–1911), Principal of the Nottingham Congregational Institute for 35 Years 1899
oil on canvas 127 x 96.5
NCM 1899-39

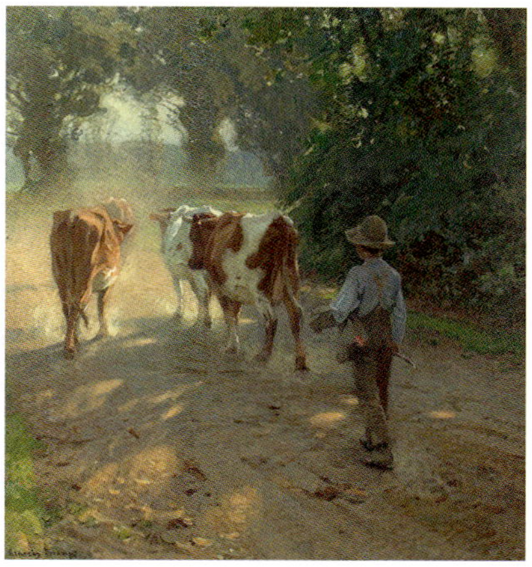

Brown, John Alfred Arnesby 1866–1955
Full Summer, Ludham, Norfolk 1902
oil on canvas 115.6 x 111.8
NCM 1902-38

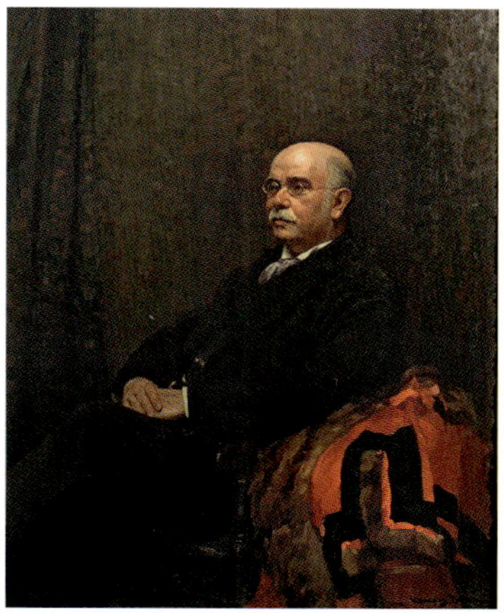

Brown, John Alfred Arnesby 1866–1955
Sir Edward Henry Fraser 1913
oil on canvas 121.9 x 104.1
NCM 1913-74

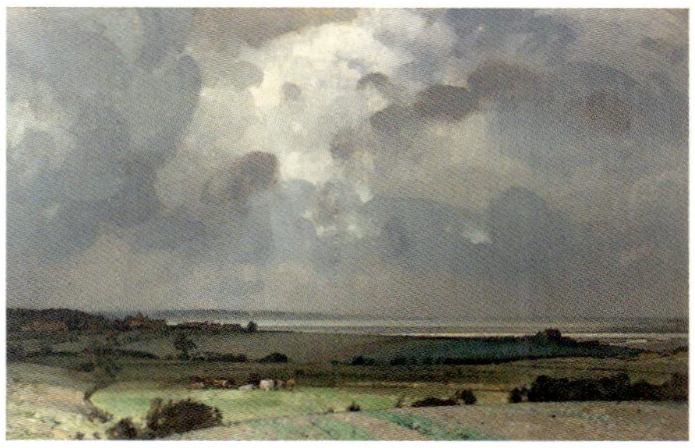

Brown, John Alfred Arnesby 1866–1955
The Estuary, Wells-next-the-Sea, Norfolk 1931
oil on canvas 87.6 x 141
NCM 1943-8

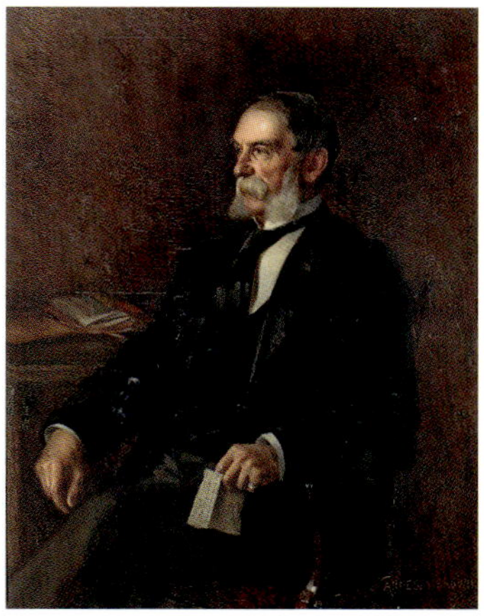

Brown, John Alfred Arnesby 1866–1955
Alderman William Lambert
oil on canvas 121.9 x 96.5
NCM 1918-61

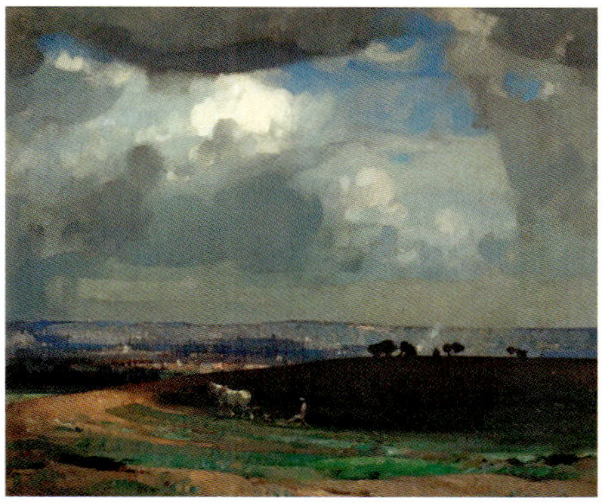

Brown, John Alfred Arnesby 1866–1955
May Morning, Nottingham
oil on canvas 100.5 x 124.5
NCM 1922-52

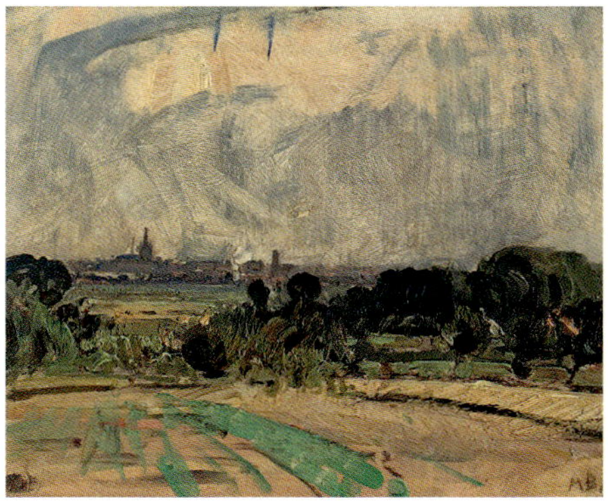

Brown, John Alfred Arnesby 1866–1955
Near Nottingham
oil on canvas 24.1 x 30.5
NCM 1967-114

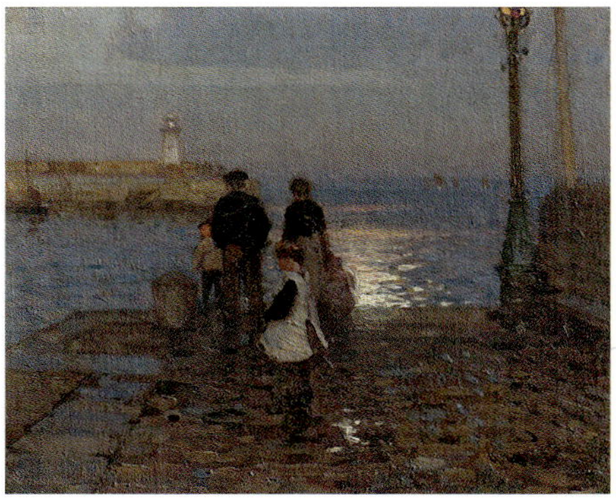

Brown, John Alfred Arnesby 1866–1955
Study for 'The Two Piers'
oil on canvas 30.5 x 36.8
NCM 1958-21

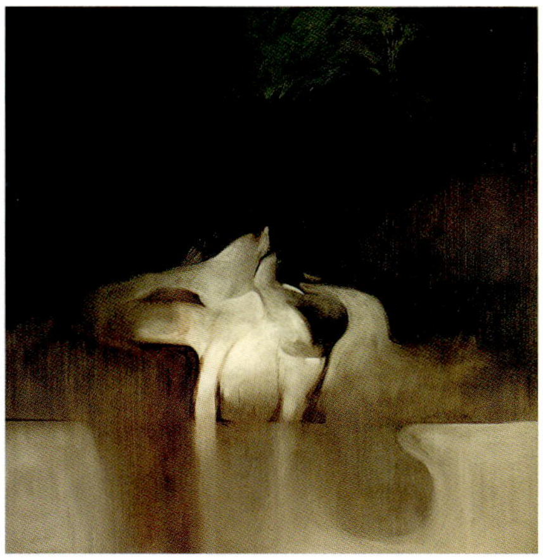

Brown, Neil Dallas 1938–2003
Bather, Still Deep
oil on board 121.9 x 121.9
NCM 1967-85

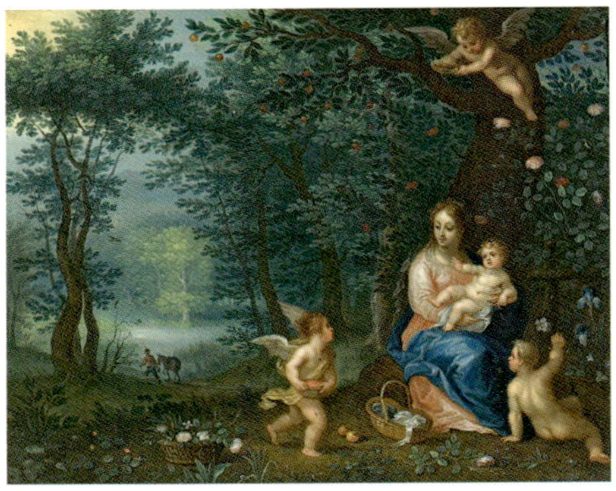

Brueghel, Jan the elder 1568–1625 & **Balen, Hendrik van I (circle of)** 1575–1632
The Rest on the Flight into Egypt early 1600s
oil on copper 23.8 x 31.1
NCM 1904-99

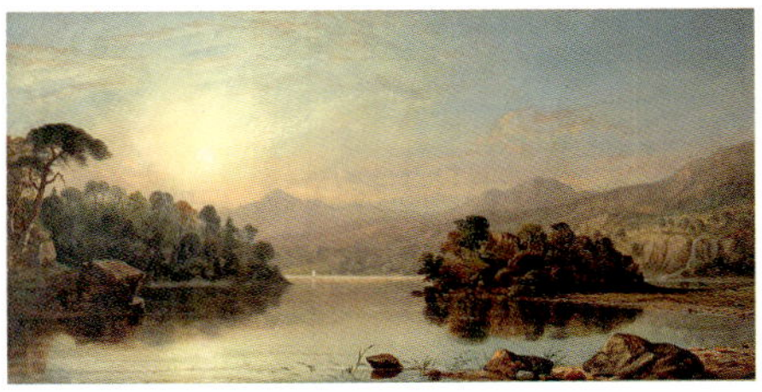

Buchanan, George F. 1800–1864
Ellen's Isle, Loch Katrine, Scotland
oil on canvas 31.1 x 62.2
NCM 1890-1173

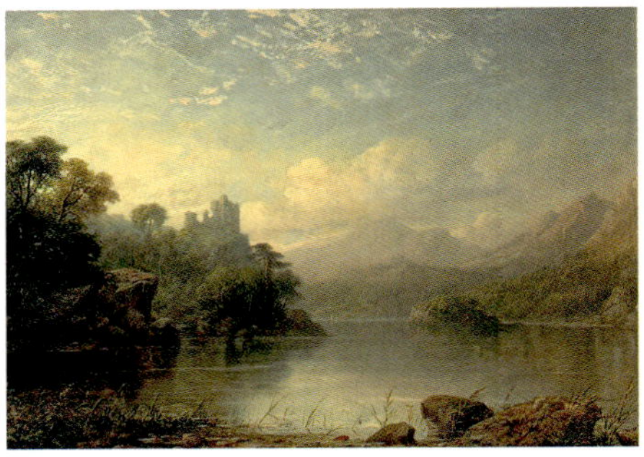

Buchanan, George F. 1800–1864
Lake Scene with Ruined Castle and Mountains
oil on canvas 63.5 x 94
NCM 1890-1201

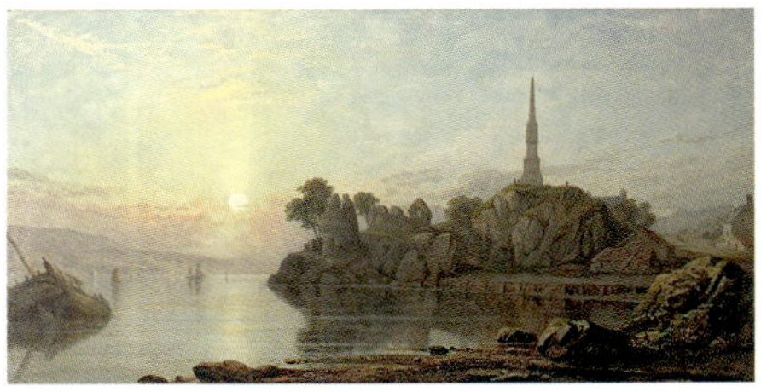

Buchanan, George F. 1800–1864
On the Clyde
oil on canvas 31.1 x 61.6
NCM 1890-1174

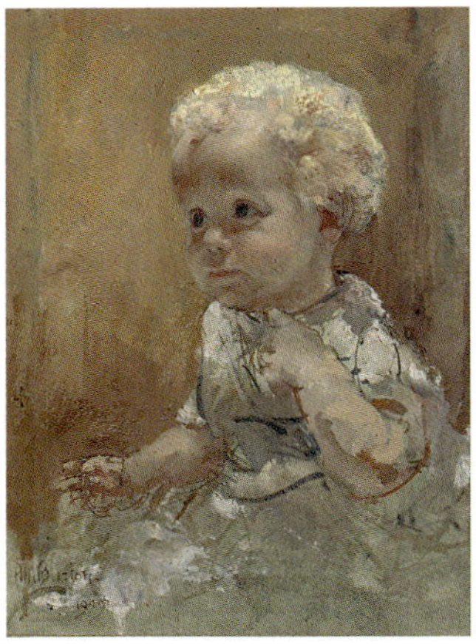

Burton, Alice Mary 1893–1968
William 1949
oil on canvas 50.8 x 40.6
NCM 1950-1

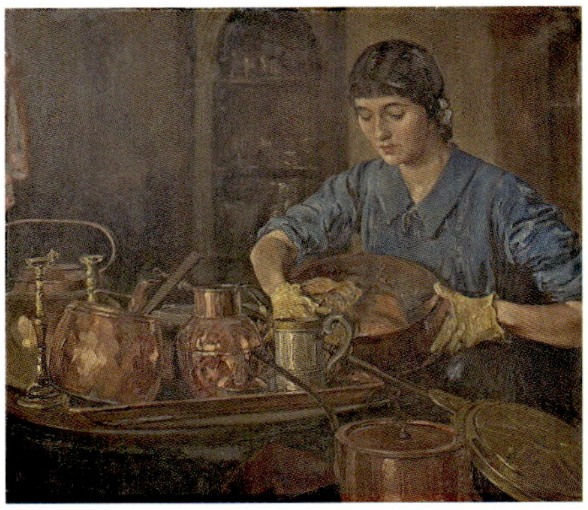

Burton, Harry Marriott 1882–1979
Pots and Pans, Natal, South Africa 1930
oil on canvas 61.6 x 74.3
NCM 1954-62

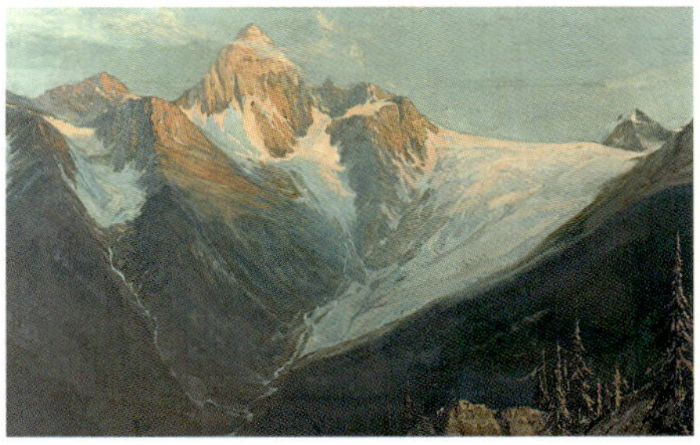

Burton, Harry Marriott 1882–1979
The Rockies, Mount Sir Donald, Canada
oil on wood 91.4 x 121.9
NCM 1946-244

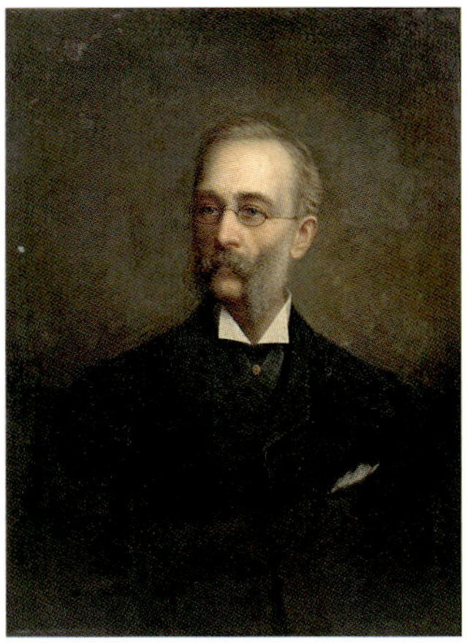

Burton, John active 1769–1836
George Bellas Rothera (c.1824–1907), Solicitor
oil on canvas 84 x 63.7
NCMG 2003-30

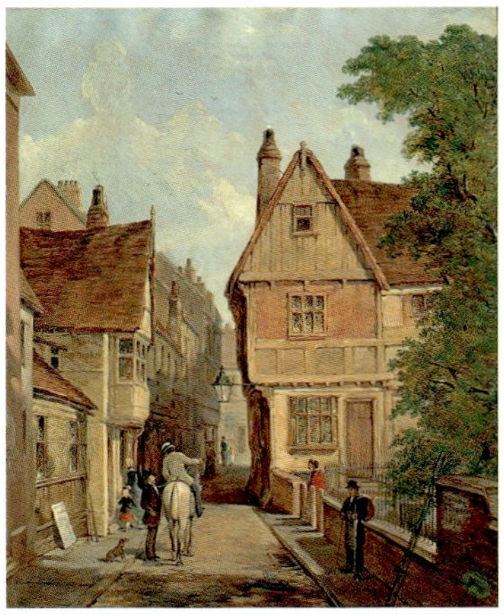

Bussey, Reuben 1818–1893
Old Houses, St Peter's Gate, Nottingham, 1842
1870
oil on canvas 61 x 50.8
NCM 1924-7

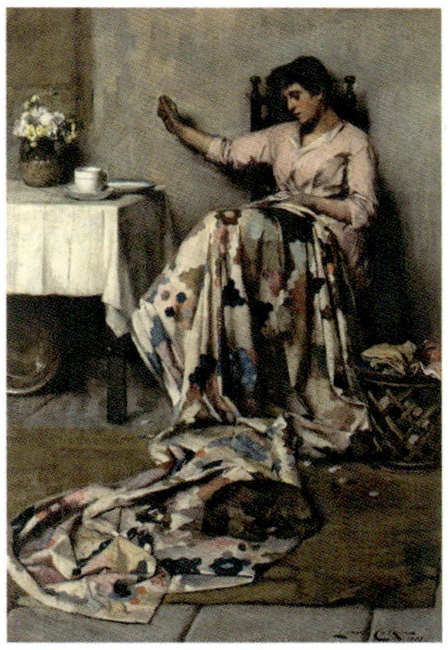

Calkin, Lance 1859–1936
The Patchwork Quilt 1887
oil on canvas 86.4 x 61
NCM 1936-21

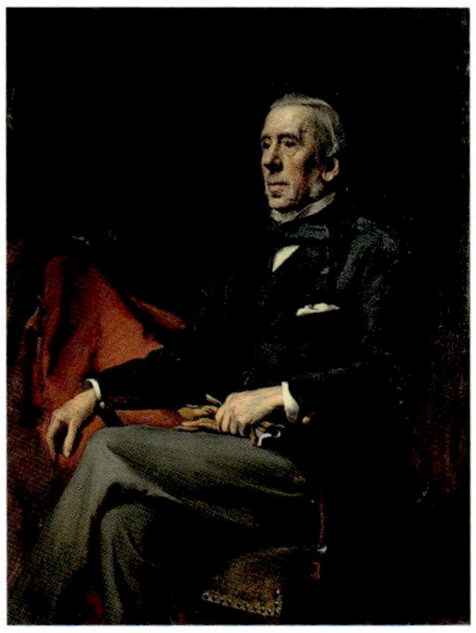

Calkin, Lance 1859–1936
Alderman John Barber, JP, Sheriff of Nottingham (1846), Mayor of Nottingham (1867–1869) 1888
oil on canvas 142.2 x 111.8
NCM 1888-259

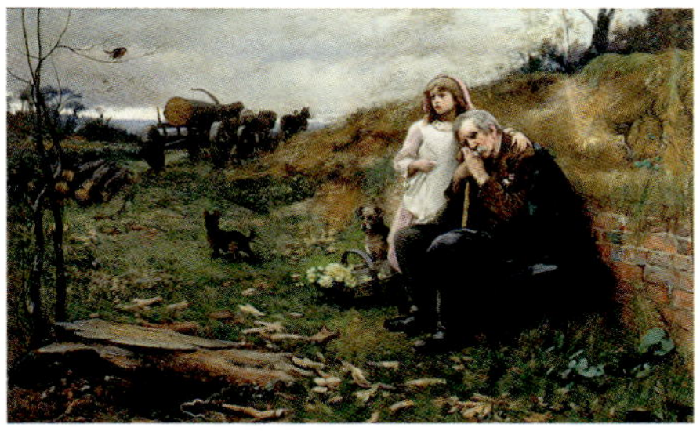

Calkin, Lance 1859–1936
'All pass away as the glimmer of day while others as fleet are born' 1888
oil on canvas 111.8 x 175.3
NCM 1889-7

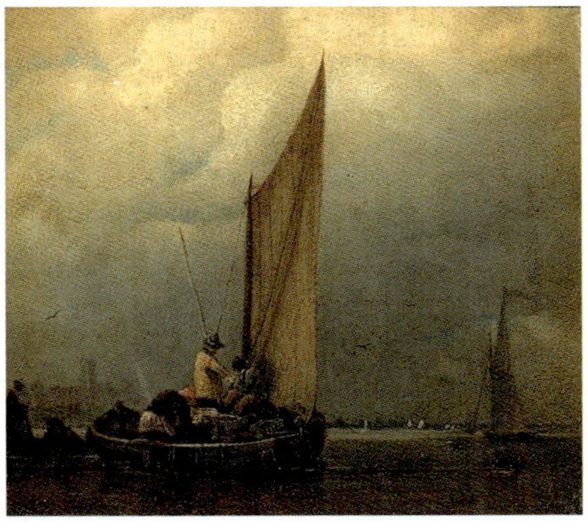

Callcott, Augustus Wall 1779–1844
A River Scene with Barges c.1825
oil on canvas 15.2 x 17.1
NCM 1904-17

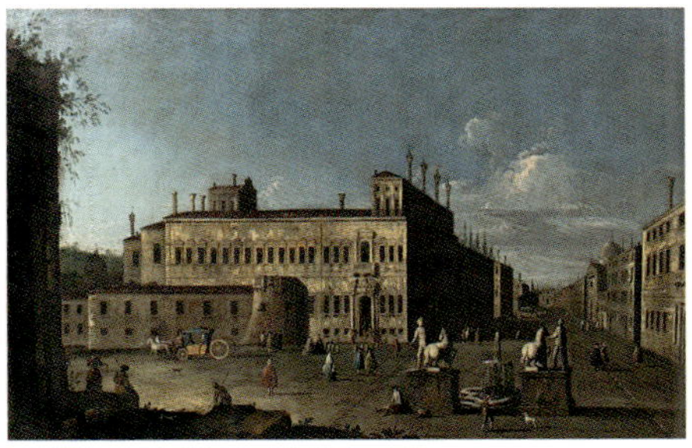

Canaletto (imitator of) 1697–1768
Piazza di Monte Cavallo, Rome, Italy
oil on canvas 71.8 x 111.4
NCM 1890-1206

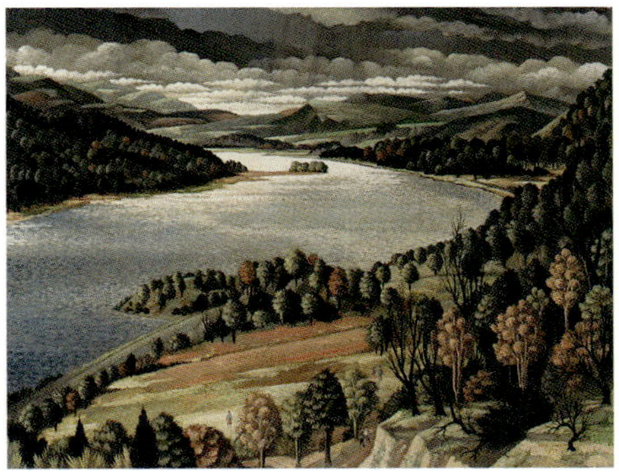

Capey, Reco 1895–1961
The Hudson from Bear Mountain Bridge, USA 1939
tempera on fabric laid on board 41.9 x 55.2
NCM 1940-20

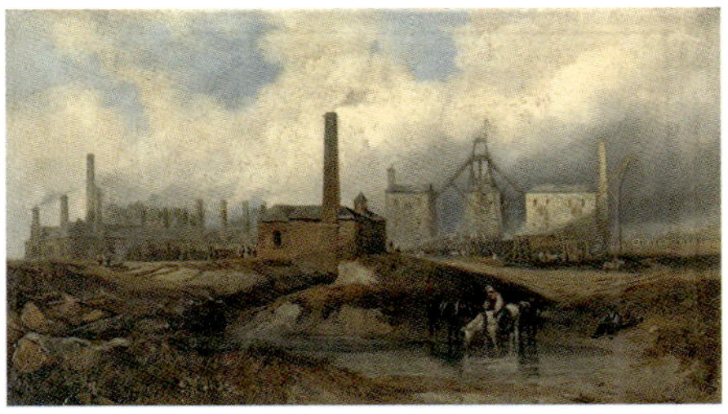

Carmichael, John Wilson 1800–1868
Industrial Scene 1833
oil on canvas 26.7 x 48.2
NCM 1938-60

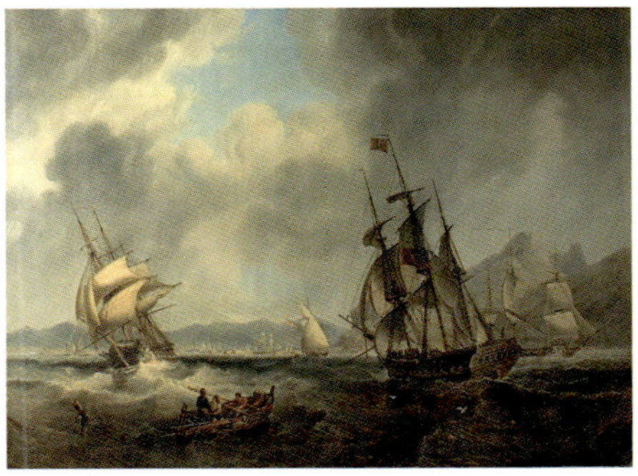

Carmichael, John Wilson 1800–1868
Scene in the Mediterranean 1842
oil on canvas 113 x 154.9
NCM 1904-18

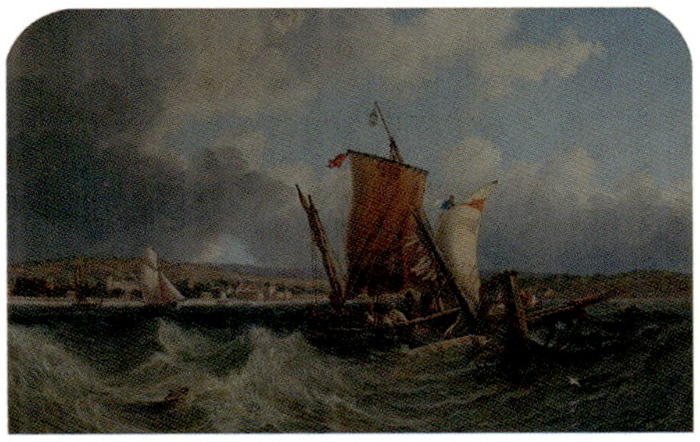

Carmichael, John Wilson 1800–1868
Shipping off North Yarmouth 1859
oil on canvas 52.1 x 81.3
NCM 1939-6

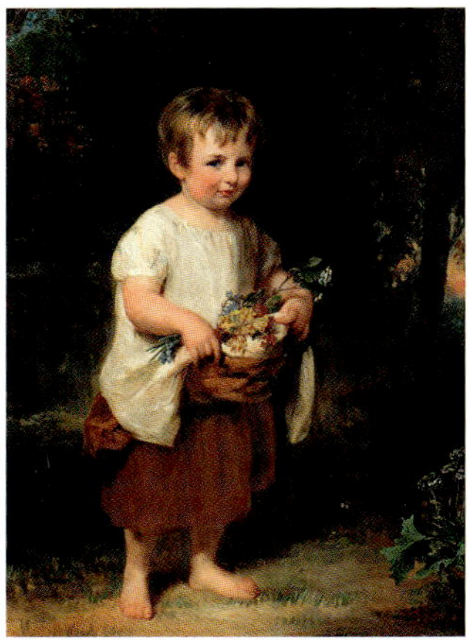

Carpenter, Margaret Sarah 1793–1872
A Spring Nosegay
oil on canvas 111.8 x 86.4
NCM 1931-43

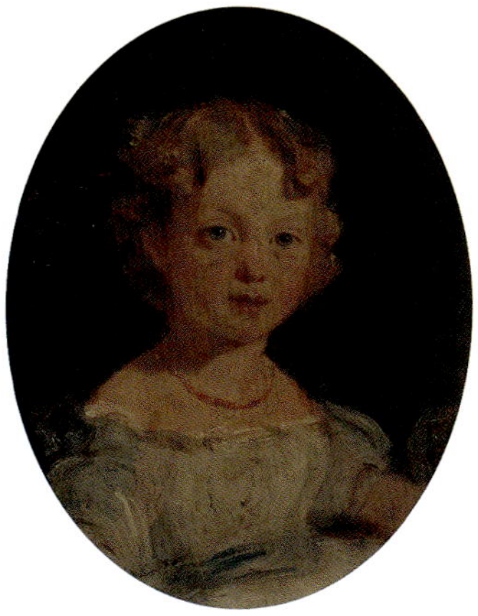

Carpenter, Margaret Sarah (attributed to) 1793–1872
Portrait of a Child
oil on canvas 27.3 x 21.6
NCM 1953-10

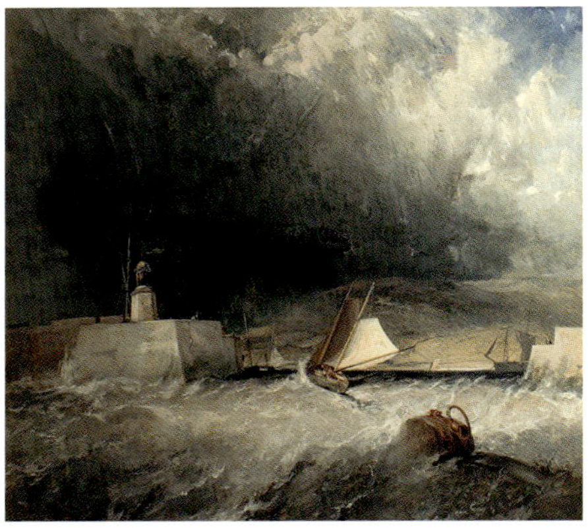

Chambers, George 1803–1840
Whitby Harbour, North Yorkshire 1836
oil on canvas 101.6 x 132.1
NCM 1904-19

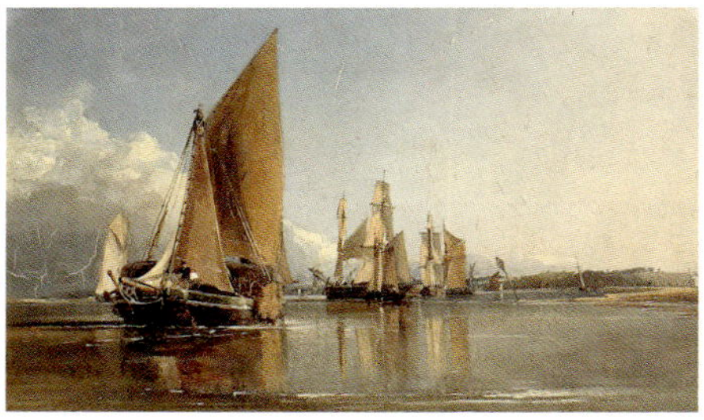

Chambers, George 1803–1840
Boats Entering the Medway
oil on canvas 33 x 53.7
NCM 1949-87

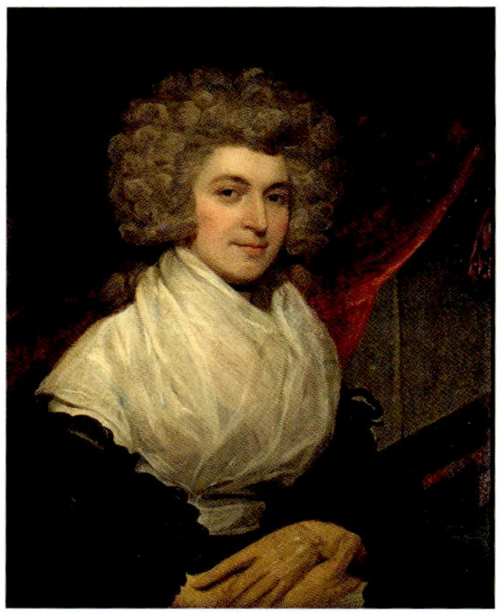

Chandler, John Westbrooke 1764–1804/1805
Portrait of a Lady
oil on canvas 76.2 x 63.5
NCM 1910-52

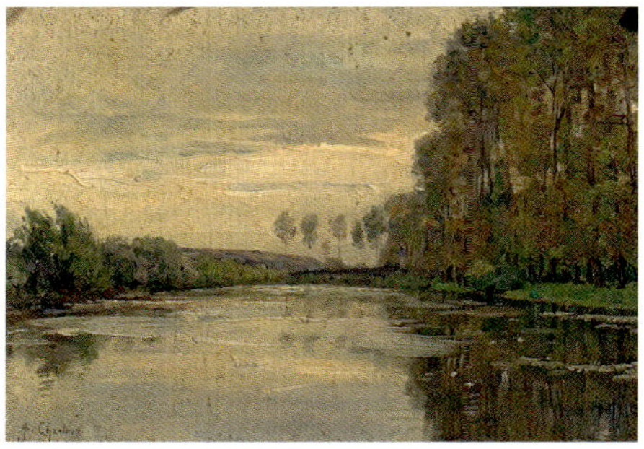

Chantron, Alexandre Jacques 1842–1918
River Scene, the Lower Loire, France
oil on board 23 x 33.5
NCM 1942-13

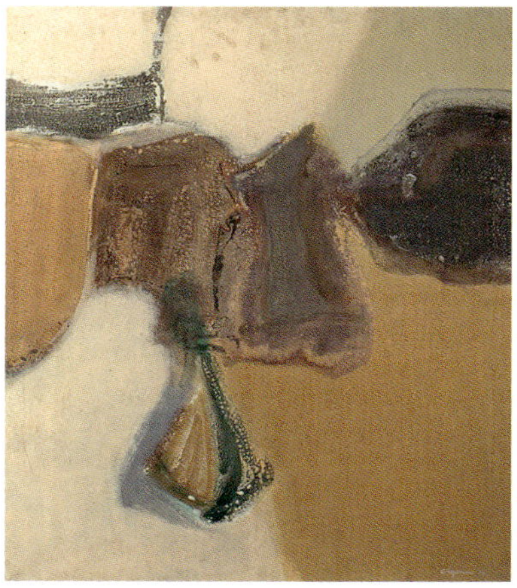

Chapman, Max 1911–1999
Emersion to Brown 1964
oil & emulsion on canvas 101.6 x 91.4
NCM 1964-309

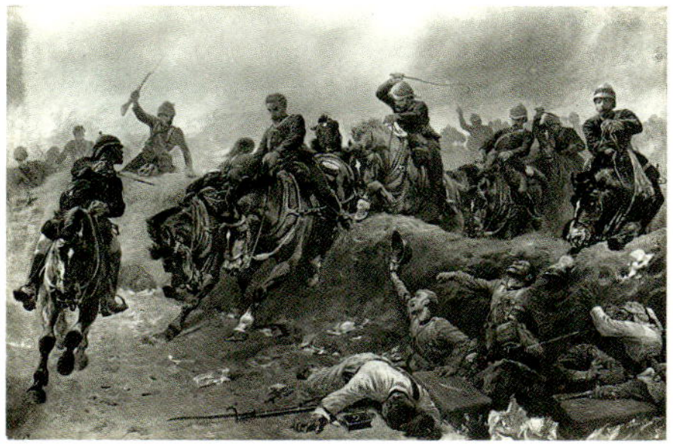

Charlton, John 1849–1917
British Artillery Entering the Enemy's Lines at Tel-el-Kebir, Egypt, 13 September 1882 1883
oil on canvas 165.1 x 248.9
NCM 1885-7

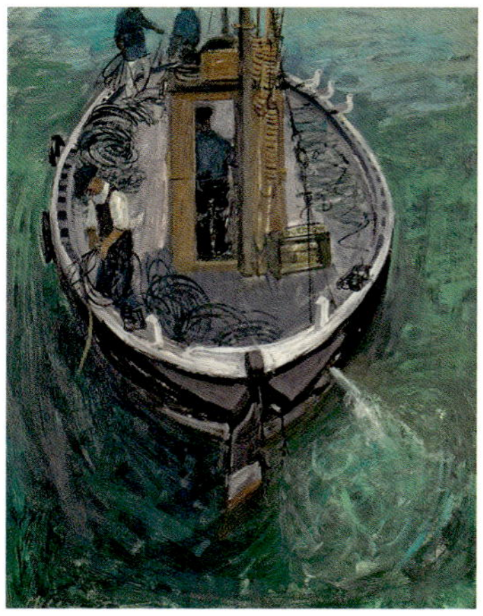

Cheese, Bernard b.1925
The 'Crissie Griggie' 1957
oil on wood 76.2 x 62.2
NCM 1957-43

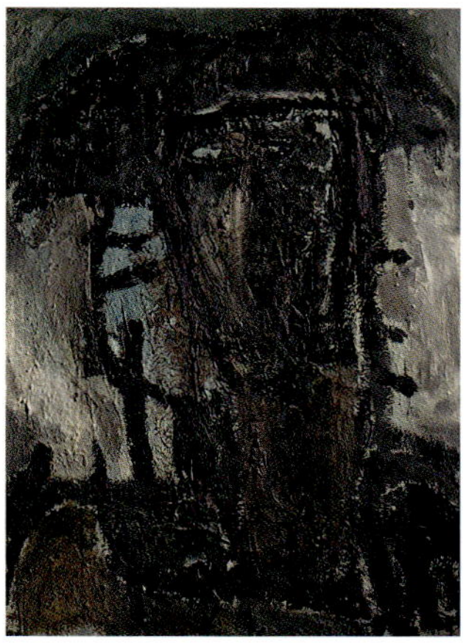

Christoforou, John b.1921
Head of a Woman c.1961
oil on wood 121.9 x 91.4
NCM 1962-75

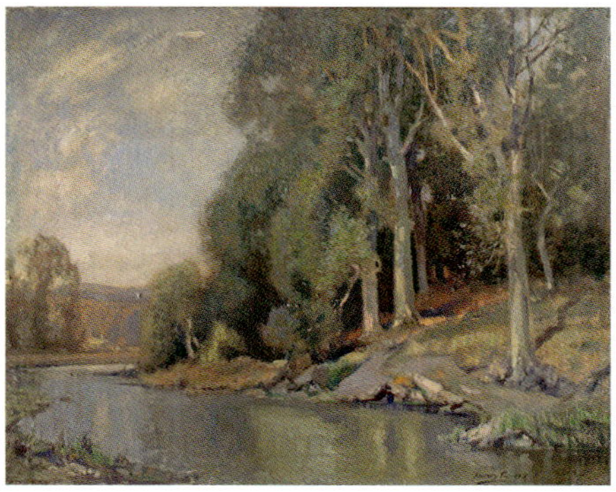

Clarke, Harry Harvey 1869–1948
The Coming of Autumn
oil on canvas 73.7 x 91.4
NCM 1909-42

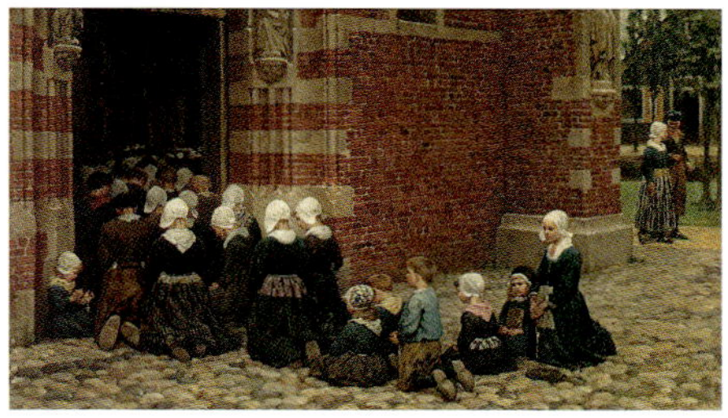

Clausen, George 1852–1944
High Mass at a Fishing Village on the Zuyder Zee, Holland 1876
oil on canvas 47 x 83.8
NCM 1906-27

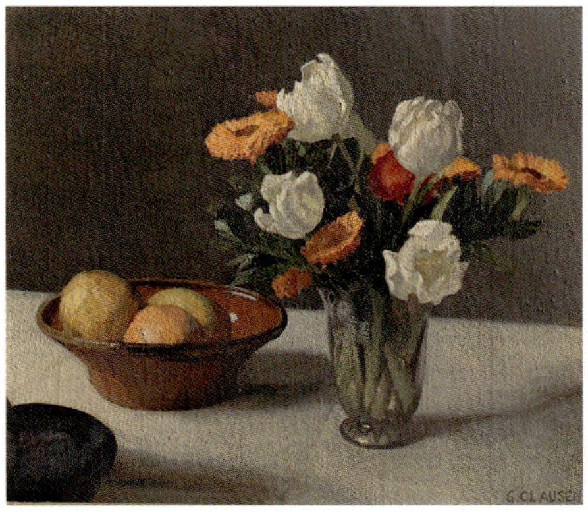

Clausen, George 1852–1944
Still Life
oil on canvas 38.1 x 45.7
NCM 1958-20

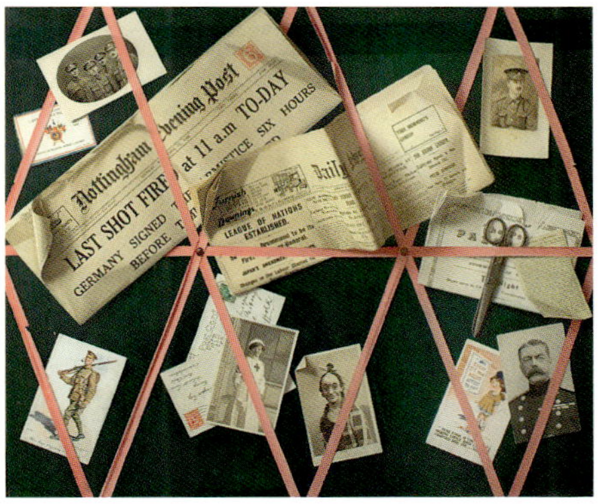

Clayton, William J. M. active 1963–1991
Time to Remember 1965
oil on canvas 63.5 x 76.2
NCM 1966-30

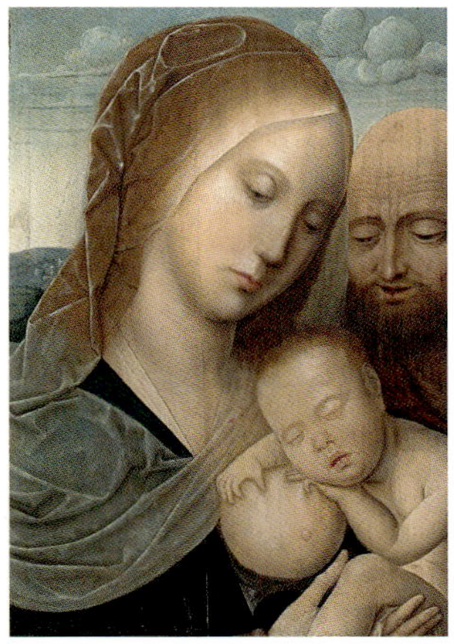

Cleve, Joos van (follower of) c.1464–c.1540
Virgin and Child with St Joseph 1500–1550
oil on wood 43.8 x 31.8
NCM 1910-57

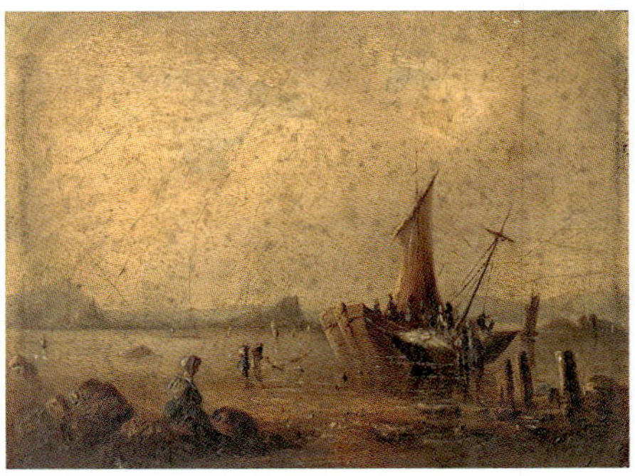

Clint, George 1770–1854
Coast Scene with Figures and Boats
oil on wood 19.1 x 26.7
NCM 1890-1214

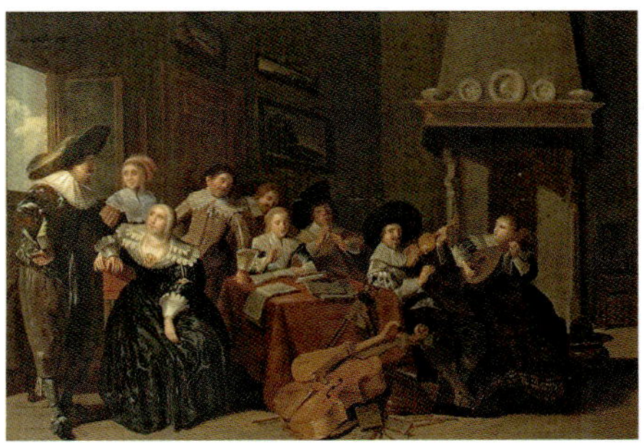

Codde, Pieter Jacobsz. (attributed to) 1599–1678
The Music Party
oil on wood 47 x 69.9
NCM 1904-89

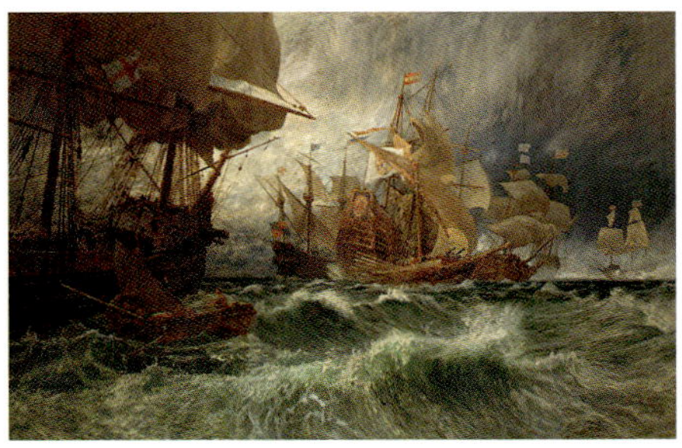

Cole, George Vicat 1833–1893
The Summons to Surrender (An Incident in the Spanish Armada)
oil on canvas 191.1 x 306.1
NCM 1898-75

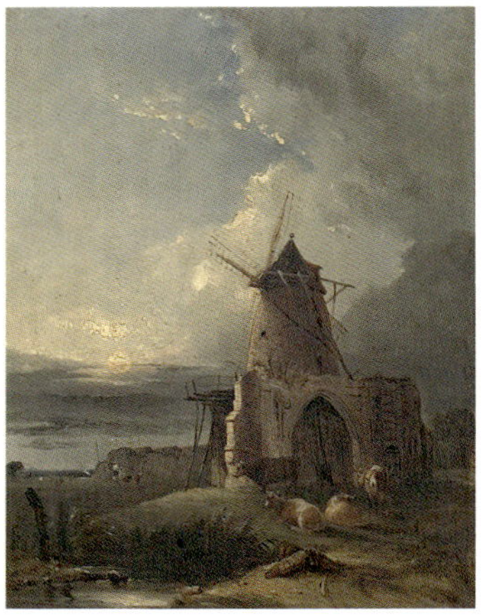

Colkett, Samuel David 1806–1863
Old Mill at Norwich, Norfolk
oil on wood 49.5 x 39.5
NCM 1890-1186

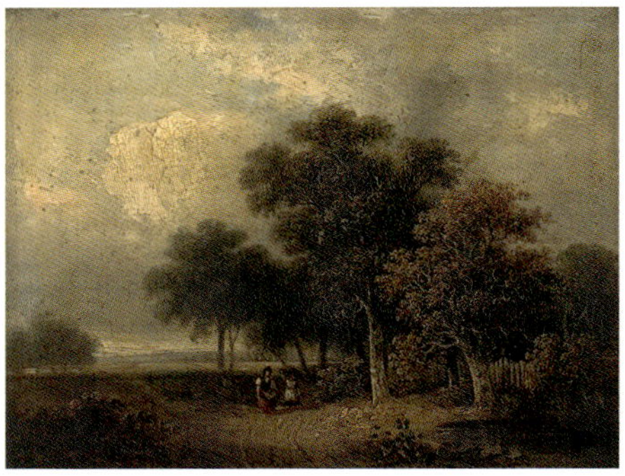

Colkett, Samuel David 1806–1863
River Scene (Trees and Figures)
oil on wood 31.4 x 41.6
NCM 1890-1168

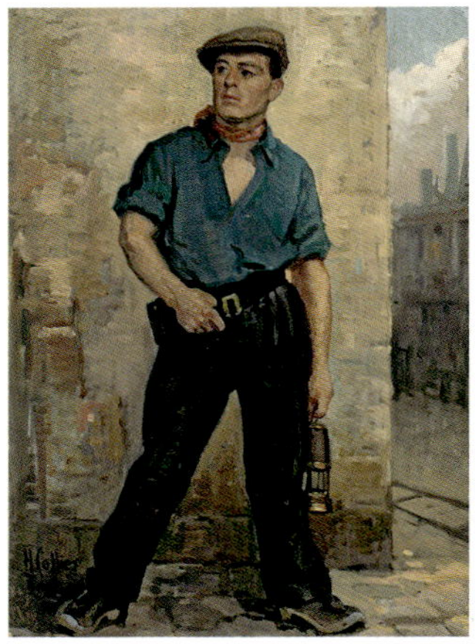

Collier, Herbert Hood 1863–1947
The Miner
oil on canvas 64.8 x 48.2
NCM 1945-41

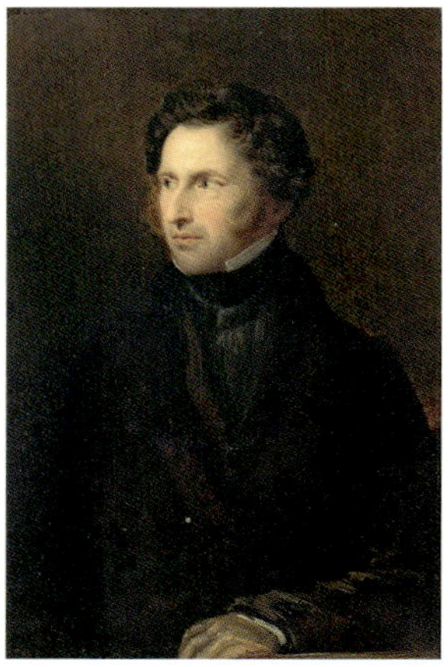

Collins, Charles Allston 1828–1873
William Collins (1788–1847)
oil on wood 34.9 x 24.8
NCM 1904-20

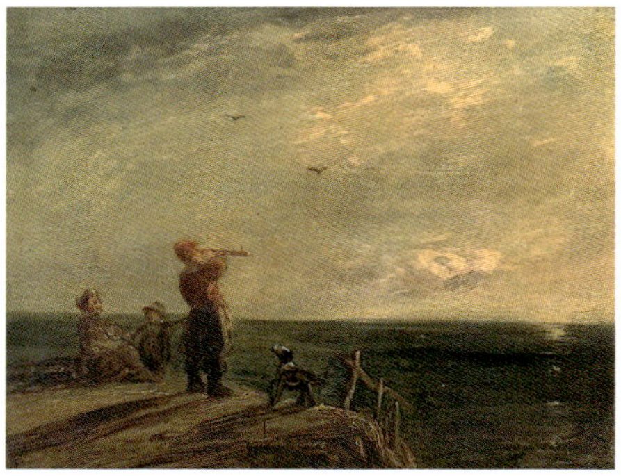

Collins, William 1788–1847
Seascape with Figures and Dog, Sunset
oil on wood 15.2 x 20.3
NCM 1904-23

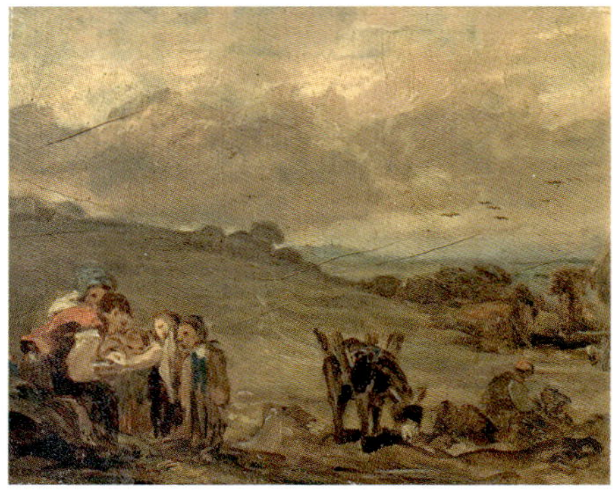

Collins, William 1788–1847
Taking out the Thorn
oil on canvas 13 x 16.5
NCM 1904-22

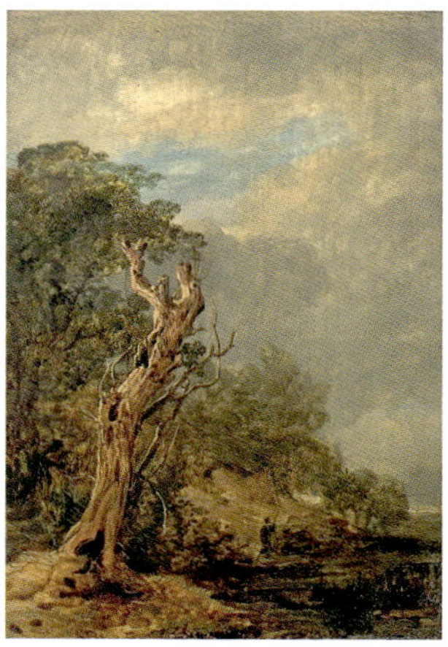

Collins, William 1788–1847
The Withered Tree
oil on wood 23.5 x 17.4
NCM 1904-21

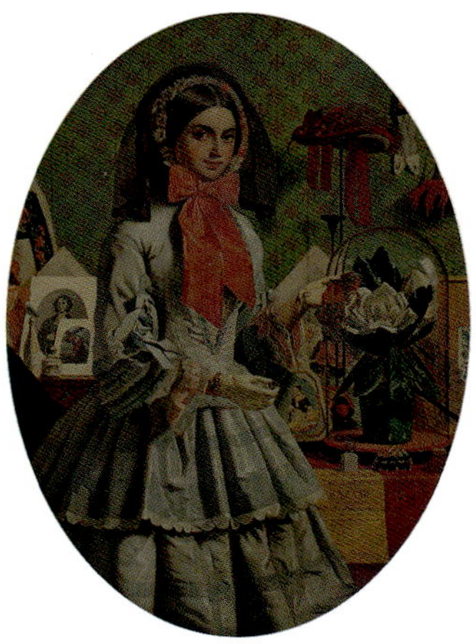

Collinson, James 1825–1881
For Sale 1857
oil on canvas 58.4 x 45.7
NCM 1959-94

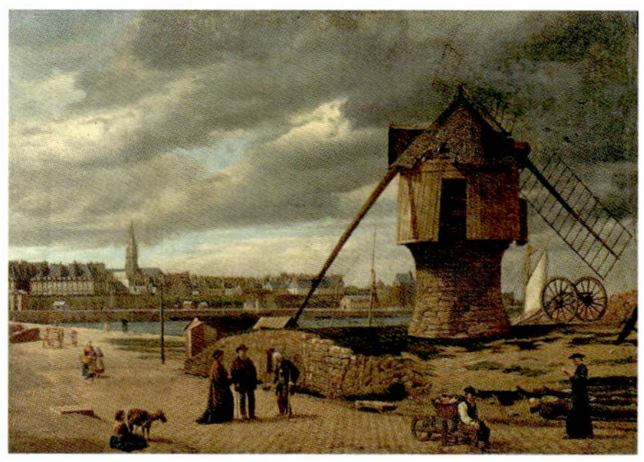

Collinson, James 1825–1881
Landscape with a Windmill, St Malo, France
1877
oil on canvas 35.6 x 51.4
NCM 1953-1

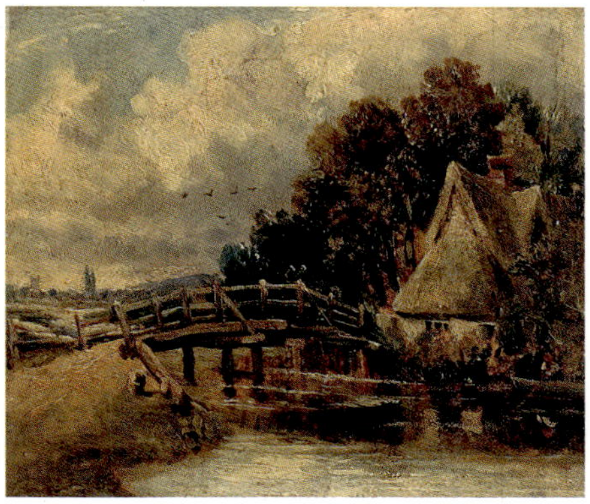

Constable, John (after) 1776–1837
On the Stour near East Bergholt, Suffolk
oil on canvas 24.1 x 29.2
NCM 1909-45

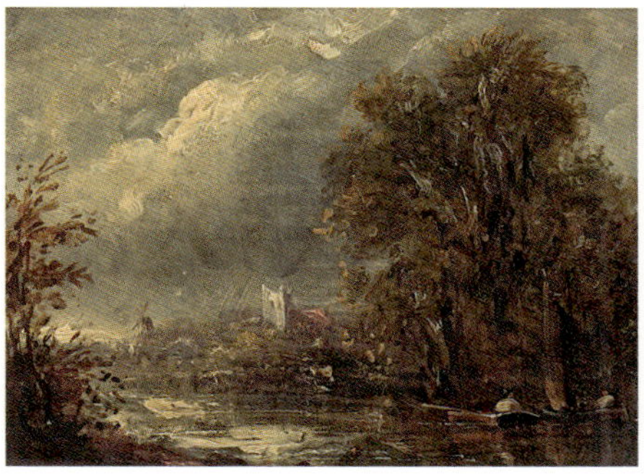

Constable, John (style of) 1776–1837
On the Stour 19th C
oil on canvas 26.7 x 36.8
NCM 1909-43

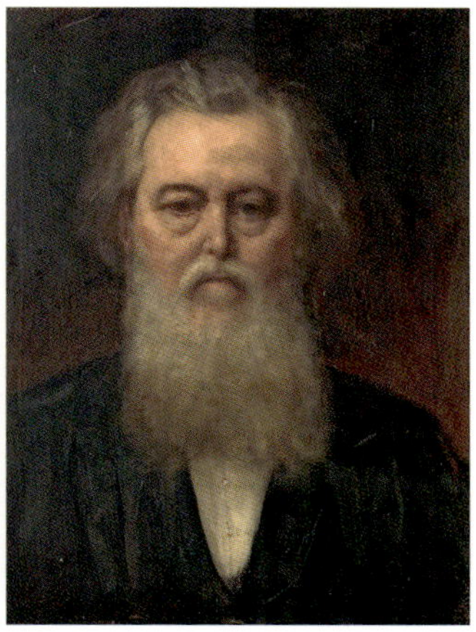

Constant, Jean Joseph Benjamin 1845–1902
Dr John Chapman (1822–1894) c.1885
oil on canvas 66 x 50.8
NCM 1932-32

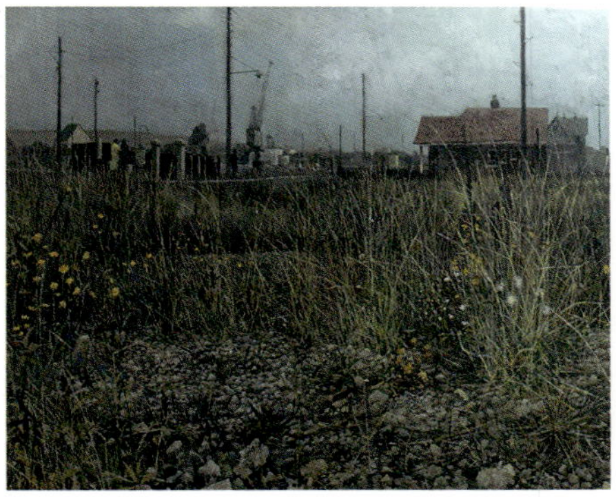

Cooke, Anthony R. b.1933
Weeds and Stones, Shoreham-by-Sea, West Sussex 1958
oil on canvas 106 x 126
NCM 1959-22

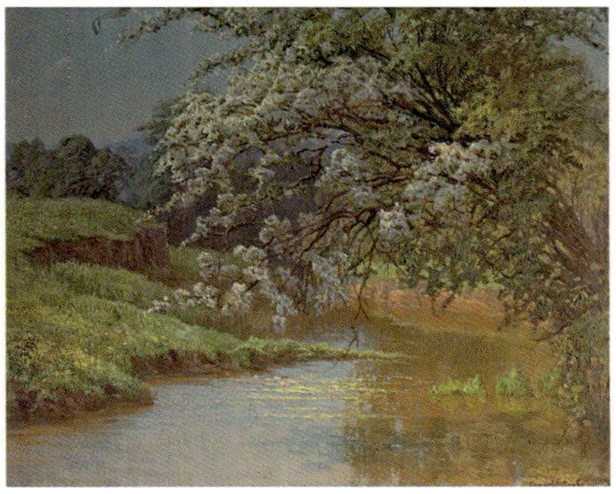

Cooke, Ernest Owen 1862–1937
May Blossom 1910
oil on canvas 77.5 x 102.9
NCM 1911-49

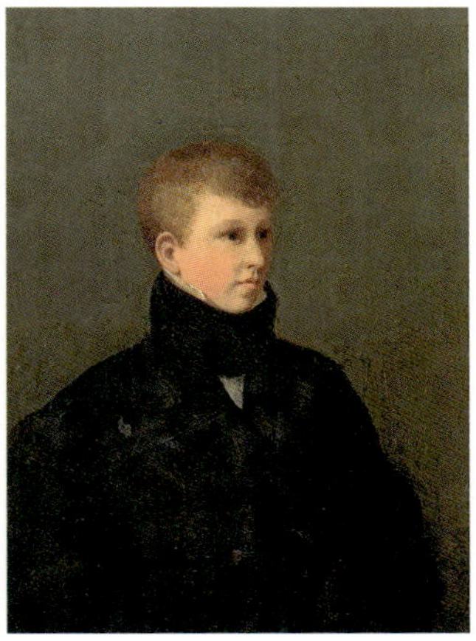

Cooper, Frederick Carter c.1795–1875
Henry Kirke White (1785–1806)
oil on wood 22.9 x 17.5
NCM 1928-281

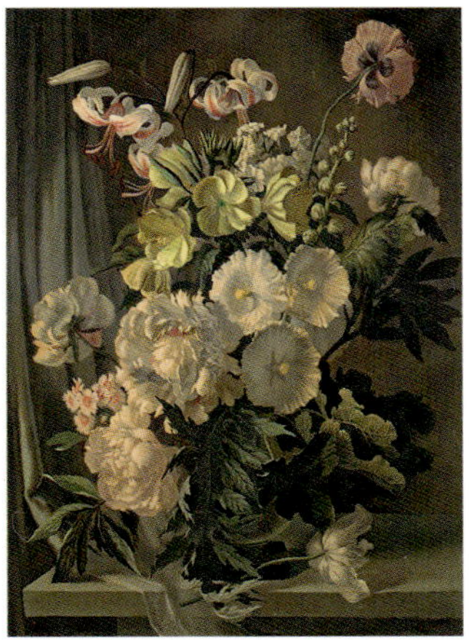

Cooper, Gerald 1898–1975
Flower Piece 1944
oil on wood 76.2 x 59.7
NCM 1944-1

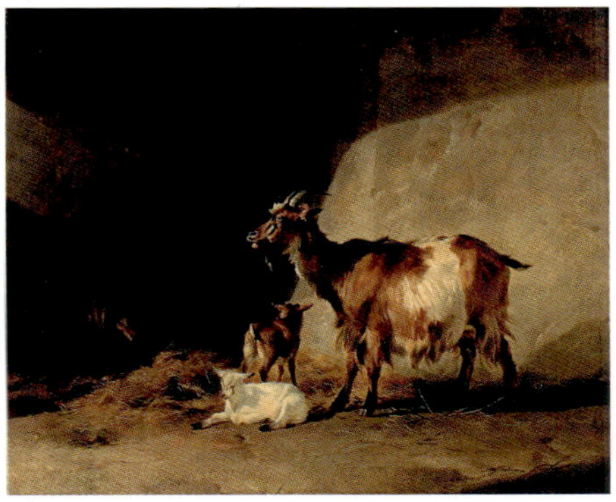

Cooper, Thomas Sidney 1803–1902
Goats and Kids in a Shed 1846
oil on wood 35.2 x 45.7
NCM 1904-26

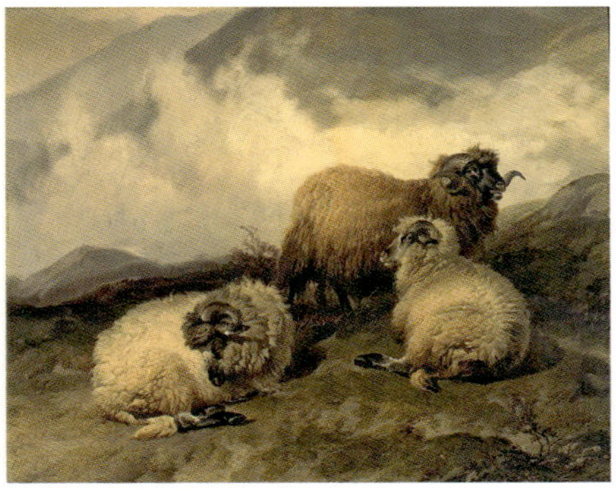

Cooper, Thomas Sidney 1803–1902
Mountain Sheep (Morning Mist Clearing Off) 1846
oil on wood 46.4 x 69.9
NCM 1904-25

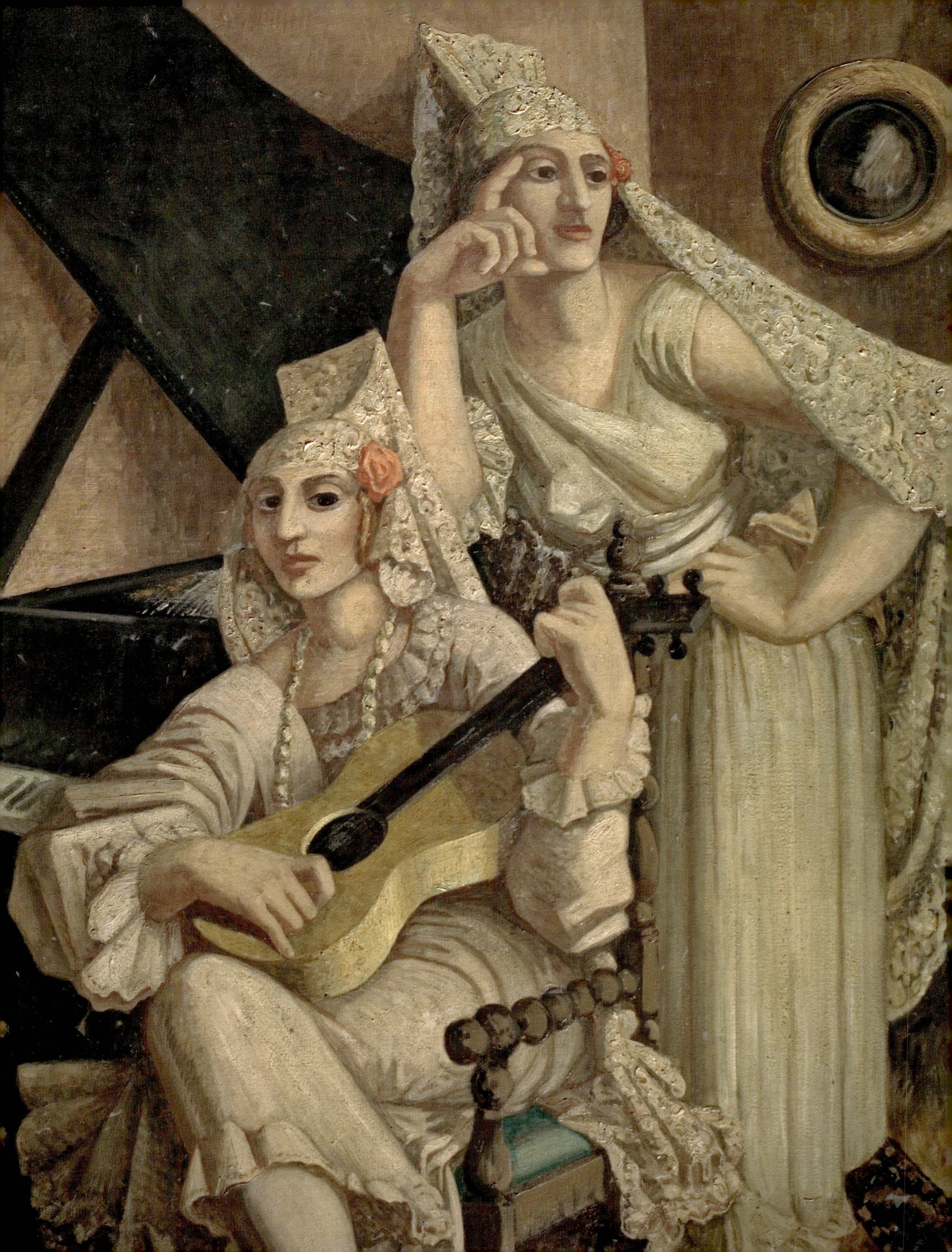

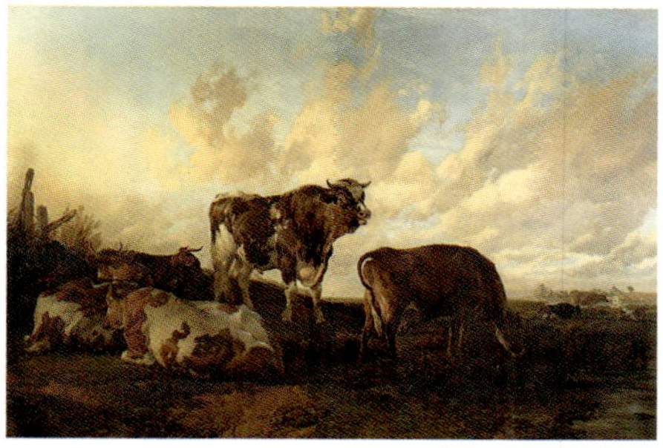

Cooper, Thomas Sidney 1803–1902
Repose in the Meadows 1851
oil on canvas 101.6 x 182.9
NCM 1941-24

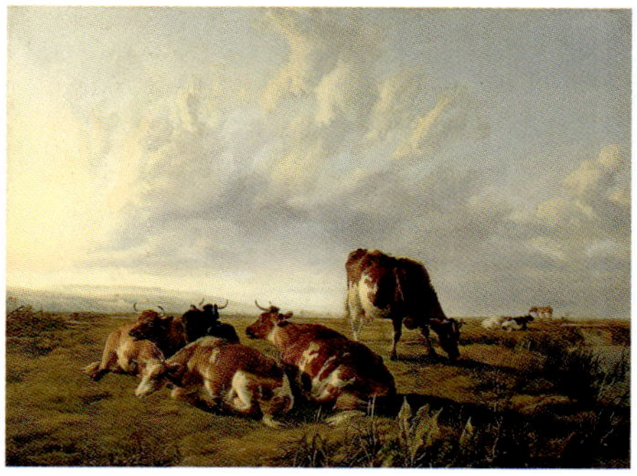

Cooper, Thomas Sidney 1803–1902
Afternoon in the Meadows 1861
oil on canvas 76.2 x 109.2
NCM 1933-248

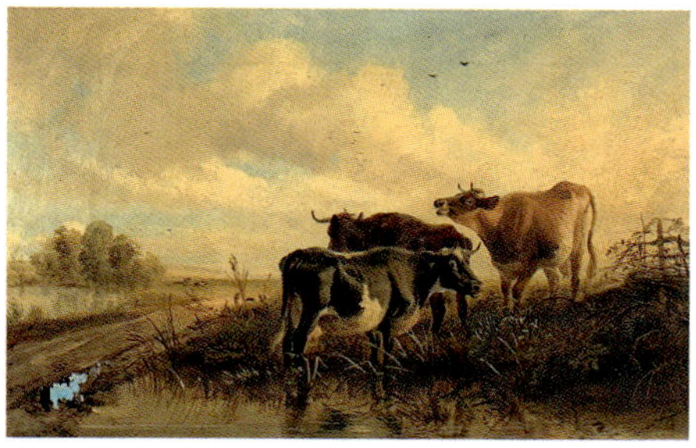

Cooper, Thomas Sidney 1803–1902
Cattle in Landscape, Evening 1862
oil on canvas 25.4 x 40.6
NCM 1904-24

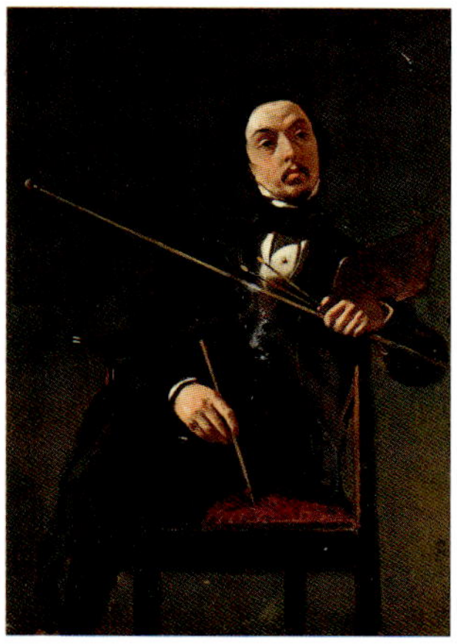

Corbould, Edward Henry 1815–1905
Edmund John Niemann (1813–1876) 1852
oil on board 35.2 x 29.2
NCM 1904-27

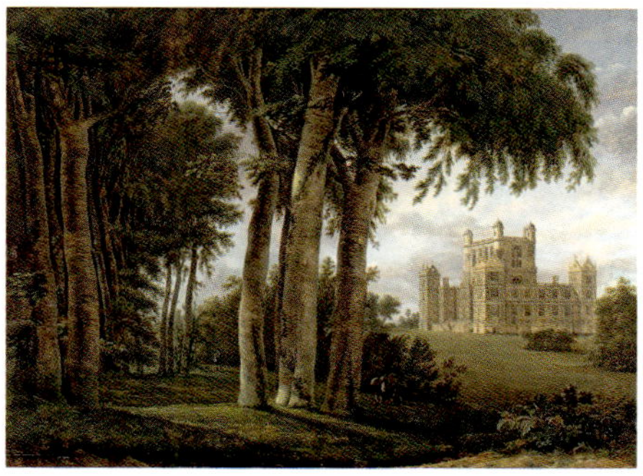

Cort, Hendrik Frans de 1742–1810
Wollaton Hall, Nottingham c.1795
oil on panel 115.5 x 158.1
NCM 1967-126

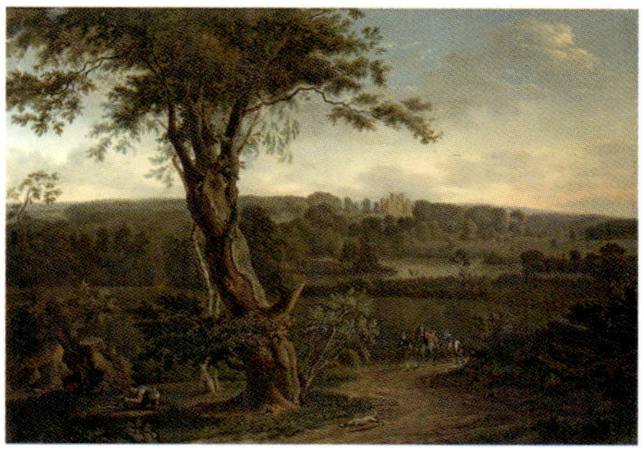

Cort, Hendrik Frans de 1742–1810
Wollaton Hall Park, Nottingham c.1795
oil on panel 111.8 x 158.7
NCM 1957-10

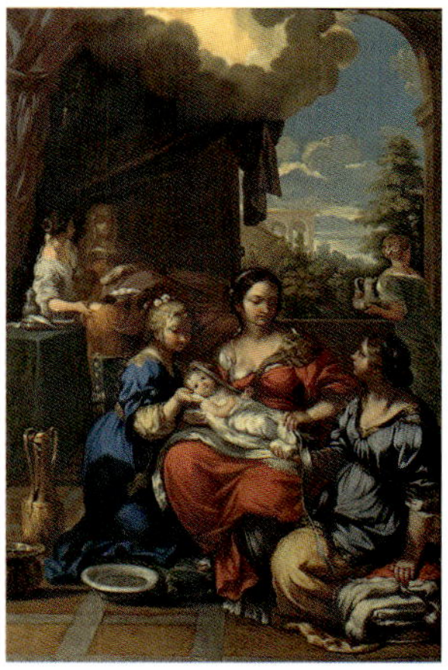

Cortona, Pietro da (after) 1596–1669
The Birth of the Virgin
oil on canvas 74.9 x 53.3
NCM 1933-251

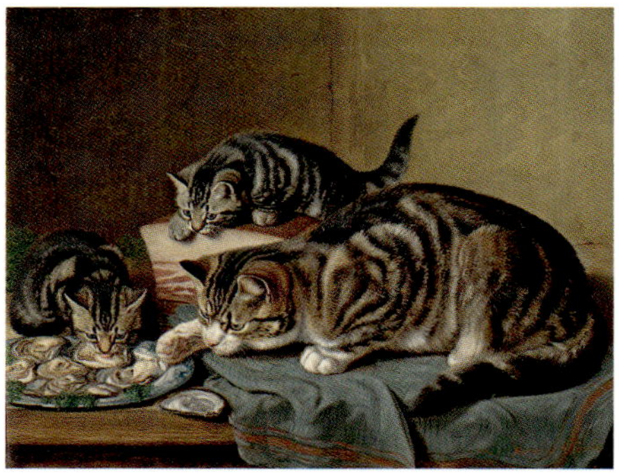

Couldery, Horatio Henri 1832–1910
An Oyster Supper 1882
oil on wood 45.7 x 61
NCM 1882-568

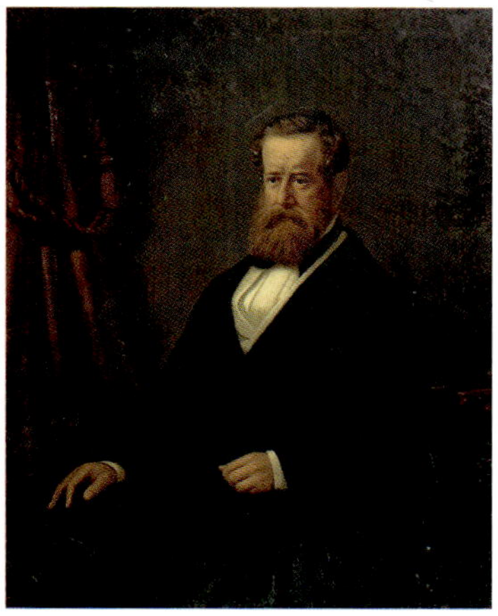

Cox, Alfred Wilson 1820–1890
Henry Pelham-Clinton (1811–1864), 5th Duke of Newcastle-under-Lyne
oil on canvas 61 x 50.8
NCM 1899-40

Facing page: Power, John Joseph Wardell, 1881–1943, *Music* (detail), Nottingham City Museums and Galleries (p. 135)

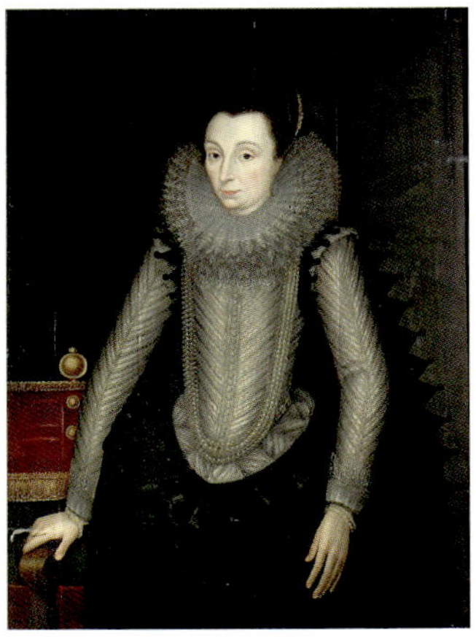

Critz, John de the elder (attributed to) 1551/1552–1642
Portrait of a Lady Called 'Countess of Nottingham' (c.1547–1603) (...) 1600–1605
oil on wood 113.6 x 85.7
NCM 1923-21

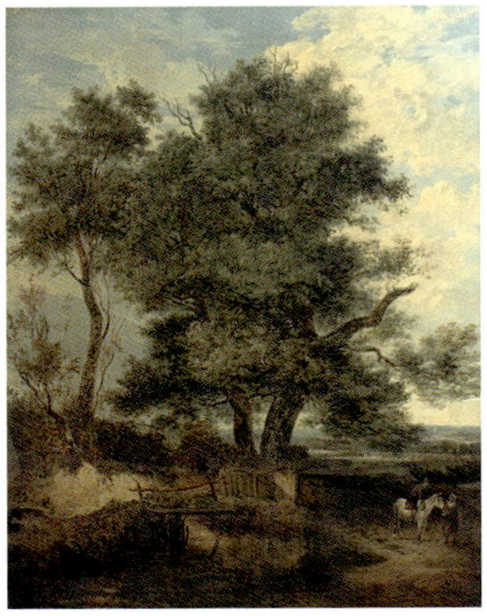

Crome, John 1768–1821
Trees by a Brook (The Willow Tree, a Horseman and a Woman on a Road) c.1818
oil on canvas 129.5 x 104.1
NCM 1955-53

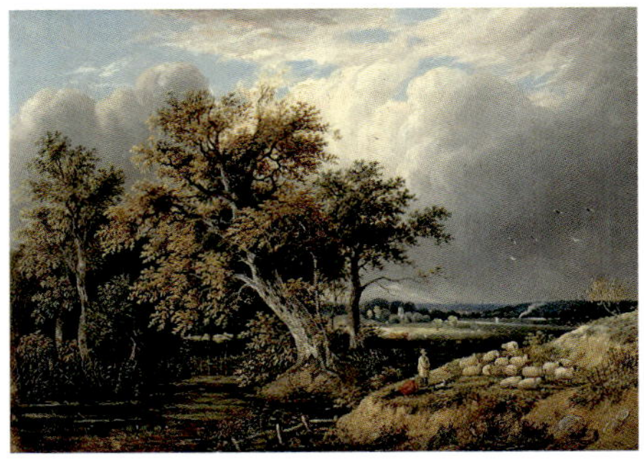

Crome, William Henry 1806–1873
Landscape with Trees and Sheep
oil on canvas 43.2 x 61
NCM 1890-1192

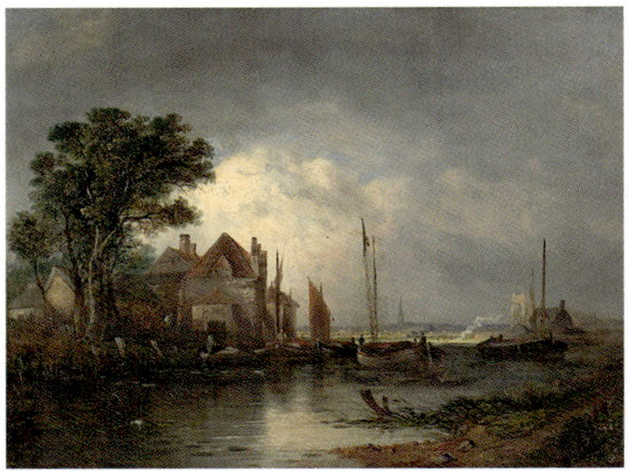

Crome, William Henry 1806–1873
River Scene with Boats
oil on canvas 45.7 x 61
NCM 1890-1177

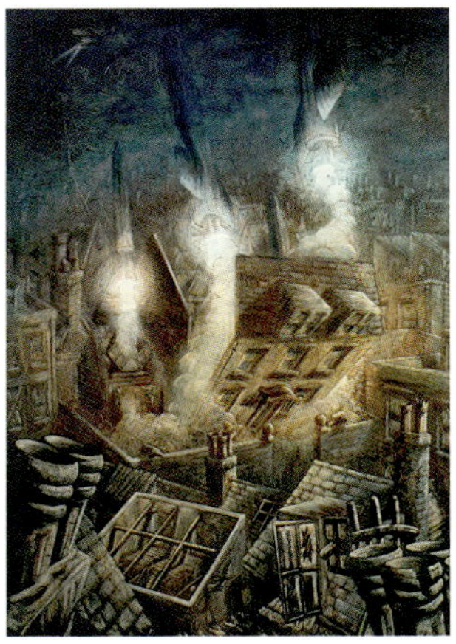

Crowley, Graham b.1950
Deadly Detached I 1987
oil on canvas 203 x 163
NCM 1989-903

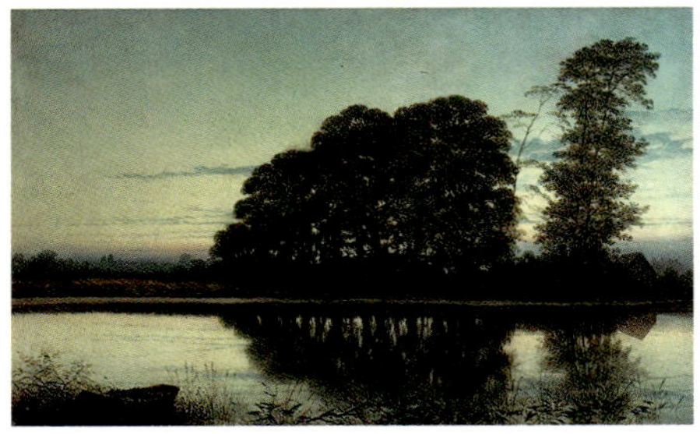

Cubley, William Harold 1814–1896
Twilight on the Trent c.1884
oil on canvas 55.9 x 91.4
NCM 1915-15

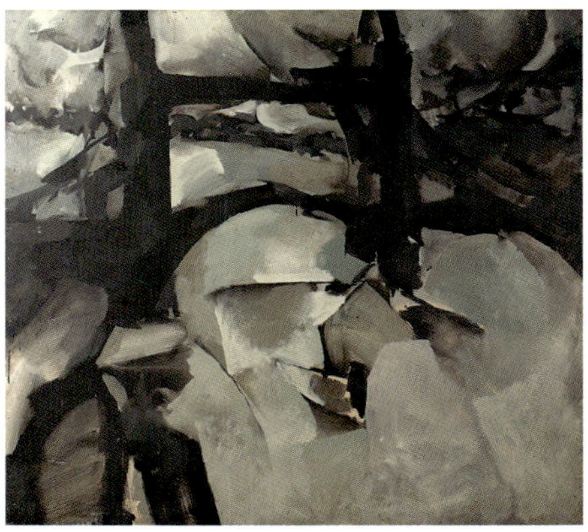

Culbert, Bill b.1935
Tower Bridge, London 1960
oil on board 111.8 x 116.2
NCM 1966-61

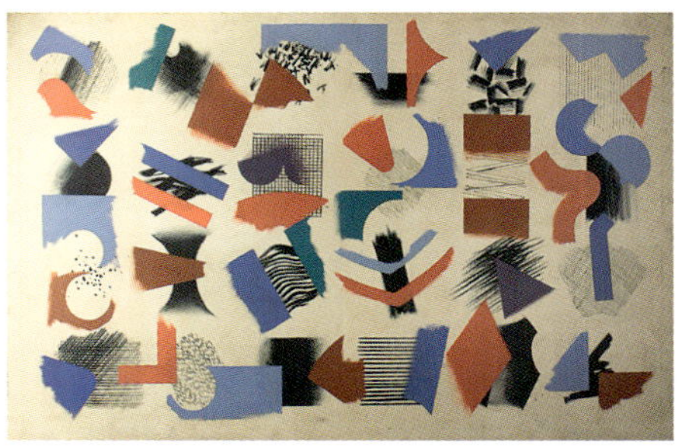

Culbert, Bill b.1935
Mediate 1963
oil on canvas 128 x 200
NCM 1966-60

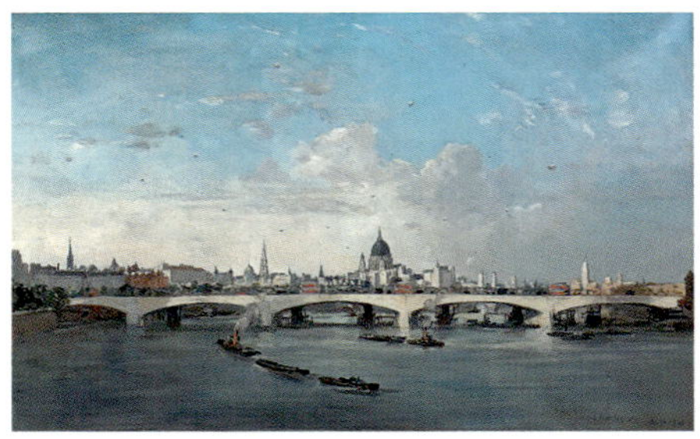

Cundall, Charles Ernest 1890–1971
Waterloo Bridge, London 1943
oil on canvas 45.7 x 76.2
NCM 1944-2

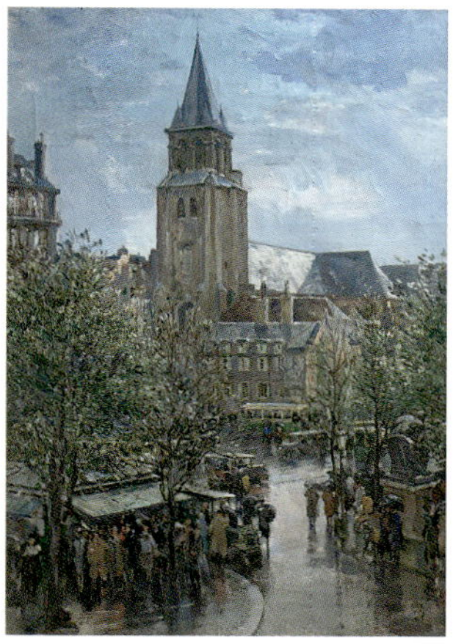

Cundall, Charles Ernest 1890–1971
The Church of St-Germain-des-Prés, Paris, France
oil on canvas 71.1 x 50.8
NCM 1943-7

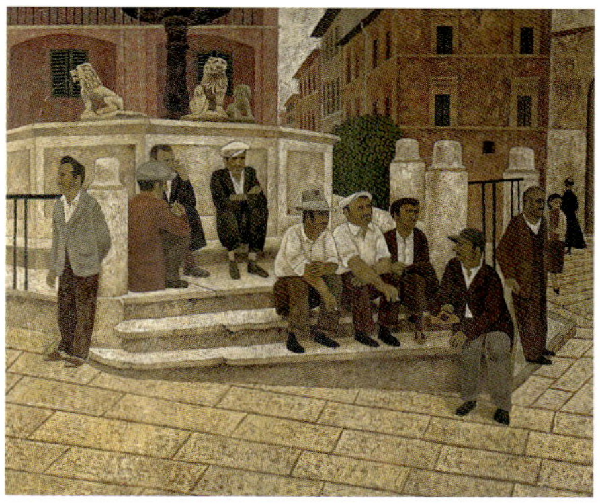

Daniels, Alfred b.1924
Town Square of Assisi, Italy
oil on wood 71.1 x 91.4
NCM 1959-92

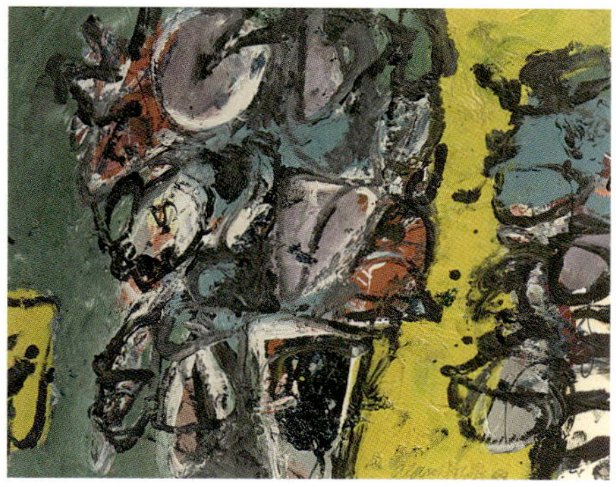

Davie, Alan b.1920
Bouquet for Couquet 1959
oil on board 41.9 x 53.3
NCM 1966-101

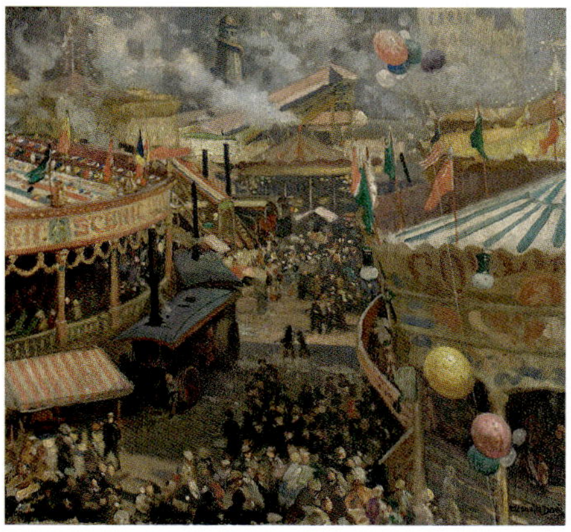

Davis, Noel Denholm 1876–1950
Nottingham Goose Fair c.1910
oil on canvas 45.7 x 50.8
NCM 1957-4

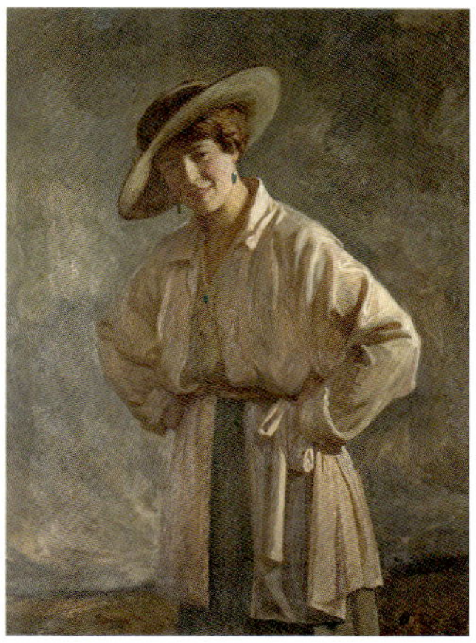

Davis, Noel Denholm 1876–1950
Lois Ball, Sister of Albert Ball, VC (later Mrs Anderson) c.1919
oil on canvas 109.9 x 79.9
NCM 1985-381

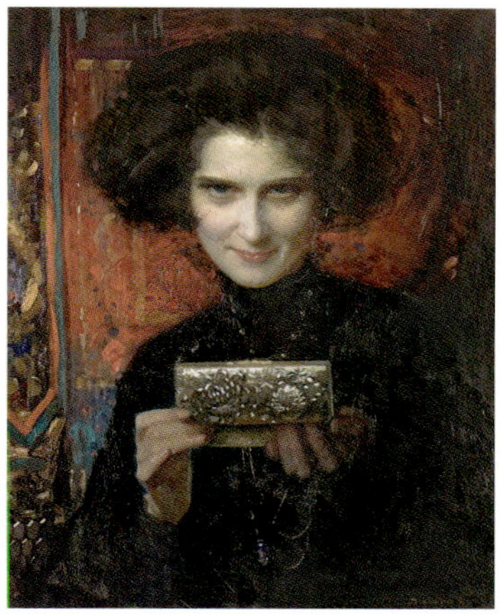

Davis, Noel Denholm 1876–1950
The Casket 1924
oil on canvas 76.2 x 61
NCM 1924-137

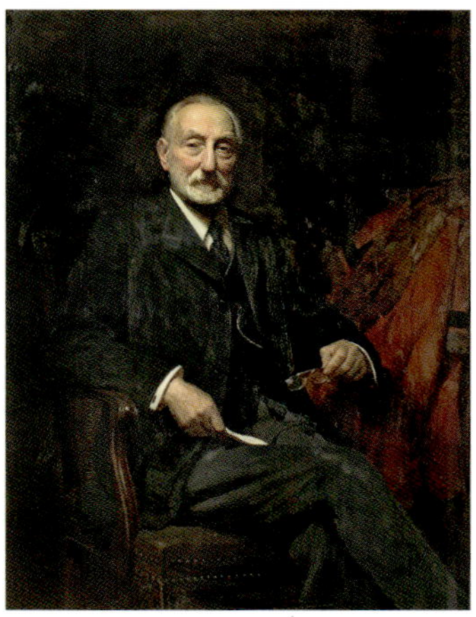

Davis, Noel Denholm 1876–1950
Alderman F. R. Radford 1925
oil on canvas 140.5 x 110.5
NCM 1990-626

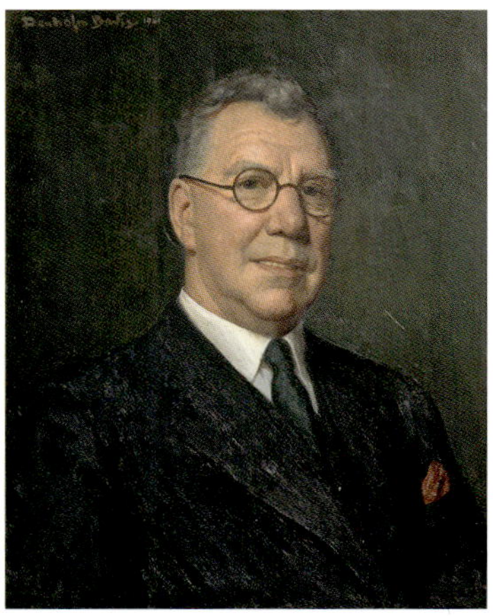

Davis, Noel Denholm 1876–1950
W. A. Spalding 1941
oil on canvas 59.5 x 49.5
NCM 1986-835

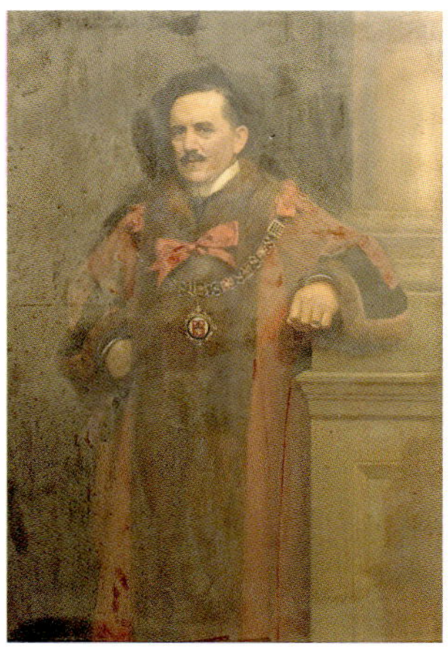

Davis, Noel Denholm 1876–1950
Albert Ball, JP, Mayor of Nottingham (1909–1910)
oil on canvas 152.5 x 107.5
NCM 1990-625

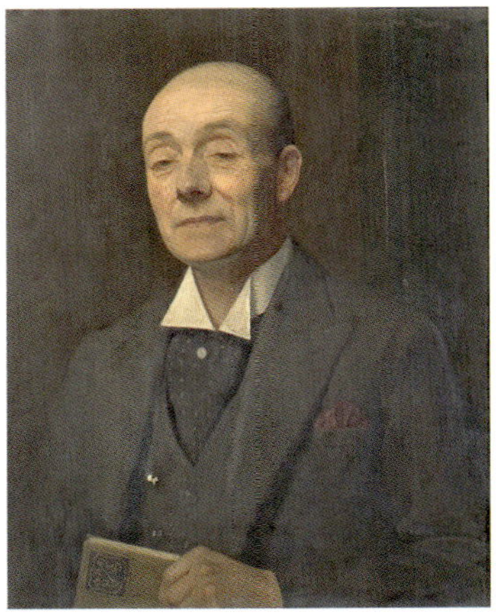

Davis, Noel Denholm 1876–1950
Edward P. Day, Master of Bingham Public Elementary School
oil on canvas 60 x 50
NCM 1993-622

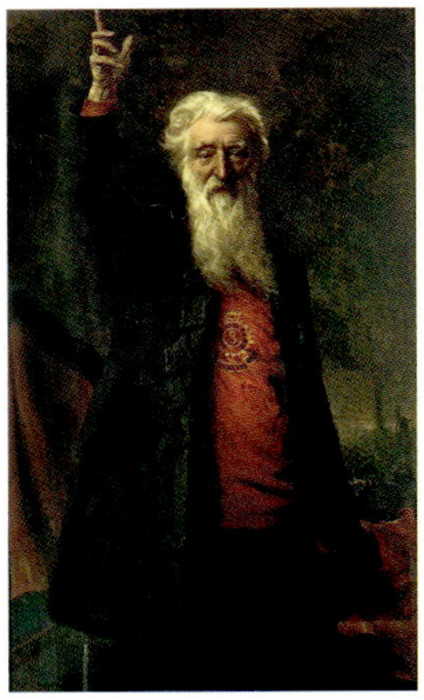

Davis, Noel Denholm 1876–1950
General William Booth (1829–1912), Founder of the Salvation Army
oil on canvas 178.4 x 101.6
NCM 1924-159

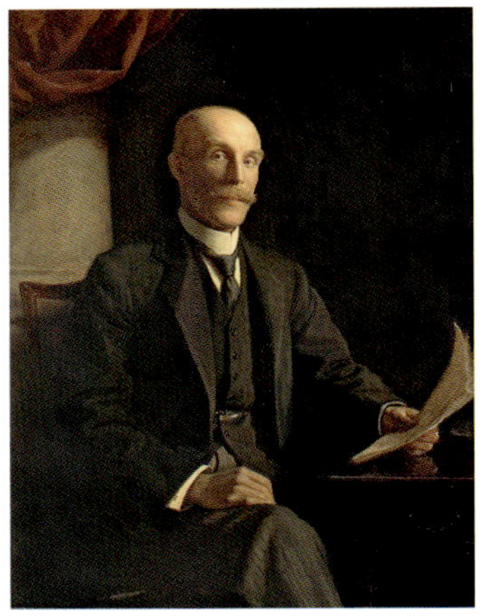

Davis, Noel Denholm 1876–1950
Sir John T. McCraith, JP
oil on canvas 124 x 100.5
NCM 1990-627

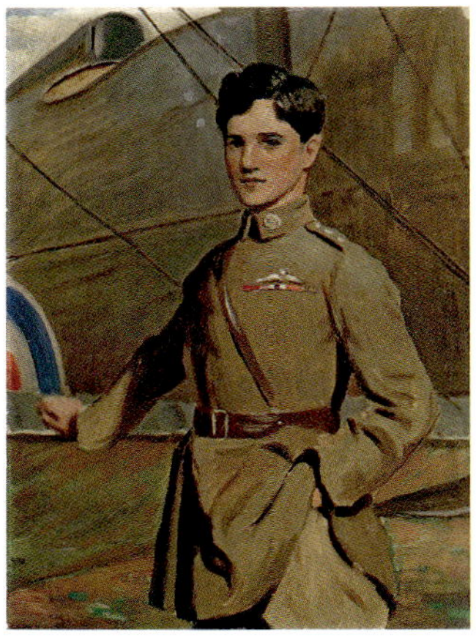

Davis, Noel Denholm 1876–1950
Study for 'Captain Albert Ball (1896–1917), VC'
oil on canvas 36.8 x 29.8
NCM 1962-76

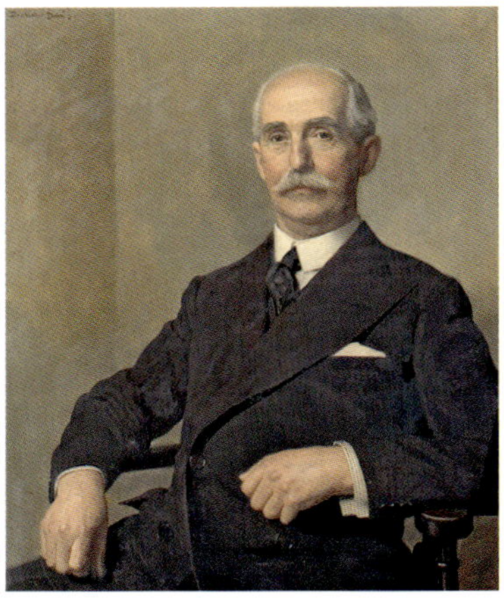

Davis, Noel Denholm 1876–1950
W. A. Spalding
oil on canvas 74 x 62.2
NCM 1986-835/(a-b)

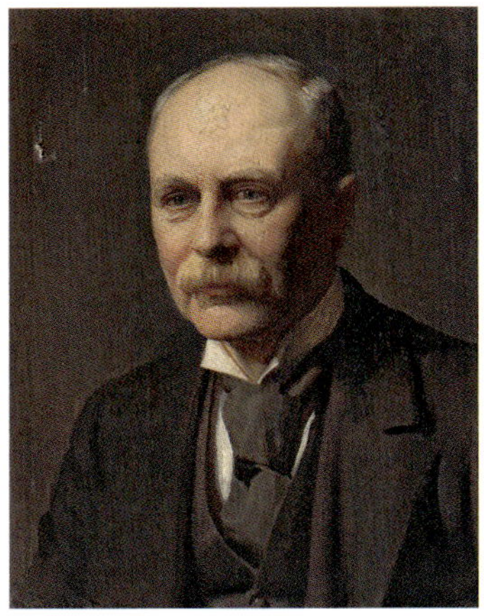

Davis, Noel Denholm 1876–1950
W. H. Hurcomb
oil on canvas 50.8 x 40.6
NCM 1967-248

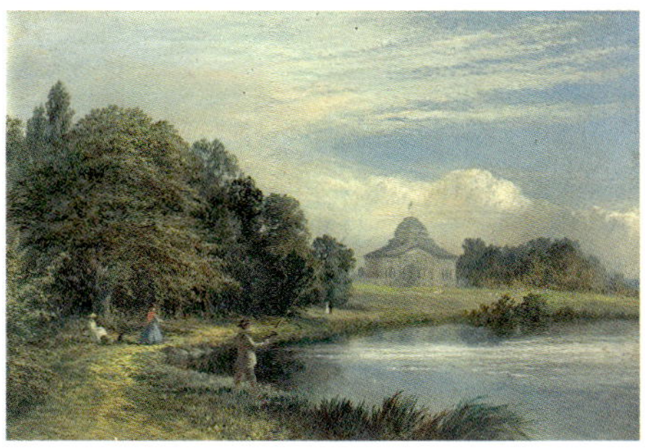

Dawson, Alfred b.1843
Nuthall Temple, Nottinghamshire 1869
oil on wood 15.2 x 22.9
NCM 1949-88

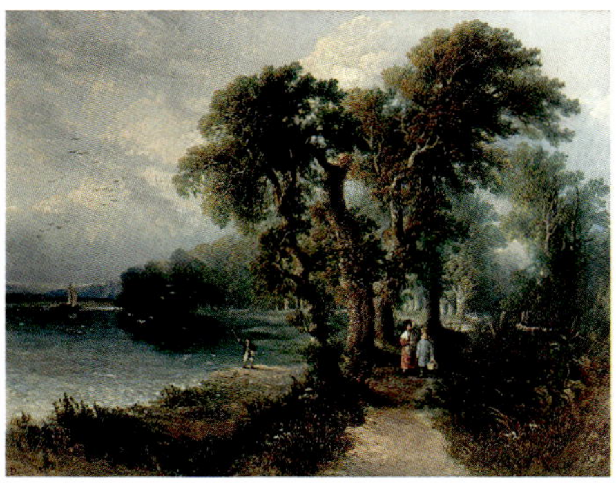

Dawson, Henry 1811–1878
Nottingham from Wilford Grove 1831
oil on canvas 67.4 x 90
NCM 1994-80

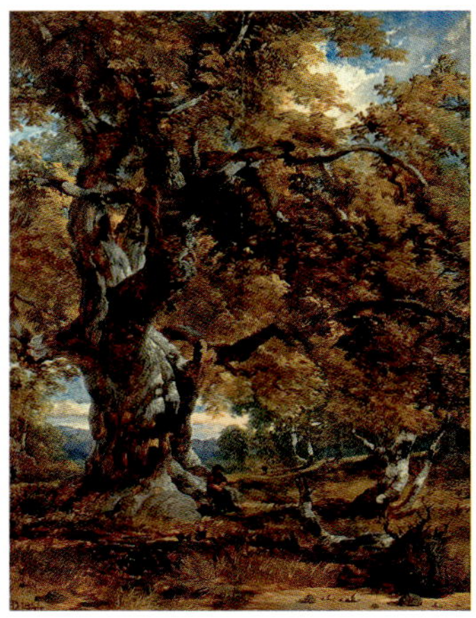

Dawson, Henry 1811–1878
The Major Oak 1844
oil on wood 76.2 x 62.9
NCM 1946-196

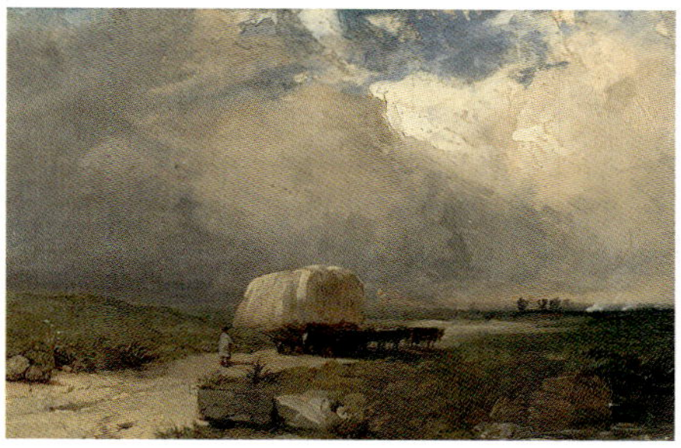

Dawson, Henry 1811–1878
The Carrier's Wagon c.1845
oil on canvas 39.4 x 59.7
NCM 1909-53

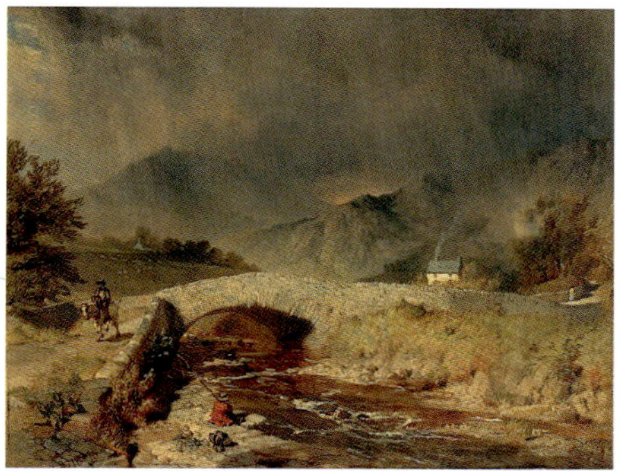

Dawson, Henry 1811–1878
Stormy Weather near Ambleside, Cumbria 1846
oil on canvas 44 x 54
NCM 1924-24

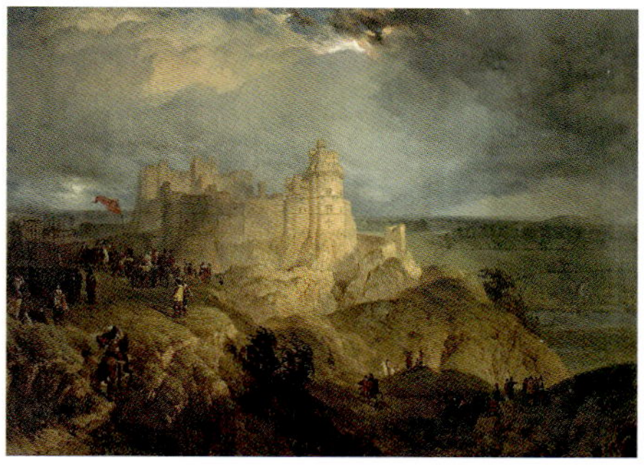

Dawson, Henry 1811–1878
Nottingham Castle (King Charles I Raising His Standard, 24 August 1642) 1847
oil on canvas 147.3 x 238.8
NCM 1912-58

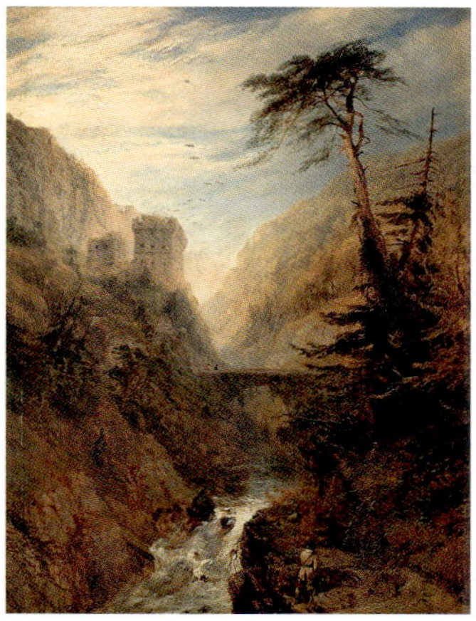

Dawson, Henry 1811–1878
A Derbyshire Dale 1849
oil on canvas 110.5 x 85.1
NCM 1940-17

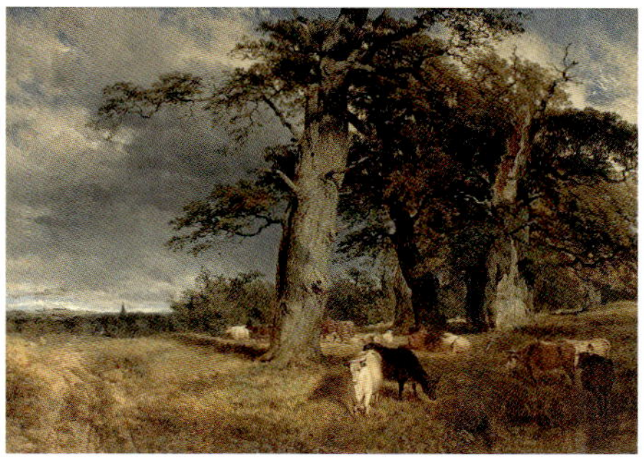

Dawson, Henry 1811–1878
Landscape in the Dukeries, Nottinghamshire 1850
oil on canvas 121.9 x 182.9
NCM 1904-8

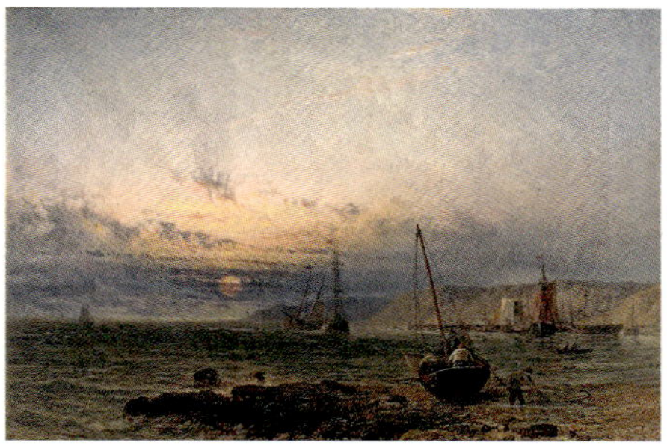

Dawson, Henry 1811–1878
Coast Scene, Sunset 1852
oil on canvas 40.6 x 60.6
NCM 1909-52

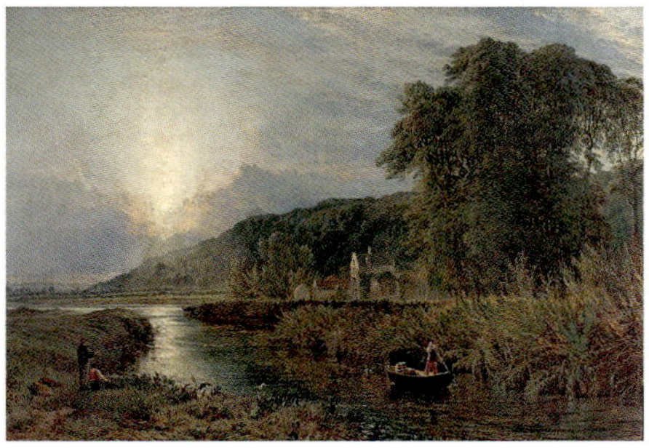

Dawson, Henry 1811–1878
The King's Mill, Castle Donington, Leicestershire 1862
oil on canvas 100.2 x 152.4
FA-X 2

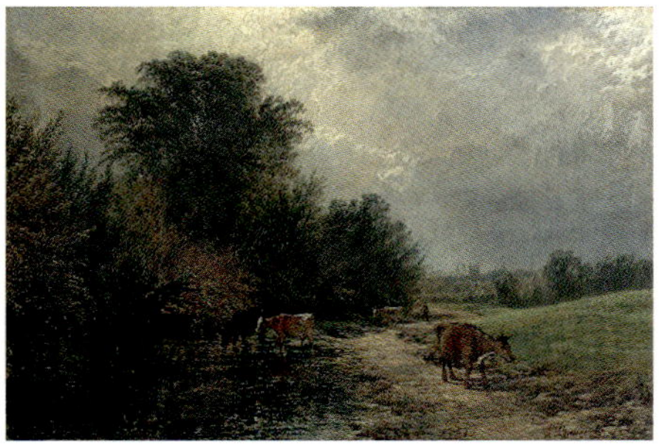

Dawson, Henry 1811–1878
Sunshine and Showers 1865
oil on canvas 40.6 x 61
NCM 1924-25

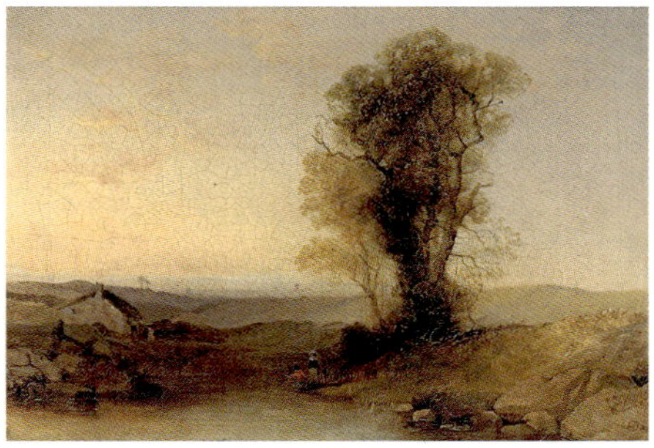

Dawson, Henry 1811–1878
Landscape
oil on canvas 30.5 x 45.7
NCM 1934-39

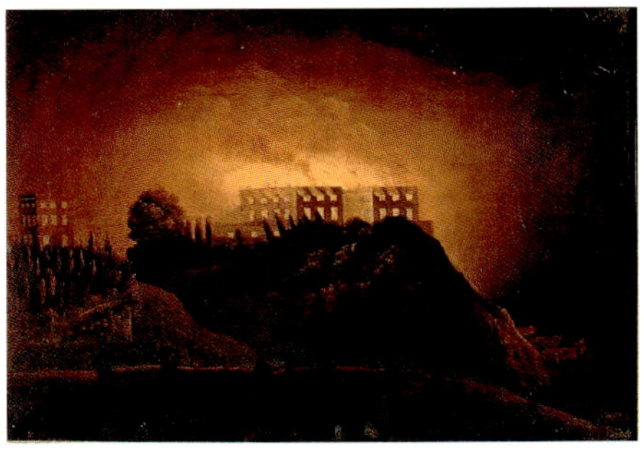

Dawson, Henry 1811–1878
Nottingham Castle on Fire, 10 October 1831
oil on canvas 47 x 67.9
NCM 1878-196

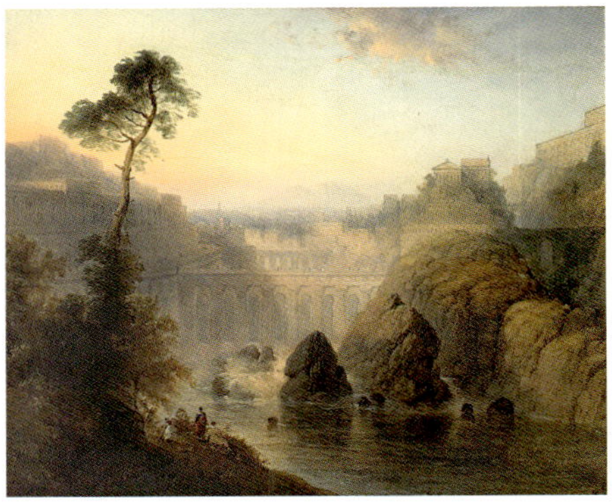

Dawson, Henry 1811–1878
On the Tiber, Italy
oil on canvas 73.7 x 91.4
NCM 1945-40

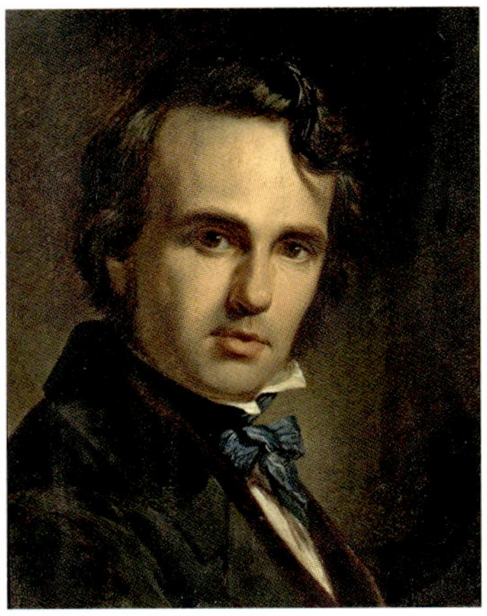

Dawson, Henry 1811–1878
Self Portrait
oil on canvas 50.8 x 40.6
NCM 1909-1

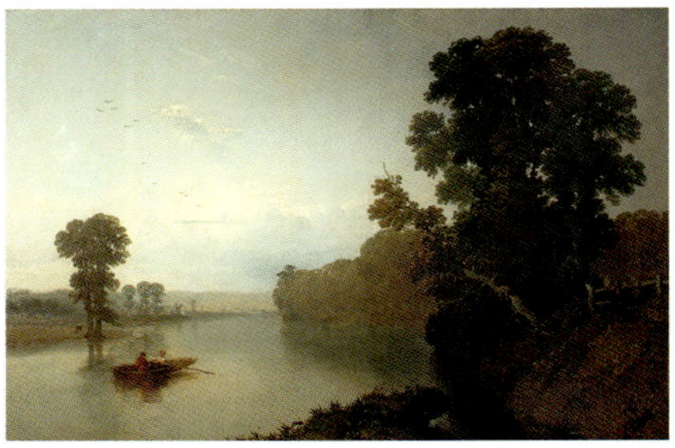

Dawson, Henry 1811–1878
The River Trent at Wilford
oil on canvas 86.3 x 132.1
NCM 1938-129

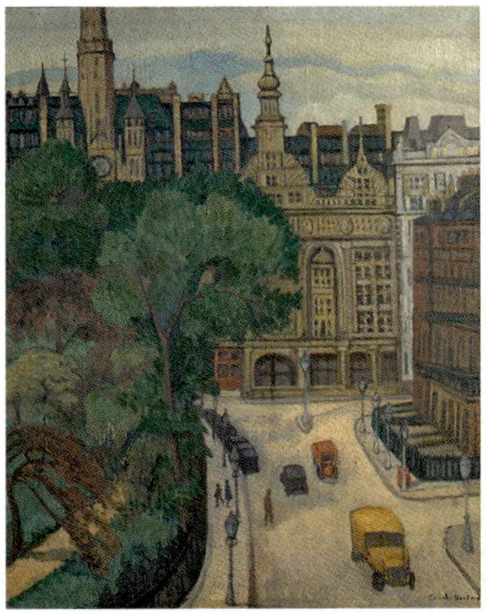

De Karlowska, Stanislawa 1876–1952
Imperial Hotel, Russell Square, London
oil on canvas 59.7 x 49.2
NCM 1968-329

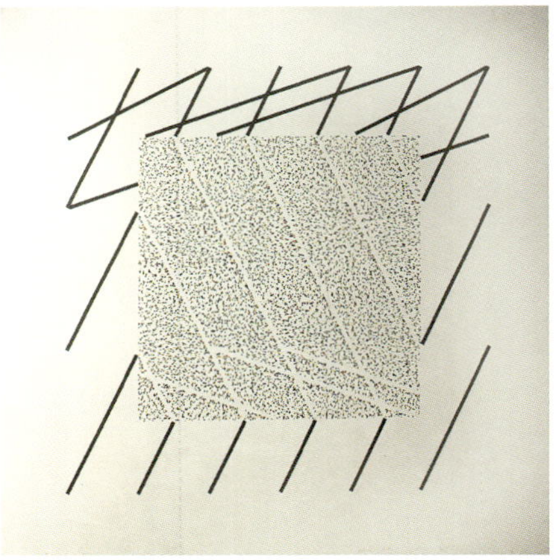

Deacon, Peter b.1945
Eclypse 2
acrylic on canvas 182.9 x 182.9
NCM 1975-227

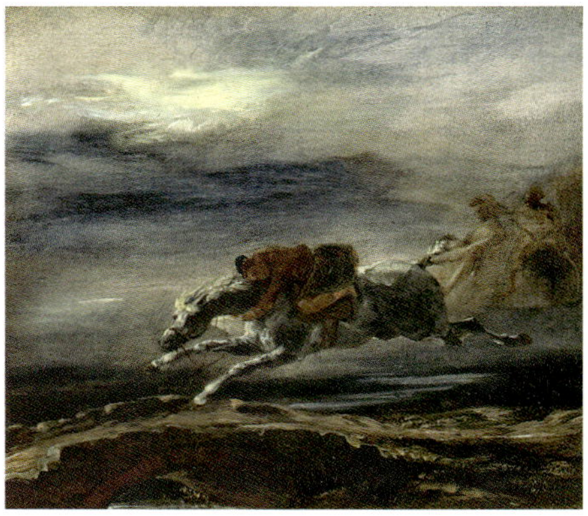

Delacroix, Eugène 1798–1863
Tam O'Shanter (after the poem by Robert Burns) 1825
oil on canvas 26.2 x 30.8
NCM 1980-195

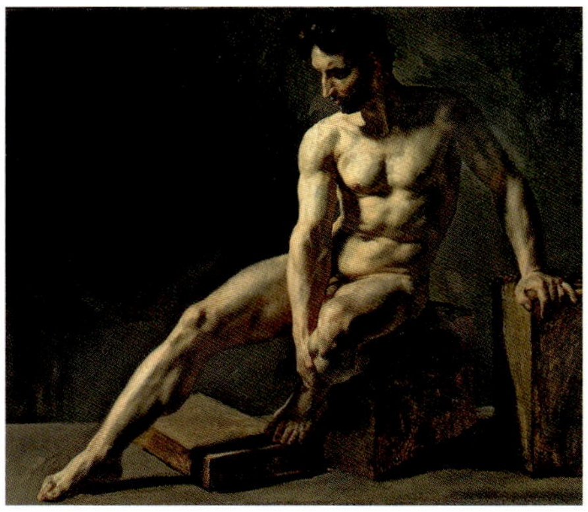

Detaille, Jean Baptiste Edouard 1848–1912
Seated Male Nude
oil on canvas 67.3 x 81.2
NCM 1941-2

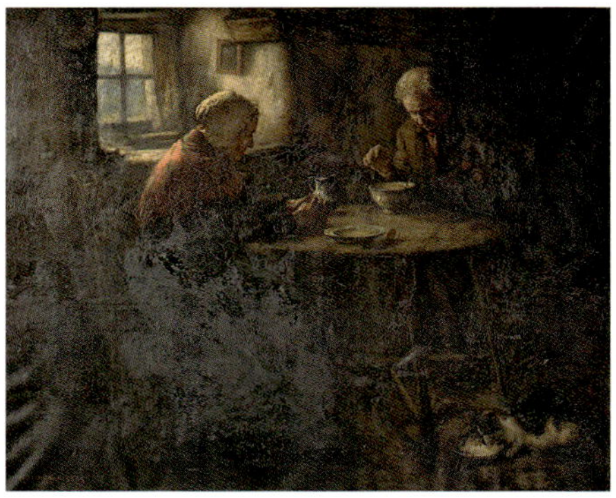

Dobson, Henry John 1858–1928
Burn's Grace
oil on canvas 101.6 x 127
NCM 1926-129

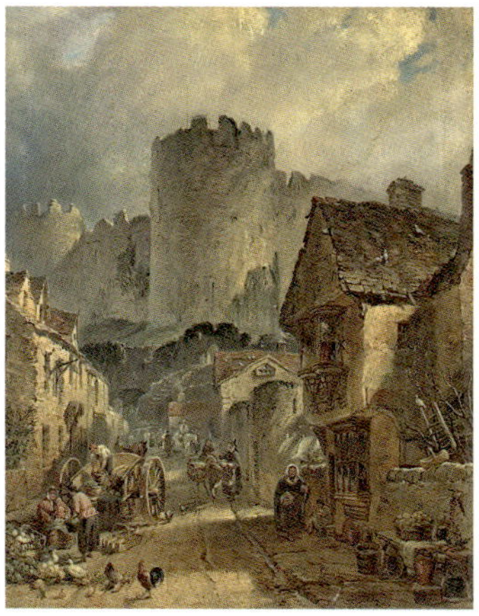

Dodd, Charles Tattershall I 1815–1878
Conway Castle, North Wales 1861
oil on canvas 61.6 x 51.4
NCM 1890-1203

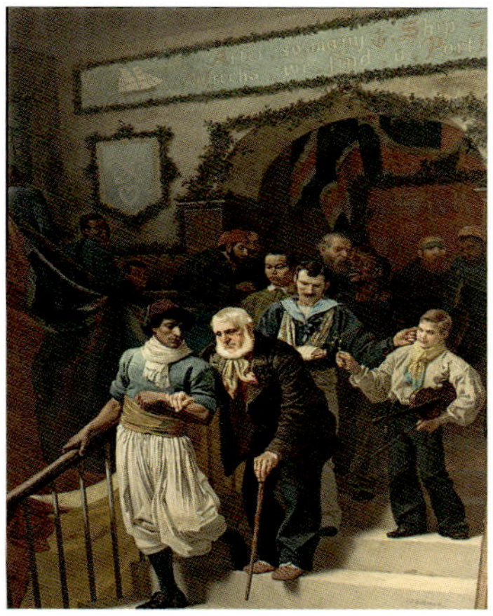

Dollman, John Charles 1851–1934
Friends in Adversity, Christmas Day at the Dreadnought Hospital, Greenwich (Coming Down to Dinner) 1880
oil on canvas 254 x 193
NCM 1882-2

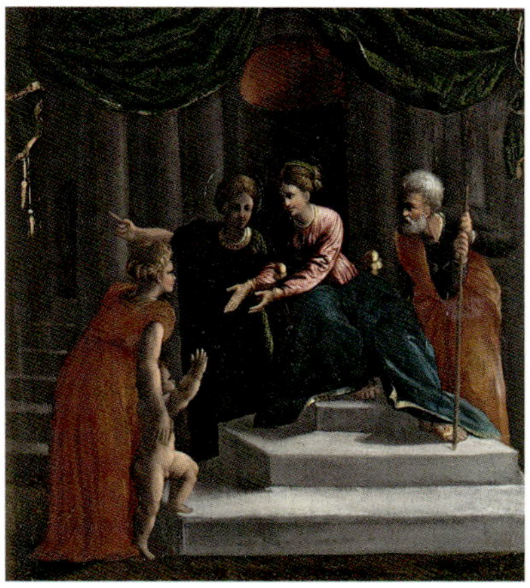

Dossi, Dosso c.1486–1542
The Christ Child Learning to Walk (Presentation in the Temple)
oil on wood 43.9 x 41.9
NCM 1910-65

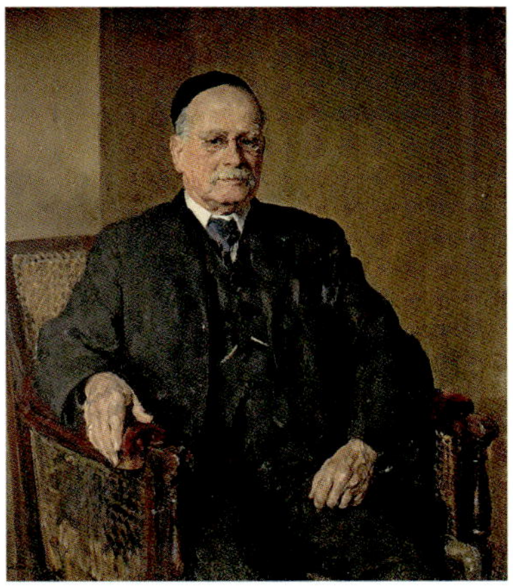

Dugdale, Thomas Cantrell 1880–1952
George Harry Wallis
oil on canvas 101.6 x 91.4
NCM 1930-1

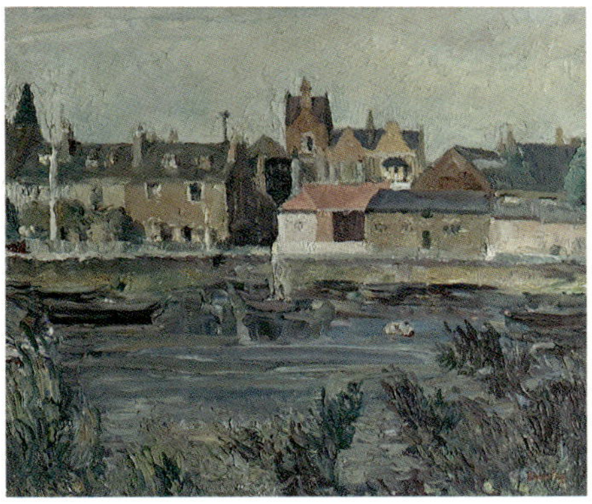

Dunlop, Ronald Ossory 1894–1973
Strand-on-the-Green, Chiswick, London
oil on canvas 63.5 x 76.2
NCM 1939-60

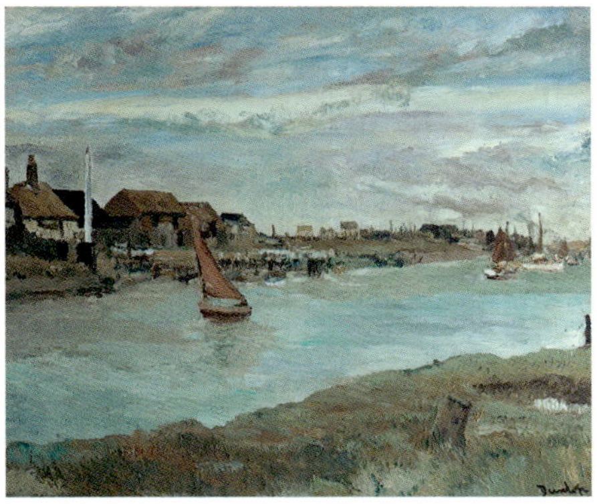

Dunlop, Ronald Ossory 1894–1973
Walberswick, Suffolk
oil on canvas 63.5 x 76.2
NCM 1939-59

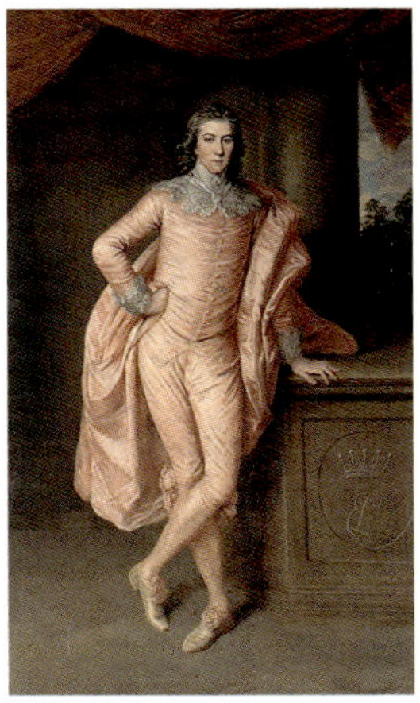

Dupont, Gainsborough 1754–1797
Henry Fiennes Pelham Clinton (1750–1778), Earl of Lincoln
oil on canvas 270 x 146
NCM 1982-642

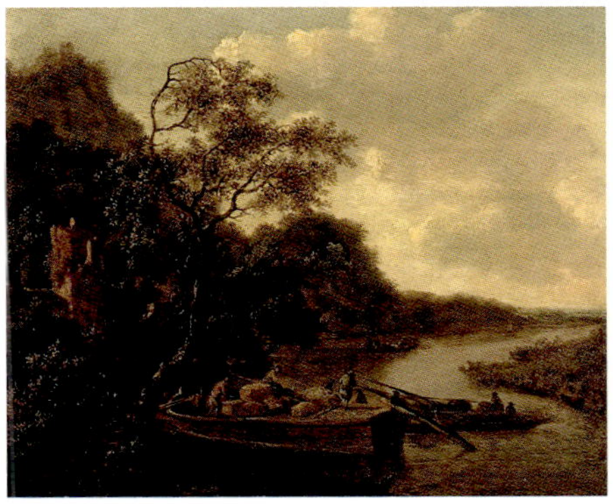

Dutch School 17th C
River Scene with Boat
oil on wood 31 x 40
NCM 1907-128

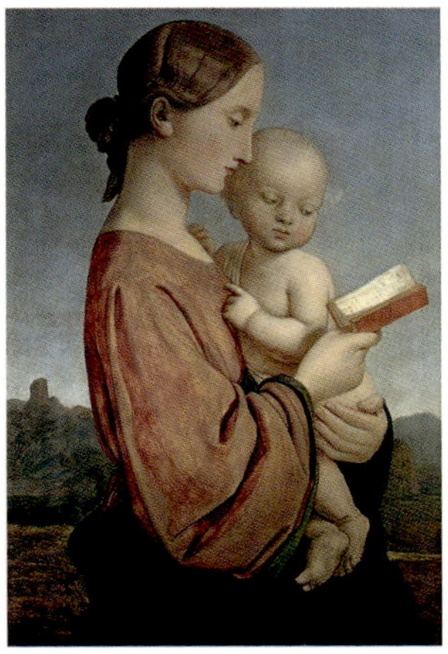

Dyce, William 1806–1864
Virgin and Child
oil on plaster 78.7 x 60.3
NCM 1910-53

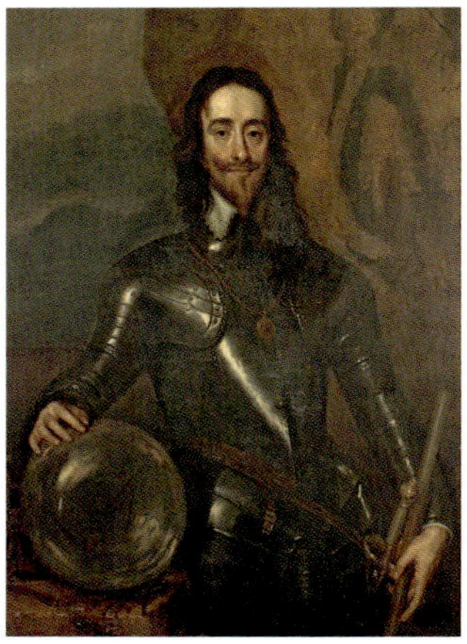

Dyck, Anthony van (after) 1599–1641
Charles I (1600–1649)
oil on canvas 128.2 x 101.6
NCM 1952-19

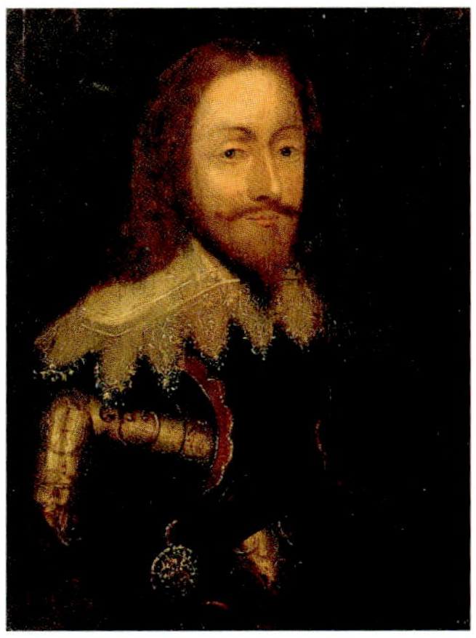

Dyck, Anthony van (after) 1599–1641
Charles I (1600–1649), in Armour Wearing the Order of the Thistle
oil on wood 31.8 x 24.1
NCM 1899-4

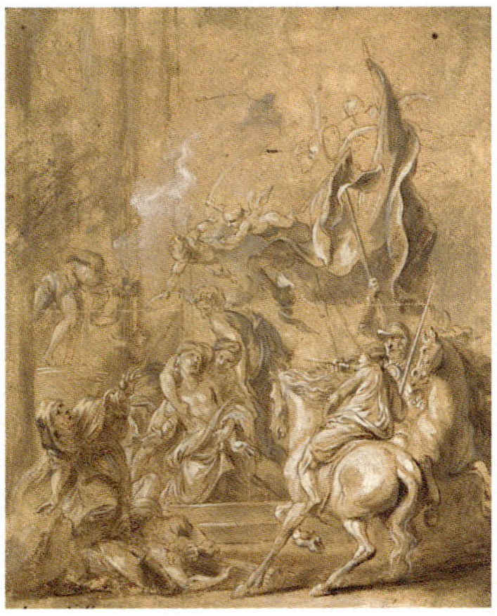

Dyck, Anthony van (after) 1599–1641
The Converion of Saul
oil & sepia on paper 23.8 x 19.7
NCM 1911-53

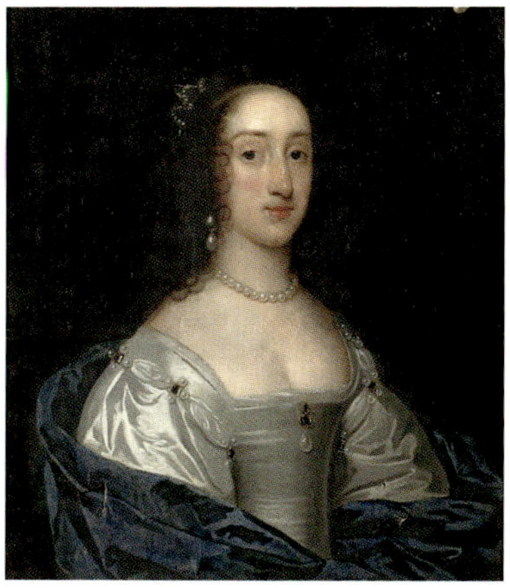

Dyck, Anthony van (attributed to) 1599–1641
Queen Henrietta Maria (1609–1669)
oil on canvas 70 x 57
FALOAN 100

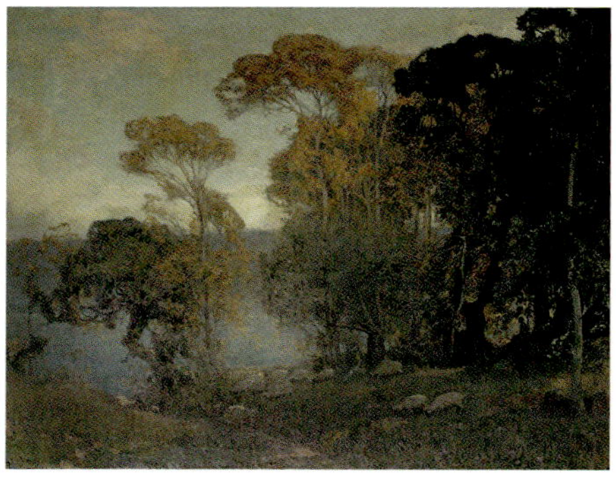

East, Alfred 1844–1913
The Shepherd's Walk, Windermere, Cumbria
oil on canvas 152.4 x 190.5
NCM 1909-23

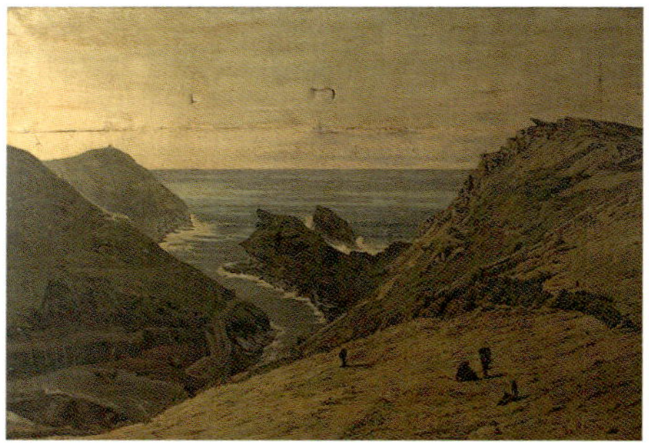

Edwards, Edwin 1823–1879
Boscastle Harbour, Cornwall
oil on canvas 121.9 x 182.9
NCM 1905-6

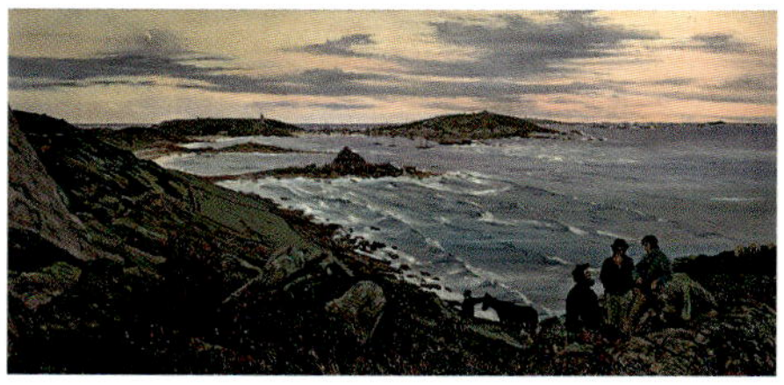

Edwards, Edwin 1823–1879
St Mary's, Scilly Isles
oil on canvas 66 x 144.8
NCM 1905-9

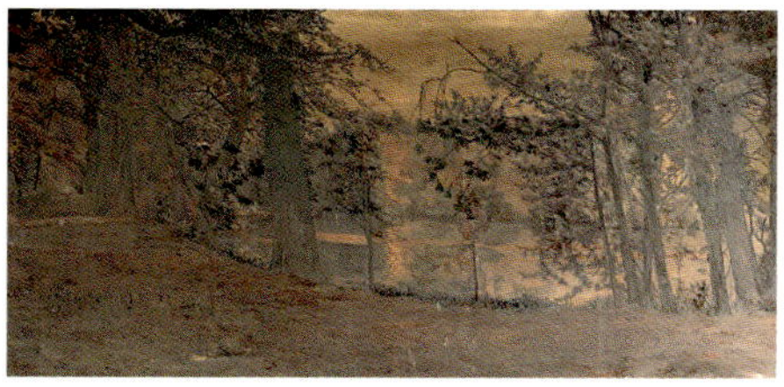

Edwards, Edwin 1823–1879
The Pond, Kempton, Middlesex
oil on canvas 87.6 x 184.2
NCM 1905-7

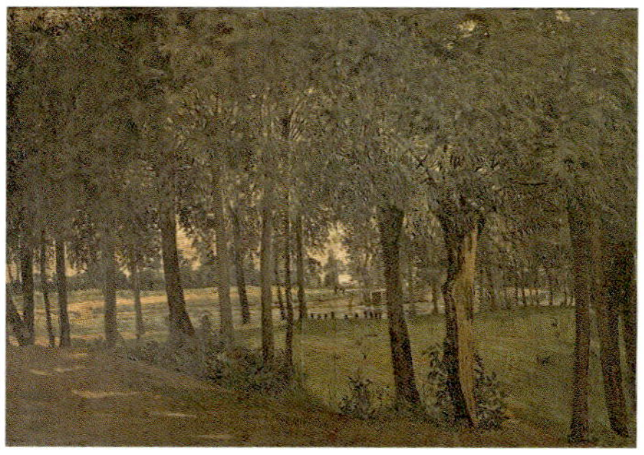

Edwards, Edwin 1823–1879
Under the Willows, Sunbury-on-Thames, Middlesex
oil on canvas 64.1 x 94
NCM 1905-8

Facing page: Davis, Noel Denholm, 1876–1950, *The Casket* (detail), 1924, Nottingham City Museums and Galleries (p. 85)

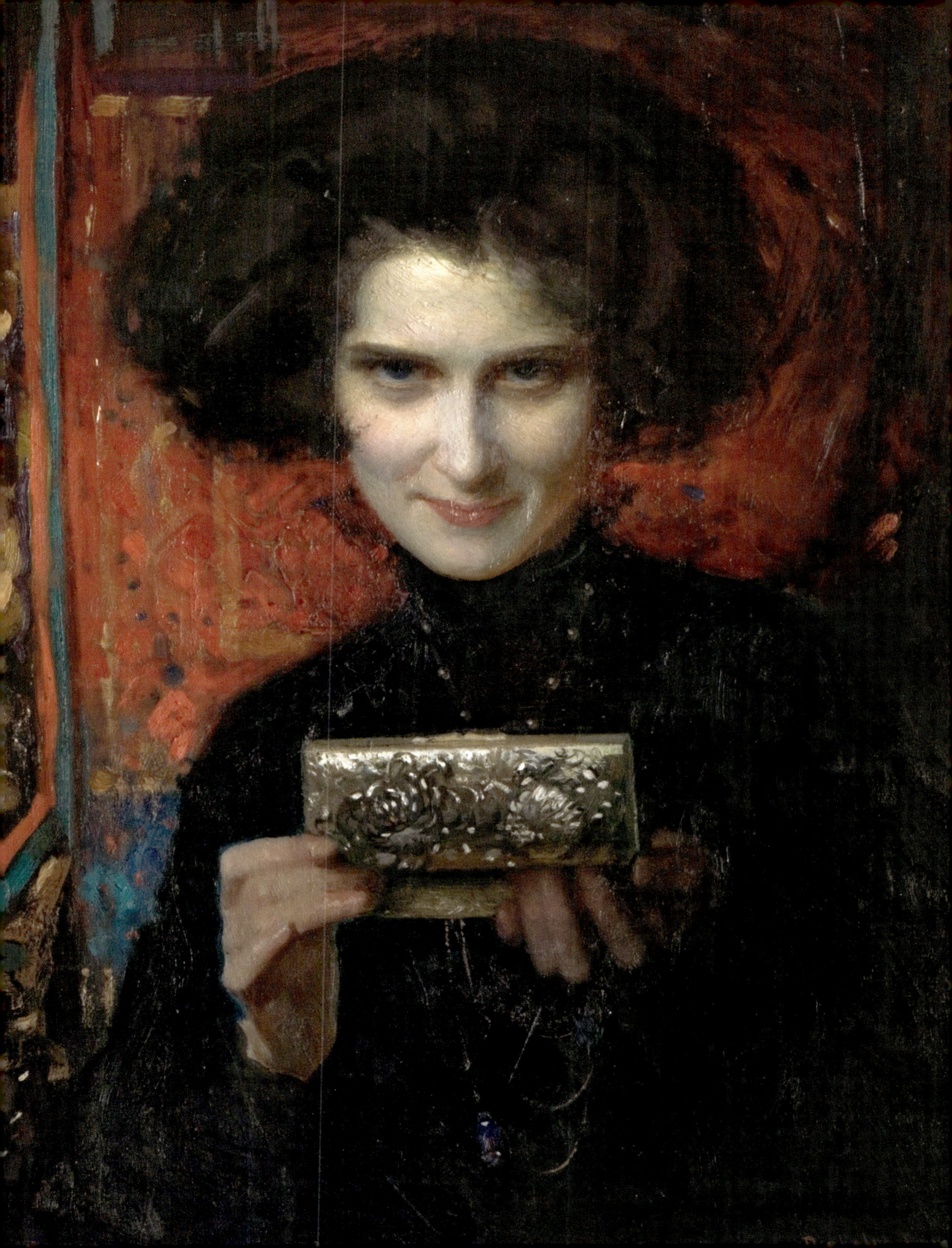

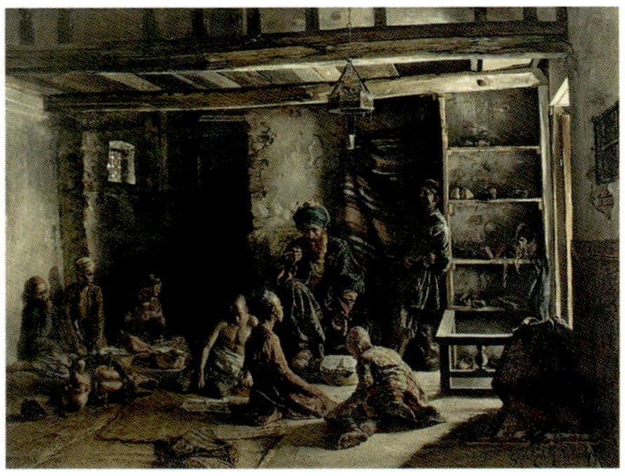

Eisenhut, Ferencz 1857–1903
An Oriental School 1885
oil on canvas 137.1 x 181.6
NCM 1932-11

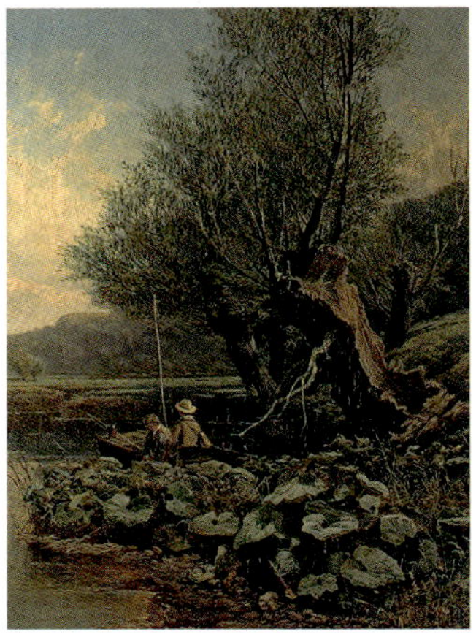

Ellis, Edwin 1841–1895
Young Anglers 1868
oil on canvas 41.9 x 35.6
NCM 1946-258

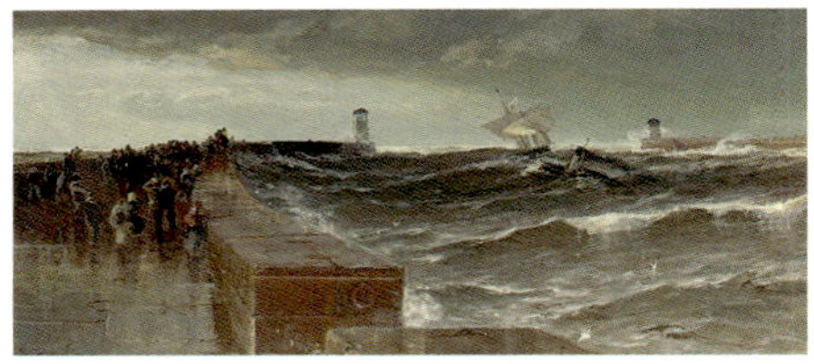

Ellis, Edwin 1841–1895
After Three Days Gale 1885
oil on canvas 102.5 x 193.5
NCM 1897-60

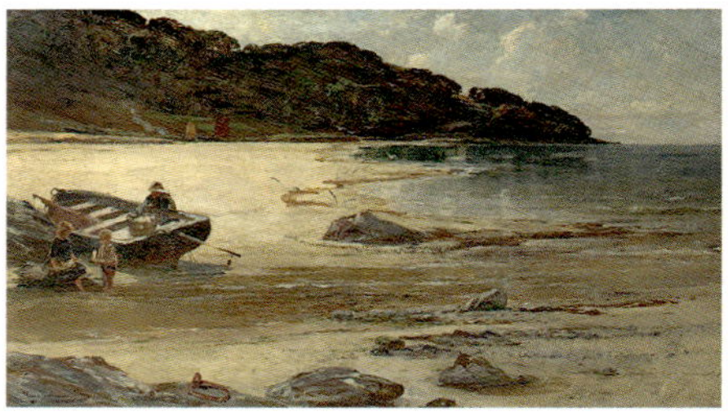

Ellis, Edwin 1841–1895
Coast Scene 1891
oil on canvas 71.1 x 127
NCM 1934-33

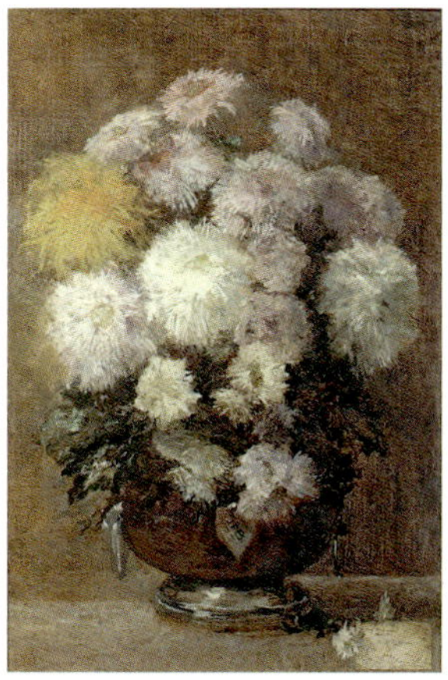

Ellis, Edwin 1841–1895
Chrysanthemums 1892
oil on canvas 77.5 x 50.8
NCM 1914-19

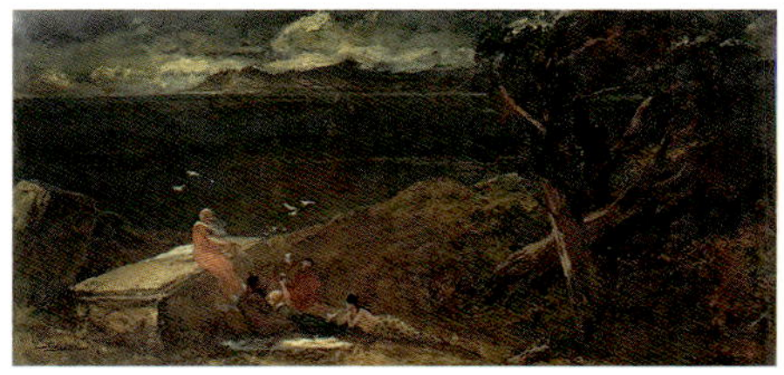

Ellis, Edwin 1841–1895
Circe (recto)
oil on canvas 71.1 x 153.7
NCM 1938-128

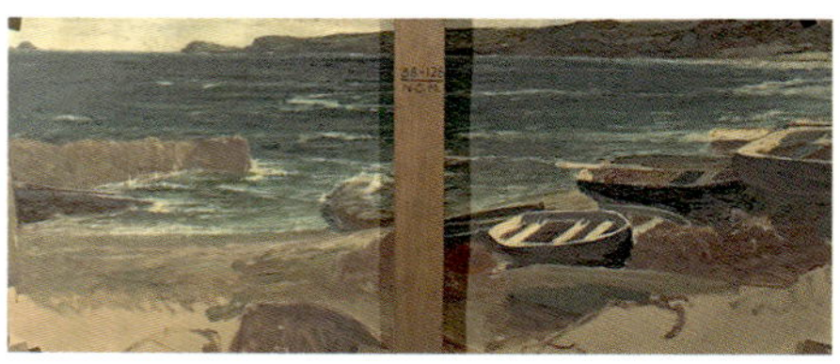

Ellis, Edwin 1841–1895
Boats on the Sand (verso)
oil on canvas 71.1 x 153.7
NCM 1938-128

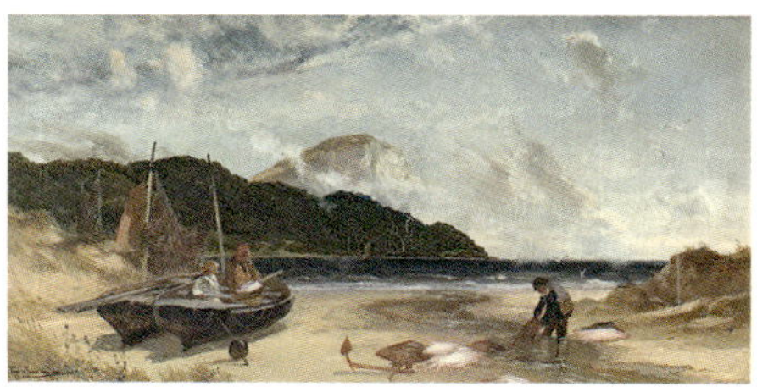

Ellis, Edwin 1841–1895
Fisherfolk
oil on canvas 45.7 x 91.4
NCM 1945-83

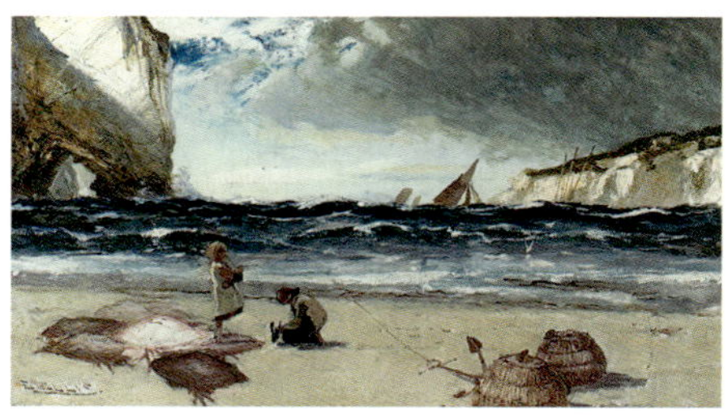

Ellis, Edwin 1841–1895
The Lobster Pots
oil on canvas 45.7 x 83.8
NCM 1945-84

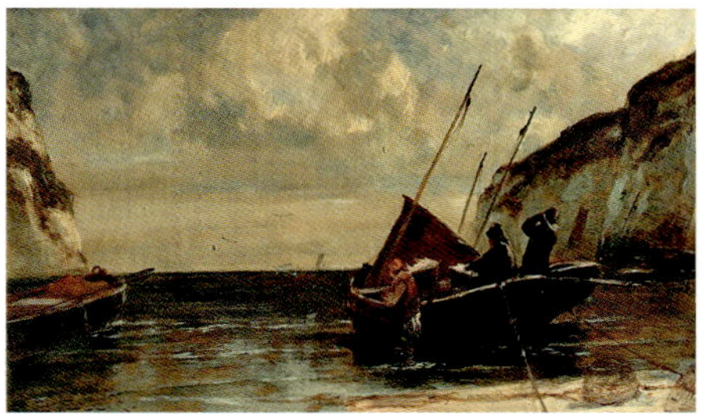

Ellis, Edwin 1841–1895
Unloading the Catch
oil on canvas 45.7 x 81.3
NCM 1946-259

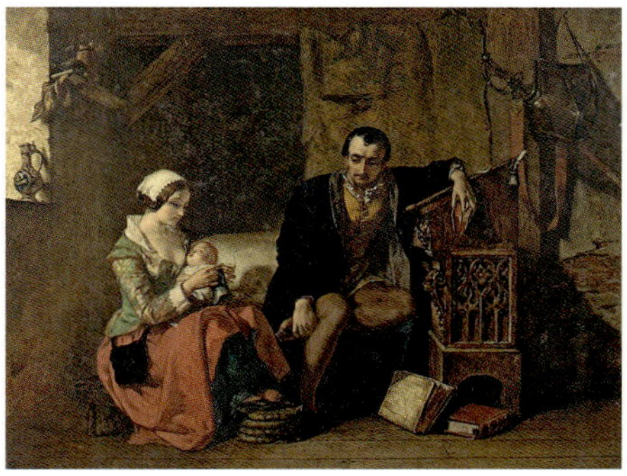

Elmore, Alfred 1815–1881
The Origin of the Stocking Loom 1847
oil on canvas 80 x 106.7
NCM 1940-28

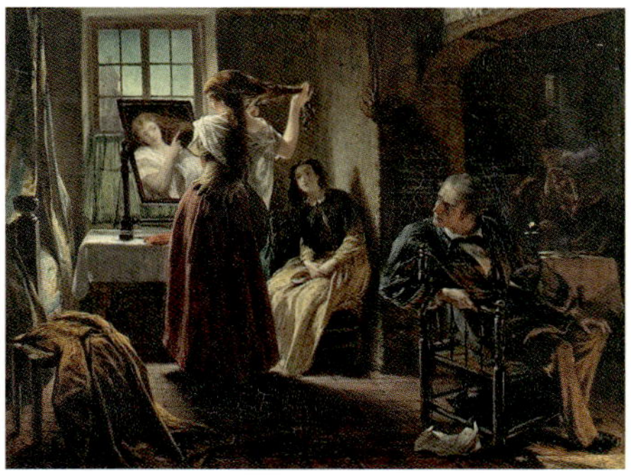

Elmore, Alfred 1815–1881
The Origin of the Combing Machine
oil on canvas 32.9 x 43.7
NCM 1968-411

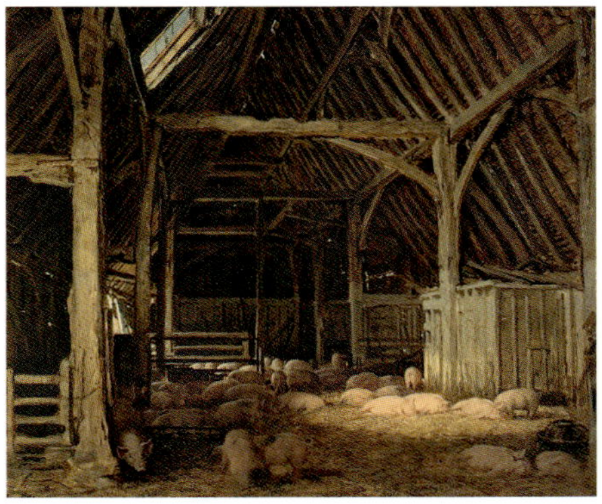

Elwell, Frederick William 1870–1958
An Interior of a Barn
oil on canvas 61.6 x 74.9
NCM 1944-3

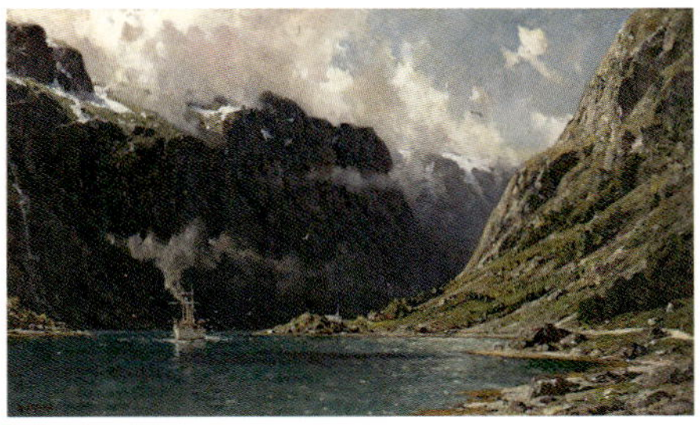

Enfield, Henry 1849–1911
Nærøyfjord, Norway 1902
oil on canvas 59.7 x 94
NCM 1902-31

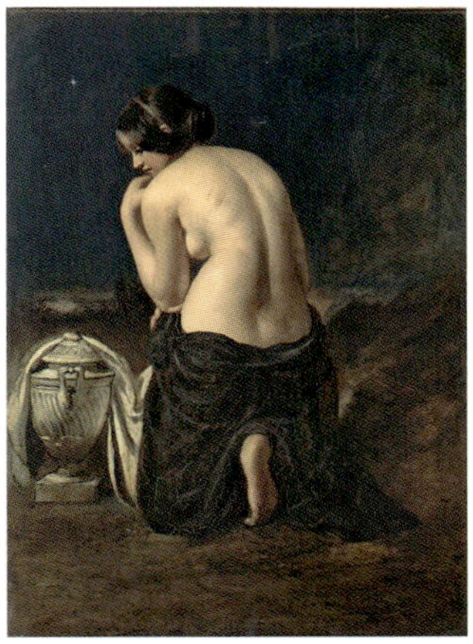

Etty, William 1787–1849
The Mourner 1842
oil on canvas 63.5 x 48.3
NCM 1904-29

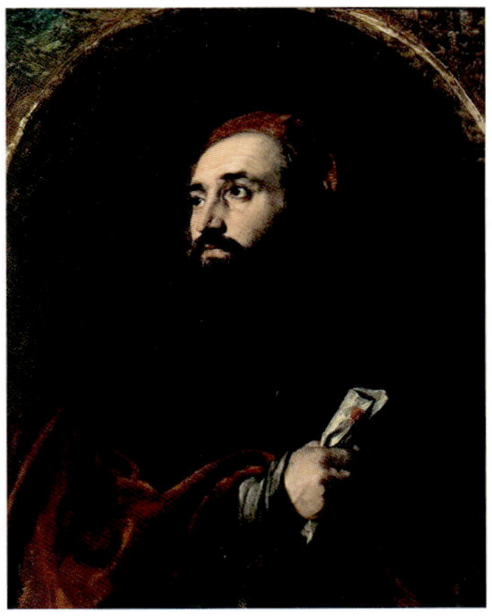

Etty, William 1787–1849
A Jew's Head
oil on canvas 76.5 x 64.1
NCM 1904-30

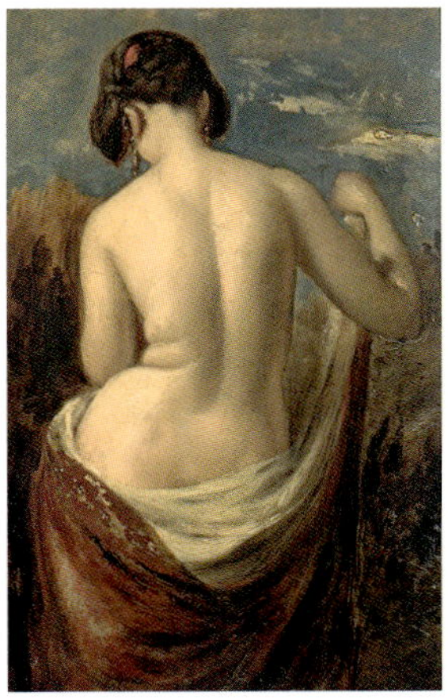

Etty, William 1787–1849
Study of a Half-Nude Figure
oil on canvas 54 x 35.6
NCM 1904-31

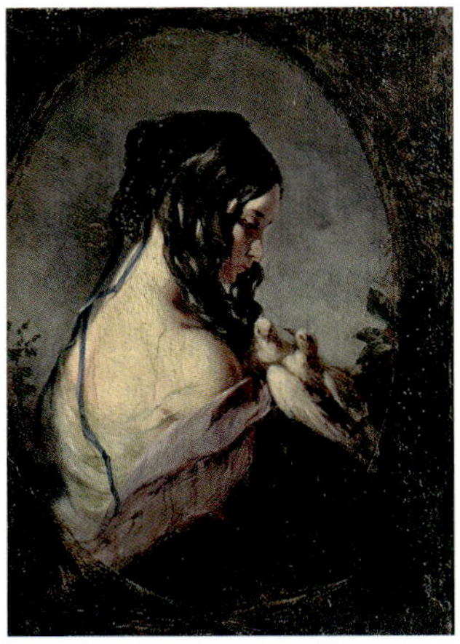

Etty, William 1787–1849
The Doves
oil on wood 28.6 x 20.3
NCM 1909-50

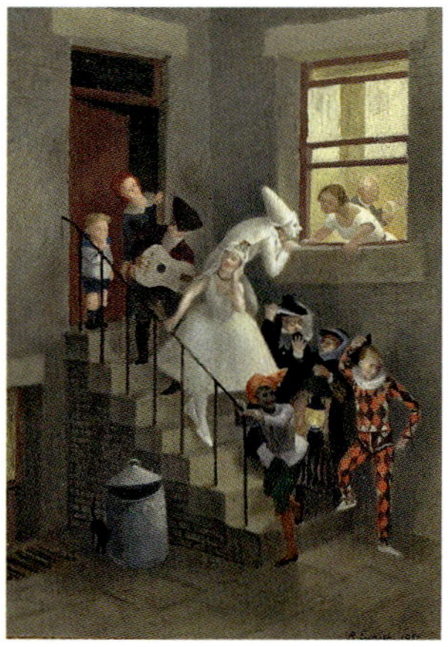

Eurich, Richard Ernst 1903–1992
The Mummers 1951
oil on board 21 x 15.9
NCM 1952-14

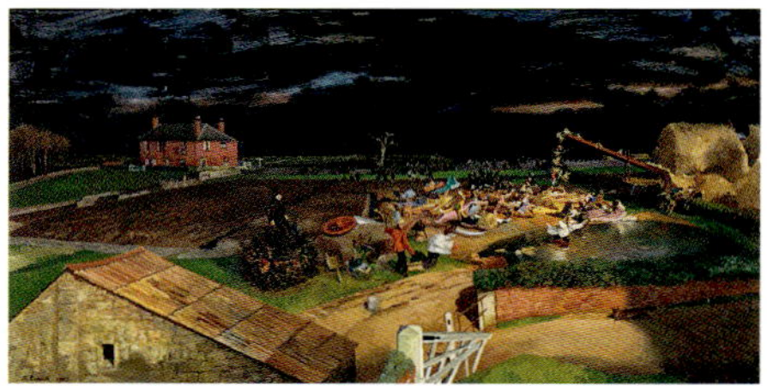

Eurich, Richard Ernst 1903–1992
Men of Straw 1957
oil on wood 50.8 x 101.6
NCM 1958-30

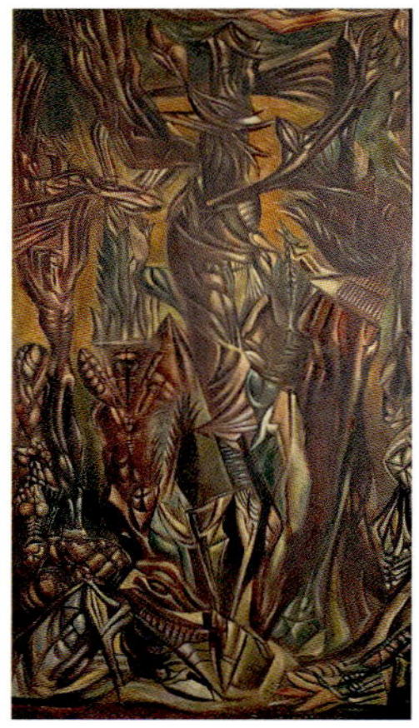

Evans, Merlyn Oliver 1910–1973
Crucifixion 1945
tempera on canvas 116.2 x 70.5
NCM 1952-17

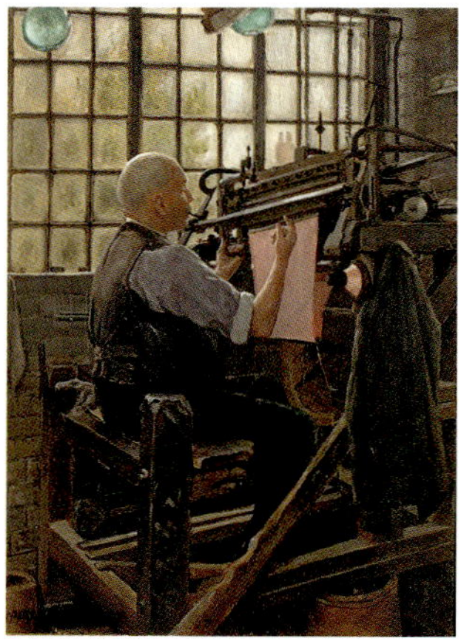

Farmer, Walter 1870–1947
The Stockinger 1911
oil on board 38.1 x 27.9
NCM 1912-67

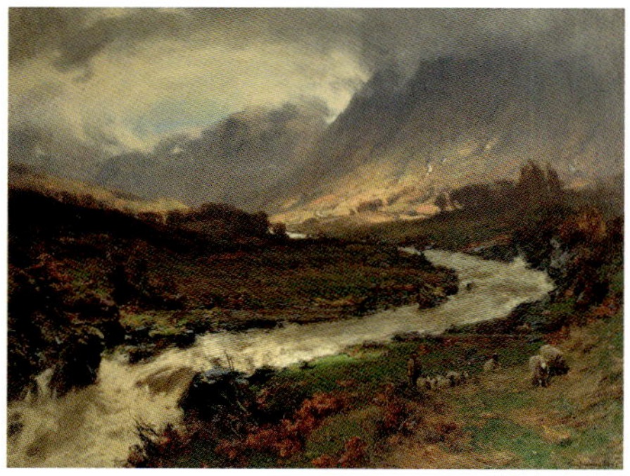

Farquharson, David 1839–1907
A Break in the Storm, Glen Lyon, Perthshire, Scotland 1891–1892
oil on canvas 122.2 x 184.2
NCM 1930-20

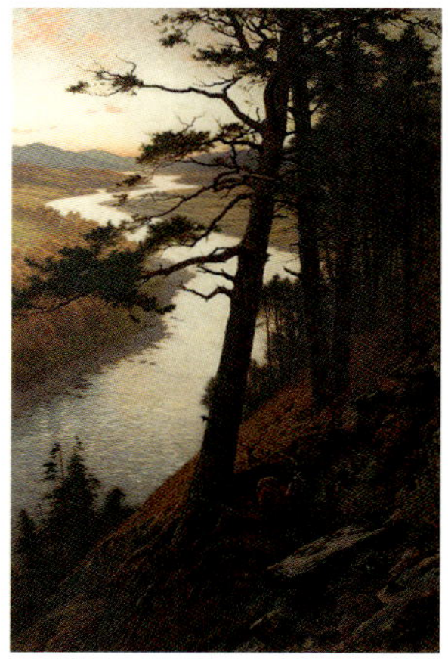

Farquharson, Joseph 1846–1935
The Winding Dee 1889
oil on canvas 182.9 x 121.9
NCM 1906-25

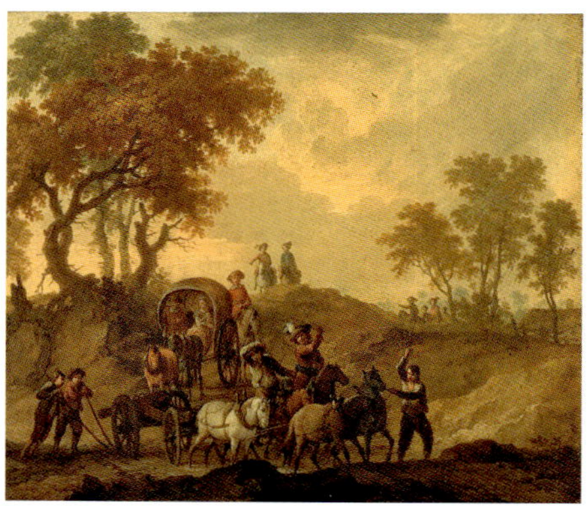

Ferg, Franz de Paula 1689–1740
Landscape with Baggage Wagon
oil on metal 16.2 x 20.3
NCM 1904-117

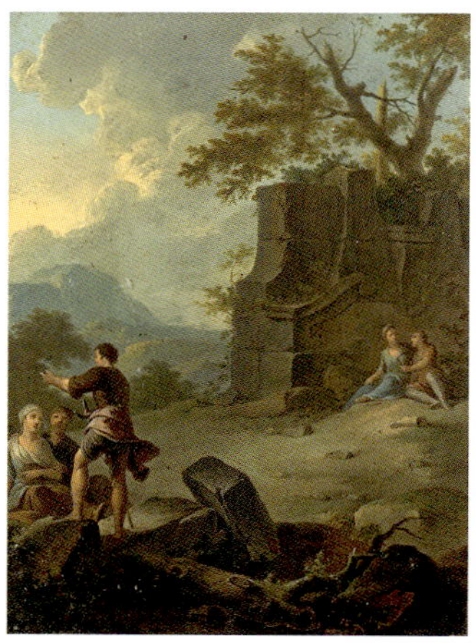

Ferg, Franz de Paula 1689–1740
Landscape with Figures and Ruins
oil on metal 26 x 21
NCM 1904-118

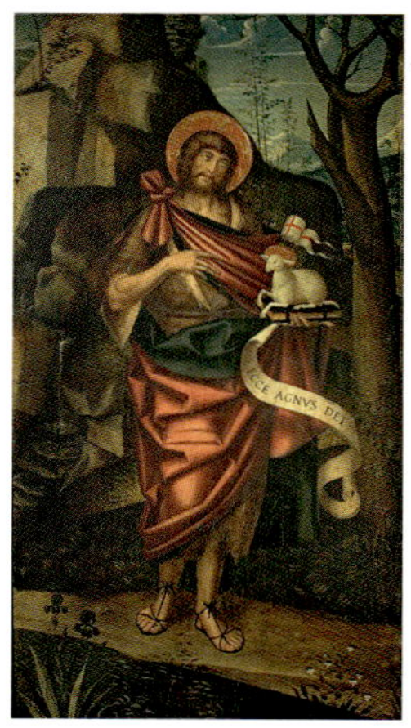

Ferrari, Defendente 1480–1485–c.1540
St John the Baptist in the Wilderness (recto) c.1520
oil on wood 154.3 x 92.1
NCM 1910-63

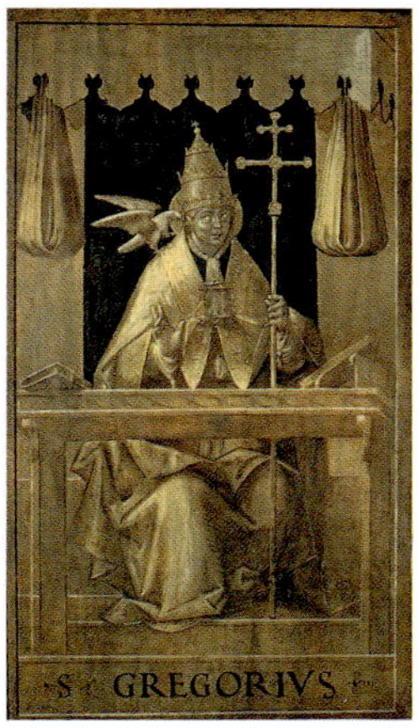

Ferrari, Defendente 1480–1485–c.1540
St Gregory in His Study (verso) c.1520
oil on wood 154.3 x 92.1
NCM 1910-63

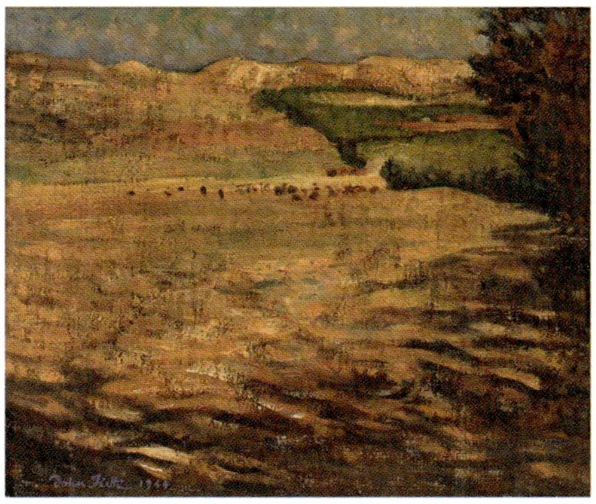

Firth, John H. S. 1912–c.1970
Orange Groves 1944
oil on canvas 33 x 40.4
NCM 1985-1173

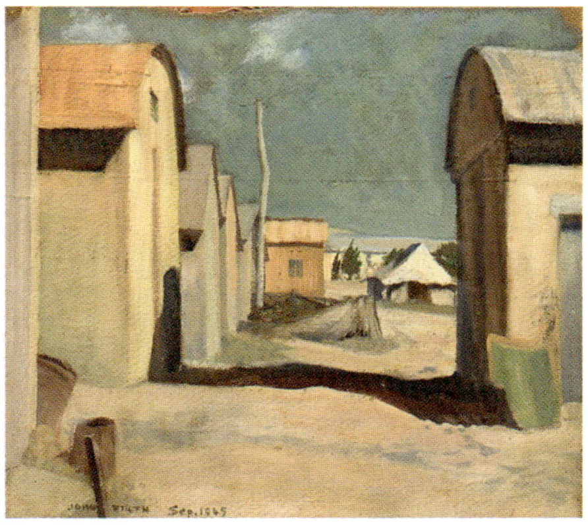

Firth, John H. S. 1912–c.1970
Deir Suneid, near Gaza, Palestine 1945
oil on canvas 26 x 30
NCM 1985-1382

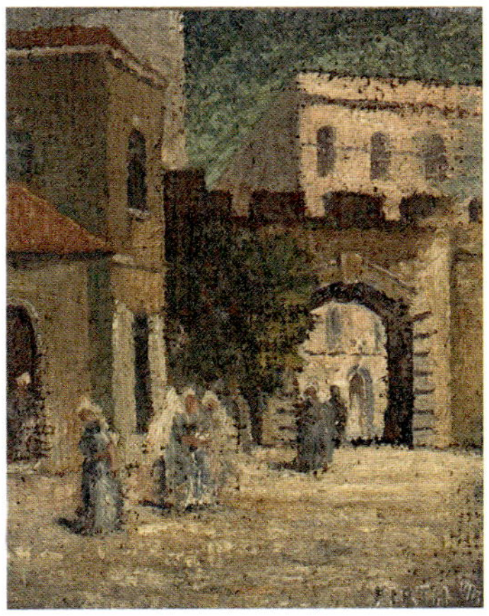

Firth, John H. S. 1912–c.1970
Inside New Gate, Jerusalem, Palestine 1947
oil on hessian 20 x 17
NCM 1985-1158

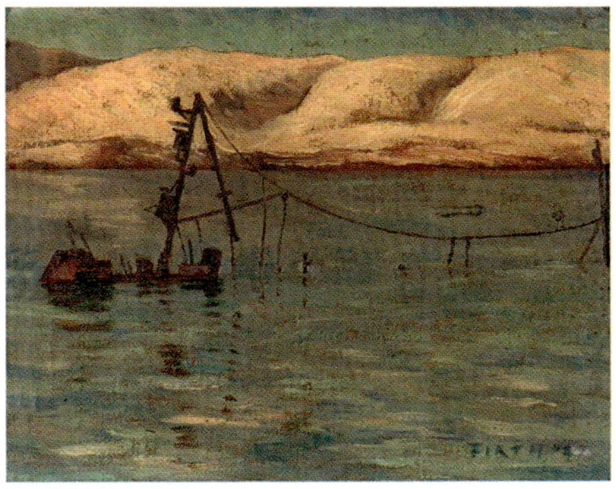

Firth, John H. S. 1912–c.1970
Postscript, Tobruk Harbour, Libya, April 1941
1947
oil on canvas 22.5 x 27
NCM 1985-1161

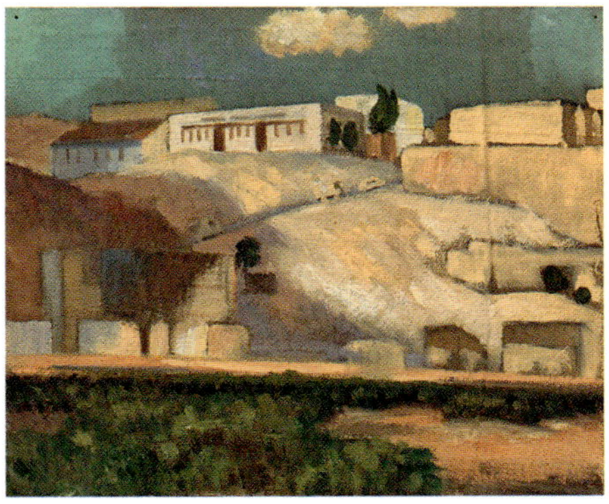

Firth, John H. S. 1912–c.1970
Scuola Benito Mussolini, Tobruk, Libya 1947
oil on canvas 21.2 x 25.5
NCM 1985-1383

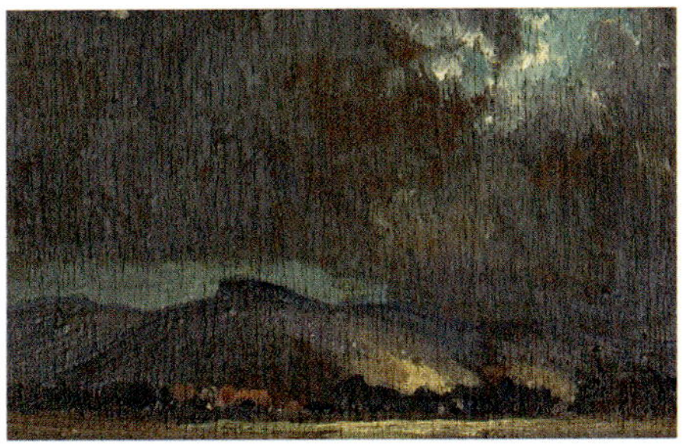

Firth, John H. S. 1912–c.1970
The South Downs 1947
oil on wood 8.5 x 15
NCM 1985-1157

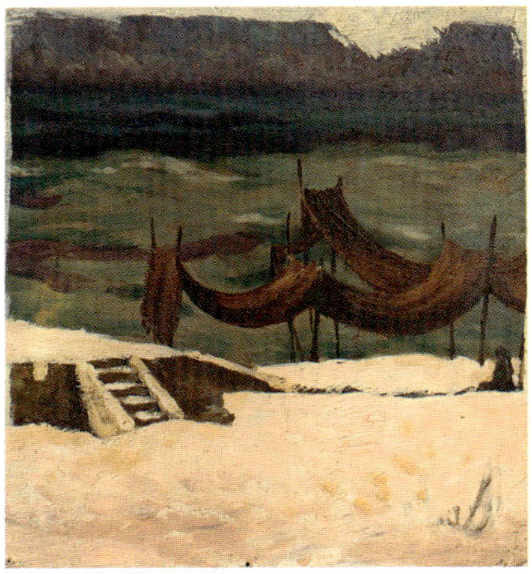

Firth, John H. S. 1912–c.1970
Drying Nets, Gaza, Palestine 1948
oil on wood 31.5 x 30
NCM 1985-1170

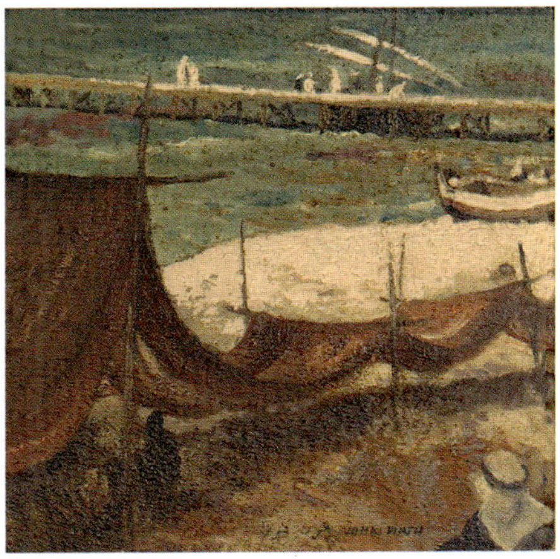

Firth, John H. S. 1912–c.1970
Gaza Pier, Palestine c.1949
oil on wood 28.5 x 28
NCM 1985-1160

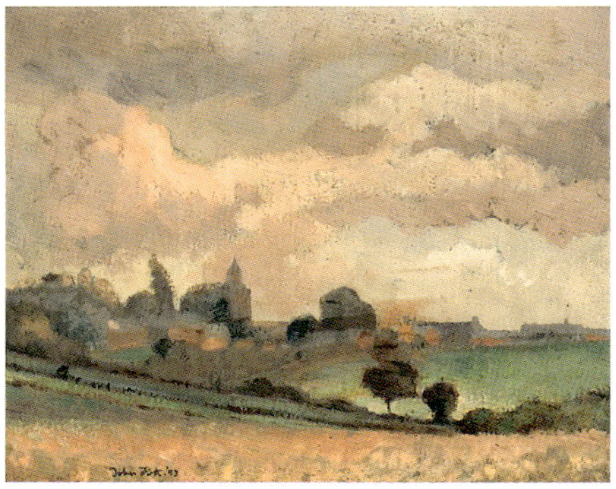

Firth, John H. S. 1912–c.1970
Landscape 1953
oil on canvas 34 x 44.5
NCM 1985-1174

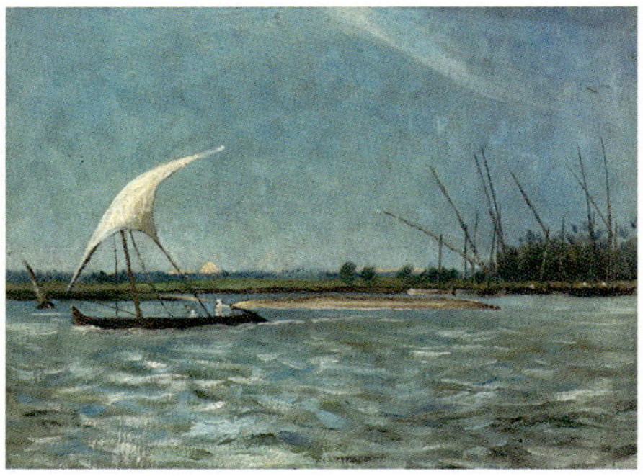

Firth, John H. S. 1912–c.1970
*Boat and Sails No.1**
oil on canvas 25.5 x 34.5
NCM 1985-1377

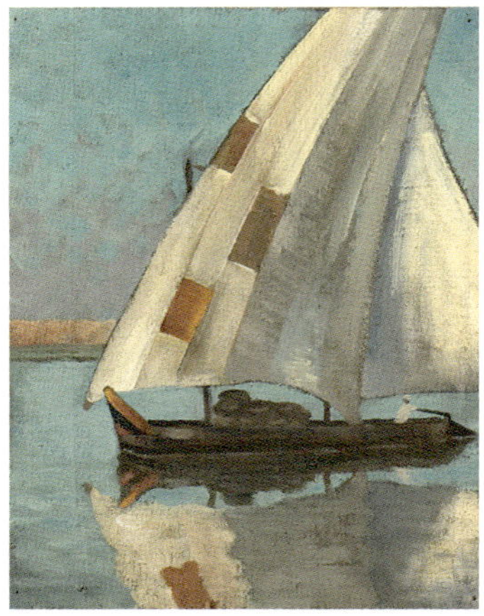

Firth, John H. S. 1912–c.1970
*Boat and Sails No.2**
oil on canvas 26 x 24
NCM 1985-1375

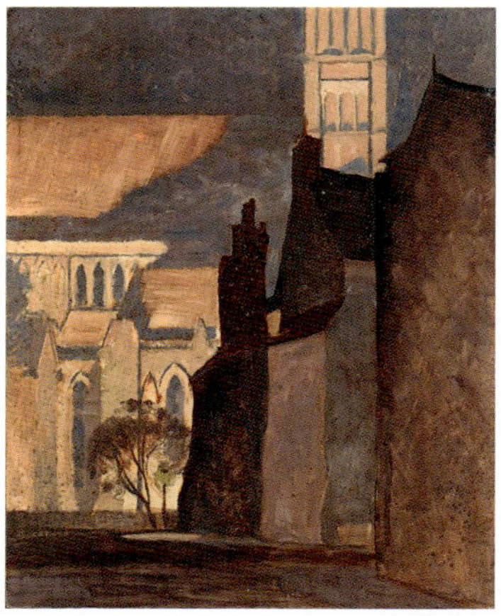

Firth, John H. S. 1912–c.1970
Lincoln (?)
oil on wood 56 x 45.3
NCM 1985-1150

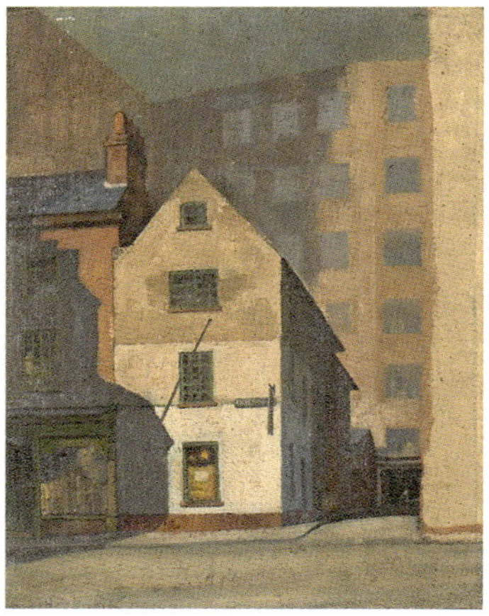

Firth, John H. S. 1912–c.1970
*Street Scene**
oil on canvas 44 x 35
NCM 1985-1334

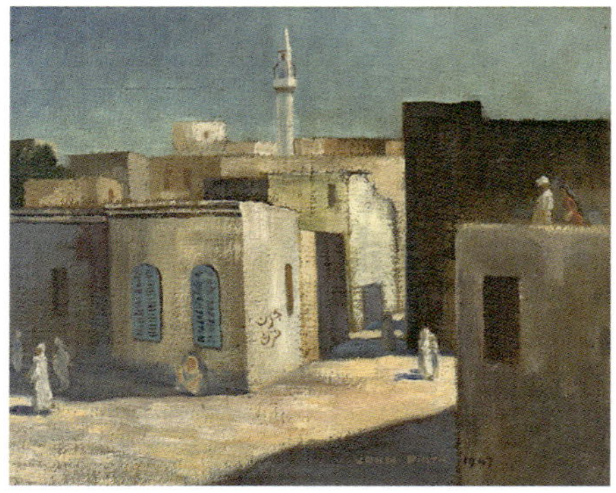

Firth, John H. S. 1912–c.1970
Zifteh, Egypt, 1947
oil on canvas 20.5 x 25
NCM 1985-1384

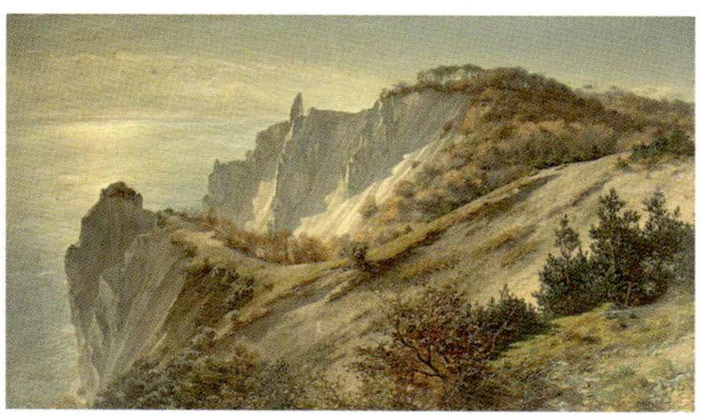

Fischer, Hans 1849–1886
Autumn View of Møns Cliff, Denmark 1882
oil on canvas 124.5 x 182.9
NCM 1908-7

Fisk, William Henry 1827–1884
Love and War (detail)
oil on canvas 373.4 x 188
NCM 1883-60

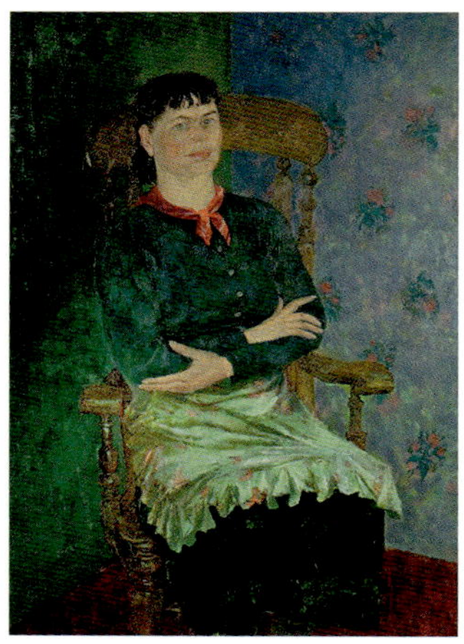

Fitton, James 1899–1982
The Painter's Wife c.1955
oil on canvas 102.9 x 77.5
NCM 1955-48

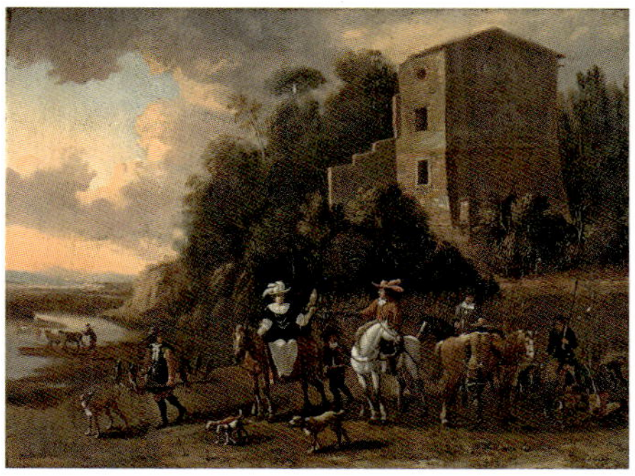

Flemish School 17th C
Hawking Party
oil on canvas 50.8 x 68.6
NCM 1890-1194

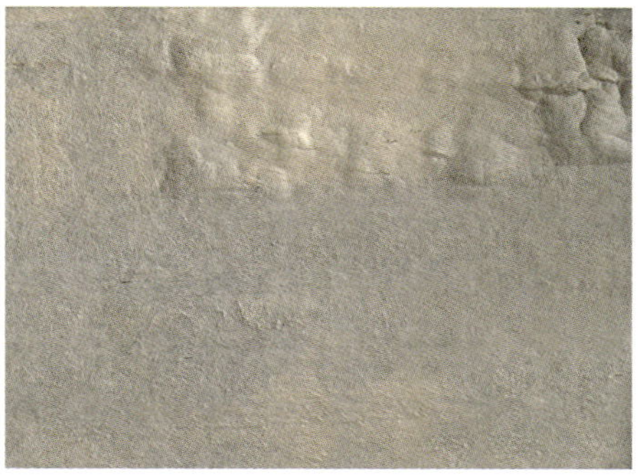

Fletcher, John Henry active 1880–1922
Nottingham Canal, London Road Bridge (Nottingham Canal, Carrington Street Bridge)
oil on board 20.3 x 28.6
NCM 1920-23

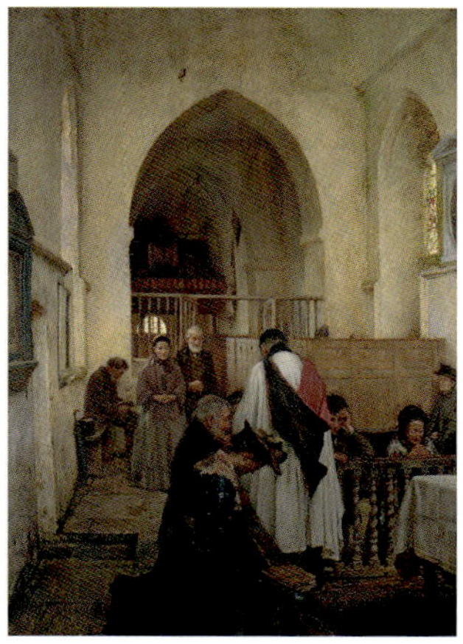

Fletcher, William Teulon Blandford 1858–1936
Sacrament Sunday 1897
oil on canvas 121.9 x 91.4
NCM 1944-26

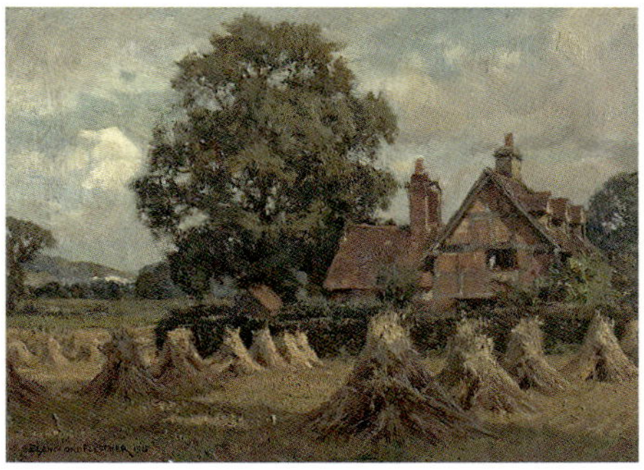

Fletcher, William Teulon Blandford 1858–1936
Bletchworth Quarry, Seen from Lower Lane Cottages, Dorking, Surrey 1915
oil on canvas 27.9 x 38.1
NCM 1950-58

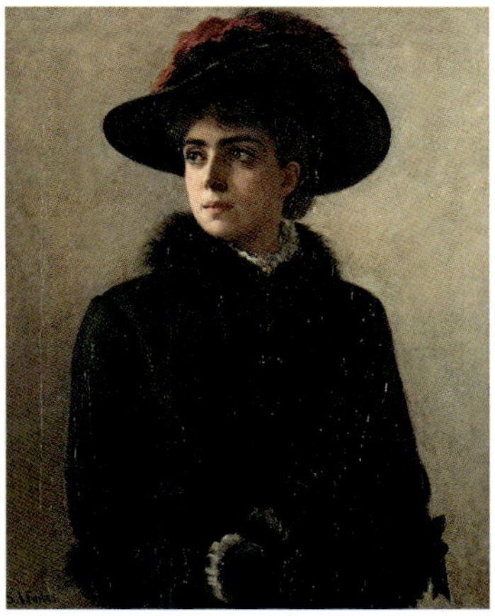

Forbes, Stanhope Alexander 1857–1947
Florence 1878
oil on canvas 74.5 x 62
FALOAN 94 (P)

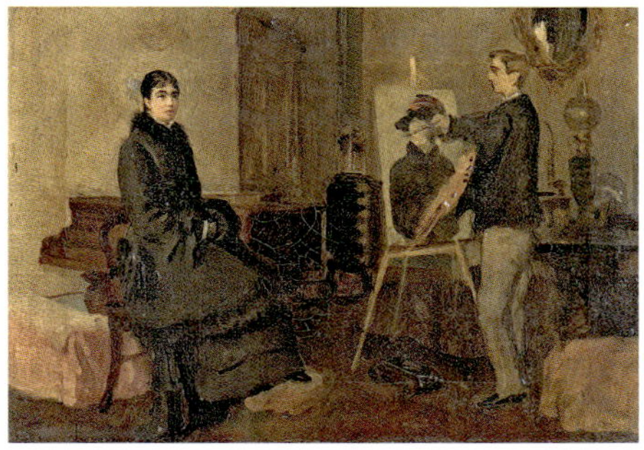

Forbes, Stanhope Alexander 1857–1947
The Artist in His Studio
oil on canvas 21 x 31
FALOAN 1/2 (1935) (P)

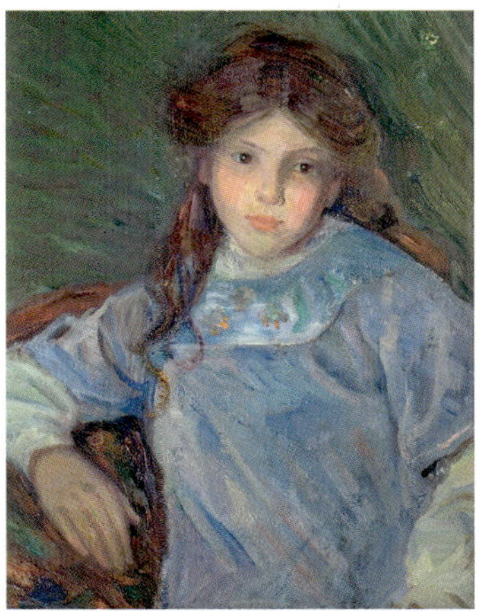

Forbes-Robertson, Janine active 1908–1912
Cecilia
oil on canvas 52.1 x 43.2
NCM 1946-229

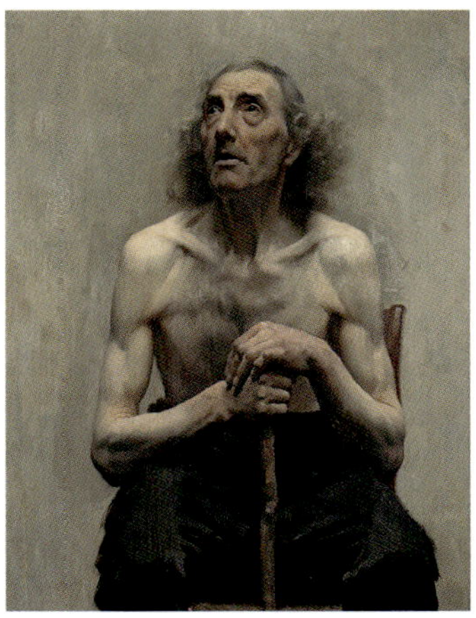

Foster, Herbert Wilson 1846–1929
The Belgian Model c.1890
oil on canvas 97.8 x 80
NCM 1941-11

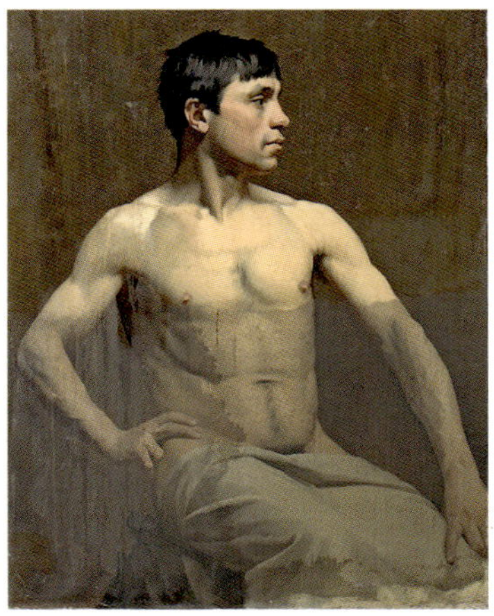

Foster, Herbert Wilson 1846–1929
The Seated Model c.1890
oil on canvas 97.8 x 80
NCM 1941-12

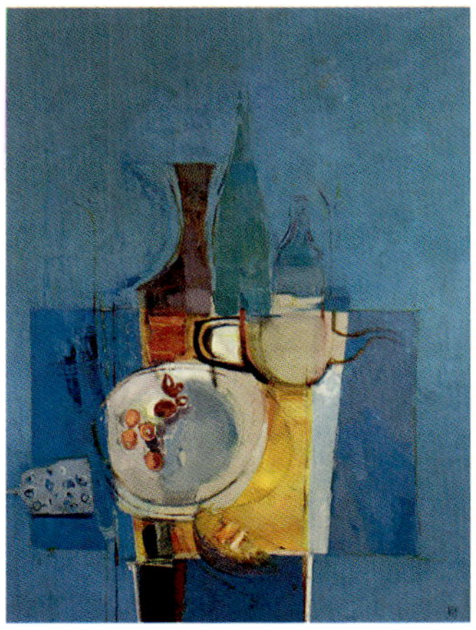

Fraser, Donald Hamilton b.1929
Still Life with Cherries 1955
oil on canvas 91.4 x 71.1
NCM 1956-87

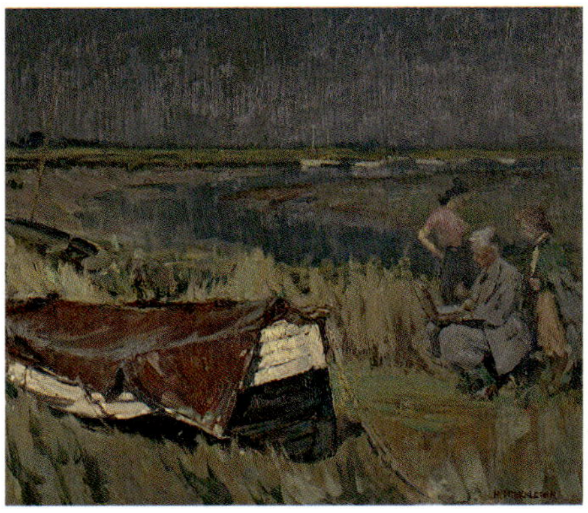

Freckleton, Harry 1890–1979
Boats 1951
oil on canvas 63.5 x 76.2
NCM 1953-112

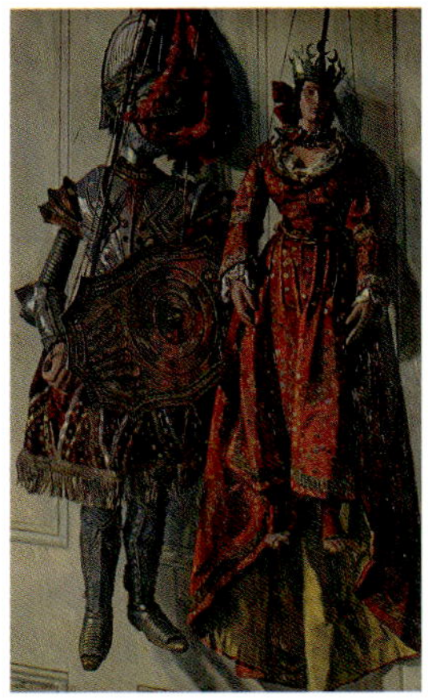

Freedman, Barnett 1901–1958
Sicilian Puppets 1933
oil on canvas 100.3 x 62.2
NCM 1935-64

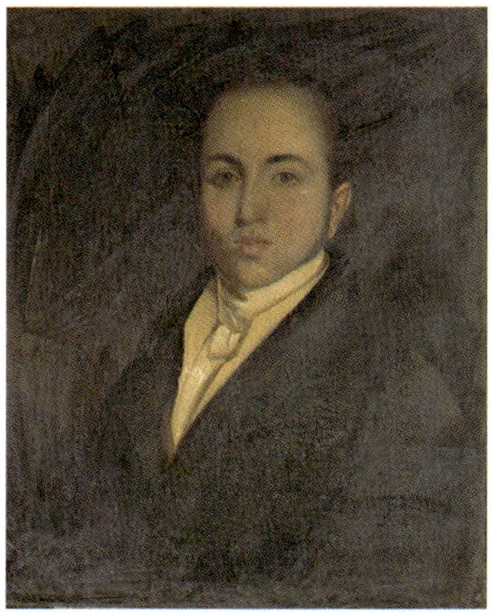

French School 19th C
Portrait of a Young Man
oil on canvas 63.5 x 51
NCM 1946-41

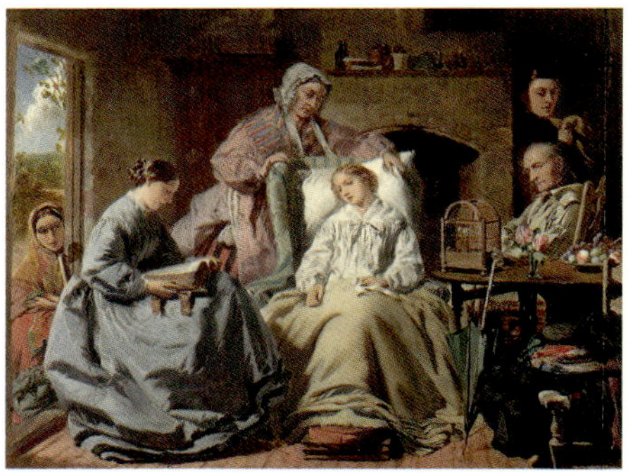

Frith, William Powell 1819–1909
The Invalid 1890
oil on board 38.1 x 45.7
NCM 1942-32

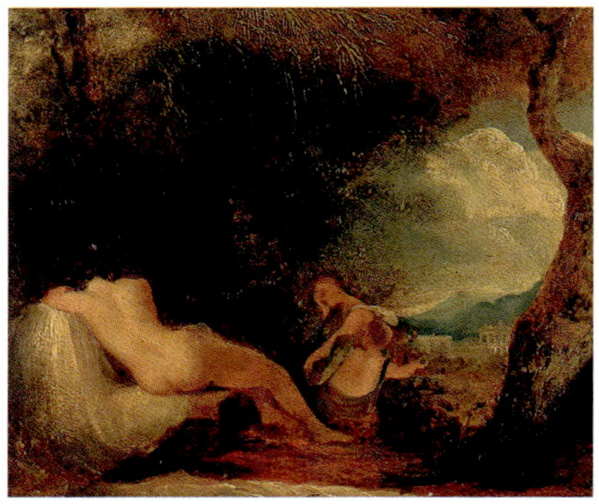

Frost, William Edward 1810–1877
Classical Subject (Venus, Cupid and Psyche)
oil on board 17.8 x 20.3
NCM 1909-51

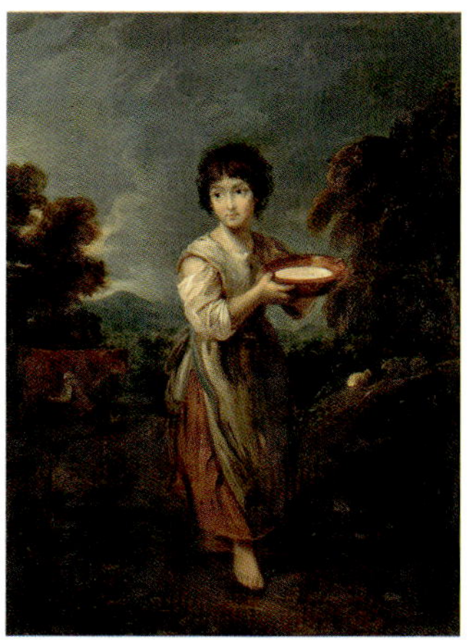

Gainsborough, Thomas (style of)
1727–1788
A Cottage Girl
oil on canvas 114.3 x 86.4
NCM 1890-1202

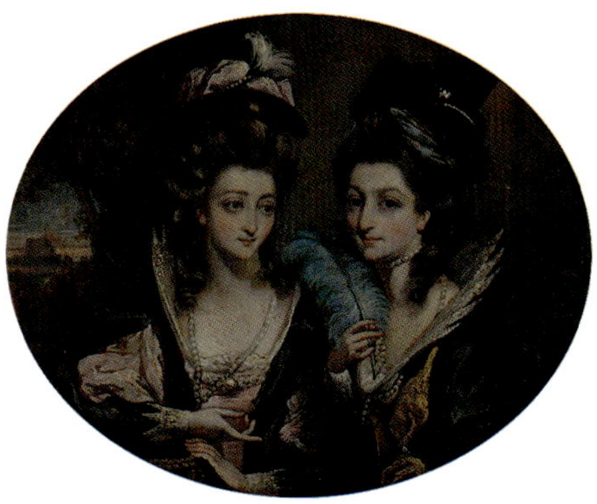

Gardner, Daniel 1750–1805
Mrs Gwynne and Mrs Bunbury as the Merry Wives of Windsor c.1779
oil on wood 24.1 x 27.3
NCM 1904-32

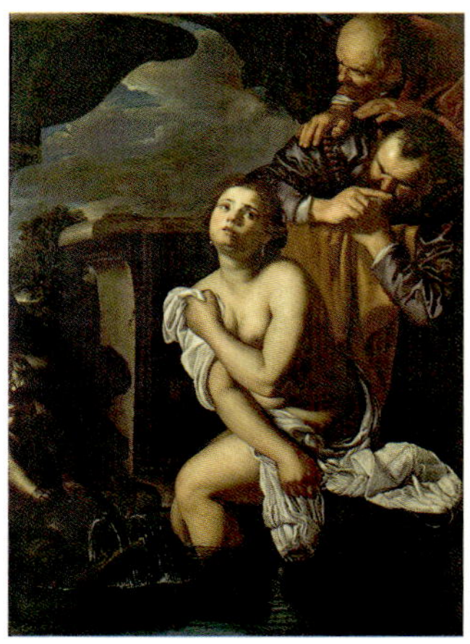

Gentileschi, Artemisia (attributed to)
1593–1651/1653
Susannah and the Elders
oil on canvas 162.5 x 121.9
NCM 1964-77

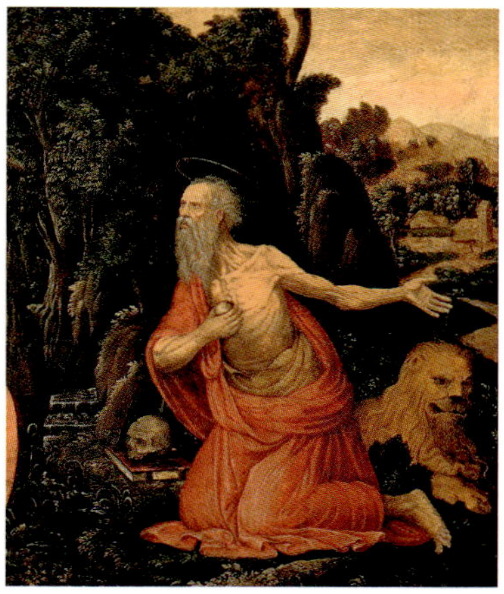

German School 16th C
St Jerome
oil on wood 68.2 x 61
NCM 1910-64

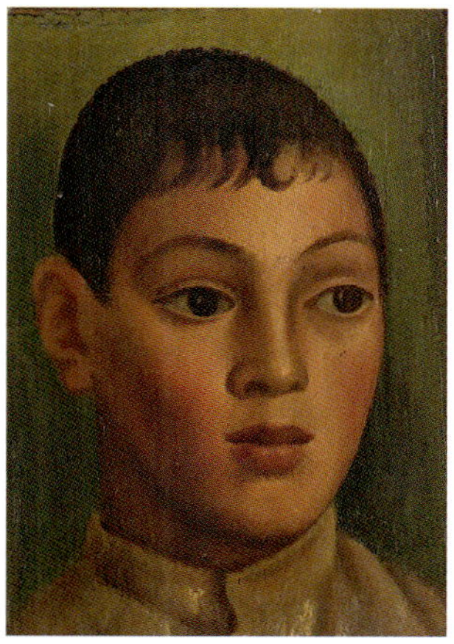

Gertler, Mark 1892–1939
Head of a Boy 1922
oil on wood 26.7 x 20.3
NCM 1938-61

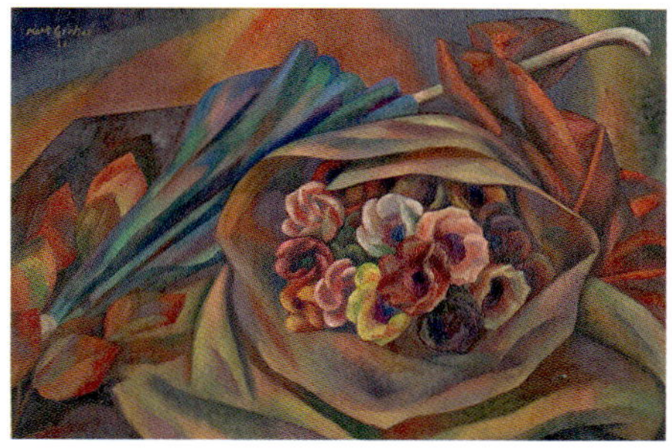

Gertler, Mark 1892–1939
Bouquet and Sunshade
oil on canvas 50.8 x 76.2
NCM 1968-328

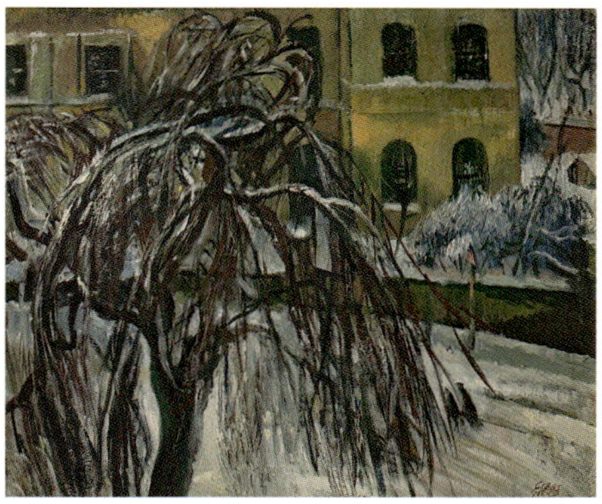

Gibbs, Evelyn 1905–1991
Clarendon Street with Tall Trees 1947
oil on canvas 63 x 76
NCM 1998-65

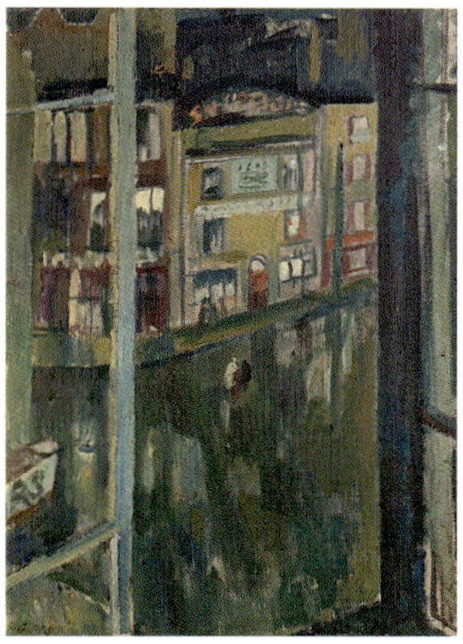

Gibbs, Evelyn 1905–1991
The Nottingham Window 1948
oil on canvas 74.5 x 54
NCM 1998-66

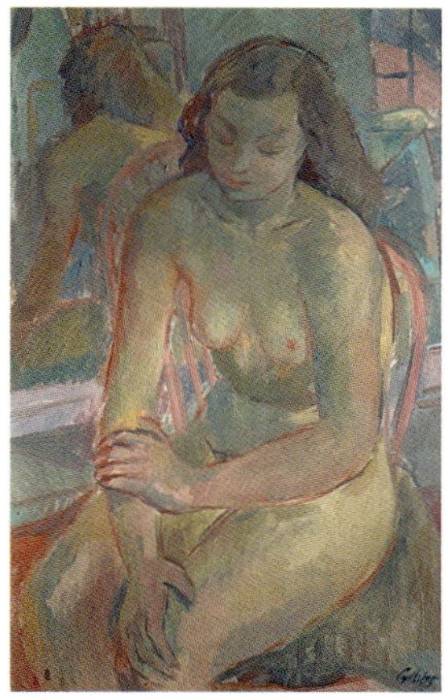

Gibbs, Evelyn 1905–1991
Female Nude 1950
oil on canvas 76.2 x 50.8
NCM 1951-56

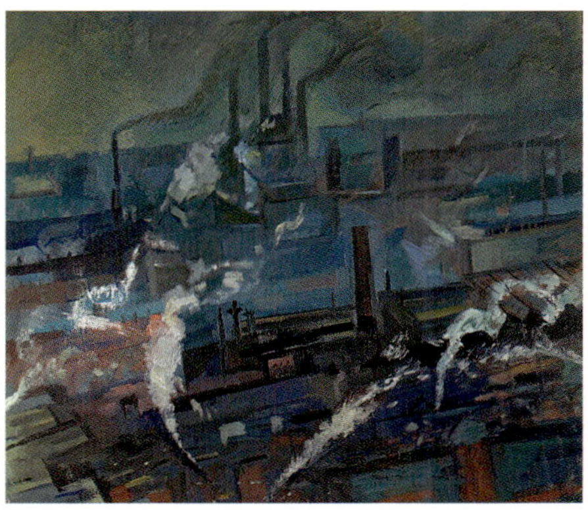

Gibbs, Evelyn 1905–1991
Industrial View 1953
oil on canvas 77.4 x 89.5
NCM 1998-67

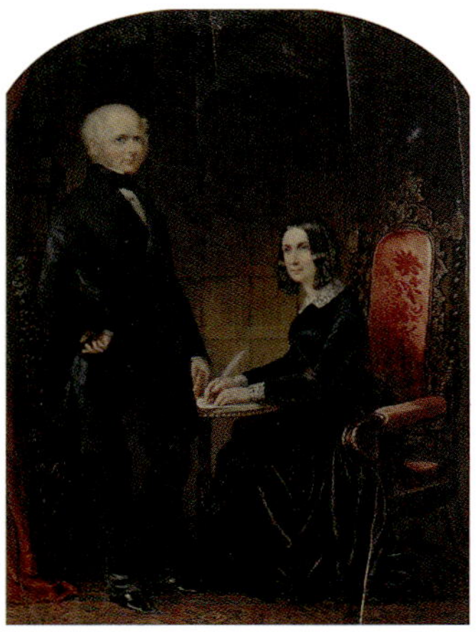

Gillies, Margaret 1803–1887
William Howitt (1792–1879), and Mary Howitt (1799–1888)
oil on ivory 41.9 x 33
NCM 1897-53

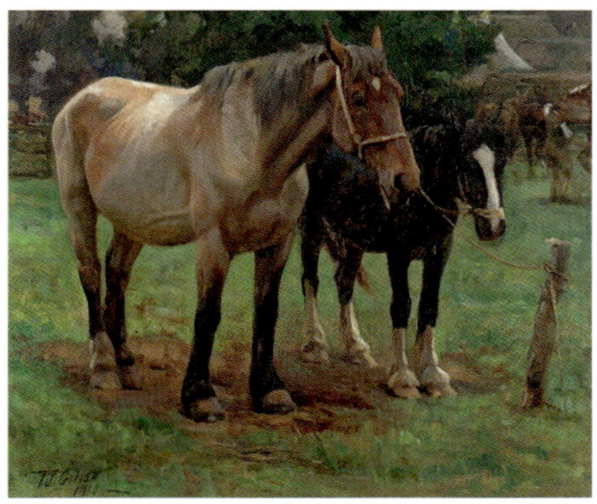

Gillott, Thomas J. 1886–1913
A Country Fair 1910
oil on canvas 50.8 x 61
NCM 1911-50

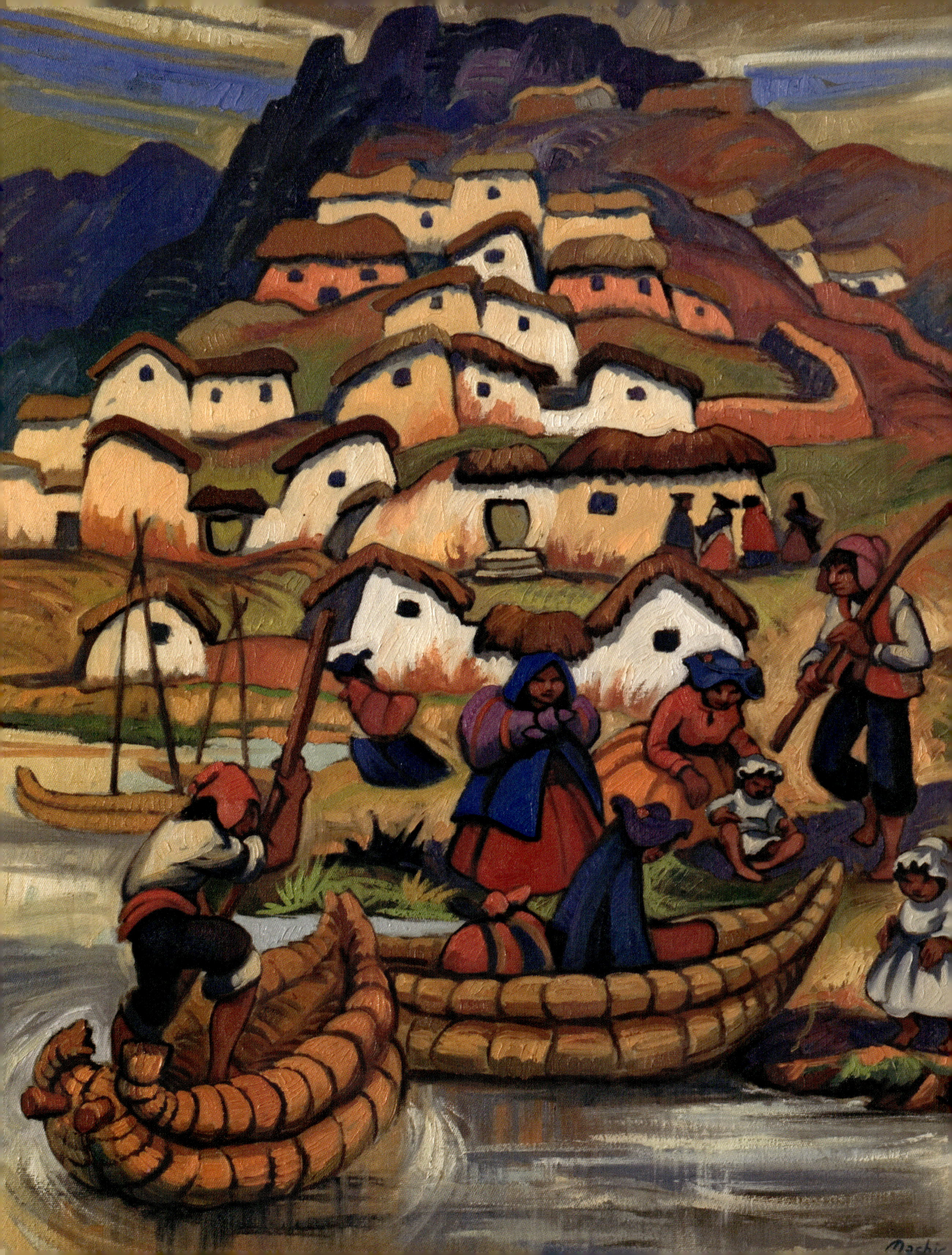

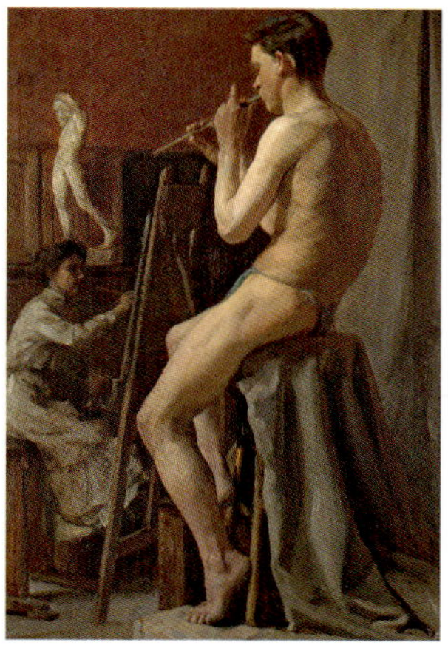

Gillott, Thomas J. 1886–1913
Life Class 1912
oil on canvas 74.9 x 54.6
NCM 1941-10

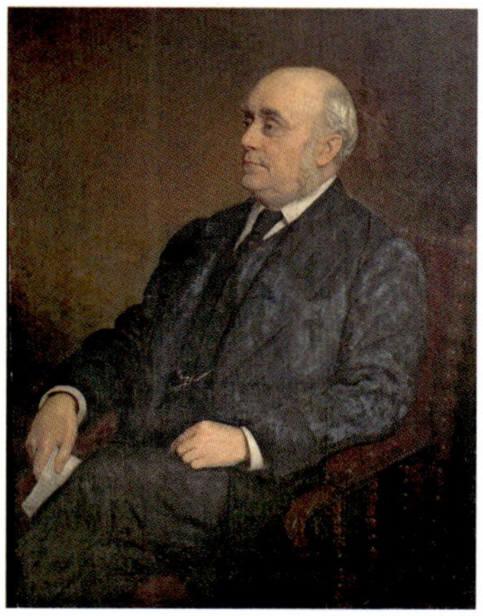

Girardot, Ernest Gustave 1840–1904
Mr Joseph Pettifor 1885
oil on canvas 111.7 x 86.3
NCM 1907-14

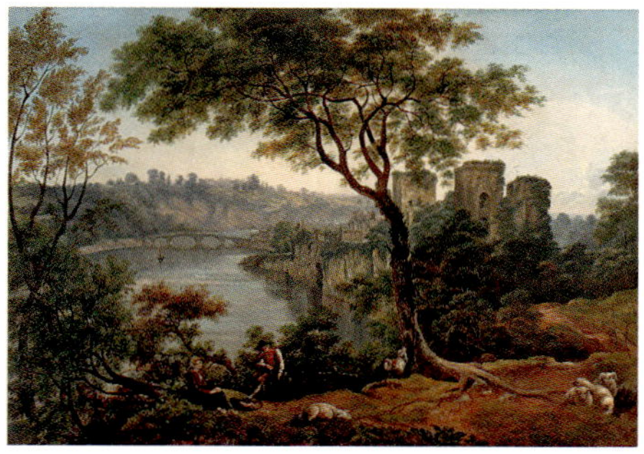

Glover, John 1767–1849
Chepstow Castle, Monmouthshire
oil on canvas 91.4 x 132.1
NCM 1897-56

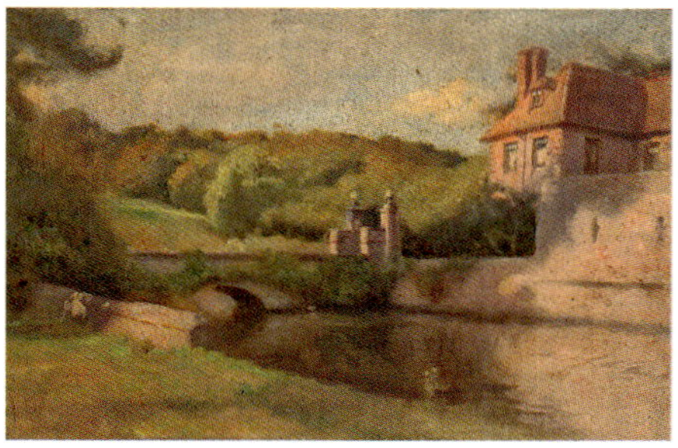

Gogin, Charles 1844–1931
Groombridge Hall, Kent
oil on board 32.4 x 48.9
NCM 1944-5

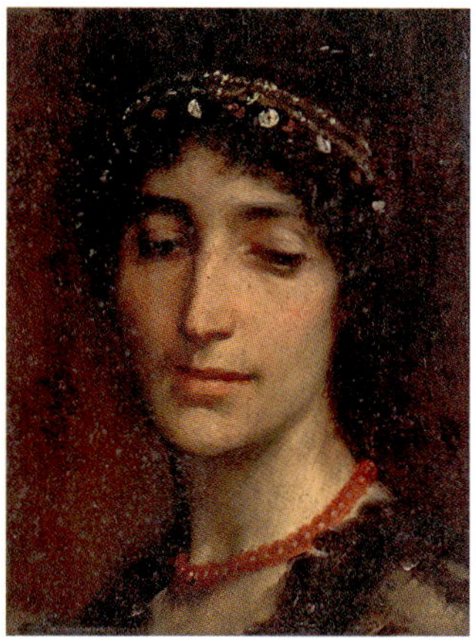

Gogin, Charles 1844–1931
Julia
oil on board 36.8 x 26.7
NCM 1944-4

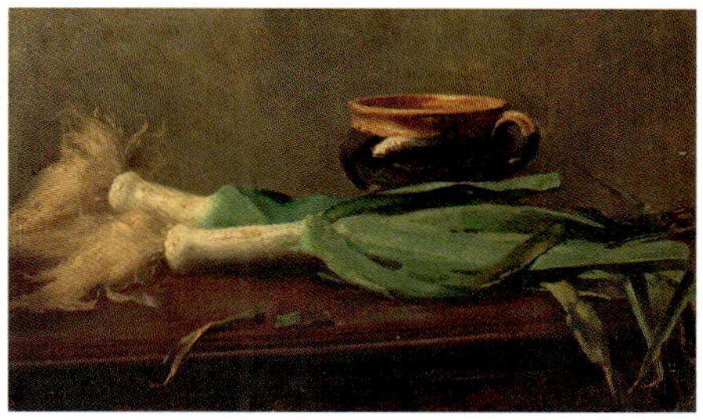

Gogin, Charles 1844–1931
Leeks
oil on canvas 38.7 x 63.5
NCM 1931-15

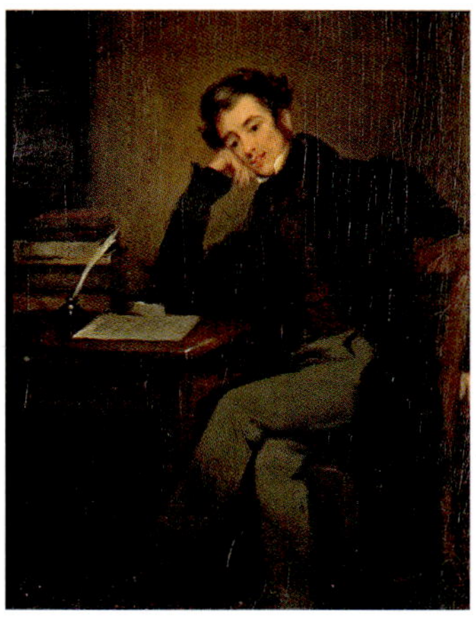

Good, Thomas Sword 1789–1872
Self Portrait
oil on wood 26 x 21.6
NCM 1904-33

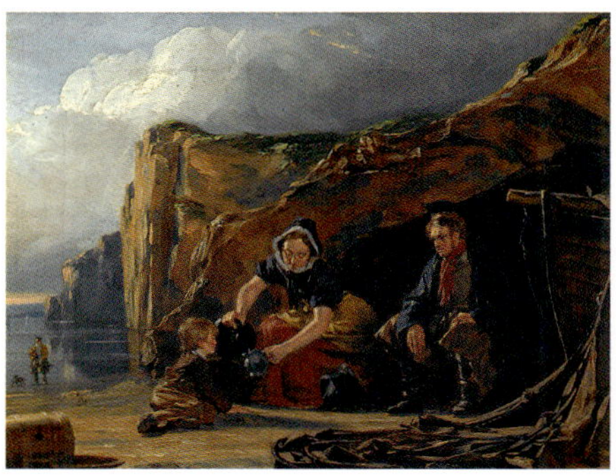

Good, Thomas Sword 1789–1872
Shore Scene with Figures
oil on canvas 22.9 x 30.5
NCM 1904-34

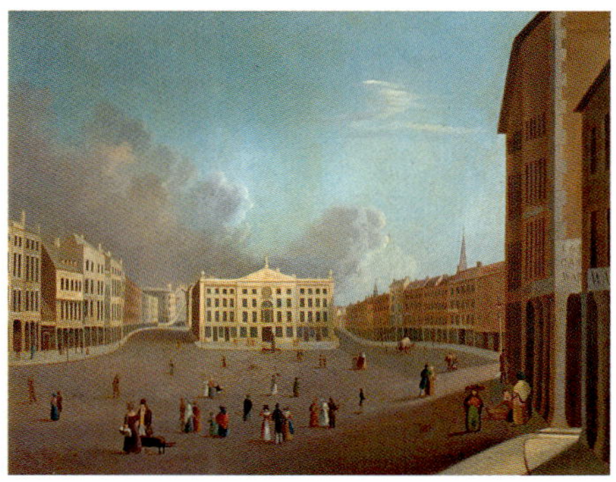

Goodacre, William 1803–1883
Nottingham Market Place c.1827
oil on wood 58 x 76
NCM 1996-478

Facing page: Machicado, Juan de la Cruz, b.1935, *Titicaca* (detail), 1989, The University of Nottingham (p. 212)

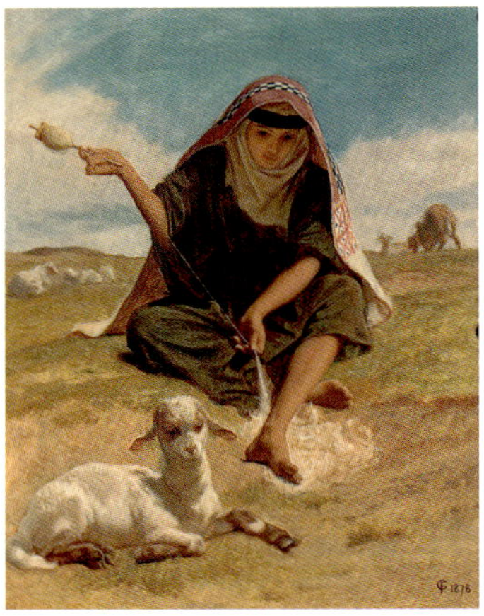

Goodall, Frederick 1822–1904
The Distaff Worker 1878
oil on canvas 55.6 x 45.1
NCM 1925-226

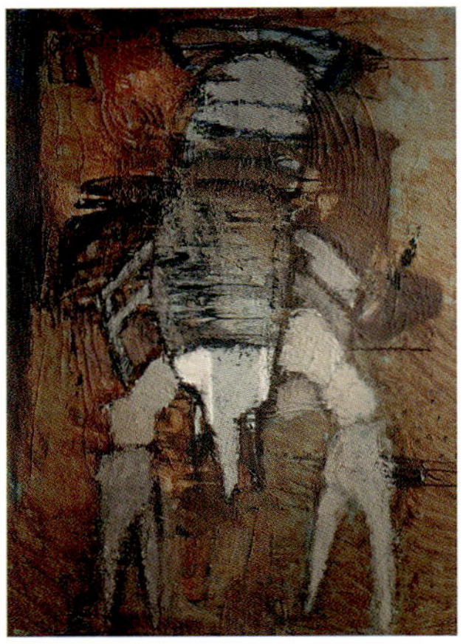

Gorski, Stefan b.1932
Crayfish 1962
oil on canvas 94 x 68.8
NCM 1962-510

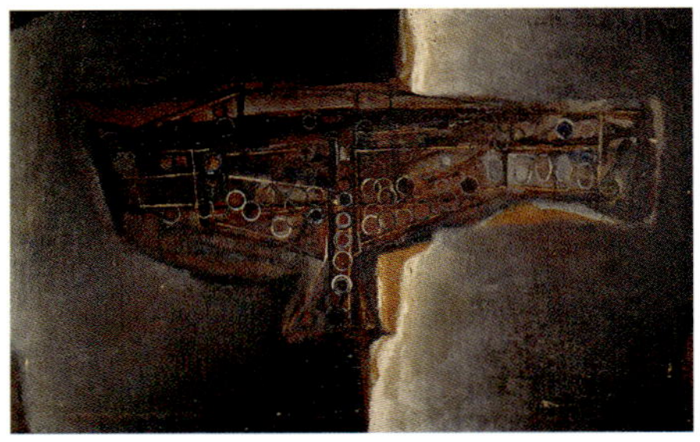

Gorski, Stefan b.1932
Birdman 1965
oil on canvas 85.7 x 137.1
NCM 1966-62

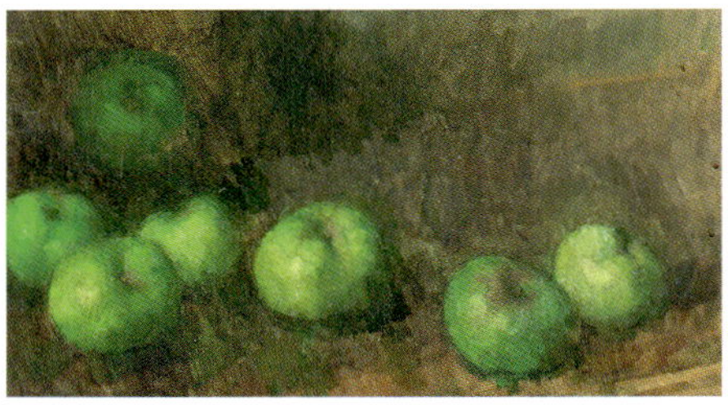

Gowing, Lawrence 1918–1991
Green Apples on a Bamboo Table 1941
oil on canvas 21.6 x 40
NCM 1944-29

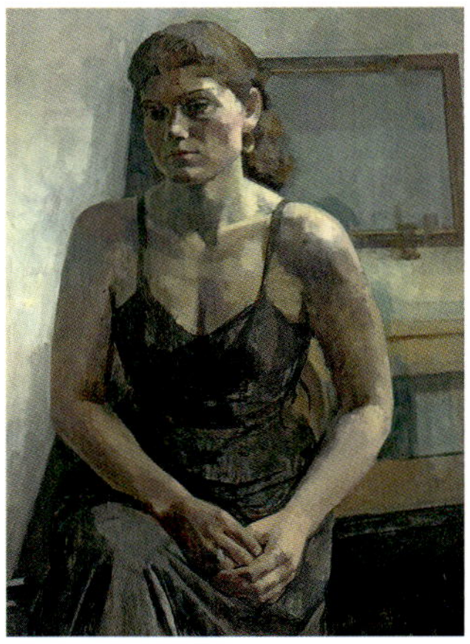

Gowing, Lawrence 1918–1991
Ilse Magdalene R. 1953
oil on canvas 91.4 x 71.1
NCM 1955-46

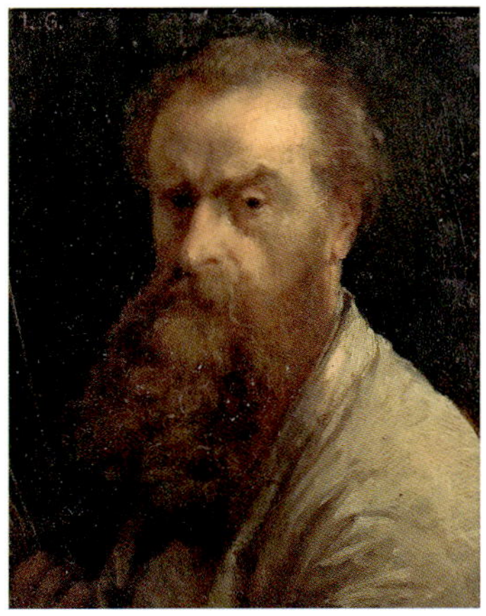

Gratia, Charles-Louis 1815–1911
Self Portrait
oil on board 22.5 x 17.4
NCM 1904-35

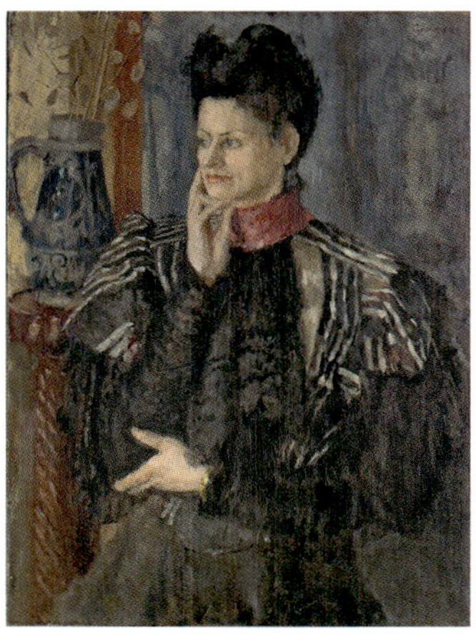

Greaves, Leonard 1918–1949
The Worth Bodice
oil on canvas 65 x 51
NCM 1952-11

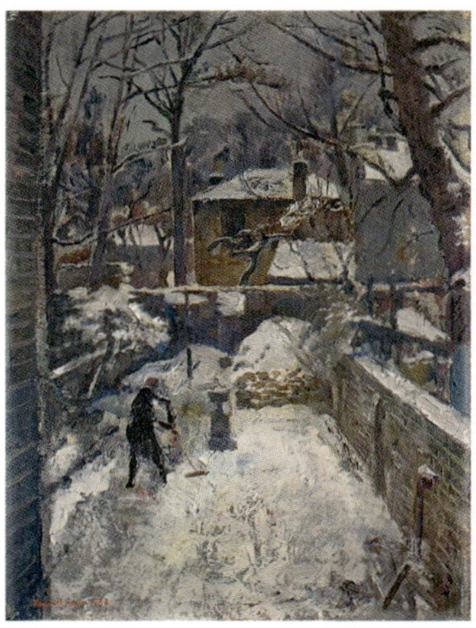

Green, Kenneth 1905–1986
Chelsea Garden under Snow (The Black Spider) 1942
oil on canvas 47 x 31.8
NCM 1942-28

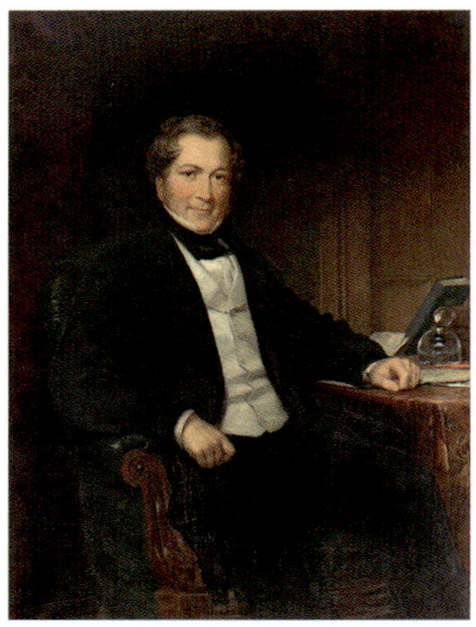

Gush, William 1813–1888
John Heathcoat (1783–1861), Inventor of the Bobbin Net Machine c.1830
oil on canvas 124.5 x 99.1
NCM 1879-128

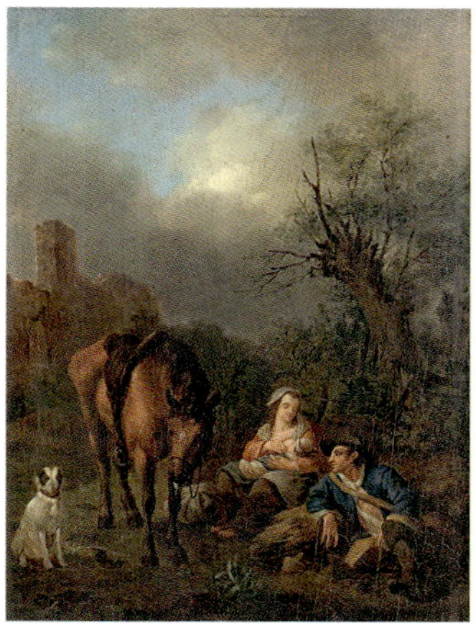

Hackaert, Jan 1629–1699
Landscape with Figures, a Horse and a Dog
oil on canvas 34.3 x 27.9
NCM 1953-105/(a)

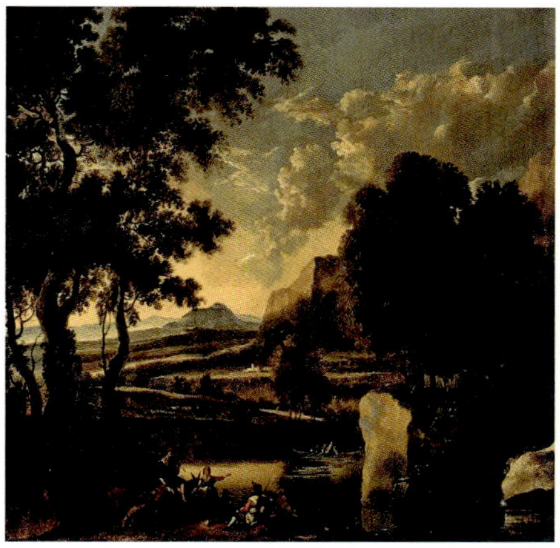

Hackaert, Jan 1629–1699
Landscape with Figures in the Foreground
oil on canvas 80 x 82.5
NCM 1953-104

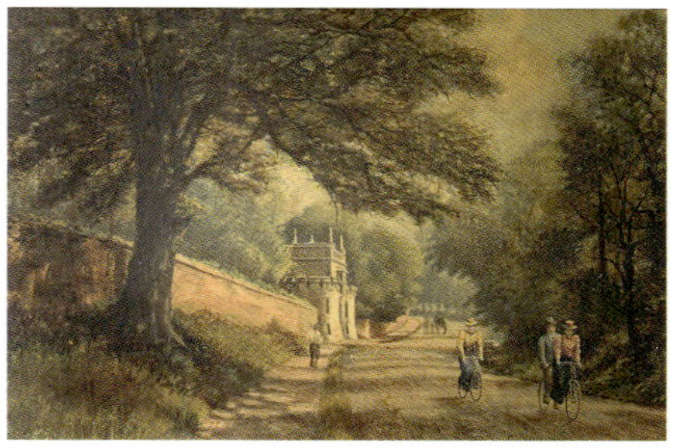

Halledine, G. H. active 20th C
The Lodge, Wollaton Park, Nottingham
oil on canvas 50.2 x 75.6
NCM 1966-98

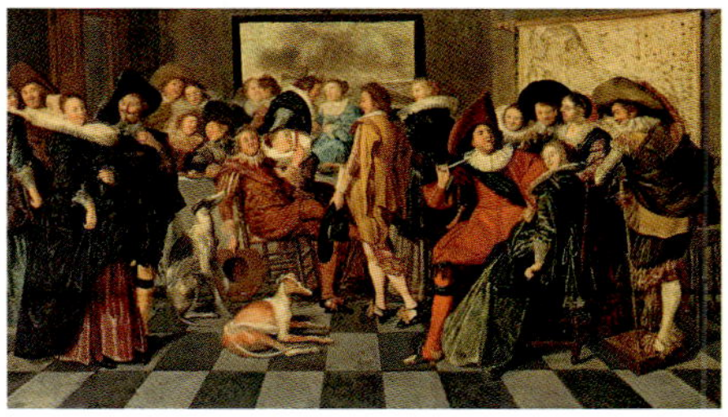

Hals, Dirck 1591–1656
A Dutch Party c.1620
oil on canvas 43.2 x 78.4
NCM 1910-55

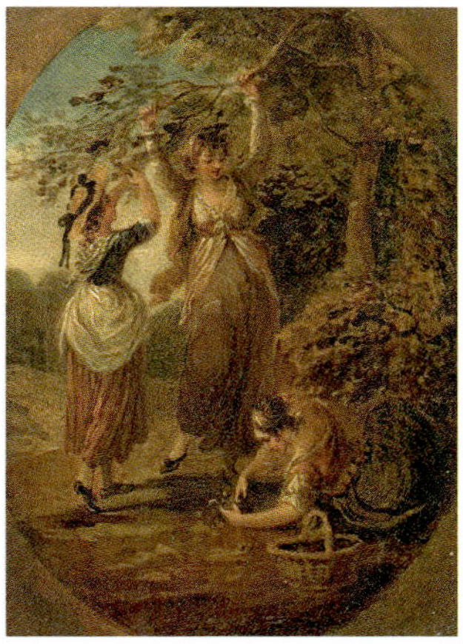

Hamilton, William 1751–1801
The Nut-Gatherers
oil on canvas 20.3 x 15.2
NCM 1904-36

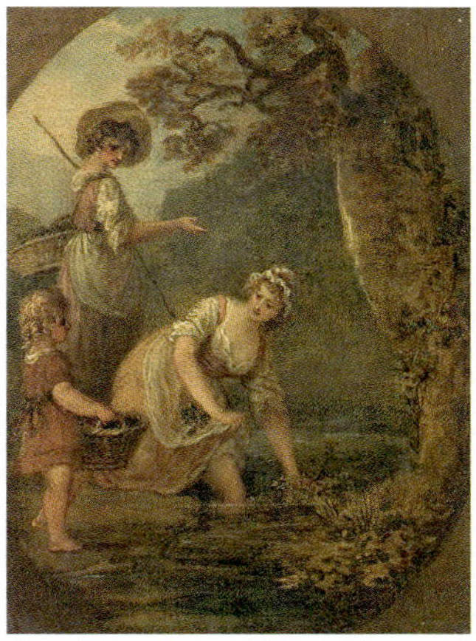

Hamilton, William 1751–1801
The Watercress-Gatherers
oil on canvas 20.3 x 15.2
NCM 1904-36/(a)

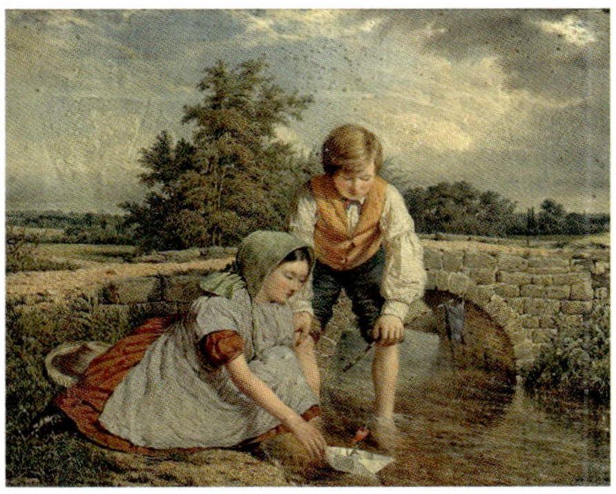

Hart, James Turpin 1835–1899
The Launch 1858
oil on canvas 35.6 x 45.7
NCM 1907-57

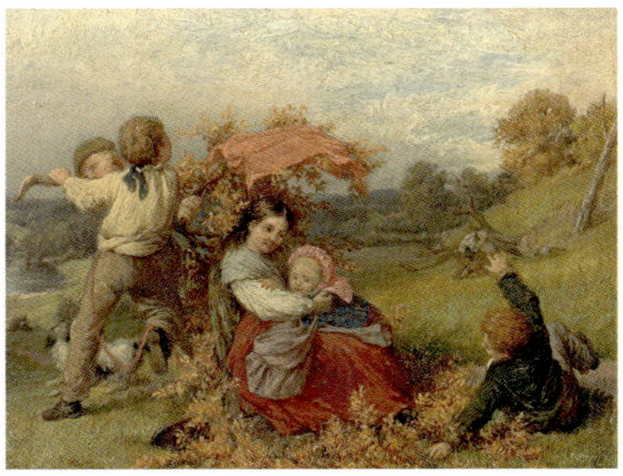

Hart, James Turpin 1835–1899
The Golden Bough c.1866
oil on wood 15.2 x 20.3
NCM 1924-28

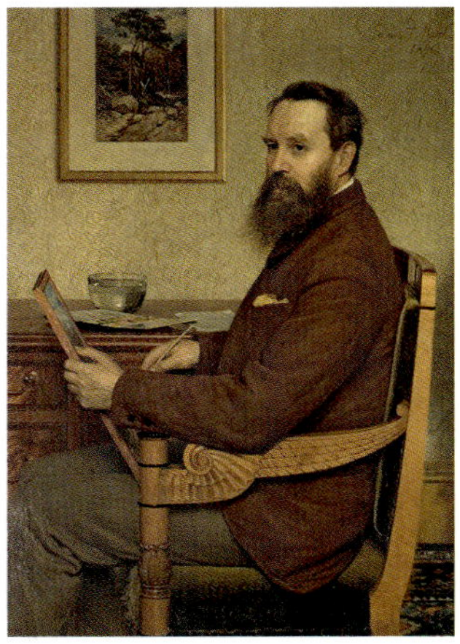

Hart, James Turpin 1835–1899
Samuel William Oscroft (1834–1924) 1890
oil on canvas 81.3 x 61
NCM 1924-20

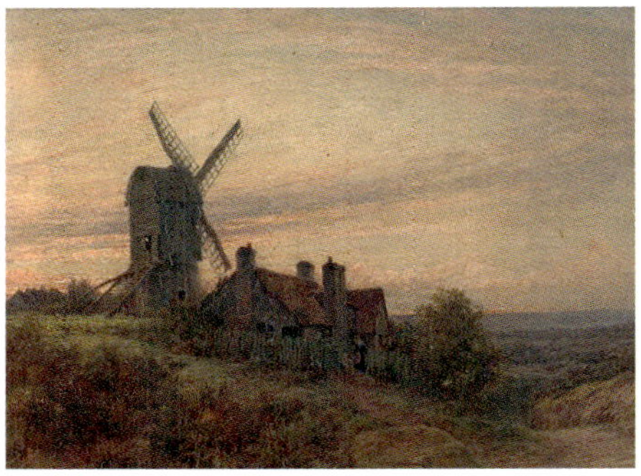

Hart, James Turpin 1835–1899
Nottingham Forest and Windmill
oil on wood 42 x 51
NCM 1989-773

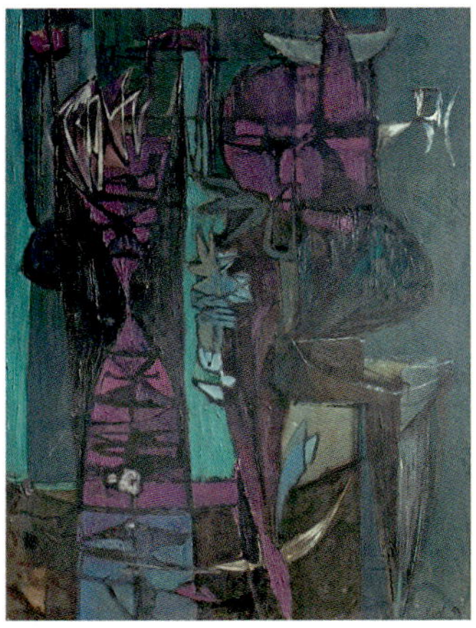

Hart, John 1921–1996
Dylan 1953
oil on canvas 91.4 x 71.1
NCM 1954-37

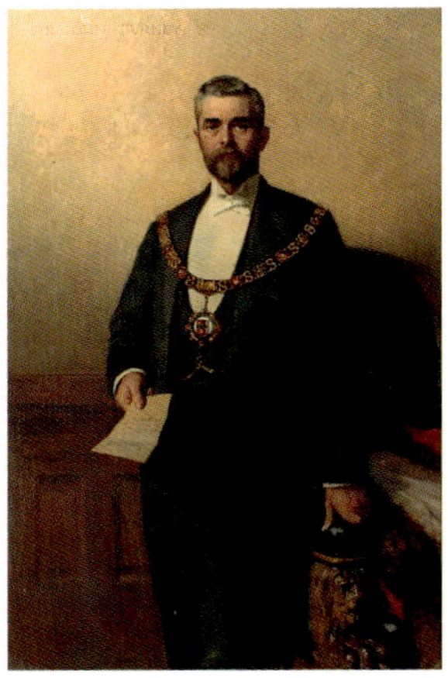

Hartley, Alfred 1855–1933
Alderman Sir John Turney, Kt 1889
oil on canvas 167.6 x 111.8
NCM 1889-400

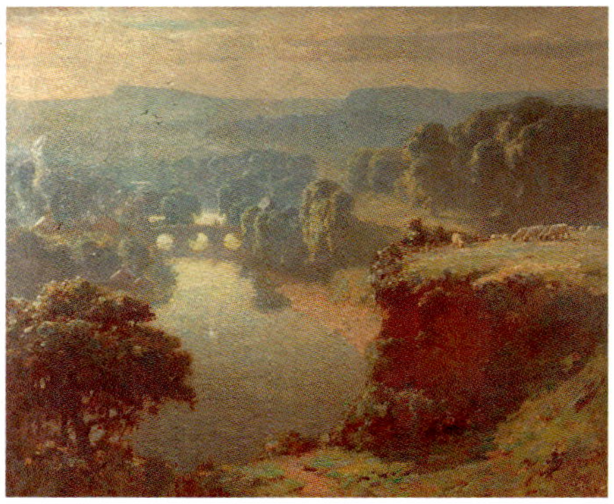

Hartley, Alfred 1855–1933
Morning, Teme Dale 1908
oil on canvas 121.9 x 152.4
NCM 1909-3

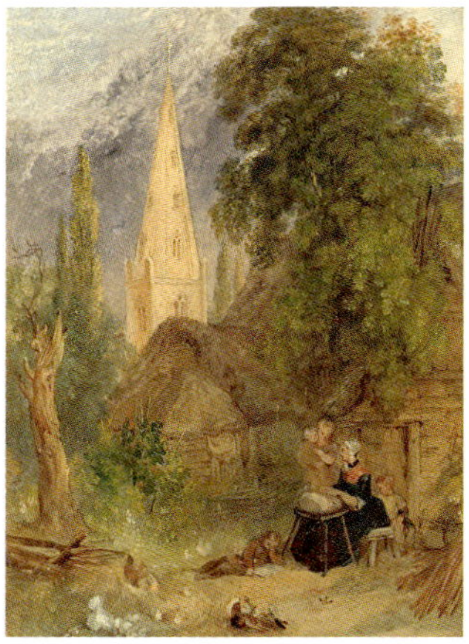

Harvey, William 1796–1866
Cottages at Olney, Buckinghamshire
oil on board 30.5 x 22.3
NCM 1904-38

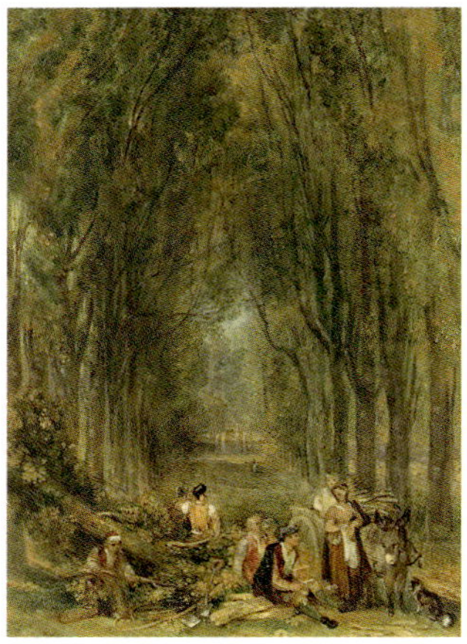

Harvey, William 1796–1866
The Lime Walk at Weston, Buckinghamshire
oil on board 30.5 x 22.9
NCM 1904-39

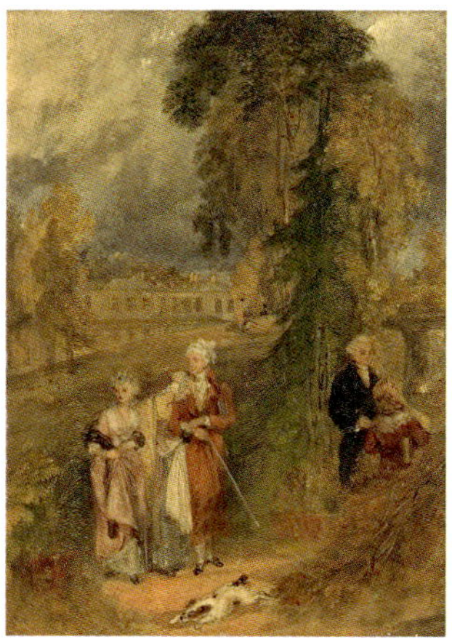

Harvey, William 1796–1866
The Residence of Hayley, Eartham, Sussex
oil on board 45.4 x 20.6
NCM 1904-37

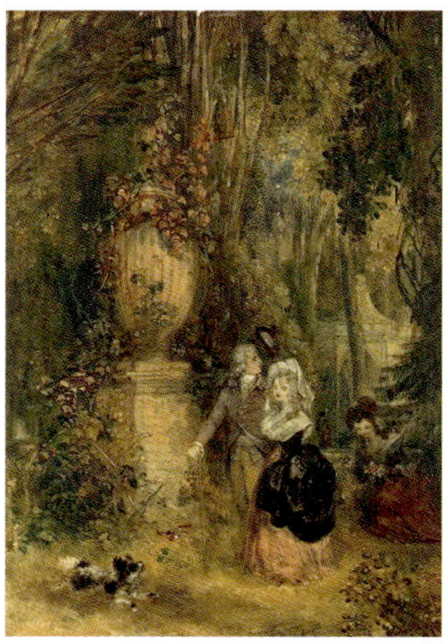

Harvey, William 1796–1866
The Wilderness at Weston, Buckinghamshire, with Pope's Monument
oil on board 30.2 x 22.5
NCM 1904-40

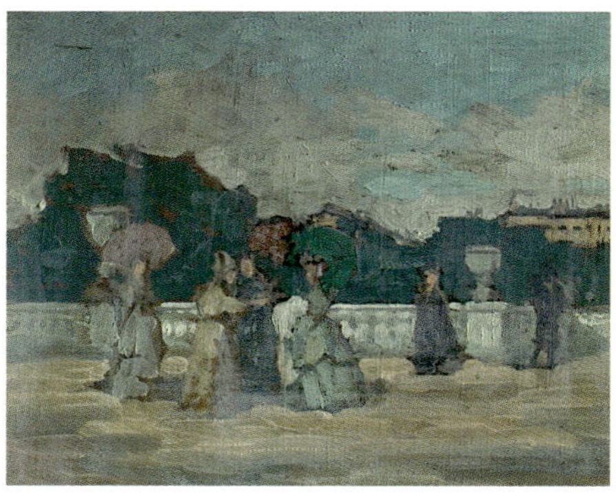

Haweis, Stephen 1878–1969
Versailles, France
oil on canvas 30.5 x 34.9
NCM 1939-67

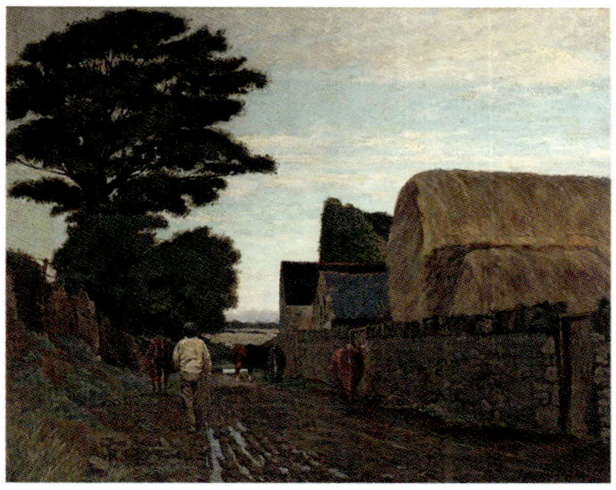

Hawksley, Arthur 1842–1915
Driving up to Milk 1881
oil on canvas 71.1 x 91.4
NCM 1916-3

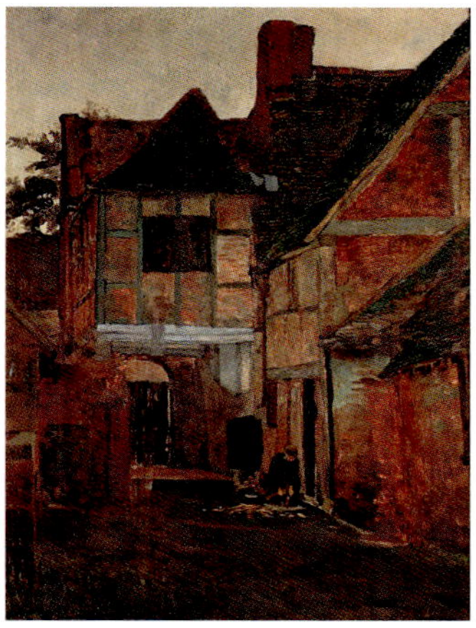

Hawksley, Arthur 1842–1915
An Old Posting Yard, Surrey 1885
oil on canvas 91.4 x 71.1
NCM 1916-2

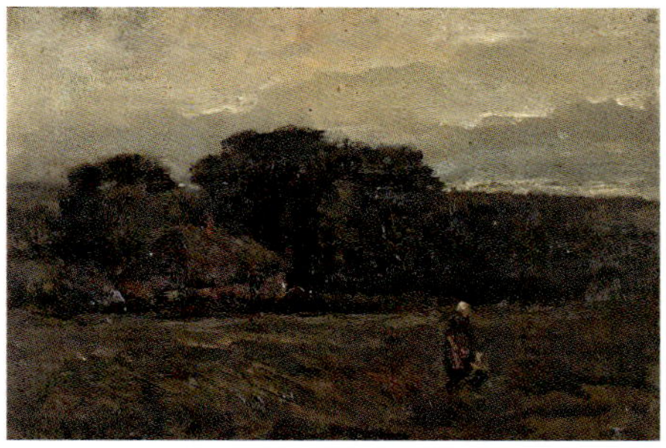

Hawksley, Arthur 1842–1915
Near Sunningdale, Berkshire
oil on canvas 30.5 x 45.7
NCM 1916-4

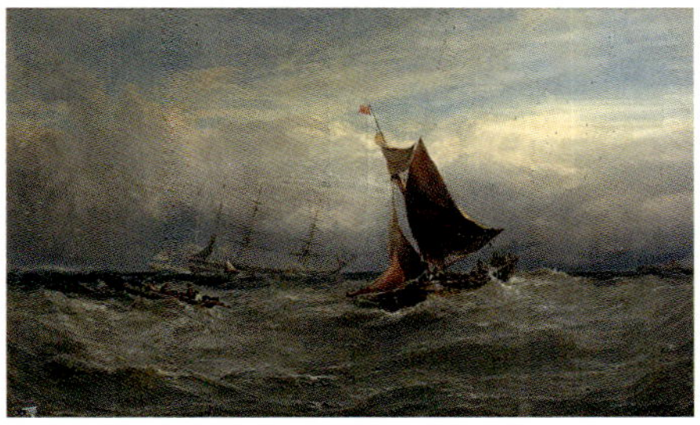

Hayes, Edwin 1819–1904
Boats in a Gale off Ostend, Belgium 1875
oil on canvas 76.2 x 127
NCM 1908-14

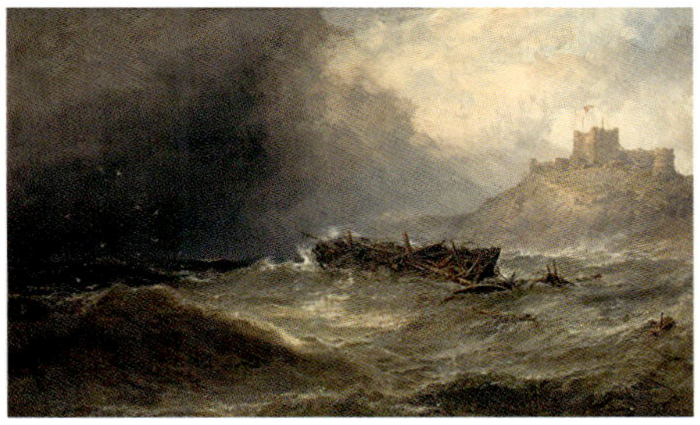

Hayes, Edwin 1819–1904
Brig Drifting Ashore off Bamborough, Northumberland (Bamborough Castle, Northumberland with a Wreck) 1875
oil on canvas 76.8 x 127.3
NCM 1908-13

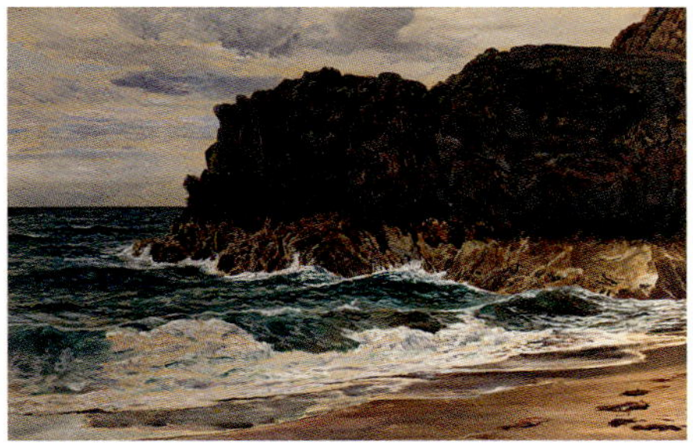

Hayes, Frederick William 1848–1918
Lighthouse Rock, Llanddwyn, North Wales
oil on paper 38.1 x 59.7
NCM 1920-52

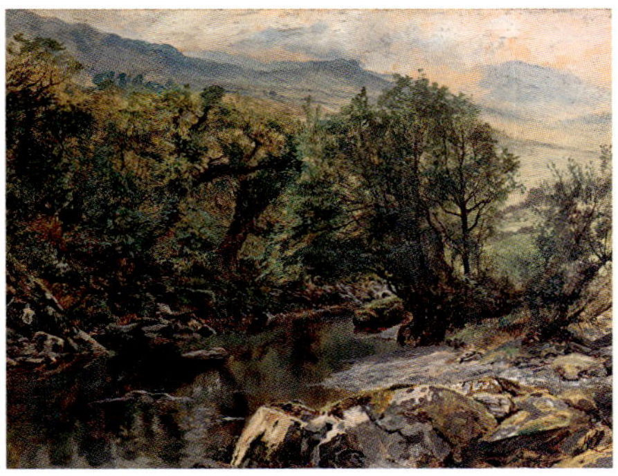

Hayes, Frederick William 1848–1918
Pool in Colwyn, North Wales
oil on paper 44.5 x 59.7
NCM 1920-51

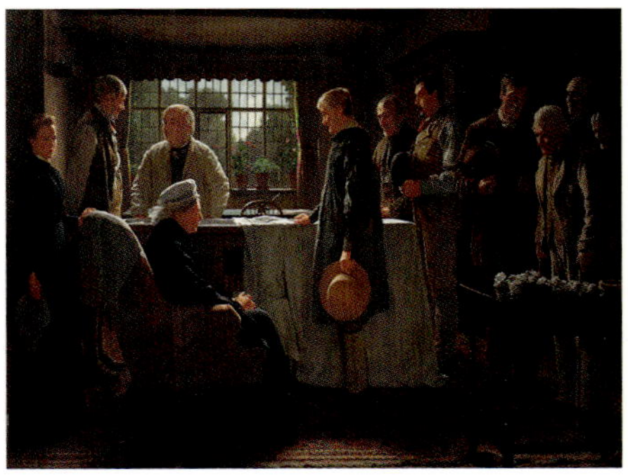

Hayllar, James 1829–1920
The Old Master 1883
oil on canvas 111.8 x 160
NCM 1885-1

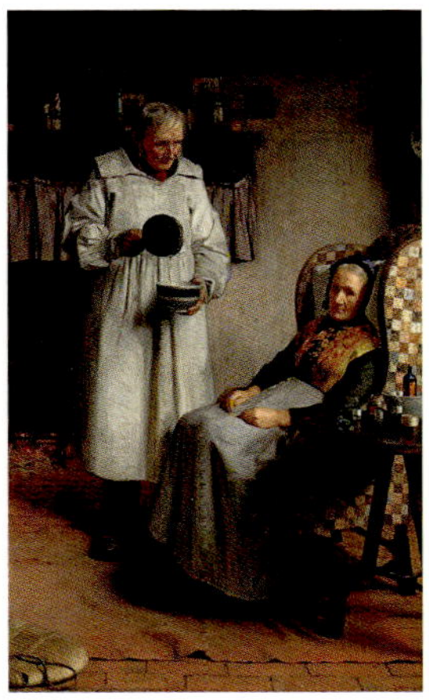

Hayllar, James 1829–1920
The Invalid
oil on canvas 91.4 x 63.5
NCM 1968-18

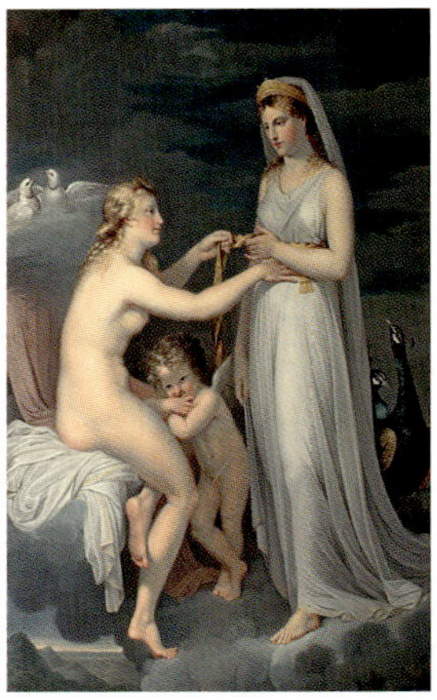

Head, Guy (attributed to) 1753–1800
Juno Borrowing the Girdle of Venus c.1771
oil on canvas 198.1 x 146.1
NCM 1894-18

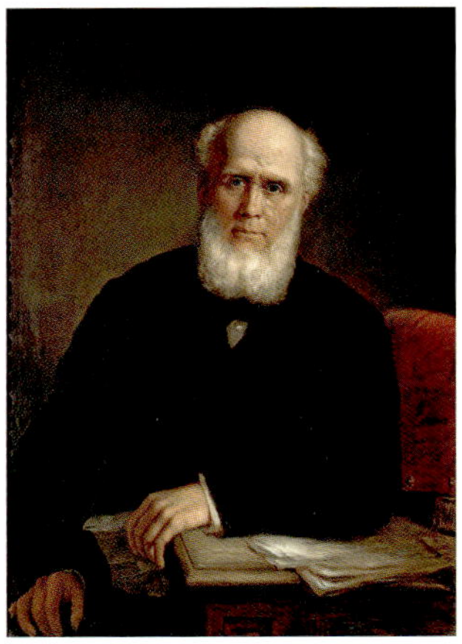

Heaphy, Thomas (after) 1775–1835
William Howitt (1792–1879)
oil on canvas 91.4 x 68.6
NCM 1890-1163

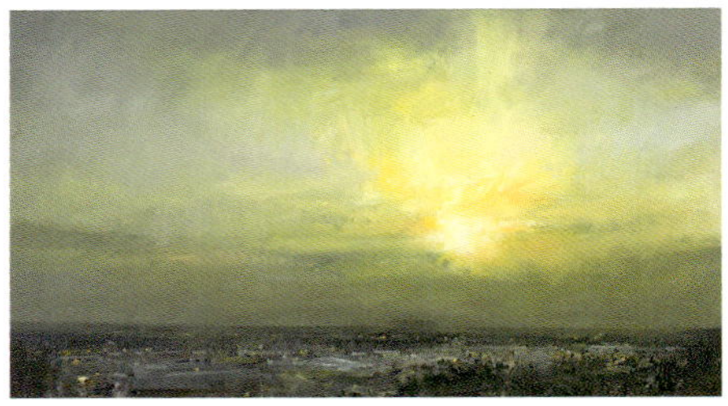

Hedderly, Nick b.1961
Nottingham, Late Afternoon 2006
oil on canvas 47.7 x 88
NCMG 2006-293

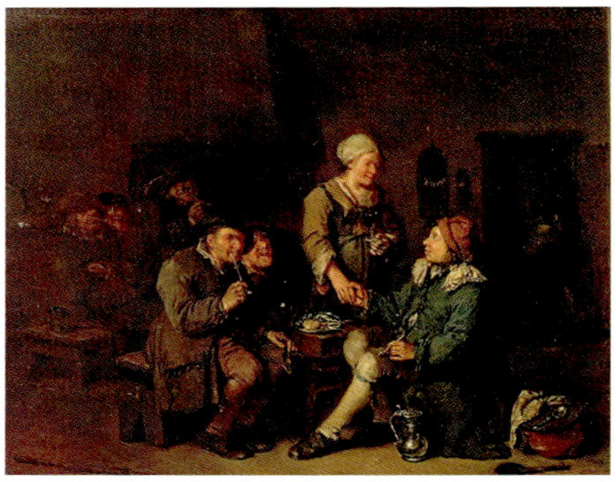

Heemskerck, Egbert van the elder
1634/1635–1704
Interior of a Tavern with Smokers
oil on wood 25.4 x 32.8
NCM 1904-103

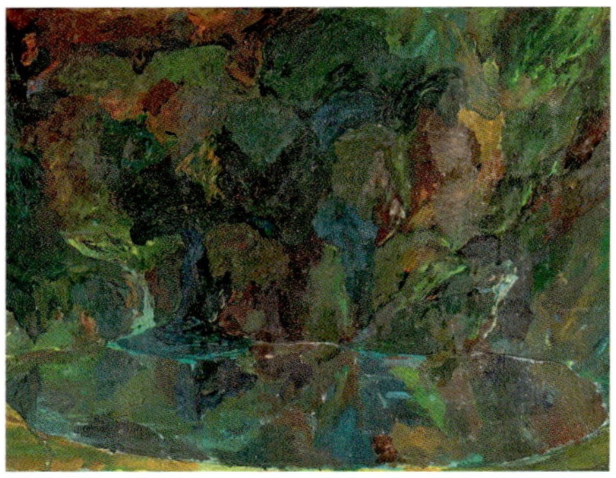

Hempton, Paul b.1946
Retreat 1972
oil on canvas 30.5 x 40.6
NCM 1973-206

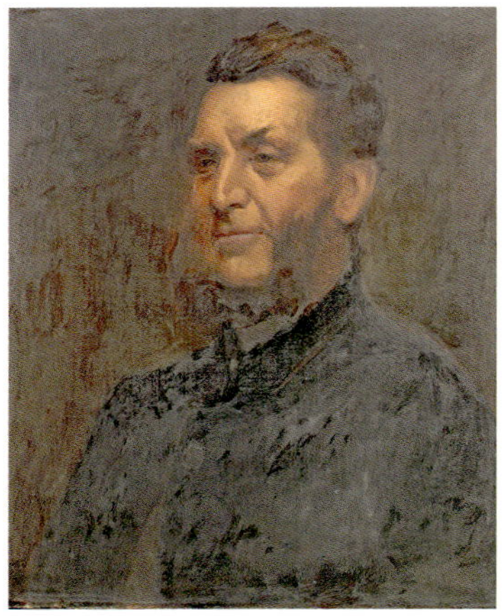

Henson, Edward c.1852–after 1891
J. Thompson 1875
oil on canvas 61 x 50.8
NCM 1878-193

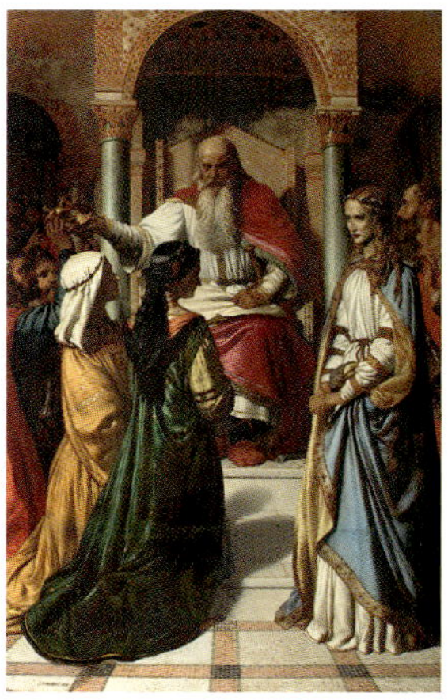

Herbert, John Rogers 1810–1890
Lear and Cordelia 1876
oil on canvas 244.2 x 170.5
FALOAN 93 (P)

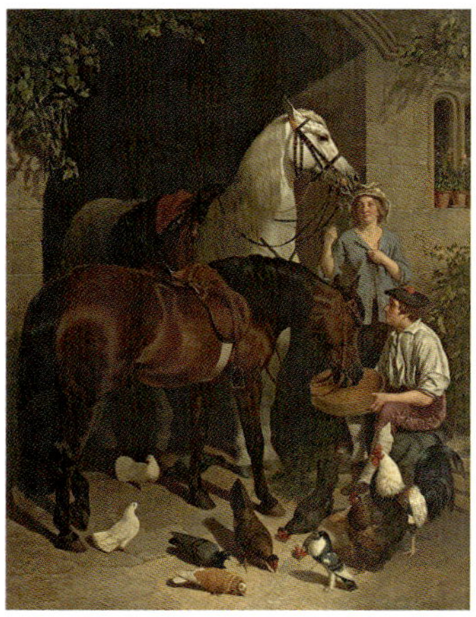

Herring, John Frederick I 1795–1865
Feeding the Horses (Horses, Figures and Poultry) 1858
oil on canvas 127 x 106.7
NCM 1941-23

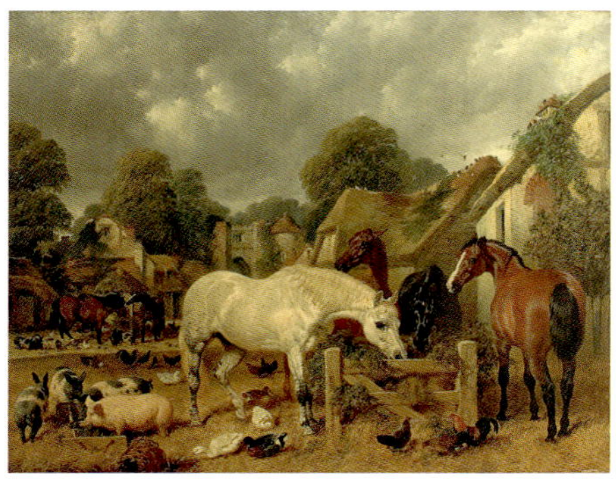

Herring, John Frederick I 1795–1865
Horses in a Paddock
oil on canvas 86.4 x 111.8
NCM 1945-82

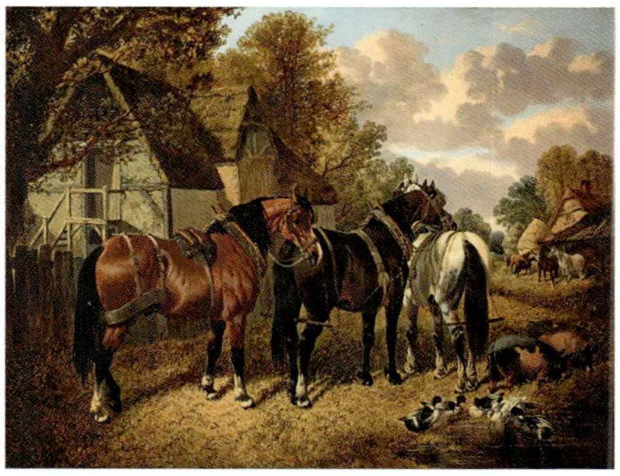

Herring, John Frederick II 1815–1907
Ready for the Plough
oil on canvas 62 x 89
NCM 1990-507

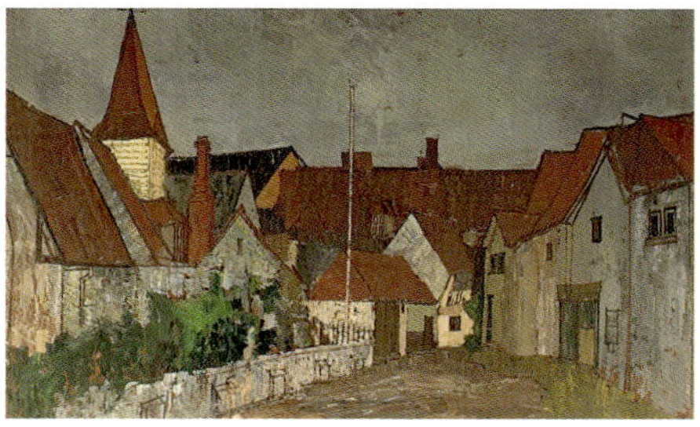

Hill, Robert W. 1932–1990
Chipping Ongar, Essex 1958
oil on wood 121.9 x 241.3
NCM 1958-29

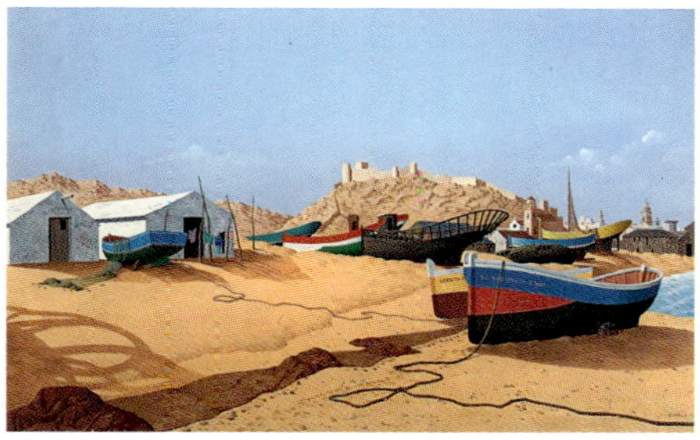

Hillier, Tristram Paul 1905–1983
Almería, Spain 1951
oil on canvas 55.9 x 91.4
NCM 1952-8

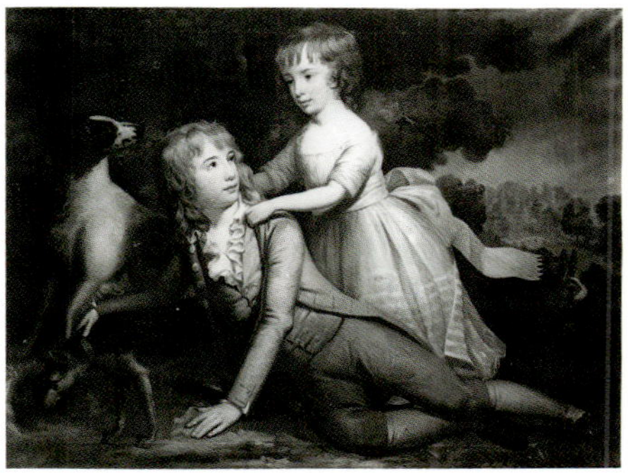

Hilton, William II 1786–1839
Jonathan and Mary Walker of Ferham
oil on canvas 99.1 x 133.4
NCM 1937-42

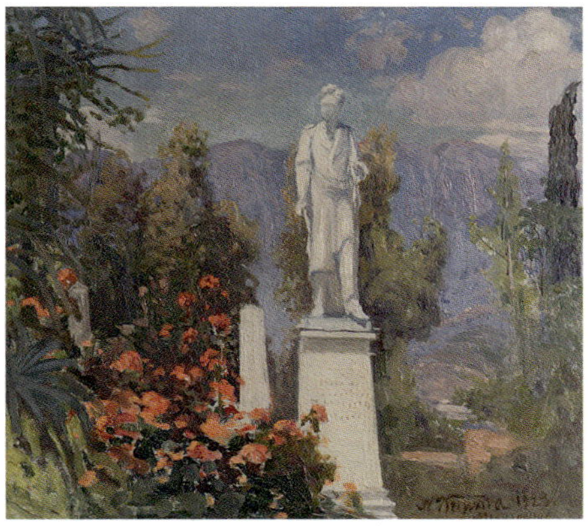

Himona, Nicolas 1865–1929
Byron's Monument at Missolonghi, Greece
1923
oil on board 29.2 x 33
NCM 1924-133

Hitchens, Ivon 1893–1979
A River Pool 1951
oil on canvas 52 x 157
NCM 1957-23

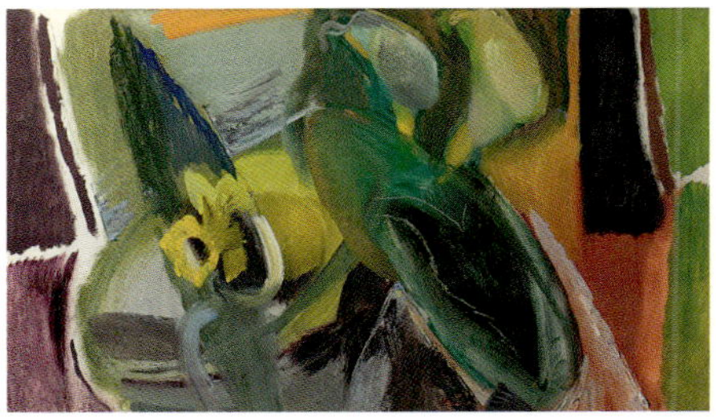

Hitchens, Ivon 1893–1979
Twelve Exercises on a Theme (Daffodils and Lilies, No.2) 1953
oil on canvas 45.7 x 76.2
NCM 1953-105

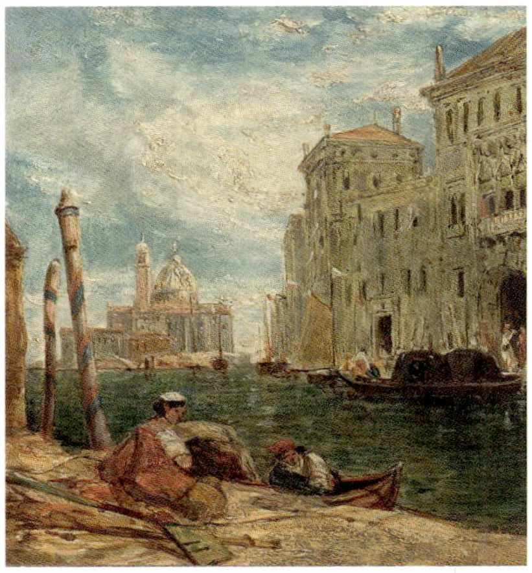

Holland, James 1800–1870
View in Venice, Italy
oil on board 22.9 x 22.9 (E)
NCM 1909-54

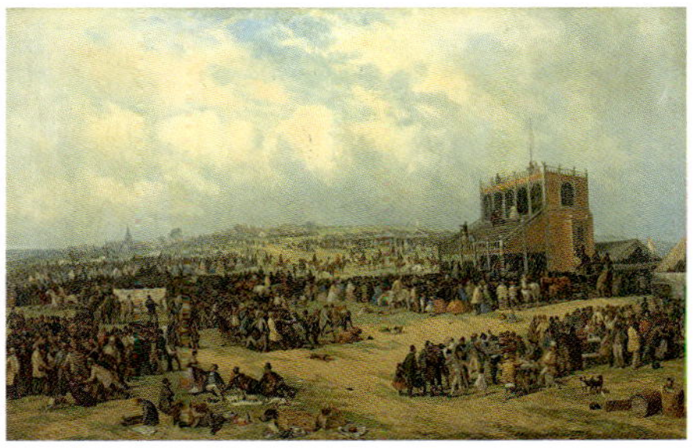

Holland, John c.1805–1880
Before the Race (Nottingham Races) 1865
oil on canvas 43.8 x 68.6
NCM 1917-1

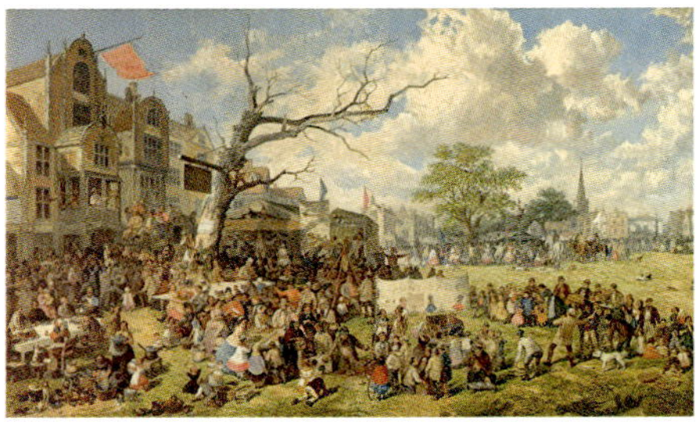

Holland, John c.1805–1880
Holiday Time (Fair Day) 1866
oil on canvas 53.3 x 91.4
NCM 1946-262

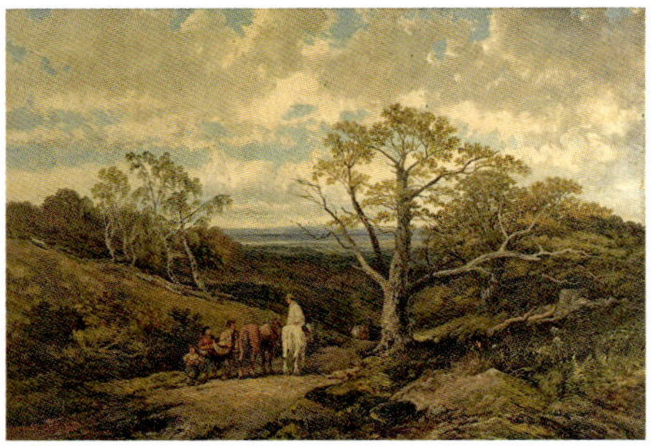

Holland, John c.1805–1880
View in Sherwood Forest (Sherwood Forest, Nottinghamshire)
oil on canvas 61 x 91.4
NCM 1902-50

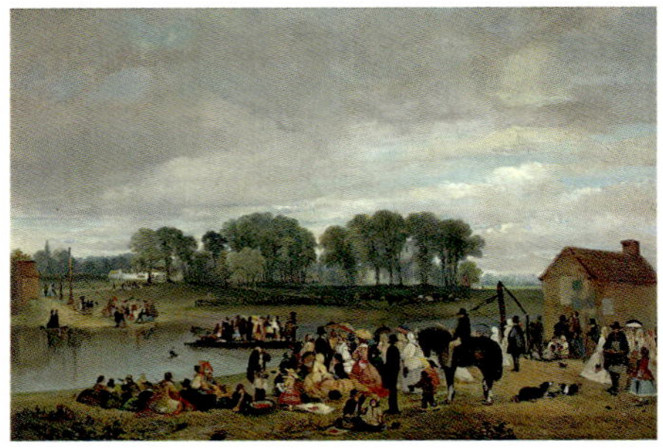

Holland, John c.1805–1880
Wilford Ferry, Nottingham (The Cherry-Eatings)
oil on canvas 61 x 91.4
NCM 1913-101

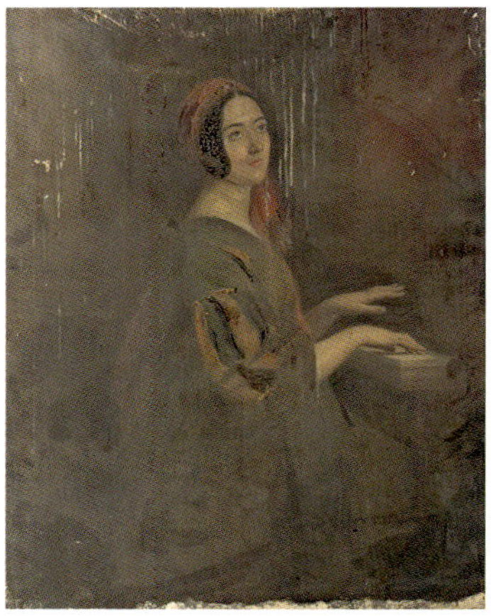

Hollins, John 1798–1855
Portrait of a Lady as St Cecilia 1841
oil on canvas 127 x 101
NCM 1882-563

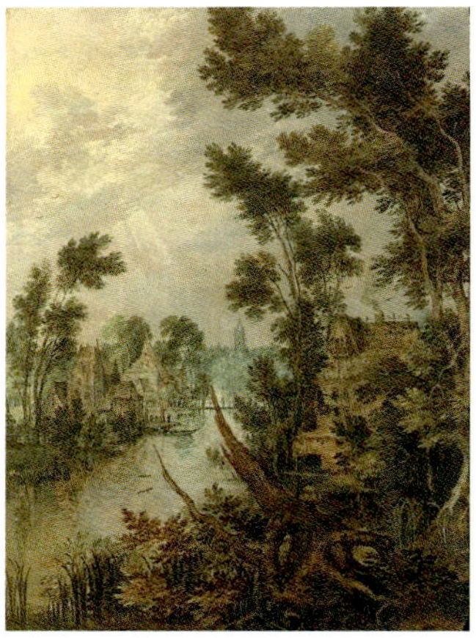

Hondecoeter, Gillis Claesz. de c.1575–1638
River Scene 1614
oil on wood 40.3 x 31.8
NCM 1900-1

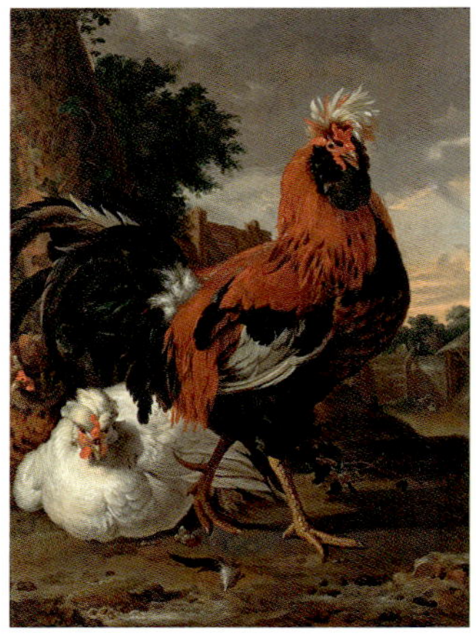

Hondecoeter, Melchior de 1636–1695
Fowl
oil on canvas 83.2 x 65.4
NCM 1904-90

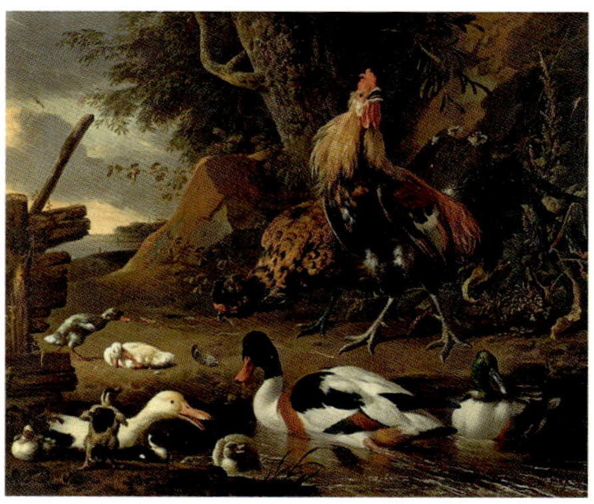

Hondecoeter, Melchior de 1636–1695
Two Fowls and Ducks on a Pond
oil on canvas 102.9 x 128.3
NCM 1939-1

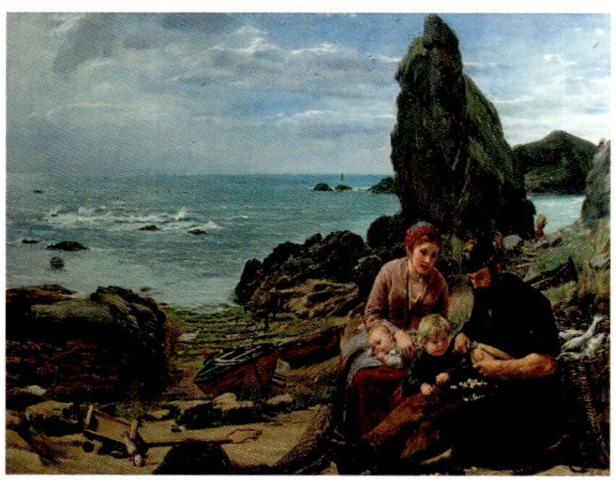

Hook, James Clarke 1819–1907
Hearts of Oak 1875
oil on canvas 95.3 x 143.5
NCM 1913-60

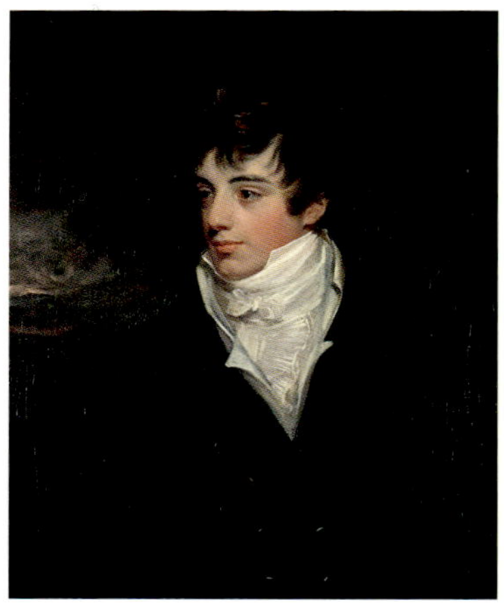

Hoppner, John 1758–1810
Henry Kirke White (1758–1810)
oil on canvas 74.9 x 62.2
NCM 1884-128

Facing page: Bonington, Richard Parkes, 1802–1828, *Ruins of the Abbey St Bertin, St Omer, France (Transept of the Abbey of St Bertin, St Omer, France)* (detail), c.1824, Nottingham City Museums and Galleries (p. 63)

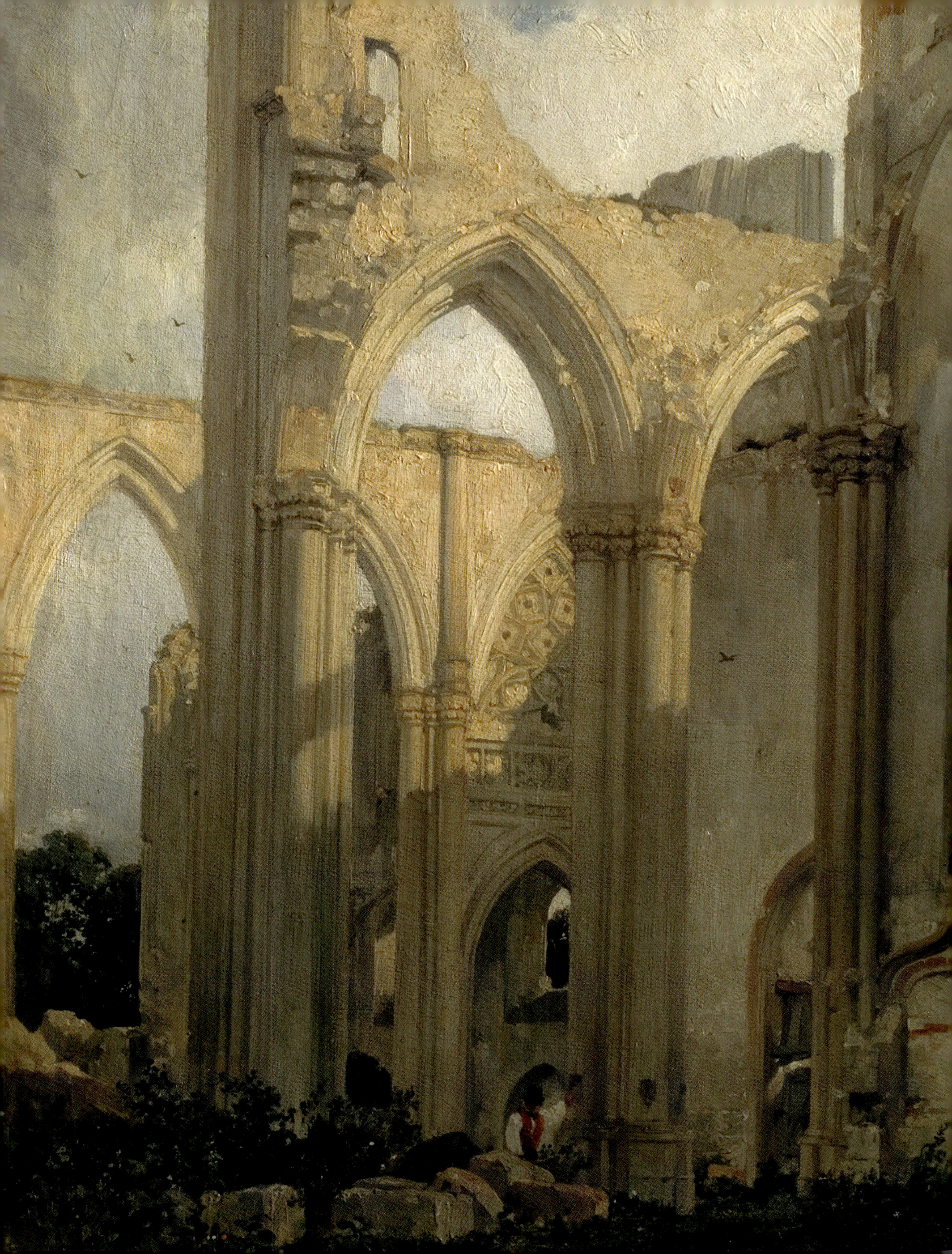

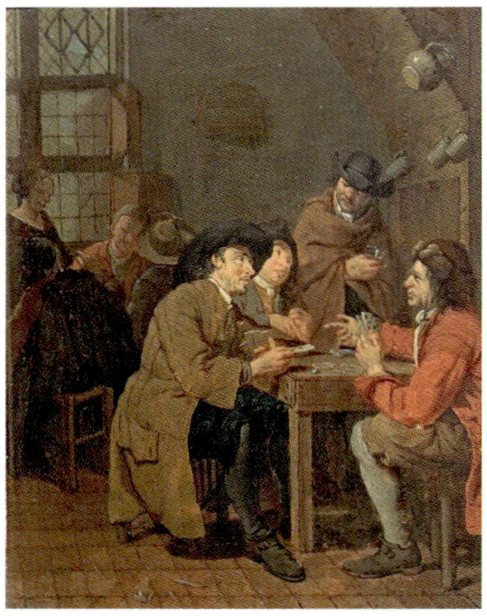

Horemans, Pieter Jacob 1700–1776
Interior, Card Playing
oil on wood 30.5 x 26.4
NCM 1904-113

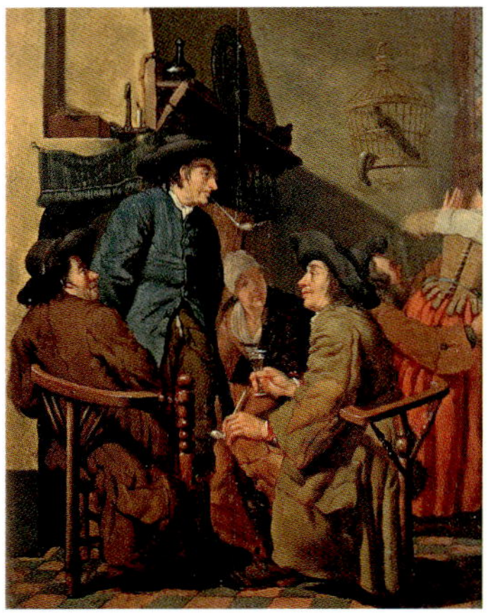

Horemans, Pieter Jacob 1700–1776
Interior, Figures Smoking
oil on wood 30.5 x 25.7
NCM 1904-114

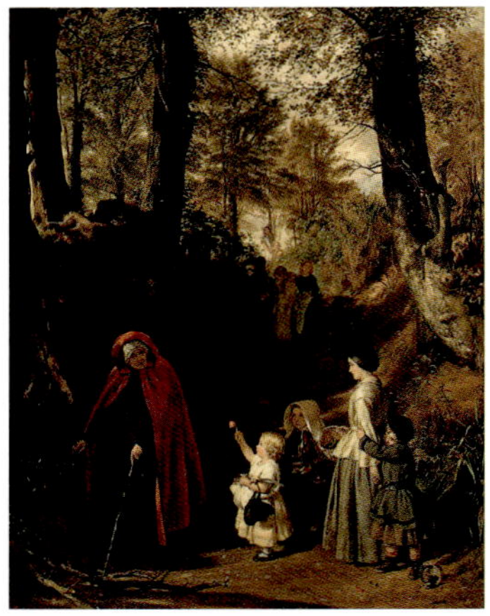

Horsley, John Callcott 1817–1903
Youth and Age 1857
oil on canvas 91.4 x 71.1
NCM 1934-128

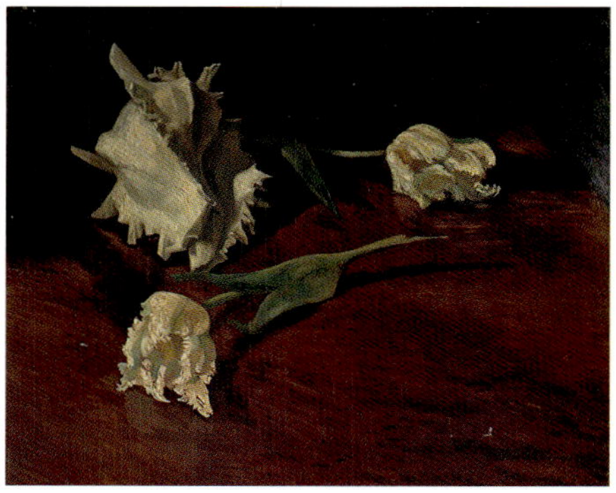

Houthuesen, Albert Anthony 1903–1979
A Shell and Flowers c.1944
oil on canvas 68.6 x 91.4
NCM 1944-32

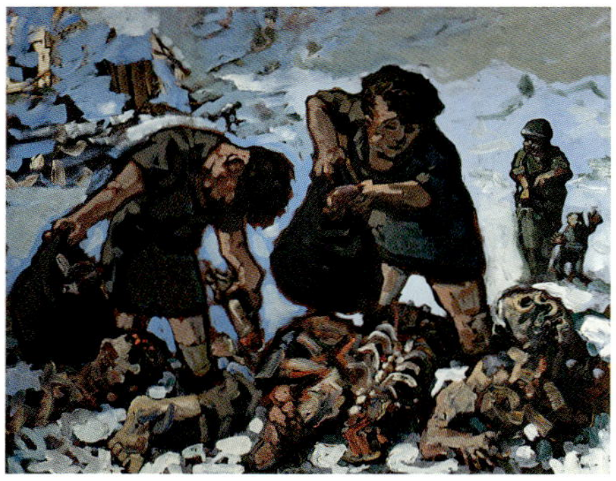

Howson, Peter b.1958
Bosnian Harvest 1994
oil on canvas 122.5 x 142.5
NCM 1995-51

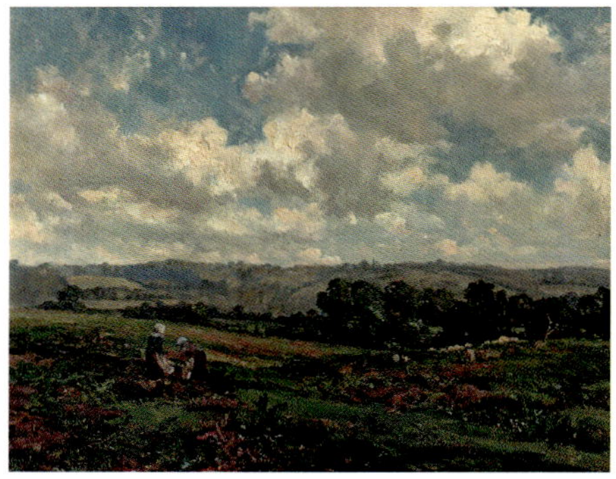

Hughes-Stanton, Herbert Edwin Pelham 1870–1937
Fields in Surrey 1890
oil on canvas 35.6 x 45.7
NCM 1933-246

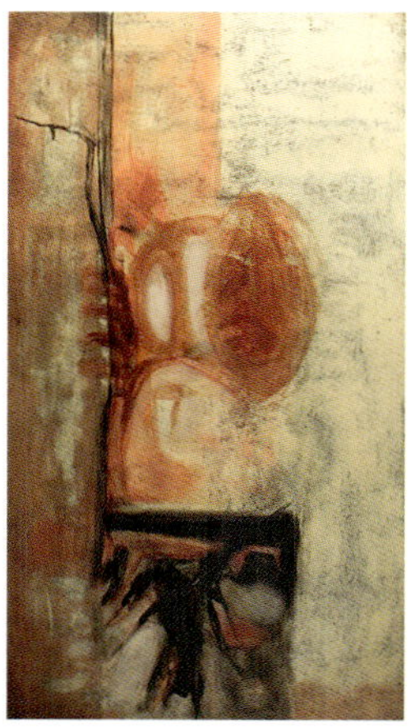

Hulbert, Thelma 1913–1995
Leaves and Red Gauze Screen
oil on wood 160 x 91.4
NCM 1966-82

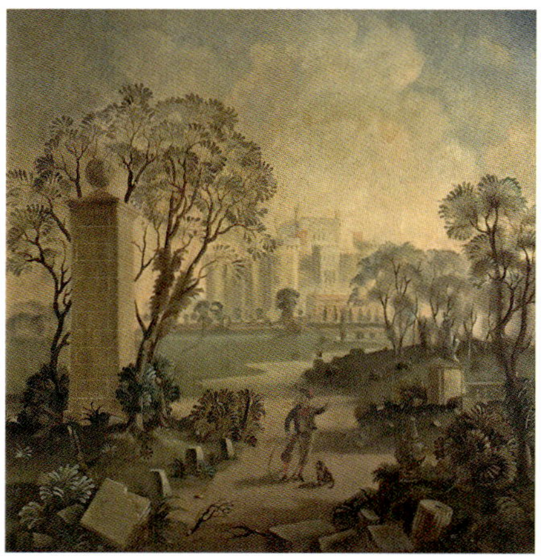

Huskinson, Leonard 1905–1974
The Little Marquess c.1936
oil on canvas 76.2 x 76.2
NCM 1936-19

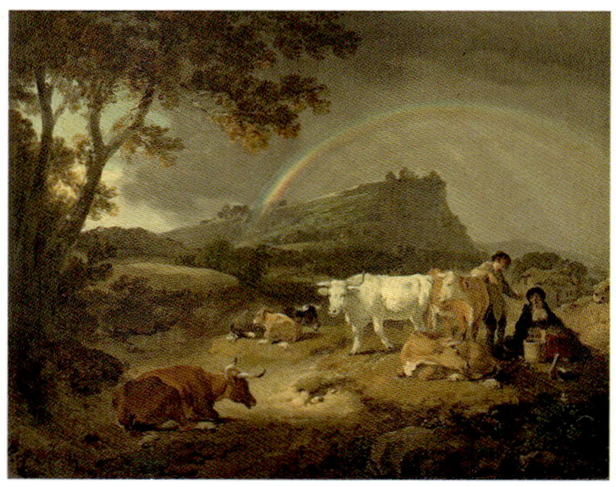

Ibbetson, Julius Caesar 1759–1817
Landscape, Beeston Castle, Cheshire, and Rainbow 1793
oil on canvas 34.9 x 45.4
NCM 1904-41

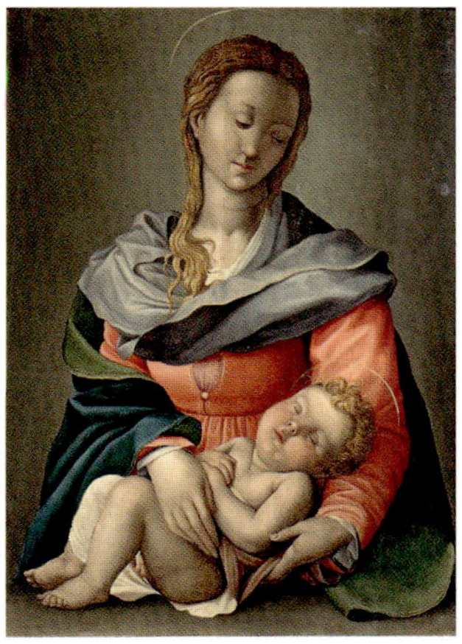

Italian (Florentine) School
Madonna and Child c.1525–1540
oil & tempera on wood 85.7 x 66
NCM 1910-62

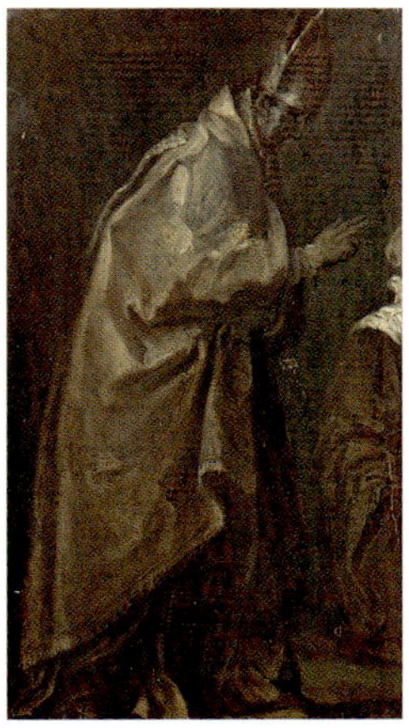

Italian (Milanese) School 17th C
A Bishop
oil on wood 40.6 x 24.1
NCM 1944-31

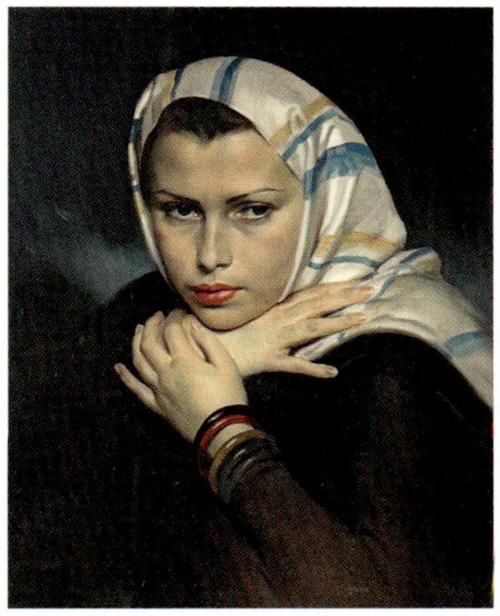

Jagger, David 1891–1958
Jewish Refugee, Vienna 1938
oil on canvas 61 x 50.8
NCM 1945-34

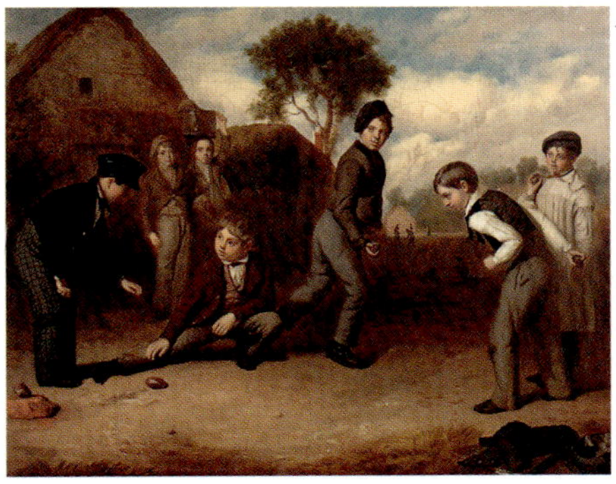

James, Robert 1809–1853
Boys Playing Duckstones c.1845
oil on canvas 59.7 x 76.2
NCM 1946-238

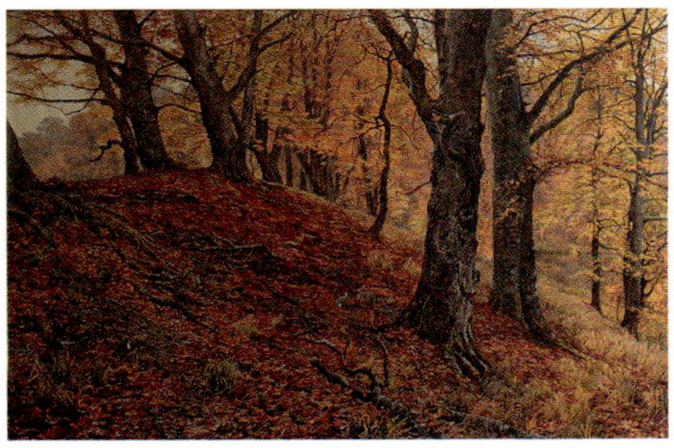

Jay, William Samuel 1843–1933
At the Fall of Leaf, Arundel Park, Sussex (Woodland Scene in Autumn) 1883
oil on canvas 106.7 x 163.8
NCM 1885-6

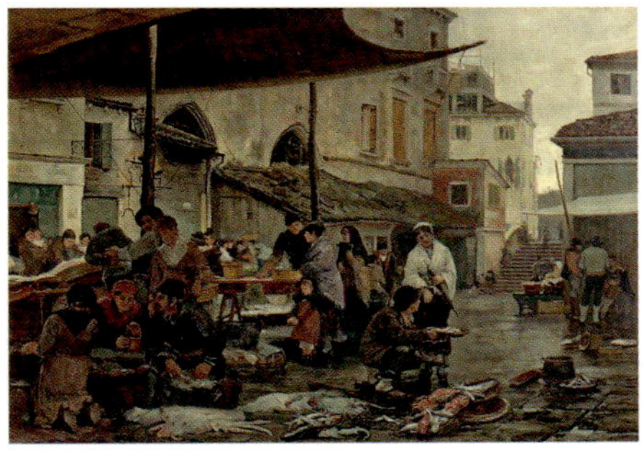

Jobbins, William H. c.1840–1893
The Fish Market, Venice, Italy 1881
oil on canvas 58.4 x 83.8
NCM 1907-76

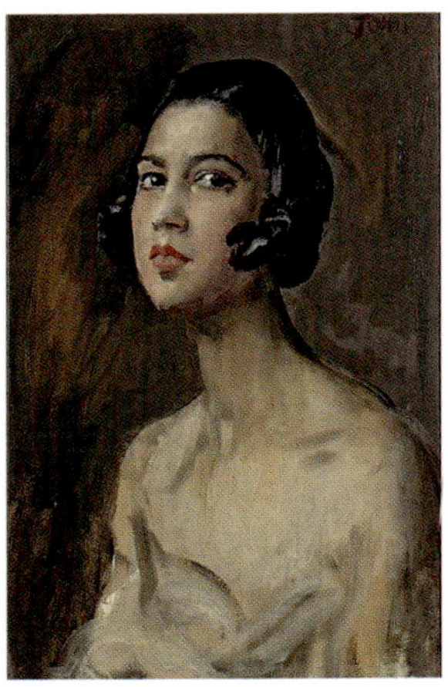

John, Augustus Edwin 1878–1961
Yvonne 1922
oil on canvas 61 x 40.6
NCM 1952-48

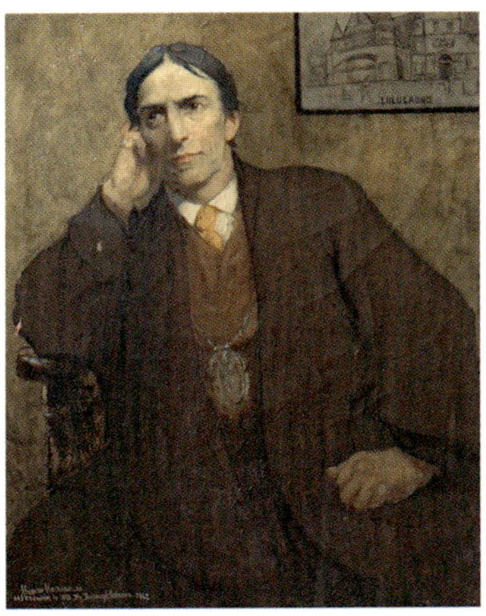

Johnson, Ernest Borough 1866–1949
Posthumous Portrait of Sir Hubert von Herkomer (1849–1914) 1942
oil on canvas 61 x 50.8
NCM 1942-33

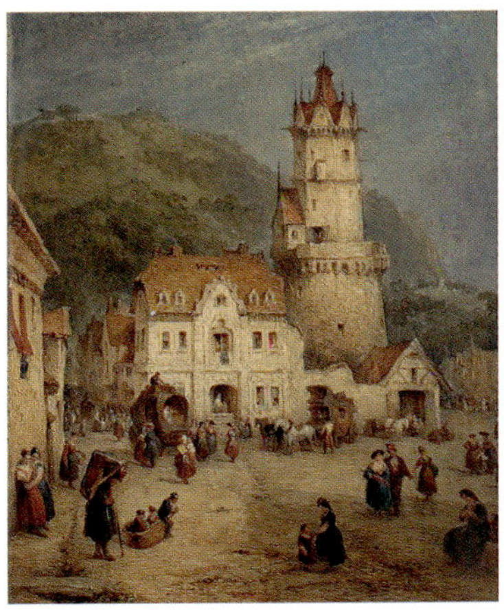

Jones, George 1786–1869
Andernach, Prussia 1863
oil on canvas 33 x 27.9
NCM 1882-85

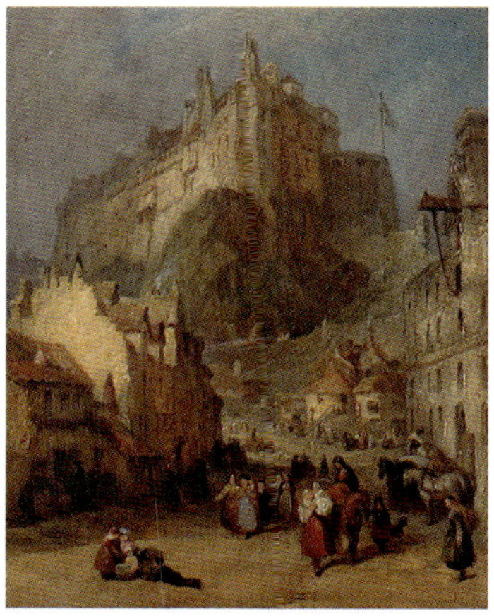

Jones, George 1786–1869
Edinburgh Castle from the Grass Market, Scotland
oil on canvas 31.1 x 26
NCM 1882-86

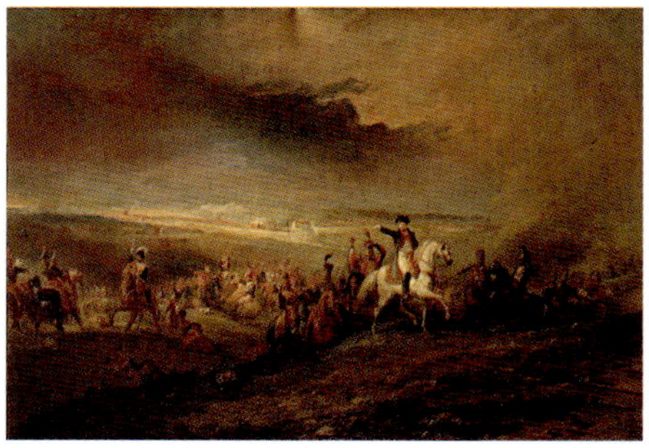

Jones, George 1786–1869
Napoleon Leaving the Field of Waterloo, 18 June 1815
oil on canvas 58.3 x 90
NCM 1882-84

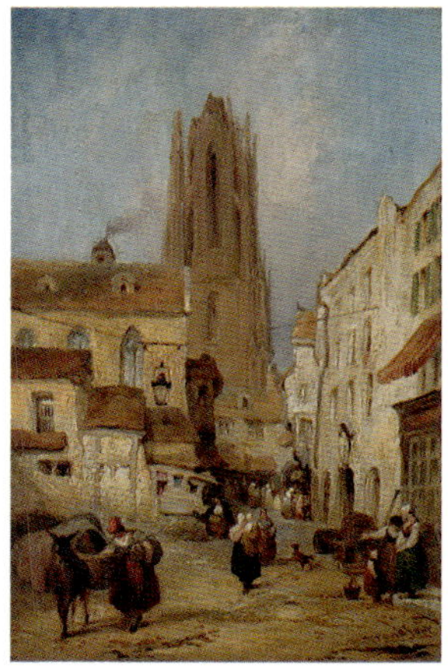

Jones, George 1786–1869
Street Scene in Frankfurt, Germany
oil on canvas 31.8 x 22.2
NCM 1882-89

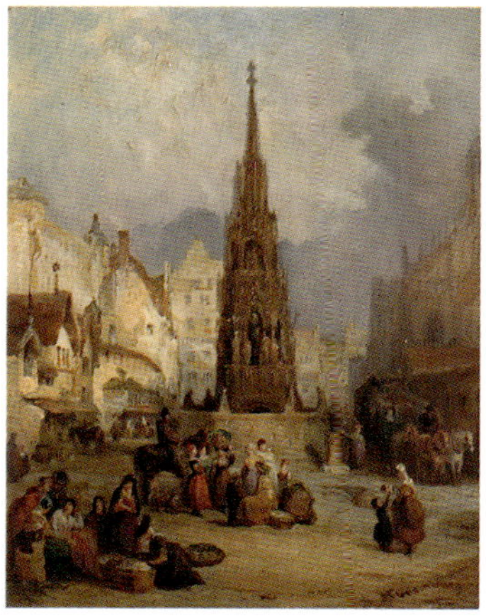

Jones, George 1786–1869
View in Nuremberg, Germany
oil on canvas 30.5 x 25.4
NCM 1882-87

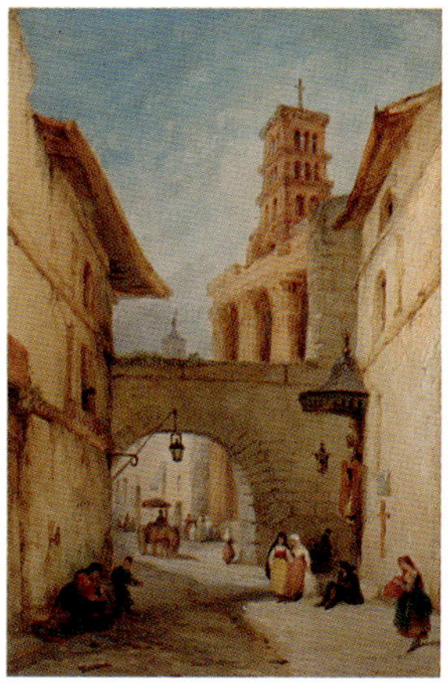

Jones, George 1786–1869
View in Rome, Italy, the Forum of Nerva
oil on canvas 30.5 x 21
NCM 1882-88

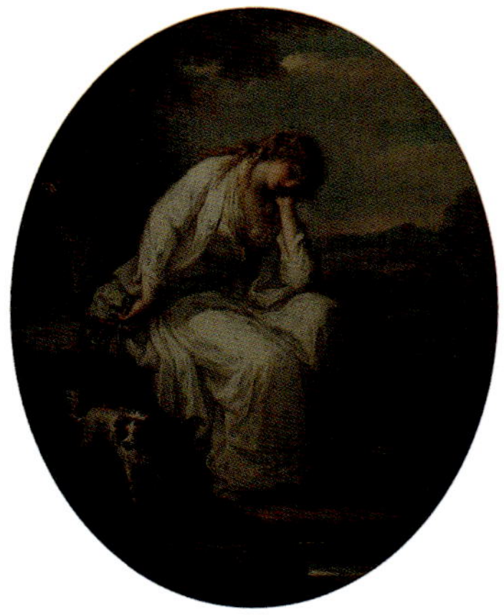

Kauffman, Angelica (after) 1740–1807
Maria
oil on canvas 30.8 x 25.4
NCM 1904-42

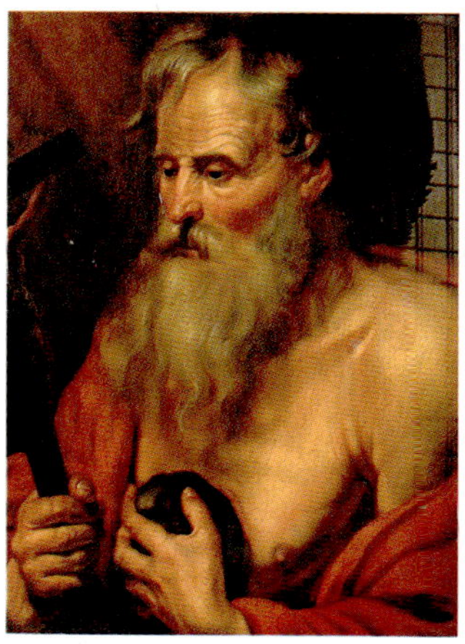

Keyser, Willem de (after) c.1647–1692
St Jerome
oil on canvas 61 x 48.2
NCM 1940-33

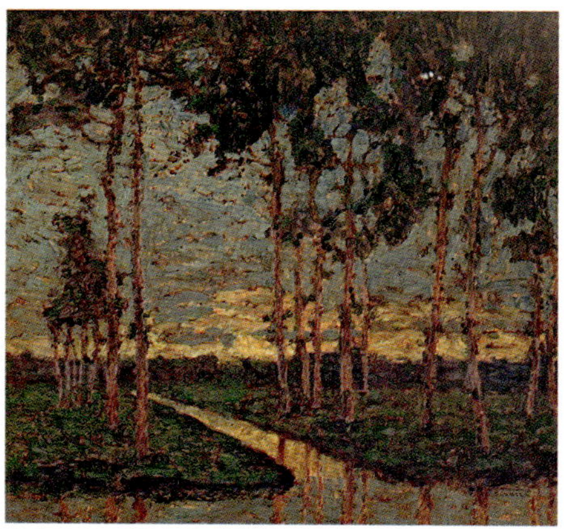

Kiddier, William 1859–1934
The Dyke 1921
oil on canvas 83.8 x 96.5
NCM 1922-10

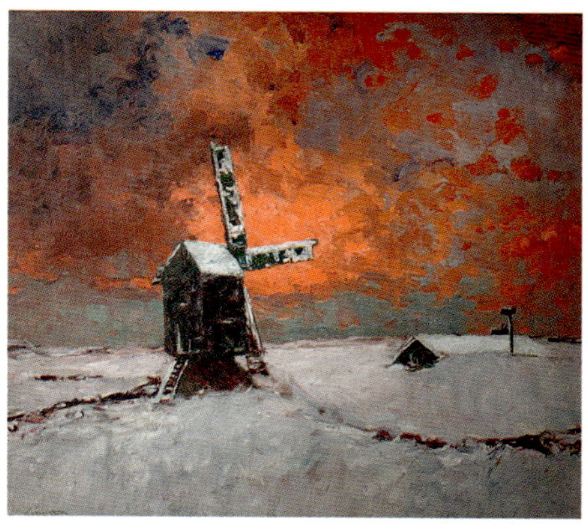

Kiddier, William 1859–1934
Snowbound Windmill c.1922
oil on canvas 85.1 x 96.5
NCM 1969-104

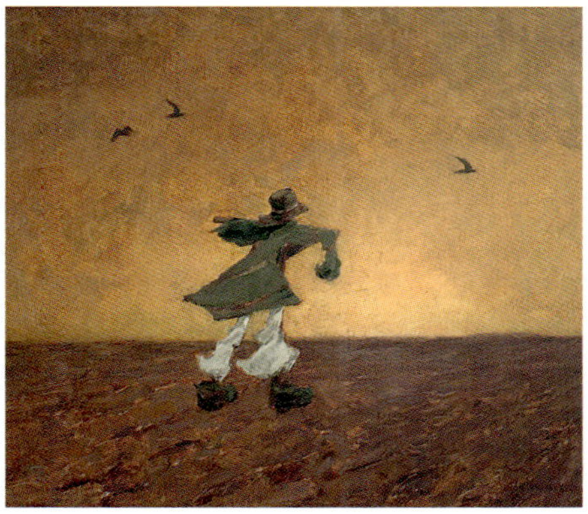

Kiddier, William 1859–1934
The Scarecrow c.1928
oil on canvas 63.5 x 76.2
NCM 1958-25

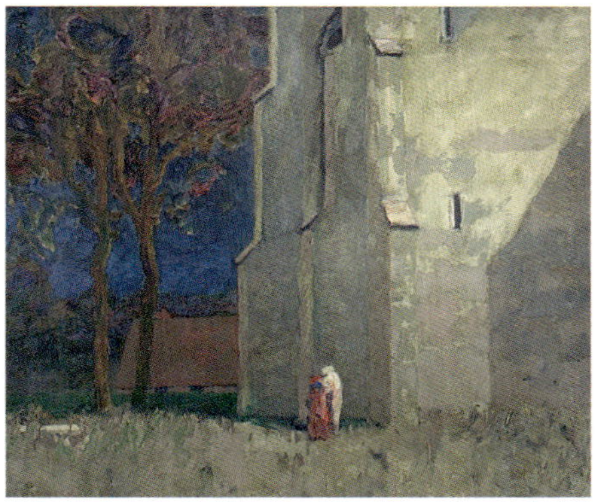

Kiddier, William 1859–1934
St Crispin
oil on canvas 63 x 74.5
NCM 1987-1034

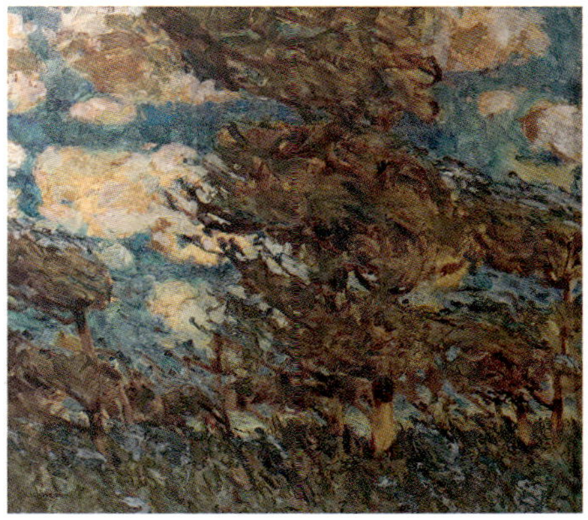

Kiddier, William 1859–1934
The West Wind
oil on canvas 84 x 96
NCM 1987-1035

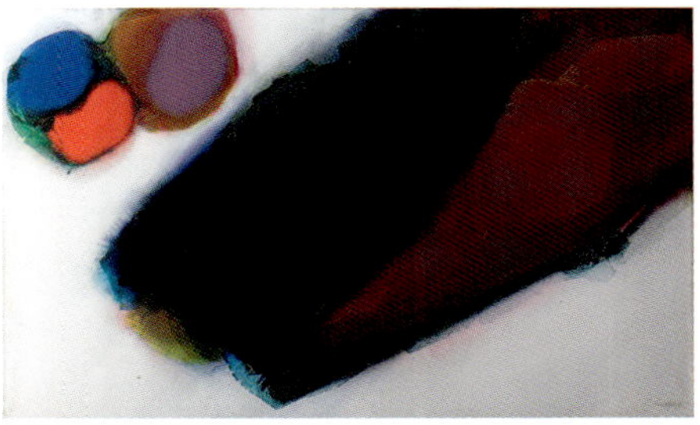

Knapp, Stefan 1921–1996
Untitled c.1964
oil & enamel on wood 40.6 x 71.1
NCM 1964-299

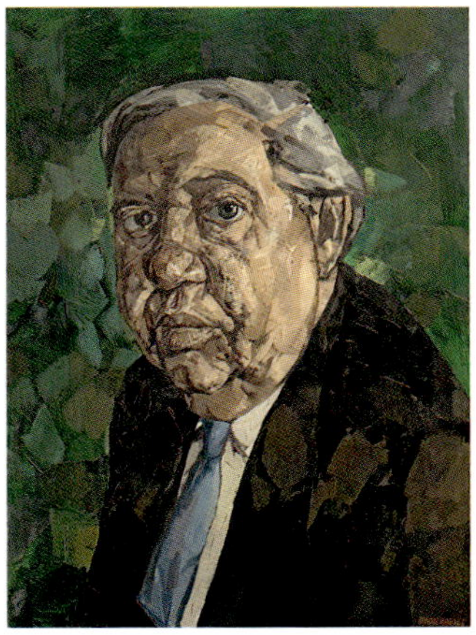

Kneale, Bryan b.1930
Charles Laughton (1899–1962) 1958–1959
oil on canvas 103.5 x 78.1
NCM 1959-96

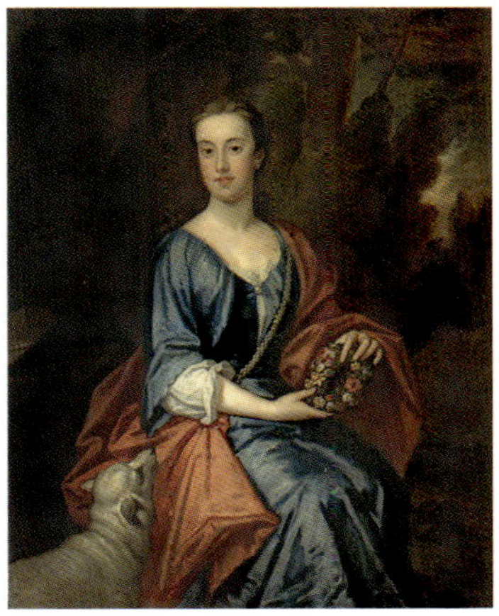

Kneller, Godfrey 1646–1723
Lady Jane Jackson (d.1731) 1713
oil on canvas 123.5 x 101
NCM 1933-250

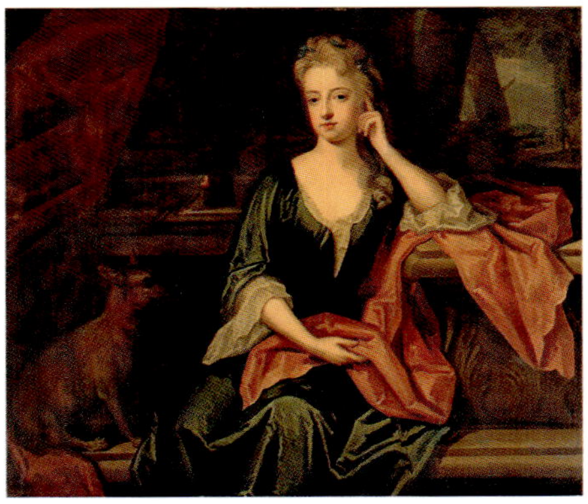

Kneller, Godfrey (school of) 1646–1723
Lady with a Dog and a Parrot 17th C
oil on canvas 107.3 x 133.4
NCM 1967-281

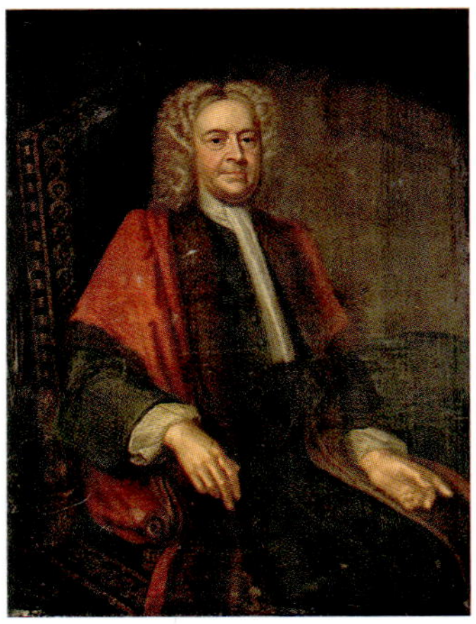

Kneller, Godfrey (school of) 1646–1723
Ralph Edge (1689–1766)
oil on canvas 127 x 101.6
NCM 1978-765

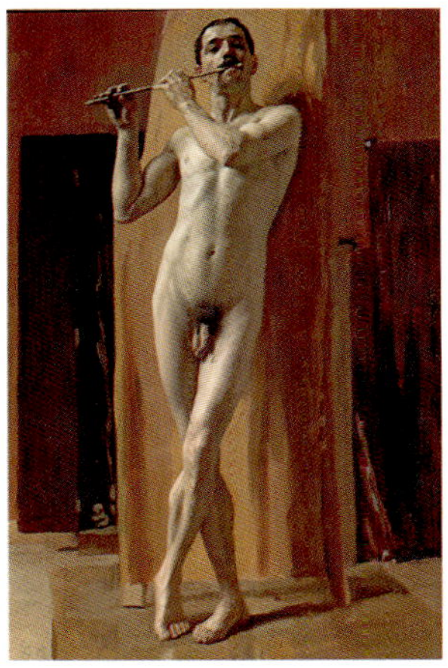

Knight, Harold 1874–1961
Standing Male Nude 1895
oil on canvas 74.9 x 53.3
NCM 1941-5

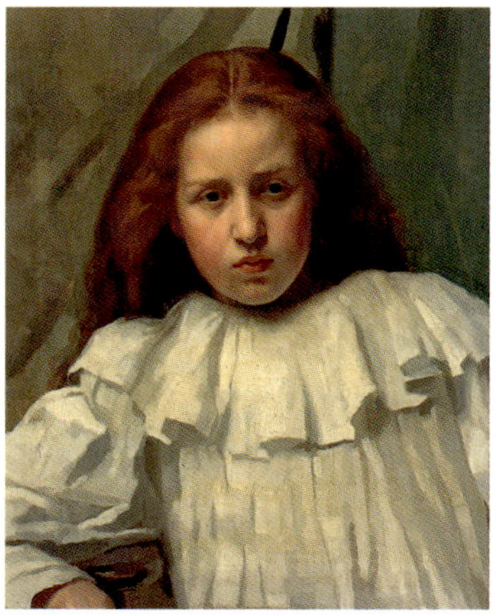

Knight, Harold 1874–1961
Girl in a White Dress c.1896
oil on canvas 61 x 50.8
NCM 1941-8

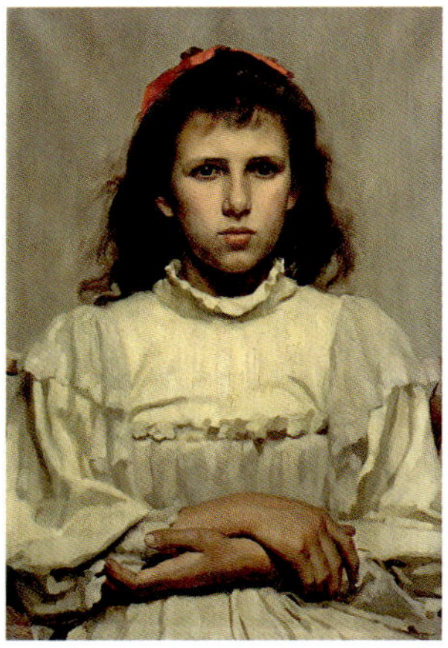

Knight, Harold 1874–1961
Girl with a Red Bow c.1896
oil on canvas 74.9 x 54.6
NCM 1941-9

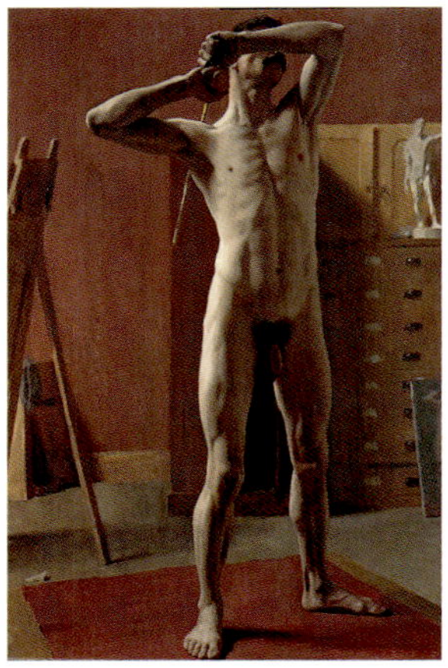

Knight, Harold 1874–1961
Standing Male Nude c.1896
oil on canvas 74.9 x 53.3
NCM 1941-3

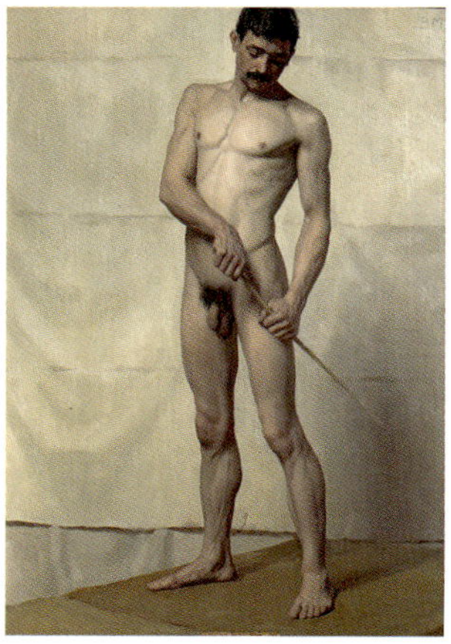

Knight, Harold 1874–1961
Standing Male Nude c.1896
oil on canvas 74.9 x 53.3
NCM 1941-4

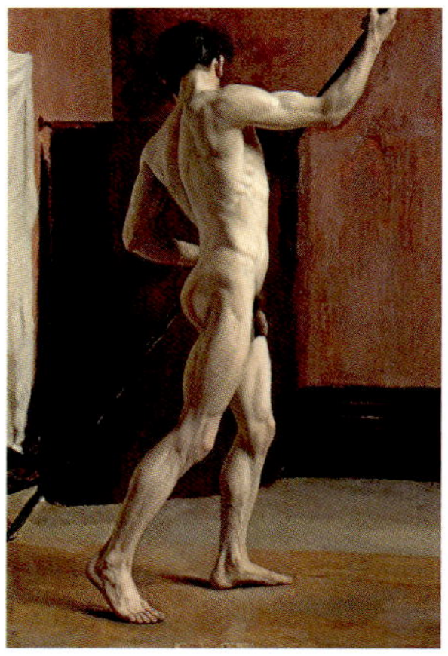

Knight, Harold 1874–1961
Standing Male Nude c.1896
oil on canvas 74.9 x 54.6
NCM 1941-6

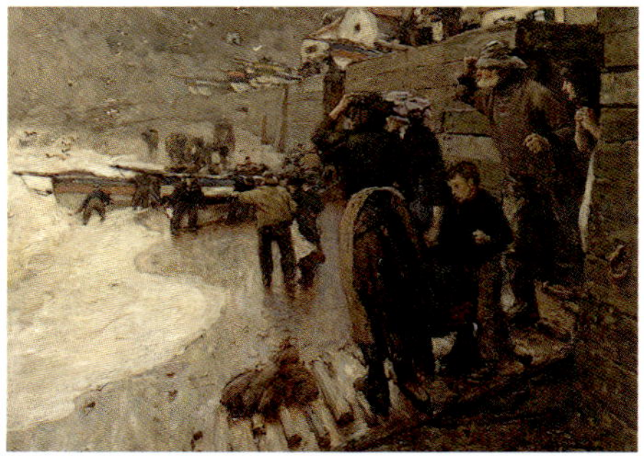

Knight, Harold 1874–1961
The Last Coble 1900
oil on canvas 92.7 x 127.6
NCM 1902-30

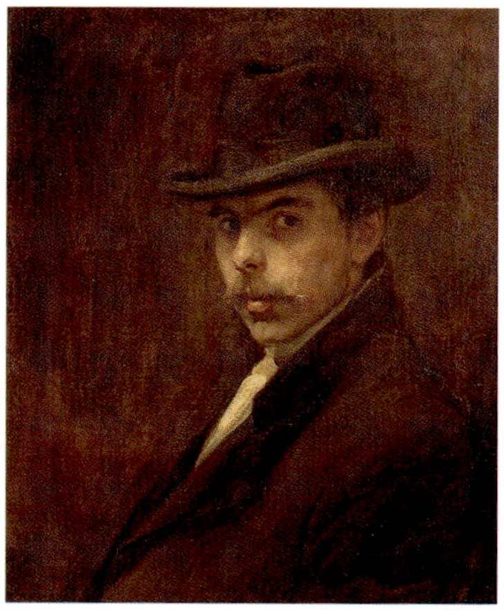

Knight, Harold 1874–1961
Wellington James Thompson 1903
oil on canvas 62 x 51.5
NCM 1992-652

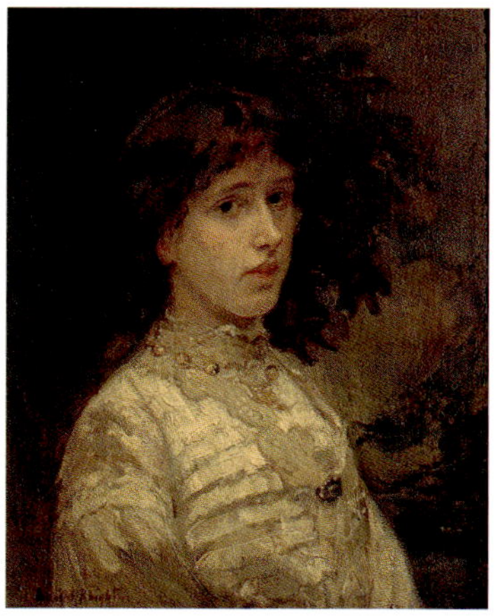

Knight, Harold 1874–1961
Mrs Rosamond Edith Thompson 1904
oil on canvas 61 x 49
NCM 1992-653

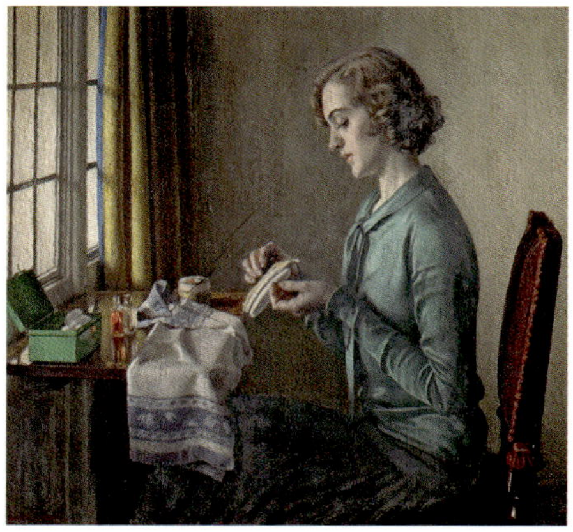

Knight, Harold 1874–1961
The Manicure 1933
oil on canvas 45.7 x 50.8
NCM 1934-60

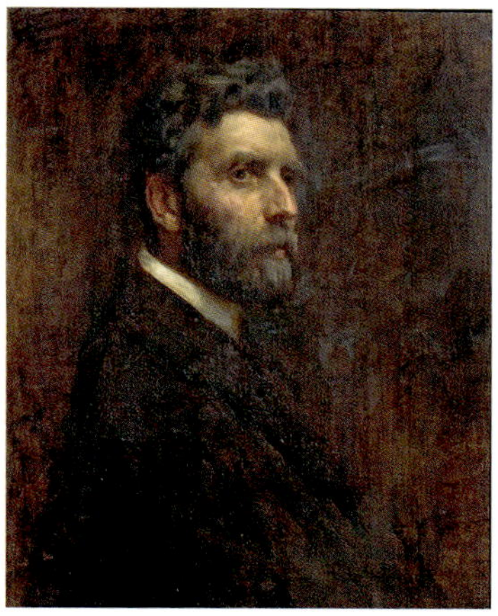

Knight, Harold 1874–1961
William Kiddier (1859–1934) 1934
oil on canvas 67.9 x 59.7
NCM 1969-177

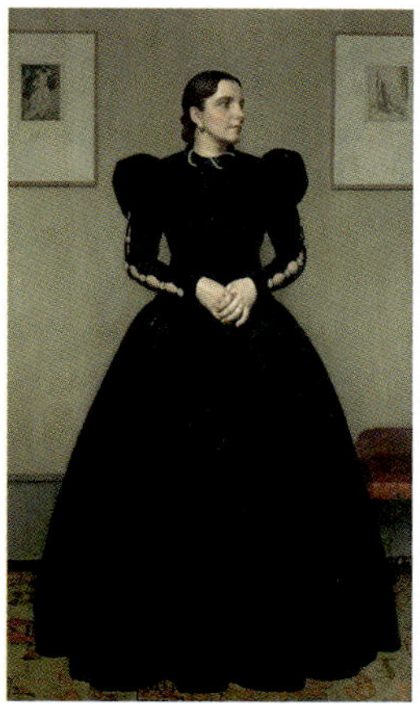

Knight, Harold 1874–1961
Ethel Bartlett, Pianist c.1935
oil on canvas 198.1 x 116.8
NCM 1954-71

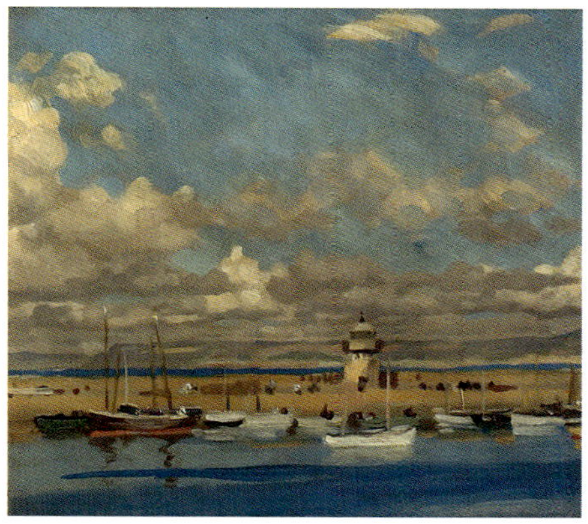

Knight, Harold 1874–1961
St Ives Bay, Cornwall
oil on canvas 30.5 x 35.6
NCM 1936-42

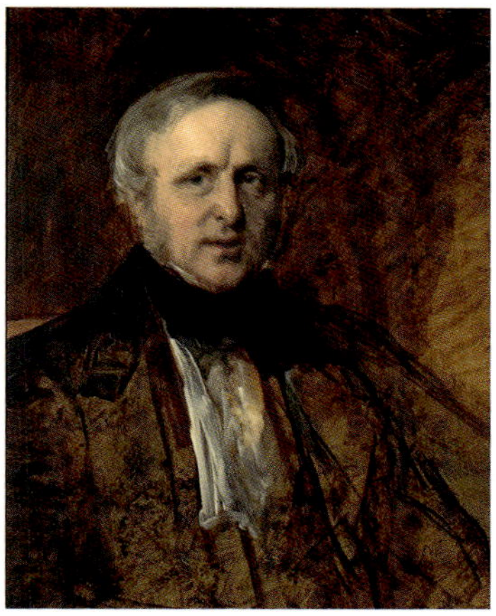

Knight, John Prescott 1803–1881
James Duffield Harding (1798–1863)
oil on canvas 68.6 x 58.4
NCM 1904-43

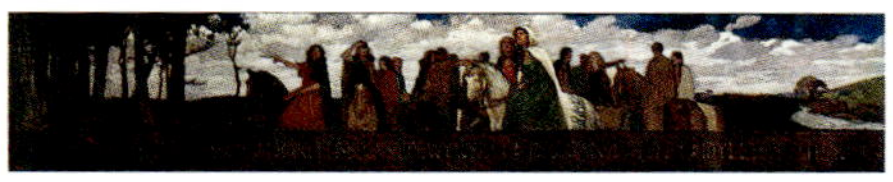

Knight, Laura 1877–1970
Idylls of the King (Pelleas and Ettare) (1 of 6)
c.1901
oil on canvas 76 x 437
NCMG 2008-1

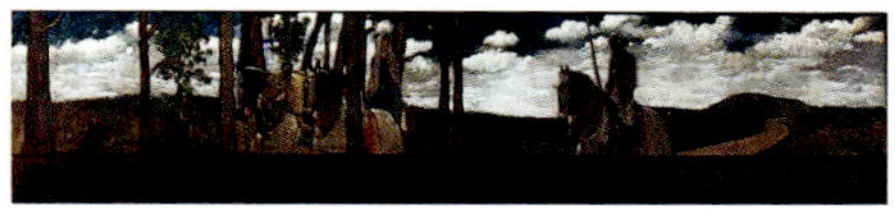

Knight, Laura 1877–1970
Idylls of the King (Enid and Geraint) (2 of 6)
c.1901
oil on canvas 76 x 437
NCMG 2008-2

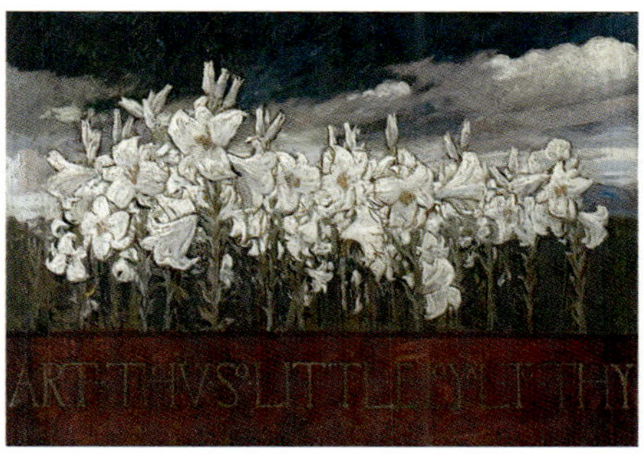

Knight, Laura 1877–1970
Idylls of the King (Balin and Balan, i) (3 of 6)
c.1901
oil on canvas 76 x 112
NCMG 2008-3

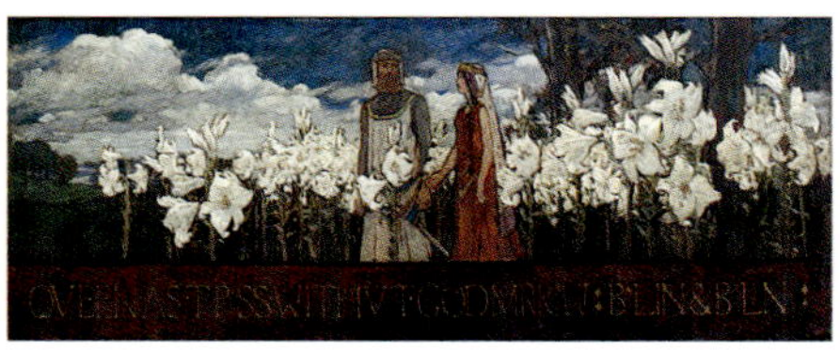

Knight, Laura 1877–1970
Idylls of the King (Balin and Balan, ii) (4 of 6)
c.1901
oil on canvas 76 x 198
NCMG 2008-4

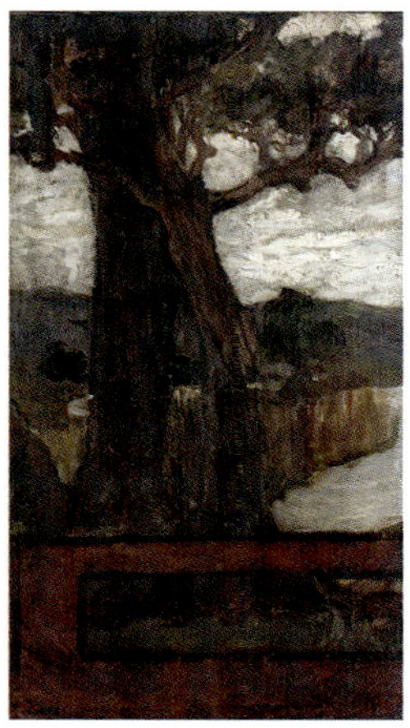

Knight, Laura 1877–1970
Tree, Idylls of the King (left panel) (5 of 6)
c.1901
oil on canvas 76 x 46
NCMG 2008-5

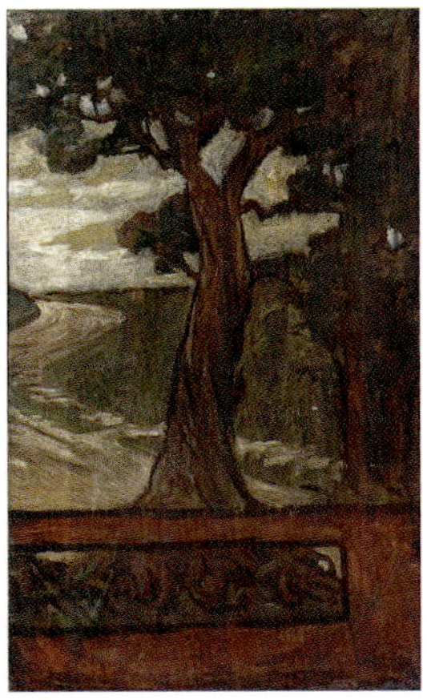

Knight, Laura 1877–1970
Tree, Idylls of the King (right panel) (6 of 6) c.1901
oil on canvas 76 x 46
NCMG 2008-6

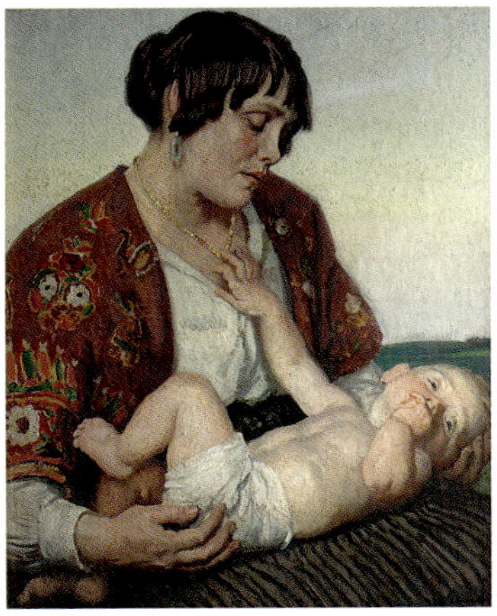

Knight, Laura 1877–1970
Motherhood c.1922
oil on canvas 77.5 x 66
NCM 1923-19

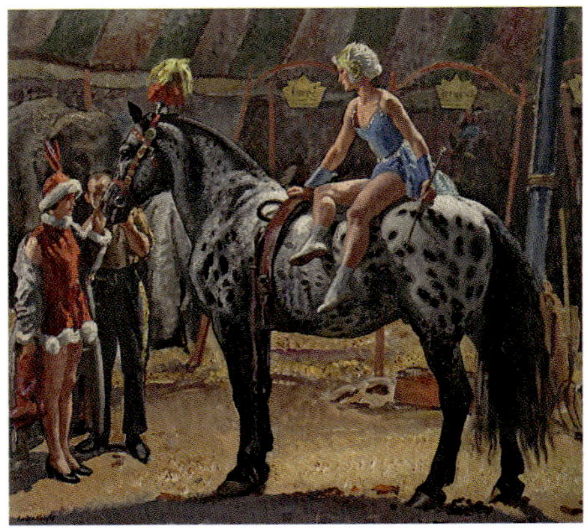

Knight, Laura 1877–1970
Elsie on 'Hassan' 1929–1930
oil on canvas 68.6 x 76.2
NCM 1930-49

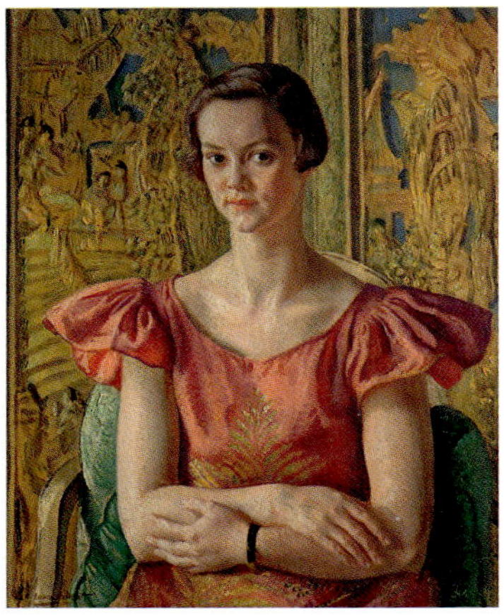

Knight, Laura 1877–1970
Miss Thompson (Miss Patricia Thompson) 1932
oil on board 76 x 63.5
NCMG 2006-294

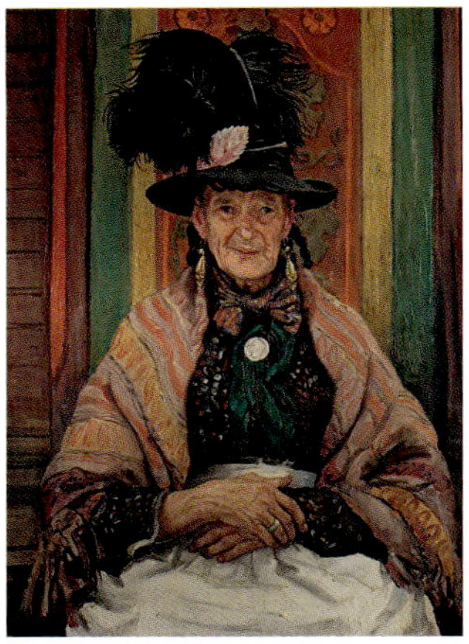

Knight, Laura 1877–1970
Fine Feathers 1939
oil on canvas 101.6 x 76.2
NCM 1949-91

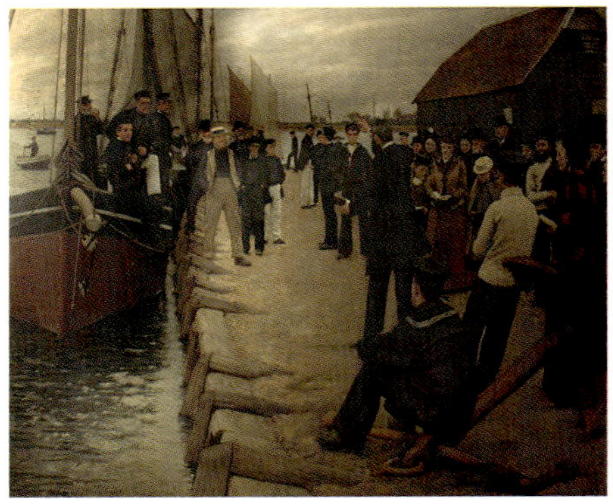

La Thangue, Henry Herbert 1859–1929
A Mission to Seamen 1891
oil on canvas 180.3 x 235
NCM 1893-9

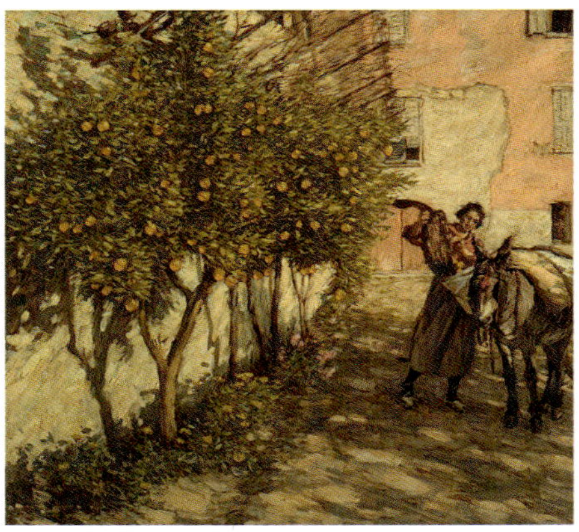

La Thangue, Henry Herbert 1859–1929
Gathering Oranges 1929
oil on canvas 71.5 x 81
NCM 1941-59

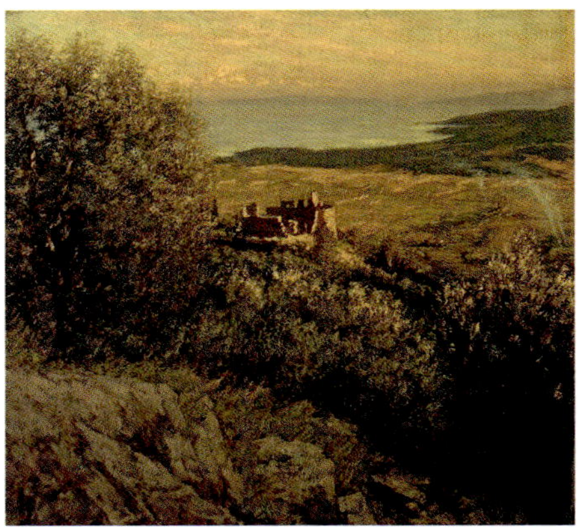

La Thangue, Henry Herbert 1859–1929
A Provençal Castle
oil on canvas 69.9 x 78.7
NCM 1941-61

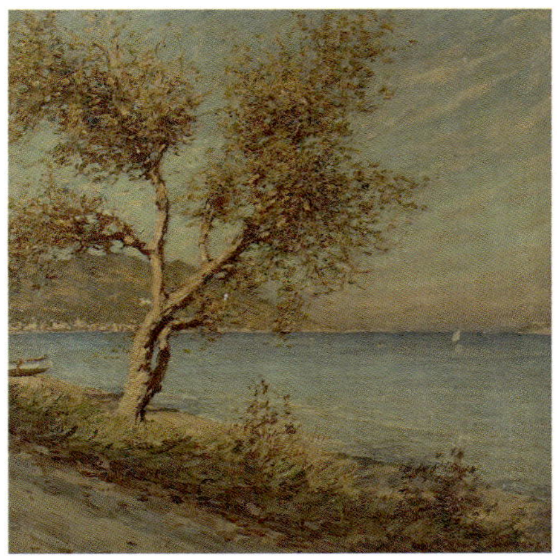

La Thangue, Henry Herbert 1859–1929
The Mulberry Tree
oil on canvas 67.3 x 73.6
NCM 1941-60

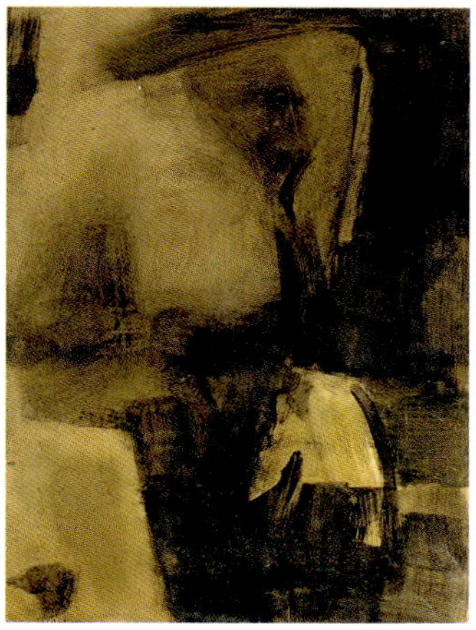

Labad, Alberto b.1940
Nude 1964
oil on paper 64.5 x 49.8
NCM 1966-68

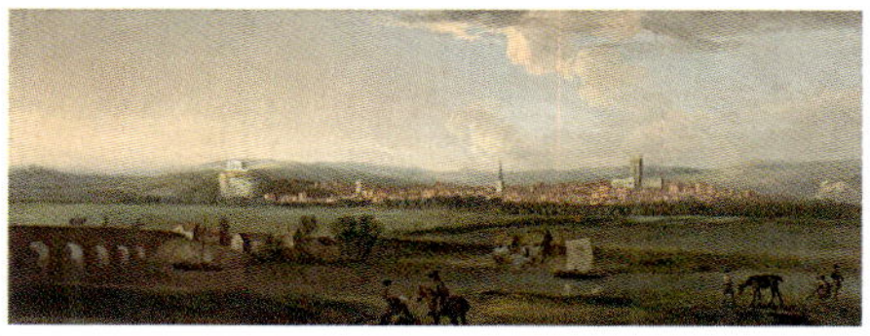

Lambert, George (style of) c.1700–1765
Nottingham from the South
oil on canvas 37.5 x 104.1
NCM 1973-389

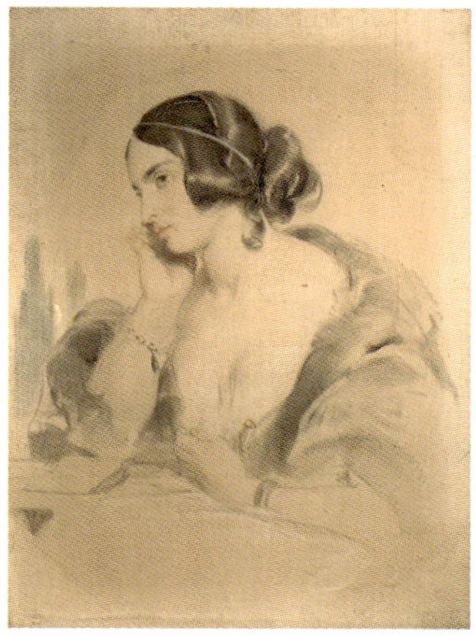

Landseer, Edwin Henry 1802–1873
The Honourable Mrs Norton c.1850
oil, charcoal & crayon on canvas 91.5 x 71.1
NCM 1941-22

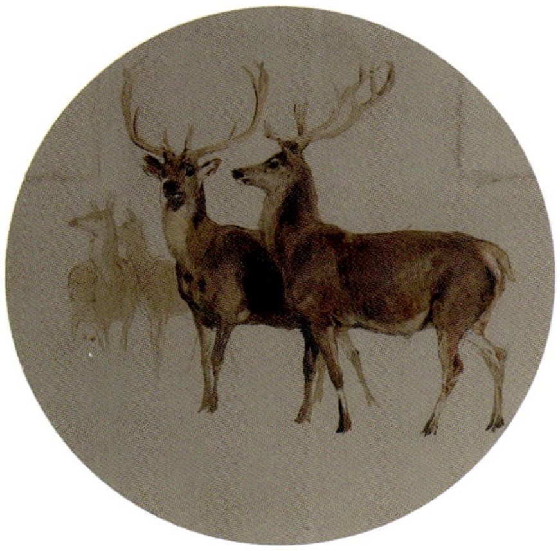

Landseer, Edwin Henry 1802–1873
Deer in a Landscape (Studies of Deer)
oil on wood 35.5
NCM 1939-56

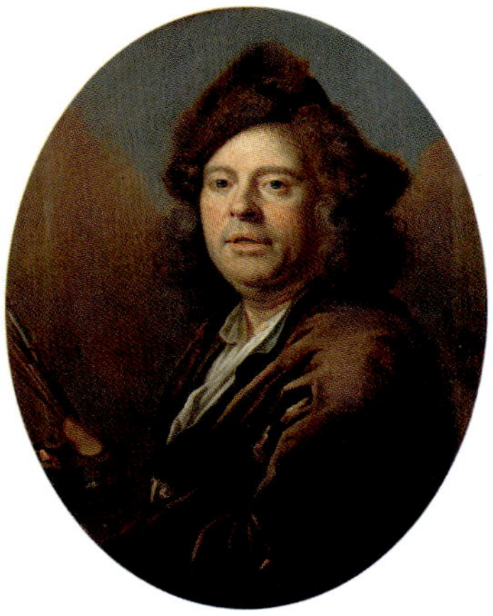

Largillière, Nicolas de 1656–1746
Jan Siberechts (1627–c.1703)
oil on canvas 69.9 x 59.7
NCM 1939-54

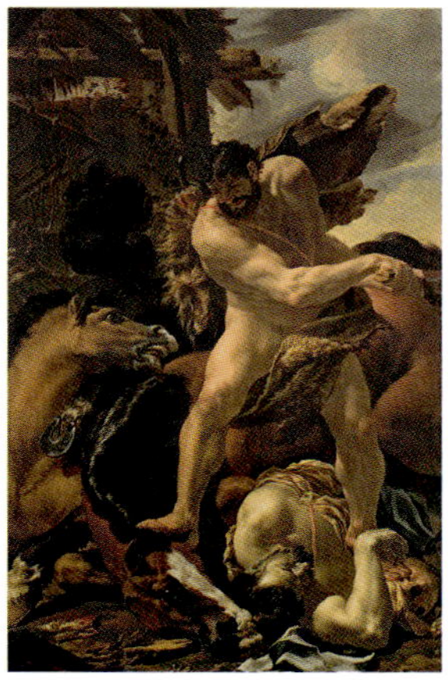

Le Brun, Charles 1619–1690
Hercules Vanquishing Diomedes 1638–1642
oil on canvas 276.9 x 179
NCM 1893-52

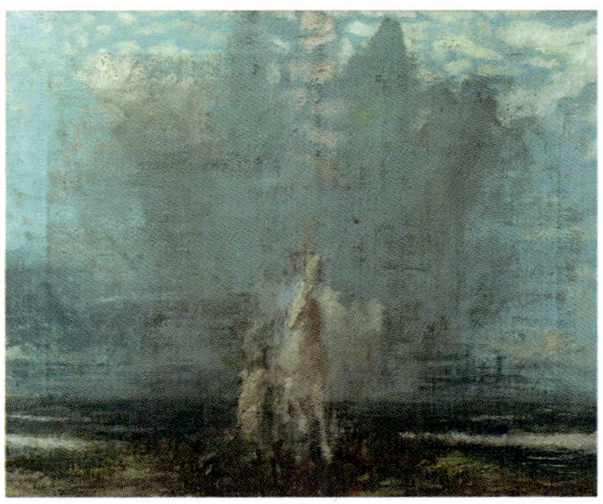

Le Brun, Christopher b.1951
Painting 1982
oil on canvas 43 x 52
NCMG 2007-137

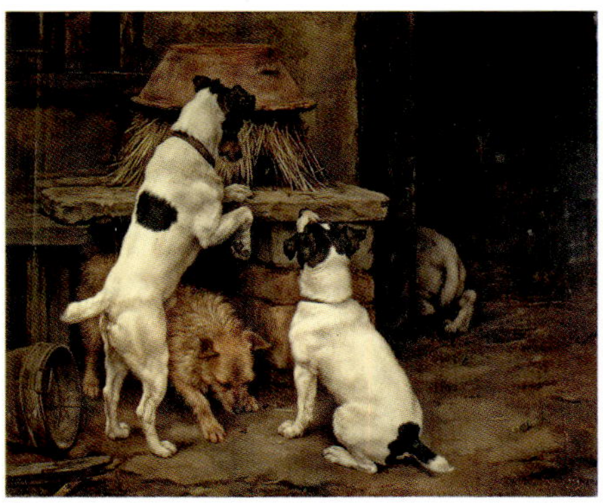

Leavers, Lucy Ann 1845–1915
Busy Bodies and Busy Bees 1892
oil on canvas 91.4 x 114.3
NCM 1892-49

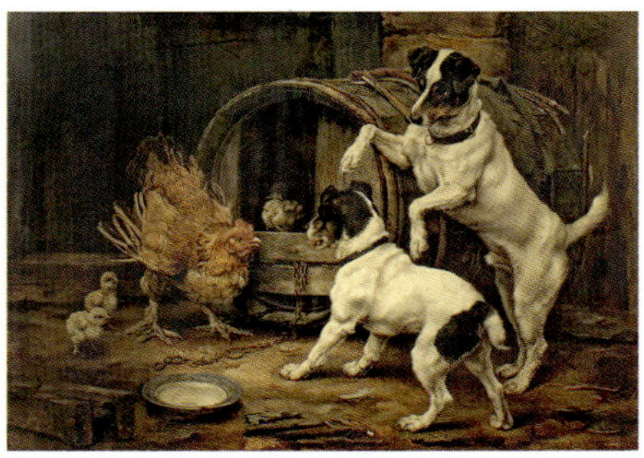

Leavers, Lucy Ann 1845–1915
An Anxious Moment 1895
oil on canvas 81.3 x 118.1
NCM 1927-36

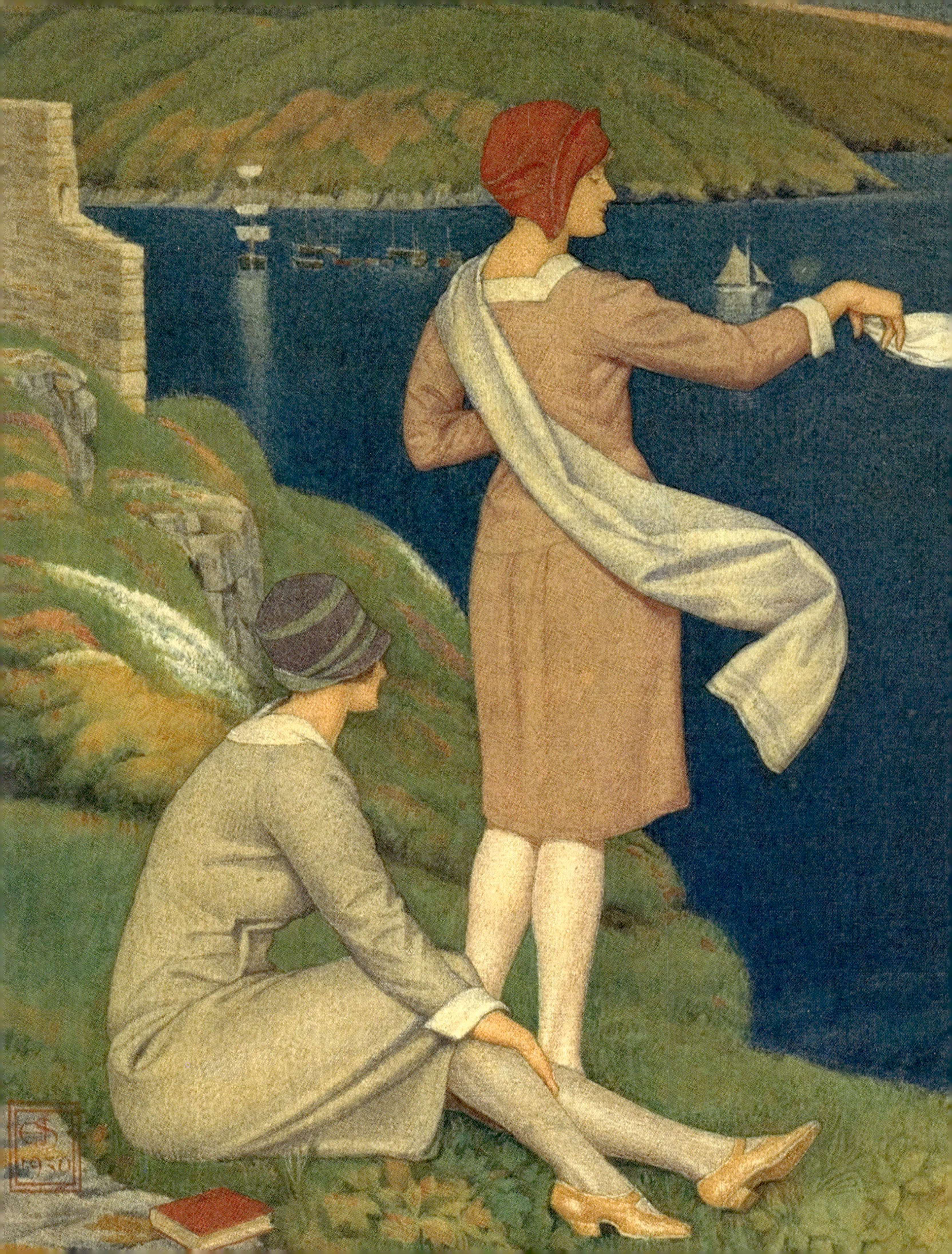
1930

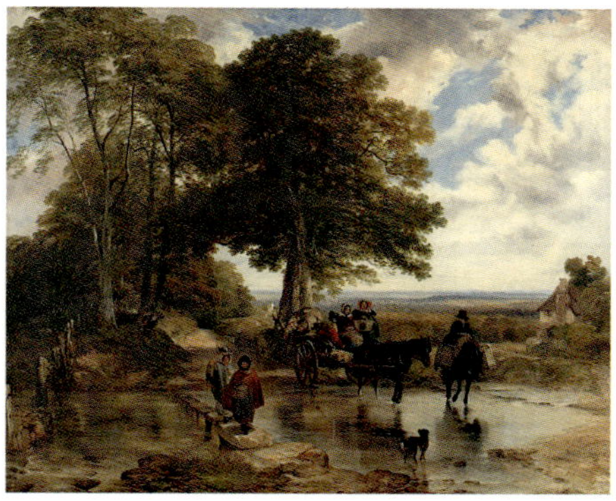

Lee, Frederick Richard 1798–1879
Market Cart at a Brook 1845
oil on canvas 102.9 x 128.3
NCM 1904-44

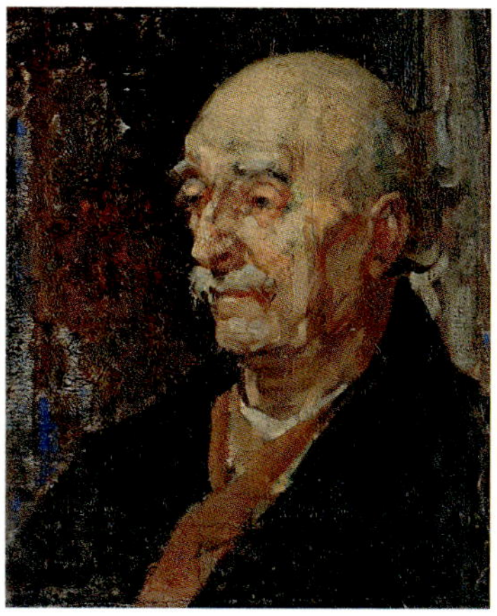

Lee-Hankey, William 1869–1952
Napoleon Danelle, Antiquaire
oil on canvas & board 48.3 x 37.5
NCM 1954-31

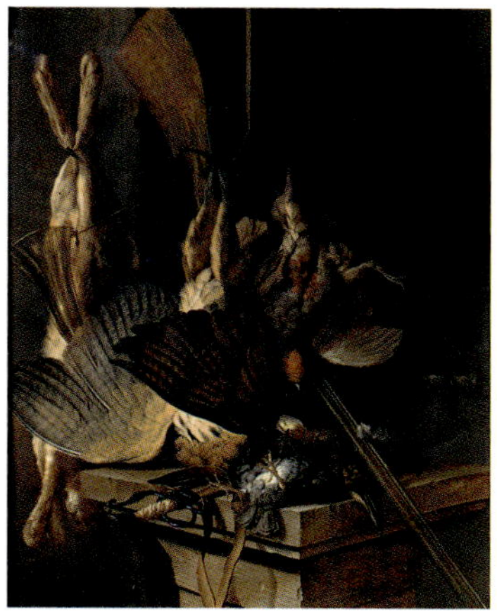

Lelienbergh, Cornelis 1626–1676
Dead Game 1657
oil on canvas 111.7 x 92.7
NCM 1904-91

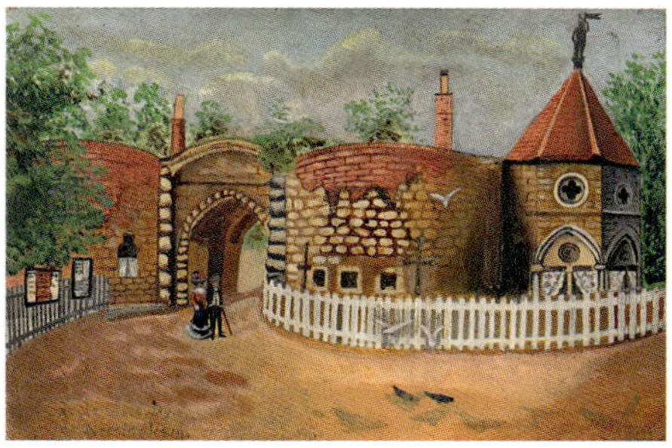

Lennox Gordon, Archie b.c.1889
Nottingham Castle Gateway 1904
oil on wood 15 x 23
FA-X 23

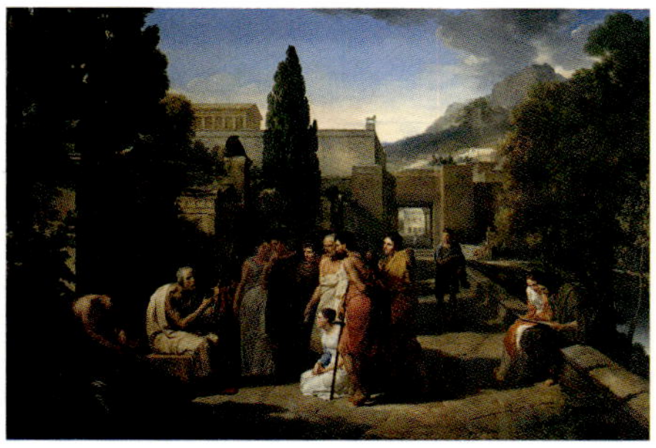

Lethière, Guillaume 1760–1832
Homer Singing His Iliad at the Gate of Athens 1811
oil on canvas 198.1 x 246.4
NCM 1884-1

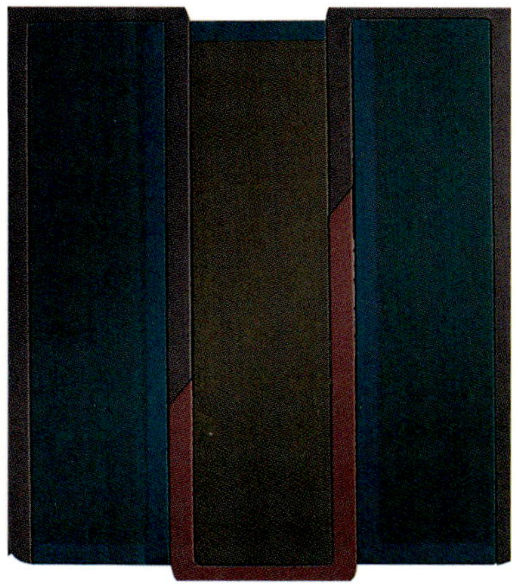

Leverett, David b.1938
Inroads 1967
oil on canvas mounted on wood 97.8 x 83.8
NCM 1968-335

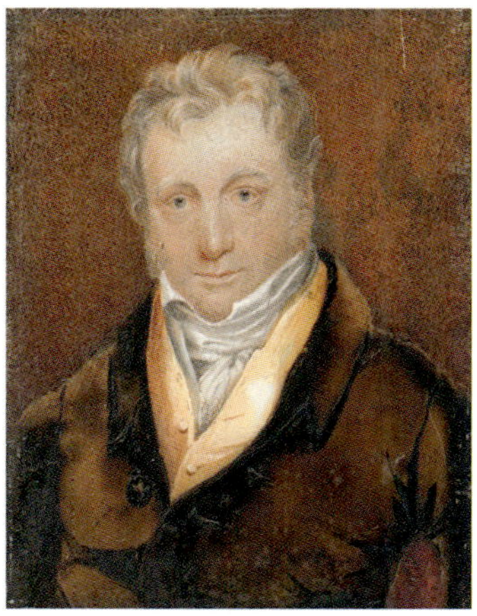

Lewis, George Robert 1782–1871
Thomas Paul Sandby, RA
oil on card 9.7 x 7.6
NCM 1945-176

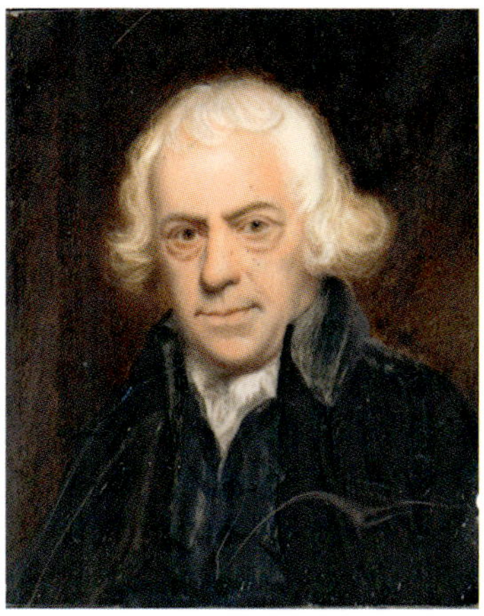

Lewis, George Robert 1782–1871
Thomas Paul Sandby, RA
oil on card 8.4 x 6.9
NCM 1945-177

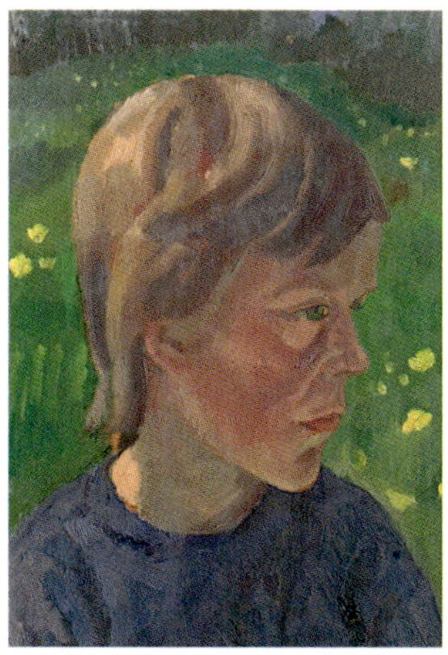

Lewis, Neville 1895–1972
Girl's Head 1927
oil on canvas 35.6 x 26.7
NCM 1927-76

Facing page: Southall, Joseph Edward, 1861–1944, *The Return* (detail), 1930, Nottingham City Museums and Galleries (p. 146)

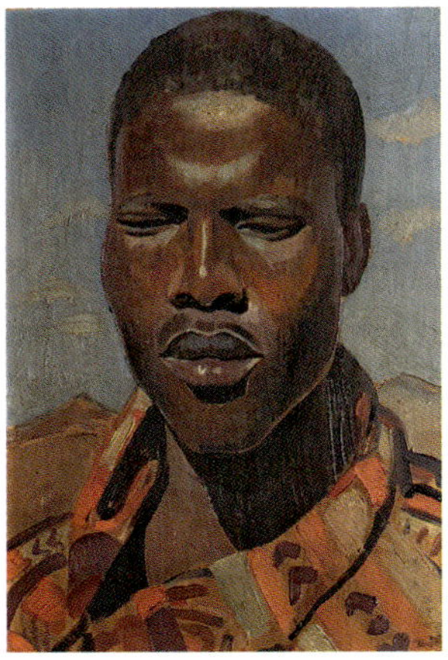

Lewis, Neville 1895–1972
The Zulu 1930
oil on wood 35.6 x 25.4
NCM 1940-34

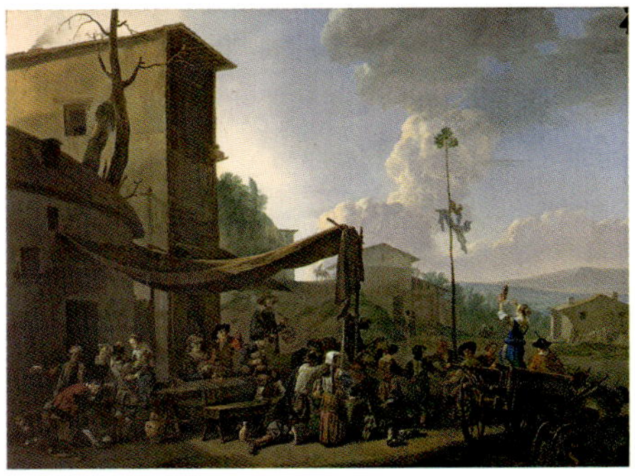

Lingelbach, Johannes 1622–1674
A Village Festival, Peasants Merrymaking Outside an Inn early 1650s
oil on canvas 87.6 x 120.6
NCM 1904-92

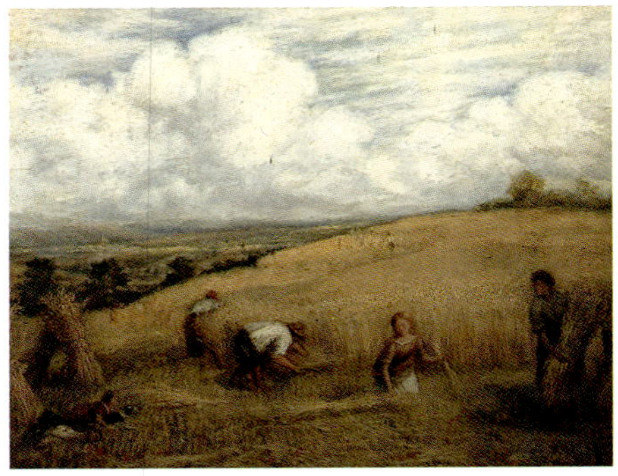

Linnell, John 1792–1882
Harvesting 1857
oil on canvas 35.6 x 45.7
NCM 1933-247

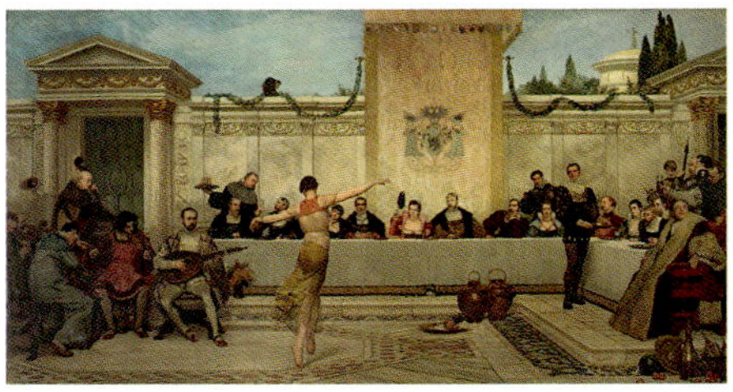

Linton, James Dromgole 1840–1916
The Banquet 1882
oil on canvas 127 x 251.5
NCM 1911-34

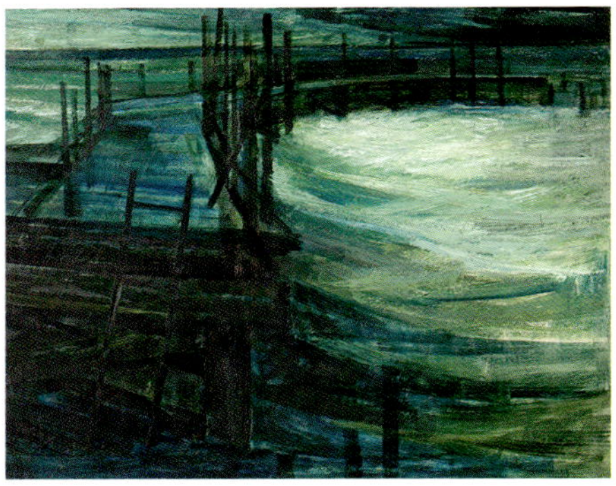

Long, John Kenneth b.1924
Derelict Pier, Swanage, Dorset 1959
oil on wood 74.3 x 96.5
NCM 1959-77

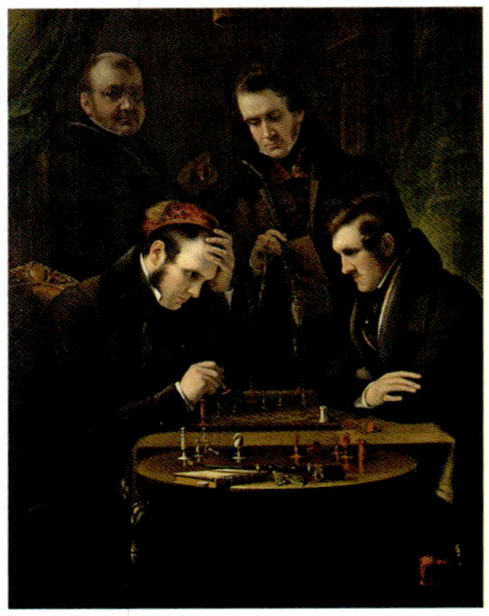

Lonsdale, James 1777–1839
The Chess Players
oil on canvas 142.2 x 111.8
NCM 1904-45

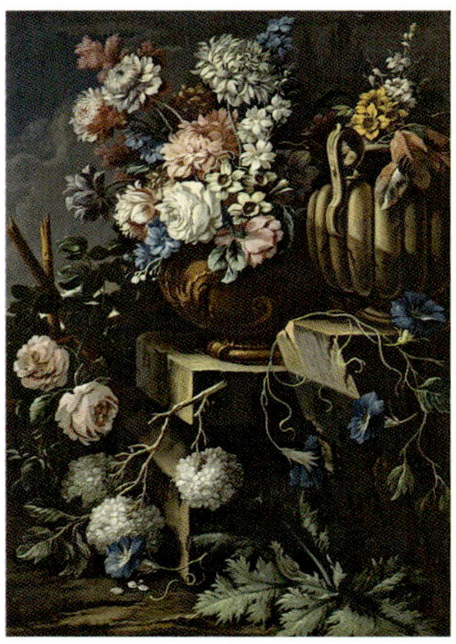

Lopez, Gasparo 1650–1732
Flower Piece
oil on canvas 76.5 x 57.1
NCM 1990-505

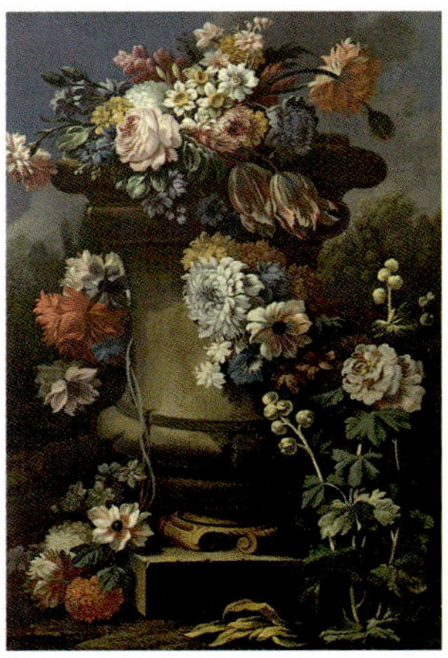

Lopez, Gasparo 1650–1732
Flower Piece
oil on canvas 76.5 x 56.5
NCM 1990-506

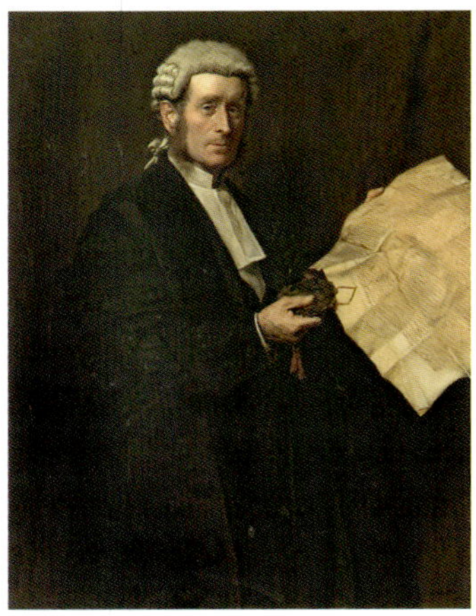

Lorimer, John Henry 1856–1936
Sir Samuel George Johnson (1831–1909), Kt 1891
oil on canvas 127 x 101.6
NCM 1893-82

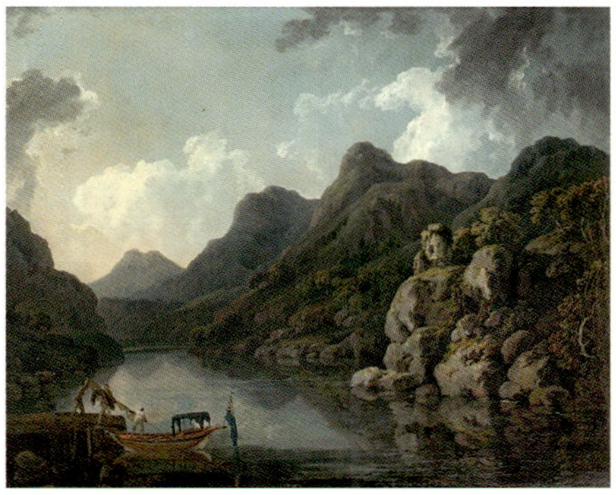

Loutherbourg, Philip James de 1740–1812
View of Snowdon with the Castle of Dolbadarn from Llanberis, North Wales 1787
oil on canvas 95 x 123
NCM 1904-46

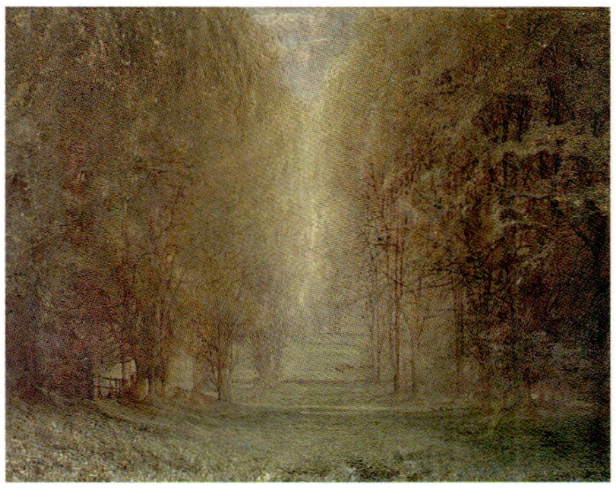

Lowe, Arthur 1866–1940
Autumn
oil on canvas 86.4 x 127
NCM 1940-26

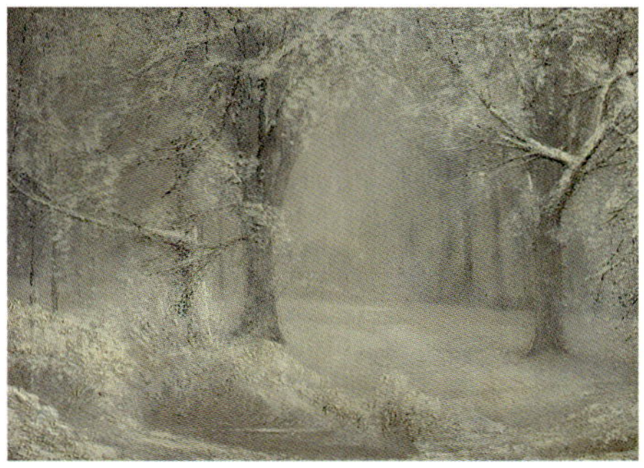

Lowe, Arthur 1866–1940
Snow
oil on canvas 66 x 91.4
NCM 1940-27

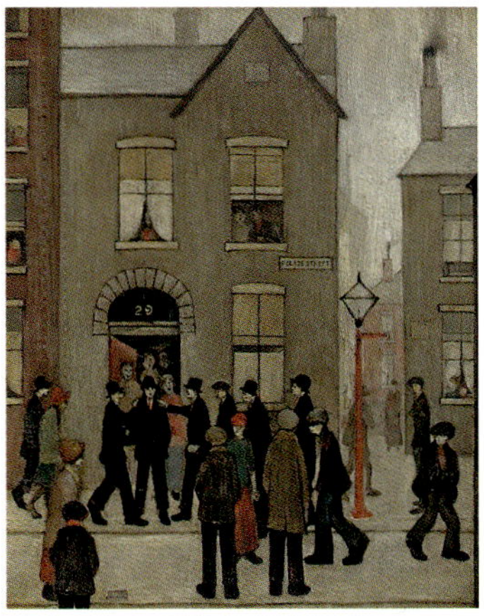

Lowry, Laurence Stephen 1887–1976
The Arrest 1927
oil on canvas 52 x 42
NCM 1952-4

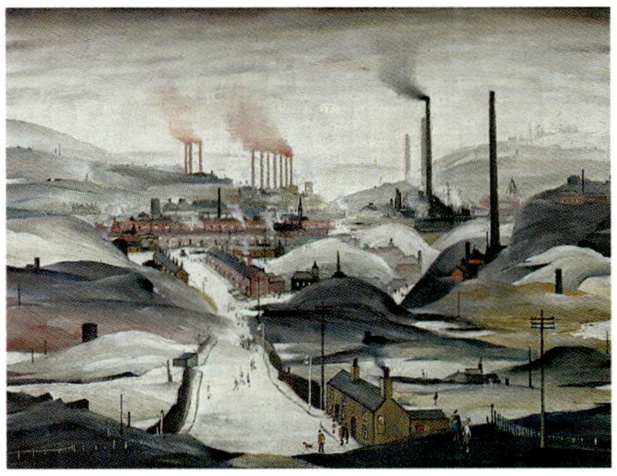

Lowry, Laurence Stephen 1887–1976
Industrial Panorama 1953
oil on canvas 58.4 x 78.7
NCM 1953-106

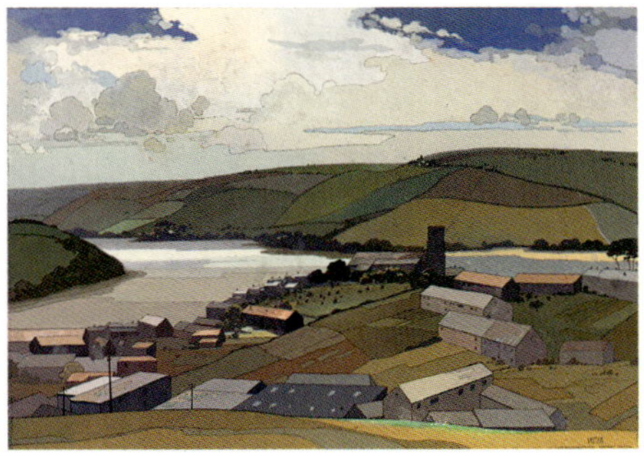

Loxton Knight, Edward 1905–1993
Salcombe, Devon
tempera on board 35.6 x 50.8
NCM 1934-127

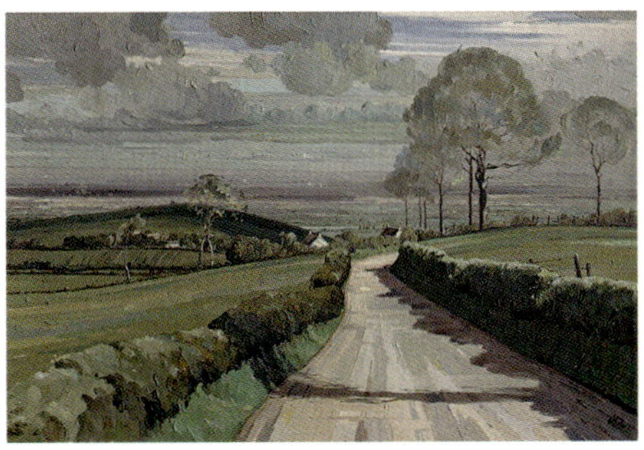

Loxton Knight, Edward 1905–1993
Spring Morning near Bristol
oil on canvas 50.8 x 76.2
NCM 1938-177

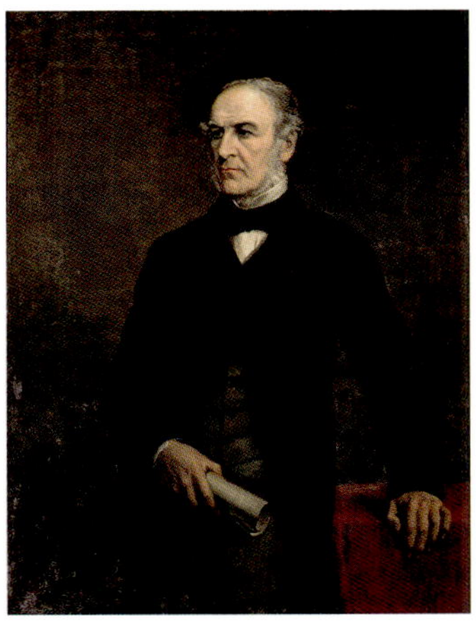

Lucy, Charles 1814–1873
The Right Honourable William E. Gladstone (1809–1898), MP c.1872
oil on canvas 129.5 x 102.2
NCM 1878-194

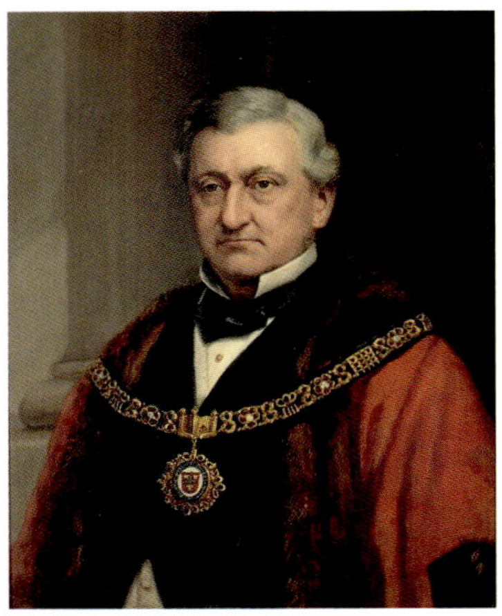

Luntley, James 1827–1887
William Parsons, Mayor of Nottingham (1863–1864) 1882
oil on canvas 76.2 x 63.5
NCM 1889-42

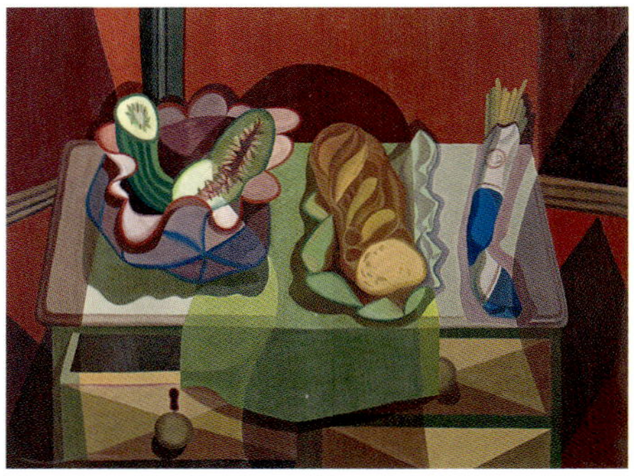

MacBryde, Robert 1913–1966
Still Life, Autumn c.1950
oil on canvas 76.2 x 101.5
NCM 1956-77

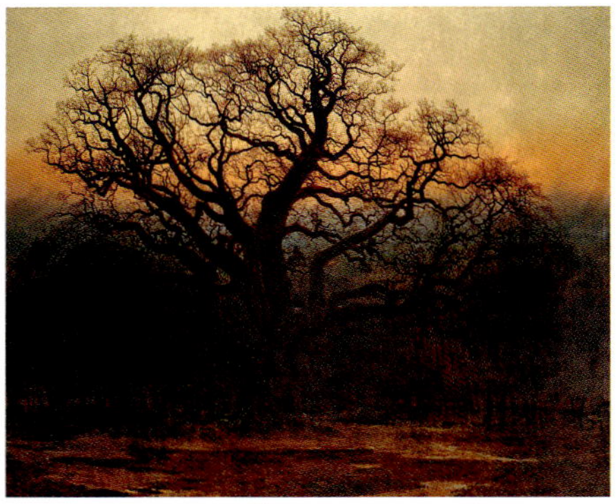

MacCallum, Andrew 1821–1902
Major Oak, Sherwood Forest, Nottinghamshire 1882
oil on canvas 266.7 x 373.4
NCM 1885-117

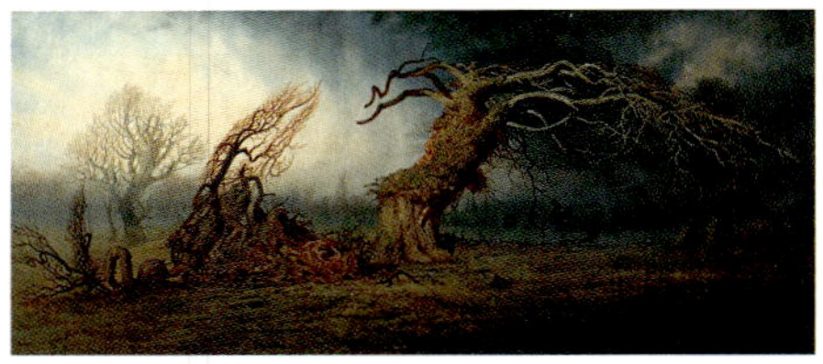

MacCallum, Andrew 1821–1902
The Blasted Tree
oil on canvas 57.1 x 129.5
NCM 1966-107

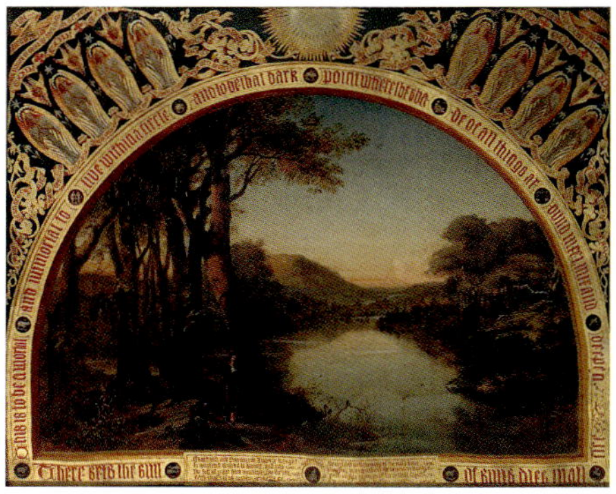

MacCallum, Andrew 1821–1902
The Opening Scene in Philip James Bailey's 'Festus'
oil on canvas 72.4 x 92.1
NCM 1901-1

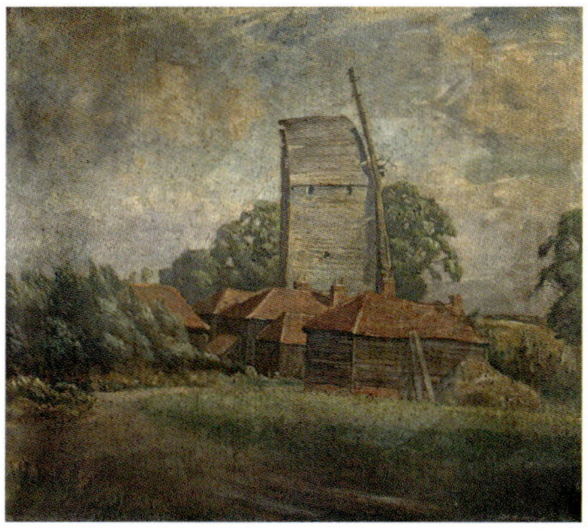

MacDougall, William Brown 1869–1936
Toot Mill, Toot Hill, Essex
oil on hessian 87.6 x 99.1
NCM 1937-39

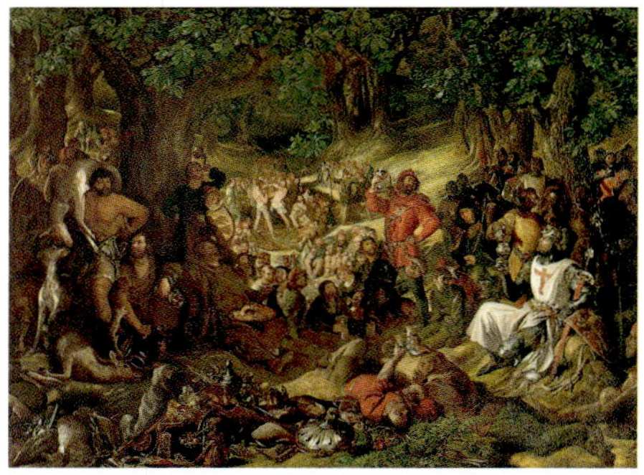

Maclise, Daniel 1806–1870
Robin Hood and His Merry Men Entertaining Richard the Lionheart in Sherwood Forest 1839
oil on canvas 111 x 155
NCM 1984-400

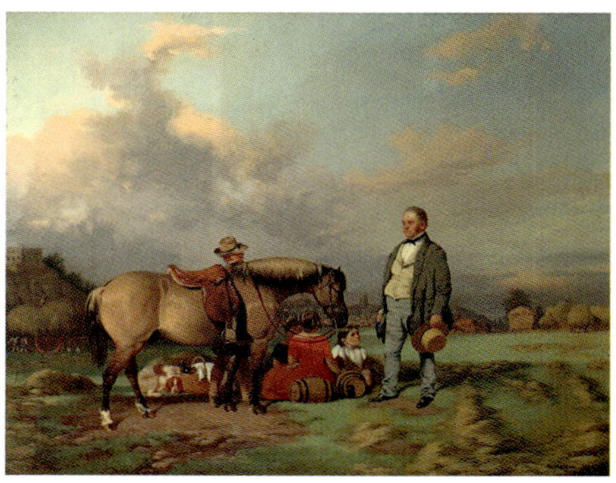

Malbon, William 1805–1877
Joseph Fenton with His Family on the Meadows, Nottingham 1840
oil on canvas 82 x 108.5
NCM 1989-908

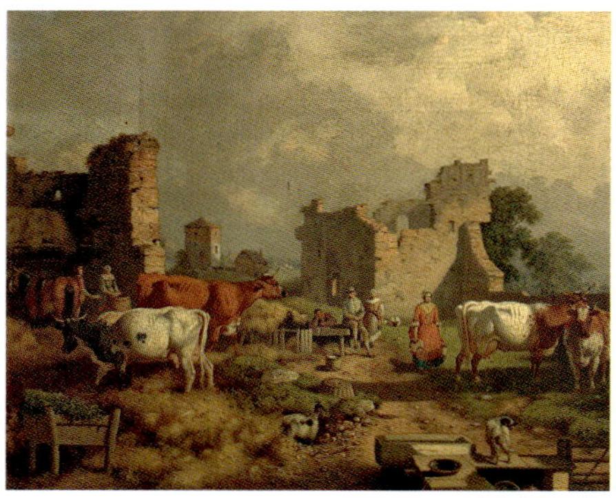

Malbon, William 1805–1877
Farmyard Scene
oil on wood 40.6 x 50.8
NCM 1901-31

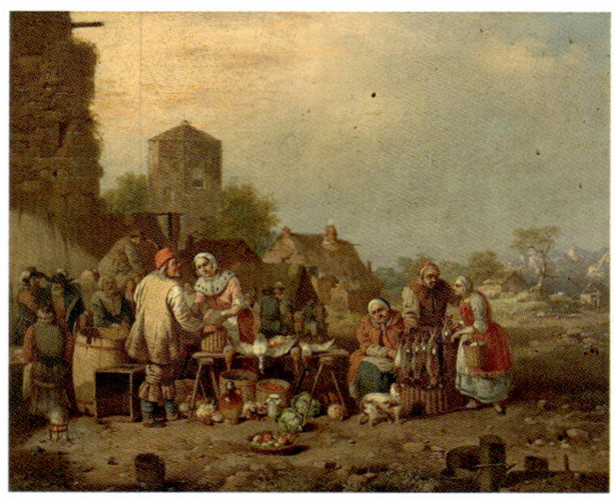

Malbon, William 1805–1877
Village Market Scene
oil on wood 40.6 x 50.8
NCM 1901-30

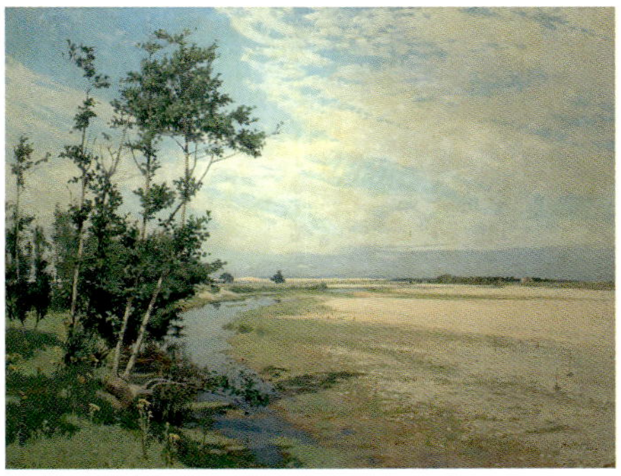

Mann, Alexander 1853–1908
Findhorn Backwater, Moray Firth, Scotland 1886
oil on canvas 127 x 154.9
NCM 1909-61

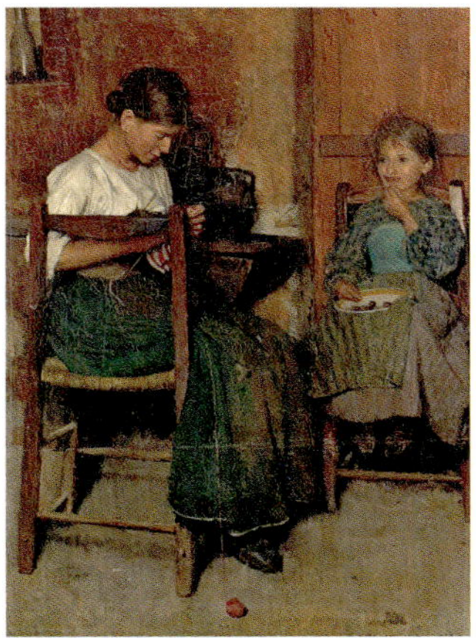

Mann, Harrington 1864–1936
Cottage Interior
oil on canvas 53.5 x 41
NCM 1987-1036

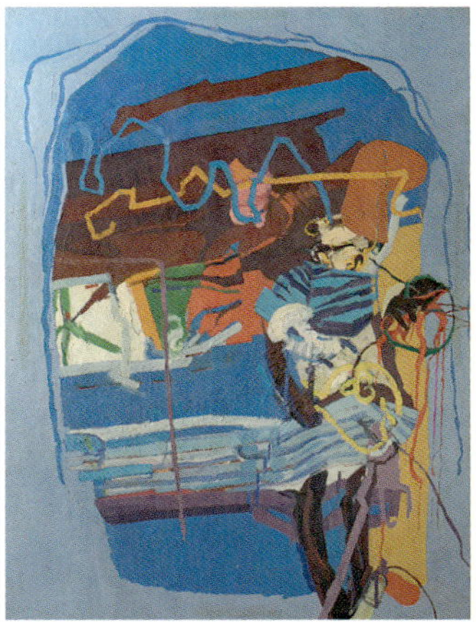

Martinez, Raymond b.1937
Blue Sentinel 1963
oil on canvas 129.5 x 100.3
NCM 1964-308

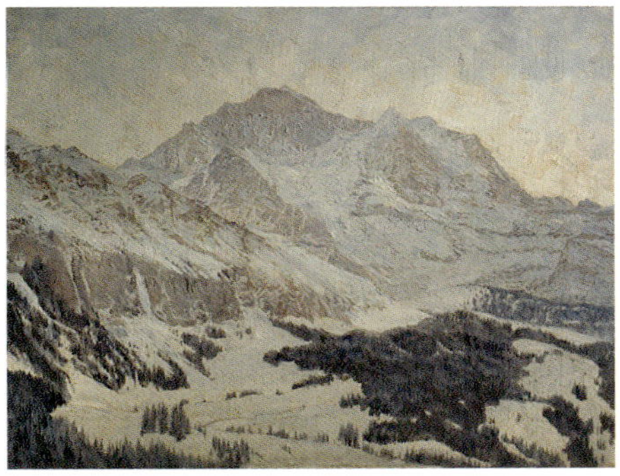

Martin-Richards, Marjorie active 1959
Jungfrau, Switzerland, Dawn
oil on canvas 76.2 x 101.6
NCM 1959-49

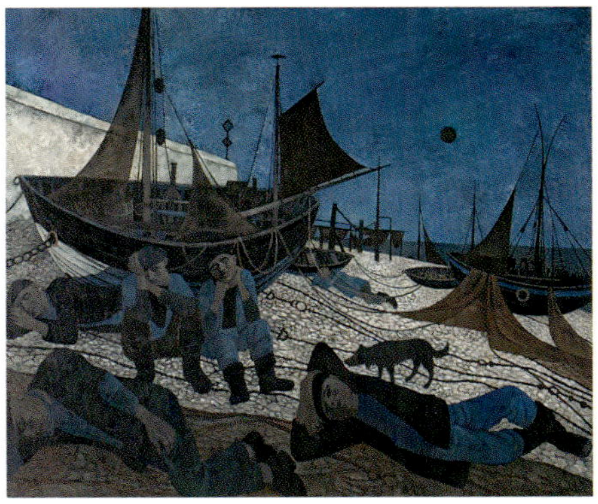

Mason, Bateson 1910–1977
Sleeping Fishermen
oil on canvas 101.6 x 121.9
NCM 1954-52

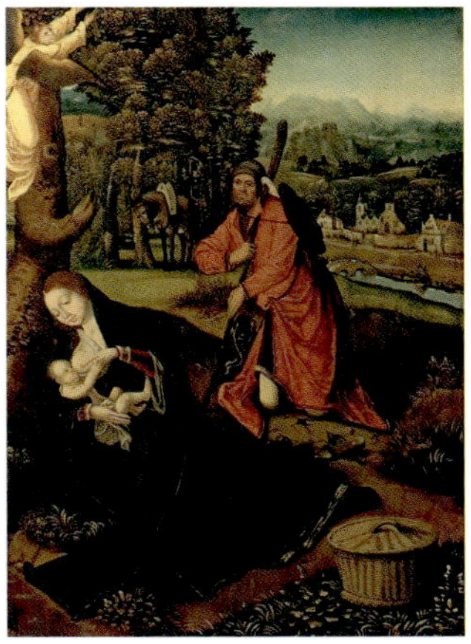

Master of the Antwerp Adoration (attributed to) active c.1520
The Rest on the Flight into Egypt (Virgin, Child and St Joseph in a Landscape)
oil on wood 62.9 x 47.6
NCM 1910-61

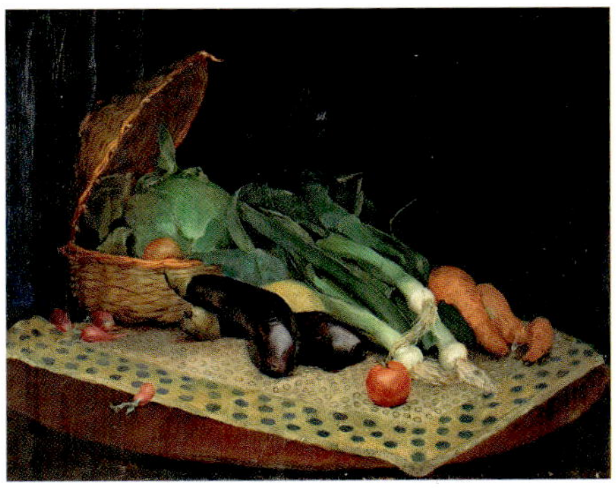

Maurice, Constance
Still Life (Vegetables)
oil on canvas 55.9 x 76.2
NCM 1931-49

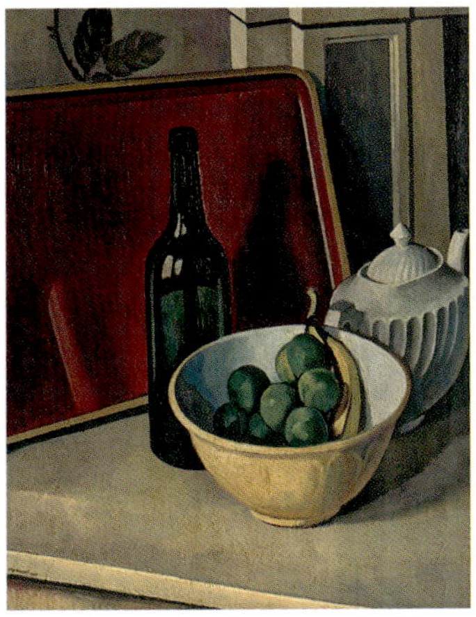

Meninsky, Bernard 1891–1950
Still Life with Yellow Bowl and Fruit 1920
oil on canvas 68.6 x 55.9
NCM 1940-35

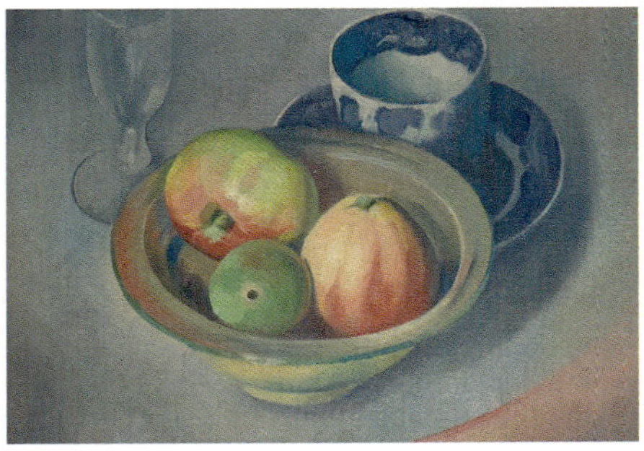

Meninsky, Bernard 1891–1950
Still Life with Apples 1927
oil on canvas 30.5 x 40.6
NCM 1927-75

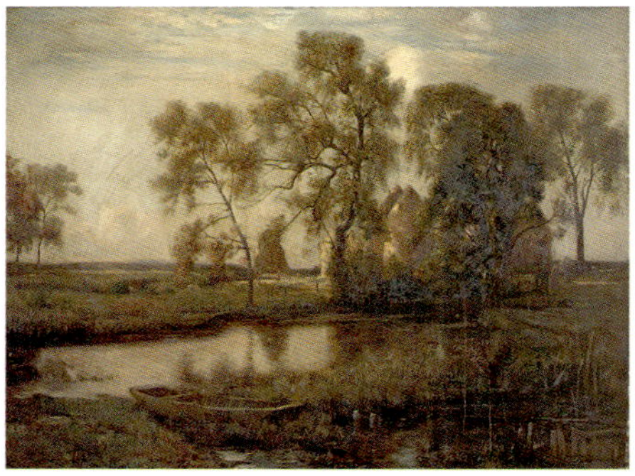

Michie, James Coutts 1861–1919
A Marshland Farm
oil on canvas 121.9 x 182.9
NCM 1924-18

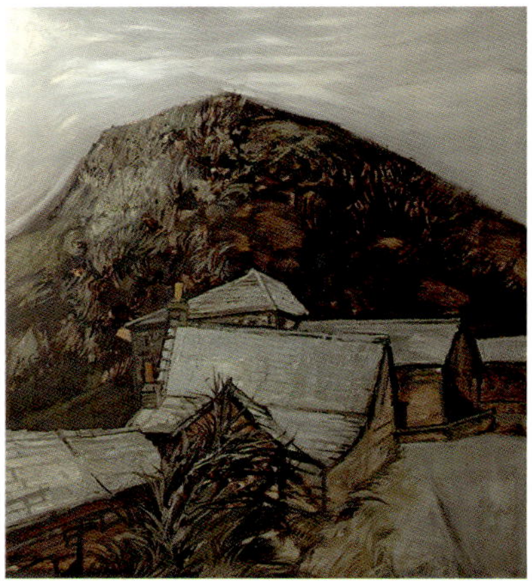

Middleditch, Edward 1923–1987
Boscastle, Cornwall 1956
oil on board 132.1 x 121.9
NCM 1956-73

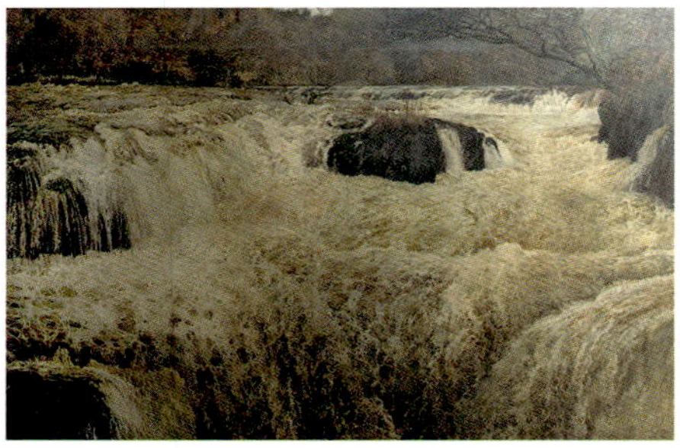

Miles, George Francis 1852–1891
Salmon Leap, Cenarth Falls, Cardiganshire, Wales 1878
oil on canvas 106.7 x 157.5
NCM 1919-11

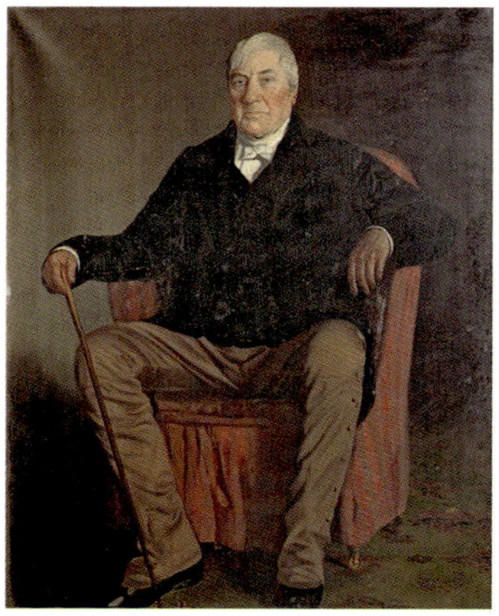

Miller, William 1796–1882
Mr Fisher 1857
oil on canvas 91.4 x 73.7
NCM 1968-401

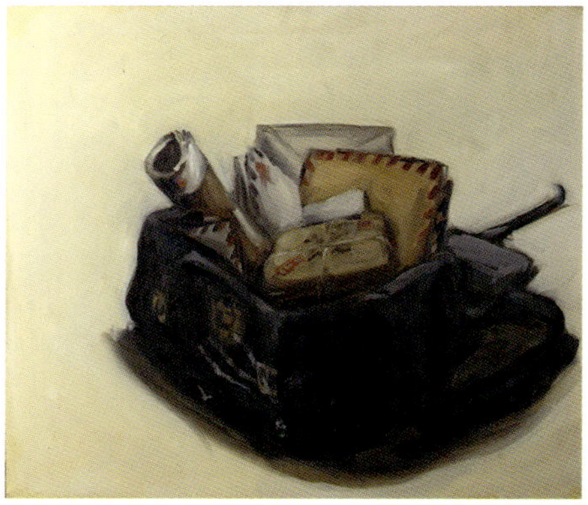

Milroy, Lisa b.1959
Mailbag 1983
oil on canvas 99 x 116
NCM 1989-906

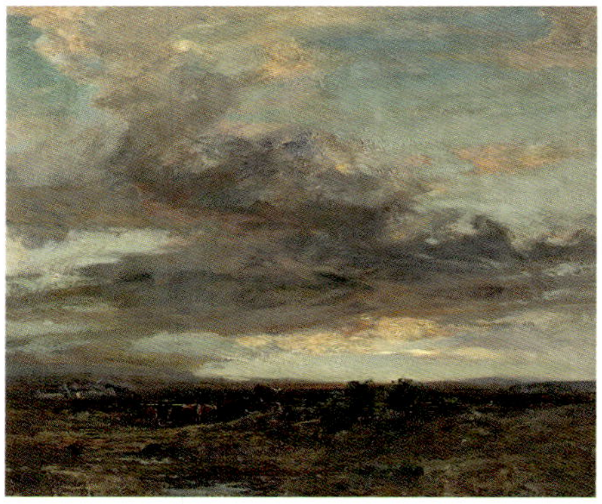

Mitchell, John Campbell 1865–1922
The Argyllshire Moor, Scotland, Sunset 1907
oil on canvas 50.8 x 61
NCM 1923-14

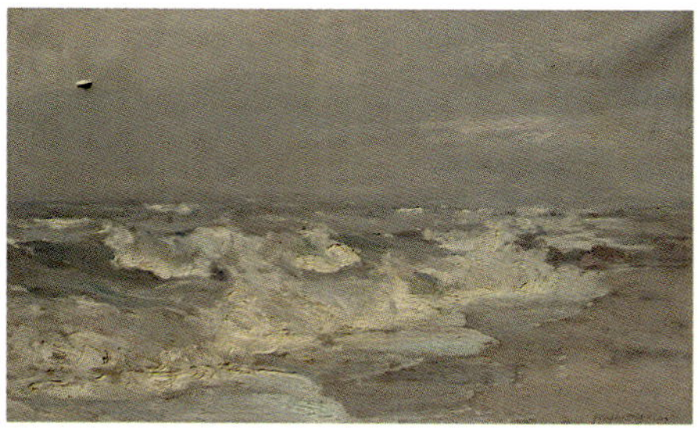

Mitchell, John Campbell 1865–1922
Wind and Rain 1907
oil on canvas 45.7 x 76.2
NCM 1923-13

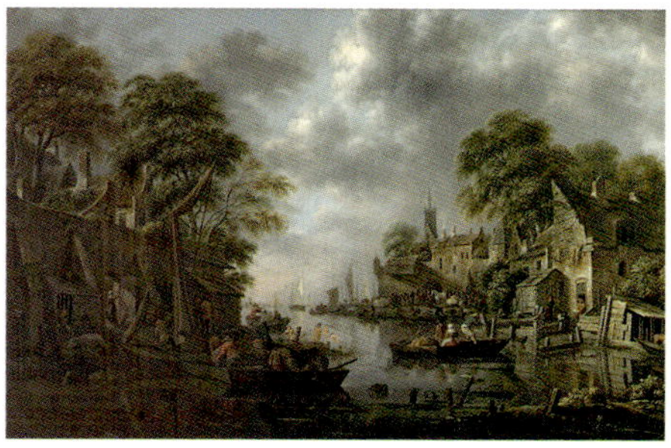

Molenaer, Klaes c.1630–1676
River Scene with Boats and Figures 1665
oil on canvas 87.9 x 139.4
NCM 1904-120

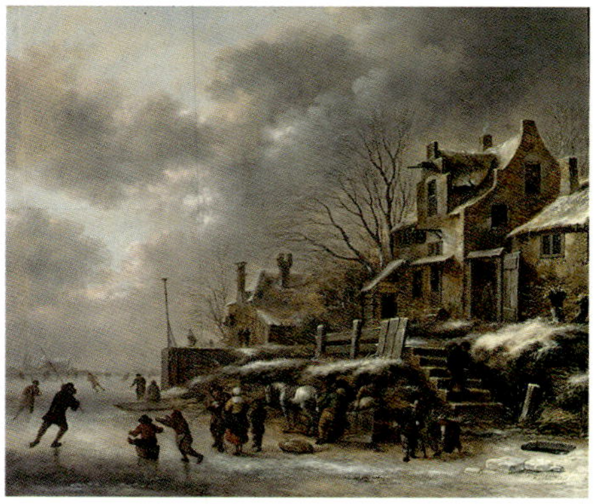

Molenaer, Klaes c.1630–1676
Winter Scene, River with Figures Skating 1671
oil on wood 44.5 x 54.6
NCM 1904-93

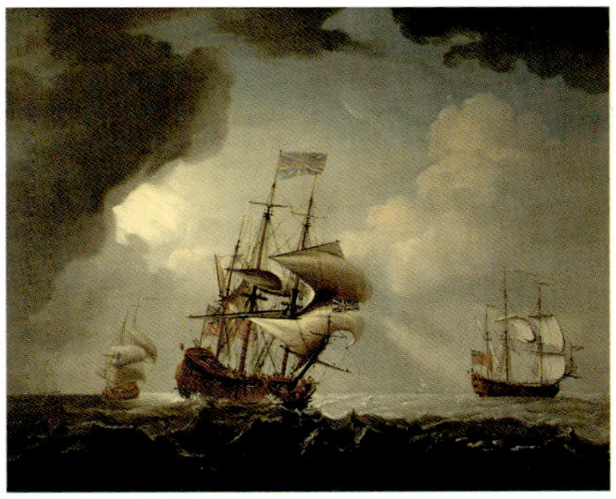

Monamy, Peter 1681–1749
Three English Men-of-War Getting Underway in a Fresh Breeze (Sea Piece)
oil on canvas 96.5 x 125
NCM 1923-15

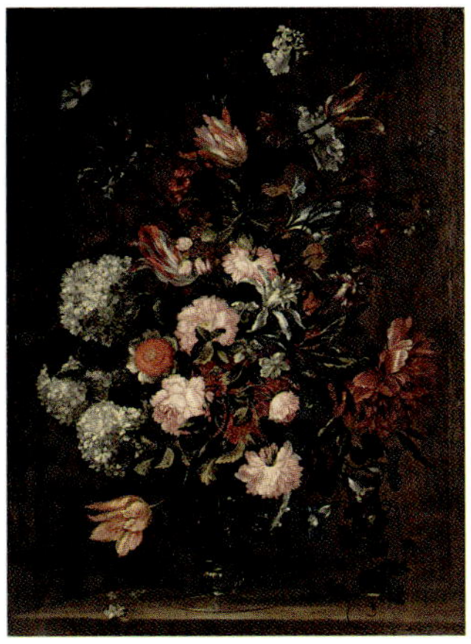

Monnoyer, Jean-Baptiste 1636–1699
Flower Piece
oil on canvas 113 x 88
NCM 1941-13

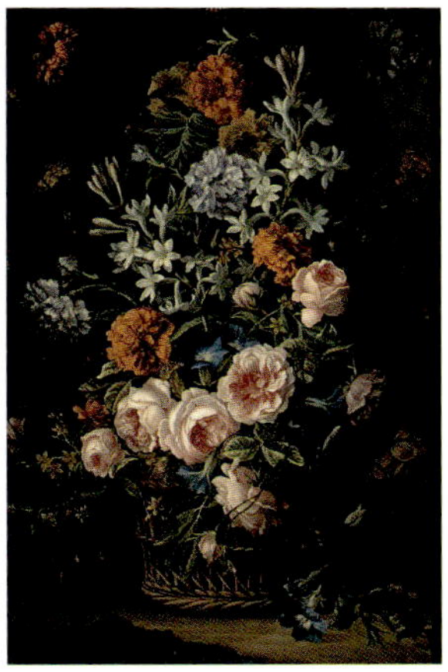

Monnoyer, Jean-Baptiste 1636–1699
Flowers in a Basket
oil on canvas 81 x 54.5
NCM 1990-504

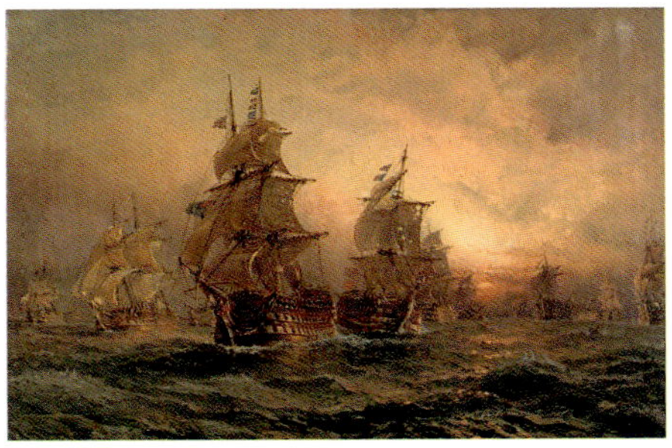

Moore, Claude Thomas Stanfield
1853–1901
The Evening of Trafalgar 1890
oil on canvas 50.8 x 76.2
NCM 1914-10

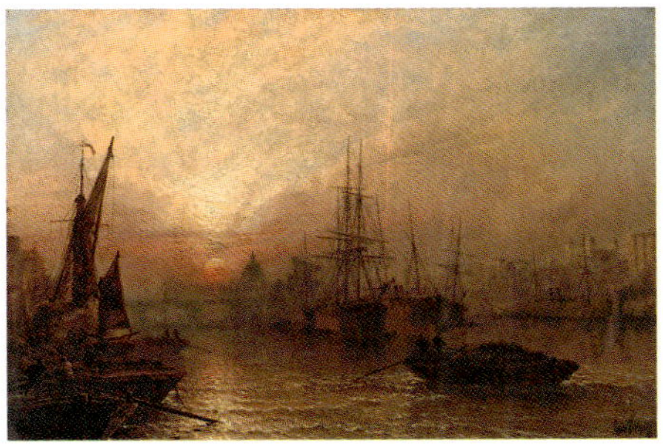

Moore, Claude Thomas Stanfield
1853–1901
The Pool of the Thames, over London's Silent Highway 1890
oil on canvas 51.1 x 76.2
NCM 1901-20

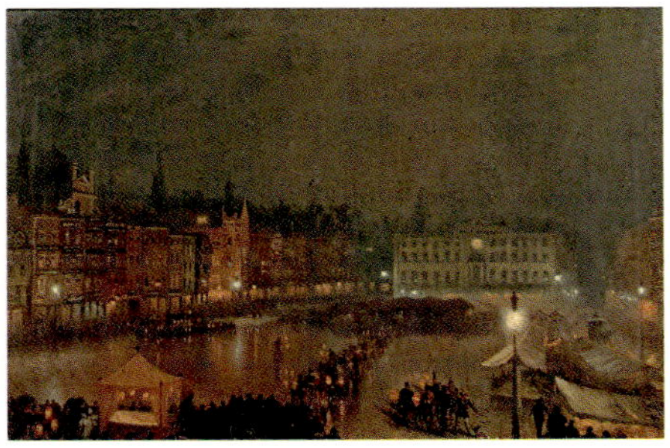

Moore, Claude Thomas Stanfield
1853–1901
Torchlight Tattoo of Robin Hood Rifles, Nottingham Market Place, 1896
oil on canvas 35.6 x 53.3
NCM 1967-237

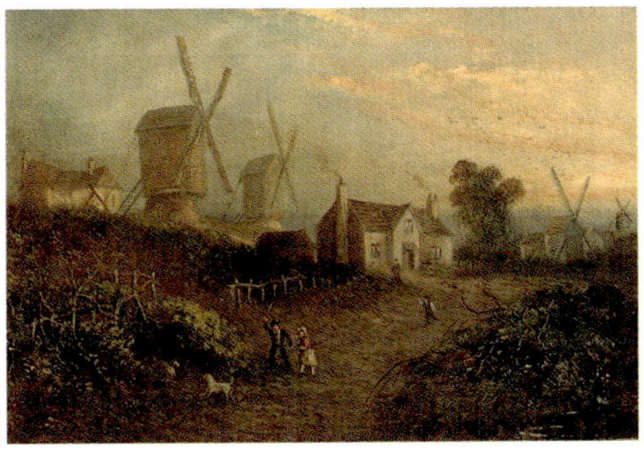

Moore, Thomas Cooper 1827–1901
Mills and Gorse Bushes in Nottingham Forest
1848
oil on canvas 26 x 39 (E)
NCM 1985-936

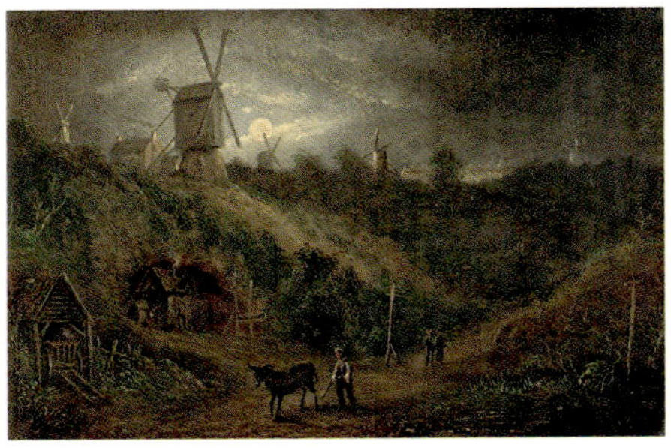

Moore, Thomas Cooper 1827–1901
The Old Ropewalk, Foot of the Gallows Hill, Nottingham Forest 1848
oil on canvas 26 x 39 (E)
NCM 1985-935

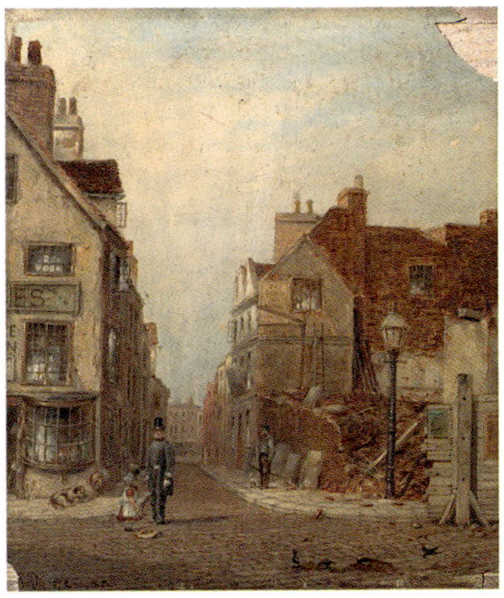

Moore, Thomas Cooper 1827–1901
Sheep Lane, Nottingham c.1885
oil on wood 17.8 x 15.6
NCM 1960-60

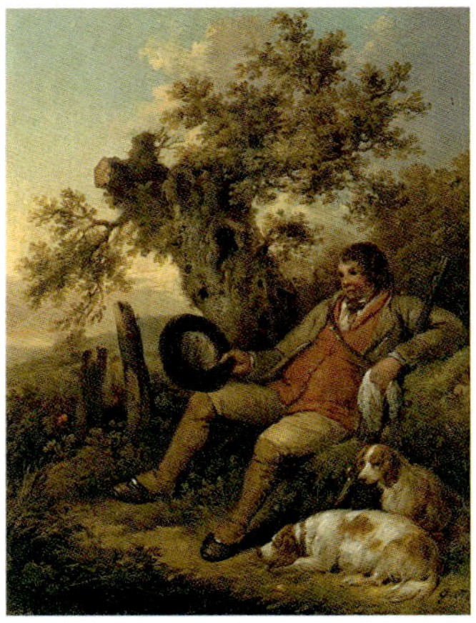

Morland, George 1763–1804
The Sportsman Resting c.1790
oil on canvas 38.1 x 30.5
NCM 1904-56

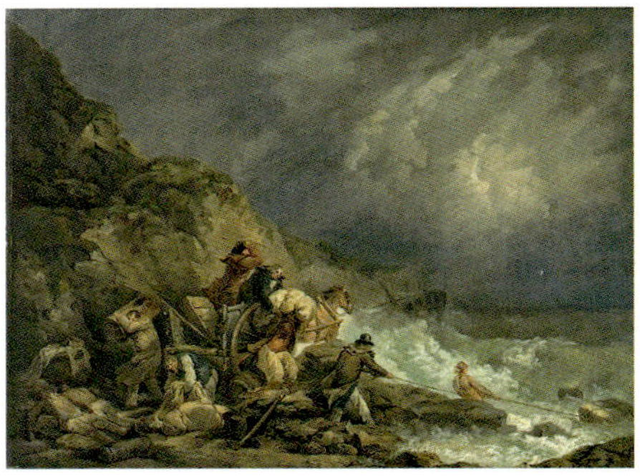

Morland, George 1763–1804
The Wreckers c.1790
oil on canvas 50.8 x 68.6
NCM 1904-53

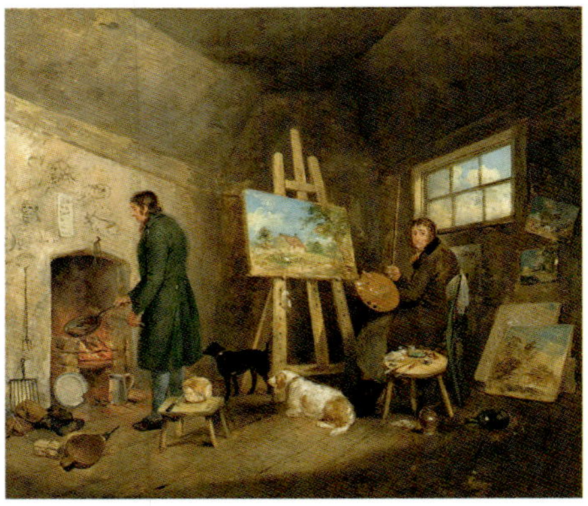

Morland, George 1763–1804
The Artist in His Studio and His Man Gibbs c.1802
oil on canvas 63.5 x 76.2
NCM 1904-55

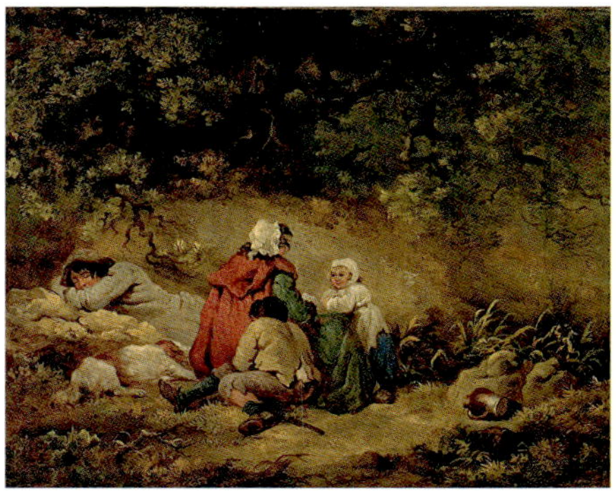

Morland, George 1763–1804
Gypsy Encampment
oil on canvas 43.8 x 55.9
NCM 1909-48

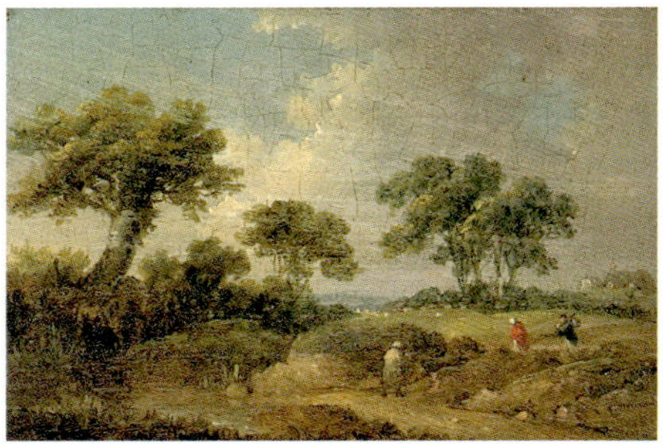

Morland, George 1763–1804
Landscape with Figures
oil on wood 10.2 x 15.2
NCM 1904-51

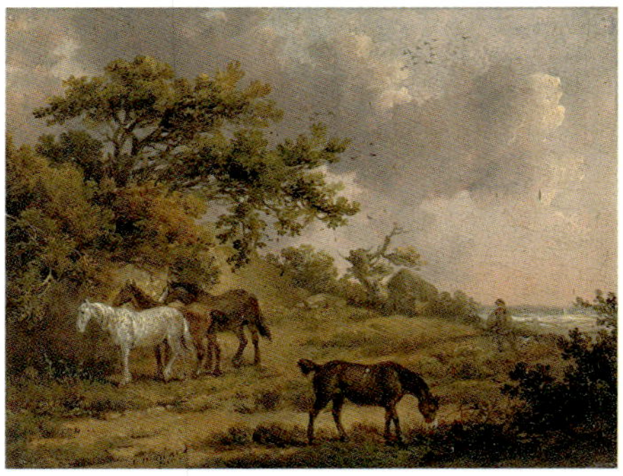

Morland, George 1763–1804
Landscape with Four Horses
oil on wood 15.2 x 20.3
NCM 1904-52

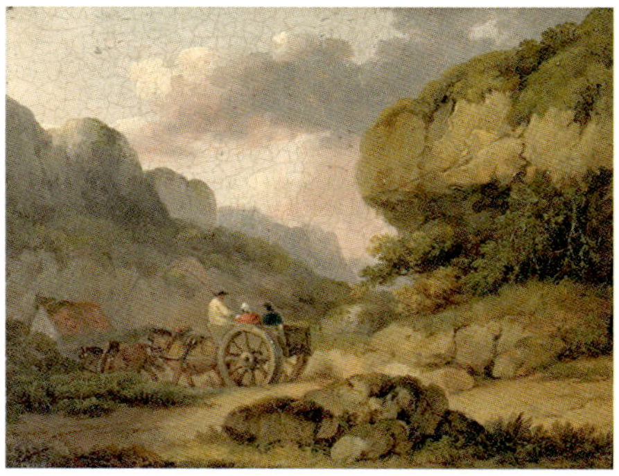

Morland, George 1763–1804
Landscape with Horses, Cart and Figures
oil on wood 15.2 x 21
NCM 1904-54

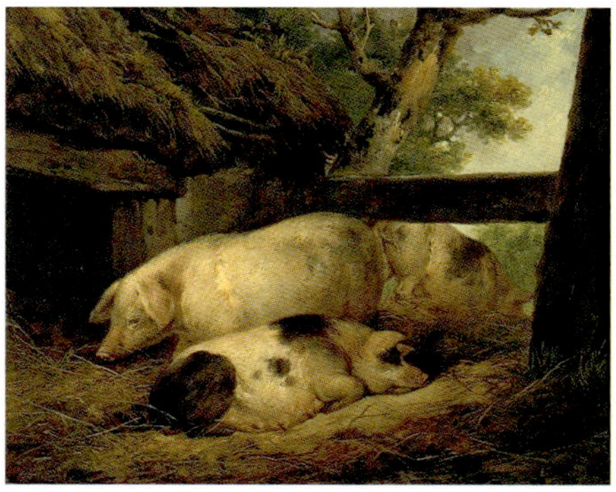

Morland, George 1763–1804
Study of Pigs
oil on wood 29.2 x 38.1
NCM 1904-50

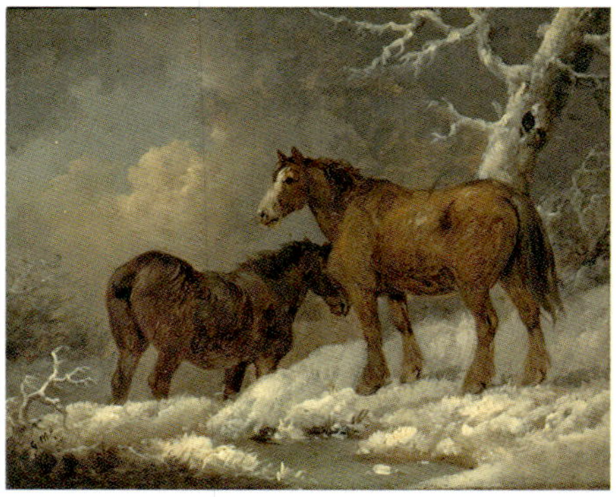

Morland, George 1763–1804
Two Horses in the Snow
oil on wood 17.8 x 23.5
NCM 1904-49

Facing page: Cleve, Joos van (follower of), c.1464–c.1540, *Virgin and Child with St Joseph* (detail), 1500–1550, Nottingham City Museums and Galleries (p. 79)

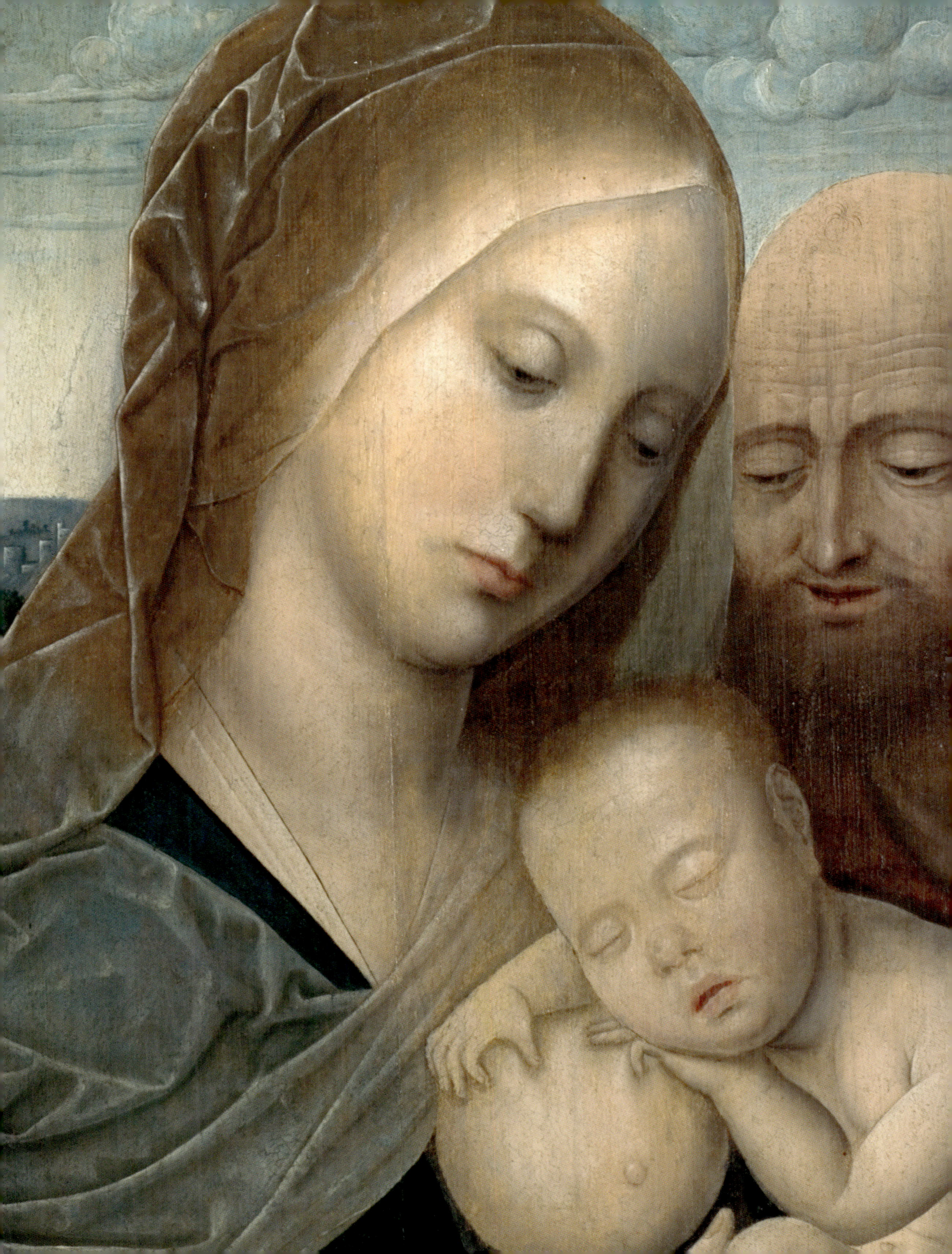

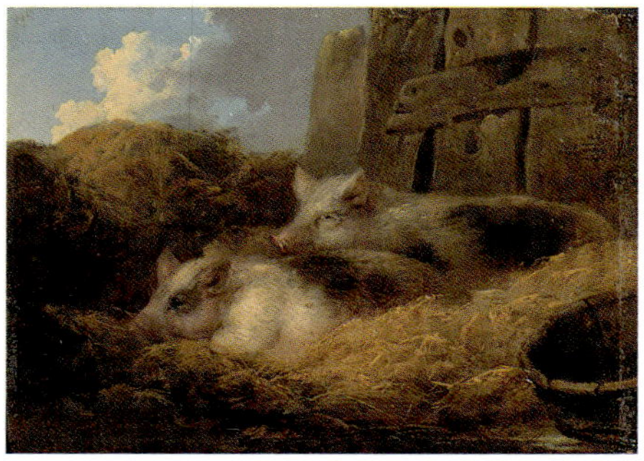

Morland, George 1763–1804
Two Pigs in Straw (Barn with Pigs)
oil on wood 19.4 x 26.7
NCM 1904-47

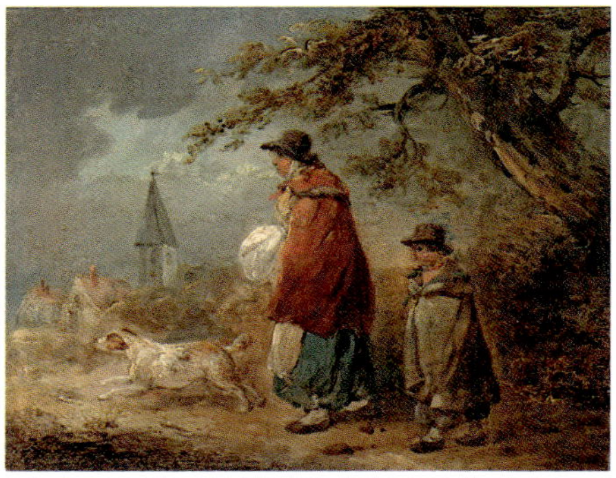

Morland, George 1763–1804
Woman, Child and Dog on a Road
oil on wood 17.1 x 21.6
NCM 1904-48

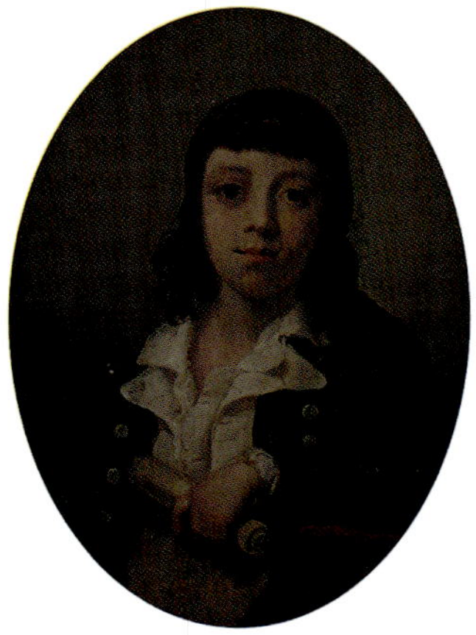

Morland, Henry Robert c.1716–1797
George Morland (1763–1804)
oil on wood 27.9 x 22.9
NCM 1904-57

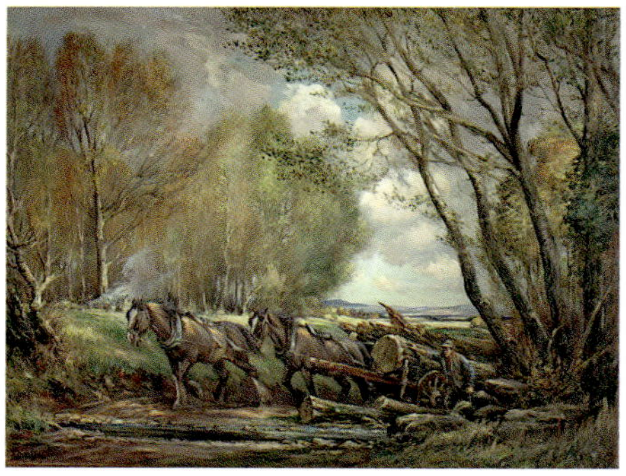

Morley, Henry 1869–1937
Hauling Timber, Stirlingshire, Scotland
oil on canvas 86.3 x 116.8
NCM 1936-37

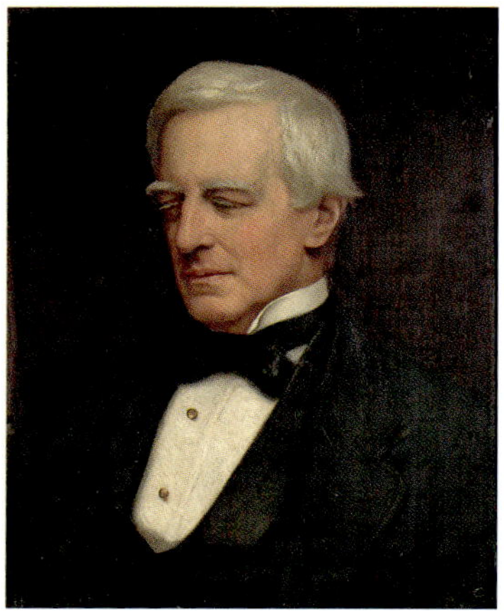

Mortlock, Ethel c.1865–1928
The Right Honourable Robert Lowe (1811–1892), Viscount Sherbrook
oil on canvas 61 x 50.8
NCM 1880-3

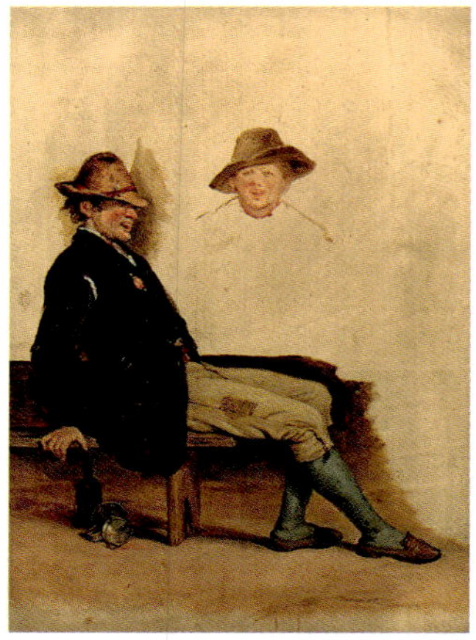

Mulready, William (follower of) 1786–1863
A Rustic Youth
oil on canvas 27 x 19.7
NCM 1945-44

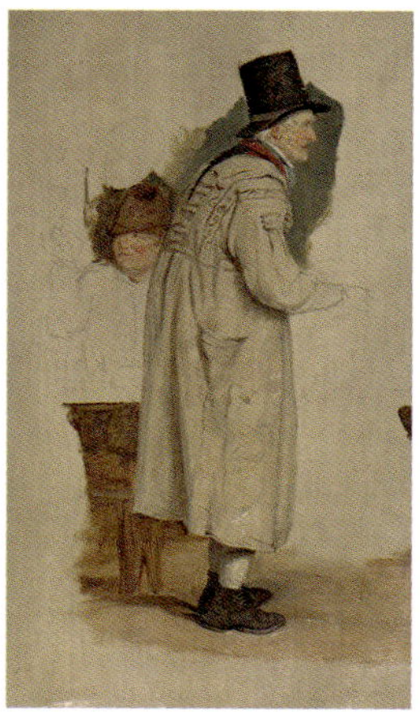

Mulready, William (follower of) 1786–1863
An Old Man in a Smock
oil on canvas 29.2 x 17.1
NCM 1945-92

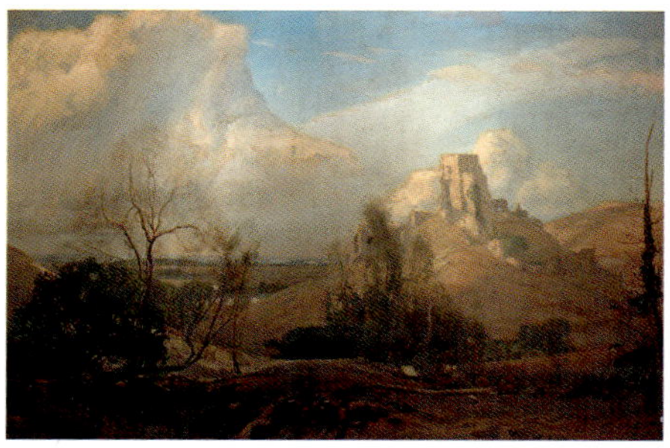

Murray, David 1849–1933
Long After, Corfe Castle, Dorset 1894
oil on canvas 180.3 x 269.2
NCM 1913-73

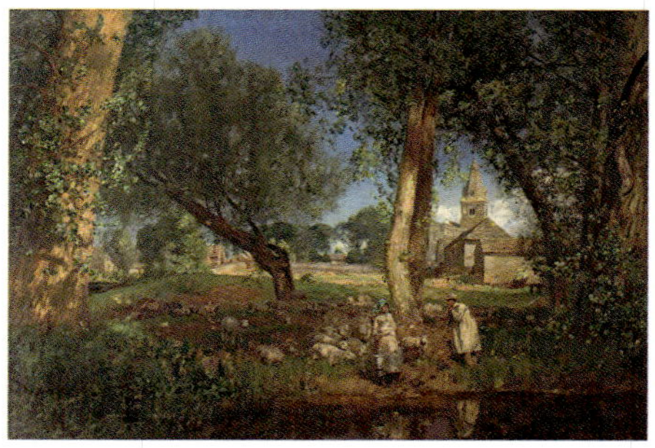

Murray, David 1849–1933
The Tithe Barns 1905
oil on canvas 121.9 x 182.9
NCM 1939-24

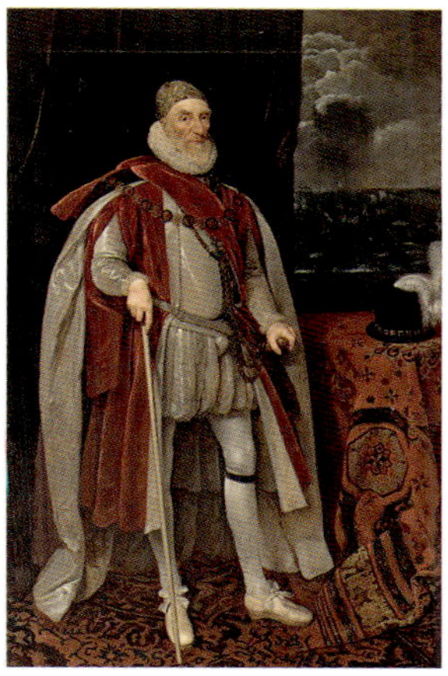

Mytens, Daniel I (studio of) c.1590–before 1648
Lord Howard of Effingham (1536–1624), 1st Earl of Nottingham 17th C
oil on canvas 243 x 155
NCM 1952-18

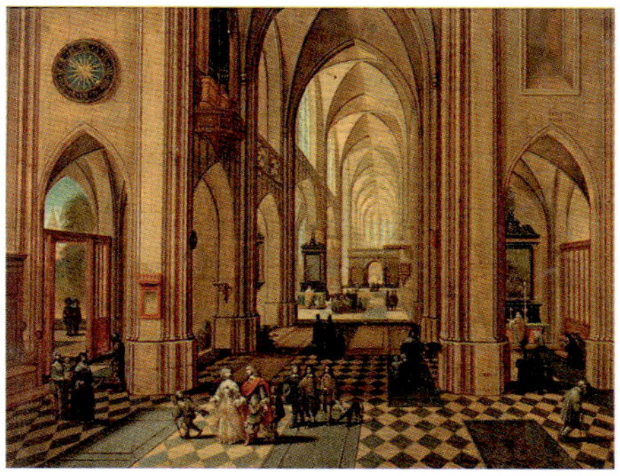

Neeffs, Peeter the elder c.1578–1656–1661 & **Vrancx, Sebastian** 1573–1647
Antwerp Cathedral
oil on wood 29.2 x 38.7
NCM 1904-115

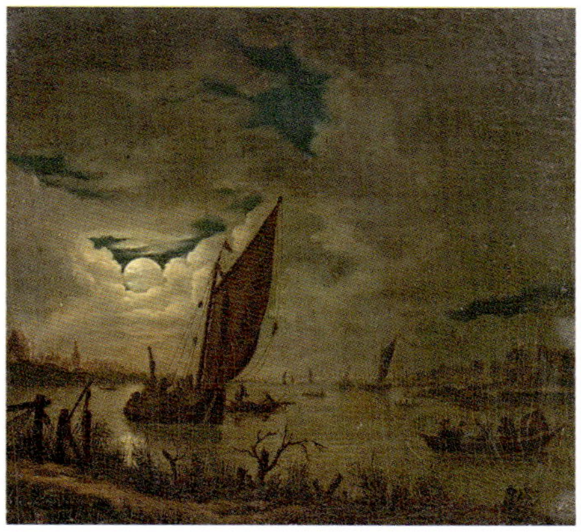

Neer, Aert van der (imitator of) 1603–1677
River Scene with Boats and Figures
oil on wood 19.7 x 21.6
NCM 1904-102

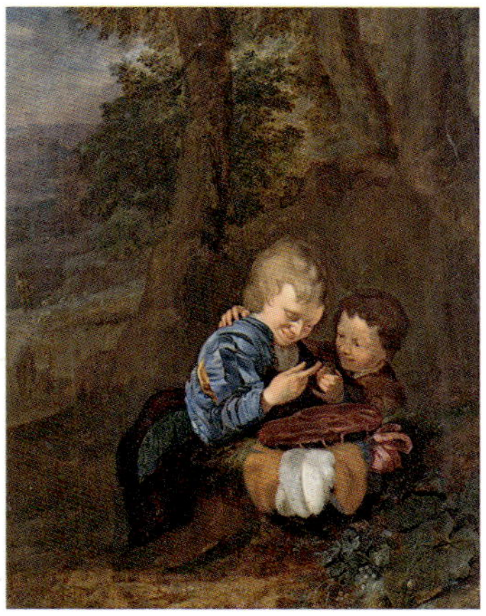

Neer, Eglon Hendrik van der 1634–1703
Two Boys with a Bird (The Birdcatchers)
oil on wood 26.4 x 20.3
NCM 1904-101

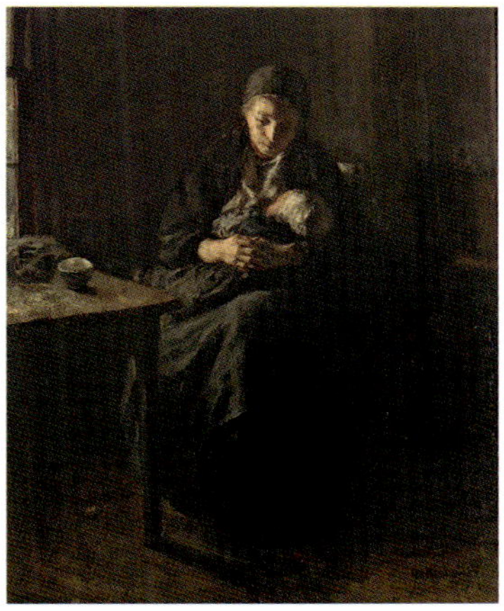

Neuhuys, Albertus Johan 1844–1914
Maternal Love (Sorrow) c.1857
oil on canvas 101.5 x 84.1
NCM 1932-43

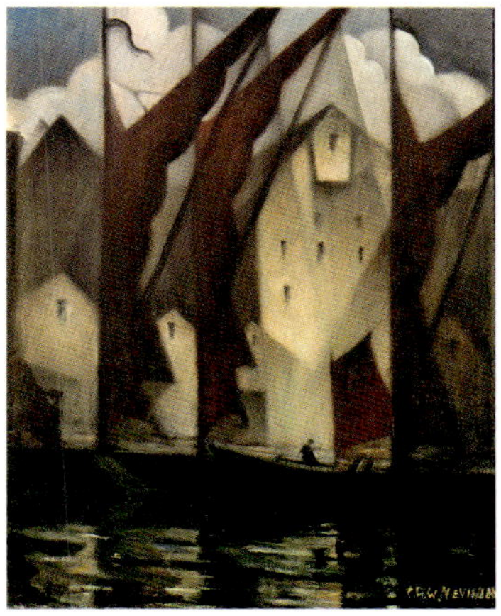

Nevinson, Christopher 1889–1946
Thameside 1941
oil on canvas 76.2 x 58.4
NCM 1942-27

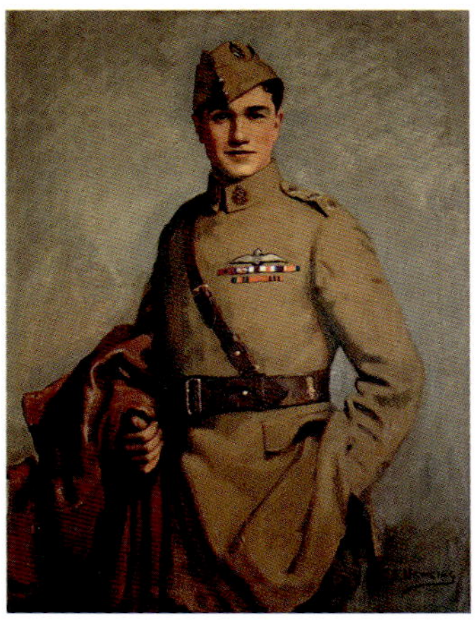

Newling, Edward active 1890–1934
Captain Albert Ball (1896–1917), VC, DSO 1921
oil on canvas 111.8 x 86.4
NCM 1922-48

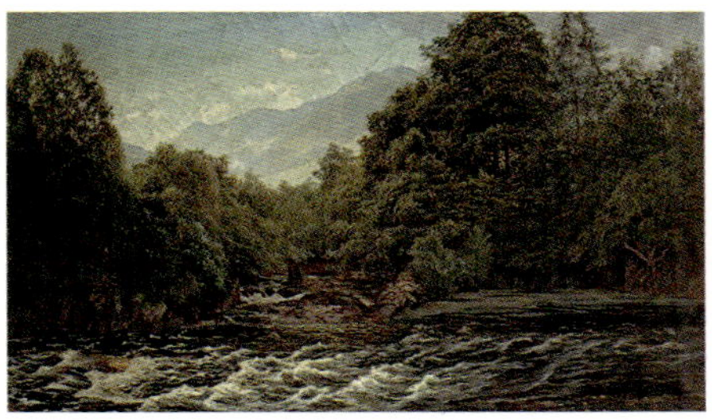

Newton, Alfred Pizzey 1830–1883
The Salmon Pool (Salmon Pool on the Spean, Scotland) 1880
oil on canvas 81.3 x 114
NCM 1919-12

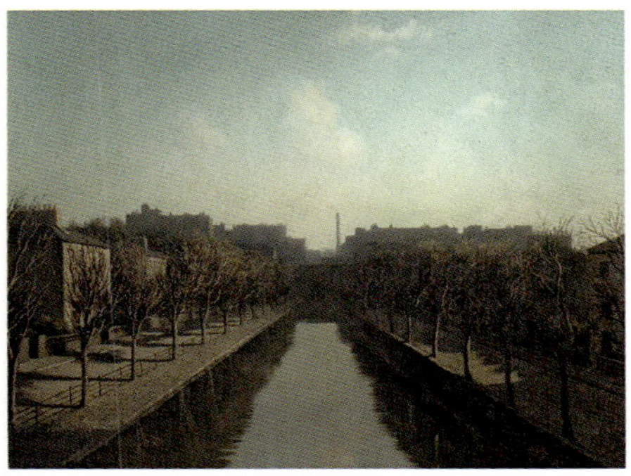

Newton, Algernon Cecil 1880–1968
Regent's Canal, Maida Vale, London 1942
oil on canvas 55.9 x 76.2
NCM 1942-19

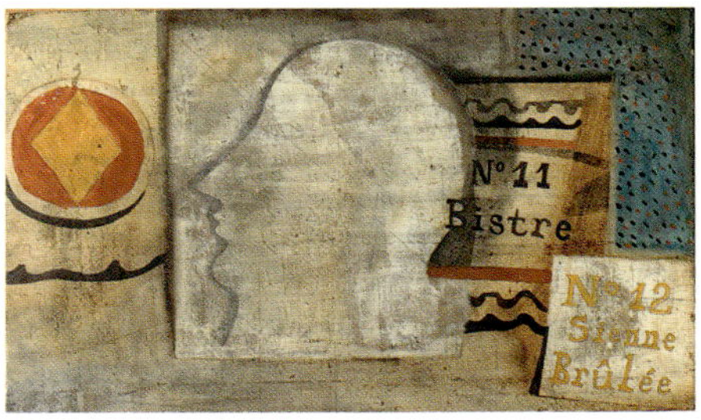

Nicholson, Ben 1894–1982
Bistre II c.1932
oil on board 44.5 x 74.9
NCM 1940-30

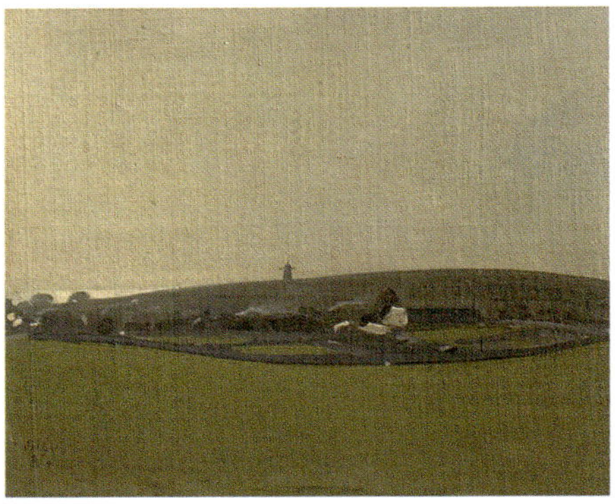

Nicholson, William 1872–1949
The Windmill, Brighton Downs (Brighton Downs, Rottingdean) 1910
oil on canvas 33 x 40.6
NCM 1957-34

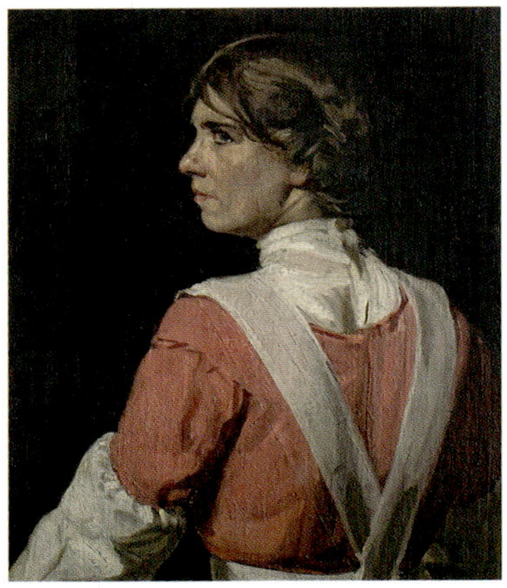

Nicholson, William 1872–1949
Miss Wish Wynne (1882–1931), Actress, in the Character of Janet Cannot for the Play 'The Great Adventure' 1913
oil on canvas 59.1 x 54.3
NCM 1933-194

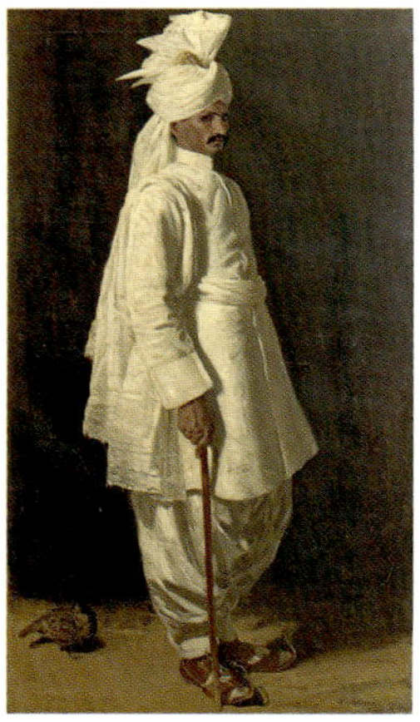

Nicholson, William 1872–1949
The Viceroy's Orderly (Ruftadur Valayar Shah) 1915
oil on canvas 198.1 x 99.1
NCM 1953-21

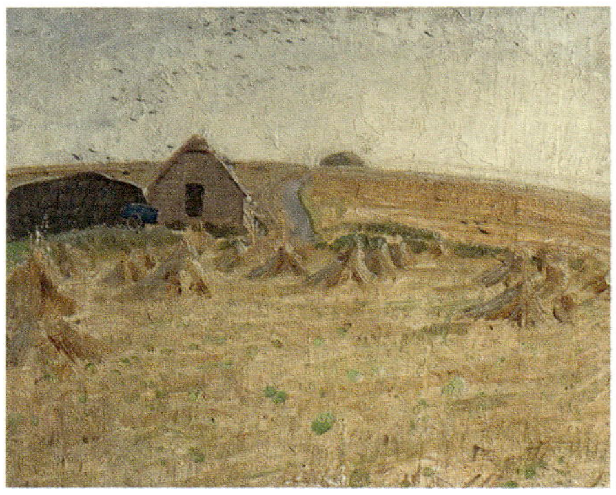

Nicholson, William 1872–1949
The Cornfield 1925
oil on canvas 33.7 x 41.3
NCM 1949-92

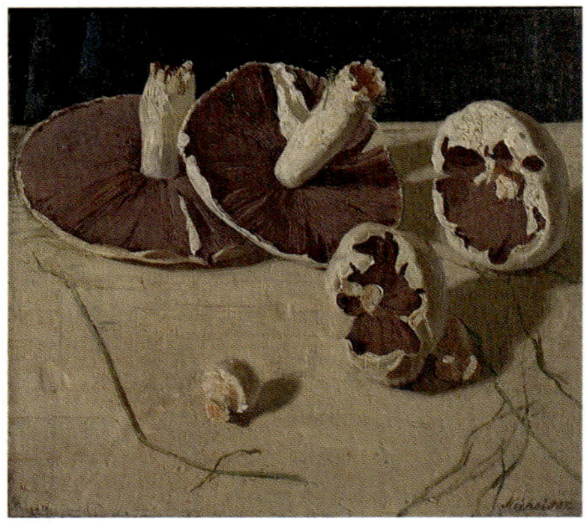

Nicholson, William 1872–1949
Mushrooms 1927
oil on canvas 50.8 x 58.4
NCM 1933-193

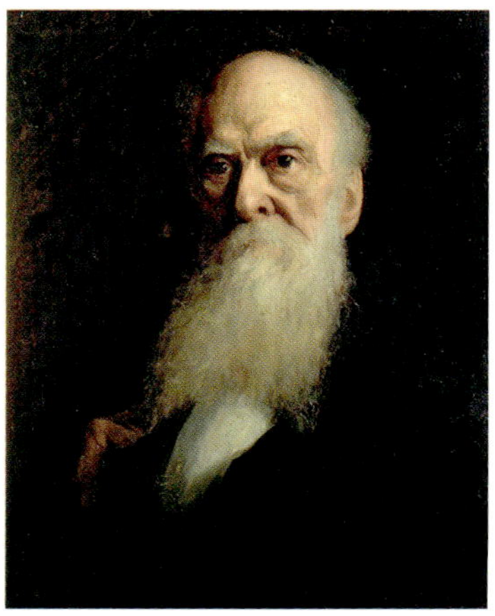

Nicholson, William 1872–1949
William Harold Cubley (1814–1896)
oil on canvas 61 x 50.8
NCM 1922-51

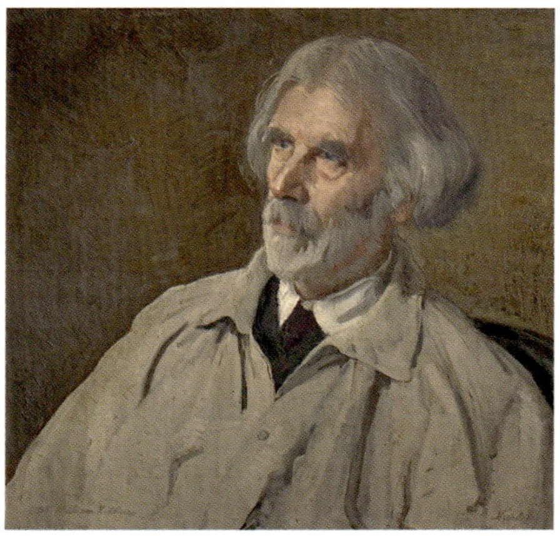

Nicholson, William 1872–1949
William Kiddier (1859–1934)
oil on wood 55.2 x 59.4
NCM 1969-178

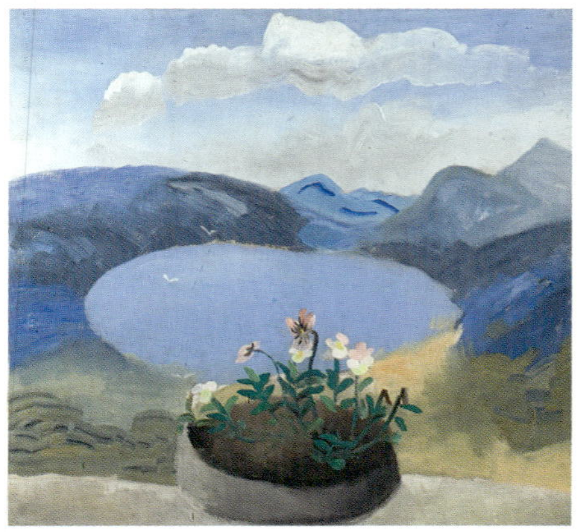

Nicholson, Winifred 1893–1981
Violas in a Window c.1920
oil on wood 52.1 x 59.7
NCM 1949-173

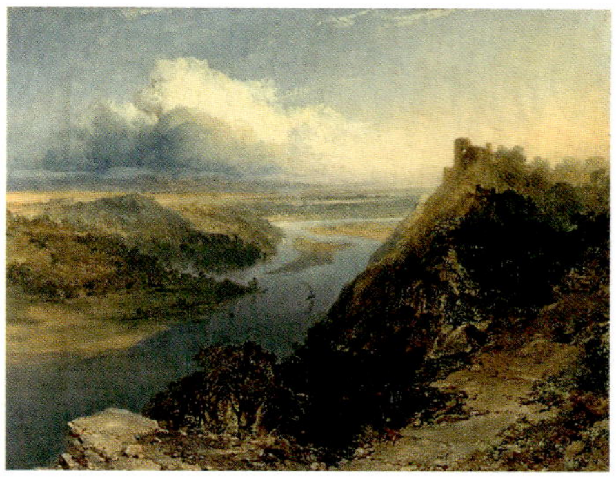

Niemann, Edmund John 1813–1876
Arundel Castle, West Sussex, and Stream 1855
oil on canvas 25.4 x 40.6
NCM 1904-58

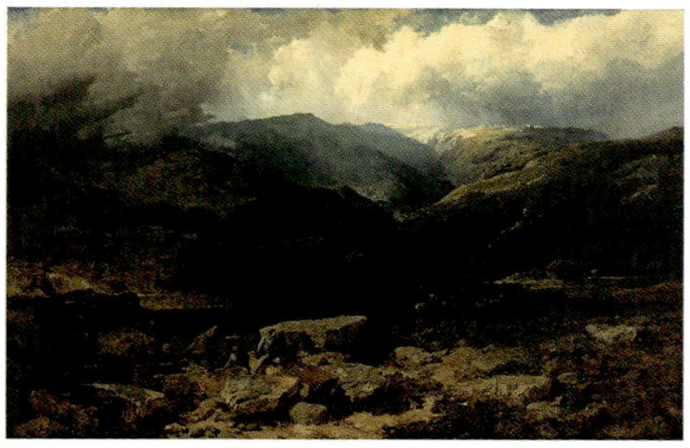

Niemann, Edmund John 1813–1876
Deer Stalking in the Highlands, a Quiet Shot 1860
oil on canvas 172.7 x 261.6
NCM 1897-65

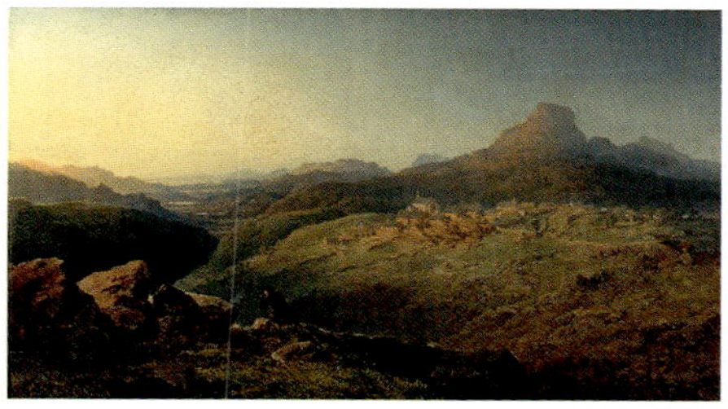

Niemann, Edmund John 1813–1876
Town and Vale of Ffestiniog, Wales
oil on canvas 63.5 x 111.7
NCM 1910-18

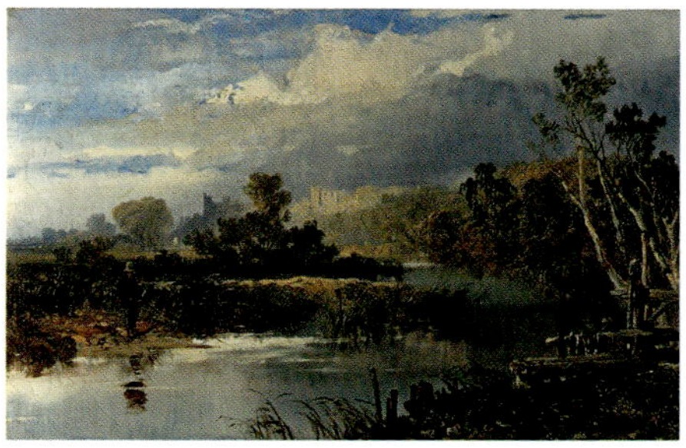

Niemann, Edmund John 1813–1876
View of Richmond, Yorkshire (Richmond Hall, Yorkshire)
oil on canvas 26 x 39
NCM 1938-160

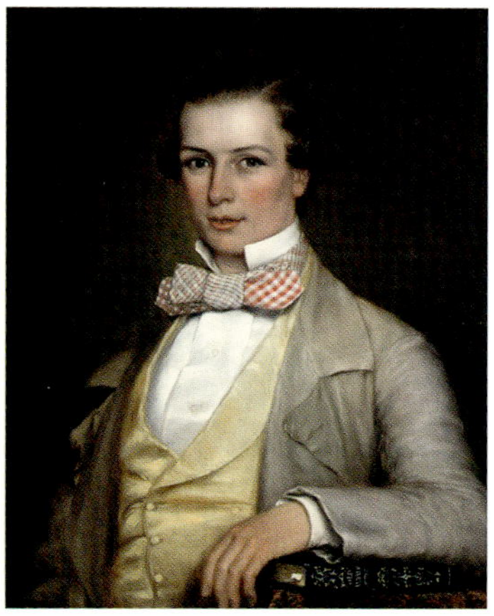

Noble, Richard Pratchett c.1814–1892
William Strover Birkin, Aged 19 1855
oil on canvas 76.2 x 63.5
NCM 1968-327

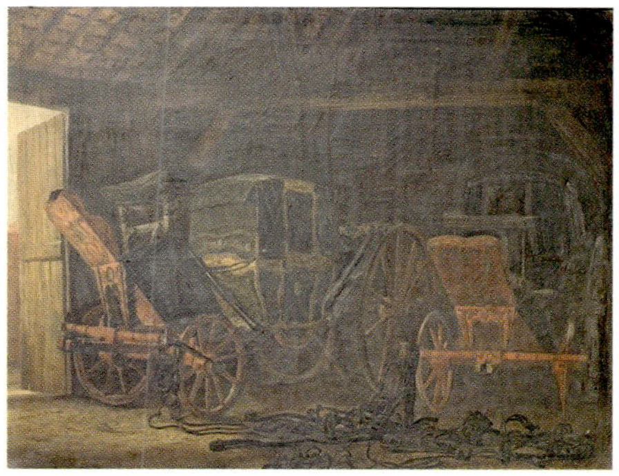

Norton, A.
Carriages
oil on canvas 74 x 96.4
FA-X 5

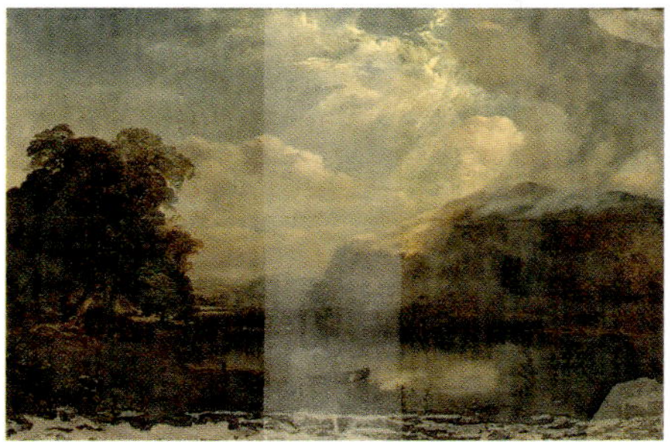

Oakes, John Wright 1820–1887
The Mouth of the River Derwent 1848
oil on canvas 94 x 125.1
NCM 1920-17

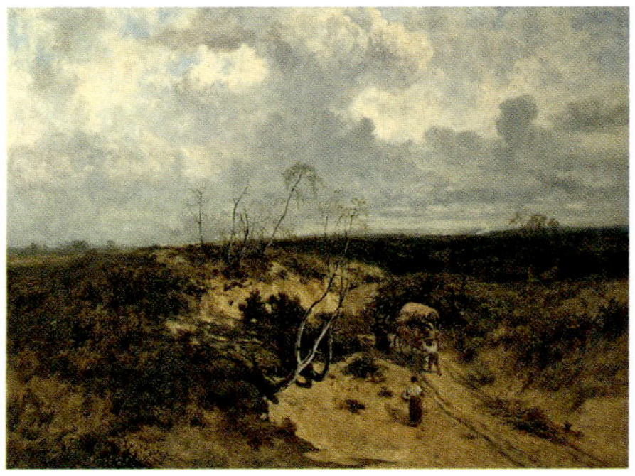

Oakes, John Wright 1820–1887
A Sandy Bit of Road 1874
oil on canvas 78.7 x 109.2
NCM 1934-38

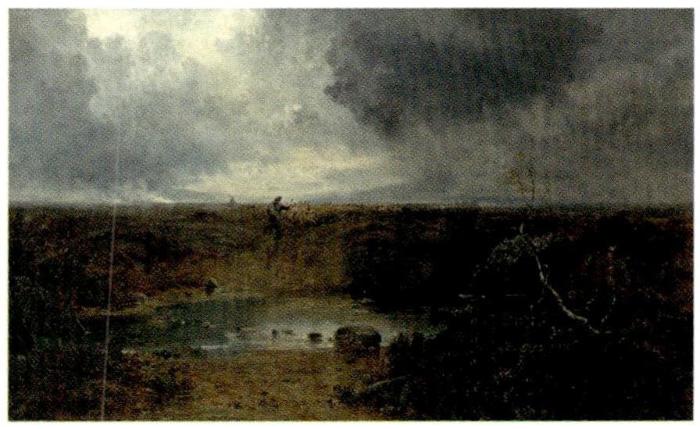

Oakes, John Wright 1820–1887
The Coming Shower
oil on canvas 55.9 x 86.4
NCM 1908-113

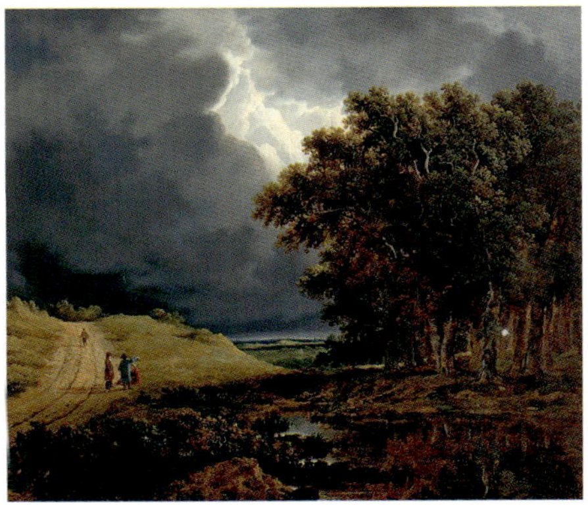

O'Connor, James Arthur 1791–1841
The Edge of a Forest, Storm Coming On 1826
oil on canvas 65.5 x 68
NCM 1904-59

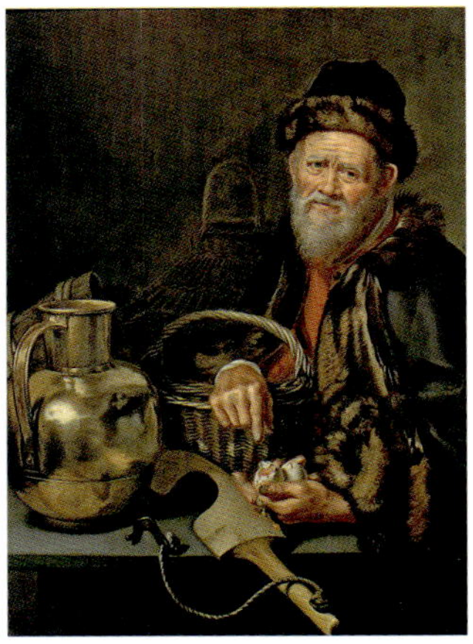

Odekerken, Willem van (attributed to)
d.1677
An Old Man with Broken Eggs
oil on wood 102.9 x 79.7
NCM 1904-88

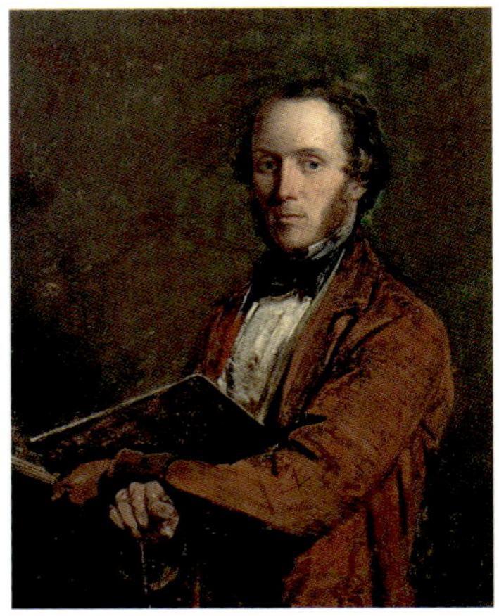

O'Neil, Henry Nelson 1817–1880
William Powell Frith (1819–1909)
oil on board 48.3 x 40.6
NCM 1904-60

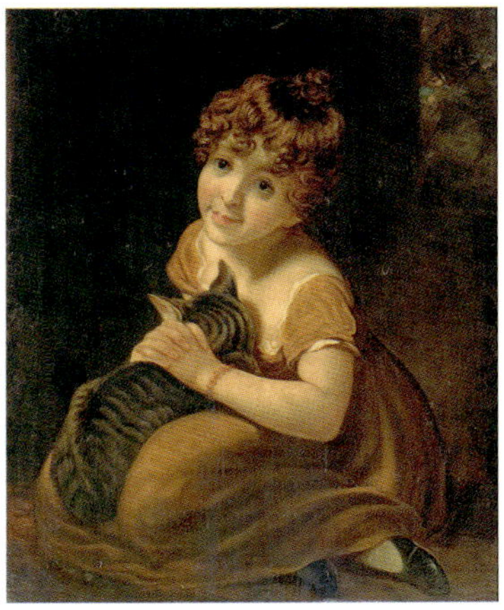

Opie, John (attributed to) 1761–1807
Girl with a Cat
oil on canvas 76.2 x 64.8
NCM 1904-61

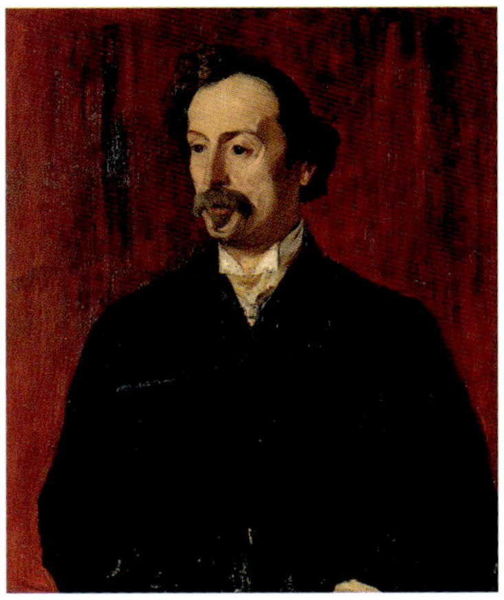

Orchardson, William Quiller 1832–1910
Self Portrait
oil on canvas 82.6 x 71.1
NCM 1904-62

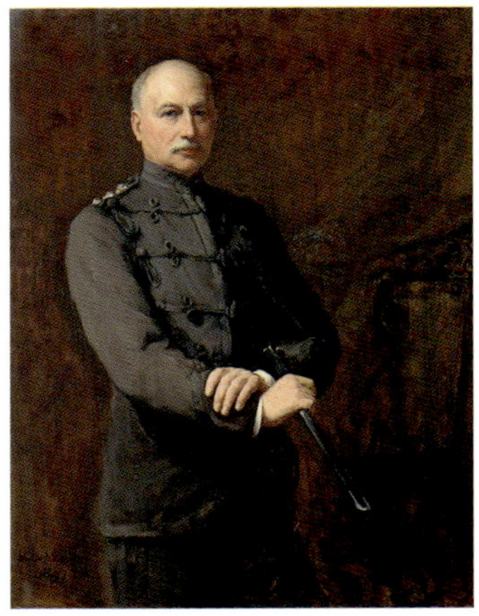

Ouless, Walter William 1848–1933
Colonel Sir Charles Seely (1859–1926) 1897
oil on canvas 125.5 x 100.4
NCM 1897-75

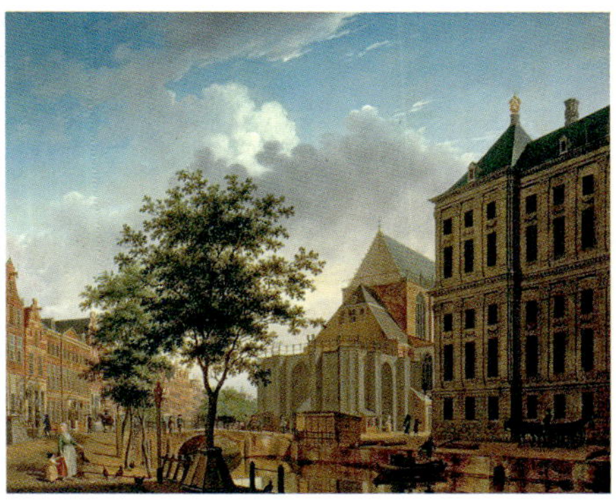

Ouwater, Isaak 1748–1793
Back of Nieuwe Kerk and Town Hall, Amsterdam, Holland
oil on canvas 51 x 66
NCM 1904-94

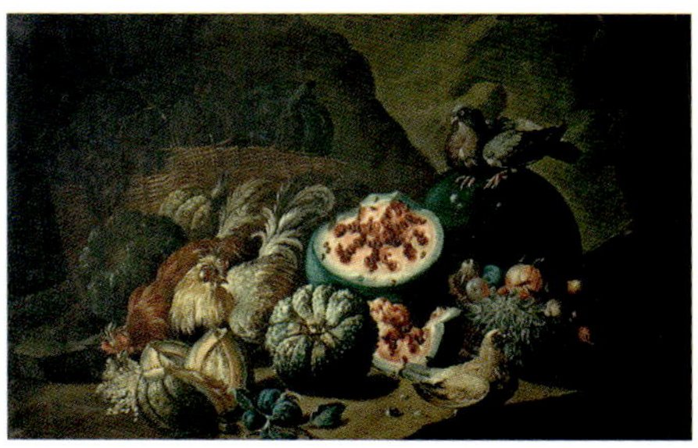

Pace del Campidoglio, Michele
1610–probably 1670
Still Life
oil on canvas 96.5 x 157.5
NCM 1942-18

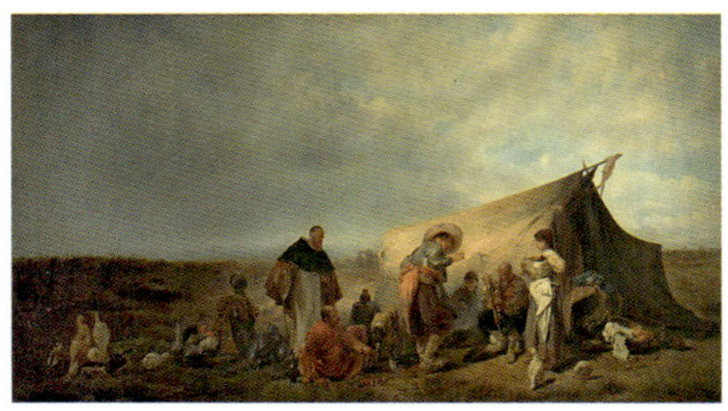

Pacsano, Enrico active early 19th C
Military Encampment
oil on canvas 81.2 x 151.1
NCM 1966-108

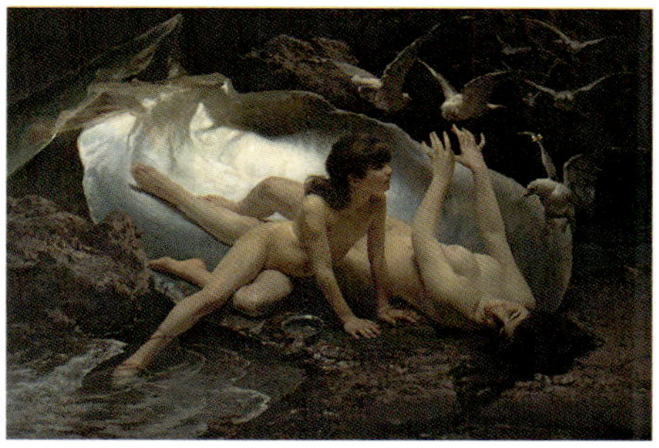

Pagliei, Gioacchino 1852–1896
The Naiads 1881
oil on canvas 144 x 213
NCM 1885-2

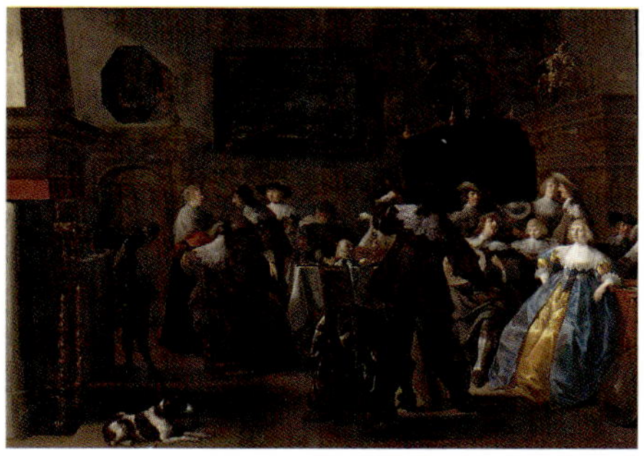

Palamedesz., Anthonie 1601–1673
Merry Company (Interior with Cavaliers and Ladies) 1630s
oil on wood 59.7 x 87.6
NCM 1904-95

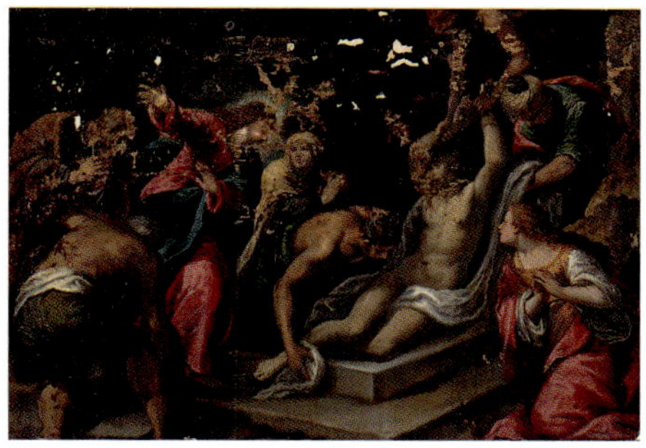

Palma, Jacopo il giovane (after) 1544/1548–1628
The Raising of Lazarus
oil on canvas 45.7 x 67
NCM 1910-56

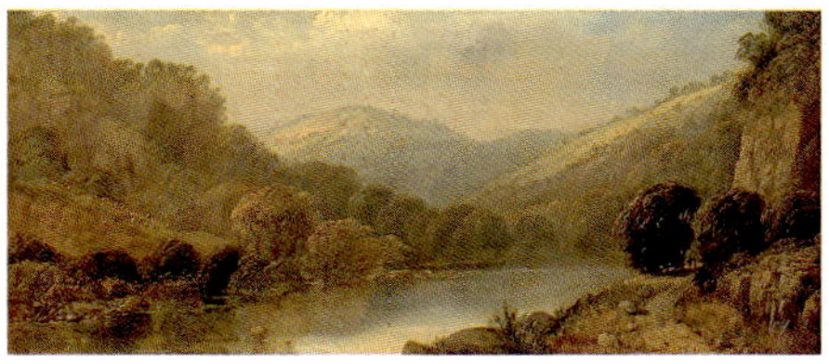

Parrott, Samuel 1797–1876
Dovedale (Spires of Dovedale, Derbyshire) 1843
oil on canvas 30.5 x 69.9
NCM 1910-30

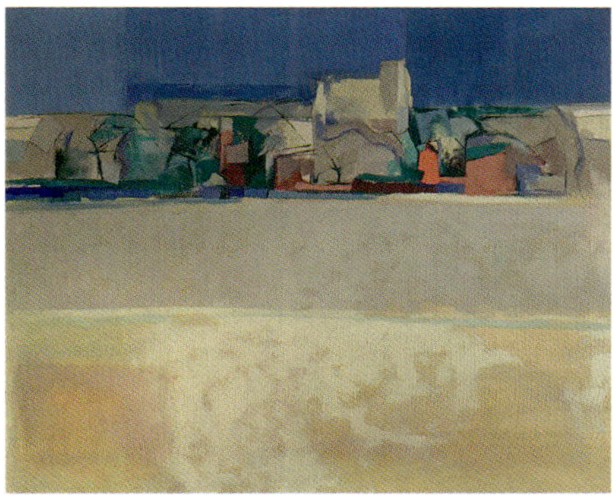

Partridge, Maurice William 1913–1973
Salthouses, Norfolk 1966
acrylic on canvas 67.5 x 85
NCM 1967-83

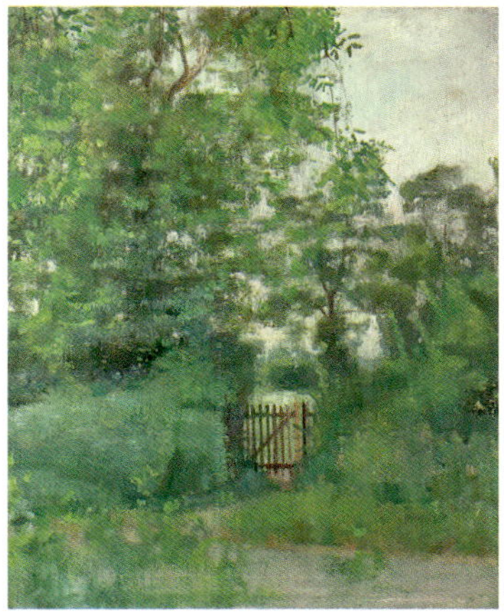

Pasmore, Victor 1908–1998
Green Landscape with Gate c.1943
oil on canvas 76.2 x 63.5
NCM 1952-12

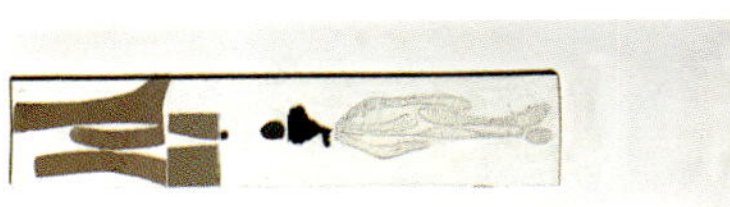

Pasmore, Victor 1908–1998
Maquette for Metamorphosis Mural 1966
oil, paper, pencil & pen on board 30 x 86.5
NCMG 2000-140

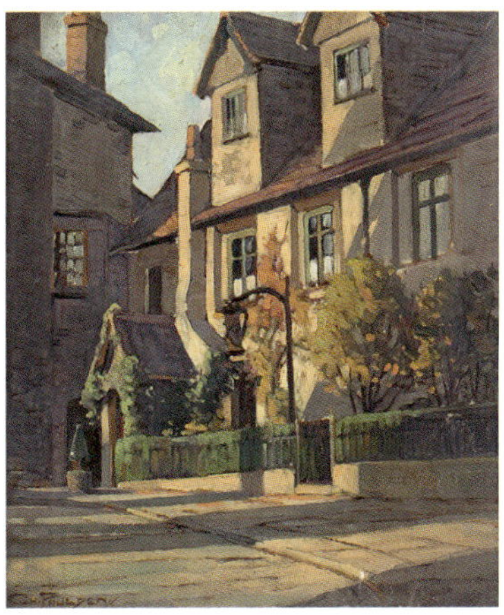

Paulden, C. H.
Dorothy Vernon House
oil on board 40 x 34.4
NCM 1988-1160

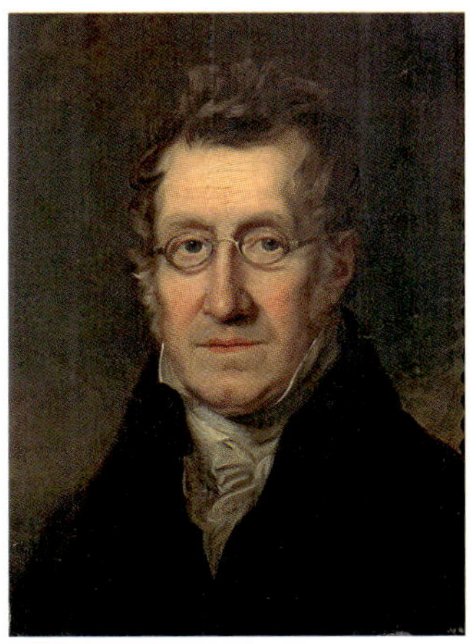

Payne, William c.1760–after 1830
Self Portrait c.1820
oil on canvas 45.1 x 35.6
NCM 1904-63

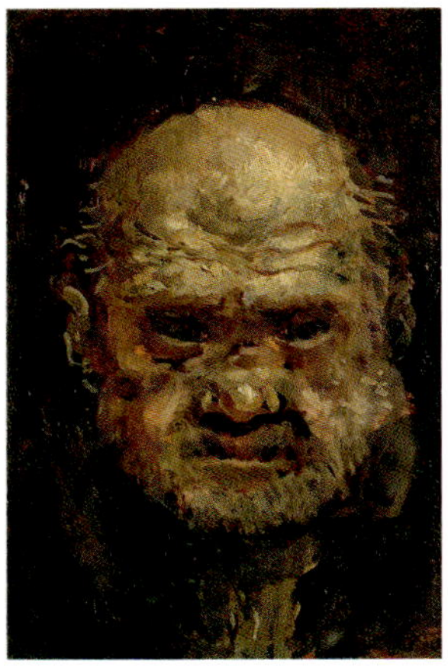

Peake, Mervyn 1911–1968
Head of an Old Man
oil on canvas 34.3 x 25.4
NCM 1949-171

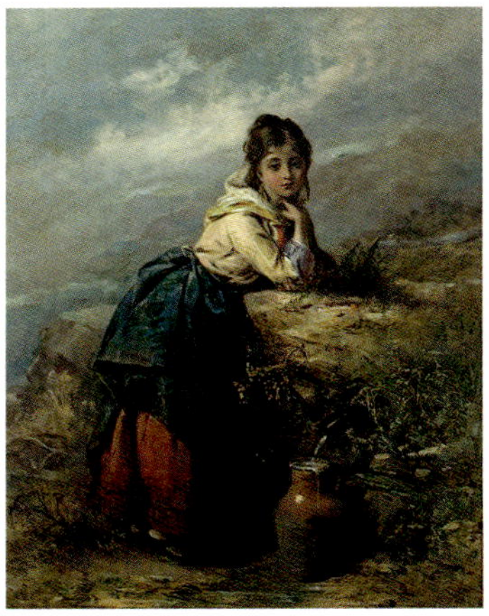

Pelham, Thomas Kent c.1831–1907
A Mountain Lassie (Girl with a Water Pot)
oil on canvas 91.4 x 71.1
NCM 1934-129

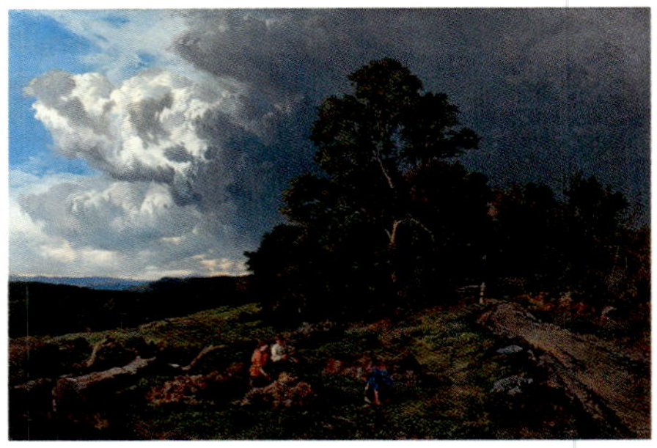

Percy, Sidney Richard 1821–1886
The Fern Gatherers 1857
oil on canvas 101.6 x 152.4
NCM 1934-32

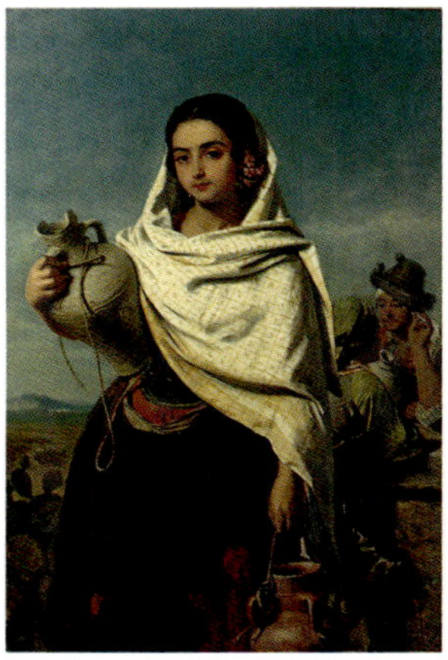

Phillip, John 1817–1867
Water-Carrier of Seville 1859
oil on canvas 137.2 x 94
NCM 1904-65

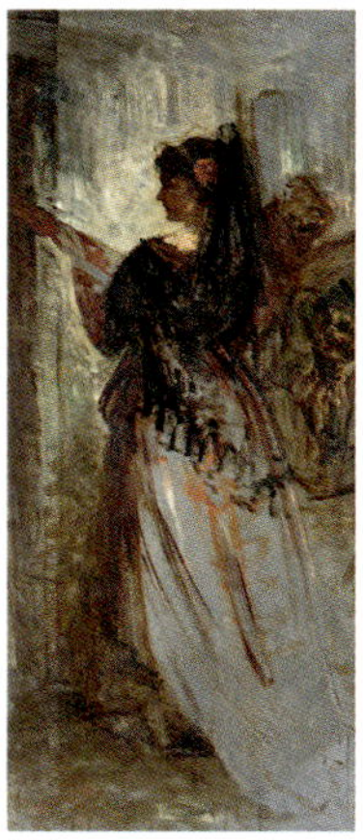

Phillip, John 1817–1867
A Lady with a Guitar
oil on canvas 113 x 49.8
NCM 1904-64

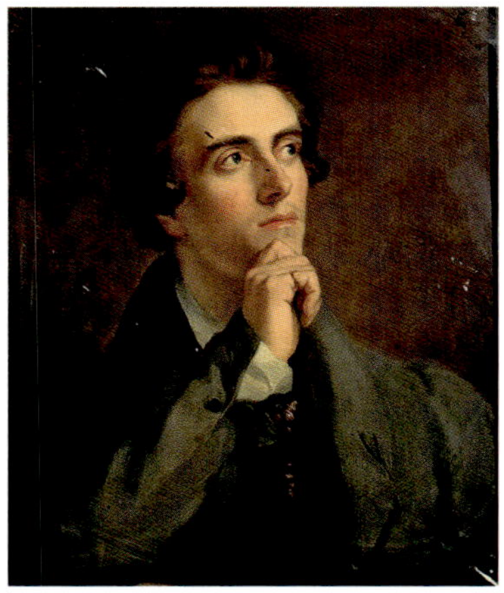

Phillips, Thomas 1770–1845
Portrait of an Unknown Man (possibly the poet John Keats or the painter Richard Parkes Bonington)
oil on canvas 63.5 x 55.9
NCM 1926-118

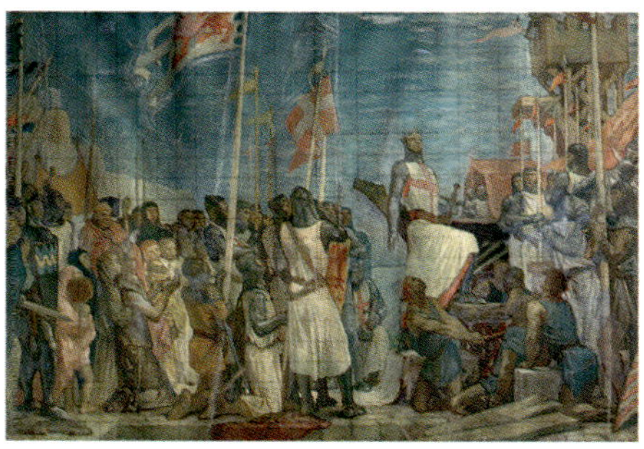

Philpot, Glyn Warren 1884–1937
Richard the Lionheart Embarks on the Third Crusade 1927
oil on canvas 74.9 x 108
NCM 1949-75

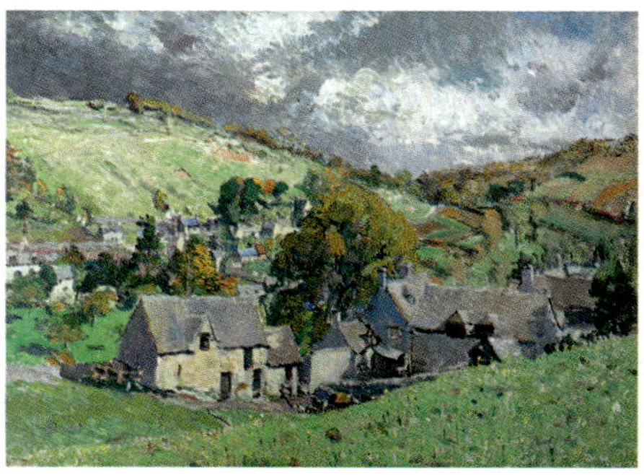

Pickard, Louise 1865–1928
A Gloucestershire Village 1919
oil on canvas 51 x 71
NCM 1924-11

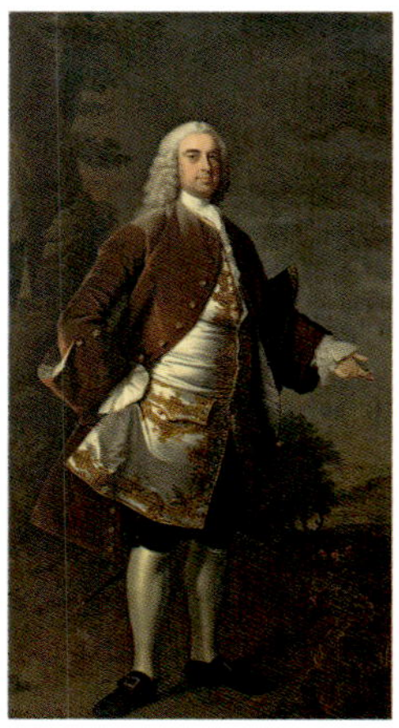

Pickering, Henry c.1720–c.1775
Sir Wolstan Dixie (1700–1767), 4th Bt, Market Bosworth 1741
oil on canvas 247.7 x 127
NCM 1953-12

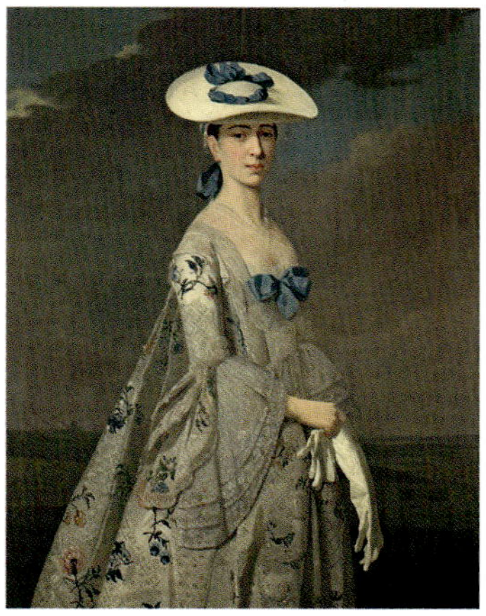

Pickering, Henry (attributed to)
c.1720–c.1775
Miss Dixie c.1750–1755
oil on canvas 121.9 x 99.1
NCM 1894-112

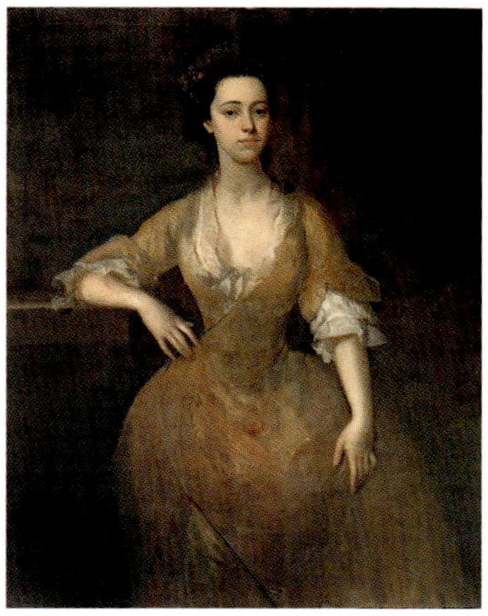

Pickering, Henry (imitator of)
c.1720–c.1775
Lady Dixie
oil on canvas 124 x 99.5
NCM 1970-23

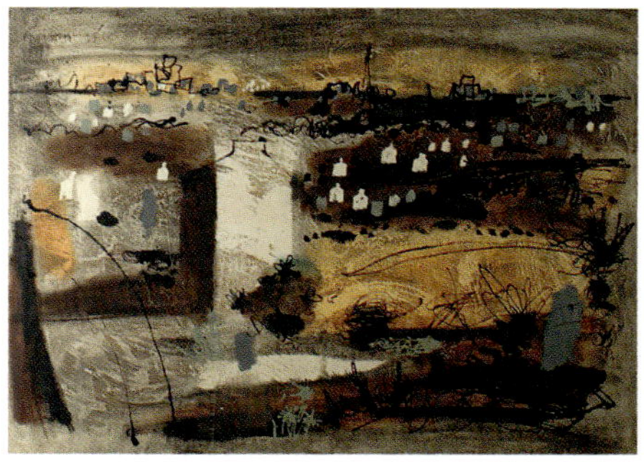

Piper, John 1903–1992
Brittany Coast, France 1963
oil on canvas 91.5 x 122
NCM 1964-1

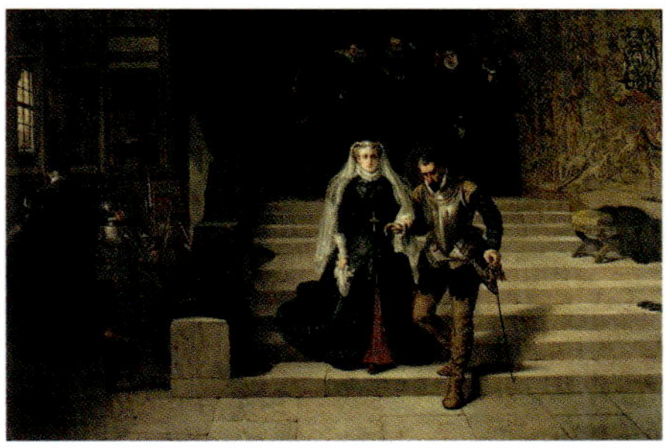

Pott, Laslett John 1837–1898
Mary, Queen of Scots, Being Led to Her Execution 1871
oil on canvas 127 x 182.9
NCM 1898-77

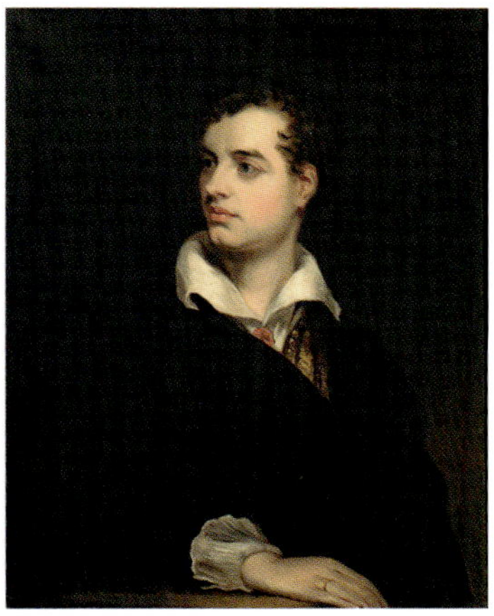

Pott, Laslett John 1837–1898
Lord Byron (1788–1824)
oil on canvas 91.4 x 72.4
NCM 1903-28

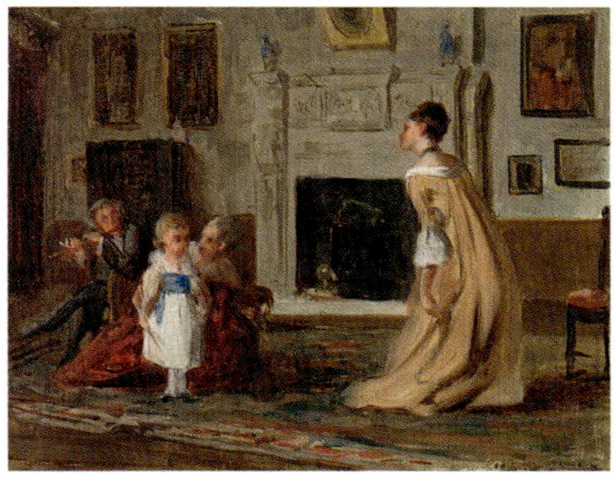

Pott, Laslett John 1837–1898
The Dancing Lesson
oil on canvas 17.1 x 22.2
NCM 1939-8

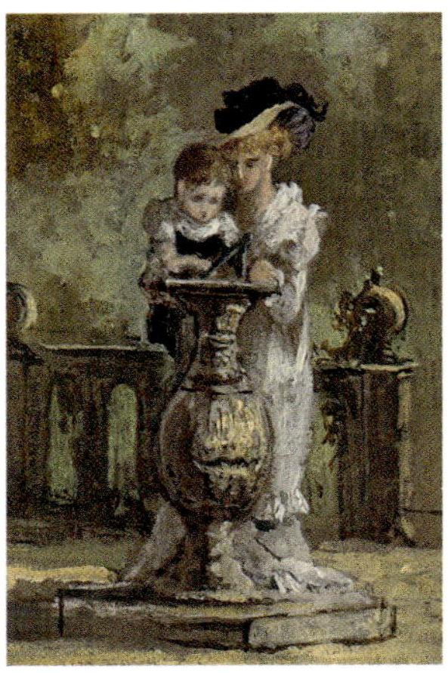

Pott, Laslett John 1837–1898
The Sundial
oil on brown paper 13.3 x 9.5
NCM 1939-7

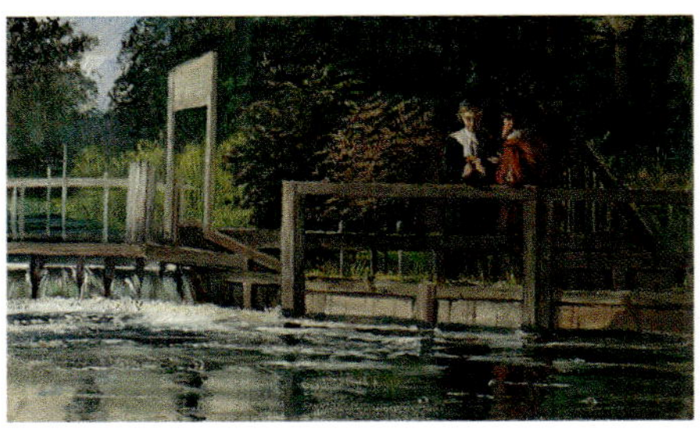

Pott, Laslett John 1837–1898
The Trysting Place
oil on canvas laid on board 17.8 x 29.8
NCM 1939-9

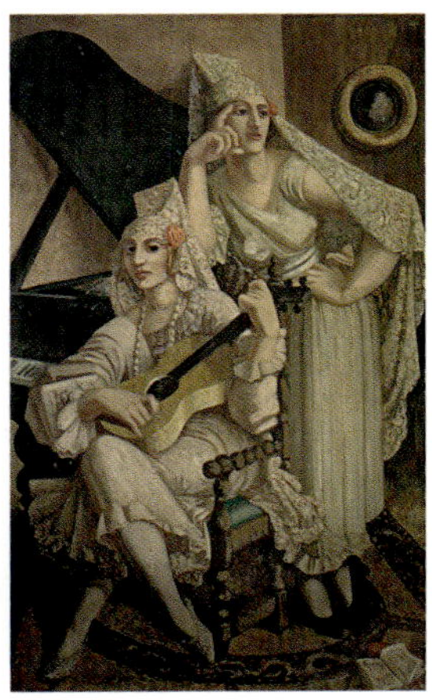

Power, John Joseph Wardell 1881–1943
Music
oil on canvas 170.2 x 106.7
NCM 1928-183

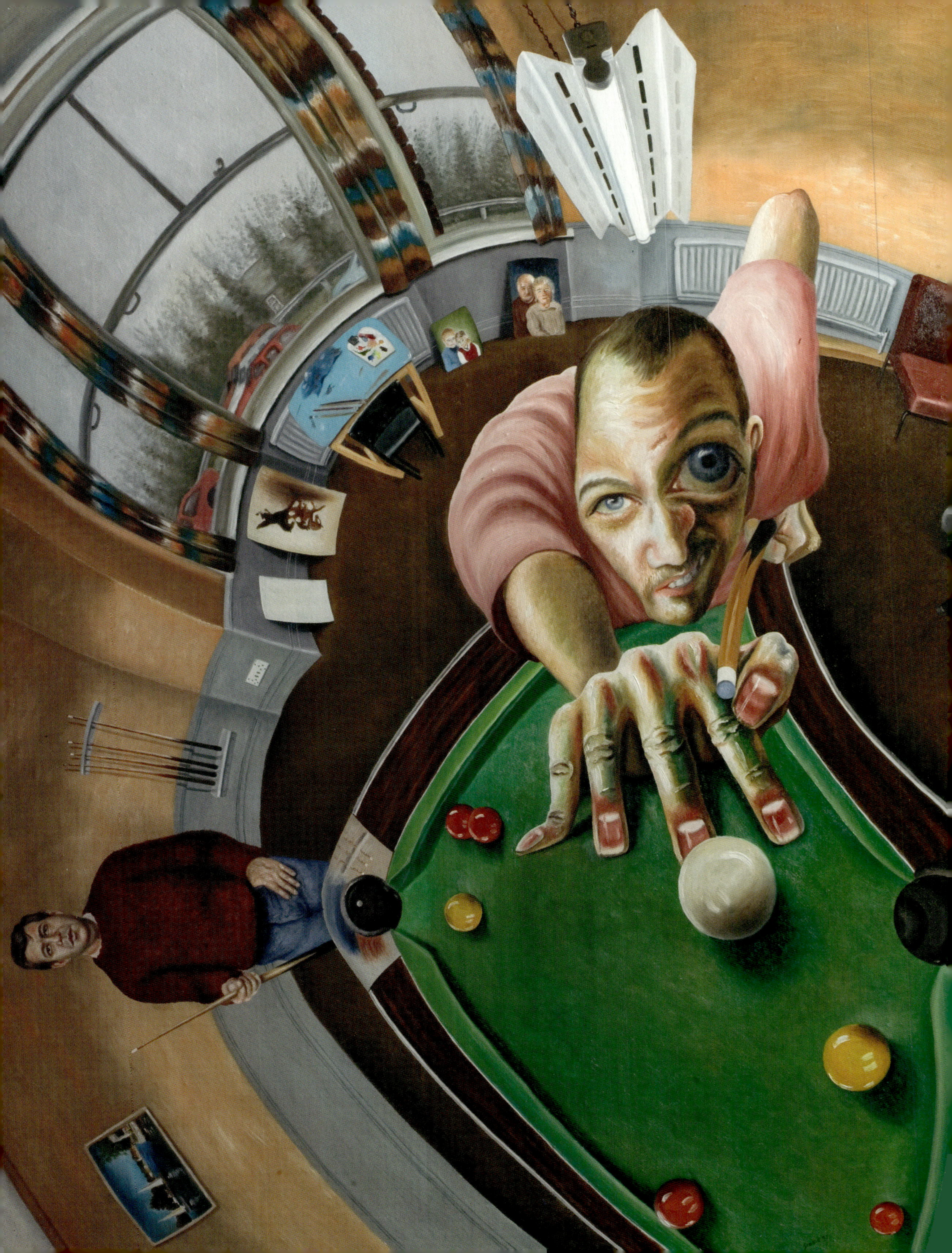

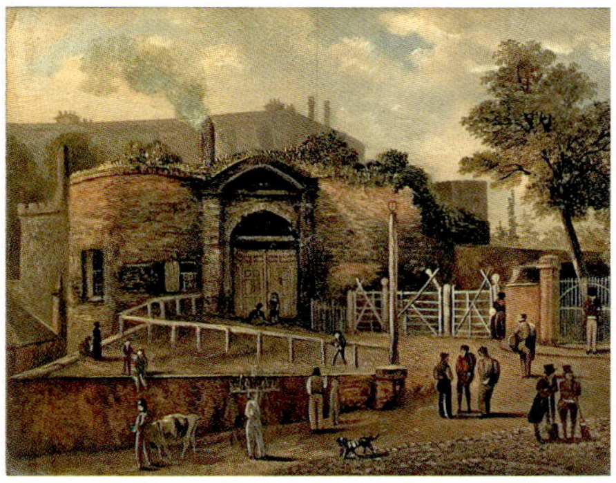

Price, Caroline Mary active 1830
View of the Castle Gateway, Nottingham
oil on board 20.3 x 27.9
NCM 1911-46

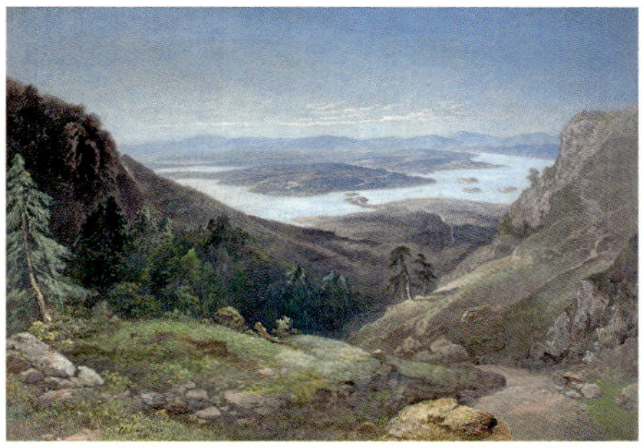

Price, Edward 1800–1885
Norway 1881
oil on canvas 62.2 x 90.2
NCM 1973-39

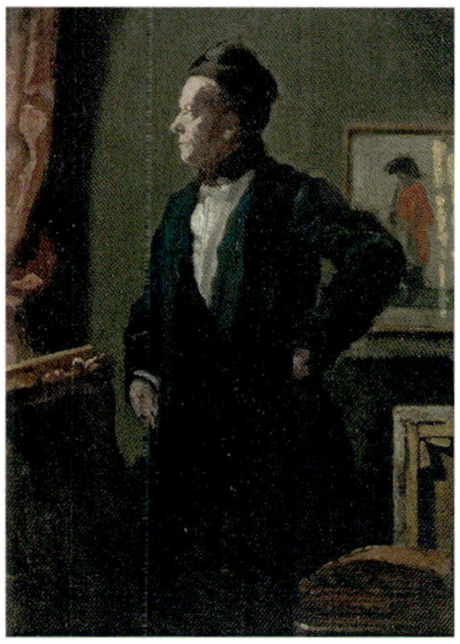

Pryde, James 1866–1941
Self Portrait as 'Scarron'
oil on canvas 40.6 x 30.5
NCM 1966-100

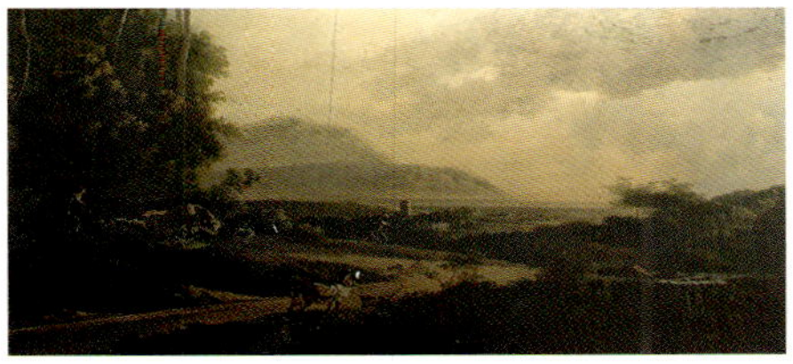

Pynacker, Adam c.1620–1673
Landscape with a Winding Roadway
oil on canvas 152.4 x 208.3
NCM 1894-19

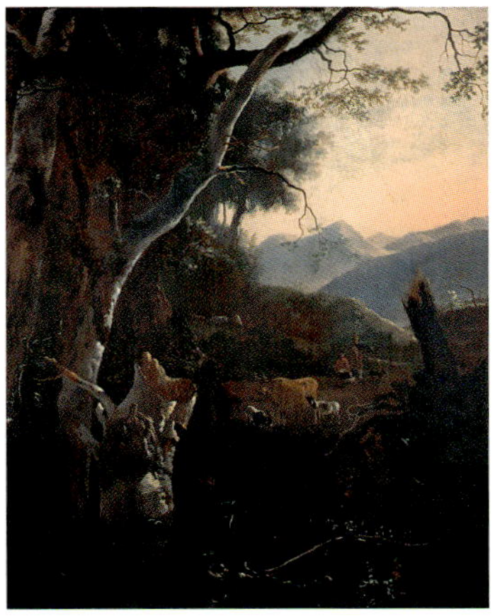

Pynacker, Adam c.1620–1673
Mountainous Landscape with Peasants, Cows and Goats
oil on canvas 90.2 x 76.2
NCM 1904-96

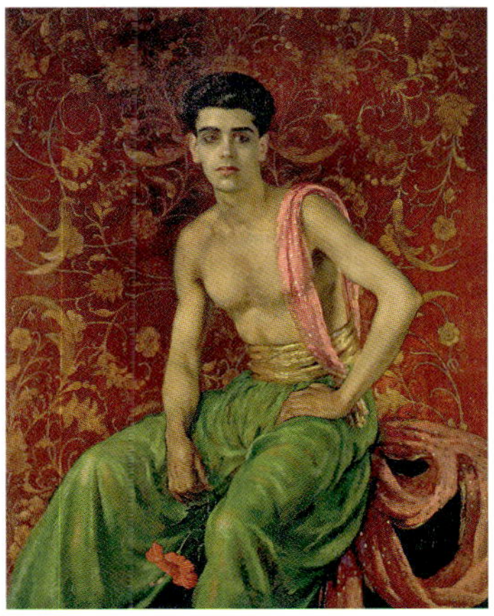

Ranken, William Bruce Ellis 1881–1941
Hibiscus Flower c.1922
oil on canvas 137.2 x 106.7
NCM 1946-309

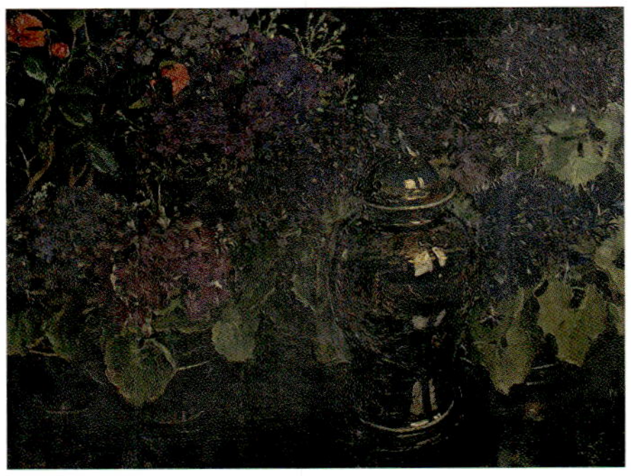

Ranken, William Bruce Ellis 1881–1941
Cinerarias
oil on canvas 91.4 x 121.9
NCM 1946-310

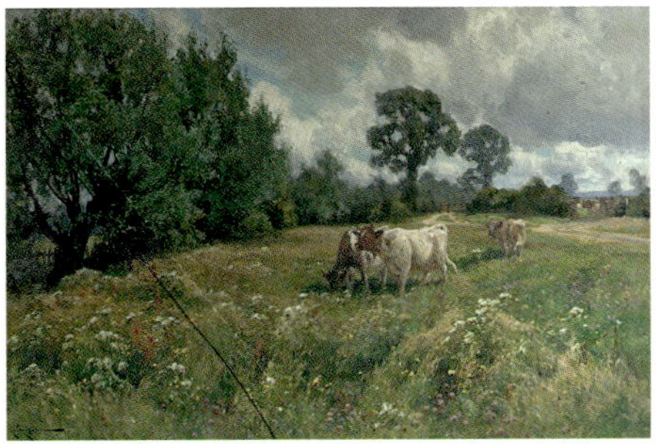

Redgate, Arthur W. 1860–1906
Trespassers 1902
oil on canvas 52.1 x 77.5
NCM 1902-32

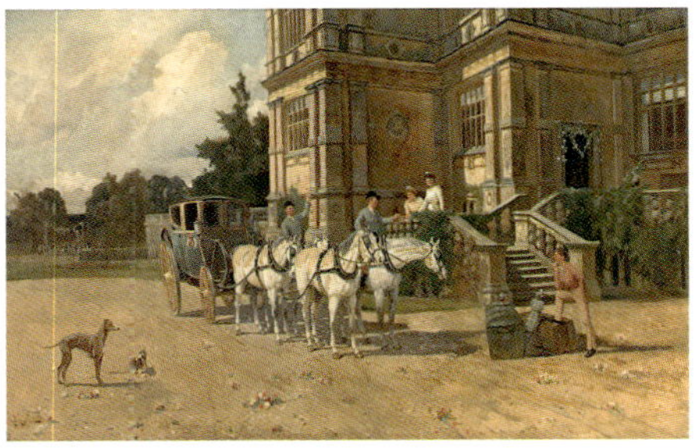

Redgate, Arthur W. 1860–1906
*Front View of Wollaton Hall, Nottingham, with Horse and Carriage**
oil on canvas 69 x 135
FA-X 26

Facing page: Scobie, Ray, active 1995–1997, *Billiard Table* (detail), 1997, Galleries of Justice, (p. 48)

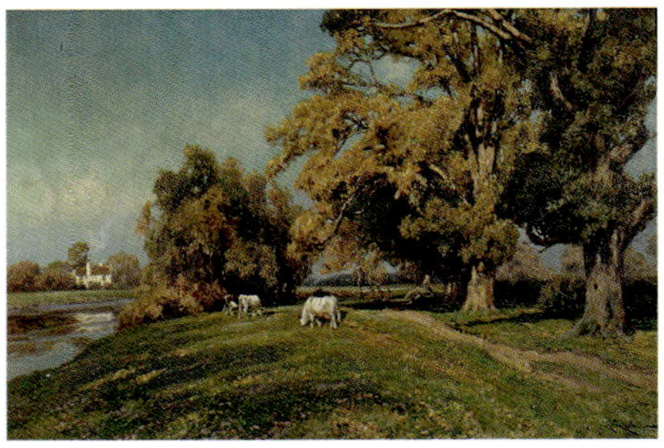

Redgate, Arthur W. 1860–1906
Grove Farm, Lenton, Nottingham
oil on canvas 61 x 95.3
NCM 1936-43/(a)

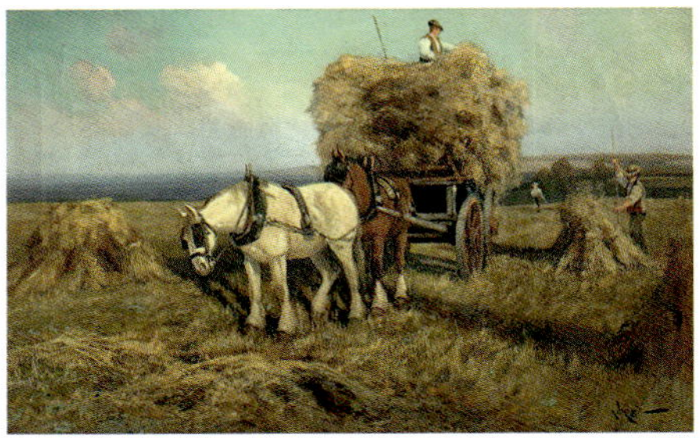

Redgate, Arthur W. 1860–1906
Loading the Harvest Wagon
oil on canvas 40.6 x 66
NCM 1946-261

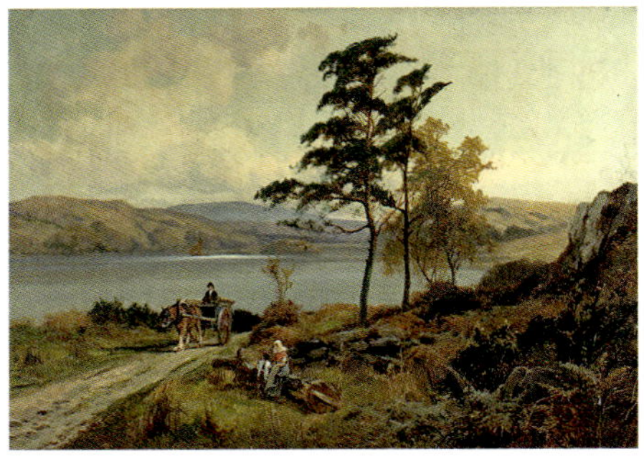

Redgate, Arthur W. 1860–1906
Near Betws-y-Coed, North Wales
oil on canvas 50.8 x 76.2
NCM 1946-260

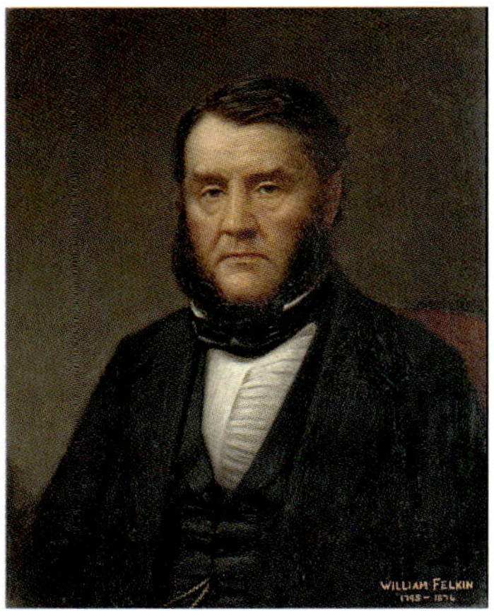

Redgate, Sylvanus 1827–1907
William Felkin (1795–1874) c.1850
oil on canvas 45.7 x 36.8
NCM 1964-67

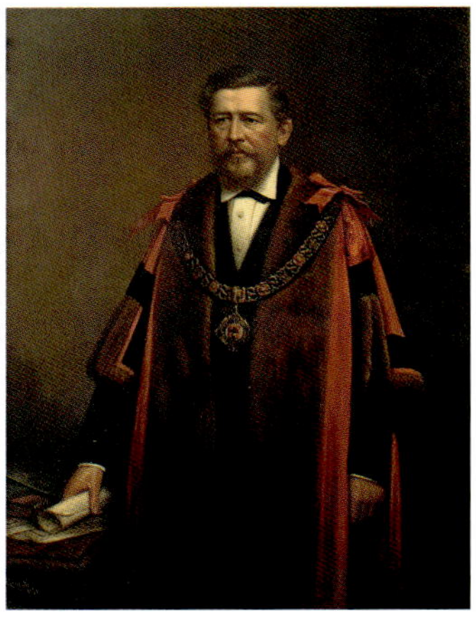

Redgate, Sylvanus 1827–1907
Alderman William George Ward 1878
oil on canvas 142.2 x 111.8
NCM 1880-2

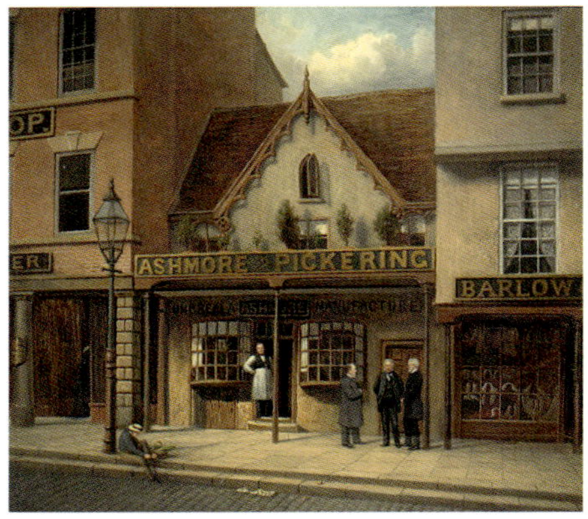

Redgate, Sylvanus 1827–1907
39, Long Row, the Market Place, Nottingham
1879
oil on canvas 67.3 x 77.5
NCM 1925-49

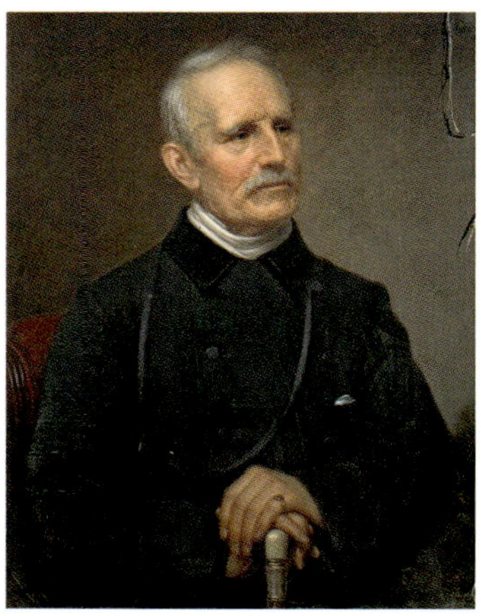

Redgate, Sylvanus 1827–1907
Major Jonathan White (b.1804), RHR (The Old Adjutant) 1883
oil on canvas 55.9 x 45.7
NCM 1883-25

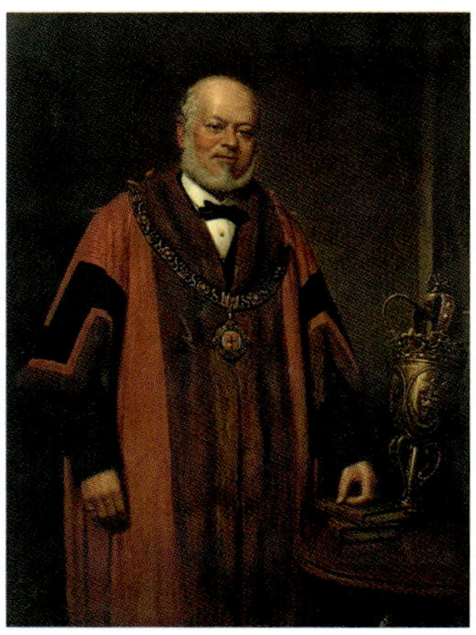

Redgate, Sylvanus 1827–1907
Alderman J. Burton
oil on canvas 142.2 x 106.7
NCM 1936-33

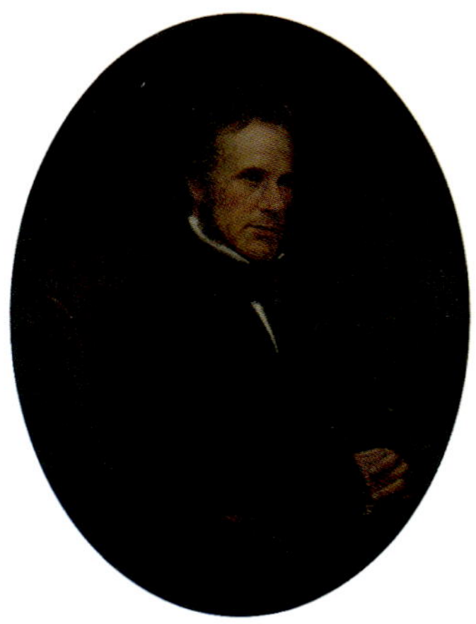

Redgate, Sylvanus 1827–1907
Henry Dawson (1811–1878)
oil on canvas 41.9 x 34.3
NCM 1901-37

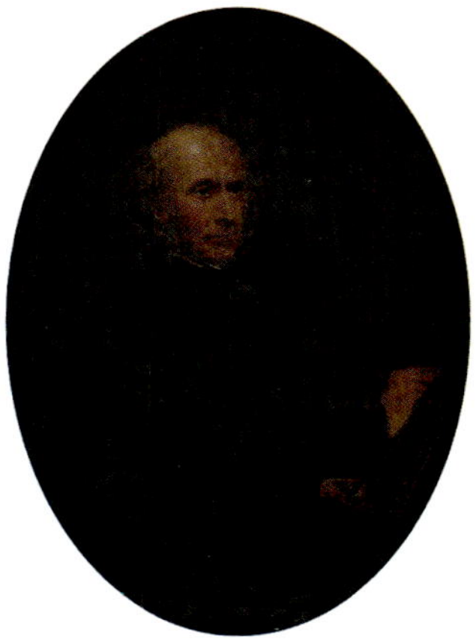

Redgate, Sylvanus 1827–1907
Josiah Gilbert
oil on board 45.7 x 35.6
NCM 1902-96

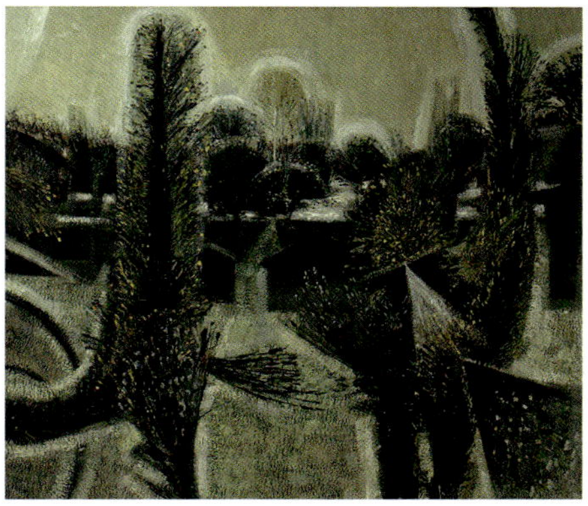

Reynolds, Alan b.1926
Evening, Just before Spring 1954
oil on board 72.4 x 91.4
NCM 1954-39

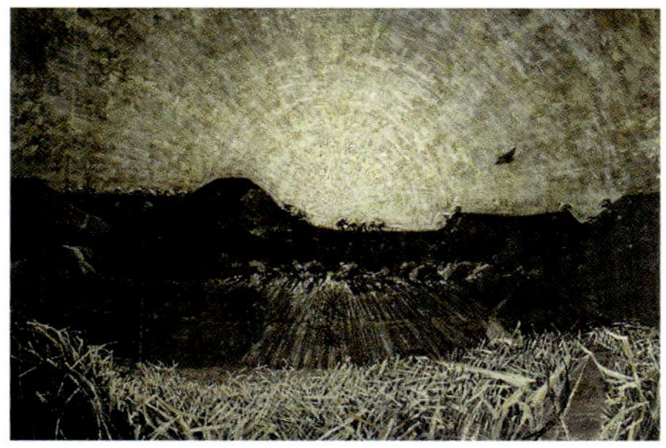

Reynolds, Alan b.1926
Sunset 1956
oil on wood 121.9 x 177.8
NCM 1958-12

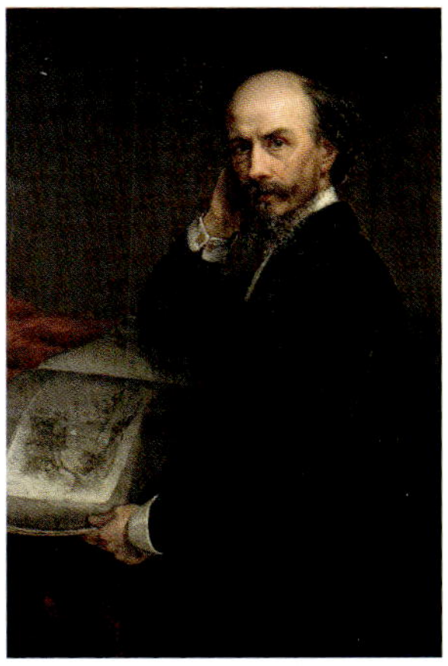

Richmond, George 1809–1896
Tom Allom (1804–1872)
oil on canvas 105.4 x 74.9
NCM 1904-66

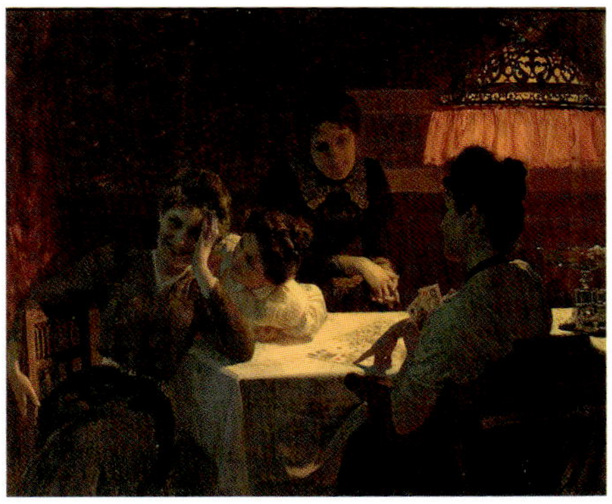

Ritzberger, Albert 1853–1915
Love's Oracle c.1900
oil on canvas 77.3 x 110
NCM 1908-37

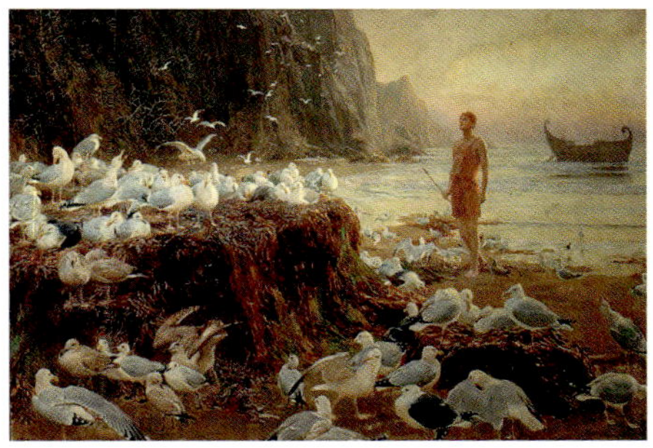

Riviere, Briton 1840–1920
An Old World Wanderer 1887
oil on canvas 108 x 172.7
NCM 1903-9

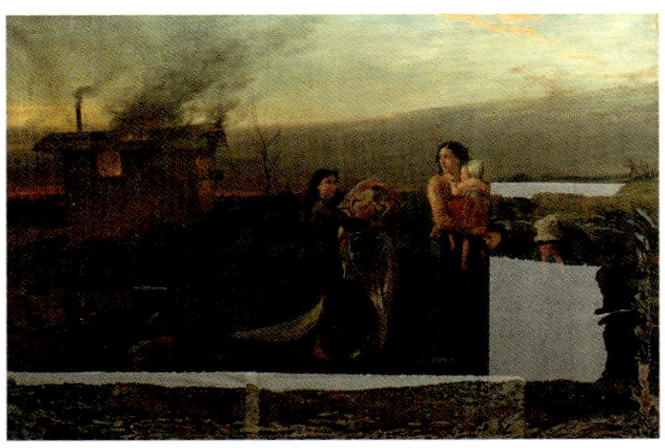

Roberts, Henry Benjamin 1831–1915
Homeless 1873
oil on canvas 121.9 x 182.9
NCM 1924-98

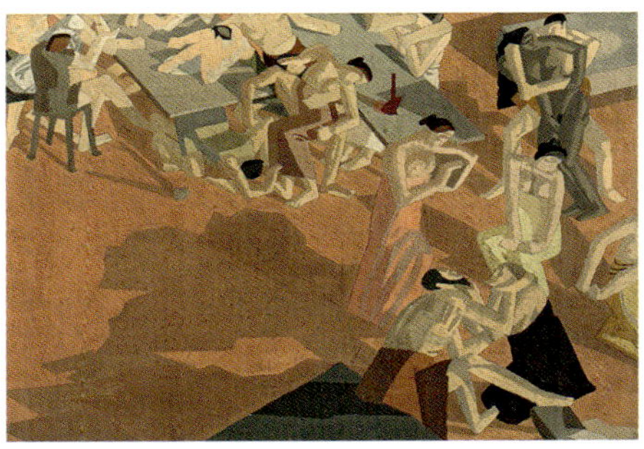

Roberts, William Patrick 1895–1980
The Return of Ulysses c.1913
oil on canvas 30.5 x 45.7
NCM 1954-45

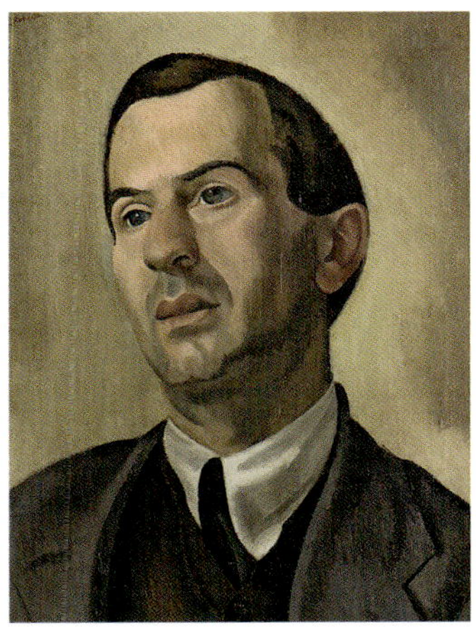

Roberts, William Patrick 1895–1980
Professor Janko Lavrin (1885–1986) 1919
oil on canvas 50.8 x 40.6
NCM 1986-1232

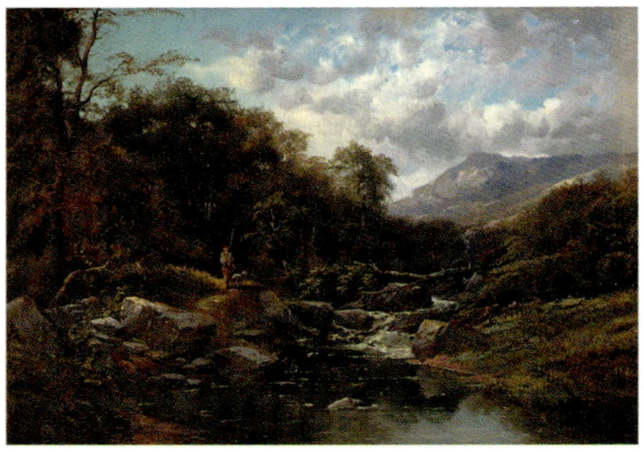

Roe, Clarence 1850–1909
A Mountain Stream
oil on canvas 45.7 x 66
NCM 1890-1169

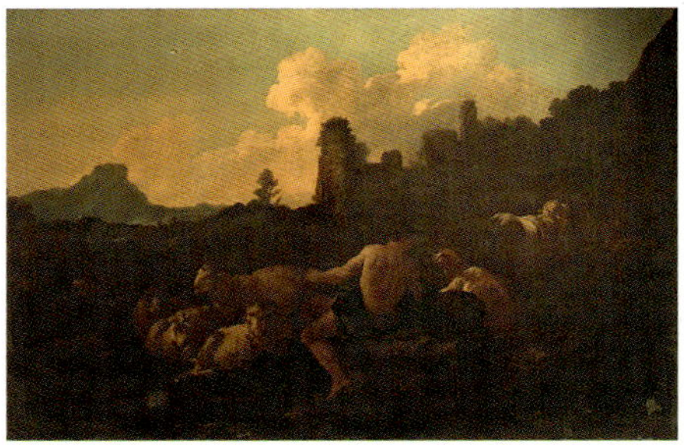

Roos, Philipp Peter 1657–1706
Landscape with Shepherd, Sheep and Dog
oil on canvas 135.9 x 210.2
NCM 1879-206

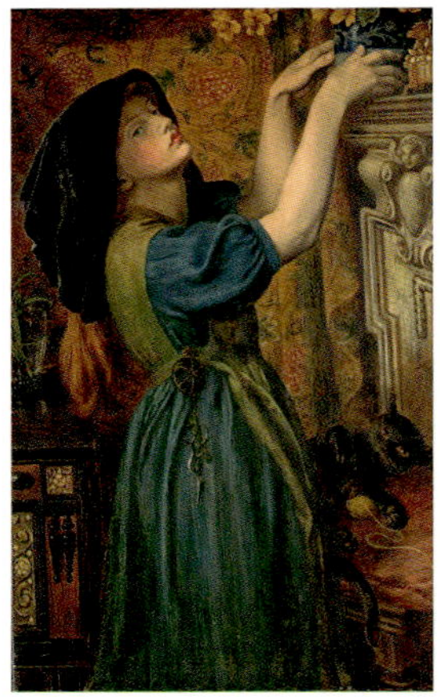

Rossetti, Dante Gabriel 1828–1882
Marigolds (The Bower Maiden, Fleur-de-Marie) 1874
oil on wood 114.3 x 73.7
NCM 1956-90

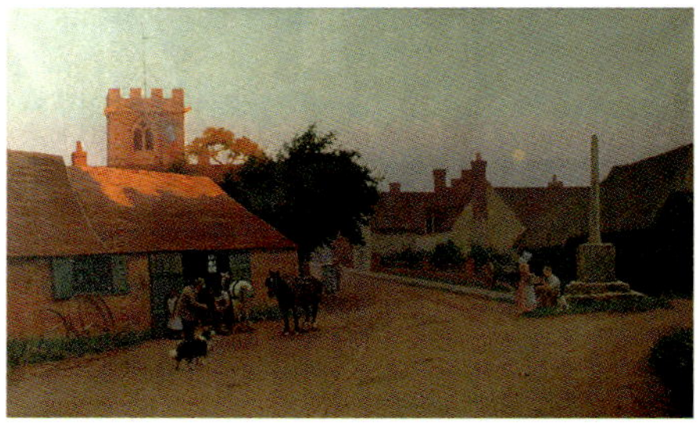

Rowe, Tom Trythall 1856–1940
Evening Glow 1909
oil on canvas 91.5 x 152.4
NCM 1909-41

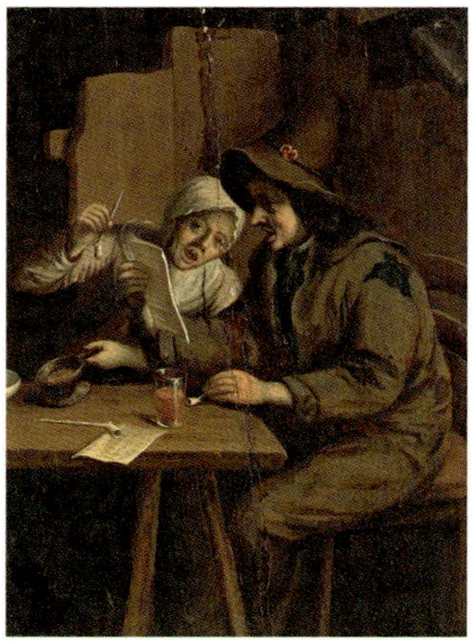

Saan, P. de
Interior, Figures at a Table, Singing
oil on wood 26 x 19.7
NCM 1904-116

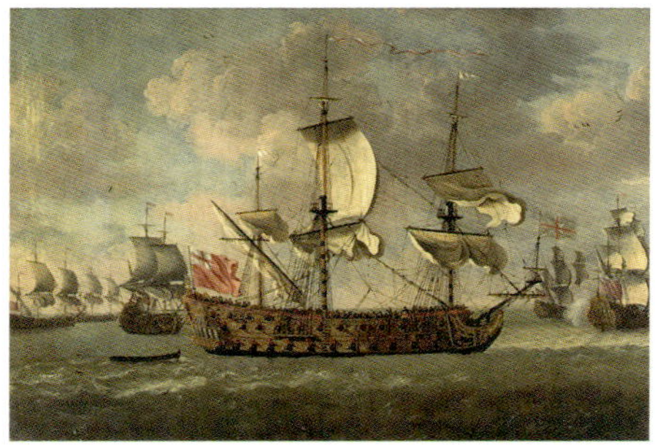

Sailmaker, Isaac c.1633–1721
HMS 'Swiftsure' 1675–1680
oil on canvas 95.3 x 139.1
NCM 1890-1207

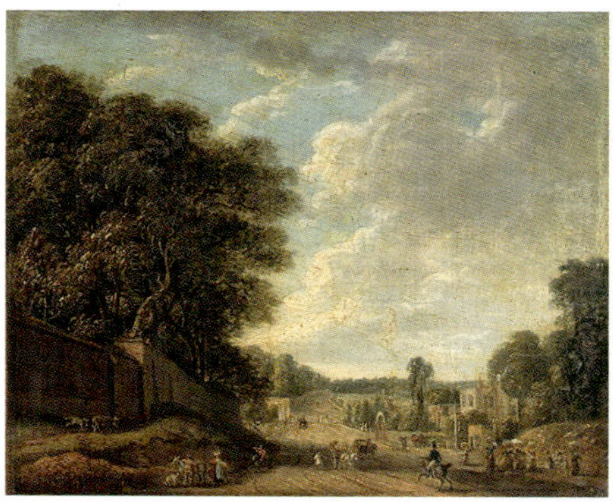

Sandby, Paul 1731–1809
Bayswater Road, London, near the Old Temple Gate (Bayswater Road at the Turnpike Gate) 1806
oil on canvas 35.6 x 44.5
NCM 1904-476

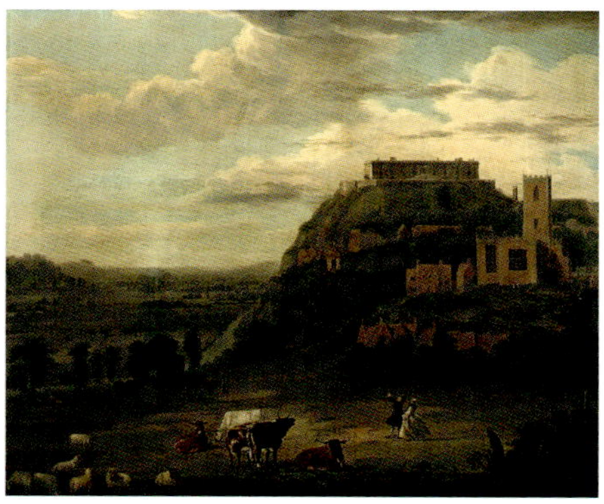

Sandby, Paul (attributed to) 1731–1809
View of Nottingham Castle with St Nicholas' Church and Houses
oil on canvas 102.9 x 125.7
NCM 1888-97

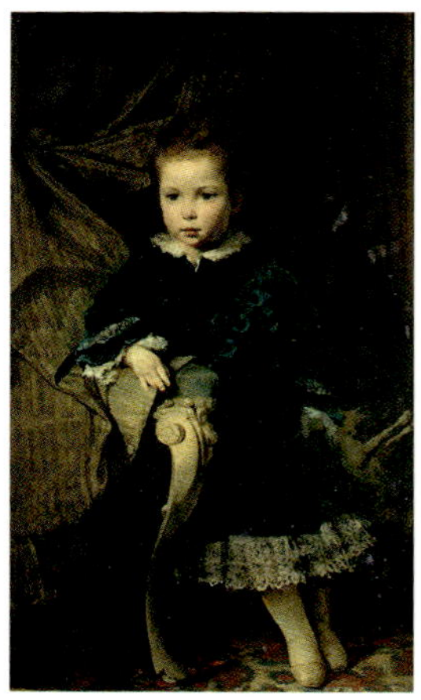

Schneider, Hermann 1847–1918
Portrait of a Child 1874
oil on canvas 91.5 x 58.5
NCM 1937-27

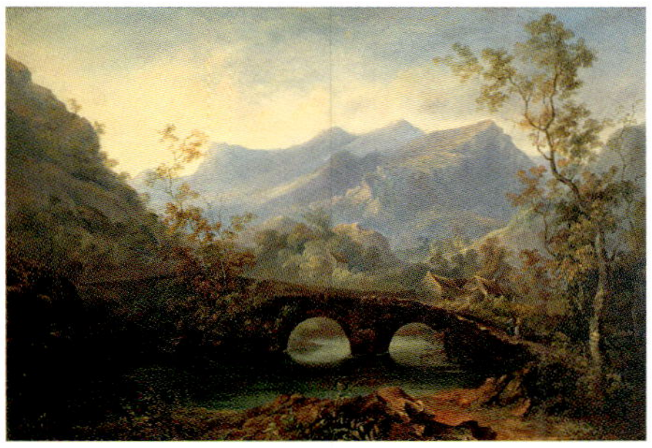

Schwanfelder, Charles Henry 1774–1837
Mountainous Landscape with River, Bridge and Cottages
oil on canvas 61 x 92
NCM 1890-1200

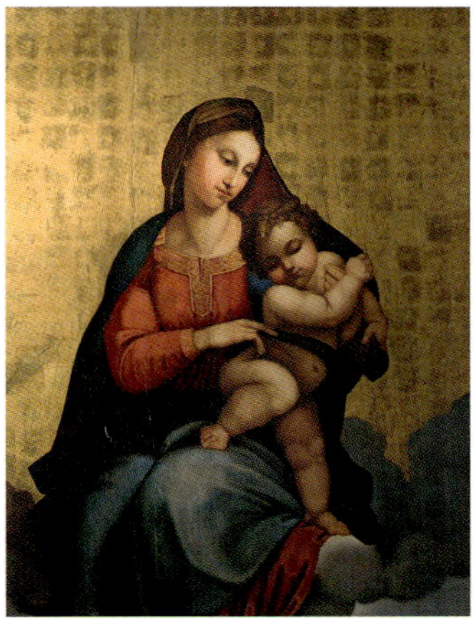

Senff, Carl Adolf 1785–1863
Virgin and Child 1819
oil & gold leaf on wood 119.4 x 100.3
NCM 1910-59

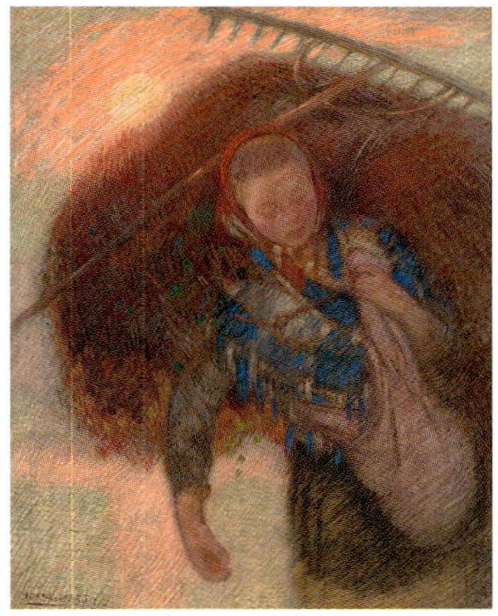

Shackleton, William 1872–1933
Study for 'The Harvesters' 1910
oil on paper laid on board 40.6 x 33
NCM 1938-143

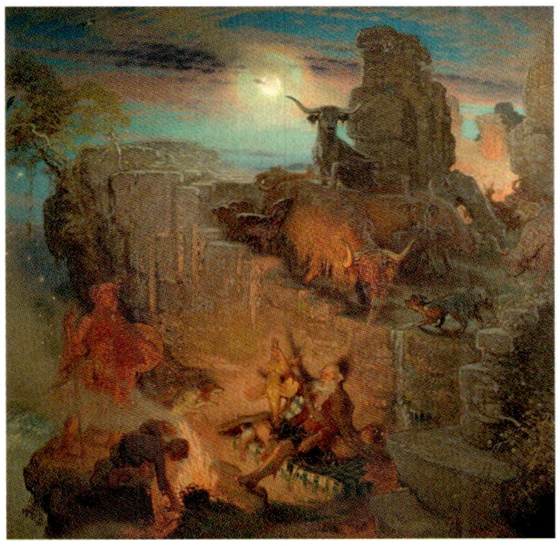

Shackleton, William 1872–1933
Highland Raiders 1918
oil on canvas 124.5 x 121.9
NCM 1938-142

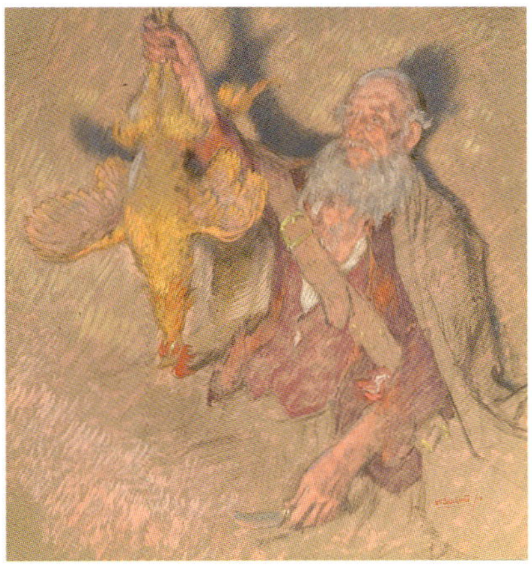

Shackleton, William 1872–1933
Study of a Man Holding a Cock for 'Highland Raiders' 1918
oil on paper 34.9 x 34.9
NCM 1938-196

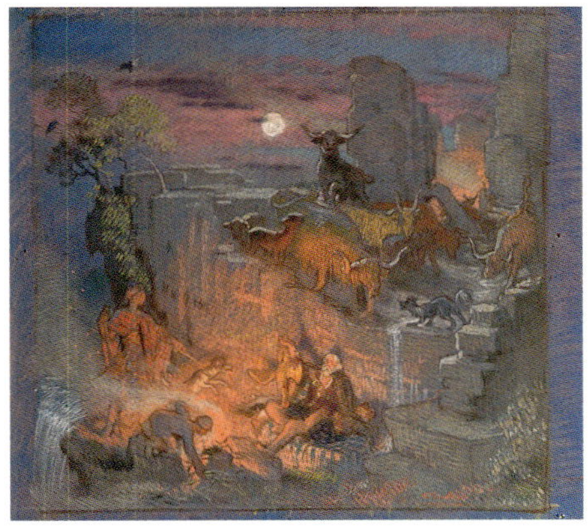

Shackleton, William 1872–1933
Study for 'Highland Raiders'
oil on paper 29.2 x 30.5
NCM 1938-188

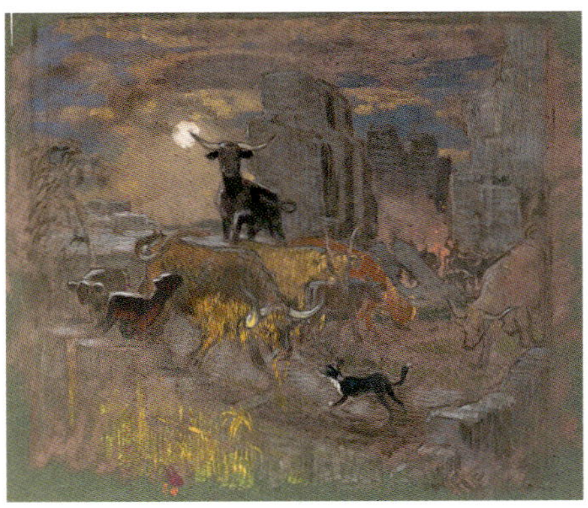

Shackleton, William 1872–1933
Study for 'Highland Raiders'
oil on paper 23.5 x 27.9
NCM 1938-190

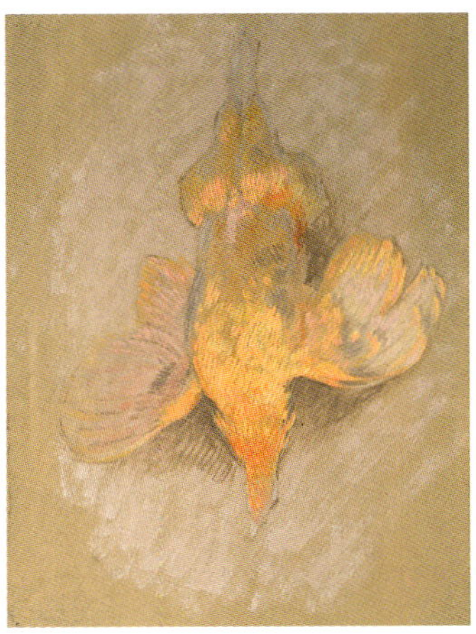

Shackleton, William 1872–1933
Study of a Fowl for 'Highland Raiders'
oil on paper 36.8 x 27.9
NCM 1938-187

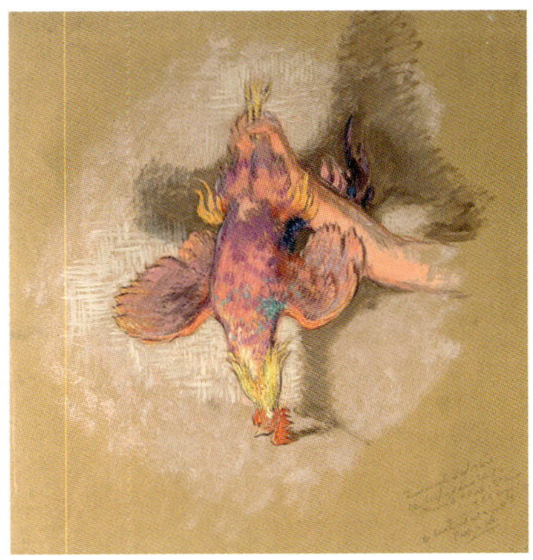

Shackleton, William 1872–1933
Study of an Arm and a Hand Holding a Fowl by the Legs for 'Highland Raiders'
oil on paper 27.9 x 27.3
NCM 1938-189

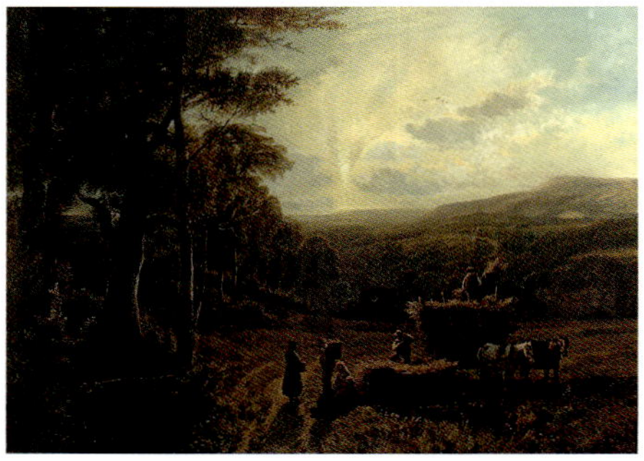

Shalders, George c.1826–1873
Near Haslemere, Surrey
oil on canvas 86.4 x 133.4
NCM 1936-8

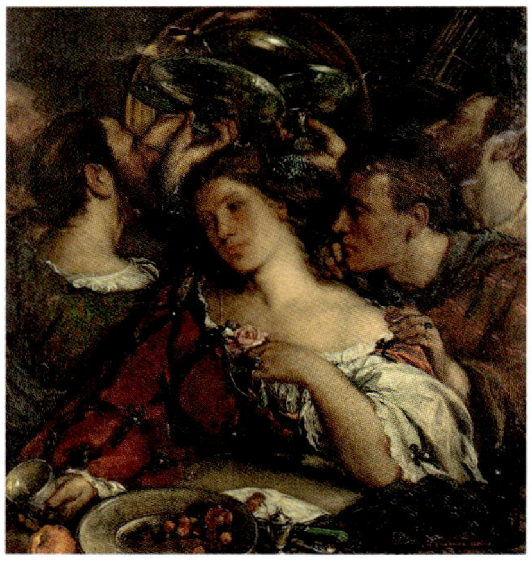

Shannon, Charles Haslewood 1863–1937
Tibullus in the House of Delia 1900–1905
oil on canvas 76.2 x 76.2
NCM 1945-1

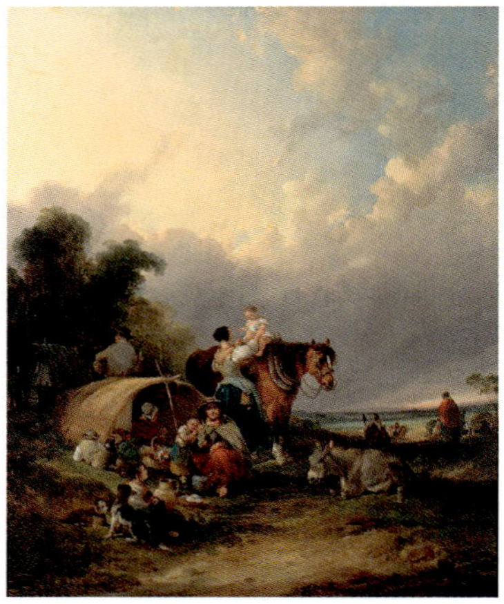

Shayer, William 1788–1879
A Gypsy Encampment
oil on canvas 100.3 x 87.6
NCM 1948-40

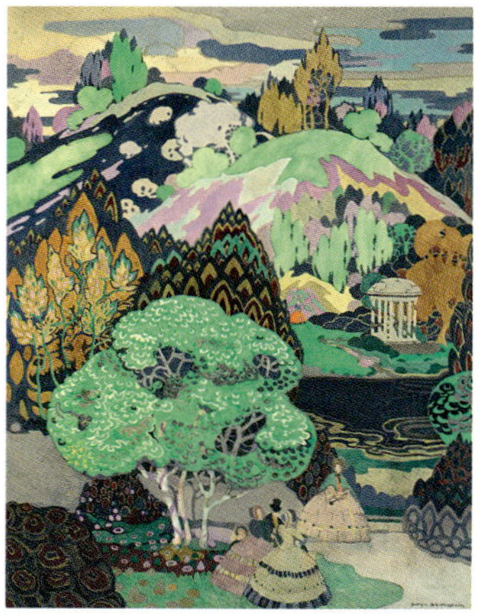

Sheringham, George 1884–1937
Ipswich Park 1919
tempera on paper 76 x 63
NCM 1938-12

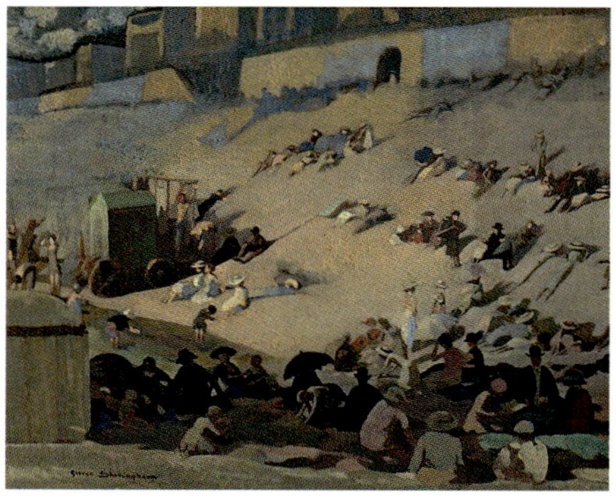

Sheringham, George 1884–1937
Brighton Beach, East Sussex
oil on canvas 30.5 x 40.6
NCM 1938-10

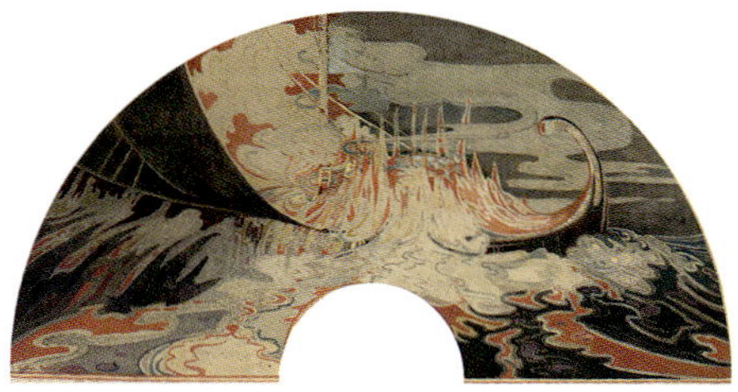

Sheringham, George 1884–1937
Fan Design (The Passing of a Viking)
tempera, watercolour & gold paint on paper 19 x 48.2
NCM 1938-15

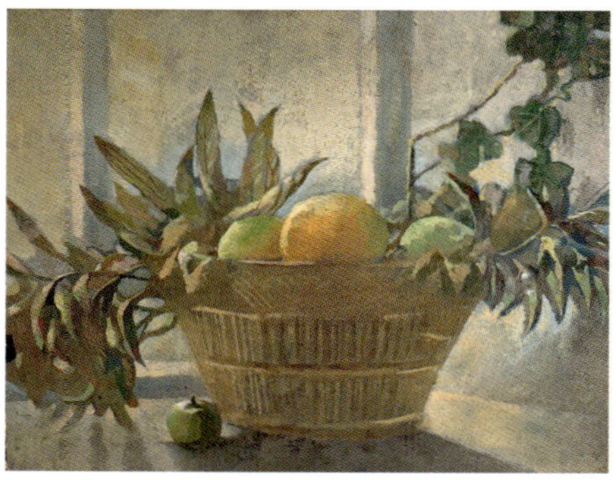

Sheringham, George 1884–1937
Fruit and Leaves in a Basket
tempera on wood 39.9 x 50.8
NCM 1973-15

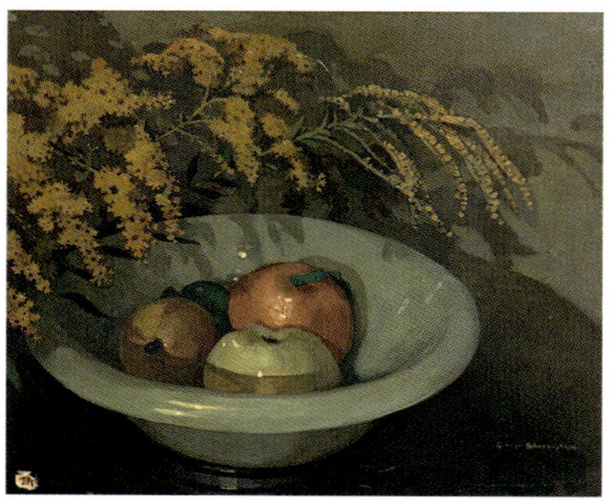

Sheringham, George 1884–1937
Fruit in a Jade Bowl
oil on wood 32.4 x 38.7
NCM 1973-331

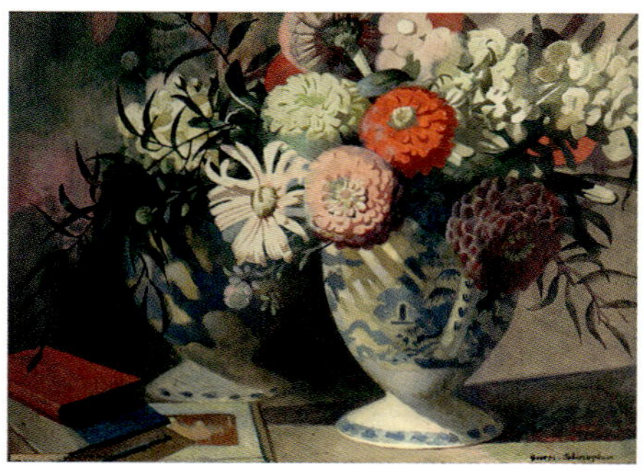

Sheringham, George 1884–1937
Reflections
tempera on wood 37.5 x 53.5
NCM 1938-11

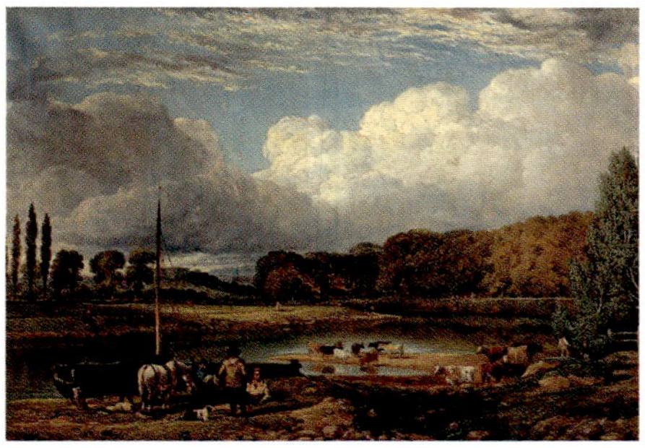

Shipham, Benjamin 1808–1872
View at Wilford, Nottingham c.1830
oil on canvas 68.6 x 99
NCM 1895-95

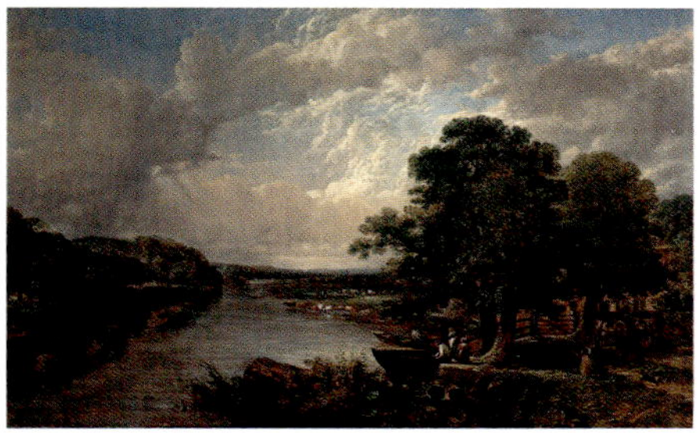

Shipham, Benjamin 1808–1872
View of the Trent at Wilford, Nottingham c.1830
oil on canvas 66 x 98
NCM 1895-95

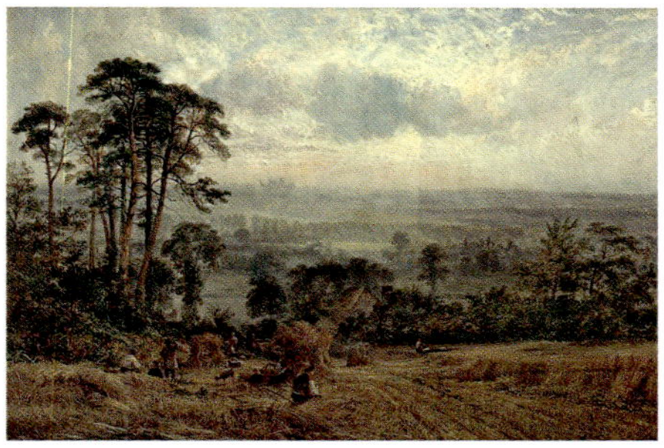

Shipham, Benjamin 1808–1872
Cornfields, Wollaton Hall, Nottingham
oil on canvas 43.2 x 63.5
NCM 1878-192

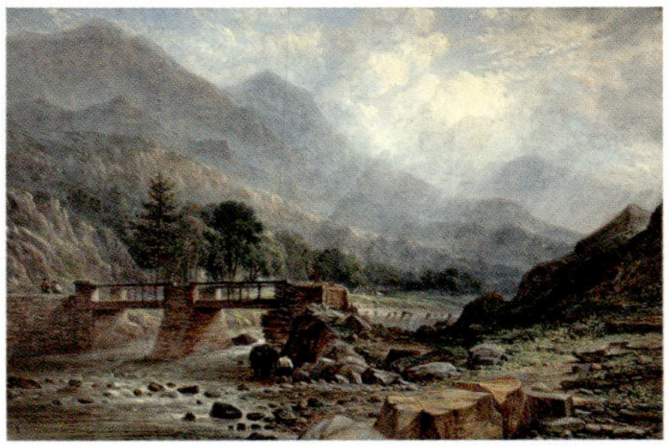

Shipham, Benjamin 1808–1872
Near Beddgelert, North Wales
oil on canvas 43.2 x 63.5
NCM 1878-191

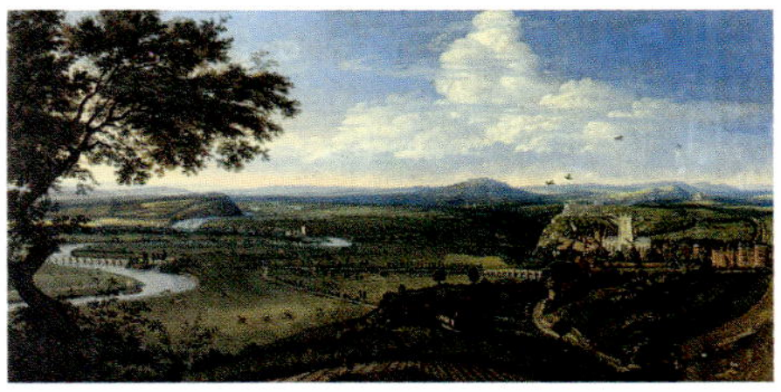

Siberechts, Jan (attributed to) 1627–c.1703
View of Nottingham from the East c.1695
oil on canvas 58.4 x 120.7
NCM 1977-515

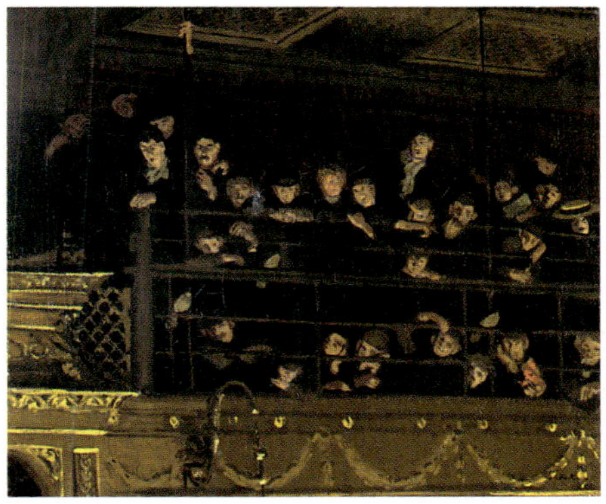

Sickert, Walter Richard 1860–1942
Noctes ambrosianae 1906
oil on canvas 63.5 x 76.2
NCM 1952-49

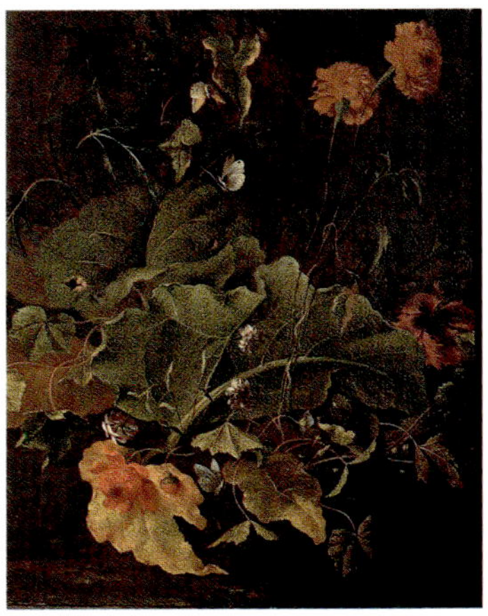

Sillett, James 1764–1840
Dock Leaves and Other Flowers c.1820
oil on canvas 57.8 x 49.5
NCM 1951-55

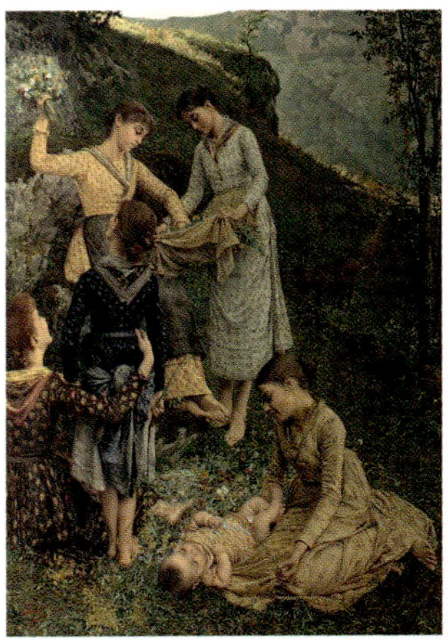

Simi, Filadelfo 1849–1923
The Flowers of Capri c.1887
oil on canvas 162.5 x 128.3
NCM 1914-22

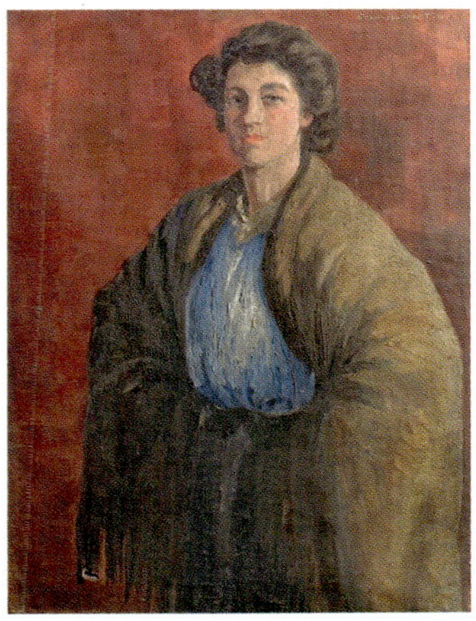

Smart, Rowley 1887–1934
Miss Muriel Pratt in the Role of Fanny in 'Hindle Wakes'
oil on canvas 91.4 x 71.1
NCM 1945-85

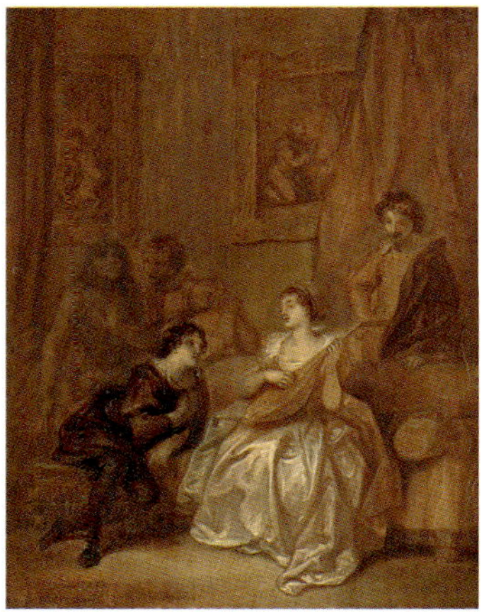

Smirke, Robert 1752–1845
Illustration to Le Strange's 'Gil Blas'
oil on wood 17.8 x 14.6
NCM 1904-68

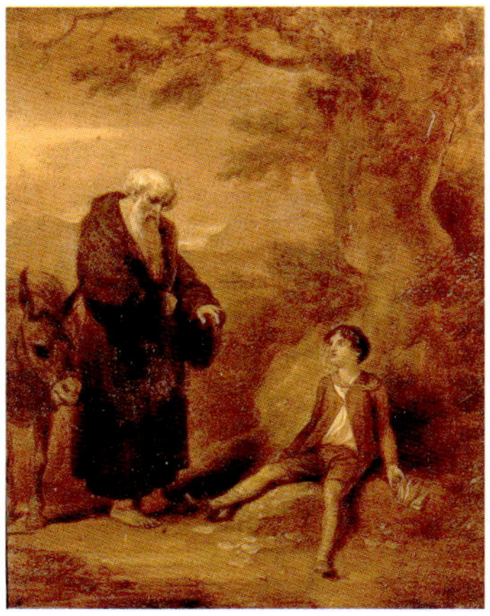

Smirke, Robert 1752–1845
Scipio and the Hermit
oil on wood 24.8 x 17.8
NCM 1904-69

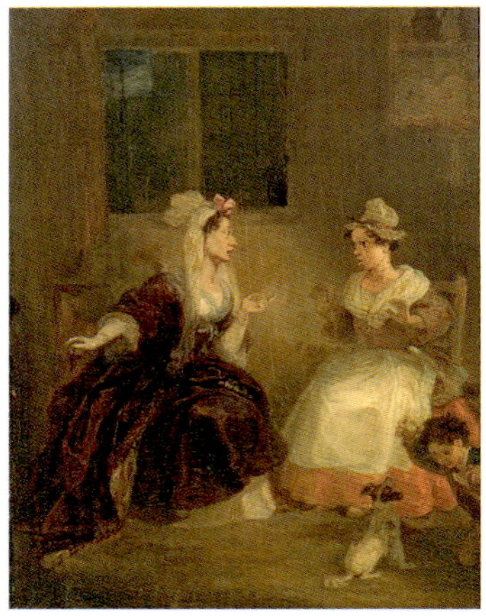

Smirke, Robert 1752–1845
The Scandal (The Keepsake)
oil on wood 25.4 x 19.1
NCM 1904-67

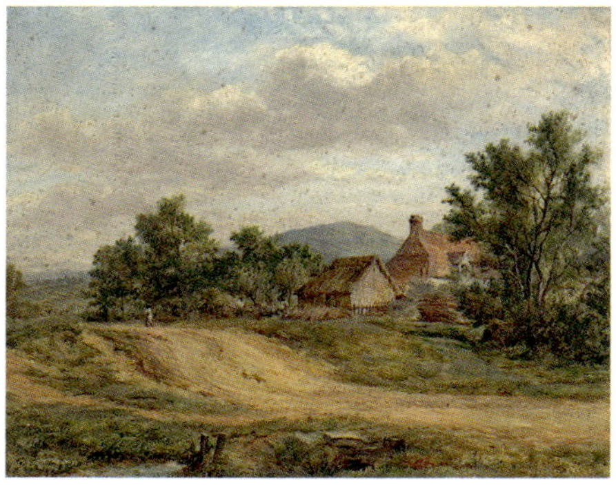

Smith, George 1829–1901
A Country Road and Cottage 1876
oil on wood 20 x 25.4
NCM 1890-1167

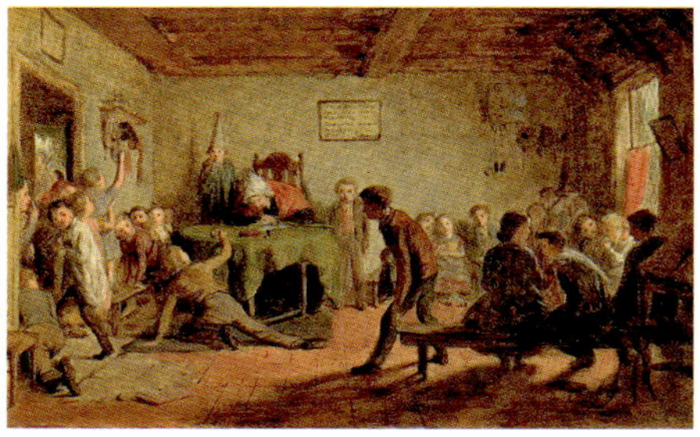

Smith, George 1829–1901
The Dame's School
oil on wood 35 x 44
NCM 1904-70

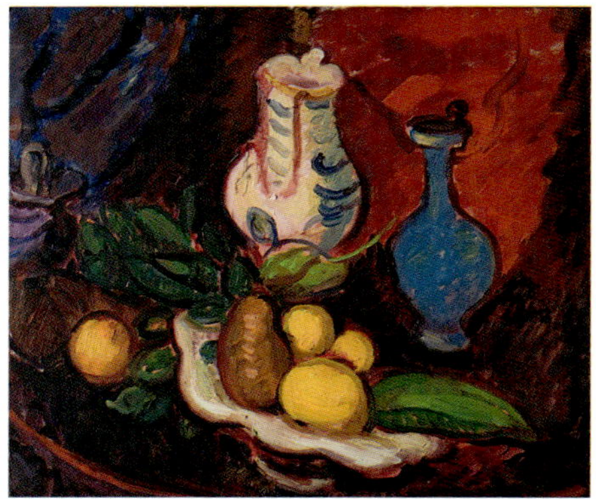

Smith, Matthew Arnold Bracy 1879–1959
Still Life with Blue and White Jugs 1950
oil on canvas 63.5 x 76.2
NCM 1952-7

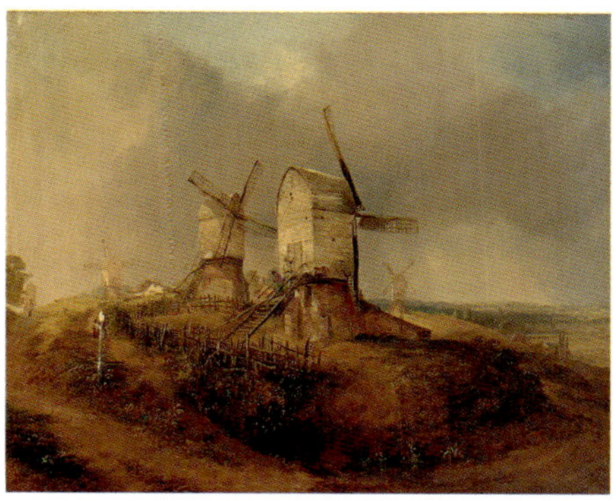

Smyth, Henry active c.1800–1860
Old Windmills on Nottingham Forest c.1830
oil on board 47 x 61.6
NCM 1920-53

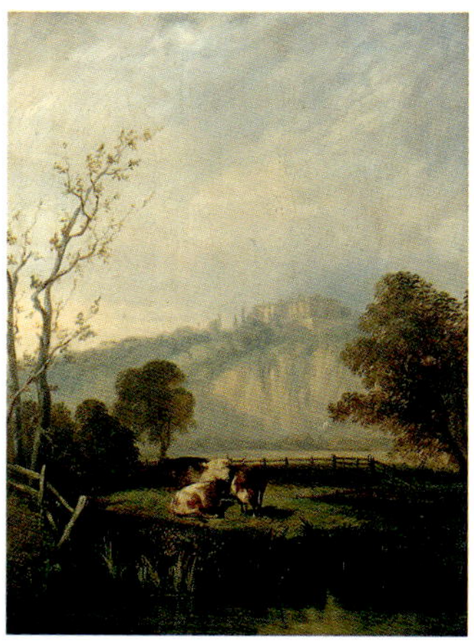

Smyth, Henry active c.1800–1860
Nottingham Meadows 1847
oil on canvas 46.4 x 36.2
NCM 1939-69

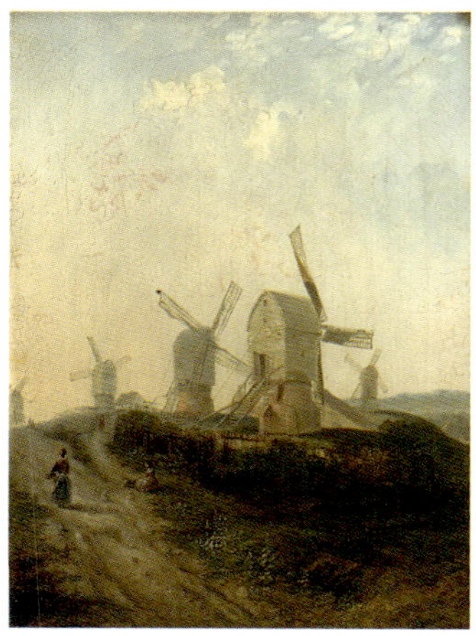

Smyth, Henry active c.1800–1860
Windmills on Nottingham Forest 1847
oil on canvas 45.7 x 35.6
NCM 1939-70

Facing page: Riviere, Briton, 1840–1920, *An Old World Wanderer* (detail), 1887, Nottingham City Museums and Galleries (p. 139)

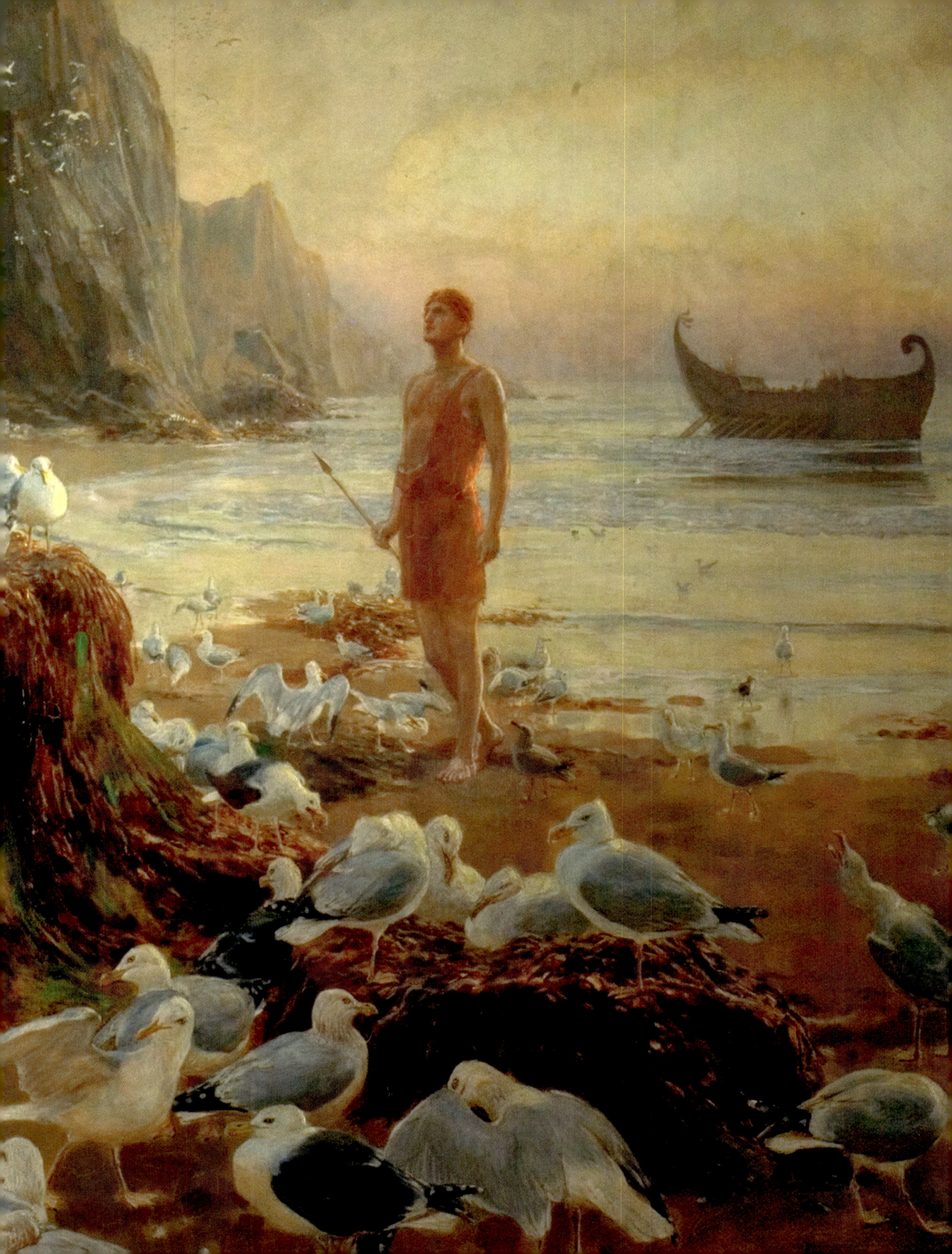

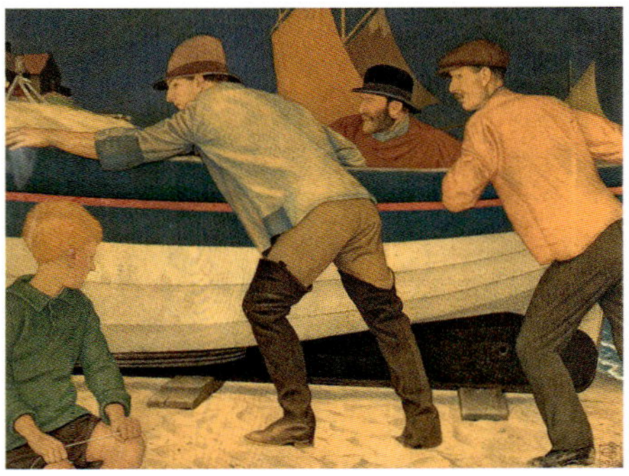

Southall, Joseph Edward 1861–1944
Up from the Sea 1920
tempera on fabric 30.5 x 41
NCM 1930-35

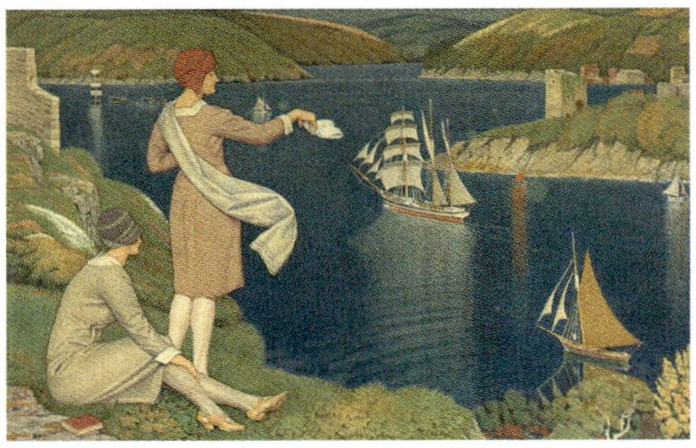

Southall, Joseph Edward 1861–1944
The Return 1930
tempera on fabric (possibly silk) 37.7 x 58.4
NCM 1948-2

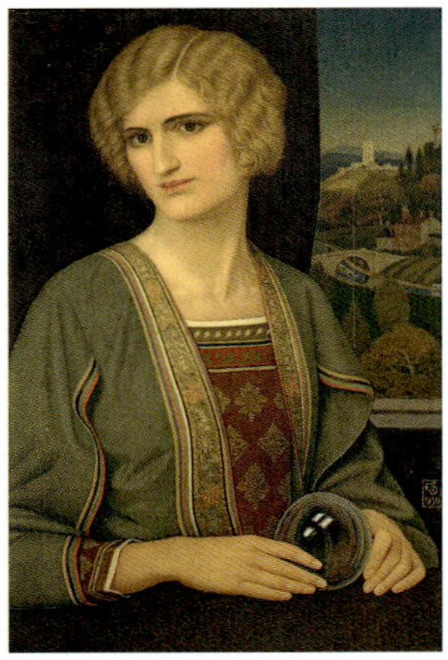

Southall, Joseph Edward 1861–1944
The Crystal
tempera on silk 65 x 44.5
NCM 1948-3

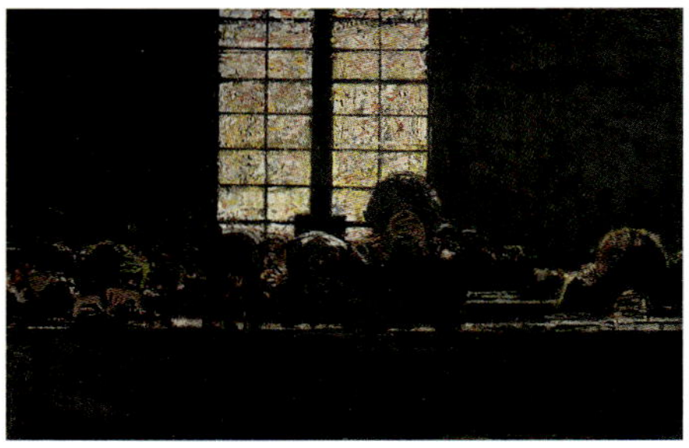

Spear, Ruskin 1911–1990
Sunday Morning 1958
oil on board 81.3 x 121.9
NCM 1958-62

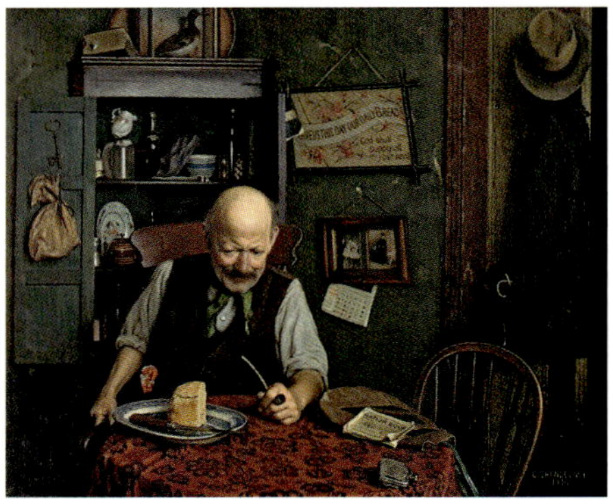

Spencelayh, Charles 1865–1958
His Daily Ration 1946
oil on canvas 50.8 x 61
NCM 1947-26

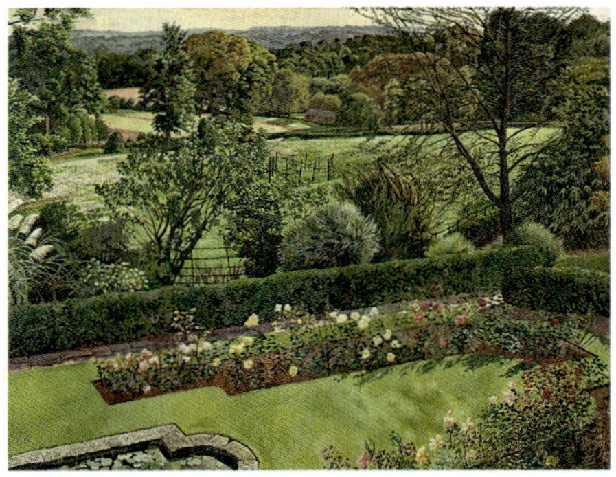

Spencer, Stanley 1891–1959
Landscape, Cookham Dean, Berkshire c.1939
oil on canvas 71.1 x 91.4
NCM 1939-14

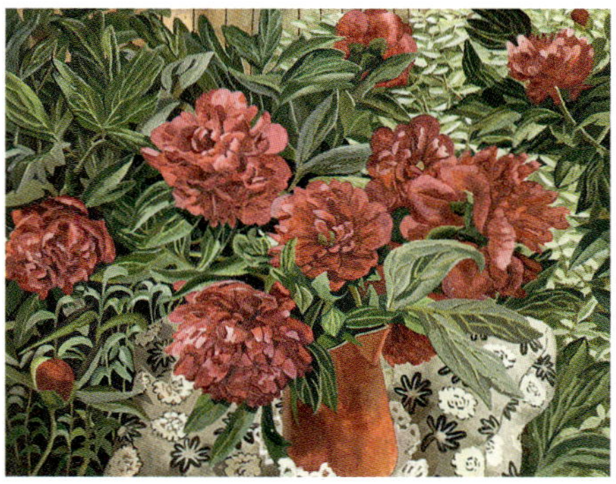

Spencer, Stanley 1891–1959
Peonies c.1939
oil on canvas 50.8 x 66
NCM 1939-15

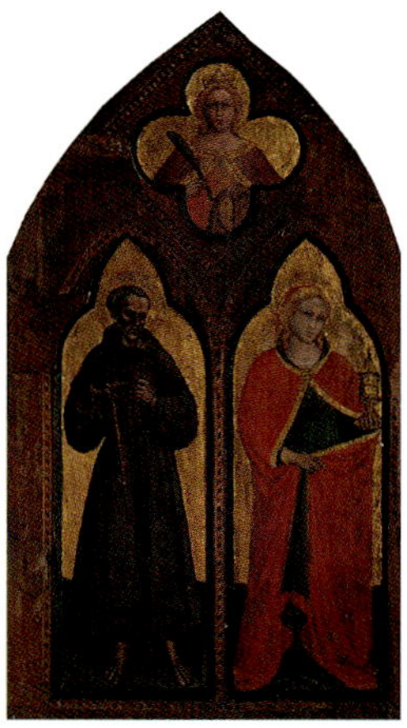

Spinello Aretino 1350/1352–1410
Blessed Gerard of Villamagna and St Mary Magdalen with St Catherine of Alexandria
1380–1390
tempera & gold leaf on wood 123.8 x 71.1
NCM 1891-133

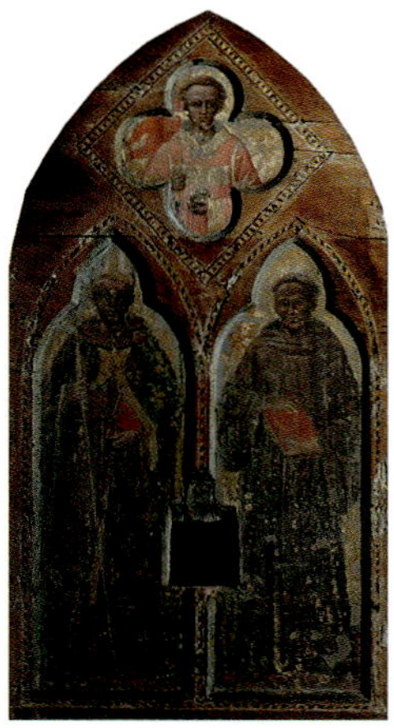

Spinello Aretino 1350/1352–1410
St Louis of Toulouse and St Anthony of Padua with St Stephen
tempera on wood 124.5 x 67.9
NCM 1891-134

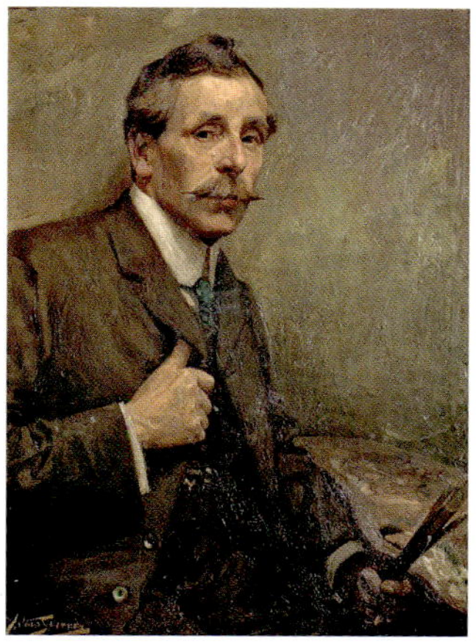

Spooner, Arthur 1873–1961
Rubens Arthur Moore (1860–c.1933) 1907
oil on canvas 90 x 69.6
NCM 1991-501

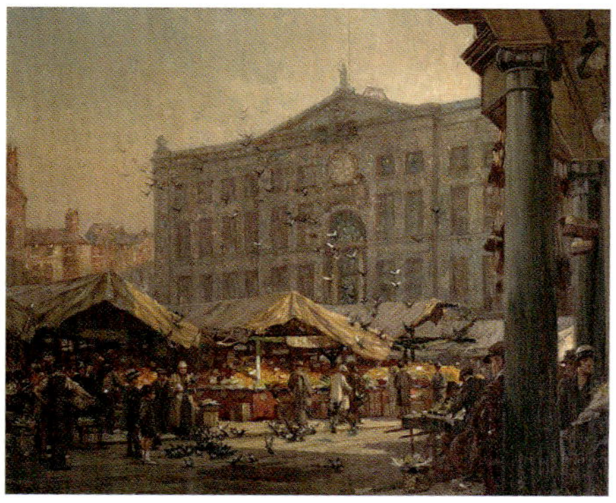

Spooner, Arthur 1873–1961
Nottingham Old Market Place c.1920
oil on canvas 112 x 132
FALOAN 97 (P)

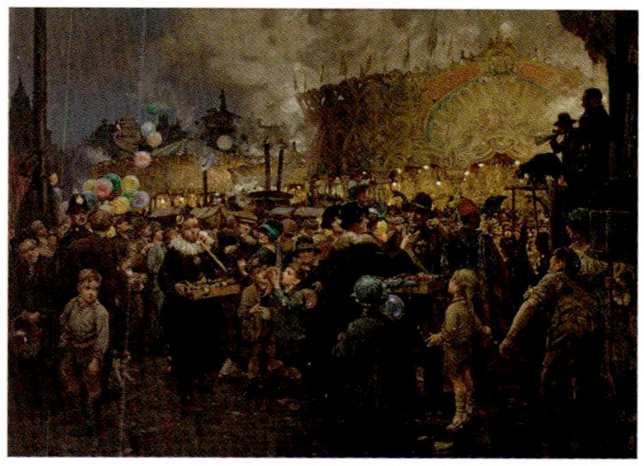

Spooner, Arthur 1873–1961
The Goose Fair, Nottingham 1926
oil on canvas 183 x 245
FALOAN 95 (P)

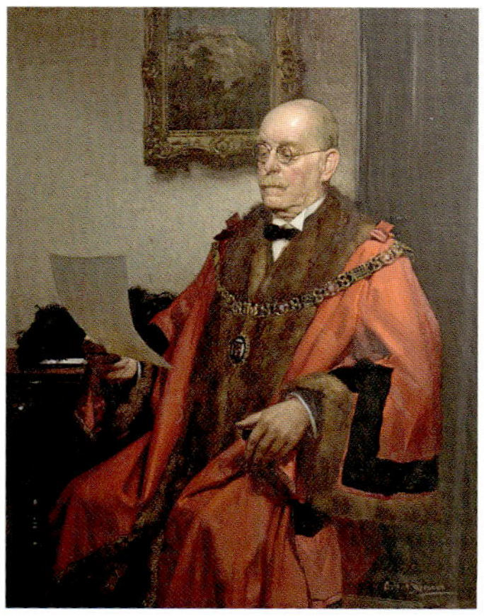

Spooner, Arthur 1873–1961
Posthumous Portrait of Alderman E. L. Manning 1937
oil on canvas 129.5 x 104.1
NCM 1937-53

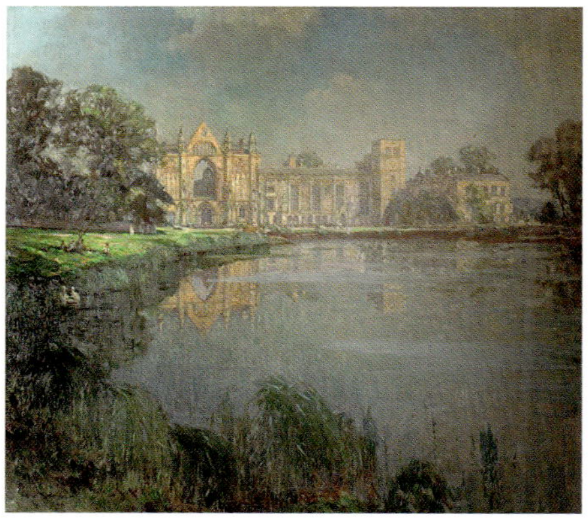

Spooner, Arthur 1873–1961
Newstead Abbey, Nottinghamshire 1944
oil on canvas 105.4 x 120.6
NCM 1944-33

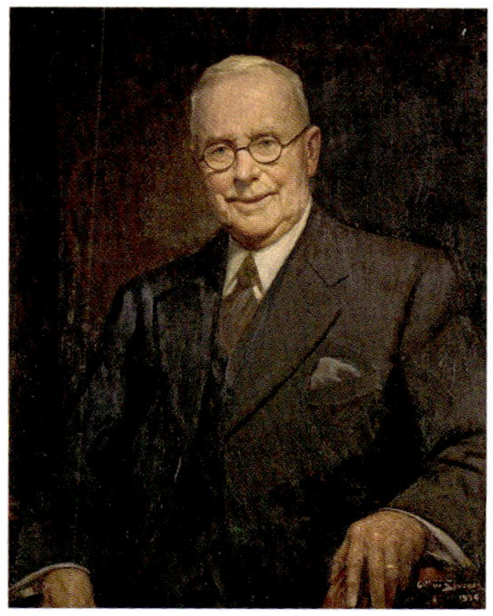

Spooner, Arthur 1873–1961
Tom Pearson (1872–1964), Founder of Pearson's of Nottingham Ltd 1954
oil on canvas 75 x 62
SHLOAN 9 (P)

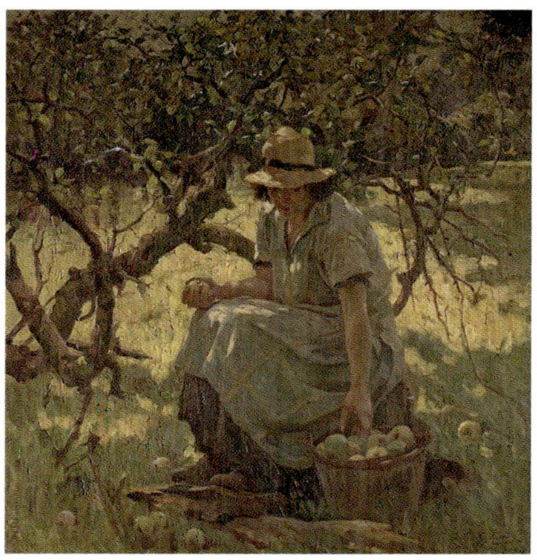

Spooner, Arthur 1873–1961
Apple Fallings
oil on canvas 91.4 x 91.4
NCM 1940-29

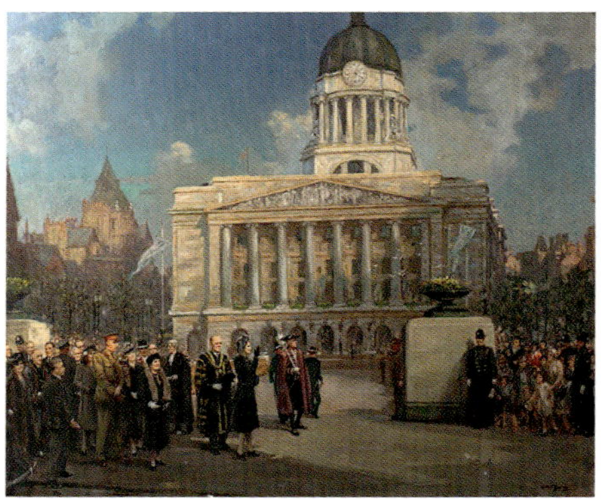

Spooner, Arthur 1873–1961
Lord Mayor and Lady Mayoress Receiving Princess Elizabeth in the Council House Square, 2 April 1946
oil on canvas 95.3 x 119.4
NCM 1948-39

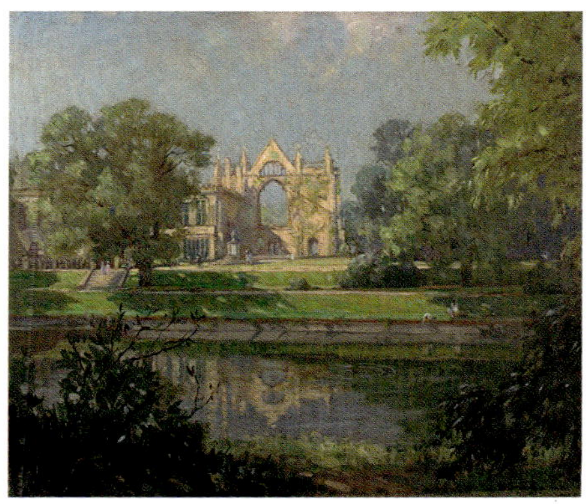

Spooner, Arthur 1873–1961
Newstead Abbey from the East, Nottinghamshire (Eagle Pond, Newstead Abbey)
oil on canvas 41.9 x 58.4
NCM 1945-17

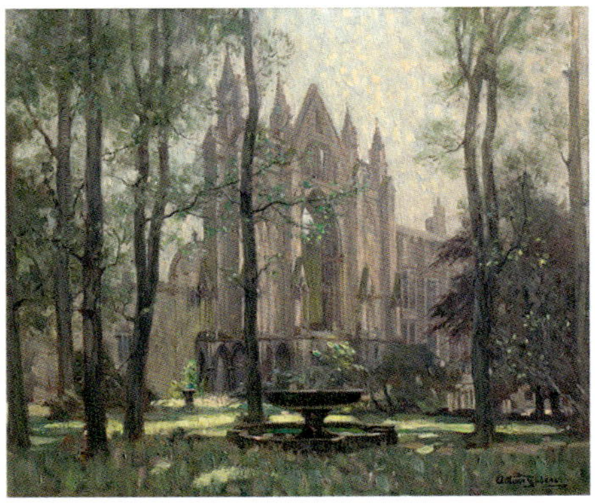

Spooner, Arthur 1873–1961
Newstead Abbey, the Monk's Wood, Nottinghamshire (Newstead Abbey, from the North West)
oil on canvas 50.8 x 81.3
NCM 1945-18

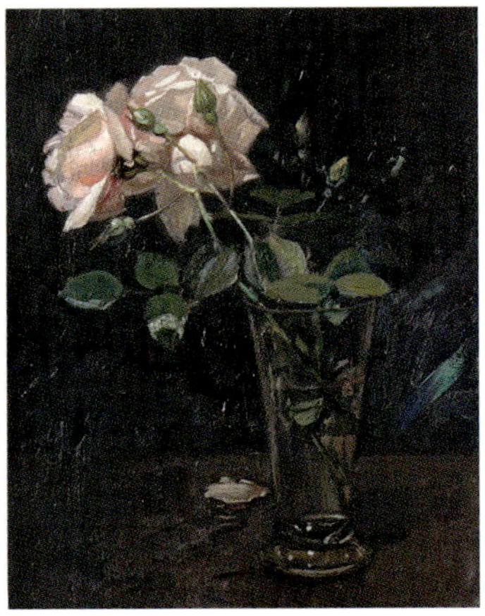

Spooner, Arthur 1873–1961
Pink Roses in a Glass Vase
oil on board 31.8 x 26.7
NCM 1973-335

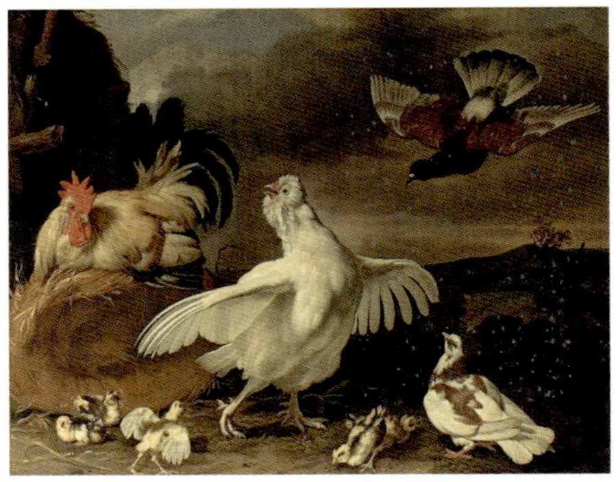

Spruyt, Johannes 1627/1628–1671
Cock and Hen with Chickens and Pigeons
oil on canvas 88.9 x 118.1
NCM 1939-2

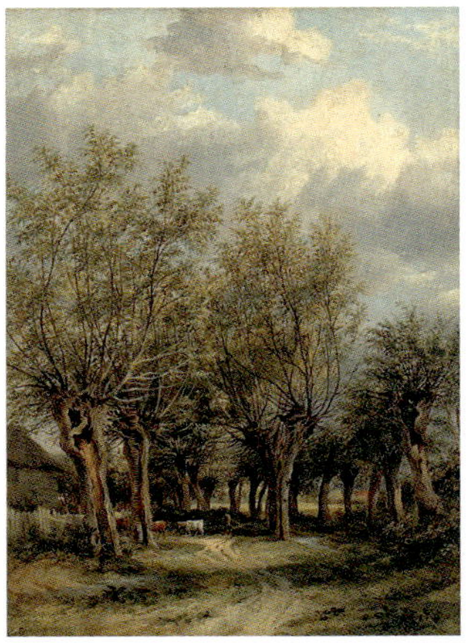

Stark, James 1794–1859
A Lane near Norwich, Norfolk c.1830
oil on wood 50.8 x 38.1
NCM 1948-41

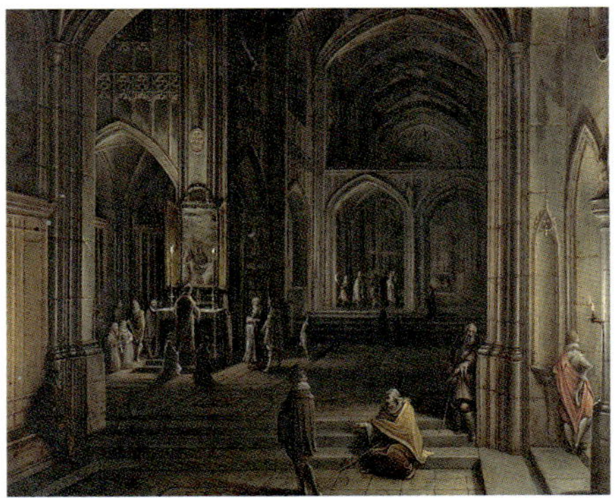

Steenwijck, Hendrick van the younger c.1580–1649
Interior of a Church 1620
oil on wood 21.6 x 26.4
NCM 1904-98

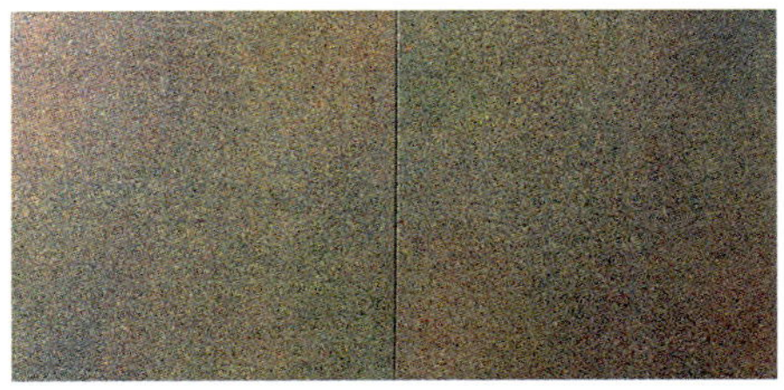

Stephenson, Ian 1934–2000
Diorama II 1967
oil & enamel on canvas 83.5 x 167.3
NCM 1976-176

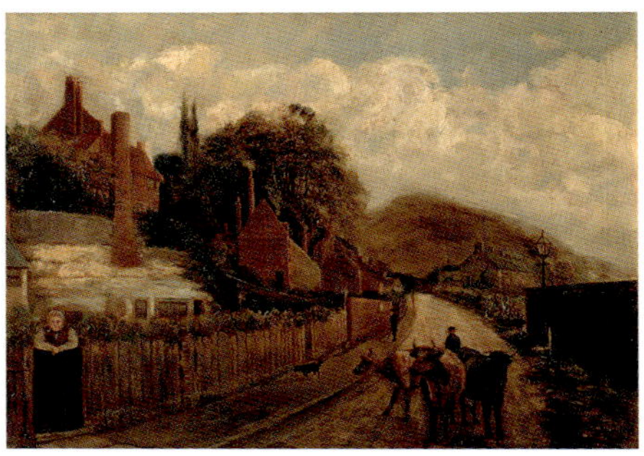

Stevenson, G. S. active 1830–1887
Sneinton Hermitage, Nottingham 1887
oil on canvas 59 x 88.3
NCM 1984-153

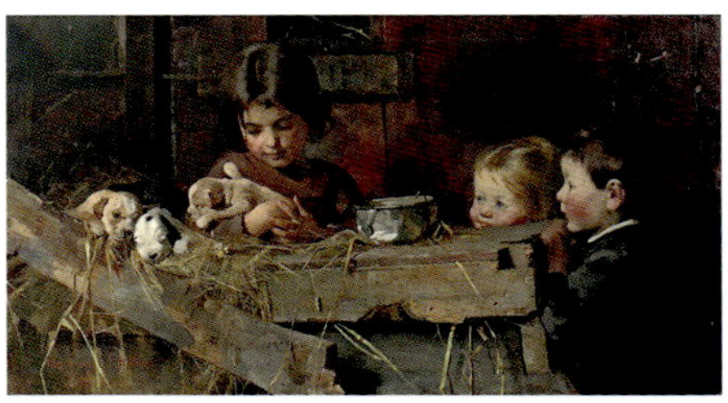

Stokes, Marianne 1855–1927
Childhood's Treasures 1886
oil on canvas 68.6 x 127
NCM 1896-67

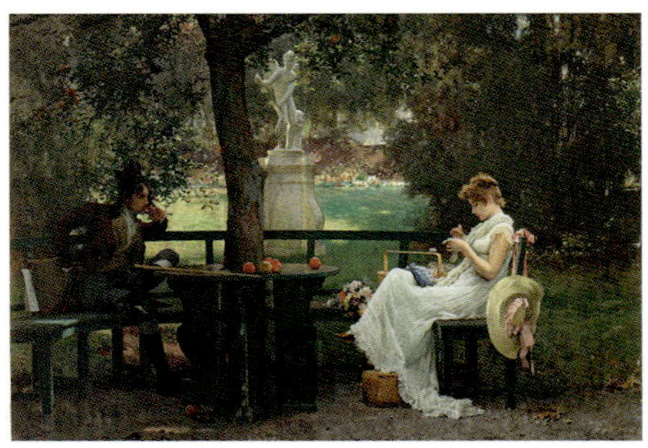

Stone, Marcus C. 1840–1921
In Love 1888
oil on canvas 111.8 x 167.7
NCM 1899-7

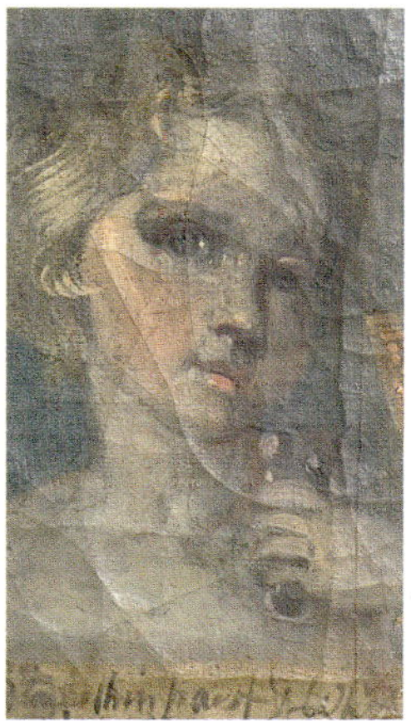

Stothard, Thomas 1755–1834
Portrait of a Child
oil on canvas 16.2 x 9.9
NCM 1890-407

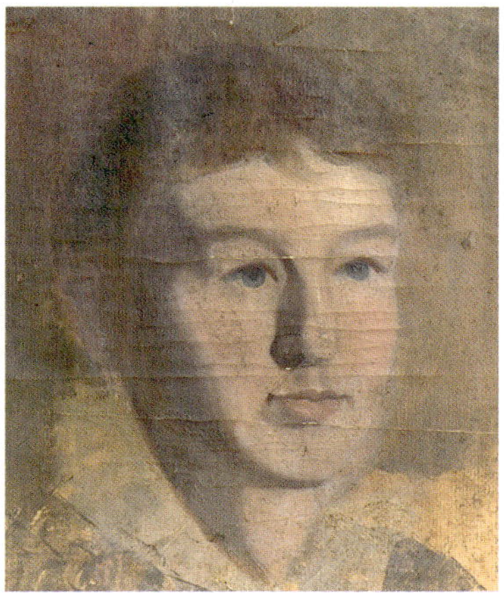

Stothard, Thomas 1755–1834
Portrait of a Young Man
oil on canvas 21.9 x 17.8
NCM 1890-411

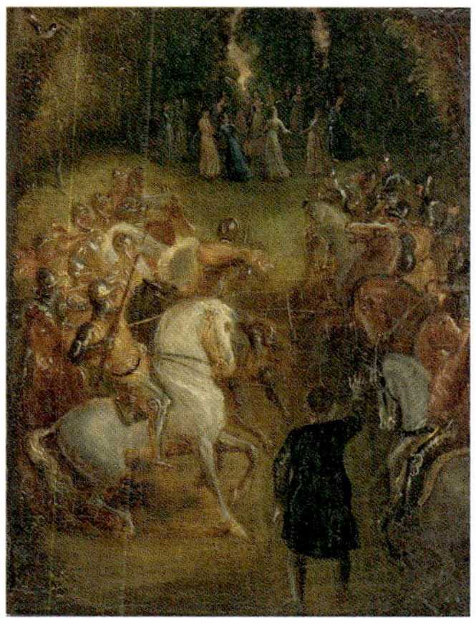

Stothard, Thomas 1755–1834
The Tournament
oil on wood 25.4 x 21.6
NCM 1904-71

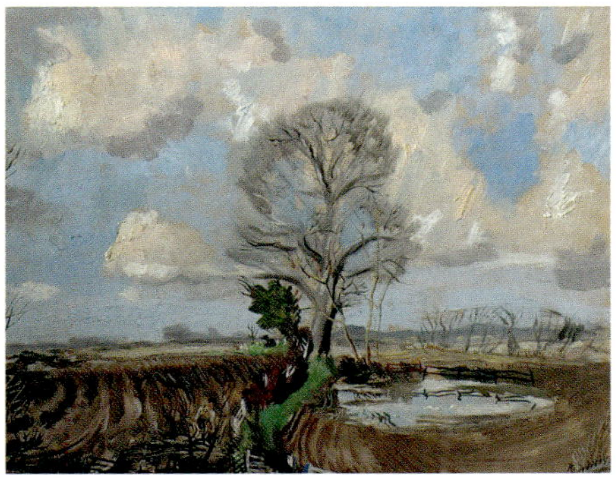

Suddaby, Rowland 1912–1972
Hedging at Cornard Tye, Suffolk 1950
oil on board 43.8 x 54.5 (E)
NCM 1950-24

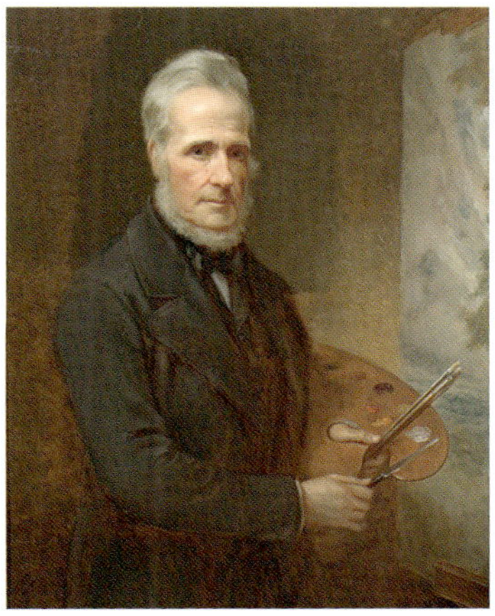

Sullivan, William Holmes 1836–1908
The Artist Henry Dawson (1811–1878)
oil on canvas 50 x 40
NCMG 2003-28

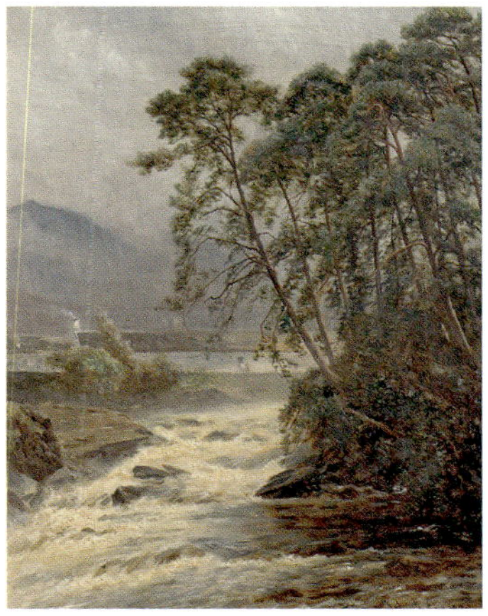

Surtees, John 1819–1915
On the Dockart, Killin, Perthshire, Scotland 1887
oil on canvas 50.8 x 40.6
NCM 1916-1

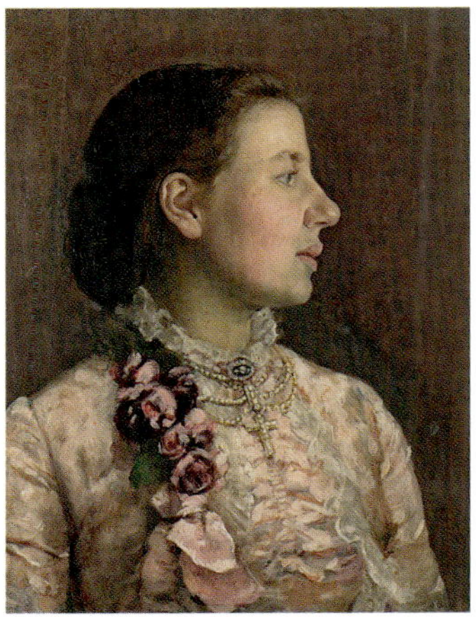

Swynnerton, Annie Louisa 1844–1933
Mrs Florence H. Musgrave
oil on canvas 49.5 x 40.6
NCM 1934-131

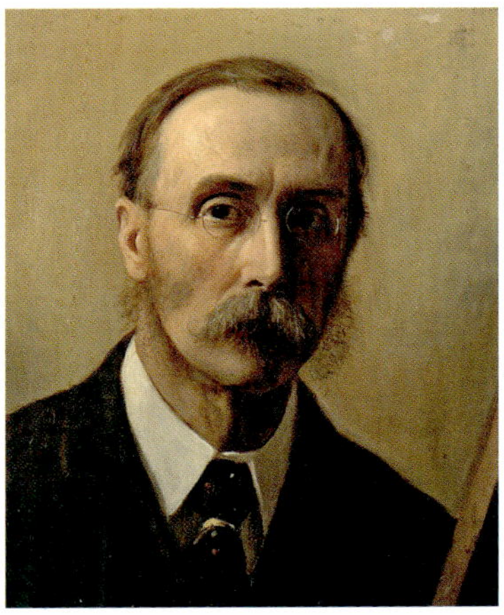

Tayler, Edward 1828–1906
Self Portrait
oil on canvas 35.6 x 30.5
NCM 1913-62

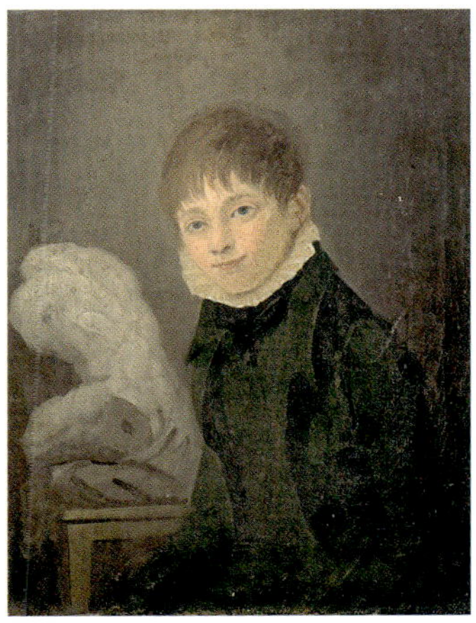

Taylor, Isaac II 1759–1829
Josiah Gilbert, Aged 16
oil on canvas 25.4 x 20.3
NCM 1939-71

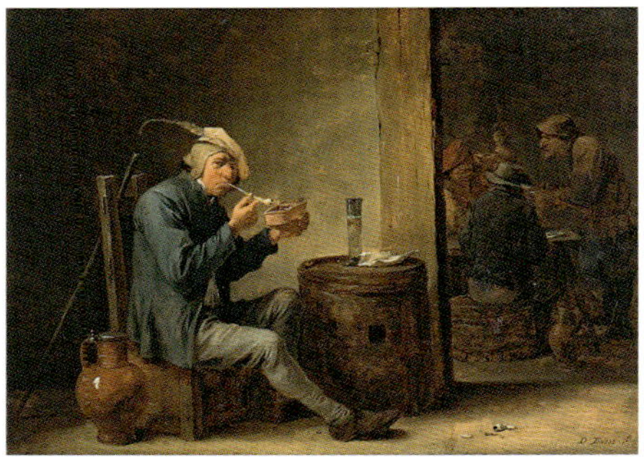

Teniers, David II 1610–1690
Peasant Smoking in an Interior (Flemish Pastimes, Interior) c.1650
oil on wood 22.9 x 33.3
NCM 1904-110

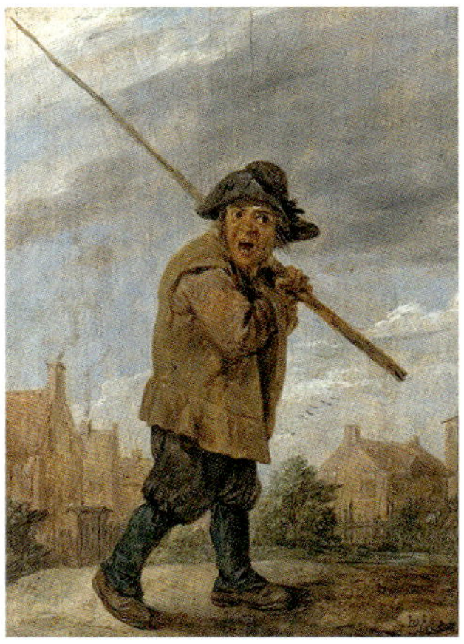

Teniers, David II 1610–1690
A Peasant Carrying a Pole
oil on wood 16.8 x 13
NCM 1904-109

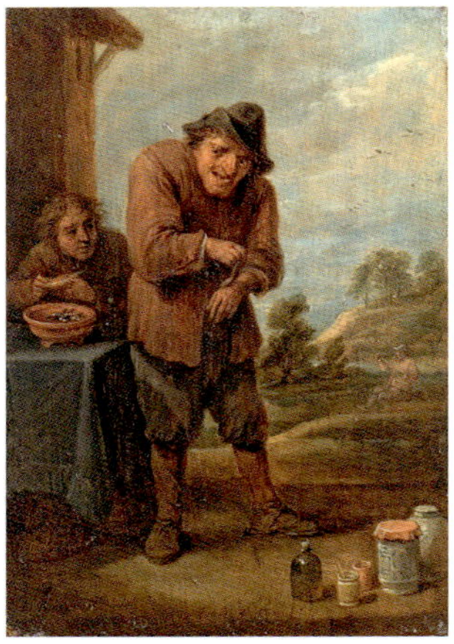

Teniers, David II 1610–1690
The Sense of Feeling
oil on wood 18.8 x 13.8
NCM 1904-112

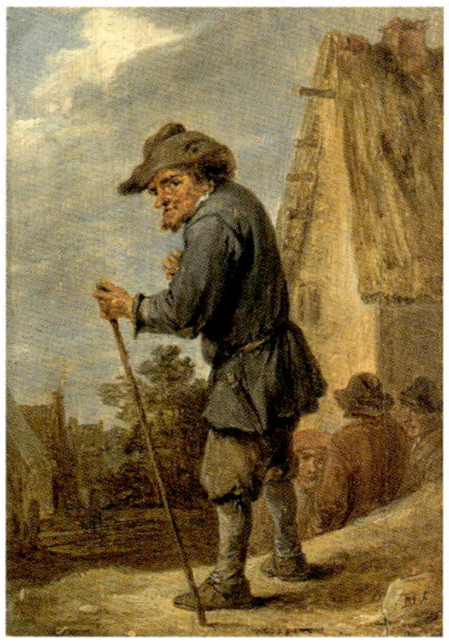

Teniers, David II 1610–1690
Village Scene with Four Peasants
oil on wood 17.8 x 12.1
NCM 1904-111

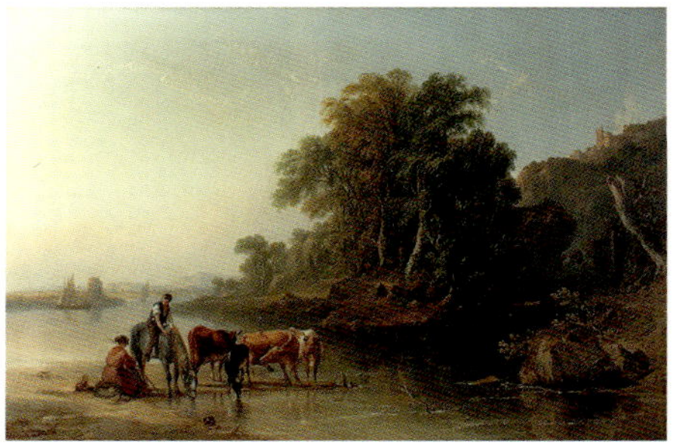

Tennant, John F. 1796–1872
The Watering Place 1840
oil on canvas 99.1 x 152.4
NCM 1933-256

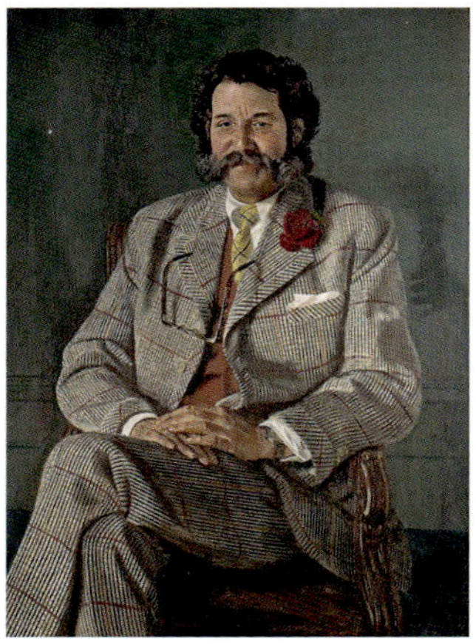

Thomson, Alfred Reginald 1894–1979
Harry Wheatcroft (1898–1977), Rose Grower 1957
oil on canvas 121.9 x 94
NCM 1957-14

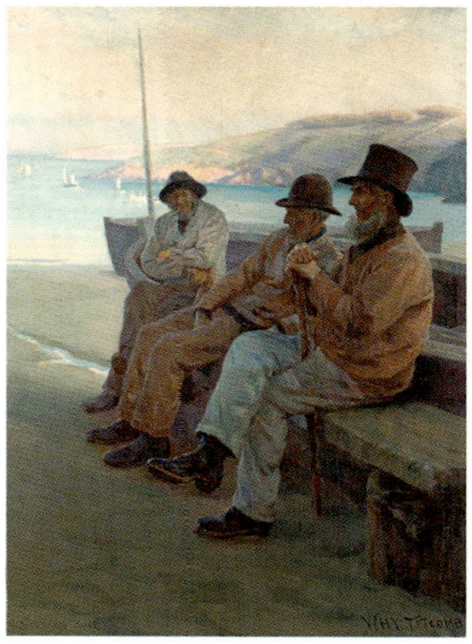

Titcomb, William Holt Yates 1858–1930
Old Sea Dogs 1891
oil on canvas 157.5 x 121.9
NCM 1895-1

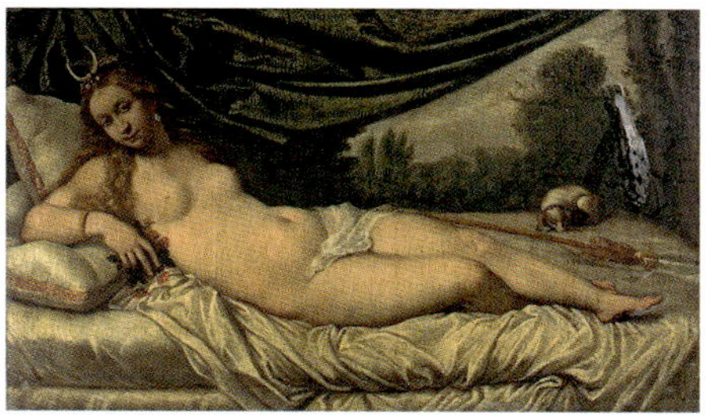

Titian (after) c.1488–1576
Diana
oil on canvas 68 x 115.5
NCM 1910-60

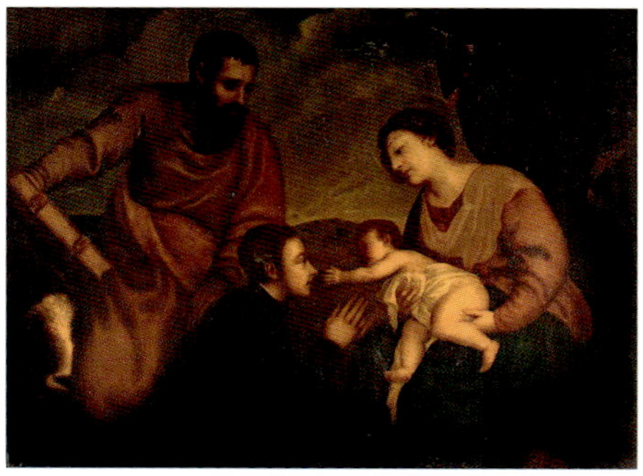

Titian (after) c.1488–1576
Madonna and Child with St Mark
oil on canvas 129.5 x 176.5
NCM 1910-58

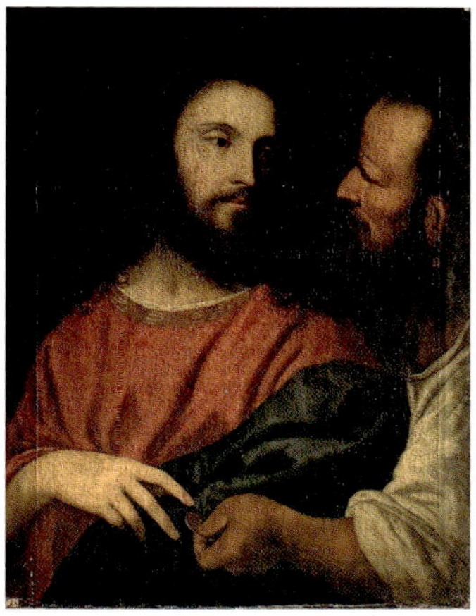

Titian (after) c.1488–1576
The Tribute Money
oil on canvas 76.2 x 63.5
NCM 1907-127

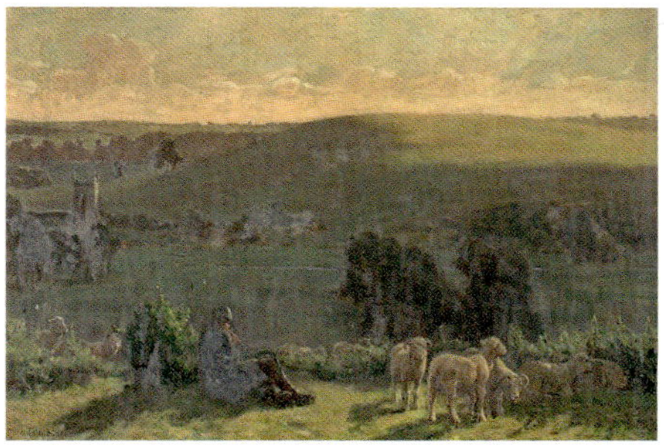

Tomson, Arthur 1858–1905
In the Down Country 1900
oil on canvas 50.8 x 76.2
NCM 1907-1

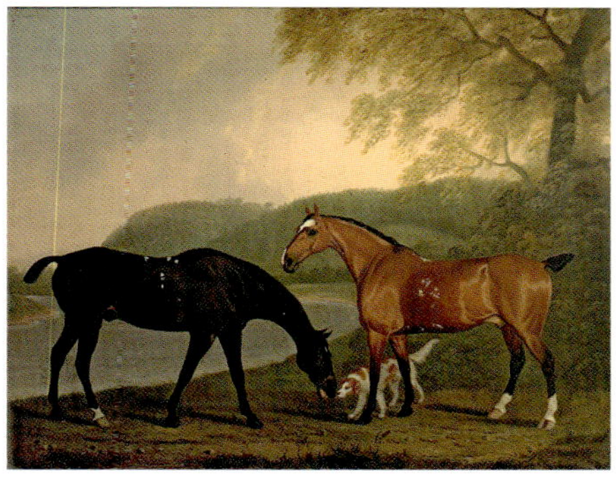

Tomson, Clifton 1775–1835
Horses and Dog in a Landscape c.1830
oil on canvas 71.8 x 94
NCM 1858-3

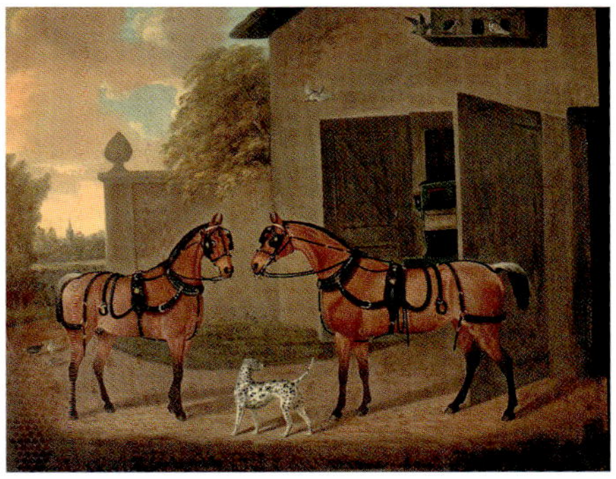

Tomson, Clifton 1775–1835
Carriages, Horses and Dogs
oil on canvas 73.7 x 91.4
NCM 1893-75

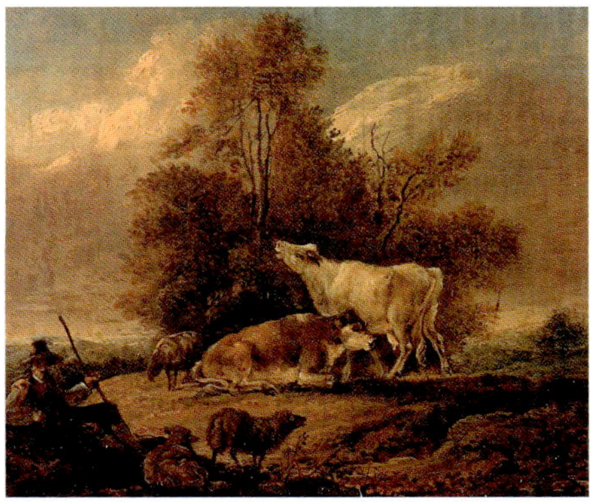

Towne, Charles 1763–1840
Landscape with Cattle and Figures
oil on wood 17.1 x 22.2
NCM 1887-1

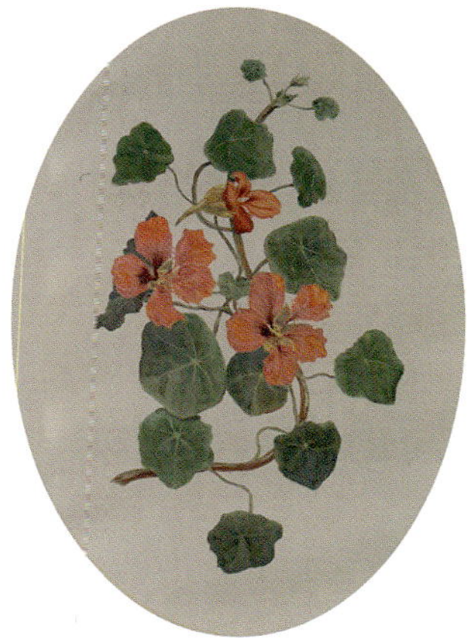

Townroe, Mary Dakeyne 1849–1941
Nasturtiums c.1870
oil on paper 48.3 x 40
NCM 1938-132

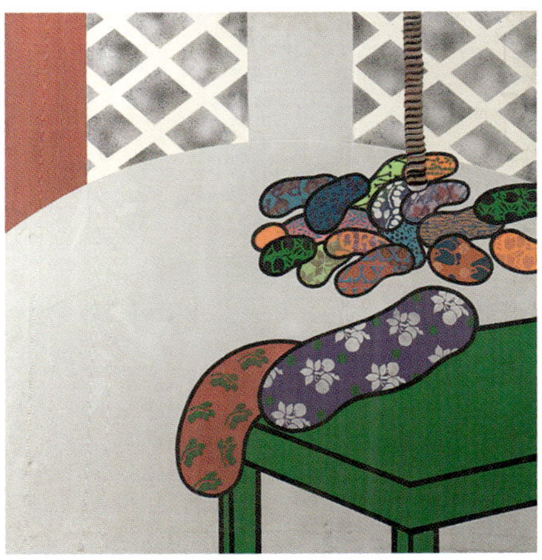

Toynton, Norman b.1939
Interior with Object 1967
acrylic on canvas 101.6 x 101.6
NCM 1969-111

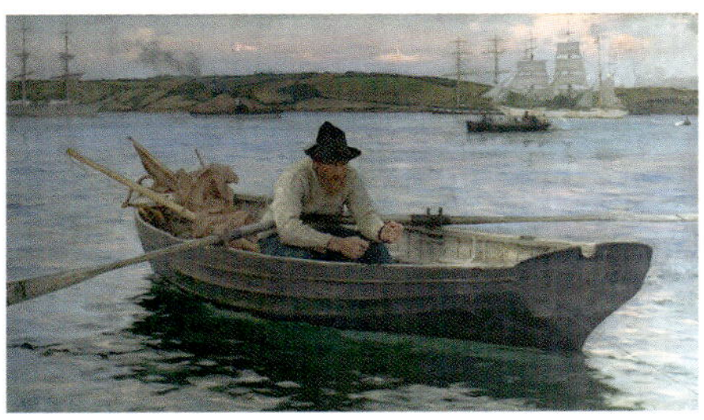

Tuke, Henry Scott 1858–1929
The Fisherman 1888–1889
oil on canvas 116.8 x 198.1
NCM 1895-2

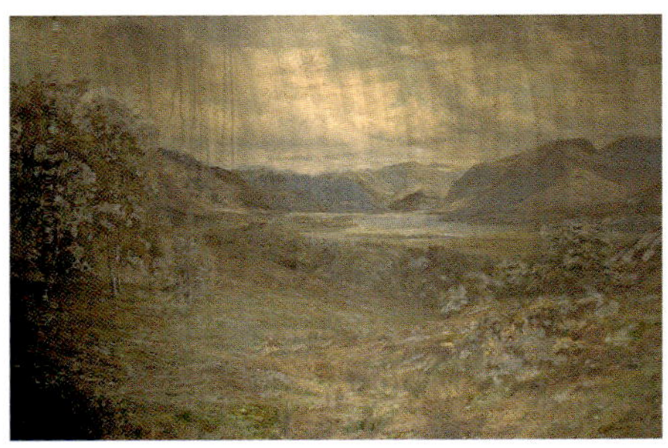

Turner, William 1789–1862
The Vale of Keswick, Cumbria
oil on canvas 101.6 x 152.4
NCM 1917-14

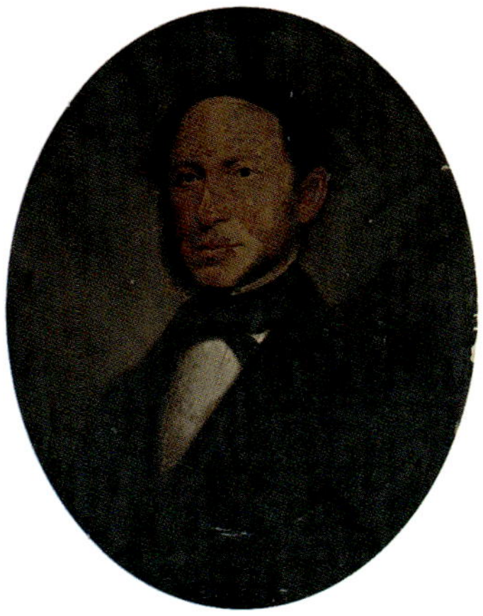

Ugolini, Giuseppe 1826–1897
Portrait of a Gentleman
oil on canvas 68.2 x 54.6
FA-X 8

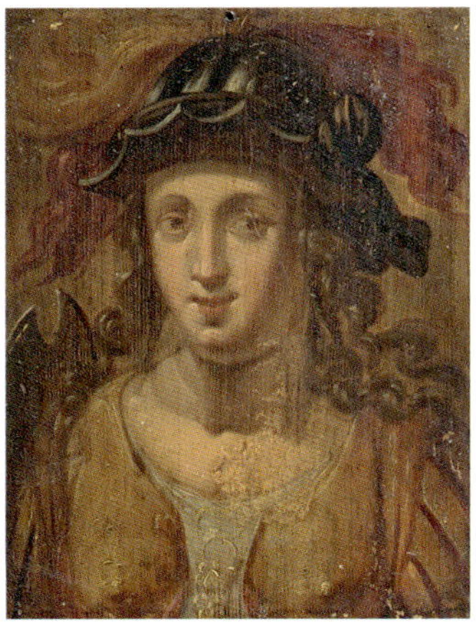

unknown artist 18th C
Armoured Woman (possibly Minerva)
oil on wood 25 x 20
FA-X 30

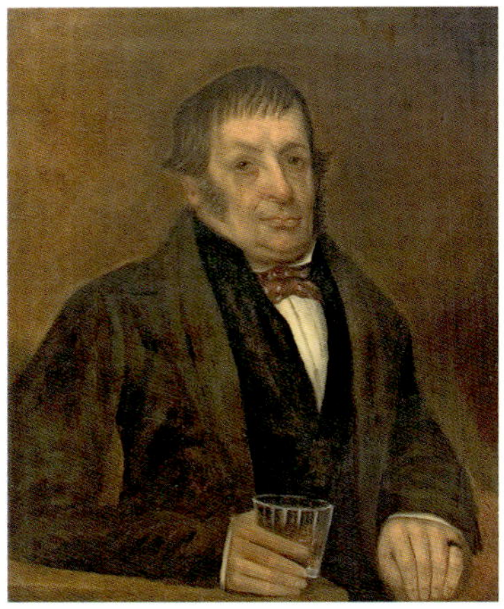

unknown artist
Mr John Burton c.1800
oil on canvas 76 x 63
NOTNH 1957.21

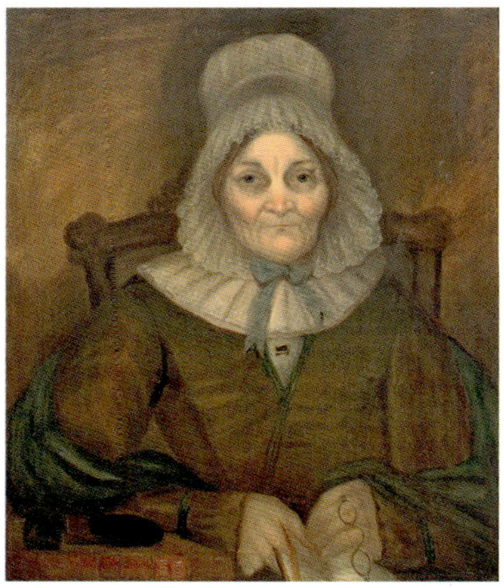

unknown artist
Mrs Hannah Burton c.1800
oil on canvas 76 x 63
NOTNH 1957.22

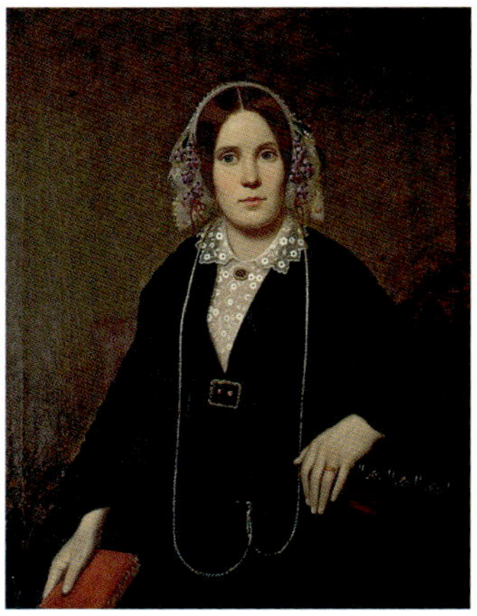

unknown artist
Portrait of a Lady of the Worthington Family
c.1845–1855
oil on canvas 90 x 69
FA-X 31

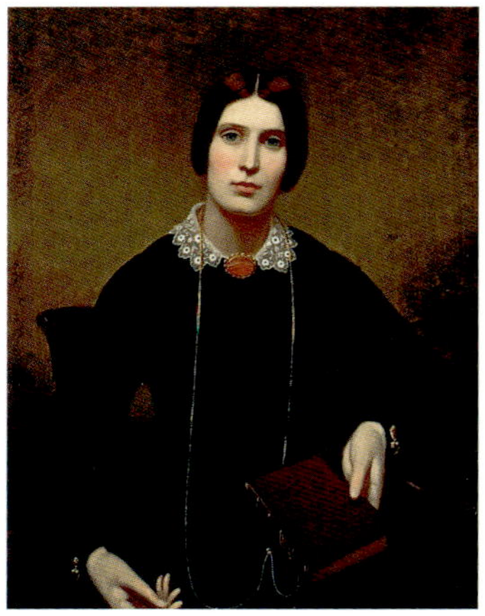

unknown artist
Portrait of a Lady of the Worthington Family Holding a Holy Bible c.1845–1855
oil on canvas 88 x 70
FA-X 32

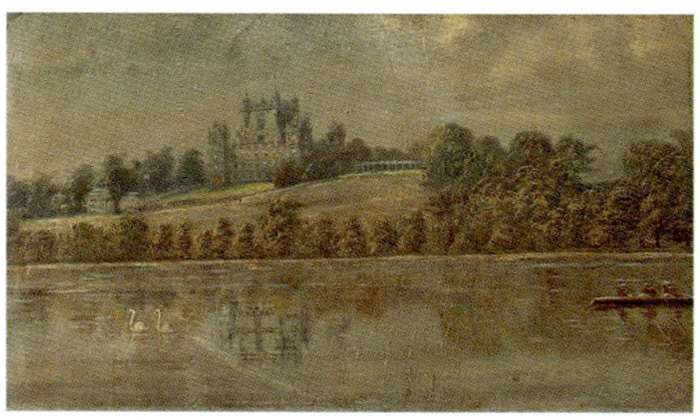

unknown artist
Wollaton Hall, Nottingham, from the Lake
c.1890
oil on canvas 27.2 x 47.3
NCM 1988-884

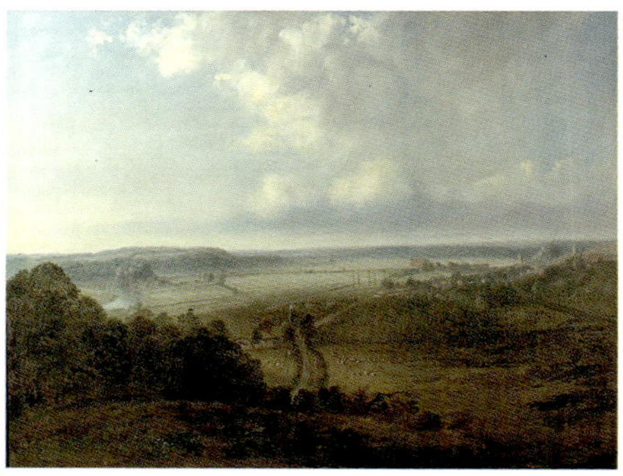

unknown artist 19th C
From Colwick Hill, Nottingham
oil on canvas 102.3 x 133.7
Public Libraries Loan

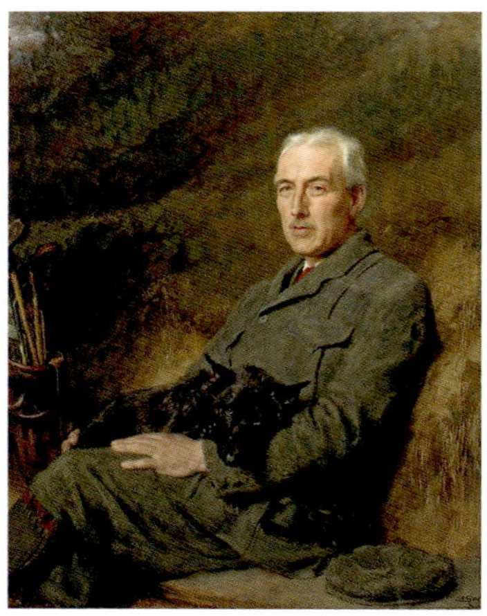

unknown artist
*Portrait of an Unidentified Gentleman with a Dog and Golf Clubs** c.1906
oil on canvas 127 x 101.6
FA-X 27

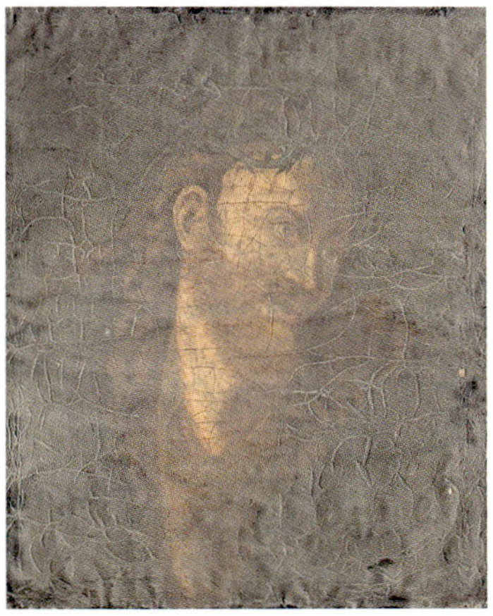

unknown artist
*Christ Crowned with Thorns**
oil on wood 41 x 39
FA-X 29

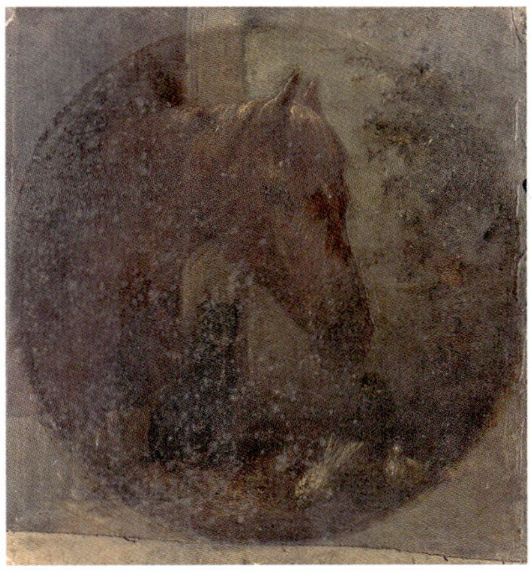

unknown artist
Head of a Horse
oil on wood 26.5 x 25
FA-X 22

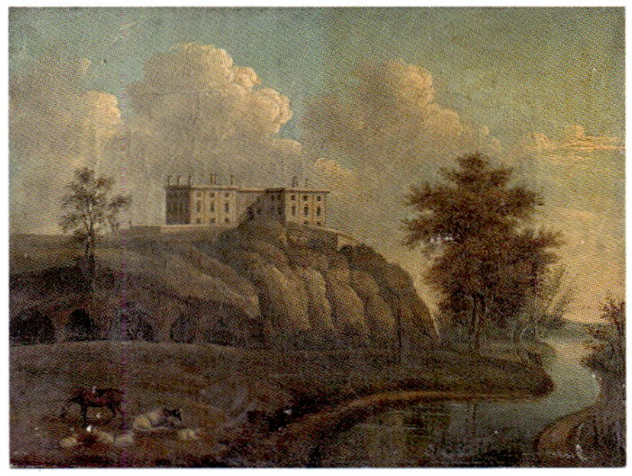

unknown artist
Nottingham Castle
oil on canvas 23 x 30.5
FA-X 21

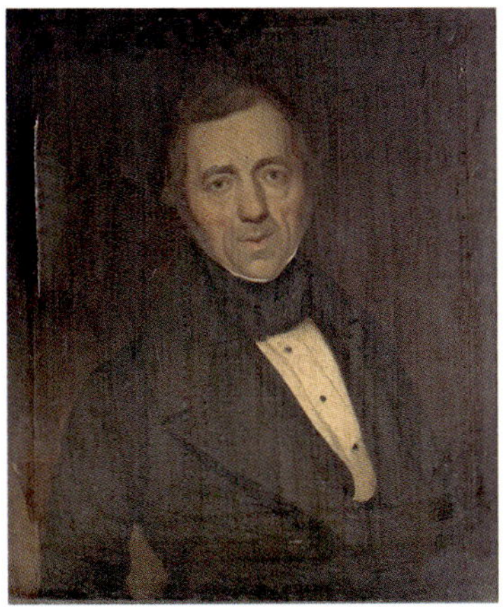

unknown artist
Portrait of a Gentleman
oil on canvas 75.9 x 63.8
FA-X 4

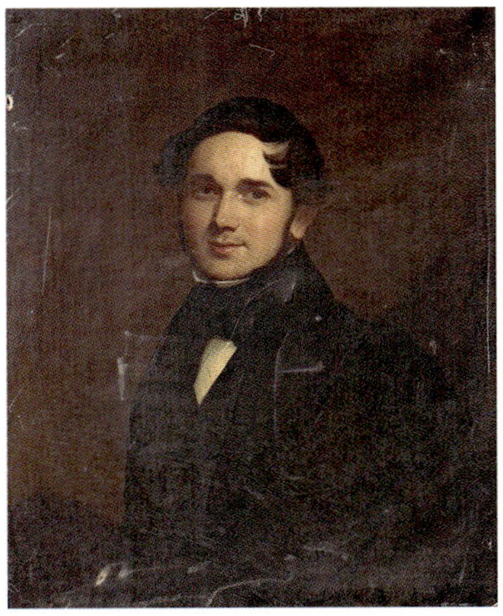

unknown artist
Portrait of a Gentleman
oil on canvas 74 x 62
FA-X 28

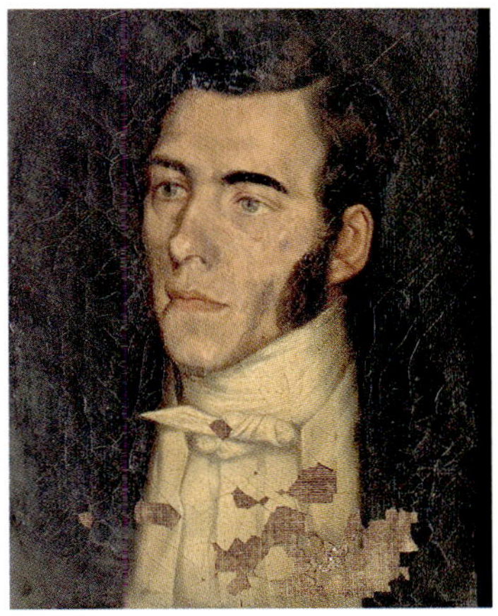

unknown artist
Portrait of a Gentleman in a White Cravat
oil on canvas 28 x 22.5
FA-X 10

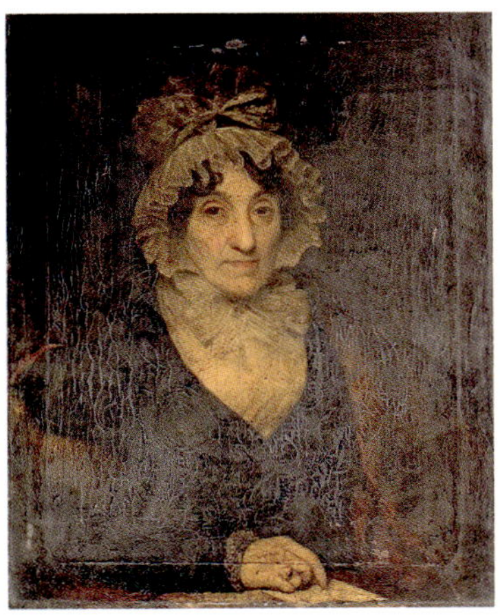

unknown artist
Portrait of a Lady in a Frilled Cap
oil on canvas 77.2 x 63.5
FA-X 6

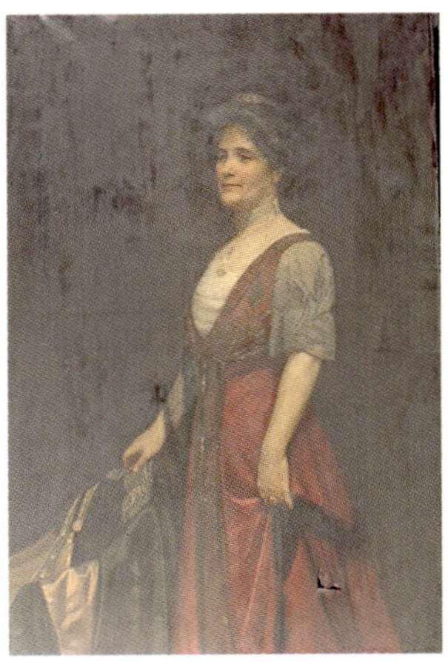

unknown artist
Portrait of a Lady with a Ruby Tiara
oil on canvas 152.4 x 110.7
FA-X 13

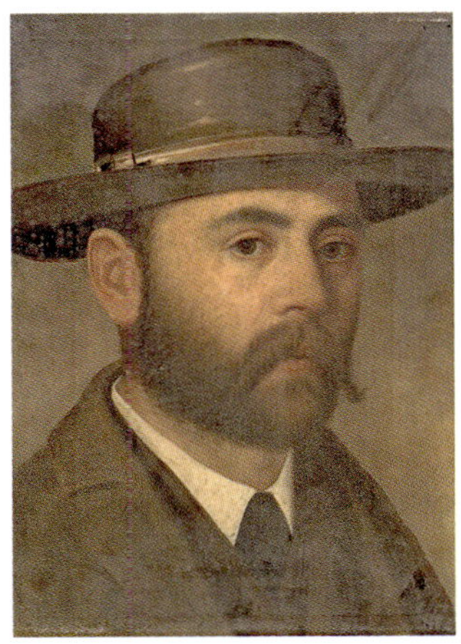

unknown artist
Portrait of a Man in a Hat
oil on canvas 42 x 32
FA-X 9

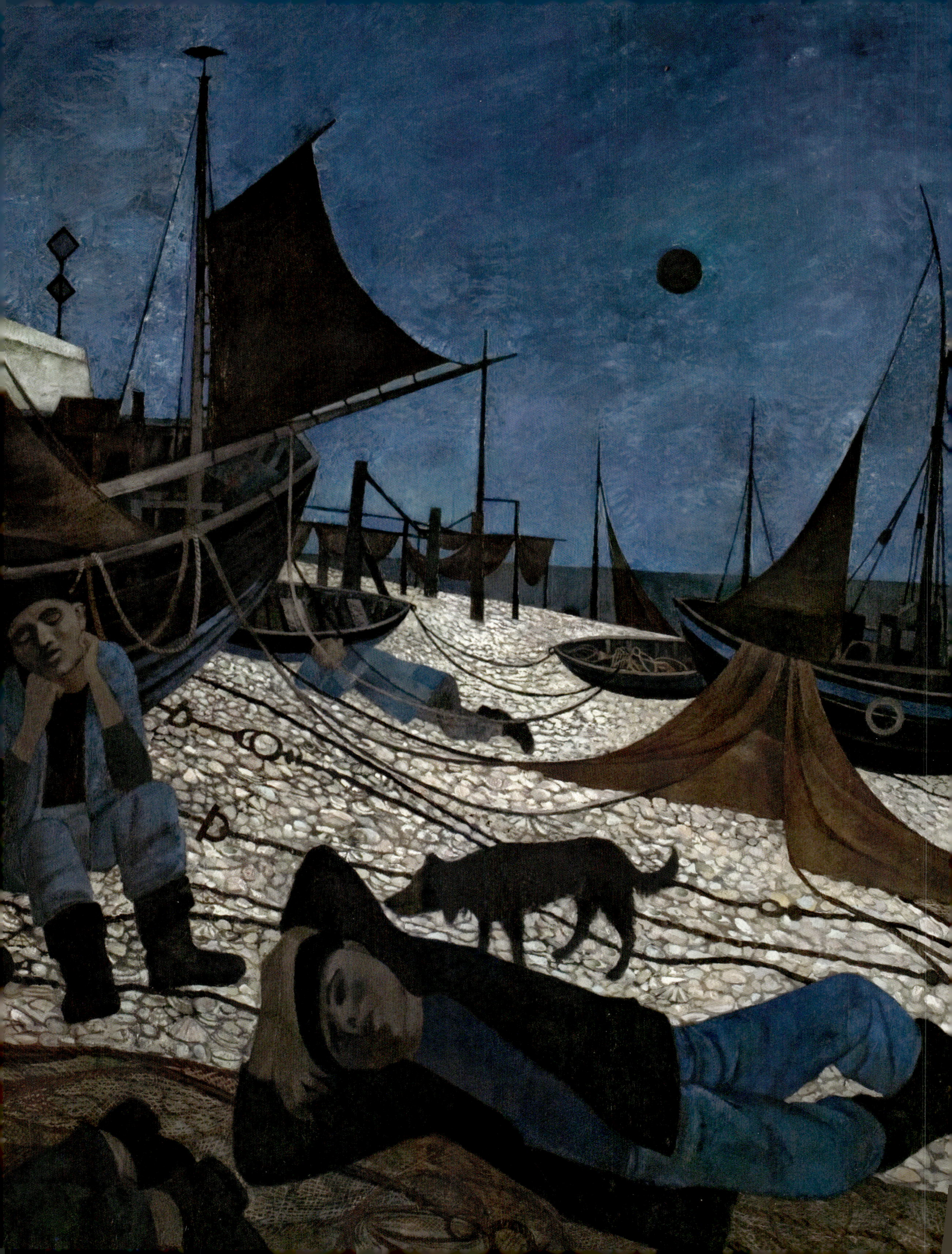

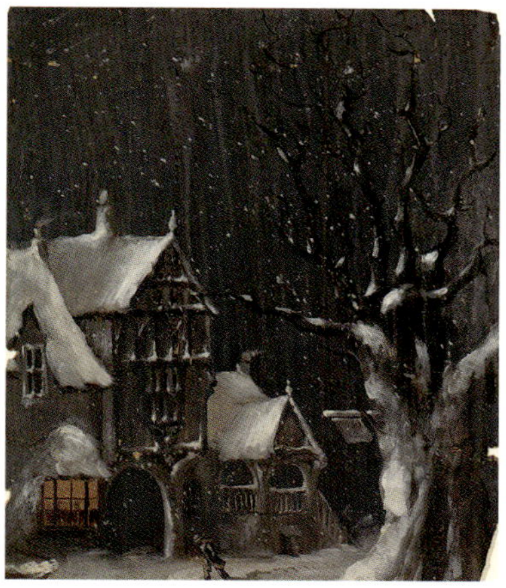

unknown artist
Punch Bowl, Nottingham
oil on paper 36 x 31.5
NCM 1983-344

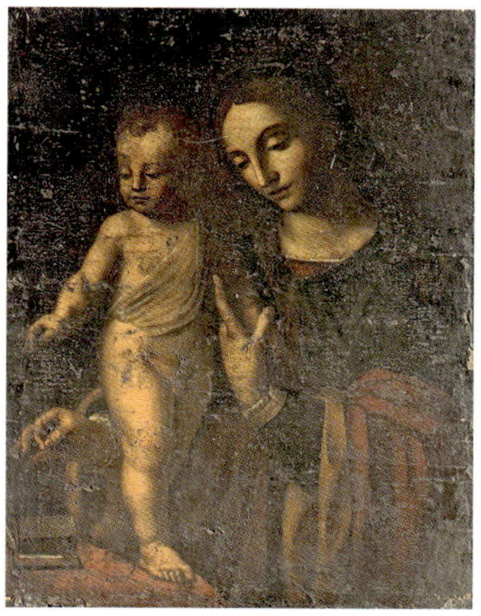

unknown artist
The Virgin and Child
oil on wood 72 x 57
FA-X 7

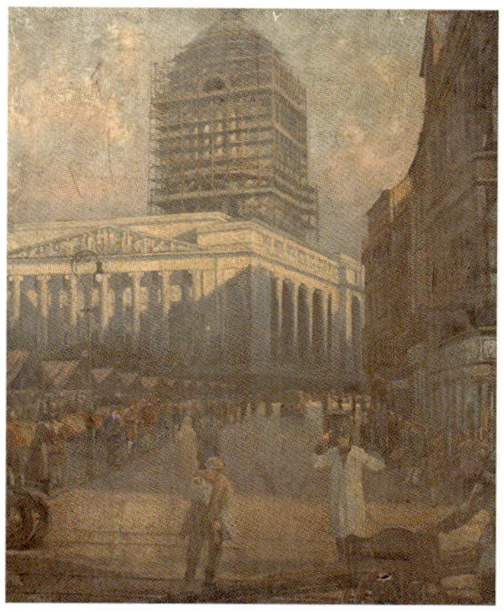

unknown artist
View of The Council House, Nottingham, from South Parade
oil on canvas 76 x 63.5
FA-X 12

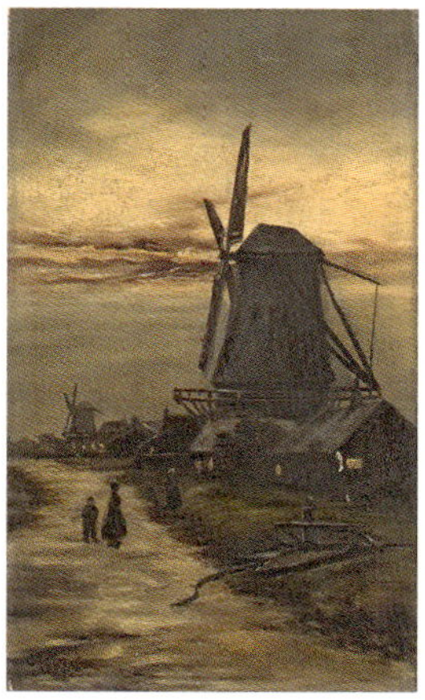

unknown artist
Windmills
oil on canvas 34.4 x 25.5
NCM 1985-927

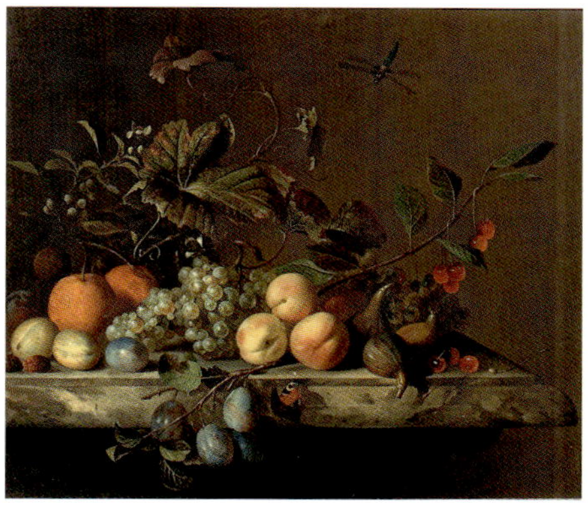

Van der Meer, Barend 1659–1702
Fruit Piece with Dragonfly 1692
oil on canvas 64.1 x 75.6
NCM 1933-254

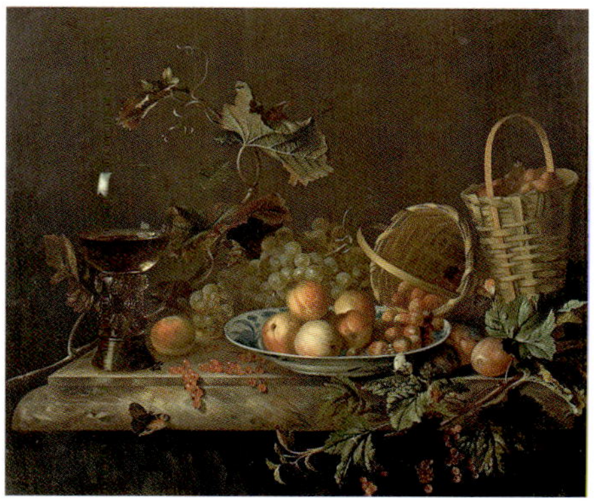

Van der Meer, Barend 1659–1702
Fruit Piece with Wine Glass 1692
oil on canvas 64.1 x 75.6
NCM 1933-253

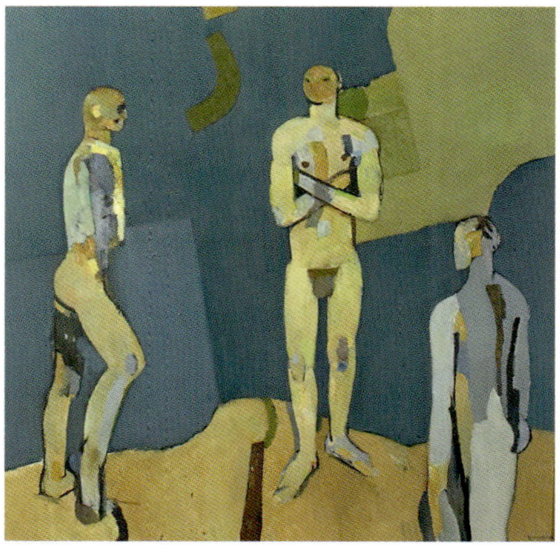

Vaughan, John Keith 1912–1977
Fourth Assembly of Figures 1956
oil on canvas 114.3 x 121.9
NCM 1960-27

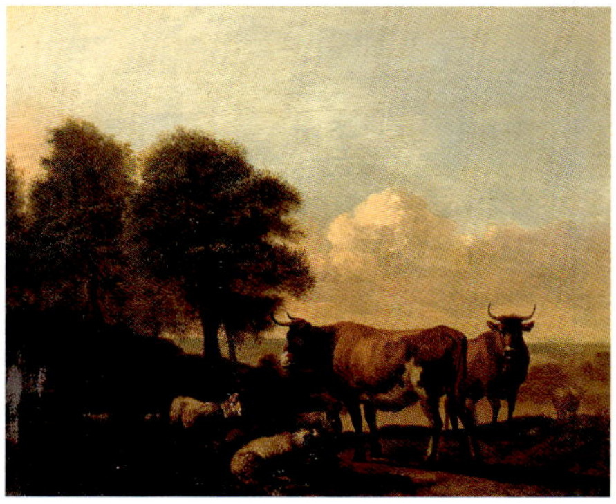

Velde, Adriaen van de 1636–1672
Landscape with Cattle
oil on wood 34.2 x 43.2
NCM 1923-16

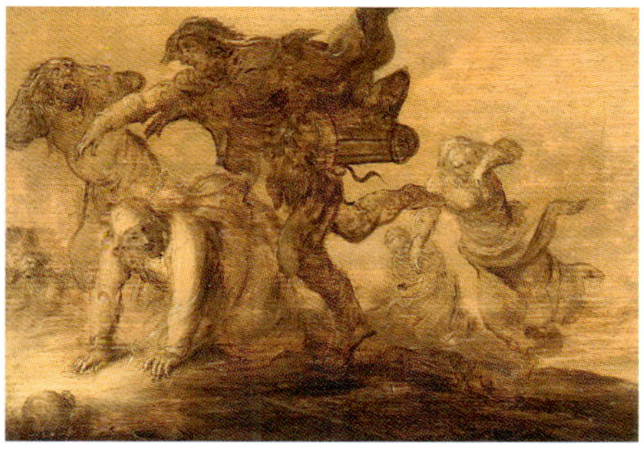

Venne, Adriaen van de 1589–1662
Peasants Fleeing (Witchcraft) c.1640
oil on wood 24.1 x 36.8
NCM 1961-318

Facing page: Mason, Bateson, 1910–1977, *Sleeping Fishermen* (detail), Nottingham City Museums and Galleries (p. 123)

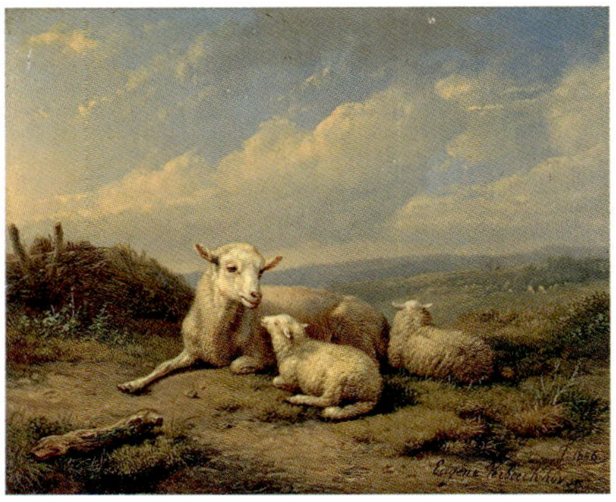

Verboeckhoven, Eugène Joseph 1799–1881
The Twins 1846
oil on wood 13.6 x 18.1
NCM 1904-104

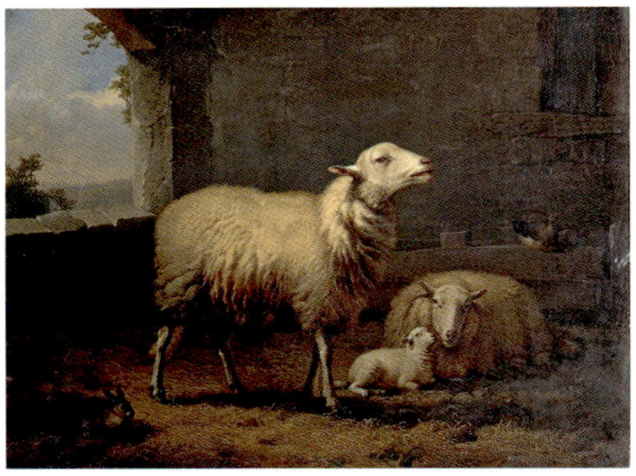

Verboeckhoven, Eugène Joseph 1799–1881
Sheep 1876
oil on canvas 61 x 78.7
NCM 1934-34

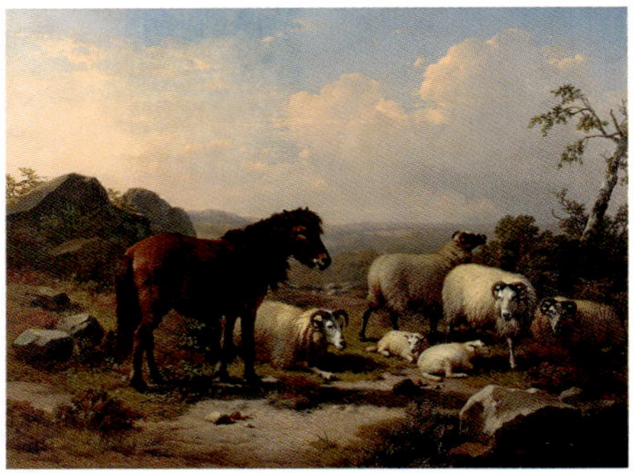

Verboeckhoven, Eugène Joseph 1799–1881
Good Friends 1878
oil on canvas 74.9 x 100.3
NCM 1946-271

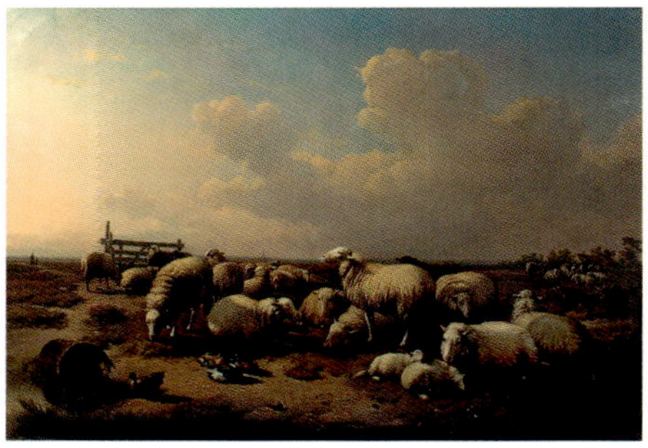

Verboeckhoven, Eugène Joseph 1799–1881
The Sheep
oil on canvas 111.5 x 162.5
NCM 1932-42

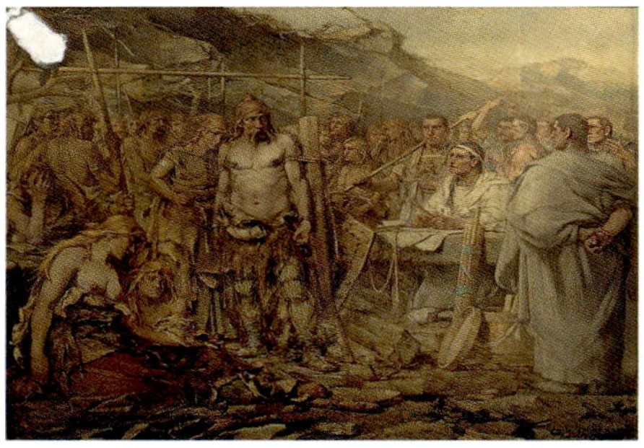

Verbrugge, Emile 1856–1936
The Aduatics Passing under the Yoke
oil on canvas 118.1 x 147.3
NCM 1937-26

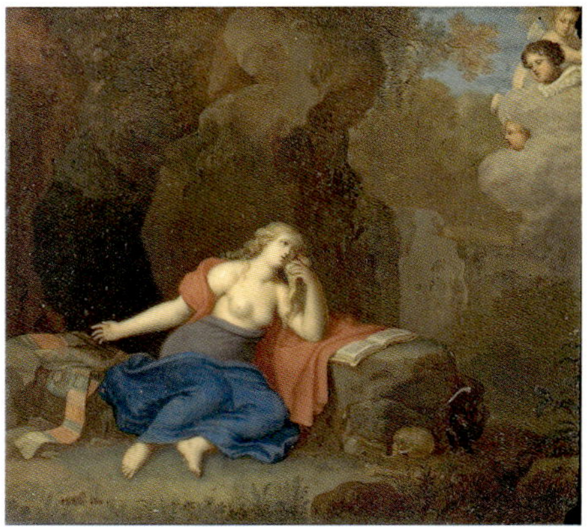

Vertangen, Daniel c.1598–1681/1684
The Penitent Magdalen in a Landscape
oil on wood 14.6 x 16.5
NCM 1904-100

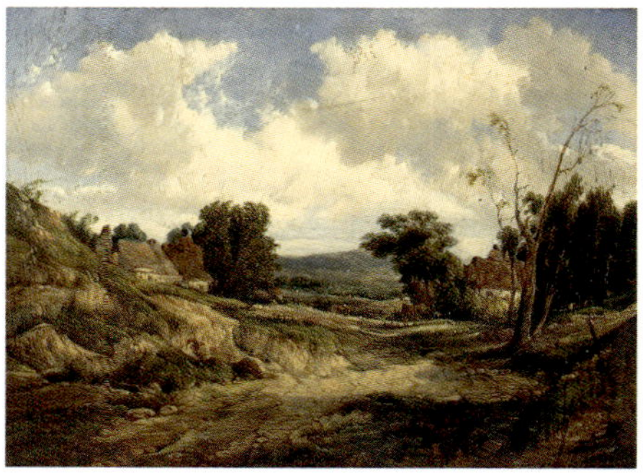

Vickers, Alfred 1786–1868
Landscape with Cottages 1864
oil on canvas 33 x 45.7
NCM 1890-1190

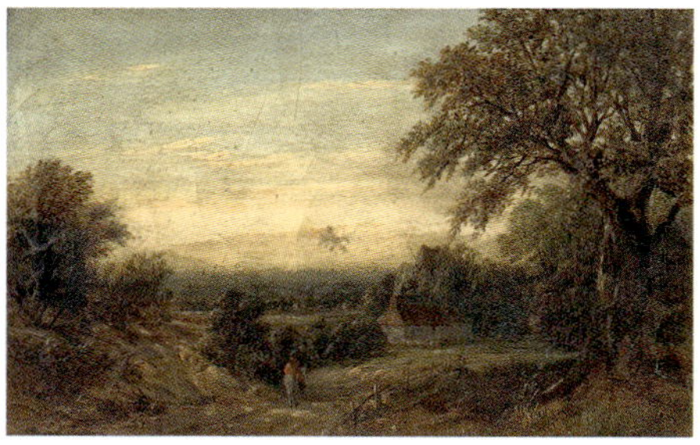

Vickers, W. active 19th C
Crossing the Heath, Evening
oil on canvas 20.3 x 30.5
NCM 1890-1213

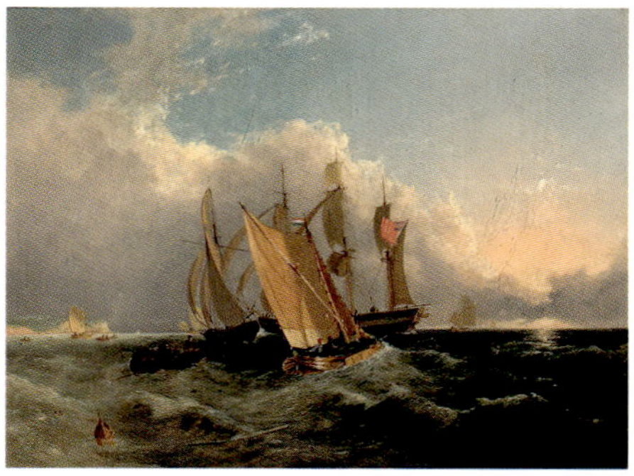

Vincent, George 1796–1831
Sea Piece 1827
oil on canvas 50.2 x 68.6
NCM 1904-73

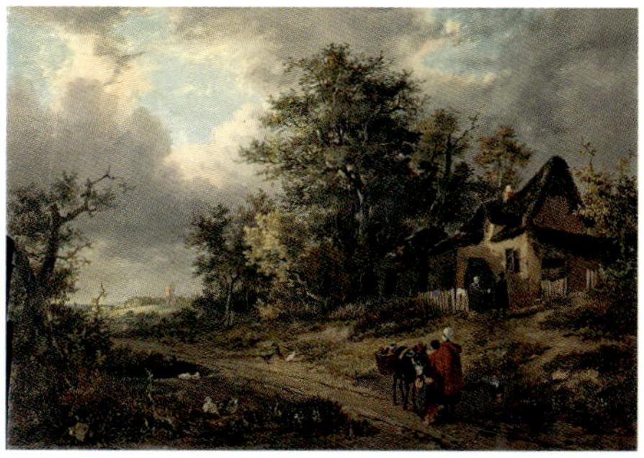

Vincent, George 1796–1831
Landscape with Cottages and Tinker 1828
oil on canvas 43.8 x 60.3
NCM 1904-74

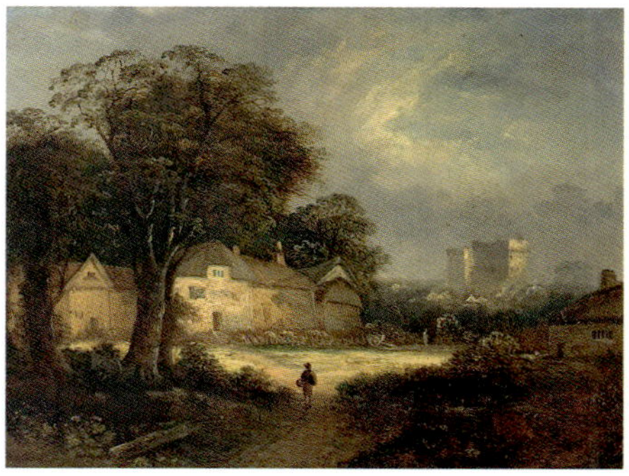

Vincent, George 1796–1831
Castle Ashby, Northamptonshire
oil on canvas 35.1 x 46.5
NCM 1890-1172

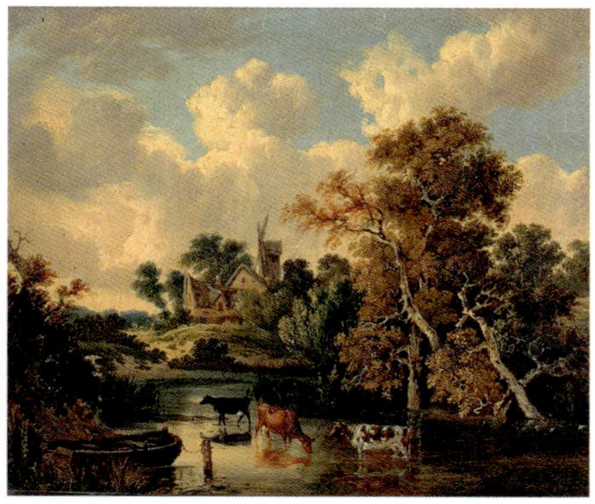

Vincent, George 1796–1831
Landscape with Cattle in a Pool
oil on wood 25.4 x 30.5
NCM 1904-75

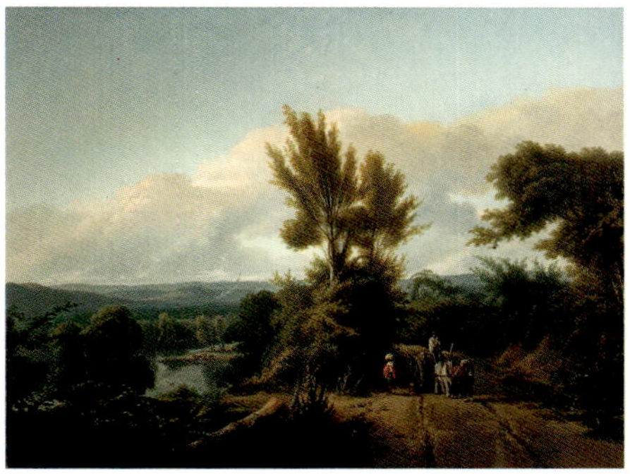

Vincent, George (attributed to) 1796–1831
Evening Twilight
oil on canvas 67.9 x 91.4
NCM 1890-1205

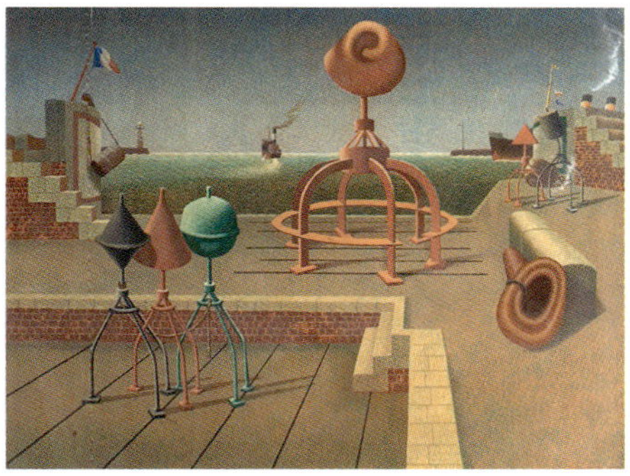

Wadsworth, Edward Alexander 1889–1949
Satellitium 1942
tempera on wood 64.8 x 88.9
NCM 1957-5

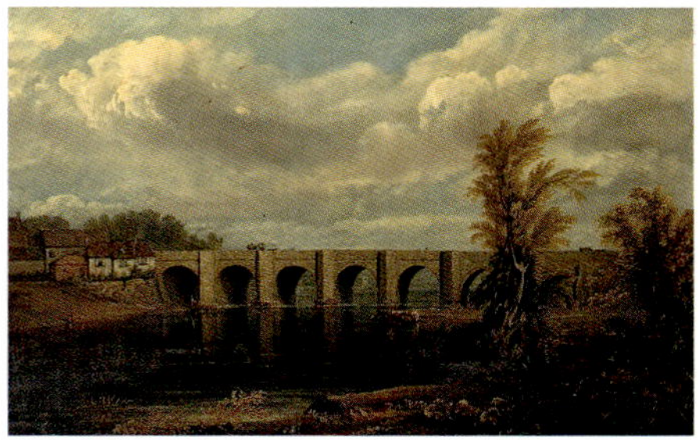

Walker, John Rawson 1796–1873
Old Trent Bridge, Nottingham 1825
oil on canvas 53.3 x 78.7
NCM 1889-73

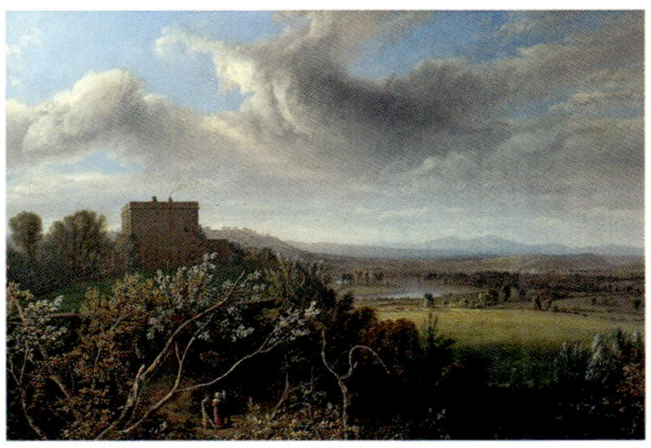

Walker, John Rawson 1796–1873
Nottingham Castle c.1832
oil on canvas 61 x 91.4
NCM 1934-41

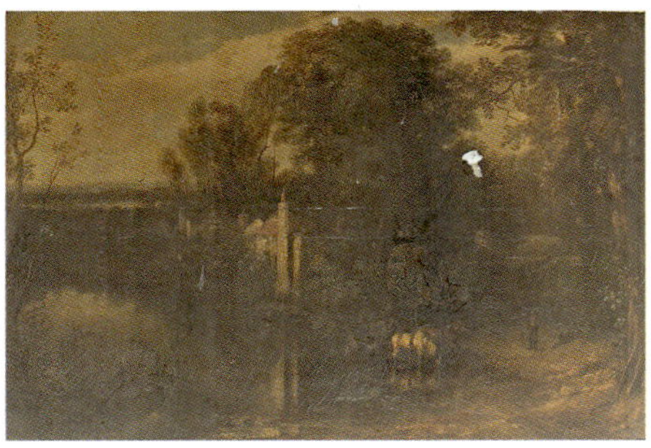

Walker, John Rawson 1796–1873
Papplewick Dam, Nottinghamshire 1844
oil on canvas 121.9 x 182.9
NCM 1922-26

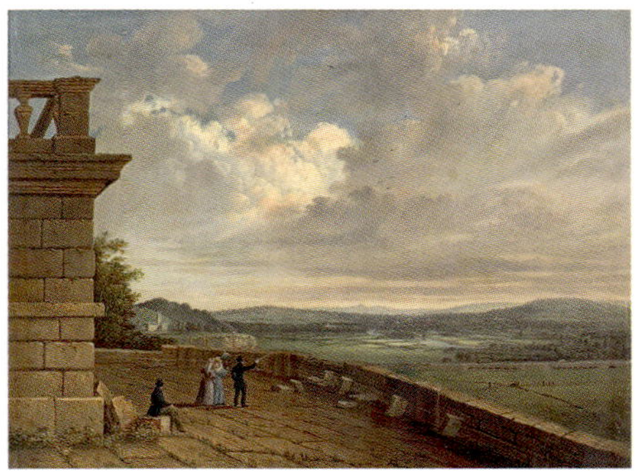

Walker, John Rawson 1796–1873
View from the Nottingham Castle Terrace Looking East c.1845
oil on canvas 55.9 x 76.8
NCM 1904-435

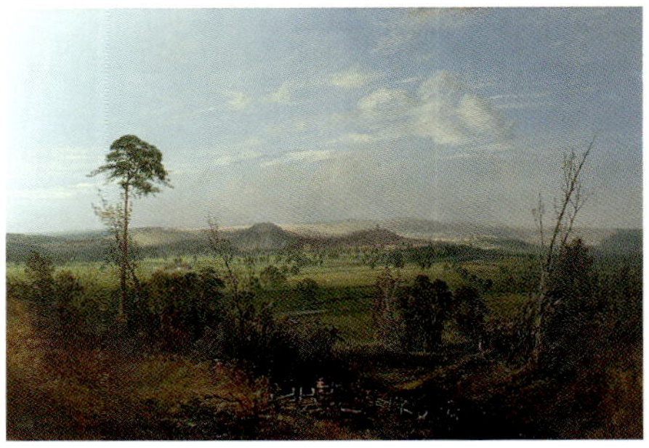

Walker, John Rawson 1796–1873
View of Nottingham from Wilford c.1850
oil on canvas 101.6 x 152.4
NCM 1913-78

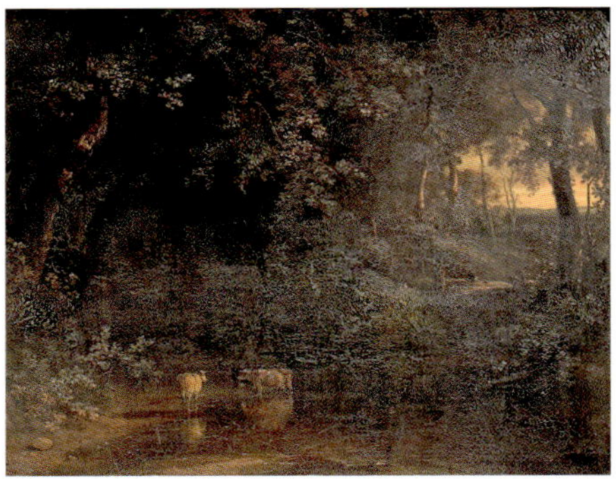

Walker, John Rawson 1796–1873
View near Linby, Nottinghamshire
oil on canvas 116.8 x 127
NCM 1898-76

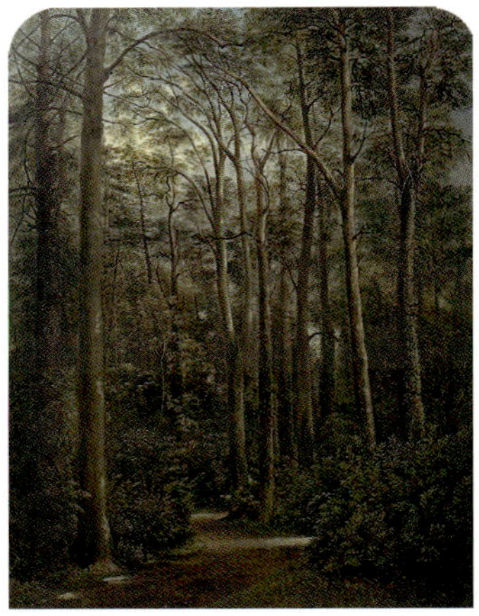

Wallis, George 1811–1891
The Wilderness 1857
oil on canvas 132.1 x 106.7
NCM 1892-50

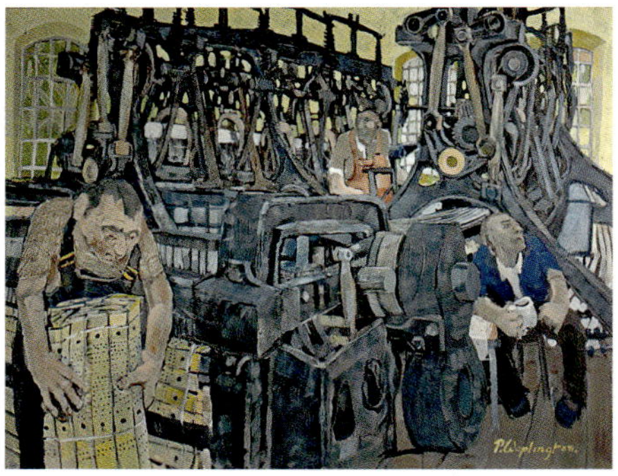

Waplington, Paul b.1938
Lace Factory
oil on canvas 91.2 x 121.5
NCM 1987-1033

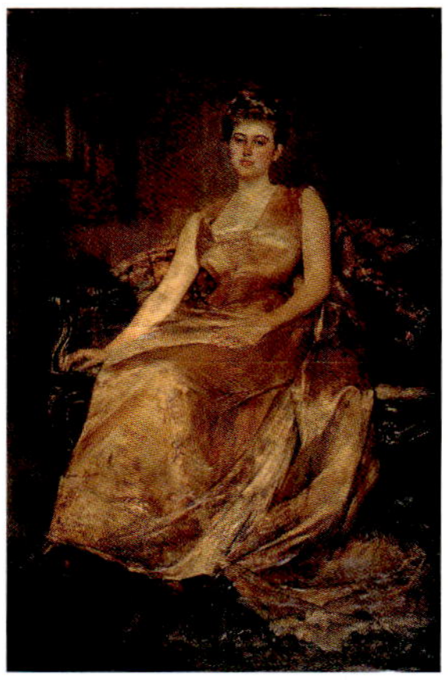

Ward, Edwin Arthur 1859–1933
Mrs Morton Jackson 1889
oil on canvas 182.9 x 121.9
NCM 1933-262

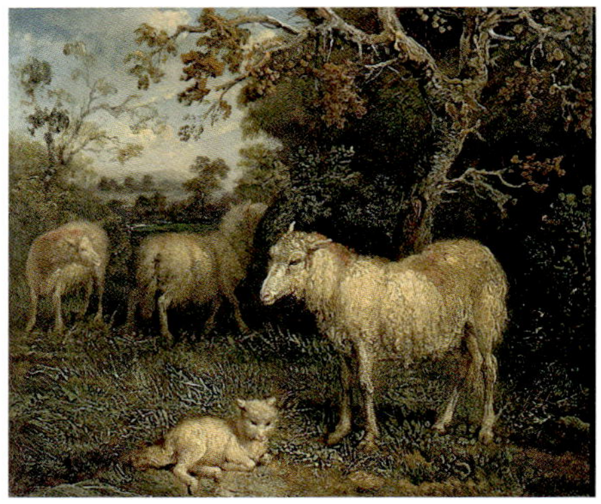

Ward, James 1769–1859
Landscape with Sheep
oil on canvas 25.4 x 30.5
NCM 1904-77

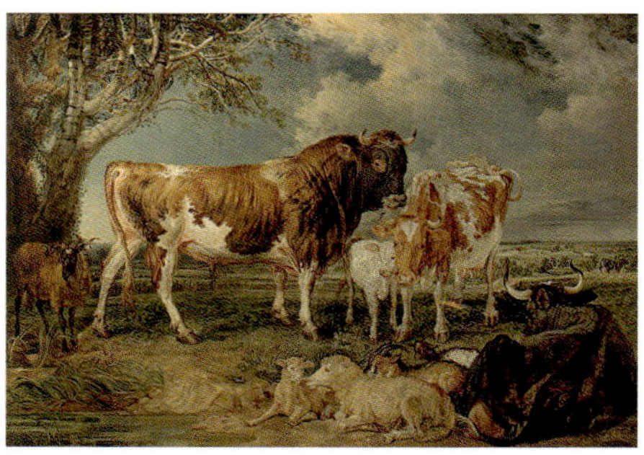

Ward, James II 1800–1884
Bull, Cow and Calf in a Landscape 1837
oil on canvas 109.2 x 161.3
NCM 1904-78

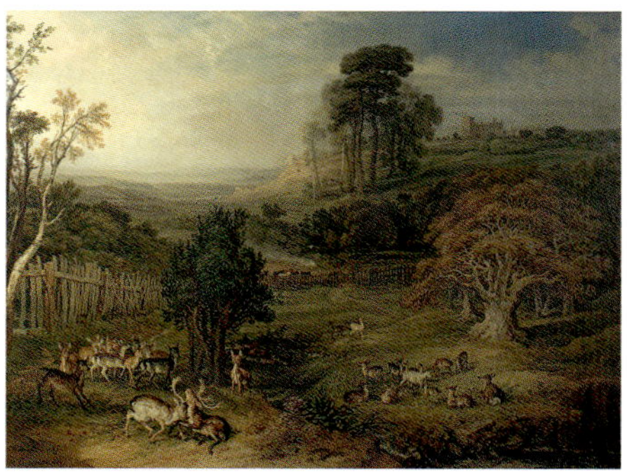

Ward, James II 1800–1884
A Dewy Morning (The Duel of the Stags) 1849
oil on canvas 124.5 x 161.9
NCM 1904-79

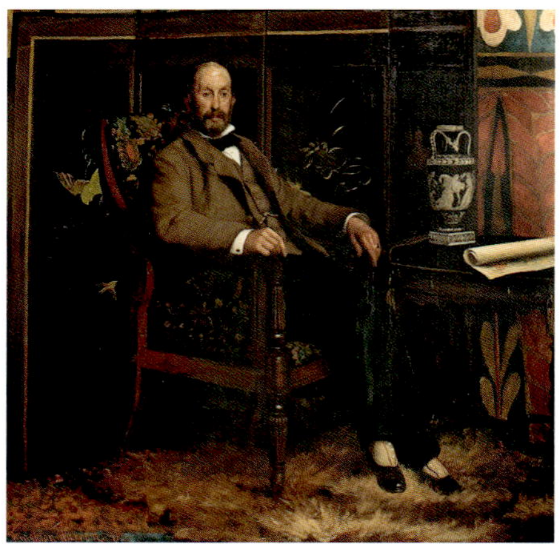

Warren, Charles Knighton b.1856
Felix Joseph (1840–1892) 1891
oil on canvas 182.9 x 208.3
NCM 1891-185

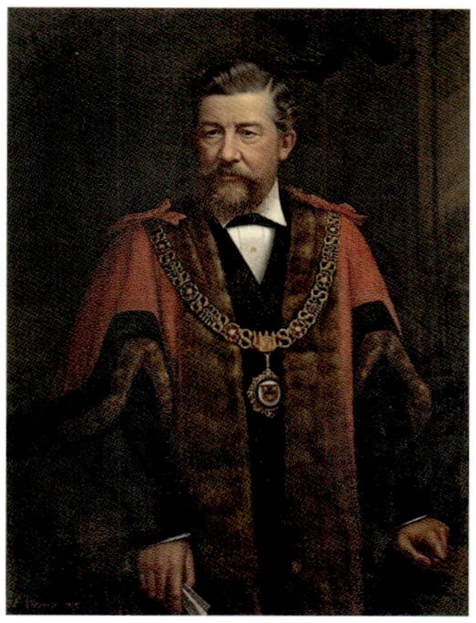

Warsop, Frederick c.1835–1895
Alderman W. G. Ward 1878
oil on canvas 112.1 x 87
NCM 1929-2

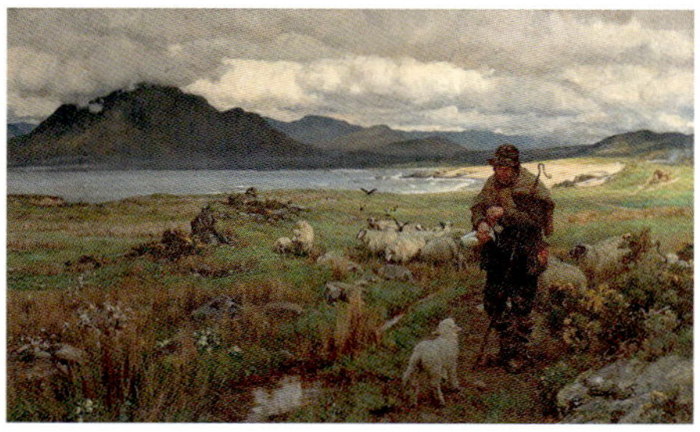

Waterlow, Ernest Albert 1850–1919
The Orphan 1888
oil on canvas 88.9 x 152.4
NCM 1913-61

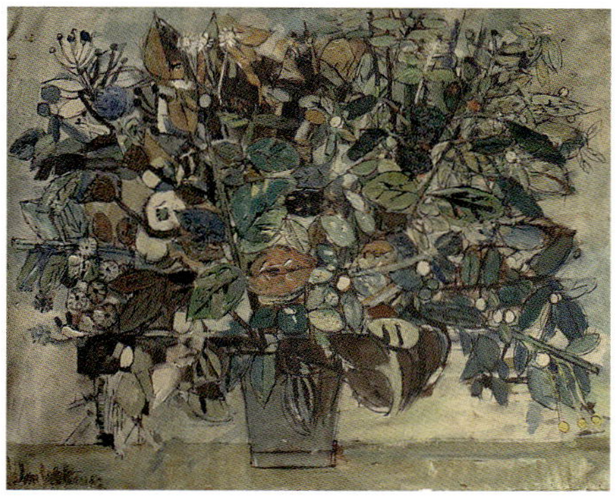

Watson, John 1923–1992
Flower Study, Autumn 1952
oil on canvas 82.6 x 106
NCM 1954-36

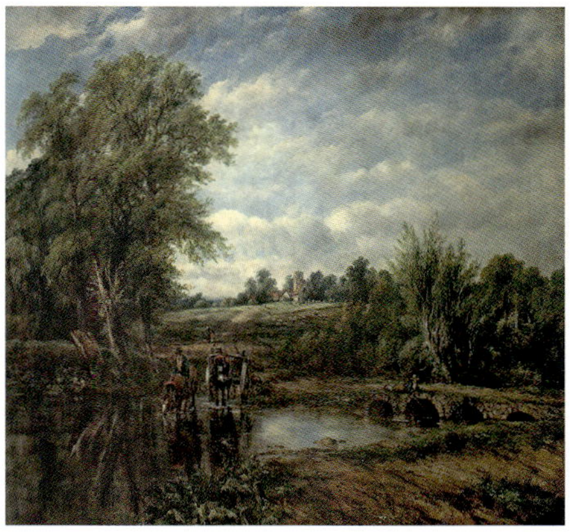

Watts, Frederick William 1800–1870
The Ford
oil on canvas 101.6 x 133.4
NCM 1933-252

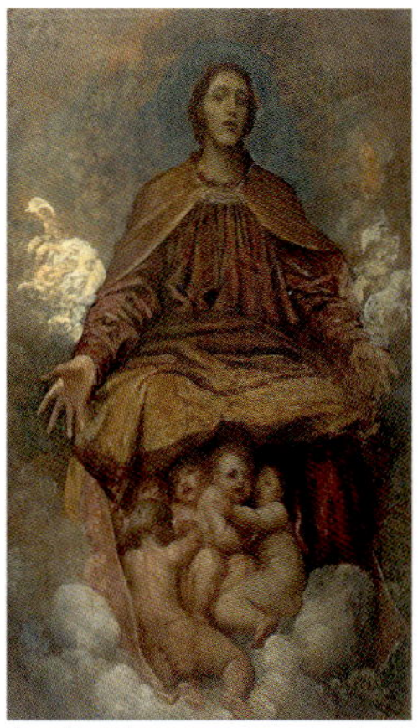

Watts, George Frederick 1817–1904
The Spirit of Christianity
oil on canvas 204.5 x 142.9
NCM 1905-69

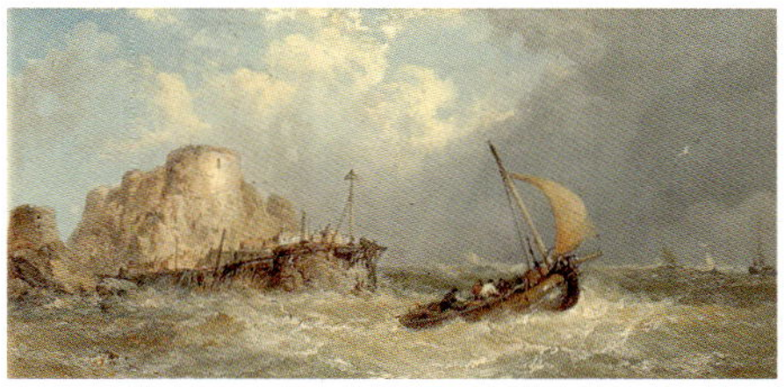

Webb, James 1825–1895
Mont Orgueil Castle, Jersey
oil on canvas 20.3 x 40.6
NCM 1904-80

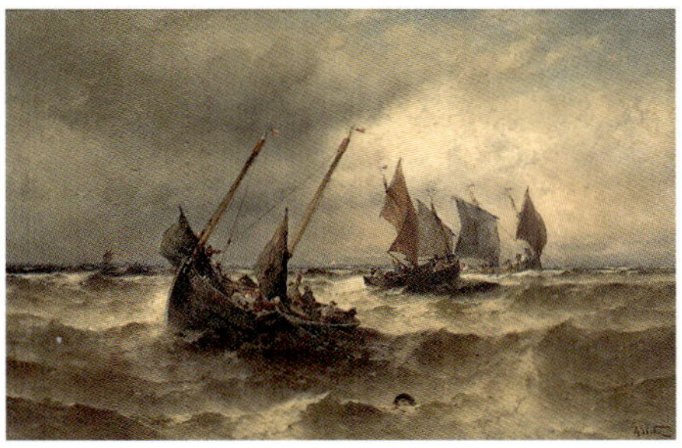

Weber, Theodor Alexander 1838–1907
Fishing Boats at Sea
oil on canvas 85.1 x 133.4
NCM 1911-48

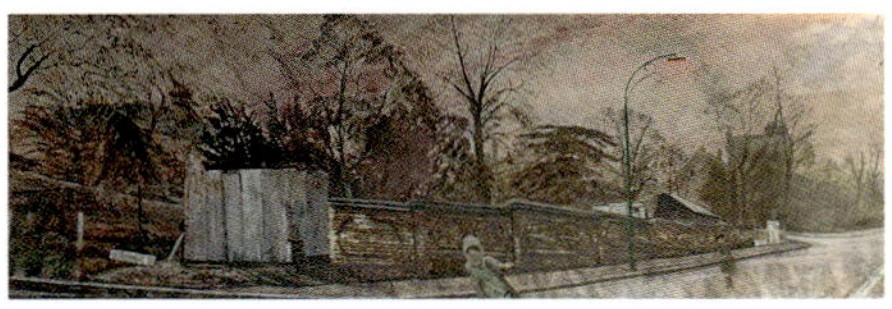

Weight, Carel Victor Morlais 1908–1997
The Moment 1955
oil on canvas 80.5 x 199.5
NCM 1958-27

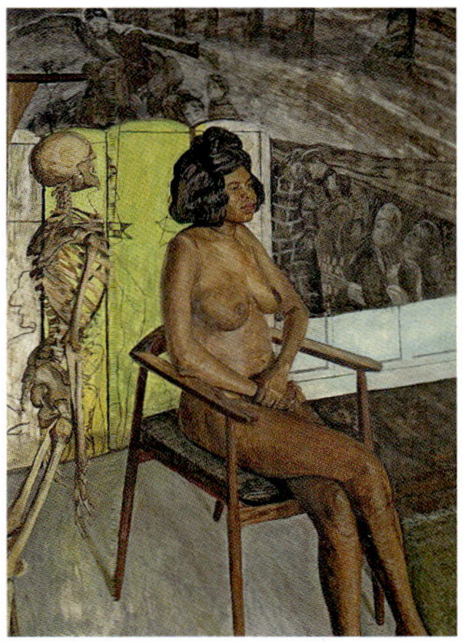

Weight, Carel Victor Morlais 1908–1997
African Girl No.2 1965
oil on canvas 101.6 x 76.2
NCM 1966-72

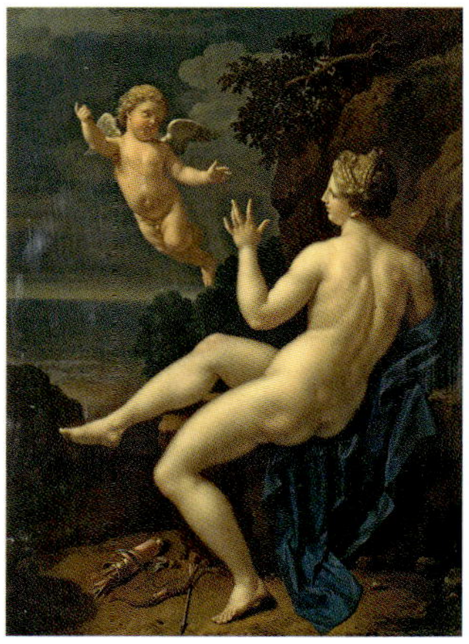

Werff, Adriaen van der 1659–1722
Venus and Cupid 1709
oil on wood 49.5 x 36.8
NCM 1953-245

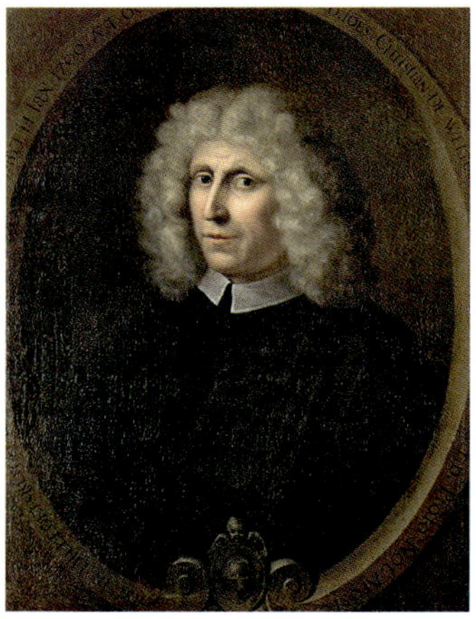

Werff, Pieter van der 1665–1722
Christian de Weerdt
oil on canvas 81.3 x 67.3
NCM 1878-217

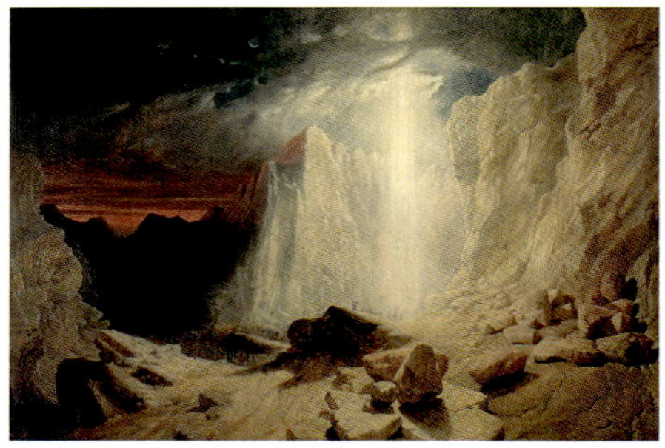

West, William 1801–1861
The Israelites Led by the Pillar of Fire by Night
c.1845
oil on canvas 66.7 x 101
NCM 1952-46

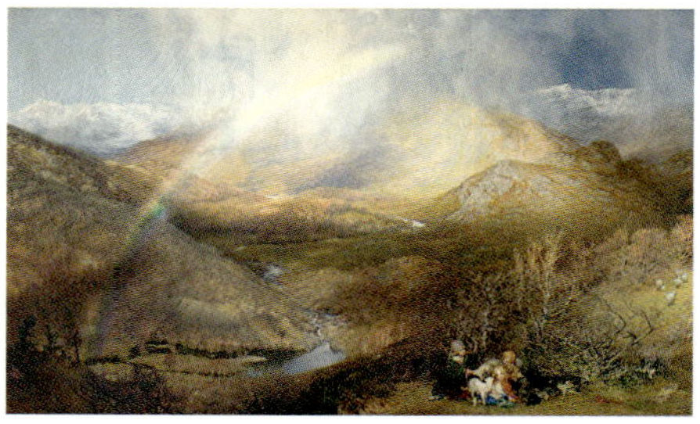

Whaite, Henry Clarence 1828–1912
The Rainbow 1862
oil on canvas 139.7 x 241.6
NCM 1893-25

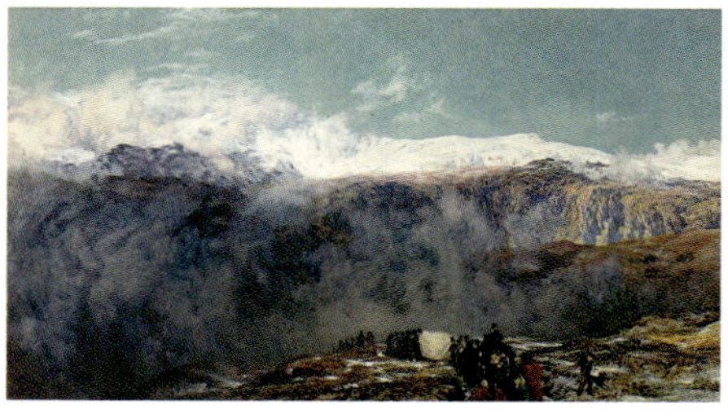

Whaite, Henry Clarence 1828–1912
A Welsh Funeral (To the Cold Earth) 1865
oil on canvas 46.4 x 83.2
NCM 1924-21

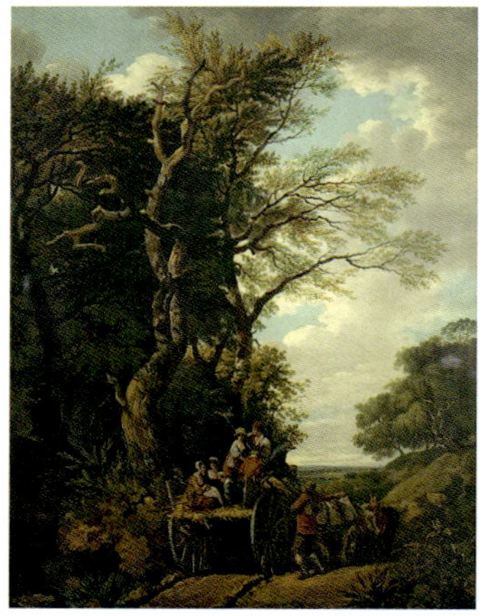

Wheatley, Francis 1747–1801
The Harvest Wagon 1774
oil on canvas 128.3 x 101.6
NCM 1904-81

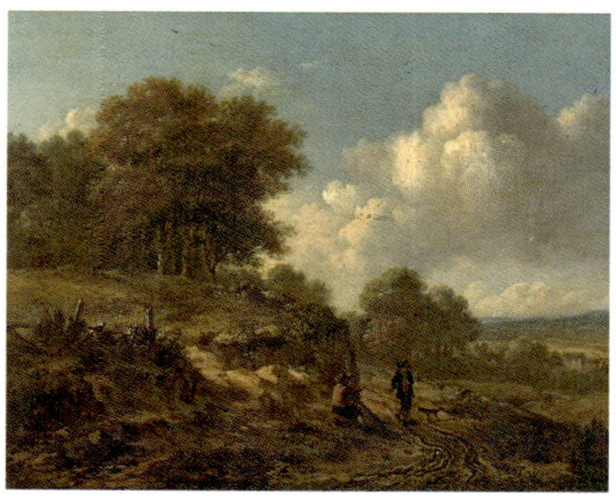

Wijnants, Jan c.1635–1684
Landscape with Peasants and a Dog
oil on wood 20.6 x 27.3
NCM 1904-108

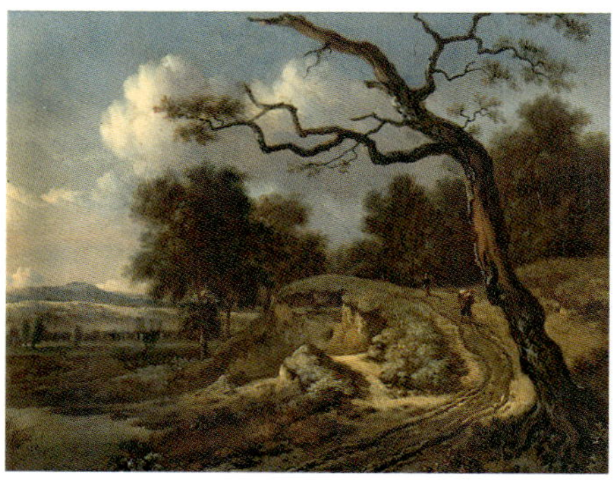

Wijnants, Jan c.1635–1684
Landscape with Peasants on a Road
oil on wood 20.3 x 26
NCM 1904-107

Wilkie, David 1785–1841
The Soldier's Grave 1813
oil on wood 19.7 x 16.5
NCM 1904-83

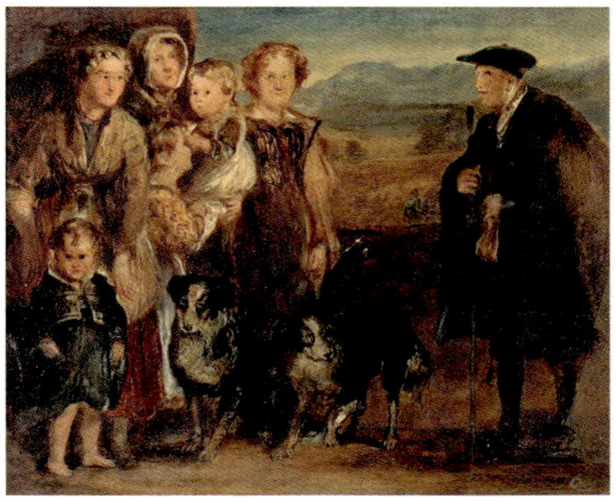

Wilkie, David 1785–1841
A Highland Family 1823
oil on wood 18.4 x 22.9
NCM 1904-84

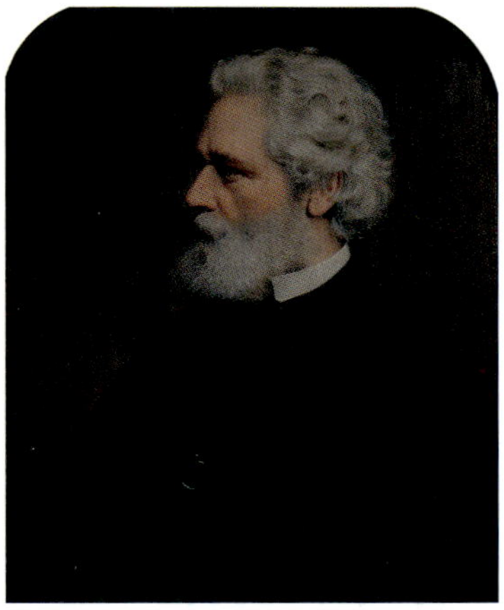

Williams, John Edgar c.1821–1891
Philip James Bailey (1816–1902) 1884
oil on canvas 76.2 x 63.5
NCM 1884-130

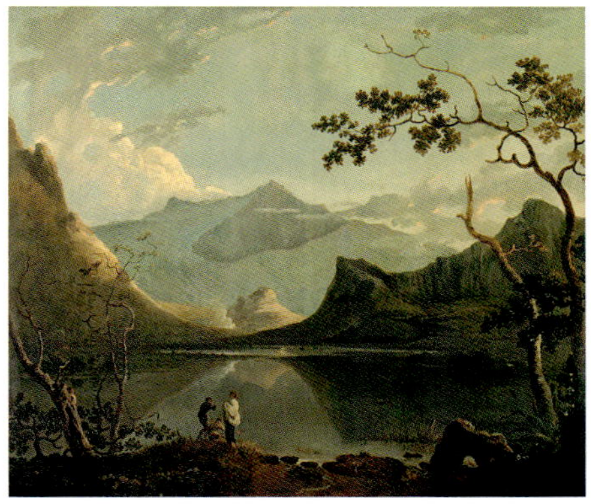

Wilson, Richard 1714–1787
Snowdon from Llyn Nantlle, North Wales
c.1765–1767
oil on canvas 104.1 x 127
NCM 1904-85

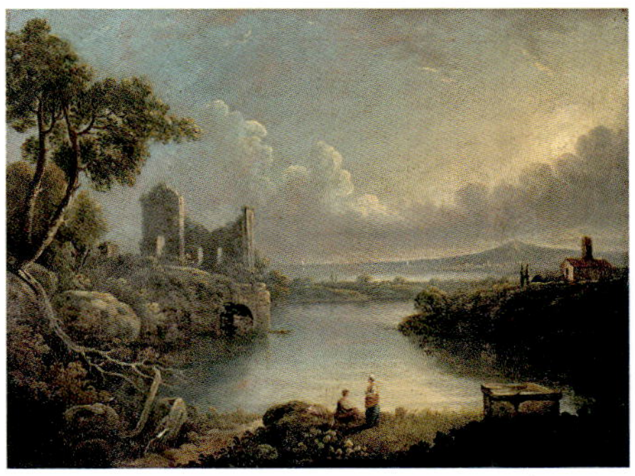

Wilson, Richard (after) 1714–1787
River Scene with Sea and Classical Ruins
oil on wood 50.8 x 68.6
NCM 1890-1182

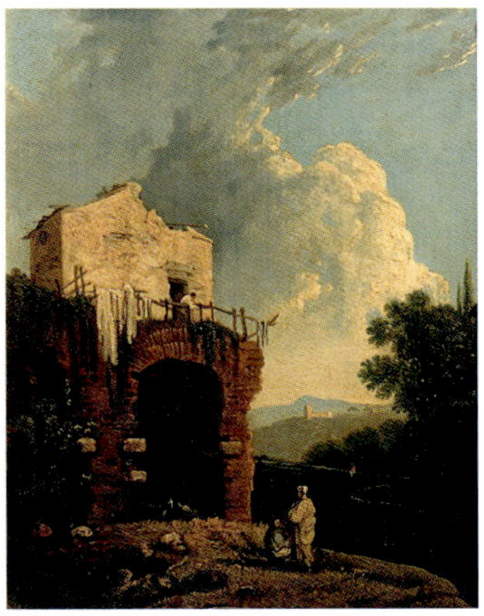

Wilson, Richard (after) 1714–1787
Ruins of a Villa near Rome (Hadrian's Villa)
oil on canvas 45 x 30
NCM 1909-46

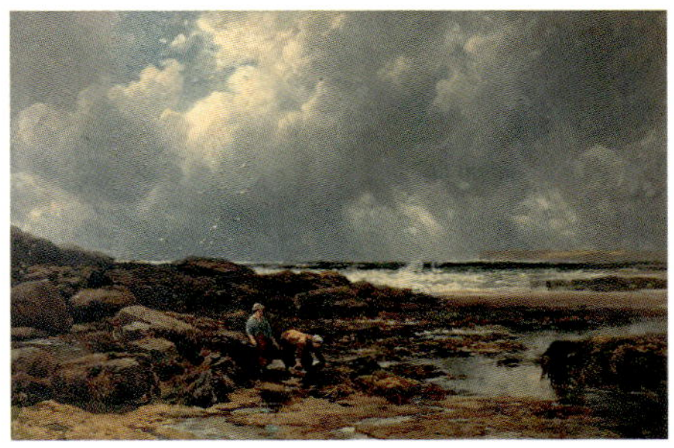

Wimperis, Edmund Morison 1835–1900
The Seaweed Gatherers
oil on canvas 50.8 x 76.2
NCM 1933-244

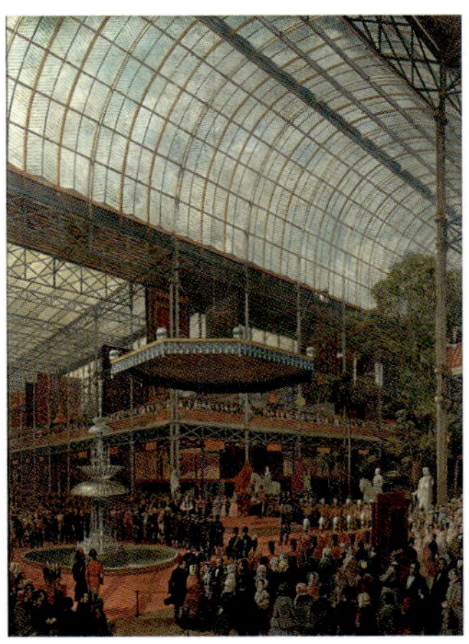

Wingfield, James Digman 1800–1872
The Opening Ceremony of the Great Exhibition, London 1851
oil on canvas 139.7 x 106.7
NCM 1882-90

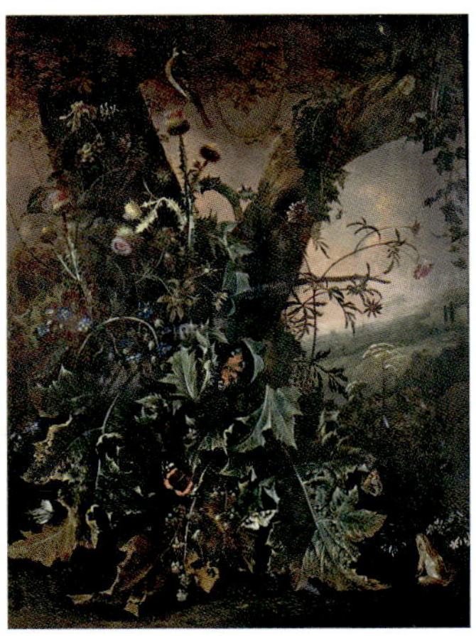

Withoos, Matthias 1627–1703
Still Life with Frog and Goldfinch (Thistles and Butterflies)
oil on canvas 85 x 67
NCM 1904-105

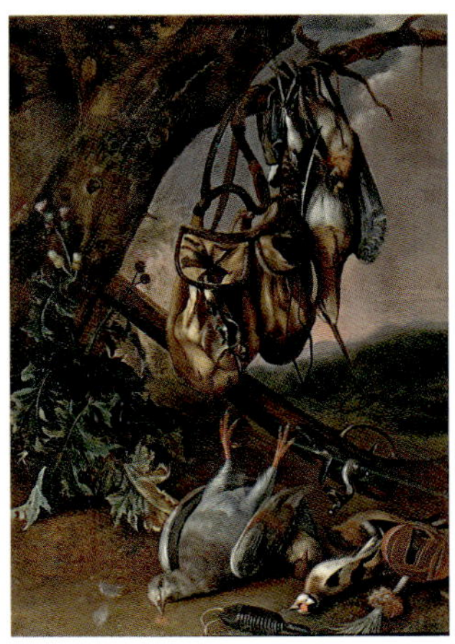

Withoos, Pieter 1654–1693
Still Life with Dead Game (Pigeon and Other Birds)
oil on canvas 78.1 x 54.6
NCM 1904-106

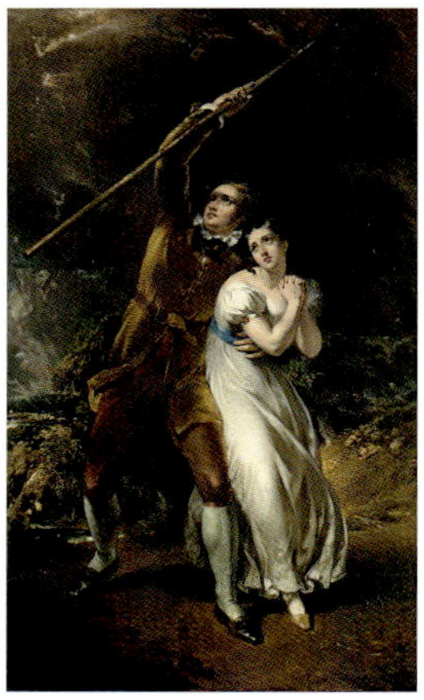

Wood, John 1801–1870
Celadon and Amelia in a Storm 1840–1849
oil on canvas 238.1 x 145.4
NCM 1887-267

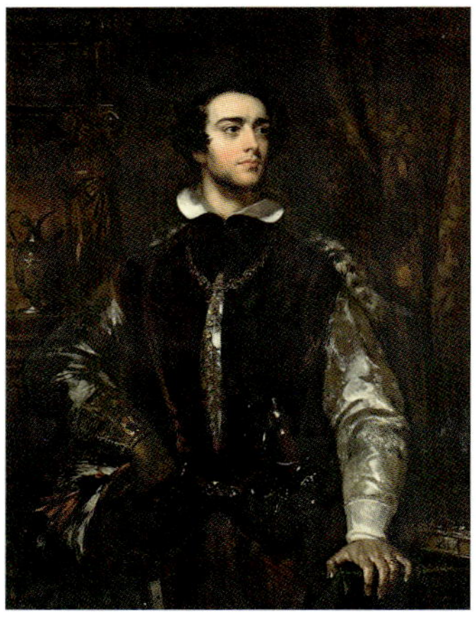

Wood, John 1801–1870
A Gentleman in an Elizabethan Costume c.1850
oil on canvas 127.6 x 102.2
NCM 1883-26

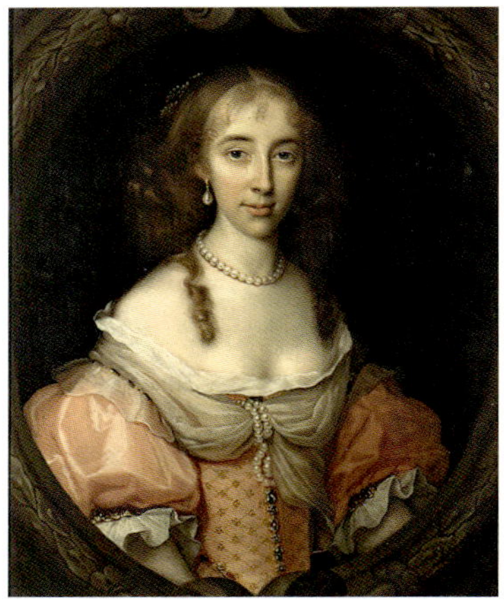

Wright, John Michael 1617–1694
Magdalen Aston, Lady Burdett 1669
oil on canvas 73.7 x 61
NCM 1957-18

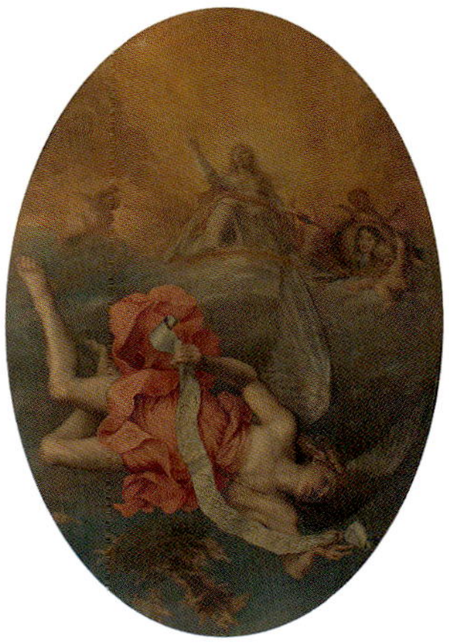

Wright, John Michael 1617–1694
Astraea Returns to Earth (The Apotheosis of Charles II)
oil on canvas 228.6 x 142.2
NCM 1953-13

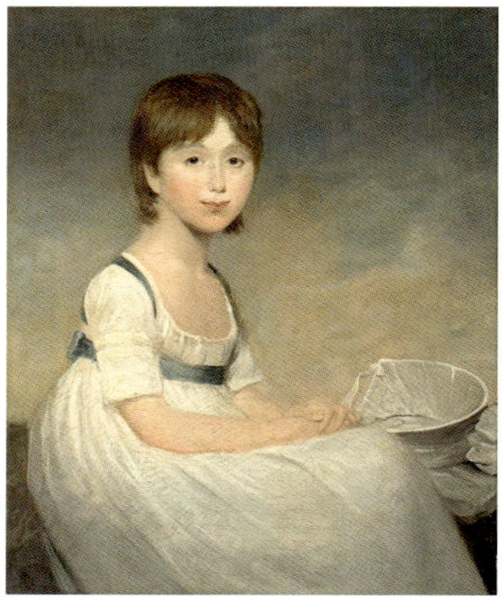

Wright, Joseph (style of) 1756–1793
Portrait of a Girl
oil on canvas 76.8 x 64.1
NCM 1890-1170

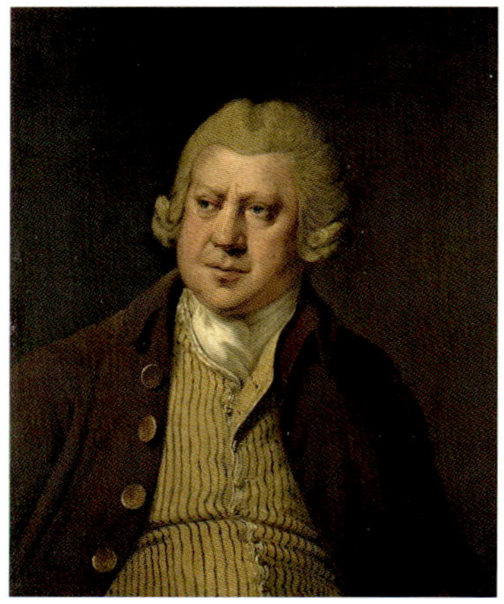

Wright, Joseph of Derby 1734–1797
Sir Richard Arkwright (1732–1792)
oil on canvas 76.2 x 63.5
NCM 1887-5

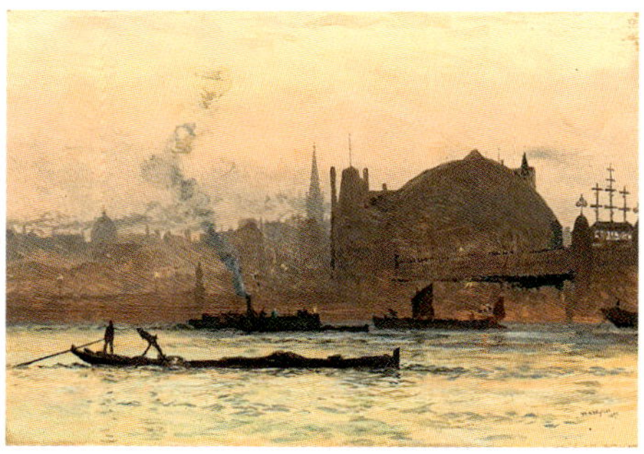

Wyllie, William Lionel 1851–1931
The Thames near Charing Cross, London 1892
oil on board 26.7 x 34.3
NCM 1946-127

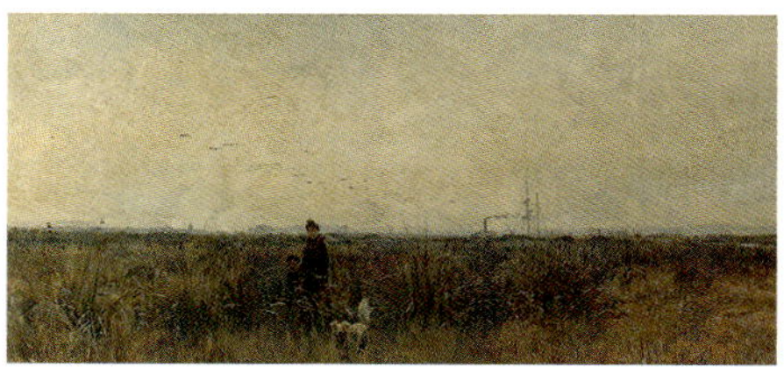

Wyllie, William Lionel 1851–1931
Romney Marsh
oil on canvas 20.3 x 41.3
NCM 1924-26

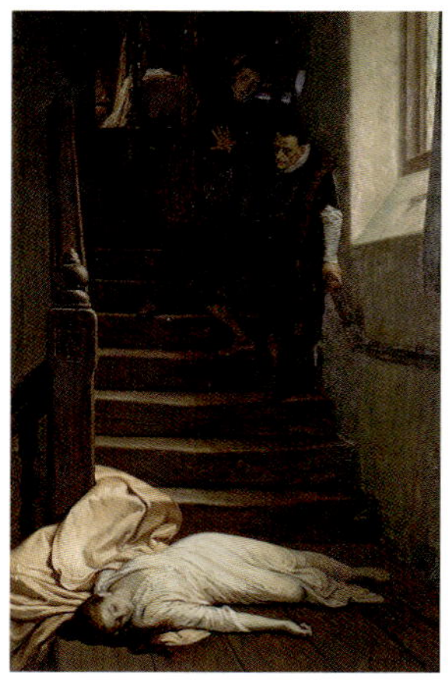

Yeames, William Frederick 1835–1918
The Death of Amy Robsart 1878
oil on canvas 87 x 61
NCM 1968-17

Facing page: Aitchison, Craigie Ronald John, b.1926, *Nude Standing in front of a Picture* (detail), 1963, Nottingham City Museums and Galleries (p. 57)

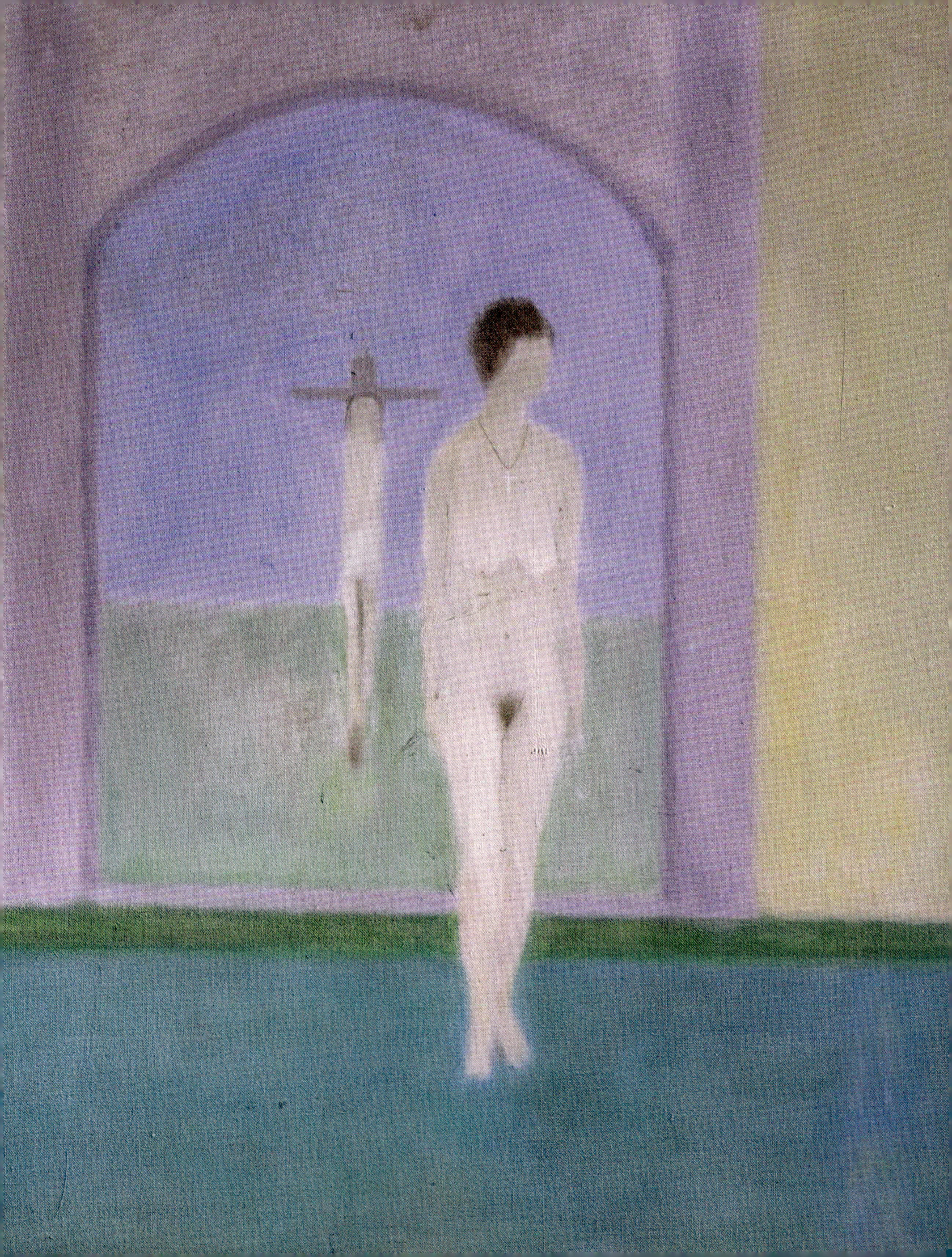

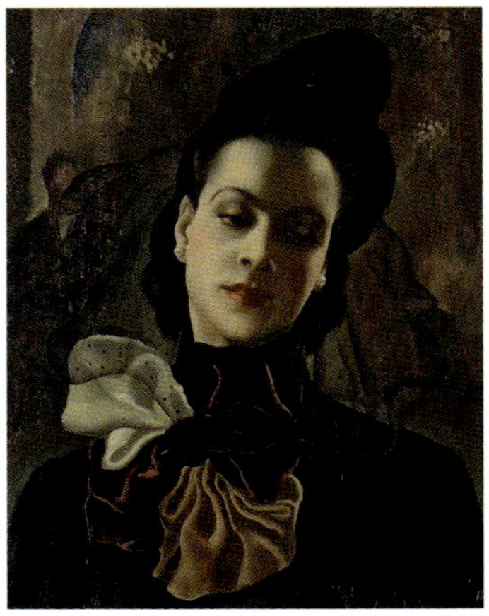

Zinkeisen, Anna Katrina 1901–1976
The Dark Lady 1938
oil on canvas 61 x 50.8
NCM 1938-147

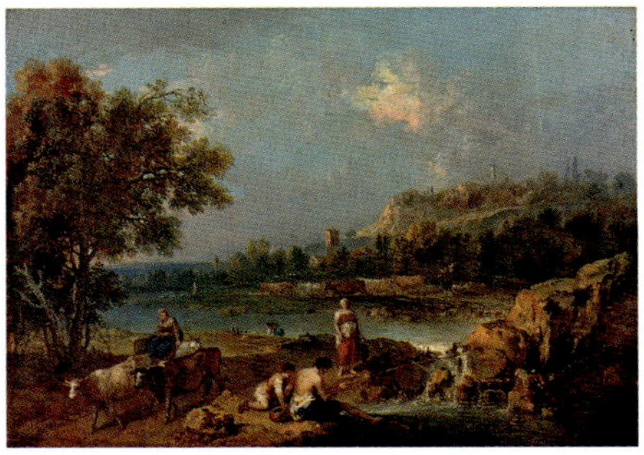

Zuccarelli, Franco 1702–1788
River Scene with Peasants
oil on wood 28.9 x 41.3
NCM 1904-86

Nottingham Magistrates' Court

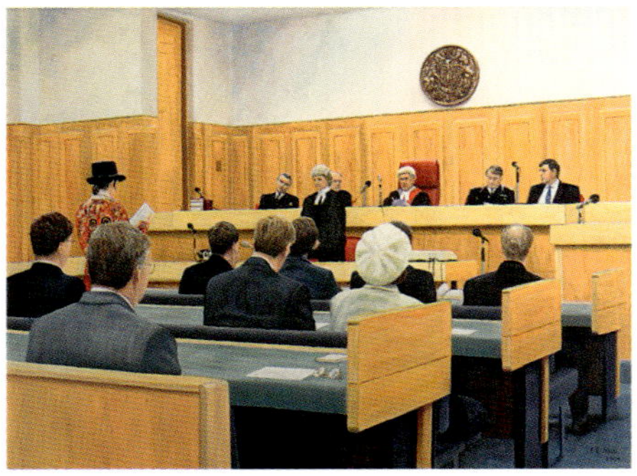

Mills, Edwin Robin
Swearing in of the New Justices (5 December 1991) 1994
oil on canvas 57 x 79.8
PCF1

Nottingham Trent University

Nottingham Trent University has a long history of collecting art and artefacts going back to the 1840s and the establishment of the Nottingham School of Design. This School of Design became one of the founding constituents of Nottingham Trent University. From the era of the Nottingham School of Design, the University holds a collection which includes student studies in anatomy, drawing exercises in ornament and an extensive lace archive.

More recently, but specifically throughout the 1990s, the University has purchased a considerable collection of paintings and works on paper from alumni, current students and members of staff of the School of Art and Design. These works are on public display across the University's estate in teaching rooms, libraries, public areas and individual offices. The purchases have all been made with University resources either by a purchasing fund held by the Vice-Chancellor or through funds allocated from time to time by the Dean of the School of Art and Design. The University has no specific purchasing policy beyond an ongoing commitment to buying works that represent the best of student endeavour. This ranges across all the art and design disciplines and is not specifically focused on the work of fine art students or lecturers. Thus, the School of Art and Design also holds examples of photography, decorative arts, fashion, knitwear and graphic design executed by students both past and present.

Professor Simon Lewis, Pro Vice-Chancellor & Head of School of Art and Design

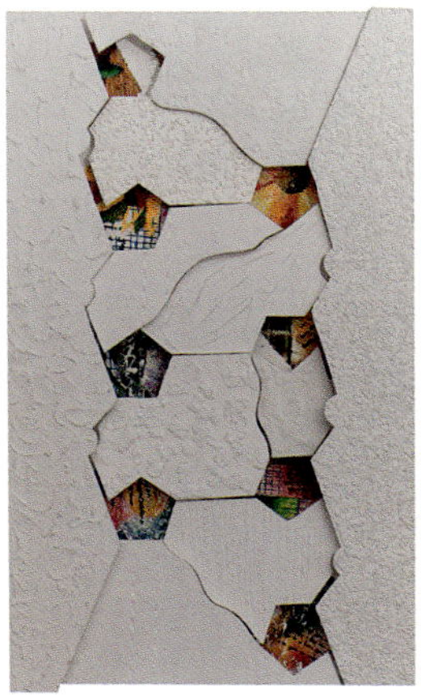

Beth, Tew
The Typical Family 2002
acrylic & mixed media (gravel, plaster & dried peas) on wood 152 x 91
BMC:144

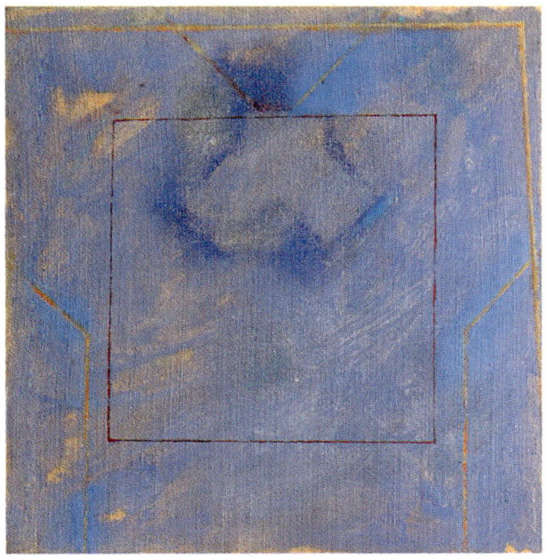

Dyer, Peter
Untitled (I)
acrylic on canvas 35 x 35
BL:131a

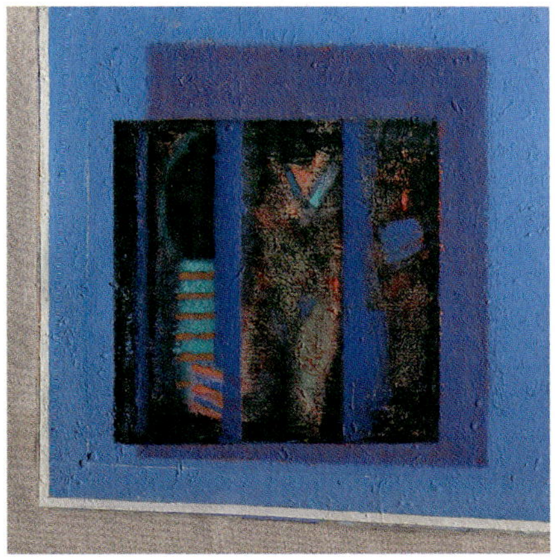

Dyer, Peter
Untitled (II)
acrylic on canvas 35 x 35
BL:131b

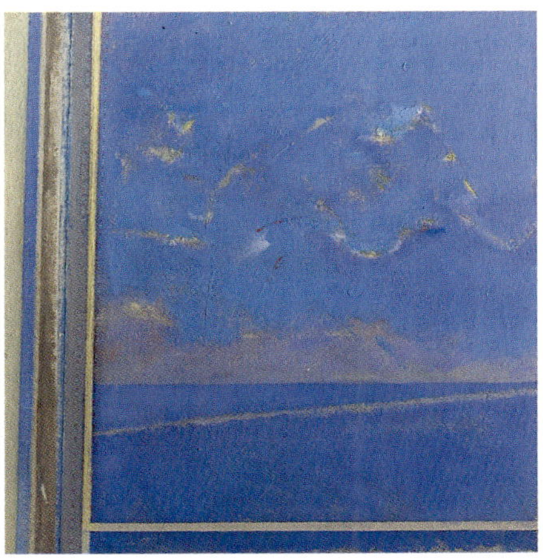

Dyer, Peter
Untitled (III)
acrylic on canvas 35 x 35
BL:131c

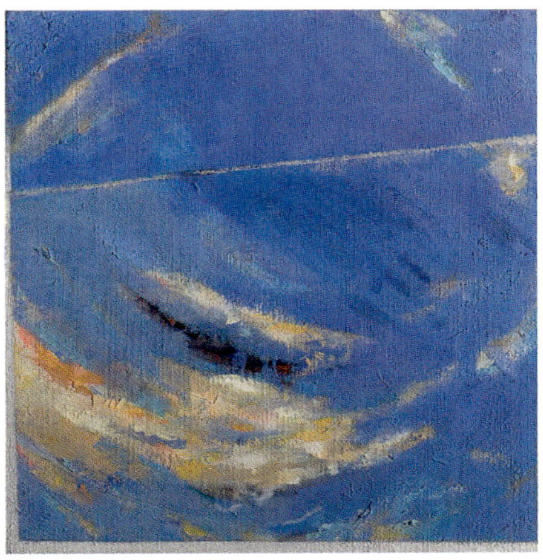

Dyer, Peter
Untitled (IV)
acrylic on canvas 35 x 35
BL:131d

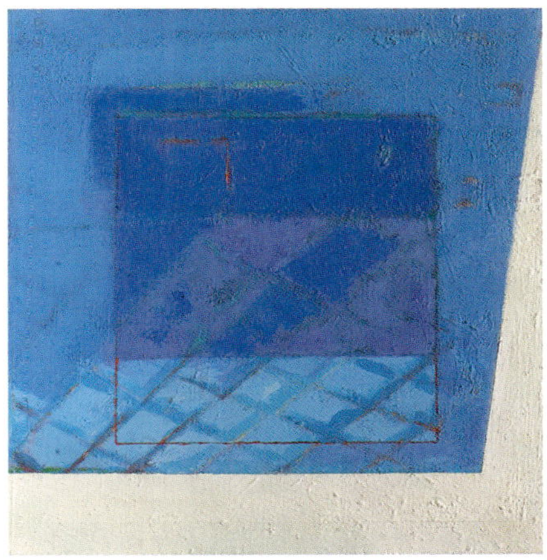

Dyer, Peter
Untitled (V)
acrylic on canvas 35 x 35
BL:131e

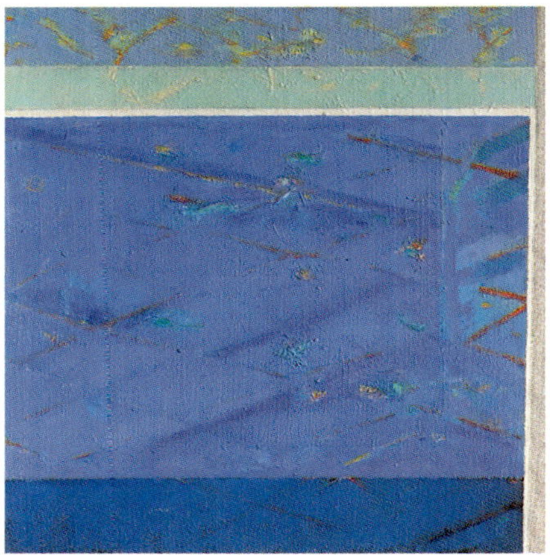

Dyer, Peter
Untitled (VI)
acrylic on canvas 35 x 35
BL:131f

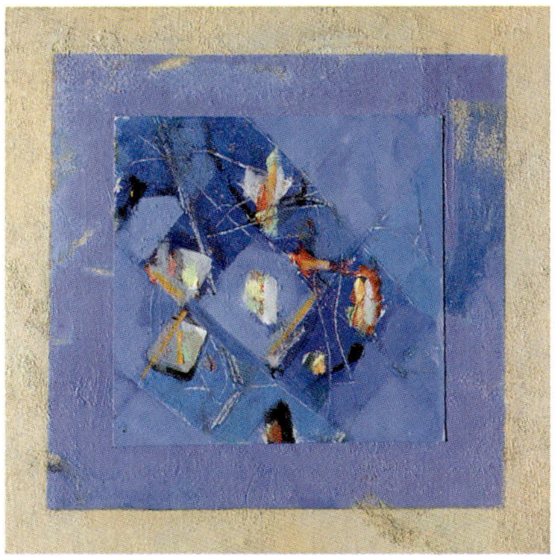

Dyer, Peter
Untitled (VII)
acrylic on canvas 35 x 35
BL:131g

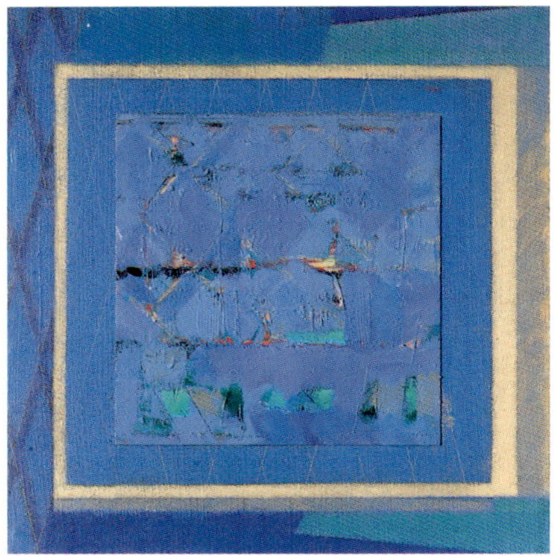

Dyer, Peter
Untitled (VIII)
acrylic on canvas 35 x 35
BL:131h

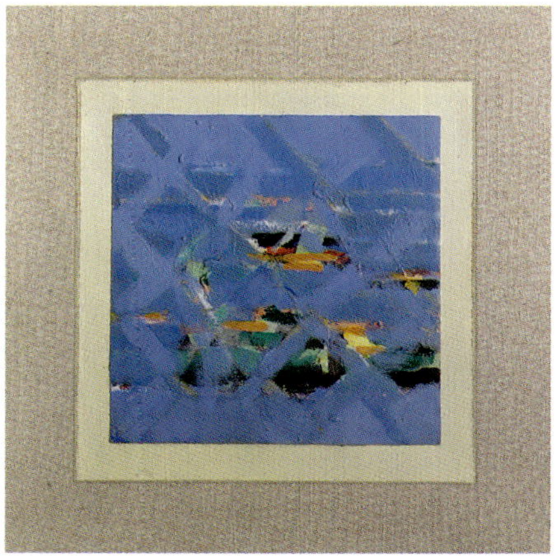

Dyer, Peter
Untitled (IX)
acrylic on canvas 35 x 35
BL:131i

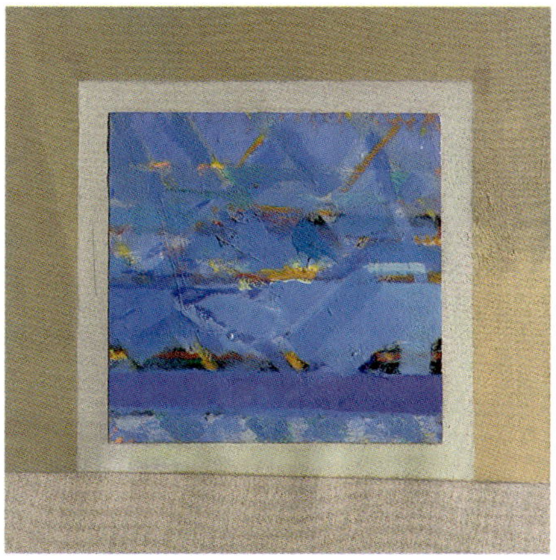

Dyer, Peter
Untitled (X)
acrylic on canvas 35 x 35
BL:131j

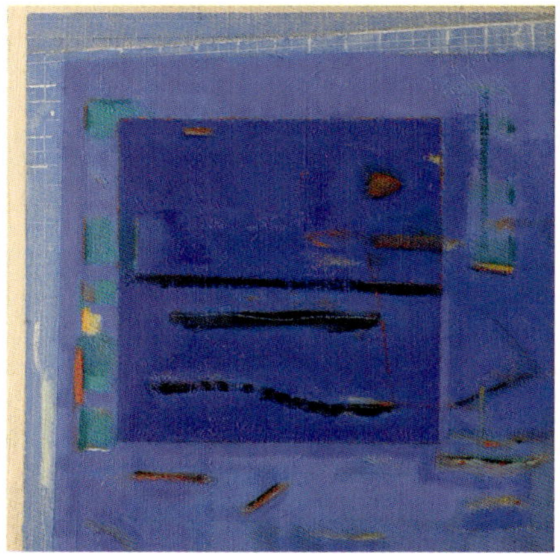

Dyer, Peter
Untitled (XI)
acrylic on canvas 35 x 35
BL:131k

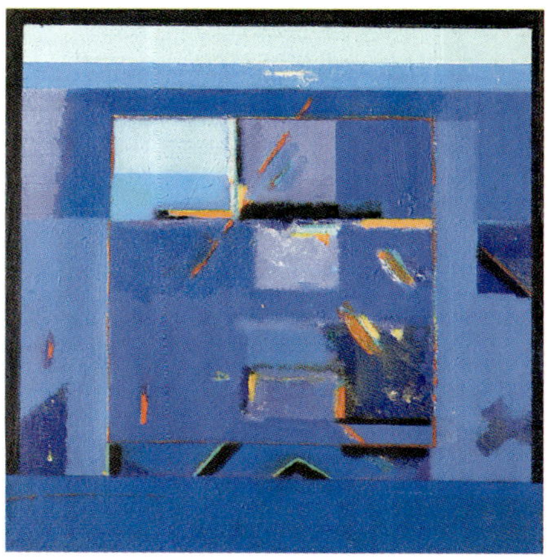

Dyer, Peter
Untitled (XII)
acrylic on canvas 35 x 35
BL:131l

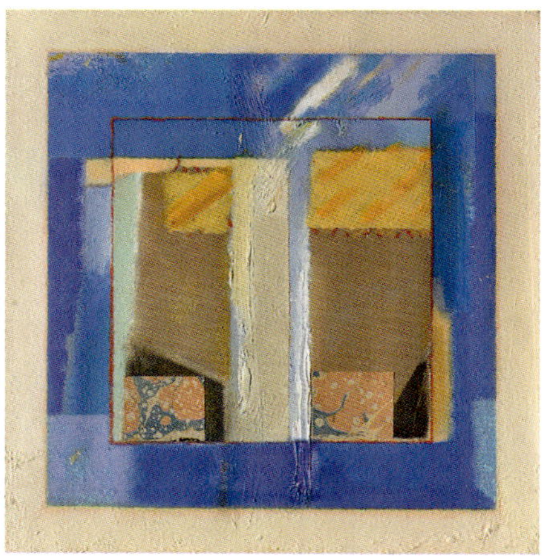

Dyer, Peter
Untitled (XIII)
acrylic on canvas 35 x 35
BL:131m

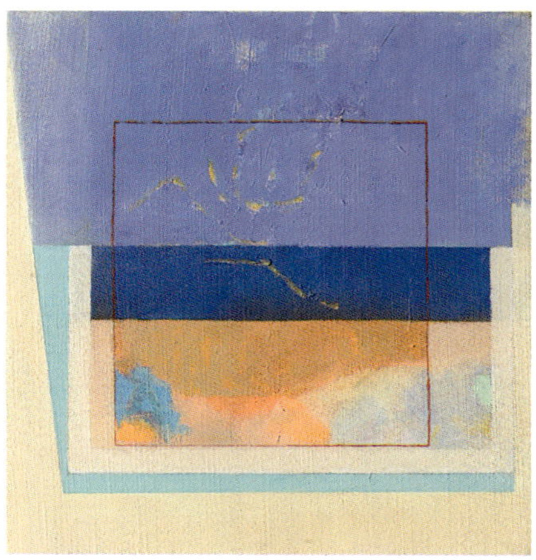

Dyer, Peter
Untitled (XIV)
acrylic on canvas 35 x 35
BL:131n

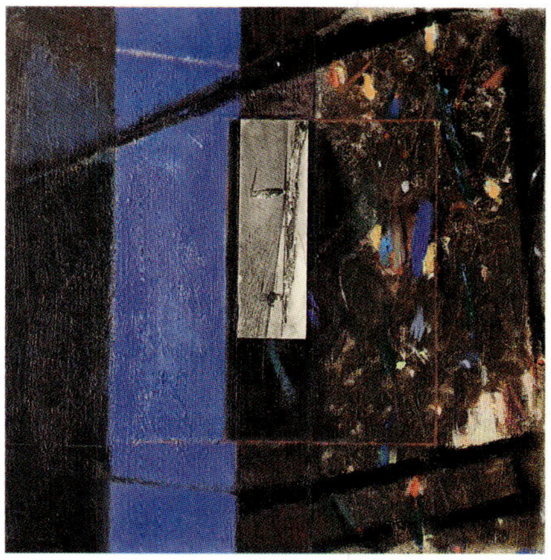

Dyer, Peter
Untitled (XV)
acrylic on canvas 35 x 35
BL:131o

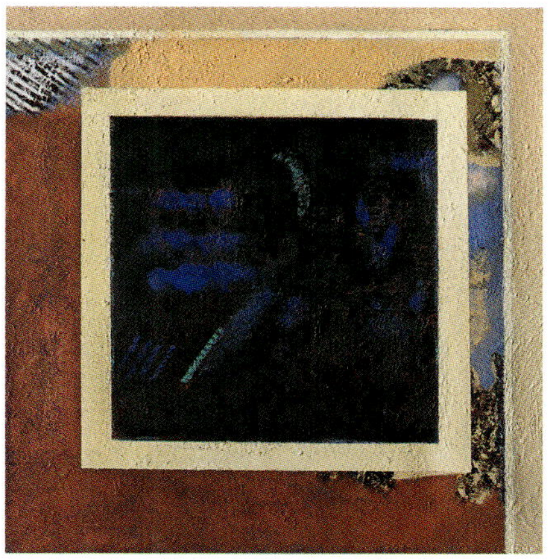

Dyer, Peter
Untitled (XVI)
acrylic on canvas 35 x 35
BL:131p

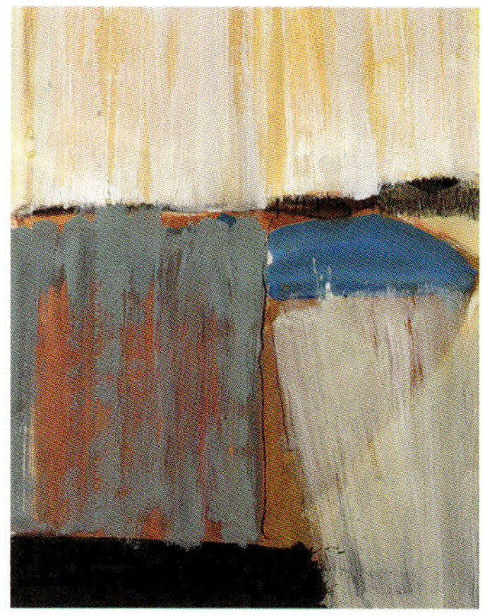

Earl, Sandra
Untitled 1995
oil on paper 75 x 54
BL:12

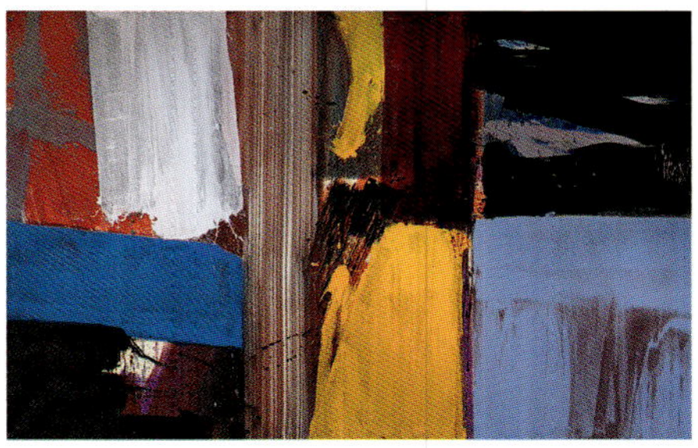

Earl, Sandra
Untitled 1995
oil on canvas 147 x 236.3
BR:73

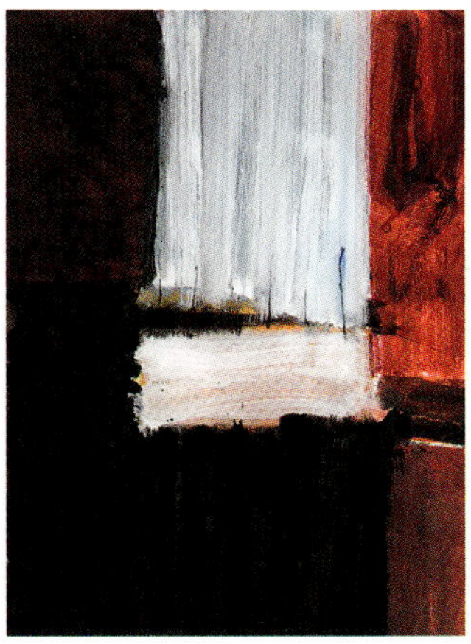

Earl, Sandra
Untitled 1995
oil on paper 75 x 54
DR:52

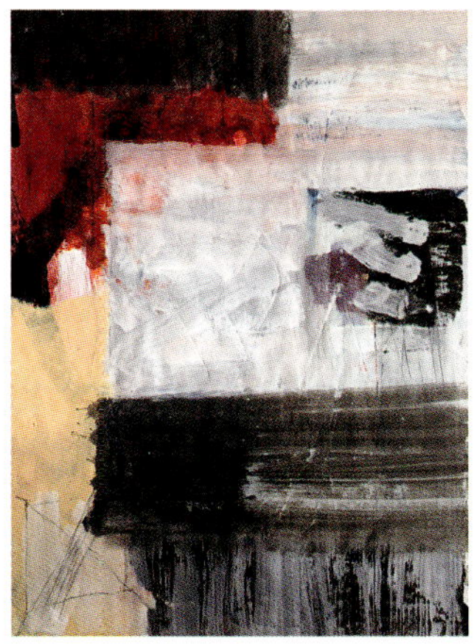

Earl, Sandra
Untitled 1995
oil on paper 75 x 54
DR:53

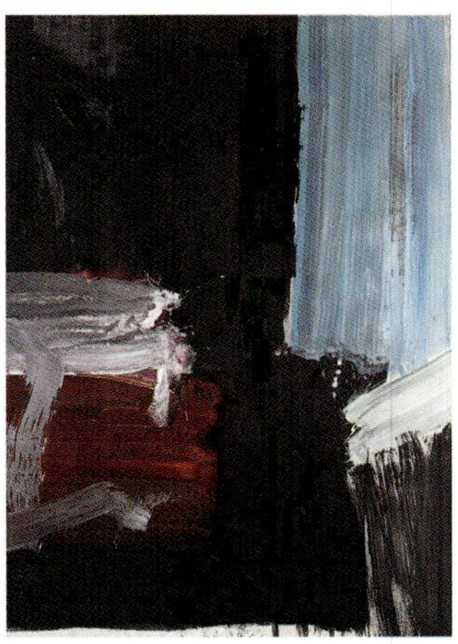

Earl, Sandra
Untitled 1995
oil on paper 75 x 54
DR:54

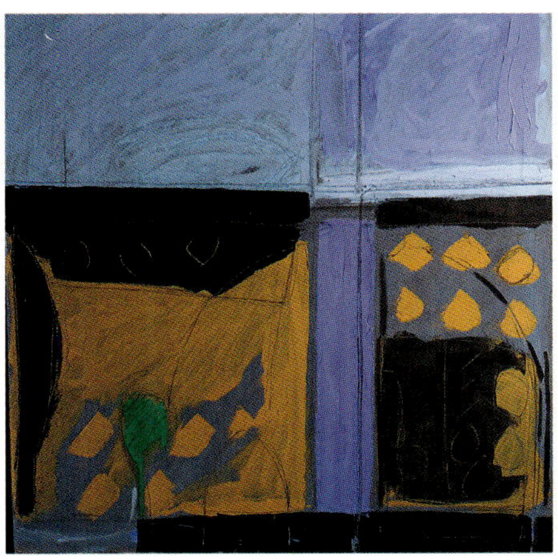

Feldman, Neil b.1947
Dunes Landscape with Window 1995
oil on canvas 71 x 71
BR:3

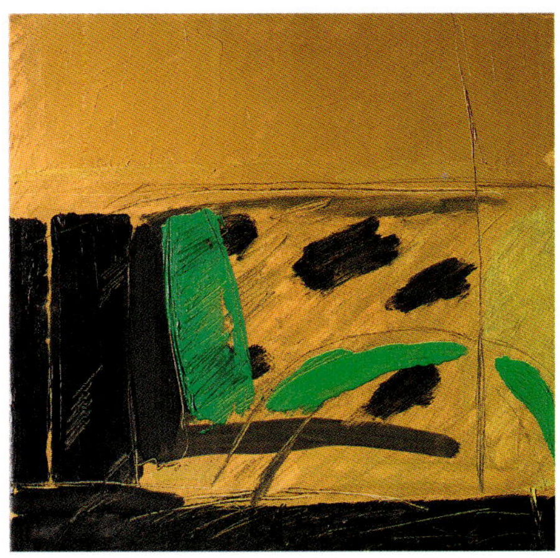

Feldman, Neil b.1947
The Hot Meadow No.2 1995
oil on canvas 38 x 38
BR:48

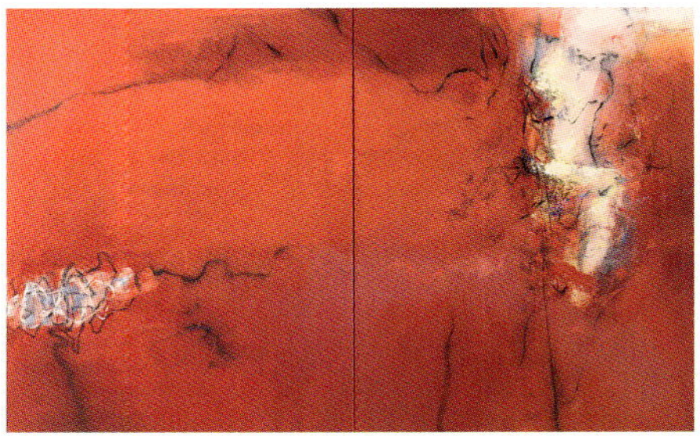

Hart, Robert b.1956
Untitled 1999
oil on canvas 152.5 x 244
BMC:89

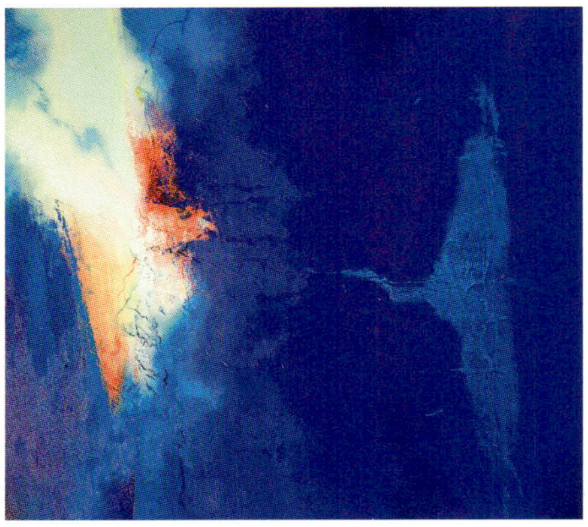

Hart, Robert b.1956
Whereness 1999
oil on canvas 199 x 238
BMC:143

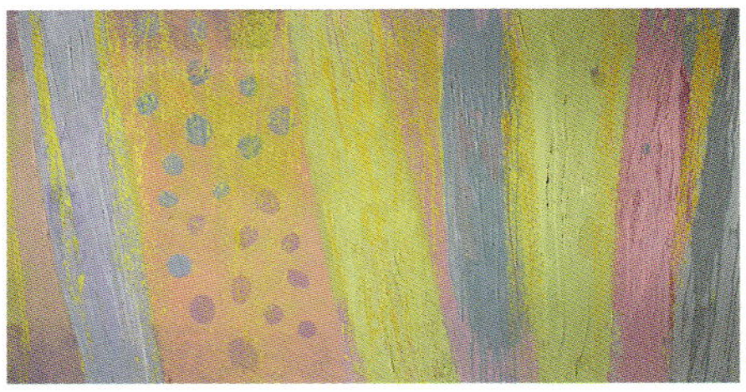

Hawthorne, Carole Diane b.1945
Stretch 1993–1994
oil on canvas 102 x 198
DR:2

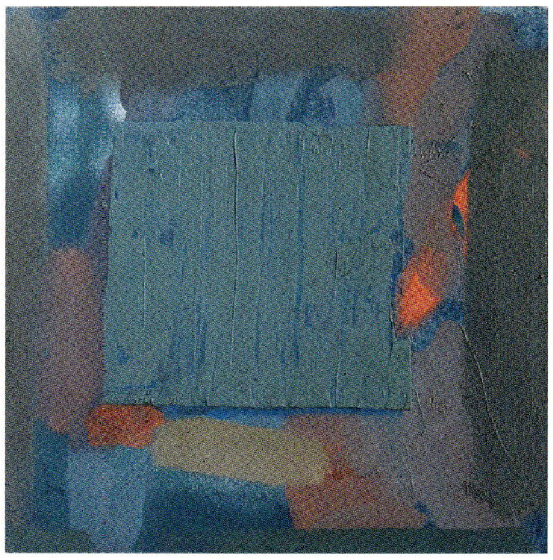

Hawthorne, Carole Diane b.1945
Square Suspended I 1995
oil on canvas 35.5 x 35.5
DR:70

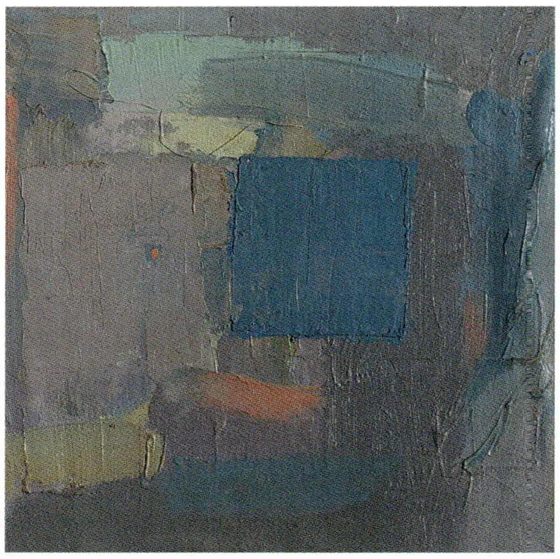

Hawthorne, Carole Diane b.1945
Square Suspended II 1995
oil on canvas 35.5 x 35.5
DR:71

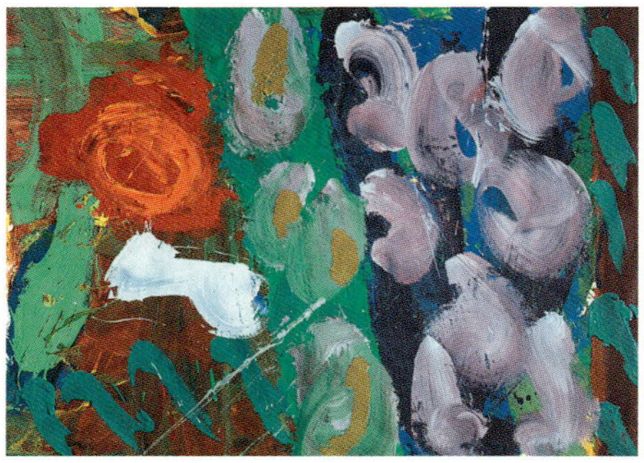

Hemsley, Antony b.1965
Lilac Time 1989
oil on paper 61 x 84
DR:1

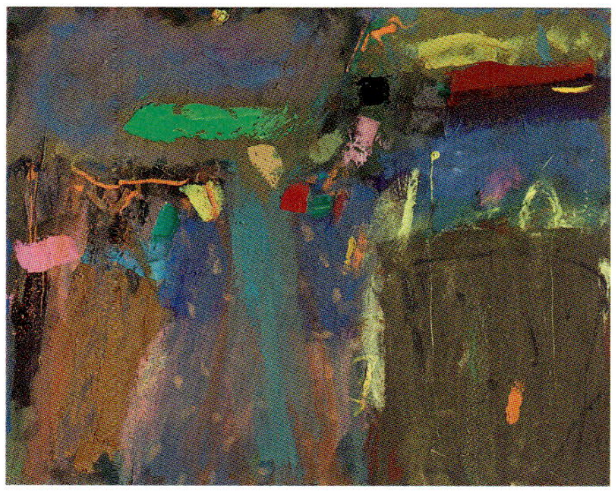

Hemsley, Antony b.1965
Steady Climb 1994
oil on canvas 101.5 x 129.5
BL:58

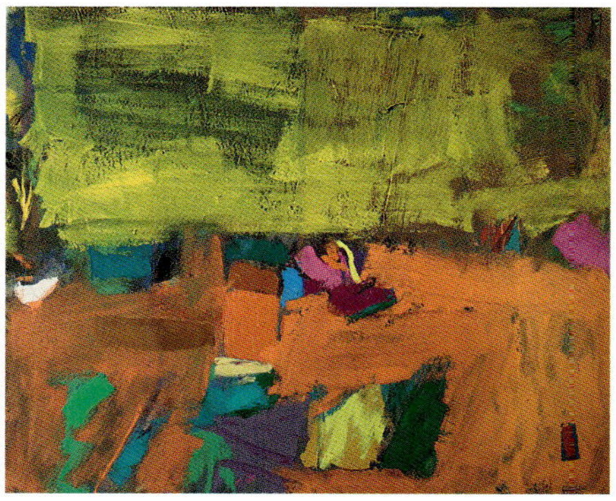

Hemsley, Antony b.1965
Winter Moor 1994
oil on canvas 126 x 160
BR:59

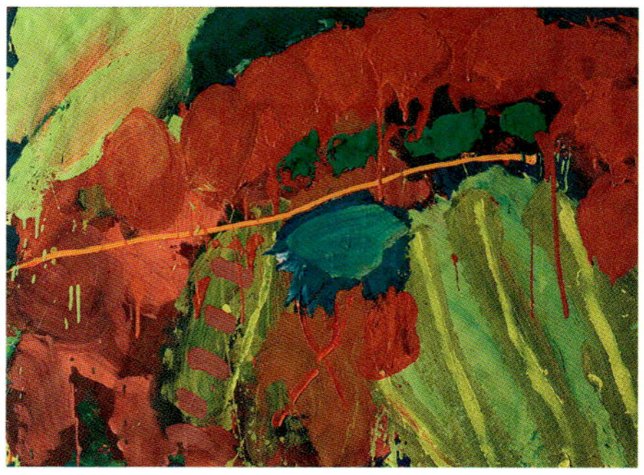

Hemsley, Antony b.1965
Rose Bowl
oil on paper 61 x 84
DR:60

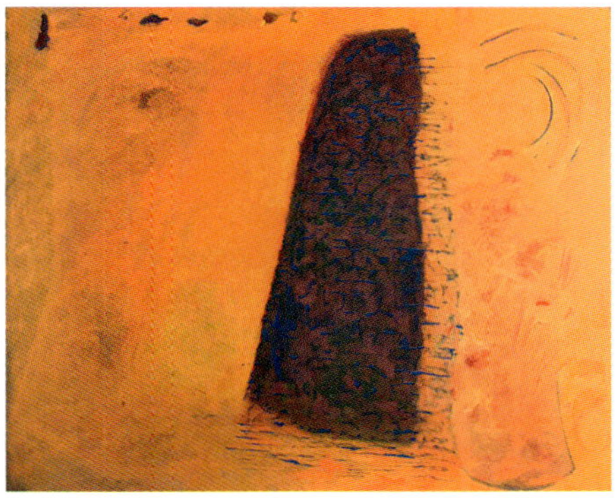

Lewis, Simon b.1945
Yellow Drift 1991
oil on canvas 185 x 246 (E)
BO:146 (P)

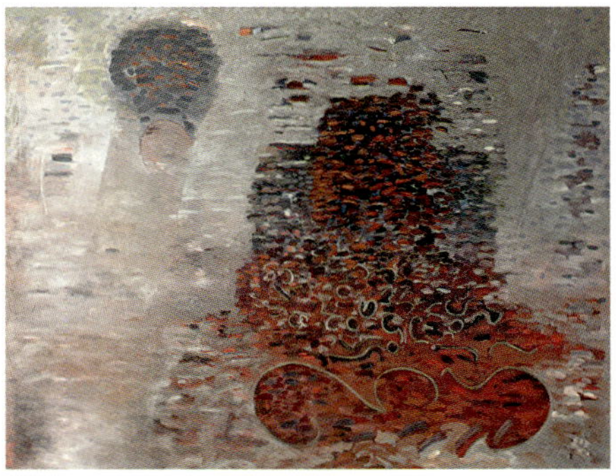

Lewis, Simon b.1945
Red Czar 1995
oil on canvas 185 x 246 (E)
BO:132 (P)

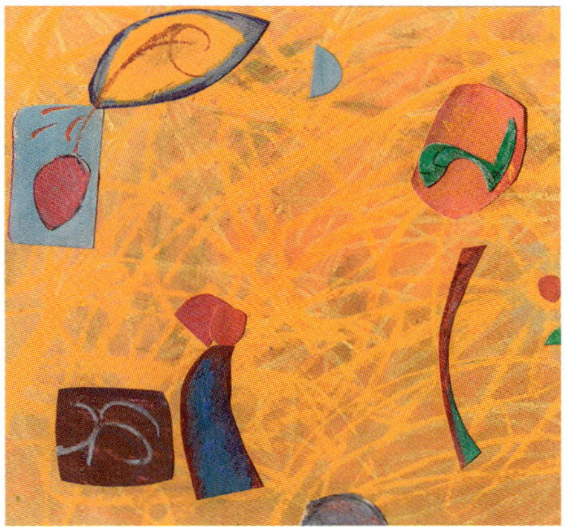

Liebert, Judith
Gather Juggling 1995
oil & mixed media collage on paper 33 x 36
DR:4

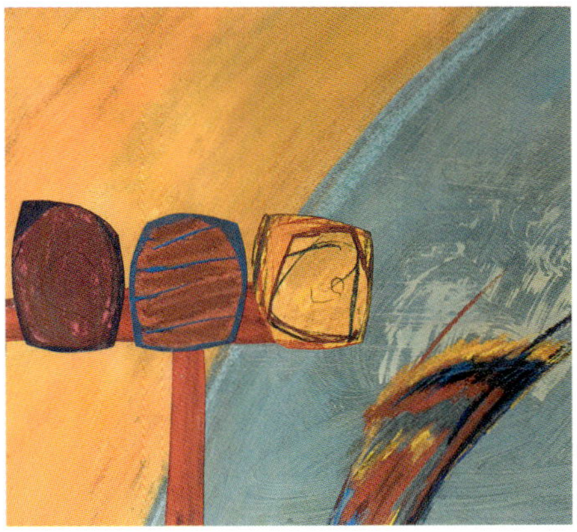

Liebert, Judith
Juggle 1 1995
oil & mixed media collage on paper 33 x 36
DR:7

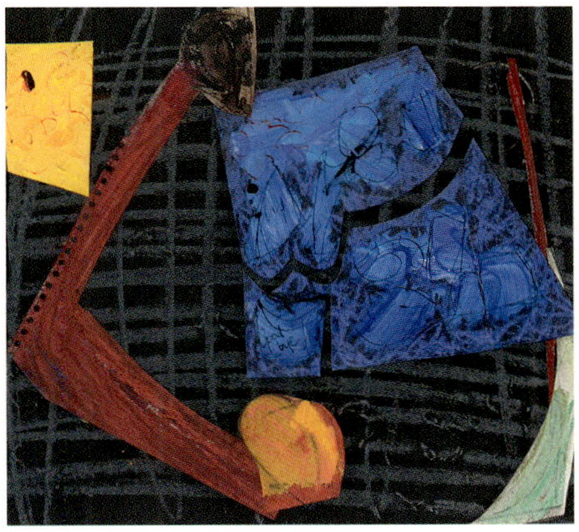

Liebert, Judith
Juggle 2 1995
oil & mixed media collage on paper 33 x 36
DR:8

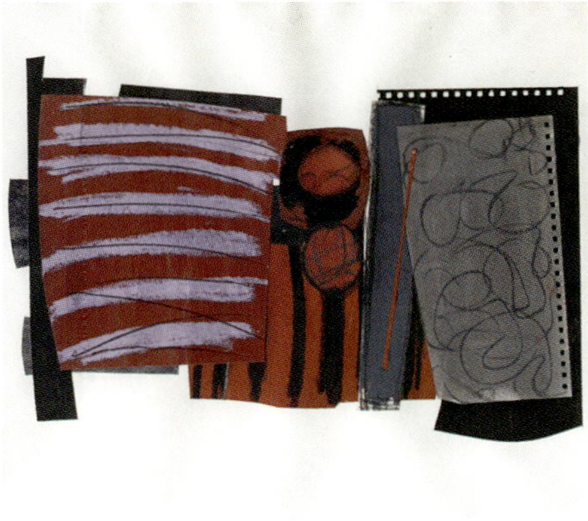

Liebert, Judith
Trio (1 of 3)
acrylic & pastel collage on paper 38.5 x 44 (E)
DR:55

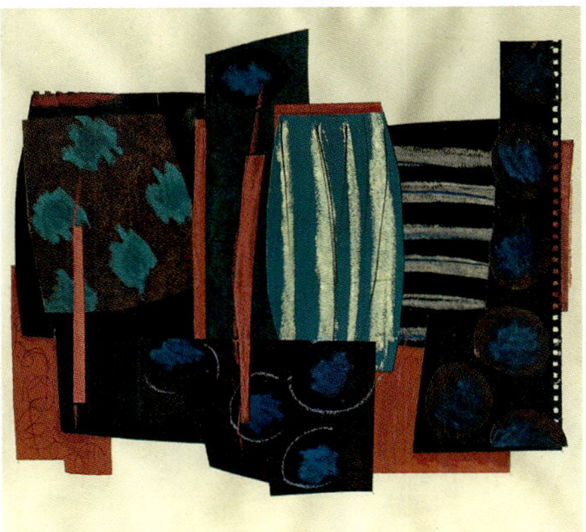

Liebert, Judith
Trio (2 of 3)
acrylic & pastel collage on paper 38.5 x 44 (E)
DR:56

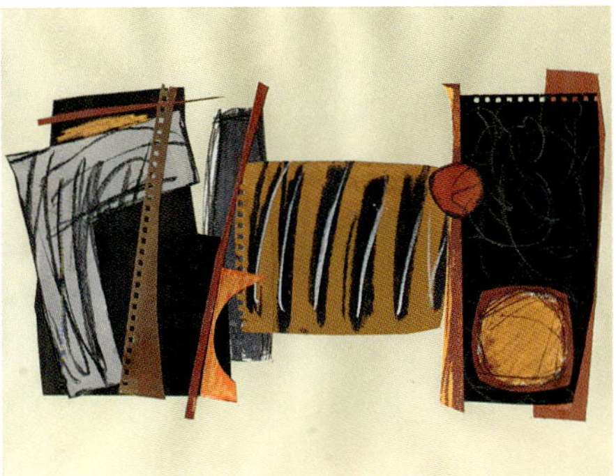

Liebert, Judith
Trio (3 of 3)
acrylic & pastel collage on paper 38.5 x 44 (E)
DR:57

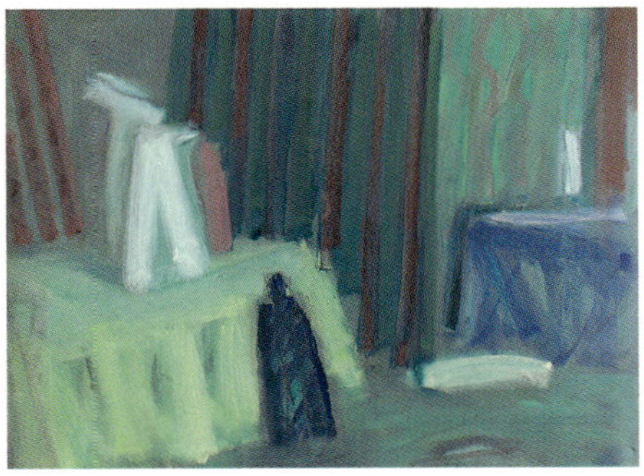

Martin, Ross active 1989–1990
Still Life 1989
oil on paper 61 x 86.2
DR:20

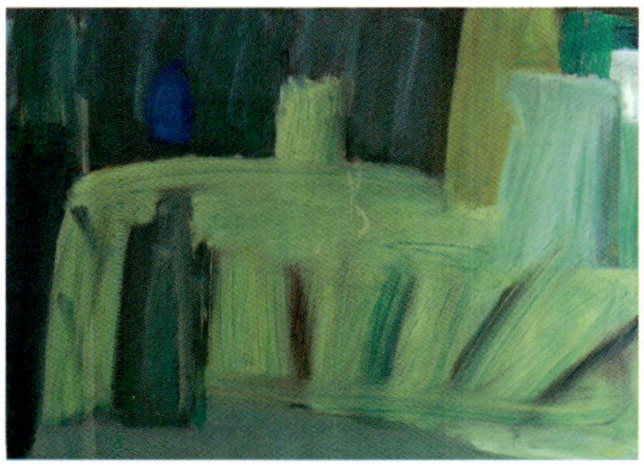

Martin, Ross active 1989–1990
Still Life 1990
oil on paper 61 x 86.2
DR:19

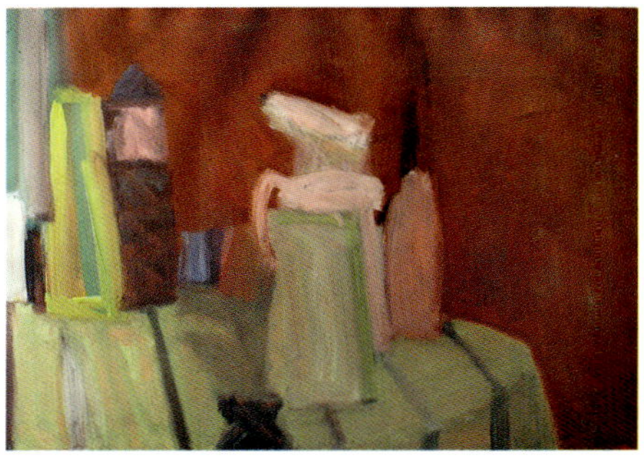

Martin, Ross active 1989–1990
Still Life 1990
oil on paper 61 x 86.2
DR:21

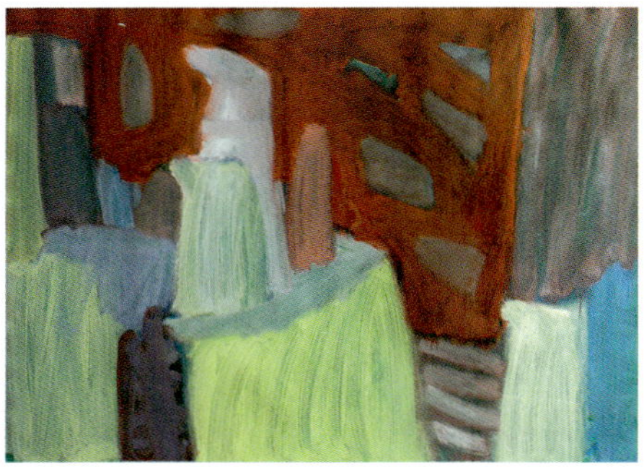

Martin, Ross active 1989–1990
Still Life 1990
oil on paper 61 x 86.2
DR:22

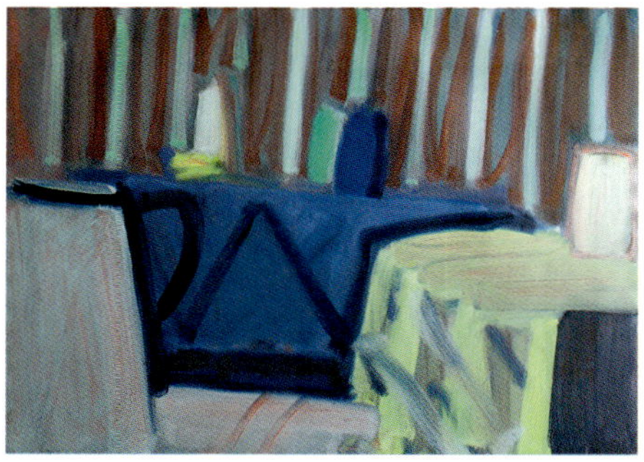

Martin, Ross active 1989–1990
Still Life 1990
oil on paper 61 x 86.2
DR:23

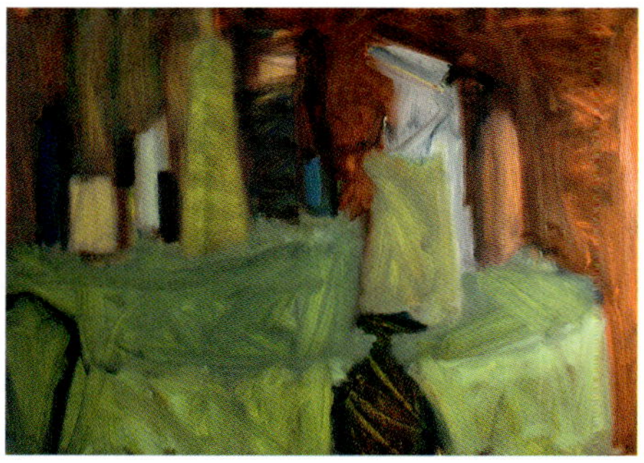

Martin, Ross active 1989–1990
Still Life 1990
oil on paper 61 x 86.2
DR:24

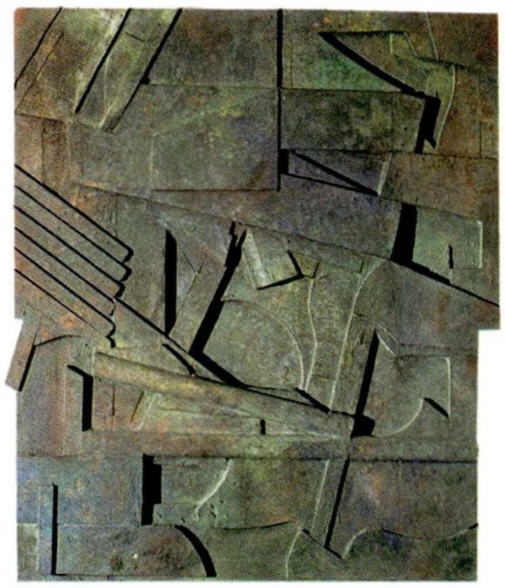

Matosic, Paul b.1955
Big Dipper 1994
powder paint & pigment on wet glue & emulsion mix on wood 104 x 89
BL:72

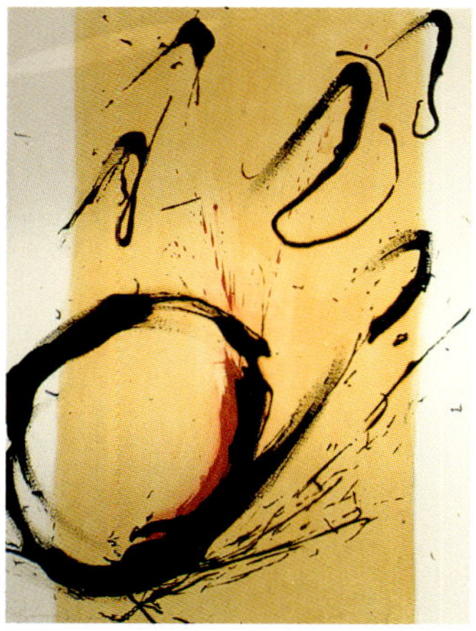

Rogan, Irene
Inspirit 1997
oil, liquid latex & varnish on canvas 137 x 114
BL:85

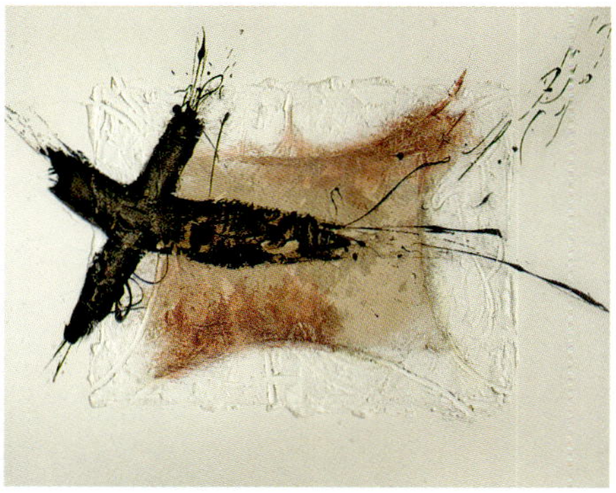

Rogan, Irene
Sum and Substance 1997
acrylic & plaster on canvas 122 x 152.5
BMC:93

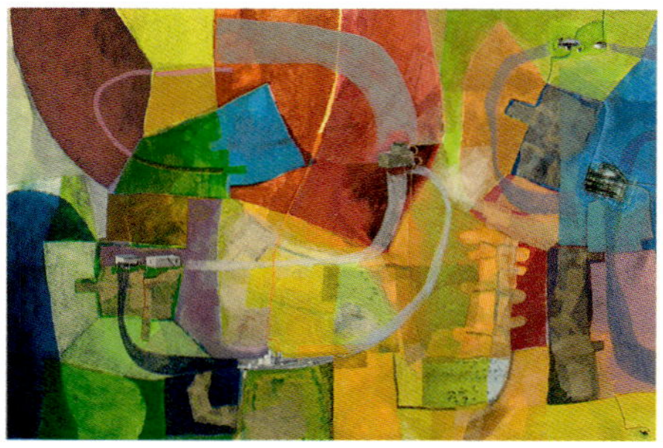

Russell, Alex b.1967
Isidore's Map (part 1) 1998
acrylic & tissue paper on board 81.2 x 122
BMC:90a

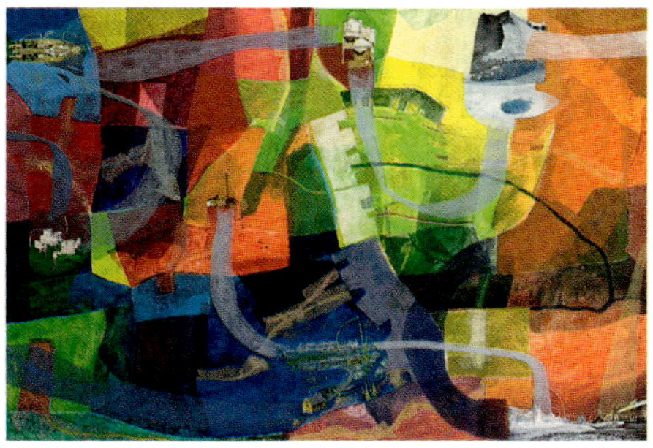

Russell, Alex b.1967
Isidore's Map (part 2) 1998
acrylic & tissue paper on board 81.2 x 122
BMC:90b

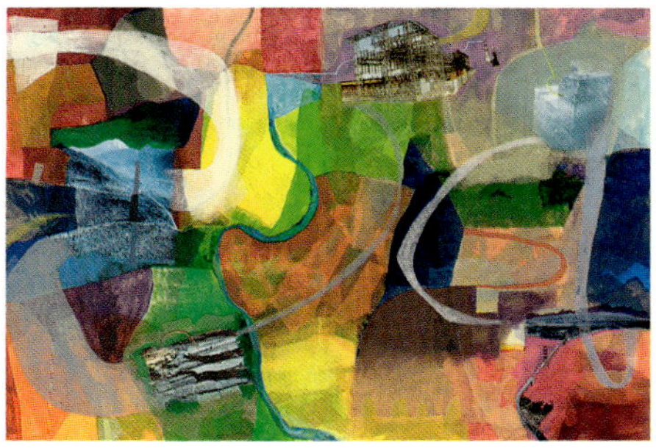

Russell, Alex b.1967
Isidore's Map (part 3) 1998
acrylic & tissue paper on board 81.3 x 122
BMC:90c

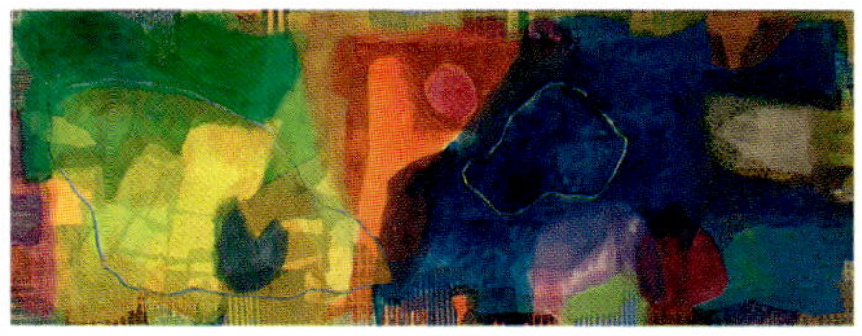

Russell, Alex b.1967
Currency 1 1999
acrylic & tissue paper on board 79 x 138
BL:84a

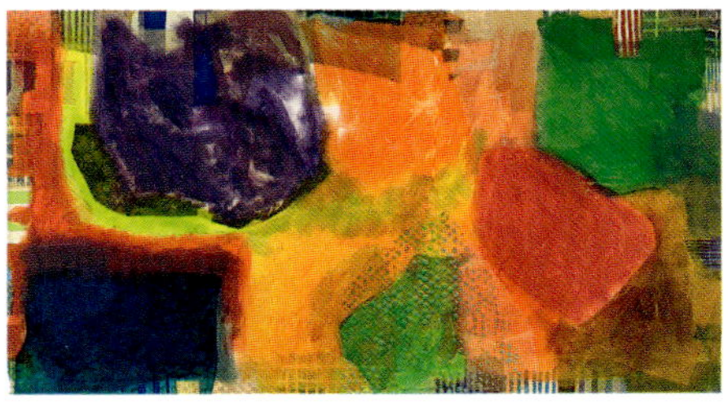

Russell, Alex b.1967
Currency 2 1999
acrylic & tissue paper on board 79 x 114
BL:84b

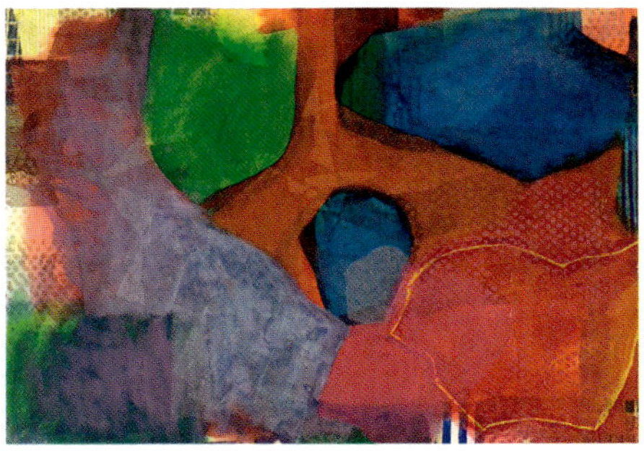

Russell, Alex b.1967
Currency 3 1999
acrylic & tissue paper on board 78 x 146
BL:84c

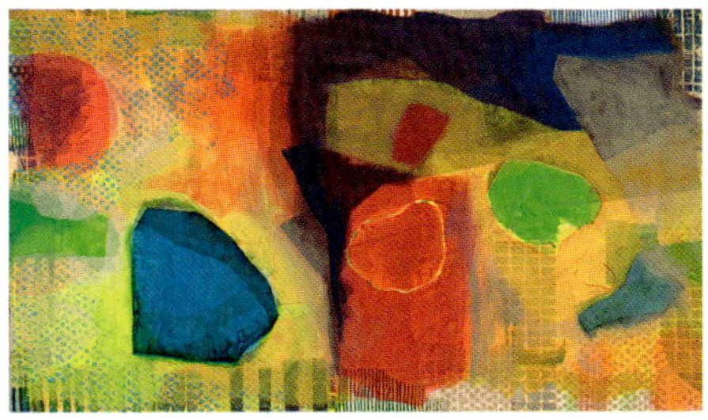

Russell, Alex b.1967
Currency 4 1999
acrylic & tissue paper on board 80 x 222
BL:84d

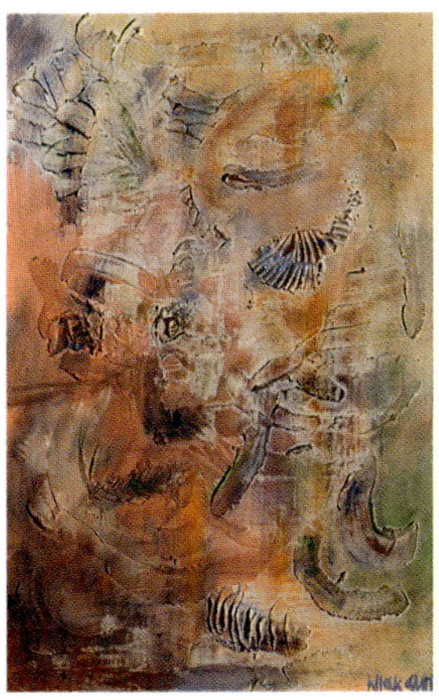

Smith, Mick
Life Begins at Faulty 2000
acrylic & plaster on MDF 90 x 60
BMC:145

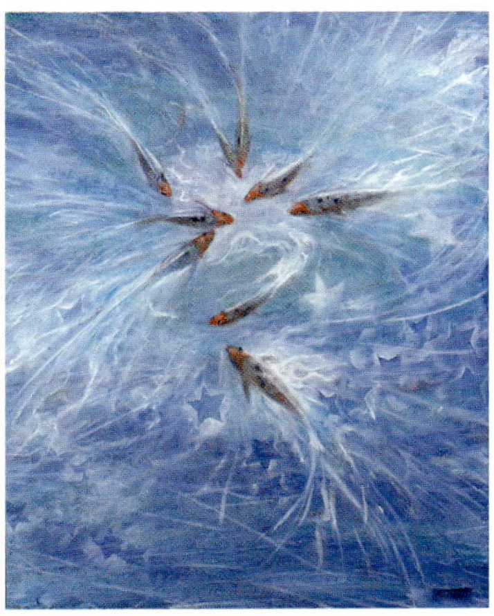

Stevenson, Wendy
Starfish 2000
acrylic, oil bars & finger technique on board 90 x 75
BMC:142

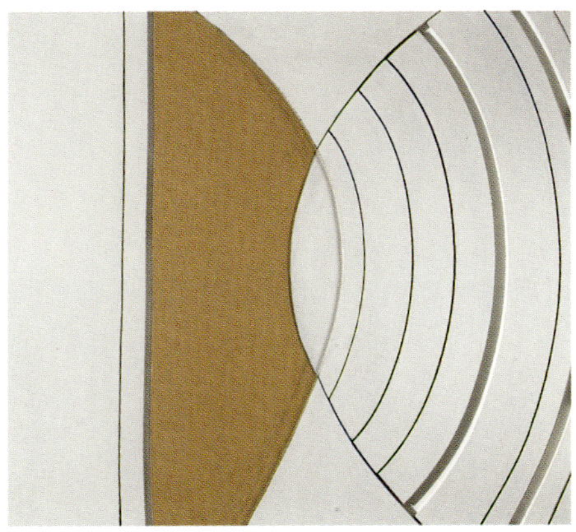

Stoddart, Rosalind b.1960
Fusion 1999
acrylic on wood 68.5 x 76
BMC:86

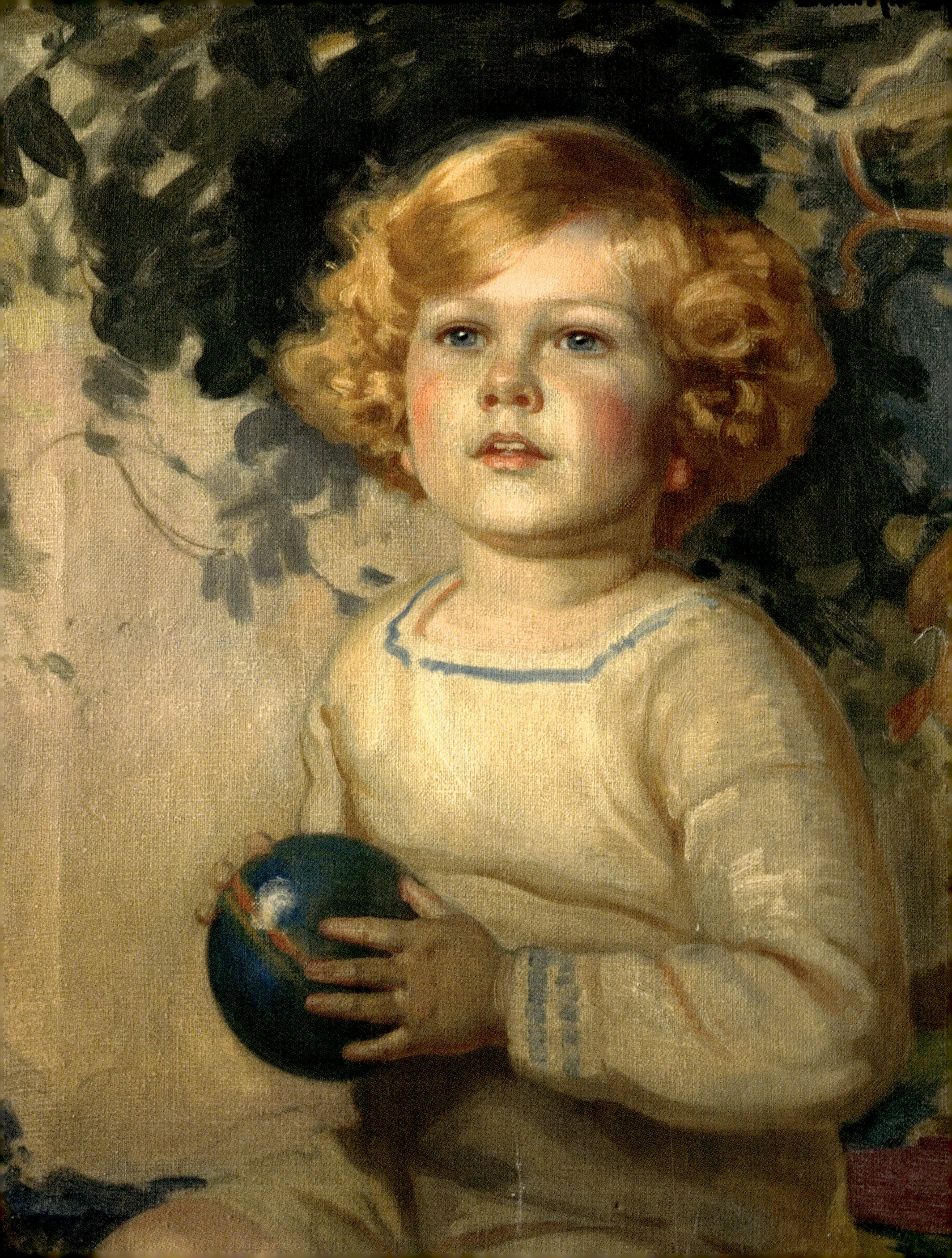

Nottinghamshire Archives

Nottinghamshire County Council set up a County Record Office in 1949 in the former Judges' Lodgings on High Pavement, Nottingham. This Georgian and Regency townhouse opposite Shire Hall (then known as County House), provided a suitable location for the display of many of the oil paintings now in the Archives Collection. They were transferred to the new Nottinghamshire Archives building on Castle Meadow Road when the service moved there in 1993.

The two main collections are of the Bristowe family of Beesthorpe and the Gilbert Cooper family. The Bristowe portraits form part of a bequest by Mrs M. H. Bristowe of Souldern House, Oxfordshire, in 1969 following the earlier deposit of her family records in 1961. The Gilbert Cooper portraits came from Nottingham City Library.

Paintings no longer form part of our acquisitions policy and are unfortunately not displayed in such appropriate surroundings as our former premises. We are therefore very pleased to be able to bring them to the attention of a wider audience through the Public Catalogue Foundation.

Mark Dorrington, Principal Archivist

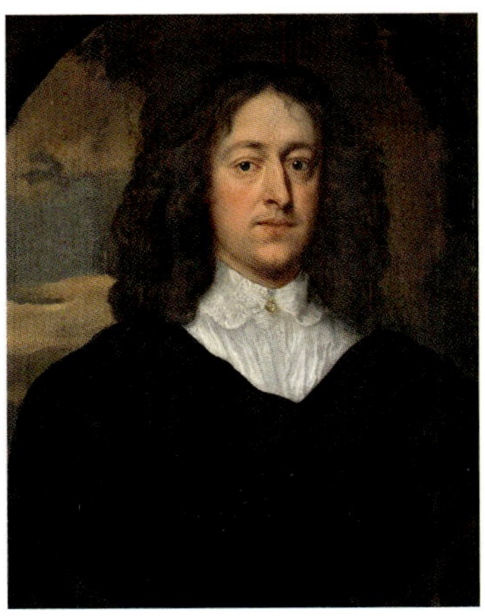

Dobson, William Charles Thomas (attributed to) 1817–1898
Thomas Bristowe of Beesthorpe and Elston (1620–1680), Clerk of the Peace (…)
oil on canvas 72 x 59.4
NA4

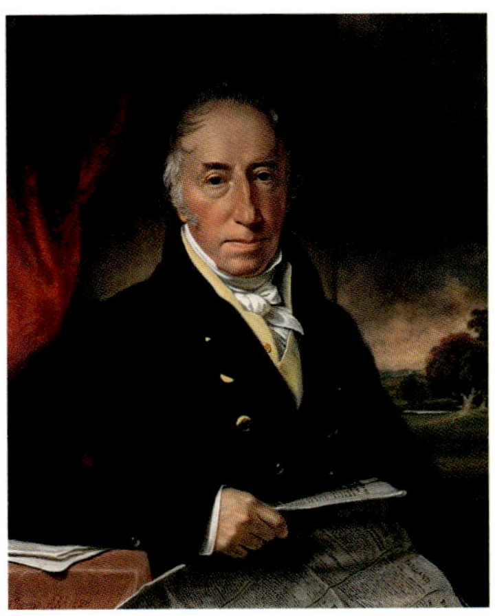

Joseph, George Francis 1764–1846
Unidentified Man from the Bristowe Family
1828
oil on canvas 74.3 x 62.3
NA40

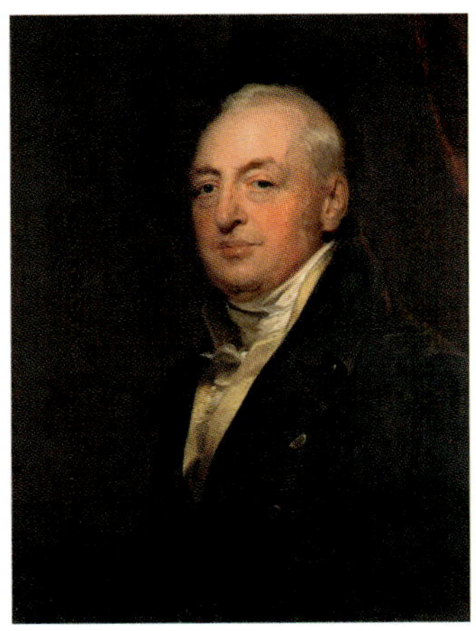

Lawrence, Thomas (attributed to)
1769–1830
John Gilbert Cooper (Gardiner) c.1820
oil on canvas 75 x 62.5
NA8

Facing page: Davis, Noel Denholm, 1876–1950, *The Honourable Henry Saville as a Child* (detail), Rushcliffe Borough Council (p. 186)

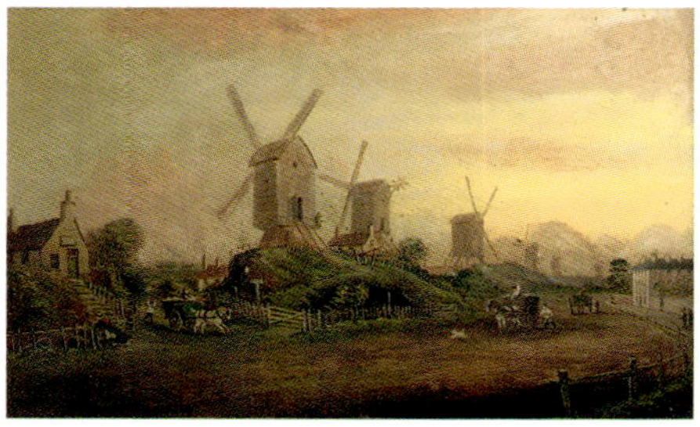

Moore, Thomas Cooper 1827–1901
Windmills on the Forest
oil on canvas 29.7 x 49
NA19

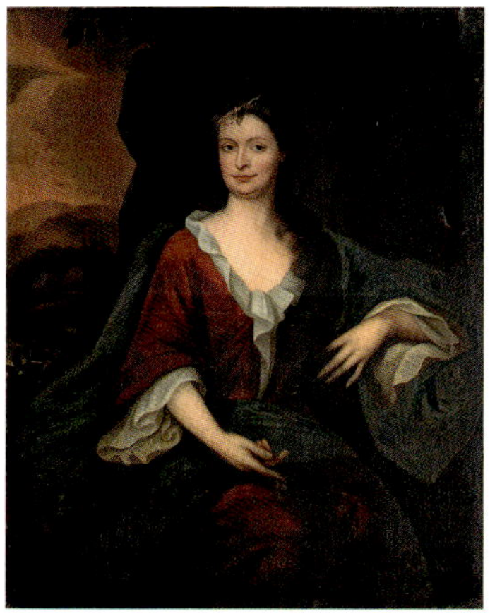

unknown artist
Anne Micclemore Cooper or Jane Beale Gilbert, Wife of Henry Gilbert c.1700
oil on canvas 125.8 x 99.6
NA9

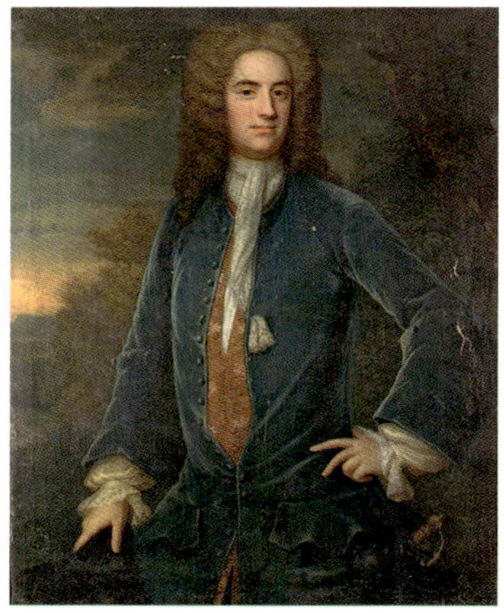

unknown artist
Cecil Cooper or Henry Gilbert c.1700
oil on canvas 123 x 98.4
NA10

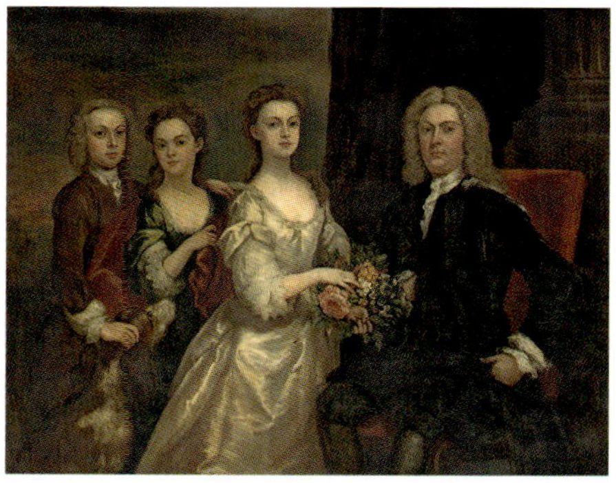

unknown artist
John Gilbert and His Children John, Elizabeth and Dorothy c.1730–1735
oil on canvas 139.5 x 180.6
NA11

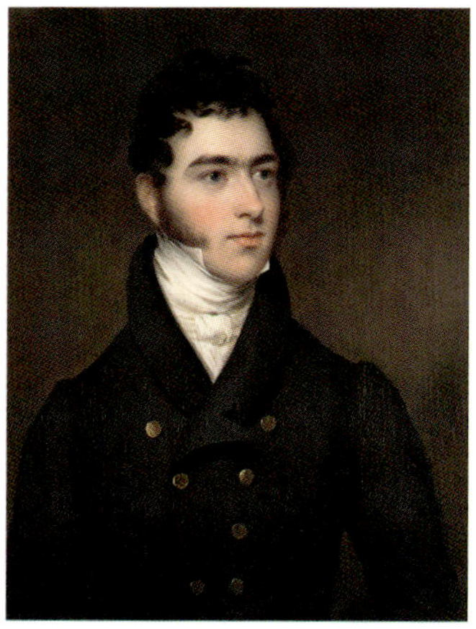

unknown artist early 19th C
Unidentified Regency Man from the Bristowe Family
oil on canvas 74.8 x 62.3
NA7

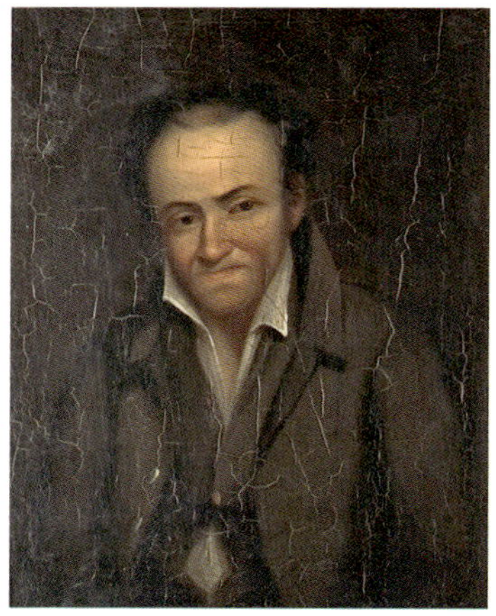

unknown artist
Benjamin Mayo 'Old General'
oil on canvas 32 x 26
NA17

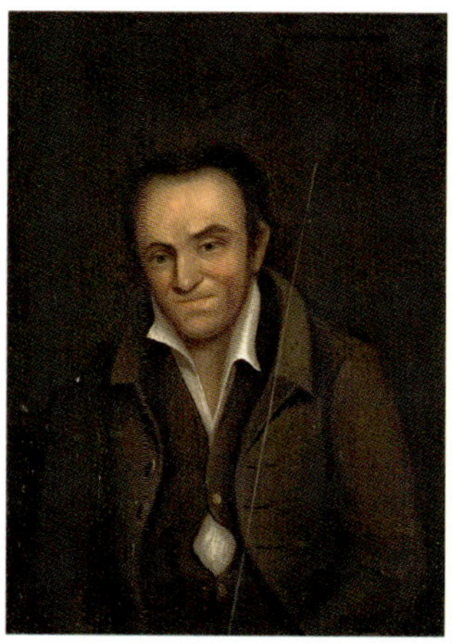

unknown artist
Benjamin Mayo 'Old General'
oil on canvas 37 x 28
NA18

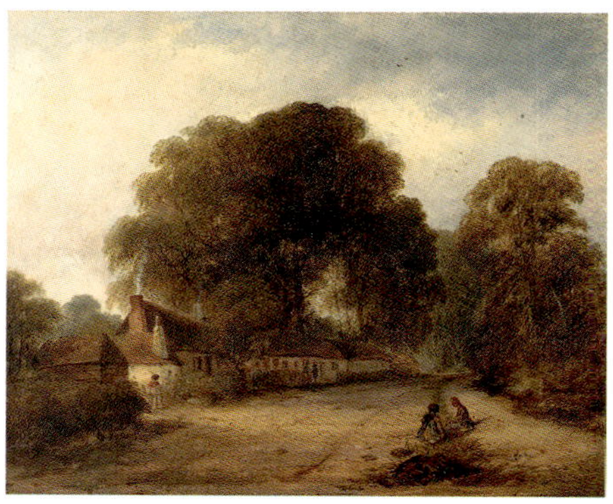

unknown artist
Clifton Grove, Nottingham
oil on canvas 46 x 59
NA20

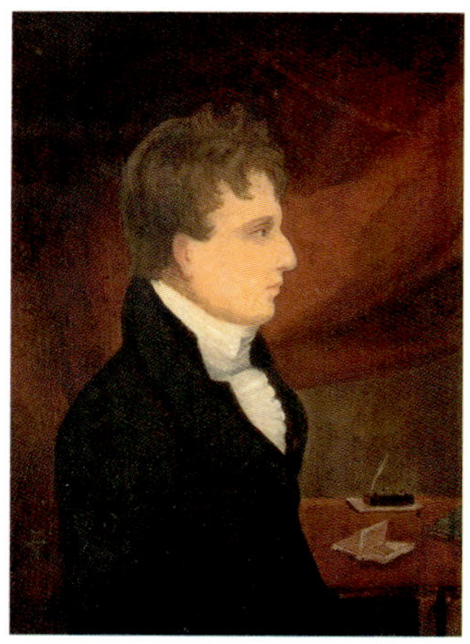

unknown artist
Henry Kirke White (1785–1806)
oil on canvas 34.6 x 26
NA12

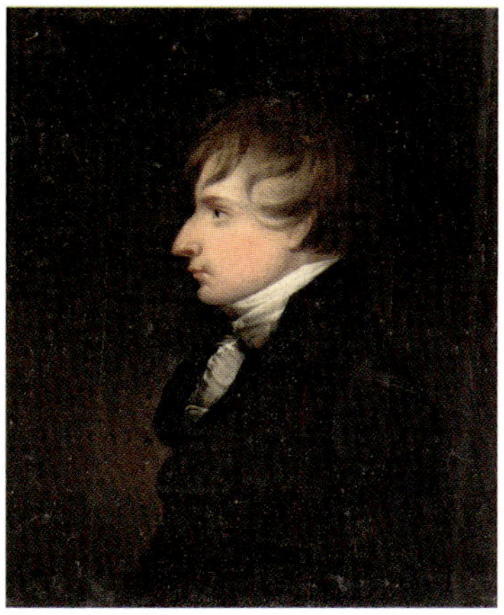

unknown artist
Henry Kirke White (1785–1806)
oil on canvas 23.5 x 20
NA15

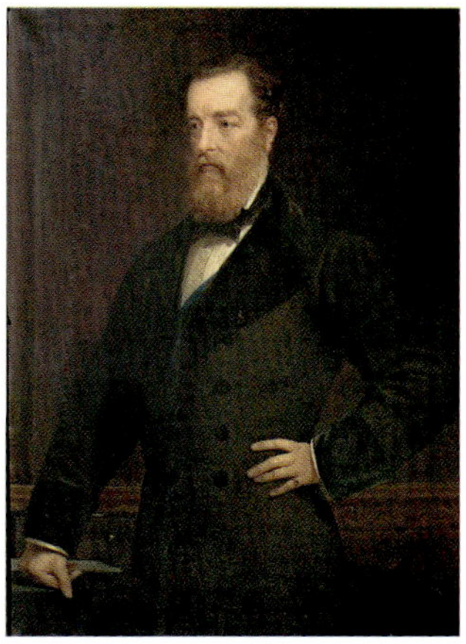

unknown artist
Henry Pelham-Clinton, 5th Duke of Newcastle, Lord Lieutenant of Nottinghamshire (1851–1864)
oil on canvas 130 x 90
NA16

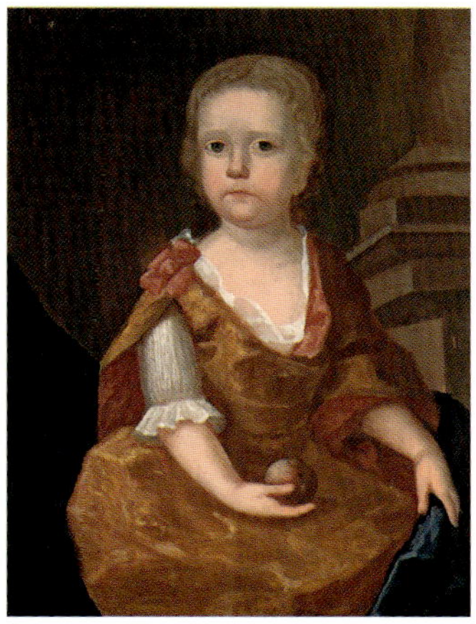

unknown artist
Jane Bristowe (1691–1696)
oil on canvas 64.5 x 52
NA1

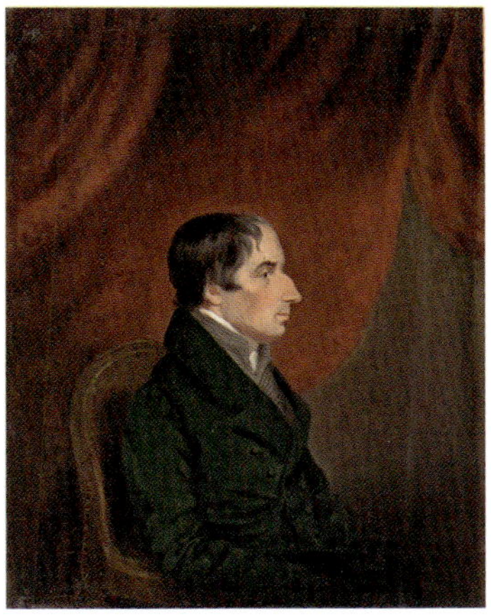

unknown artist
John White (1747–1822)
oil on canvas 28 x 22
NA13

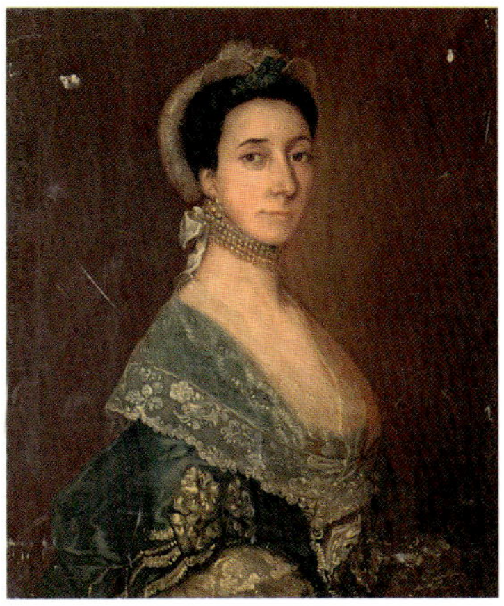

unknown artist
Mary Bristowe (1732–1793)
oil on canvas 76 x 63.5
NA2

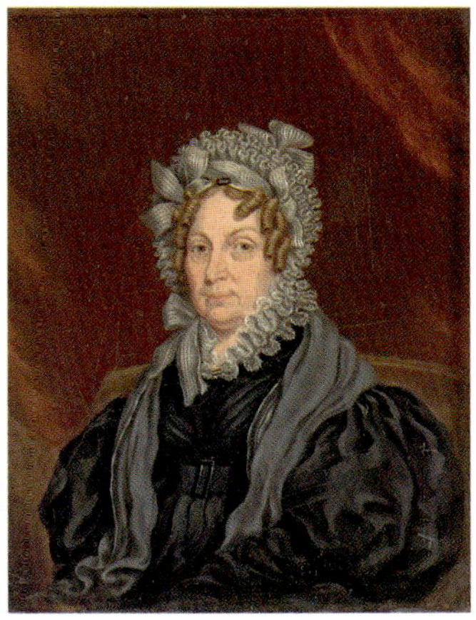

unknown artist
Mary White (c.1756–1833)
oil on canvas 28 x 22
NA14

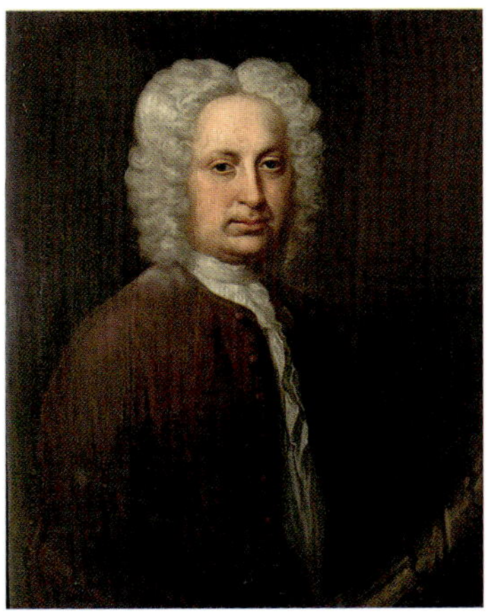

unknown artist
Samuel Bristowe of Twyford (1694–1761)
oil on canvas 74 x 61.3
NA3

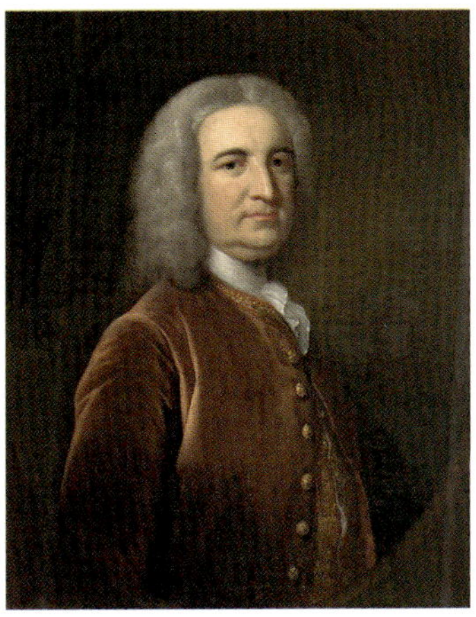

unknown artist
William Bristowe of Beesthorpe (1695–1770)
oil on canvas 74.4 x 61.5
NA5

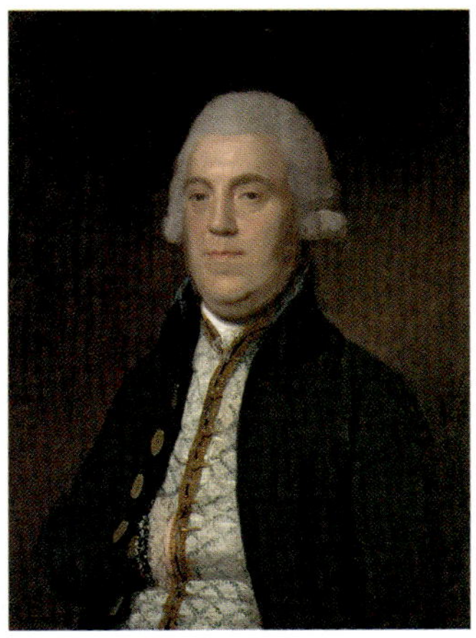

Wright, Joseph of Derby (attributed to)
1734–1797
Samuel Bristowe of Twyford and Beesthorpe (1736–1818)
oil on canvas 73.5 x 61.1
NA6

Nottinghamshire County Cricket Club

The small collection of paintings at the Nottinghamshire County Cricket Club is housed in the members' pavilion at Trent Bridge, Nottingham. The pavilion is the oldest 'grand' pavilion extant in England being built in 1886, older even than the pavilions at Lord's Cricket Ground or The Oval in London.

The members' principal meeting place at the pavilion is the Long Room and the attached bar. The seven oils found here have, like all the other cricket 'memorabilia' owned by the Club, been given by members or friends of the Club. The main collection includes over 7,000 books and some 150 historic bats, plus a large collection of photographs, which date back to the 1850s.

Six of the seven paintings are portraits, five being of famous Nottinghamshire cricketers and the sixth portraying the first Honorary Secretary of the Club, John Johnson. The other oil *Playing Out Time in a Difficult Light* is by Francis Cunningham Batson and it depicts a batsman's perspective on the ground at Fairford in Gloucestershire established by the well-known American artist E. A. Abbey. Abbey formed his own cricket team 'Artists C. C.', which flourished in the first years of the twentieth century, and Francis Batson, who played county cricket for Wiltshire, was the team's leading batsman.

The portrait of Mordecai Sherwin was presented to him by his admirers in about 1890. Sherwin kept wicket for Nottinghamshire and England and captained the county for two seasons. The portrait originally hung in the pub 'The Craven Arms', in Woodborough Road, Nottingham. Sherwin owned this pub and he died there in 1910.

The portrait of Joe Hardstaff was presented to the Club by his son following the cricketer's death in 1988. Hardstaff was the outstanding batsman for Nottinghamshire in the 1930s and 1940s, when he regularly played for England.

John Gunn's portrait, by his grandson, was executed a few years prior to his death which occurred in 1963. Gunn, along with his father William and his brother George, played for England.

Mrs Mary Bissett Brown left the portrait of Richard Daft to the Club in her will of August 1997. She had claimed to be the last direct descendant of Richard Daft, but the executors of the will were unable to give any details of her family history. The artist George Francis Miles lived in the adjacent village to Daft.

The library which houses much archive material at Trent Bridge is open to the public. The Club are happy to show visitors the paintings in the Long Room; however, as the room is used for functions it is wise to make an appointment prior to visiting.

Peter Wynne-Thomas, Archivist

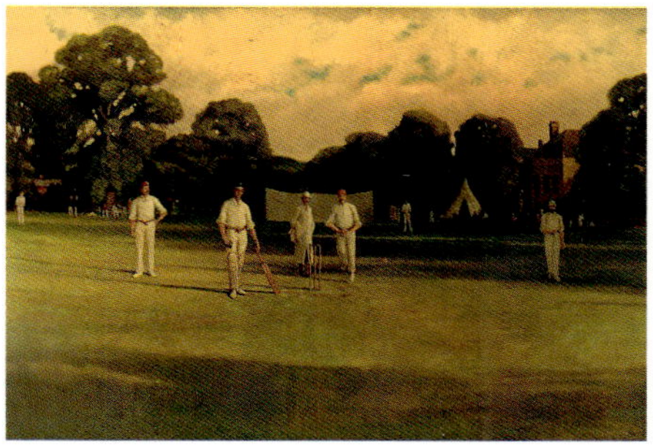

Batson, Francis Cunningham 1858–1931
Playing Out Time in a Difficult Light c.1902
oil on canvas 122 x 175
1

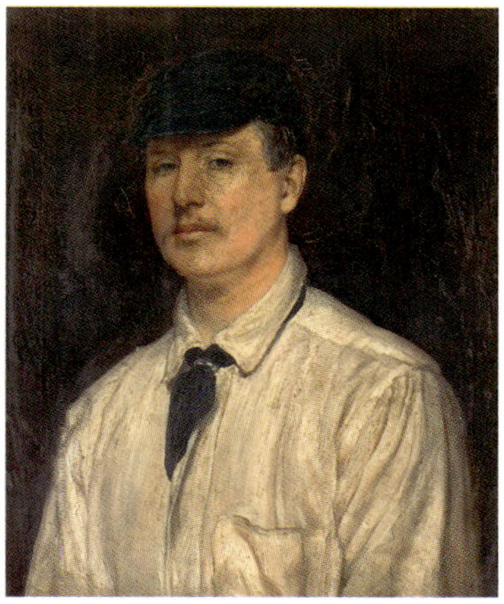

Miles, George Francis 1852–1891
Richard Daft (1835–1900), Captain of Nottinghamshire County Cricket Club (1871–1880) c.1875
oil on canvas 61 x 39
4

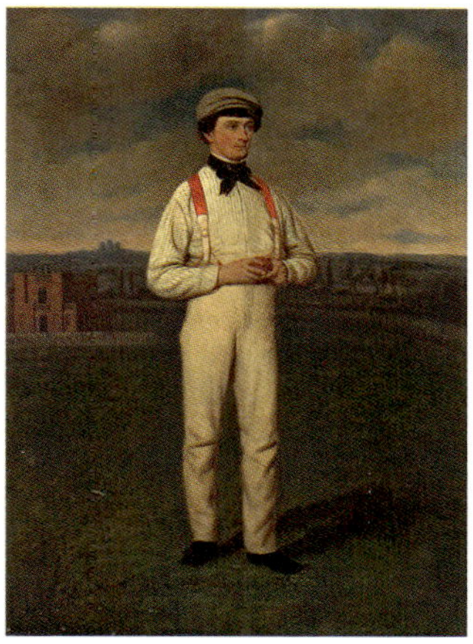

Redgate, Sylvanus 1827–1907
James Grundy (1827–1873)
oil on canvas 76 x 54
5

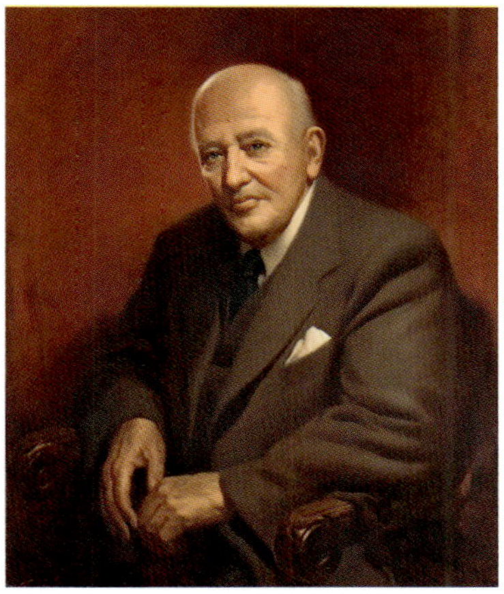

Townsend, John b.1930
John Richard Gunn (1876–1963)
oil on canvas 76 x 60
6

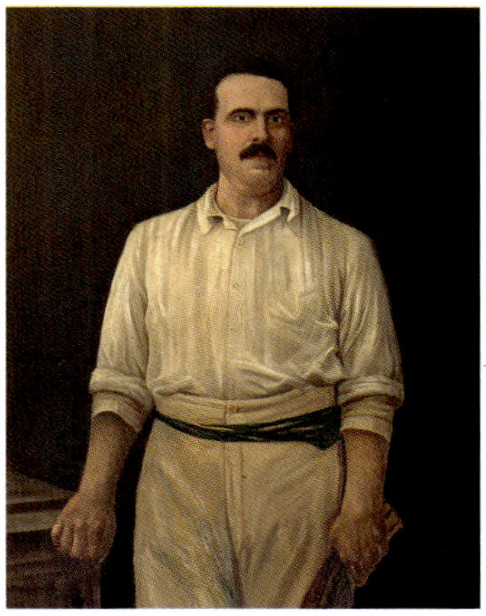

unknown artist
Mordecai Sherwin (1851–1910) c.1890
oil on canvas 129 x 104
2

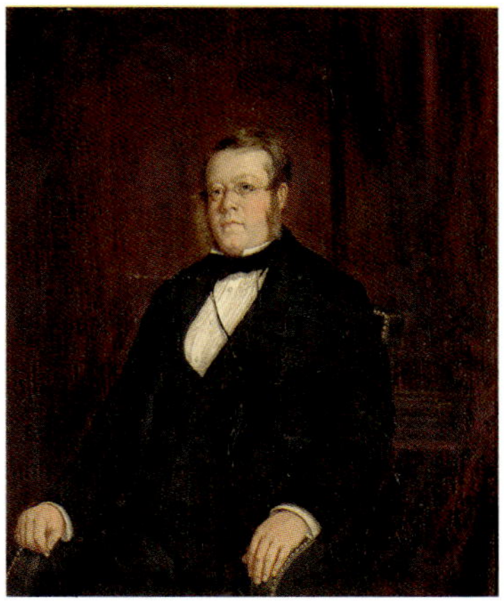

unknown artist
John Johnson (1810–1877), First Honorary Secretary to the Nottinghamshire County Cricket Club (1859–1867)
oil on canvas 32.5 x 29
7

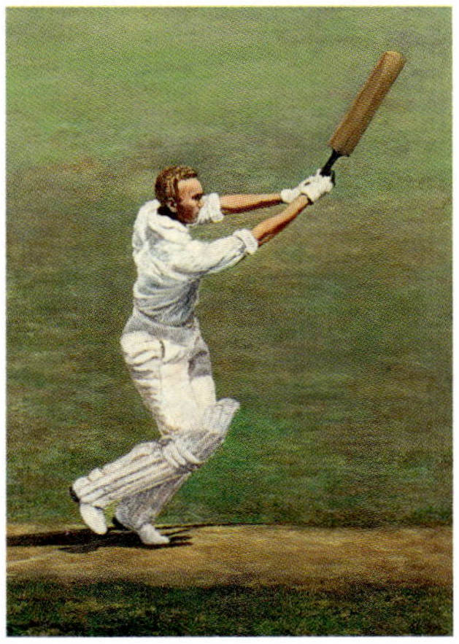

unknown artist
Joseph Hardstaff, Junior (1911–1988)
oil on canvas 56 x 40
3

Nottinghamshire County Football Club

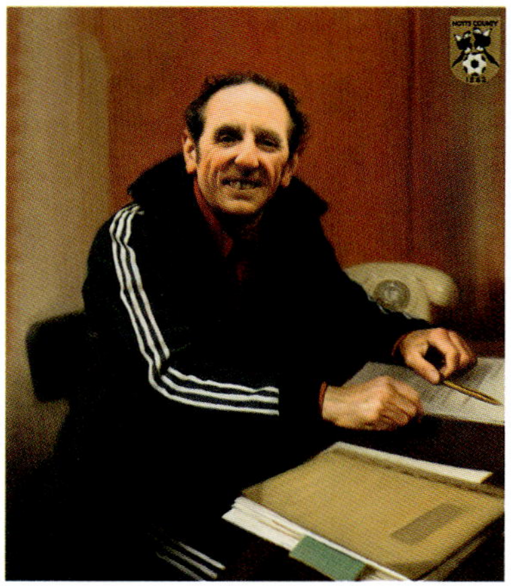

Townsend, John b.1930
Jimmy Sirrel, Nottinghamshire County Football Club's Legendary Manager (1969–1975, 1977–1982, & 1984–1987) 2007
oil on canvas 103 x 86
FC1

Nottinghamshire County Hall

Nottinghamshire County Council has an extensive collection of artefacts from all over the world, the majority of which are gifts to the County from visiting delegations. This diverse collection has been put together over many years and is continually growing. Items from the Collection are periodically exhibited at County Hall and libraries.

The Collection includes a large number of paintings, charcoal sketches and an interesting selection of oil works. Many of the oil paintings are hung throughout County Hall and include portraits of distinguished previous chairmen of the Authority, which line the main stairwell of County Hall. These pieces are not only a pictorial record of the councillors between 1914 and 2001, but they also display a broad variety of painting styles. The most recent painting by D. Todd is *Councillor Dennis Pettitt, Leader of the County Council (1981–2001)*, whose portrait is characterised by bold brushstrokes and use of colour.

There is also a varied collection of local scenes, notably of the River Trent, reflecting its vital importance to Nottingham's industrial heritage as a trading link to both east coast ports and to central England via the canal network. Many of the scenes feature river crossings, especially Trent Bridge, linking the city and county, and Wilford Ferry.

Newstead Abbey is another significant subject. This imposing building was home to the Romantic poet and writer, Lord Byron, whose work was often inspired by the Abbey's brooding Gothic features and its picturesque grounds.

Artist Robert O'Rourke was commissioned in 2003 to capture the spirit of Rufford Country Park and its Cistercian Abbey. The Scheduled Ancient Monument and its extensive grounds were once part of the country estate of the Savile family. Today it houses a sculpture garden, galleries and a craft centre, having been bought by the County Council in 1952.

John Allin, Chairman of Nottinghamshire County Council

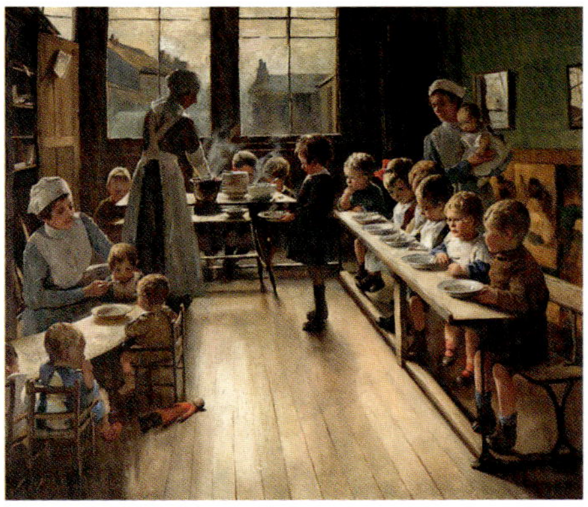

Bates, Marjorie Christine 1883–1962
Turn of the Century Nursery Scene
oil on canvas 38 x 47
CH0394

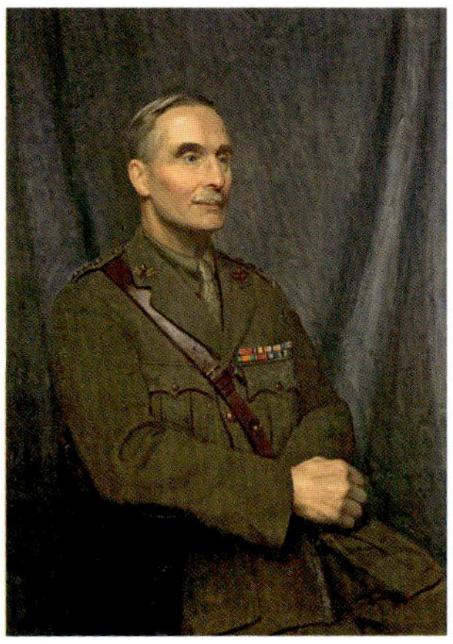

Davis, Noel Denholm 1876–1950
Alderman Thomas Phillip Barber, Chairman of the County Council (1932–1946)
oil on canvas 41 x 31 (E)
CH0115

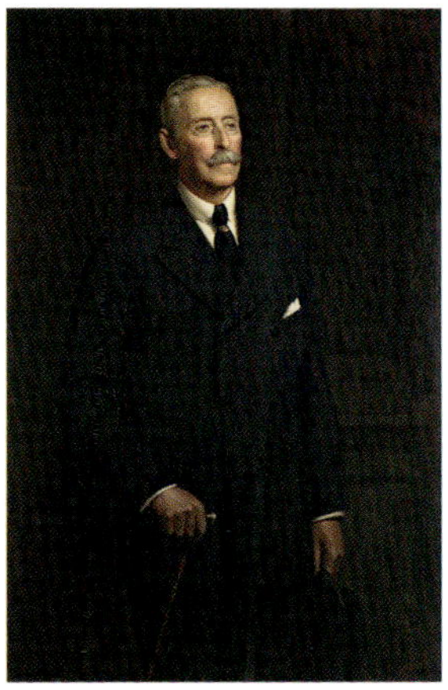

Davis, Noel Denholm 1876–1950
Colonel Sir Lancelot Rolleston, KCB, DSO, TD, DL, JP, Chairman of Nottinghamshire County Council and Quarter Sessions (1928–1932)
oil on canvas 41 x 31 (E)
CH0109

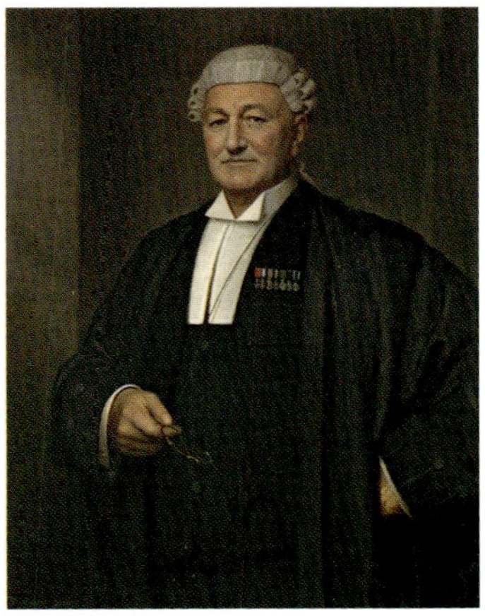

Davis, Noel Denholm 1876–1950
K. Tweedale Meaby, CBE, DL, Clerk of the Peace (1921–1954)
oil on canvas 41 x 31 (E)
CH0119

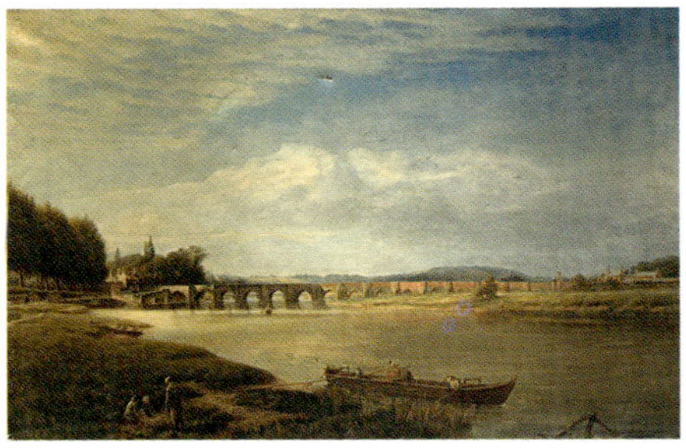

Doubleday, Matthew c.1828–1900
Old Trent Bridge 1873
oil on canvas 31 x 47
CH0030

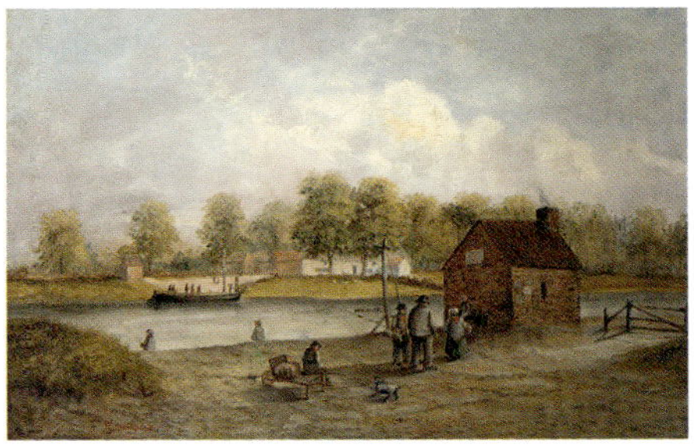

Edwards, Edwin 1823–1879
Fishing by the River at Wilford Ferry, Nottingham, Barge in the Background
oil on canvas 42.5 x 66
CH0023

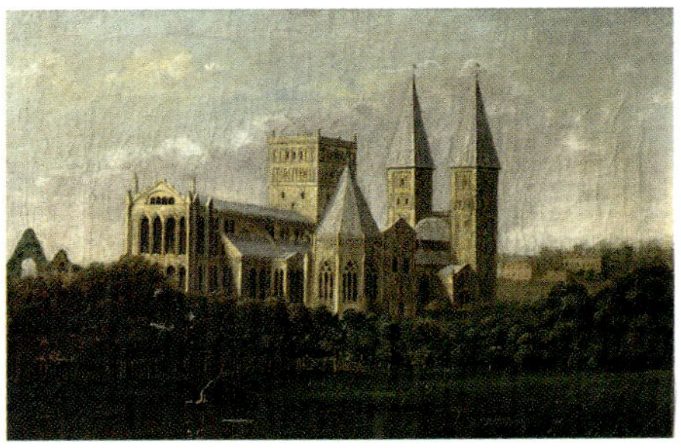

Frost, T.
Southwell Minster, Nottinghamshire 1778
oil on canvas 10 x 16
CH0367

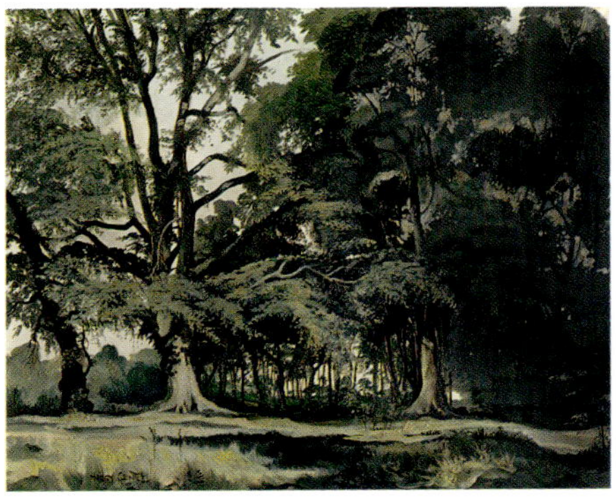

Gentle, Harry
Scene in Clumber Park, Worksop, Nottinghamshire
oil on board 51.5 x 67
reg1

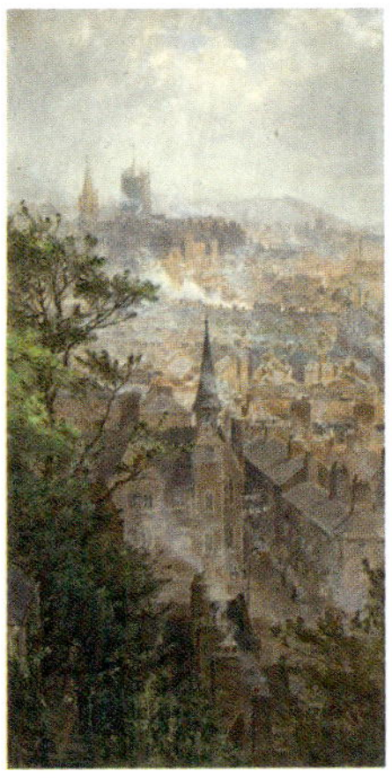

Hammond, Thomas William 1854–1935
Rooftop View over City Churches, Nottingham
oil on canvas 30 x 16
CH0335

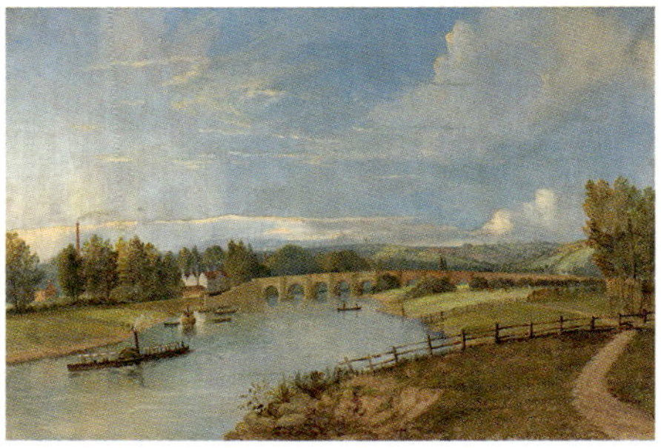

Hingsley, W. C.
Old Trent Bridge with Steamer, from the North Bank 1872
oil on canvas 21 x 31
CH0293

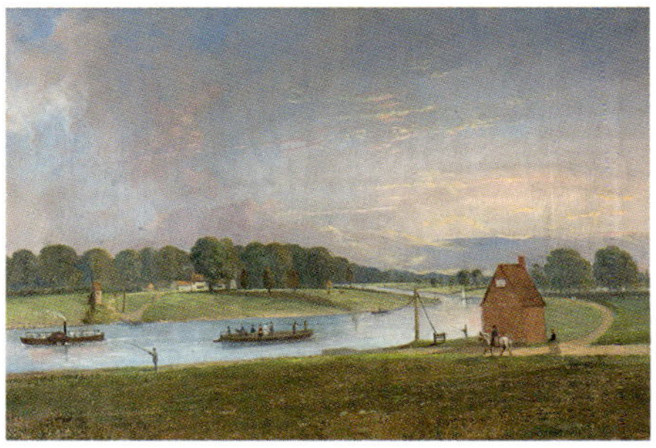

Hingsley, W. C.
Wilford Ferry, from the North Bank, 1872
oil on canvas 21 x 31
CH0287

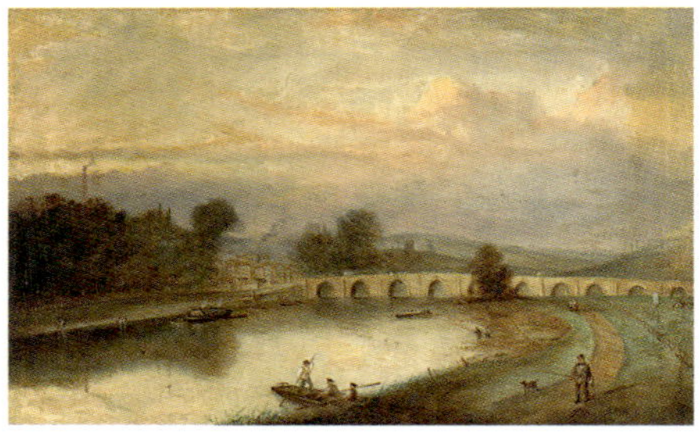

Moore, Thomas Cooper 1827–1901
Trent Bridge, Nottingham, with Ferry
oil on canvas 16 x 26
CH0203

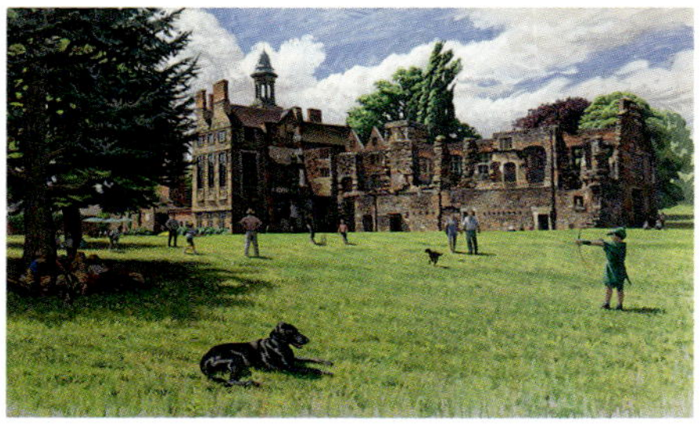

O'Rourke, Robert active 2003
Rufford Abbey, Nottinghamshire, from the Lawns
oil on canvas 127 x 200
chtemp2

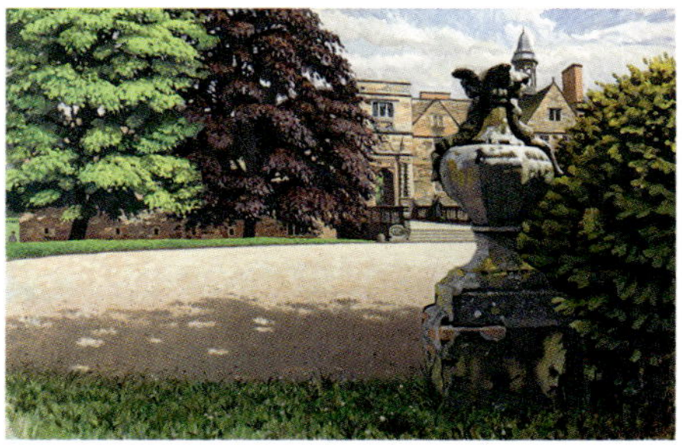

O'Rourke, Robert active 2003
Rufford Abbey, Nottinghamshire, from the Turning Circle
oil on canvas 100 x 147
chtemp1

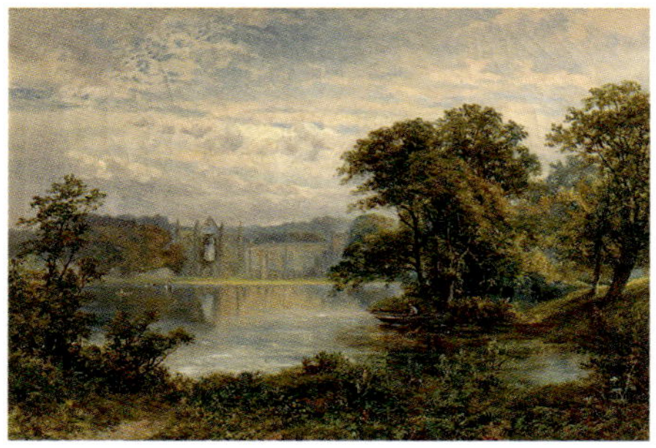

Payne, David (attributed to) c.1844–1891
Newstead Abbey, Nottinghamshire, View from the Lake
oil on canvas 20 x 30
CH0235

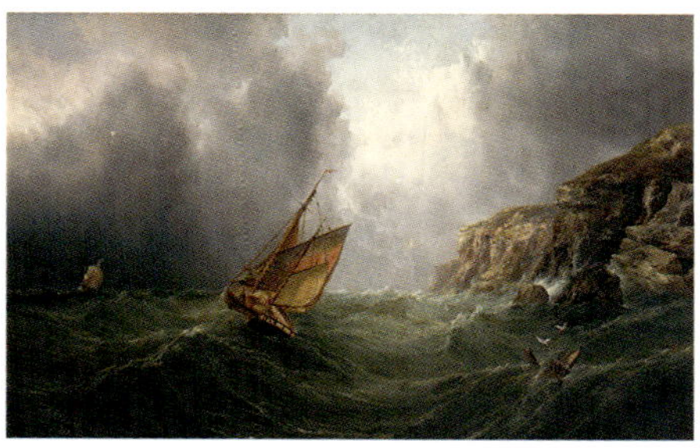

Redmore, Henry 1820–1887
A Coastal Scene with a Cliff, a Fishing Boat and a Merchantman in a Storm 1878
oil on canvas 29 x 40
CH0021

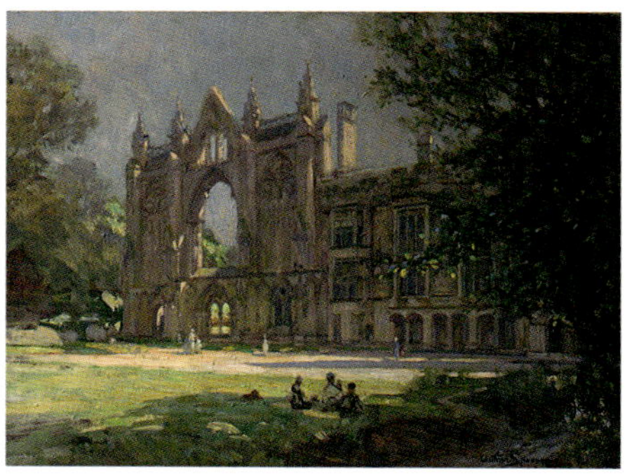

Spooner, Arthur 1873–1961
Newstead Abbey, Nottinghamshire, View from the Lawn, with Figures in Sunlight and Shade
1944
oil on canvas 18 x 25
CH0400

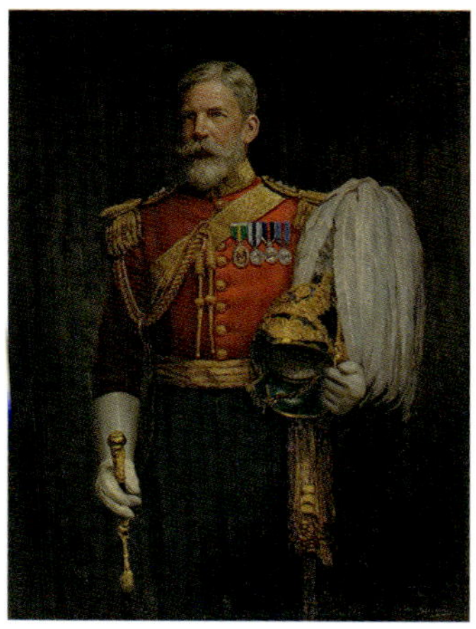

Spooner, Arthur 1873–1961
The Right Honourable Lord Belper, First Chairman of Nottinghamshire County Council
oil on canvas 41 x 31 (E)
CH0107

Facing page: Nicholson, William, 1872–1949, *Miss Wish Wynne (1882–1931), Actress, in the Character of Janet Cannot for the Play 'The Great Adventure'* (detail), Nottingham City Museums and Galleries (p. 130)

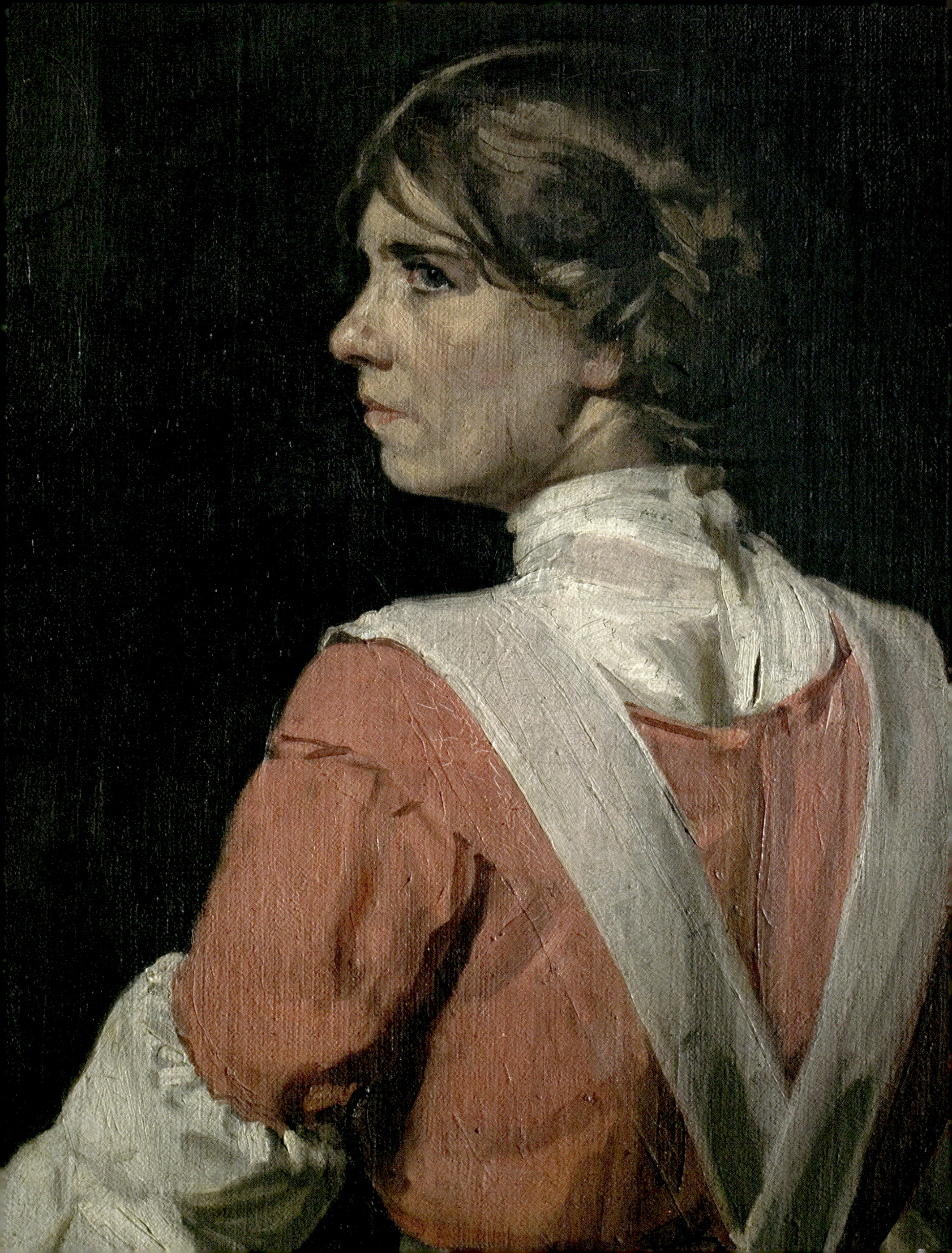

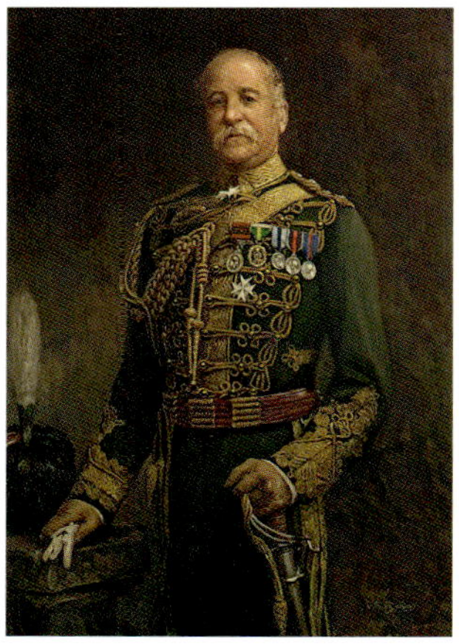

Spooner, Arthur 1873–1961
The Right Honourable Viscount Galway, CB, Chairman of the County Council (1914–1928)
oil on canvas 41 x 31 (E)
CH0116

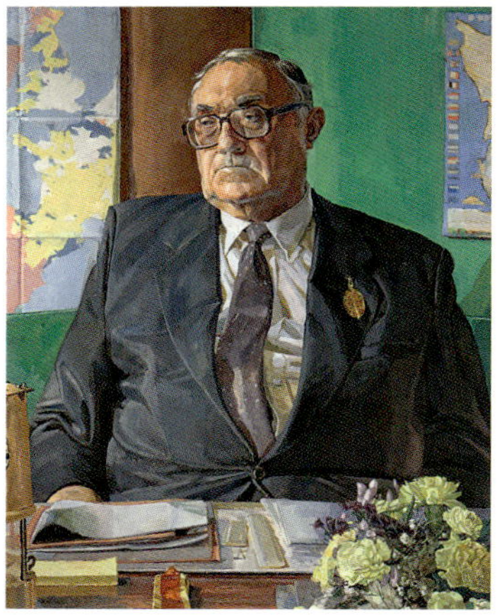

Todd, D.
Councillor Dennis Pettitt, Leader of the County Council (1981–2001)
oil on canvas 41 x 31 (E)
CH0121

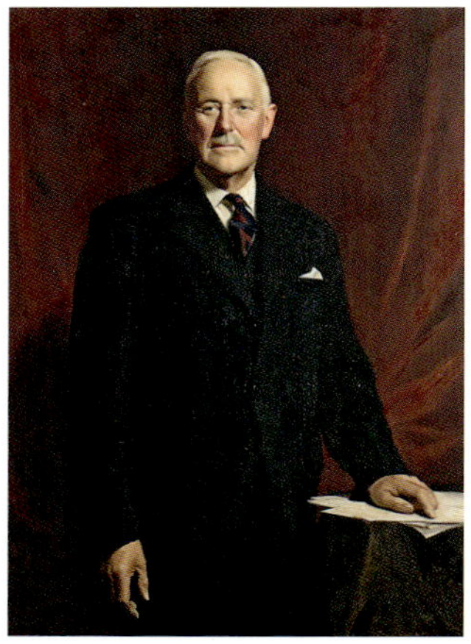

Townsend, John b.1930
Alderman Colonel Sydney Farr, MC, DL, JP, Chairman of the County Council (1962–1963) 1963
oil on canvas 41 x 31 (E)
CH0114

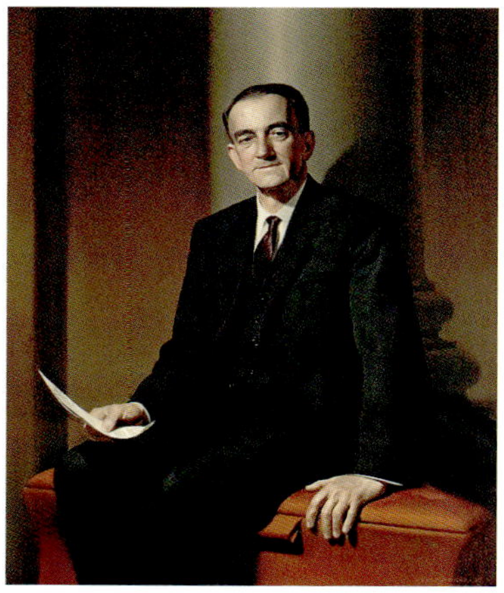

Townsend, John b.1930
Alderman Sir Frank Small, CBE, DL, JP, Chairman of the County Council (1963–1967) 1965
oil on canvas 41 x 31 (E)
CH0113

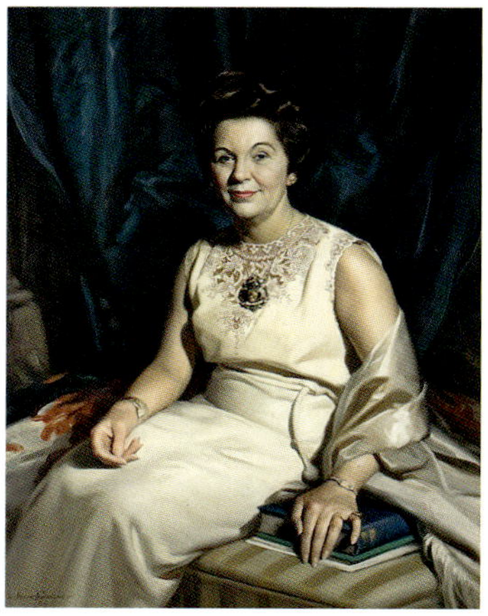

Townsend, John b.1930
Alderman Mrs Anne Yates, CBE, JP, Chairman of the County Council (1968–1974) 1969
oil on canvas 41 x 31 (E)
CH0112

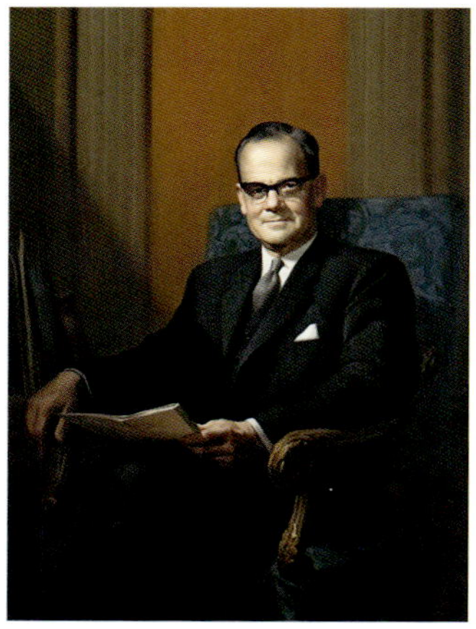

Townsend, John b.1930
Alderman Albert James Pounder, JP, Chairman of the County Council (1967–1968)
oil on canvas 41 x 31 (E)
CH0111

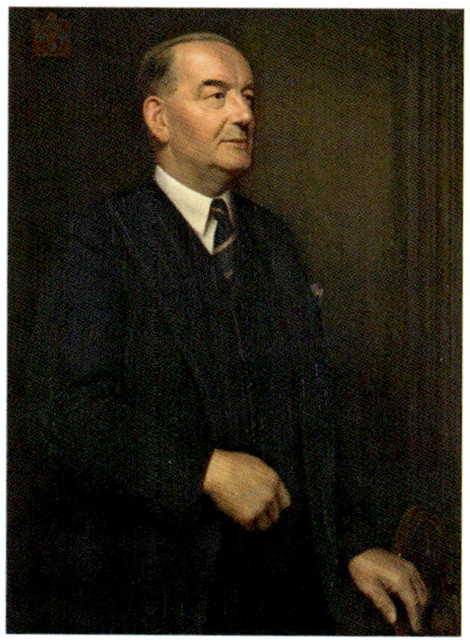

Townsend, John b.1930
Alderman William Bayliss, CE, JP, Chairman of the County Council (1946–1962)
oil on canvas 41 x 31 (E)
CH0110

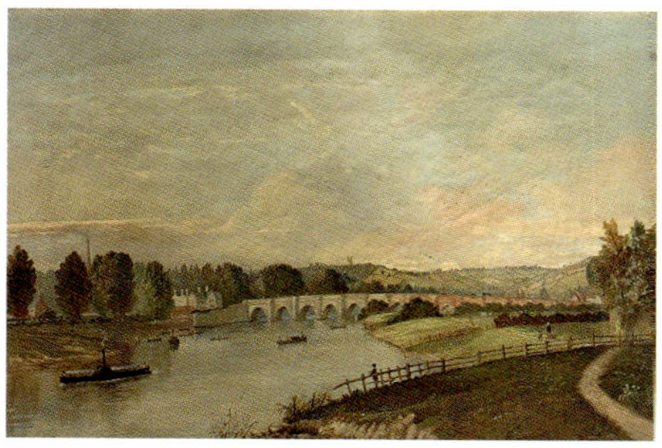

unknown artist
Old Trent Bridge Steamer and Figures c.1890
oil on canvas 21 x 31
CH0375

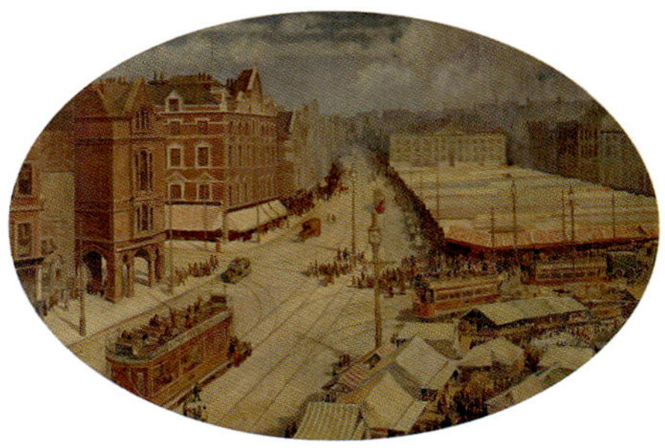

unknown artist
Nottingham Market Square, Pre-Council House Dome, on Market Day, with Trams in View
oil on canvas 24 x 38
CH0234

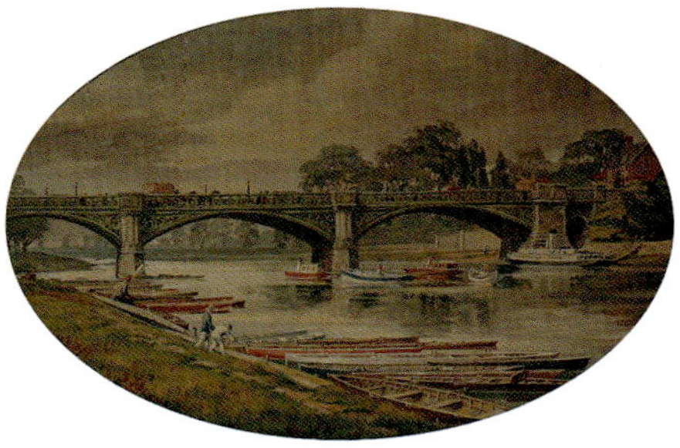

unknown artist
Trent Bridge Pre-Embankment, with Rowing Boats and Steam Boats
oil on canvas 24 x 38
CH0240

Nottinghamshire County Library Service

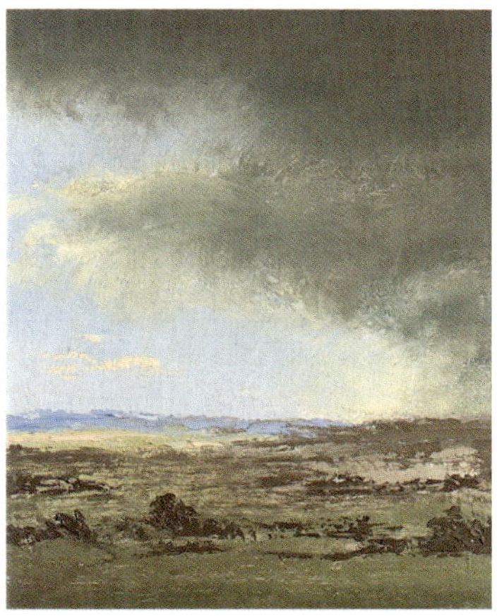

Burton, Marjorie E. active 1980
Approaching Storm
oil on canvas 30 x 25
RTLIB3

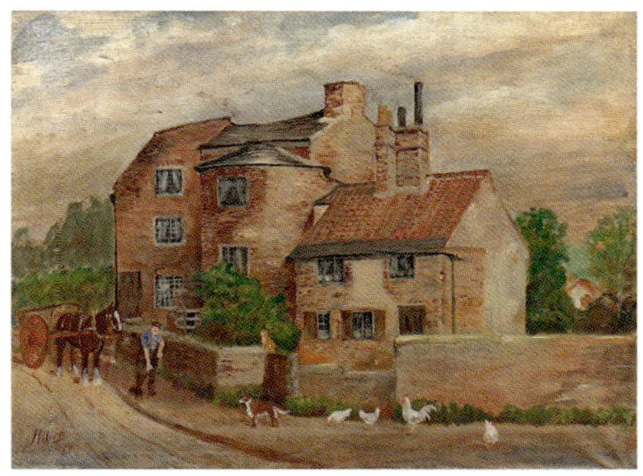

Elliot, W. J. active 1924–1966
Round House, Hallam Lane, Arnold, Nottinghamshire 1924
oil on canvas 38 x 51.2
ALIB3

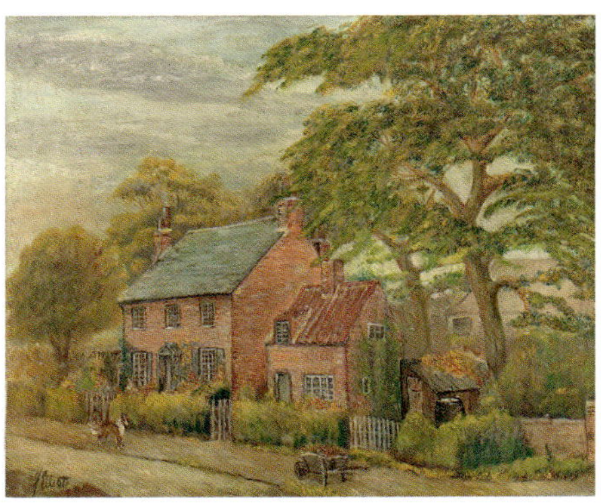

Elliot, W. J. active 1924–1966
Higginbottom's Cottage, Hallam Lane, Arnold, Nottinghamshire c.1965
oil on canvas 41 x 51
ALIB2

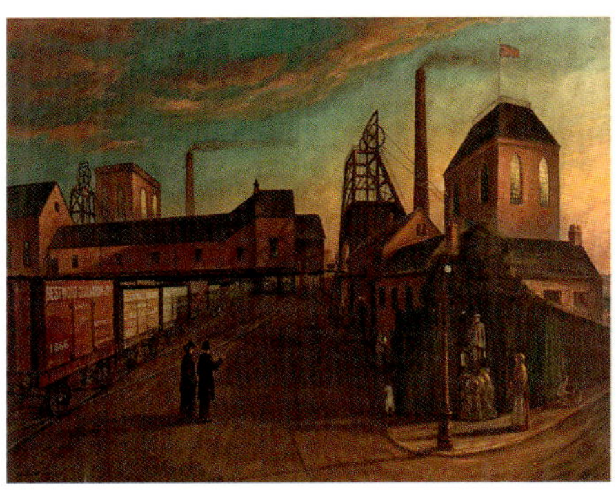

Lacey, Elias b.1871
Bestwood Pit, Nottinghamshire 1926
oil on canvas 77 x 102.4
HKLIB4

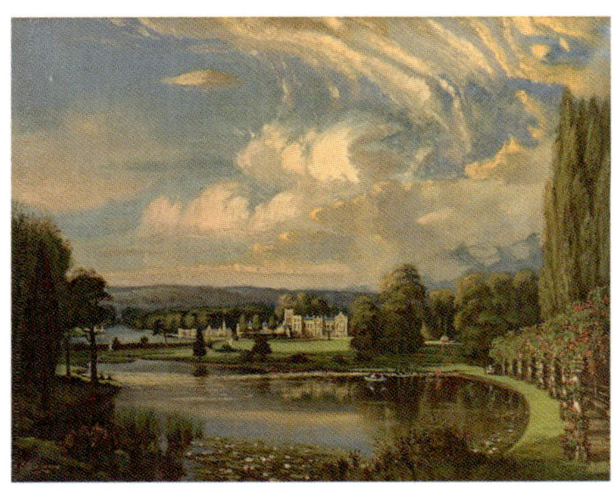

Lacey, Elias b.1871
South Front and Lake of Newstead Abbey, Nottinghamshire 1937
oil on canvas 75.4 x 100
HKLIB3

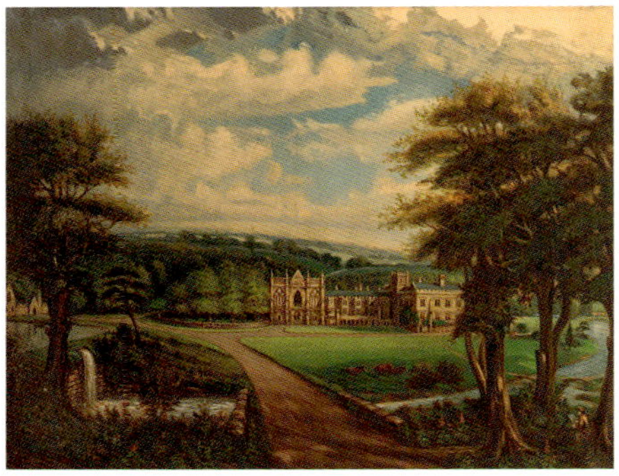

Lacey, Elias b.1871
West Front of Newstead Abbey, Nottinghamshire 1937
oil on canvas 75.4 x 100
HKLIB2

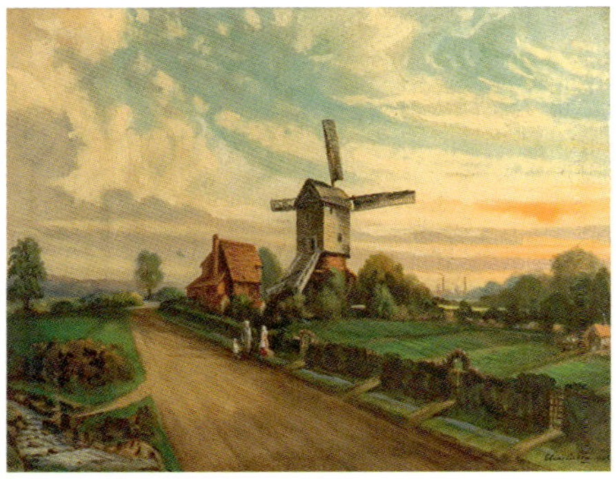

Lacey, Elias b.1871
Old Sandy Lane Mill, 'Club Mill', Nottinghamshire 1943
oil on canvas 44 x 66
HKLIB1

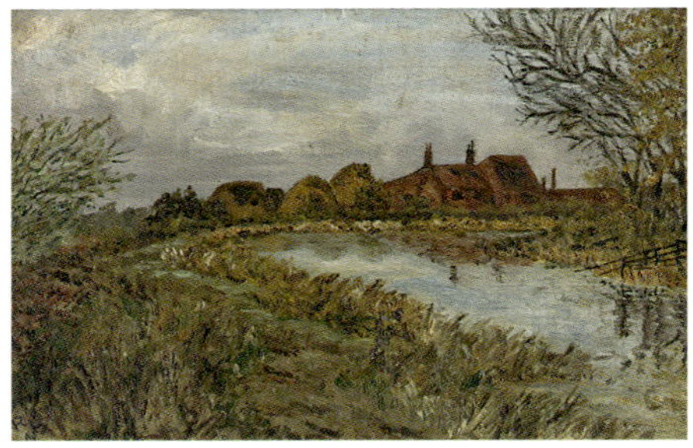

Laming, Ruth
A Scene along the Canal Bank, near Ladybridge, Bolton, Lancashire 1955
oil on canvas 27 x 42
RTLIB6

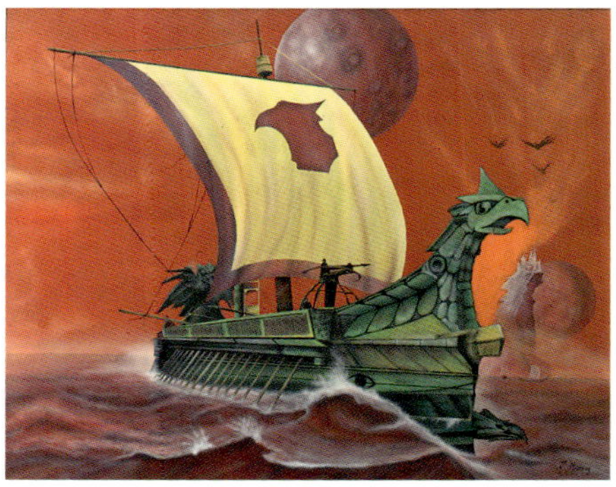

Murray, Trevor
*Dragon Ship** 1981
acrylic on board 54 x 69
RHLIB2

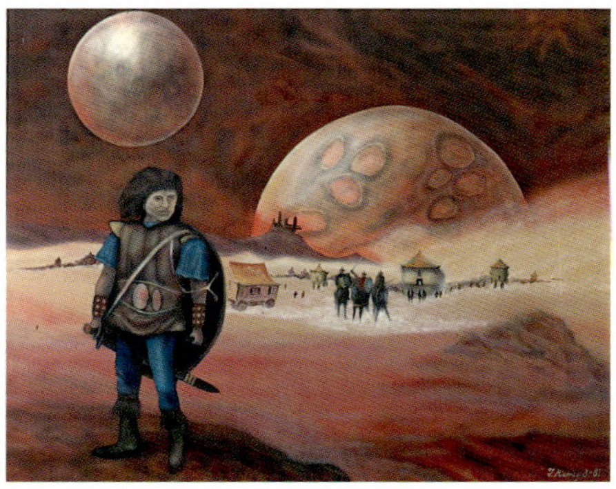

Murray, Trevor
*Man on Mars** 1981
acrylic on board 54 x 69
RHLIB1

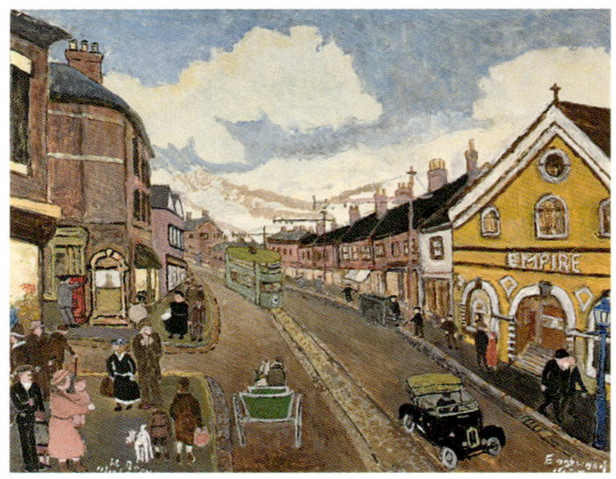

Reeve, Walter
Nottingham Road, Eastwood, 1920s c.1985
oil on board 34.5 x 44.3
EWLIB1

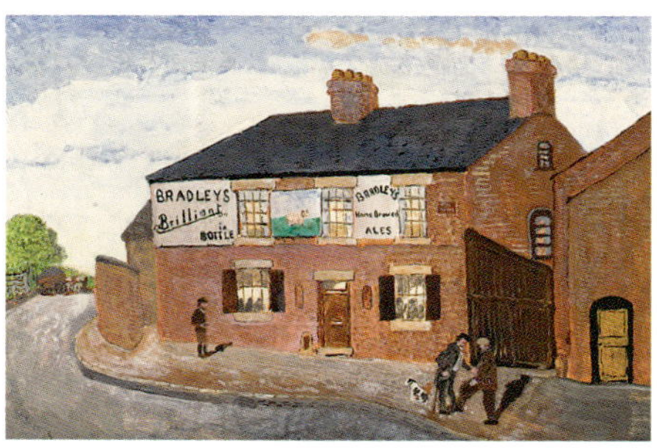

Reeve, Walter
Bradley's Brewery (now the 'Ram Inn'), Eastwood, Nottinghamshire
oil on board 28.5 x 45.5
EWLIB2

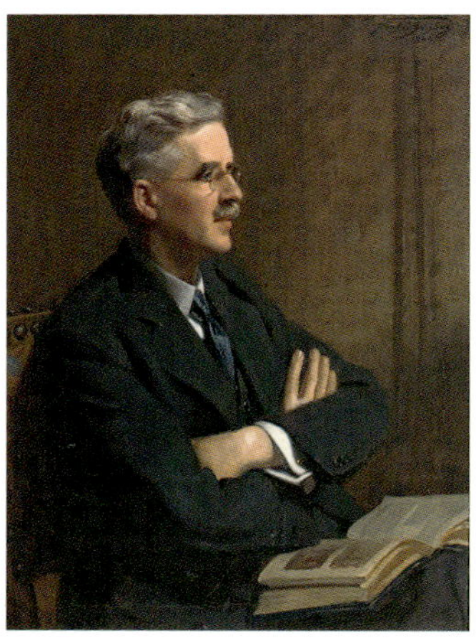

Salisbury, Frank O. 1874–1962
Arthur Mee (1875–1943), Editor of 'The Children's Newspaper'
oil on canvas 89 x 69
SPLIB1

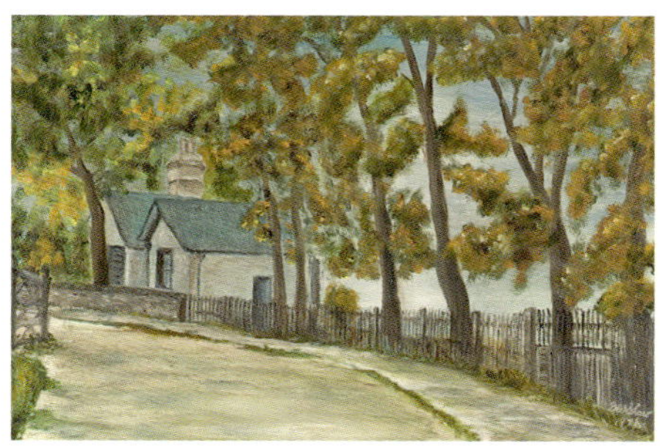

Shaw, Don W.
Arno Vale, Nottinghamshire 1976
oil on canvas 31 x 47
ALIB1

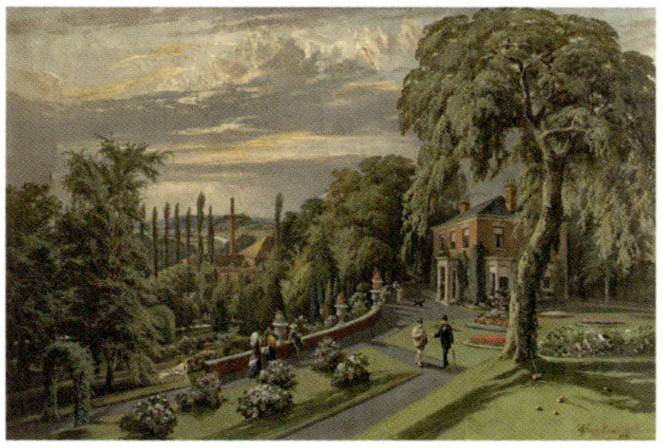

Shaw, Frank
Bolham Manor, Ladybridge, Nottinghamshire
1886
oil on canvas 61 x 91.5
RTLIB1

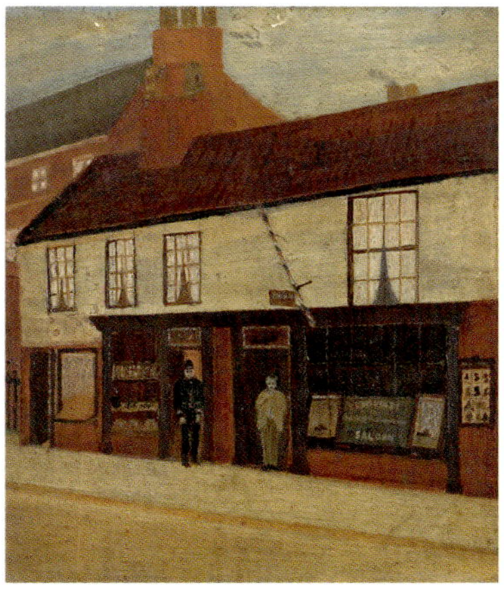

unknown artist
Arnfield's Book and Paper Shop, Smedley's Barber's Shop, Carolgate, Retford, Nottinghamshire 1900
oil on board 28 x 25
RTLIB2

Nottinghamshire Police

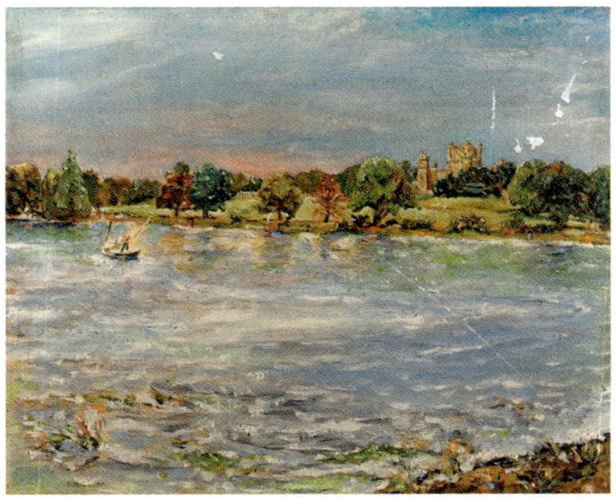

unknown artist
*View of Wollaton Hall, Nottingham, from the Lake**
oil on canvas 40 x 50
centralPS1

Rushcliffe Borough Council

The Borough of Rushcliffe lies immediately south of the City of Nottingham and the River Trent and extends across towards Newark in the North East and Loughborough in the South West. Although parts of the Borough lie close to Nottingham, Rushcliffe has a strong identity of its own with a combination of delightful rural villages and leafy suburbs. It has a vibrant cultural life and is a popular place to visit with huge numbers of people attracted to the Borough's legendary sporting facilities: Trent Bridge Cricket Ground, Nottingham Forest Football Club and the National Watersports Centre.

Rushcliffe Borough Council's art collection currently consists of over 80 pieces, of those 16 paintings are in oils and included in this catalogue. The Collection has been assembled over a period of 40 years with most pieces inherited from the former Council's of West Bridgford Urban District, Bingham Rural District, and part of Basford Rural District when they merged to form Rushcliffe in April 1974.

The Collection features work donated by a number of former members of the Nottingham Society of Artists, including Noel Denholm Davis and Winifred D. Boynton. There are also three pieces by Herbert Wilson Foster, a former student at the Nottingham School of Art and a Minton porcelain decorator. In 1893 his painting *The Procession of the May Queen* was exhibited at the Royal Academy. When he died at his home in West Bridgford in 1929, the Principal of the Nottingham School of Art, Mr J. Else, was quoted in the obituary which appeared in the *Nottingham Evening Post* as stating, 'Mr Foster was one of the most distinguished life masters in the country'.

Rushcliffe Borough Council would like to thank the Public Catalogue Foundation for including our Collection in this publication and allowing it to become better known.

Allen Graham, Chief Executive

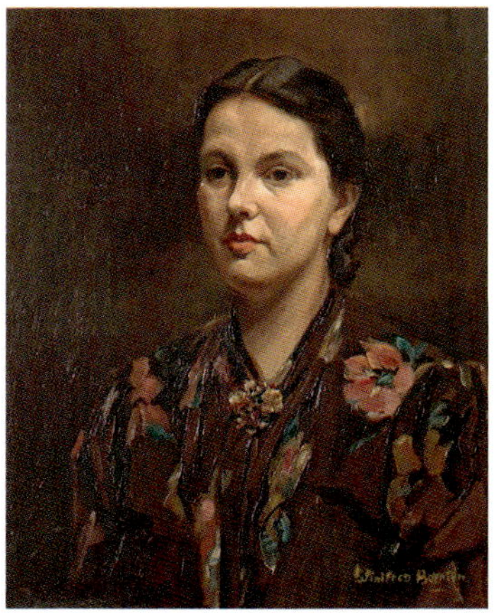

Boynton, Winifred D. active c.1938–1940
Portrait of a Lady c.1938–1939
oil on canvas laid on board 59 x 47
RC:006

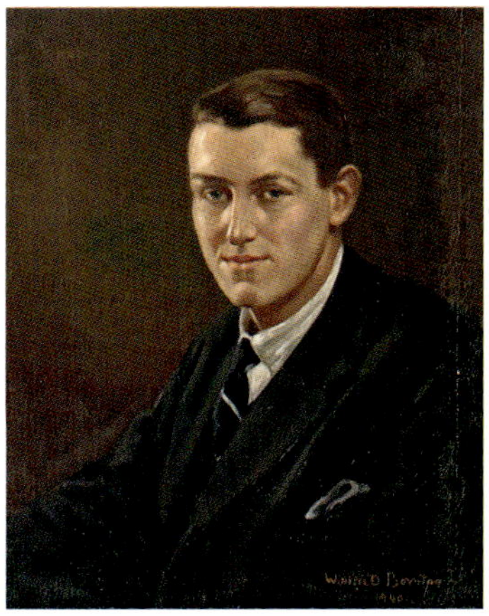

Boynton, Winifred D. active c.1938–1940
On Active Service (Arnold Boynton Hall, lost at sea in HMS 'Exmouth', 21 January 1940) 1940
oil on canvas laid on board 60.4 x 49.3
RC:005

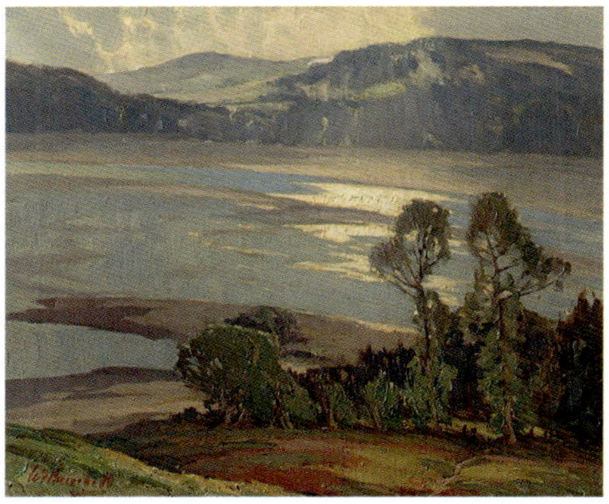

Burchell, William F.
The Solway
oil on canvas 41.8 x 52
RC:003

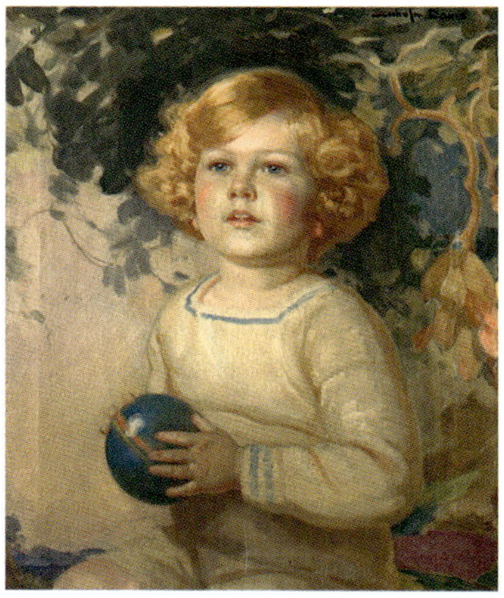

Davis, Noel Denholm 1876–1950
The Honourable Henry Saville as a Child
oil on canvas 56 x 48
RC:017

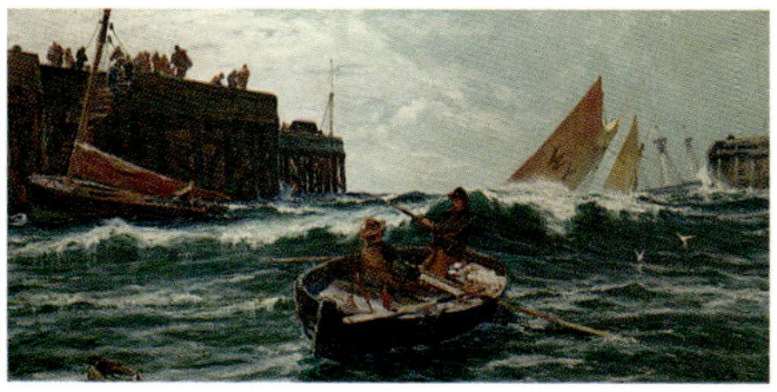

Ellis, Edwin 1841–1895
The Approaching Storm, Whitby, North Yorkshire
oil on canvas 54.5 x 110
RC:011

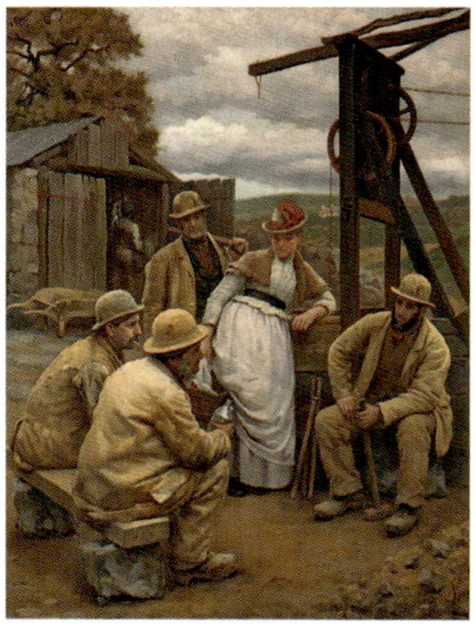

Foster, Herbert Wilson 1846–1929
Tea Break 1889
oil on canvas 89.5 x 69
RC:013

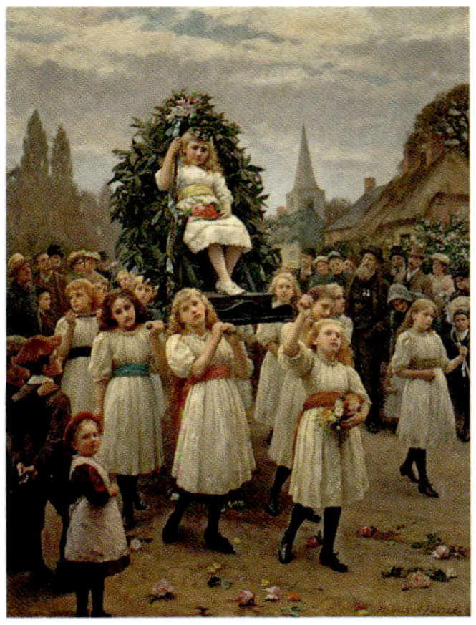

Foster, Herbert Wilson 1846–1929
The Procession of the May Queen 1893
oil on canvas 181 x 142
RC:015

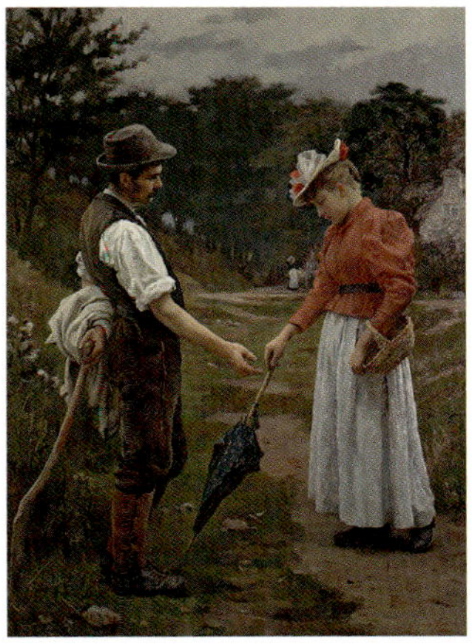

Foster, Herbert Wilson 1846–1929
Country Courtship 1895
oil on canvas 90 x 69
RC:010

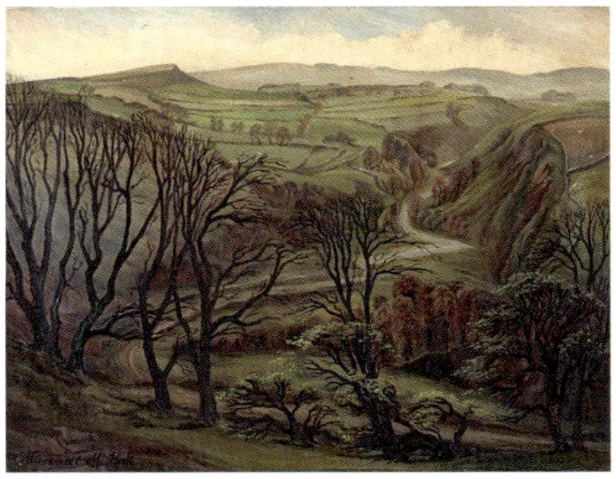

Hall, Margaret M.
Early March
oil on board 29.5 x 40
RC:009

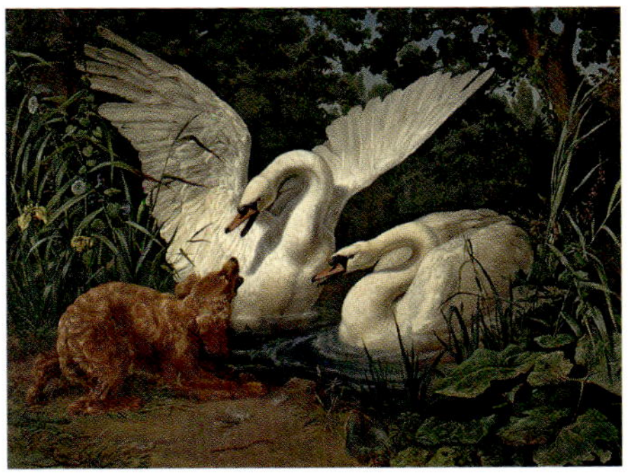

Lachenwitz, F. Sigmund 1820–1868
Two Swans Startled by a Hound 1846
oil on canvas 117 x 160
RC:016

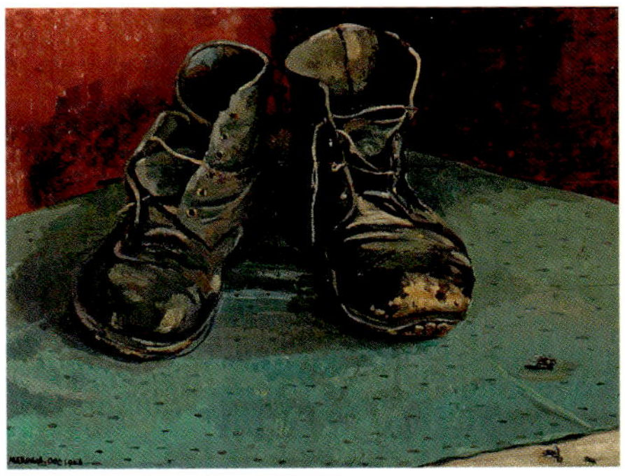

Makinson, Trevor b.1926
From Dunkirk (Sam's Boots) 1943
oil on board 28 x 38.5
RC:004

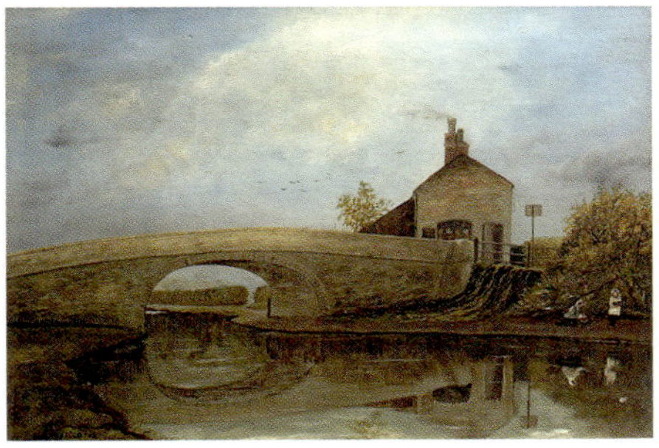

Mayfield, F.
The Old Bridge, Lady Bay, Nottingham 1862
oil on canvas 24.6 x 34.6
RC:002

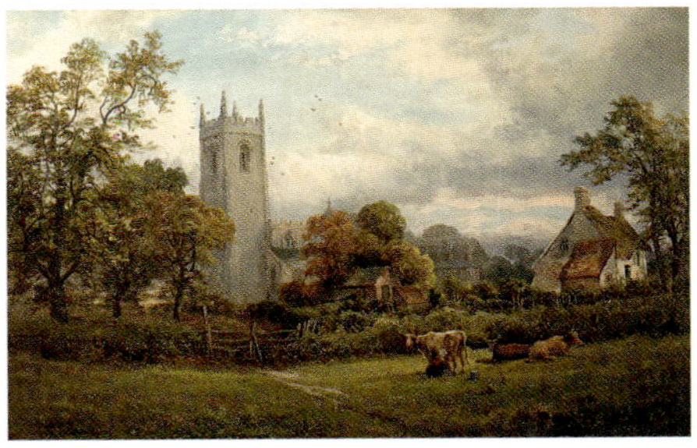

Payne, David c.1844–1891
Milking Time late 1880s
oil on canvas 49 x 79
RC:001

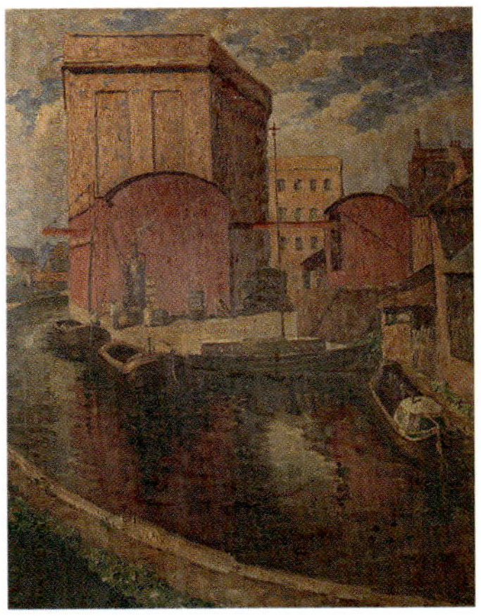

Smart, Hilda Elizabeth 1900–1992
Trent Navigation Wharf 1925
oil on canvas 100 x 79
RC:007 (P)

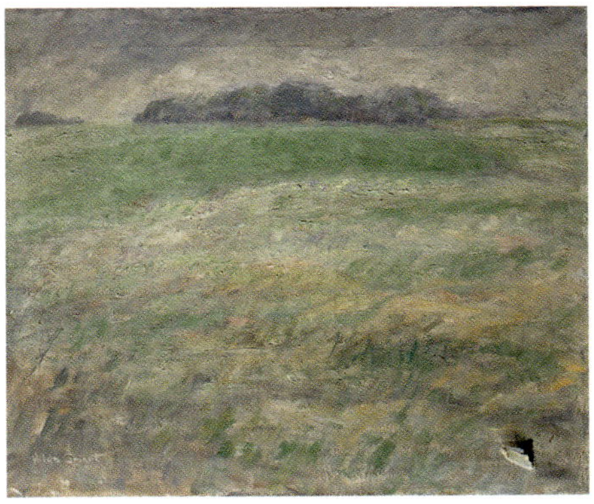

Smart, Hilda Elizabeth 1900–1992
Summer Rain
oil on canvas 54 x 65
RC:008 (P)

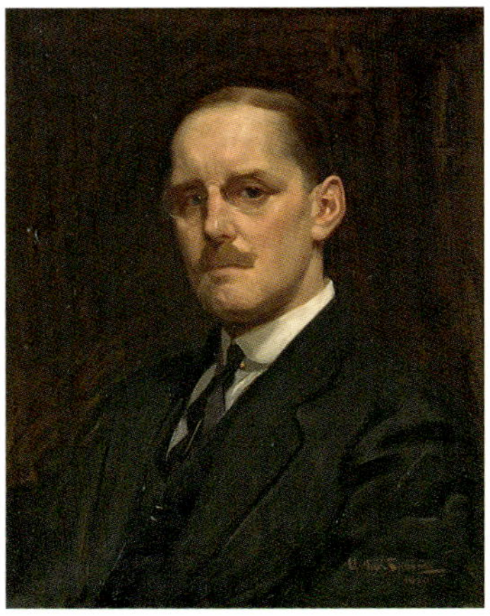

Spooner, Arthur 1873–1961
Portrait of a Gentleman 1920
oil on canvas 59 x 49
RC:014

The Congregational Memorial Hall Trust (1978) Limited

The Congregational Memorial Hall Trust (1978) Limited (formerly the Congregational Memorial Hall on Farringdon Street, London), has as its key purpose to maintain and upkeep the Congregational Library, to continue the Congregational Lecture, and to make grants to the United Reformed Church, Congregational Federation and the Evangelical Fellowship of Congregational Churches. The Trust has a collection of portraits of which the majority are housed within the offices of the Congregational Federation Nottingham. This Collection includes a broad range of portraits, with relevance not only from a Congregational viewpoint, but some also to Nottinghamshire history.

In the painting attributed to George Hayter, Lord John Russell (1792–1878) and Lord Holland (1773–1840) are portrayed side by side. Russell will always be remembered as being the champion of the great Reform Bill of 1832. The motion by Lord Russell that the repeal of the Test and Corporation Acts be considered was of even greater interest. Supported by a large number of petitions, he persuaded the House of Commons in 1828 to repeal these despised acts. Lord Holland, seated beside him, was a friend of Lord Byron and has a Nottingham connection in that he became the Nottingham Recorder in 1809.

The portrait by an unknown artist of *Samuel Morley (1809–1886), MP*, depicts an important figure in local history. Samuel Morley was born in Hackney. His father was a Nottingham tradesman in the hosiery business who worshipped in a North London Congregational Church. He became MP for Nottingham in 1865 but was unseated. He then became MP for Bristol, retaining this seat until his retirement in 1885. He was a loyal supporter of Gladstone and principal proprietor of the *Daily News*. Morley always treated his work people well, especially in regard to pensions. He was very generous in supporting Congregational causes, and gave £6,000 (the second largest single donation) towards the erection of the Congregational Memorial Hall. He also gave over £14,000 towards the erection of 24 new chapels, these gifts being conditional on the chapels being free of ornate trappings. It is believed that he felt the Castle Gate Chapel in Nottingham was too ornate, and his donation for this chapel was relatively small by his standards. In 1858 Morley became Treasurer of the Home Missionary Society, and whilst he did not believe in separating Home and Foreign missions, he continually emphasised that the stronger churches were at home, the more foreign missions would prosper. His strong leadership helped to build up Congregationalism during the second half of the nineteenth century.

James Alexander Mitchell's portrait by an unknown artist also depicts a prominent local figure. Mitchell was born in Edinburgh and at the close of a successful school career he proceeded to the Crossley Orphanage, Halifax as an Assistant Minister. After three years at the orphanage he entered New College to prepare for the Congregational ministry obtaining the 'Mills Scholarship'. On leaving college he became Assistant Minister at Rusholme, Manchester and in 1878 became pastor at Friarlane Church, Nottingham, where he remained for 15 years. In addition to his church duties he undertook lectureship on Church History at the Congregational Institute. In 1893 he moved to St Helen's Congregational Church and in 1903 he was appointed Secretary of the Congregational Union. His theological position was such to be ever open to conviction, keenly alive to the advance in Biblical criticism he was nevertheless evangelical to the core.

Reverend Michael Heaney, General Secretary

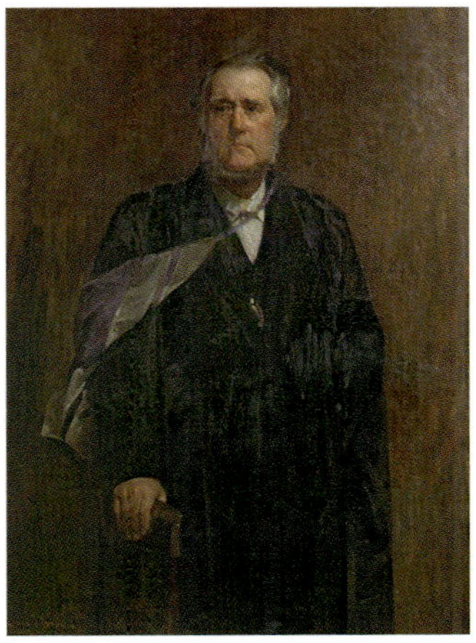

Brown, John Alfred Arnesby 1866–1955
Dr Paton (1830–1911) 1899
oil on canvas 127 x 96
PCF2

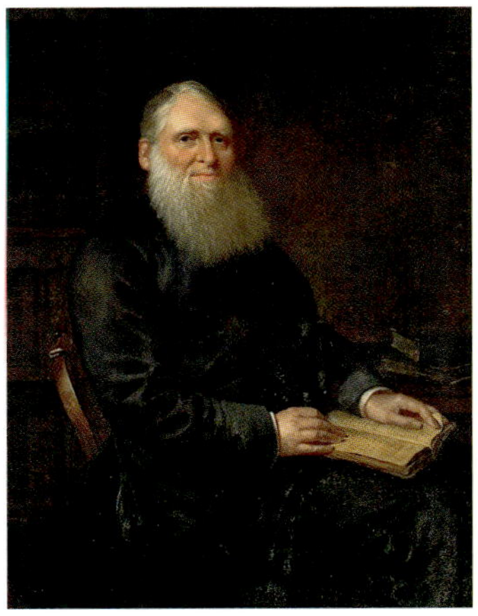

Caledfryn, Ap 1837–1915
Thomas Rees (1815–1885)
oil on canvas 125 x 99
CMHT. 15

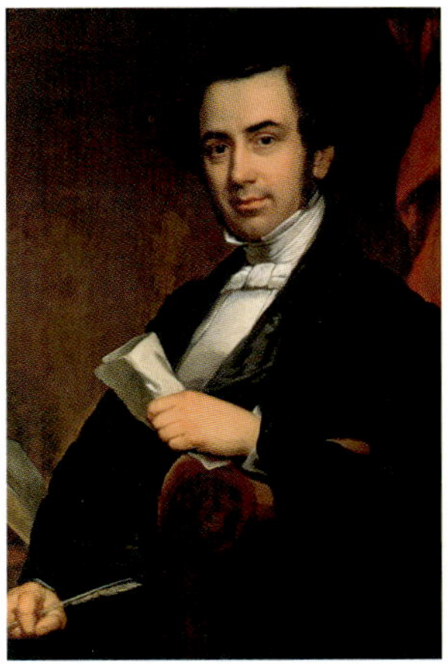

Grant, Francis (style of) 1803–1878
John Legge Poore (1816–1867)
oil on canvas 89.5 x 62
CMHT. 19

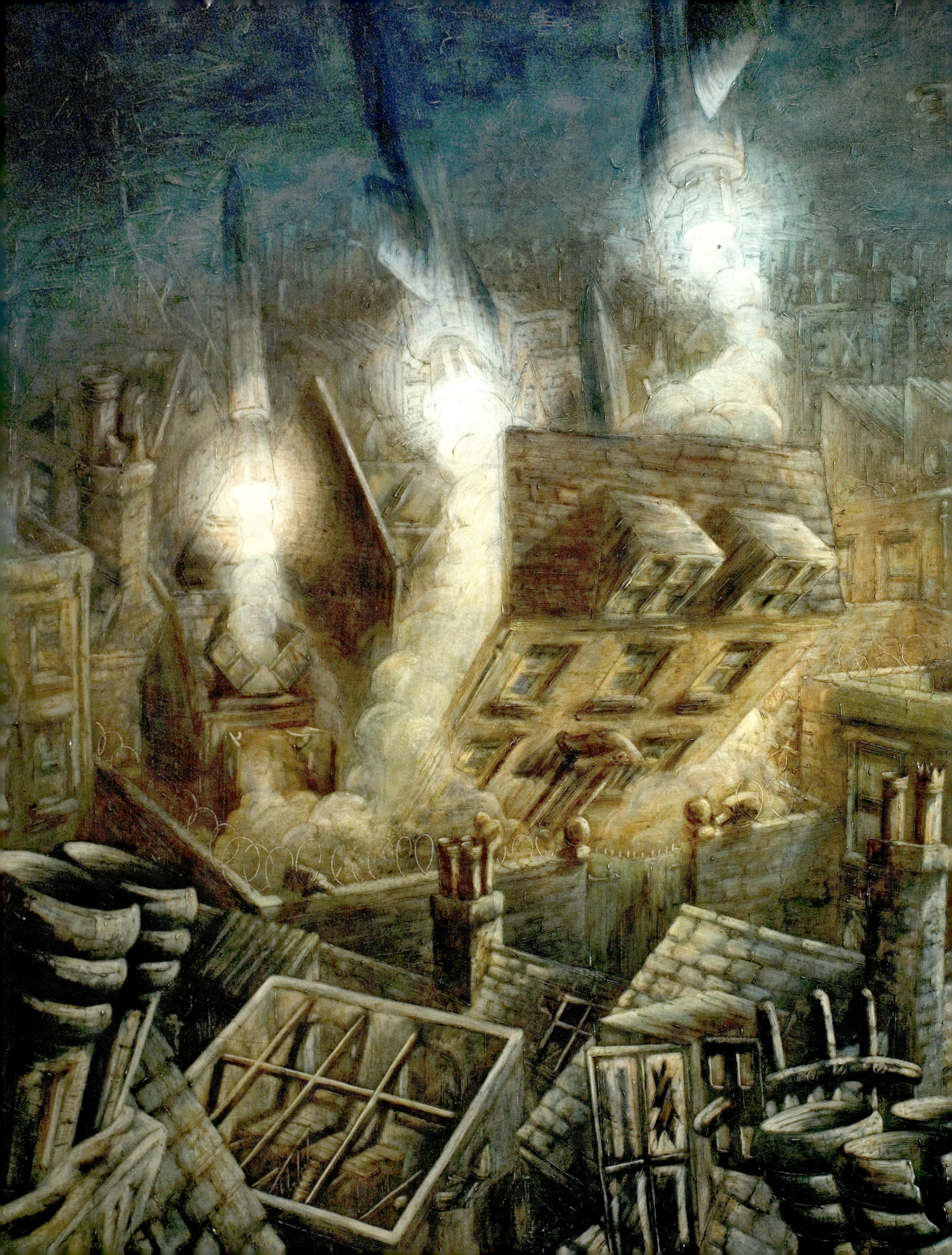

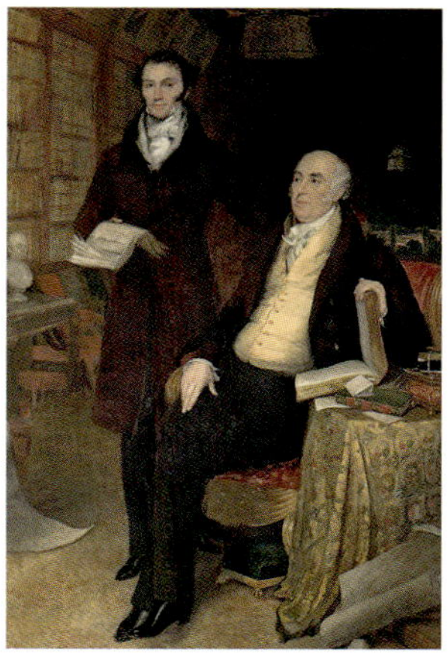

Hayter, George (attributed to) 1792–1871
Lord John Russell (1792–1878), and Lord Holland (1773–1840)
oil on canvas 200 x 138
CMHT. 54

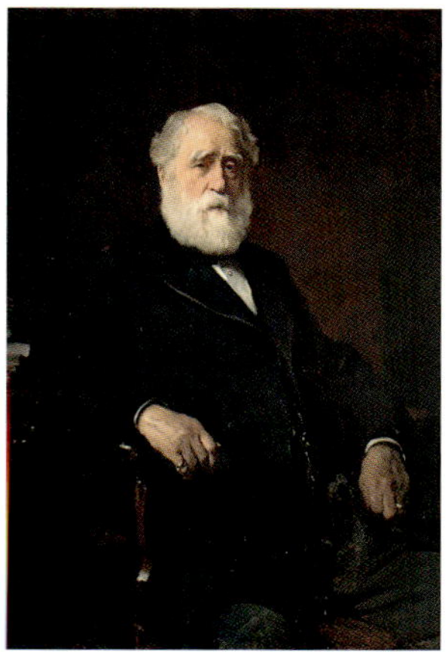

Holl, Frank 1845–1888
James Spicer (1807–1888)
oil on canvas 125.5 x 99
CMHT. 16

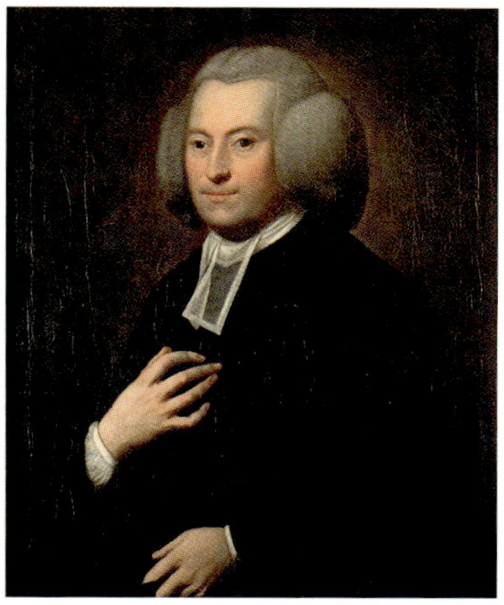

Hudson, Thomas 1701–1779
John Stafford (1728–1800)
oil on canvas 73 x 61
CMHT. 01

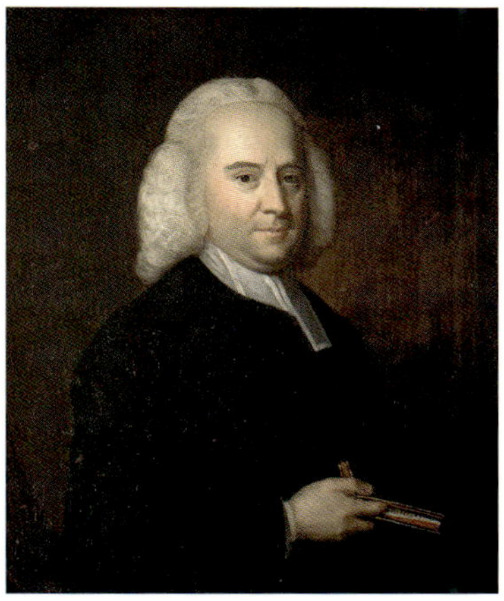

Hudson, Thomas (school of) 1701–1779
John Howe (1630–1705)
oil on canvas 73.5 x 62.5
CMHT. 51

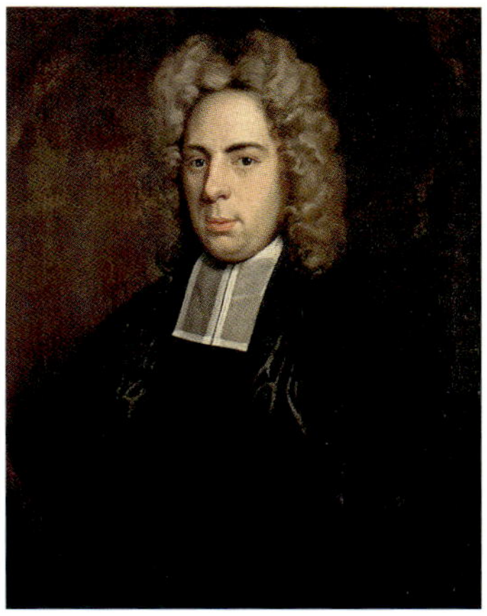

Jervas, Charles (attributed to) c.1675–1739
Isaac Watts (1674–1748)
oil on canvas 73.5 x 60.4
CMHT. 03

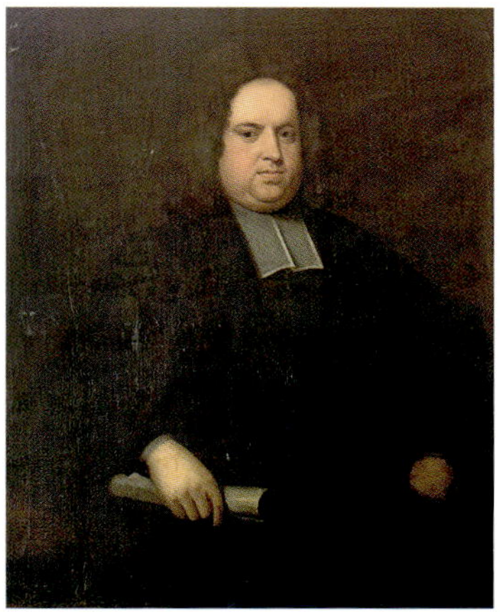

Kneller, Godfrey (follower of) 1646–1723
Matthew Henry (1662–1714)
oil on canvas 102.5 x 84.6
CMHT. 05

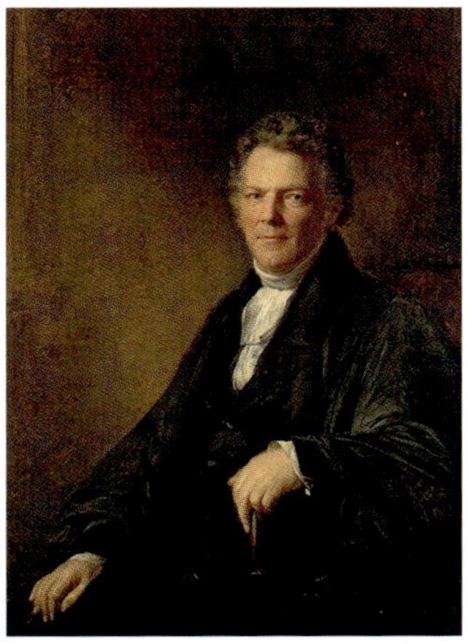

Linnell, John 1792–1882
John Leifchild (1780–1862)
oil on canvas 109 x 81.5
CMHT. 50

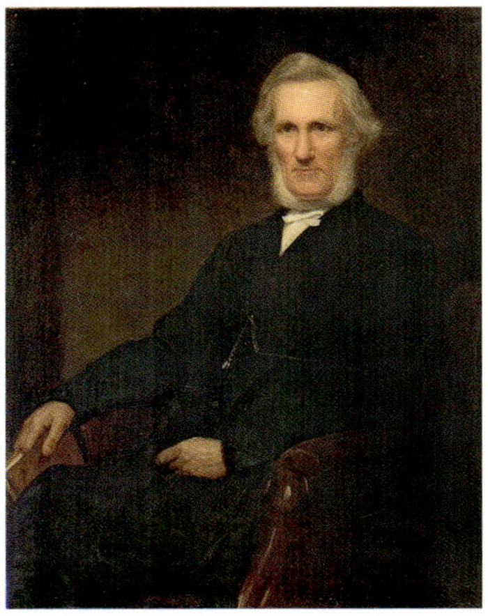

Napier, John James 1831–1877
Alexander Raleigh (1817–1875)
oil on canvas 110.2 x 90
CMHT. 21

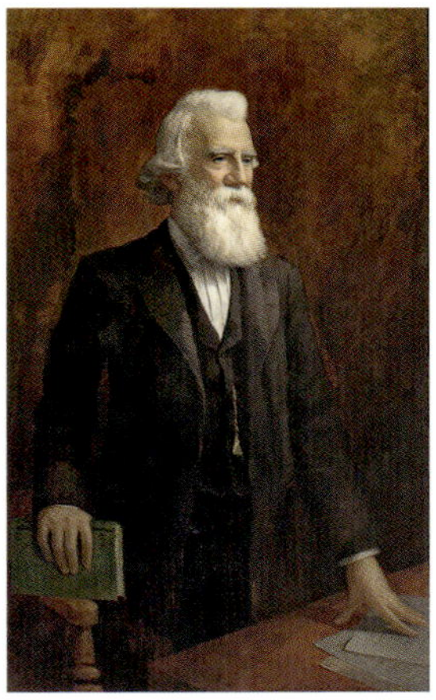

Ogilvie, Frank Stanley 1858–after 1935
Alexander Hannay (1822–1890) 1891
oil on canvas 170 x 103
CMHT. 48

Facing page: Crowley, Graham, b.1950, *Deadly Detached I* (detail), 1987, Nottingham City Museums and Galleries (p. 84)

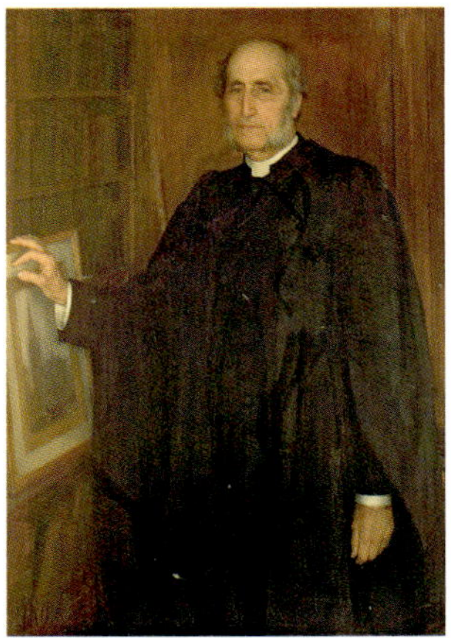

Olivier, Herbert Arnould 1861–1952
Christopher John Newman Hall (1816–1902)
oil on canvas 125.5 x 99
CMHT. 56

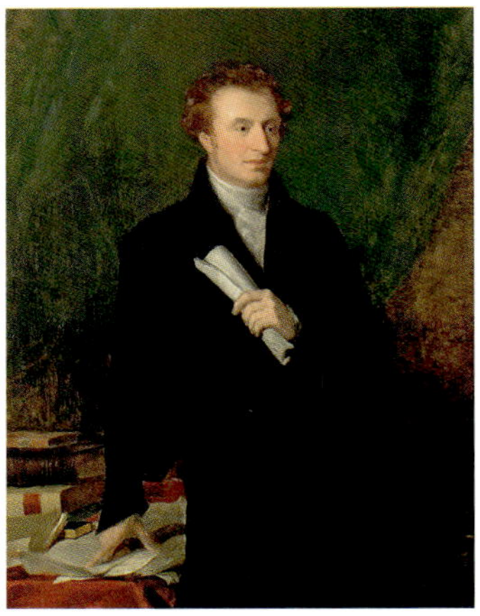

Pickersgill, Henry William (circle of) 1782–1875
John Blackburn (1792–1855)
oil on canvas 121 x 97
CMHT. 55

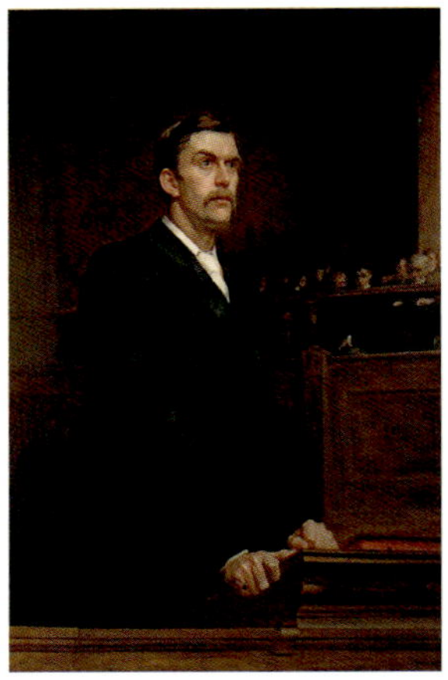

Riviere, Hugh Goldwin 1869–1956
Charles Sylvester Horne (1865–1914), MA, MP 1904
oil on canvas 135 x 92.5
CMHT. 34

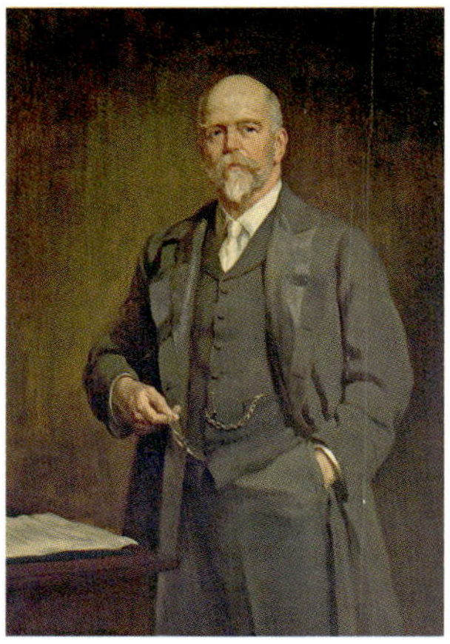

Riviere, Hugh Goldwin 1869–1956
Albert Spicer (1847–1934), Bt, PC, JP
oil on canvas 123 x 84.5
CMHT. 27

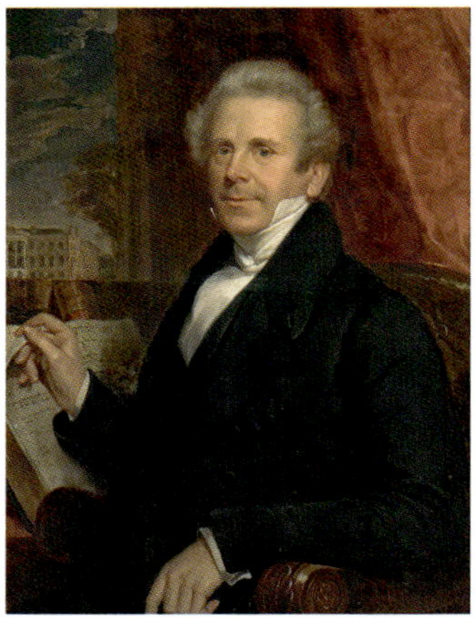

Room, Henry 1802–1850
Ebenezer Henderson (1784–1858)
oil on canvas 90 x 70
CMHT. 18

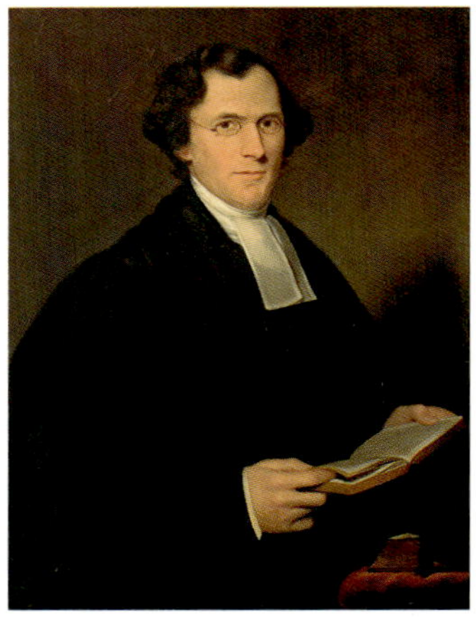

Room, Henry 1802–1850
Edward Mannering (1801–1875)
oil on canvas 90 x 70
CMHT. 23

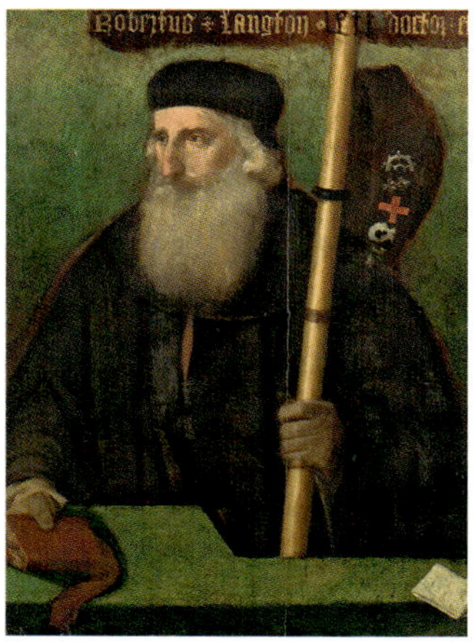

unknown artist
Robritus Langton c.1650
oil on wood 81 x 63
PCF3

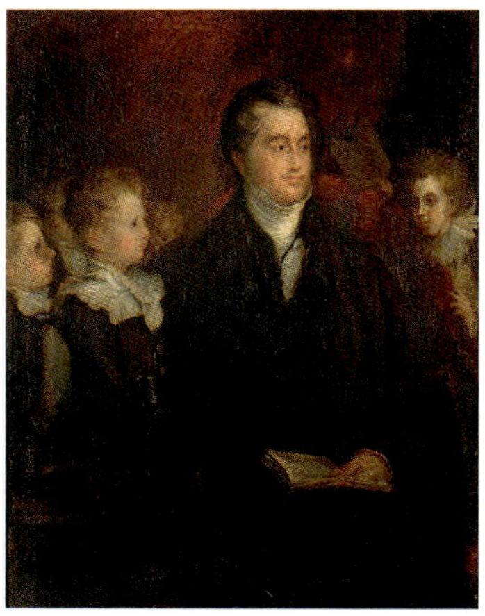

unknown artist
Alexander Fletcher (1787–1860)
oil on canvas 74 x 61
CMHT. 13

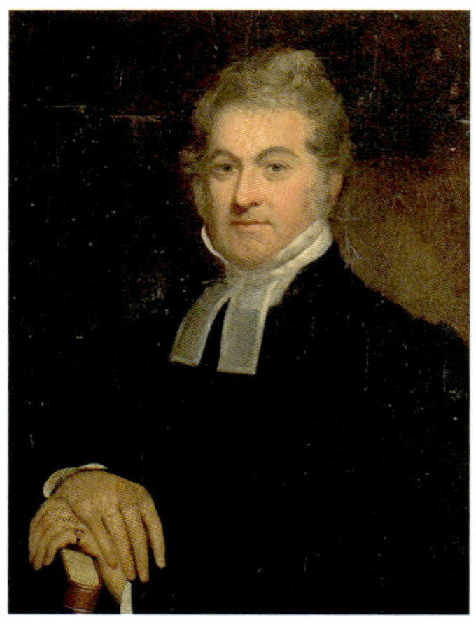

unknown artist
Alexander Fletcher (1787–1860)
oil on canvas 79 x 61
CMHT. 14

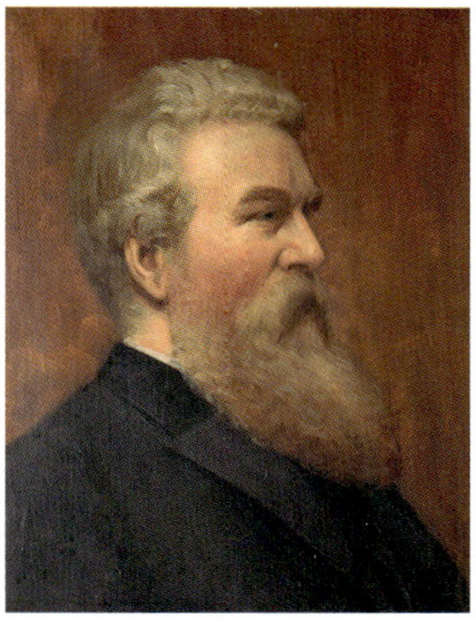

unknown artist
Alexander Mackennal (1835–1904)
oil on canvas 50 x 39
CMHT. 31

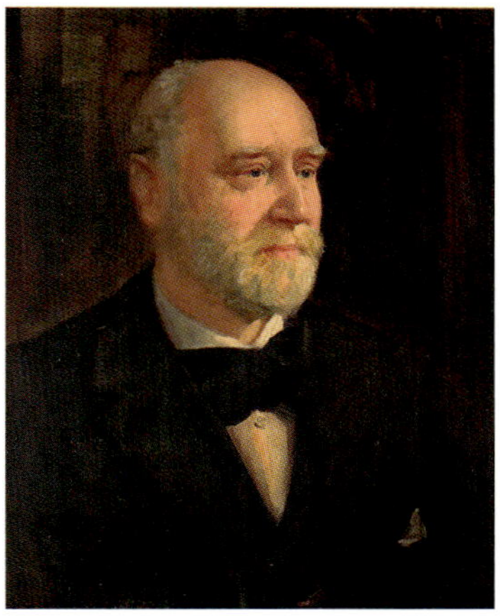

unknown artist
Bernard Joseph Snell (1856–1934), MA, BSc
oil on canvas 64.5 x 54
CMHT. 38

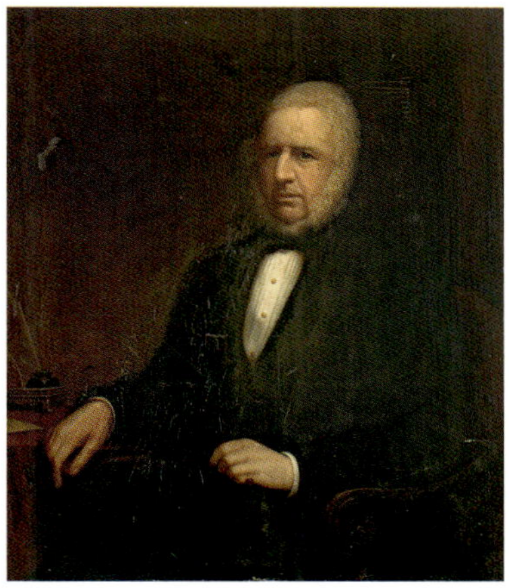

unknown artist
Charles Reed (1819–1881), MP
oil on canvas 101.5 x 89.3
CMHT. 32

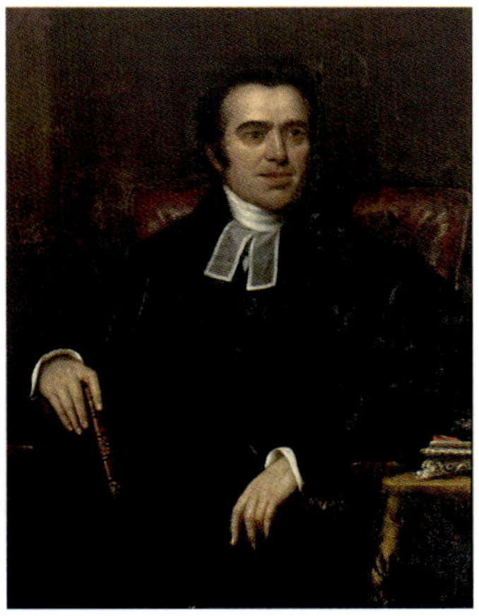

unknown artist
George Collison (1772–1847)
oil on canvas 105 x 82
CMHT. 26

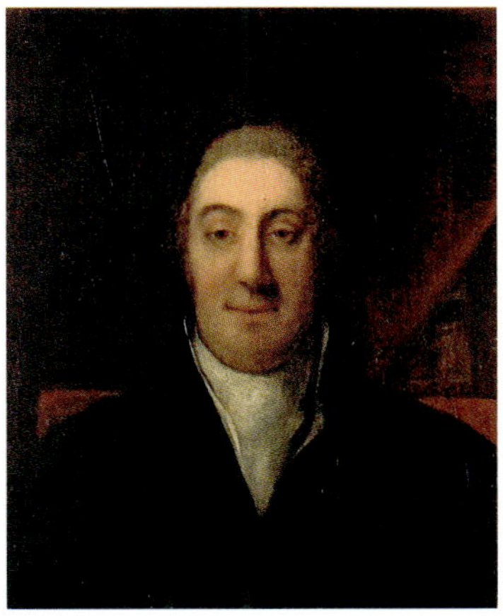

unknown artist
Isaac Stockton Keith (1755–1813)
oil on canvas 60 x 50
CMHT. 22

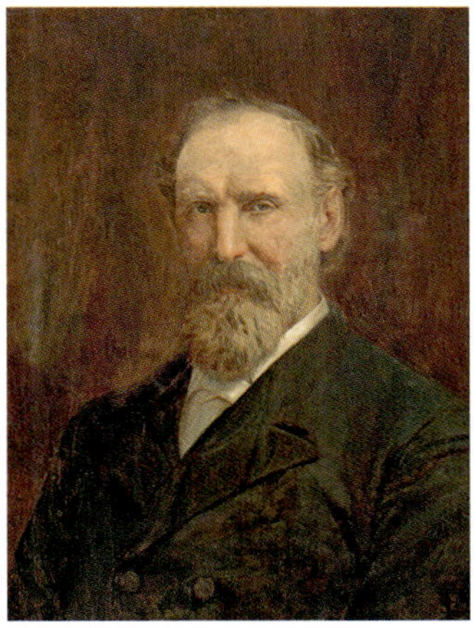

unknown artist
James Alexander Mitchell (1849–1919)
oil on canvas 64 x 49.5
CMHT. 02

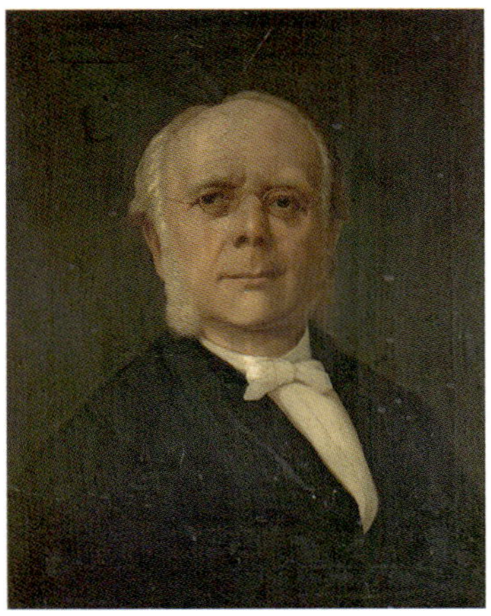

unknown artist
James Guinness Rogers (1822–1911)
oil on canvas 59 x 48
CMHT. 08

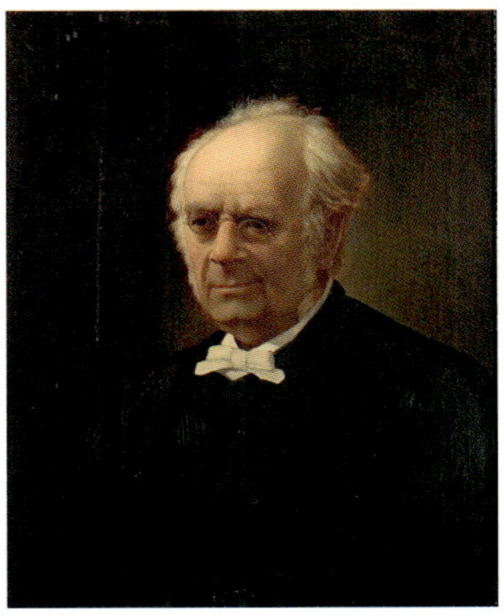

unknown artist
James Guinness Rogers (1822–1911)
oil on canvas 59 x 50
CMHT. 09

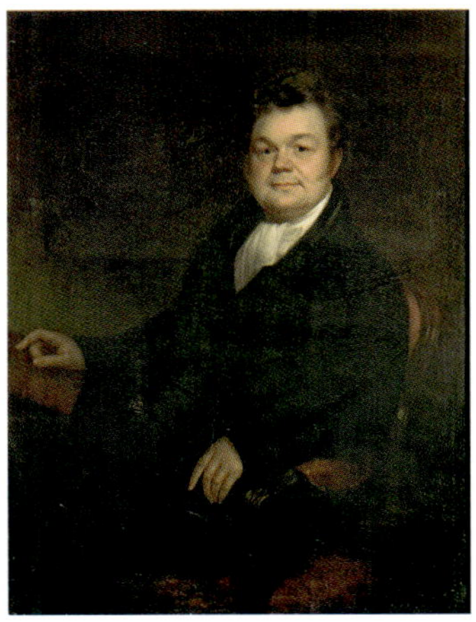

unknown artist
John Angell James (1785–1859)
oil on canvas 113 x 88
CMHT. 25

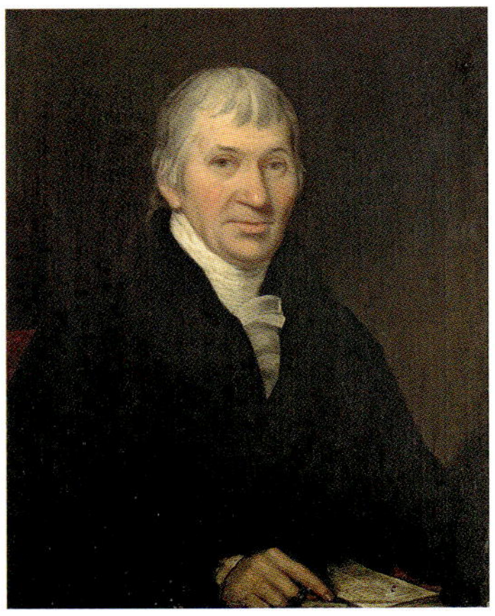

unknown artist
John Clayton Junior (1780–1865)
oil on canvas 74.5 x 61.5
CMHT. 20

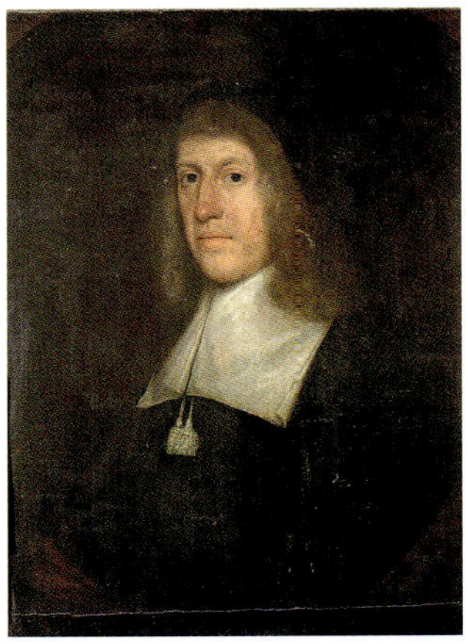

unknown artist
John Owen (1616–1683)
oil on canvas 74.5 x 57
CMHT. 47

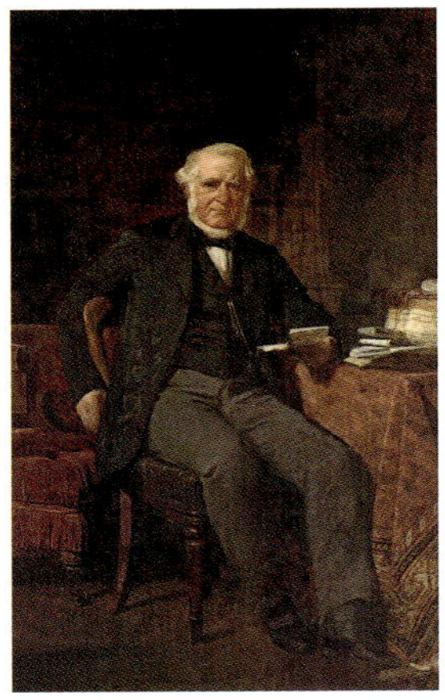

unknown artist
John Remington Mills (1798–1879)
oil on canvas 195 x 120
CMHT. 49

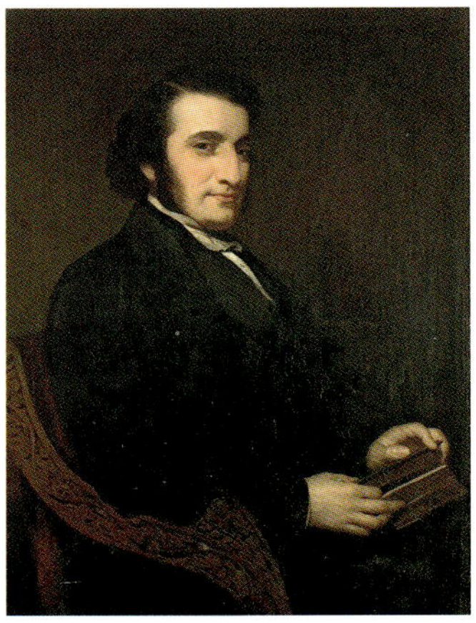

unknown artist
John Stoughton (1807–1897)
oil on canvas 90.4 x 70
CMHT. 04

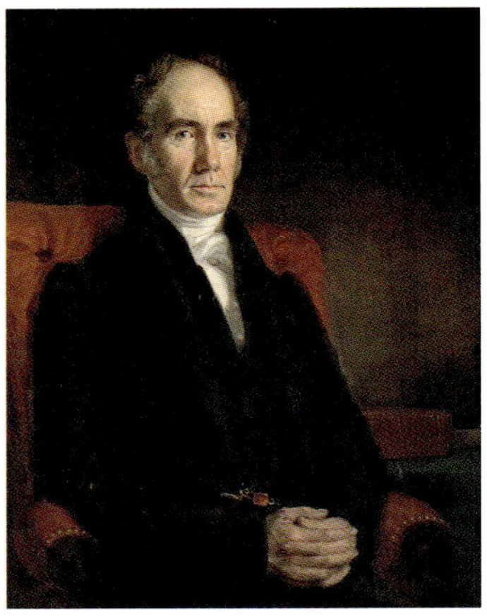

unknown artist
Ralph Wardlaw (1779–1853)
oil on canvas 88.5 x 72.5
CMHT. 36

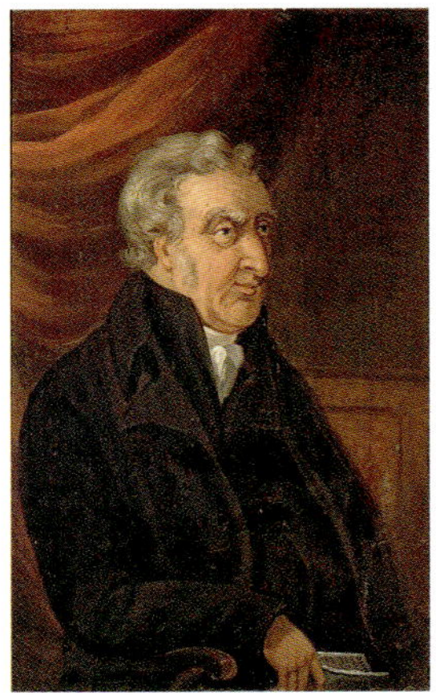

unknown artist
Rowland Hill (1744–1833)
oil on canvas 36 x 22.5
CMHT. 10

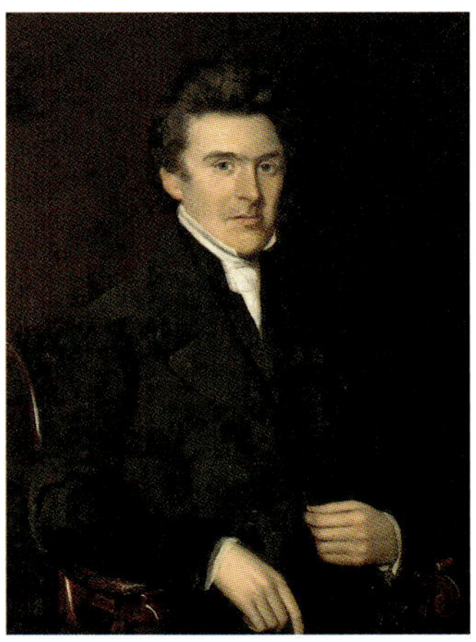

unknown artist
Samuel Martin (1817–1878)
oil on canvas 89.7 x 69.2
CMHT. 24

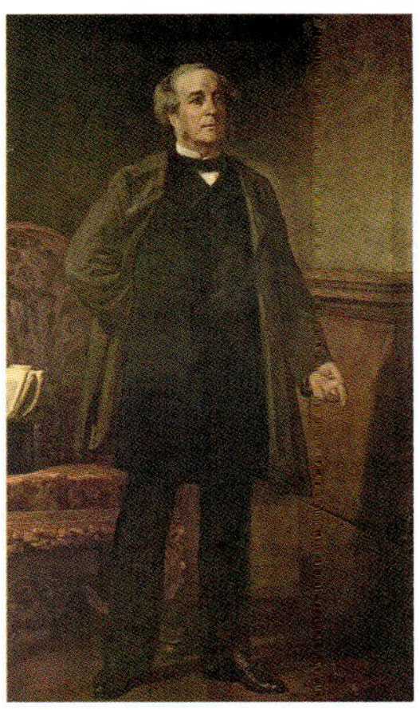

unknown artist
Samuel Morley (1809–1886), MP
oil on canvas 200 x 123.5
CMHT. 35

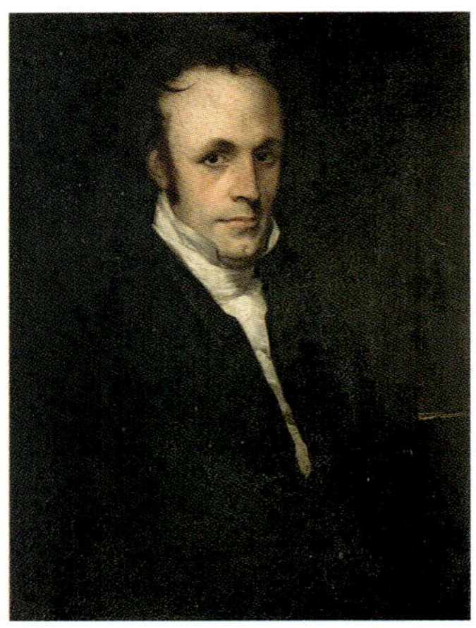

unknown artist
Thomas Binney (1798–1874)
oil on canvas 70.7 x 55
CMHT. 12

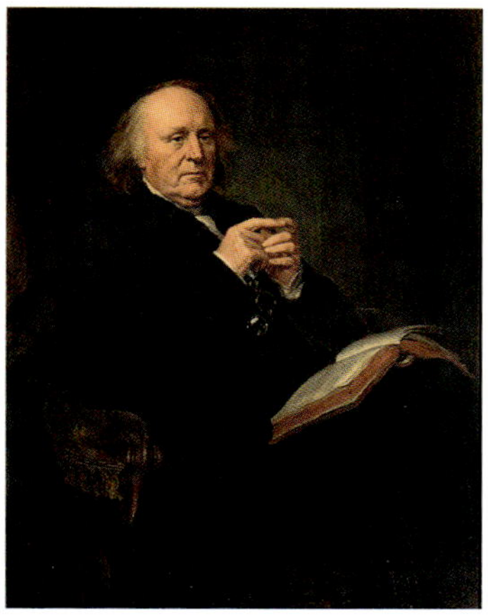

unknown artist
Thomas Binney (1798–1874)
oil on canvas 125.5 x 99.5
CMHT. 29

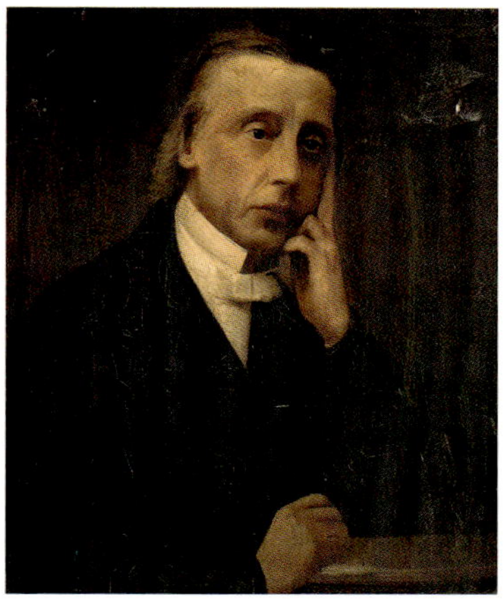

unknown artist
Thomas Toke Lynch (1818–1871)
oil on canvas 70 x 60
PCF1

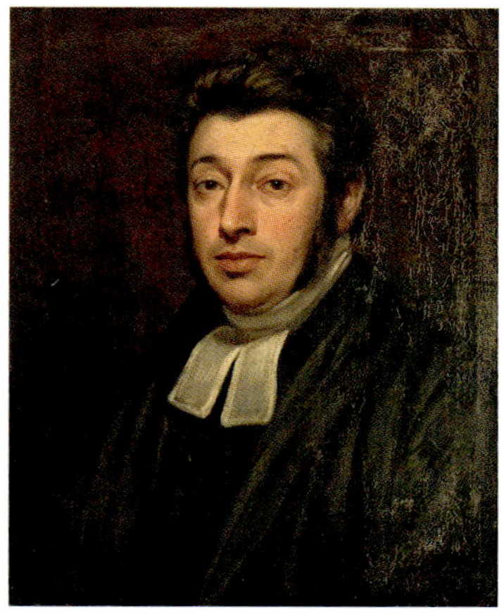

unknown artist
William Campbell (1799–1878)
oil on canvas 64 x 53.5
CMHT. 07

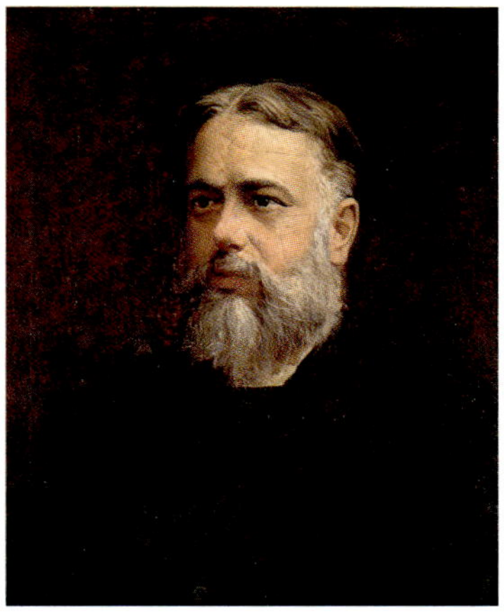

unknown artist
William James Woods (1850–1903), BA
oil on canvas 59.5 x 49
CMHT. 06

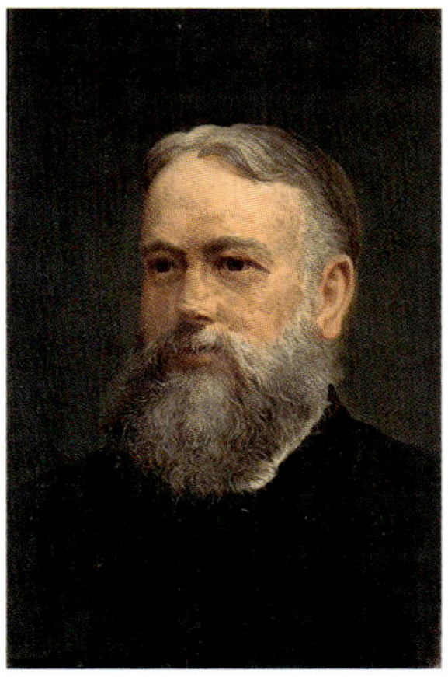

unknown artist
William James Woods (1850–1903), BA
oil on canvas 36 x 24
CMHT. 11

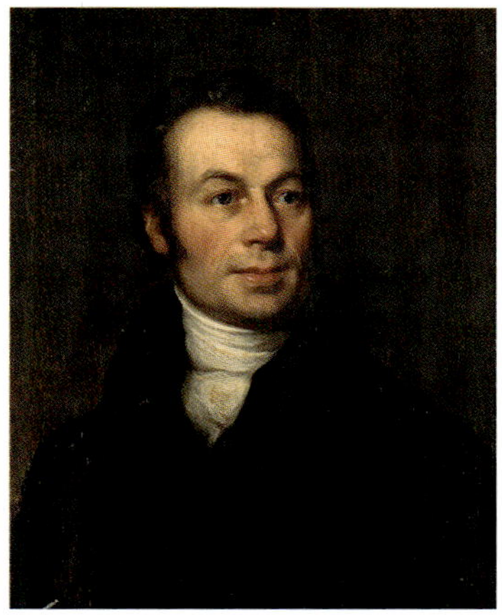

unknown artist
William Roby (1766–1830)
oil on canvas 58 x 48.5
CMHT. 40

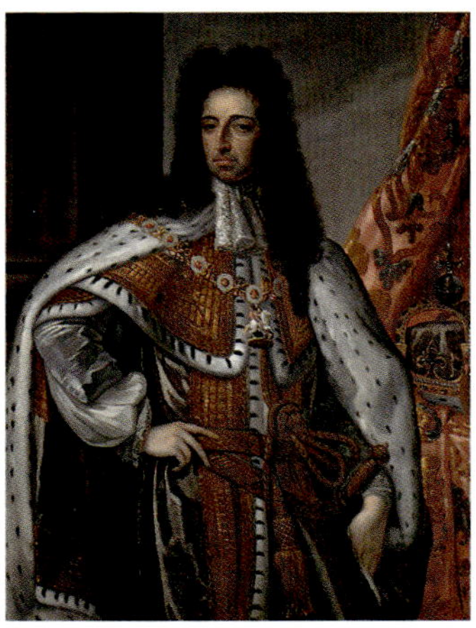

Wissing, Willem 1656–1687
King William III (1650–1702)
oil on canvas 120 x 97.5
CMHT. 52

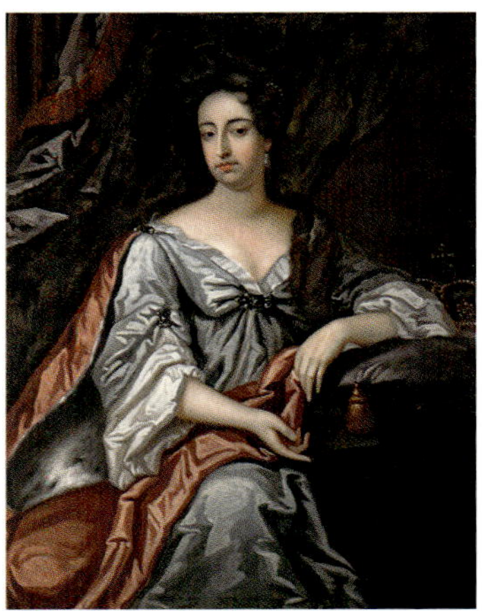

Wissing, Willem 1656–1687
Queen Mary II (1662–1692)
oil on canvas 120 x 97.5
CMHT. 53

The Council House

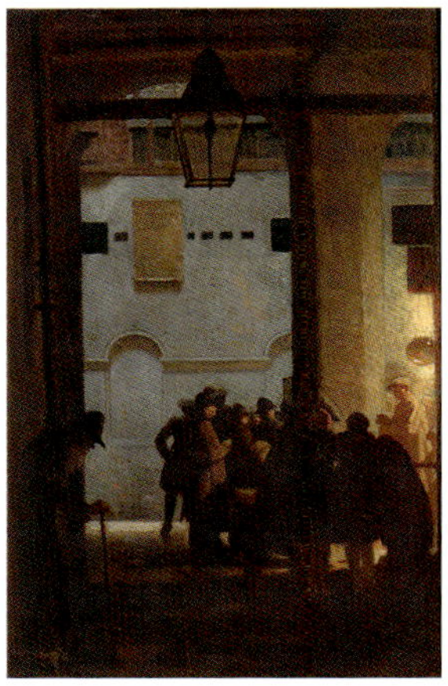

Davis, Noel Denholm 1876–1950
The Shambles, Old Exchange, Nottingham 1928
oil on canvas 59.5 x 39
PCF1

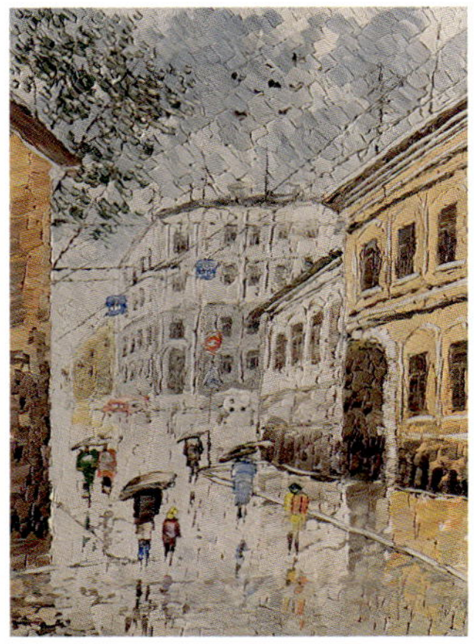

Krit, D. (attributed to)
Munck 1996
oil on canvas 39 x 30
PCF2

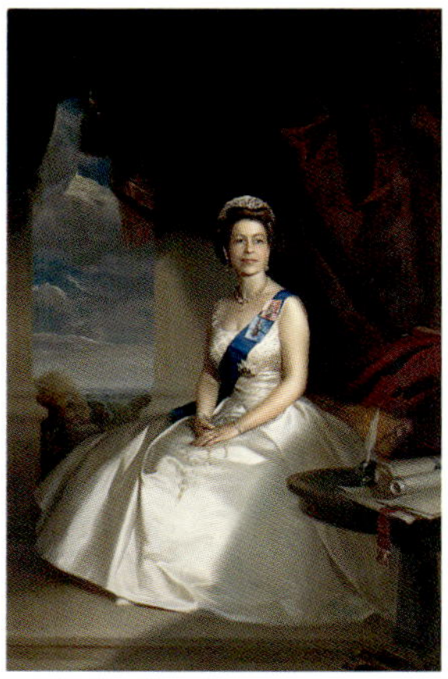

Townsend, John b.1930
Queen Elizabeth II (b.1926) 1970
oil on canvas 240 x 140.5
PCF3

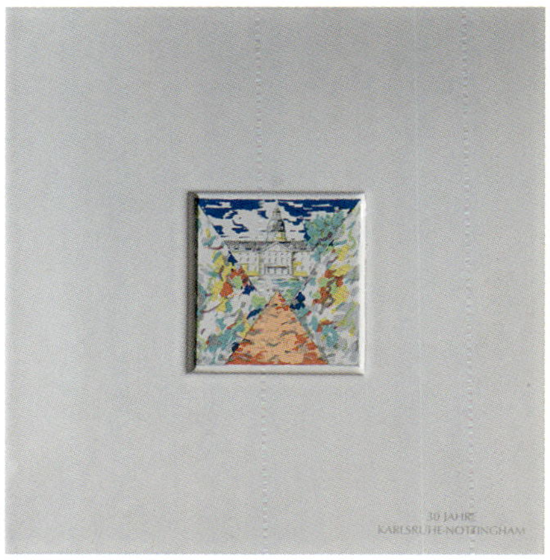

unknown artist
30 Years, Karlsruhe-Nottingham
oil on ceramic 33 x 33
PCF4

The Sherwood Rangers Yeomanry Regimental Association

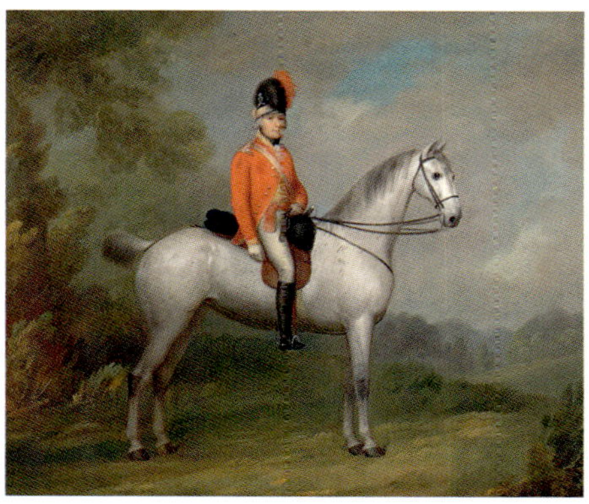

Boultbee, John 1753–1812
Captain Ichabod Wright of Mapperley (1767–1862), Formed the First Nottingham Troop in 1794 1803
oil on canvas 49.8 x 59
TAca.01

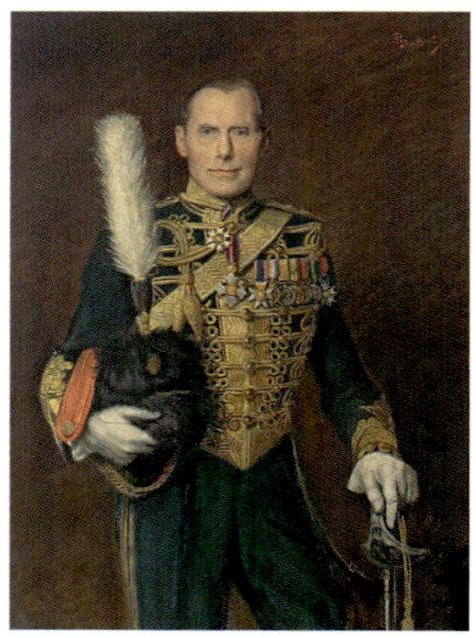

Lewis, Reginald b.1901
Colonel the Lord Barnby of Blyth, CMG, CBE, MVO, TD, Commanding Officer, the Sherwood Rangers Yeomanry (1920–1928), (...)
oil on canvas 119 x 89
TAca.02

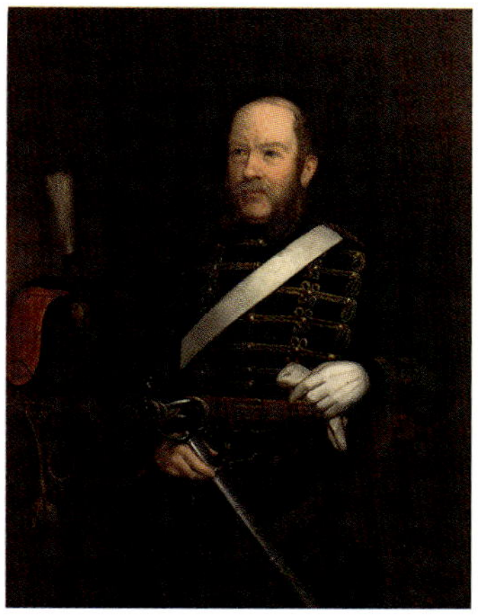

unknown artist
Quartermaster Bousfield (1815–1890)
oil on canvas 126 x 97.8
TAca.03

The University of Nottingham

The University of Nottingham art collection consists of some 526 items covering a broad range of subjects and media which have been acquired through purchase, gift and bequest. The works are distributed across the four main campuses at Nottingham in academic schools, halls of residence and principal administration buildings. There is no permanent gallery or storage space for the Collection. The Djanogly Art Gallery, the university-funded art gallery at the Lakeside Arts Centre, is a temporary exhibition space organising a year-round programme of contemporary and historic loan exhibitions. For further information on the programme see www.lakesidearts.org.uk

The two principal coherent parts of the Collection, which include oil and acrylic paintings, are the Newcastle Bequest (of which the largest concentration is displayed in the Trent Building) and the Lakeside Arts Centre Collection displayed in the Arts Centre and Music Department.

Documentation of the collections currently exists as an unpublished skeleton catalogue held by the Visual Arts Officer at the Djanogly Art Gallery.

The University of Nottingham first accepted charge of the family papers of the Duke of Newcastle in 1955. They are among the country's pre-eminent surviving family archives and are probably most familiar to historians for their value in studying British political history and colonial affairs in the eighteenth and nineteenth centuries. The addition of the Newcastle family portraits in 1991–1992 added a new dimension to the Collection.

Over the centuries the Dukes of Newcastle acquired a collection of exceptional interest. The Clumber Collection has been dispersed in recent times, but a significant core remained the property of the Dukes of Newcastle. The 9th Duke hoped that the family pictures which survived would be maintained by an institution able to care for and exhibit them. The bequest has made it possible to study a family's papers alongside the family portraits and to research social history as revealed in historical portraiture, domestic letters, diaries and personal papers.

The collection of 34 items includes portraits from the sixteenth to the twentieth centuries including works by Godfrey Kneller and Thomas Lawrence.

For further information regarding this bequest see the exhibition catalogue produced by the University of Nottingham Art Gallery in 1992, *The Newcastles of Clumber: A Gift to the University of Nottingham.*

In 1992 the Art Gallery at The University of Nottingham moved to its present purpose-built premises at the south entrance to University Park. At this time it was renamed the Djanogly Art Gallery after its principal benefactor Sir Harry Djanogly. Year after year the Gallery has built up a small collection of contemporary art to adorn the walls of the Lakeside Arts Centre and adjacent Music Department. The purchases, made with relatively modest sums of money, have tended to be from artists whose work has featured in exhibitions held by the Gallery or from artists working in the Nottingham and East Midlands region. At present the Collection consists of 98 items.

Neil Walker, Visual Arts Officer, Djanogly Art Gallery

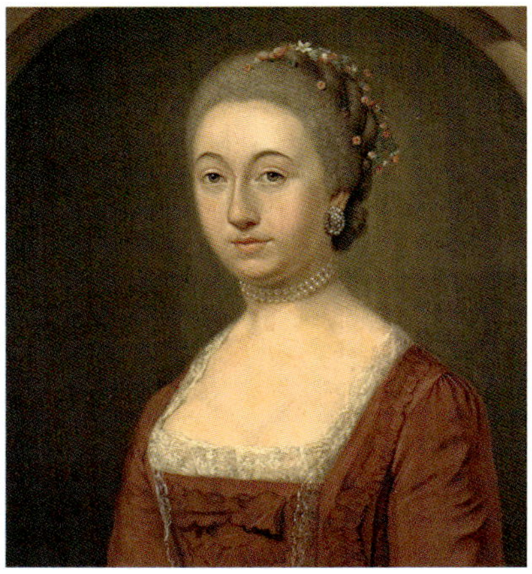

Alexander, Cosmo 1724–1772
Mrs Thomas Hope 1763
oil on canvas 54.5 x 53
UON.076

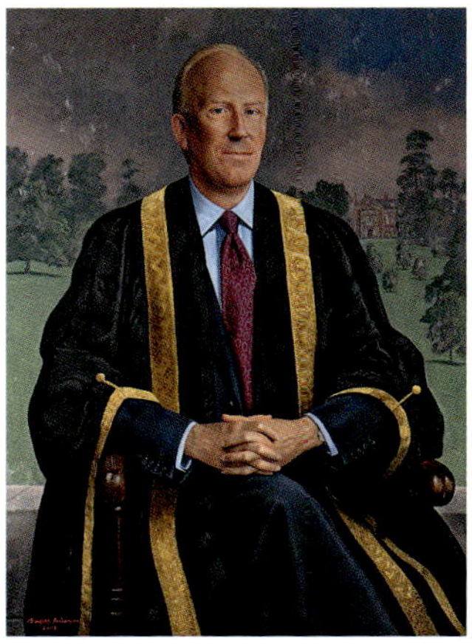

Anderson, Douglas Hardinge b.1934
Julian Ronald Haylock, BSc, FRSA, President of the Council (1996–2003) 2003
oil on canvas 98.5 x 74.5
UON.023

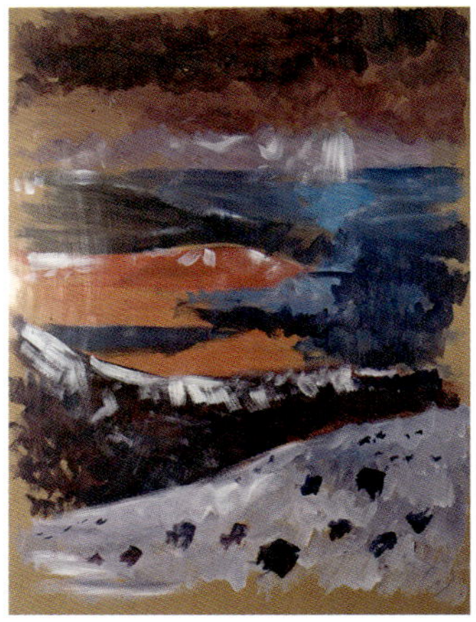

Arnfield, Nick 1961–1999
Light on Cornish Sea
acrylic on board 103 x 78.5
UON.024

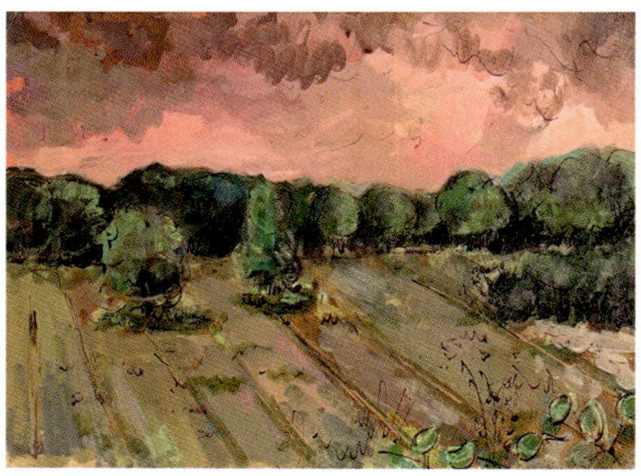

Arnfield, Nick 1961–1999
Pink Sky (1), *Hertfordshire*
acrylic on board 30 x 42
UON.005

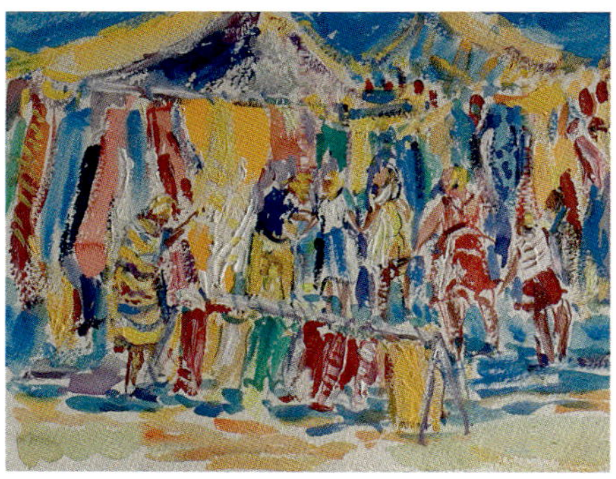

Arnfield, Marjorie 1930–2001
Street Market, Lascala 1998
acrylic on paper mounted on board 27.5 x 38
UON.054

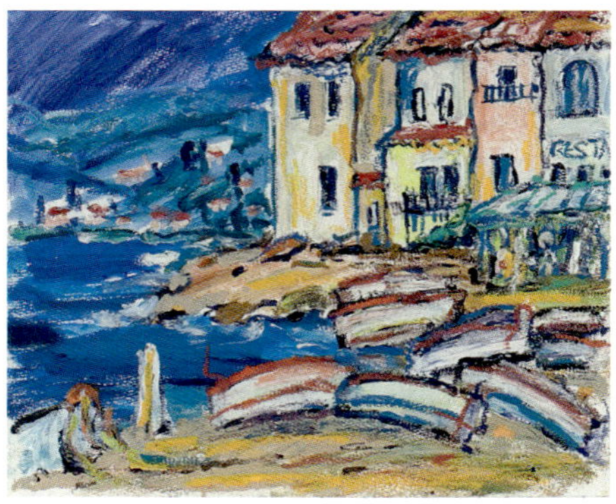

Arnfield, Marjorie 1930–2001
Cadaqués, Spain (1) 2000
acrylic on paper mounted on board 40 x 51
UON.053

Facing page: Knight, Laura, 1877–1970, *Motherhood* (detail), c.1922, Nottingham City Museums and Galleries (p. 116)

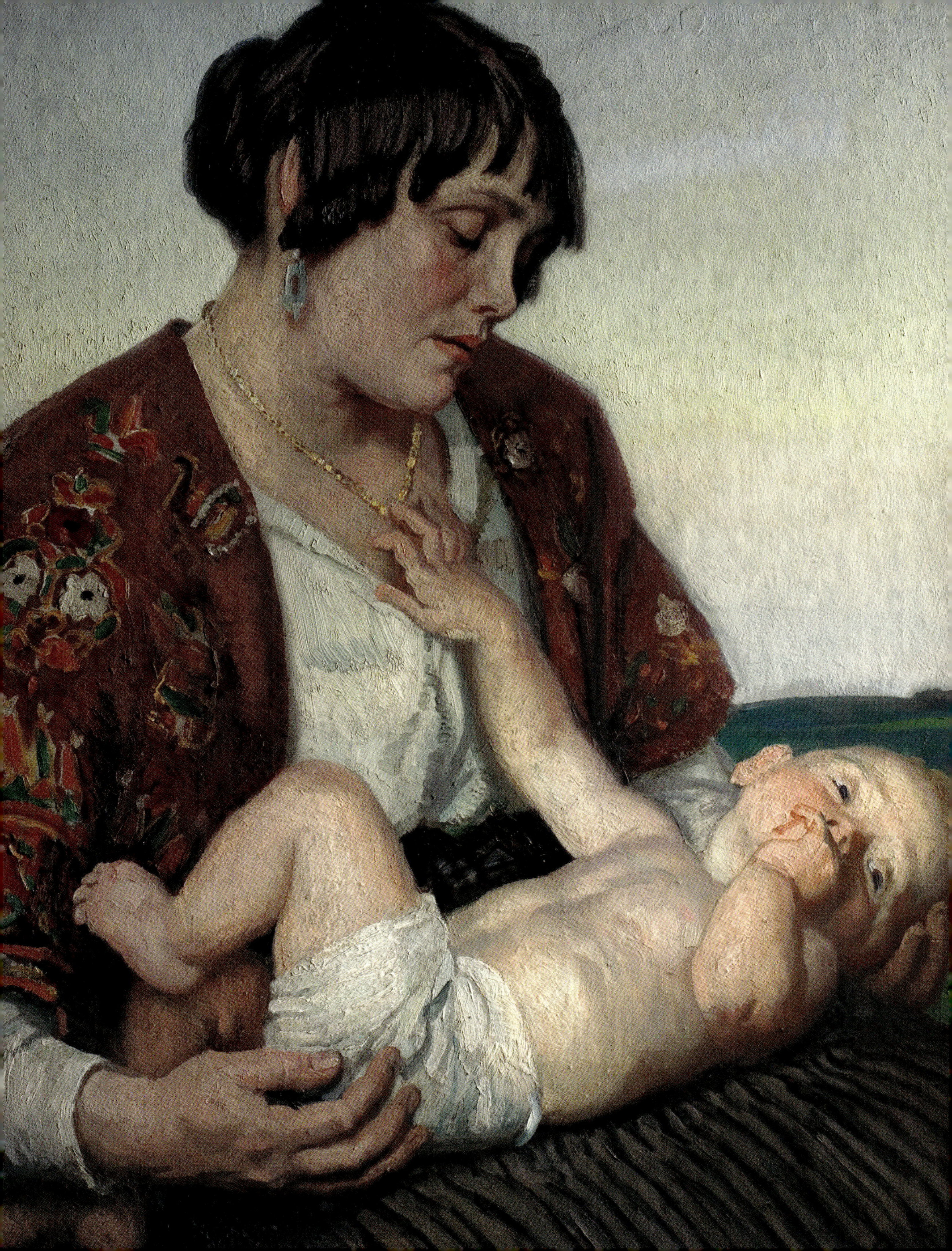

Barke, Christopher
Black Abstract 2000
oil on board 61 x 61
UON.055

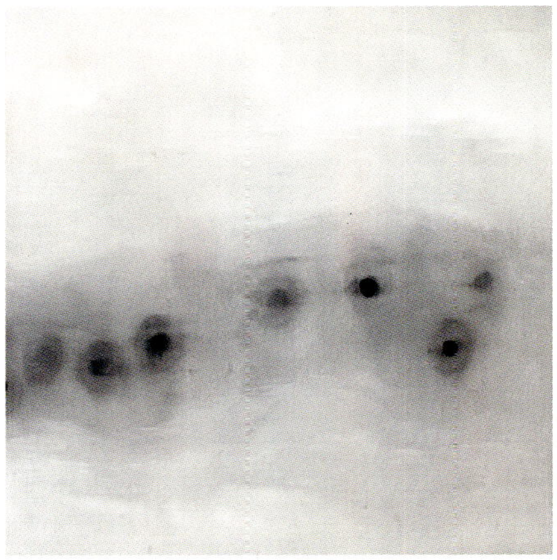

Barke, Christopher
White Abstract 2000
oil on canvas over board 61 x 61
UON.056

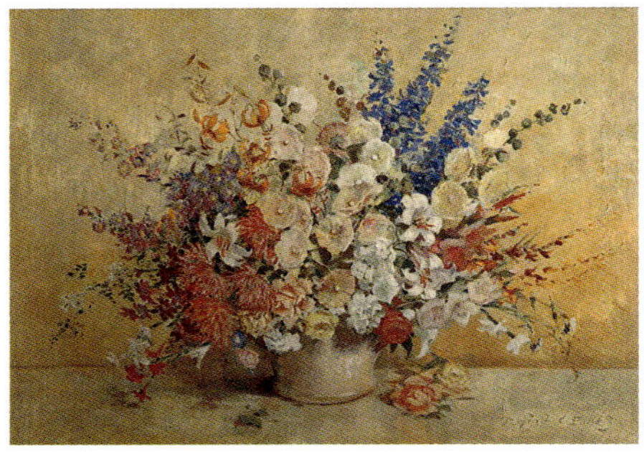

Bates, Marjorie Christine 1883–1962
Flower Still Life
oil on canvas 86 x 126
UON.153

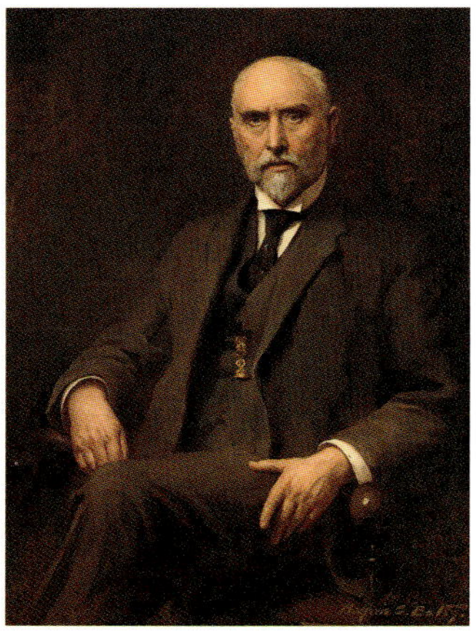

Bates, Marjorie Christine 1883–1962
William Henry Revis, Esq. (d.1923)
oil on canvas 110 x 85
UON.006

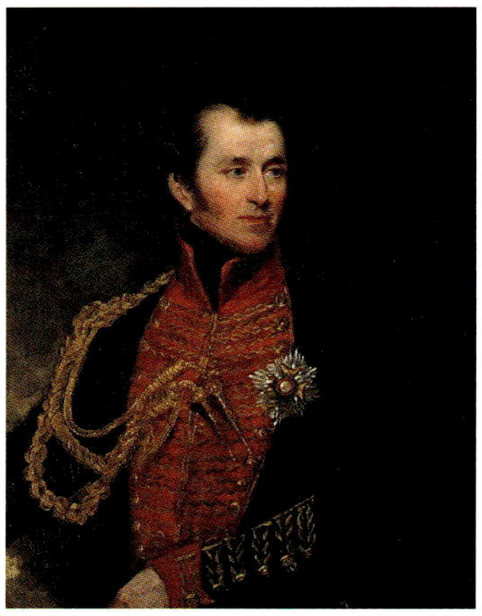

Beechey, William (school of) 1753–1839
General Sir William Henry Clinton (1769–1846)
oil on canvas 89 x 68.5
UON.077

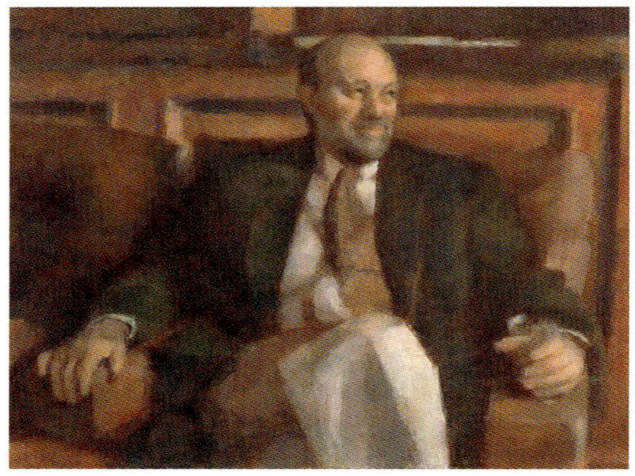

Bennett, Chris b.1957
Mr W. Ian Hooker, Warden of Lenton and Wortley Hall (1980–2006)
acrylic on canvas 58 x 68 (E)
UON.163

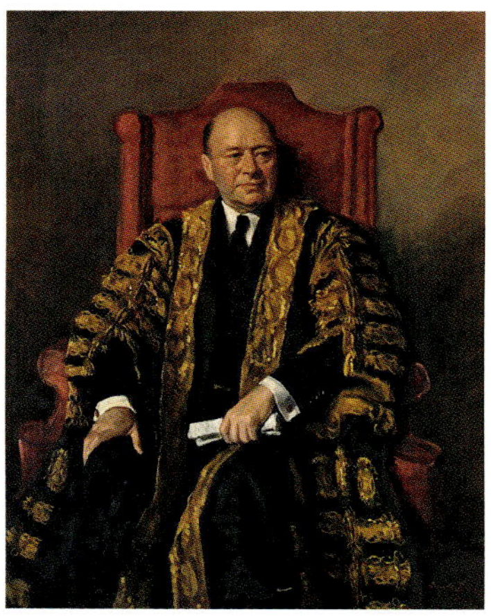

Birley, Oswald Hornby Joseph 1880–1952
The Right Honourable Lord Trent (1889–1956), Chancellor of the University (1948–1954)
oil on canvas 138 x 112
UON.026

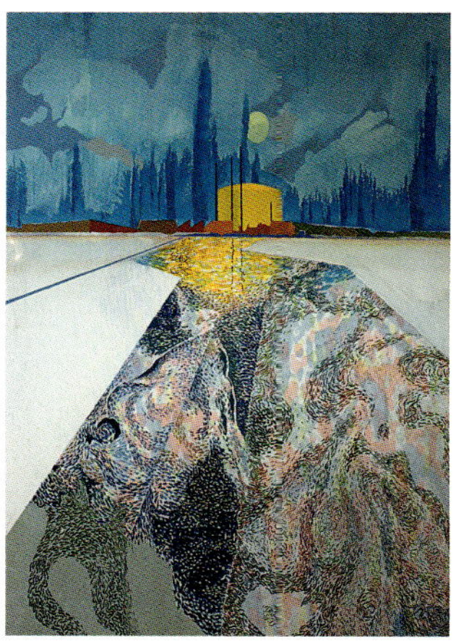

Birrell, William
The Canal 1970
acrylic on canvas 120 x 108
UON.122

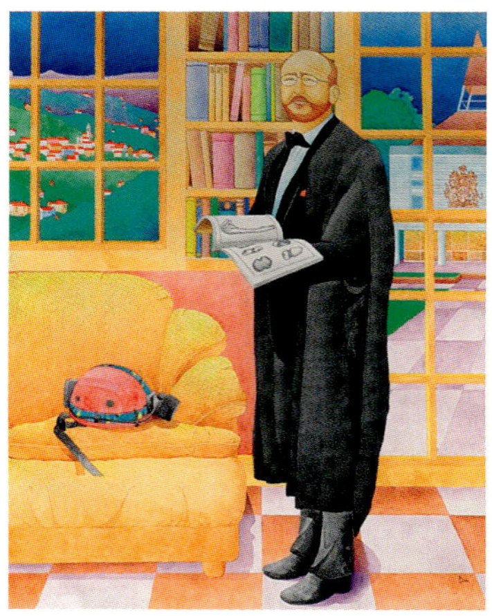

Bixio, Roberto b.1947
Dr Mark Pearce 2007
oil & acrylic on canvas 110 x 90
UON.169

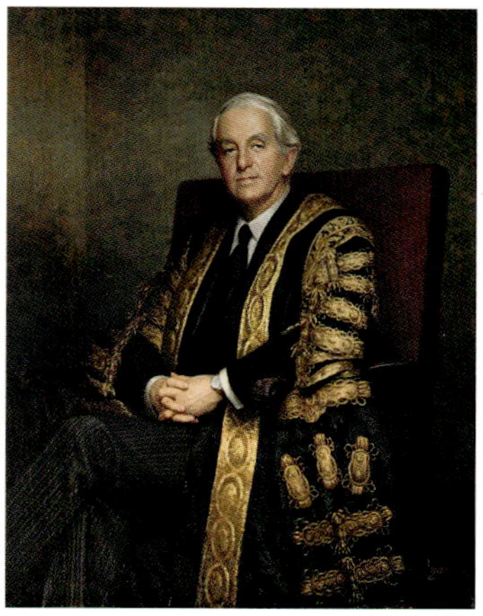

Boden, Leonard 1911–1999
Sir Francis Hill (1899–1980), Chancellor of the University (1972–1978)
oil on canvas 126 x 100
UON.027

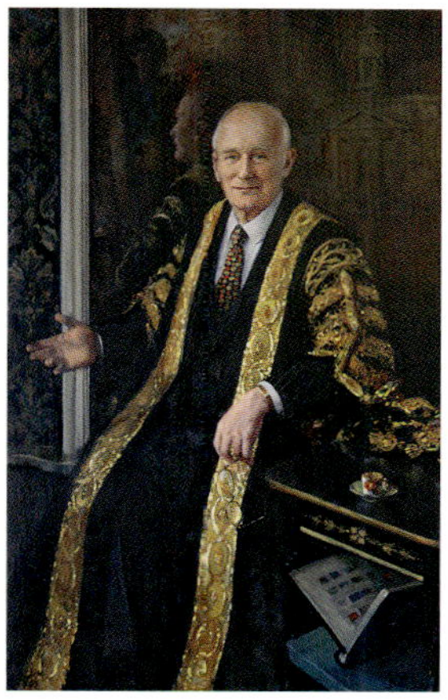

Bond, Jane b.1939
Lord Ronald Dearing (b.1930) 2000
oil on canvas 150 x 97
UON.028

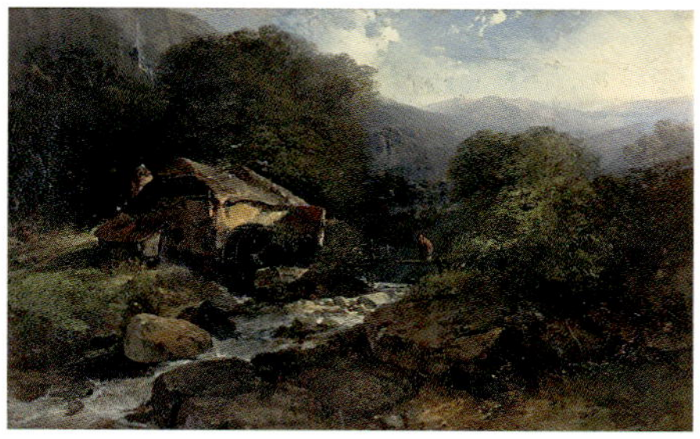

Bright, Henry 1814–1873
Welsh Landscape with a Watermill
oil on canvas 34 x 56
UON.007

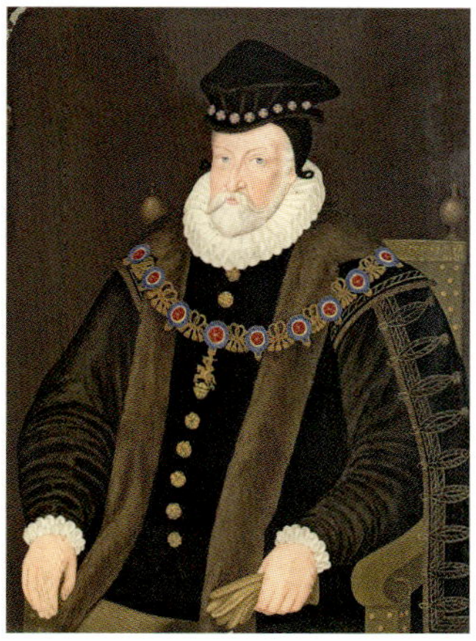

British (English) School 16th C
Edward Fiennes de Clinton (1512–1585), KG (later 1st Earl of Lincoln)
oil on enamel 18 x 14.3
UON.136

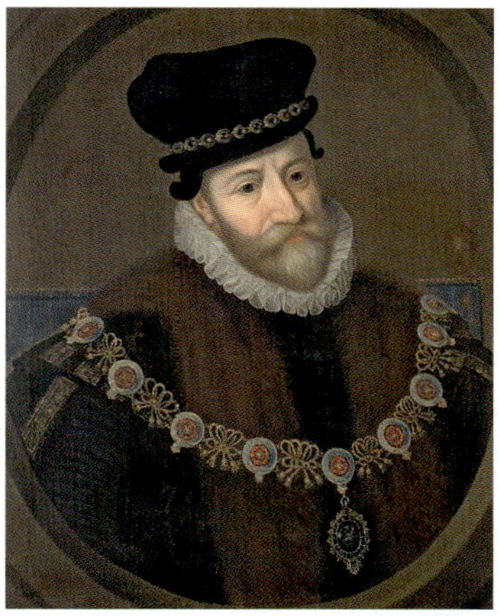

British (English) School 16th C
Edward Fiennes de Clinton (1512–1585), KG (later 1st Earl of Lincoln)
oil on canvas 74 x 61
UON.140

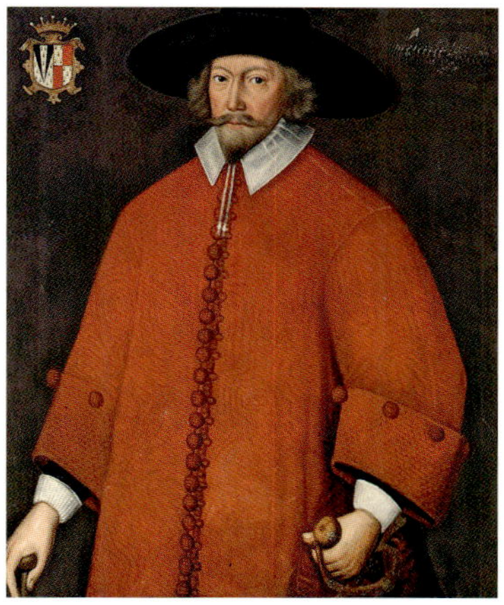

British (English) School
John Holles (c.1565–1637), 1st Earl Clare
1600–1637
oil on canvas 97.8 x 84.5
UON.034

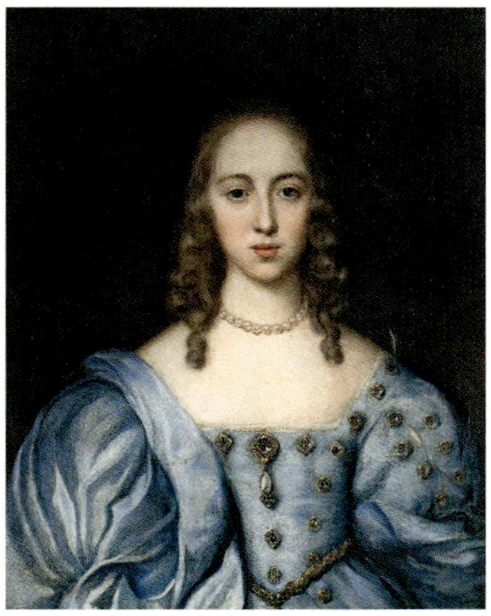

British (English) School 17th C
Bridget, 4th Countess of Lincoln
oil on canvas 70.5 x 57.5
UON.035

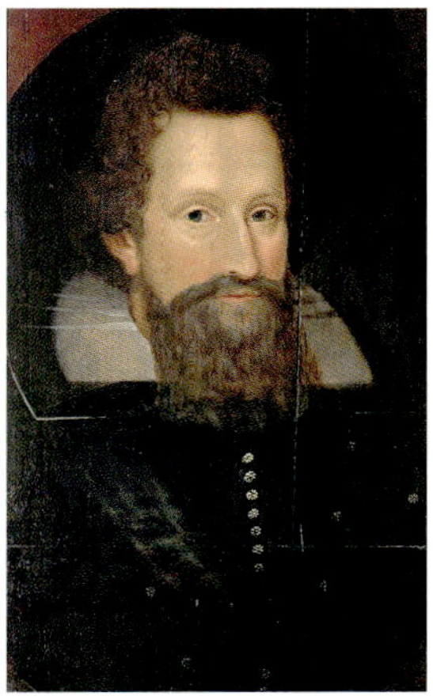

British (English) School 17th C
Portrait of a Man in a White Lace Collar
oil on panel 58 x 37
UON.085

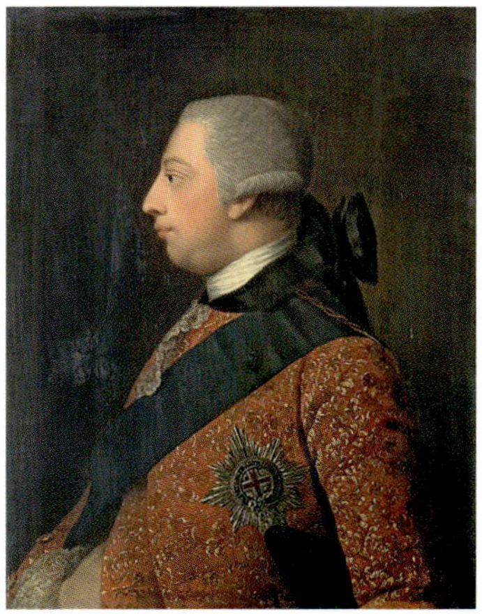

British (English) School 18th C
Portrait of a Man in Profile in a Red Jacket and a Black Sash
oil on board 75.5 x 62
UON.086

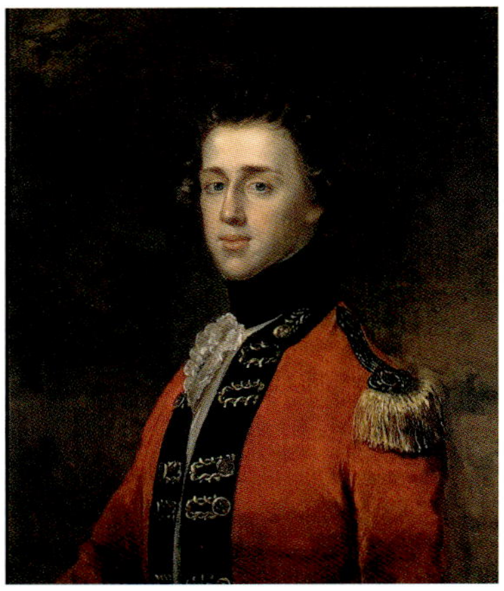

British (English) School 18th C
Thomas Pelham-Clinton (1752–1795) (later 10th Earl of Lincoln and 3rd Duke of Newcastle-under-Lyne)
oil on canvas 73.7 x 61
UON.168

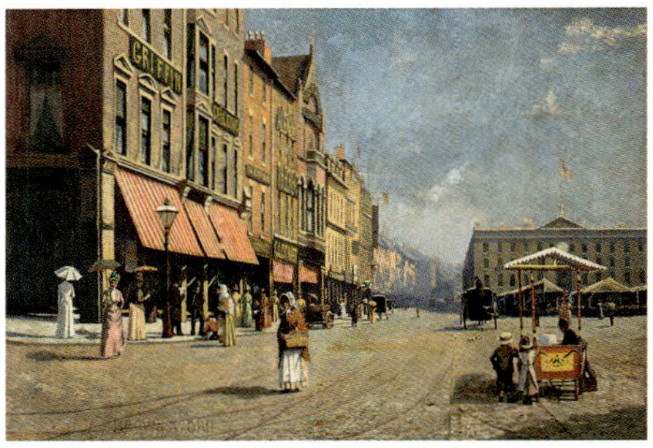

Brownsword, Harry A. 1862–1920
Old Market Square, Nottingham, 1889
oil on canvas 100.5 x 151.5
UON.008

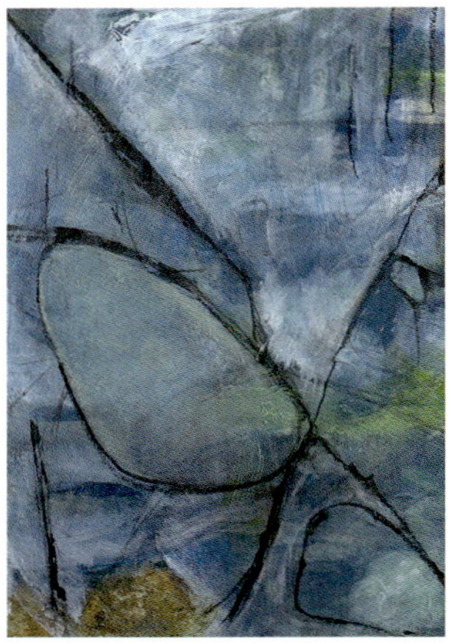

Buckingham, Jennie Beatrice b.1968
Boulder (III) 1997
acrylic on paper 58 x 40.5
UON.069

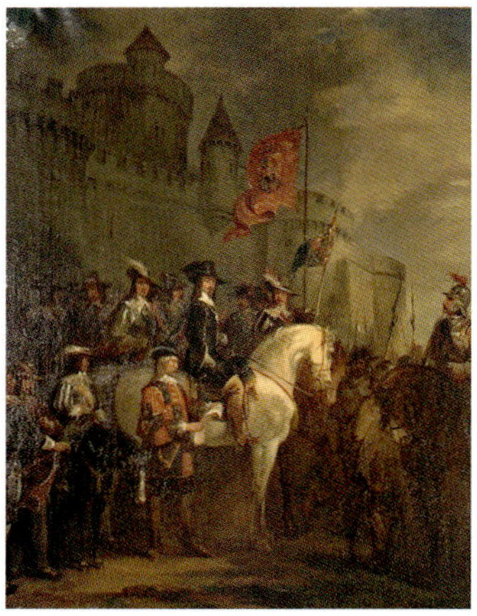

Bussey, Reuben 1818–1893
Charles I Raising His Standard at Nottingham Castle
oil on canvas 120 x 100 (E)
UON.166

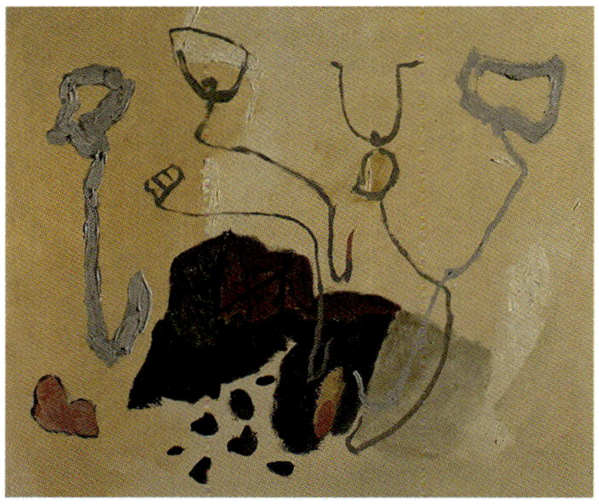

Cockrill, Maurice b.1936
Generation (Ochre Series) 1993
oil on canvas 50.5 x 61
UON.070

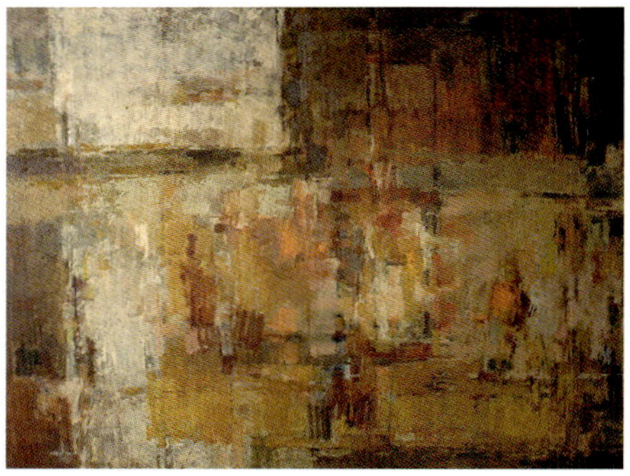

Cohen, Harold b.1928
Still Life 1956
oil on board 90.2 x 120.5
UON.125

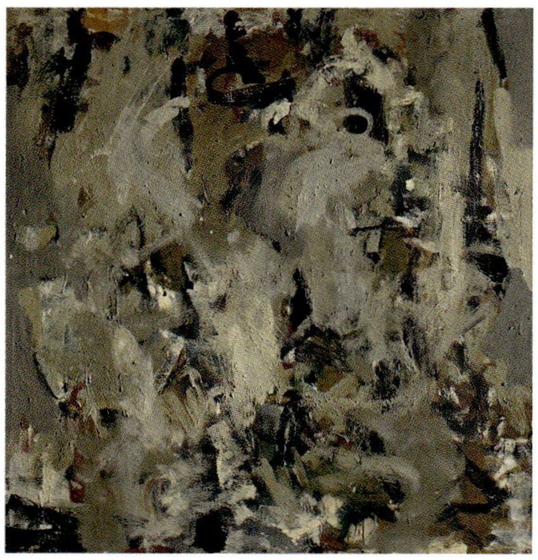

Cohen, Harold b.1928
Untitled 1958
oil on canvas 140 x 140
UON.109

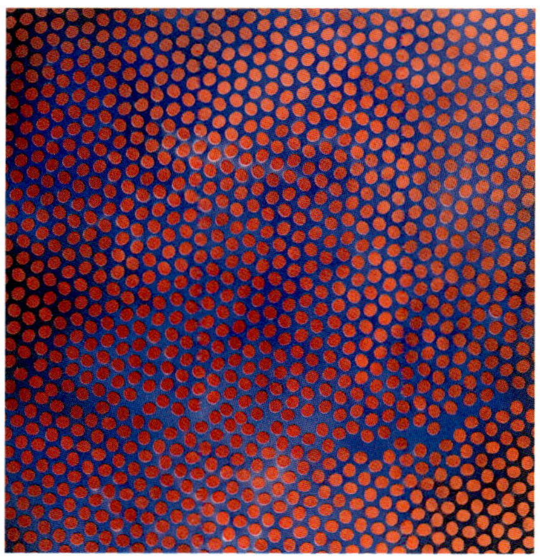

Cohen, Harold b.1928
Gandalf 1967
oil on canvas 126.5 x 126.5
UON.009

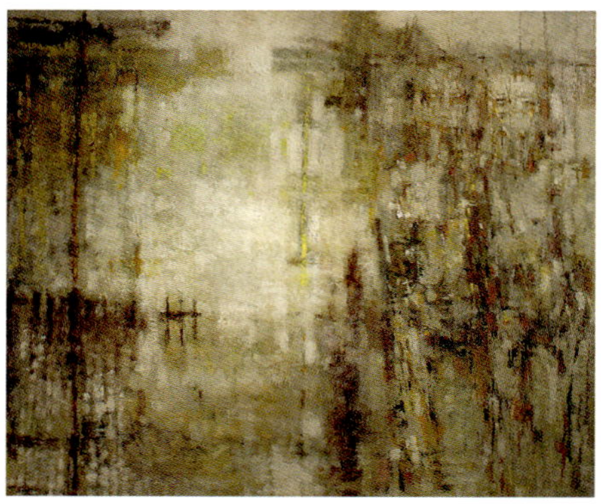

Cohen, Harold b.1928
Flood
oil on board 96.5 x 122
UON.105

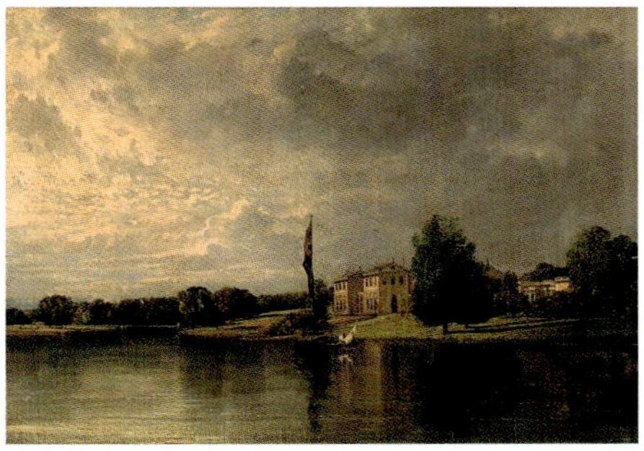

Collins, William 1788–1847
The South and East Front of Clumber House, Nottinghamshire
oil on canvas 59 x 83
UON.096

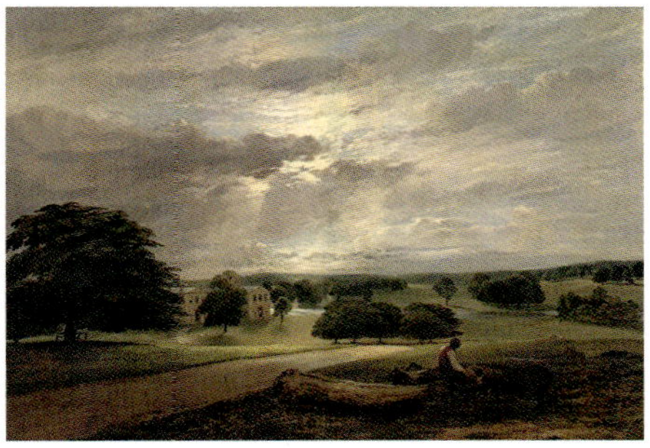

Collins, William 1788–1847
The West Front of Clumber House, Nottinghamshire
oil on canvas 59 x 83
UON.097

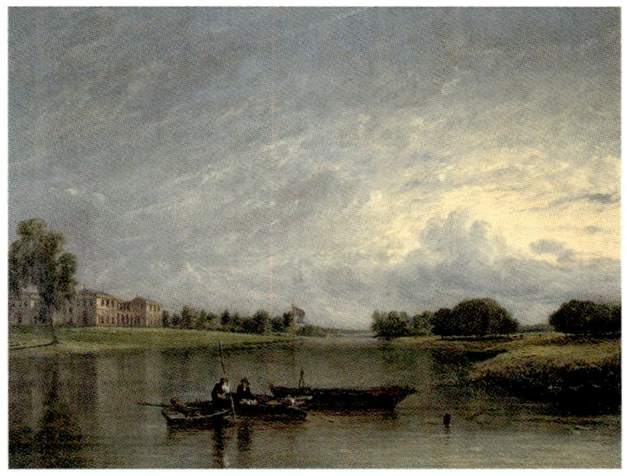

Collins, William 1788–1847
View of the South and West Fronts of Clumber House, Nottinghamshire
oil on canvas 58.5 x 106.7
UON.078

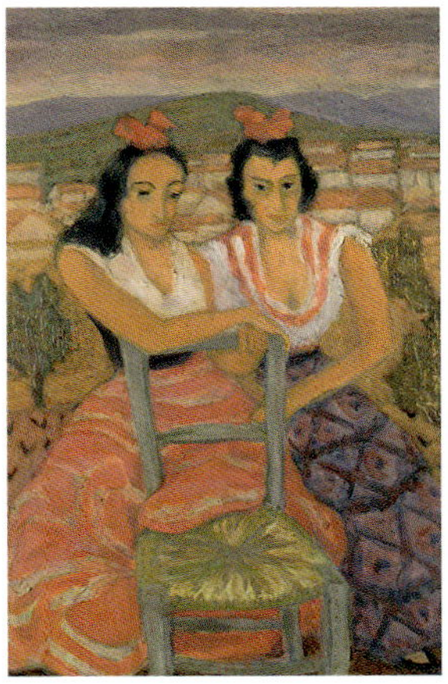

Colvile, Harry Morton 1905–1992
Andalusian Women
oil on canvas 80 x 53
UON.089

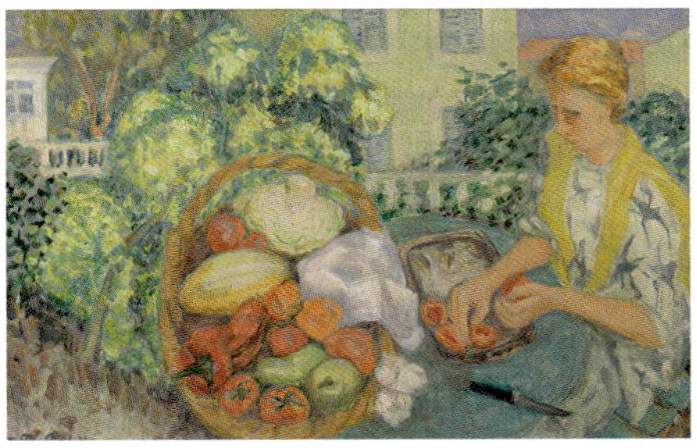

Colvile, Harry Morton 1905–1992
Girl in a Riviera Garden
oil on canvas 64 x 102
UON.091

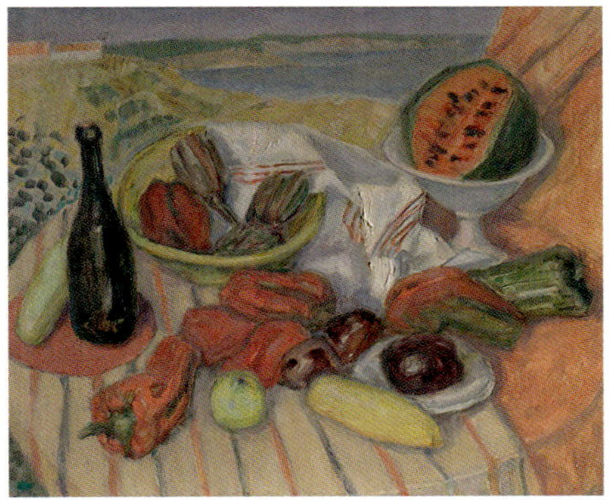

Colvile, Harry Morton 1905–1992
Mediterranean Fruit
oil on canvas 58.5 x 72
UON.088

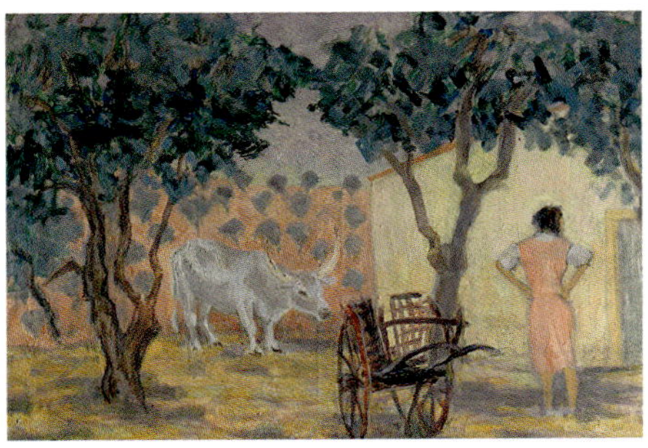

Colvile, Harry Morton 1905–1992
Spanish Ox and Cart
oil on canvas 52 x 80
UON.090

Cooper, Samuel (school of) 1609–1672
William Cavendish (c.1593–1676) (later 1st Duke of Newcastle upon Tyne)
oil on copper 8.9 x 4.4
UON.018

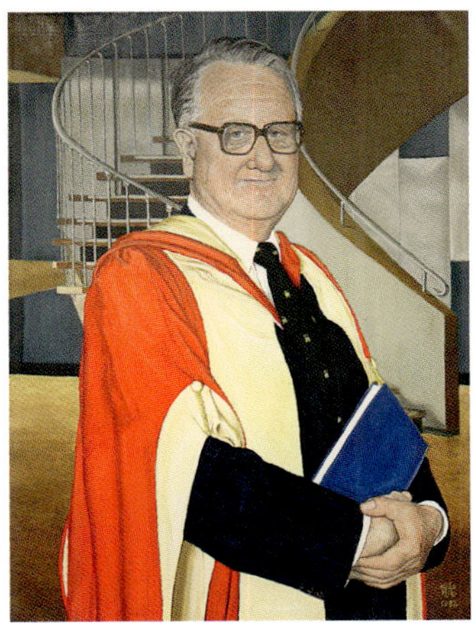

Cowlishaw, Tony b.1944
Professor David Greenfield (1917–2005), Foundation Dean of Nottingham Medical School, University of Nottingham 1983
oil on canvas 89.5 x 70
UON.177

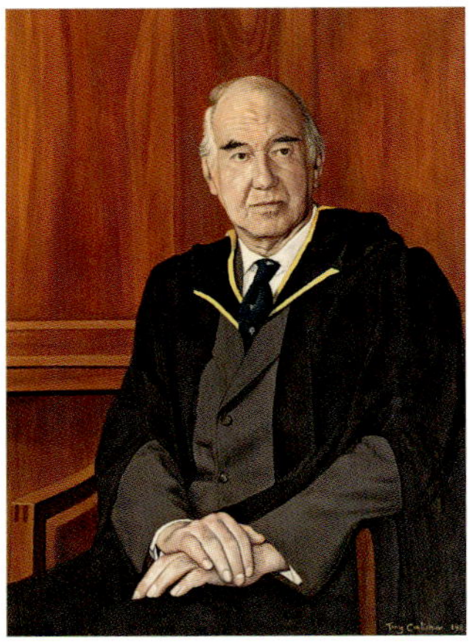

Cowlishaw, Tony b.1944
Frank Arnold Barnes (1920–2003), Warden of Derby Hall (1963–1985) 1985
oil on canvas 106 x 74 (E)
UON.099

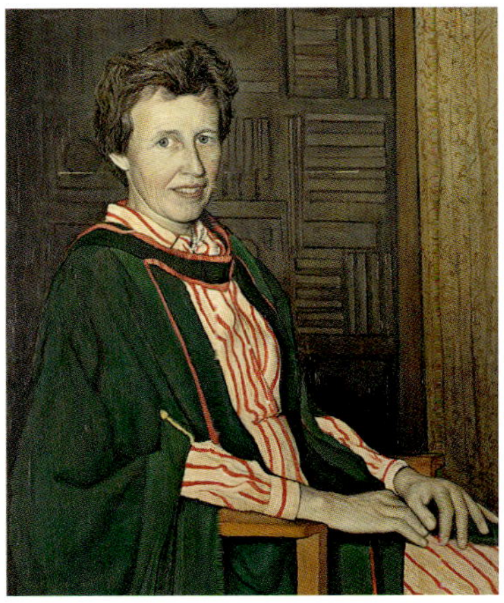

Cowlishaw, Tony b.1944
Dr Virginia van der Lande, Founder and Warden of Ancaster Hall (1966–1986) 1986
oil on canvas 100 x 85
UON.126

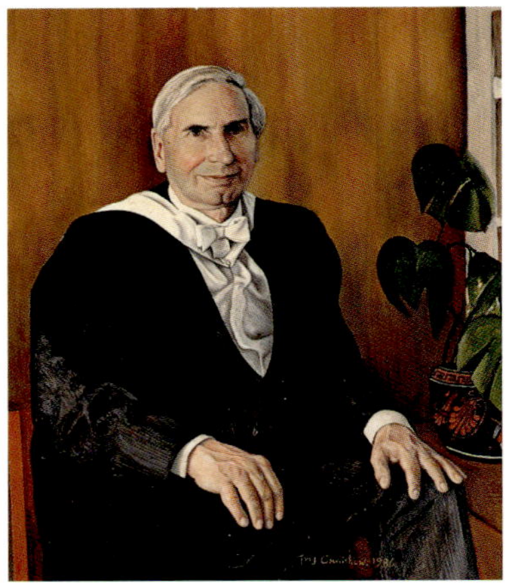

Cowlishaw, Tony b.1944
W. R. Chalmers (d.2004), MA, Warden of Sherwood Hall (1964–1986) 1986
oil on canvas 120 x 100 (E)
UON.172

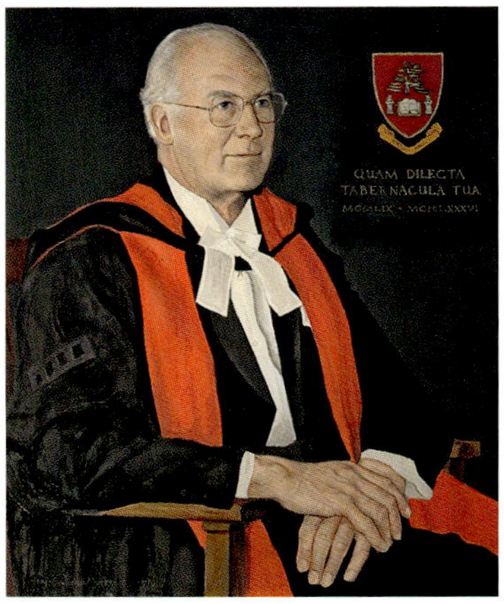

Cowlishaw, Tony b.1944
Dr Waterhouse, Warden of Wortley Hall until 1984 1987
oil on canvas 105 x 100 (E)
UON.106

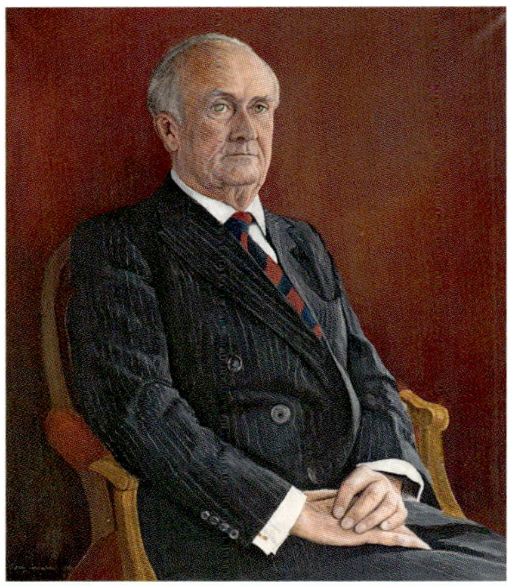

Cowlishaw, Tony b.1944
Charles Manners (1919–1999), 10th Duke of Rutland 1988
oil on canvas 104 x 79
UON.173

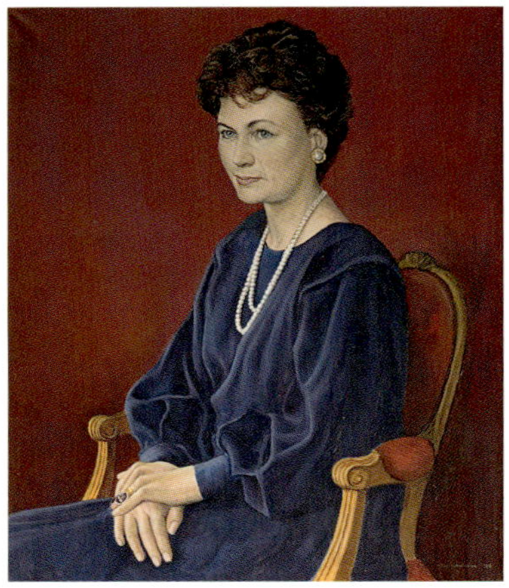

Cowlishaw, Tony b.1944
Frances Helen Sweeney (b.1937), Duchess of Rutland 1988
oil on canvas 104 x 79
UON.174

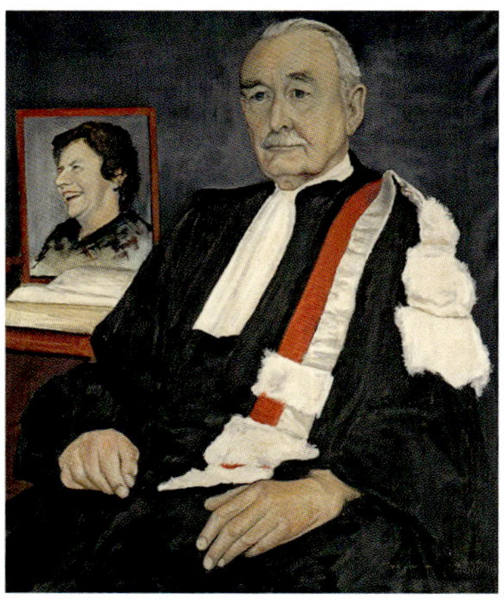

Cowlishaw, Tony b.1944
Dr Lucas 1988
oil on canvas 104 x 97 (E)
UON.107

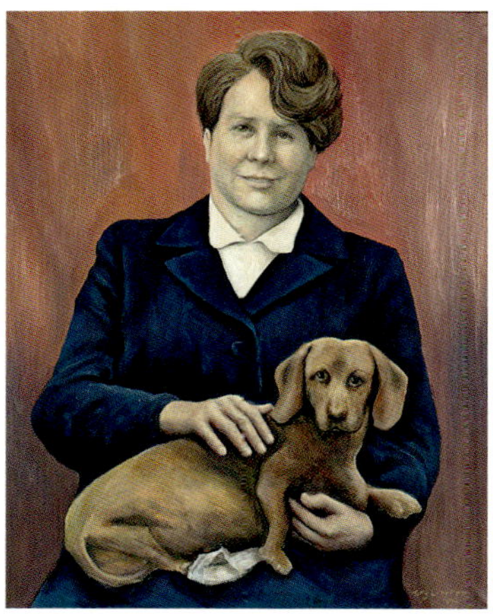

Cowlishaw, Tony b.1944
Audrey Beecham (1915–1989), Warden of Nightingale Hall (1950–1980) 1990
oil on canvas 113 x 97.7
UON.110

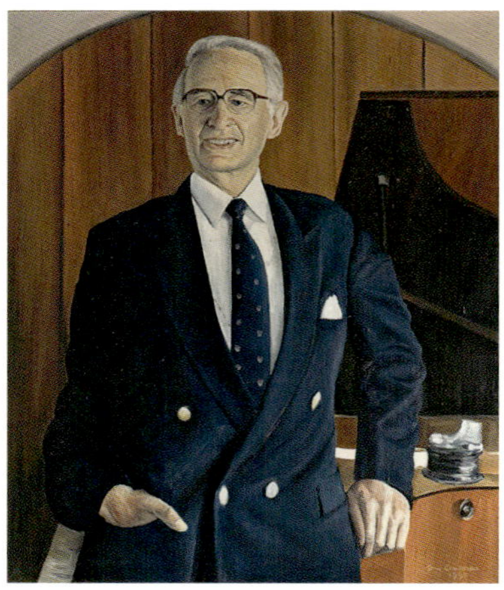

Cowlishaw, Tony b.1944
D. E. Varley, Warden of Rutland Hall (1967–1989) 1990
oil on canvas 104 x 79
UON.175

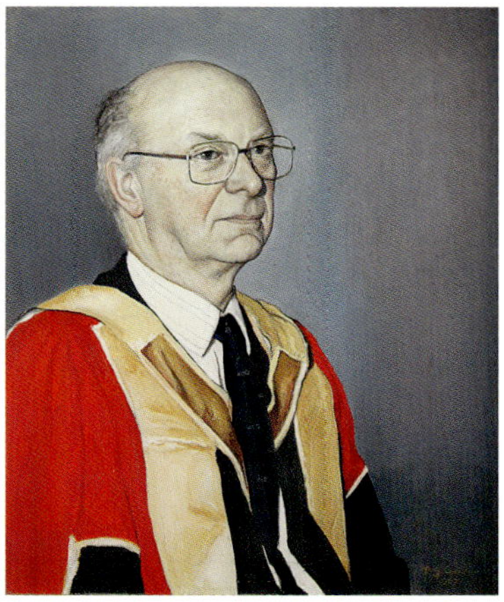

Cowlishaw, Tony b.1944
Professor Wilfred Heginbottom c.1990
oil on canvas 69.5 x 59.6
UON.176

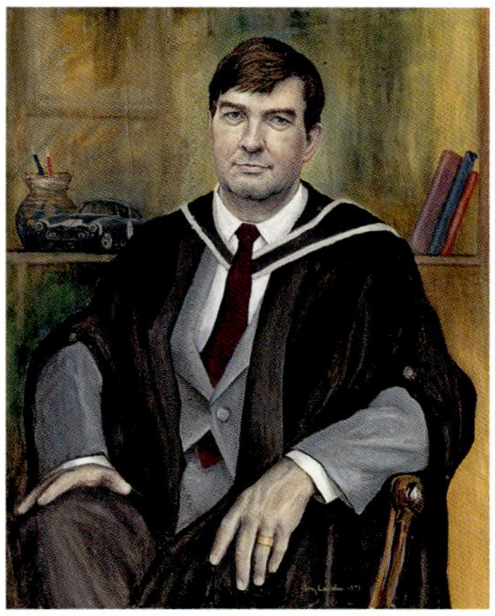

Cowlishaw, Tony b.1944
P. F. McGoldrick, MSc, Warden of Sherwood Hall (1986–1991) 1993
oil on canvas 120 x 100 (E)
UON.170

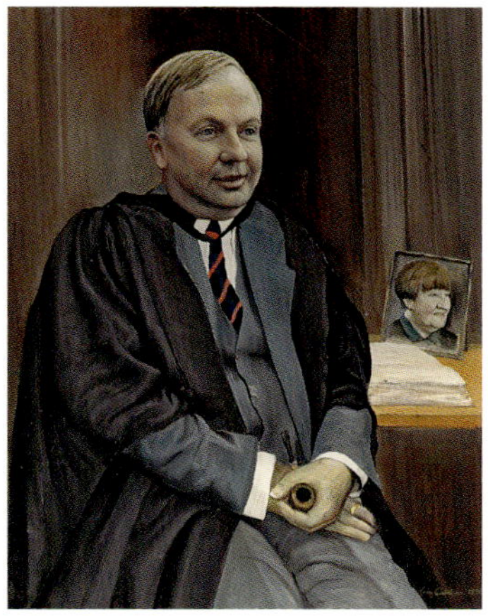

Cowlishaw, Tony b.1944
Dr P. Morris, MA, PhD, Warden of Sherwood Hall (1992–1995) 1996
oil on canvas 120 x 100 (E)
UON.171

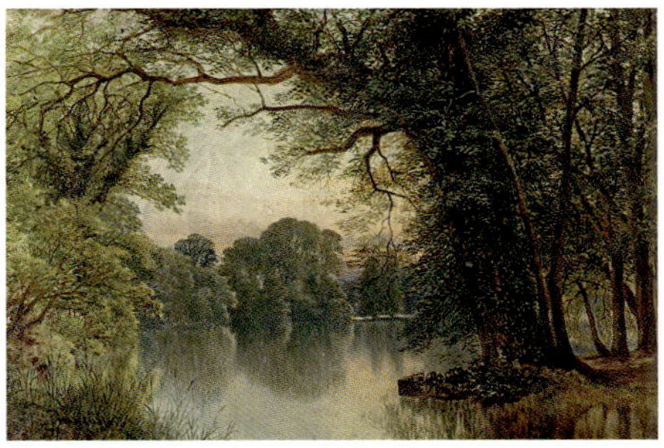

Cubley, William Harold 1814–1896
The Lake, Highfields, Nottingham 1884
oil on canvas 34.2 x 51.5
UON.029

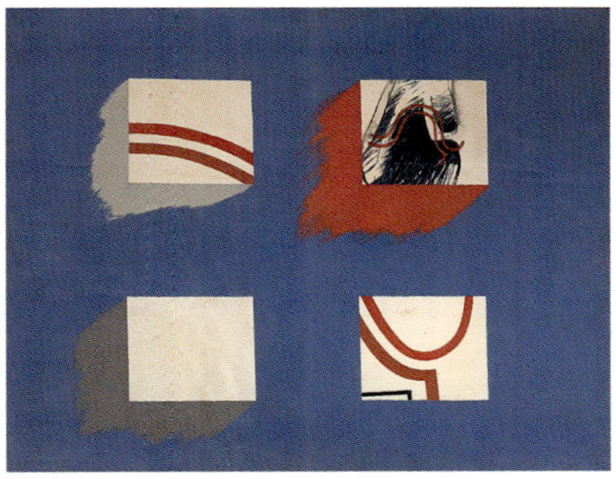

Culbert, Bill b.1935
Transit 1964
acrylic on wood 47 x 62
UON.167

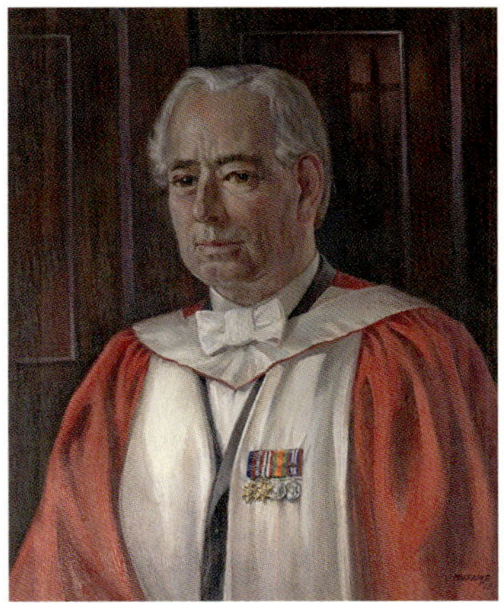

Darking, Harry Fred 1911–1999
Reverend Dr William Neil, MA, BD, PhD, DD, Warden of Hugh Stewart Hall (1953–1975)
1975
oil on canvas 60 x 50
UON.165

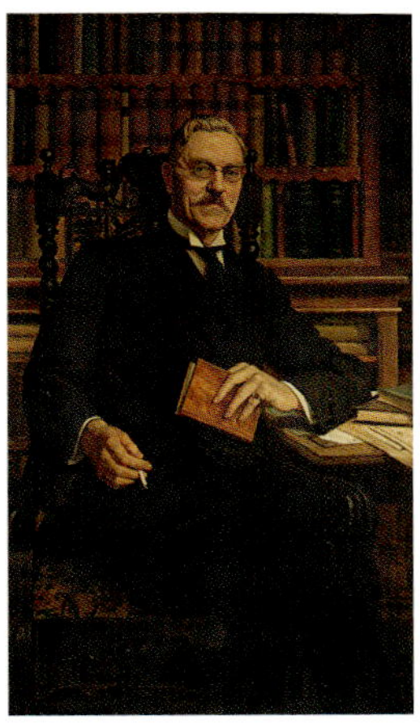

Davis, Noel Denholm 1876–1950
Alderman Edmund Huntsman, Member of the College Council (1917–1921), Chairman of the College Council (1921–1939) 1930
oil on canvas 152 x 90
UON.031

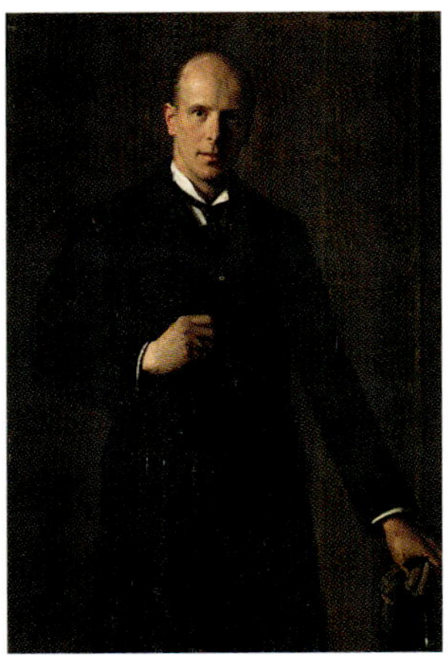

Davis, Noel Denholm 1876–1950
Cecil Roberts, Esq. (1892–1976)
oil on canvas 122 x 84
UON.032

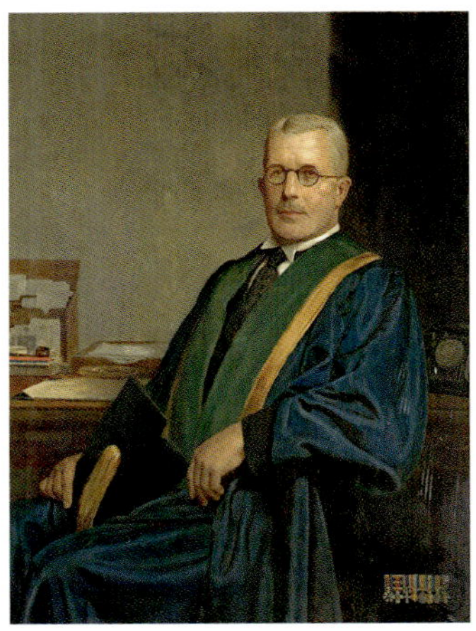

Davis, Noel Denholm 1876–1950
Hugh Stewart (1884–1934), Principal of University College Nottingham (1929–1934)
oil on canvas 110 x 85
UON.164

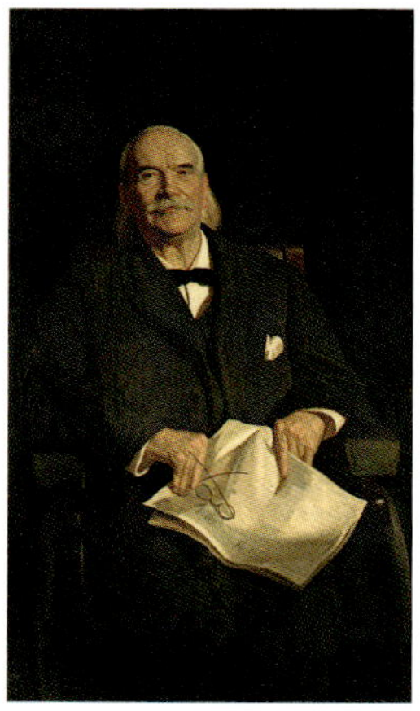

Davis, Noel Denholm 1876–1950
Sir Jesse Boot (1850–1931), Bt, JP (later 1st Baron Trent)
oil on canvas 150 x 90
UON.030

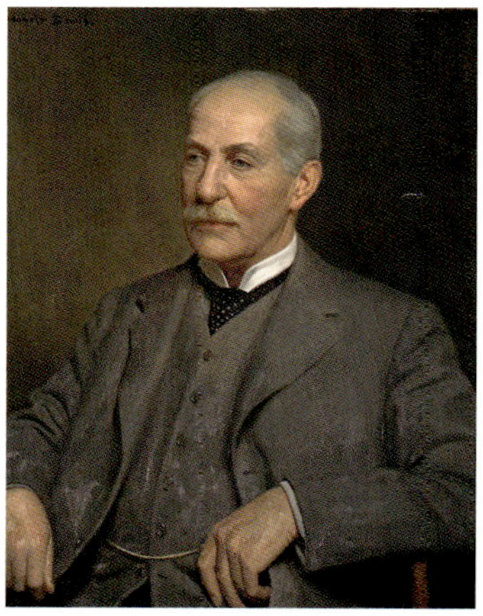

Davis, Noel Denholm 1876–1950
Sir Louis Pearson (d.1943), CBE, DLJP
oil on canvas 75 x 62
UON.123

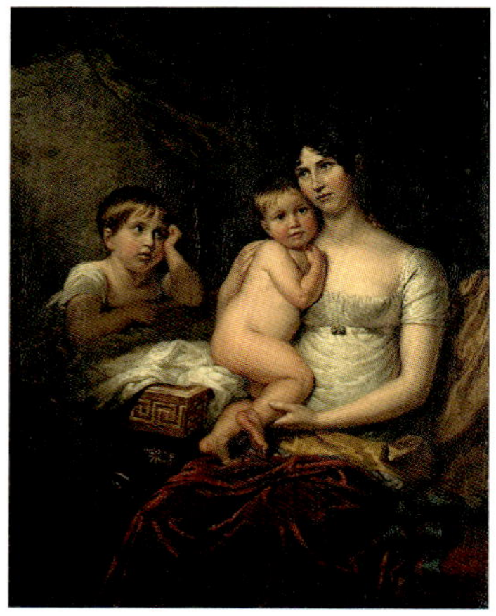

Dawe, George 1781–1829
Mrs Thomas Hope (d.1851), with Her Sons Henry Thomas (1808–1862), and Charles (1810–1817)
oil on canvas 127.6 x 104
UON.033

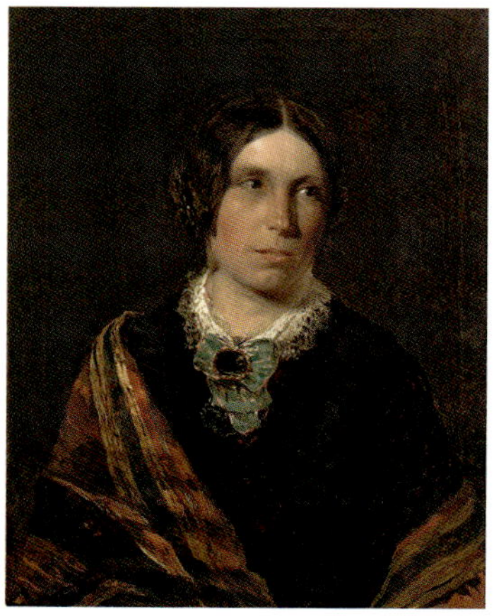

Dawson, Henry 1811–1878
Portrait of the Artist's Wife, Elizabeth Dawson, née Whittle
oil on canvas 59.8 x 49.7
UON.011

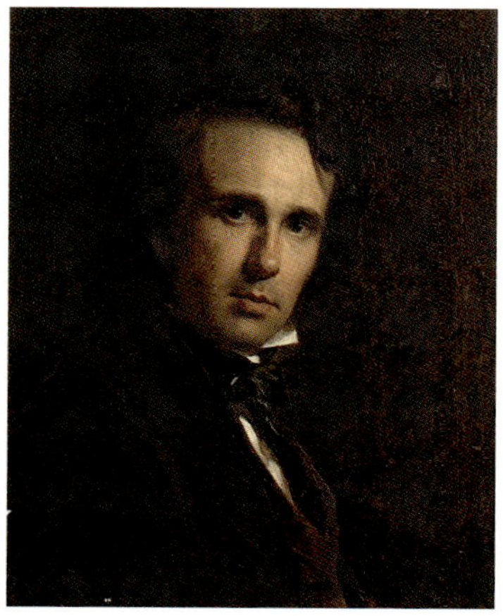

Dawson, Henry 1811–1878
Self Portrait
oil on canvas 59.8 x 49.7
UON.010

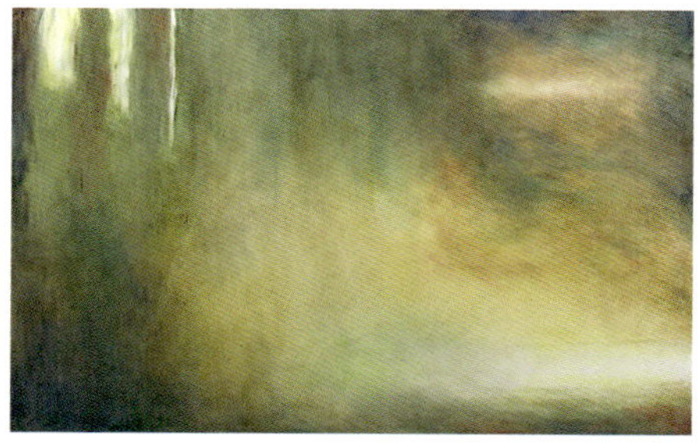

de Castella, Hubert active 1999–2000
Staircase 1999
oil on canvas 114 x 183
UON.057

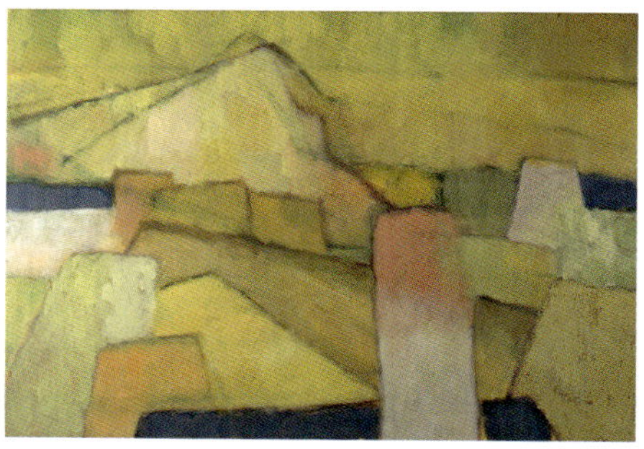

de Castella, Hubert active 1999–2000
Mont Saint-Michel, Normandy, France 2000
oil on canvas 60.2 x 90
UON.058

Di Stefano, Arturo b.1955
Beach Scene 1998
oil on paper 50 x 58
UON.079

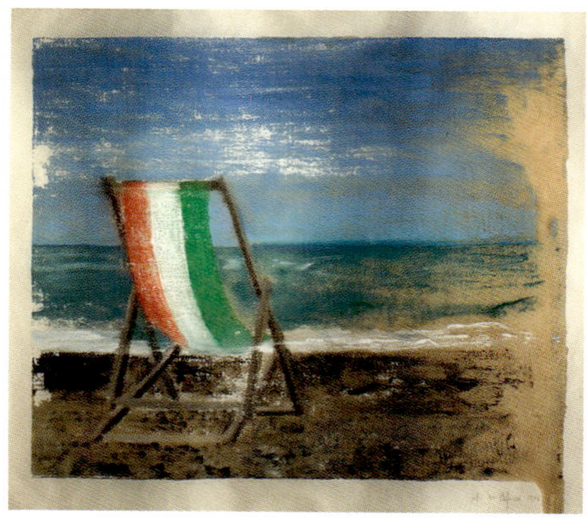

Di Stefano, Arturo b.1955
Deck Chair 1998
oil on paper 50 x 59
UON.119

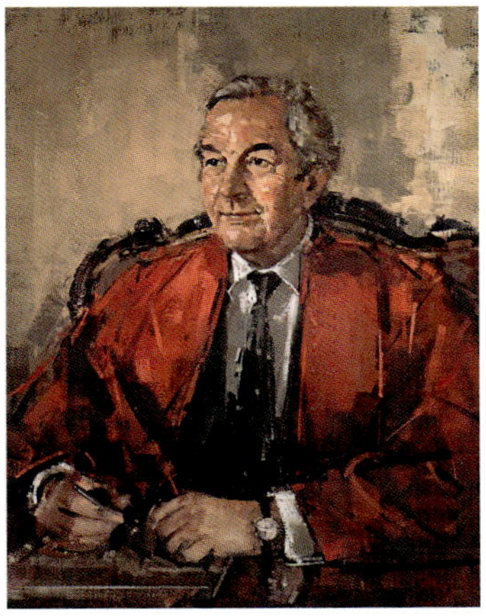

Evans, William 1911–1978
Sir William John Hughes Butterfield (1920–2000), OBE, MA, DM, MD, LLD, FRCP, Vice-Chancellor (1971–1975)
oil on canvas 95.5 x 77
UON.036

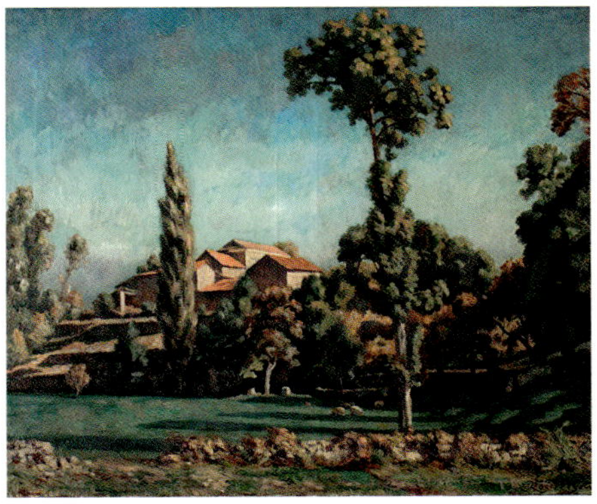

Fry, Roger Eliot 1866–1934
La fontaine noire
oil on canvas 64.5 x 80
UON.111

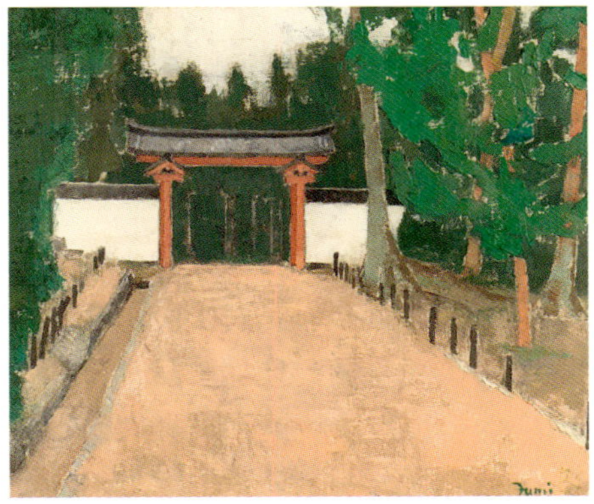

Fumi
Daigoji Temple, Kyoto, Japan
oil on canvas 40.7 x 48.3
UON.013

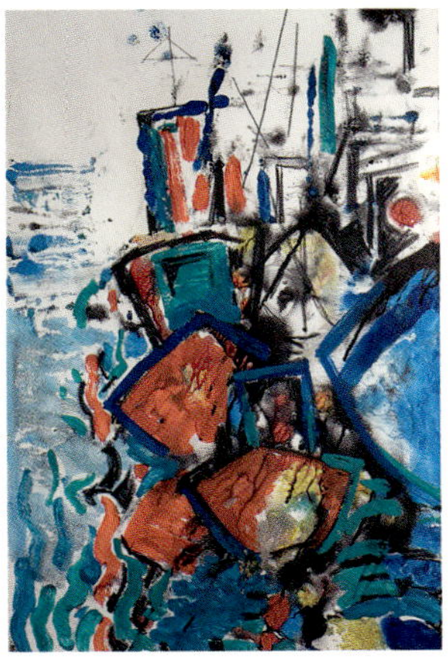

Glover, Carole
Quayside 1991
oil on paper 47.5 x 32.5
UON.127

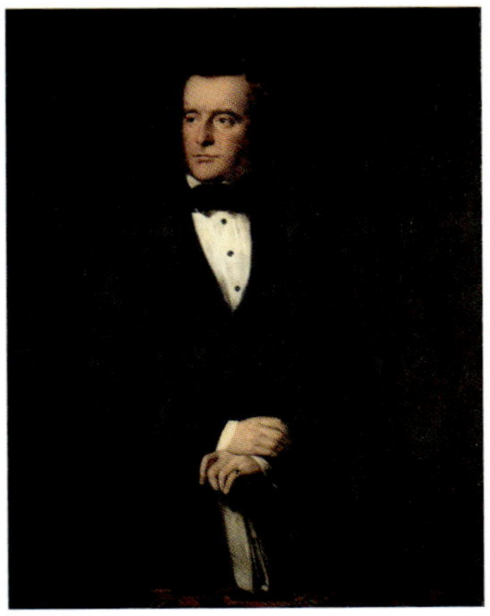

Gordon, John Watson 1788–1864
Henry Pelham Fiennes Pelham-Clinton (1811–1864), 5th Duke of Newcastle-under-Lyne 1855
oil on canvas 125.4 x 100.4
UON.037

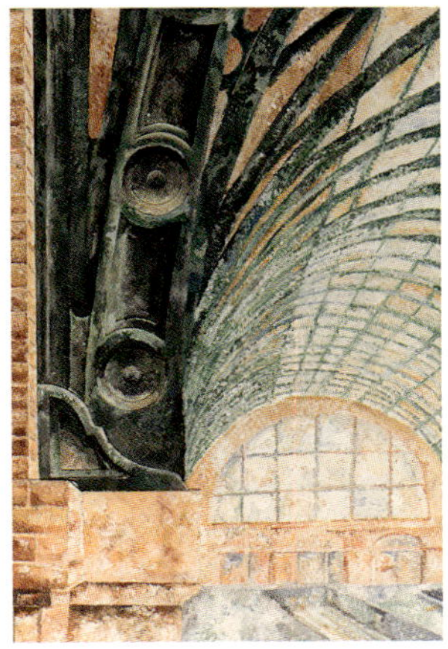

Gratton, Lucinda b.1976
King's Cross I (St Pancras), London 1994
acrylic & card on paper 69.3 x 48.7
UON.112

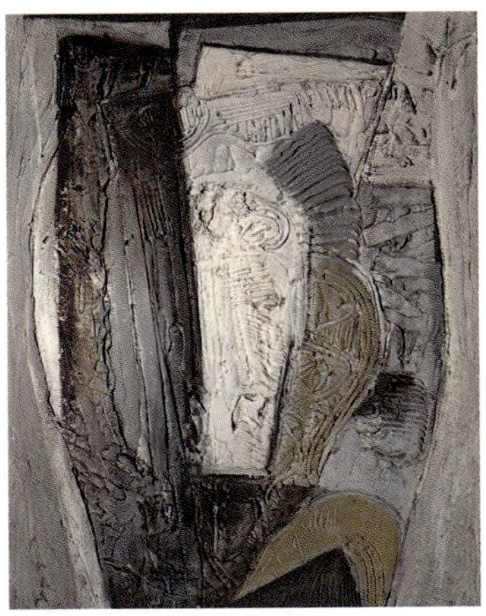

Grici, Claude
Untitled 1960
oil & cement on board 101 x 81
UON.158

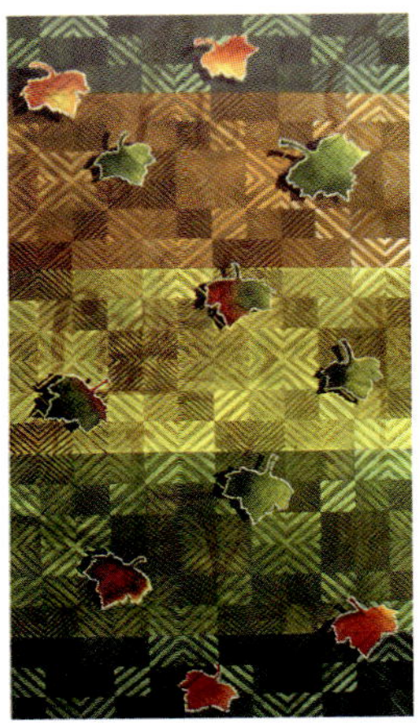

Hampson, Derek b.1952
George Green 1993
acrylic on canvas 480 x 240 (E)
UON.179

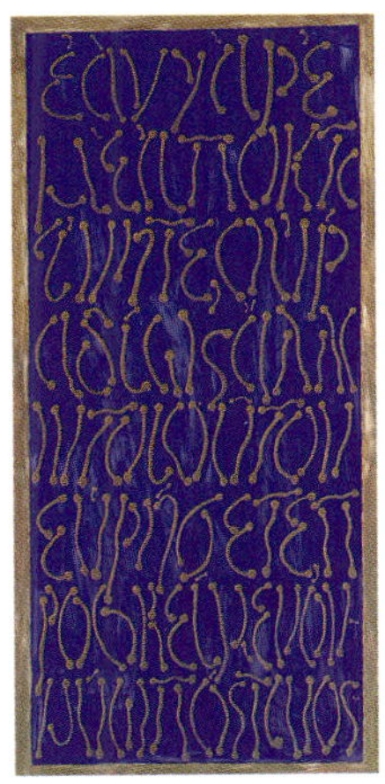

Hampson, Derek b.1952
The Great and the Good (The Roots of Democracy) (left panel of triptych) 1993
acrylic on canvas 300 x 130 (E)
UON.101a

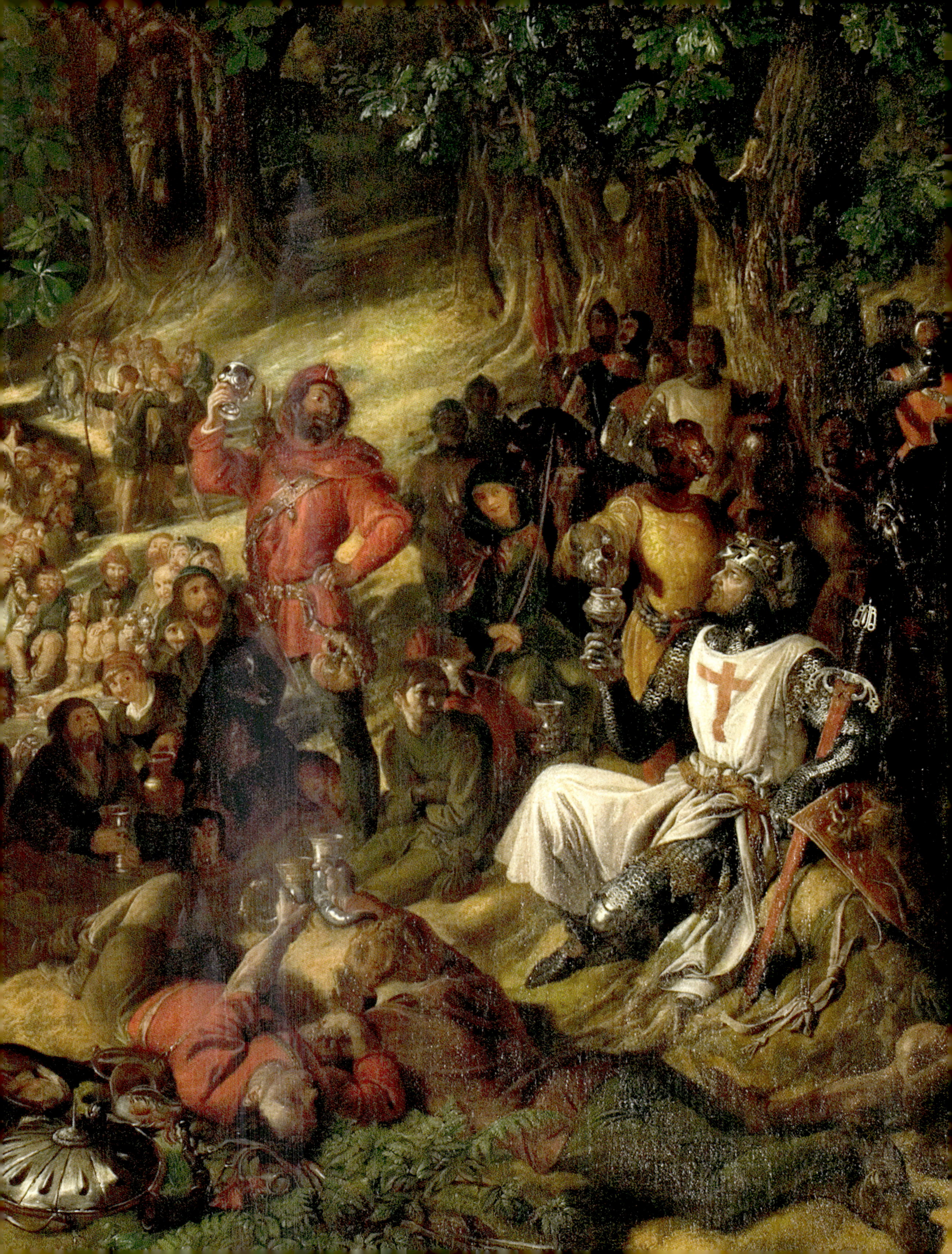

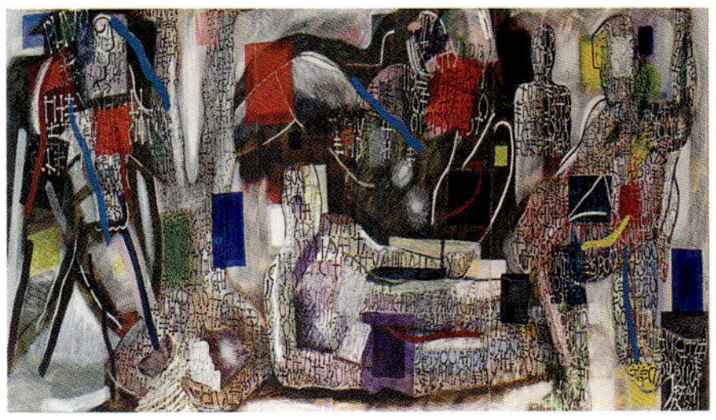

Hampson, Derek b.1952
The Great and the Good (The Roots of Democracy) (centre panel of triptych) 1993
acrylic on canvas 300 x 696 (E)
UON.101b

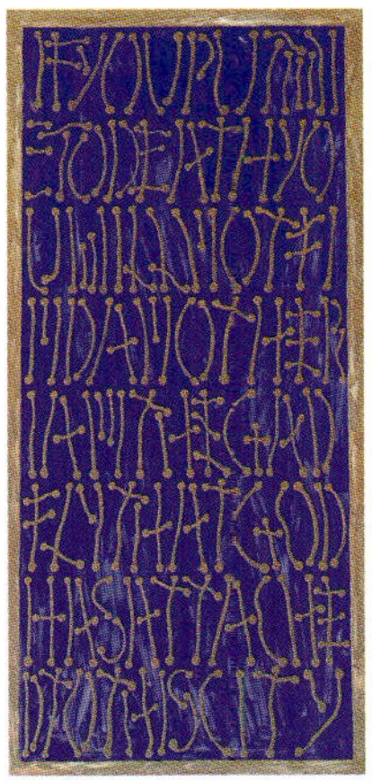

Hampson, Derek b.1952
The Great and the Good (The Roots of Democracy) (right panel of triptych) 1993
acrylic on canvas 300 x 130 (E)
UON.101c

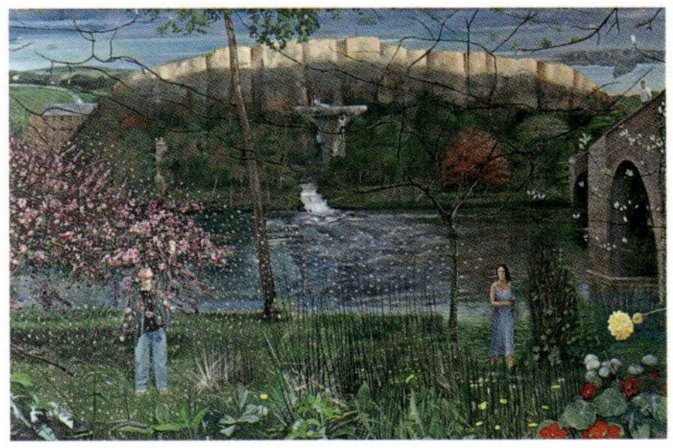

Hampson, Derek b.1952
The Loves of the Plants 2003
acrylic on canvas 132 x 208
UON.100

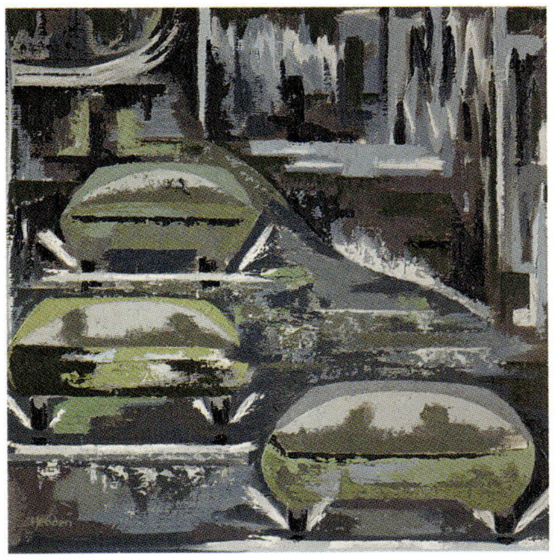

Hebden, Rosemary
Night Drive 1963
oil on board 61 x 61
UON.098

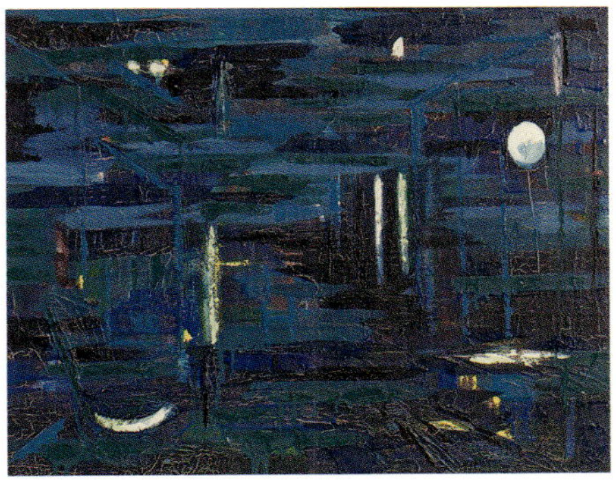

Hebden, Rosemary
Strange Vista 1963
acrylic on board 38.6 x 50.6
UON.015

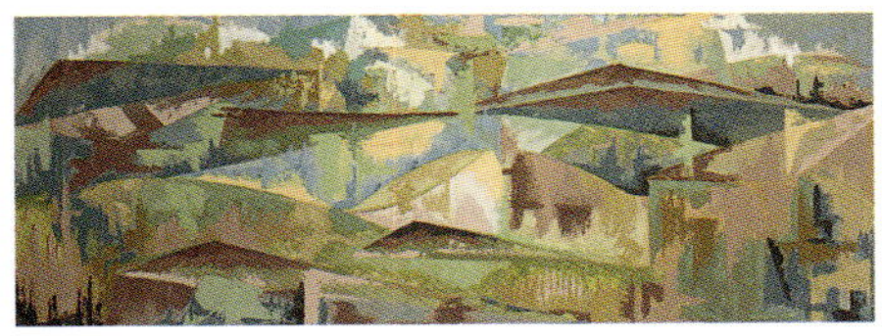

Hebden, Rosemary
Essential Landscape
acrylic on board 44 x 120
UON.157

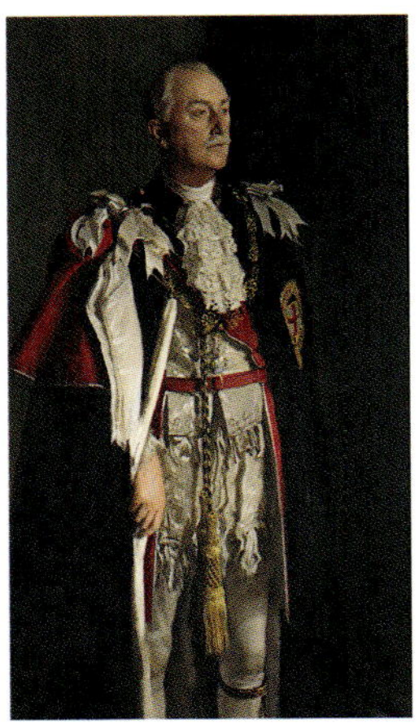

Hepple, Norman 1908–1994
The 7th Duke of Portland (1893–1977), Chancellor of the University (1954–1971) 1958
oil on canvas 170 x 100
UON.038

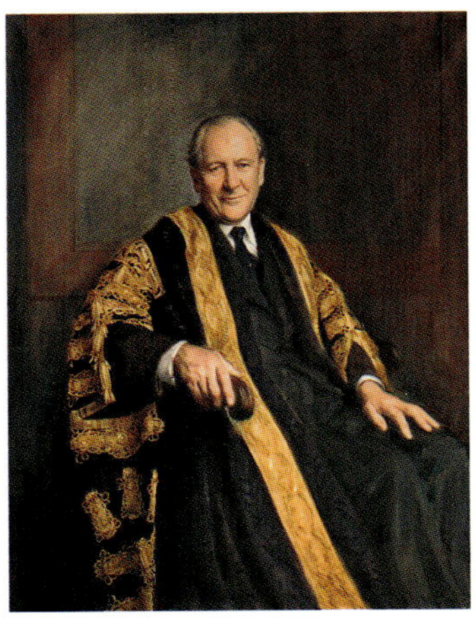

Hepple, Norman 1908–1994
Sir Gordon Hobday (b.1916), 4th Chancellor of the University (1978–1993) 1980
oil on canvas 125 x 100
UON.039

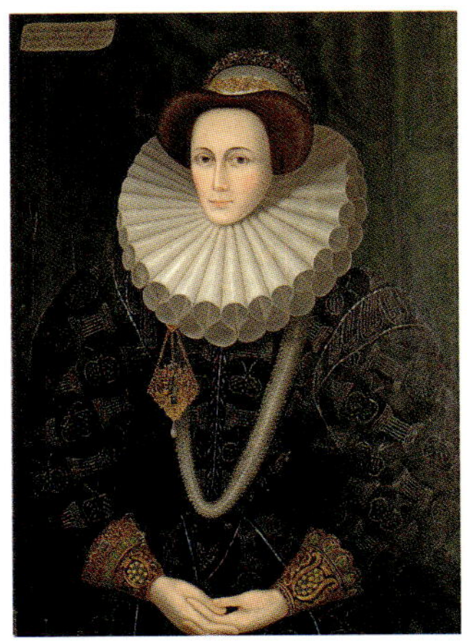

Hewetson, Richard active 19th C
Frances Clinton, Lady Chandos (d.1623) (copy of an earlier painting)
oil on panel 90.2 x 67.3
UON.128

Facing page: Maclise, Daniel, 1806–1870, *Robin Hood and His Merry Men Entertaining Richard the Lionheart in Sherwood Forest* (detail), 1839, Nottingham City Museums and Galleries (p. 122)

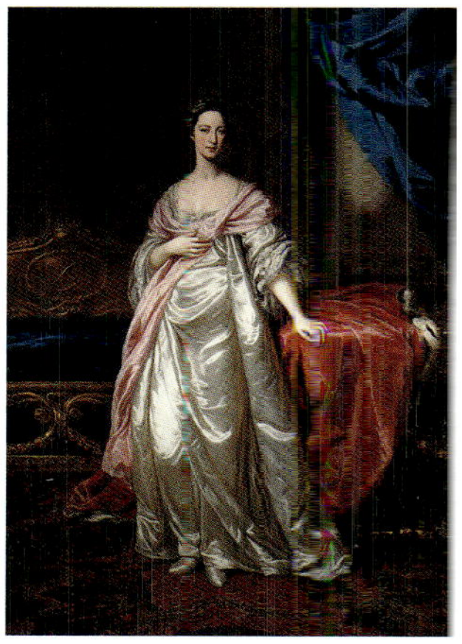

Hoare, William 1706–1792
Catherine Pelham-Clinton (1727–1760), Countess of Lincoln
oil on canvas 233 x 170
UON.041

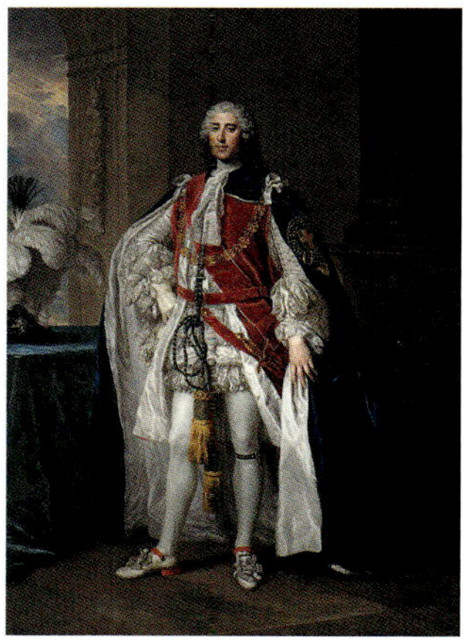

Hoare, William 1706–1792
Henry Pelham-Clinton (1720–1794), KG, 9th Earl of Lincoln (later 2nd Duke of Newcastle-under-Lyne)
oil on canvas 233 x 170
UON.040

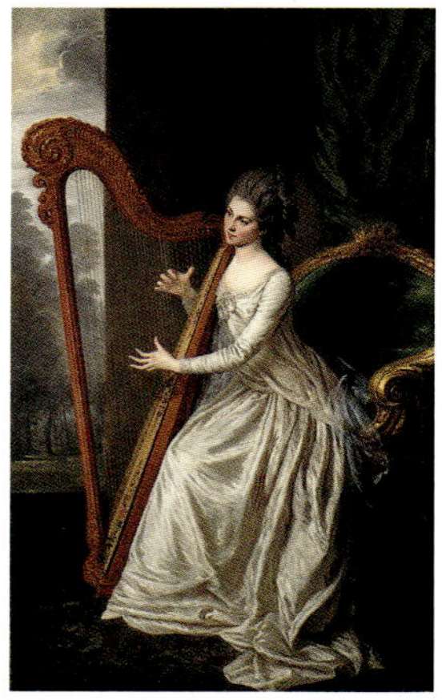

Hoare, William 1706–1792
Lady Frances Seymour Conway (1751–1820), Countess of Lincoln
oil on canvas 235.3 x 147.9
UON.043

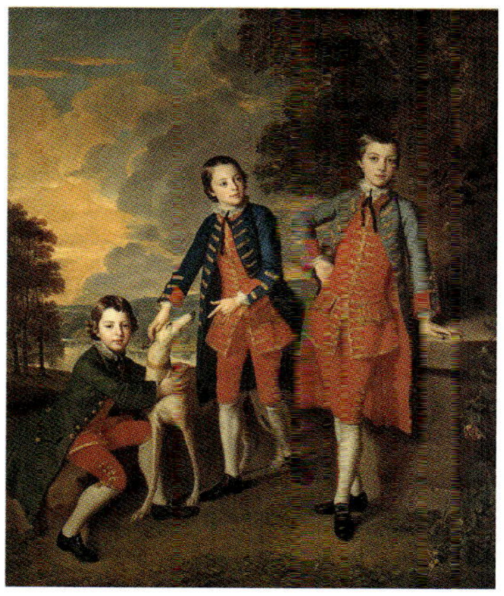

Hoare, William 1706–1792
The Children of the 2nd Duke of Newcastle-under-Lyne, Henry (1750–1778), Thomas (1752–1795) and John (1755–1781)
oil on canvas 207.8 x 180
UON.042

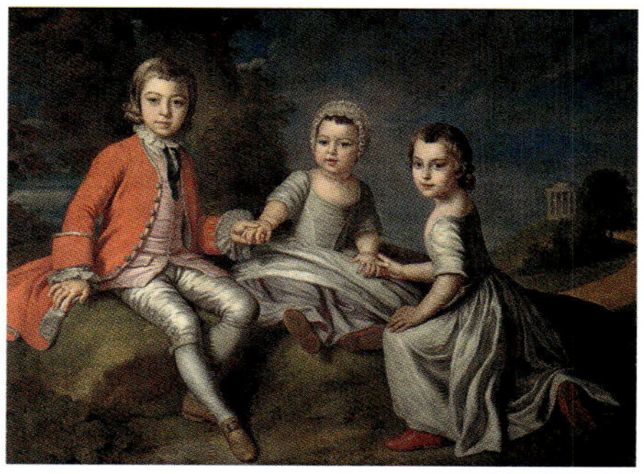

Hoare, William 1706–1792
The Children of the 2nd Duke of Newcastle-under-Lyne, Henry (1750–1778), Thomas (1752–1795) and John (1755–1781)
oil on canvas 116.4 x 160
UON.081

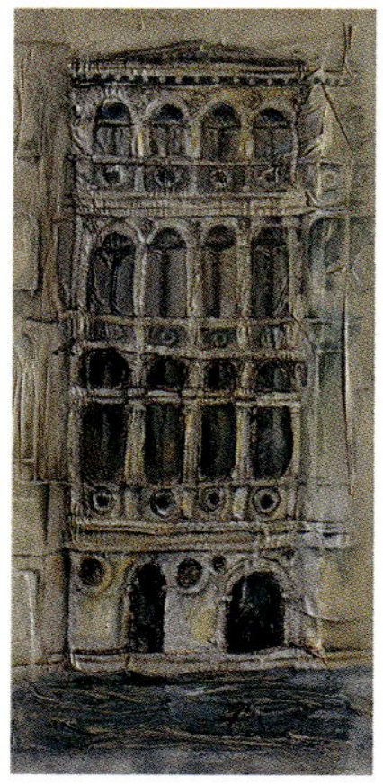

Hunt, Doreen
Palazzo, Grand Canal, Venice, Italy
acrylic & mixed media on cloth 49 x 24
UON.149

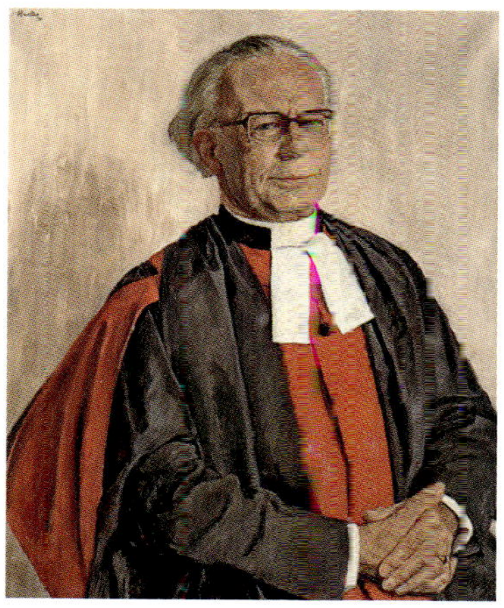

Hunter, Norma
Dr Trueman Dicken (1919–2000), Warden of Lenton Hall (1965–1980) 1981
oil on canvas 65 x 55
UON.108

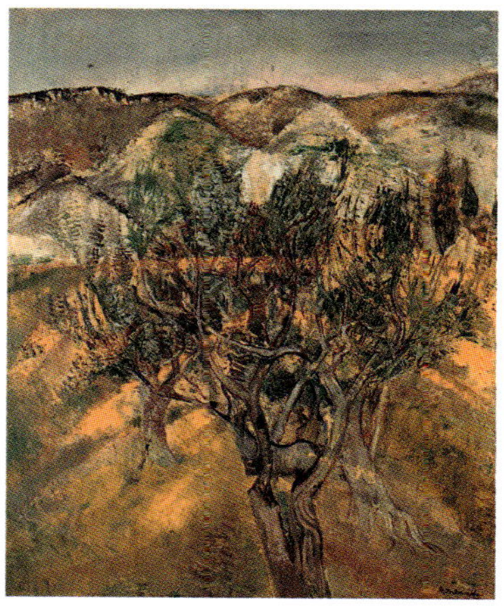

Inlander, Henry 1925–1983
Olive Trees 1956
acrylic on canvas 69 x 59
UON.044

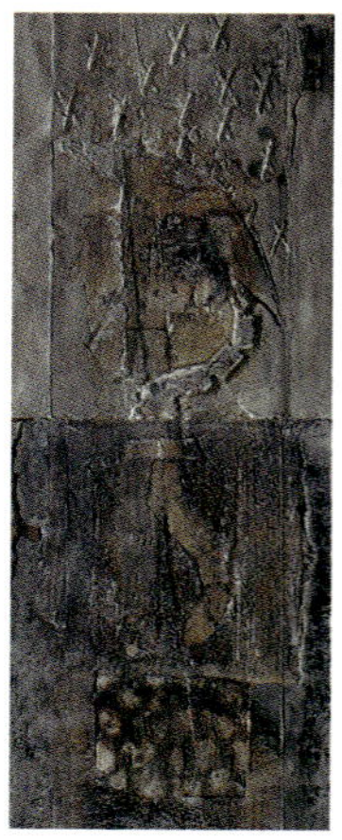

Jones, Chris
Version (left panel of triptych) 1986
acrylic & mixed media on paper 21 x 10 (E)
UON.145a

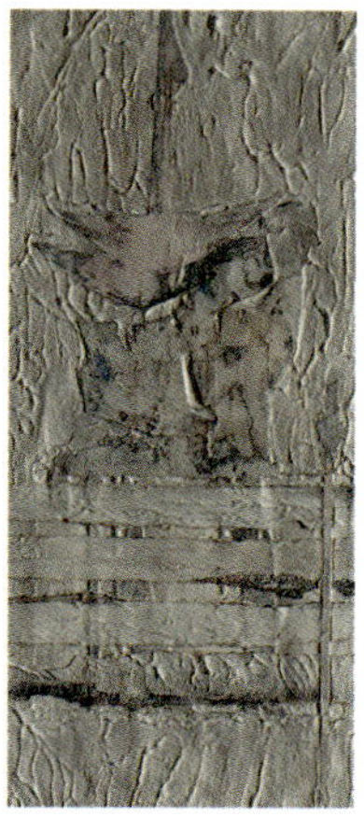

Jones, Chris
The Blessed (centre panel of triptych) 1986
acrylic & mixed media on paper 20 x 10 (E)
UON.146

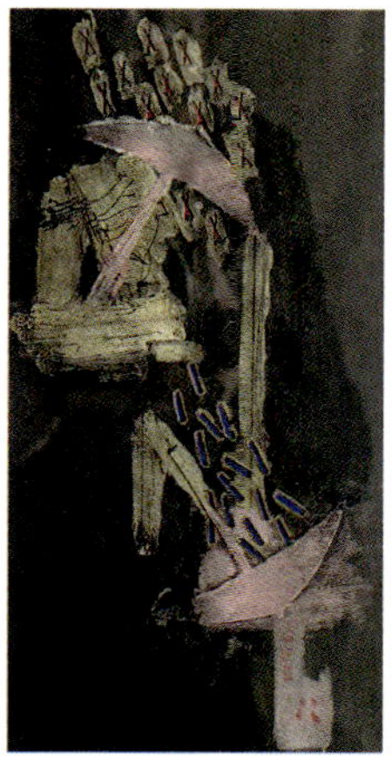

Jones, Chris
Proverb (right panel of triptych) 1986
acrylic & mixed media on paper 20 x 11 (E)
UON.147

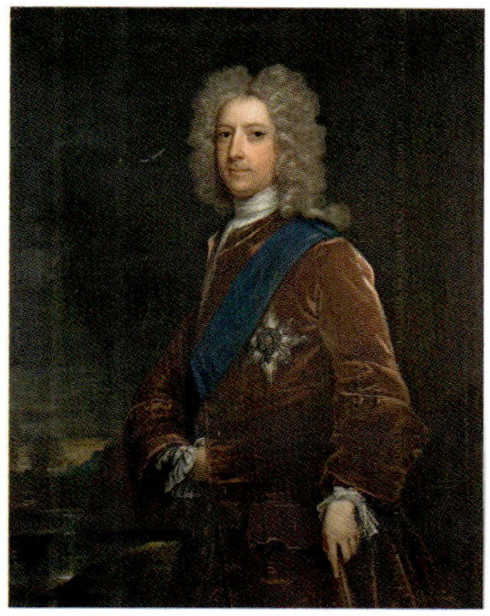

Kneller, Godfrey 1646–1723
Henry Fiennes Clinton (1684–1728), 7th Earl of Lincoln
oil on canvas 124.2 x 98.9
UON.045

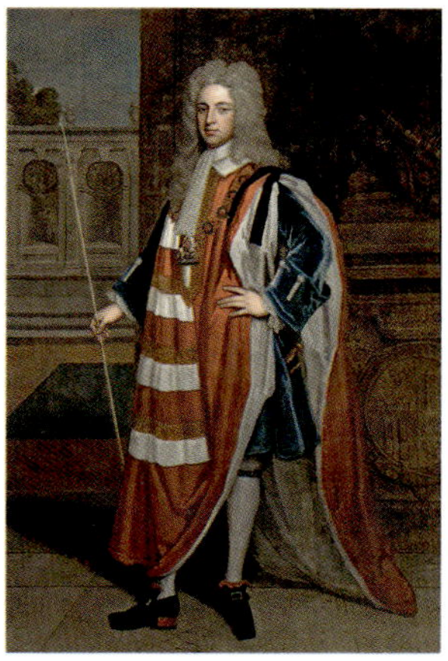

Kneller, Godfrey 1646–1723
Thomas Pelham-Holles (1693–1768), KG, 4th Duke of Newcastle upon Tyne (later 1st Duke of Newcastle-under-Lyne)
oil on canvas 210.8 x 146
UON.082

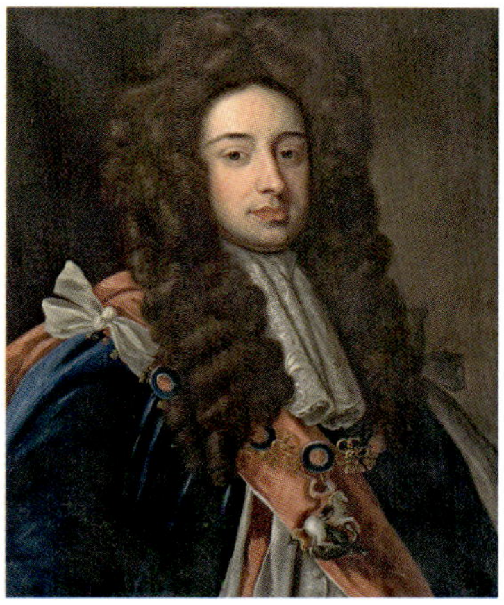

Kneller, Godfrey (after) 1646–1723
John Holles (1662–1711), 4th Earl of Clare and 3rd Duke of Newcastle upon Tyne, KG
oil on canvas 76 x 63
UON.083

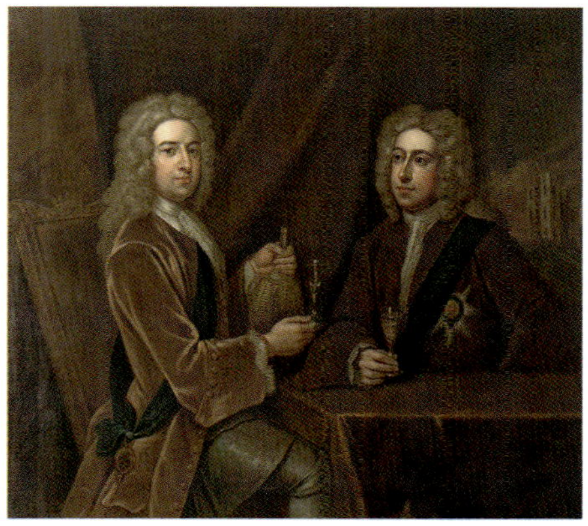

Kneller, Godfrey (after) 1646–1723
Thomas Pelham-Holles (1693–1768), 1st Duke of Newcastle-under-Lyne with Henry Fiennes Clinton (1684–1728), 7th Earl of Lincoln, KG
oil on canvas 124.5 x 145
UON.084

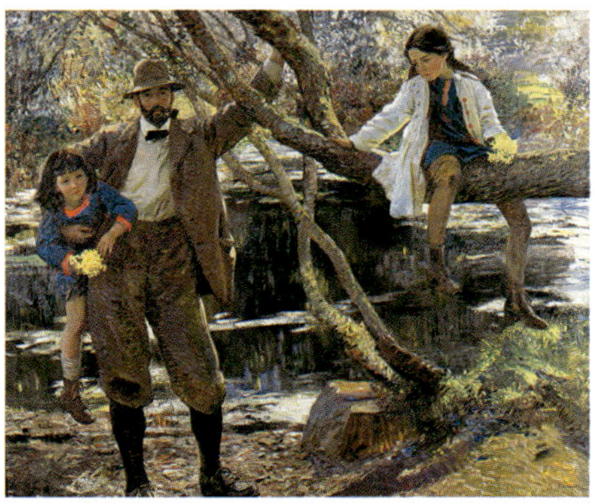

Knight, Laura 1877–1970
Lamorna Birch (1869–1955), and His Daughters 1934
oil on canvas 215 x 261
UON.071

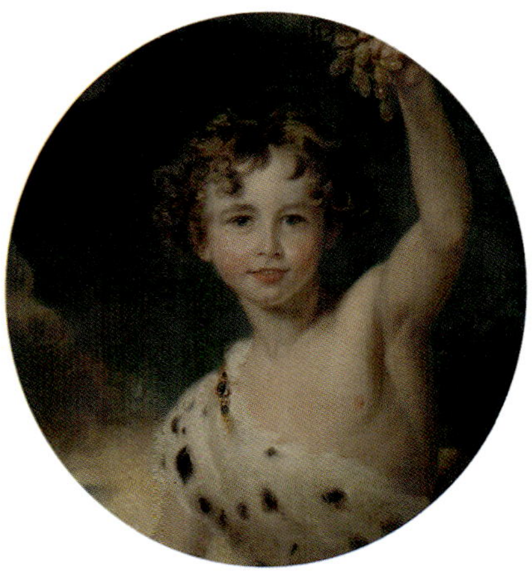

Lawrence, Thomas 1769–1830
Charles Hope (1810–1817), as Bacchus
oil on canvas 60
UON.129

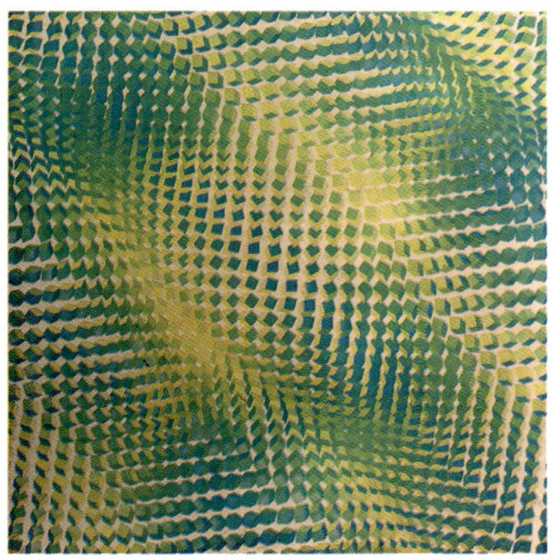

Lees, Stewart Marshall
Sunrise
oil on canvas mounted on board 151 x 153
UON.002

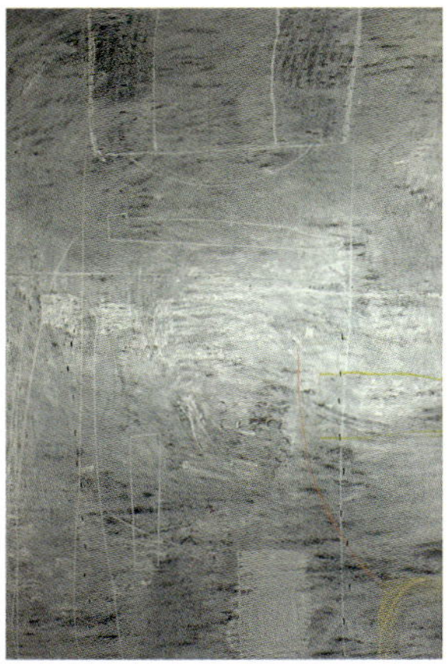

Macaskill, Duncan
Useful Verbs 1996
acrylic & chalk on board 160 x 110.5
UON.072

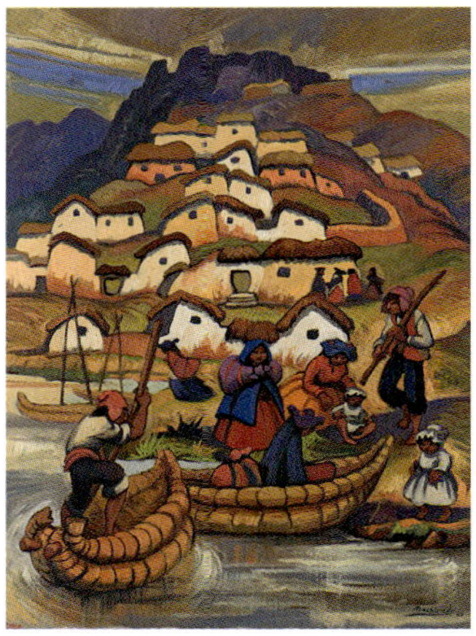

Machicado, Juan de la Cruz b.1935
Titicaca 1989
oil on canvas 92 x 72
UON.092

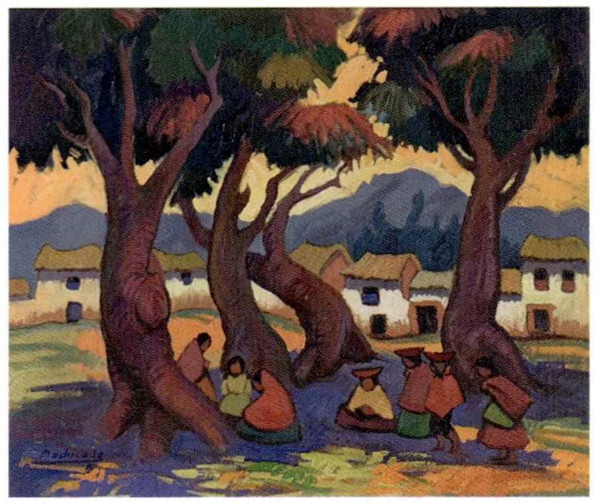

Machicado, Juan de la Cruz b.1935
Village 1990
oil on canvas 52 x 62
UON.093

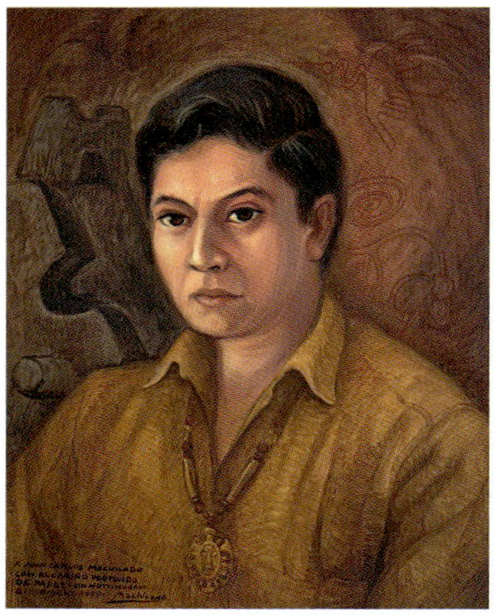

Machicado, Juan de la Cruz b.1935
Portrait of the Artist's Son, Juan Carlos 1992
oil on canvas 61 x 50
UON.095

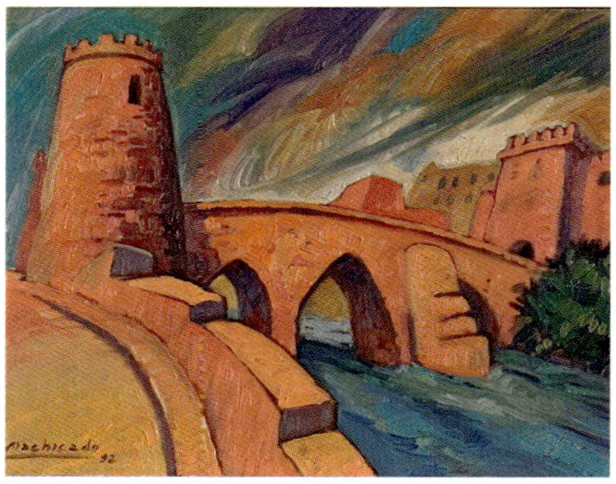

Machicado, Juan de la Cruz b.1935
River Fortress 1992
oil on canvas 32 x 40
UON.094

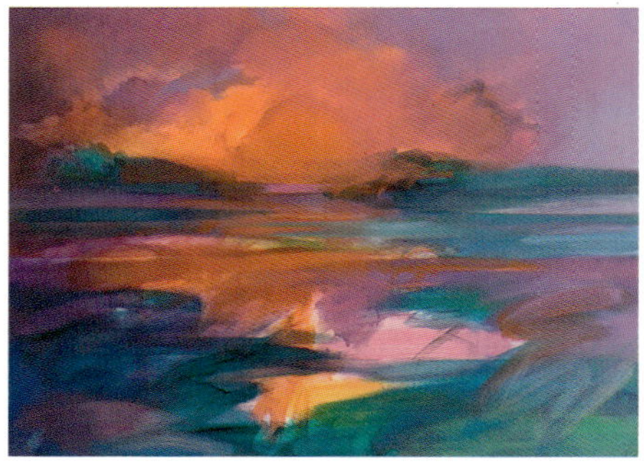

Malaysian School 20th C
*Sunset (Reflections on Water)**
oil on canvas 90.5 x 126
UON.004

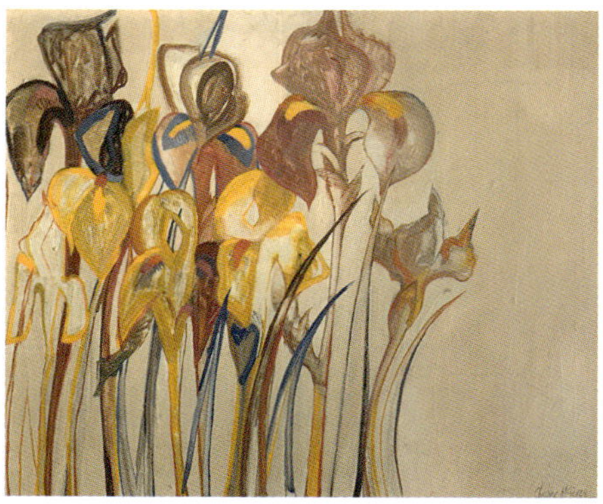

McGegan, Christine Mary 1923–1989
Irises c.1969
oil on board 61 x 77
UON.161

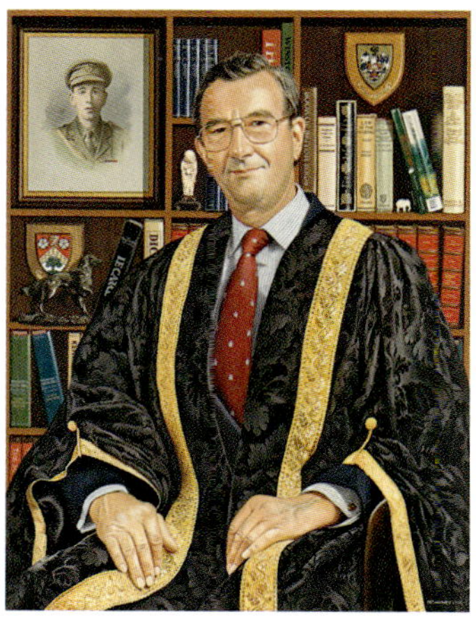

Mundy, William Percy b.1936
Roger John Godfrey, LLB, LLD, President of the Council (1983–1993)
oil on canvas 75 x 60
UON.046

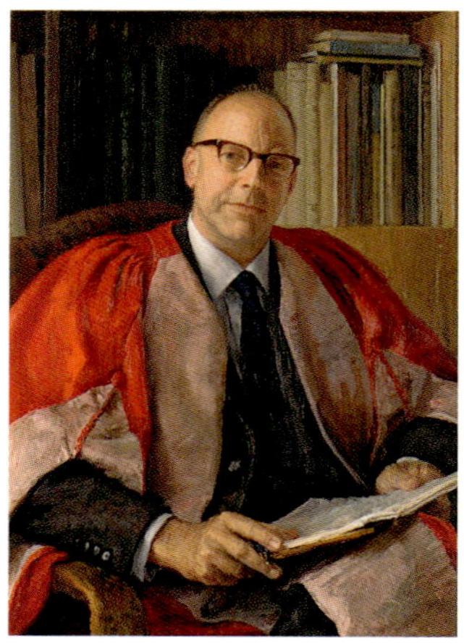

Nanaway, William E.
Sir Frederick Sydney Dainton (1914–1997), MA, LLD, ScD, DSc, DTech, FRS, Vice-Chancellor (1965–1970)
oil on canvas 100.4 x 75.3
UON.047

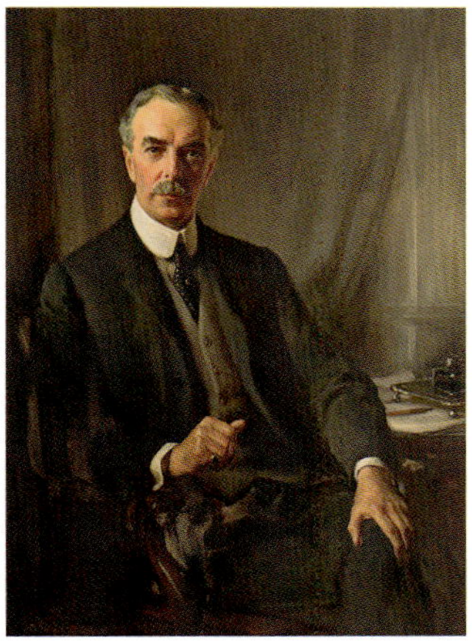

Neale, George Hall 1863–1940
Portrait of an Unknown Man
oil on canvas 118 x 87.3
UON.014

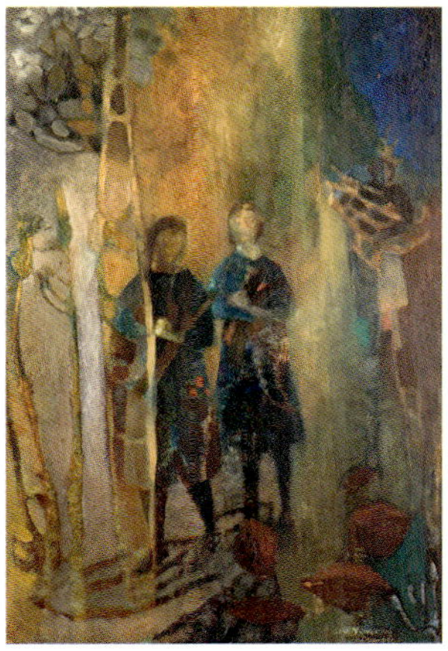

Newcomb, Mary 1922–2008
The Homing Wives 1957
oil on board 74.6 x 53.3
UON.113

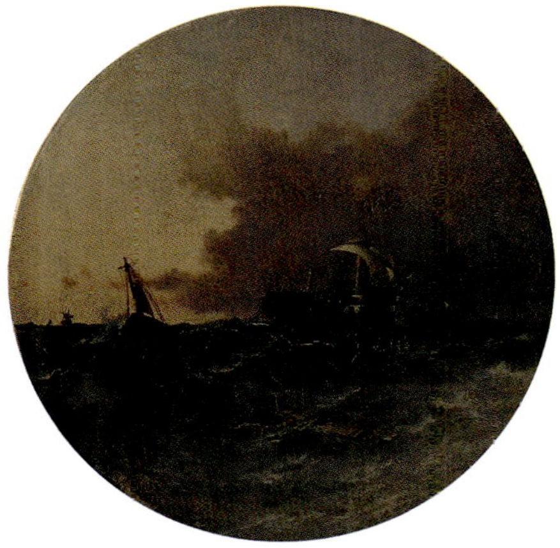

Niemann, Edmund John 1813–1876
Storm at Sea 1858
oil on board 46
UON.048

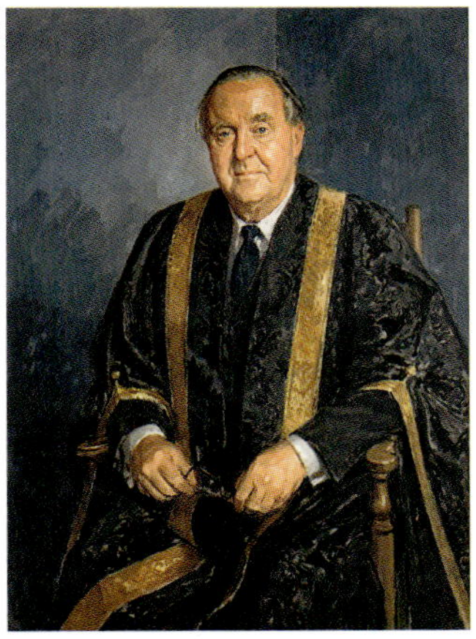

Noakes, Michael b.1933
Paul Francis Granger, LLD, FCA, President of the Council (1968–1975)
oil on canvas 101 x 75.3
UON.049

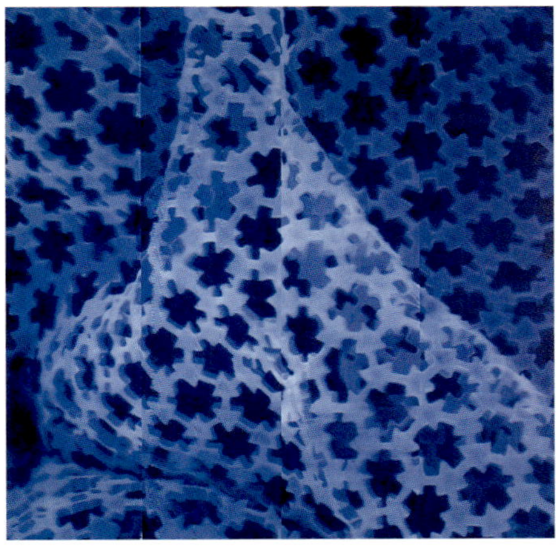

Nolan, Gavin b.1977
Blue Abstract 1999
oil on board 183 x 183
UON.067

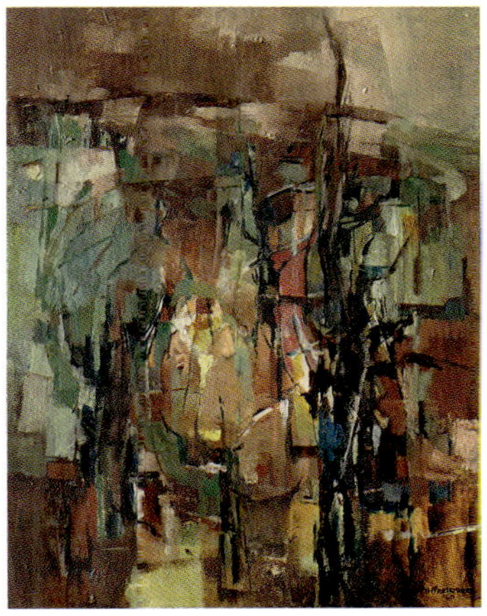

Partridge, Maurice William 1913–1973
Pembroke 1960
acrylic on canvas 75.7 x 60.3
UON.062

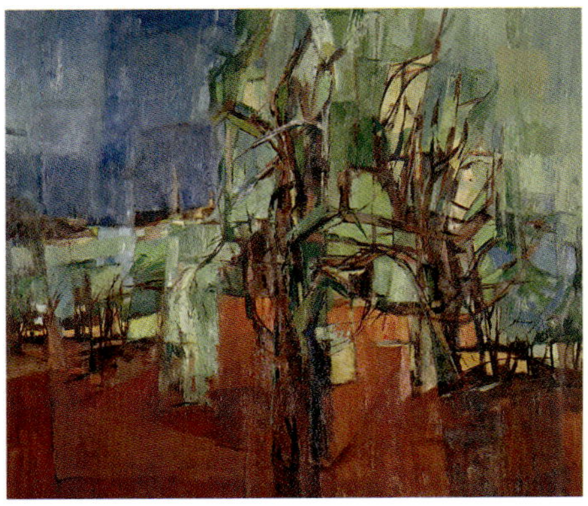

Partridge, Maurice William 1913–1973
Untitled 1961
oil on board 74 x 89
UON.150

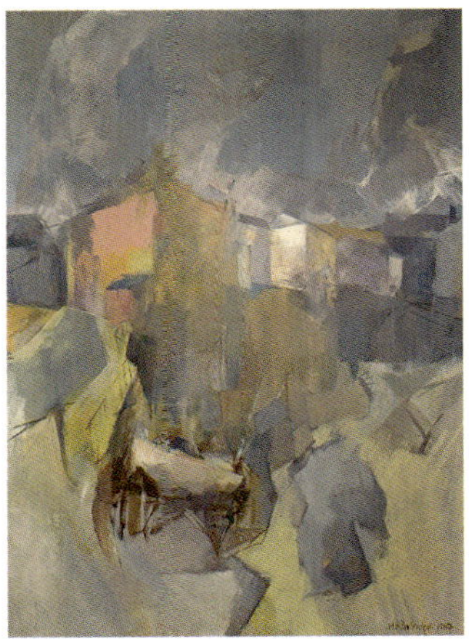

Partridge, Maurice William 1913–1973
Newlyn Old Harbour, Cornwall 1967
oil on canvas 100.5 x 74.6
UON.066

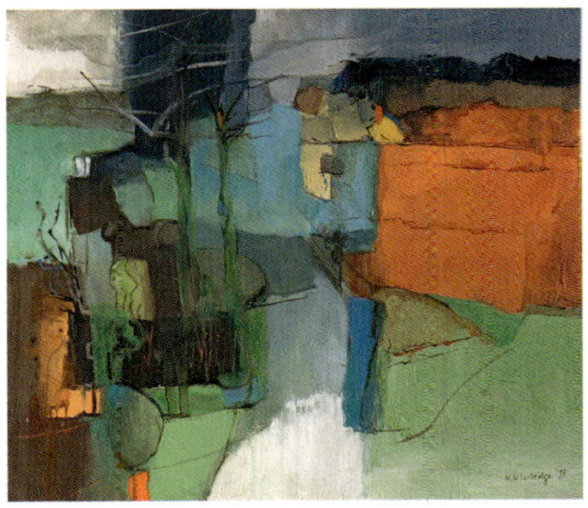

Partridge, Maurice William 1913–1973
Near Ancaster, Lincolnshire 1973
acrylic on canvas 50 x 60.2
UON.064

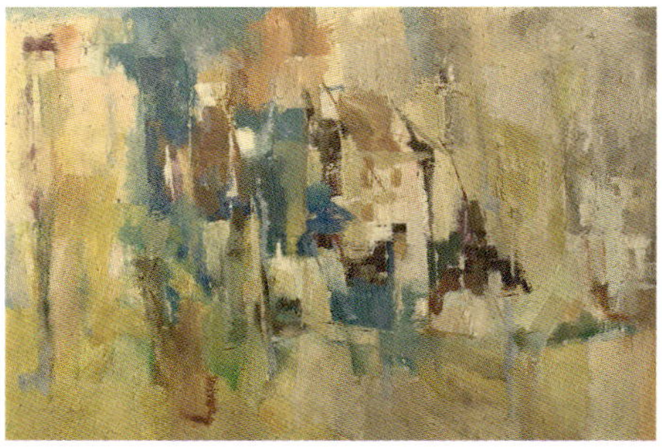

Partridge, Maurice William 1913–1973
Abstract with Buildings
oil on board 52 x 77
UON.155

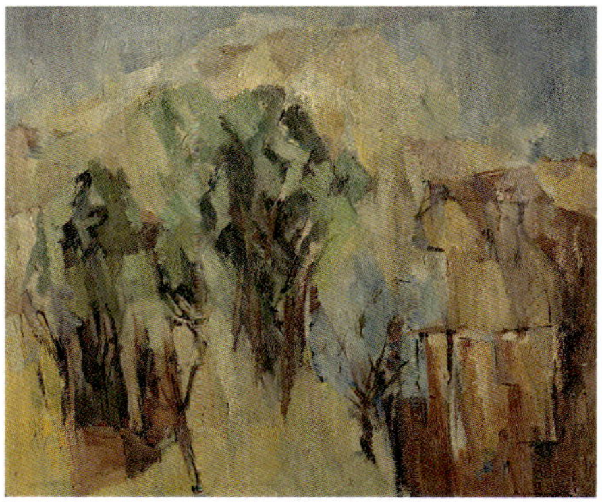

Partridge, Maurice William 1913–1973
Istrian Landscape, Croatia
oil on canvas 76 x 92
UON.159

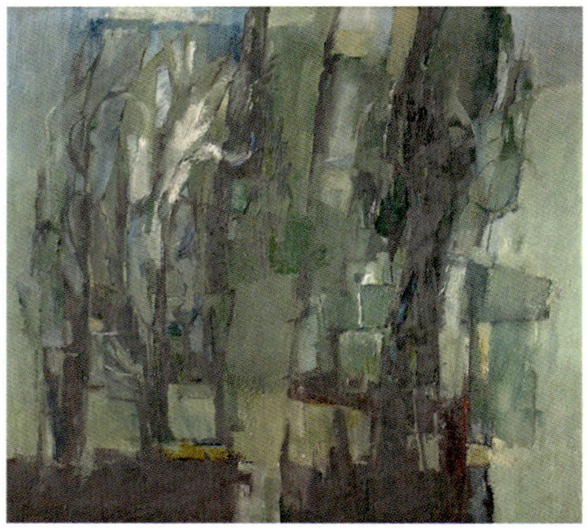

Partridge, Maurice William 1913–1973
Landscape
acrylic on board 74.5 x 90
UON.102

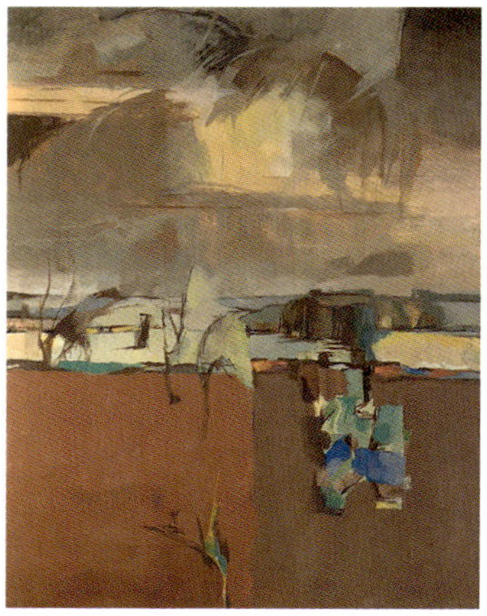

Partridge, Maurice William 1913–1973
Landscape with Trees on Red Square
acrylic on canvas 60 x 49
UON.156

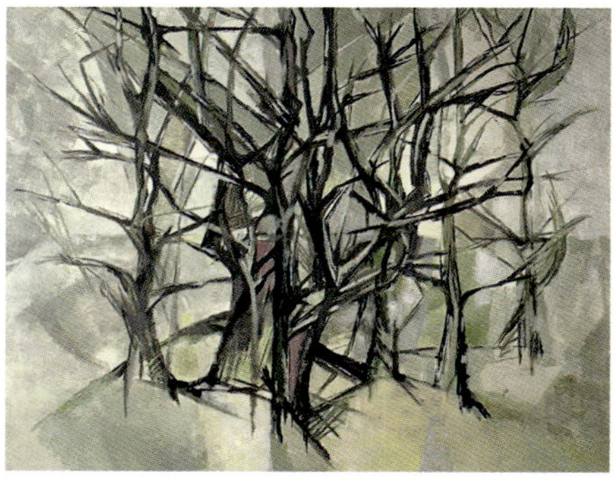

Partridge, Maurice William 1913–1973
Near Wortley Hall, South Yorkshire
acrylic on board 60 x 75
UON.059

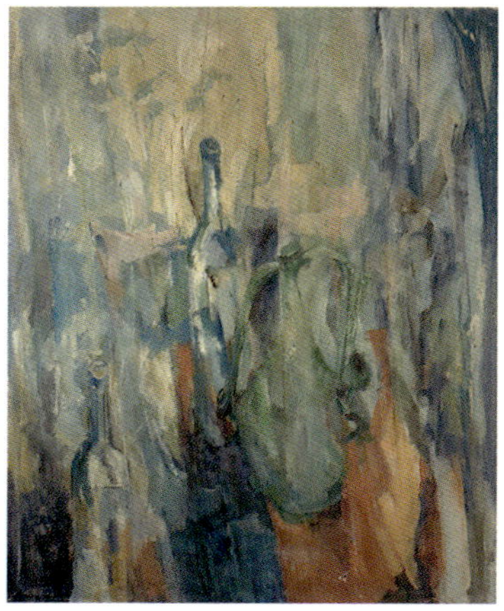

Partridge, Maurice William 1913–1973
Still Life with Bottles
oil on canvas 92 x 76
UON.160

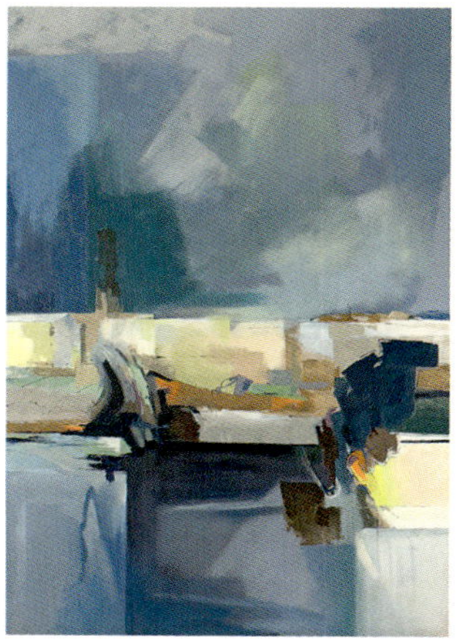

Partridge, Maurice William 1913–1973
The Trent Building
acrylic on canvas 151.1 x 106
UON.065

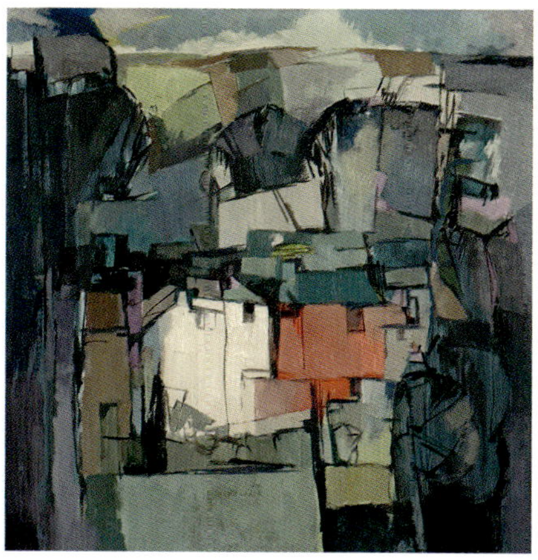

Partridge, Maurice William 1913–1973
Untitled
acrylic on board 75 x 75
UON.060

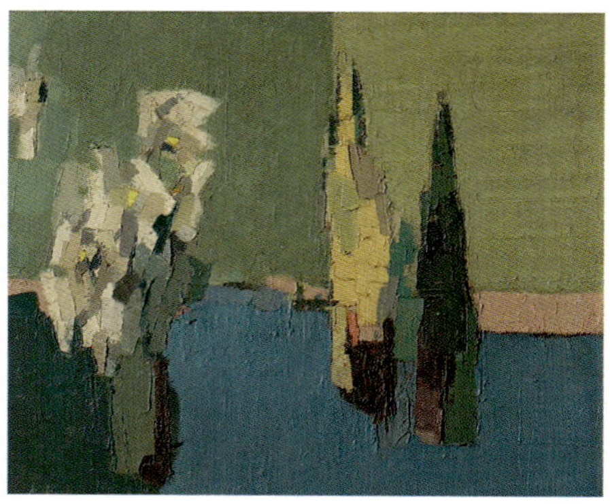

Partridge, Maurice William 1913–1973
Untitled
acrylic on board 60.5 x 75.7
UON.061

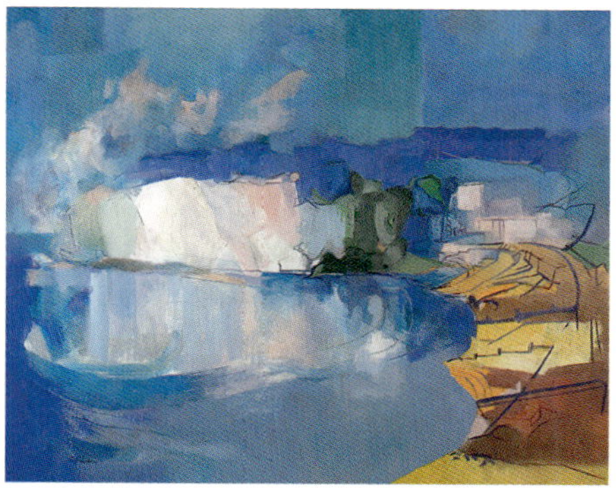

Partridge, Maurice William 1913–1973
White Cliffs
acrylic on canvas 71 x 90.5
UON.063

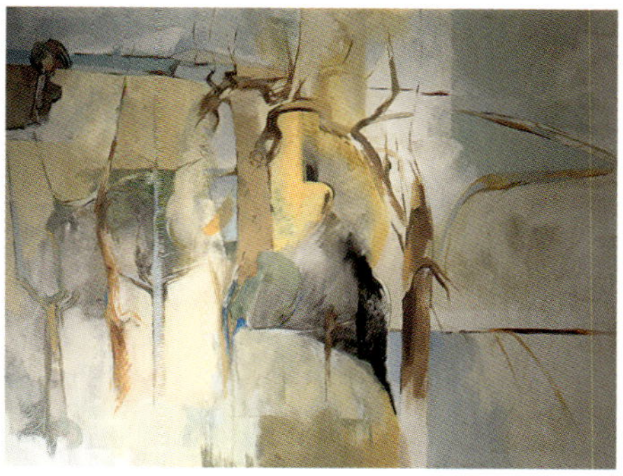

Partridge, Maurice William 1913–1973
Winter Landscape
oil on canvas 90 x 130 (E)
UON.130

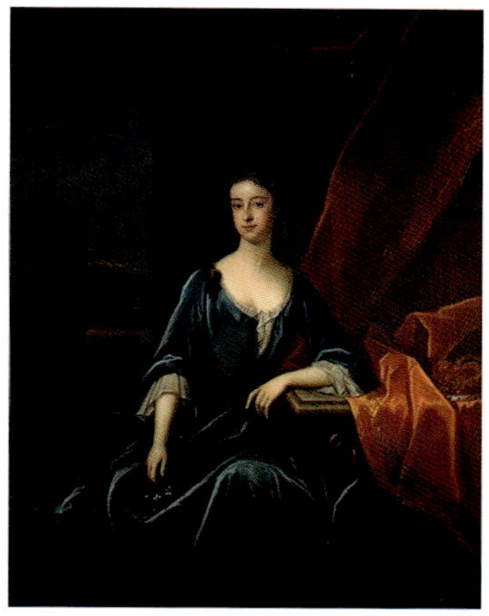

Richardson, Jonathan the elder
1664/1665–1745
Henrietta Pelham-Holles (d.1776), 1st Duchess of Newcastle-under-Lyne
oil on canvas 162.5 x 131
UON.050

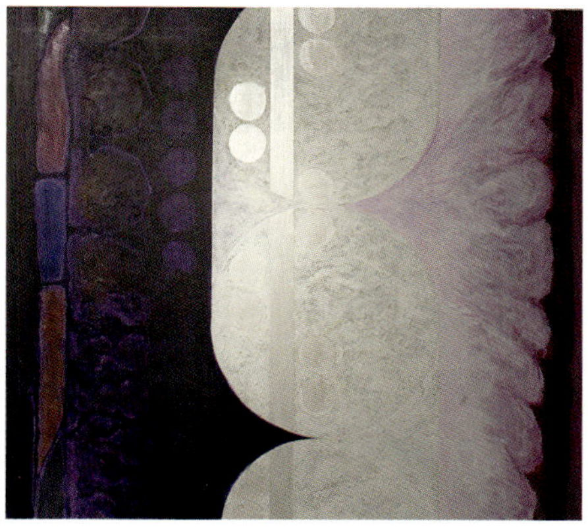

Roberts, John Horrocks b.1931
Untitled
acrylic & mixed media on board 106 x 121.5
UON.114

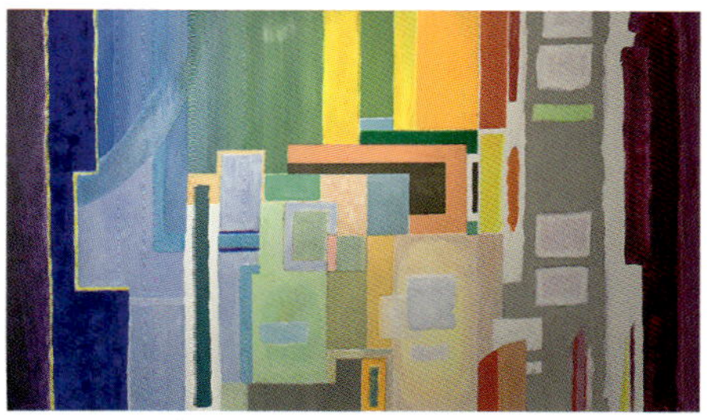

Roberts, John Horrocks b.1931
Untitled
acrylic on board 107 x 182.5
UON.115

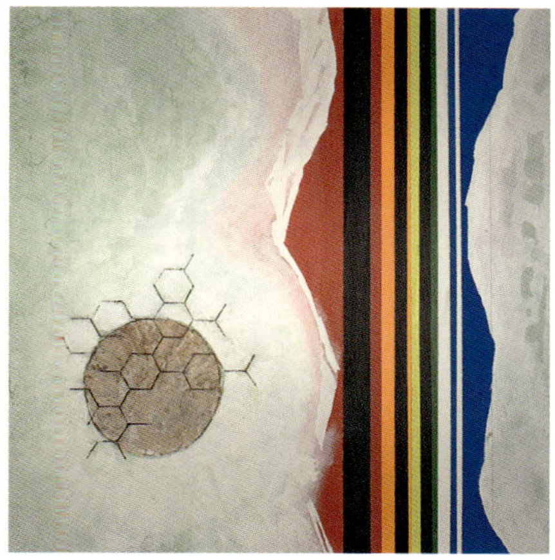

Roberts, John Horrocks b.1931
Untitled
acrylic on board 120.5 x 120
UON.116

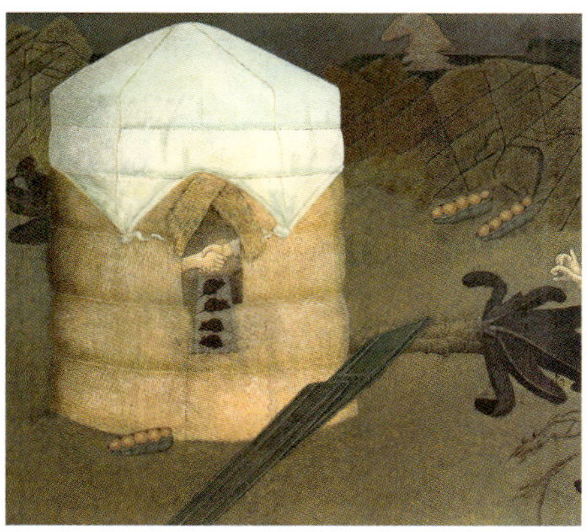

Robson, Gavin b.1950
The Park
oil on canvas 70.6 x 81
UON.017

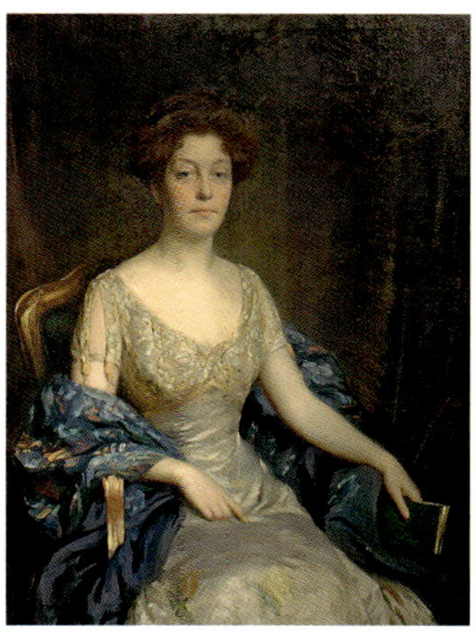

Ronaldson, Thomas Martine 1881–1942
Kathleen (1872–1955), 7th Duchess of Newcastle-under-Lyne
oil on canvas 108.4 x 84.6
UON.117

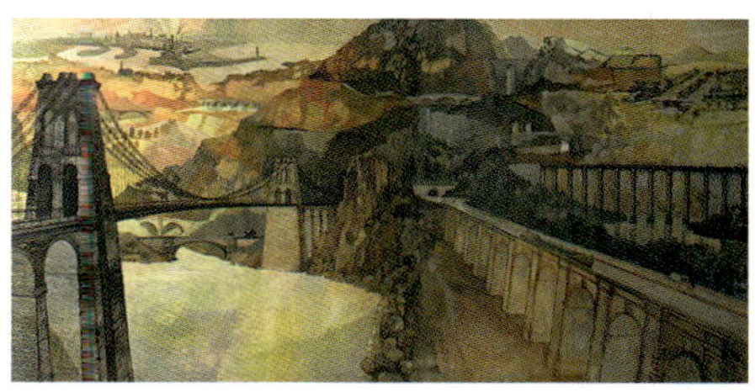

Rosoman, Leonard Henry b.1913
Composite Painting of the Works of Thomas Telford 1958
oil on canvas 365.8 x 731.5
UON.131

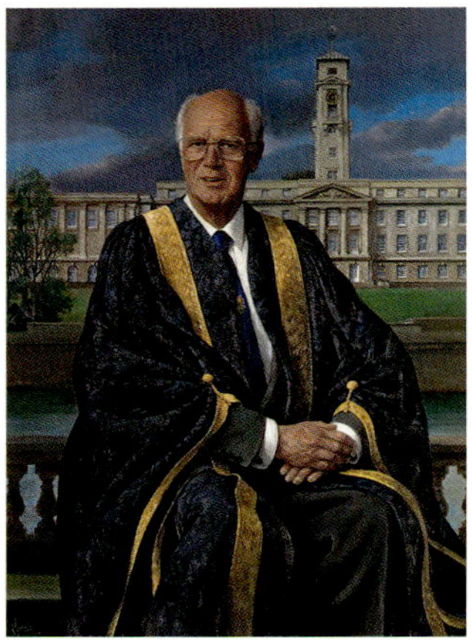

Sancha, Carlos Luis 1920–2001
Dr David J. Atkin, LLD, FIBF, President of the Council (1993–1996) 1997
oil on canvas 100 x 74.5
UON.051

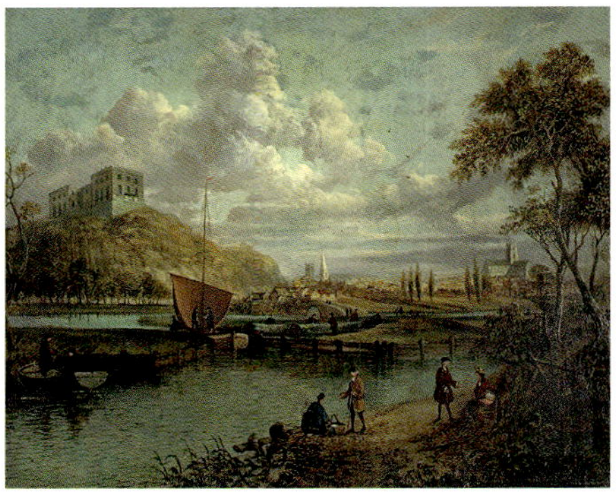

Sandby, Paul (school of) 1731–1809
A Panorama of Nottingham from the Canal
oil on canvas 89 x 119
UON.118

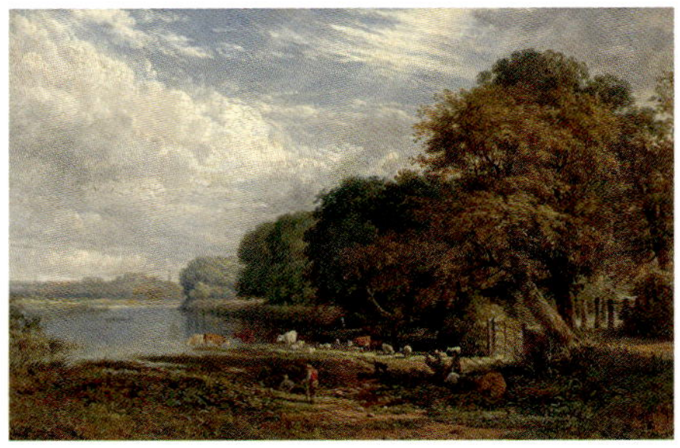

Shipham, Benjamin (attributed to) 1808–1872
Distant View of Nottingham from the Trent at Clifton Grove
oil on canvas 41 x 61
UON.012

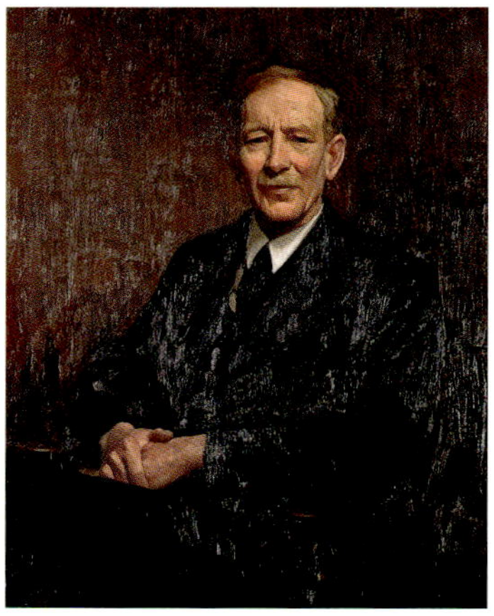

Spooner, Arthur 1873–1961
Frank H. Jacob, MD, FRCP
oil on canvas 89 x 73
UON.124

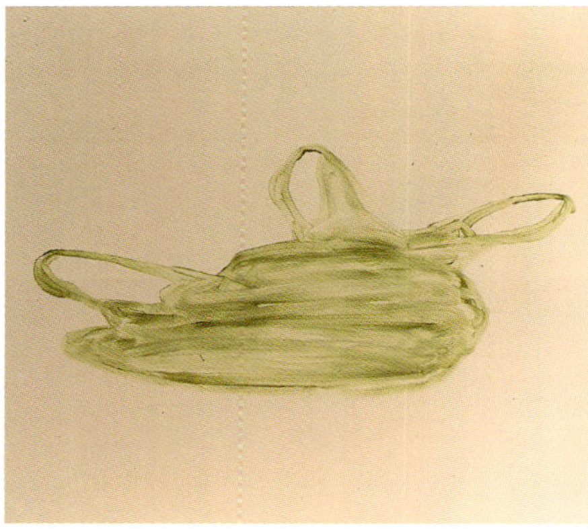

Sprawson, Derek b.1955
First 1999
oil on canvas 81.5 x 91.5
UON.020

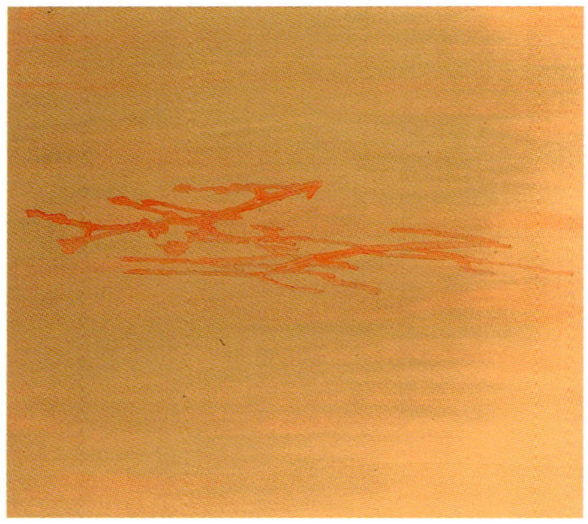

Sprawson, Derek b.1955
Fruit 1999
oil on canvas 81.5 x 91.5
UON.019

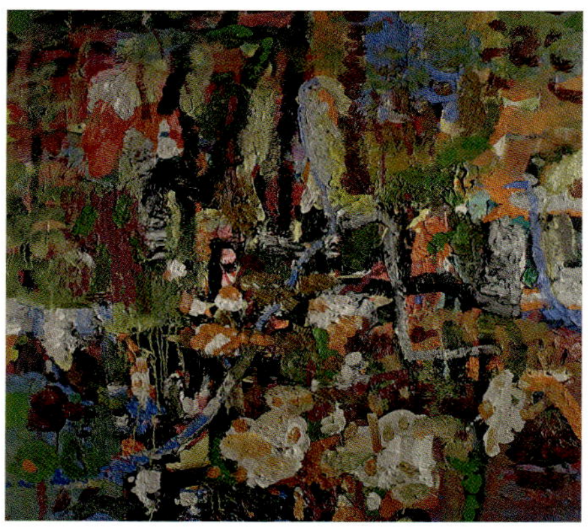

Sprawson, Derek b.1955
Phial
oil on canvas 122 x 137
UON.075

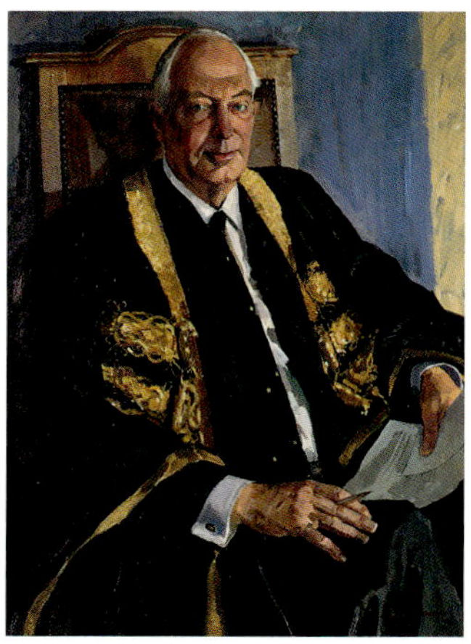

Stubley, Trevor b.1932
Basil Charles Leicester Weedon (1923–2003), CBE, DSc, PhD, DTech, LLD, ARCS, DIC, CChem, FRSC, FRS, Vice-Chancellor (...)
oil on canvas 100 x 75
UON.025

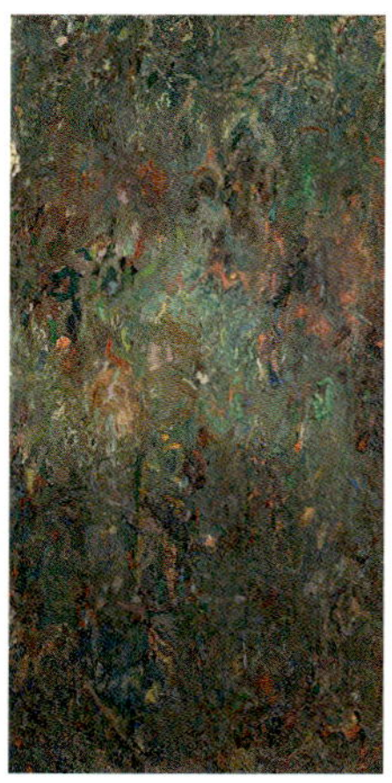

Taborn, David b.1947
Chine 1980
oil on canvas 183 x 98
UON.132

Facing page: Jagger, David, 1891–1958, *Jewish Refugee, Vienna* (detail), (1939), Nottingham City Museums and Galleries (p. 111)

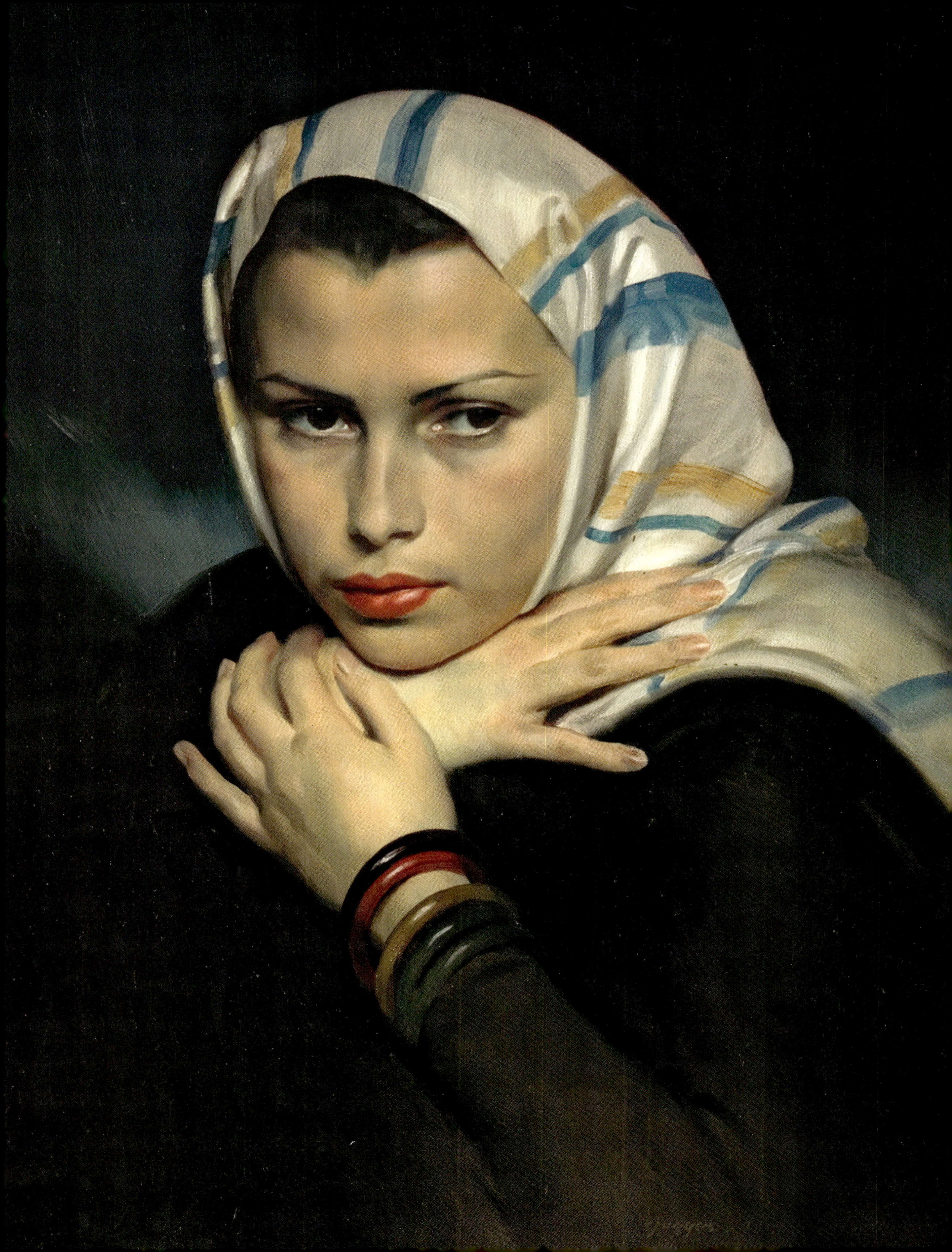

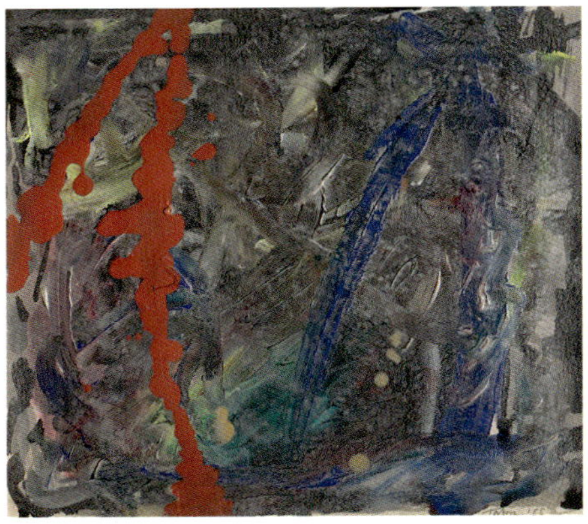

Taborn, David b.1947
Untitled 1988
acrylic & mixed media on paper 30.7 x 35.4
UON.120

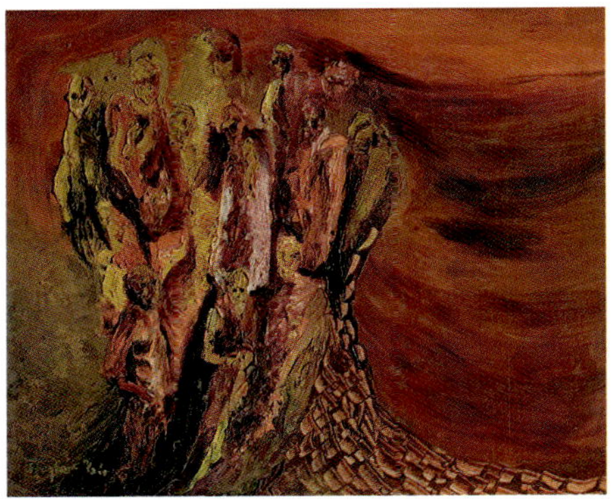

Taylor, S.
Group of Figures in Reds 1966
oil on canvas 60 x 74.5
UON.103

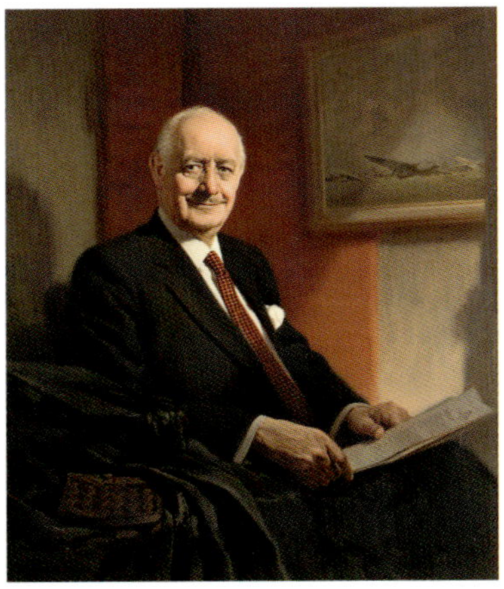

Townsend, John b.1930
John Madocks, CBE, DL, Bursar (1967–1987)
oil on canvas 104.5 x 89.5
UON.001

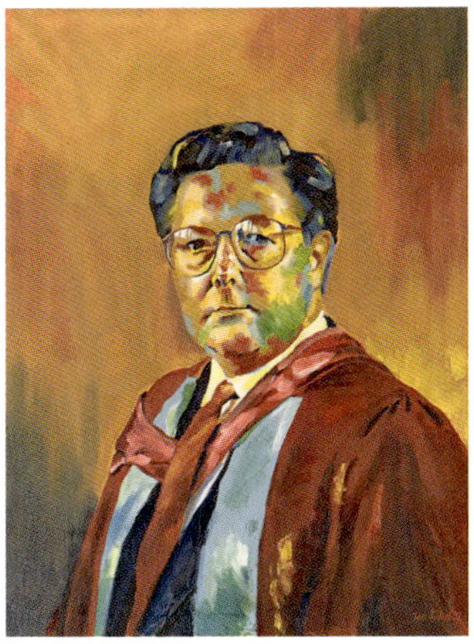

Trickett, Rob
Professor Douglas James Davies (b.1947), Warden of Derby Hall (1985–1997) 1999
oil on canvas 100 x 73 (E)
UON.104

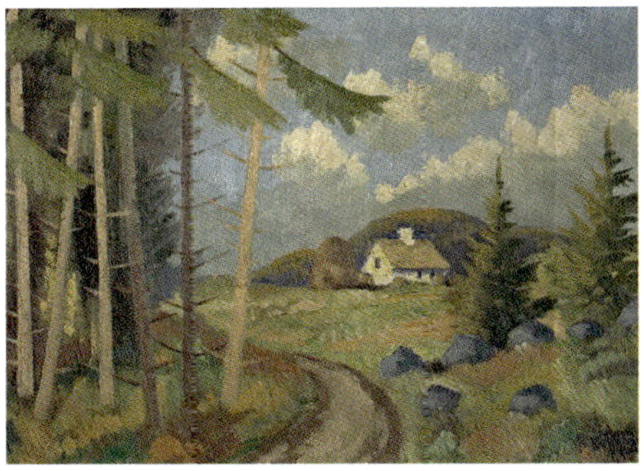

unknown artist
Landscape with Trees and Cottages
oil on hessian 64.5 x 90
UON.154

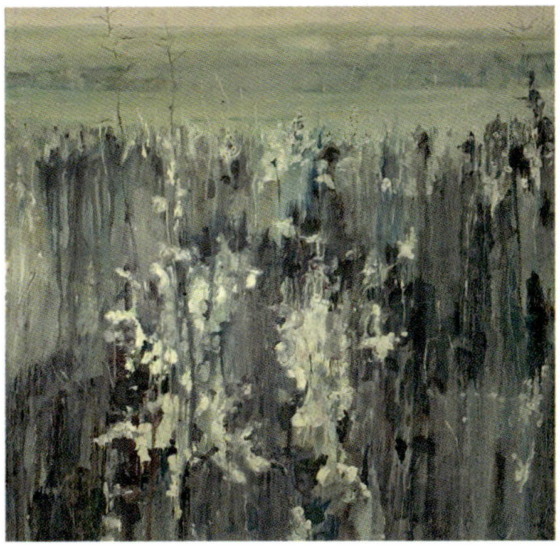

unknown artist
Meadow Landscape
oil on canvas mounted on board 100 x 101
UON.162

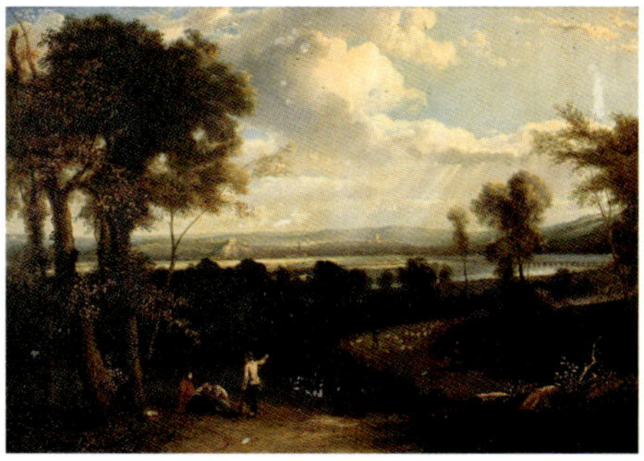

Walker, John Rawson 1796–1873
View of Nottingham from Clifton (South Prospect of Nottingham Castle) 1863
oil on canvas 85 x 121
UON.133

Warburton, Stella
Moment Painting No.2 (Ashby Parva) (left panel of diptych) 1999
acrylic & mixed media on canvas 120 x 90
UON.152a

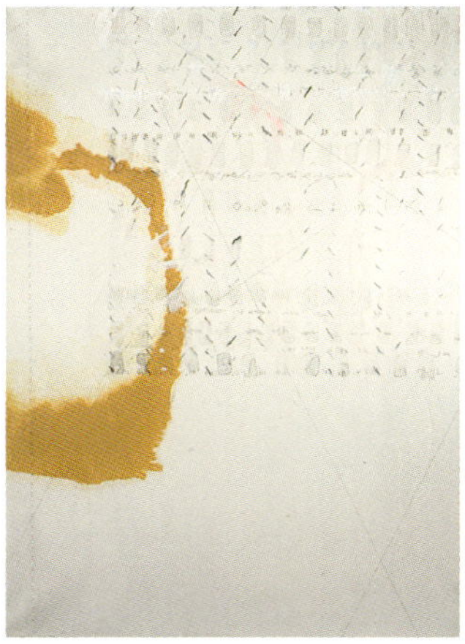

Warburton, Stella
Moment Painting No.2 (Ashby Parva) (right panel of diptych) 1999
acrylic & mixed media on canvas 120 x 90
UON.152b

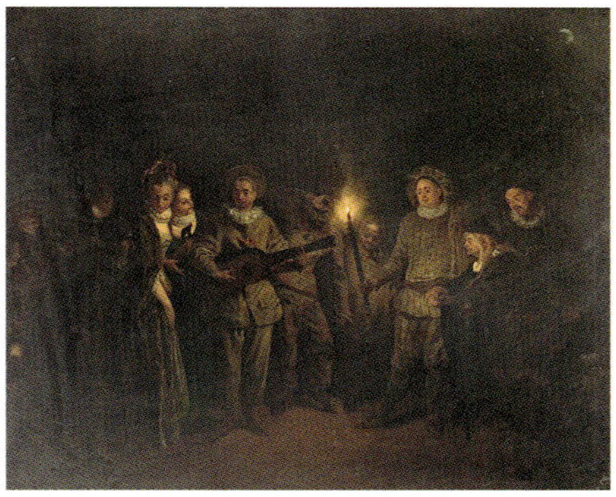

Watteau, Jean-Antoine (after) 1684–1721
A Music Party
oil on canvas 38 x 48
UON.087

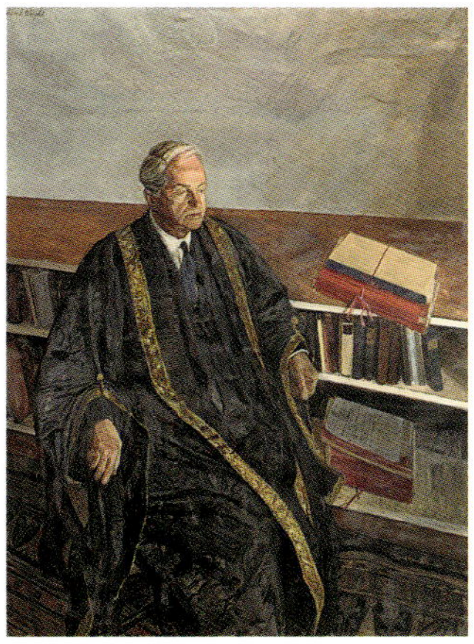

Weight, Carel Victor Morlais 1908–1997
Sir Francis Hill (1899–1980), President of Council (1948–1967)
oil on canvas 120 x 90.5
UON.022

Willetts, David b.1939
Garden
acrylic on wood 30 x 39
UON.074

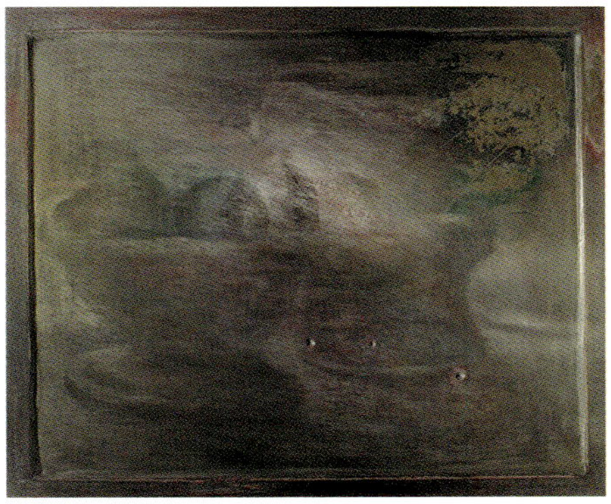

Willetts, David b.1939
Still Life with Fruit Bowl
acrylic on wood 49.5 x 61
UON.073

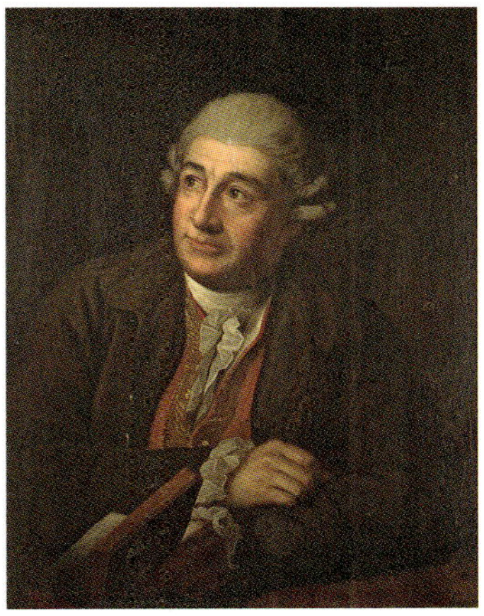

Zoffany, Johann (after) 1733–1810
David Garrick (1717–1779)
oil on canvas 73.5 x 58.5
UON.052

The Worcestershire and Sherwood Foresters Museum (The Sherwood Foresters Collection) of the Mercian Regiment

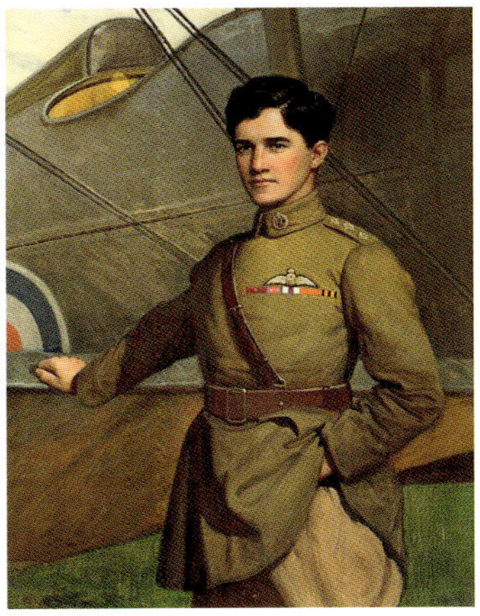

Davis, Noel Denholm 1876–1950
Captain Albert Ball (1896–1917), VC 1917
oil on canvas 134.6 x 104.1
NCM 1990-624

Bassetlaw District Council

Bassetlaw Museum is based in Amcott House, a late eighteenth-century townhouse in the centre of Retford, North Nottinghamshire. The Museum was opened in 1986 and its Collection, incorporating the collection of the former Worksop Museum, encompasses a wide range of archaeological, photographic and social history artefacts and a small fine and decorative art collection. In 1994 the Museum opened the Percy Laws Art Gallery which is housed in a modern extension, and since then has hosted a number of exhibitions by local artists and photographers, as well as showing its own works of art. The core of the art collection is a group of oils and watercolours by James Walsham Baldock, a resident of Worksop in the nineteenth century. Raised on a farm by his grandfather, his work depicts the local countryside and rural themes such as hunting.

The art collection also covers more contemporary works, such as *Two Standing Forms by a Palisade II* by Graham Sutherland (a gouache painting and therefore not included in the present catalogue), and paintings by local artists who have held exhibitions in the gallery.

It is not possible to display any one group of works permanently as we have limited space, but many of the Baldock paintings are out on show as part of a Victorian room setting.

The Collection has grown through the generosity of local and national donors and to some extent by purchases made over the years by the local authority, Bassetlaw District Council. However, limited resources place many works beyond our means. Where possible, we will continue to collect artworks by local artists, both historical and more contemporary.

Samantha Glasswell, Curator

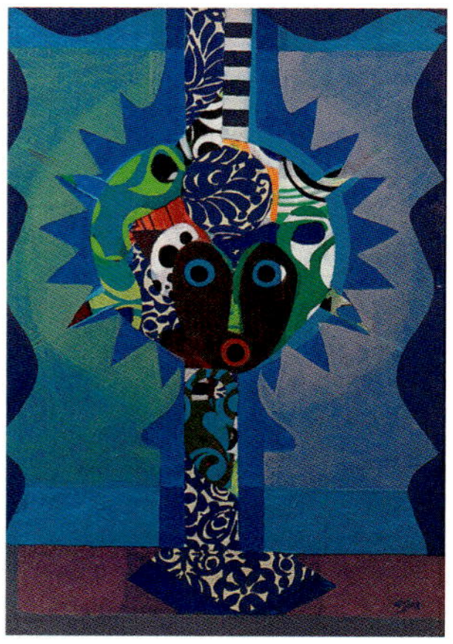

Agar, Eileen 1899–1991
The Magician 1980
acrylic on canvas 74.8 x 54.4
RETBM : A129

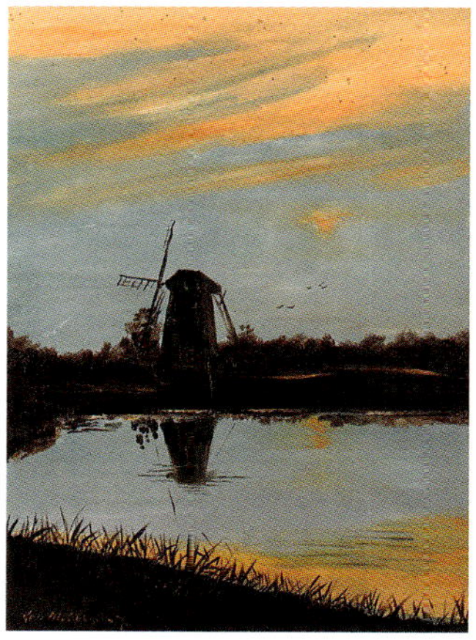

Allsebrook, Kenneth
Windmill 1970
oil on board 40.5 x 30.5
RETBM : 2005.1275

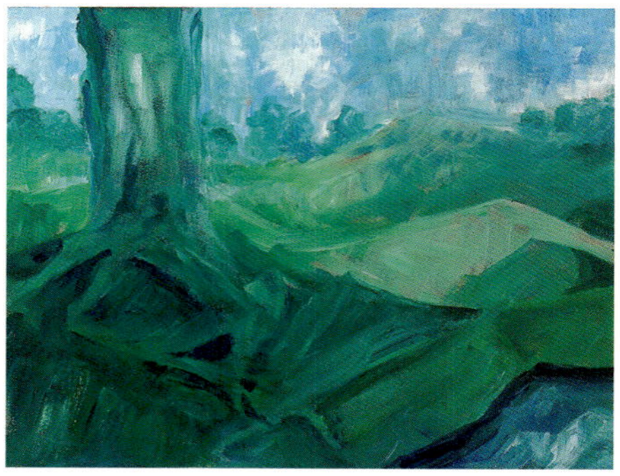

Ashton, Garry John b.1954
Tree Roots 2005
oil on canvas 30.5 x 40.5
RETBM : art.2006.2051

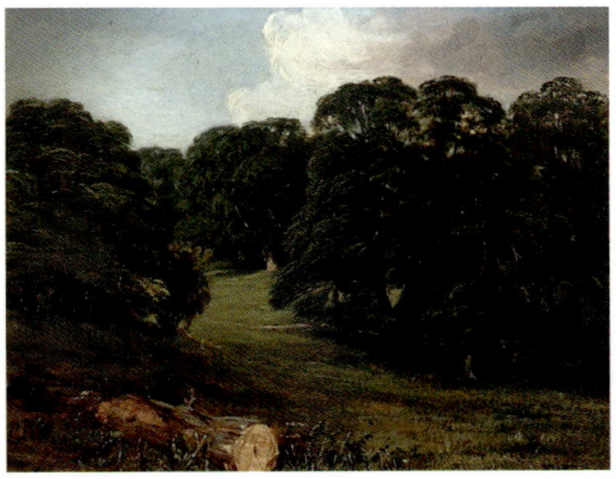

Baldock, James Walsham 1822–1898
In Welbeck Park, Nottinghamshire 1857
oil on board 18.4 x 24
RETBM : A25

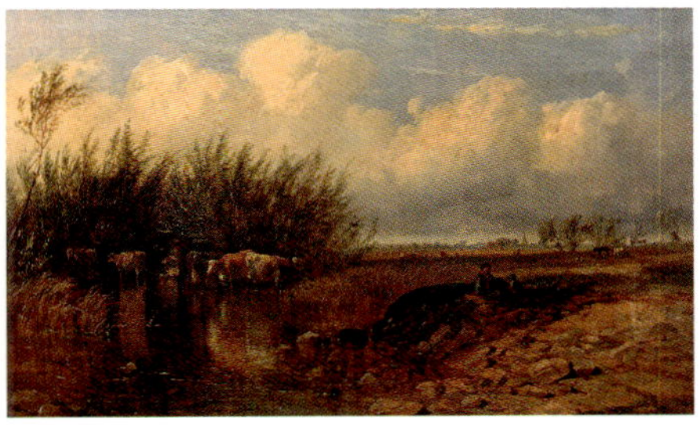

Baldock, James Walsham 1822–1898
Landscape with a Boy and Cattle 1857
oil on canvas 30.5 x 51.2
RETBM : A5

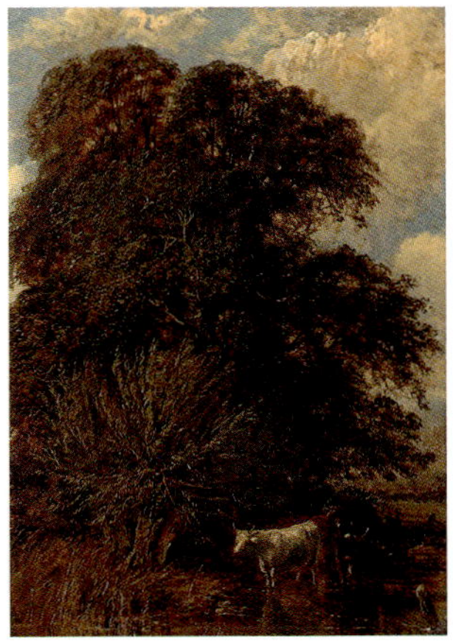

Baldock, James Walsham 1822–1898
Cows in the Shadow of a Tree 1861
oil on board 30 x 21
RETBM : A24

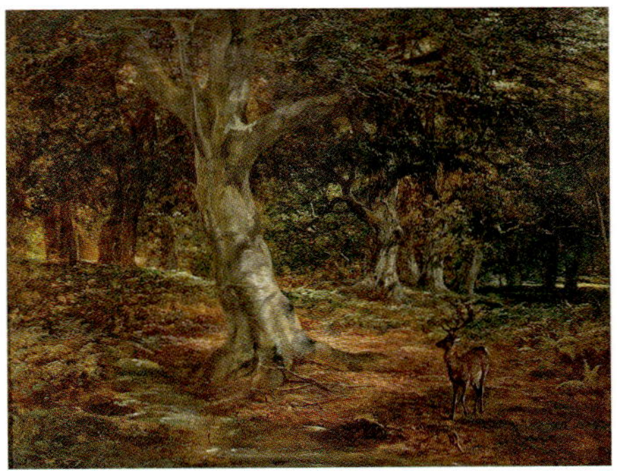

Baldock, James Walsham 1822–1898
Forest Scene with Deer 1863
oil on canvas 32 x 41
RETBM : A6

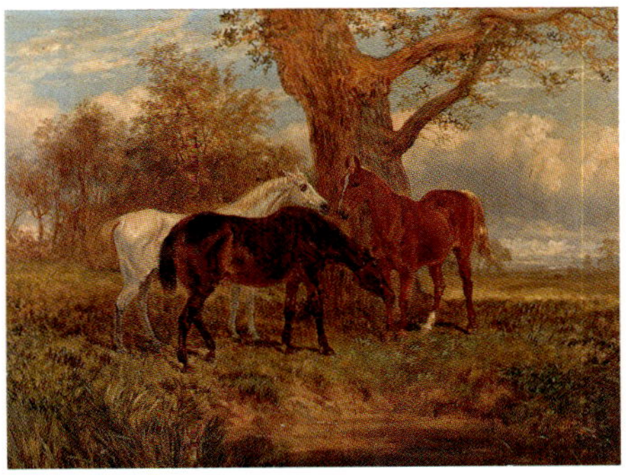

Baldock, James Walsham 1822–1898
Study of Three Horses in a Landscape 1879
oil on canvas 30.5 x 41
RETBM : A7

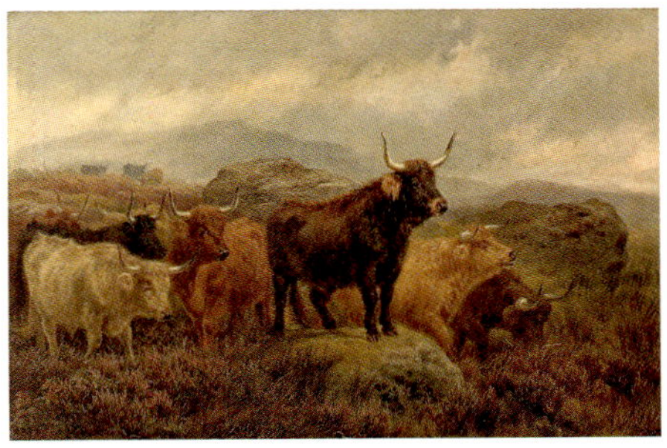

Baldock, James Walsham 1822–1898
On the Scottish Moors 1889
oil on canvas 59 x 85.2
RETBM : A42

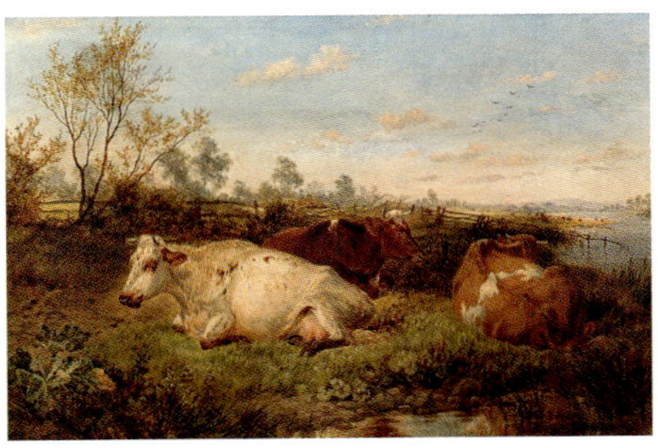

Baldock, James Walsham 1822–1898
Study of Cattle 1890
oil on canvas 30.5 x 45
RETBM : A3

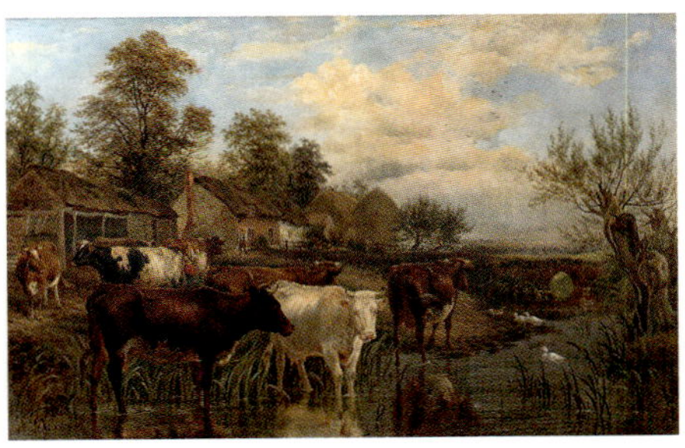

Baldock, James Walsham 1822–1898
Lady Lea Farm 1892
oil on canvas 75 x 120.4
RETBM : A43

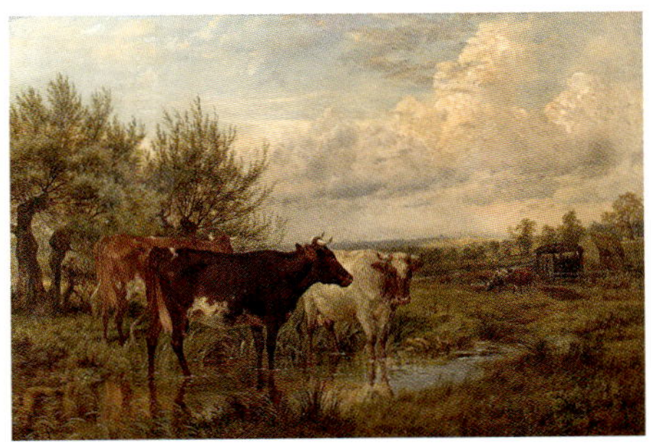

Baldock, James Walsham 1822–1898
Landscape near Worksop Manor Park, Nottinghamshire 1894
oil on canvas 59.8 x 90.1
RETBM : A44

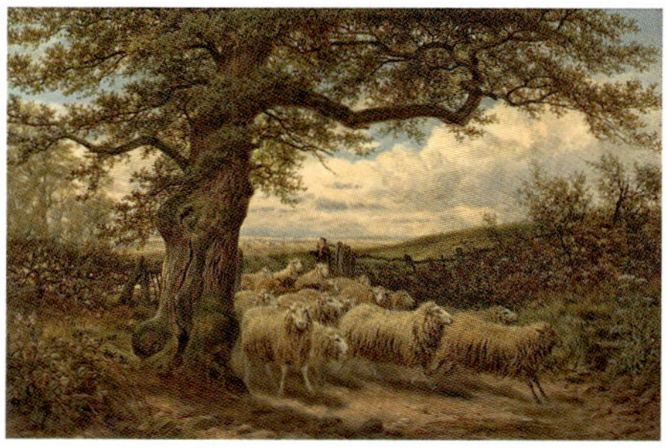

Baldock, James Walsham 1822–1898
Sheep and Shepherd 1895
oil on canvas 50 x 74
RETBM : A21

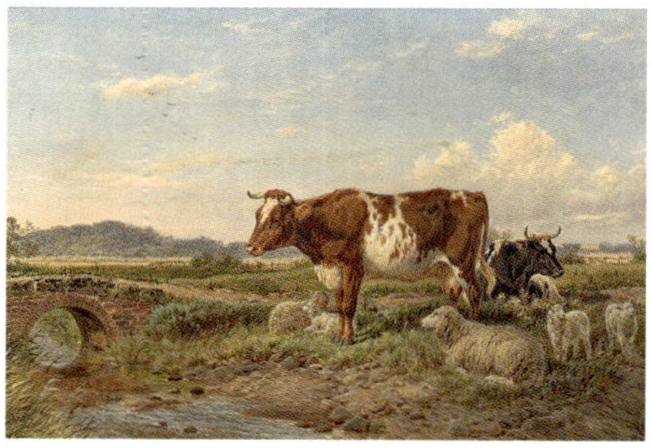

Baldock, James Walsham 1822–1898
A Quiet Day in the Trent Valley
oil on canvas 29 x 44
RETBM : A1

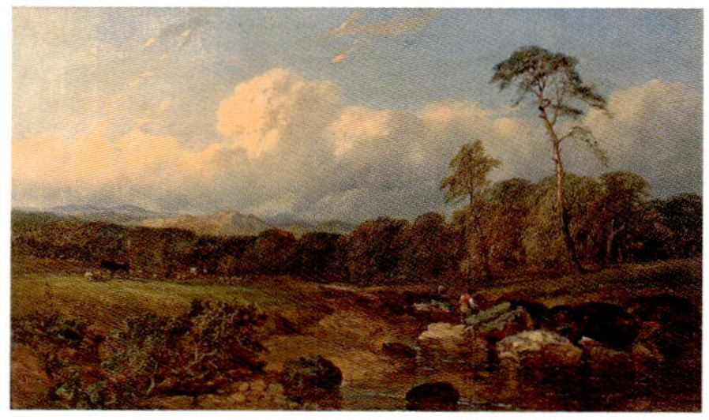

Baldock, James Walsham 1822–1898
Landscape with Men and Cattle
oil on canvas 31 x 51
RETBM : A15

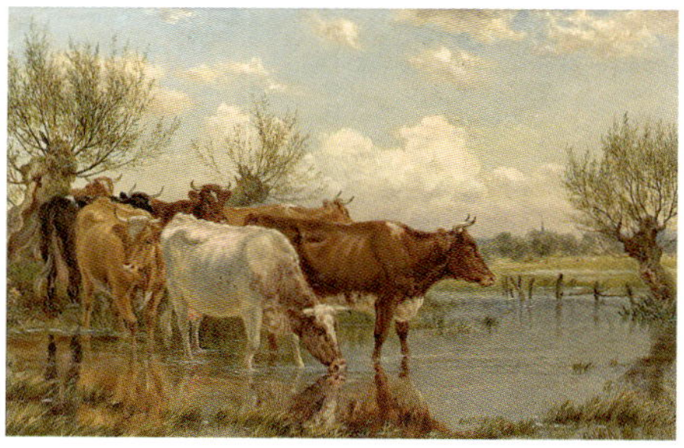

Baldock, James Walsham 1822–1898
Study of Cattle at a Pond
oil on canvas 30.5 x 45
RETBM : A4

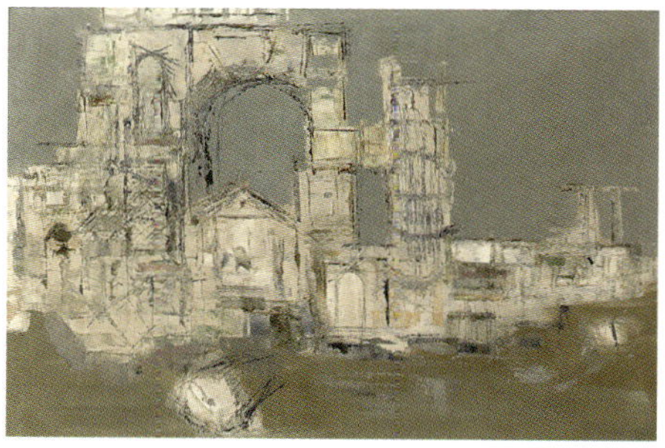

Barker, Kit 1916–1988
Ruins at Hadrian's Villa, Tivoli, Rome, Italy
oil on canvas 43.5 x 65.5
RETBM : A115

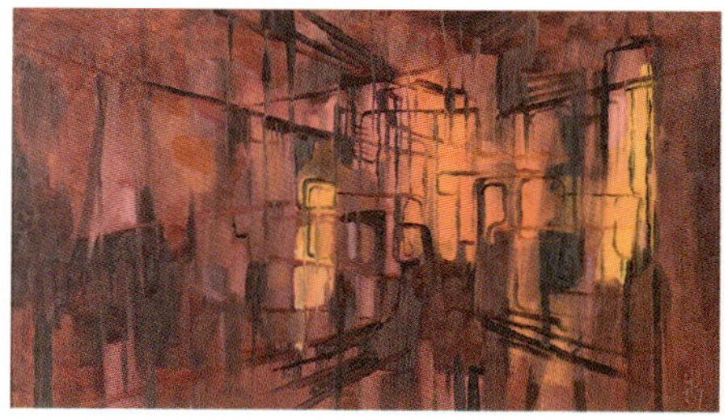

Barker, L.
City Lights 1967
oil on plywood 42 x 74
RETBM : A60

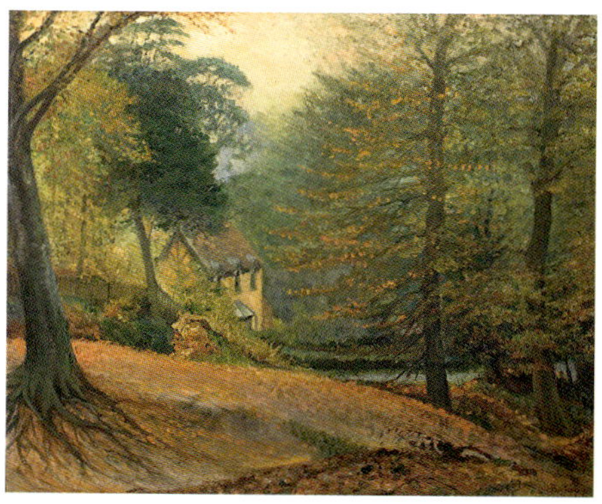

Bartrop, Darwin Holdsworth b.1882
Rock Cottage, Worksop, Nottinghamshire 1946
oil on board 76.5 x 92
RETBM : A106

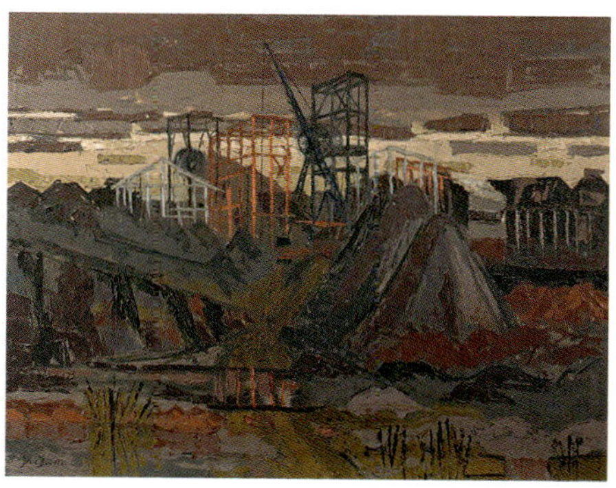

Bowett, Druie 1924–1998
Manton Colliery, Nottinghamshire 1962
oil on canvas 95 x 123.5
RETBM : A119

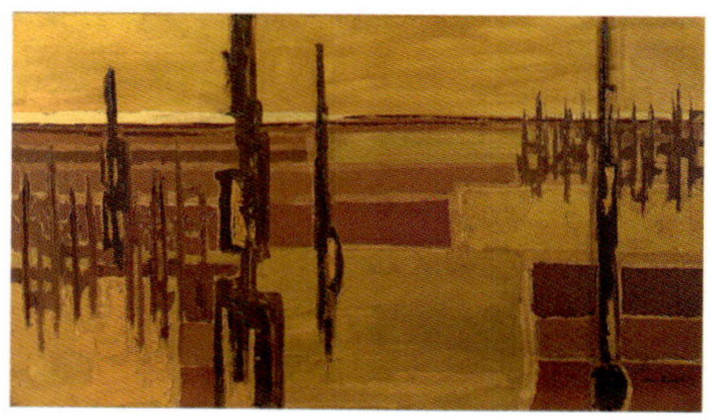

Bowett, Druie 1924–1998
Brown and Yellow Painting 1963
oil on canvas 77.5 x 137.5
RETBM : A120

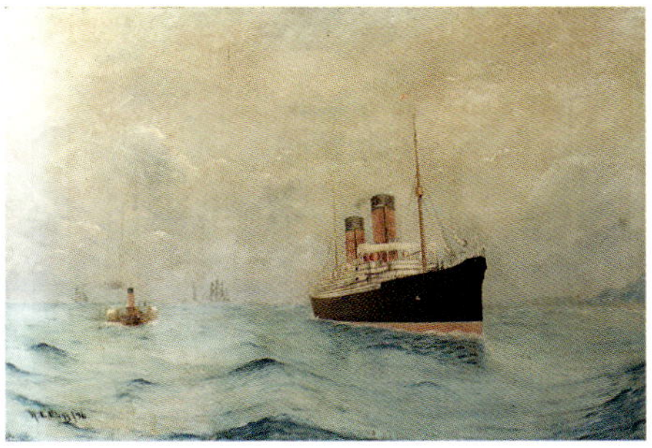

Clegg, William George 1863–1940
'Campania' 1896
oil on canvas 76 x 114
RETBM : art.2006.2050

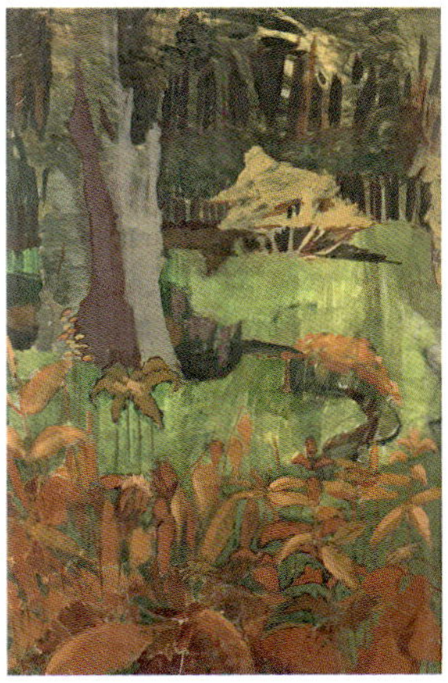

Davis, W. Gronow
Japanese Landscape
oil on board 90 x 59.5
RETBM : A111

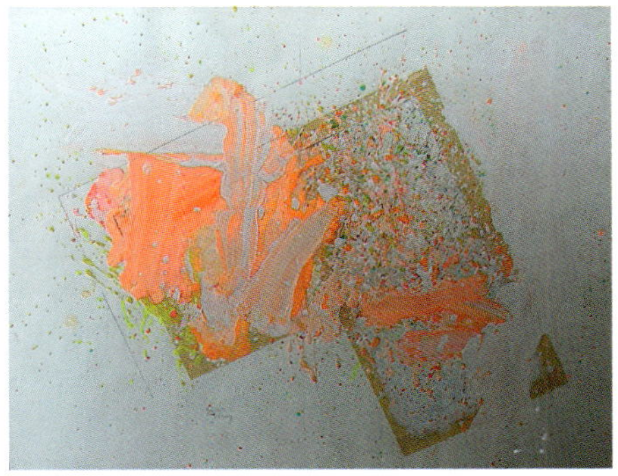

Delaney, Barbara b.1941
Dec II 1975
acrylic & mixed media on paper
62 x 76.9 (E)
RETBM : A70

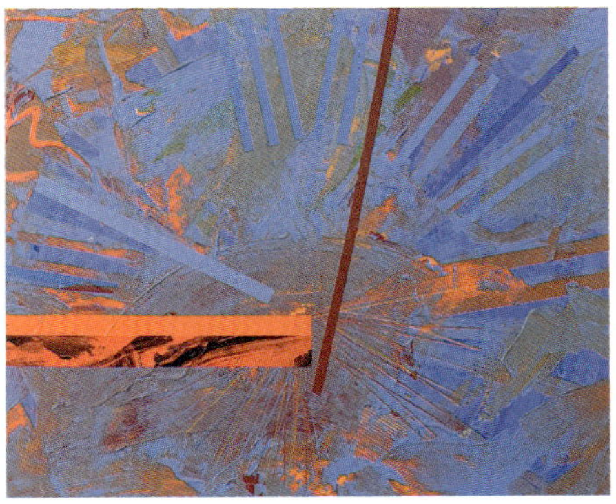

Delaney, Barbara b.1941
34516 1994
acrylic & mixed media on canvas 61 x 76
RETBM : A147

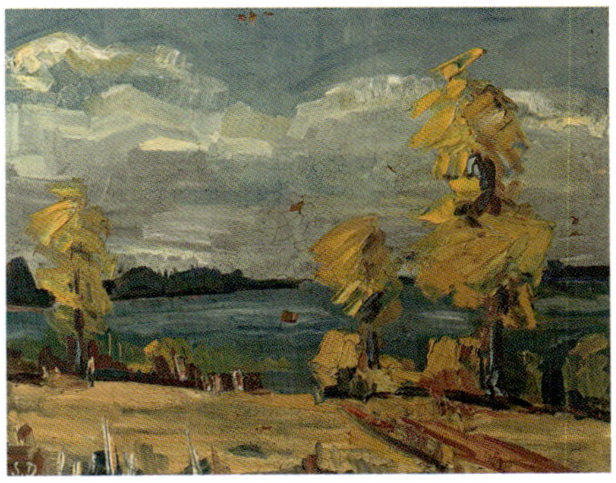

Downar, S.
2 Clumber 9 1967
acrylic on board 45 x 58
RETBM : A117

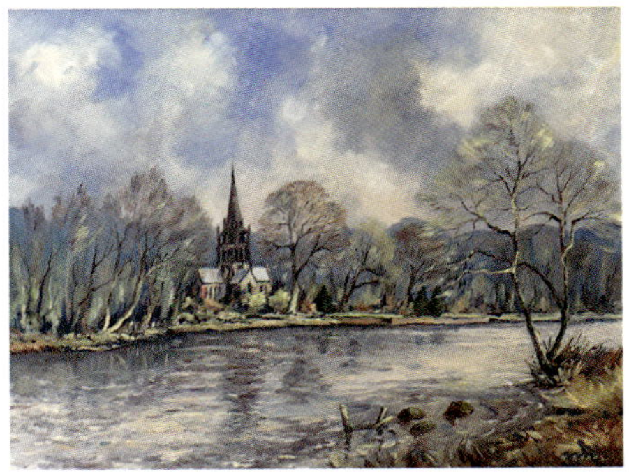

Evans, Norman
Springtime in Clumber, Nottinghamshire 1993
oil on canvas 45 x 59
RETBM : A133

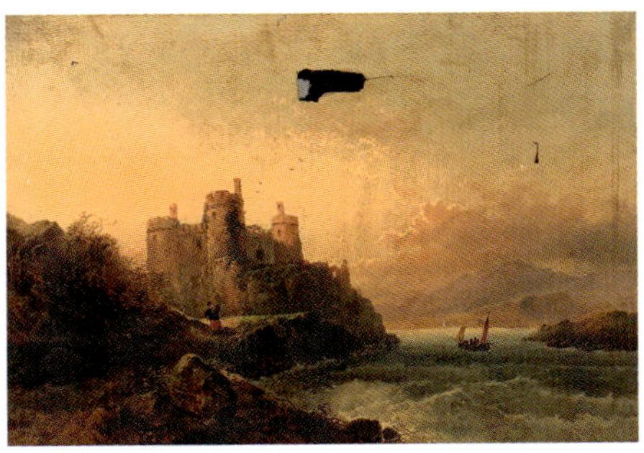

Forbes, D. (attributed to)
*Seascape With Ruins**
oil on canvas 59.6 x 90
RETBM : A41

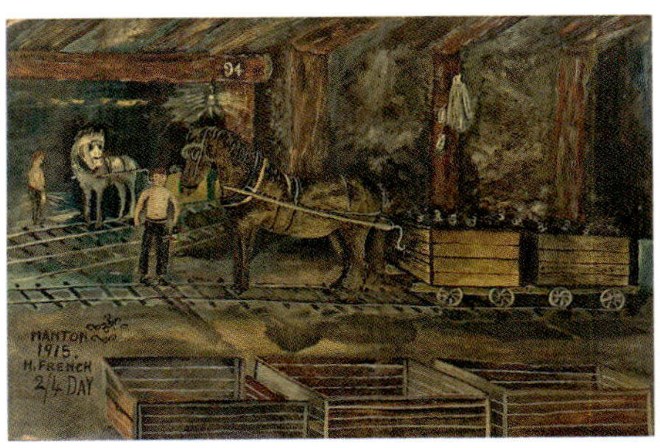

French, H.
Manton Colliery, Nottinghamshire 1915
oil on Daler board 50 x 61
RETBM : art.1994.61

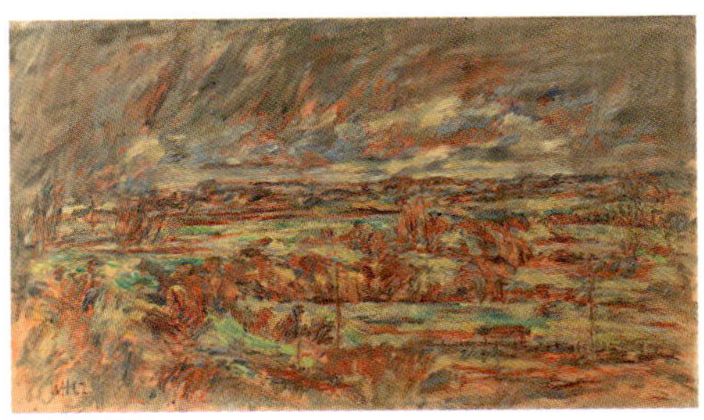

Hartwell, William John 1922–1995
Landscape near Buckenham, Suffolk 1962
oil on board 59.5 x 105
RETBM : A112

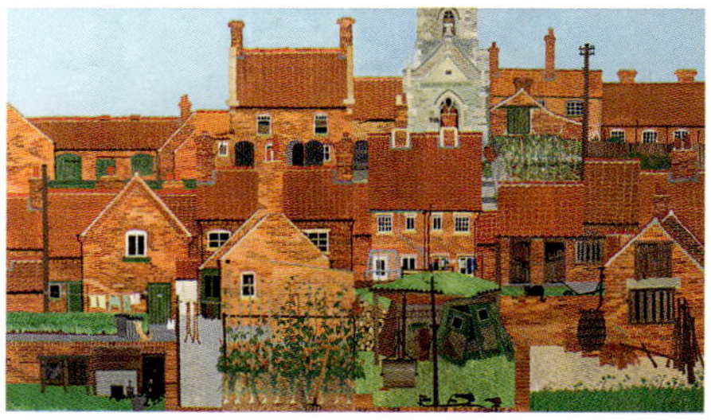

Hayward, Liz b.1949
Bothamsall's Buildings, Nottinghamshire 1983
oil on board 55 x 101
RETBM : A85

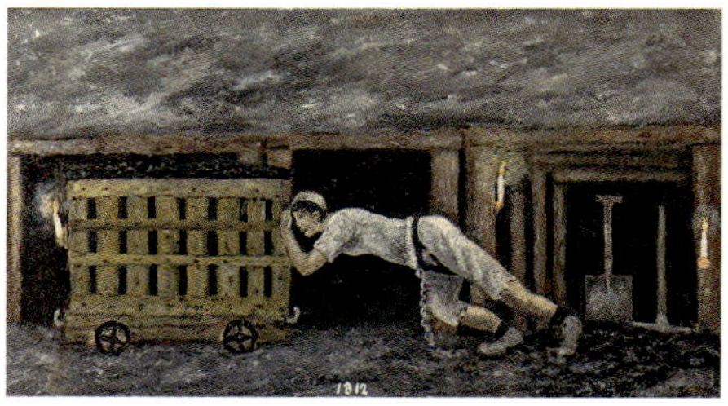

Hector, G. active 2006
1812
oil on wood 34.4 x 64
RETBM : art.2006.1697

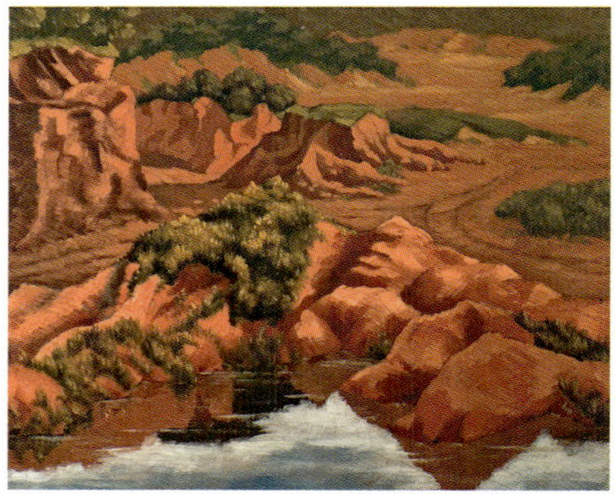

Hicken, Harry d.2000
Gateford Quarry, Nottinghamshire 1959
oil on board 60 x 74
RETBM : 2006.2343

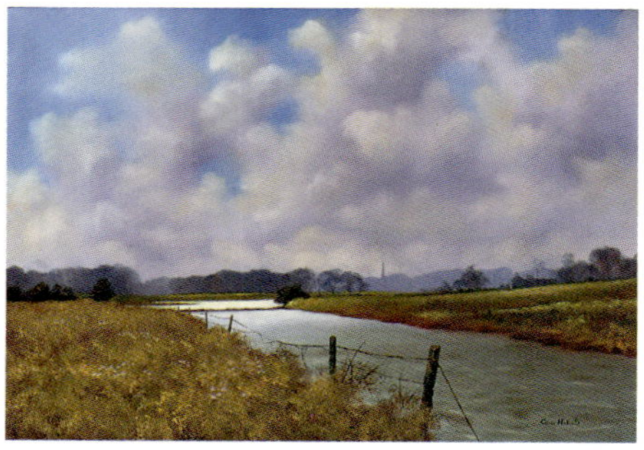

Holmes, Alan
The Poulter below Clumber, Nottinghamshire
oil on board 40.5 x 58.6
PCF1

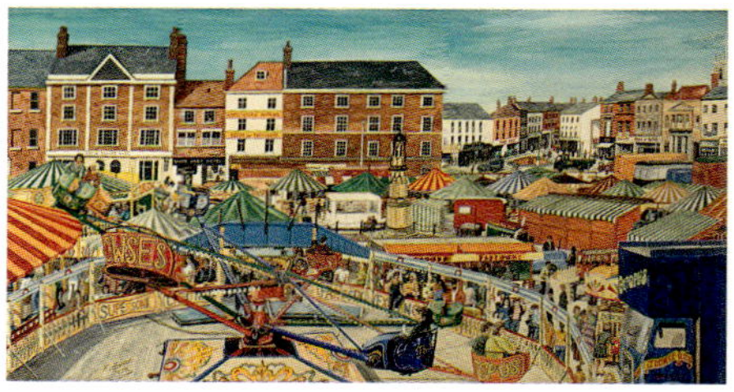

Hudson, Keith
Retford Fair, Nottinghamshire 1979
acrylic on board 42 x 80
PCF2

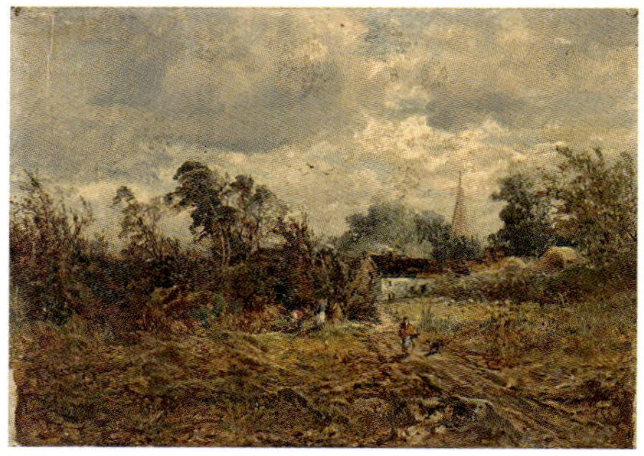

Hudson, Robert 1852–1884
Edwinstowe Church, Nottinghamshire 1876
oil on canvas 25.2 x 35.5
RETBM : A72

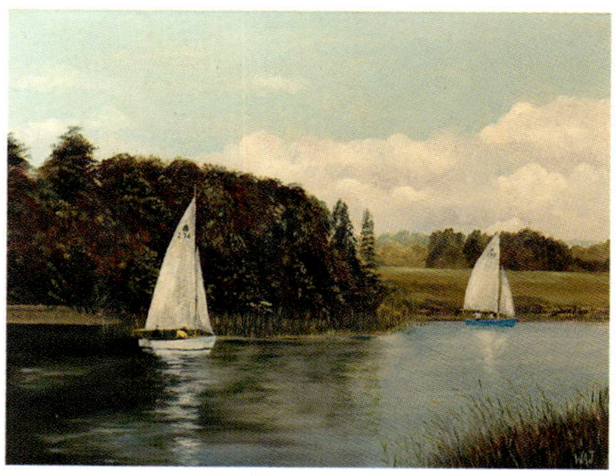

Jones, W. A. active 1968–1969
Sailing at Welbeck, Nottinghamshire 1969
oil on board 45 x 60
RETBM : A110

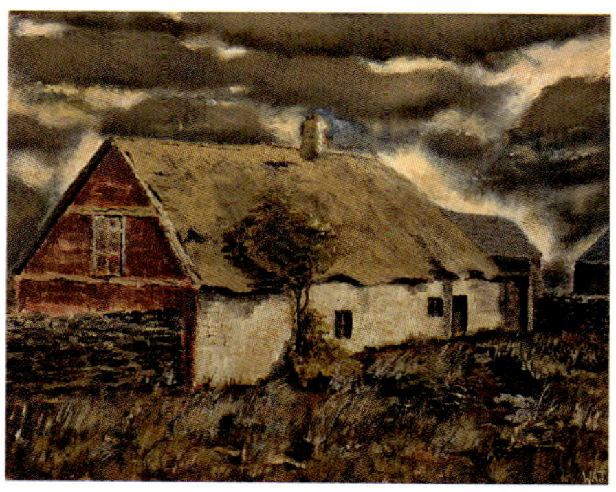

Jones, W. A. active 1968–1969
Molly Leigh's Cottage, Burslem, Staffordshire
oil on hardboard 49.5 x 64
RETBM : A81

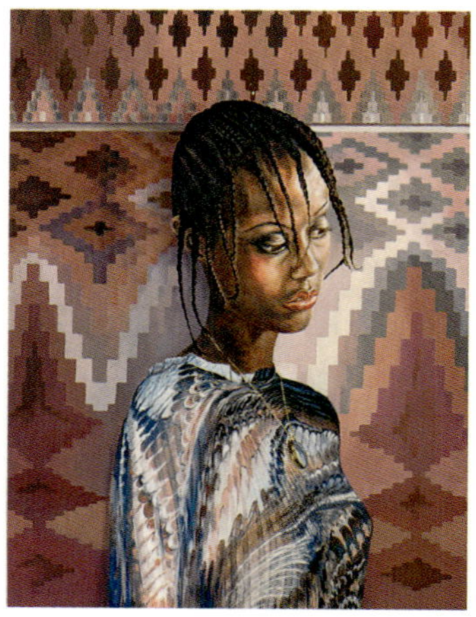

Kempson, Mary
Negro Lady 1978
oil on hardboard 54.1 x 44
RETBM : A65

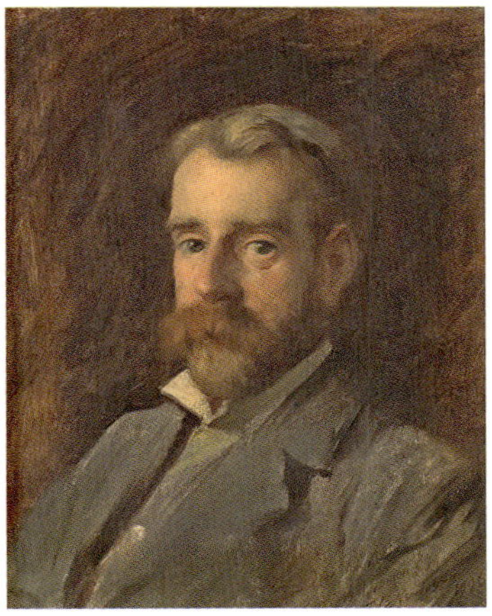

Kennington, Thomas Benjamin 1856–1916
T. W. Denman (1832–1907) 1906
oil on canvas 34 x 28
RETBM : A31L (P)

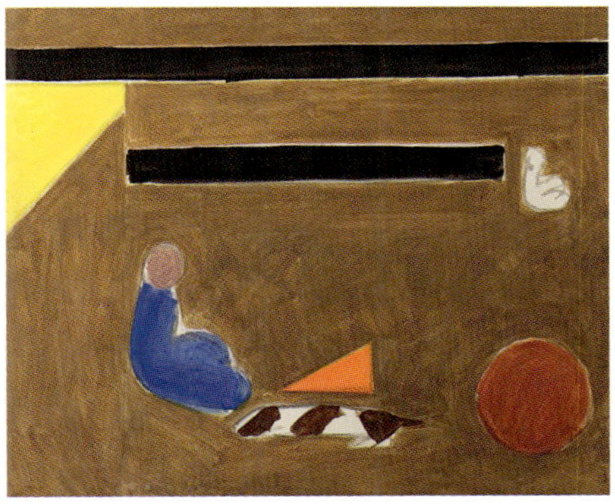

Kinley, Peter 1926–1988
Fireside 1975
oil on canvas 61 x 76
RETBM : A69

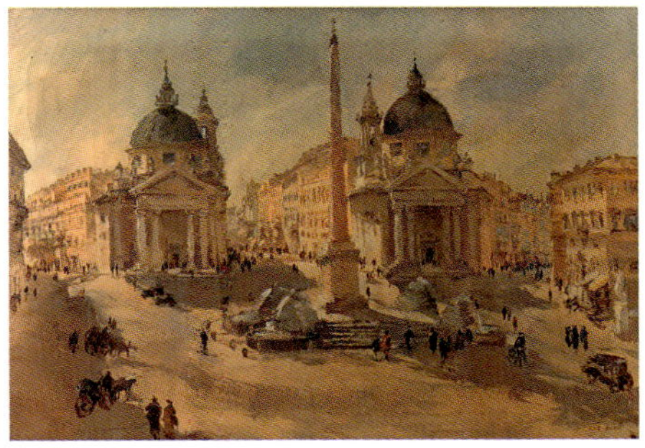

Kirk, Eve 1900–1969
Piazza del Popolo, Rome, Italy
oil on canvas 50.4 x 74.5
RETBM : A100

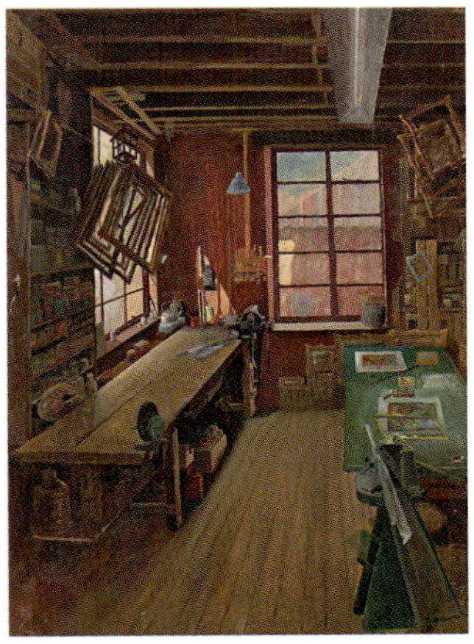

Laws, Percy S. 1892–1972
Interior of Percy Laws' Workshop
oil on canvas 100 x 75
RETBM : A144

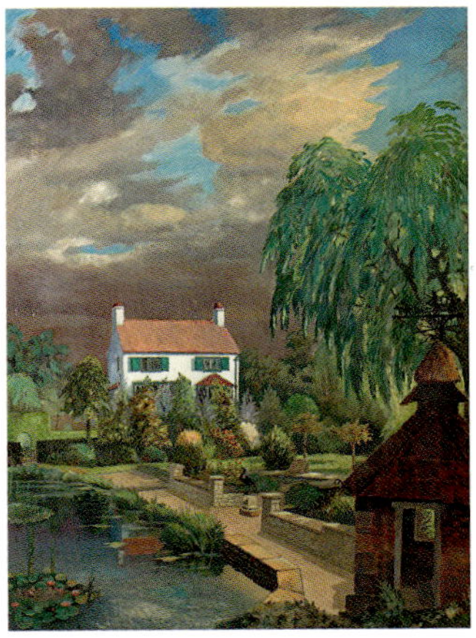

Laws, Percy S. 1892–1972
Quaker's Cottage and Garden, South Leverton, Nottinghamshire
oil on canvas 100.5 x 75
RETBM : A145

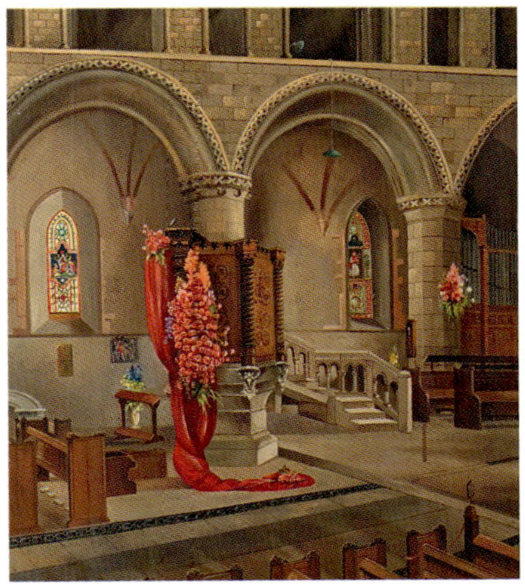

Mallender, L. active 1938–1973
Interior, Worksop Priory, Nottinghamshire
1966
oil on hardboard 68 x 56.4
RETBM : A54

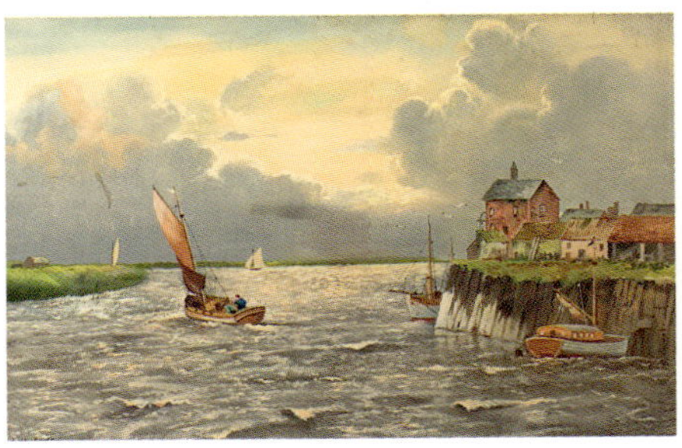

Mallender, L. active 1938–1973
Braydon Water, Yarmouth, Suffolk 1970
oil on hardboard 51 x 80.9
RETBM : A53

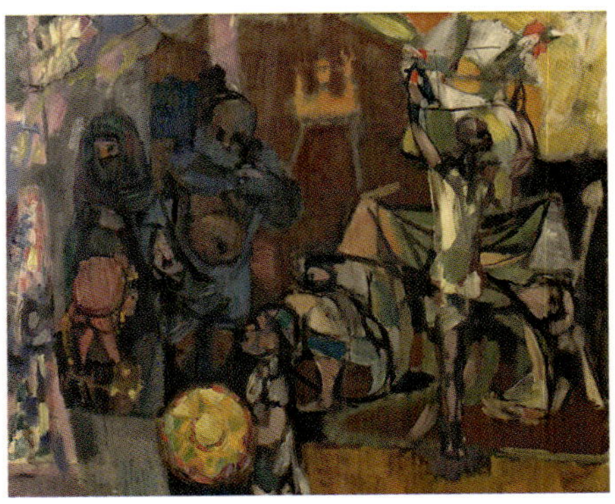

Medley, Robert 1905–1994
Beggars, Bird Carriers, Sweet Seller 1948
oil on canvas 70.5 x 90.5
RETBM : A61

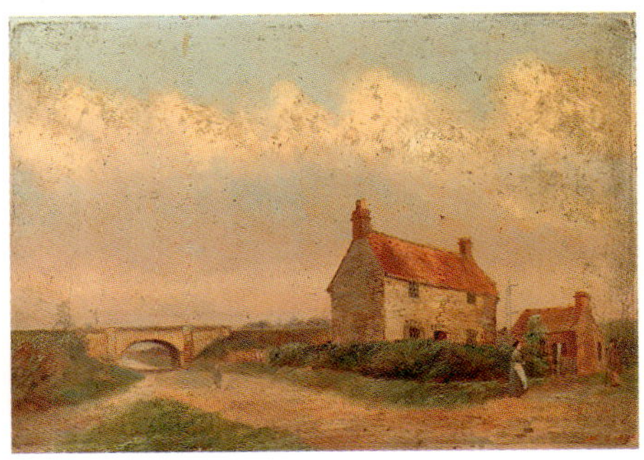

Milnes, B.
Kilton Farm Cottages, Worksop, Nottinghamshire 1899
oil on board 23.2 x 33.7
RETBM : A131

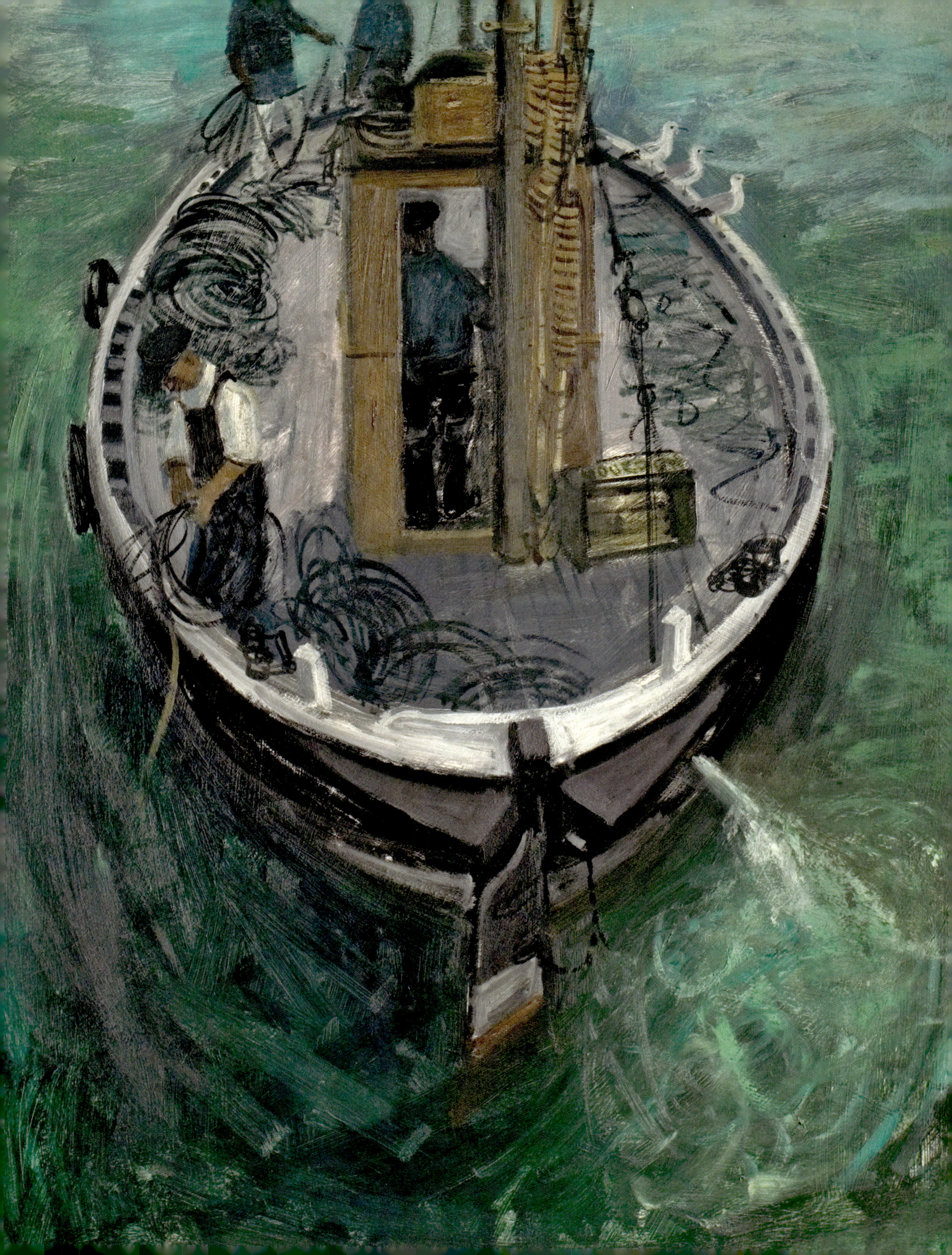

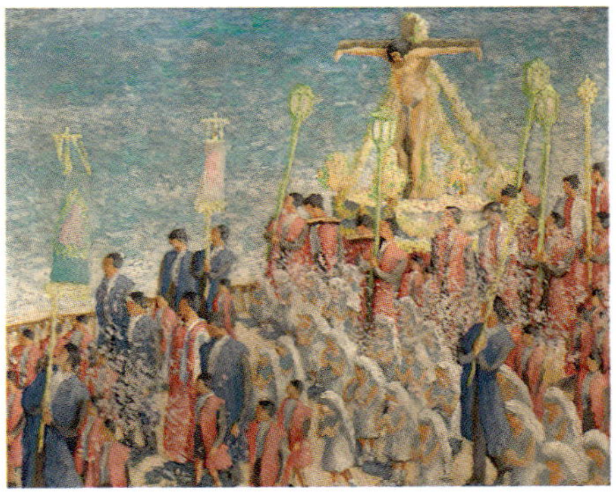

O'Dea, Eric
Corpus Christi 1938
oil on canvas 40.6 x 50.7
RETBM : A48

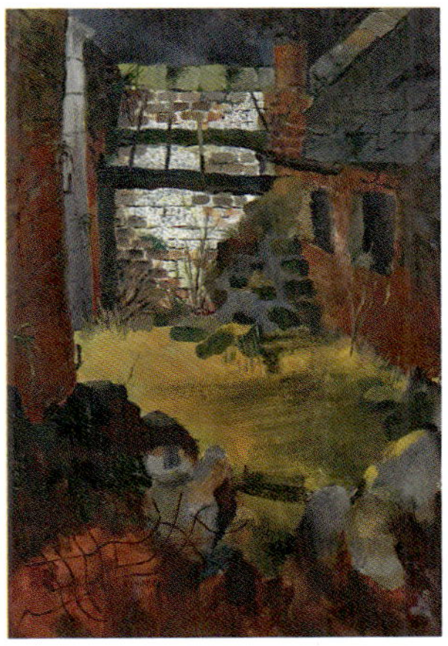

Penrose, J. E.
Workhouse, Worksop, Nottinghamshire 1946–1947
oil on canvas 48.5 x 34
RETBM : 2005.966

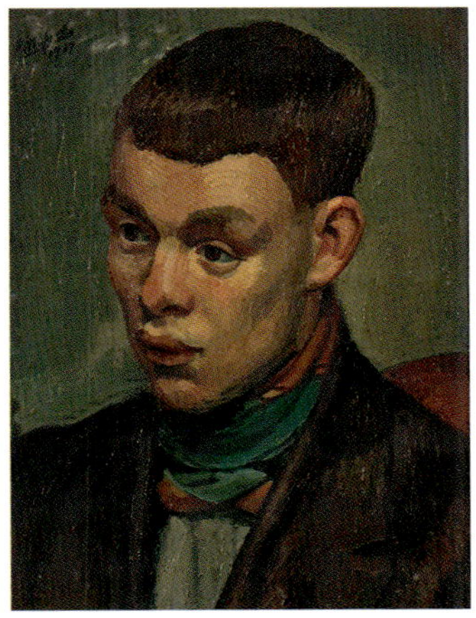

Pitchforth, Roland Vivian 1895–1982
Boy's Head 1927
oil on canvas 46 x 35.5
RETBM : A50

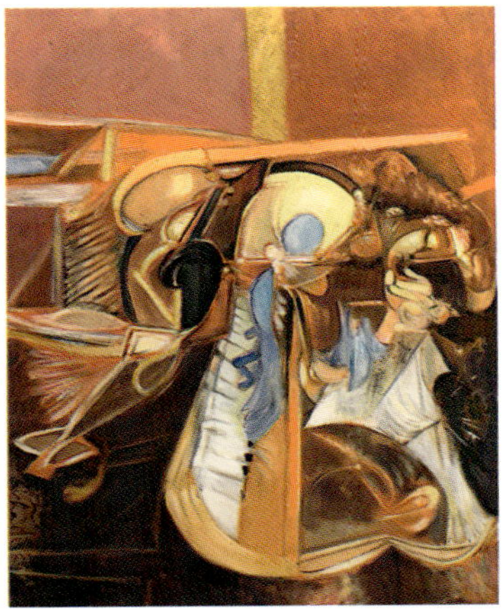

Richards, Ceri Geraldus 1903–1971
St Cecilia 1949
oil on canvas 96.8 x 79
RETBM : A47

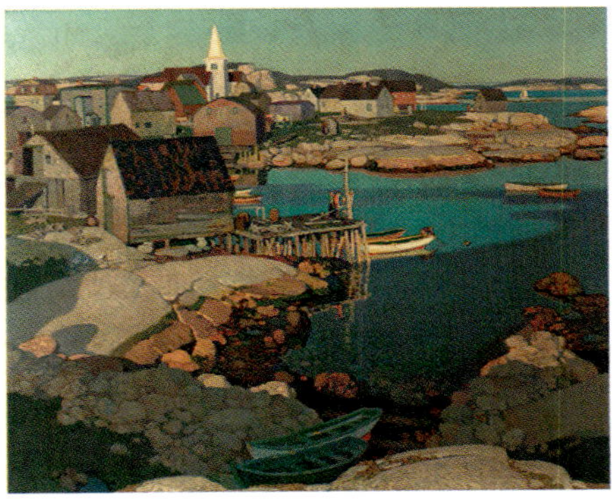

Royle, Stanley 1888–1961
Evening Light, Fishing Village of Prospect, Nova Scotia, Canada 1941
oil on canvas 99.8 x 129.2
RETBM : A113

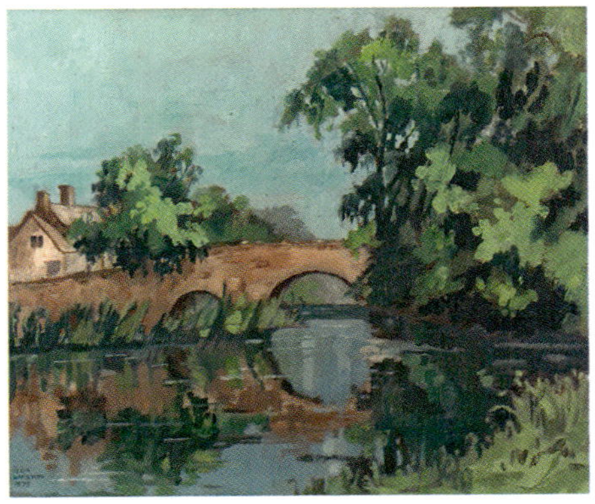

Shipston, Olga
Red Bridge 3 1973
oil on board 40 x 47.5
RETBM : A58

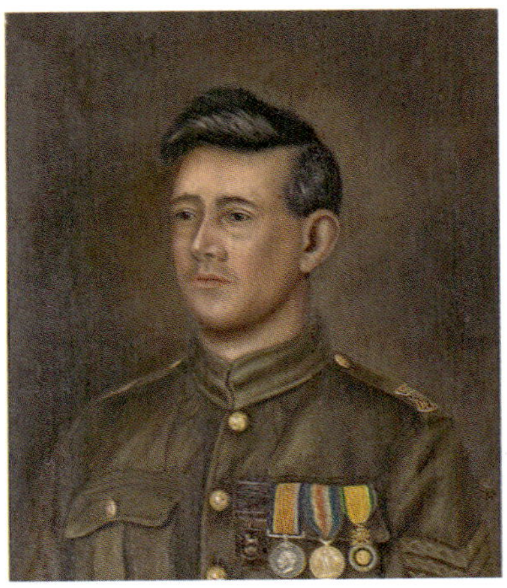

Smith, Herbert
Sergeant William Henry Johnson (1890–1945), VC 1925
oil on canvas 90.1 x 72.6
RETBM : A101

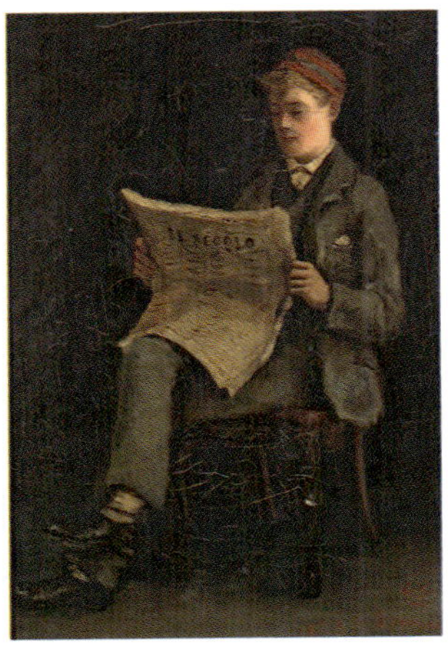

Spencer, Augustus 1860–1924
Boy Reading a Newspaper 1883
oil on canvas 36.5 x 26
RETBM : A76

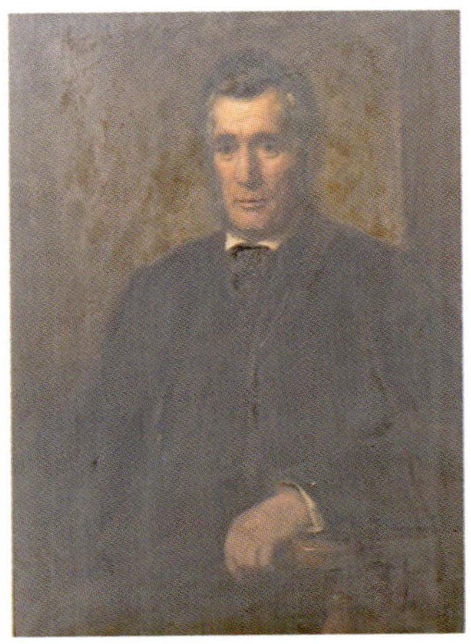

unknown artist
John Jones, CC (Manager of Shirebrook Colliery) 1898
oil on canvas 99.8 x 74.2
RETBM : A123

Facing page: Cheese, Bernard, b.1925, *The 'Crissie Griggie'* (detail), 1957, Nottingham City Museums and Galleries (p. 78)

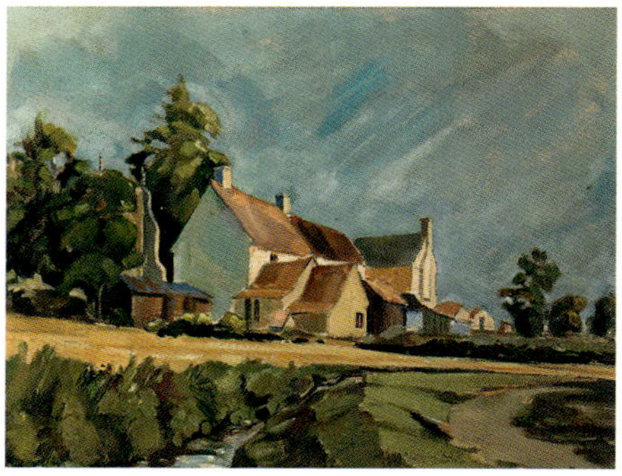

Waller, W. R.
Rattlesden, Suffolk 1969
oil on board 45 x 60
RETBM : A68

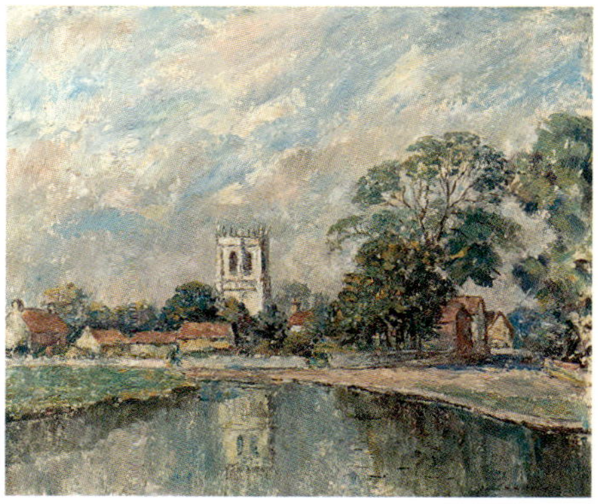

Warmby, Byron Winston 1902–1978
The Mill Pond, Tickhill, South Yorkshire
oil on board 48.3 x 59
RETBM : A108

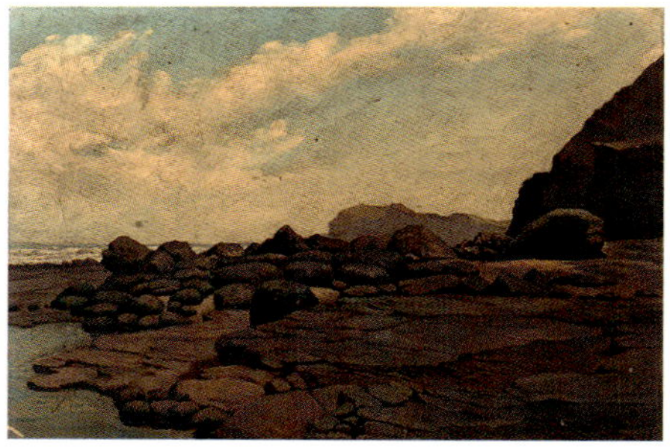

Whall, Charles Albert b.1849
Whitby Scaur Rocks, North Yorkshire 1882
oil on canvas 35.7 x 54.5
RETBM : A37

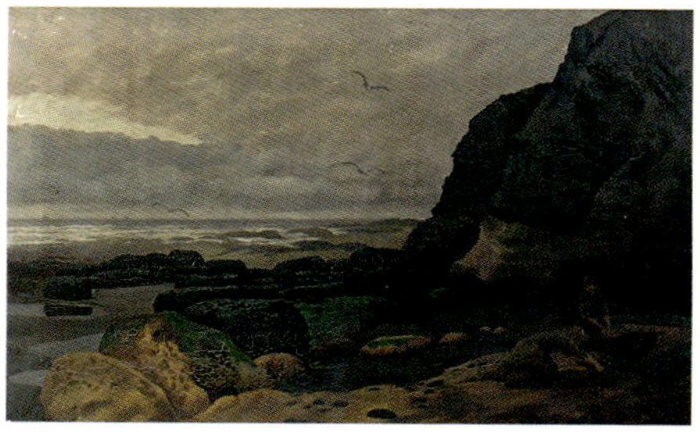

Whall, Charles Albert b.1849
Whitby Scaur, North Yorkshire 1894
oil on canvas 77 x 127.7
RETBM : A45

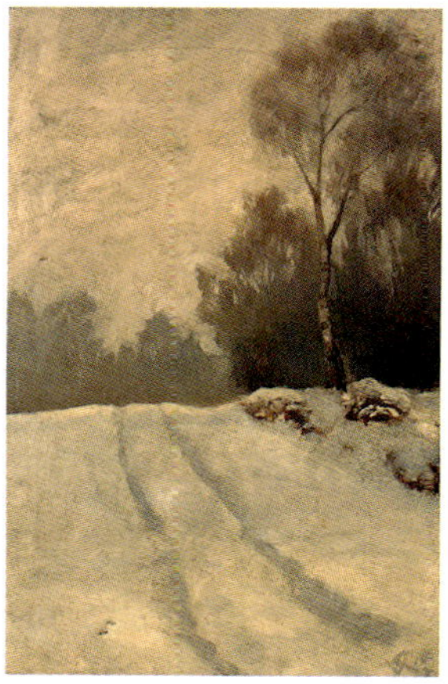

Whall, Charles Albert b.1849
Drinking Pit Lane 1897
oil on canvas 61.4 x 40.5
RETBM : A49

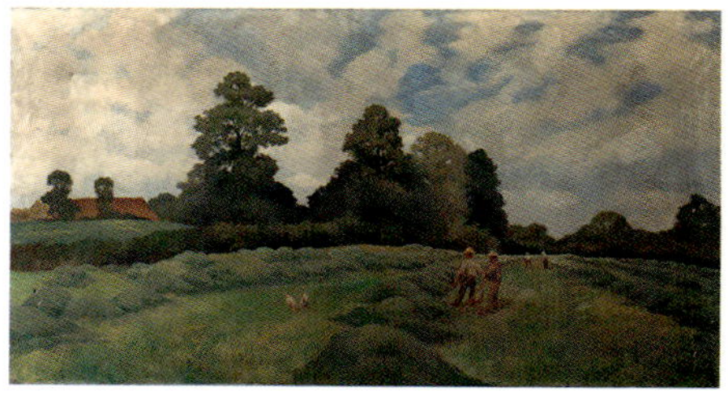

Whall, Charles Albert b.1849
Haymaking at Shibbings Meadows 1907
oil on canvas 68.8 x 130.2
RETBM : A46

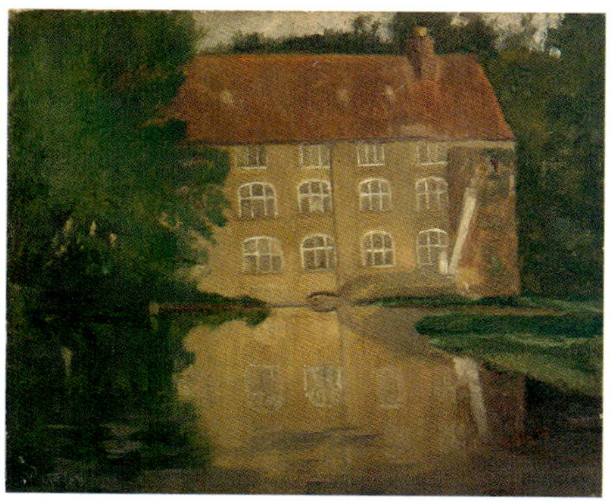

Whall, Charles Albert b.1849
Beard's Mill, Worksop, Nottinghamshire 1908
oil on canvas 23.2 x 28.1 (E)
RETBM : A96

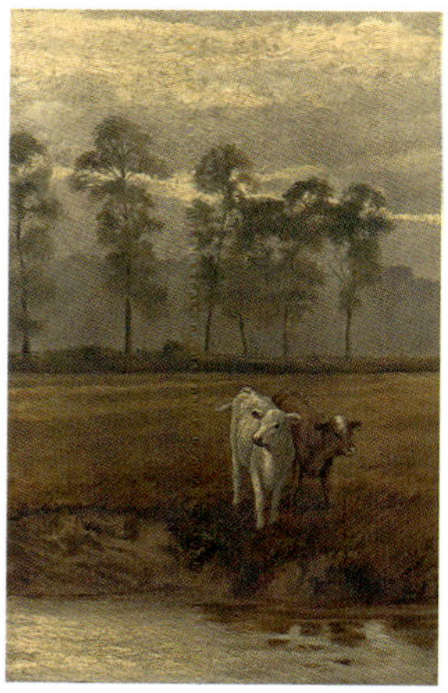

Whall, Charles Albert (attributed to) b.1849
Landscape with Cattle
oil on canvas 46 x 30.5
RETBM : A103

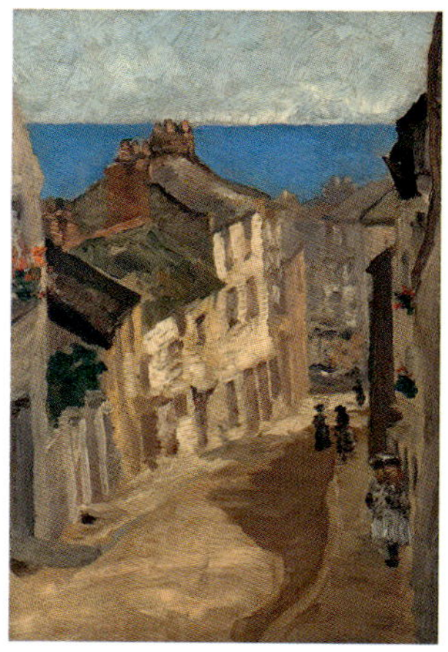

Whall, Charles Albert (attributed to) b.1849
Lyme Regis, Dorset
oil on canvas 36 x 25.5
RETBM : A107

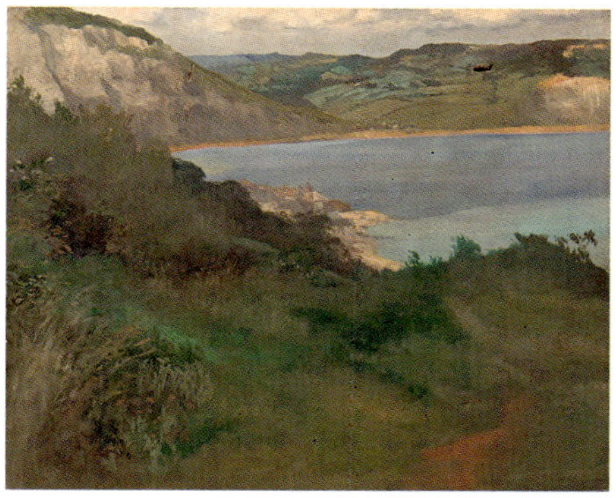

Whall, Charles Albert (attributed to) b.1849
Marine Scene, Sidmouth, Devon
oil on canvas 40.6 x 51
RETBM : A122

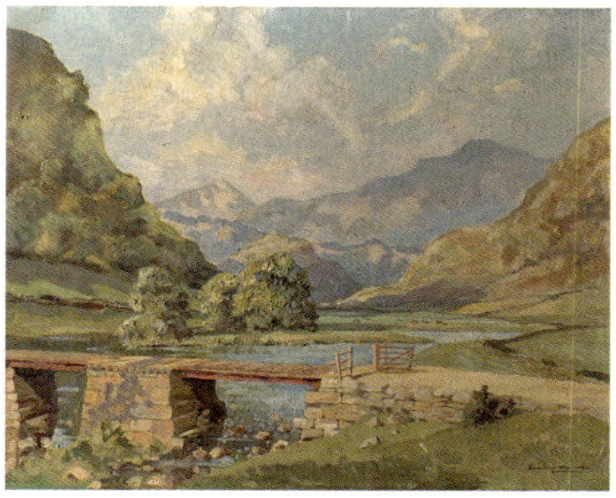

Whitton, Stanley
Llyn Dinas, near Beddgelert, North Wales
oil on canvas 53.8 x 66.1
RETBM : A99

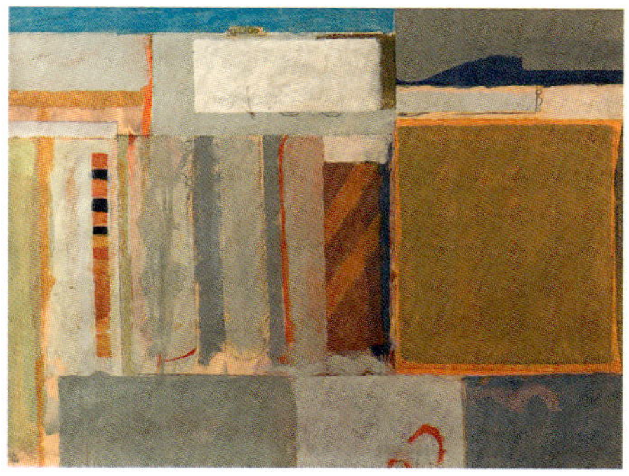

Wood, Alan b.1935
Kirkstall 1964
acrylic on paper 54.5 x 73.2
RETBM : A114

Retford Town Hall

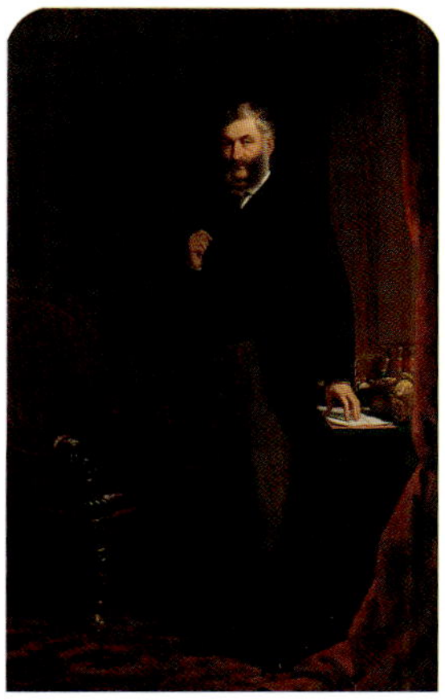

Crighton, Hugh Ford 1824–1886
John Smith, Esq., Mayor of East Retford (1864–1865 & 1867–1868) 1868
oil on canvas 270 x 145.5
RTH03

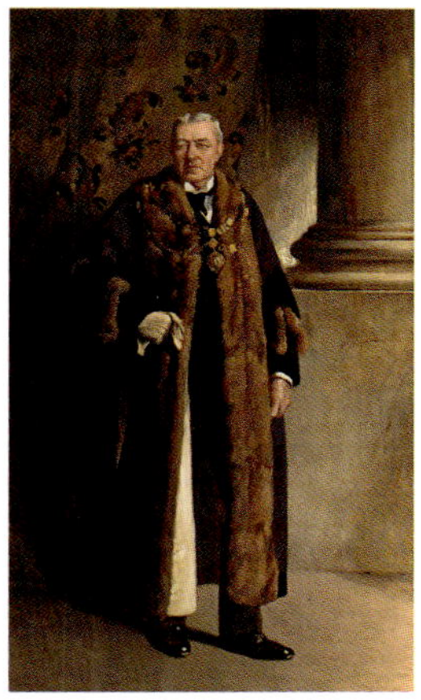

Hall, Frederick 1860–1948
J. W. Holmes, Esq., Mayor of East Retford (1886, 1891 & 1901) 1919
oil on canvas 264 x 139
RTH04

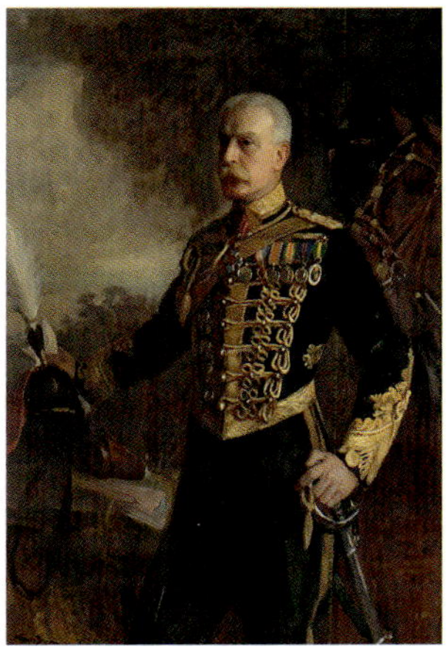

Harrison-Brown, H.
Colonel Whittaker (?) 1912–1913
oil on canvas 142 x 110
RTH01

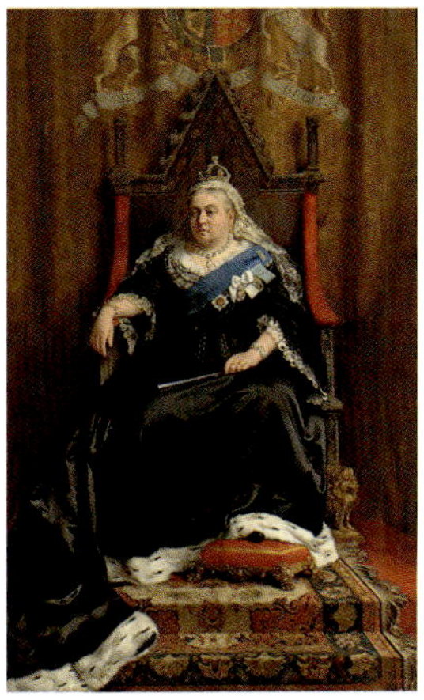

Kennington, Thomas Benjamin 1856–1916
Queen Victoria (1819–1901) 1898
oil on canvas 237 x 144.5
RTH07

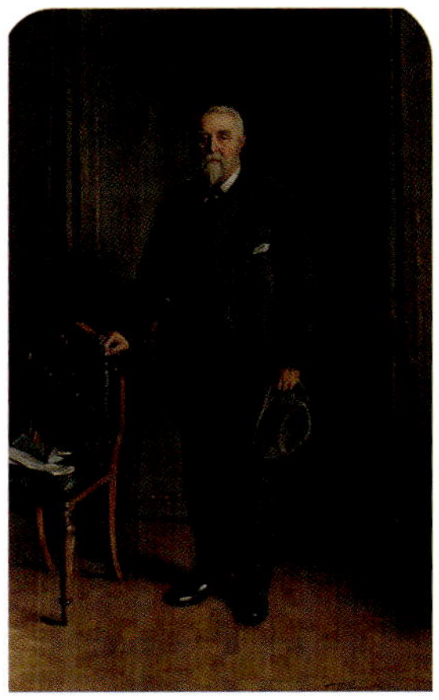

Kennington, Thomas Benjamin 1856–1916
Thomas William Denman, Esq., JP, Town Councillor (1866–1871), Alderman (1878–1905), and Mayor of East Retford (…) 1906
oil on canvas 270 x 145.5
RTH05

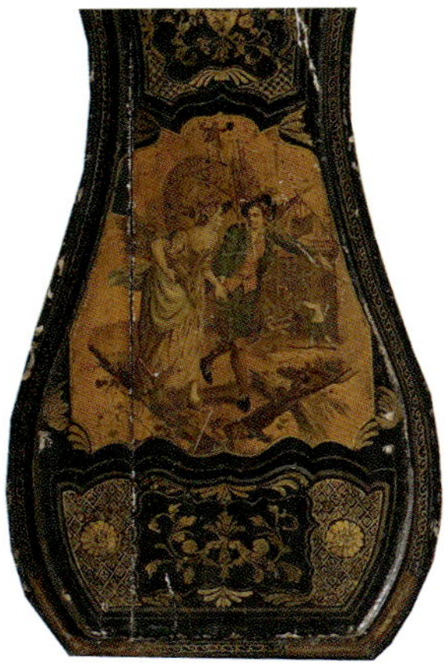

unknown artist
William Sterck Clock c.1760
oil on wood 104 x 60
RTH temp1

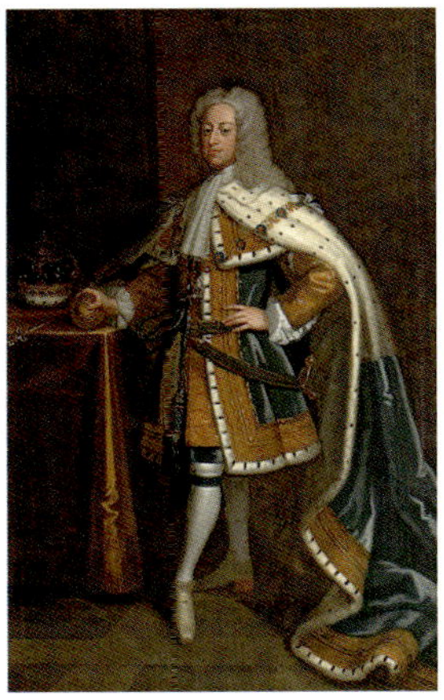

unknown artist
George II (1683–1760)
oil on canvas 256 x 144
RTH06

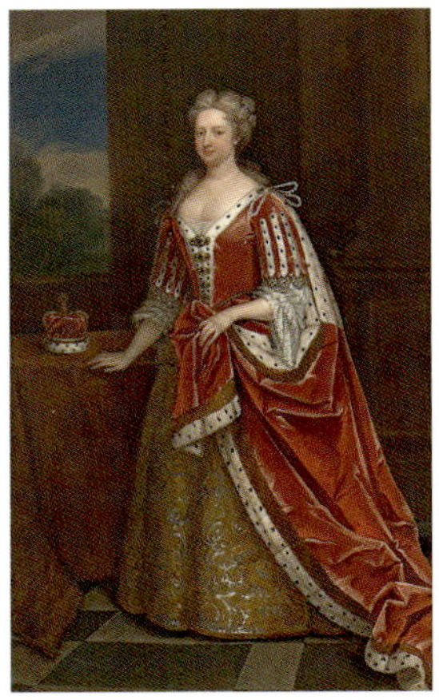

unknown artist
Caroline Wilhelmina of Brandenburg-Ansbach (1683–1737), Consort to George II
oil on canvas 226 x 143
RTH08

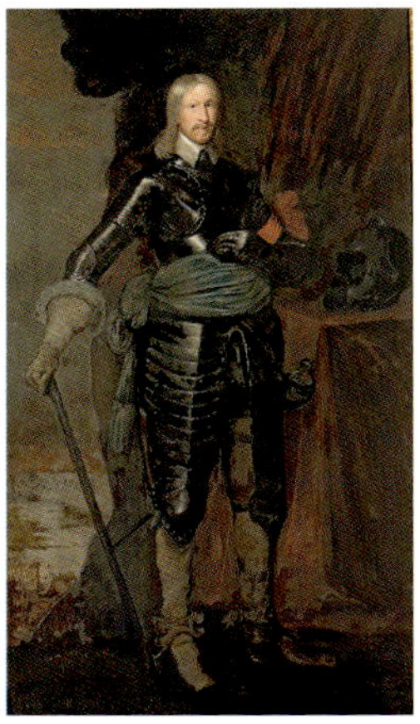

unknown artist
Colonel Francis Thornhach of Fenton (1617–1648), MP for East Retford
oil on canvas 220 x 125
RTH02

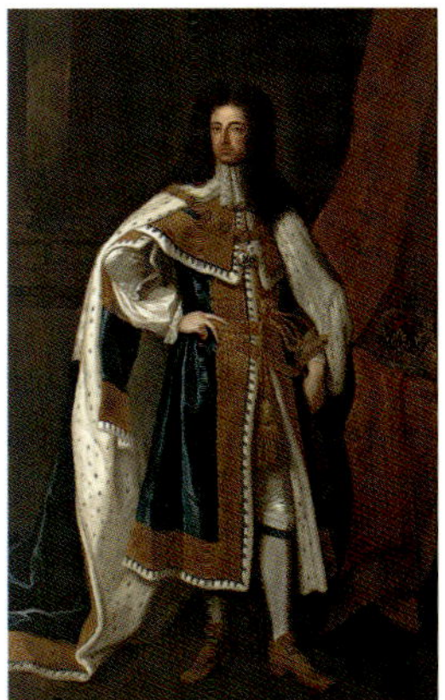

unknown artist
William III (1650–1702), Reigned with Mary During Their Short Lives
oil on canvas 256 x 142
RTH10

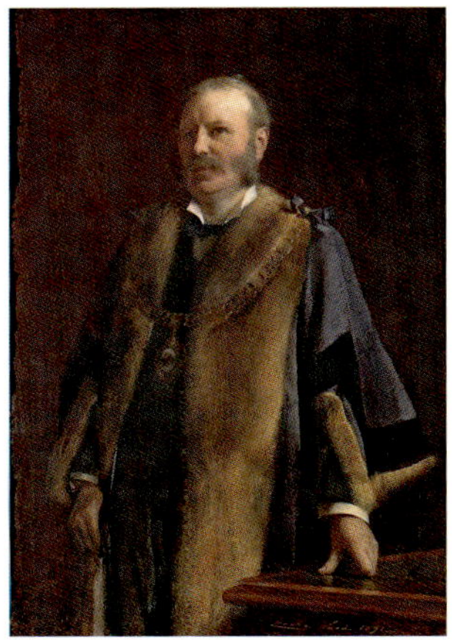

Ward, Edwin Arthur 1859–1933
Thomas Bescoby, Mayor (1890) 1891
oil on canvas 180 x 90
RTH09

Ruddington Parish Council

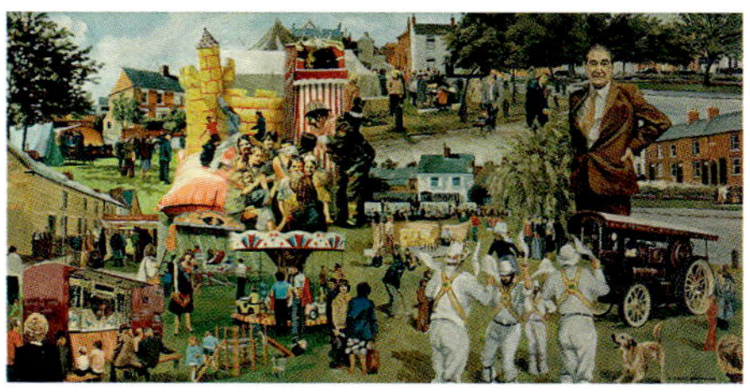

Heaton, Roger
Silver Jubilee 1981
oil on canvas 60 x 120.5
OP1

Ruddington Village Museum

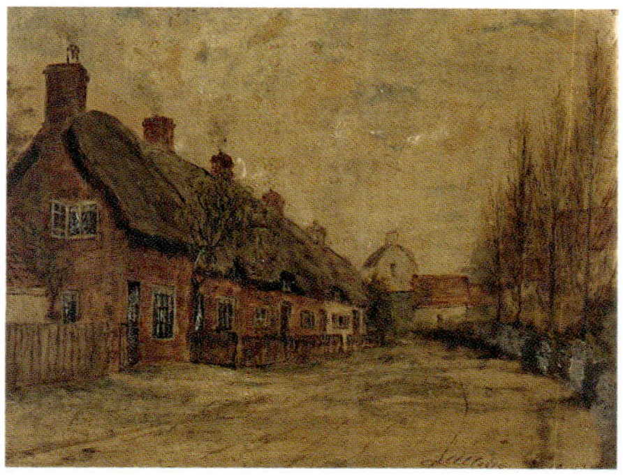

Cooke, Jill
Scene at Wilford, Nottingham 1914
oil on canvas 22.3 x 30
69.106

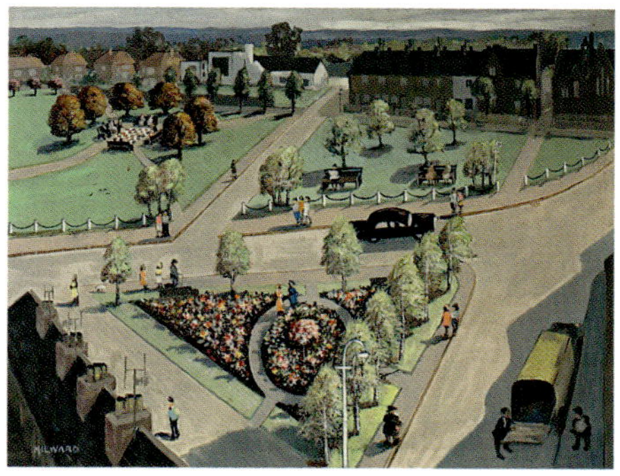

Milward
Ruddington Village Green, Nottinghamshire c.1960
oil on board 45.5 x 60
2008.01

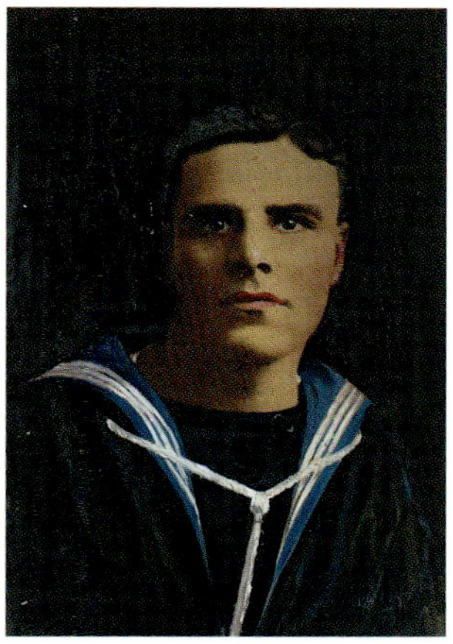

Milward, William
E. Tillotson as a Boy Sailor 1919
oil on canvas 35 x 24
91.78

Southwell Town Council

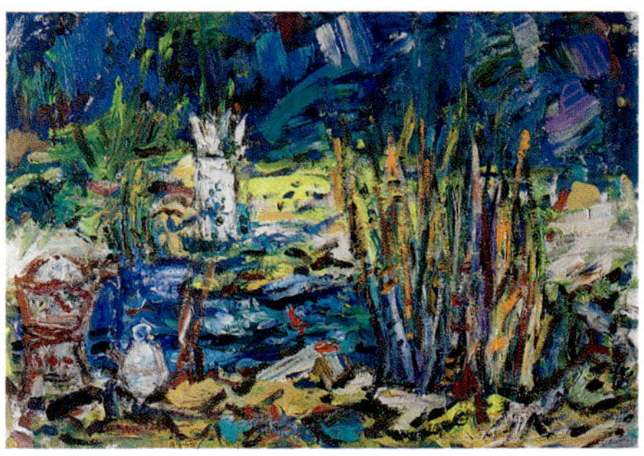

Arnfield, Marjorie 1930–2001
Conservatory, Blackhouse Park, Sunderland, Tyne and Wear c.1950
oil on canvas 52 x 77
STC:02

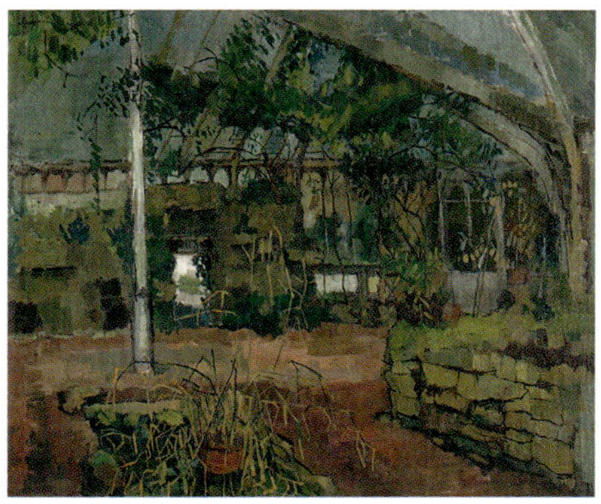

Arnfield, Marjorie 1930–2001
Water Gardens, Westhorpe, Suffolk 2002
oil on canvas 49 x 72
STC:01

Sherwood Forest Hospitals NHS Foundation Trust

Sherwood Forest Hospitals NHS Foundation Trust, which runs King's Mill and Newark Hospitals, possesses a varied collection of art across these two sites. The Trust is keen to incorporate art and design into the hospitals to provide a colourful and visually striking distraction in many environments, such as visitor waiting rooms, outpatient clinics and children's play areas. The bulk of the Collection was assembled through donations from appeals, patients or members of staff. In the early 1990s, the Art in Health organisation provided some vibrant copies of original paintings by well-known artists, now displayed in the X-Ray Department at King's Mill. Several brightly coloured abstracts were purchased to liven up the main entrance and create a more relaxed and friendly atmosphere. *Blue Flax* and *Bonnieux, Provence, France* are from a larger collection of works, consisting mostly of watercolours, given by the estate of Marjorie Arnfield in 2006.

With the Foundation's ongoing redevelopment scheme, due to be completed in 2011, the Trust hopes to add to its Collection, highlighting the value and importance of art in the health sector.

Angharad Jones, Nottinghamshire Co-ordinator for The Public Catalogue Foundation

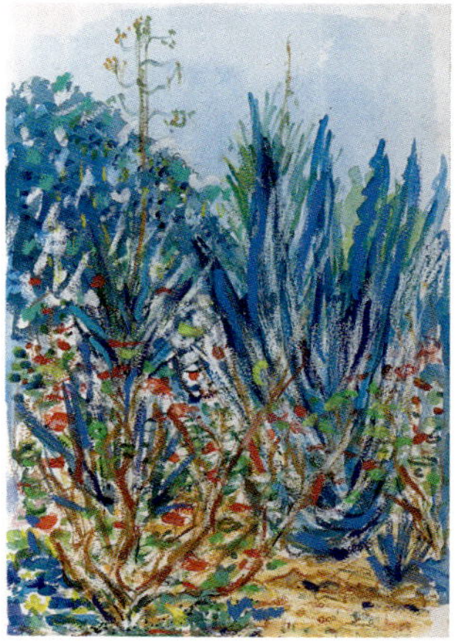

Arnfield, Marjorie 1930–2001
Blue Flax
oil & mixed media on paper 54 x 44
KM:MA4

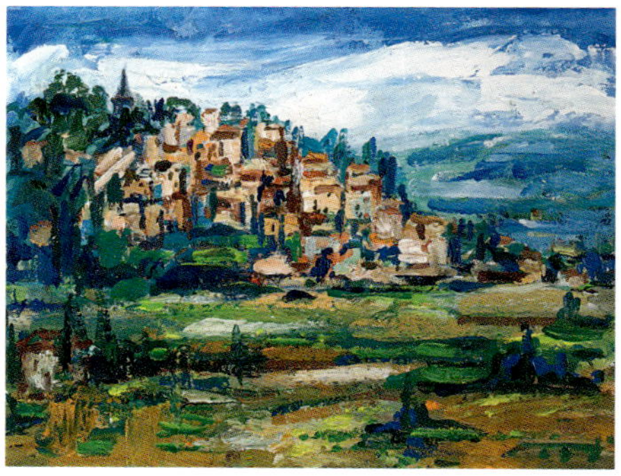

Arnfield, Marjorie 1930–2001
Bonnieux, Provence, France
acrylic on board 41 x 51
KM:MA15

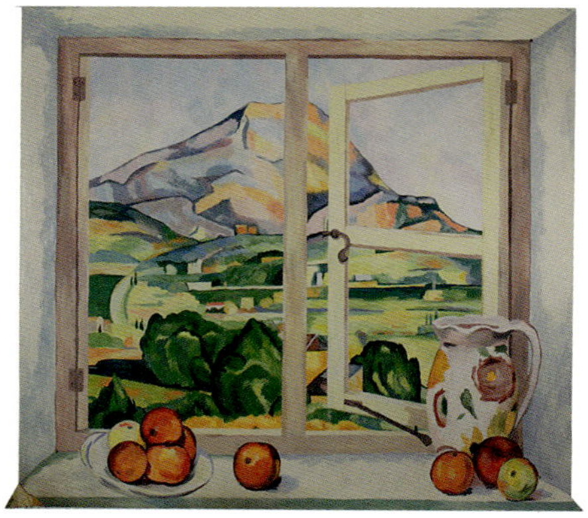

Cézanne, Paul (copy after) 1839–1906
Mont St Michel
oil on plywood 122 x 138
KM38

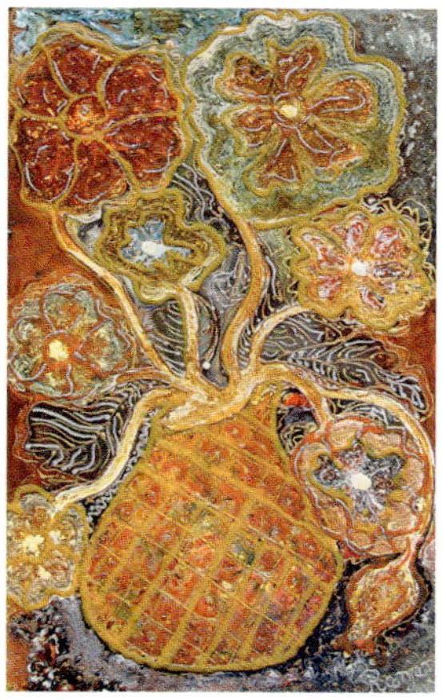

Chowdhary, Ranjan b.1955
Flower Basket 2004
acrylic on glass 68.5 x 43.1
KM57

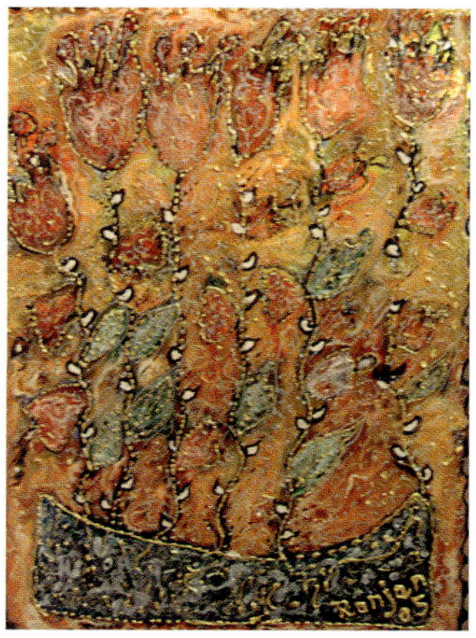

Chowdhary, Ranjan b.1955
Flowers in Abstract 1 2005
acrylic on glass 48.2 x 38.1
KM58

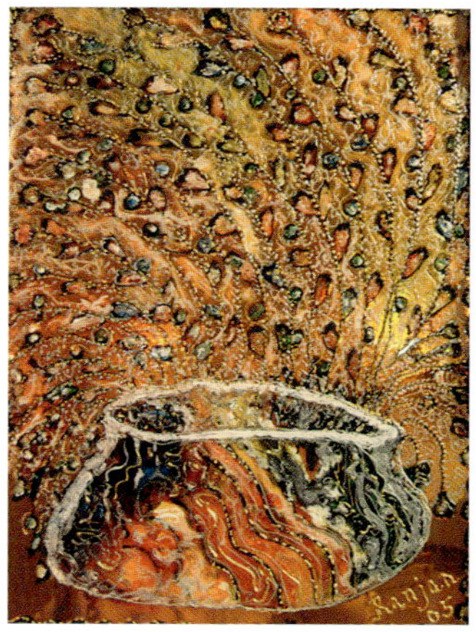

Chowdhary, Ranjan b.1955
Flowers in Abstract 2 2005
acrylic on glass 48.2 x 38.1
KM59

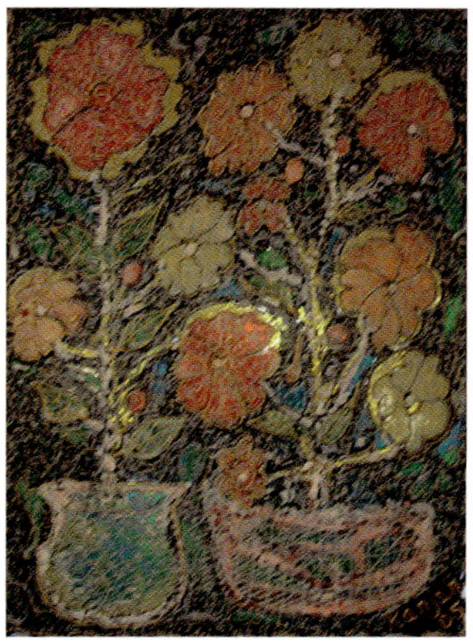

Chowdhary, Ranjan b.1955
Flowers in Abstract 3 2005
acrylic on glass 48.2 x 38.1
KM60

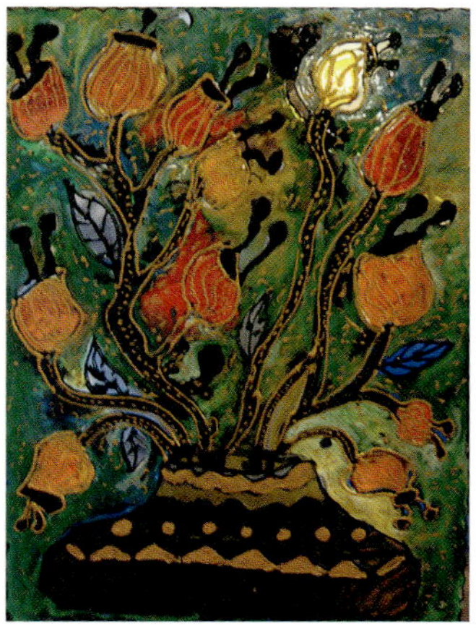

Chowdhary, Ranjan b.1955
Flowers in Abstract 4 2005
acrylic on glass 48.2 x 38.1
KM61

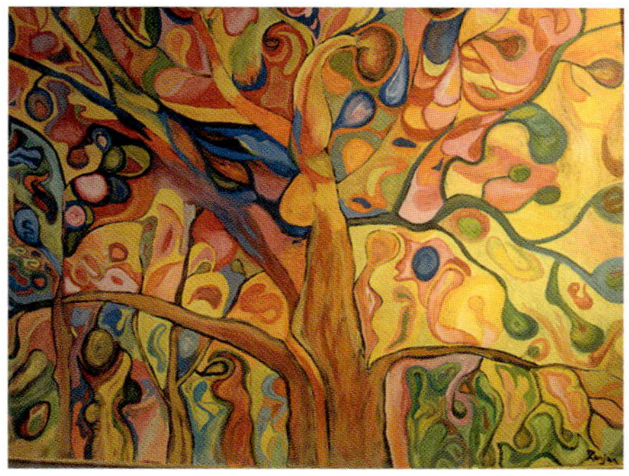

Chowdhary, Ranjan b.1955
Nature's Delight 2005
oil on canvas 93.9 x 121 (E)
KM56

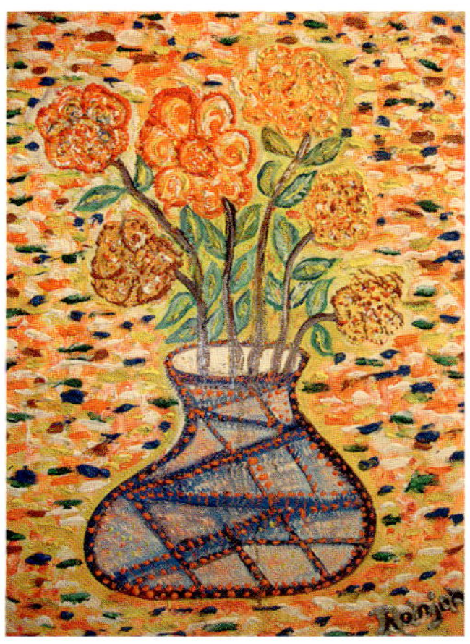

Chowdhary, Ranjan b.1955
Colours in Nature 2007
oil on canvas 60.9 x 45.7
NWK9

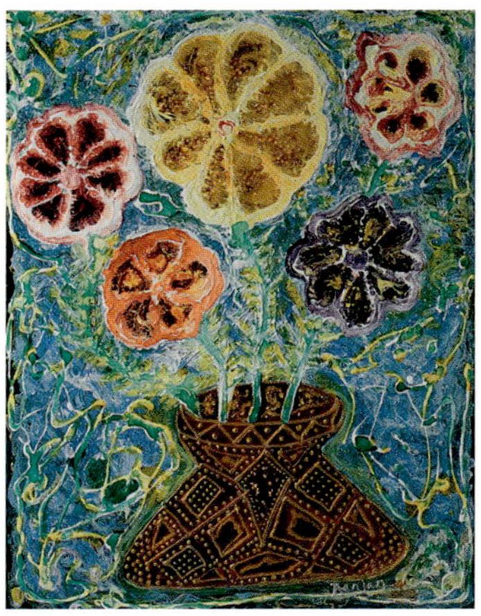

Chowdhary, Ranjan b.1955
Flower Vase 2007
acrylic on glass 50 x 39
NWK8

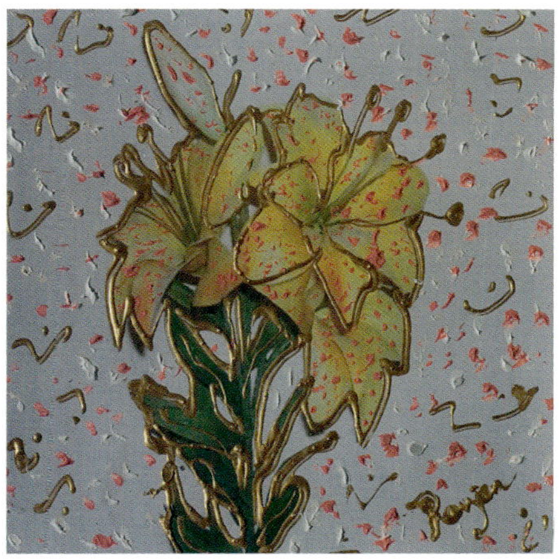

Chowdhary, Ranjan b.1955
Iris No.1 2007
acrylic on paper 16 x 16
NWK5

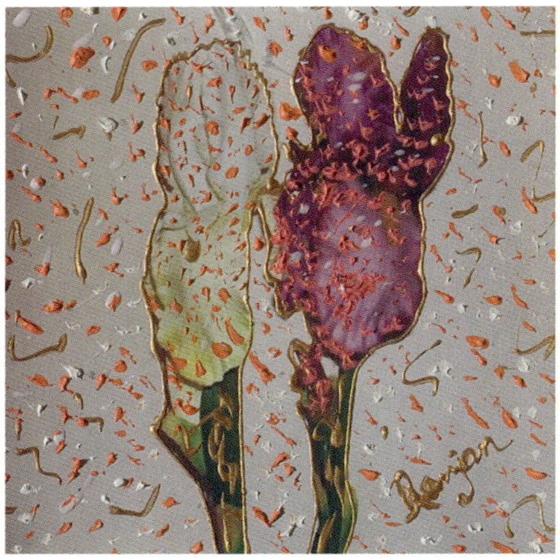

Chowdhary, Ranjan b.1955
Iris No.2 2007
acrylic on paper 16 x 16
NWK6

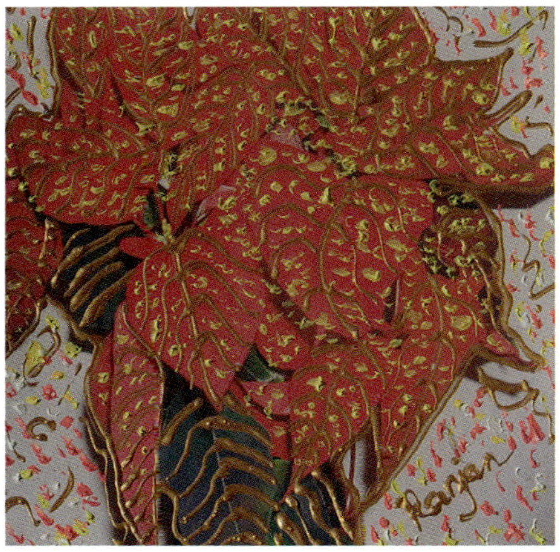

Chowdhary, Ranjan b.1955
Poinsettia 2007
acrylic on paper 16 x 16
NWK7

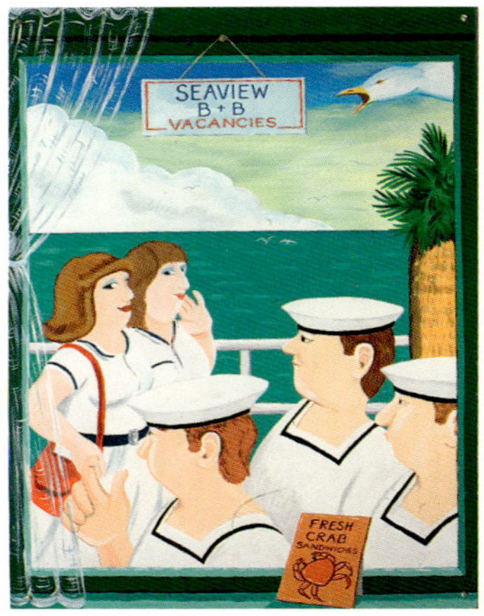

Cook, Beryl (copy after) 1926–2008
*Sailors**
oil on plywood 89.5 x 70
KM53

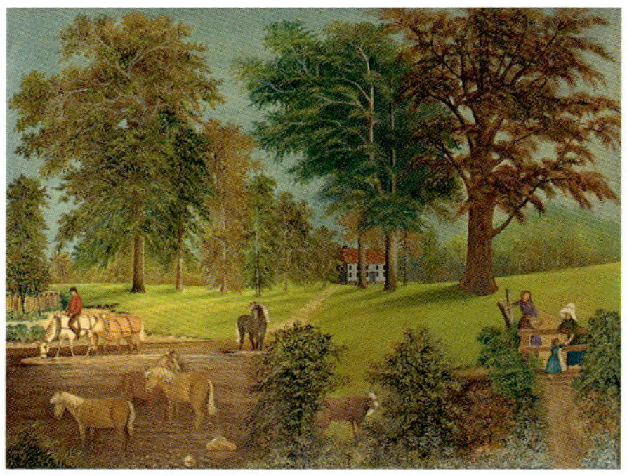

Dabrowski, Stanislaw 1882–1973
*Farmyard Scene** 1949
oil on canvas 88 x 120
NWK2

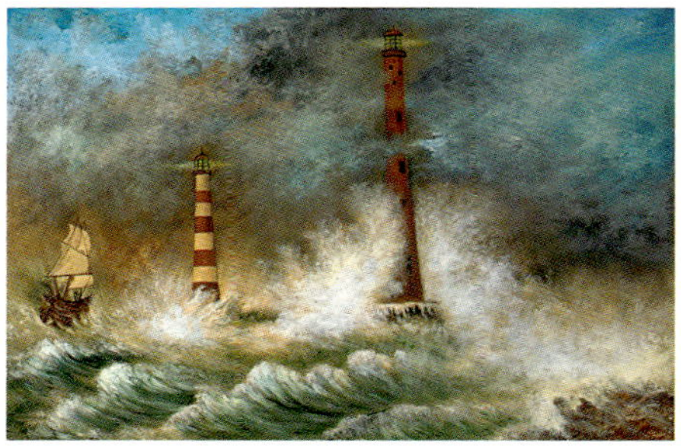

Dabrowski, Stanislaw 1882–1973
*Lighthouse Storm**
oil on canvas 70 x 117
NWK3

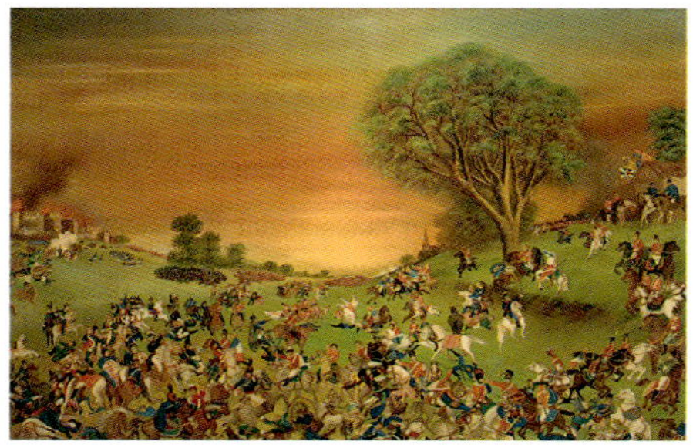

Dabrowski, Stanislaw 1882–1973
The Battle of Waterloo, 18 June 1815
oil on board 120 x 182
NWK1

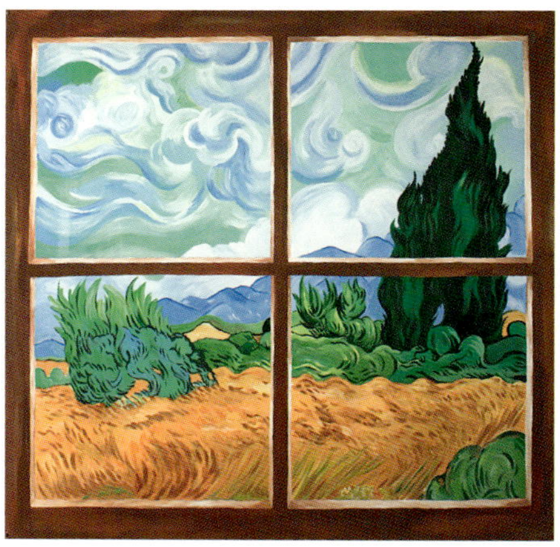

Gogh, Vincent van (copy after) 1853–1890
A Wheatfield, with Cypresses 1996
oil on plywood 110 x 122.5
KM46

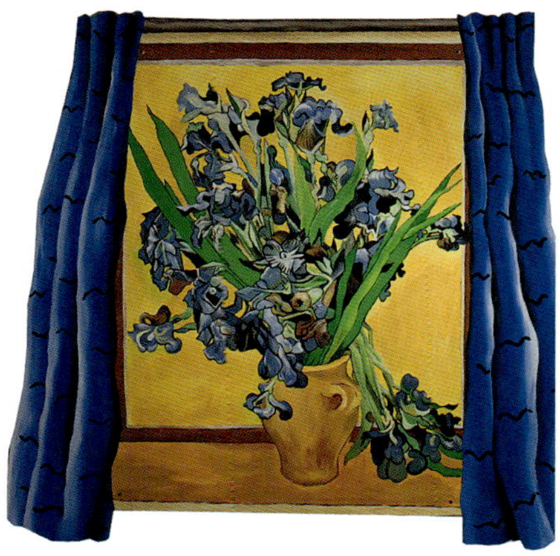

Gogh, Vincent van (copy after) 1853–1890
Irises 1996
oil on plywood 130 x 123(E)
KM44

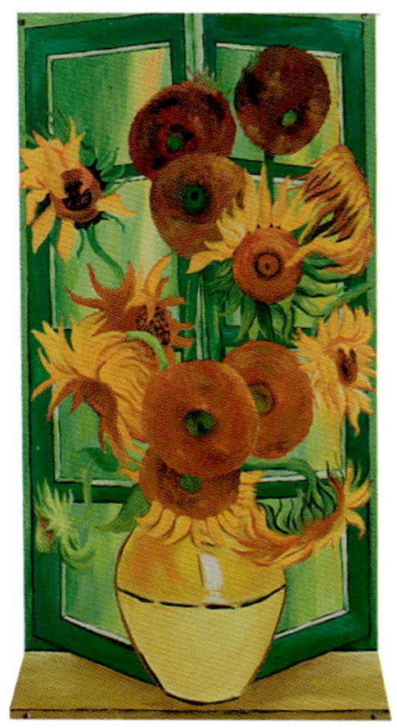

Gogh, Vincent van (copy after) 1853–1890
Sunflowers 1996
oil on plywood 90 x 49
KM48

Facing page: Spooner, Arthur, 1873–1961, *The Goose Fair, Nottingham* (detail), 1926, Nottingham City Museums and Galleries (p. 147)

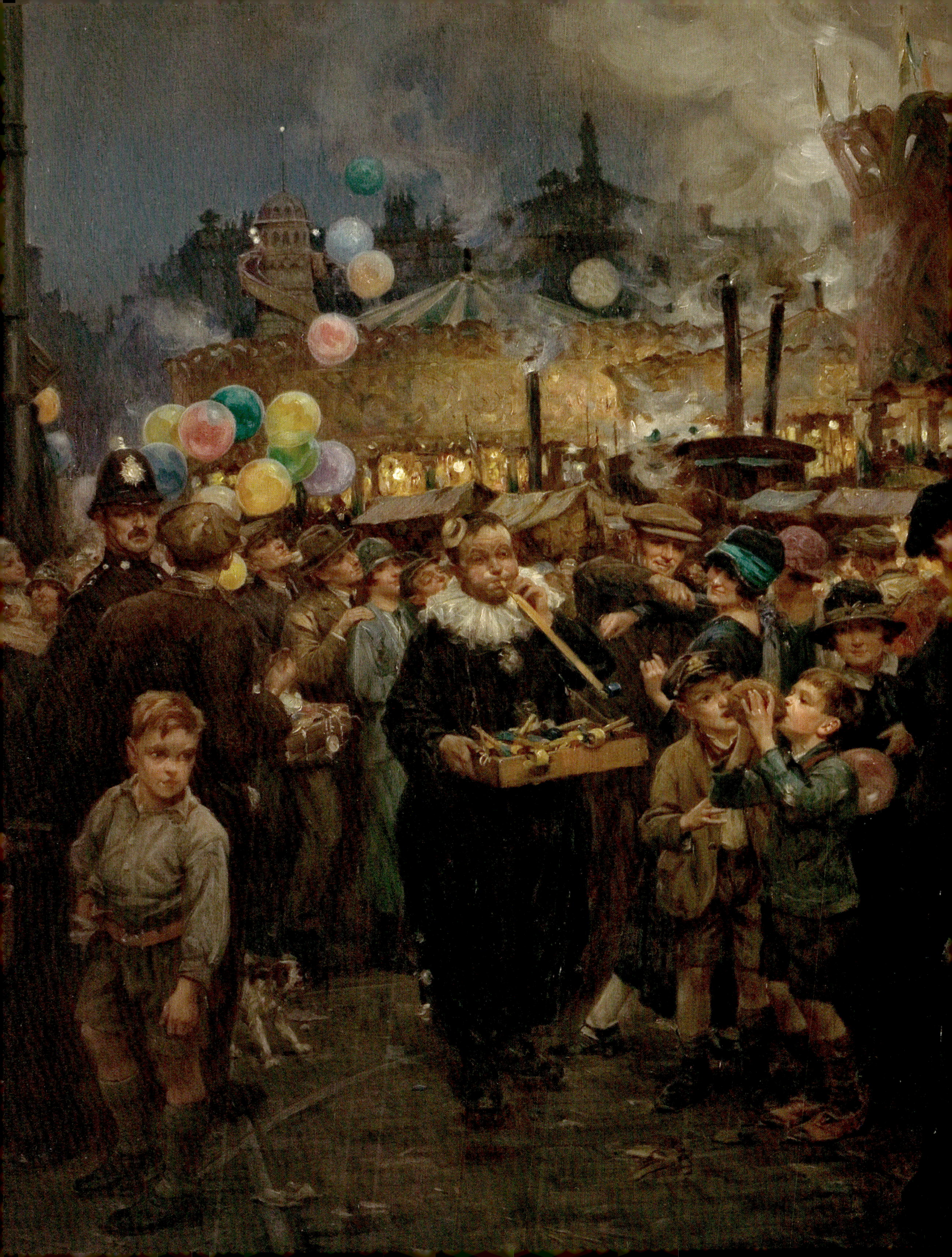

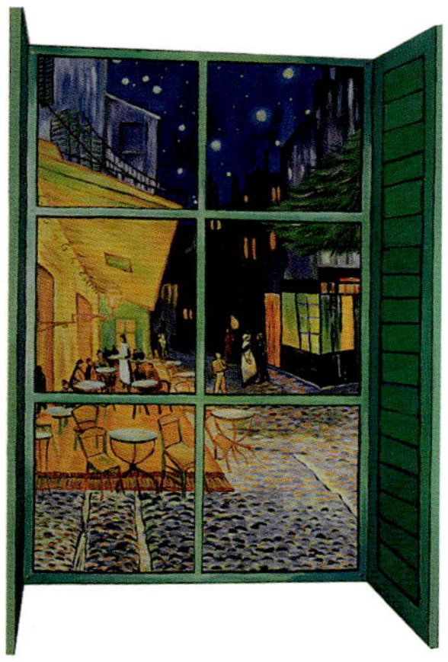

Gogh, Vincent van (copy after) 1853–1890
The Café Terrace on the Place Forum, Arles, at Night 1996
oil on plywood 122 x 85
KM47

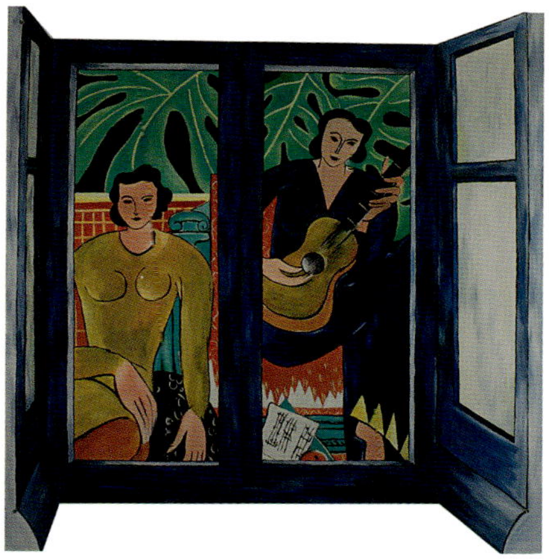

Matisse, Henri (copy after) 1869–1954
Music 1996
oil on plywood 122 x 122.5
KM49

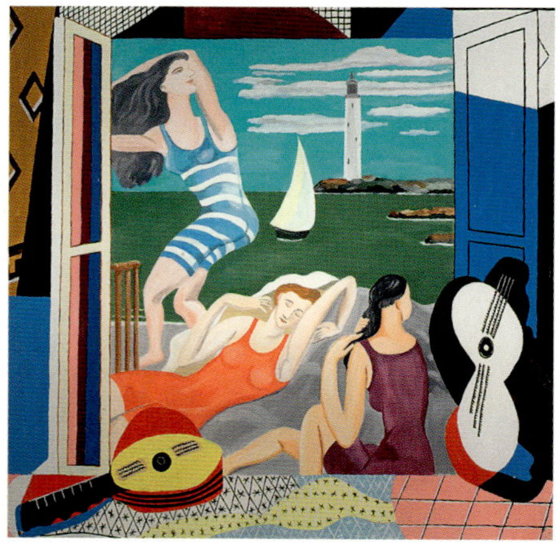

Picasso, Pablo (copy after) 1881–1973
Les baigneuses
oil on plywood 120 x 122
KM54

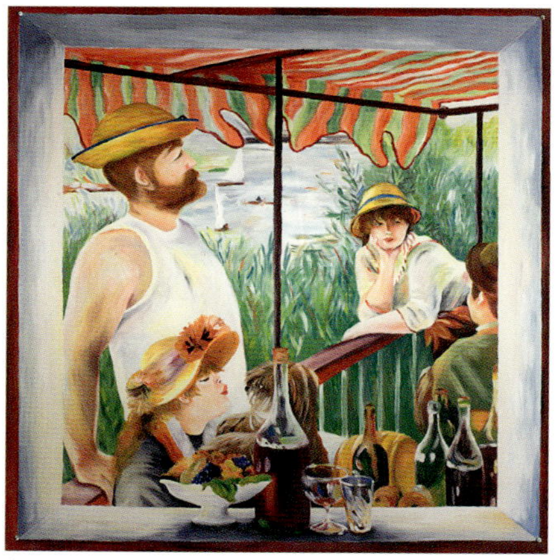

Renoir, Pierre-Auguste (copy after) 1841–1919
Luncheon of the Boating Party 1996
oil on plywood 100 x 100
KM39

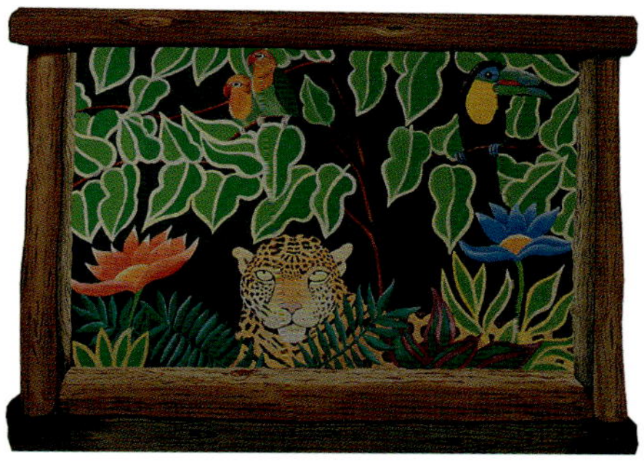

Rousseau, Henri (copy after) 1844–1910
Leopard in the Jungle 1996
oil on plywood 128 x 168 (E)
KM41

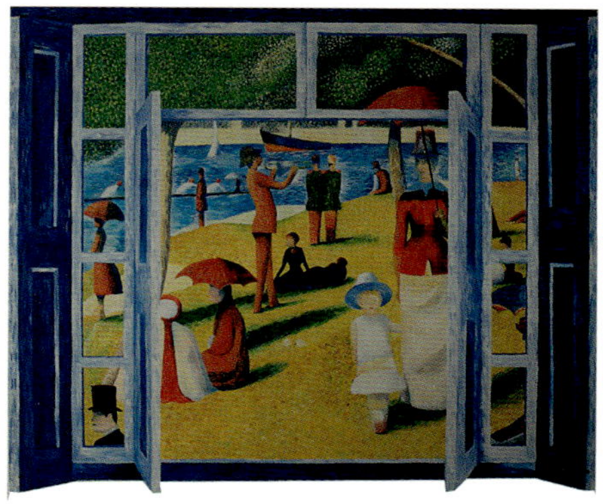

Seurat, Georges (copy after) 1859–1891
A Sunday Afternoon on the Island of La Grande Jatte 1996
oil on plywood 100 x 122
KM50

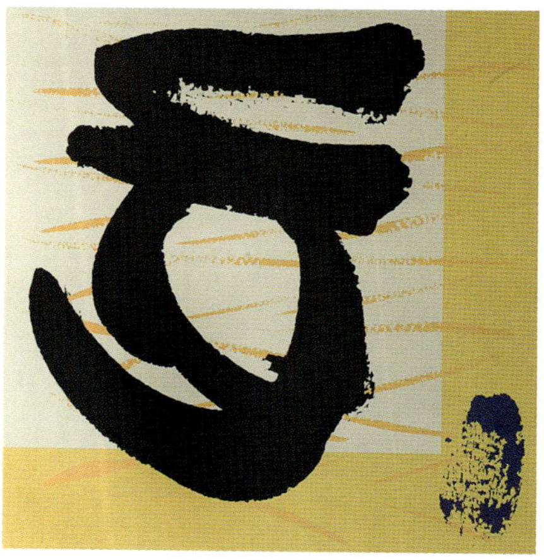

unknown artist
*Abstract No.11**
acrylic on canvas 50 x 50
KM11

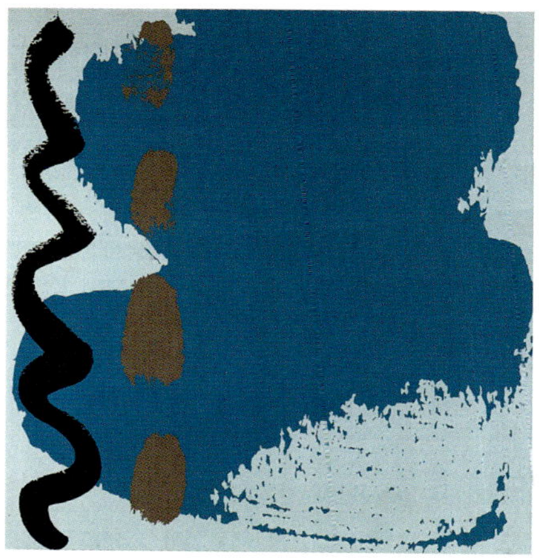

unknown artist
*Abstract No.12**
acrylic on canvas 50 x 50
KM12

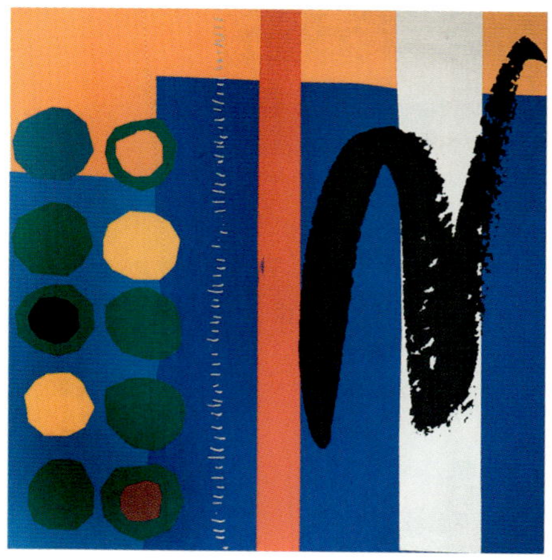

unknown artist
*Abstract No.13**
acrylic on canvas 50 x 50
KM13

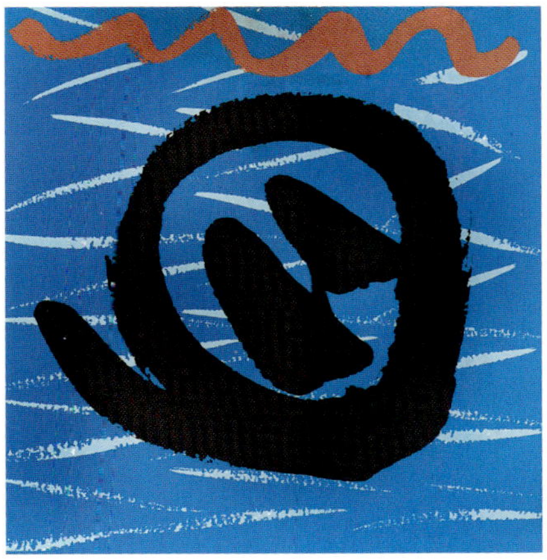

unknown artist
*Abstract No.14**
acrylic on canvas 50 x 50
KM14

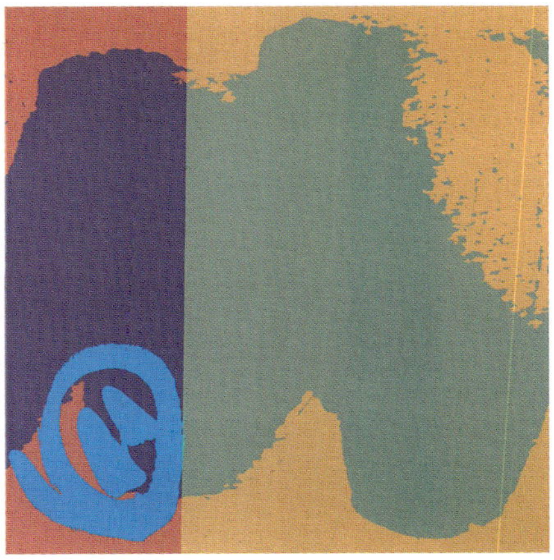

unknown artist
*Abstract No.15**
acrylic on canvas 50 x 50
KM15

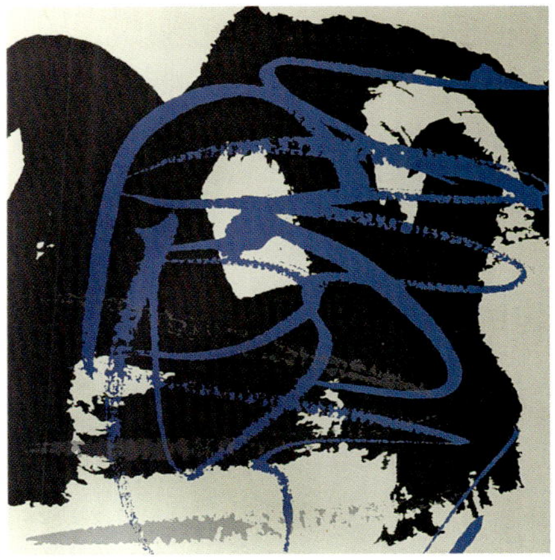

unknown artist
*Abstract No.16**
acrylic on canvas 50 x 50
KM16

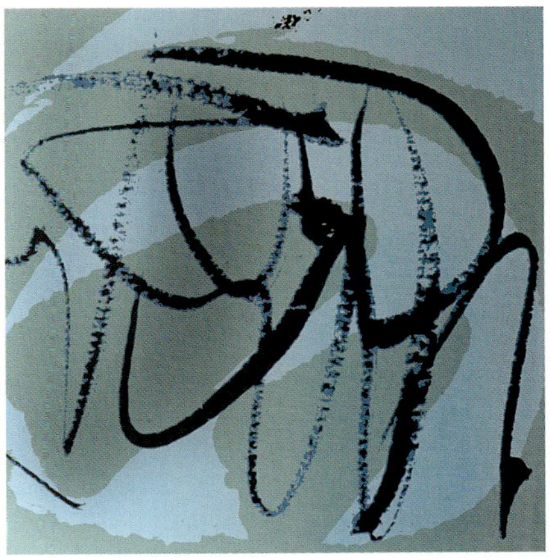

unknown artist
*Abstract No.17**
acrylic on canvas 50 x 50
KM17

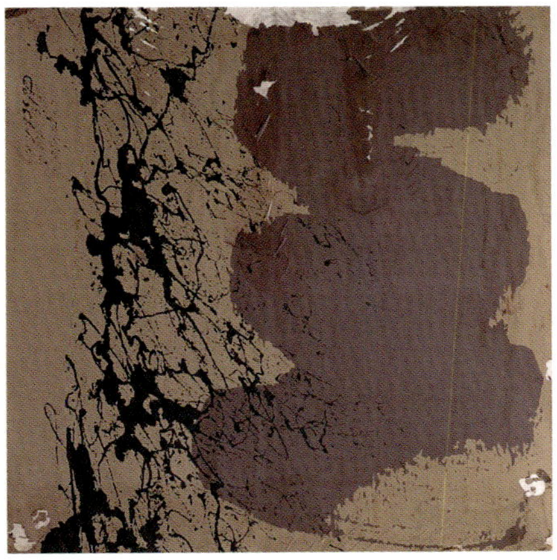

unknown artist
*Abstract No.18**
acrylic on canvas 50 x 50
KM18

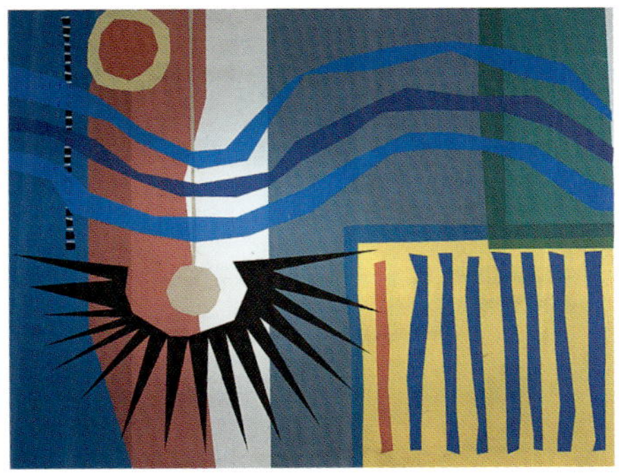

unknown artist
*Abstract No.22**
acrylic on canvas 115 x 150
KM22

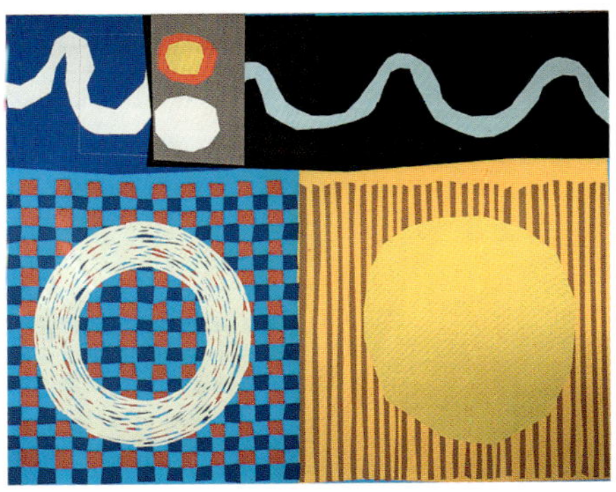

unknown artist
*Abstract No.23**
acrylic on canvas 115 x 150
KM23

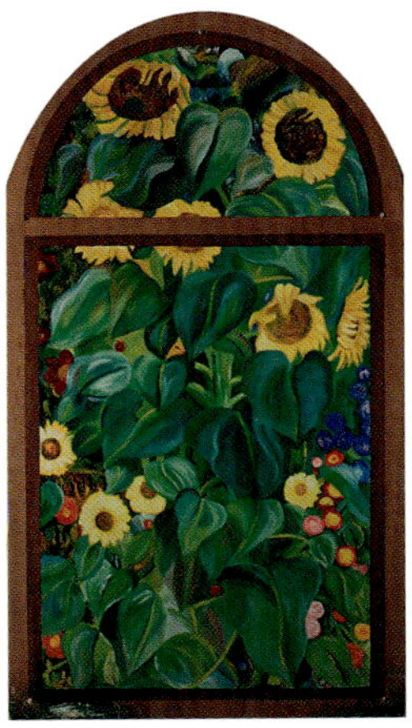

unknown artist
Sunflowers
oil on plywood 122 x 70
KM37

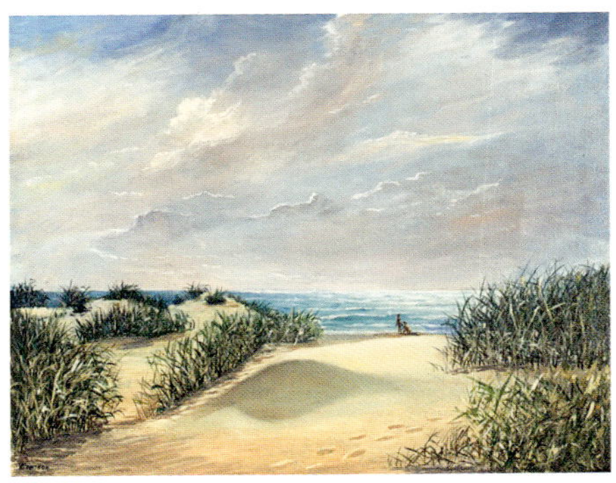

Weston, C.
*Sand Dunes**
oil on canvas 45 x 60
NWK4

British Horological Institute

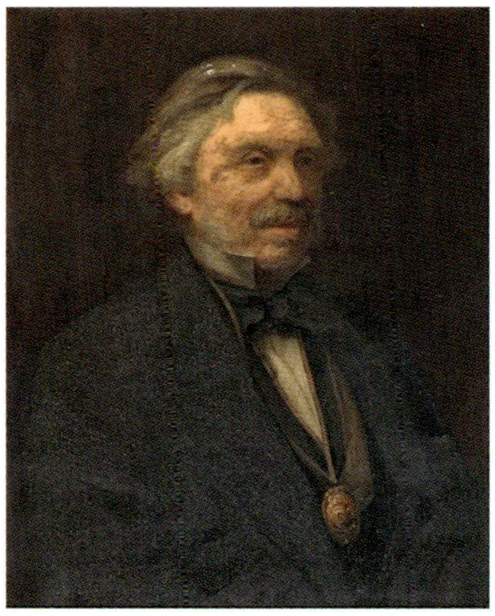

Carey, Charles William 1862–1943
John Jones of the Strand (1815–1909), Watchmaker of the Strand
oil on canvas 74 x 60
UP1

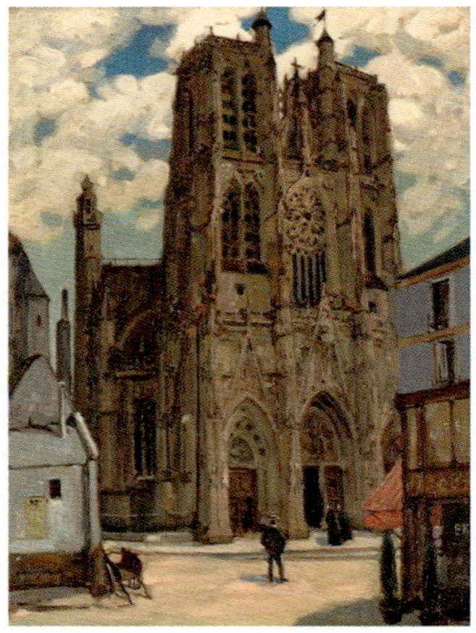

Formier, Alexander (attributed to)
Abbeville Church, Normandy, France 1905
oil on canvas 89 x 70
UP4 (P)

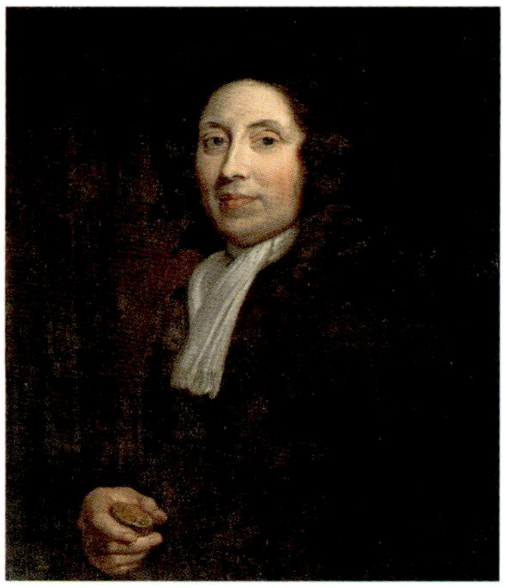

Kneller, Godfrey (attributed to) 1646–1723
Thomas Tompion (1638–1713), 'Father of English Clockmaking'
oil on canvas 73 x 63
UP3

Kneller, Godfrey (school of) 1646–1723
Alan Brodrick (c.1656–1728), 1st Viscount Midleton c.1717
oil on canvas 130 x 110 (E)
UP5 (P)

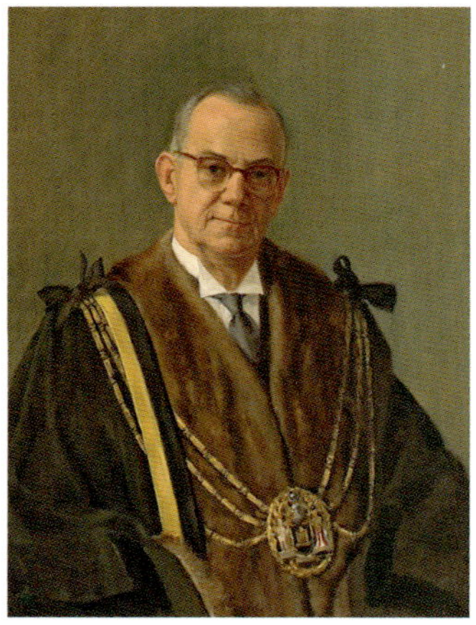

unknown artist
Michael Laurence Bateman (1893–1966), Vice-President and Past Chairman of the British Horological Institute
oil on canvas 76 x 62.5
UP2

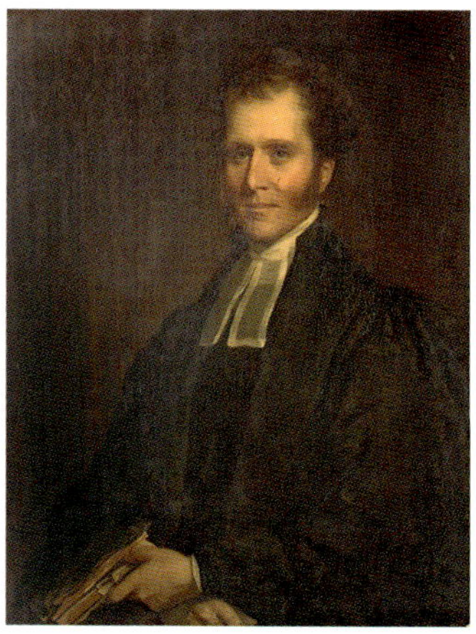

unknown artist
William John (1798–1870), 7th Viscount Midleton, Dean of Exeter
oil on canvas 75 x 69 (E)
UP6 (P)

Creswell Crags Museum and Education Centre

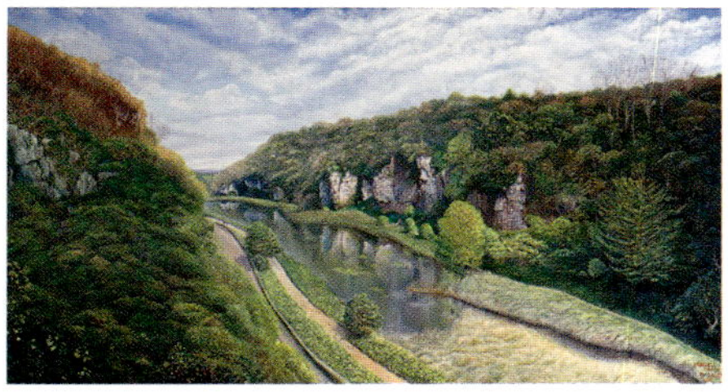

Hyatt, John A.
Creswell Crags, Nottinghamshire 2002
oil on canvas 64.5 x 125
CC:01

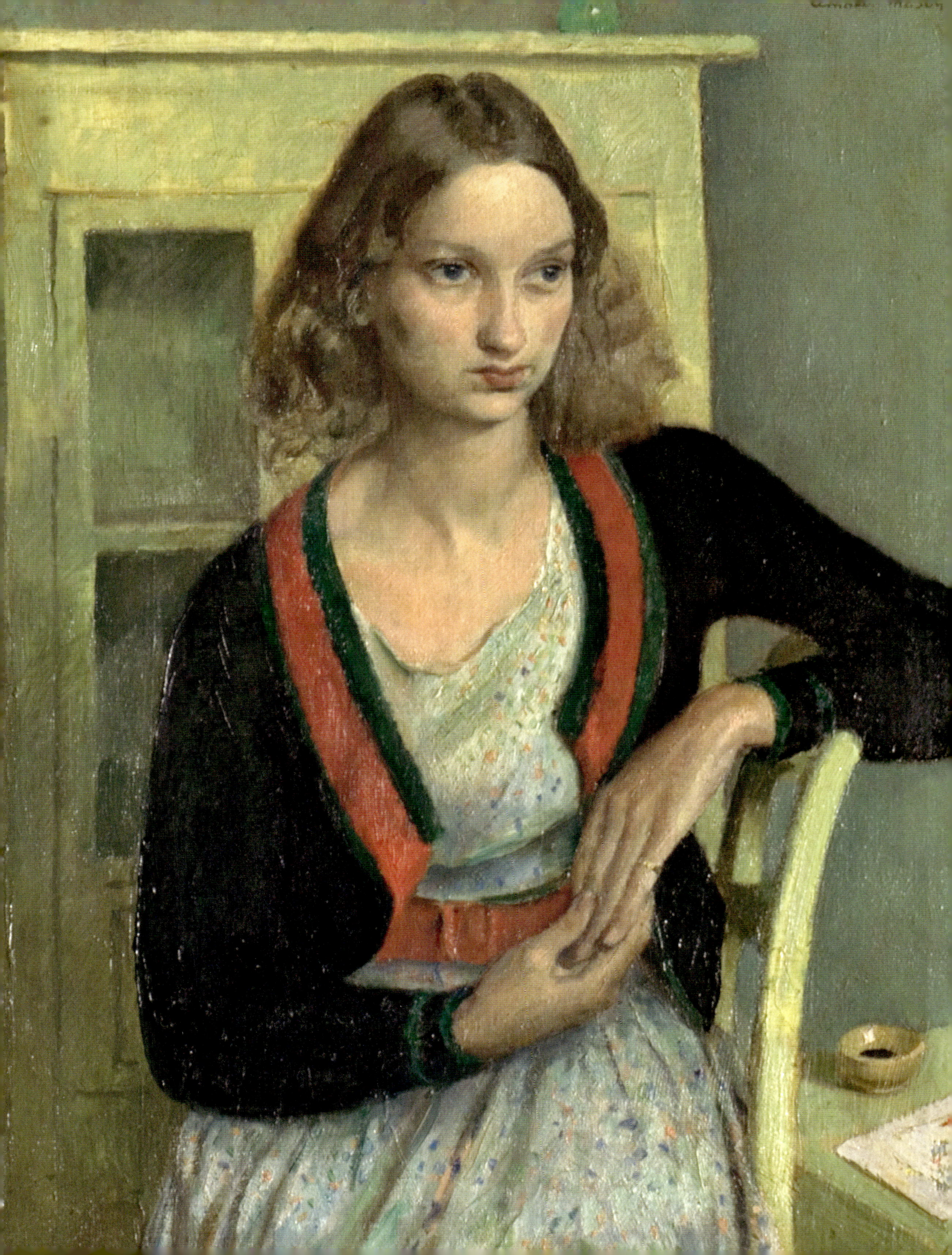

Paintings Without Reproductions

This section lists all the paintings that have not been included in the main pages of the catalogue. They were excluded as it was not possible to photograph them for this project. Additional information relating to acquisition credit lines or loan details is also included. For this reason the information below is not repeated in the Further Information section.

Djanogly City Academy Nottingham

unknown artist *Landscape*, oil on canvas, DCA:013, not available at the time of photography

Nottingham City Museums and Galleries

Barrett, Thomas 1845–1924, *On the Shore*, 20.3 x 30.5, oil on canvas, NCM 1946-242, not available at the time of photography

Gamble, F. Lorence *The Castle and the Duke of Newcastle's Wharf*, oil on canvas, NCMB 1975-374, not available at the time of photography

Knight, Harold 1874–1961, *Standing Male Nude*, 74.9 x 54.6, oil on canvas, NCM 1941-7, not available at the time of photography

Steenwijck, Hendrick van the elder c.1550–1603, *Interior of a Church*, 17.1 x 12.4, oil on wood, NCM 1904-97, not available at the time of photography

unknown artist *Players*, 8.4 x 6.4, oil on canvas, NCMB 1976-458, not available at the time of photography

Ward, James 1769–1859, *Coast Scene, Storm*, 23.5 x 34.9, oil on canvas, NCM 1904-76, not available at the time of photography

Rushcliffe Borough Council

Lowe, Arthur 1866–1940, *The Vale of Belvoir: Pulling the Boat*, oil on board, RC:012, not available at the time of photography

The University of Nottingham

Bell, Vanessa 1879–1961, *W. J. H. (Sebastian) Sprott, Professor of Psychology and Sociology as a Young Student at Charleston*, 1921, oil on canvas, PCF6, not available at the time of photography

Bowen, Siân b.1959, *Double Summertime (Cone Flower VI)*, 134, not available at the time of photography

Brooks, Sally *Grapefruit 3D Form*, 135, not available at the time of photography

Cowlishaw, Tony b.1944, *Professor Francis O'Grady, Foundation Professor of Medical Microbiology, University of Nottingham*, 1982, oil on canvas, UON.178, not available at the time of photography

Davis, Noel Denholm 1876–1950, *George Spencer, Member of College Council (1924–1939), Vice-President of College (1930–1946)*, 127 x 101.5, oil on canvas, PCF1, not available at the time of photography

Davis, Noel Denholm 1876–1950, *H. F. Lancashire, JP, Member of College Council (1917–1926), Vice-President of College (1926–1928)*, 127 x 101.5 , oil on canvas, PCF2, not available at the time of photography

Halliday, Trevor b.1939, *Mythological Scene*, 137, not available at the time of photography

Hempton, Paul b.1946, *Night into Day*, 101.5 x 113.5, oil on canvas, PCF5, not available at the time of photography

Lees, Stewart Marshall *Blue*, 152.5 x 152.5, oil on canvas on board, PCF3, not available at the time of photography

Lees, Stewart Marshall *Untitled*, 152.5 x 152.5, oil on canvas on board, PCF4, not available at the time of photography

Measures, David b.1937, *West Porlock, Somerset*, 138, not available at the time of photography

Robson, Gavin b.1950, *Untitled*, 139, not available at the time of photography

Bassetlaw District Council

Farrar, S. *Clumber Bridge*, 60.7 x 89.3, oil on board, RETBM : A109, not available at the time of photography

STOLEN

Nottingham City Museums and Galleries

Barber, Thomas 1771–1843, *The Cow Drinks, Nottingham Park*, 40.6 x 61, oil on canvas, NCM 1892-60

Facing page: Mason, Arnold, 1885–1963, *Portrait of a Woman* (detail), 1931, Newark and Sherwood Museum Service (p. 24)

Further Information

The paintings listed in this section have additional information relating to one or more of the five categories outlined below. This extra information is only provided where it is applicable and where it exists. Paintings listed in this section follow the same order as in the illustrated pages of the catalogue.

I The full name of the artist if this was too long to display in the illustrated pages of the catalogue. Such cases are marked in the catalogue with a (...).

II The full title of the painting if this was too long to display in the illustrated pages of the catalogue. Such cases are marked in the catalogue with a (...).

III Acquisition information or acquisition credit lines as well as information about loans, copied from the records of the owner collection.

IV Artist copyright credit lines where the copyright owner has been traced. Exhaustive efforts have been made to locate the copyright owners of all the images included within this catalogue and to meet their requirements. Any omissions or mistakes brought to our attention will be duly attended to and corrected in future publications.

V The credit line of the lender of the transparency if the transparency has been borrowed. Bridgeman images are available subject to any relevant copyright approvals from the Bridgeman Art Library at www.bridgeman.co.uk

Gedling Borough Council

Dodd, Charles J. B. *Jane Torvill and Christopher Dean, Ice Dancing*, gift from an unknown source
Shelton, Beryl *Camellias*, gift from an unknown source
Wheatley, Grahame b.1943, *Self Portrait**, gift from an unknown source
Zirbes, P. *Rothenburg Town Hall, Germany*, gift from an unknown source

Ashfield District Council

unknown artist *Ada Lovelace (1815–1852)*, acquired from an unknown source

Langwith Whaley Thorns Heritage Centre

Salt, Les 1916–1986, *Holy Cross Church, Upper Langwith, Derbyshire*, gift, 2007, acquired as part of the John Hyatt Collection
Simons, Stephen b.1984, *Pithead Sunset*, gift from the artist, 2008, acquired as part of the John Hyatt Collection, © the artist
Trolley, Arthur 1914–1985, *The Hay Wain* (after John Constable), gift from the son of the artist, 2007, acquired as part of the John Hyatt Collection

Mansfield District Council

Barker, Wright 1864–1941, *Tree and Rabbits*, transferred, 1987
Barker, Wright 1864–1941, *Deer in a Forest*, transferred, 1987
Barker, Wright 1864–1941, *Horses in a Paddock**, unknown provenance
Barron, Dennis active 1999–2001, *Baron Taylor of Mansfield (1895–1991), MP for Mansfield (1941–1966)*, unknown provenance
Bertrand, James 1823–1887, *Lady on the Beach*, gift from W. H. Thompson
Birks, J. *Sebastian Sales, Official Town Crier for Mansfield (1827–1853)*, gift from the Mansfield Brewery Company to the Old Mansfield Society, presented to the Museum from an unknown source
Bissill, George William 1896–1973, *Zell's Farm, Winter, Hampshire*, gift from V. W. Wright, 1956
Blood, Gerry 1932–2005, *Newstead Abbey, December*, purchased by the Mansfield Corporation, 1965
Bray, Julian b.1965, *Sally Twinkles*, purchased from the artist, 2008, © the artist
Bretland, Thomas W. 1802–1874, *Horse Owned by Mr Robert White*, bequeathed from an anonymous source
Bretland, Thomas W. 1802–1874, *Tethered Horse and Hunt*, bequeathed from an anonymous source
Bywater, J. E. *Major Oak*, gift from Mr H. Hodgkins, 1960
Bywater, J. E. *Oak*, gift from Mr H. Hodgkins
Carter, Frank *Albert Sorby Buxton (1867–1932)*, unknown provenance
Clark, Heath Richard b.1970, *Window II*, purchased from an anonymous source, 2000, © the artist
Coker, Peter 1926–2004, *Still Life with Chicken*, allocated by the Contemporary Art Society, 1965, © Peter Coker, RA
Cook, Margaret C. b.c.1897, *Posthumous Portrait of Albert Sorby Buxton (1867–1932)*, gift from Mr J. Craven
Cooke, Stanley b.1913, *Quarry at Mansfield*, gift from the artist, 1955, © the artist/www.bridgeman.co.uk
Gilbert, A. *Castle Gateway, Nottingham*, unknown provenance
Hall, R. active 1971, *Goods Marshalling Yard, Mansfield, London, Midland and Scottish Railway*, gift from the artist, 1971
Hall, R. active 1971, *Goods Shed, Mansfield, London, Midland and Scottish Railway*, gift from the artist, 1971
Hall, R. active 1971, *The Platelayers, Mansfield, London, Midland and Scottish Railway*, gift from the artist, 1971
Hall, R. active 1971, *The Signal Box, Mansfield, London, Midland and Scottish Railway*, gift from the artist, 1971
Hampson, John b.1898, *Fireman's Cabin*, gift from the artist
Hampson, John b.1898, *Water Level*, gift from the artist
Harbord, R. C. *Old Oaks in Sherwood Forest*, purchased from an anonymous source, 1972
Hill, Chas G. *James Sorby (b.1794)*, unknown provenance
Holloway, Robert 1896–1976, *Old Mansfield, Nottinghamshire*, purchased from an anonymous source, 1970, © the artist's estate
Hooch, Pieter de (copy of) 1629–1684, *The Courtyard of a House in Delft*, transferred, 1987
Jones, Tom *Early Autumn, Sherwood Forest, Nottinghamshire*, unknown provenance
Kidger, C. W. *The Old Bridge, Baslow, Derbyshire*, purchased, 1962
Lane, H. S. *Reed Mill, Mansfield, Nottinghamshire*, gift from Mrs N. Gabbitas, 1972
Moore, Thomas Cooper (attributed to) 1827–1901, *Harbour and Ships*, unknown provenance
Paulson, Ann 1808–1866, *Victory Arch*, gift from Mrs Talbot Coke, 1900
Paulson, Ann 1808–1866, *Apples and Flowers*, bequeathed from an anonymous source
Payne, David c.1844–1891, *Newstead Abbey, Nottinghamshire*, unknown provenance
Pickin, E. M. (attributed to) *After the Shipwreck*, transferred, 1987
Powell, Ella Ffolliott c.1887–1943, *Home Guard*, unknown provenance
Race, W. *Grimbsy Trawlers Leaving the Humber*, purchased by the Mansfield Corporation, 1957
Royce active 19th C, *Landscape with Watermill*, unknown provenance
Sutton, Hector McDonald 1903–1992, *Royal Ballet*, gift from Mr J. Sutton
Sutton, Hector McDonald 1903–1992, *Brookhill Colliery, Pinxton, Derbyshire*, gift from Mr J. Noble, 2000
Sutton, Hector McDonald 1903–1992, *King John's Palace, Clipstone, Nottinghamshire*, purchased from an anonymous source
Tucker, R. *Pleasley, Nottinghamshire*, gift from Mr J. Tucker, 1965
Tyndall, W. Castell *Jackson's Mill, Mansfield, Nottinghamshire*, gift from Mrs M. Clay, 1964
unknown artist early 19th C, *Mr Mumford, Former Squire of Mansfield*, gift from Mr M. Mumford, 1982
unknown artist *A Lady in a Black Dress*, transferred, 1987
unknown artist *Buck Gates, Thoresby Estate, Nottinghamshire*, gift from Mr H. Hodgkins, 1960
unknown artist *Clumber House, Nottinghamshire*, gift from Mr H. Hodgkins, 1960
unknown artist *Gypsy Boy*, bequeathed from an anonymous source, 1951
unknown artist *Gypsy Girl*, bequeathed from an anonymous source, 1951
unknown artist *Lodge Gates, Thoresby Estate, Nottinghamshire*, gift from Mr H. Hodgkins, 1960
unknown artist *Man and Woman*,

transferred, 1987
unknown artist *Oak in Sherwood Forest No.1**, gift from Mrs Taylor, 2008
unknown artist *Oak in Sherwood Forest No.2**, gift from Mrs Taylor, 2008
unknown artist *Old Man at a Desk*, transferred, 1987
unknown artist *Portrait of an Unknown Man*, unknown provenance
unknown artist *Welbeck Abbey, Nottinghamshire*, gift from Mr H. Hodgkins, 1960
Wilkinson, Norman 1878–1972, *Castle**, unknown provenance, © the Norman Wilkinson estate
Wilkinson, Norman 1878–1972, *Castle and Moat*, unknown provenance, © the Norman Wilkinson estate

Mansfield Fire Station Museum

Barron, Dennis active 1999–2001, *The Old Borough of Mansfield Fire Station* (built in 1939), commissioned, c.1999, to commemorate the opening of the old Mansfield Fire Station by Sir Vivian L. Henderson, MC, DL, JP, Chairman of the Fire Commission, 1936
Barron, Dennis active 1999–2001, *The New Mansfield Fire Station* (built in 1997), commissioned to commemorate the opening of the new Mansfield Fire Station by The Duchess of Gloucester, 1997
unknown artist *Fire Insurance Badge* (1)*, gift from a private source in Southampton, along with the remnants of the Merryweather Collection, c.1990
unknown artist *Fire Insurance Badge* (2)*, gift from a private source in Southampton, along with the remnants of the Merryweather Collection, c.1990
unknown artist *Fire Insurance Badge* (3)*, gift from a private source in Southampton, along with the remnants of the Merryweather Collection, c.1990
Walton, Amy *Captain Merryweather*, gift from a private source in Southampton, along with the remnants of the Merryweather Collection, c.1990

Nottinghamshire County Teaching Primary Care Trust

Arnfield, Marjorie 1930–2001, *Breaking the Coal (c. 1920)*, purchased, c.1998, © the artist's estate
Arnfield, Marjorie 1930–2001, *Rufford Colliery Demolition*, purchased, c.1998, © the artist's estate
Arnfield, Marjorie 1930–2001, *Desolation, Pleasley Colliery, Nottinghamshire*, purchased, c.1998, © the artist's estate
Arnfield, Marjorie 1930–2001, *The Last Shift*, purchased, c.1998, © the artist's estate
Grace *Cottage Scene**, gift from an anonymous source
Grace *Washed Ashore**, gift from an anonymous source
Grace *Waterfall**, gift from an anonymous source
Humphrey, J. *The Hay Wain* (copy of John Constable), gift from an anonymous source
Lambert *Chatsworth House, Derbyshire*, gift from an anonymous source, in memory of Alice K. Slaney, 'The Daffodil Lady', 1965–1985
unknown artist *Ploughing the Field**, gift from an anonymous source

Portland College

Evans, E. S. *Two of The Duke Of Portland's Racehorses* (one of a pair), on long-term loan from the Portland Collection, 1950
Evans, E. S. *Two of The Duke Of Portland's Racehorses* (one of a pair), on long-term loan from the Portland Collection, 1950
Gresley, Harold 1892–1967, *Dovedale, Derbyshire*, gift from Colonel P. C. Cooper-Parry, © the artist's estate
László, Philip Alexius de 1869–1937, *The Duchess of Portland*, on long-term loan from the Portland Collection, 1950
Spooner, Arthur 1873–1961, *Welbeck during The Great War* (one of a pair), on long-term loan from the Portland Collection, 1950
Spooner, Arthur 1873–1961, *Welbeck during The Great War* (one of a pair), on long-term loan from the Portland Collection, 1950

Newark and Sherwood Museum Service

Bell, Vanessa 1879–1961, *Jocelyn's Farm, Ripe, East Sussex*, gift from the Contemporary Art Society, 1956, © 1961 estate of Vanessa Bell courtesy Henrietta Garnett
Benner, William 1884–1964, *Newark Market Place, Nottinghamshire*, bequeathed by Mrs Bloom, 1974
Brannan, Peter 1926–1994, *Street Scene, Newark, Nottinghamshire*, gift from the artist, 1989, © the artist's estate
Brannan, Peter 1926–1994, *Street Scene, Newark, Nottinghamshire*, gift from the artist, 1989, © the artist's estate
British (English) School *Lady Ossington (1806–1889)*, purchased at auction with the assistance of grant aid, 1981
British (English) School 19th C, *Portrait of a Man in Black*, gift
British (English) School 19th C, *Portrait of an Old Man*, gift
British (English) School late 19th C, *Winter Snow Scene*, gift
British (English) School *Hills and Lake*, gift
British (English) School *Mountain and Lake Scene*
British (English) School *William Ewart Gladstone (1809–1898), MP for Newark (1832), Prime Minister (1868–1874, 1880–1886 & 1892–1894)*, gift
Coleridge, Francis George 1838–1923, *Hen*, gift, 1965
Coleridge, Francis George 1838–1923, *Cockbird*, gift, 1966
Coyne, Douglas 1930–2008, *Still Life with Geraniums, Two Bottles and Fruit*, purchased by the Museum Committee, 1950, © the artist's estate
Cubley, Henry Hadfield 1858–1934, *The Old Shop, Newark, Nottinghamshire*, gift, 1954
Cubley, Henry Hadfield 1858–1934, *Three Cattle on Open Land*, on loan from Mrs D. Ablewhite, 2007
Cubley, Henry Hadfield (attributed to) 1858–1934, *Cattle on a Country Road*, gift
Cubley, Henry Hadfield (copy of) 1858–1934, *Norton Hall*, on loan from Mrs D. Ablewhite, 2007
Cubley, William Harold 1814–1896, *William Ewart Gladstone (1809–1898), MP for Newark (1832), Prime Minister (1868–1874, 1880–1886 & 1892–1894)*, gift from Colonel T. W. Ford, 1947; on loan to Newark Town Hall
Cubley, William Harold 1814–1896, *Frederick Thesiger*, gift, 1965
Cubley, William Harold 1814–1896, *A Study in Black and White of William Ewart Gladstone (1809–1898), MP for Newark (1832), Prime Minister (1868–1874, 1880–1886 & 1892–1894)*, gift from G. T. Branston, presented by Miss Cubley, 1937
Cubley, William Harold 1814–1896, *Flint's Dockyard, Newark, 1850*, gift
Cubley, William Harold 1814–1896, *The Terrace, Haddon Hall, Derbyshire*, gift from Miss Cubley
Cubley, William Harold 1814–1896, *Dorothy Vernon's Doorway, Haddon Hall, Derbyshire*
Cubley, William Harold 1814–1896, *Killin, Perthshire, Scotland*, gift
Cubley, William Harold 1814–1896, *In the Vale of Gwynant, Wales*, gift
Cubley, William Harold 1814–1896, *Joseph Gilstrap (1775–1869)*, gift, 1991
Cubley, William Harold 1814–1896, *Near Lake Ogwen, Wales*, gift
Cubley, William Harold 1814–1896, *Newark Castle, Nottinghamshire*, gift from Alderman H. H. Cubley, c.1920
Cubley, William Harold 1814–1896, *Newark Castle, Nottinghamshire, with Sebastopol Cannon*, gift from Alderman H. H. Cubley
Cubley, William Harold 1814–1896, *Self Portrait*, gift to Newark Corporation by the artist's daughter, 1903; donated by Newark Corporation, 1957; on loan to Newark Town Hall
Cubley, William Harold 1814–1896, *Sunset at Bridlington, East Yorkshire*, gift
Cubley, William Harold 1814–1896, *The Chapel, Haddon Hall, Derbyshire*, gift from the son of H. H. Cubley, 1920s
Cubley, William Harold 1814–1896, *The Crypt, Knaresborough Castle, Yorkshire*, gift from Alderman H. H. Cubley
Cubley, William Harold 1814–1896, *The Keep, Newark Castle, Nottinghamshire*, gift
Cubley, William Harold 1814–1896, *The Old Churchyard, Betws-y-Coed, Wales*, gift from Alderman H. H. Cubley
Cubley, William Harold 1814–1896, *View of the River Trent*, gift
Cubley, William Harold 1814–1896, *View of the River Trent and the Old Pack Horse*, gift
Forbes, Stanhope Alexander 1857–1947, *Grosvenor Hodgkinson (1818–1881)*, gift, 1937, © the artist's estate/www.bridgeman.co.uk
Ganesco, Alexandre 1910–1979, *Horse Race*, gift from the Contemporary Art Society, 1963
Gibbon, Sidney 1895–1988, *Forum Fantasy*, purchased by the Museum Committee, 1952
Grant, E. E. d.c.1970, *Paintworks*, purchased by the Museum committee, 1970
Grant, E. E. d.c.1970, *The Farm*, gift from the artist, 1957
Guttuso, Renato 1912–1987, *The Raft of the Medusa* (copy after Eugène Delacroix), gift from the Contemporary Art Society, 1962, © DACS 2008
Hall, Lilian Iris 'Betty' *Willie Hall*, gift, 1990s
Knowles, William Pitcairn c.1846–c.1904, *Heath and Woodlands*, purchased from Mrs Butt, 1938
Mason, Arnold 1885–1963, *Portrait of a Woman*, gift from the Contemporary Art Society, 1963, © the artist's estate
Morrocco, Alberto 1917–1998, *Low Tide*, gift from the Contemporary Art Society, 1952, © the artist's estate
Moynihan, Rodrigo 1910–1990, *Rain Clouds, Beached Boats*, gift from the Contemporary Art Society, 1944, © the artist's estate
Nicholson, William 1872–1949, *Flower Piece*, gift from the Contemporary Art Society, 1950, © Elizabeth Banks
Nicholson, Winifred 1893–1981, *Primula stellata*, gift from the Contemporary Art Society, 1952, © trustees of Winifred Nicholson
Oliver, Peter 1927–2006, *The Strand, Jersey*, gift from the Contemporary Art Society 1958; presented, 1959, © the artist's estate
Ramsay, Patricia 1886–1974, *Sea Fans, Bermuda*, gift from the Contemporary Art Society, 1954, © the artist's estate
Spooner, Arthur 1873–1961, *Mrs J. R. Hole*, gift from an anonymous donor, 1992
Spooner, Arthur 1873–1961, *The Daughter of J. Hole*, gift from an anonymous donor, 1992
Talbot, William c.1823–1907, *Longstone Bridge and Watermill, Derbyshire*, gift from Mr L. H. Abbott, Esq., 1965
unknown artist *Post Mill, Tolney Lane, Newark, Nottinghamshire*, purchased from G. W. Ford & Son, 1937
Walker, Ethel 1861–1951, *Beached Dinghies on a Storm-Tossed Shore, (Robin Hood's Bay, North Yorkshire)*, gift from the Contemporary Art Society, 1938, © the artist's estate/www.bridgeman.co.uk
Wehrschmidt, Daniel Albert 1861–1932, *Sydney Pierrepont (1826–1900), 3rd Earl Manvers*, purchased with the assistance of the Victoria and Albert Museum Purchase Grant Fund, 1990

Newark Town Council

Adeney, William Bernard 1878–1966, *Tunley Bottom*, purchased from the Contemporary Art Society, 1946
Bearpark, John Victor b.1946, *Gill's Garden*, gift from the artist, 2002, © the artist
Brannan, Peter 1926–1994, *View of a Town*, gift, 1974, © the artist's estate
Brannan, Peter 1926–1994, *The Mount School, Newark, Nottinghamshire*, on loan from Mr T. T. Trickett, © the artist's estate
Buckner, Richard 1812–1883, *Lady Elizabeth Gilstrap (1822–1891)*, unknown provenance
Chowne, Gerard 1875–1917, *Honeysuckle*, gift from the Contemporary Art Society, 1954
Cubley, Henry Hadfield 1858–1934, *Autumn, Albury Park, Surrey*, purchased, 2008
Cubley, Henry Hadfield 1858–1934, *Barmouth Bay, West Wales*, gift from the Newark Drainage Board, 2007
Cubley, Henry Hadfield 1858–1934, *The Timber Clearing at Matlock, Derbyshire*, purchased
Cubley, William Harold 1814–1896, *Becher Tidd Pratt (1826–1901)*, unknown provenance
Dobson, William 1611–1646, *Sir Richard Willis (1614–1690)*, gift from Mr T. Haywood, 1958
Fuller, Leonard John 1891–1973, *John H. Knight (1886–1976)*, gift from the sitter, 1959

Herbert, John Rogers 1810–1890, *Sir William Gilstrap (1816–1896)*, unknown provenance
Isaac, Susan b.1961, *Market Place, Newark, Nottinghamshire*, purchased, 2007 , © the artist
Kiddey, Robert 1900–1984, *Hilda Walker*, gift from Mrs Hilda Walker, 1955, © Robert Kiddey Estate
Kiddey, Robert 1900–1984, *Night*, gift from Mr and Mrs P. Kiddey, 2001, © Robert Kiddey Estate
Knight, Harold 1874–1961, *Thomas Earp (1830–1910), Mayor of Newark*, gift, 1903, © reproduced with permission of the estate of Dame Laura Knight, DBE, RA, 2008. All rights reserved
Nicholson, William 1872–1949, *Still Life*, gift from G. T. Branston, Esq., 1937, © Elizabeth Banks
Nicholson, William 1872–1949, *Music*, gift from G. T. Branston, Esq., 1937, © Elizabeth Banks
Nicholson, William 1872–1949, *Boy with the Caroline Mug*, on loan from Newark College, Lincoln, 2005, © Elizabeth Banks
Nicholson, William 1872–1949, *Chrysanthemums*, gift from Newark and Sherwood District Council, 1974, © Elizabeth Banks
Nicholson, Winifred 1893–1981, *Boigneville, Île-de-France, France*, on loan from Newark College, Lincoln, 2005, © trustees of Winifred Nicholson
Paul, Joseph (attributed to) 1804–1887, *Bridge Street, Newark, Nottinghamshire*, purchased, 1976
Paul, Joseph (attributed to) 1804–1887, *Corner of Market Place, Newark, Nottinghamshire*, gift from Mr J. B. Eastwood, 1973
Paul, Joseph (attributed to) 1804–1887, *View of Beaumond Cross, Newark, Nottinghamshire*, gift to Newark Town Council, 1974
Paul, Joseph (attributed to) 1804–1887, *View of Kirkgate, Newark, Nottinghamshire*, gift from Mr J. B. Eastwood, 1973
Paul, Joseph (attributed to) 1804–1887, *View of Market Place, Newark, Nottinghamshire*, gift from Mr Snowden, restored thanks to Newark Community Arts, 2001
Paul, Joseph (attributed to) 1804–1887, *View of the Parish Church, Newark, Nottinghamshire*, gift from Mr J. B. Eastwood, 1973
Spencer, Stanley 1891–1959, *Poppies*, gift from the Contemporary Art Society, 1942, © estate of Stanley Spencer/ DACS 2008
Spooner, Arthur 1873–1961, *William Arthur (1857–1943), 6th Duke of Portland, KG, Lord Lieutenant of Nottinghamshire*, gift from the sitter, 1928
Spooner, Arthur 1873–1961, *Godfrey Tallents (1849–1917), Town Clerk*, gift from Major H. Tallents, DSO, c.1928
Spooner, Arthur 1873–1961, *Percy John Charles Staniland (1880–1961), MBE, JP*, gift from the sitter, 1949
Spooner, Arthur 1873–1961, *Richard Pursey Blatherwick (1880–1971), JP*, gift from the sitter, 1949
Sulimow, Jurij b.1952, *Sandomierz, Poland*, gift from the town of Sandomierz, Poland, celebrating twinning, 2006
Townsend, Ernest 1880–1944, *William Edward Knight (1845–1934), JP, Councillor (1883), Alderman (1904), and Mayor of Newark (1889 & 1915–1918)*, unknown provenance
unknown artist *John Clay (1602–1669)*, on loan from Mrs S. M. Wade-Gery
unknown artist *Lady in Blue*, gift from Mrs J. P. Darwin, 1934
unknown artist *John Hole (b.c.1772), Mayor of Newark (1822)*, gift from J. Hole, 1959
unknown artist *Portrait of an Unknown Gentleman*, unknown provenance
Walton, Henry 1746–1813, *Edward Cooper*, unknown provenance
Wilkinson, David *17th and 21st Lancers*, purchased from the artist, 1985
Yates, Edward *Joseph Gilstrap Branston (1838–1926)*, gift from an unknown source, 1927

The Holocaust Centre

Hancock, K. B. *Camp Train**
unknown artist *Jewish Candles**

Newstead Abbey

Barber, Thomas 1771–1843, *Joseph Murray (1737–1820)*, gift from Charles Ian Fraser, 1931
Barraud, Henry 1811–1874, *'Lord, have mercy upon us'*, gift from Charles Ian Fraser, 1931
Barraud, Henry 1811–1874, *'We praise thee, O Lord'*, gift from Charles Ian Fraser, 1931
Bell, John 1823–1881, *Newstead Abbey, Nottinghamshire, from the Upper Lake*, purchased from Jonathan Gatty with the assistance of the Victoria and Albert Museum Purchase Grant Fund, the Museum's Purchase Fund and the Thorpe Perry Bequest, 1977
British (English) School late 17th C, *Portrait of a Young Woman in White Satin*, gift from Charles Ian Fraser, 1931
British (English) School early 18th C, *Portrait of a Young Woman in a Blue Wrap*, gift from Charles Ian Fraser, 1931
British (English) School 18th C, *Young Woman in a Blue Dress*, on loan from the Gray Trust, 1978
Byron, Richard 1724–1811, *East View of Newstead Abbey, Nottinghamshire, and the Great Garden*, purchased from Mr W. H. Gordon-Smith with the assistance of the Museum and Galleries Commission/Victoria and Albert Museum Purchase Grant Fund, The Friends of Nottingham Museum and The Friends of Newstead Abbey (MONKS), 1998
Chaffin, Donald *George Gordon, Lord Byron (1788–1824)*, gift from Miss Mary Lander, 1975
Chalon, Henry Bernard 1771–1849, *'Nettle'*, gift from Mrs H. V. Currie, 1952
Collins, James Edgell 1819–1895, *Colonel Gerald Littlehales Goodlake (1832–1890)*, gift from Charles Ian Fraser, 1931
Collins, James Edgell 1819–1895, *Colonel Gerald Littlehales Goodlake (1832–1890), Coldstream Guards (1857)*, gift from Charles Ian Fraser, 1931
Corbould, Alfred c.1821–1874, *Portrait of the Artist's Daughter*, gift from Charles Ian Fraser, 1931
Corbould, Alfred c.1821–1874, *After the Lion Hunt (W. F. Webb and Captain W. Codrington, South Africa)*, gift from Charles Ian Fraser, 1931
Corbould, Alfred c.1821–1874, *White Horse and Retriever*, gift from Charles Ian Fraser, 1931
Curran, Amelia 1775–1847, *Claire Clairmont (1798–1879)*, gift from Lieutenant-Colonel K. Edgcumbe, 1938
Dahl, Michael I 1656/1659–1743, *Frances, Lady Byron (d.1757), Third Wife of the 4th Lord Byron*, purchased from Historical Portraits Ltd with the assistance of the Museums and Galleries Commission/Victoria and Albert Museum Purchase Grant Fund and the National Art Collections Fund, 1993
Dahl, Michael I (after) 1656/1659–1743, *Penelope, Lady Herbert (1620–1647)*, gift from Charles Ian Fraser, 1931
Dyck, Anthony van (after) 1599–1641, *Lady Elizabeth Thimbelby and Dorothy, Viscountess Andover*, gift from Charles Ian Fraser, 1931
Dyck, Anthony van (after) 1599–1641, *Thomas Howard (1585–1646), Earl of Arundel and His Son Lord Maltravers (1607–1624)*, gift from Charles Ian Fraser, 1931
Gainsborough, Thomas (after) 1727–1788, *Woman and Child at a Ford*, gift from Mrs H. V. Currie, 1952
Geefs, Fanny 1807–1883, *Katherine Mary Webb Palmer (1824–1890)* (later Lady Lambert), gift from Charles Ian Fraser, 1931
Halls, John James 1776–1853, *John Hanson (d.1841)*, gift from Madame S. Mennessier, 1982
Houckgeest, Joachim Ottensz. c.1585–before 1645, *Sir Nicholas Byron (d.1596)*, purchased from Gooden and Fox with the assistance of the Victoria and Albert Museum Purchase Grant Fund, 1962
Houckgeest, Joachim Ottensz. c.1585–before 1645, *Sir Thomas Byron (d.1643)*, purchased from Gooden and Fox with the assistance of the Victoria and Albert Museum Purchase Grant Fund, 1962
Kneller, Godfrey (after) 1646–1723, *George I (1660–1727)*, gift from Charles Ian Fraser, 1931
Kneller, Godfrey (after) 1646–1723, *William III (1650–1702)*, gift from Charles Ian Fraser, 1931
Lawrence, Thomas (style of) 1769–1830, *Portrait of a Boy*, bequeathed by Herbert C. Roe, 1937
Lonsdale, James 1777–1839, *Augustus Frederick (1773–1843), Duke of Sussex*, gift from Charles Ian Fraser, 1931
Lonsdale, James 1777–1839, *Louisa Wildman (1800–1879)*, gift from Mrs Augustus Darling, 1896
Lonsdale, James 1777–1839, *Thomas Wildman (1787–1859)*, gift from Mrs Augustus Darling, 1896
Luker, William c.1820–1892, *Stag Hunt in Scotland*, gift from Charles Ian Fraser, 1931
Luker, William (attributed to) c.1820–1892, *The Turkish Pony 'Bobby', the Cock from Sebastopol, the Cow from the Valley of Baidar, and the Pigeon from Colonel Zarhoski (Commandant of Fort Constatine)*, gift from Charles Ian Fraser, 1931
Luker, William (attributed to) c.1820–1892, *The Toy*, gift from Charles Ian Fraser, 1931
Lytton, Neville Stephen 1879–1951, *Ralph, 2nd Earl of Lovelace (1839–1906)*, on loan from the 5th Earl of Lytton, 1989
Masson, Hippolyte d.1878, *Marguerite, Countess of Blessington (1789–1849)*, bequeathed by Herbert C. Roe, 1937
Phillips, Thomas 1770–1845, *6th Lord Byron (1788–1824)*, gift from Charles Ian Fraser, 1931
Phillips, Thomas 1770–1845, *Mary Chaworth Musters (1786–1832)*, bequeathed by Herbert C. Roe, 1937
Phillips, Thomas (after) 1770–1845, *6th Lord Byron (1788–1824)*, gift from the Countess of Munster, 1947
Phillips, Thomas (after) 1770–1845, *6th Lord Byron (1788–1824)*, bequeathed by Herbert C. Roe, 1937
Phillips, Thomas (attributed to) 1770–1845, *Thomas Wildman (1787–1859)*, gift from Charles Ian Fraser, 1931
Pickersgill, Henry William 1782–1875, *Countess Teresa Guiccioli (c.1800–1873)*, on loan from a private collection, 2007
Ramsay, Allan 1713–1784, *George III (1738–1820)*, gift from Charles Ian Fraser, 1931
Ramsay, James 1786–1854, *Portrait of a Lady*, gift from Baroness D'Erlanger, 1936
Reynolds, Joshua 1723–1792, *Admiral the Honourable John Byron (?) (1723–1786)*, purchased from Sotheby's with the assistance of a grant from the National Arts Collection Fund, 1978
Ross, William Charles 1794–1860, *Frederick Webb (1790–1846)*, gift from Charles Ian Fraser, 1931
Sanders, George (after) 1774–1846, *6th Lord Byron (1788–1824), and His Servant Robert Rushton (1793–1833)*, gift from Mrs E. MacDonald, 1960
Stewardson, Thomas 1781–1859, *Mrs Catherine Gordon Byron (1765–1811)*, on loan from a private collection, 2003
Taylor, George William *Newstead Abbey, Nottinghamshire, from Upper Lake*, gift from Mrs D. M. Wilson, 1955
Tillemans, Peter 1684–1734, *Spruce' and 'Bell'*, purchased by private treaty from the owner, Johnny Bute, through Christie's, with the assistance of the National Art Collections Fund and the Museums and Galleries Commission/Victoria and Albert Museum Purchase Grant Fund, 1999
Tillemans, Peter 1684–1734, *Two Racehorses with Grooms and Hounds in the Park at Newstead Abbey, Nottinghamshire*, purchased by private treaty from the owner, Johnny Bute, through Christie's, with the assistance of the National Art Collections Fund and the Museums and Galleries Commission/Victoria and Albert Museums Purchase Grant Fund, 1999
Tillemans, Peter 1684–1734, *East View of Newstead Abbey, Nottinghamshire*, purchased from Historical Portraits Ltd with the assistance of the Heritage Lottery Fund and the Museum Galleries Commission/Victoria and Albert Museum Purchase Grant Fund, 2000
Tillemans, Peter 1684–1734, *West View of Newstead Abbey, Nottinghamshire*, purchased from Historical Portraits Ltd with the assistance of the Heritage Lottery Fund and the Museum Galleries Commission/Victoria and Albert Museum Purchase Grant Fund, 2000
Tillemans, Peter 1684–1734, *Newstead Abbey, Nottinghamshire, West Aspect*, gift from Charles Ian Fraser, 1931
Tomson, Clifton 1775–1835, *Lord Byron's Dog 'Boatswain' (1803–1808) (The Newfoundland)*, gift from Charles Ian Fraser, 1931
Tomson, Clifton 1775–1835, *Lord Byron's Dog 'Lyon' (The Wolf Dog)*, gift from Charles Ian Fraser, 1931
unknown artist 17th C, *A Gentleman of the Byron Family*, gift from Charles Ian Fraser, 1931
unknown artist 18th C, *Brother John of Algarve, Portugal (1701–1758)*, gift from Charles Ian Fraser, 1931

unknown artist 19th C, *West View of Newstead Abbey, Nottinghamshire, Including a Boating Party on the Upper Lake*, purchased from Jonathan Gatty, 1977
unknown artist *Apollo Flaying Marsyas*, bequeathed by Miss M. M. Johnstone, 1965
unknown artist *Gerald Littlehales Goodlake (1832–1890)*, gift from Charles Ian Fraser, 1931
unknown artist *Head of Christ on a Cloth*, gift from Charles Ian Fraser, 1931
unknown artist *Head of Christ with Figures of Saints*, gift from Charles Ian Fraser, 1931
unknown artist *Newstead Abbey, Nottinghamshire, from the South*, gift from Charles Ian Fraser, 1931
unknown artist *Portrait of an Unidentified Lady*
unknown artist *Victorian Foxhunt* (far left panel from a folded screen), gift from Mr Alan Redman, c.1970
unknown artist *Victorian Foxhunt* (left panel from a folded screen), gift from Mr Alan Redman, c.1970
unknown artist *Victorian Foxhunt* (right panel from a folded screen), gift from Mr Alan Redman, c.1970
unknown artist *Victorian Foxhunt* (far right panel from a folded screen), gift from Mr Alan Redman, c.1970
Vivian, Jane active 1861–1877, *Grand Canal, Venice, Italy*, purchased from H. Ford, 1944
Wainewright, Thomas Francis 1794–1883, *6th Lord Byron (1788–1824)*, gift from Baroness D'Erlanger, 1936
Walker, John Rawson 1796–1873, *The Original Sketch for the Grand Staircase at Newstead Abbey, Nottinghamshire*, purchased from Mr D. N. Brocklehurst, 2000
Waplington, Gilbert b.1873, *Bulwell Wood Hall, Nottinghamshire*, gift from John Fyson, 1979
Webster, Moses (after) 1792–1870, *West View of Newstead Abbey, Nottinghamshire*, gift from Jonathon Gatty, 1977
Westall, Richard (attributed to) 1765–1836, *6th Lord Byron (1788–1824)*, purchased from Elkin Matthews Ltd, 1938
Winck, Christian (attributed to) 1738–1797, *Christ Rising from the Tomb and Roman Soldiers Fleeing*, gift from Charles Ian Fraser, 1931
Wissing, Willem (after) 1656–1687, *Mrs Knott*, gift from Charles Ian Fraser, 1931
Wright, John Michael (after) 1617–1694, *Charles II (1630–1685)*, gift from Charles Ian Fraser, 1931

Castle College Nottingham

Reynolds, S. *Rainy Street Scene**, acquired from the County archives, 1982
unknown artist *Watermill**, acquired from the County archives, 1982

Djanogly City Academy Nottingham

Cheall, John b.1965, *Shower, Loughborough, Leicestershire*, purchased by Sir Harry Djanogly, 1989, © the artist
unknown artist *Alan Sillitoe (b.1928), Author of 'Saturday Night and Sunday Morning'**, commissioned, c.2000
unknown artist *Art Teacher**, commissioned, c.2000
unknown artist *Dancer**, commissioned, c.2000
unknown artist *Edward Elgar (1857–1954), Composer**, commissioned, c.2000
unknown artist *Installation (1)**, purchased by Sir Harry Djanogly, 1989
unknown artist *Installation (2)**, purchased by Sir Harry Djanogly, 1989
unknown artist *Installation (3)**, purchased by Sir Harry Djanogly, 1989
unknown artist *Installation (4)**, purchased by Sir Harry Djanogly, 1989
unknown artist *Installation (5)**, purchased by Sir Harry Djanogly, 1989
unknown artist *Installation (6)**, purchased by Sir Harry Djanogly, 1989
unknown artist *John Wayne (1907–1979)**, purchased by Sir Harry Djanogly, 1989
unknown artist *River View** (panel 1 of 4), commissioned, c.2000
unknown artist *River View** (panel 2 of 4), commissioned, c.2000
unknown artist *River View** (panel 3 of 4), commissioned, c.2000
unknown artist *River View** (panel 4 of 4), commissioned, c.2000
unknown artist *School Choir** (panel 1 of 3), commissioned, c.2000
unknown artist *School Choir** (panel 2 of 3), commissioned, c.2000
unknown artist *School Choir** (panel 3 of 3), commissioned, c.2000
unknown artist *Scrap Yard*, purchased by Sir Harry Djanogly, 1989

Galleries of Justice

Brickland *PINXIT* (triptych left panel), gift as part of the HM Prison Service Collection, c.1998
Brickland *PINXIT* (triptych centre panel), gift as part of the HM Prison Service Collection, c.1998
Brickland *PINXIT* (right panel of triptych), gift as part of the HM Prison Service Collection, c.1998
Ross, William A. *Segregation Cell*, gift as part of the HM Prison Service Collection, c.1998
Ross, William A. *Egyptian Mummy*, gift as part of the HM Prison Service Collection, c.1998
Scobie, Ray active 1995–1997, *House Painter*, gift as part of the HM Prison Service Collection, c.1998
Scobie, Ray active 1995–1997, *Billiard Table*, gift as part of the HM Prison Service Collection, c.1998
unknown artist *Bang Up*, gift as part of the HM Prison Service Collection, c.1998
unknown artist *Ghostly Figure*, gift as part of the HM Prison Service Collection, c.1998
unknown artist *Man behind Bars*, gift as part of the HM Prison Service Collection, c.1998

Government Office for the East Midlands

Collaku, B. Y. *Ocean and Earth No.1**, purchased, 2005
Collaku, B. Y. *Ocean and Earth No.2**, purchased, 2005
Collaku, B. Y. *Red Earth**, purchased, 2005
unknown artist *Brown and Cream**, purchased, 2005
unknown artist *Brown, Gold and Blue**, purchased, 2005
unknown artist *Brown, Gold and Orange No.1**, purchased, 2005
unknown artist *Brown, Gold and Orange No.2**, purchased, 2005
unknown artist *Brown, Gold and Orange No.3**, purchased, 2005
unknown artist *Brown, Gold and Orange No.4**, purchased, 2005
unknown artist *Brown, Gold, Orange and Cream**, purchased, 2005

Nottingham Central Library

Ball, Henry 1894–1966, *St Paul's Church* (recto), untraced gift
Ball, Henry (attributed to) 1894–1966, *Sketch of an Unidentified Woman** (verso), untraced gift
Burrows, Sarah Elisabeth *Oaklands Mill, Sneinton, Nottingham*, untraced gift
Bussey, Reuben 1818–1893, *Farmyard Scene, Sutton-in-Ashfield, Nottinghamshire**, on long-term loan from Sutton-in-Ashfield Library
Cox, E. *Clifton Village Green, Nottingham*, presented to the library, 1996
Dawson, Henry 1811–1878, *Nottingham Castle Gateway*, gift from W. A. Lewitt
Goodwin, Albert 1845–1932, *Mansfield Road, Nottingham*, untraced gift
Goodwin, Albert 1845–1932, *Mount Street East, Nottingham*, untraced gift
Goodwin, Albert 1845–1932, *The 'Salutation Inn', Nottingham*, untraced gift
Goodwin, Albert (attributed to) 1845–1932, *Charlotte Street, Nottingham*, untraced gift
Hallam, J. C. *High Street, Hucknall, Nottinghamshire**, untraced gift
Hode, T. *The Birthplace of Henry Kirke White, Cheapside, Nottingham*, untraced gift
Johnson, A. *Nottingham Canal, View One Kilometre East between Carrington Street Bridge*, untraced gift
Johnson, A. *Nottingham Canal, View One Kilometre East from Carrington Street Bridge towards Wood Bridge, Trent Street*, untraced gift
Johnson, A. *Wilford Ferry, Nottinghamshire*, untraced gift
Moore, Thomas Cooper 1827–1901, *Lenton Boatyard, Nottingham*, untraced gift
Moore, Thomas Cooper (attributed to) 1827–1901, *River Trent, View From the North Bank near Wilford, Nottinghamshire*, purchased from J. Orton, Eton College, 1968 then donated to the library by an unknown source
Moore, Thomas Cooper (attributed to) 1827–1901, *The 'Leather Bottle Inn', Hockley, Essex*, untraced gift
Moore, Thomas Cooper (attributed to) 1827–1901, *Old Trent Bridge, West Aspect, Nottingham*, gift from Miss Helen Shipstone
Moore, Thomas Cooper (attributed to) 1827–1901, *The Ancient Chapel Bar*, untraced gift
unknown artist *River Trent, View at Colwick, Nottinghamshire*, untraced gift
unknown artist *Major Oak*, painted for a library event by a local communities librarian, 2007
unknown artist *Cottages at Clifton, Nottinghamshire*, untraced gift
unknown artist *Mrs M. A. Musters, née Chaworth*, gift from W. A. Briscoe, c.1930
unknown artist *Portrait of an Unidentified Gentleman*, donated from Hucknall Library, Nottingham, c.2003
Waplington, Paul b.1938, *The Lace Draughting Room*, untraced gift
Xhaferin *The Romanians Departing**, untraced gift

Nottingham City Museums and Galleries

Adnams, Marion 1898–1995, *Spring in the Cemetery*, purchased from the artist, 1956
Adnams, Marion 1898–1995, *Three Stones*, purchased from the Midland Group Gallery, 1971
Aitchison, Craigie Ronald John b.1926, *Nude Standing in front of a Picture*, gift from the Contemporary Art Society, 1986, © the artist/www.bridgeman.co.uk
Allori, Cristofano (after) 1577–1621, *Judith with the Head of Holofernes*, gift from Mrs Sidney Cartwright, 1873–1874
Armfield, Maxwell Ashby 1882–1972, *Shell and Comma Butterfly*, purchased from the Medici Society Ltd, London, 1957, © the artist's estate/www.bridgeman.co.uk
Artaud, William 1763–1823, *George Coldham, Town Clerk of Nottingham*, purchased from Nottingham Corporation (?), 1879
Atkinson, John Augustus 1775–1833, *Soldiers Refreshing*, bequeathed by Mr Richard Godson Millns, 1904
Bacon, John Henry Frederick 1865–1914, *'Suscipe me Domine' ('Receive Me O Lord')*, gift from Mr J. S. Derbyshire, 1919
Baker, Thomas 1809–1869, *Entrance to Colwick Woods, Nottinghamshire*, purchased from Mr W. Pease, 1913
Ball, Henry 1894–1966, *Portrait of the Artist's Father (A Quiet Hour)*, purchased from Henry Ball, Esq., 1956
Banner, Delmar Harmond 1896–1983, *Clement Fothergill Pitman (d.1973), Art Director and Curator of Nottingham Castle Museum (1930–1959)*, gift from Mr Clement Fothergill Pitman, 1960, © the artist's estate
Banner, Delmar Harmond 1896–1983, *Coniston Fells from Upper Eskdale, Cumberland (Grey Friar, Old Man, Dow Crag, Hardknott and Upper Eskdale from Black Apron, November)*, gift from the artist, 1939, © the artist's estate
Barber, Thomas 1771–1843, *Lord Denman (1779–1854)*, purchased, 1879
Barber, Thomas 1771–1843, *The Trent at Wilford*, bequeathed by the executors of the estate of Mr J. R. Wild, 1909
Barber, Thomas 1771–1843, *Self Portrait*, bequeathed by the executors of the estate of Mr J. R. Wild, 1909
Barber, Thomas 1771–1843, *Benjamin Mayo (c.1779–1843), the Old General*, gift from Mrs H. Storer Birkin, 1873–1874
Barber, Thomas 1771–1843, *David Love (1750–1827), Ballad-Writer*, bequeathed by the executors of the estate of Lieutenant-Colonel F. Rayner, 1946
Barber, Thomas 1771–1843, *Henry Kirke White (1785–1806), Poet*, gift from the executors of the estate of Mr Thomas Walker, 1894
Barber, Thomas 1771–1843, *Jonathan Dunn (1771–1857)*, purchased from Mrs C. H. A. Roe, 1922
Barber, Thomas 1771–1843, *Thomas Stevenson*, gift from Mr Thomas Stevenson Junior, 1893
Barber, Thomas 1771–1843, *View across Nottingham Park with Lenton Priory in the Distance*, purchased from Miss Amenia (?) Barber, 1892

Barber, Thomas 1771–1843, *William Chapman (1812–1874)*, gift from Mr George Dudgeon, 1894
Barber, Thomas (attributed to) 1798–1826, *John Rawson Walker (1796–1893)*, purchased from Miss Rawson Walker, 1898
Barber, Thomas (attributed to) 1798–1826, *Miss Elizabeth Hoare* (later Mrs J. Rawson Walker), purchased from Miss Rawson Walker, 1898
Barker, John Edward 1889–1953, *Kitchen Still Life*, purchased from the Piccadilly Gallery, 1958
Barker, Thomas 1769–1847, *Mountainous Landscape*, bequeathed by Mr Henry Lammin, 1890
Barker, Thomas (imitator of) 1769–1847, *Landscape with Two Figures*, bequeathed by Mr Richard Godson Millns, 1904
Barker, Thomas Jones 1815–1882, *Landscape with Cattle*, bequeathed by Mr Henry Lammin, 1890
Barret, George 1732–1784, *Llanberis Lake and Dolbadarn Castle, North Wales*, bequeathed by Mr Richard Godson Millns, 1904
Barrett, Thomas 1845–1924, *Snow Piece, Bulwell Forest, Nottinghamshire*, bequeathed by Mr Henry Lammin, 1890
Bates, David 1841–1921, *Broadheath Common*, bequeathed by Samuel William Oscroft, 1924
Bayliss, Wyke 1835–1906, *Interior of St Mark's Basilica, Venice, Italy*, purchased from the artist, 1882
Beechey, William 1753–1839, *A Child of Paul Sandby*, bequeathed by Lady Fanny E. J. Rich, 1945
Beechey, William 1753–1839, *Portrait of a Young Girl*, bequeathed by Lady Fanny E. J. Rich, 1945
Beechey, William 1753–1839, *The Children of Paul Sandby*, bequeathed by Lady Fanny E. J. Rich, 1945
Beechey, William 1753–1839, *Thomas Paul Sandby (1766–c.1832)*, bequeathed by Lady Fanny E. J. Rich, 1945
Beeton, Alan 1880–1942, *The Black Porcelain Fish (The Bronze Fish)*, gift from Mrs George Sheringham, 1939
Bega, Cornelis Pietersz. 1631/1632–1664, *The Dwarf Fiddler*, bequeathed by Mr Richard Godson Millns, 1904
Belleroche, Albert de 1864–1944, *A Girl with a Racquet*, purchased from the artist's widow, Countess Julie de Belleroche, 1952
Benner, William 1884–1964, *After the Blitz, near Trivett's Works from Cliff Road, Nottingham* (painted after the night of enemy aerial attack, 8–9 May 1941), purchased from the artist, 1943
Benyon, Margaret b.1940, *Untitled*, purchased, 1969, © the artist
Ben-Zenou, Helena b.1970, *The Imposition (Prospect Room, Wollaton Hall, February 2006)*, purchased, 2006, © the artist
Bevan, Tony b.1951, *Condition*, presented by the Contemporary Art Society, 1988, © the artist
Bilbie, James Lees 1860–1945, *An Earnest Movement in Andante (Charles Heywood, Violinist)*, gift from Mrs Bilbie, the artist's widow, 1946
Bilbie, James Lees 1860–1945, *Deepening Shades*, purchased from the artist, 1890, © Nottingham City Museums and Galleries
Bilbie, James Lees 1860–1945, *Hayfield near Trent Baths at Nottingham*, gift from Mrs Mary Dakeyne Townroe, 1938
Bird, Edward 1772–1819, *The Recruit*, bequeathed by Mr Richard Godson Millns, 1904
Birley, Oswald Hornby Joseph 1880–1952, *Colonel William Frank Wheatley (d.1923)*, gift from Miss Pearl Wheatley, via the Art Exhibitions Bureau, 1954, © the artist's estate
Blaas, Eugen von 1843–1931, *The Offer*, bequeathed by T. E. Beaumont, 1899
Blaas, Eugen von 1843–1931, *Accepted*, bequeathed by T. E. Beaumont, 1899
Blache, Christian Vigilius 1838–1920, *Cape North, Iceland*, purchased from the artist, 1885
Black, Arthur John 1855–1936, *Mrs Mary E. Pennel (Portrait of a Seated Woman Dressed in Black with Red Flowers on Her Lap)*, gift from Mrs Mary E. Pennel, 1945
Black, Arthur John 1855–1936, *A Winter Scene*, gift from Mr S. C. Turner via the National Art Collections Fund
Black, Arthur John 1855–1936, *Girl Haymaking*, gift from Mrs E. Manning, 1936
Bogdany, Jakob c.1660–1724, *Two Iceland Falcons*, bequeathed by Mrs Elizabeth Holbrooke, 1939
Bomberg, David 1890–1957, *The Moorish Wall, Cyprus*, purchased from the artist's widow, Mrs Lilian S. C. Bomberg, 1967, © the artist's family
Bonington, Richard 1768–1835, *Nottingham Meadows from the Rock Cliff, Where Lenton Road Turns into Park Valley (Nottingham Park from Castle Rock)*, gift from Mr Fred W. Dobson, Esq., JP, 1905
Bonington, Richard 1768–1835, *Portrait of One of the Donor's Family (Hodges)*, gift from Mrs C. E. Hodges, 1963
Bonington, Richard Parkes 1802–1828, *Le Château de la Duchesse de Berry*, on loan from the Acceptance in Lieu of Tax Scheme, Her Majesty's Government, Department of Culture, Media and Sport, 2004
Bonington, Richard Parkes 1802–1828, *Ruins of the Abbey St Bertin, St Omer, France (Transept of the Abbey of St Bertin, St Omer, France)*, purchased from Mr James Orrock, 1907
Bonington, Richard Parkes 1802–1828, *Don Quixote in His Study*, purchased from Messrs Arthur Tooth & Sons Ltd, 1958
Bonington, Richard Parkes 1802–1828, *The Grand Canal, Venice, Italy*, purchased from Messrs Arthur Tooth & Sons Ltd, 1958
Bonington, Richard Parkes 1802–1828, *Quentin Durward at Liège, Belgium*, purchased from Messrs Arthur Tooth & Sons Ltd with the assistance of the Museums, Libraries and Archives Council/Victoria and Albert Museum Purchase Grant Fund, 1974
Bonington, Richard Parkes (after) 1802–1828, *Meditation*, gift from Mr James Orrock, 1909
Bonington, Richard Parkes (attributed to) 1802–1828, *Fisherfolk on the Coast of Normandy, France*, purchased from Messrs Christie, Manson and Wood from the sale of the property of James Ross, 1927
Bonington, Richard Parkes (attributed to) 1802–1828, *Self Portrait*, purchased, 1884
Bonington, Richard Parkes (imitator of) 1802–1828, *Scene on the Coast of Normandy, France (The Old Castle of Dieppe on the Coast of Normandy)*, purchased from Lockwood Auctioneers, 1895
Bonington, Richard Parkes (imitator of) 1802–1828, *Coast Scene*, purchased from Mrs A. Boyton, 1925
Bonington, Richard Parkes (imitator of) 1802–1828, *The Piazza, San Marco, Venice, Italy (View of the Piazza of San Marco and the Campanile)*, purchased from the Lockwood Bros Auctioneers, 1892
Bonington, Richard Parkes (imitator of) 1802–1828, *Self Portrait*, purchased from Mr P. M. Turner, 1927
Booth, James William 1867–1953, *Homeward Bound*, gift from Miss Helen Shipstone, 1932
Booth, James William 1867–1953, *End O'Day*, gift from Miss Helen Shipstone, 1933
Both, Jan c.1618–1652 & **Both, Andries Dirksz.** 1611/1612–1641 *Landscape with Figures*, bequeathed by Mr Henry Lammin, 1890
Boudin, Eugène Louis 1824–1898, *The Fortifications at Antibes, France*, gift from Her Majesty's Government, Treasury, 1975
Bough, Samuel 1822–1878, *The Thames at Chiswick, London*, bequeathed by Mr Richard Godson Millns, 1904
Bradbury, W. *Druidical Remains, Nottingham Park*, gift from Mrs A. G. Hamlet, 1960
Bradbury, W. *Nottingham Castle from the Park Bowling Green*, gift from Mrs A. G. Hamlet, 1960
Bradley, Robert 1813–1880, *View of the Old Trent Bridge Inn, West Bridgford, Nottingham*, purchased from Neale & Son Auctioneers, via J. Ward & Son, 1911
Brennand-Wood, Michael b.1952, *You Are Here* (joined diptych), acquired through the Contemporary Art Society Special Collections Scheme, 2001
Bretland, Thomas W. 1802–1874, *Portrait of the Horse, Which Belonged to Major Burton at the Balaklava Charge*, gift from Miss Elizabeth Ingham Bretland, 1899
Brett, John 1830–1902, *Golden Prospects, St Catherine's Well, Land's End, Cornwall*, purchased from Messrs Wallis & Son, 1913
Bright, Henry 1814–1873, *Newstead Abbey, Nottinghamshire*, purchased from Sotheby's, via E. J. Laws, 1963
Bright, Henry 1814–1873, *Norfolk Broads with Boats*, bequeathed by Mr Richard Godson Millns, 1904
Bristow, Edmund 1787–1876, *Gypsies Striking Camp*, bequeathed by Mr Richard Godson Millns, 1904
Bristow, Edmund 1787–1876, *Landscape with Cattle and Sheep*, bequeathed by Mr Richard Godson Millns, 1904
British (English) School 17th C, *John Pym (1584–1643)*, gift from Samuel Hickling Gell (pawnbroker, clothier, silversmith, and jeweller), 1879
British (English) School 17th C, *Lady Sophia Chaworth*, bequeathed by Reverend Tolhurst, 1953
British (English) School 17th C, *William Cavendish (1640–1707), 1st Duke of Devonshire*, purchased from Nottingham Corporation (?), 1879
British (English) School *William Elliot (1707–1792)*, purchased from Sotheby's Olympia, 2002
British (English) School *View of the Ancient Gateway and Castle, Nottingham*, purchased from the sale of the property of Dr Thomas Wright, 1910
British (English) School *View of the Footpath to Lenton across Nottingham Park*, purchased from the sale of the property of Dr Thomas Wright, 1910
British (English) School 18th C, *Portrait of a Lady*, bequeathed by Miss Elizabeth Beatson, 1937
British (English) School 18th C, *Portrait of a Man* (thought to be Dr Robert Thoroton, 1623–1678), purchased from Messrs Ford & Son from the collection of Chauntrey House, Newark, 1898
British (English) School 18th C, *Ruins near Tivoli, Italy*, bequeathed by Samuel William Oscroft, 1924
British (English) School 18th C, *Thomas Hawksley (1666–1749), Mayor of Nottingham (1715)*, gift from Mrs G. M. Davis, 1951
British (English) School *Nottingham Castle from the Meadows*, gift from H. Pfundst, 1884
British (English) School *Robert Davison*, gift from Mr John Steegman, Esq., 1959
British (English) School *Portrait of an Officer* (probably Major William Wylde, 1803–1808, OC, Southwell Volunteer Infantry), purchased from Mr E. Dickinson of the Military Historical Society, 1984
British (English) School *Mrs Birkhead, née Eliza Davison*, gift from Mr John Steegman, Esq., 1959
British (English) School *View of Nottingham Castle and Rock, Looking East*, gift from Mr Charles T. Jacoby, 1890
British (English) School *View of Nottingham Castle from the Meadows*, gift from Mr E. Crosland, 1889
British (English) School 19th C, *A Woodland Scene with a Cottage*, bequeathed by Mr Henry Lammin, 1890
British (English) School 19th C, *A Woodland Stream*, bequeathed by Mr Henry Lammin, 1890
British (English) School 19th C, *An Oak in Moccas Park, Herefordshire*, bequeathed by Harry Lammin, 1890
British (English) School 19th C, *Cottage near East Bergholt, Suffolk*, gift from Mr James Orrock, 1909
British (English) School 19th C, *Grasmere, Westmorland, Cumbria*, bequeathed by Mr Henry Lammin, 1890
British (English) School 19th C, *Hampstead Heath, London*, bequeathed by Mr Henry Lammin, 1890
British (English) School 19th C, *John Churchill (1650–1722), Duke of Marlborough*, gift from Mr J. Henry Jacoby, 1899
British (English) School 19th C, *John Leavers*, gift from Mrs Mary H. Case, 1970
British (English) School 19th C, *Lady in a Frilled Cap*, purchased from the Midland Group of Artists, 1966
British (English) School 19th C, *Landscape, Cottage and Stream with a Figure and a House*, bequeathed by Mr Henry Lammin, 1890
British (English) School 19th C, *Landscape near the Coast (View of a Mansion with the Sea in the Distance)*, bequeathed by Mr Henry Lammin, 1890
British (English) School 19th C, *Landscape, Trees and Cottages*, bequeathed by Mr Henry Lammin, 1890
British (English) School 19th C, *Mountainous Landscape, Evening*, bequeathed by Mr Henry Lammin, 1890
British (English) School 19th C, *Mountainous Landscape, Morning*, bequeathed by Mr Henry Lammin, 1890
British (English) School 19th C, *Norham Castle, Northumberland*, bequeathed by Mr Henry Lammin, 1890

British (English) School 19th C, *Nottingham Castle Gateway*, gift from Mr John Dable, 1963
British (English) School 19th C, *Ploughing and Dibbling Beans*, bequeathed by Mr Henry Lammin, 1890
British (English) School 19th C, *Portrait of a Gentleman*, gift from Earl Manvers, 1878
British (English) School 19th C, *Portrait of a Gentleman*, bequeathed by Mr Richard Godson Millns, 1904
British (English) School 19th C, *Portrait of a Lady*, bequeathed by Miss Elizabeth Beatson, 1937
British (English) School 19th C, *Ringland Hills, Costessy, Norwich*, bequeathed by Mr Richard Godson Millns, 1904
British (English) School 19th C, *River Scene, Boy Driving Sheep*, bequeathed by Mr Richard Godson Millns, 1904
British (English) School 19th C, *River Scene with Shipping*, bequeathed by Mr Henry Lammin, 1890
British (English) School 19th C, *River Scene with Shipping*, bequeathed by Mr Henry Lammin, 1890
British (English) School 19th C, *Wood Scene, Stream and Figures*, bequeathed by Mr Henry Lammin, 1890
British (English) School *Head of a Woman in Profile*, purchased from Mr J. Levin, 1942
British (English) School *Nottingham Castle on Fire, 1831*, gift from Mrs Marjery Jones, 1963
British (English) School *Portrait of a Woman with a Finger on Her Cheek*, unknown provenance
British (English) School *River and Sheep*, bequeathed by Samuel William Oscroft, 1924
British (Norwich) School 19th C, *Lad's Lane, Boy's Hill, Cheltenham*, bequeathed by Mr Henry Lammin, 1890
British (Norwich) School 19th C, *Landscape, Trees in the Foreground, Lake and Hills in the Distance*, bequeathed by Mr Henry Lammin, 1890
British (Norwich) School 19th C, *Landscape with Cottage and Stream*, bequeathed by Mr Henry Lammin, 1890
British (Norwich) School 19th C, *Old Mill, Norwich, Norfolk*, bequeathed by Mr Henry Lammin, 1890
British (Norwich) School 19th C, *River Scene (Cottage and Trees)*, bequeathed by Mr Henry Lammin, 1890
British (Norwich) School 19th C, *The Homestead*, bequeathed by Mr Henry Lammin, 1890
British (Norwich) School 19th C, *Woodland Scene with Bridge and Cattle*, bequeathed by Mr Henry Lammin, 1890
British (Norwich) School 19th C, *Woodland Scene with Cottage*, bequeathed by Mr Henry Lammin, 1890
British (Norwich) School 19th C, *Woodland Scene with Stream and Cottages*, bequeathed by Mr Henry Lammin, 1890
Bronzino, Agnolo (imitator of) 1503–1572, *Portrait of an Infanta of Spain*, gift from Mr James Alfred Jacoby, 1893
Brown, Ford Madox 1821–1893, *Cromwell and the Vaudois (Cromwell, Protector of the Protestants of the Vaudois)*, purchased from the Fine Art Society, 1937
Brown, Ford Madox (attributed to) 1821–1893, *Manfred in the Chamois Hunter's Hut*, bequeathed by Mr J. R. Holliday, 1927
Brown, John Alfred Arnesby 1866–1955, *Haymaking* (recto), purchased from Neale & Son Auctioneers, from the sale of the property of G. H. Wallis, 1936
Brown, John Alfred Arnesby 1866–1955, *Poppy Field* (verso), purchased from Neale & Son Auctioneers, from the sale of the property of G. H. Wallis, 1936
Brown, John Alfred Arnesby 1866–1955, *Dr John Brown Paton (1830–1911), Principal of the Nottingham Congregational Institute for 35 Years*, gift from Messrs Blackburne and Johnstone, 1899
Brown, John Alfred Arnesby 1866–1955, *Full Summer, Ludham, Norfolk*, purchased from the artist, 1902
Brown, John Alfred Arnesby 1866–1955, *Sir Edward Henry Fraser*, gift from subscribers, 1913
Brown, John Alfred Arnesby 1866–1955, *The Estuary, Wells-next-the-Sea, Norfolk*, purchased from Lord Plender, 1943
Brown, John Alfred Arnesby 1866–1955, *Alderman William Lambert*, bequeathed by Mrs W. Lambert, 1918
Brown, John Alfred Arnesby 1866–1955, *May Morning, Nottingham*, purchased from the artist, 1922
Brown, John Alfred Arnesby 1866–1955, *Near Nottingham*, purchased from M. Newman Ltd, 1967
Brown, John Alfred Arnesby 1866–1955, *Study for 'The Two Piers'*, purchased from the Fine Art Society, 1958
Brown, Neil Dallas 1938–2003, *Bather, Still Deep*, purchased from the Piccadilly Gallery with the assistance of a Calouste Gulbenkian Foundation grant, 1967, © the artist's estate
Brueghel, Jan the elder 1568–1625 & **Balen, Hendrik van I (circle of)** 1575–1632 *The Rest on the Flight into Egypt*, bequeathed by Mr Richard Godson Millns, 1904
Buchanan, George F. 1800–1864, *Ellen's Isle, Loch Katrine, Scotland*, bequeathed by Mr Henry Lammin, 1890
Buchanan, George F. 1800–1864, *Lake Scene with Ruined Castle and Mountains*, bequeathed by Mr Henry Lammin, 1890
Buchanan, George F. 1800–1864, *On the Clyde*, bequeathed by Mr Henry Lammin, 1890
Burton, Alice Mary 1893–1968, *William*, purchased from the artist, via the Royal Portrait Society, 1950
Burton, Harry Marriott 1882–1979, *Pots and Pans, Natal, South Africa*, gift from the artist, 1954
Burton, Harry Marriott 1882–1979, *The Rockies, Mount Sir Donald, Canada*, gift from Miss Florence Burton, 1946
Burton, John active 1769–1836, *George Bellas Rothera (c.1824–1907), Solicitor*, gift from Mr Ian Rothera, 2003
Bussey, Reuben 1818–1893, *Old Houses, St Peter's Gate, Nottingham, 1842*, gift from Mr J. T. Goodwin, 1925
Calkin, Lance 1859–1936, *The Patchwork Quilt*, purchased from G. H. Wallis, 1936
Calkin, Lance 1859–1936, *Alderman John Barber, JP, Sheriff of Nottingham (1846), Mayor of Nottingham (1867–1869)*, gift from Nottingham Corporation, presented by the Magistrates, Alderman, members of the Town Council and the principal officials of the Borough of Nottingham on the occasion of the opening of the Nottingham Guildhall, 1888
Calkin, Lance 1859–1936, *'All pass away as the glimmer of day while others as fleet are born'*, purchased from the artist, 1889
Callcott, Augustus Wall 1779–1844, *A River Scene with Barges*, bequeathed by Mr Richard Godson Millns, 1904
Canaletto (imitator of) 1697–1768, *Piazza di Monte Cavallo, Rome, Italy*, bequeathed by Mr Henry Lammin, 1890
Capey, Reco 1895–1961, *The Hudson from Bear Mountain Bridge, USA*, purchased from the artist, via the Royal Academy of Arts, 1940
Carmichael, John Wilson 1800–1868, *Industrial Scene*, gift from Mrs Mary Dakeyne Townroe, 1938
Carmichael, John Wilson 1800–1868, *Scene in the Mediterranean*, bequeathed by Mr Richard Godson Millns, 1904
Carmichael, John Wilson 1800–1868, *Shipping off North Yarmouth*, gift from Mr R. S. Lymbery, 1939
Carpenter, Margaret Sarah 1793–1872, *A Spring Nosegay*, bequeathed by Mr H. Bradley, via Messrs Browne Son & Jacobson, 1931
Carpenter, Margaret Sarah (attributed to) 1793–1872, *Portrait of a Child*, purchased from Mr W. A Lewitt, Esq., 1953
Chambers, George 1803–1840, *Whitby Harbour, North Yorkshire*, bequeathed by Mr Richard Godson Millns, 1904
Chambers, George 1803–1840, *Boats Entering the Medway*, bequeathed by Mr C. W. Gowthorpe, 1949
Chandler, John Westbrooke 1764–1804/1805, *Portrait of a Lady*, gift from Sir Kenneth A. Muir Mackenzie, 1910
Chantron, Alexandre Jacques 1842–1918, *River Scene, the Lower Loire, France*, purchased from Mr J. Levin, 1942
Chapman, Max 1911–1999, *Emersion to Brown*, purchased from the Molton Gallery, under the terms of the Calouste Gulbenkian Foundation Grant, 1964
Charlton, John 1849–1917, *British Artillery Entering the Enemy's Lines at Tel-el-Kebir, Egypt, 13 September 1882*, purchased from Mr John Charlton, 1885, on long-term loan to the Royal School of Artillery, Larkhill, Salisbury
Cheese, Bernard b.1925, *The 'Crissie Griggie'*, purchased from the Art Exhibitions Bureau, 1957, © the artist
Christoforou, John b.1921, *Head of a Woman*, gift from the Contemporary Art Society, 1962, © ADAGP, Paris and DACS, London 2008
Clarke, Harry Harvey 1869–1948, *The Coming of Autumn*, gift from the Holbrook Trust, Trustees of the William S. Holbrook Bequest, 1909
Clausen, George 1852–1944, *High Mass at a Fishing Village on the Zuyder Zee, Holland*, bequeathed by the executors of the estate of Mr Henry Hirsch, 1906, © Clausen estate
Clausen, George 1852–1944, *Still Life*, purchased from the Fine Art Society, 1958, © Clausen estate
Clayton, William J. M. active 1963–1991, *Time to Remember*, gift from Councillor L. Whitehouse, 1965
Cleve, Joos van (follower of) c.1464–c.1540, *Virgin and Child with St Joseph*, gift from Sir Kenneth A. Muir Mackenzie, 1910
Clint, George 1770–1854, *Coast Scene with Figures and Boats*, bequeathed by Mr Henry Lammin, 1890
Codde, Pieter Jacobsz. (attributed to) 1599–1678, *The Music Party*, bequeathed by Mr Richard Godson Millns, 1904
Cole, George Vicat 1833–1893, *The Summons to Surrender (An Incident in the Spanish Armada)*, gift from Colonel Sir Charles Seely, 1898
Colkett, Samuel David 1806–1863, *Old Mill at Norwich, Norfolk*, bequeathed by Mr Henry Lammin, 1890
Colkett, Samuel David 1806–1863, *River Scene (Trees and Figures)*, bequeathed by Mr Henry Lammin, 1890
Collier, Herbert Hood 1863–1947, *The Miner*, purchased from the Nottingham Society of Artists exhibition, 1945
Collins, Charles Allston 1828–1873, *William Collins (1788–1847)*, bequeathed by Mr Richard Godson Millns, 1904
Collins, William 1788–1847, *Seascape with Figures and Dog, Sunset*, bequeathed by Mr Richard Godson Millns, 1904
Collins, William 1788–1847, *Taking out the Thorn*, bequeathed by Mr Richard Godson Millns, 1904
Collins, William 1788–1847, *The Withered Tree*, bequeathed by Mr Richard Godson Millns, 1904
Collinson, James 1825–1881, *For Sale*, purchased from Sotheby's, via Messrs Thomas Agnew & Sons Ltd, London, 1959
Collinson, James 1825–1881, *Landscape with a Windmill, St Malo, France*, purchased from Mr A. M. Poxon, Esq., 1953
Constable, John (after) 1776–1837, *On the Stour near East Bergholt, Suffolk*, gift from Mr James Orrock, 1909
Constable, John (style of) 1776–1837, *On the Stour*, gift from Mr James Orrock, 1909
Constant, Jean Joseph Benjamin 1845–1902, *Dr John Chapman (1822–1894)*, gift from Mr H. B. Matthews, 1932
Cooke, Anthony R. b.1933, *Weeds and Stones, Shoreham-by-Sea, West Sussex*, purchased from a student's exhibition at the Royal Academy School, 1959
Cooke, Ernest Owen 1862–1937, *May Blossom*, bequeathed by the Holbrook Trust, Trustees of the William S. Holbrook Bequest, 1911
Cooper, Frederick Carter c.1795–1875, *Henry Kirke White (1785–1806)*, gift from Mr R. L. Walker, 1928
Cooper, Gerald 1898–1975, *Flower Piece*, purchased from the artist, via a Royal Academy exhibition, 1944
Cooper, Thomas Sidney 1803–1902, *Goats and Kids in a Shed*, bequeathed by Mr Richard Godson Millns, 1904
Cooper, Thomas Sidney 1803–1902, *Mountain Sheep (Morning Mist Clearing Off)*, bequeathed by Mr Richard Godson Millns, 1904
Cooper, Thomas Sidney 1803–1902, *Repose in the Meadows*, gift from Mrs Eric Snell and Helena K. Mackness, 1941
Cooper, Thomas Sidney 1803–1902, *Afternoon in the Meadows*, gift from Miss Helen Shipstone, 1933
Cooper, Thomas Sidney 1803–1902, *Cattle in Landscape, Evening*, bequeathed by Mr Richard Godson Millns, 1904
Corbould, Edward Henry 1815–1905, *Edmund John Niemann (1813–1876)*, bequeathed by Mr Richard Godson Millns, 1904

Cort, Hendrik Frans de 1742–1810, *Wollaton Hall, Nottingham*, purchased from Bonfiglioli Ltd with the assistance of the Victoria and Albert Museum Purchase Grant, 1967
Cort, Hendrik Frans de 1742–1810, *Wollaton Hall Park, Nottingham*, purchased from Messrs Thomas Agnew & Sons, 1957
Cortona, Pietro da (after) 1596–1669, *The Birth of the Virgin*, gift from Miss Helen Shipstone, 1933
Couldery, Horatio Henri 1832–1910, *An Oyster Supper*, gift from Charles T. Jacoby, 1882
Cox, Alfred Wilson 1820–1890, *Henry Pelham-Clinton (1811–1864), 5th Duke of Newcastle-under-Lyne*, gift from Mr George J. Hine, 1899
Critz, John de the elder (attributed to) 1551/1552–1642, *Portrait of a Lady Called 'Countess of Nottingham' (c.1547–1603) (Catherine Carey)*, gift from Mr Frederick W. Dobson, JP, 1923
Crome, John 1768–1821, *Trees by a Brook (The Willow Tree, a Horseman and a Woman on a Road)*, purchased with the assistance of the National Art Collections Fund, via the Ernest E. Cook Bequest, 1955
Crome, William Henry 1806–1873, *Landscape with Trees and Sheep*, bequeathed by Mr Henry Lammin, 1890
Crome, William Henry 1806–1873, *River Scene with Boats*, bequeathed by Mr Henry Lammin, 1890
Crowley, Graham b.1950, *Deadly Detached I*, purchased from the Ed Totah Gallery with the assistance of the Museums, Libraries and Archives Council/Victoria and Albert Museum Purchase Grant Fund, 1989, © courtesy of Beaux Arts
Cubley, William Harold 1814–1896, *Twilight on the Trent*, gift from Dr H. J. Spencer, Esq., 1914
Culbert, Bill b.1935, *Tower Bridge*, purchased with the assistance of a Gulbenkian Grant from the University of Nottingham Art Department, bought under the terms of the Calouste Gulbenkian Foundation Grant, 1966, © the artist
Culbert, Bill b.1935, *Mediate*, purchased with the assistance of a Gulbenkian Grant from the University of Nottingham Art Department, bought under the terms of the Calouste Gulbenkian Foundation Grant, 1966, © the artist
Cundall, Charles Ernest 1890–1971, *Waterloo Bridge, London*, purchased from the artist, via a Royal Academy exhibition, 1944, © the artist's estate/www.bridgeman.co.uk
Cundall, Charles Ernest 1890–1971, *The Church of St-Germain-des-Prés, Paris, France*, purchased from Messrs Pease, 1943, © the artist's estate/www.bridgeman.co.uk
Daniels, Alfred b.1924, *Town Square of Assisi, Italy*, gift from the Contemporary Art Society, 1959, © the artist
Davie, Alan b.1920, *Bouquet for Couquet*, purchased from Christie, Manson and Woods, 1966, © the artist
Davis, Noel Denholm 1876–1950, *Nottingham Goose Fair*, gift from Mrs F. G. Blythen, 1957
Davis, Noel Denholm 1876–1950, *Lois Ball, Sister of Albert Ball, VC* (later Mrs Anderson), gift from Mrs Cynthia Morris, 1985
Davis, Noel Denholm 1876–1950, *The Casket*, gift from the Trustees of the William S. Holbrook Bequest, 1924
Davis, Noel Denholm 1876–1950, *Alderman F. R. Radford*, unknown provenance
Davis, Noel Denholm 1876–1950, *W. A. Spalding*, bequeathed by Denis Burington Spalding, 1986
Davis, Noel Denholm 1876–1950, *Albert Ball, JP, Mayor of Nottingham (1909–1910)*, unknown provenance
Davis, Noel Denholm 1876–1950, *Edward P. Day, Master of Bingham Public Elementary School*, gift from Bingham Library, via Mrs Margaret Beeby, 1993
Davis, Noel Denholm 1876–1950, *General William Booth (1829–1912), Founder of the Salvation Army*, gift from an anonymous source, via the artist, 1924
Davis, Noel Denholm 1876–1950, *Sir John T. McCraith, JP*, unknown provenance
Davis, Noel Denholm 1876–1950, *Study for 'Captain Albert Ball (1896–1917), VC'*, gift from County Councillor H. M. Woolley, 1962
Davis, Noel Denholm 1876–1950, *W. A. Spalding*, bequeathed by Denis Burington Spalding, 1986
Davis, Noel Denholm 1876–1950, *W. H. Hurcomb*, bequeathed by Mrs M. E. Pearson, 1967
Dawson, Alfred b.1843, *Nuthall Temple, Nottinghamshire*, purchased from Mrs D. M. Williams, 1949
Dawson, Henry 1811–1878, *Nottingham from Wilford Grove*, purchased from David Fisher, 1994
Dawson, Henry 1811–1878, *The Major Oak*, purchased from Max de Beer, 1946
Dawson, Henry 1811–1878, *The Carrier's Wagon*, gift from Mr James Orrock, 1909
Dawson, Henry 1811–1878, *Stormy Weather near Ambleside, Cumbria*, bequeathed by Samuel William Oscroft, 1924
Dawson, Henry 1811–1878, *Nottingham Castle (King Charles I Raising His Standard, 24 August 1642)*, purchased from Mrs Clara Colls, 1912
Dawson, Henry 1811–1878, *A Derbyshire Dale*, gift from the family of the late Mrs E. M. Day, 1940
Dawson, Henry 1811–1878, *Landscape in the Dukeries, Nottinghamshire*, purchased from the Shepherd Bros, 1904
Dawson, Henry 1811–1878, *Coast Scene, Sunset*, gift from Mr James Orrock, 1909
Dawson, Henry 1811–1878, *The King's Mill, Castle Donington, Leicestershire*
Dawson, Henry 1811–1878, *Sunshine and Showers*, bequeathed by Samuel William Oscroft, 1924
Dawson, Henry 1811–1878, *Landscape*, gift from Sir George Hill, Director of the British Museum, 1934
Dawson, Henry 1811–1878, *Nottingham Castle on Fire, 10 October 1831*, gift from Mr J. A. Preston, 1875–1876
Dawson, Henry 1811–1878, *On the Tiber, Italy*, gift from the YMCA, Nottingham, 1945
Dawson, Henry 1811–1878, *Self Portrait*, purchased from Mr S. Clifford, 1909
Dawson, Henry 1811–1878, *The River Trent at Wilford*, purchased from Neale & Son Auctioneers, 1938
De Karlowska, Stanislawa 1876–1952, *Imperial Hotel, Russell Square, London*, gift from the artist's children, Mr Robert Alexander Polhill Bevan and Mrs E. H. Baty, 1968, © the artist's estate/www.bridgeman.co.uk
Deacon, Peter b.1945, *Eclypse 2*, purchased, 1975
Delacroix, Eugène 1798–1863, *Tam O'Shanter* (after the poem by Robert Burns), purchased from Sotheby's with the assistance of the Museums, Libraries and Archives Council/Victoria and Albert Museum Purchase Grant Fund, 1980
Detaille, Jean Baptiste Edouard 1848–1912, *Seated Male Nude*, gift from Nottingham College of Art and Crafts, via the Principal A. H. Rodway, 1941
Dobson, Henry John 1858–1928, *Burn's Grace*, bequeathed by Mr George Thomas Nelson, 1926
Dodd, Charles Tattershall I 1815–1878, *Conway Castle, North Wales*, bequeathed by Mr Henry Lammin, 1890
Dollman, John Charles 1851–1934, *Friends in Adversity, Christmas Day at the Dreadnought Hospital, Greenwich (Coming Down to Dinner)*, purchased from the artist, possibly via Mr C. B. Cox, 1882
Dossi, Dosso c.1486–1542, *The Christ Child Learning to Walk (Presentation in the Temple)*, gift from Sir Kenneth A. Muir Mackenzie, 1910
Dugdale, Thomas Cantrell 1880–1952, *George Harry Wallis*, purchased from the artist, 1930, © Joanna Dunham
Dunlop, Ronald Ossory 1894–1973, *Strand-on-the-Green, Chiswick, London*, purchased from Miss Winifred Broadhead, 1939
Dunlop, Ronald Ossory 1894–1973, *Walberswick, Suffolk*, purchased from Miss Winifred Broadhead, 1939
Dupont, Gainsborough 1754–1797, *Henry Fiennes Pelham Clinton (1750–1778), Earl of Lincoln*, gift from Her Majesty's Government through the Acceptance in Lieu Scheme, 1982
Dutch School 17th C, *River Scene with Boat*, bequeathed by Mrs Fanny Peach, 1907
Dyce, William 1806–1864, *Virgin and Child*, gift from Sir Kenneth A. Muir Mackenzie, 1910
Dyck, Anthony van (after) 1599–1641, *Charles I (1600–1649)*, purchased from Messrs Leggatt Bros, 1952
Dyck, Anthony van (after) 1599–1641, *Charles I (1600–1649), in Armour Wearing the Order of the Thistle*, gift from Mr J. Henry Jacoby, 1899
Dyck, Anthony van (after) 1599–1641, *The Converion of Saul*, gift from Mr Alfred Heald, Philadelphia, USA, 1911
Dyck, Anthony van (attributed to) 1599–1641, *Queen Henrietta Maria (1609–1669)*, bequeathed by Cecil Roberts, on loan from Nottingham Central Library, 2004
East, Alfred 1844–1913, *The Shepherd's Walk, Windermere, Cumbria*, purchased from Shepherd Bros in the Milburn sale, 1909
Edwards, Edwin 1823–1879, *Boscastle Harbour, Cornwall*, gift from Mrs E. Ruth Edwards, 1905
Edwards, Edwin 1823–1879, *St Mary's, Scilly Isles*, gift from Mrs E. Ruth Edwards, 1905
Edwards, Edwin 1823–1879, *The Pond, Kempton, Middlesex*, gift from Mrs E. Ruth Edwards, 1905
Edwards, Edwin 1823–1879, *Under the Willows, Sunbury-on-Thames, Middlesex*, gift from Mrs E. Ruth Edwards, 1905
Eisenhut, Ferencz 1857–1903, *An Oriental School*, gift from Mrs N. Hill, 1932
Ellis, Edwin 1841–1895, *Young Anglers*, gift from Captain Fletcher, 1946
Ellis, Edwin 1841–1895, *After Three Days Gale*, purchased from Mrs M. E. Fox, 1897
Ellis, Edwin 1841–1895, *Coast Scene*, gift from the executors of the estate of Miss Helen Shipstone, 1934
Ellis, Edwin 1841–1895, *Chrysanthemums*, gift from Mrs E. L. Manning, 1914
Ellis, Edwin 1841–1895, *Circe* (recto), purchased from Neale & Son Auctioneers, 1938
Ellis, Edwin 1841–1895, *Boats on the Sand* (verso), purchased from Neale & Son Auctioneers, 1938
Ellis, Edwin 1841–1895, *Fisherfolk*, purchased from Mr George F. W. Ellis, 1945
Ellis, Edwin 1841–1895, *The Lobster Pots*, purchased from Mr George F. W. Ellis, 1945
Ellis, Edwin 1841–1895, *Unloading the Catch*, gift from Captain Fletcher, 1946
Elmore, Alfred 1815–1881, *The Origin of the Stocking Loom*, purchased from Mr A. C. P. Coggan, 1940
Elmore, Alfred 1815–1881, *The Origin of the Combing Machine*, bequeathed by Percy Sampson, 1968
Elwell, Frederick William 1870–1958, *An Interior of a Barn*, purchased from the artist, via a Royal Academy exhibition, 1944
Enfield, Henry 1849–1911, *Nærøyfjord, Norway*, bequeathed by the Holbrook Trust, Trustees of the William S. Holbrook Bequest, 1902
Etty, William 1787–1849, *The Mourner*, bequeathed by Mr Richard Godson Millns, 1904
Etty, William 1787–1849, *A Jew's Head*, bequeathed by Mr Richard Godson Millns, 1904
Etty, William 1787–1849, *Study of a Half-Nude Figure*, bequeathed by Mr Richard Godson Millns, 1904
Etty, William 1787–1849, *The Doves*, gift from Mr James Orrock, 1909
Eurich, Richard Ernst 1903–1992, *The Mummers*, purchased from the Redfern Gallery, 1952, © the artist's estate/www.bridgeman.co.uk
Eurich, Richard Ernst 1903–1992, *Men of Straw*, purchased from the artist, via the Royal Academy of Arts, 1958, © the artist's estate/www.bridgeman.co.uk
Evans, Merlyn Oliver 1910–1973, *Crucifixion*, purchased, 1952
Farmer, Walter 1870–1947, *The Stockinger*, bequeathed by the Holbrook Trust, Trustees of the William S. Holbrook Bequest, 1911
Farquharson, David 1839–1907, *A Break in the Storm, Glen Lyon, Perthshire, Scotland*, gift from Frederick Acton, Esq., 1930
Farquharson, Joseph 1846–1935, *The Winding Dee*, purchased from the Philo L. Mills Sale, 1906
Ferg, Franz de Paula 1689–1740, *Landscape with Baggage Wagon*, bequeathed by Mr Richard Godson Millns, 1904
Ferg, Franz de Paula 1689–1740, *Landscape with Figures and Ruins*, bequeathed by Mr Richard Godson Millns, 1904
Ferrari, Defendente 1480–1485–c.1540, *St John the Baptist in the Wilderness* (recto), gift from Sir Kenneth A. Muir Mackenzie, 1910
Ferrari, Defendente 1480–1485–c.1540, *St Gregory in His Study* (verso), gift from Sir Kenneth A.

Muir Mackenzie, 1910
Firth, John H. S. 1912–c.1970, *Orange Groves*, gift from Mr Hugh Mountney, 1985
Firth, John H. S. 1912–c.1970, *Deir Suneid, near Gaza, Palestine*, gift from Mr Hugh Mountney, 1985
Firth, John H. S. 1912–c.1970, *Inside New Gate, Jerusalem, Palestine*, gift from Mr Hugh Mountney, 1985
Firth, John H. S. 1912–c.1970, *Postscript, Tobruk Harbour, Libya, April 1941*, gift from Mr Hugh Mountney, 1985
Firth, John H. S. 1912–c.1970, *Scuola Benito Mussolini, Tobruk, Libya*, gift from Mr Hugh Mountney, 1985
Firth, John H. S. 1912–c.1970, *The South Downs*, gift from Mr Hugh Mountney, 1985
Firth, John H. S. 1912–c.1970, *Drying Nets, Gaza, Palestine*, gift from Mr Hugh Mountney, 1985
Firth, John H. S. 1912–c.1970, *Gaza Pier, Palestine*, gift from Mr Hugh Mountney, 1985
Firth, John H. S. 1912–c.1970, *Landscape*, gift from Mr Hugh Mountney, 1985
Firth, John H. S. 1912–c.1970, *Boat and Sails No.1**, gift from Mr Hugh Mountney, 1985
Firth, John H. S. 1912–c.1970, *Boat and Sails No.2**, gift from Mr Hugh Mountney, 1985
Firth, John H. S. 1912–c.1970, *Lincoln (?)*, gift from Mr Hugh Mountney, 1985
Firth, John H. S. 1912–c.1970, *Street Scene**, gift from Mr Hugh Mountney, 1985
Firth, John H. S. 1912–c.1970, *Zifteh, Egypt, 1947*, gift from Mr Hugh Mountney, 1985
Fischer, Hans 1849–1886, *Autumn View of Møns Cliff, Denmark*, bequeathed by R. Wilkinson-Smith, 1908
Fisk, William Henry 1827–1884, *Love and War* (detail), gift from the Nottingham Arts Society, via G. H. Wallis and W. H. Fisk, 1884
Fitton, James 1899–1982, *The Painter's Wife*, purchased from the Royal Academy of Arts, 1955, © the artist's estate
Flemish School 17th C, *Hawking Party*, bequeathed by Mr Henry Lammin, 1890
Fletcher, John Henry active 1880–1922, *Nottingham Canal, London Road Bridge (Nottingham Canal, Carrington Street Bridge)*, gift from Mr W. Kiddier, 1920
Fletcher, William Teulon Blandford 1858–1936, *Sacrament Sunday*, gift from the artist's widow, Mrs W. T. B. Fletcher, 1944
Fletcher, William Teulon Blandford 1858–1936, *Bletchworth Quarry, Seen from Lower Lane Cottages, Dorking, Surrey*, gift from the artist's widow, Mrs W. T. B. Fletcher, 1950
Forbes, Stanhope Alexander 1857–1947, *Florence*, on long-term loan from a private collection, 1935, © the artist's estate/www.bridgeman.co.uk
Forbes, Stanhope Alexander 1857–1947, *The Artist in His Studio*, on long-term loan from a private collection, 1935, © the artist's estate/www.bridgeman.co.uk
Forbes-Robertson, Janine active 1908–1912, *Cecilia*, gift from the Contemporary Art Society, 1946
Foster, Herbert Wilson 1846–1929, *The Belgian Model*, gift from Nottingham College of Art and Crafts, via the Principal A. H. Rodway, 1941
Foster, Herbert Wilson 1846–1929, *The Seated Model*, gift from Nottingham College of Art and Crafts, via the Principal A. H. Rodway, 1942
Fraser, Donald Hamilton b.1929, *Still Life with Cherries*, gift from the Contemporary Art Society, 1956, © Donald Hamilton Fraser
Freckleton, Harry 1890–1979, *Boats*, gift from the Holbrook Trust, Trustees of the William S. Holbrook Bequest, 1953
Freedman, Barnett 1901–1958, *Sicilian Puppets*, gift from the Contemporary Art Society, 1935, © V. C. Freedman and descendants
French School 19th C, *Portrait of a Young Man*, bequeathed by the executors of the estate of Lieutenant-Colonel F. Rayner, 1946
Frith, William Powell 1819–1909, *The Invalid*, purchased from Reverend Thomas R. Griffin, 1942
Frost, William Edward 1810–1877, *Classical Subject (Venus, Cupid and Psyche)*, gift from Mr James Orrock, 1909
Gainsborough, Thomas (style of) 1727–1788, *A Cottage Girl*, bequeathed by Mr Henry Lammin, 1890
Gardner, Daniel 1750–1805, *Mrs Gwynne and Mrs Bunbury as the Merry Wives of Windsor*, bequeathed by Mr Richard Godson Millns, 1904
Gentileschi, Artemisia (attributed to) 1593–1651/1653, *Susannah and the Elders*, gift from Leon H. Willson, 1964
German School 16th C, *St Jerome*, gift from Sir Kenneth A. Muir Mackenzie, 1910
Gertler, Mark 1892–1939, *Head of a Boy*, gift from the Contemporary Art Society, 1938, © by permission of Luke Gertler
Gertler, Mark 1892–1939, *Bouquet and Sunshade*, bequeathed by Thomas Balston, via the National Art Collections Fund, 1968, © by permission of Luke Gertler
Gibbs, Evelyn 1905–1991, *Clarendon Street with Tall Trees*, gift from Pauline M. Lucas, Trustee of Sir Hugh Willatt, 1998, © the artist's estate
Gibbs, Evelyn 1905–1991, *The Nottingham Window*, gift from Pauline M. Lucas, Trustee of Sir Hugh Willatt, 1998, © the artist's estate
Gibbs, Evelyn 1905–1991, *Female Nude*, purchased from the artist, 1951, © the artist's estate
Gibbs, Evelyn 1905–1991, *Industrial View*, gift from Pauline M. Lucas, Trustee of Sir Hugh Willatt, 1998, © the artist's estate
Gillies, Margaret 1803–1887, *William Howitt (1792–1879), and Mary Howitt (1799–1888)*, gift from Miss Margaret Howitt, daughter of William and Mary Howitt, 1897
Gillott, Thomas J. 1886–1913, *A Country Fair*, bequeathed by the Holbrook Trust, Trustees of the William S. Holbrook Bequest, 1911
Gillott, Thomas J. 1886–1913, *Life Class*, gift from the Nottingham College of Art and Crafts, via the Principal A. H. Rodway, 1941
Girardot, Ernest Gustave 1840–1904, *Mr Joseph Pettifor*, bequeathed by Miss Pettifor, 1907
Glover, John 1767–1849, *Chepstow Castle, Monmouthshire*, gift from Mr James Ward, 1897
Gogin, Charles 1844–1931, *Groombridge Hall, Kent*, gift from the artist's widow, Mrs Alma Gogin, 1944
Gogin, Charles 1844–1931, *Julia*, gift from the artist's widow, Mrs Alma Gogin, 1944
Gogin, Charles 1844–1931, *Leeks*, gift from the artist's widow, Mrs Alma Gogin, 1931
Good, Thomas Sword 1789–1872, *Self Portrait*, bequeathed by Mr Richard Godson Millns, 1904
Good, Thomas Sword 1789–1872, *Shore Scene with Figures*, bequeathed by Mr Richard Godson Millns, 1904
Goodacre, William 1803–1883, *Nottingham Market Place*, purchased from Neales Auctioneers with the assistance of the Museums, Libraries and Archives Council/Victoria and Albert Museum Purchase Grant Fund, 1996
Goodall, Frederick 1822–1904, *The Distaff Worker*, gift from Mr F. H. Alton, 1925
Gorski, Stefan b.1932, *Crayfish*, purchased from the artist, 1962
Gorski, Stefan b.1932, *Birdman*, purchased from the artist, via Yorak Sottyorick, 1966
Gowing, Lawrence 1918–1991, *Green Apples on a Bamboo Table*, gift from the Contemporary Art Society, 1944, © estate of Sir Lawrence Gowing
Gowing, Lawrence 1918–1991, *Ilse Magdalene R.*, purchased from the Leicester Galleries, 1955, © estate of Sir Lawrence Gowing
Gratia, Charles-Louis 1815–1911, *Self Portrait*, bequeathed by Mr Richard Godson Millns, 1904
Greaves, Leonard 1918–1949, *The Worth Bodice*, gift from the Contemporary Art Society, 1952
Green, Kenneth 1905–1986, *Chelsea Garden under Snow (The Black Spider)*, purchased from the artist, via a Royal Academy exhibition, 1942, © the artist's estate
Gush, William 1813–1888, *John Heathcoat (1783–1861), Inventor of the Bobbin Net Machine*, gift from Miss Heathcoat, 1879
Hackaert, Jan 1629–1699, *Landscape with Figures, a Horse and a Dog*, gift from Dr H. Mary Browning, 1953
Hackaert, Jan 1629–1699, *Landscape with Figures in the Foreground*, gift from Dr H. Mary Browning, 1953
Halledine, G. H. active 20th C, *The Lodge, Wollaton Park, Nottingham*, purchased from Henry Spencer & Sons, 1966
Hals, Dirck 1591–1656, *A Dutch Party*, gift from Sir Kenneth A. Muir Mackenzie, 1910
Hamilton, William 1751–1801, *The Nut-Gatherers*, bequeathed by Mr Richard Godson Millns, 1904
Hamilton, William 1751–1801, *The Watercress-Gatherers*, bequeathed by Mr Richard Godson Millns, 1904
Hart, James Turpin 1835–1899, *The Launch*, purchased from Mr C. Tagent, 1907
Hart, James Turpin 1835–1899, *The Golden Bough*, bequeathed by Samuel William Oscroft, 1924
Hart, James Turpin 1835–1899, *Samuel William Oscroft (1834–1924)*, bequeathed by Samuel William Oscroft, 1924
Hart, James Turpin 1835–1899, *Nottingham Forest and Windmill*, purchased from Neales Auctioneers, 1989
Hart, John 1921–1996, *Dylan*, purchased from the Midland Group Gallery, 1954
Hartley, Alfred 1855–1933, *Alderman Sir John Turney, Kt*, gift from the Nottingham Corporation, 1889
Hartley, Alfred 1855–1933, *Morning, Teme Dale*, purchased from Alfred (?) Hartley, 1909
Harvey, William 1796–1866, *Cottages at Olney, Buckinghamshire*, bequeathed by Mr Richard Godson Millns, 1904
Harvey, William 1796–1866, *The Lime Walk at Weston, Buckinghamshire*, bequeathed by Mr Richard Godson Millns, 1904
Harvey, William 1796–1866, *The Residence of Hayley, Eartham, Sussex*, bequeathed by Mr Richard Godson Millns, 1904
Harvey, William 1796–1866, *The Wilderness at Weston, Buckinghamshire, with Pope's Monument*, bequeathed by Mr Richard Godson Millns, 1904
Haweis, Stephen 1878–1969, *Versailles, France*, gift from Mrs George Sheringham, the artist's widow, 1939
Hawksley, Arthur 1842–1915, *Driving up to Milk*, gift from Mrs Arthur Hawksley, 1916
Hawksley, Arthur 1842–1915, *An Old Posting Yard, Surrey*, gift from Mrs Arthur Hawksley, 1916
Hawksley, Arthur 1842–1915, *Near Sunningdale, Berkshire*, gift from Mrs Arthur Hawksley, 1916
Hayes, Edwin 1819–1904, *Boats in a Gale off Ostend, Belgium*, purchased from the executors of the estate of Mr R. Wilkinson Smith, 1908
Hayes, Edwin 1819–1904, *Brig Drifting Ashore off Bamborough, Northumberland (Bamborough Castle, Northumberland with a Wreck)*, purchased from the executors of the estate of Mr R. Wilkinson Smith, 1908
Hayes, Frederick William 1848–1918, *Lighthouse Rock, Llanddwyn, North Wales*, gift from the artist's widow, Mrs Frederick William Hayes, via her son Mr Gerald R. Hayes, 1920
Hayes, Frederick William 1848–1918, *Pool in Colwyn, North Wales*, gift from the artist's widow, via Mrs Frederick William Hayes, via her son Mr Gerald R. Hayes, 1920
Hayllar, James 1829–1920, *The Old Master*, purchased from the artist, 1885
Hayllar, James 1829–1920, *The Invalid*, gift from Mr P. N. Gunsaker, 1968
Head, Guy (attributed to) 1753–1800, *Juno Borrowing the Girdle of Venus*, gift from Mr William Bradshaw, 1894
Heaphy, Thomas (after) 1775–1835, *William Howitt (1792–1879)*, gift from Mr A. A. Watts, Esq., 1890
Hedderly, Nick b.1961, *Nottingham, Late Afternoon*, purchased from the artist, 2006, © the artist
Heemskerck, Egbert van the elder 1634/1635–1704, *Interior of a Tavern with Smokers*, bequeathed by Mr Richard Godson Millns, 1904
Hempton, Paul b.1946, *Retreat*, purchased from the artist, 1973, © the artist
Henson, Edward c.1852–after 1891, *J. Thompson*, gift from Mrs Sidney Maria Cartwright
Herbert, John Rogers 1810–1890, *Lear and Cordelia*, on long-term loan from Miss Herbert
Herring, John Frederick I 1795–1865, *Feeding the Horses (Horses, Figures and Poultry)*, purchased from the executors of the estate of Sir Thomas Shipstone, 1941
Herring, John Frederick I 1795–1865, *Horses in a Paddock*, gift from Miss S. Fisher, 1945
Herring, John Frederick II 1815–1907, *Ready for the Plough*, bequeathed by Mrs Sadie Margaret Griffin, 1990
Hill, Robert W. 1932–1990, *Chipping Ongar, Essex*, purchased from the Royal Academy of Arts, 1958
Hillier, Tristram Paul 1905–1983,

Almeria, Spain, purchased from Messrs Arthur Tooth & Sons Ltd, 1952, © the artist's estate
Hilton, William II 1786–1839, *Jonathan and Mary Walker of Ferham*, bequeathed by Miss Elizabeth Beatson, 1937, on long-term loan to the Rotherham Museum, South Yorkshire
Himona, Nicolas 1865–1929, *Byron's Monument at Missolonghi, Greece*, gift from the Duke of Portland, 1924
Hitchens, Ivon 1893–1979, *A River Pool*, purchased from Messrs Ernest Brown & Phillips Ltd, 1957, © Ivon Hitchens' estate/Jonathan Clark & Co.
Hitchens, Ivon 1893–1979, *Twelve Exercises on a Theme (Daffodils and Lilies, No.2)*, purchased from the Art Exhibitions Bureau, 1953, © Ivon Hitchens' estate/Jonathan Clark & Co.
Holland, James 1800–1870, *View in Venice, Italy*, gift from Mr James Orrock, 1909
Holland, John c.1805–1880, *Before the Race (Nottingham Races)*, gift from the Duke of Portland, 1917
Holland, John c.1805–1880, *Holiday Time (Fair Day)*, purchased from Mr Maurice Dodd, 1946
Holland, John c.1805–1880, *View in Sherwood Forest (Sherwood Forest, Nottinghamshire)*, gift from Mr James Ward, 1902
Holland, John c.1805–1880, *Wilford Ferry, Nottingham (The Cherry-Eatings)*, purchased from Mr George W. Keep, 1913
Hollins, John 1798–1855, *Portrait of a Lady as St Cecilia*, gift from Mrs Robert Holland, 1882
Hondecoeter, Gillis Claesz. de c.1575–1638, *River Scene*, gift from Charles T. Jacoby, 1901
Hondecoeter, Melchior de 1636–1695, *Fowl*, bequeathed by Mr Richard Godson Millns, 1904
Hondecoeter, Melchior de 1636–1695, *Two Fowls and Ducks on a Pond*, bequeathed by Mrs Elizabeth Holbrooke, 1939
Hook, James Clarke 1819–1907, *Hearts of Oak*, purchased from Christie's through the sale of the property of George McCullough, 1913
Hoppner, John 1758–1810, *Henry Kirke White (1758–1810)*, gift from Mr Watson Fothergill, 1884
Horemans, Pieter Jacob 1700–1776, *Interior, Card Playing*, bequeathed by Mr Richard Godson Millns, 1904
Horemans, Pieter Jacob 1700–1776, *Interior, Figures Smoking*, bequeathed by Mr Richard Godson Millns, 1904
Horsley, John Callcott 1817–1903, *Youth and Age*, purchased, 1934
Houthuesen, Albert Anthony 1903–1979, *A Shell and Flowers*, purchased from the artist, 1944, © reproduced by permission of the trustees of the Albert Houthuesen Trust
Howson, Peter b.1958, *Bosnian Harvest*, purchased from Flowers East Gallery with the assistance of the Museums and Galleries Commission and the Victoria and Albert Museum Purchase Grant Fund, 1995, © the artist
Hughes-Stanton, Herbert Edwin Pelham 1870–1937, *Fields in Surrey*, gift from Miss Helen Shipstone, 1933
Hulbert, Thelma 1913–1995, *Leaves and Red Gauze Screen*, purchased from the Redfern Gallery by means of a fund created with the assistance of the Calouste Gulbenkian Foundation Grant, 1966
Huskinson, Leonard 1905–1974, *The Little Marquess*, purchased from the artist, 1936
Ibbetson, Julius Caesar 1759–1817, *Landscape, Beeston Castle, Cheshire, and Rainbow*, bequeathed by Mr Richard Godson Millns, 1904
Italian (Florentine) School *Madonna and Child*, gift from Sir Kenneth A. Muir Mackenzie, 1910
Italian (Milanese) School 17th C, *A Bishop*, purchased from Dr Llewellyn Davies, 1944
Jagger, David 1891–1958, *Jewish Refugee, Vienna*, purchased from the artist, 1945, © the artist's estate
James, Robert 1809–1853, *Boys Playing Duckstones*, gift from Mrs D. Foster, 1946
Jay, William Samuel 1843–1933, *At the Fall of Leaf, Arundel Park, Sussex (Woodland Scene in Autumn)*, purchased from the artist, 1885
Jobbins, William H. c.1840–1893, *The Fish Market, Venice, Italy*, purchased from Neale & Son Auctioneers, from the sale of the property of William Windle, 1907
John, Augustus Edwin 1878–1961, *Yvonne*, purchased from Messrs Arthur Tooth & Sons Ltd, 1952, © the artist's estate/www.bridgeman.co.uk
Johnson, Ernest Borough 1866–1949, *Posthumous Portrait of Sir Hubert von Herkomer (1849–1914)*, gift from Mr Frank Burton, 1942
Jones, George 1786–1869, *Andernach, Prussia*, gift from Mrs George Jones, 1882
Jones, George 1786–1869, *Edinburgh Castle from the Grass Market, Scotland*, gift from Mrs George Jones, 1882
Jones, George 1786–1869, *Napoleon Leaving the Field of Waterloo, 18 June 1815*, gift from Mrs George Jones, 1882
Jones, George 1786–1869, *Street Scene in Frankfurt, Germany*, gift from Mrs George Jones, 1882
Jones, George 1786–1869, *View in Nuremberg, Germany*, gift from Mrs George Jones, 1882
Jones, George 1786–1869, *View in Rome, Italy, the Forum of Nerva*, gift from Mrs George Jones, 1882
Kauffman, Angelica (after) 1740–1807, *Maria*, bequeathed by Mr Richard Godson Millns, 1904
Keyser, Willem de (after) c.1647–1692, *St Jerome*, gift from Miss E. M. Bond, 1940
Kiddier, William 1859–1934, *The Dyke*, gift from Mr Cecil Roberts, 1922
Kiddier, William 1859–1934, *Snowbound Windmill*, bequeathed by the artist's daughter, Miss Alice Kiddier, care of Lloyd's Bank, 1969
Kiddier, William 1859–1934, *The Scarecrow*, bequeathed by the artist's daughter, Miss Alice Kiddier, 1958
Kiddier, William 1859–1934, *St Crispin*, purchased from the executors of the estate of Miss Alice Kiddier, 1969
Kiddier, William 1859–1934, *The West Wind*, unknown provenance
Knapp, Stefan 1921–1996, *Untitled*, purchased, 1964
Kneale, Bryan b.1930, *Charles Laughton (1899–1962)*, purchased from the Royal Academy of Arts, 1959, © the artist
Kneller, Godfrey 1646–1723, *Lady Jane Jackson (d.1731)*, gift from Miss Helen Shipstone, 1933
Kneller, Godfrey (school of) 1646–1723, *Lady with a Dog and a Parrot*, bequeathed by Mrs H. R. Savidge, 1967
Kneller, Godfrey (school of) 1646–1723, *Ralph Edge (1689–1766)*, bequeathed by Miss Emily Mary Edge, 1978
Knight, Harold 1874–1961, *Standing Male Nude*, gift from the Nottingham College of Art and Crafts, via the Principal A. H. Rodway, 1941, © reproduced with permission of the estate of Dame Laura Knight, DBE, RA, 2008. All rights reserved
Knight, Harold 1874–1961, *Girl in a White Dress*, gift from the Nottingham College of Art and Crafts, via the Principal A. H. Rodway, 1941, © reproduced with permission of the estate of Dame Laura Knight, DBE, RA, 2008. All rights reserved
Knight, Harold 1874–1961, *Girl with a Red Bow*, gift from the Nottingham College of Art and Crafts, via the Principal A. H. Rodway, 1941, © reproduced with permission of the estate of Dame Laura Knight, DBE, RA, 2008. All rights reserved
Knight, Harold 1874–1961, *Standing Male Nude*, gift from the Nottingham College of Art and Crafts, via the Principal A. H. Rodway, 1941, © reproduced with permission of the estate of Dame Laura Knight, DBE, RA, 2008. All rights reserved
Knight, Harold 1874–1961, *Standing Male Nude*, gift from the Nottingham College of Art and Crafts, via the Principal A. H. Rodway, 1941, © reproduced with permission of the estate of Dame Laura Knight, DBE, RA, 2008. All rights reserved
Knight, Harold 1874–1961, *Standing Male Nude*, gift from Nottingham College of Art and Crafts, via Principal A. H. Rodway, 1941, © reproduced with permission of the estate of Dame Laura Knight, DBE, RA, 2008. All rights reserved
Knight, Harold 1874–1961, *The Last Coble*, gift from the Holbrook Trust, Trustees of the William S. Holbrook Bequest, 1902, © reproduced with permission of the estate of Dame Laura Knight, DBE, RA, 2008. All rights reserved
Knight, Harold 1874–1961, *Wellington James Thompson*, gift from Mrs Rosamond Ellen Fraser, 1992, © reproduced with permission of the estate of Dame Laura Knight, DBE, RA, 2008. All rights reserved
Knight, Harold 1874–1961, *Mrs Rosamond Edith Thompson*, gift from Mrs Rosamond Ellen Fraser, 1992, © reproduced with permission of the estate of Dame Laura Knight, DBE, RA, 2008. All rights reserved
Knight, Harold 1874–1961, *The Manicure*, purchased from the artist, 1934, © reproduced with permission of the estate of Dame Laura Knight, DBE, RA, 2008. All rights reserved
Knight, Harold 1874–1961, *William Kiddier (1859–1934)*, bequeathed by Miss Alice Kiddier, 1969
Knight, Harold 1874–1961, *Ethel Bartlett, Pianist*, purchased from the artist, 1954, © Nottingham City Museums and Galleries
Knight, Harold 1874–1961, *St Ives Bay, Cornwall*, purchased from Mr C. F. K. Smith, 1936, © reproduced with permission of the estate of Dame Laura Knight, DBE, RA, 2008. All rights reserved
Knight, John Prescott 1803–1881, *James Duffield Harding (1798–1863)*, bequeathed by Mr Richard Godson Millns, 1904
Knight, Laura 1877–1970, *Idylls of the King (Pelleas and Ettare)* (1 of 6), purchased with the assistance of the Heritage Lottery Fund and the Museums, Libraries and Archives Council/Victoria and Albert Museum Purchase Grant Fund, 2008, © reproduced with permission of the estate of Dame Laura Knight, DBE, RA, 2008. All rights reserved
Knight, Laura 1877–1970, *Idylls of the King (Enid and Geraint)* (2 of 6), purchased with the assistance of the Heritage Lottery Fund and the Museums, Libraries and Archives Council/Victoria and Albert Museum Purchase Grant Fund, 2008, © reproduced with permission of the estate of Dame Laura Knight, DBE, RA, 2008. All rights reserved
Knight, Laura 1877–1970, *Idylls of the King (Balin and Balan, i)* (3 of 6), purchased with the assistance of the Heritage Lottery Fund and the Museums, Libraries and Archives Council/Victoria and Albert Museum Purchase Grant Fund, 2008, © reproduced with permission of the estate of Dame Laura Knight, DBE, RA, 2008. All rights reserved
Knight, Laura 1877–1970, *Idylls of the King (Balin and Balan, ii)* (4 of 6), purchased with the assistance of the Heritage Lottery Fund and the Museums, Libraries and Archives Council/Victoria and Albert Museum Purchase Grant Fund, 2008, © reproduced with permission of the estate of Dame Laura Knight, DBE, RA, 2008. All rights reserved
Knight, Laura 1877–1970, *Tree, Idylls of the King* (left panel) (5 of 6), purchased with the assistance of the Heritage Lottery Fund and the Museums, Libraries and Archives Council/Victoria and Albert Museum Purchase Grant Fund, 2008, © reproduced with permission of the estate of Dame Laura Knight, DBE, RA, 2008. All rights reserved
Knight, Laura 1877–1970, *Tree, Idylls of the King* (right panel) (6 of 6), purchased with the assistance of the Heritage Lottery Fund and the Museums, Libraries and Archives Council/Victoria and Albert Museum Purchase Grant Fund, 2008, © reproduced with permission of the estate of Dame Laura Knight, DBE, RA, 2008. All rights reserved
Knight, Laura 1877–1970, *Motherhood*, purchased from Messrs William Marchant & Co, 1923, © Nottingham City Museums and Galleries
Knight, Laura 1877–1970, *Elsie on 'Hassan'*, purchased from Ernest Brown & Phillips, Leicester Galleries, 1930, © Nottingham City Museums and Galleries
Knight, Laura 1877–1970, *Miss Thompson (Miss Patricia Thompson)*, purchased from Mrs Eva Spence, 2005, © reproduced with permission of the estate of Dame Laura Knight, DBE, RA, 2008. All rights reserved
Knight, Laura 1877–1970, *Fine Feathers*, purchased from the artist, 1949
La Thangue, Henry Herbert 1859–1929, *A Mission to Seamen*, purchased from the artist, 1893
La Thangue, Henry Herbert 1859–1929, *Gathering Oranges*, bequeathed by the artist's widow, Mrs K. La Thangue, 1941
La Thangue, Henry Herbert 1859–1929, *A Provençal Castle*, bequeathed by the artist's widow, Mrs K. La Thangue, 1941
La Thangue, Henry Herbert 1859–1929, *The Mulberry Tree*, bequeathed by the artist's widow, Mrs K. La Thangue, 1941

Labad, Alberto b.1940, *Nude*, gift from R. L. Beckett, Esq., 1965, © the artist
Lambert, George (style of) c.1700–1765, *Nottingham from the South*, purchased from William Darby, New Bond Street, London, with the assitance of the Victoria and Albert Museum Purchase Grant Fund, 1973
Landseer, Edwin Henry 1802–1873, *The Honourable Mrs Norton*, gift from the Duke of Albans to the Nottingham Art School, gift to Nottingham Castle Museum and Art Gallery, 1941
Landseer, Edwin Henry 1802–1873, *Deer in a Landscape (Studies of Deer)*, bequeathed by Miss Ada Percy, via J. C. Irving, Esq., 1939
Largillière, Nicolas de 1656–1746, *Jan Siberechts (1627–c.1703)*, gift from Miss F. M. Cameron, 1939
Le Brun, Charles 1619–1690, *Hercules Vanquishing Diomedes*, gift from Colonel C. J. Wright, 1893
Le Brun, Christopher b.1951, *Painting*, gift from the Contemporary Art Society from the Nancy Bafour Bequest, 2007, © the artist
Leavers, Lucy Ann 1845–1915, *Busy Bodies and Busy Bees*, gift from Alderman John Renals, JP, 1892
Leavers, Lucy Ann 1845–1915, *An Anxious Moment*, gift from Mr Mornington Cannon in memory of his wife Nelley Gray, daughter of the late Alderman Bennet of Nottingham, 1927
Lee, Frederick Richard 1798–1879, *Market Cart at a Brook*, bequeathed by Mr Richard Godson Millns, 1904
Lee-Hankey, William 1869–1952, *Napoleon Danelle, Antiquaire*, gift from the artist's widow Mrs Edith Lee-Hankey, 1954
Lelienbergh, Cornelis 1626–1676, *Dead Game*, bequeathed by Mr Richard Godson Millns, 1904
Lennox Gordon, Archie b.c.1889, *Nottingham Castle Gateway*, gift from the artist's son, Mr R. Lennox Gordon, Esq., 1967
Lethière, Guillaume 1760–1832, *Homer Singing His Iliad at the Gate of Athens*, purchased from Mrs M. G. Grissell, 1884
Leverett, David b.1938, *Inroads*, purchased from an exhibition at the Redfern Gallery with the assistance the Calouste Gulbenkian Foundation Grant, 1968
Lewis, George Robert 1782–1871, *Thomas Paul Sandby, RA*, bequeathed by Lady Fanny E. J. Rich, 1945
Lewis, George Robert 1782–1871, *Thomas Paul Sandby, RA*, bequeathed by Lady Fanny E. J. Rich, 1945
Lewis, Neville 1895–1972, *Girl's Head*, gift from the Contemporary Art Society, 1927, © the artist's estate
Lewis, Neville 1895–1972, *The Zulu*, gift from the Contemporary Art Society, 1940, © the artist's estate
Lingelbach, Johannes 1622–1674, *A Village Festival, Peasants Merrymaking Outside an Inn*, bequeathed by Mr Richard Godson Millns, 1904
Linnell, John 1792–1882, *Harvesting*, gift from Miss Helen Shipstone, 1933
Linton, James Dromgole 1840–1916, *The Banquet*, purchased from the sale of the property of Charles Jacoby, 1911
Long, John Kenneth b.1924, *Derelict Pier, Swanage, Dorset*, purchased from the artist, 1959
Lonsdale, James 1777–1839, *The Chess Players*, bequeathed by Mr Richard Godson Millns, 1904
Lopez, Gasparo 1650–1732, *Flower Piece*, bequeathed by Mrs Sadie Margaret Griffin, 1990
Lopez, Gasparo 1650–1732, *Flower Piece*, bequeathed by Mrs Sadie Margaret Griffin, 1990
Lorimer, John Henry 1856–1936, *Sir Samuel George Johnson (1831–1909), Kt*, gift from an anonymous subscriber, 1893
Loutherbourg, Philip James de 1740–1812, *View of Snowdon with the Castle of Dolbadarn from Llanberis, North Wales*, bequeathed by Mr Richard Godson Millns, 1904
Lowe, Arthur 1866–1940, *Autumn*, purchased from Mrs A. Lowe, 1940
Lowe, Arthur 1866–1940, *Snow*, purchased from Mrs A. Lowe, 1940
Lowry, Laurence Stephen 1887–1976, *The Arrest*, purchased from Messrs Alex Reid & Lefevre, Lefevre Gallery, 1952, © courtesy of the estate of L. S. Lowry
Lowry, Laurence Stephen 1887–1976, *Industrial Panorama*, purchased from Messrs Alex Reid & Lefevre at the Lefevre Gallery, 1953, © courtesy of the estate of L. S. Lowry
Loxton Knight, Edward 1905–1993, *Salcombe, Devon*, purchased from the Brook Street Art Gallery, London, 1934
Loxton Knight, Edward 1905–1993, *Spring Morning near Bristol*, purchased from the Brook Street Art Galleries, 1938
Lucy, Charles 1814–1873, *The Right Honourable William E. Gladstone (1809–1898), MP*, bequeathed by W. J. Ward, 1978
Luntley, James 1827–1887, *William Parsons, Mayor of Nottingham (1863–1864)*, gift from Mr F. W. Parsons, JP, 1889
MacBryde, Robert 1913–1966, *Still Life, Autumn*, purchased with the aid of the Contemporary Art Society, 1956
MacCallum, Andrew 1821–1902, *Major Oak, Sherwood Forest, Nottinghamshire*, gift from the artist, 1885
MacCallum, Andrew 1821–1902, *The Blasted Tree*, purchased from Geoffrey H. Dixon, Esq., 1966
MacCallum, Andrew 1821–1902, *The Opening Scene in Philip James Bailey's 'Festus'*, gift from the artist, 1901
MacDougall, William Brown 1869–1936, *Toot Mill, Toot Hill, Essex*, gift from Miss Agnes Watson, 1937
Maclise, Daniel 1806–1870, *Robin Hood and His Merry Men Entertaining Richard the Lionheart in Sherwood Forest*, purchased from the Gavin Graham Gallery with the assistance of the Museums, Libraries and Archives Council/ Victoria and Albert Museum Purchase Grant Fund, 1984
Malbon, William 1805–1877, *Joseph Fenton with His Family on the Meadows, Nottingham*, purchased from Neales Auctioneers with the assistance of the Museums, Libraries and Archives Council/Victoria and Albert Museum Purchase Grant Fund, 1989
Malbon, William 1805–1877, *Farmyard Scene*, gift from Mrs E. Renals, 1901
Malbon, William 1805–1877, *Village Market Scene*, gift from Mrs E. Renals, 1901
Mann, Alexander 1853–1908, *Findhorn Backwater, Moray Firth, Scotland*, purchased from the Alexander Mann Exhibition, 1909
Mann, Harrington 1864–1936, *Cottage Interior*, unknown provenance
Martinez, Raymond b.1937, *Blue Sentinel*, purchased from Alex Reid & Lefevre Ltd with the assistance of the Calouste Gulbenkian Foundation, 1964, © the artist
Martin-Richards, Marjorie active 1959, *Jungfrau, Switzerland, Dawn*, gift from the artist, 1959
Mason, Bateson 1910–1977, *Sleeping Fishermen*, purchased from the Contemporary Art Society, via the Grundy Art Gallery, Blackpool, 1954
Master of the Antwerp Adoration (attributed to) active c.1520, *The Rest on the Flight into Egypt (Virgin, Child and St Joseph in a Landscape)*, gift from Sir Kenneth A. Muir Mackenzie, 1910
Maurice, Constance *Still Life (Vegetables)*, gift from the Contemporary Art Society, 1931
Meninsky, Bernard 1891–1950, *Still Life with Yellow Bowl and Fruit*, gift from the Contemporary Art Society, 1940, © the artist's estate
Meninsky, Bernard 1891–1950, *Still Life with Apples*, gift from the Contemporary Art Society, 1927, © the artist's estate
Michie, James Coutts 1861–1919, *A Marshland Farm*, gift from Mrs J. Coutts Michie, 1924
Middleditch, Edward 1923–1987, *Boscastle, Cornwall*, purchased from the Royal Academy of Arts, 1956, © the estate of Edward Middleditch, courtesy James Hyman Gallery, London
Miles, George Francis 1852–1891, *Salmon Leap, Cenarth Falls, Cardiganshire, Wales*, gift from Miss E. M. Davy, 1919
Miller, William 1796–1882, *Mr Fisher*, bequeathed by Miss G. M. Fisher-Gilsthorpe, 1968
Milroy, Lisa b.1959, *Mailbag*, gift from the Contemporary Art Society, 1989, © Lisa Milroy
Mitchell, John Campbell 1865–1922, *The Argyllshire Moor, Scotland, Sunset*, gift from Mr A. E. Anderson, via the National Art Collections Fund, 1923
Mitchell, John Campbell 1865–1922, *Wind and Rain*, gift from Mr A. E. Anderson, via the National Art Collections Fund, 1923
Molenaer, Klaes c.1630–1676, *River Scene with Boats and Figures*, bequeathed by Mr Richard Godson Millns, 1905
Molenaer, Klaes c.1630–1676, *Winter Scene, River with Figures Skating*, bequeathed by Mr Richard Godson Millns, 1904
Monamy, Peter 1681–1749, *Three English Men-of-War Getting Underway in a Fresh Breeze (Sea Piece)*, gift from Miss C. L. Buckle, executrix for Miss Broadhurst's estate, 1923
Monnoyer, Jean-Baptiste 1636–1699, *Flower Piece*, gift from the Nottingham College of Art and Crafts, via the Principal A. H. Rodway, 1941
Monnoyer, Jean-Baptiste 1636–1699, *Flowers in a Basket*, bequeathed by Mrs Sadie Margaret Griffin, 1990
Moore, Claude Thomas Stanfield 1853–1901, *The Evening of Trafalgar*, gift from Mr F. R. Pickerill, 1914
Moore, Claude Thomas Stanfield 1853–1901, *The Pool of the Thames, over London's Silent Highway*, purchased from the Holbrook Trust, Trustees of the William S. Holbrook Bequest, 1901
Moore, Claude Thomas Stanfield 1853–1901, *Torchlight Tattoo of Robin Hood Rifles, Nottingham Market Place, 1896*, purchased from Mr Henry C. Hall, 1967
Moore, Thomas Cooper 1827–1901, *Mills and Gorse Bushes in Nottingham Forest*, purchased from Neales Auctioneers, 1985
Moore, Thomas Cooper 1827–1901, *The Old Ropewalk, Foot of the Gallows Hill, Nottingham Forest*, purchased from Neales Auctioneers, 1985
Moore, Thomas Cooper 1827–1901, *Sheep Lane, Nottingham*, anonymous gift, 1960
Morland, George 1763–1804, *The Sportsman Resting*, bequeathed by Mr Richard Godson Millns, 1904
Morland, George 1763–1804, *The Wreckers*, bequeathed by Mr Richard Godson Millns, 1904
Morland, George 1763–1804, *The Artist in His Studio and His Man Gibbs*, bequeathed by Mr Richard Godson Millns, 1904
Morland, George 1763–1804, *Gypsy Encampment*, gift from Mr James Orrock, 1909
Morland, George 1763–1804, *Landscape with Figures*, bequeathed by Mr Richard Godson Millns, 1904
Morland, George 1763–1804, *Landscape with Four Horses*, bequeathed by Mr Richard Godson Millns, 1904
Morland, George 1763–1804, *Landscape with Horses, Cart and Figures*, bequeathed by Mr Richard Godson Millns, 1904
Morland, George 1763–1804, *Study of Pigs*, bequeathed by Mr Richard Godson Millns, 1904
Morland, George 1763–1804, *Two Horses in the Snow*, bequeathed by Mr Richard Godson Millns, 1904
Morland, George 1763–1804, *Two Pigs in Straw (Barn with Pigs)*, bequeathed by Mr Richard Godson Millns, 1904
Morland, George 1763–1804, *Woman, Child and Dog on a Road*, bequeathed by Mr Richard Godson Millns, 1904
Morland, Henry Robert c.1716–1797, *George Morland (1763–1804)*, bequeathed by Mr Richard Godson Millns, 1904
Morley, Henry 1869–1937, *Hauling Timber, Stirlingshire, Scotland*, gift from Henry Morley, 1936
Mortlock, Ethel c.1865–1928, *The Right Honourable Robert Lowe (1811–1892), Viscount Sherbrook*, gift from Mrs G. Chaworth Musters, 1880
Mulready, William (follower of) 1786–1863, *A Rustic Youth*, gift from Mr James H. Bingham, 1945
Mulready, William (follower of) 1786–1863, *An Old Man in a Smock*, gift from Mr James H. Bingham, 1945
Murray, David 1849–1933, *Long After, Corfe Castle, Dorset*, gift from Mrs J. Coutts Michie, via Dolman & Sons, 1913
Murray, David 1849–1933, *The Tithe Barns*, gift from Sir Edwin Cooper, RA, Trustee to the late Sir David Murray, RA, 1939
Mytens, Daniel I (studio of) c.1590–before 1648, *Lord Howard of Effingham (1536–1624), 1st Earl of Nottingham*, purchased from Lady Lucas, 1952
Neeffs, Peeter the elder c.1578–1656-1661 & **Vrancx, Sebastian** 1573–1647 *Antwerp Cathedral*, bequeathed by Mr Richard Godson Millns, 1904
Neer, Aert van der (imitator of) 1603–1677, *River Scene with Boats and Figures*, bequeathed by Mr Richard Godson Millns, via Bourlet & Sons, London, 1904
Neer, Eglon Hendrik van der 1634–1703, *Two Boys with a Bird*

(The Birdcatchers), bequeathed by Mr Richard Godson Millns, 1904
Neuhuys, Albertus Johan 1844–1914, *Maternal Love (Sorrow)*, gift from Miss Helen Shipstone, 1932
Nevinson, Christopher 1889–1946, *Thameside*, purchased from the artist, via the Council for the Enlargement of Music and the Arts exhibition, 1941, © the artist's estate/www.bridgeman.co.uk
Newling, Edward active 1890–1934, *Captain Albert Ball (1896–1917), VC, DSO*, gift from Alderman Albert Ball, JP, 1922
Newton, Alfred Pizzey 1830–1883, *The Salmon Pool (Salmon Pool on the Spean, Scotland)*, gift from Miss E. M. Davy, 1919
Newton, Algernon Cecil 1880–1968, *Regent's Canal, Maida Vale, London*, purchased from the artist, via a Royal Academy exhibition, 1942
Nicholson, Ben 1894–1982, *Bistre II*, gift from Alderman Ernest Archibald and J. P. Braddock, 1940, © Angela Verren Taunt 2008. All rights reserved, DACS
Nicholson, William 1872–1949, *The Windmill, Brighton Downs (Brighton Downs, Rottingdean)*, purchased from the Leger Galleries, through J. Leger & Son, 1957, © Elizabeth Banks
Nicholson, William 1872–1949, *Miss Wish Wynne (1882–1931), Actress, in the Character of Janet Cannot for the Play 'The Great Adventure'*, gift from Miss Helen Shipstone, 1933, © Elizabeth Banks
Nicholson, William 1872–1949, *The Viceroy's Orderly (Ruftadur Valayar Shah)*, purchased from Roland, Browse and Delbanco, 1953, © Elizabeth Banks
Nicholson, William 1872–1949, *The Cornfield*, purchased from Roland, Browse and Delbanco, 1949, © Elizabeth Banks
Nicholson, William 1872–1949, *Mushrooms*, purchased from the Beaux Arts Galleries, via Major S. Lessore, 1933, © Elizabeth Banks
Nicholson, William 1872–1949, *William Harold Cubley (1814–1896)*, gift from Miss J. A. Cubley, 1922, © Elizabeth Banks
Nicholson, William 1872–1949, *William Kiddier (1859–1934)*, bequeathed by Miss Alice Kiddier, 1969, © Elizabeth Banks
Nicholson, Winifred 1893–1981, *Violas in a Window*, gift from the Contemporary Art Society, 1949, © trustees of Winifred Nicholson
Niemann, Edmund John 1813–1876, *Arundel Castle, West Sussex, and Stream*, bequeathed by Mr Richard Godson Millns, 1904
Niemann, Edmund John 1813–1876, *Deer Stalking in the Highlands, a Quiet Shot*, bequeathed by Mr Edward Cope, JP, 1897
Niemann, Edmund John 1813–1876, *Town and Vale of Ffestiniog, Wales*, bequeathed by Sir James Alfred Jacoby, via Messrs Wells & Hind, 1910
Niemann, Edmund John 1813–1876, *View of Richmond, Yorkshire (Richmond Hall, Yorkshire)*, gift from Mr J. H. Bingham, 1938
Noble, Richard Pratchett c.1814–1892, *William Strover Birkin, Aged 19*, purchased from Ernest A. Spinks, 1968
Norton, A. *Carriages*, unknown provenance
Oakes, John Wright 1820–1887, *The Mouth of the River Derwent*, gift from the sons of the late Mr W. M. Rook, 1920
Oakes, John Wright 1820–1887, *A Sandy Bit of Road*, gift from Sir George Hill, 1934
Oakes, John Wright 1820–1887, *The Coming Shower*, purchased from the sale of the property of William Goddard, 1908
O'Connor, James Arthur 1791–1841, *The Edge of a Forest, Storm Coming On*, bequeathed by Mr Richard Godson Millns, 1904
Odekerken, Willem van (attributed to) d.1677, *An Old Man with Broken Eggs*, bequeathed by Mr Richard Godson Millns, 1904
O'Neil, Henry Nelson 1817–1880, *William Powell Frith (1819–1909)*, bequeathed by Mr Richard Godson Millns, 1904
Opie, John (attributed to) 1761–1807, *Girl with a Cat*, bequeathed by Mr Richard Godson Millns, 1904
Orchardson, William Quiller 1832–1910, *Self Portrait*, bequeathed by Mr Richard Godson Millns, 1904
Ouless, Walter William 1848–1933, *Colonel Sir Charles Seely (1859–1926)*, gift from a Nottingham Corporation, 1897
Ouwater, Isaak 1748–1793, *Back of Nieuwe Kerk and Town Hall, Amsterdam, Holland*, bequeathed by Mr Richard Godson Millns, 1904
Pace del Campidoglio, Michele 1610–probably 1670, *Still Life*, gift from L. J. and J. Levin, 1942
Pacsano, Enrico active early 19th C, *Military Encampment*, gift from Mrs Harpham, 1966
Pagliei, Gioacchino 1852–1896, *The Naiads*, purchased from Abraham Dixon, 1885
Palamedesz., Anthonie 1601–1673, *Merry Company (Interior with Cavaliers and Ladies)*, bequeathed by Mr Richard Godson Millns, 1904
Palma, Jacopo il giovane (after) 1544/1548–1628, *The Raising of Lazarus*, gift from Sir Kenneth A. Muir Mackenzie, 1910
Parrott, Samuel 1797–1876, *Dovedale (Spires of Dovedale, Derbyshire)*, gift from Mr P. B. Fleet, Esq., 1910
Partridge, Maurice William 1913–1973, *Salthouses, Norfolk*, purchased, 1967
Pasmore, Victor 1908–1998, *Green Landscape with Gate*, gift from the Contemporary Art Society, 1952, © Victor Pasmore estate
Pasmore, Victor 1908–1998, *Maquette for Metamorphosis Mural*, gift from the Contemporary Art Society in memory of Nancy Balfour, 2000, © Victor Pasmore estate
Paulden, C. H. *Dorothy Vernon House*, gift from the Thoroton Society, 1931
Payne, William c.1760–after 1830, *Self Portrait*, bequeathed by Mr Richard Godson Millns, 1904
Peake, Mervyn 1911–1968, *Head of an Old Man*, gift from the Contemporary Art Society, 1949, © the artist's estate
Pelham, Thomas Kent c.1831–1907, *A Mountain Lassie (Girl with a Water Pot)*, purchased, 1934
Percy, Sidney Richard 1821–1886, *The Fern Gatherers*, gift from the executors of the estate of Miss Helen Shipstone, 1933
Phillip, John 1817–1867, *Water-Carrier of Seville*, bequeathed by Mr Richard Godson Millns, 1904
Phillip, John 1817–1867, *A Lady with a Guitar*, bequeathed by Mr Richard Godson Millns, 1904
Phillips, Thomas 1770–1845, *Portrait of an Unknown Man* (possibly the poet John Keats or the painter Richard Parkes Bonington), gift from Mr F. W. Dobson, 1926
Philpot, Glyn Warren 1884–1937, *Richard the Lionheart Embarks on the Third Crusade*, purchased from the artist's sister, Miss Daisy Philpot, 1949
Pickard, Louise 1865–1928, *A Gloucestershire Village*, gift from the Contemporary Art Society, 1924
Pickering, Henry c.1720–c.1775, *Sir Wolstan Dixie (1700–1767), 4th Bt, Market Bosworth*, purchased from Lady Dixie, 1953
Pickering, Henry (attributed to) c.1720–c.1775, *Miss Dixie*, gift from Mr J. Henry Jacoby, 1894
Pickering, Henry (imitator of) c.1720–c.1775, *Lady Dixie*, purchased from Sir Wolston Dixie, 1970
Piper, John 1903–1992, *Brittany Coast, France*, purchased from Marlborough Fine Art Ltd, 1964, © the artist's estate
Pott, Laslett John 1837–1898, *Mary, Queen of Scots, Being Led to Her Execution*, purchased from the Shepherd Bros, 1898
Pott, Laslett John 1837–1898, *Lord Byron (1788–1824)*, gift from Mr T. J. Birkin, Esq., 1903
Pott, Laslett John 1837–1898, *The Dancing Lesson*, gift from the artist's daughter, Mrs Katherine Prichard, 1939
Pott, Laslett John 1837–1898, *The Sundial*, gift from the artist's daughter, Mrs Katherine Prichard, 1939
Pott, Laslett John 1837–1898, *The Trysting Place*, gift from the artist's daughter, Mrs Katherine Prichard, 1939
Power, John Joseph Wardell 1881–1943, *Music*, gift from the Contemporary Art Society, 1928
Price, Caroline Mary active 1830, *View of the Castle Gateway, Nottingham*, gift from Mr John Storer Beveridge, 1911
Price, Edward 1800–1885, *Norway*, bequeathed by Miss K. M. W. Hoe, 1973
Pryde, James 1866–1941, *Self Portrait as 'Scarron'*, purchased from Christie, Manson & Woods, 1966
Pynacker, Adam c.1620–1673, *Landscape with a Winding Roadway*, gift from Mr John Henry Walter, 1894
Pynacker, Adam c.1620–1673, *Mountainous Landscape with Peasants, Cows and Goats*, bequeathed by Mr Richard Godson Millns, 1904
Ranken, William Bruce Ellis 1881–1941, *Hibiscus Flower*, gift from the artist's sister, Mrs Ernest Thesiger, 1946
Ranken, William Bruce Ellis 1881–1941, *Cinerarias*, purchased from the artist's sister, Mrs Ernest Thesiger, 1946
Redgate, Arthur W. 1860–1906, *Trespassers*, bequeathed by the Holbrook Trust, Trustees of the William S. Holbrook Bequest, 1910
Redgate, Arthur W. 1860–1906, *Front View of Wollaton Hall, Nottingham, with Horse and Carriage**, unknown provenance
Redgate, Arthur W. 1860–1906, *Grove Farm, Lenton, Nottingham*, purchased from Mrs D. Stevens, 1936
Redgate, Arthur W. 1860–1906, *Loading the Harvest Wagon*, gift from Captain Fletcher, 1946
Redgate, Arthur W. 1860–1906, *Near Betws-y-Coed, North Wales*, gift from Captain Fletcher, 1946
Redgate, Sylvanus 1827–1907, *William Felkin (1795–1874)*, bequeathed by Mrs Laura Felkin, 1964
Redgate, Sylvanus 1827–1907, *Alderman William George Ward*, purchased from the artist, 1880
Redgate, Sylvanus 1827–1907, *39, Long Row, the Market Place, Nottingham*, gift from Mr Edwin E. Tew, 1925
Redgate, Sylvanus 1827–1907, *Major Jonathan White (b.1804), RHR (The Old Adjutant)*, purchased from the artist, 1883
Redgate, Sylvanus 1827–1907, *Alderman J. Burton*, gift from Mrs Burton, 1933
Redgate, Sylvanus 1827–1907, *Henry Dawson (1811–1878)*, gift from Mr William Bradshaw, 1901
Redgate, Sylvanus 1827–1907, *Josiah Gilbert*, purchased, 1902
Reynolds, Alan b.1926, *Evening, Just before Spring*, purchased from the Redfern Gallery, 1954, © the artist
Reynolds, Alan b.1926, *Sunset*, purchased from the Leicester Galleries, 1958, © the artist
Richmond, George 1809–1896, *Tom Allom (1804–1872)*, bequeathed by Mr Richard Godson Millns, 1904
Ritzberger, Albert 1853–1915, *Love's Oracle*, bequeathed by Henry Clark, 1908
Riviere, Briton 1840–1920, *An Old World Wanderer*, anonymous gift via Professor Frank Clowes, University of Nottingham Department of Chemistry, 1903
Roberts, Henry Benjamin 1831–1915, *Homeless*, gift from the family of the late Mr William Winter Lewis, 1924
Roberts, William Patrick 1895–1980, *The Return of Ulysses*, gift from the Contemporary Art Society, 1954, © William Roberts Society
Roberts, William Patrick 1895–1980, *Professor Janko Lavrin (1885–1986)*, gift from John Lavrin, 1986, © William Roberts Society
Roe, Clarence 1850–1909, *A Mountain Stream*, bequeathed by Mr Henry Lammin, 1890
Roos, Philipp Peter 1657–1706, *Landscape with Shepherd, Sheep and Dog*, gift from Mr Frederick Chatfield Smith, MP, 1880
Rossetti, Dante Gabriel 1828–1882, *Marigolds (The Bower Maiden, Fleur-de-Marie)*, purchased from Edward J. H. Cross, 1956
Rowe, Tom Trythall 1856–1940, *Evening Glow*, gift from the Holbrook Trust, Trustees of the William S. Holbrook Bequest, 1909
Saan, P. de *Interior, Figures at a Table, Singing*, bequeathed by Mr Richard Godson Millns, 1904
Sailmaker, Isaac c.1633–1721, *HMS 'Swiftsure'*, bequeathed by Mr Henry Lammin, 1890
Sandby, Paul 1731–1809, *Bayswater Road, London, near the Old Temple Gate (Bayswater Road at the Turnpike Gate)*, bequeathed by Mr William Arnold Sandby, via Messrs Last & Goodford, 1905
Sandby, Paul (attributed to) 1731–1809, *View of Nottingham Castle with St Nicholas' Church and Houses*, gift from the Duke of Newcastle,1888
Schneider, Hermann 1847–1918, *Portrait of a Child*, gift from Sir Arthur Black, Kt, 1937
Schwanfelder, Charles Henry 1774–1837, *Mountainous Landscape with River, Bridge and Cottages*, bequeathed by Mr Harry Lammin, 1890
Senff, Carl Adolf 1785–1863, *Virgin and Child*, gift from Sir Kenneth A. Muir Mackenzie, 1910
Shackleton, William 1872–1933, *Study for 'The Harvesters'*, gift from the artist's widow, Mrs May Shackleton, 1938

Shackleton, William 1872–1933, *Highland Raiders*, gift from the artist's widow, Mrs May Shackleton, 1938
Shackleton, William 1872–1933, *Study of a Man Holding a Cock for 'Highland Raiders'*, gift from the artist's widow, Mrs May Shackleton, 1938
Shackleton, William 1872–1933, *Study for 'Highland Raiders'*, gift from the artist's widow, Mrs May Shackleton, 1938
Shackleton, William 1872–1933, *Study for 'Highland Raiders'*, gift from the artist's widow, Mrs May Shackleton, 1938
Shackleton, William 1872–1933, *Study of a Fowl for 'Highland Raiders'*, gift from the artist's widow, Mrs May Shackleton, 1938
Shackleton, William 1872–1933, *Study of an Arm and a Hand Holding a Fowl by the Legs for 'Highland Raiders'*, gift from the artist's widow, Mrs May Shackleton, 1938
Shalders, George c.1826–1873, *Near Haslemere, Surrey*, bequeathed by Mr H. H. L. Sands, 1936
Shannon, Charles Haslewood 1863–1937, *Tibullus in the House of Delia*, purchased, 1945
Shayer, William 1788–1879, *A Gypsy Encampment*, gift from Mr Frederick John Nettlefold, Esq., 1948
Sheringham, George 1884–1937, *Ipswich Park*, purchased from the artist's widow, Mrs George Sheringham, 1938
Sheringham, George 1884–1937, *Brighton Beach, East Sussex*, purchased from the artist's widow, Mrs George Sheringham, 1938
Sheringham, George 1884–1937, *Fan Design (The Passing of a Viking)*, purchased from the artist's widow, Mrs George Sheringham, 1938
Sheringham, George 1884–1937, *Fruit and Leaves in a Basket*, gift from Clement F. Pitman, 1973
Sheringham, George 1884–1937, *Fruit in a Jade Bowl*, bequeathed by Mr Clement F. Pitman, 1973
Sheringham, George 1884–1937, *Reflections*, purchased from the artist's widow, Mrs George Sheringham, 1938
Shipham, Benjamin 1808–1872, *View at Wilford, Nottingham*
Shipham, Benjamin 1808–1872, *View of the Trent at Wilford, Nottingham*, gift from Mr Duncan S. Hepburn, 1895
Shipham, Benjamin 1808–1872, *Cornfields, Wollaton Hall, Nottingham*, gift from Mrs Sidney Cartwright, 1873–1874
Shipham, Benjamin 1808–1872, *Near Beddgelert, North Wales*, gift from Mrs Sidney Cartwright, 1873–1874
Siberechts, Jan (attributed to) 1627–c.1703, *View of Nottingham from the East*, purchased from Ernest A. Spinks with the assistance of a grant from the National Art Collections Fund, 1977
Sickert, Walter Richard 1860–1942, *Noctes ambrosianae*, purchased from Messrs Arthur Tooth & Sons Ltd, 1952, © estate of Walter R. Sickert/DACS 2008
Sillett, James 1764–1840, *Dock Leaves and Other Flowers*, purchased from the Fine Art Society, 1951
Simi, Filadelfo 1849–1923, *The Flowers of Capri*, bequeathed by Alfred Bradley, via the executors of his estate, 1914
Smart, Rowley 1887–1934, *Miss Muriel Pratt in the Role of Fanny in 'Hindle Wakes'*, gift from Muriel Pratt, via Hunt, Dicking & Willat, 1945
Smirke, Robert 1752–1845, *Illustration to Le Strange's 'Gil Blas'*, bequeathed by Mr Richard Godson Millns, 1904
Smirke, Robert 1752–1845, *Scipio and the Hermit*, bequeathed by Mr Richard Godson Millns, 1904
Smirke, Robert 1752–1845, *The Scandal (The Keepsake)*, bequeathed by Mr Richard Godson Millns, 1904
Smith, George 1829–1901, *A Country Road and Cottage*, bequeathed by Mr Henry Lammin, 1890
Smith, George 1829–1901, *The Dame's School*, bequeathed by Mr Richard Godson Millns, 1904
Smith, Matthew Arnold Bracy 1879–1959, *Still Life with Blue and White Jugs*, purchased from Messrs Arthur Tooth & Sons Ltd, 1952, © by permission of the copyright holder
Smyth, Henry active c.1800–1860, *Old Windmills on Nottingham Forest*, purchased from Mr T. R. Smith, 1920
Smyth, Henry active c.1800–1860, *Nottingham Meadows*, gift from Miss Annie Laurie Gilbert, 1939
Smyth, Henry active c.1800–1860, *Windmills on Nottingham Forest*, gift from Miss Annie Laurie Gilbert, 1939
Southall, Joseph Edward 1861–1944, *Up from the Sea*, gift from W. A. Cadbury, 1930, © reproduced with permission of the Barrow family
Southall, Joseph Edward 1861–1944, *The Return*, bequeathed by Mrs Southall, 1948, © reproduced with permission of the Barrow family
Southall, Joseph Edward 1861–1944, *The Crystal*, bequeathed by Mrs Southall, 1948, © reproduced with permission of the Barrow family
Spear, Ruskin 1911–1990, *Sunday Morning*, purchased from the Contemporary Art Society Exhibition, 1958, © the artist's estate/www.bridgeman.co.uk
Spencelayh, Charles 1865–1958, *His Daily Ration*, purchased from the Royal Academy of Arts, 1947, © the artist's estate/www.bridgeman.co.uk
Spencer, Stanley 1891–1959, *Landscape, Cookham Dean, Berkshire*, purchased from Messrs Arthur Tooth & Sons Ltd, 1939, © estate of Stanley Spencer/ DACS 2008
Spencer, Stanley 1891–1959, *Peonies*, purchased from Messrs Arthur Tooth & Sons Ltd, 1938, © estate of Stanley Spencer/ DACS 2008
Spinello Aretino 1350/1352–1410, *Blessed Gerard of Villamagna and St Mary Magdalen with St Catherine of Alexandria*, bequeathed by Viscountess Galway of Serlby, 1891
Spinello Aretino 1350/1352–1410, *St Louis of Toulouse and St Anthony of Padua with St Stephen*, bequeathed by Viscountess Galway of Serlby, 1891
Spooner, Arthur 1873–1961, *Rubens Arthur Moore (1860–c.1933)*, gift from Mr Brian Heason, 1991
Spooner, Arthur 1873–1961, *Nottingham Old Market Place*, on loan from Sir Harry Djanogly
Spooner, Arthur 1873–1961, *The Goose Fair, Nottingham*, on loan from Sir Harry Djanogly
Spooner, Arthur 1873–1961, *Posthumous Portrait of Alderman E. L. Manning*, purchased from the artist, 1937
Spooner, Arthur 1873–1961, *Newstead Abbey, Nottinghamshire*, purchased from the artist, 1944
Spooner, Arthur 1873–1961, *Tom Pearson (1872–1964), Founder of Pearson's of Nottingham Ltd*, on loan from Pearson Bros Ltd, 1988
Spooner, Arthur 1873–1961, *Apple Fallings*, purchased from Alderman Ernest Archibald Braddock, JP, 1940
Spooner, Arthur 1873–1961, *Lord Mayor and Lady Mayoress Receiving Princess Elizabeth in the Council House Square, 2 April 1946*, purchased from the artist, 1948
Spooner, Arthur 1873–1961, *Newstead Abbey from the East, Nottinghamshire (Eagle Pond, Newstead Abbey)*, purchased from the artist, 1945
Spooner, Arthur 1873–1961, *Newstead Abbey, the Monk's Wood, Nottinghamshire (Newstead Abbey, from the North West)*, purchased from the artist, 1945
Spooner, Arthur 1873–1961, *Pink Roses in a Glass Vase*, bequeathed by Mr Clement F. Pitman, 1973
Spruyt, Johannes 1627/1628–1671, *Cock and Hen with Chickens and Pigeons*, bequeathed by Mrs Elizabeth Holbrooke, 1939
Stark, James 1794–1859, *A Lane near Norwich, Norfolk*, gift from Mr Frederick John Nettlefold, Esq., 1948
Steenwijck, Hendrick van the younger c.1580–1649, *Interior of a Church*, bequeathed by Mr Richard Godson Millns, 1904
Stephenson, Ian 1934–2000, *Diorama II*, gift from the Contemporary Art Society, 1976, © the artist's estate
Stevenson, G. S. active 1830–1887, *Sneinton Hermitage, Nottingham*, purchased from Mr Miles, 1984
Stokes, Marianne 1855–1927, *Childhood's Treasures*, purchased from W. A. Michael, 1896
Stone, Marcus C. 1840–1921, *In Love*, bequeathed by Mr T. E. Beaumont, 1899
Stothard, Thomas 1755–1834, *Portrait of a Child*, gift from Mr Felix Joseph, 1890
Stothard, Thomas 1755–1834, *Portrait of a Young Man*, gift from Mr Felix Joseph, 1890
Stothard, Thomas 1755–1834, *The Tournament*, bequeathed by Mr Richard Godson Millns, 1904
Suddaby, Rowland 1912–1972, *Hedging at Cornard Tye, Suffolk*, purchased from Messrs Ernest Brown & Phillips Ltd, 1950, © the artist's estate
Sullivan, William Holmes 1836–1908, *The Artist Henry Dawson (1811–1878)*, purchased from Mellors & Kirk, 2003
Surtees, John 1819–1915, *On the Dockart, Killin, Perthshire, Scotland*, gift from Misses Jane, Kate and Rosa Wallis, 1916
Swynnerton, Annie Louisa 1844–1933, *Mrs Florence H. Musgrave*, bequeathed by Mrs F. H. Musgrave, 1934
Tayler, Edward 1828–1906, *Self Portrait*, gift from the son of the artist, Mr J. Edward Tayler, Esq., 1913
Taylor, Isaac II 1759–1829, *Josiah Gilbert, Aged 16*, gift from Miss Annie Laurie Gilbert, 1939
Teniers, David II 1610–1690, *Peasant Smoking in an Interior (Flemish Pastimes, Interior)*, bequeathed by Mr Richard Godson Millns, 1904
Teniers, David II 1610–1690, *A Peasant Carrying a Pole*, bequeathed by Mr Richard Godson Millns, 1904
Teniers, David II 1610–1690, *The Sense of Feeling*, bequeathed by Mr Richard Godson Millns, via Bourlet & Sons, London, 1904
Teniers, David II 1610–1690, *Village Scene with Four Peasants*, bequeathed by Mr Richard Godson Millns, 1904
Tennant, John F. 1796–1872, *The Watering Place*, gift from Miss Helen Shipstone, 1933
Thomson, Alfred Reginald 1894–1979, *Harry Wheatcroft (1898–1977), Rose Grower*, purchased from the Royal Academy of Arts, 1957
Titcomb, William Holt Yates 1858–1930, *Old Sea Dogs*, purchased from the artist, 1894
Titian (after) c.1488–1576, *Diana*, gift from Sir Kenneth A. Muir Mackenzie, 1910
Titian (after) c.1488–1576, *Madonna and Child with St Mark*, gift from Sir Kenneth A. Muir Mackenzie, 1910
Titian (after) c.1488–1576, *The Tribute Money*, bequeathed by Mrs Fanny Peach, 1907
Tomson, Arthur 1858–1905, *In the Down Country*, gift from Mrs Arthur Tomson, via John Baillie, Esq., 1907
Tomson, Clifton 1775–1835, *Horses and Dog in a Landscape*, purchased from Mr George Harry Wallis, 1898
Tomson, Clifton 1775–1835, *Carriages, Horses and Dogs*, purchased from Mr Walker, 1893
Towne, Charles 1763–1840, *Landscape with Cattle and Figures*, bequeathed by Mr R. Wallace Walsh, 1887
Townroe, Mary Dakeyne 1849–1941, *Nasturtiums*, gift from the artist, 1938
Toynton, Norman b.1939, *Interior with Object*, purchased from the 56 Group by means of the fund created with the assistance of the Calouste Gulbenkian Foundation Grant, 1969, © the artist
Tuke, Henry Scott 1858–1929, *The Fisherman*, purchased from the artist, 1895
Turner, William 1789–1862, *The Vale of Keswick, Cumbria*, gift from the Holbrook Trust, Trustees of the William S. Holbrook Bequest, 1917
Ugolini, Giuseppe 1826–1897, *Portrait of a Gentleman*, unknown provenance
unknown artist 18th C, *Armoured Woman* (possibly Minerva), unknown provenance
unknown artist *Mr John Burton*, gift from Mrs Bernard Stevenson, 1957
unknown artist *Mrs Hannah Burton*, gift from Mrs Bernard Stevenson, 1957
unknown artist *Portrait of a Lady of the Worthington Family*, bequeathed by Mrs E. Worthington
unknown artist *Portrait of a Lady of the Worthington Family Holding a Holy Bible*, bequeathed by Mrs E. Worthington
unknown artist *Wollaton Hall, Nottingham, from the Lake*, gift from David Benfield, 1988
unknown artist 19th C, *From Colwick Hill, Nottingham*, on long-term loan from Nottingham Public Libraries
unknown artist *Portrait of an Unidentified Gentleman with a Dog and Golf Clubs**, unknown provenance
unknown artist *Christ Crowned with Thorns**, unknown provenance
unknown artist *Head of a Horse*, unknown provenance
unknown artist *Nottingham Castle*, unknown provenance
unknown artist *Portrait of a Gentleman*, unknown provenance

unknown artist *Portrait of a Gentleman*, unknown provenance
unknown artist *Portrait of a Gentleman in a White Cravat*, unknown provenance
unknown artist *Portrait of a Lady in a Frilled Cap*, unknown provenance
unknown artist *Portrait of a Lady with a Ruby Tiara*
unknown artist *Portrait of a Man in a Hat*, unknown provenance
unknown artist *Punch Bowl, Nottingham*, gift from Mrs D. Langham, 1983
unknown artist *The Virgin and Child*, unknown provenance
unknown artist *View of The Council House, Nottingham, from South Parade*, unknown provenance
unknown artist *Windmills*, gift from Mrs Barbara Smith, 1985
Van der Meer, Barend 1659–1702, *Fruit Piece with Dragonfly*, gift from Miss Helen Shipstone, 1933
Van der Meer, Barend 1659–1702, *Fruit Piece with Wine Glass*, gift from Miss Helen Shipstone, 1933
Vaughan, John Keith 1912–1977, *Fourth Assembly of Figures*, purchased from the Matthiesen Gallery Ltd, 1960, © the estate of Keith Vaughan/DACS 2008
Velde, Adriaen van de 1636–1672, *Landscape with Cattle*, gift from Miss C. L. Buckle, executor of the estate of Miss Broadhurst, 1923
Venne, Adriaen van de 1589–1662, *Peasants Fleeing (Witchcraft)*, purchased from Mrs Sybil Fisher, 1961
Verboeckhoven, Eugène Joseph 1799–1881, *The Twins*, bequeathed by Mr Richard Godson Millns, 1904
Verboeckhoven, Eugène Joseph 1799–1881, *Sheep*, gift from the executors of the estate of Miss Helen Shipstone, 1934
Verboeckhoven, Eugène Joseph 1799–1881, *Good Friends*, gift from Lieutenant-Commander and Mrs Mackness, 1946
Verboeckhoven, Eugène Joseph 1799–1881, *The Sheep*, gift from Miss Helen Shipstone, 1932
Verbrugge, Emile 1856–1936, *The Aduatics Passing under the Yoke*, gift from Sir Arthur Black, Kt, 1937
Vertangen, Daniel c.1598–1681/1684, *The Penitent Magdalen in a Landscape*, bequeathed by Mr Richard Godson Millns, 1904
Vickers, Alfred 1786–1868, *Landscape with Cottages*, bequeathed by Mr Henry Lammin, 1890
Vickers, W. active 19th C, *Crossing the Heath, Evening*, bequeathed by Mr Henry Lammin, 1890
Vincent, George 1796–1831, *Sea Piece*, bequeathed by Mr Richard Godson Millns, 1904
Vincent, George 1796–1831, *Landscape with Cottages and Tinker*, bequeathed by Mr Richard Godson Millns, 1904
Vincent, George 1796–1831, *Castle Ashby, Northamptonshire*, bequeathed by Mr Henry Lammin, 1890
Vincent, George 1796–1831, *Landscape with Cattle in a Pool*, bequeathed by Mr Richard Godson Millns, 1904
Vincent, George (attributed to) 1796–1831, *Evening Twilight*, bequeathed by Mr Henry Lammin, 1890
Wadsworth, Edward Alexander 1889–1949, *Satellitium*, purchased Messrs Arthur Tooth & Sons Ltd, 1957, © estate of Edward Wadsworth 2008. All rights reserved, DACS
Walker, John Rawson 1796–1873, *Old Trent Bridge, Nottingham*, purchased from Mr James Ward, 1889
Walker, John Rawson 1796–1873, *Nottingham Castle*, bequeathed by Miss F. Percy, via Messrs Larkeno Company, Newark, Nottinghamshire, 1934
Walker, John Rawson 1796–1873, *Papplewick Dam, Nottinghamshire*, bequeathed by A. Joynes Butler, JP, 1922
Walker, John Rawson 1796–1873, *View from the Nottingham Castle Terrace Looking East*, purchased from Mr Charles Wood, 1904
Walker, John Rawson 1796–1873, *View of Nottingham from Wilford*, gift from Miss H. M. Hopkins, 1913
Walker, John Rawson 1796–1873, *View near Linby, Nottinghamshire*, gift from Miss Locke, 1898
Wallis, George 1811–1891, *The Wilderness*, gift from the children of the artist, 1892
Waplington, Paul b.1938, *Lace Factory*, purchased from the artist, 1987
Ward, Edwin Arthur 1859–1933, *Mrs Morton Jackson*, bequeathed by the artist, 1933
Ward, James 1769–1859, *Landscape with Sheep*, bequeathed by Mr Richard Godson Millns, 1904
Ward, James II 1800–1884, *Bull, Cow and Calf in a Landscape*, bequeathed by Mr Richard Godson Millns, 1904
Ward, James II 1800–1884, *A Dewy Morning (The Duel of the Stags)*, bequeathed by Mr Richard Godson Millns, 1904
Warren, Charles Knighton b.1856, *Felix Joseph (1840–1892)*, gift from Nottingham Corporation, c.1891
Warsop, Frederick c.1835–1895, *Alderman W. G. Ward*, gift from A. Armitage, JP, 1929
Waterlow, Ernest Albert 1850–1919, *The Orphan*, purchased from Christie's from the sale of the property of George McCullock, 1913
Watson, John 1923–1992, *Flower Study, Autumn*, purchased from the Midland Group Gallery, 1954, © the artist's estate
Watts, Frederick William 1800–1870, *The Ford*, gift from Miss Helen Shipstone, 1933
Watts, George Frederick 1817–1904, *The Spirit of Christianity*, bequeathed by the artist, 1904
Webb, James 1825–1895, *Mont Orgueil Castle, Jersey*, bequeathed by Mr Richard Godson Millns, 1904
Weber, Theodor Alexander 1838–1907, *Fishing Boats at Sea*, bequeathed by Mrs John Watson, 1911
Weight, Carel Victor Morlais 1908–1997, *The Moment*, purchased from the Royal Academy, 1958, © the estate of the artist
Weight, Carel Victor Morlais 1908–1997, *African Girl No.2*, purchased from the University of Nottingham Fine Art Department, 1966, © the estate of the artist
Werff, Adriaen van der 1659–1722, *Venus and Cupid*, gift from Miss Helen Shipstone, 1933
Werff, Pieter van der 1665–1722, *Christian de Weerdt*, gift from Mr Carl Sipman, 1878
West, William 1801–1861, *The Israelites Led by the Pillar of Fire by Night*, purchased from Mrs Lucy West, 1952
Whaite, Henry Clarence 1828–1912, *The Rainbow*, purchased from Reverend Harry Ward, 1893
Whaite, Henry Clarence 1828–1912, *A Welsh Funeral (To the Cold Earth)*, bequeathed by Samuel William Oscroft, 1924
Wheatley, Francis 1747–1801, *The Harvest Wagon*, bequeathed by Mr Richard Godson Millns, 1904
Wijnants, Jan c.1635–1684, *Landscape with Peasants and a Dog*, bequeathed by Mr Richard Godson Millns, 1904
Wijnants, Jan c.1635–1684, *Landscape with Peasants on a Road*, bequeathed by Mr Richard Godson Millns, 1904
Wilkie, David 1785–1841, *The Soldier's Grave*, bequeathed by Mr Richard Godson Millns, 1904
Wilkie, David 1785–1841, *A Highland Family*, bequeathed by Mr Richard Godson Millns, 1904
Williams, John Edgar c.1821–1891, *Philip James Bailey (1816–1902)*, gift from W. F. Rock, 1884
Wilson, Richard 1714–1787, *Snowdon from Llyn Nantlle, North Wales*, bequeathed by Mr Richard Godson Millns, 1904
Wilson, Richard (after) 1714–1787, *River Scene with Sea and Classical Ruins*, bequeathed by Mr Henry Lammin, 1890
Wilson, Richard (after) 1714–1787, *Ruins of a Villa near Rome (Hadrian's Villa)*, gift from Mr James Orrock, 1909
Wimperis, Edmund Morison 1835–1900, *The Seaweed Gatherers*, gift from Miss Helen Shipstone, 1933
Wingfield, James Digman 1800–1872, *The Opening Ceremony of the Great Exhibition, London*, purchased from Shepherd Bros, 1882
Withoos, Matthias 1627–1703, *Still Life with Frog and Goldfinch (Thistles and Butterflies)*, bequeathed by Mr Richard Godson Millns, 1904
Withoos, Pieter 1654–1693, *Still Life with Dead Game (Pigeon and Other Birds)*, bequeathed by Mr Richard Godson Millns, 1904
Wood, John 1801–1870, *Celadon and Amelia in a Storm*, gift from the artist's sister, Miss Elizabeth Wood, 1887
Wood, John 1801–1870, *A Gentleman in an Elizabethan Costume*, gift from the artist's sister, Miss Elizabeth Wood, 1883
Wright, John Michael 1617–1694, *Magdalen Aston, Lady Burdett*, purchased from Messrs Thomas Agnew & Sons, Ltd, 1957
Wright, John Michael 1617–1694, *Astraea Returns to Earth (The Apotheosis of Charles II)*, purchased from Mrs Day, 1953
Wright, Joseph (style of) 1756–1793, *Portrait of a Girl*, bequeathed by Mr Henry Lammin, 1890
Wright, Joseph of Derby 1734–1797, *Sir Richard Arkwright (1732–1792)*, purchased, 1887
Wyllie, William Lionel 1851–1931, *The Thames near Charing Cross, London*, gift from Ralph Carr, on behalf of the family of the late Mr and Mrs Thomas Parker, 1946
Wyllie, William Lionel 1851–1931, *Romney Marsh*, bequeathed by Samuel William Oscroft, 1924
Yeames, William Frederick 1835–1918, *The Death of Amy Robsart*, gift from Mr P. N. Gunsaker, 1968
Zinkeisen, Anna Katrina 1901–1976, *The Dark Lady*, purchased from the Royal Academy of Arts, 1938, © the artist's estate
Zuccarelli, Franco 1702–1788, *River Scene with Peasants*, bequeathed by Mr Richard Godson Millns, 1904

Nottingham Magistrates' Court

Mills, Edwin Robin *Swearing in of the New Justices (5 December 1991)*, gift from the artist to the Nottingham Bench, 1994

Nottingham Trent University

Beth, Tew *The Typical Family*
Dyer, Peter *Untitled (I)*
Dyer, Peter *Untitled (II)*
Dyer, Peter *Untitled (III)*
Dyer, Peter *Untitled (IV)*
Dyer, Peter *Untitled (V)*
Dyer, Peter *Untitled (VI)*
Dyer, Peter *Untitled (VII)*
Dyer, Peter *Untitled (VIII)*
Dyer, Peter *Untitled (IX)*
Dyer, Peter *Untitled (X)*
Dyer, Peter *Untitled (XI)*
Dyer, Peter *Untitled (XII)*
Dyer, Peter *Untitled (XIII)*
Dyer, Peter *Untitled (XIV)*
Dyer, Peter *Untitled (XV)*
Dyer, Peter *Untitled (XVI)*
Earl, Sandra *Untitled*, purchased, 1995
Earl, Sandra *Untitled*, purchased, 1995
Earl, Sandra *Untitled*, purchased, 1995
Earl, Sandra *Untitled*, purchased, 1995
Earl, Sandra *Untitled*, purchased, 1995
Feldman, Neil b.1947, *Dunes Landscape with Window*, purchased, 1995, © the artist
Feldman, Neil b.1947, *The Hot Meadow No.2*, purchased, 1995, © the artist
Hart, Robert b.1956, *Untitled*, commissioned, 1999, © the artist
Hart, Robert b.1956, *Whereness*, commissioned, 1999, © the artist
Hawthorne, Carole Diane b.1945, *Stretch*, purchased, 1995, © the artist
Hawthorne, Carole Diane b.1945, *Square Suspended I*, purchased, 1995, © the artist
Hawthorne, Carole Diane b.1945, *Square Suspended II*, purchased, 1995, © the artist
Hemsley, Antony b.1965, *Lilac Time*, purchased, 1995
Hemsley, Antony b.1965, *Steady Climb*, purchased, 1995
Hemsley, Antony b.1965, *Winter Moor*, purchased, 1995
Hemsley, Antony b.1965, *Rose Bowl*, purchased, 1995
Lewis, Simon b.1945, *Yellow Drift*, on long-term loan from the artist, © the artist
Lewis, Simon b.1945, *Red Czar*, on long-term loan from the artist, © the artist
Liebert, Judith *Gather Juggling*, purchased, 1995
Liebert, Judith *Juggle 1*, purchased, 1995
Liebert, Judith *Juggle 2*, purchased, 1995
Liebert, Judith *Trio* (1 of 3), purchased, 1995
Liebert, Judith *Trio* (2 of 3), purchased, 1995
Liebert, Judith *Trio* (3 of 3), purchased, 1995
Martin, Ross active 1989–1990, *Still Life*, purchased, 1992
Martin, Ross active 1989–1990, *Still Life*, purchased, 1992
Martin, Ross active 1989–1990, *Still Life*, purchased, 1992
Martin, Ross active 1989–1990, *Still Life*, purchased, 1992
Martin, Ross active 1989–1990, *Still Life*, purchased, 1992
Martin, Ross active 1989–1990, *Still Life*, purchased, 1992
Matosic, Paul b.1955, *Big Dipper*, purchased, 1995, © the artist
Rogan, Irene *Inspirit*, purchased, 1998
Rogan, Irene *Sum and Substance*, purchased, 1999

Russell, Alex b.1967, *Isidore's Map (part 1)*, purchased, 1999, © the artist
Russell, Alex b.1967, *Isidore's Map (part 2)*, purchased, 1999, © the artist
Russell, Alex b.1967, *Isidore's Map (part 3)*, purchased, 1999, © the artist
Russell, Alex b.1967, *Currency 1*, purchased, 1999, © the artist
Russell, Alex b.1967, *Currency 2*, purchased, 1999, © the artist
Russell, Alex b.1967, *Currency 3*, purchased, 1999, © the artist
Russell, Alex b.1967, *Currency 4*, purchased, 1999, © the artist
Smith, Mick *Life Begins at Faulty*, purchased from an exhibition of local artists at a Nottingham Craft Centre, 2000
Stevenson, Wendy *Starfish*, acquired, 2000
Stoddart, Rosalind b.1960, *Fusion*, purchased in sponsorship for the artist's sculpture residency at the National Trust property, Lyveden New Bield, Northamptonshire, 1999, © the artist

Nottinghamshire Archives

Dobson, William Charles Thomas (attributed to) 1817–1898, *Thomas Bristowe of Beesthorpe and Elston (1620–1680), Clerk of the Peace of Nottinghamshire (1654–1659)*, bequeathed by Mrs M. H. Bristowe of Souldern House, Oxfordshire, 1969
Joseph, George Francis 1764–1846, *Unidentified Man from the Bristowe Family*, bequeathed by Mrs M. H. Bristowe of Souldern House, Oxfordshire, 1969
Lawrence, Thomas (attributed to) 1769–1830, *John Gilbert Cooper (Gardiner)*, on loan via Mrs M. Annis from Nottingham Public Library, 1956
Moore, Thomas Cooper 1827–1901, *Windmills on the Forest*, on long-term loan from an unknown provenance
unknown artist *Anne Micclemore Cooper or Jane Beale Gilbert, Wife of Henry Gilbert*, on long-term loan from Nottingham Public Library, 1956
unknown artist *Cecil Cooper or Henry Gilbert*, on long-term loan from Nottingham Public Library, 1956
unknown artist *John Gilbert and His Children John, Elizabeth and Dorothy*, on long-term loan from Nottingham Public Library, 1956
unknown artist early 19th C, *Unidentified Regency Man from the Bristowe Family*, bequeathed by Mrs M. H. Bristowe of Souldern House, Oxfordshire, 1969
unknown artist *Benjamin Mayo 'Old General'*, on long-term loan from an unknown provenance
unknown artist *Benjamin Mayo 'Old General'*, on long-term loan from an unknown provenance
unknown artist *Clifton Grove, Nottingham*, on long-term loan from an unknown provenance
unknown artist *Henry Kirke White (1785–1806)*, on long-term loan from an unknown provenance
unknown artist *Henry Kirke White (1785–1806)*, on long-term loan from an unknown provenance
unknown artist *Henry Pelham-Clinton, 5th Duke of Newcastle, Lord Lieutenant of Nottinghamshire (1851–1864)*, originally a gift from T. I. Birkin on behalf of his father Richard Birkin, 1899, on loan to the library from an unknown provenance
unknown artist *Jane Bristowe (1691–1696)*, bequeathed by Mrs M. H. Bristowe of Souldern House, Oxfordshire, 1969
unknown artist *John White (1747–1822)*, on long-term loan from an unknown provenance
unknown artist *Mary Bristowe (1732–1793)*, bequeathed by Mrs M. H. Bristowe of Souldern House, Oxfordshire, 1969
unknown artist *Mary White (c.1756–1833)*, on long-term loan from an unknown provenance
unknown artist *Samuel Bristowe of Twyford (1694–1761)*, bequeathed by Mrs M. H. Bristowe of Souldern House, Oxfordshire, 1969
unknown artist *William Bristowe of Beesthorpe (1695–1770)*, bequeathed by Mrs M. H. Bristowe of Souldern House, Oxfordshire, 1969
Wright, Joseph of Derby (attributed to) 1734–1797, *Samuel Bristowe of Twyford and Beesthorpe (1736–1818)*, bequeathed by Mrs M. H. Bristowe of Souldern House, Oxfordshire, 1969

Nottinghamshire County Cricket Club

Batson, Francis Cunningham 1858–1931, *Playing Out Time in a Difficult Light*, gift from the artist, 1906
Miles, George Francis 1852–1891, *Richard Daft (1835–1900), Captain of Nottinghamshire County Cricket Club (1871–1880)*, bequeathed by Mrs Mary Bissett Brown, a relative of the sitter, 1997
Redgate, Sylvanus 1827–1907, *James Grundy (1827–1873)*, gift from Mrs James Grundy
Townsend, John b.1930, *John Richard Gunn (1876–1963)*, gift from an unknown source
unknown artist *Mordecai Sherwin (1851–1910)*, gift from an unknown source
unknown artist *John Johnson (1810–1877), First Honorary Secretary to the Nottinghamshire County Cricket Club (1859–1867)*, gift from an unknown source
unknown artist *Joseph Hardstaff, Junior (1911–1988)*, gift from the Hardstaff Family, 1990

Nottinghamshire County Football Club

Townsend, John b.1930, *Jimmy Sirrel, Nottinghamshire County Football Club's Legendary Manager (1969–1975, 1977–1982, & 1984–1987)*, commissioned by the Nottingham County Supporters Trust, 2007

Nottinghamshire County Hall

Bates, Marjorie Christine 1883–1962, *Turn of the Century Nursery Scene*, gift
Davis, Noel Denholm 1876–1950, *Alderman Thomas Phillip Barber, Chairman of the County Council (1932–1946)*
Davis, Noel Denholm 1876–1950, *Colonel Sir Lancelot Rolleston, KCB, DSO, TD, DL, JP, Chairman of Nottinghamshire County Council and Quarter Sessions (1928–1932)*, presented on the occasion of the 50th anniversary of the sitter's marriage, 1932
Davis, Noel Denholm 1876–1950, *K. Tweedale Meaby, CBE, DL, Clerk of the Peace (1921–1954)*
Doubleday, Matthew c.1828–1900, *Old Trent Bridge*
Edwards, Edwin 1823–1879, *Fishing by the River at Wilford Ferry, Nottingham, Barge in the Background*, gift
Frost, T. *Southwell Minster, Nottinghamshire*
Gentle, Harry *Scene in Clumber Park, Worksop, Nottinghamshire*, gift from the artist
Hammond, Thomas William 1854–1935, *Rooftop View over City Churches, Nottingham*, gift
Hingsley, W. C. *Old Trent Bridge with Steamer, from the North Bank*, gift from Miss D. Joynes
Hingsley, W. C. *Wilford Ferry, from the North Bank, 1872*, gift
Moore, Thomas Cooper 1827–1901, *Trent Bridge, Nottingham, with Ferry*
O'Rourke, Robert active 2003, *Rufford Abbey, Nottinghamshire, from the Lawns*, commissioned by Nottinghamshire County Council, 2003
O'Rourke, Robert active 2003, *Rufford Abbey, Nottinghamshire, from the Turning Circle*, commissioned by Nottinghamshire County Council, 2003
Payne, David (attributed to) c.1844–1891, *Newstead Abbey, Nottinghamshire, View from the Lake*
Redmore, Henry 1820–1887, *A Coastal Scene with a Cliff, a Fishing Boat and a Merchantman in a Storm*
Spooner, Arthur 1873–1961, *Newstead Abbey, Nottinghamshire, View from the Lawn, with Figures in Sunlight and Shade*
Spooner, Arthur 1873–1961, *The Right Honourable Lord Belper, First Chairman of Nottinghamshire County Council*
Spooner, Arthur 1873–1961, *The Right Honourable Viscount Galway, CB, Chairman of the County Council (1914–1928)*
Todd, D. *Councillor Dennis Pettitt, Leader of the County Council (1981–2001)*
Townsend, John b.1930, *Alderman Colonel Sydney Farr, MC, DL, JP, Chairman of the County Council (1962–1963)*
Townsend, John b.1930, *Alderman Sir Frank Small, CBE, DL, JP, Chairman of the County Council (1963–1967)*
Townsend, John b.1930, *Alderman Mrs Anne Yates, CBE, JP, Chairman of the County Council (1968–1974)*
Townsend, John b.1930, *Alderman Albert James Pounder, JP, Chairman of the County Council (1967–1968)*
Townsend, John b.1930, *Alderman William Bayliss, CE, JP, Chairman of the County Council (1946–1962)*
unknown artist *Old Trent Bridge Steamer and Figures*
unknown artist *Nottingham Market Square, Pre-Council House Dome, on Market Day, with Trams in View*
unknown artist *Trent Bridge Pre-Embankment, with Rowing Boats and Steam Boats*

Nottinghamshire County Library Service

Burton, Marjorie E. *Approaching Storm*, gift from the artist, 1980
Elliot, W. J. active 1924–1966, *Round House, Hallam Lane, Arnold, Nottinghamshire*, gift from the artist
Elliot, W. J. active 1924–1966, *Higginbottom's Cottage, Hallam Lane, Arnold, Nottinghamshire*, gift from the artist, 1966
Lacey, Elias b.1871, *Bestwood Pit, Nottinghamshire*, gift from the artist
Lacey, Elias b.1871, *South Front and Lake of Newstead Abbey, Nottinghamshire*, gift from the artist
Lacey, Elias b.1871, *West Front of Newstead Abbey, Nottinghamshire*, gift from the artist
Lacey, Elias b.1871, *Old Sandy Lane Mill, 'Club Mill', Nottinghamshire*, gift from the artist
Laming, Ruth *A Scene along the Canal Bank, near Ladybridge, Bolton, Lancashire*, gift, 1971
Murray, Trevor *Dragon Ship**, gift from R. M. Riley to Ravenshead Library
Murray, Trevor *Man on Mars**, gift from R. M. Riley to Ravenshead Library
Reeve, Walter *Nottingham Road, Eastwood, 1920s*, gift from the artist's wife, c.1995
Reeve, Walter *Bradley's Brewery (now the 'Ram Inn'), Eastwood, Nottinghamshire*, gift from the artist's wife, c.1995
Salisbury, Frank O. 1874–1962, *Arthur Mee (1875–1943), Editor of 'The Children's Newspaper'*, gift to the library to commemorate the sitter's 50 years in journalism, © estate of Frank O. Salisbury/DACS 2008
Shaw, Don W. *Arno Vale, Nottinghamshire*, gift from the artist
Shaw, Frank *Bolham Manor, Ladybridge, Nottinghamshire*, gift from Miss Ashworth to Retford Library
unknown artist *Arnfield's Book and Paper Shop, Smedley's Barber's Shop, Carolgate, Retford, Nottinghamshire*, gift

Nottinghamshire Police

unknown artist *View of Wollaton Hall, Nottinghamshire, from the Lake**, gift

Rushcliffe Borough Council

Boynton, Winifred D. active c.1938–1940, *Portrait of a Lady*, gift from the artist
Boynton, Winifred D. active c.1938–1940, *On Active Service (Arnold Boynton Hall, lost at sea in HMS 'Exmouth', 21 January 1940)*
Burchell, William F. *The Solway*, gift from the artist
Davis, Noel Denholm 1876–1950, *The Honourable Henry Saville as a Child*, gift from the artist
Ellis, Edwin 1841–1895, *The Approaching Storm, Whitby, North Yorkshire*
Foster, Herbert Wilson 1846–1929, *Tea Break*
Foster, Herbert Wilson 1846–1929, *The Procession of the May Queen*, gift from Reverend L. Foster, 1951
Foster, Herbert Wilson 1846–1929, *Country Courtship*, gift from Mrs Foster
Hall, Margaret M. *Early March*
Lachenwitz, F. Sigmund 1820–1868, *Two Swans Startled by a Hound*
Makinson, Trevor b.1926, *From Dunkirk (Sam's Boots)*, gift to West Bridgford Urban District Council
Mayfield, F. *The Old Bridge, Lady Bay, Nottingham*
Payne, David c.1844–1891, *Milking Time*
Smart, Hilda Elizabeth 1900–1992, *Trent Navigation Wharf*, on long-term loan from the family of the artist, c.1992
Smart, Hilda Elizabeth 1900–1992, *Summer Rain*, on long-term loan from the family of the artist, c.1992
Spooner, Arthur 1873–1961, *Portrait of a Gentleman*

The Congregational Memorial Hall Trust (1978) Limited

Brown, John Alfred Arnesby 1866–1955, *Dr Paton (1830–1911)*, acquired as part of the Memorial Hall Trust Collection
Caledfryn, Ap 1837–1915, *Thomas Rees (1815–1885)*, acquired as part of the Memorial Hall Trust Collection
Grant, Francis (style of) 1803–1878, *John Legge Poore (1816–1867)*, acquired as part of the Memorial Hall Trust Collection
Hayter, George (attributed to) 1792–1871, *Lord John Russell (1792–1878), and Lord Holland (1773–1840)*, acquired as part of the Memorial Hall Trust Collection
Holl, Frank 1845–1888, *James Spicer (1807–1888)*, acquired as part of the Memorial Hall Trust Collection
Hudson, Thomas 1701–1779, *John Stafford (1728–1800)*, acquired as part of the Memorial Hall Trust Collection
Hudson, Thomas (school of) 1701–1779, *John Howe (1630–1705)*, acquired as part of the Memorial Hall Trust Collection
Jervas, Charles (attributed to) c.1675–1739, *Isaac Watts (1674–1748)*, acquired as part of the Memorial Hall Trust Collection
Kneller, Godfrey (follower of) 1646–1723, *Matthew Henry (1662–1714)*, acquired as part of the Memorial Hall Trust Collection
Linnell, John 1792–1882, *John Leifchild (1780–1862)*, acquired as part of the Memorial Hall Trust Collection
Napier, John James 1831–1877, *Alexander Raleigh (1817–1875)*, acquired as part of the Memorial Hall Trust Collection
Ogilvie, Frank Stanley 1858–after 1935, *Alexander Hannay (1822–1890)*, acquired as part of the Memorial Hall Trust Collection
Olivier, Herbert Arnould 1861–1952, *Christopher John Newman Hall (1816–1902)*, acquired as part of the Memorial Hall Trust Collection, © the artist's estate
Pickersgill, Henry William (circle of) 1782–1875, *John Blackburn (1792–1855)*, acquired as part of the Memorial Hall Trust Collection
Riviere, Hugh Goldwin 1869–1956, *Charles Sylvester Horne (1865–1914), MA, MP*, acquired as part of the Memorial Hall Trust Collection, © the artist's estate
Riviere, Hugh Goldwin 1869–1956, *Albert Spicer (1847–1934), Bt, PC, JP*, acquired as part of the Memorial Hall Trust Collection, © the artist's estate
Room, Henry 1802–1850, *Ebenezer Henderson (1784–1858)*, acquired as part of the Memorial Hall Trust Collection
Room, Henry 1802–1850, *Edward Mannering (1801–1875)*, acquired as part of the Memorial Hall Trust Collection
unknown artist *Robritus Langton*, acquired as part of the Memorial Hall Trust Collection
unknown artist *Alexander Fletcher (1787–1860)*, acquired as part of the Memorial Hall Trust Collection
unknown artist *Alexander Fletcher (1787–1860)*, acquired as part of the Memorial Hall Trust Collection
unknown artist *Alexander Mackennal (1835–1904)*, acquired as part of the Memorial Hall Trust Collection
unknown artist *Bernard Joseph Snell (1856–1934), MA, BSc*, acquired as part of the Memorial Hall Trust Collection
unknown artist *Charles Reed (1819–1881), MP*, acquired as part of the Memorial Hall Trust Collection
unknown artist *George Collison (1772–1847)* , acquired as part of the Memorial Hall Trust Collection
unknown artist *Isaac Stockton Keith (1755–1813)*, acquired as part of the Memorial Hall Trust Collection
unknown artist *James Alexander Mitchell (1849–1919)*, acquired as part of the Memorial Hall Trust Collection
unknown artist *James Guinness Rogers (1822–1911)*, acquired as part of the Memorial Hall Trust Collection
unknown artist *James Guinness Rogers (1822–1911)*, acquired as part of the Memorial Hall Trust Collection
unknown artist *John Angell James (1785–1859)*, acquired as part of the Memorial Hall Trust Collection
unknown artist *John Clayton Junior (1780–1865)*, acquired as part of the Memorial Hall Trust Collection
unknown artist *John Owen (1616–1683)*, acquired as part of the Memorial Hall Trust Collection
unknown artist *John Remington Mills (1798–1879)*, acquired as part of the Memorial Hall Trust Collection
unknown artist *John Stoughton (1807–1897)*, acquired as part of the Memorial Hall Trust Collection
unknown artist *Ralph Wardlaw (1779–1853)*, acquired as part of the Memorial Hall Trust Collection
unknown artist *Rowland Hill (1744–1833)*, acquired as part of the Memorial Hall Trust Collection
unknown artist *Samuel Martin (1817–1878)*, acquired as part of the Memorial Hall Trust Collection
unknown artist *Samuel Morley (1809–1886), MP*, acquired as part of the Memorial Hall Trust Collection
unknown artist *Thomas Binney (1798–1874)*, acquired as part of the Memorial Hall Trust Collection
unknown artist *Thomas Binney (1798–1874)*, acquired as part of the Memorial Hall Trust Collection
unknown artist *Thomas Toke Lynch (1818–1871)*, acquired as part of the Memorial Hall Trust Collection
unknown artist *William Campbell (1799–1878)*, acquired as part of the Memorial Hall Trust Collection
unknown artist *William James Woods (1850–1903), BA*, acquired as part of the Memorial Hall Trust Collection
unknown artist *William James Woods (1850–1903)*, acquired as part of the Memorial Hall Trust Collection
unknown artist *William Roby (1766–1830)*, acquired as part of the Memorial Hall Trust Collection
Wissing, Willem 1656–1687, *King William III (1650–1702)*, acquired as part of the Memorial Hall Trust Collection
Wissing, Willem 1656–1687, *Queen Mary II (1662–1692)*, acquired as part of the Memorial Hall Trust Collection

The Council House

Davis, Noel Denholm 1876–1950, *The Shambles, Old Exchange, Nottingham*, gift from the Rotary Club to Nottingham City Council, 1952
Krit, D. (attributed to) *Munck*
Townsend, John b.1930, *Queen Elizabeth II (b.1926)*, gift from Lewis H. Colton to Nottingham City Council, 1970
unknown artist *30 Years, Karlsruhe-Nottingham*, gift to Nottingham City Council, c.1990

The Sherwood Rangers Yeomanry Regimental Association

Boultbee, John 1753–1812, *Captain Ichabod Wright of Mapperley (1767–1862), Formed the First Nottingham Troop in 1794*, gift from an unknown source
Lewis, Reginald b.1901, *Colonel the Lord Barnby of Blyth, CMG, CBE, MVO, TD, Commanding Officer, the Sherwood Rangers Yeomanry (1920–1928), Honourary Colonel (1948–1954)*, gift from the executors of late Lord Barnby, 1987
unknown artist *Quartermaster Bousfield (1815–1890)*, gift from an unknown source

The University of Nottingham

Alexander, Cosmo 1724–1772, *Mrs Thomas Hope*, gift from the Trustees of the Newcastle (Clumber) Collection, 1991–1992
Anderson, Douglas Hardinge b.1934, *Julian Ronald Haylock, BSc, FRSA, President of the Council (1996–2003)*, commissioned, 2003, © the artist
Arnfield, Nick 1961–1999, *Light on Cornish Sea*, purchased, 2001, © the artist's estate
Arnfield, Nick 1961–1999, *Pink Sky (1), Hertfordshire*, purchased, 2001, © the artist's estate
Arnfield, Marjorie 1930–2001, *Street Market, Lascala*, purchased, 2001, © the artist's estate
Arnfield, Marjorie 1930–2001, *Cadaqués, Spain (1)*, purchased, 2001, © the artist's estate
Barke, Christopher *Black Abstract*, purchased from the Loughborough University School of Art and Design for the University of Nottingham School of Pharmacy Collection, 2000
Barke, Christopher *White Abstract*, purchased from the Loughborough University School of Art and Design for the University of Nottingham School of Pharmacy Collection, 2000
Bates, Marjorie Christine 1883–1962, *Flower Still Life*, gift from Mrs Jane Forman-Hardy
Bates, Marjorie Christine 1883–1962, *William Henry Revis, Esq. (d.1923)*, unknown acquisition
Beechey, William (school of) 1753–1839, *General Sir William Henry Clinton (1769–1846)*, gift from the Trustees of the Newcastle (Clumber) Collection, 1991–1992
Bennett, Chris b.1957, *Mr W. Ian Hooker, Warden of Lenton and Wortley Hall (1980–2006)*, commissioned, © the artist
Birley, Oswald Hornby Joseph 1880–1952, *The Right Honourable Lord Trent (1889–1956), Chancellor of the University (1948–1954)*, commissioned, © the artist's estate
Birrell, William *The Canal*, gift to the University of Nottingham Medical School (Queen's Medical Centre) by the staff of the Department of Physiology to mark its inauguration, 1970
Bixio, Roberto b.1947, *Dr Mark Pearce*, purchased, 2007, © the artist
Boden, Leonard 1911–1999, *Sir Francis Hill (1899–1980), Chancellor of the University (1972–1978)*, commissioned, © the artist's estate
Bond, Jane b.1939, *Lord Ronald Dearing (b.1930)*, commissioned, © the artist
Bright, Henry 1814–1873, *Welsh Landscape with a Watermill*, unknown acquisition
British (English) School 16th C, *Edward Fiennes de Clinton (1512–1585), KG* (later 1st Earl of Lincoln), gift from the Trustees of the Newcastle (Clumber) Collection, 1991–1992
British (English) School 16th C, *Edward Fiennes de Clinton (1512–1585), KG* (later 1st Earl of Lincoln), gift from the Trustees of the Newcastle (Clumber) Collection, 1991–1992
British (English) School *John Holles (c.1565–1637), 1st Earl Clare*, gift from the Trustees of the Newcastle (Clumber) Collection, 1991–1992
British (English) School 17th C, *Bridget, 4th Countess of Lincoln*, gift from the Trustees of the Newcastle (Clumber) Collection, 1991–1992
British (English) School 17th C, *Portrait of a Man in a White Lace Collar*, unknown acquisition
British (English) School 18th C, *Portrait of a Man in Profile in a Red Jacket and a Black Sash*, unknown acquisition
British (English) School 18th C, *Thomas Pelham-Clinton (1752–1795)* (later 10th Earl of Lincoln and 3rd Duke of Newcastle-under-Lyne), gift from the Trustees of the Newcastle (Clumber) Collection, 1991–1992
Brownsword, Harry A. 1862–1920, *Old Market Square, Nottingham, 1889*, gift to the University of Nottingham Fine Art Department by Sir Alan Drury, FRS, 1975
Buckingham, Jennie Beatrice b.1968, *Boulder (III)*, purchased, 1998, © the artist
Bussey, Reuben 1818–1893, *Charles I Raising His Standard at Nottingham Castle*, unknown acquisition method
Cockrill, Maurice b.1936, *Generation (Ochre Series)*, purchased, 1996, © the artist
Cohen, Harold b.1928, *Still Life*, © the artist
Cohen, Harold b.1928, *Untitled*, © the artist
Cohen, Harold b.1928, *Gandalf*, unknown acquisition, © the artist
Cohen, Harold b.1928, *Flood*, gift, 1956–1959, © the artist
Collins, William 1788–1847, *The South and East Front of Clumber House, Nottinghamshire*, gift from the Trustees of the Newcastle (Clumber) Collection, 1991–1992
Collins, William 1788–1847, *The West Front of Clumber House, Nottinghamshire*, gift from the Trustees of the Newcastle (Clumber) Collection, 1991–1992
Collins, William 1788–1847, *View of the South and West Fronts of Clumber House, Nottinghamshire*, gift from the Trustees of the Newcastle (Clumber) Collection, 1991–1992
Colvile, Harry Morton 1905–1992, *Andalusian Women*, purchased from the artist
Colvile, Harry Morton 1905–1992, *Girl in a Riviera Garden*, purchased from the artist
Colvile, Harry Morton 1905–1992, *Mediterranean Fruit*, purchased from the artist
Colvile, Harry Morton 1905–1992, *Spanish Ox and Cart*, purchased from the artist
Cooper, Samuel (school of) 1609–1672, *William Cavendish (c.1593–1676)* (later 1st Duke of Newcastle upon Tyne), gift from the Trustees of the Newcastle (Clumber) Collection, 1991–1992
Cowlishaw, Tony b.1944, *Professor David Greenfield (1917–2005), Foundation Dean of Nottingham*

Medical School, University of Nottingham, commissioned, © the artist
Cowlishaw, Tony b.1944, *Frank Arnold Barnes (1920–2003), Warden of Derby Hall (1963–1985)*, commissioned, 1985, © the artist
Cowlishaw, Tony b.1944, *Dr Virginia van der Lande, Founder and Warden of Ancaster Hall (1966–1986)*, commissioned, 1986, © the artist
Cowlishaw, Tony b.1944, *W. R. Chalmers (d.2004), MA, Warden of Sherwood Hall (1964–1986)*, commissioned, 1986, © the artist
Cowlishaw, Tony b.1944, *Dr Waterhouse, Warden of Wortley Hall until 1984*, commissioned, 1987, © the artist
Cowlishaw, Tony b.1944, *Charles Manners (1919–1999), 10th Duke of Rutland*, commissioned, © the artist
Cowlishaw, Tony b.1944, *Frances Helen Sweeney (b.1937), Duchess of Rutland*, commissioned, © the artist
Cowlishaw, Tony b.1944, *Dr Lucas*, commissioned, 1988, © the artist
Cowlishaw, Tony b.1944, *Audrey Beecham (1915–1989), Warden of Nightingale Hall (1950–1980)*, commissioned, 1990, © the artist
Cowlishaw, Tony b.1944, *D. E. Varley, Warden of Rutland Hall (1967–1989)*, commissioned, 1990, © the artist
Cowlishaw, Tony b.1944, *Professor Wilfred Heginbottom*, commissioned, © the artist
Cowlishaw, Tony b.1944, *P. F. McGoldrick, MSc, Warden of Sherwood Hall (1986–1991)*, commissioned, 1993, © the artist
Cowlishaw, Tony b.1944, *Dr P. Morris, MA, PhD, Warden of Sherwood Hall (1992–1995)*, commissioned, 1996, © the artist
Cubley, William Harold 1814–1896, *The Lake, Highfields, Nottingham*, unknown acquisition method
Culbert, Bill b.1935, *Transit*, gift from the Commonwealth Institute to the University of Nottingham Fine Art Department, © the artist
Darking, Harry Fred 1911–1999, *Reverend Dr William Neil, MA, BD, PhD, DD, Warden of Hugh Stewart Hall (1953–1975)*, commissioned
Davis, Noel Denholm 1876–1950, *Alderman Edmund Huntsman, Member of the College Council (1917–1921), Chairman of the College Council (1921–1939)*, commissioned
Davis, Noel Denholm 1876–1950, *Cecil Roberts, Esq. (1892–1976)*, commissioned
Davis, Noel Denholm 1876–1950, *Hugh Stewart (1884–1934), Principal of University College Nottingham (1929–1934)*
Davis, Noel Denholm 1876–1950, *Sir Jesse Boot (1850–1931), Bt, JP* (later 1st Baron Trent), commissioned
Davis, Noel Denholm 1876–1950, *Sir Louis Pearson (d.1943), CBE, DLJP*, commissioned
Dawe, George 1781–1829, *Mrs Thomas Hope (d.1851), with Her Sons Henry Thomas (1808–1862), and Charles (1810–1817)*, gift from the Trustees of the Newcastle (Clumber) Collection, 1991–1992
Dawson, Henry 1811–1878, *Portrait of the Artist's Wife, Elizabeth Dawson, née Whittle*, gift from Elizabeth and Peter Reddick, 1994
Dawson, Henry 1811–1878, *Self Portrait*, gift from Elizabeth and Peter Reddick, 1994
de Castella, Hubert active 1999–2000, *Staircase*, purchased from the Loughborough University School of Art and Design for the University of Nottingham School of Pharmacy Collection, 1999
de Castella, Hubert active 1999–2000, *Mont Saint-Michel, Normandy, France*, purchased from the Loughborough University School of Art and Design for the University of Nottingham School of Pharmacy Collection, 1999
Di Stefano, Arturo b.1955, *Beach Scene*, purchased, 1999, © the artist
Di Stefano, Arturo b.1955, *Deck Chair*, purchased, 1999, © the artist
Evans, William 1911–1978, *Sir William John Hughes Butterfield (1920–2000), OBE, MA, DM, MD, LLD, FRCP, Vice-Chancellor (1971–1975)*, commissioned
Fry, Roger Eliot 1866–1934, *La fontaine noire*, unknown acquisition method
Fumi *Daigoji Temple, Kyoto, Japan*, unknown acquisition method
Glover, Carole b.1942, *Quayside*, purchased, 1997, © the artist
Gordon, John Watson 1788–1864, *Henry Pelham Fiennes Pelham-Clinton (1811–1864), 5th Duke of Newcastle-under-Lyne*, gift from the Trustees of the Newcastle (Clumber) Collection, 1991–1992
Gratton, Lucinda b.1976, *King's Cross I (St Pancras), London*, purchased, 1998, © the artist
Grici, Claude *Untitled*, unknown acquisition
Hampson, Derek b.1952, *George Green*, commissioned to commemorate the bicentenary of the mathematician George Green's birth, 1993, © the artist
Hampson, Derek b.1952, *The Great and the Good (The Roots of Democracy)* (left panel of triptych), commissioned to celebrate the 30th anniversary of the opening of Derby Hall, University of Nottingham, 1993, © the artist
Hampson, Derek b.1952, *The Great and the Good (The Roots of Democracy)* (centre panel of triptych), commissioned to celebrate the 30th anniversary of the opening of Derby Hall, University of Nottingham, 1993, © the artist
Hampson, Derek b.1952, *The Great and the Good (The Roots of Democracy)* (right panel of triptych), commissioned to celebrate the 30th anniversary of the opening of Derby Hall, University of Nottingham, 1993, © the artist
Hampson, Derek b.1952, *The Loves of the Plants*, commissioned to celebrate the 40th anniversary of the opening of Derby Hall, University of Nottingham, 2003, © the artist
Hebden, Rosemary *Night Drive*, unknown acquisition
Hebden, Rosemary *Strange Vista*, purchased by Mary Cannell from Nottingham College of Education, 1963
Hebden, Rosemary *Essential Landscape*, unknown acquisition
Hepple, Norman 1908–1994, *The 7th Duke of Portland (1893–1977), Chancellor of the University (1954–1971)*, commissioned, © the artist's estate/www.bridgeman.co.uk
Hepple, Norman 1908–1994, *Sir Gordon Hobday (b.1916), 4th Chancellor of the University (1978–1993)*, commissioned, © the artist's estate/www.bridgeman.co.uk
Hewetson, Richard active 19th C, *Frances Clinton, Lady Chandos (d.1623) (copy of an earlier painting)*, gift from the Trustees of the Newcastle (Clumber) Collection, 1991–1992
Hoare, William 1706–1792, *Catherine Pelham-Clinton (1727–1760), Countess of Lincoln*, gift from the Trustees of the Newcastle (Clumber) Collection, 1991–1992
Hoare, William 1706–1792, *Henry Fiennes-Clinton Pelham Clinton (1720–1794), KG, 9th Earl of Lincoln* (later 2nd Duke of Newcastle-under-Lyne), gift from the Trustees of the Newcastle (Clumber) Collection, 1991–1992
Hoare, William 1706–1792, *Lady Frances Seymour Conway (1751–1820), Countess of Lincoln*, gift from the Trustees of the Newcastle (Clumber) Collection, 1991–1992
Hoare, William 1706–1792, *The Children of the 2nd Duke of Newcastle-under-Lyne, Henry (1750–1778), Thomas (1752–1795) and John (1755–1781)*, gift from the Trustees of the Newcastle (Clumber) Collection, 1991–1992
Hoare, William 1706–1792, *The Children of the 2nd Duke of Newcastle-under-Lyne, Henry (1750–1778), Thomas (1752–1795) and John (1755–1781)*, gift from the Trustees of the Newcastle (Clumber) Collection, 1991–1992
Hunt, Doreen *Palazzo, Grand Canal, Venice, Italy*, purchased, 1996 (?)
Hunter, Norma *Dr Trueman Dicken (1919–2000), Warden of Lenton Hall (1965–1980)*, commissioned
Inlander, Henry 1925–1983, *Olive Trees*, purchased, 1956, © the artist's estate
Jones, Chris *Version* (left panel of triptych), purchased, 1996
Jones, Chris *The Blessed* (centre panel of triptych), purchased, 1996
Jones, Chris *Proverb* (right panel of triptych), purchased, 1996
Kneller, Godfrey 1646–1723, *Henry Fiennes Clinton (1684–1728), 7th Earl of Lincoln*, gift from the Trustees of the Newcastle (Clumber) Collection, 1991–1992
Kneller, Godfrey 1646–1723, *Thomas Pelham-Holles (1693–1768), KG, 4th Duke of Newcastle upon Tyne* (later 1st Duke of Newcastle-under-Lyne), gift from the Trustees of the Newcastle (Clumber) Collection, 1991–1992
Kneller, Godfrey (after) 1646–1723, *John Holles (1662–1711), 4th Earl of Clare and 3rd Duke of Newcastle upon Tyne, KG*, gift from the Trustees of the Newcastle (Clumber) Collection, 1991–1992
Kneller, Godfrey (after) 1646–1723, *Thomas Pelham-Holles (1693–1768), 1st Duke of Newcastle-under-Lyne with Henry Fiennes Clinton (1684–1728), 7th Earl of Lincoln, KG*, gift from the Trustees of the Newcastle (Clumber) Collection, 1991–1992
Knight, Laura 1877–1970, *Lamorna Birch (1869–1955), and His Daughters*, gift from Dame Laura Knight to the University of Nottingham, 1968, © reproduced with permission of the estate of Dame Laura Knight, DBE, RA, 2008. All rights reserved
Lawrence, Thomas 1769–1830, *Charles Hope (1810–1817), as Bacchus*, gift from the Trustees of the Newcastle (Clumber) Collection, 1991–1992
Lees, Stewart Marshall *Sunrise*, unknown acquisition
Macaskill, Duncan *Useful Verbs*, purchased, 1996
Machicado, Juan de la Cruz b.1935, *Titicaca*, purchased from the artist, 1992, © the artist
Machicado, Juan de la Cruz b.1935, *Village*, purchased from the artist, 1992, © the artist
Machicado, Juan de la Cruz b.1935, *Portrait of the Artist's Son, Juan Carlos*, purchased from the artist, 1992, © the artist
Machicado, Juan de la Cruz b.1935, *River Fortress*, purchased from the artist, 1992, © the artist
Malaysian School 20th C, *Sunset (Reflections on Water)**, gift from the Sultan Azlan Shar of Malaysia, 1993
McGegan, Christine Mary 1923–1989, *Irises*, unknown acquisition, © the artist's estate
Mundy, William Percy b.1936, *Roger John Godfrey, LLB, LLD, President of the Council (1983–1993)*, commissioned, 1996, © William P. Mundy
Nanaway, William E. *Sir Frederick Sydney Dainton (1914–1997), MA, LLD, ScD, DSc, DTech, FRS, Vice-Chancellor (1965–1970)*, commissioned
Neale, George Hall 1863–1940, *Portrait of an Unknown Man*, unknown acquisition
Newcomb, Mary 1922–2008, *The Homing Wives*, purchased, 1999, © the artist's estate
Niemann, Edmund John 1813–1876, *Storm at Sea*, unknown acquisition method
Noakes, Michael b.1933, *Paul Francis Granger, LLD, FCA, President of the Council (1968–1975)*, commissioned, © the artist
Nolan, Gavin b.1977, *Blue Abstract*, purchased from the Loughborough University School of Art and Design for the University of Nottingham School of Pharmacy Collection, 1999
Partridge, Maurice William 1913–1973, *Pembroke*, gift from the artist, Lord Trent Professor of Pharmaceutical Chemistry, Head of Department of Pharmacy (1967–1973) for the University of Nottingham School of Pharmacy Collection
Partridge, Maurice William 1913–1973, *Untitled*, presented by Mary F. Robertson to the School of Pharmacy, 2008
Partridge, Maurice William 1913–1973, *Newlyn Old Harbour, Cornwall*, gift from the son of Lord Trent Professor of Pharmaceutical Chemistry, Head of Department of Pharmacy (1967–1973), for the University of Nottingham School of Pharmacy Collection, presented by the family in memory of Professor and Mrs J. Crossland, c.2003
Partridge, Maurice William 1913–1973, *Near Ancaster, Lincolnshire*, gift from the artist, Lord Trent Professor of Pharmaceutical Chemistry, Head of Department of Pharmacy (1967–1973) for the University of Nottingham School of Pharmacy Collection
Partridge, Maurice William 1913–1973, *Abstract with Buildings*, unknown acquisition method
Partridge, Maurice William 1913–1973, *Istrian Landscape, Croatia*, unknown acquisition method
Partridge, Maurice William 1913–1973, *Landscape*, unknown acquisition method
Partridge, Maurice William 1913–1973, *Landscape with Trees on Red Square*, unknown acquisition method
Partridge, Maurice William 1913–1973, *Near Wortley Hall, South Yorkshire*, gift from the widow of Lord Trent Professor of Pharmaceutical Chemistry, Head of the Department of Pharmacy (1967–1973), for the University of Nottingham School of Pharmacy Collection
Partridge, Maurice William 1913–1973, *Still Life with Bottles*, unknown acquisition
Partridge, Maurice William 1913–1973, *The Trent Building*, gift from

the artist, Lord Trent Professor of Pharmaceutical Chemistry, Head of Department of Pharmacy (1967–1973) to the University of Nottingham School of Pharmacy collection
Partridge, Maurice William 1913–1973, *Untitled*, gift from the artist, Lord Trent Professor of Pharmaceutical Chemistry, Head of Department of Pharmacy (1967–1973) for the University of Nottingham School of Pharmacy Collection
Partridge, Maurice William 1913–1973, *Untitled*, gift from the artist, Lord Trent Professor of Pharmaceutical Chemistry, Head of Department of Pharmacy (1967–1973) for the University of Nottingham School of Pharmacy Collection
Partridge, Maurice William 1913–1973, *White Cliffs*, gift from the widow of the artist, Lord Trent Professor of Pharmaceutical Chemistry, Head of Department of Pharmacy (1967–1973), for the University of Nottingham School of Pharmacy Collection
Partridge, Maurice William 1913–1973, *Winter Landscape*, gift to the University of Nottingham Collection for the Hallward Library, presented by Professor Monica Partridge, 1988
Richardson, Jonathan the elder 1664/1665–1745, *Henrietta Pelham-Holles (d.1776), 1st Duchess of Newcastle-under-Lyne*, gift from the Trustees of the Newcastle (Clumber) Collection, 1991–1992
Roberts, John Horrocks b.1931, *Untitled*, unknown acquisition, © the artist
Roberts, John Horrocks b.1931, *Untitled*, unknown acquisition, © the artist
Roberts, John Horrocks b.1931, *Untitled*, unknown acquisition, © the artist
Robson, Gavin b.1950, *The Park*, acquired, possibly 1975–1977
Ronaldson, Thomas Martine 1881–1942, *Kathleen (1872–1955), 7th Duchess of Newcastle-under-Lyne*, gift from the Trustees of the Newcastle (Clumber) Collection, 1991–1992, © the artist's estate
Rosoman, Leonard Henry b.1913, *Composite Painting of the Works of Thomas Telford*, commissioned by the Institute of Civil Engineers for a bicentenary exhibition held in 1957 in honour of its first president, Thomas Telford, who accepted the presidency in 1820, purchased by the University of Nottingham, 1958, © the artist
Sancha, Carlos Luis 1920–2001, *Dr David J. Atkin, LLD, FIBF, President of the Council (1993–1996)*, commissioned
Sandby, Paul (school of) 1731–1809, *A Panorama of Nottingham from the Canal*, unknown acquisition
Shipham, Benjamin (attributed to) 1808–1872, *Distant View of Nottingham from the Trent at Clifton Grove*, unknown acquisition
Spooner, Arthur 1873–1961, *Frank H. Jacob, MD, FRCP*, unknown acquisition
Sprawson, Derek b.1955, *First*, purchased, 1999, © the artist
Sprawson, Derek b.1955, *Fruit*, purchased, 1999, © the artist
Sprawson, Derek b.1955, *Phial*, purchased, 1996, © the artist
Stubley, Trevor b.1932, *Basil Charles Leicester Weedon (1923–2003), CBE, DSc, PhD, DTech, LLD, ARCS, DIC, CChem, FRSC, FRS, Vice-Chancellor (1975–1988)*, commissioned, © the artist
Taborn, David b.1947, *Chine*, purchased by the Physics Department to celebrate its centenary with the aid of a grant from East Midlands Arts, 1981, © the artist
Taborn, David b.1947, *Untitled*, purchased, 1998, © the artist
Taylor, S. *Group of Figures in Reds*, unknown acquisition
Townsend, John b.1930, *John Madocks, CBE, DL, Bursar (1967–1987)*, gift
Trickett, Rob *Professor Douglas James Davies (b.1947), Warden of Derby Hall (1985–1997)*, commissioned
unknown artist *Landscape with Trees and Cottages*, unknown acquisition
unknown artist *Meadow Landscape*, unknown acquisition
Walker, John Rawson 1796–1873, *View of Nottingham from Clifton (South Prospect of Nottingham Castle)*, acquired as part of the University of Nottingham Collection, c.1937
Warburton, Stella *Moment Painting No.2 (Ashby Parva)* (left panel of diptych), purchased from the Loughborough University School of Art and Design for The University of Nottingham School of Pharmacy Collection, 1999
Warburton, Stella *Moment Painting No.2 (Ashby Parva)* (right panel of diptych), purchased from the Loughborough University School of Art and Design for the University of Nottingham School of Pharmacy Collection, 1999
Watteau, Jean-Antoine (after) 1684–1721, *A Music Party*, unknown acquisition
Weight, Carel Victor Morlais 1908–1997, *Sir Francis Hill (1899–1980), President of Council (1948–1967)*, commissioned, © the estate of the artist
Willetts, David b.1939, *Garden*, purchased, 1996, © the artist
Willetts, David b.1939, *Still Life with Fruit Bowl*, purchased, 1996, © the artist
Zoffany, Johann (after) 1733–1810, *David Garrick (1717–1779)*, acquired, c.1987

The Worcestershire and Sherwood Foresters Museum (The Sherwood Foresters Collection) of the Mercian Regiment

Davis, Noel Denholm 1876–1950, *Captain Albert Ball (1896–1917), VC*, gift to Nottingham Corporation from County Councillor H. M. Woolley, 1962; transferred to Nottingham City Museums and Galleries for display with The Sherwood Foresters Collection, 1990

Bassetlaw District Council

Agar, Eileen 1899–1991, *The Magician*, gift via the artist from the Contemporary Art Society, 1988, © the artist's estate, courtesy Redfern Gallery
Allsebrook, Kenneth *Windmill*, gift from the artist, 1970
Ashton, Garry John b.1954, *Tree Roots*, purchased from the artist, 2006, © the artist
Baldock, James Walsham 1822–1898, *In Welbeck Park, Nottinghamshire*, bequeathed by Leonard Towne, 1953, gift from Worksop Museum, 1984
Baldock, James Walsham 1822–1898, *Landscape with a Boy and Cattle*, gift from Worksop Museum, 1984
Baldock, James Walsham 1822–1898, *Cows in the Shadow of a Tree*, bequeathed by Leonard Towne, 1953, gift from Worksop Museum, 1984
Baldock, James Walsham 1822–1898, *Forest Scene with Deer*, gift from Worksop Museum, 1984
Baldock, James Walsham 1822–1898, *Study of Three Horses in a Landscape*, gift from Worksop Museum, 1984
Baldock, James Walsham 1822–1898, *On the Scottish Moors*, gift from Worksop Museum, 1984
Baldock, James Walsham 1822–1898, *Study of Cattle*, gift from Worksop Museum, 1984
Baldock, James Walsham 1822–1898, *Lady Lea Farm*, gift from Worksop Museum, 1984
Baldock, James Walsham 1822–1898, *Landscape near Worksop Manor Park, Nottinghamshire*, gift from Worksop Museum, 1984
Baldock, James Walsham 1822–1898, *Sheep and Shepherd*, gift from Worksop Museum, 1984
Baldock, James Walsham 1822–1898, *A Quiet Day in the Trent Valley*, gift from Worksop Museum, 1984
Baldock, James Walsham 1822–1898, *Landscape with Men and Cattle*, gift from Worksop Museum, 1984
Baldock, James Walsham 1822–1898, *Study of Cattle at a Pond*, gift from Worksop Museum, 1984
Barker, Kit 1916–1988, *Ruins at Hadrian's Villa, Tivoli, Rome, Italy*, gift from Worksop Museum via the Contemporary Art Society, 1984, © the artist's estate
Barker, L. *City Lights*, gift from Worksop Museum, 1984
Bartrop, Darwin Holdsworth b.1882, *Rock Cottage, Worksop, Nottinghamshire*, gift from Worksop Museum, 1984
Bowett, Druie 1924–1998, *Manton Colliery, Nottinghamshire*, gift from Worksop Museum via Hillards Ltd, 1984, © the artist's estate
Bowett, Druie 1924–1998, *Brown and Yellow Painting*, gift from Worksop Museum via Hadfield, Cawkwell, Davidson & Partners (Architects) to Simons Construction Group Ltd, 1984, © the artist's estate
Clegg, William George 1863–1940, *'Campania'*, gift from Vivian Allen, 2006, © the artist's estate
Davis, W. Gronow *Japanese Landscape*, gift from Worksop Museum, 1984
Delaney, Barbara b.1941, *Dec II*, gift from Worksop Museum via the Contemporary Art Society, 1984, © the artist
Delaney, Barbara b.1941, *34516*, purchased from the artist following an exhibition of her work, 1997, © the artist
Downar, S. *2 Clumber 9*, gift from Worksop Museum, 1984
Evans, Norman *Springtime in Clumber, Nottinghamshire*, purchased from the artist, 1993
Forbes, D. (attributed to) *Seascape With Ruins**, gift from Worksop Museum, 1984
French, H. *Manton Colliery, Nottinghamshire*, acquired from J. Burling, 1994
Hartwell, William John 1922–1995, *Landscape near Buckenham, Suffolk*, gift from Worksop Museum via the Contemporary Art Society, 1984
Hayward, Liz b.1949, *Bothamsall's Buildings, Nottinghamshire*, purchased from the artist, 1984, © the artist
Hector, G. *1812*, gift from the artist, 2006
Hicken, Harry d.2000, *Gateford Quarry, Nottinghamshire*, gift from Mrs Cashmore, 2006
Holmes, Alan *The Poulter below Clumber, Nottinghamshire*, unknown provenance
Hudson, Keith *Retford Fair, Nottinghamshire*, unknown provenance
Hudson, Robert 1852–1884, *Edwinstowe Church, Nottinghamshire*, gift from Worksop Museum, 1984
Jones, W. A. active 1968–1969, *Sailing at Welbeck, Nottinghamshire*, purchased from the artist, 1969; gift from Worksop Museum, 1984
Jones, W. A. active 1968–1969, *Molly Leigh's Cottage, Burslem, Staffordshire*, purchased from the artist, 1968; gift from Worksop Museum, 1984
Kempson, Mary *Negro Lady*, gift from Worksop Museum, 1984
Kennington, Thomas Benjamin 1856–1916, *T. W. Denman (1832–1907)*, on long-term loan from Mr and Mrs K. Siddons, 1984
Kinley, Peter 1926–1988, *Fireside*, gift from the Contemporary Art Society, 1979, © the artist's estate
Kirk, Eve 1900–1969, *Piazza del Popolo, Rome, Italy*, gift from Worksop Museum via the Contemporary Art Society, 1984
Laws, Percy S. 1892–1972, *Interior of Percy Laws' Workshop*, purchased from Mr G. L. Morley, 1997
Laws, Percy S. 1892–1972, *Quaker's Cottage and Garden, South Leverton, Nottinghamshire*, purchased from Mr G. L. Morley, 1998
Mallender, L. active 1938–1973, *Interior, Worksop Priory, Nottinghamshire*, gift from Worksop Museum, 1984
Mallender, L. active 1938–1973, *Braydon Water, Yarmouth, Suffolk*, gift from Worksop Museum, 1984
Medley, Robert 1905–1994, *Beggars, Bird Carriers, Sweet Seller*, gift from the Contemporary Art Society, 1949, © James Hyman Fine Art on behalf of the estate of Robert Medley
Milnes, B. *Kilton Farm Cottages, Worksop, Nottinghamshire*, gift from Worksop Museum via Mr F. Owen, 1990
O'Dea, Eric *Corpus Christi*, gift from Worksop Museum via the Contemporary Art Society, 1984
Penrose, J. E. *Workhouse, Worksop, Nottinghamshire*, donated by Jennifer Masters, 2005
Pitchforth, Roland Vivian 1895–1982, *Boy's Head*, gift from Worksop Museum via the Contemporary Art Society, 1984, © the artist's estate
Richards, Ceri Geraldus 1903–1971, *St Cecilia*, gift from the Contemporary Art Society, 1952, © estate of Ceri Richards/DACS 2008
Royle, Stanley 1888–1961, *Evening Light, Fishing Village of Prospect, Nova Scotia, Canada*, gift from Worksop Museum, 1984, © the artist's estate/www.bridgeman.co.uk
Shipston, Olga *Red Bridge 3*, gift from Worksop Museum, 1984
Smith, Herbert *Sergeant William Henry Johnson (1890–1945), VC*, gift from Worksop Corporation, 1984
Spencer, Augustus 1860–1924, *Boy Reading a Newspaper*, gift from Worksop Museum, 1984
unknown artist *John Jones, CC (Manager of Shirebrook Colliery)*, gift from an unknown provenance
Waller, W. R. *Rattlesden, Suffolk*, gift from Worksop Museum, 1984
Warmby, Byron Winston 1902–1978, *The Mill Pond, Tickhill, South Yorkshire*, gift from Worksop Museum, 1984

Whall, Charles Albert b.1849, *Whitby Scaur Rocks, North Yorkshire*, gift from Worksop Museum via Mrs Whall, 1984
Whall, Charles Albert b.1849, *Whitby Scaur, North Yorkshire*, gift from Worksop Museum via Mrs Whall, 1984
Whall, Charles Albert b.1849, *Drinking Pit Lane*, gift from Worksop Museum via Mrs Whall, 1984
Whall, Charles Albert b.1849, *Haymaking at Shibbings Meadows*, gift from Worksop Museum via Mrs Whall, 1984
Whall, Charles Albert b.1849, *Beard's Mill, Worksop, Nottinghamshire*, bequeathed by Miss Beard, 1953, gift from Worksop Museum, 1984
Whall, Charles Albert (attributed to) b.1849, *Landscape with Cattle*, gift from Worksop Museum via Mrs Whall, 1984
Whall, Charles Albert (attributed to) b.1849, *Lyme Regis, Dorset*, gift from Worksop Museum via Mrs Whall, 1984
Whall, Charles Albert (attributed to) b.1849, *Marine Scene, Sidmouth, Devon*, gift from Worksop Museum via Mrs Whall, 1984
Whitton, Stanley *Llyn Dinas, near Beddgelert, North Wales*, purchased, 1973
Wood, Alan b.1935, *Kirkstall*, gift from the Contemporary Art Society, 1972

Retford Town Hall

Crighton, Hugh Ford 1824–1886, *John Smith, Esq., Mayor of East Retford (1864–1865 & 1867–1868)*, gift by public subscription, 1868
Hall, Frederick 1860–1948, *J. W. Holmes, Esq., Mayor of East Retford (1886, 1891 & 1901)*, gift by public subscription, © the artist's estate/ www.bridgeman.co.uk
Harrison-Brown, H. *Colonel Whittaker (?)*
Kennington, Thomas Benjamin 1856–1916, *Queen Victoria (1819–1901)*, commissioned for the commemoration of the Diamond Jubilee, 1867, gift from Alderman Denman to the Town of East Retford, 1898
Kennington, Thomas Benjamin 1856–1916, *Thomas William Denman, Esq., JP, Town Councillor (1866–1871), Alderman (1878–1905), and Mayor of East Retford (1883–1884)*
unknown artist *William Sterck Clock*, gift to the Corporation of East Retford from Councillor and Mrs Eris C. Spencer, Mayor and Mayoress, 1937
unknown artist *George II (1683–1760)*
unknown artist *Caroline Wilhelmina of Brandenburg-Ansbach (1683–1737), Consort to George II*
unknown artist *Colonel Francis Thornhach of Fenton (1617–1648), MP for East Retford*
unknown artist *William III (1650–1702), Reigned with Mary During Their Short Lives*
Ward, Edwin Arthur 1859–1933, *Thomas Bescoby, Mayor (1890)*

Ruddington Parish Council

Heaton, Roger *Silver Jubilee*, commissioned to commemorate HRH The Queen's Silver Jubliee, 1977

Ruddington Village Museum

Cooke, Jill *Scene at Wilford, Nottingham*, gift from an unknown source, 1969
Milward *Ruddington Village Green, Nottinghamshire, c.1960*, gift from Ruddington Library, 2007
Milward, William *E. Tillotson as a Boy Sailor*, gift from Mr A. Rappitt, 1991

Southwell Town Council

Arnfield, Marjorie 1930–2001, *Conservatory, Blackhouse Park, Sunderland, Tyne and Wear*, gift from the artist, © the artist's estate
Arnfield, Marjorie 1930–2001, *Water Gardens, Westhorpe, Suffolk*, gift from the artist, © the artist's estate

Sherwood Forest Hospitals NHS Foundation Trust

Arnfield, Marjorie 1930–2001, *Blue Flax*, gift from the estate of the artist, 2006, © the artist's estate, www.marjoriearnfield.co.uk
Arnfield, Marjorie 1930–2001, *Bonnieux, Provence, France*, gift from the estate of the artist, 2006, © the artist's estate, www.marjoriearnfield.co.uk
Cézanne, Paul (copy after) 1839–1906, *Mont St Michel*, gift from the Art in Health organisation, c.1996
Chowdhary, Ranjan b.1955, *Flower Basket*, gift from the artist to King's Mill Hospital, 2004, © the artist
Chowdhary, Ranjan b.1955, *Flowers in Abstract 1*, gift from the artist to King's Mill Hospital, 2005, © the artist
Chowdhary, Ranjan b.1955, *Flowers in Abstract 2*, gift from the artist to King's Mill Hospital, 2005, © the artist
Chowdhary, Ranjan b.1955, *Flowers in Abstract 3*, gift from the artist to King's Mill Hospital, 2005, © the artist
Chowdhary, Ranjan b.1955, *Flowers in Abstract 4*, gift from the artist to King's Mill Hospital, 2005, © the artist
Chowdhary, Ranjan b.1955, *Nature's Delight*, gift from the artist to King's Mill Hospital, 2005, © the artist
Chowdhary, Ranjan b.1955, *Colours in Nature*, gift from the artist to Newark Community Hospital, 2008, © the artist
Chowdhary, Ranjan b.1955, *Flower Vase*, gift from the artist to Newark Community Hospital, 2008, © the artist
Chowdhary, Ranjan b.1955, *Iris No.1*, gift from the artist to Newark Community Hospital, 2008, © the artist
Chowdhary, Ranjan b.1955, *Iris No.2*, gift from the artist to Newark Community Hospital, 2008, © the artist
Chowdhary, Ranjan b.1955, *Poinsettia*, gift from the artist to Newark Community Hospital, 2008, © the artist
Cook, Beryl (copy after) 1926–2008, *Sailors**, gift from the Art in Health organisation, c.1996
Dabrowski, Stanislaw 1882–1973, *Farmyard Scene**, gift from the artist, before 2001
Dabrowski, Stanislaw 1882–1973, *Lighthouse Storm**, gift from the artist
Dabrowski, Stanislaw 1882–1973, *The Battle of Waterloo, 18 June 1815*, gift from the artist, before 2001
Gogh, Vincent van (copy after) 1853–1890, *A Wheatfield, with Cypresses*, gift from the Art in Health organisation, c.1996
Gogh, Vincent van (copy after) 1853–1890, *Irises*, gift from the Art in Health organisation, c.1996
Gogh, Vincent van (copy after) 1853–1890, *Sunflowers*, gift from the Art in Health organisation, c.1996
Gogh, Vincent van (copy after) 1853–1890, *The Café Terrace on the Place Forum, Arles, at Night*, gift from the Art in Health organisation, c.1996
Matisse, Henri (copy after) 1869–1954, *Music*, gift from the Art in Health organisation, c.1996
Picasso, Pablo (copy after) 1881–1973, *Les baigneuses*, gift from the Art in Health organisation, c.1996
Renoir, Pierre-Auguste (copy after) 1841–1919, *Luncheon of the Boating Party*, gift from the Art in Health organisation, c.1996
Rousseau, Henri (copy after) 1844–1910, *Leopard in the Jungle*, gift from the Art in Health organisation, c.1996
Seurat, Georges (copy after) 1859–1891, *A Sunday Afternoon on the Island of La Grande Jatte*, gift from the Art in Health organisation, c.1996
unknown artist *Abstract No.11**, purchased, late 1990s
unknown artist *Abstract No.12**, purchased, late 1990s
unknown artist *Abstract No.13**, purchased, late 1990s
unknown artist *Abstract No.14**, purchased, late 1990s
unknown artist *Abstract No.15**, purchased, late 1990s
unknown artist *Abstract No.16**, purchased, late 1990s
unknown artist *Abstract No.17**, purchased, late 1990s
unknown artist *Abstract No.18**, purchased, late 1990s
unknown artist *Abstract No.22**, purchased, late 1990s
unknown artist *Abstract No.23**, purchased, late 1990s
unknown artist *Sunflowers*, gift from the Art in Health organisation, c.1996
Weston, C. *Sand Dunes**, gift from the artist

British Horological Institute

Carey, Charles William 1862–1943, *John Jones of the Strand (1815–1909), Watchmaker of the Strand*, commissioned by the members of the British Horological Institute, c.1900
Formier, Alexander (attributed to) *Abbeville Church, Normandy, France*, on loan from a private collector
Kneller, Godfrey (attributed to) 1646–1723, *Thomas Tompion (1638–1713), 'Father of English Clockmaking'*, gift from James Lund, c.1875
Kneller, Godfrey (school of) 1646–1723, *Alan Brodrick (c.1656–1728), 1st Viscount Midleton*, on loan from a private collector
unknown artist *Michael Laurence Bateman (1893–1966), Vice-President and Past Chairman of the British Horological Institute*, bequeathed, c.1966
unknown artist *William John (1798–1870), 7th Viscount Midleton, Dean of Exeter*, on loan from a private collector

Creswell Crags Museum and Education Centre

Hyatt, John A. *Creswell Crags, Nottinghamshire*, donated by the artist to the education centre, 2002

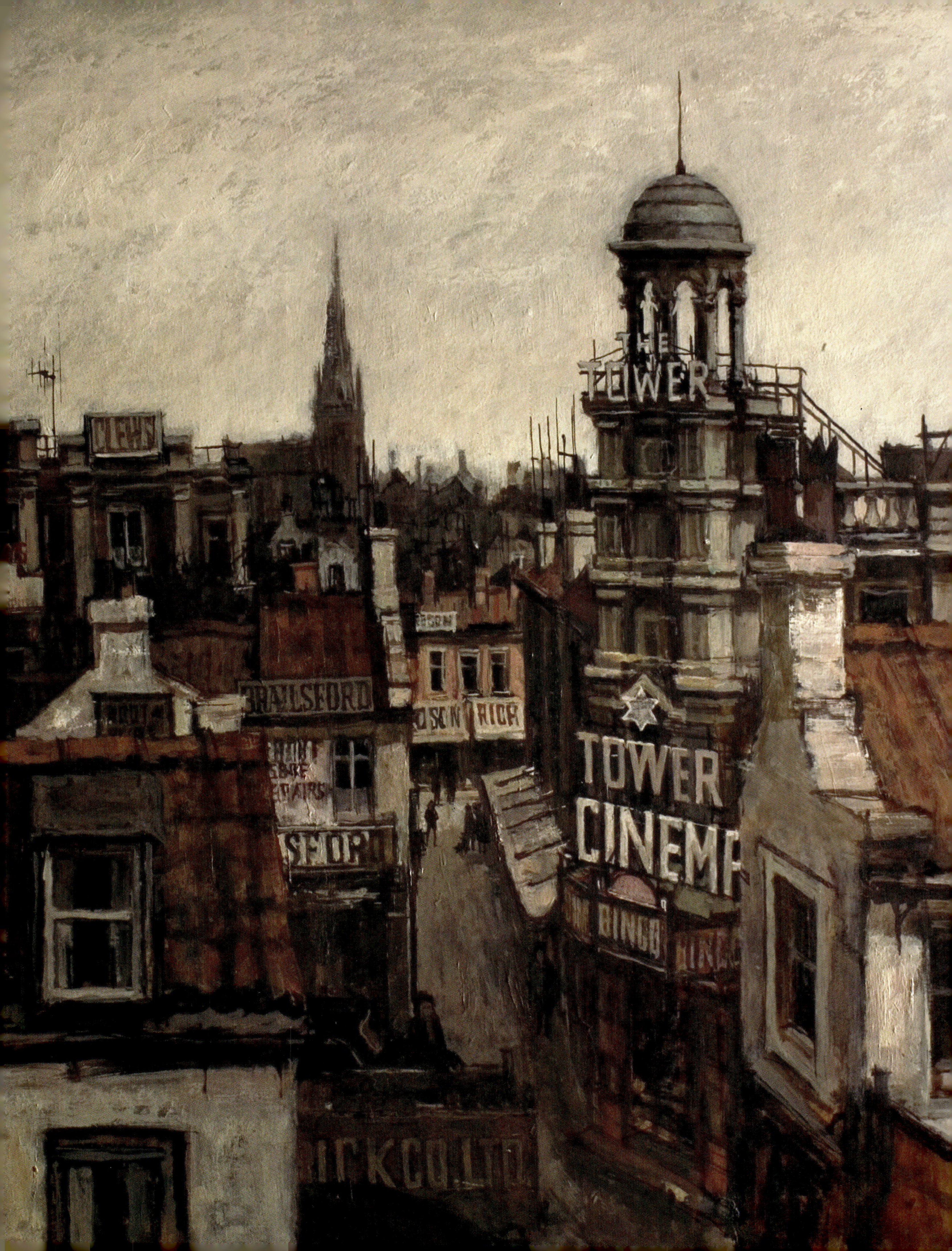
THE TOWER
TOWER
BINGO

Collection Addresses

Arnold

Gedling Borough Council
Civic Centre, Arnot Hill Park, Arnold NG5 6LU
Telephone 0115 9013901

Kirkby-in-Ashfield

Ashfield District Council
Urban Road, Kirkby-in-Ashfield NG17 8DA
Telephone 01623 450000

Mansfield

Langwith Whaley Thorns Heritage Centre
Methodist Chapel, West Street, Langwith
Mansfield NG20 9BW
Telephone 01623 747601

Mansfield District Council:

> Mansfield District Council
> Civic Centre, Chesterfield Road South
> Mansfield NG19 7BH
> Telephone 01623 463463
>
> Mansfield Museum & Art Gallery
> Leeming Street, Mansfield NG18 1NG
> Telephone 01623 463088

Mansfield Fire Station Museum
Rosemary Street, Mansfield NG19 6AB
Telephone 01623 666999

Nottinghamshire County Teaching Primary Care Trust:

> Nottinghamshire County Teaching Primary
> Care Trust
> Ransom Hall, Southwell Road West
> Rainworth, Mansfield NG21 0ER
> Telephone 01623 414114
>
> Ashfield Community Hospital
> Portland Street, Kirkby-in-Ashfield NG17 7AE
> Telephone 01623 785050
>
> Mansfield Community Hospital
> Stockwell Gate, Mansfield NG18 5QJ
> Telephone 01623 785091

Portland College
Nottingham Road, Mansfield NG18 4TJ
Telephone 01623 499100

Newark-on-Trent

Newark and Sherwood Museum Service
Newark Millgate Museum, 48 Millgate, Newark NG24 4TS
Telephone 01636 655730

Newark Town Council:

> Newark Town Hall Museum & Art Gallery
> Market Place, Newark NG24 1DU
> Telephone 01636 680333

The Holocaust Centre
Laxton, Newark NG22 0PA
Telephone 01623 836627

Newstead

Newstead Abbey
Newstead Abbey Park NG15 8NA
Telephone 01623 455900

Nottingham

Castle College Nottingham
Maid Marian Way, Nottingham NG1 6AB
Telephone 0115 8842203

Djanogly City Academy Nottingham
Sherwood Rise, Nottingham Road, Nottingham NG7 7AR
Telephone 0115 9424422

Galleries of Justice
High Pavement, Lace Market, Nottingham NG1 1HN
Telephone 0115 9520555

Government Office for the East Midlands
The Belgrave Centre, Stanley Place, Talbot Street
Nottingham NG1 5GG
Telephone 0115 9719971

Nottingham Central Library
Angel Row, Nottingham NG1 6HP
Telephone 0115 9152873

Facing page: Brannan, Peter, 1926–1994, *View of a Town* (detail), 1968, Newark Town Council (p. 27)

Nottingham City Museums and Galleries:

Nottingham City Museums and Galleries
Castle Place, Nottingham NG1 6EL
Telephone 0115 9153672

Nottingham Castle Museum and Art Gallery
Friar Lane, Off Maid Marian Way
Nottingham NG1 6EL
Telephone 0115 9153 700

Nottingham Industrial Museum
Wollaton Park, Courtyard Stables, Wollaton
Nottingham NG8 2AE
Telephone 0115 9153900

Nottingham Natural History Museum
Wollaton Hall, Wollaton, Nottingham NG8 2AE
Telephone 0115 9153900

The Museum of Nottingham Life at
Brewhouse Yard
Castle Boulevard, Nottingham NG7 1FB
Telephone 0115 9153600

Wollaton Hall
Wollaton, Nottingham NG8 2AE
Telephone 0115 9153900

Nottingham Magistrates' Court
Carrington Street, Nottingham NG2 1EE
Telephone 0115 9558111

Nottingham Trent University
Burton Street, Nottingham NG1 4BU
Telephone 0115 9418418

Nottinghamshire Archives
County House, Castle Meadow Road
Nottingham NG2 1AG
Telephone 0115 9504524

Nottinghamshire County Cricket Club
Trent Bridge Ground, Nottingham NG2 6AG
Telephone 0115 9823000

Nottinghamshire County Football Club
Meadow Lane, Nottingham NG2 3HJ
Telephone 0115 9529000

Nottinghamshire County Hall
West Bridgford, Nottingham NG2 7QP
Telephone 0115 9823823

Nottinghamshire County Library Service:

Nottinghamshire County Library Service
County Hall, West Bridgford
Nottingham NG2 7QP
Telephone 0115 9774401

Arnold Library
Front Street, Arnold NG5 7EE
Telephone 0115 9202247

Eastwood Library
Wellington Place, Eastwood NG16 3GB
Telephone 01773 712209

Hucknall Library
South Street, Hucknall NG15 7BS
Telephone 0115 9632035

Ravenshead Library
Milton Court, Ravenshead NG15 9BD
Telephone 01623 794634

Retford Library
Churchgate, Retford DN22 6PE
Telephone 01777 708724

Stapleford Library
Church Street, Stapleford NG9 8GA
Telephone 0115 9399178

Nottinghamshire Police
City Division, Central Police Station
North Church Street, Nottingham NG1 4BH
Telephone 0115 9482999

Rushcliffe Borough Council
Civic Centre, Pavilion Road, West Bridgford
Nottingham NG2 5FE
Telephone 0115 9819911

The Congregational Memorial Hall Trust (1978) Limited
8 Castle Gate, Nottingham NG1 7AS
Telephone 0115 9111460

The Council House
Old Market Square, Nottingham NG1 2DT
Telephone 0115 9155012

The Sherwood Rangers Yeomanry Regimental Association:

Sherwood Rangers Yeomanry Museum
TA Centre, Cavendish Drive, Carlton
Nottingham NG4 3DX
Telephone 0115 9618722

The University of Nottingham
Djanogly Art Gallery, Lakeside Arts Centre
University Park, Nottingham NG7 2RD
Telephone 0115 9513192

The Worcestershire and Sherwood Foresters Museum (The Sherwood Foresters Collection) of the Mercian Regiment
c/o Nottingham Castle, Friar Lane, Off Maid Marian Way
Nottingham NG1 6EL
Telephone 0115 9465415

Retford

Bassetlaw District Council:

Bassetlaw Museum and Percy Laws Memorial Gallery
Amcott House, 40 Grove Street
Retford DN22 6LD
Telephone 01777 713749

Retford Town Hall
17b The Square, Retford DN22 6DB
Telephone 01777 713861

Ruddington

Ruddington Parish Council
St Peter's Rooms, Church Street, Ruddington NG11 6HA
Telephone 0115 9146660

Ruddington Village Museum
St Peter's Rooms, Church Street, Ruddington NG11 6HA
Telephone 0115 9146645

Southwell

Southwell Town Council
The Old Court House, The Burgage, Southwell NG25 0EP
Telephone 01636 816103

Sutton-in-Ashfield

Sherwood Forest Hospitals NHS Foundation Trust:

King's Mill Hospital
Mansfield Road, Sutton-in-Ashfield NG17 4JL
Telephone 01623 622515

Newark Hospital
Boundary Road, Newark NG24 4DE
Telephone 01636 681681

Upton

British Horological Institute:

Upton Hall Museum of Time
Upton Hall, Upton NG23 5TE
Telephone 01636 813795

Worksop

Creswell Crags Museum and Education Centre
Crags Road, Welbeck, Worksop S80 3LH
Telephone 01909 720378

Index of Artists

In this catalogue, artists' names and the spelling of their names follow the preferred presentation of the name in the Getty Union List of Artist Names (ULAN) as of February 2004, if the artist is listed in ULAN.

The page numbers next to each artist's name below direct readers to paintings that are by the artist; are attributed to the artist; or, in a few cases, are more loosely related to the artist being, for example, 'after', 'the circle of' or copies of a painting by the artist. The precise relationship between the artist and the painting is listed in the catalogue.

Adeney, William Bernard (1878–1966) 27
Adnams, Marion (1898–1995) 57
Agar, Eileen (1899–1991) 220
Aitchison, Craigie Ronald John (b.1926) 57, 163
Alexander, Cosmo (1724–1772) 198
Allori, Cristofano (1577–1621) 57
Allsebrook, Kenneth 220
Anderson, Douglas Hardinge (b.1934) 198
Armfield, Maxwell Ashby (1882–1972) 57
Arnfield, Marjorie (1930–2001) 14, 15, 198, 232, 233
Arnfield, Nick (1961–1999) 198
Artaud, William (1763–1823) 57
Ashton, Garry John (b.1954) 220
Atkinson, John Augustus (1775–1833) 57
Bacon, John Henry Frederick (1865–1914) 57
Baker, Thomas (1809–1869) 57
Baldock, James Walsham (1822–1898) 221, 222
Balen, Hendrik van I (1575–1632) 76
Ball, Henry (1894–1966) 51, 58
Banner, Delmar Harmond (1896–1983) 58
Barber, Thomas (1771–1843) 34, 46, 58, 59, 241
Barke, Christopher 200
Barker, John Edward (1889–1953) 59
Barker, Kit (1916–1988) 222
Barker, L. 222
Barker, Thomas (1769–1847) 59
Barker, Thomas Jones (1815–1882) 60
Barker, Wright (1864–1941) 5
Barraud, Henry (1811–1874) 34
Barret, George (1732–1784) 60
Barrett, Thomas (1845–1924) 60, 241
Barron, Dennis (active 1999–2001) 6, 14
Bartrop, Darwin Holdsworth (b.1882) 222
Bates, David (1841–1921) 60
Bates, Marjorie Christine (1883–1962) 179, 200
Batson, Francis Cunningham (1858–1931) 177
Bayliss, Wyke (1835–1906) 60
Bearpark, John Victor (b.1946) 27
Beechey, William (1753–1839) 60, 200
Beeton, Alan (1880–1942) 61
Bega, Cornelis Pietersz. (1631/1632–1664) 61
Bell, John (1823–1881) 34
Bell, Vanessa (1879–1961) 18, 241
Belleroche, Albert de (1864–1944) 61
Benner, William (1884–1964) 18, 61
Bennett, Chris (b.1957) 200
Benyon, Margaret (b.1940) 61
Ben-Zenou, Helena (b.1970) 61
Bertrand, James (1823–1887) 6
Beth, Tew 165
Bevan, Tony (b.1951) 61
Bilbie, James Lees (1860–1945) 61, 62
Bird, Edward (1772–1819) 62
Birks, J. 6
Birley, Oswald Hornby Joseph (1880–1952) 62, 200
Birrell, William 200
Bissill, George William (1896–1973) 6
Bixio, Roberto (b.1947) 200
Blaas, Eugen von (1843–1931) 62
Blache, Christian Vigilius (1838–1920) 62
Black, Arthur John (1855–1936) 62
Blood, Gerry (1932–2005) 6
Boden, Leonard (1911–1999) 201
Bogdany, Jakob (c.1660–1724) 63
Bomberg, David (1890–1957) 63
Bond, Jane (b.1939) 201
Bonington, Richard (1768–1835) 63
Bonington, Richard Parkes (1802–1828) 63, 65, 109
Booth, James William (1867–1953) 65
Both, Andries Dirksz. (1611/1612–1641) 66
Both, Jan (c.1618–1652) 66
Boudin, Eugène Louis (1824–1898) 66
Bough, Samuel (1822–1878) 66
Boultbee, John (1753–1812) 196
Bowen, Siân (b.1959) 241
Bowett, Druie (1924–1998) 222
Boynton, Winifred D. (active c.1938–1940) 186
Bradbury, W. 66
Bradley, Robert (1813–1880) 66
Brannan, Peter (1926–1994) 18, 27, 260
Bray, Julian (b.1965) 6
Brennand-Wood, Michael (b.1952) 66
Bretland, Thomas W. (1802–1874) 6, 66
Brett, John (1830–1902) 66
Brickland 48
Bright, Henry (1814–1873) 67, 201

Bristow, Edmund (1787–1876) 67
British (English) School 18, 20, 34, 67–72, 201, 202
British (Norwich) School 72, 74
Bronzino, Agnolo (1503–1572) 74
Brooks, Sally 241
Brown, Ford Madox (1821–1893) 74
Brown, John Alfred Arnesby (1866–1955) 74, 75, 189
Brown, Neil Dallas (1938–2003) 75
Brownsword, Harry A. (1862–1920) 202
Brueghel, Jan the elder (1568–1625) 76
Buchanan, George F. (1800–1864) 76
Buckingham, Jennie Beatrice (b.1968) 202
Buckner, Richard (1812–1883) 27
Burchell, William F. 186
Burrows, Sarah Elisabeth 51
Burton, Alice Mary (1893–1968) 76
Burton, Harry Marriott (1882–1979) 76
Burton, John (active 1769–1836) 76
Burton, Marjorie E. (active 1980) 183
Bussey, Reuben (1818–1893) 51, 76, 202
Byron, Richard (1724–1811) 34
Bywater, J. E. 6, 7
Caledfryn, Ap (1837–1915) 189
Calkin, Lance (1859–1936) 77
Callcott, Augustus Wall (1779–1844) 77
Canaletto (1697–1768) 77
Capey, Reco (1895–1961) 77
Carey, Charles William (1862–1943) 238
Carmichael, John Wilson (1800–1868) 77
Carpenter, Margaret Sarah (1793–1872) 78
Carter, Frank 7
Cézanne, Paul (1839–1906) 232
Chaffin, Donald 34
Chalon, Henry Bernard (1771–1849) 35
Chambers, George (1803–1840) 78
Chandler, John Westbrooke (1764–1804/1805) 78
Chantron, Alexandre Jacques (1842–1918) 78
Chapman, Max (1911–1999) 78
Charlton, John (1849–1917) 78
Cheall, John (b.1965) 44
Cheese, Bernard (b.1925) 78, 226
Chowdhary, Ranjan (b.1955) 233, 234
Chowne, Gerard (1875–1917) 27
Christoforou, John (b.1921) 79
Clark, Heath Richard (b.1970) 7
Clarke, Harry Harvey (1869–1948) 79
Clausen, George (1852–1944) 79
Clayton, William J. M. (active 1963–1991) 79
Clegg, William George (1863–1940) 223
Cleve, Joos van (c.1464–c.1540) 79, 127
Clint, George (1770–1854) 79
Cockrill, Maurice (b.1936) 202
Codde, Pieter Jacobsz. (1599–1678) 79
Cohen, Harold (b.1928) 202
Coker, Peter (1926–2004) 7
Cole, George Vicat (1833–1893) 79
Coleridge, Francis George (1838–1923) 20
Colkett, Samuel David (1806–1863) 80
Collaku, B. Y. 49
Collier, Herbert Hood (1863–1947) 80
Collins, Charles Allston (1828–1873) 80
Collins, James Edgell (1819–1895) 35
Collins, William (1788–1847) 80, 203
Collinson, James (1825–1881) 80
Colvile, Harry Morton (1905–1992) 203
Constable, John (1776–1837) 4, 15, 81
Constant, Jean Joseph Benjamin (1845–1902) 81
Cook, Beryl (1926–2008) 234
Cook, Margaret C. (b.c.1897) 7
Cooke, Anthony R. (b.1933) 81
Cooke, Ernest Owen (1862–1937) 81
Cooke, Jill 231
Cooke, Stanley (b.1913) 7
Cooper, Frederick Carter (c.1795–1875) 81
Cooper, Gerald (1898–1975) 81
Cooper, Samuel (1609–1672) 203
Cooper, Thomas Sidney (1803–1902) 81, 83
Corbould, Alfred (c.1821–1874) 35
Corbould, Edward Henry (1815–1905) 83
Cort, Hendrik Frans de (1742–1810) 83
Cortona, Pietro da (1596–1669) 83
Couldery, Horatio Henri (1832–1910) 83
Cowlishaw, Tony (b.1944) 203–205, 241
Cox, Alfred Wilson (1820–1890) 83
Cox, E. 51
Coyne, Douglas (1930–2008) 20
Crighton, Hugh Ford (1824–1886) 229
Critz, John de the elder (1551/1552–1642) 84
Crome, John (1768–1821) 84
Crome, William Henry (1806–1873) 84
Crowley, Graham (b.1950) 84, 190
Cubley, Henry Hadfield (1858–1934) 20, 27
Cubley, William Harold (1814–1896) 21–23, 28, 84, 205
Culbert, Bill (b.1935) 84, 205
Cundall, Charles Ernest (1890–1971) 84, 85
Curran, Amelia (1775–1847) 35
Dabrowski, Stanislaw (1882–1973) 234
Dahl, Michael I (1656/1659–1743) 35
Daniels, Alfred (b.1924) 85
Darking, Harry Fred (1911–1999) 205
Davie, Alan (b.1920) 85
Davis, Noel Denholm (1876–1950) 85, 86, 91, 172, 179, 186, 196, 205, 206, 219, 241
Davis, W. Gronow 223
Dawe, George (1781–1829) 206
Dawson, Alfred (b.1843) 86
Dawson, Henry (1811–1878) 51, 86–88, 206
de Castella, Hubert (active 1999–2000) 206
De Karlowska, Stanislawa (1876–1952) 88
Deacon, Peter (b.1945) 88
Delacroix, Eugène (1798–1863) 23, 88
Delaney, Barbara (b.1941) 223
Detaille, Jean Baptiste Edouard (1848–1912) 88
Di Stefano, Arturo (b.1955) 206
Dobson, Henry John (1858–1928) 88
Dobson, William (1611–1646) 28
Dobson, William Charles Thomas (1817–1898) 173
Dodd, Charles J. B. 3

Dodd, Charles Tattershall I (1815–1878) 89
Dollman, John Charles (1851–1934) 89
Dossi, Dosso (c.1486–1542) 89
Doubleday, Matthew (c.1828–1900) 179
Downar, S. 223
Dugdale, Thomas Cantrell (1880–1952) 89
Dunlop, Ronald Ossory (1894–1973) 89
Dupont, Gainsborough (1754–1797) 89
Dutch School 89
Dyce, William (1806–1864) 89
Dyck, Anthony van (1599–1641) 36, 90
Dyer, Peter 165–167
Earl, Sandra 167
East, Alfred (1844–1913) 90
Edwards, Edwin (1823–1879) 90, 179
Eisenhut, Ferencz (1857–1903) 92
Elliot, W. J. (active 1924–1966) 183
Ellis, Edwin (1841–1895) 92, 93, 186
Elmore, Alfred (1815–1881) 93
Elwell, Frederick William (1870–1958) 93
Enfield, Henry (1849–1911) 93
Etty, William (1787–1849) 93
Eurich, Richard Ernst (1903–1992) 94
Evans, E. S. 16
Evans, Merlyn Oliver (1910–1973) 94
Evans, Norman 223
Evans, William (1911–1978) 207
Farmer, Walter (1870–1947) 94
Farquharson, David (1839–1907) 94
Farquharson, Joseph (1846–1935) 94
Farrar, S. 241
Feldman, Neil (b.1947) 167
Ferg, Franz de Paula (1689–1740) 94
Ferrari, Defendente (1480–1485–c.1540) 94, 95
Firth, John H. S. (1912–c.1970) 95, 96
Fischer, Hans (1849–1886) 96
Fisk, William Henry (1827–1884) 96
Fitton, James (1899–1982) 64, 96
Flemish School 97
Fletcher, John Henry (active 1880–1922) 97
Fletcher, William Teulon Blandford (1858–1936) 97
Forbes, D. 223
Forbes, Stanhope Alexander (1857–1947) 23, 97
Forbes-Robertson, Janine (active 1908–1912) 97
Formier, Alexander 238
Foster, Herbert Wilson (1846–1929) 19, 97, 186, 187
Fraser, Donald Hamilton (b.1929) 98
Freckleton, Harry (1890–1979) 98
Freedman, Barnett (1901–1958) 98
French, H. 223
French School 98
Frith, William Powell (1819–1909) 98
Frost, T. 179
Frost, William Edward (1810–1877) 98
Fry, Roger Eliot (1866–1934) 207
Fuller, Leonard John (1891–1973) 28
Fumi 207
Gainsborough, Thomas (1727–1788) 36, 98
Gamble, F. Lorence 241
Ganesco, Alexandre (1910–1979) 23
Gardner, Daniel (1750–1805) 98
Geefs, Fanny (1807–1883) 36
Gentileschi, Artemisia (1593–1651/1653) 98
Gentle, Harry 179
German School 99
Gertler, Mark (1892–1939) 99
Gibbon, Sidney (1895–1988) 23
Gibbs, Evelyn (1905–1991) 99
Gilbert, A. 7
Gillies, Margaret (1803–1887) 99
Gillott, Thomas J. (1886–1913) 99, 101
Girardot, Ernest Gustave (1840–1904) 101
Glover, Carole 207
Glover, John (1767–1849) 101
Gogh, Vincent van (1853–1890) 234, 236
Gogin, Charles (1844–1931) 101
Good, Thomas Sword (1789–1872) 101
Goodacre, William (1803–1883) 101
Goodall, Frederick (1822–1904) 102
Goodwin, Albert (1845–1932) 52
Gordon, John Watson (1788–1864) 207
Gorski, Stefan (b.1932) 102
Gowing, Lawrence (1918–1991) 102
Grace 15
Grant, E. E. (d.c.1970) 23
Grant, Francis (1803–1878) 189
Gratia, Charles-Louis (1815–1911) 102
Gratton, Lucinda (b.1976) 207
Greaves, Leonard (1918–1949) 102
Green, Kenneth (1905–1986) 102
Gresley, Harold (1892–1967) 16
Grici, Claude 207
Gush, William (1813–1888) 102
Guttuso, Renato (1912–1987) 23
Hackaert, Jan (1629–1699) 103
Hall, Frederick (1860–1948) 229
Hall, Lilian Iris 'Betty' 23
Hall, Margaret M. 187
Hall, R. (active 1971) 7, 8
Hallam, J. C. 52
Halledine, G. H. (active 20th C) 103
Halliday, Trevor (b.1939) 241
Halls, John James (1776–1853) 36
Hals, Dirck (1591–1656) 103
Hamilton, William (1751–1801) 103
Hammond, Thomas William (1854–1935) 179
Hampson, Derek (b.1952) 207, 209
Hampson, John (b.1898) 8
Hancock, K. B. 32
Harbord, R. C. 8
Harrison-Brown, H. 229
Hart, James Turpin (1835–1899) 103, 104
Hart, John (1921–1996) 104
Hart, Robert (b.1956) 168
Hartley, Alfred (1855–1933) 104
Hartwell, William John (1922–1995) 223
Harvey, William (1796–1866) 104
Haweis, Stephen (1878–1969) 104

Hawksley, Arthur (1842–1915) 105
Hawthorne, Carole Diane (b.1945) 168
Hayes, Edwin (1819–1904) 105
Hayes, Frederick William (1848–1918) 105
Hayllar, James (1829–1920) 105
Hayter, George (1792–1871) 191
Hayward, Liz (b.1949) 224
Head, Guy (1753–1800) 106
Heaphy, Thomas (1775–1835) 106
Heaton, Roger 230
Hebden, Rosemary 209
Hector, G. (active 2006) 224
Hedderly, Nick (b.1961) 106
Heemskerck, Egbert van the elder (1634/1635–1704) 106
Hempton, Paul (b.1946) 106, 241
Hemsley, Antony (b.1965) 168
Henson, Edward (c.1852–after 1891) 106
Hepple, Norman (1908–1994) 209
Herbert, John Rogers (1810–1890) 28, 106
Herring, John Frederick I (1795–1865) 106, 107
Hewetson, Richard (active 19th C) 209
Hicken, Harry (d.2000) 224
Hill, Chas G. 8
Hill, Robert W. (1932–1990) 107
Hillier, Tristram Paul (1905–1983) 107
Hilton, William II (1786–1839) 107
Himona, Nicolas (1865–1929) 107
Hingsley, W. C. 180
Hitchens, Ivon (1893–1979) 107
Hoare, William (1706–1792) 210
Hode, T. 52
Holl, Frank (1845–1888) 191
Holland, James (1800–1870) 107
Holland, John (c.1805–1880) 107, 108
Holloway, Robert (1896–1976) 8
Holmes, Alan 224
Hondecoeter, Gillis Claesz. de (c.1575–1638) 108
Hondecoeter, Melchior de (1636–1695) 108
Hooch, Pieter de (1629–1684) 8
Hook, James Clarke (1819–1907) 108
Hoppner, John (1758–1810) 108
Horemans, Pieter Jacob (1700–1776) 110
Horsley, John Callcott (1817–1903) 110
Houckgeest, Joachim Ottensz. (c.1585–before 1645) 36
Houthuesen, Albert Anthony (1903–1979) 110
Howson, Peter (b.1958) 110
Hudson, Keith 224
Hudson, Robert (1852–1884) 224
Hudson, Thomas (1701–1779) 191
Hughes-Stanton, Herbert Edwin Pelham (1870–1937) 110
Hulbert, Thelma (1913–1995) 110
Humphrey, J. 15
Hunt, Doreen 210
Hunter, Norma 210
Huskinson, Leonard (1905–1974) 110
Hyatt, John A. 239
Ibbetson, Julius Caesar (1759–1817) 110
Inlander, Henry (1925–1983) 210
Isaac, Susan (b.1961) 28
Italian (Florentine) School 111
Italian (Milanese) School 111
Jagger, David (1891–1958) 111, 217
James, Robert (1809–1853) 111
Jay, William Samuel (1843–1933) 111
Jervas, Charles (c.1675–1739) 191
Jobbins, William H. (c.1840–1893) 111
John, Augustus Edwin (1878–1961) 111
Johnson, A. 52
Johnson, Ernest Borough (1866–1949) 111
Jones, Chris 210, 211
Jones, George (1786–1869) 111, 112
Jones, Tom 8
Jones, W. A. (active 1968–1969) 224
Joseph, George Francis (1764–1846) 10, 173
Kauffman, Angelica (1740–1807) 112
Kempson, Mary 224
Kennington, Thomas Benjamin (1856–1916) 225, 229
Keyser, Willem de (c.1647–1692) 112
Kiddey, Robert (1900–1984) 28
Kiddier, William (1859–1934) 112, 113
Kidger, C. W. 9
Kinley, Peter (1926–1988) 225
Kirk, Eve (1900–1969) 225
Knapp, Stefan (1921–1996) 113
Kneale, Bryan (b.1930) 113
Kneller, Godfrey (1646–1723) 36, 113, 191, 211, 238
Knight, Harold (1874–1961) 28, 113–115, 241
Knight, John Prescott (1803–1881) 115
Knight, Laura (1877–1970) 115, 116, 199, 211
Knowles, William Pitcairn (c.1846–c.1904) 24
Krit, D. 196
La Thangue, Henry Herbert (1859–1929) 116
Labad, Alberto (b.1940) 117
Lacey, Elias (b.1871) 183, 184
Lachenwitz, F. Sigmund (1820–1868) 187
Lambert 15
Lambert, George (c.1700–1765) 117
Laming, Ruth 184
Landseer, Edwin Henry (1802–1873) 117
Lane, H. S. 9
Largillière, Nicolas de (1656–1746) 117
László, Philip Alexius de (1869–1937) 16
Lawrence, Thomas (1769–1830) 38, 173, 211
Laws, Percy S. (1892–1972) 225
Le Brun, Charles (1619–1690) vi, 117
Le Brun, Christopher (b.1951) 117
Leavers, Lucy Ann (1845–1915) 117
Lee, Frederick Richard (1798–1879) 119
Lee-Hankey, William (1869–1952) 119
Lees, Stewart Marshall 211, 241
Lelienbergh, Cornelis (1626–1676) 119
Lennox Gordon, Archie (b.c.1889) 119
Lethière, Guillaume (1760–1832) 119
Leverett, David (b.1938) 119
Lewis, George Robert (1782–1871) 119
Lewis, Neville (1895–1972) 119, 120
Lewis, Reginald (b.1901) 196
Lewis, Simon (b.1945) 169

Liebert, Judith 169
Lingelbach, Johannes (1622–1674) 120
Linnell, John (1792–1882) 120, 191
Linton, James Dromgole (1840–1916) 28, 120
Long, John Kenneth (b.1924) 120
Lonsdale, James (1777–1839) 38, 120
Lopez, Gasparo (1650–1732) 120
Lorimer, John Henry (1856–1936) 120
Loutherbourg, Philip James de (1740–1812) 121
Lowe, Arthur (1866–1940) 121, 241
Lowry, Laurence Stephen (1887–1976) 121
Loxton Knight, Edward (1905–1993) 121
Lucy, Charles (1814–1873) 121
Luker, William (c.1820–1892) 38
Luntley, James (1827–1887) 121
Lytton, Neville Stephen (1879–1951) 38
Macaskill, Duncan 212
MacBryde, Robert (1913–1966) 122
MacCallum, Andrew (1821–1902) 122
MacDougall, William Brown (1869–1936) 122
Machicado, Juan de la Cruz (b.1935) 100, 212
Maclise, Daniel (1806–1870) 122, 208
Makinson, Trevor (b.1926) 187
Malaysian School 212
Malbon, William (1805–1877) 122
Mallender, L. (active 1938–1973) 225
Mann, Alexander (1853–1908) 123
Mann, Harrington (1864–1936) 123
Martin, Ross (active 1989–1990) 169, 170
Martinez, Raymond (b.1937) 123
Martin-Richards, Marjorie (active 1959) 123
Mason, Arnold (1885–1963) 24, 240
Mason, Bateson (1910–1977) 123, 154
Masson, Hippolyte (d.1878) 38
Master of the Antwerp Adoration (active c.1520) 123
Matisse, Henri (1869–1954) 236
Matosic, Paul (b.1955) 170
Maurice, Constance 123
Mayfield, F. 187
McGegan, Christine Mary (1923–1989) 212
Measures, David (b.1937) 241
Medley, Robert (1905–1994) 225
Meninsky, Bernard (1891–1950) 123
Michie, James Coutts (1861–1919) 124
Middleditch, Edward (1923–1987) 124
Miles, George Francis (1852–1891) 124, 177
Miller, William (1796–1882) 124
Mills, Edwin Robin 164
Milnes, B. 225
Milroy, Lisa (b.1959) 124
Milward 231
Milward, William 231
Mitchell, John Campbell (1865–1922) 124
Molenaer, Klaes (c.1630–1676) 124
Monamy, Peter (1681–1749) 125
Monnoyer, Jean-Baptiste (1636–1699) 125
Moore, Claude Thomas Stanfield (1853–1901) 125
Moore, Thomas Cooper (1827–1901) 9, 53, 125, 174, 180
Morland, George (1763–1804) 126, 128
Morland, Henry Robert (c.1716–1797) 128
Morley, Henry (1869–1937) 128
Morrocco, Alberto (1917–1998) 24
Mortlock, Ethel (c.1865–1928) 128
Moynihan, Rodrigo (1910–1990) 24
Mulready, William (1786–1863) 128
Mundy, William Percy (b.1936) 212
Murray, David (1849–1933) 128
Murray, Trevor 184
Mytens, Daniel I (c.1590–before 1648) 129
Nanaway, William E. 212
Napier, John James (1831–1877) 191
Neale, George Hall (1863–1940) 213
Neeffs, Peeter the elder (c.1578–1656–1661) 129
Neer, Aert van der (1603–1677) 129
Neer, Eglon Hendrik van der (1634–1703) 129
Neuhuys, Albertus Johan (1844–1914) 129
Nevinson, Christopher (1889–1946) 129
Newcomb, Mary (1922–2008) 213
Newling, Edward (active 1890–1934) 129
Newton, Alfred Pizzey (1830–1883) 129
Newton, Algernon Cecil (1880–1968) 129
Nicholson, Ben (1894–1982) 130
Nicholson, William (1872–1949) 24, 29, 30, 130, 181
Nicholson, Winifred (1893–1981) 24, 30, 130
Niemann, Edmund John (1813–1876) 131, 213
Noakes, Michael (b.1933) 213
Noble, Richard Pratchett (c.1814–1892) 131
Nolan, Gavin (b.1977) 213
Norton, A. 131
Oakes, John Wright (1820–1887) 131
O'Connor, James Arthur (1791–1841) 132
O'Dea, Eric 227
Odekerken, Willem van (d.1677) 132
Ogilvie, Frank Stanley (1858–after 1935) 191
Oliver, Peter (1927–2006) 24
Olivier, Herbert Arnould (1861–1952) 192
O'Neil, Henry Nelson (1817–1880) 132
Opie, John (1761–1807) 132
Orchardson, William Quiller (1832–1910) 132
O'Rourke, Robert (active 2003) 180
Ouless, Walter William (1848–1933) 132
Ouwater, Isaak (1748–1793) 132
Pace del Campidoglio, Michele (1610–probably 1670) 132
Pacsano, Enrico (active early 19th C) 132
Pagliei, Gioacchino (1852–1896) 133
Palamedesz., Anthonie (1601–1673) 133
Palma, Jacopo il giovane (1544/1548–1628) 133
Parrott, Samuel (1797–1876) 133
Partridge, Maurice William (1913–1973) 133, 213–215
Pasmore, Victor (1908–1998) 133
Paul, Joseph (1804–1887) 30, 31
Paulden, C. H. 133
Paulson, Ann (1808–1866) 9
Payne, David (c.1844–1891) 9, 180, 187
Payne, William (c.1760–after 1830) 133
Peake, Mervyn (1911–1968) 134
Pelham, Thomas Kent (c.1831–1907) 134
Penrose, J. E. 227

Percy, Sidney Richard (1821–1886) 134
Phillip, John (1817–1867) 134
Phillips, Thomas (1770–1845) 39, 134
Philpot, Glyn Warren (1884–1937) 134
Picasso, Pablo (1881–1973) 236
Pickard, Louise (1865–1928) 134
Pickering, Henry (c.1720–c.1775) 134, 135
Pickersgill, Henry William (1782–1875) 39, 192
Pickin, E. M. 9
Piper, John (1903–1992) 135
Pitchforth, Roland Vivian (1895–1982) 227
Pott, Laslett John (1837–1898) 135
Powell, Ella Ffolliott (c.1887–1943) 9
Power, John Joseph Wardell (1881–1943) 82, 135
Price, Caroline Mary (active 1830) 137
Price, Edward (1800–1885) 137
Pryde, James (1866–1941) 137
Pynacker, Adam (c.1620–1673) 137
Race, W. 9
Ramsay, Allan (1713–1784) 39
Ramsay, James (1786–1854) 39
Ramsay, Patricia (1886–1974) 24
Ranken, William Bruce Ellis (1881–1941) 137
Redgate, Arthur W. (1860–1906) 137, 138
Redgate, Sylvanus (1827–1907) 138, 139, 177
Redmore, Henry (1820–1887) 180
Reeve, Walter 184
Renoir, Pierre-Auguste (1841–1919) 236
Reynolds, Alan (b.1926) 139
Reynolds, Joshua (1723–1792) 39
Reynolds, S. 43
Richards, Ceri Geraldus (1903–1971) 227
Richardson, Jonathan the elder (1664/1665–1745) 215
Richmond, George (1809–1896) 139
Ritzberger, Albert (1853–1915) 139
Riviere, Briton (1840–1920) 139, 145
Riviere, Hugh Goldwin (1869–1956) 192
Roberts, Henry Benjamin (1831–1915) 139
Roberts, John Horrocks (b.1931) 215
Roberts, William Patrick (1895–1980) 55, 139
Robson, Gavin (b.1950) 215, 241
Roe, Clarence (1850–1909) 140
Rogan, Irene 170
Ronaldson, Thomas Martine (1881–1942) 215
Room, Henry (1802–1850) 192
Roos, Philipp Peter (1657–1706) 140
Rosoman, Leonard Henry (b.1913) 215
Ross, William A. 48
Ross, William Charles (1794–1860) 40
Rossetti, Dante Gabriel (1828–1882) 140
Rousseau, Henri (1844–1910) 236
Rowe, Tom Trythall (1856–1940) 140
Royce (active 19th C) 11
Royle, Stanley (1888–1961) 37
Russell, Alex (b.1967) 170, 171
Saan, P. de 140
Sailmaker, Isaac (c.1633–1721) 140
Salisbury, Frank O. (1874–1962) 184
Salt, Les (1916–1986) 4
Sancha, Carlos Luis (1920–2001) 216
Sandby, Paul (1731–1809) 140, 216
Sanders, George (1774–1846) 40
Schneider, Hermann (1847–1918) 140
Schwanfelder, Charles Henry (1774–1837) 141
Scobie, Ray (active 1995–1997) 48, 136
Senff, Carl Adolf (1785–1863) 141
Seurat, Georges (1859–1891) 236
Shackleton, William (1872–1933) 141
Shalders, George (c.1826–1873) 142
Shannon, Charles Haslewood (1863–1937) 142
Shaw, Don W. 184
Shaw, Frank 185
Shayer, William (1788–1879) 142
Shelton, Beryl 3
Sheringham, George (1884–1937) 142
Shipham, Benjamin (1808–1872) 143, 216
Shipston, Olga 227
Siberechts, Jan (1627–c.1703) 143
Sickert, Walter Richard (1860–1942) 143
Sillett, James (1764–1840) 143
Simi, Filadelfo (1849–1923) 143
Simons, Stephen (b.1984) 4
Smart, Hilda Elizabeth (1900–1992) 187
Smart, Rowley (1887–1934) 143
Smirke, Robert (1752–1845) 144
Smith, George (1829–1901) 144
Smith, Herbert 227
Smith, Matthew Arnold Bracy (1879–1959) 144
Smith, Mick 171
Smyth, Henry (active c.1800–1860) 144
Southall, Joseph Edward (1861–1944) 118, 146
Spear, Ruskin (1911–1990) 146
Spencelayh, Charles (1865–1958) 146
Spencer, Augustus (1860–1924) 227
Spencer, Stanley (1891–1959) 31, 146
Spinello Aretino (1350/1352–1410) 146
Spooner, Arthur (1873–1961) 16, 24, 25, 31, 147, 148, 180, 182, 188, 216, 235
Sprawson, Derek (b.1955) 216
Spruyt, Johannes (1627/1628–1671) 148
Stark, James (1794–1859) 148
Steenwijck, Hendrick van the elder (c.1550–1603) 241
Steenwijck, Hendrick van the younger (c.1580–1649) 148
Stephenson, Ian (1934–2000) 148
Stevenson, G. S. (active 1830–1887) 148
Stevenson, Wendy 171
Stewardson, Thomas (1781–1859) 40
Stoddart, Rosalind (b.1960) 171
Stokes, Marianne (1855–1927) 148
Stone, Marcus C. (1840–1921) 148
Stothard, Thomas (1755–1834) 149
Stubley, Trevor (b.1932) 216
Suddaby, Rowland (1912–1972) 149
Sulimow, Jurij (b.1952) 31
Sullivan, William Holmes (1836–1908) 149
Surtees, John (1819–1915) 149
Sutton, Hector McDonald (1903–1992) 11
Swynnerton, Annie Louisa (1844–1933) 149

Taborn, David (b.1947) 216, 218
Talbot, William (c.1823–1907) 25
Tayler, Edward (1828–1906) 149
Taylor, George William 40
Taylor, Isaac II (1759–1829) 149
Taylor, S. 218
Teniers, David II (1610–1690) 150
Tennant, John F. (1796–1872) 150
Thomson, Alfred Reginald (1894–1979) 150
Tillemans, Peter (1684–1734) 40
Titcomb, William Holt Yates (1858–1930) 150
Titian (c.1488–1576) 150, 151
Todd, D. 182
Tomson, Arthur (1858–1905) 151
Tomson, Clifton (1775–1835) 41, 151
Towne, Charles (1763–1840) 151
Townroe, Mary Dakeyne (1849–1941) 151
Townsend, Ernest (1880–1944) 31
Townsend, John (b.1930) 177, 178, 182, 196, 218
Toynton, Norman (b.1939) 151
Trickett, Rob 218
Trolley, Arthur (1914–1985) 4
Tucker, R. 11
Tuke, Henry Scott (1858–1929) 151
Turner, William (1789–1862) 151
Tyndall, W. Castell 11
Ugolini, Giuseppe (1826–1897) 152
Van der Meer, Barend (1659–1702) 155
Vaughan, John Keith (1912–1977) 155
Velde, Adriaen van de (1636–1672) 155
Venne, Adriaen van de (1589–1662) 155
Verboeckhoven, Eugène Joseph (1799–1881) 156
Verbrugge, Emile (1856–1936) 156
Vertangen, Daniel (c.1598–1681/1684) 156
Vickers, Alfred (1786–1868) 156
Vickers, W. (active 19th C) 156
Vincent, George (1796–1831) 156, 157
Vivian, Jane (active 1861–1877) 42
Vrancx, Sebastian (1573–1647) 129
Wadsworth, Edward Alexander (1889–1949) 157
Wainewright, Thomas Francis (1794–1883) 42
Walker, Ethel (1861–1951) 25
Walker, John Rawson (1796–1873) 42, 157, 158, 218
Waller, W. R. 228
Wallis, George (1811–1891) 158
Walton, Amy 14
Walton, Henry (1746–1813) 32
Waplington, Gilbert (b.1873) 43
Waplington, Paul (b.1938) ii, 54, 158
Warburton, Stella 218
Ward, Edwin Arthur (1859–1933) 158, 230
Ward, James (1769–1859) 158
Ward, James II (1800–1884) 158
Warmby, Byron Winston (1902–1978) 228
Warren, Charles Knighton (b.1856) 158
Warsop, Frederick (c.1835–1895) 159
Waterlow, Ernest Albert (1850–1919) 159
Watson, John (1923–1992) 159
Watteau, Jean-Antoine (1684–1721) 219
Watts, Frederick William (1800–1870) 159
Watts, George Frederick (1817–1904) 159
Webb, James (1825–1895) 159
Weber, Theodor Alexander (1838–1907) 159
Webster, Moses (1792–1870) 43
Wehrschmidt, Daniel Albert (1861–1932) 25
Weight, Carel Victor Morlais (1908–1997) 1, 159, 219
Werff, Adriaen van der (1659–1722) 160
Werff, Pieter van der (1665–1722) 160
West, William (1801–1861) 160
Westall, Richard (1765–1836) 43
Weston, C. 237
Whaite, Henry Clarence (1828–1912) 160
Whall, Charles Albert (b.1849) 228, 229
Wheatley, Francis (1747–1801) 160
Wheatley, Grahame (b.1943) 3, 73
Whitton, Stanley 229
Wijnants, Jan (c.1635–1684) 160
Wilkie, David (1785–1841) 160, 161
Wilkinson, David 32
Wilkinson, Norman (1878–1972) 13
Willetts, David (b.1939) 219
Williams, John Edgar (c.1821–1891) 161
Wilson, Richard (1714–1787) 161
Wimperis, Edmund Morison (1835–1900) 161
Winck, Christian (1738–1797) 43
Wingfield, James Digman (1800–1872) 161
Wissing, Willem (1656–1687) 43, 195
Withoos, Matthias (1627–1703) 161
Withoos, Pieter (1654–1693) 161
Wood, Alan (b.1935) 229
Wood, John (1801–1870) 162
Wright, John Michael (1617–1694) 43, 162
Wright, Joseph (1756–1793) 162
Wright, Joseph of Derby (1734–1797) 162, 175
Wyllie, William Lionel (1851–1931) 162
Xhaferin 54
Yates, Edward 32
Yeames, William Frederick (1835–1918) 162
Zinkeisen, Anna Katrina (1901–1976) 164
Zirbes, P. 3
Zoffany, Johann (1733–1810) 219
Zuccarelli, Franco (1702–1788) 164

Supporters of The Public Catalogue Foundation

Master Patrons

The Public Catalogue Foundation is greatly indebted to the following Master Patrons who have helped it in the past or are currently working with it to raise funds for the publication of their county catalogues. All of them have given freely of their time and have made an enormous contribution to the work of the Foundation.

Peter Andreae *(Hampshire)*
Sir Henry Aubrey-Fletcher, Bt, Lord Lieutenant of Buckinghamshire *(Buckinghamshire)*
Sir Nicholas Bacon, DL, High Sheriff of Norfolk *(Norfolk)*
The Hon. Mrs Bayliss, JP, Lord Lieutenant of Berkshire *(Berkshire)*
Ian Bonas *(County Durham)*
Peter Bretherton *(West Yorkshire: Leeds)*
Sir Hugo Brunner, KCVO, JP, Lord Lieutenant of Oxfordshire *(Oxfordshire)*
Lady Butler *(Warwickshire)*
Richard Compton *(North Yorkshire)*
George Courtauld, DL, Vice Lord Lieutenant of Essex *(Essex)*
The Marquess of Downshire *(North Yorkshire)*
Jenny Farr, MBE, DL *(Nottinghamshire)*
John Fenwick *(Tyne & Wear Museums)*
Mark Fisher, MP *(Staffordshire)*
Patricia Grayburn, MBE, DL *(Surrey)*
Algy Heber-Percy, Lord Lieutenant of Shropshire *(Shropshire)*
The Lady Mary Holborow, Lord Lieutenant of Cornwall *(Cornwall)*
Sarah Holman *(Warwickshire)*
Tommy Jowitt *(West Yorkshire)*
Sir Michael Lickiss *(Cornwall)*
Lord Marlesford, DL *(Suffolk)*
Loraine Morgan-Brinkhurst *(Somerset)*
Lady Sarah Nicholson *(County Durham)*
Sir John Riddell, Lord Lieutenant of Northumberland *(Northumberland)*
The Most Hon. The Marquess of Salisbury, PC, DL *(Hertfordshire)*
Julia Somerville *(Government Art Collection)*
Tim Stevenson, OBE, Lord Lieutenant of Oxfordshire *(Oxfordshire)*
Phyllida Stewart-Roberts, OBE, Lord Lieutenant of East Sussex *(East Sussex)*
Lady Juliet Townsend *(Northamptonshire)*
Leslie Weller, DL *(West Sussex)*

Financial support

The Public Catalogue Foundation is particularly grateful to the following organisations and individuals who have given it generous financial support since the project started in 2003.

National Sponsor

Christie's

Benefactors
(£10,000–£50,000)

The 29th May 1961 Charitable Trust
City of Bradford Metropolitan District Council
Deborah Loeb Brice Foundation
The Bulldog Trust
A. & S. Burton 1960 Charitable Trust
Christie's
The John S. Cohen Foundation
Covent Garden London
Department for Culture, Media and Sport
Sir Harry Djanogly, CBE
Mr Lloyd Dorfman
Fenwick Ltd
The Foyle Foundation
Hampshire County Council
The Charles Hayward Foundation
Peter Harrison Foundation
Hiscox plc
David Hockney CH, RA
ICAP plc
Michael Jacobson
Kent County Council
The Linbury Trust
The Manifold Trust
Robert Warren Miller
The Monument Trust
Miles Morland
National Gallery Trust
Stavros S. Niarchos Foundation
Norfolk County Council
Northern Rock Foundation
Nottingham City Council
Provident Financial
P. F. Charitable Trust
The Pilgrim Trust
RAB Capital plc
The Radcliffe Trust
Renaissance West Midlands
Renaissance Yorkshire
Saga Group Ltd
The Bernard Sunley Charitable Foundation
University College, London
University of Leeds
Garfield Weston Foundation
Mr & Mrs A. H. Wilkinson

Series Patrons
(Minimum donation of £2,500)

James & Lindsay Adam
Harry Bott
Janey Buchan
Dr Peter Cannon-Brookes
Bushey Museum in memory of Lavender Watson
Mr Lloyd Dorfman
Lord Douro
Jenny Farr, MBE, DL
Mrs Greta Fenston
The FIRS Trust
Glasgow Museums
Patricia Grayburn, MBE DL
G. Laurence Harbottle
R. K. Harrison
Paul & Fiona Hart
Paul & Kathrine Haworth
The Lady Hind Trust
Patrik Holden & Lin Hinds
Neil Honebon
Michael Jacobson
Grace Jenkins
Dr David Johnson, DL
The Keatley Trust
John Kendall, Esq.
Michael A. Lambert, CBE
David & Amanda Leathers
Miles Morland
North East Regional Museums Hub
Nottingham Civic Society
Richard & Amika Oldfield
Renaissance East Midlands
Adam Sedgwick
Sir Harry & Lady Soloman
Stuart M. Southall
Chloe Teacher
University of Surrey
David & Cissy Walker
Tony Wilkinson
Mr & Mrs Jo Windsor
Mr & Mrs Charles Wyvill

Catalogue Patrons
(£1,000–£10,000)

The 29th May 1961 Charitable Trust
ACE Study Tours
Adams & Remers
Marcus & Kate Agius
The AIM Foundation
John Alston, CBE
Amberley Castle
Chairman of Cornwall County Council, Mrs Doris Anson, OBE JP
Archant Ltd
G. F. Armitage Family Charitable Trust

Mr Ian Askew
Aurelius Charitable Trust
The Bacon Charitable Trust
Barlow Robbins LLP
Mr James & Lady Emma Barnard
Basingstoke and Deane Borough Council
Birmingham Common Good Trust
Sir Christopher Bland
The Charlotte Bonham-Carter Charitable Trust
H. R. Pratt Boorman Family Foundation
The Bowerman Charitable Trust
Viscountess Boyd Charitable Trust
Bramdean Asset Management LLP
Peter Bretherton
Mrs T. Brotherton-Ratcliffe
Mr & Mrs Patrick Burgess
Mr & Mrs Mark Burrell
Arnold J. Burton Charitable Trust
Bushey Museum in memory of Lavender Watson
C. J. R. & Mrs C. L. Calderwood
Chichester District Council
The Timothy Colman Charitable Trust
The Helen Jean Cope Trust
Cornwall County Council
Mr S. J. D. Corsan
Graeme Cottam & Gloriana Marks de Chabris
Coutts Charitable Trust
David Crane Trust
Elaine Craven, Earl Street Employment Consultants Ltd
Harriett Cullen
Culture North East
De La Rue Charitable Trust
Mr Robert Dean
Deborah Gage (Works of Art) Ltd
J. N. Derbyshire Trust
The Duke of Devonshire's Charitable Trust
Lord Douro
Professor Patrick & Dr Grace Dowling
Dunn Family Charitable Trust
East Sussex County Council
Eastbourne Borough Council
EEMLAC, through the Association for Suffolk Museums
Lord & Lady Egremont
Sir John & Lady Elliott
Andrew & Lucy Ellis
Essex County Council
Mrs Jenny Farr, MBE, DL
John Feeney Charitable Trust
Marc Fitch Fund
Elizabeth & Val Fleming
The Follett Trust
Christopher & Catherine Foyle
Lewis & Jacqueline Golden
Gorringes
Charles Gregson
The Gulland Family
David Gurney
Philip Gwyn
Sir Ernest Hall
The Hartnett Charitable Trust
Hazlitt, Gooden & Fox Ltd
Heartwood Wealth Management Ltd
The Lady Hind Trust
The Friends of Historic Essex
Hobart Charitable Trust
David Hockney CH, RA
Patrick Holden & Lin Hinds
David & Prue Hopkinson
Isle of Wight Council
The J. and S. B. Charitable Trust
Alan & Penny Jerome
Tommy Jowitt
The Keatley Trust
Kent Messenger Group
Kirklees Council
Garrett Kirk, Jr
The Friends of the Laing Art Gallery
Lord Lea of Crondall, OBE
The Leche Trust
Leeds Art Collections Fund
Leeds City Council
Leeds Philosophical and Literary Society
Mark & Sophie Lewisohn
Tom Lugg & the Lane Family
The Orr Mackintosh Foundation
Maidstone Borough Council
The Marlay Group
Marshall Charitable Trust
The Piet Mendels Foundation
The Mercers' Company
MLA East of England
MLA North East of England
Mr Paul Myners
Rupert Nabarro
Newcastle City Council
Bryan Norman
Nottingham Civic Society

Oakmoor Trust
The Orr Mackintosh Foundation
The Owen Family Trust
Sir Idris Pearce
The Pennycress Trust
Mrs Margaret Pollett
The Portland Family
Portsmouth City Council
Provident Financial plc
Mr John Rank
Rathbone Investment Management Ltd
The Hans and Märit Rausing Charitable Trust
Roger & Jane Reed
Renaissance North East
Renaissance South East
Renaissance South West
Michael Renshall, CBE, MA, FCA
Sir Miles & Lady Rivett-Carnac
Rothschild Foundation
Royal Cornwall Museum
The Friends of the Royal Pavilion, Art Gallery & Museums, Brighton
Russell New
Scarfe Charitable Trust
Shaftesbury PLC
The Shears Foundation
Smith & Williamson
South West of England Regional Development Agency
Caroline M. Southall
Stuart M. Southall
Southampton City Council
The Friends of Southampton's Museums, Archives and Galleries
The Jessie Spencer Trust
Mrs Andrew Stewart-Roberts, OBE
Mr Peter Stormonth Darling
Strutt and Parker
Suffolk County Council, through the Association for Suffolk Museums
The Friends of Sunderland Museums
Surrey County Council
The John Swire 1989 Charitable Trust
The Tanner Trust
Tennants Auctioneers
Tesco Charity Trust
The Thistle Trust
Trusthouse Charitable Foundation
TWM Business Partners
Tyne & Wear Museums
University College Falmouth
University of Essex
Wakefield Metropolitan District Council
The Walland Trust Fund
John Wates Charitable Trust
Leslie Weller, DL
The Welton Foundation
West Sussex County Council
Wilkin & Sons Ltd
Peter Wolton Charitable Trust
Michael J. Woodhall, FRICS
The Friends of York Art Gallery (E. J. Swift Bequest)